PRO FOOTBALL
GUIDE

1985 EDITION

Editors/Pro Football Guide
HOWARD BALZER
DAVE SLOAN

President-Chief Executive Officer
RICHARD WATERS

Editor
TOM BARNIDGE

Director of Books and Periodicals
RON SMITH

Published by

The Sporting News

1212 North Lindbergh Boulevard
P.O. Box 56 — St. Louis, Mo. 63166

Copyright © 1985
The Sporting News Publishing Company
a Times Mirror company

ISSN 0732-1902   ISBN 0-89204-189-7

TABLE OF CONTENTS

ON THE COVER: Miami Dolphins quarterback Dan Marino set a new standard by which NFL quarterbacks are judged with records for most touchdown passes (48), most yards (5,084) and most 300-yard passing games (9) in 1984.

Photograph by Kevin W. Reece

THE NATIONAL FOOTBALL LEAGUE

WELLINGTON MARA
President
National Football
Conference

PETE ROZELLE
Commissioner
National Football
League

LAMAR HUNT
President
American Football
Conference

COMMISSIONER'S OFFICE

PETE ROZELLE, Commissioner
DON WEISS, Executive Director
JOE RHEIN, Director of Administration
JOHN SCHOEMER, Treasurer
JAY MOYER, Executive V.P./Counsel to Commissioner
JAN VAN DUSER, Director of Operations
JIM HEFFERNAN, Director of Public Relations
JOE BROWNE, Director of Communications
VAL PINCHBECK, Jr., Director of Broadcasting
WARREN WELSH, Director of Security
CHARLES R. JACKSON, Assistant Director of Security
JOEL BUSSERT, Director of Player Personnel
ART McNALLY, Supervisor of Officials
JACK READER, Assistant Supervisor of Officials
NICK SKORICH, Assistant Supervisor of Officials
JIM STEEG, Director of Special Events
SUSAN McCANN, Assistant Director of Special Events
TOM SULLIVAN, Controller
JAMES NOEL, Assistant Counsel

AMERICAN FOOTBALL CONFERENCE

LAMAR HUNT, President
AL WARD, Assistant to the President
PETER ABITANTE, Director of Information

NATIONAL FOOTBALL CONFERENCE

WELLINGTON MARA, President
BILL GRANHOLM, Assistant to the President
DICK MAXWELL, Director of Information

LEAGUE OFFICES
410 Park Avenue
New York, New York 10022

TELEPHONE (Area Code 212)
Commissioner's Office: 758-1500

NATIONAL FOOTBALL LEAGUE

FINAL STANDINGS OF THE TEAMS—1984

AMERICAN CONFERENCE

EASTERN DIVISION

	W.	L.	T.	Pct.	Pts.	Opp.
*Miami	14	2	0	.875	513	298
New England	9	7	0	.563	362	352
New York Jets	7	9	0	.438	332	364
Indianapolis	4	12	0	.250	239	414
Buffalo	2	14	0	.125	250	454

CENTRAL DIVISION

	W.	L.	T.	Pct.	Pts.	Opp.
*Pittsburgh	9	7	0	.563	387	310
Cincinnati	8	8	0	.500	339	339
Cleveland	5	11	0	.313	250	297
Houston	3	13	0	.188	240	437

WESTERN DIVISION

	W.	L.	T.	Pct.	Pts.	Opp.
*Denver	13	3	0	.813	353	241
†Seattle	12	4	0	.750	418	282
†L.A. Raiders	11	5	0	.688	368	278
Kansas City	8	8	0	.500	314	324
San Diego	7	9	0	.438	394	413

*Division champion.
†Wild-card team.

NATIONAL CONFERENCE

EASTERN DIVISION

	W.	L.	T.	Pct.	Pts.	Opp.
*Washington	11	5	0	.688	426	310
†New York Giants	9	7	0	.563	299	301
Dallas	9	7	0	.563	308	308
St. Louis	9	7	0	.563	423	345
Philadelphia	6	9	1	.406	278	320

CENTRAL DIVISION

	W.	L.	T.	Pct.	Pts.	Opp.
*Chicago	10	6	0	.625	325	248
Green Bay	8	8	0	.500	390	309
Tampa Bay	6	10	0	.375	335	380
Detroit	4	11	1	.281	283	408
Minnesota	3	13	0	.188	276	484

WESTERN DIVISION

	W.	L.	T.	Pct.	Pts.	Opp.
*San Francisco	15	1	0	.938	475	227
†L.A. Rams	10	6	0	.625	346	316
New Orleans	7	9	0	.438	298	361
Atlanta	4	12	0	.250	281	382

*Division champion.
†Wild-card team.

AFC PLAYOFFS

WILD CARD
Seattle 13, Los Angeles Raiders 7

SEMIFINALS
Miami 31, Seattle 10
Pittsburgh 24, Denver 17

NFC PLAYOFFS

WILD CARD
New York Giants 16, Los Angeles Rams 13

SEMIFINALS
San Francisco 21, New York Giants 10
Chicago 23, Washington 19

AFC CHAMPIONSHIP
Miami 45, Pittsburgh 28

NFC CHAMPIONSHIP
San Francisco 23, Chicago 0

NFL CHAMPIONSHIP
San Francisco 38, Miami 16

NATIONAL FOOTBALL LEAGUE CHAMPIONS

Year—Team	Coach
1921—Chicago Staleys†	George Halas
1922—Canton Bulldogs	Guy Chamberlin
1923—Canton Bulldogs	Guy Chamberlin
1924—Cleveland Bulldogs‡	Guy Chamberlin
1925—Chicago Cardinals	Norman Barry
1926—Frankford Yellowjackets	Guy Chamberlin
1927—New York Giants	Earl Potteiger
1928—Providence Steamrollers	Jim Conzelman
1929—Green Bay Packers	Curly Lambeau
1930—Green Bay Packers	Curly Lambeau
1931—Green Bay Packers	Curly Lambeau
1932—Chicago Bears	Ralph Jones
1933—Chicago Bears	George Halas
1934—New York Giants	Steve Owen
1935—Detroit Lions	Potsy Clark
1936—Green Bay Packers	Curly Lambeau
1937—Washington Redskins	Ray Flaherty
1938—New York Giants	Steve Owen
1939—Green Bay Packers	Curly Lambeau
1940—Chicago Bears	George Halas
1941—Chicago Bears	George Halas
1942—Washington Redskins	Ray Flaherty
1943—Chicago Bears	Luke Johnsos & Hunk Anderson
1944—Green Bay Packers	Curly Lambeau
1945—Cleveland Rams	Adam Walsh
1946—Chicago Bears	George Halas
1947—Chicago Cardinals	Jim Conzelman
1948—Philadelphia Eagles	Greasy Neale
1949—Philadelphia Eagles	Greasy Neale
1950—Cleveland Browns	Paul Brown
1951—Los Angeles Rams	Joe Stydahar
1952—Detroit Lions	Buddy Parker
1953—Detroit Lions	Buddy Parker
1954—Cleveland Browns	Paul Brown
1955—Cleveland Browns	Paul Brown
1956—New York Giants	Jim Lee Howell
1957—Detroit Lions	George Wilson
1958—Baltimore Colts	Weeb Ewbank
1959—Baltimore Colts	Weeb Ewbank
1960—Philadelphia Eagles	Buck Shaw
1961—Green Bay Packers	Vince Lombardi
1962—Green Bay Packers	Vince Lombardi
1963—Chicago Bears	George Halas
1964—Cleveland Browns	Blanton Collier
1965—Green Bay Packers	Vince Lombardi
1966—Green Bay Packers*	Vince Lombardi
1967—Green Bay Packers*	Vince Lombardi
1968—Baltimore Colts	Don Shula
1969—Minnesota Vikings	Bud Grant
1970—Baltimore Colts	Don McCafferty
1971—Dallas Cowboys	Tom Landry
1972—Miami Dolphins	Don Shula
1973—Miami Dolphins	Don Shula
1974—Pittsburgh Steelers	Chuck Noll
1975—Pittsburgh Steelers	Chuck Noll
1976—Oakland Raiders	John Madden
1977—Dallas Cowboys	Tom Landry
1978—Pittsburgh Steelers	Chuck Noll
1979—Pittsburgh Steelers	Chuck Noll
1980—Oakland Raiders	Tom Flores
1981—San Francisco 49ers	Bill Walsh
1982—Washington Redskins	Joe Gibbs
1983—Los Angeles Raiders	Tom Flores
1984—San Francisco 49ers	Bill Walsh

†Later called the Chicago Bears.
‡Franchise moved from Canton.
*Won AFL-NFL Championship Game.

ATLANTA FALCONS
(Western Division, National Conference)

Dan Henning

Chairman of the Board—Rankin M. Smith, Sr.
President—Rankin M. Smith, Jr.
Executive Vice-President—Eddie LeBaron
General Manager—Tom Braatz
Pro Personnel—Bill Jobko
Head Coach—Dan Henning (2 years: 11-21)

Assistant Coaches:
Offensive Coordinator/Off. Line—Larry Beightol
Strength and Conditioning—George Dostal
Running Backs—Sam Elliott
Special Teams—Ted Fritsch
Receivers—Bob Harrison
Linebackers—Bobby Jackson
Asst. Research/Development—Joe Madden
Defensive Coordinator—John Marshall
Assistant Offensive Line—Garry Puetz
Asst. Head Coach/Def. Line—Dan Sekanovich
Defensive Backs—Jack Stanton
Public Relations Director—Charlie Dayton
(Office Phone: 945-1111—Area Code 404)

Offices—I-85 & Suwanee Rd., Suwanee, Ga. 30174
Stadium—Atlanta-Fulton County Stadium (Capacity: 59,709)
Team Colors—Red, Black, White and Silver
Training Site—Atlanta Falcon Complex, Suwanee, Ga.

1985 SCHEDULE
(All times local. All games Sunday unless noted otherwise.)

Sept. 8	DETROIT	1:00
Sept. 15	at San Francisco	1:00
Sept. 22	DENVER	1:00
Sept. 29	at Los Angeles Rams	1:00
Oct. 6	SAN FRANCISCO	1:00
Oct. 13	at Seattle	1:00
Oct. 20	NEW ORLEANS	1:00
Oct. 27	at Dallas	12:00
Nov. 3	WASHINGTON	1:00
Nov. 10	at Philadelphia	1:00
Nov. 17	LOS ANGELES RAMS	1:00
Nov. 24	at Chicago	12:00
Dec. 1	LOS ANGELES RAIDERS	4:00
Dec. 8	at Kansas City	12:00
Dec. 15	MINNESOTA	1:00
Dec. 22	at New Orleans	12:00

1984 RESULTS—(Won 4, Lost 12)

Falcons	Opp.		Att.
36 New Orleans	28	(A)	66,652
24 Detroit (OT)	27	(H)	49,878
20 Minnesota	27	(A)	53,955
42 Houston	10	(H)	45,248
5 San Francisco	14	(A)	57,990
30 Los Angeles Rams	28	(A)	47,832
7 New York Giants	19	(H)	50,268
10 Los Angeles Rams	24	(H)	52,861
10 Pittsburgh	35	(A)	55,971
14 Washington	27	(A)	51,301
13 New Orleans	17	(H)	40,590
7 Cleveland	23	(H)	28,280
14 Cincinnati	35	(A)	44,678
17 San Francisco	35	(H)	29,644
6 Tampa Bay	23	(A)	33,808
26 Philadelphia	10	(H)	15,582

1984 GAMES STARTED

16 games: Stacey Bailey, Cliff Benson, James Britt, Rick Bryan, Arthur Cox, Buddy Curry, Kenny Johnson, Tom Pridemore, John Scully, Don Smith, R.C. Thielemann.

15 games: Bobby Butler, Alfred Jackson.

14 games: Mike Kenn, Al Richardson, Gerald Riggs.

13 games: Brett Miller, Mike Pitts, Jeff Van Note.

11 games: Steve Bartkowski, David Frye.

8 games: Dan Benish, Gary Burley.

7 games: John Rade.

5 games: Mike Moroski.

3 games: Dan Dufour, Joe Pellegrini, Andrew Provence.

2 games: Lynn Cain, Eric Sanders.

1 game: Floyd Hodge, Gerald Small.

ATLANTA FALCONS 1985 VETERAN ROSTER

No.	Name	Pos.	Ht.	Wt.	NFL Exp.	Birth-date	College	Games in '84	How Acquired
31	Andrews, William	RB	6-0	213	6	12-25-55	Auburn	*0	D3a, '79
16	Archer, David	QB	6-2	203	2	2-15-62	Iowa State	2	OFA, '84
39	Austin, Cliff	RB	6-0	190	3	3- 2-60	Clemson	15	FA, '84
82	Bailey, Stacey	WR	6-0	157	4	2-10-60	San Jose State	16	D3, '82
10	†Bartkowski, Steve	QB	6-4	218	11	11-12-52	California	11	D1, '75
69	Benish, Dan	DT	6-5	265	3	11-21-61	Clemson	15	OFA, '83
87	Benson, Cliff	TE	6-4	234	2	8-28-61	Purdue	16	D5, '84
53	Benson, Thomas	LB	6-2	235	2	9- 6-61	Oklahoma	16	D2a, '84
26	Britt, James	CB	6-0	185	3	9-12-60	Louisiana State	16	D2, '83
77	Bryan, Rick	DE	6-4	260	2	3-20-62	Oklahoma	16	D1, '84
73	Burley, Gary	DT	6-3	290	10	12- 8-52	Pittsburgh	12	T-Cin, '84
23	Butler, Bobby	CB	5-11	175	5	5-28-59	Florida State	15	D1, '81
21	Cain, Lynn	RB	6-1	205	7	10-16-55	Southern California	15	D4, '79
25	Case, Scott	S	6-0	178	2	5-17-62	Oklahoma	16	D2, '84
70	Chapman, Mike	C-G	6-4	250	2	2-10-61	Texas	4	FA, '84
88	Cox, Arthur	TE	6-2	255	3	2- 5-61	Texas Southern	16	OFA, '83
89	Curran, William	WR	5-11	175	4	12-30-59	UCLA	14	OFA, '82
50	Curry, Buddy	LB	6-4	228	6	6- 4-58	North Carolina	16	D2, '80
71	†Dufour, Dan	T-C	6-5	280	3	10-18-60	UCLA	6	OFA, '83
58	Frye, David	LB	6-2	213	3	6-21-61	Purdue	16	OFA, '83
34	†Gaison, Blane	S	6-1	188	5	5-13-58	Hawaii	15	OFA, '81
1	Giacomarro, Ralph	P	6-1	194	3	1-17-61	Penn State	16	D10, '83
75	Harris, Roy	DT	6-2	266	2	3-26-61	Florida	15	OFA, '84
30	Haworth, Steve	S	6-0	188	3	9-16-61	Oklahoma	5	FA, '83
83	Hodge, Floyd	WR	6-0	195	4	7-18-59	Utah	12	OFA, '81
8	Holly, Bob	QB	6-2	205	4	6- 1-60	Princeton	*0	FA, '84
85	Jackson, Alfred	WR	6-0	190	8	8- 3-55	Texas	16	D7, '78
51	Jackson, Jeff	LB	6-1	228	2	10- 9-61	Auburn	16	D8, '84
81	Johnson, Billy	WR	5-9	177	10	1-27-52	Widener	6	FA, '82
37	Johnson, Kenny	S	5-11	172	6	1- 7-58	Mississippi State	16	D5a, '80
78	Kenn, Mike	T	6-7	266	8	2- 9-56	Michigan	14	D1, '78
54	†Kuykendall, Fulton	LB	6-4	228	11	6-10-53	UCLA	16	D6, '75
80	Landrum, Mike	TE	6-2	231	2	11- 6-61	Southern Mississippi	15	OFA, '84
55	Levenick, Dave	LB	6-3	220	3	5-29-59	Wisconsin	8	D12, '82
18	†Luckhurst, Mick	K	6-2	183	5	3-31-58	California	16	OFA, '81
52	Malancon, Rydell	LB	6-1	219	2	1-10-62	Louisiana State	7	D4, '84
49	Matthews, Allama	TE	6-2	230	3	8-24-61	Vanderbilt	6	D12, '83
62	Miller, Brett	T	6-7	285	3	10- 2-58	Iowa	15	D5, '83
15	†Moroski, Mike	QB	6-4	203	7	9- 4-57	Cal-Davis	16	D6, '79
64	†Pellegrini, Joe	G-C	6-4	258	4	4- 8-57	Harvard	15	FA, '84
74	Pitts, Mike	DT	6-5	270	3	9-25-60	Alabama	14	D1, '83
27	Pridemore, Tom	S	5-11	186	8	4-29-56	West Virginia	16	D9, '78
72	Provence, Andrew	DE	6-3	260	3	3- 8-61	South Carolina	16	D3, '83
59	Rade, John	LB	6-1	225	3	8-31-60	Boise State	7	D8, '83
56	Richardson, Al	LB	6-3	222	6	9-23-57	Georgia Tech	16	D8, '80
42	Riggs, Gerald	RB	6-1	230	4	11- 6-60	Arizona State	15	D1, '82
67	†Sanders, Eric	T	6-7	280	5	10-22-58	Nevada-Reno	10	D5, '81
61	Scully, John	G	6-6	255	5	8- 2-58	North Dame	16	D4, '81
41	†Seay, Virgil	WR	5-8	180	5	1- 1-58	Troy State	*14	FA, '84
48	Small, Gerald	CB	5-11	192	8	8-10-56	San Jose State	16	T-Mia, '84
65	†Smith, Don	DE	6-5	270	7	5- 9-57	Miami, Fla.	16	D1, '79
84	Stamps, Sylvester	RB	5-7	166	2	2-24-61	Jackson State	10	OFA, '84
68	†Thielemann, R.C.	G	6-4	262	9	8-12-55	Arkansas	16	D2, '77
86	Tuttle, Perry	WR	6-0	180	4	8- 2-59	Clemson	*8	W-TB, '84
32	Tyrrell, Tim	RB	6-1	201	2	2-19-61	Northern Illinois	11	OFA, '84
57	Van Note, Jeff	C	6-2	250	17	2- 7-46	Kentucky	16	D11, '69
	Washington, Joe	RB	5-10	179	9	9-24-53	Oklahoma	*7	T-Was, '85

*Andrews missed '84 season due to injury; Holly active for 4 games with Atlanta, 7 with Philadelphia in '84 but did not play; Seay played 11 games with Washington, 3 with Atlanta in '84; Tuttle played 3 games with Tampa Bay, 5 with Atlanta in '84; Washington played 7 games with Washington in '84.

†Option playout; subject to developments.

Also played with Falcons in '84—T Warren Bryant (4 games), RB Rodney Tate (7), LB Johnny Taylor (2), RB Richard Williams (1), DE Jeff Yeates (8).

D—Draft; T—Trade; W—Waivers; FA—Free Agent; OFA—Original Free Agent.

ATLANTA FALCONS
1985 DRAFT CHOICES

(Number following name designates order of selection among 336 players drafted.)

Round and Player	Position		College
1. FRALIC, Bill from Houston through Minnesota (a)	2	T	Pittsburgh
1. Choice to Minnesota (a)			
2. Choice to Washington (b)			
2. GANN, Mike from St. Louis (c)	45	DE	Notre Dame
3. Choice to Minnesota (a)			
4. HARRY, Emile	89	WR	Stanford
5. Choice to St. Louis (c)			
6. Choice to Miami (d)			
6. PLEASANT, Reggie from New Orleans (e)	152	DB	Clemson
7. Choice to Cincinnati (f)			
8. LEE, Ashley	201	DB	Virginia Tech
8. WASHINGTON, Ronnie from New England (g)	215	LB	N.E. Louisiana
9. MOON, Micah	228	LB	North Carolina
10. MARTIN, Brent	257	C	Stanford
11. AYRES, John	284	DB	Illinois
12. WHISENHUNT, Ken	313	TE	Georgia Tech

(a) Vikings acquired pick from Oilers in switch of first-round positions, April 9, 1985; Falcons acquired pick for 1st and 3rd round picks, April 30, 1985.

(b) Traded pick, 2nd round pick and 6th round pick in 1986 for running back Joe Washington and 1st and 2nd round picks in 1986, April 30, 1985.

(c) Acquired pick for 2nd and 5th round picks, April 30, 1985.

(d) Traded pick and offensive lineman Ronnie Lee for cornerback Gerald Small, August 26, 1984.

(e) Acquired pick for tight end Junior Miller, August 26, 1984.

(f) Traded pick for nose tackle Gary Burley, August 23, 1984.

(g) Acquired pick for cornerback Rod McSwain, August 27, 1984.

ATLANTA FALCONS
1985 ROOKIE AND FIRST-YEAR ROSTER

(1) Indicates player in previous NFL camp.
(2) Indicates player with USFL game experience.
(3) Indicates player in previous USFL camp.
(4) Indicates player with CFL game experience.
(5) Indicates player in previous CFL camp.
　　All others classified as rookies.

Name	Pos.	Hgt.	Wgt.	Birth-date	College	How Acquired
Ayres, John	CB	5-11	183	9- 6-63	Illinois	D11
Bailey, Eric	TE	6-5	227	5-12-63	Kansas State	FA
Bennett, Ben (2)	QB	6-1	196	5- 5-62	Duke	D6 '84
Best, Chuck	LB	6-1	240	11-22-61	New Mexico	FA
Cason, Wendell	CB	5-11	183	1-22-63	Oregon	FA
Davis, Chucky (4)	RB	6-0	213	4-21-61	Wisconsin	FA
Dean, Melvin	CB	5-10	175	9- 9-63	Pittsburgh	FA
Fralic, Bill	T	6-5	285	10-31-62	Pittsburgh	D1
Gann, Mike	DE	6-5	256	10-19-63	Notre Dame	D2
Gay, Stan (1)	DB	5-10	180	12- 6-60	Alabama	*FA '83
Goff, Willard	DT	6-3	265	10-17-61	West Texas State	FA
Greene, Tiger	CB	5-10	184	2-15-62	Western Carolina	FA
Harry, Emile	WR	5-10	168	4- 5-63	Stanford	D4
Heeres, Greg	QB	6-3	194	5-30-63	Hope, Mich.	FA
Holmes, Don	WR	5-10	180	4- 1-63	Mesa, Colo.	D12 '84
Jefferson, Don	CB	6-1	195	8-26-63	Florida A&M	FA
Jones, Cedric (2)	RB	5-9	185	2-18-63	Florida State	FA
Jones, Michael	WR	5-11	170	6-13-62	Wisconsin	FA
Jones, Nathan	S	6-0	195	1-14-62	Arkansas	FA
Kiewel, Jeff (2)	OT	6-4	252	9-27-60	Arizona	FA
Lee, Ashley	S	6-1	196	4- 2-61	Virginia Tech	D8
Llewellyn, Nick	G	6-1	264	3- 1-62	Missouri	FA
Lowe, Marshall	WR	6-0	183	4- 6-61	Alcorn State	FA
Mack, Tracey	LB	6-0	214	12-29-61	Missouri	FA
Martin, Brent	C	6-3	268	6- 5-63	Stanford	D10
McDonald, Terry	LB	6-1	218	11-29-63	San Jose State	FA
Moon, Micah	LB	6-1	230	11-15-62	North Carolina	D9
Noirfalise, Harold	RB	6-2	215	12-26-61	Missouri Southern	FA
Norman, Tommy (2)	WR	5-11	174	10-25-64	Jackson State	D11 '84
Pleasant, Reggie	CB	5-9	175	5- 2-62	Clemson	D6
Price, Arthur	LB	6-2	220	5-17-62	Wisconsin	FA
Radloff, Wayne (2)	C	6-5	263	5-17-61	Georgia	FA
Shanks, Austin	WR	5-10	162	6-28-62	San Diego State	FA
Simmons, Ricky (2)	WR	5-11	185	1-29-61	Nebraska	FA
Smoldt, Dave	TE	6-2	229	11- 7-61	Iowa State	FA
Speed, Henry	OT	...	.....	....	....	FA
Sullivan, Randy	RB	5-10	198	9-26-62	Moorhead	FA
Taylor, John	LB	6-2	239	6-21-60	Hawaii	*FA '84
Thomasson, Leon	CB	6-0	185	6-20-63	Texas Southern	FA
Walker, Don	TE	6-2	228	6-21-63	Alcorn State	FA
Walker, Greg	T	6-4	254	1-19-63	Mississippi	FA
Wallace, Mike	WR	6-0	185	5-10-63	Kansas State	FA
Ward, Alvin	G	6-1	260	10-24-62	Miami	FA
Washington, Ronnie	LB	6-1	234	7-29-63	NE Louisiana State	D8a
Whisenhunt, Ken	TE	6-2	226	2-28-62	Georgia Tech	D12
Young, Almon	G	6-2	275	7- 3-62	Bethune-Cookman	FA

*Gay missed '84 season due to injury; Taylor played 2 games with Atlanta in '84.

BUFFALO BILLS
(Eastern Division, American Conference)

Kay Stephenson

President—Ralph C. Wilson, Jr.
Executive Vice-President—Patrick J. McGroder, Jr.
Vice-President/Head Coach—Kay Stephenson (2 years: 10-22)
Vice-President for Player Personnel—Norm Pollom
Vice-President, Administration and G.M.—Terry Bledsoe
Vice-President, Public Relations—L. Budd Thalman
 (Office Phone: 648-1800—Area Code 716)
Assistant Coaches:
 Tight Ends—Art Asselta
 Asst. Head Coach/Def. Coord.—Hank Bullough
 Quarterbacks—Kay Dalton
 Linebackers—Monte Kiffin
 Receivers—Bob Leahy
 Defensive Backs—Dick Mosley
 Running Backs—Elijah Pitts
 Offensive Coordinator/Off. Line—Jim Ringo
 Strength and Conditioning—Jim Speros
 Defensive Line—Ardell Wiegandt
Offices: One Bills Drive, Orchard Park, N. Y. 14127
Stadium—Rich Stadium (Capacity: 80,290)
Team Colors—Royal Blue, White and Scarlet
Training Site—Fredonia State University, Fredonia, N. Y.

1985 SCHEDULE
(All times local.
All games Sunday unless noted otherwise.)

Sept. 8	SAN DIEGO	4:00
Sept. 15	at New York Jets	1:00
Sept. 22	NEW ENGLAND	1:00
Sept. 29	MINNESOTA	1:00
Oct. 6	at Indianapolis	12:00
Oct. 13	at New England	1:00
Oct. 20	INDIANAPOLIS	1:00
Oct. 27	at Philadelphia	1:00
Nov. 3	CINCINNATI	1:00
Nov. 10	HOUSTON	1:00
Nov. 17	at Cleveland	1:00
Nov. 24	MIAMI	1:00
Dec. 1	at San Diego	1:00
Dec. 8	NEW YORK JETS	1:00
Dec. 15	at Pittsburgh	1:00
Dec. 22	at Miami	1:00

1984 RESULTS—(Won 2, Lost 14)

Bills		Opp.		Att.
17	New England	21	(H)	48,528
7	St. Louis	37	(A)	35,785
17	Miami	21	(H)	65,455
26	New York Jets	28	(H)	48,330
17	Indianapolis	31	(A)	60,032
17	Philadelphia	27	(H)	37,555
28	Seattle	31	(A)	59,034
7	Denver	37	(H)	31,204
7	Miami	38	(A)	58,824
10	Cleveland	13	(H)	33,343
10	New England	38	(A)	43,313
14	Dallas	3	(H)	74,391
14	Washington	41	(A)	51,513
21	Indianapolis	15	(H)	20,693
17	New York Jets	21	(A)	45,378
21	Cincinnati	52	(A)	55,771

1984 GAMES STARTED

16 games: Jon Borchardt, Joe Devlin, Byron Franklin, Will Grant, Ken Johnson, Ken Jones, Eugene Marve, Charles Romes, Fred Smerlas, Darryl Talley.

15 games: Greg Bell, Steve Freeman, Jim Haslett, Booker Moore, Ben Williams.

14 games: Jim Ritcher.

13 games: Preston Dennard.

11 games: Joe Ferguson, Don Wilson.

10 games: Brian Carpenter.

9 games: Tony Hunter.

8 games: Lucius Sanford.

7 games: Buster Barnett.

6 games: Chris Keating.

5 games: Joe Dufek, Rod Kush.

3 games: Stan David, Julius Dawkins, Lucious Smith.

2 games: Rodney Bellinger, Tim Vogler.

1 game: Martin Bayless, Mark Brammer, Sean McNanie, Speedy Neal, Gary Thompson.

BUFFALO BILLS 1985 VETERAN ROSTER

No.	Name	Pos.	Ht.	Wt.	NFL Exp.	Birth-date	College	Games in '84	How Acquired
75	†Acker, Bill	NT	6-3	255	6	11- 7-56	Texas	15	FA, '83
50	Azelby, Joe	LB	6-1	225	2	3- 5-62	Harvard	14	D10, '84
84	Barnett, Buster	TE	6-5	235	5	11-24-58	Jackson State	16	D11, '81
43	Bayless, Martin	S	6-2	195	2	10-11-62	Bowling Green	*16	FA, '84
28	Bell, Greg	RB	5-10	210	2	8- 1-62	Notre Dame	16	D1, '84
36	Bellinger, Rodney	CB	5-8	181	2	6- 4-62	Miami, Fla.	10	D3, '84
86	Brammer, Mark	TE	6-3	235	6	5- 3-58	Michigan State	12	D3, '80
81	Brookins, Mitchell	WR	5-11	196	2	12-10-60	Illinois	16	D4, '84
80	Butler, Jerry	WR	6-0	178	6	10-12-57	Clemson	*0	D1a, '79
30	Carpenter, Brian	CB	5-10	170	4	11-27-60	Michigan	*16	T-Was, '84
63	Cross, Justin	T	6-6	265	4	4-29-59	Western State, Colo.	7	D10, '81
59	David, Stan	LB	6-3	210	2	2-17-62	Texas Tech	16	D7, '84
89	†Dawkins, Julius	WR	6-1	196	3	1- 4-61	Pittsburgh	16	D12, '83
83	Dennard, Preston	WR	6-1	183	8	11-28-55	New Mexico	16	T-Ram, '84
70	Devlin, Joe	T	6-5	250	9	2-23-54	Iowa	16	D2a, '76
19	†Dufek, Joe	QB	6-4	215	3	8-23-61	Yale	5	FA, '83
85	Franklin, Byron	WR	6-1	185	4	9- 4-58	Auburn	16	D2a, '81
22	†Freeman, Steve	S	5-11	185	11	5- 8-53	Mississippi State	15	W-NE, '75
53	Grant, Will	C	6-3	255	8	3- 7-54	Kentucky	16	D10, '78
	Hargrove, James	RB	6-2	228	2	11-13-57	Wake Forest	*0	FA, '85
	Hartnett, Perry	G	6-5	275	3	4-28-60	Southern Methodist	*0	FA, '85
55	†Haslett, Jim	LB	6-3	232	7	12- 9-56	Indiana, Pa.	15	D2a, '79
25	Hill, Rod	CB	6-0	188	3	3-14-59	Kentucky State	2	T-Dal, '84
87	Hunter, Tony	TE	6-4	237	3	5-22-60	Notre Dame	11	D1, '83
91	Johnson, Ken	DE	6-5	253	7	3-25-55	Knoxville College	16	D4, '79
48	Johnson, Lawrence	CB	5-11	204	6	9-11-57	Wisconsin	*16	T-Cle, '84
	Jones, Bobby	WR	5-11	185	7	7-12-55	Millikin	*0	FA, '85
72	Jones, Ken	T	6-5	260	10	12- 1-52	Arkansas State	16	D2, '76
52	†Keating, Chris	LB	6-2	233	7	10-12-57	Maine	16	OFA, '79
4	Kidd, John	P	6-3	201	2	8-22-61	Northwestern	16	D5, '84
10	†Kofler, Matt	QB	6-3	192	4	8-30-59	San Diego State	16	D2, '82
42	†Kush, Rod	S	6-0	188	6	1-31-53	Nebraska-Omaha	16	D5, '79
61	Lynch, Tom	G	6-5	250	9	5-24-55	Boston College	16	T-Sea, '81
54	Marve, Eugene	LB	6-2	230	4	8-14-60	Saginaw Valley State	16	D3, '82
95	McNanie, Sean	DE	6-5	252	2	9- 9-61	San Diego State	15	D3a, '84
34	Moore, Booker	FB	5-11	224	4	6-23-59	Penn State	15	D1, '81
88	Mosley, Mike	WR	6-1	186	4	6-30-58	Texas A&M	4	D3, '81
41	Neal, Speedy	FB	6-2	254	2	8-26-62	Miami, Fla.	12	D3b, '84
13	Nelson, Chuck	K	5-11	175	3	2-23-60	Washington	7	FA, '84
38	Nixon, Jeff	S	6-3	190	5	10-13-56	Richmond	*0	D4a, '79
49	Norris, Ulysses	TE	6-4	232	7	1-15-57	Georgia	14	W-Det, '84
58	Potter, Steve	LB	6-3	235	5	11- 6-57	Virginia	10	FA, '84
79	Prater, Dean	DE	6-4	245	4	9-28-58	Oklahoma State	13	FA, '84
40	†Riddick, Robb	RB	6-0	195	4	4-26-57	Millersville State, Pa.	16	D9, '81
51	Ritcher, Jim	G	6-3	251	6	5-21-58	North Carolina State	14	D1, '80
26	Romes, Charles	CB	6-1	190	9	12-16-54	North Carolina Central	16	D12, '77
57	Sanford, Lucius	LB	6-2	216	8	2-14-56	Georgia Tech	8	D4, '78
76	Smerlas, Fred	NT	6-3	270	7	4- 8-57	Boston College	16	D2, '79
56	Talley, Darryl	LB	6-4	235	3	7-10-60	West Virginia	16	D2, '83
65	†Vogler, Tim	C	6-3	245	7	10- 2-56	Ohio State	16	OFA, '79
60	Wenglikowski, Al	LB	6-1	220	2	8- 3-60	Pittsburgh	5	FA, '84
27	White, Craig	WR	6-1	194	2	10- 8-61	Missouri	14	D11, '84
77	Williams, Ben	DE	6-3	260	10	9- 1-54	Mississippi	15	D3, '76
23	†Williams, Van	RB	6-0	208	3	3-15-59	Carson-Newman	16	D4, '82
21	Wilson, Donald	S	6-2	190	2	7-21-61	North Carolina State	16	OFA, '84

*Butler and Nixon missed '84 season due to injuries; Bayless played 3 games with St. Louis, 13 with Buffalo in '84; Carpenter played 3 games with Washington, 13 with Buffalo in '84; L. Johnson played 6 games with Cleveland, 10 with Buffalo in '84; Hargrove last active with Cincinnati in '81 and Boston (USFL) in '83; Hartnett last active with Chicago in '82 and Chicago (USFL) in '84; B. Jones last active with Cleveland in '83.

†Option playout; subject to developments.

Also played with Bills in '84—G Jon Borchardt (16 games), K Joe Danelo (9), QB Joe Ferguson (12), LB Trey Junkin (2), LB Mark Merrill (2), WR John Mistler (1), CB Lucious Smith (4), CB Gary Thompson (8), S Marco Tongue (1), DE Scott Virkus (2), CB Lenny Walterscheid (3).

D—Draft; T—Trade; W—Waivers; FA—Free Agent; OFA—Original Free Agent.

BUFFALO BILLS
1985 DRAFT CHOICES

(Number following name designates order of selection among 336 players drafted.)

Round and Player		Position	College
1. SMITH, Bruce	1	DE	Virginia Tech
1. BURROUGHS, Derrick from Green Bay (a)	14	DB	Memphis State
2. TRAYNOWICZ, Mark	29	T	Nebraska
2. BURKETT, Chris from Green Bay (a)	42	WR	Jackson State
3. REICH, Frank	57	QB	Maryland
3. GARNER, Hal from Cleveland (b)	63	LB	Utah State
4. REED, Andre	86	WR	Kutztown, Pa.
4. HELLESTRAE, Dale from San Francisco (c)	112	T	SMU
5. Choice to Los Angeles Rams (d)			
5. TEAL, Jimmy from Dallas (e)	130	WR	Texas A & M
6. HAMBY, Mike	141	DT	Utah State
7. PITTS, Ron	169	DB	UCLA
8. ROBINSON, Jacque	197	RB	Washington
9. JONES, Glenn	225	DB	Norfolk State
10. BABYAR, Chris	253	G	Illinois
11. SEAWRIGHT, James	282	LB	South Carolina
12. Choice to Washington (f)			
12. WOODSIDE, Paul from Seattle (g)	333	K	West Virginia

(a) Acquired picks for 1st round pick and 4th round pick in 1986, April 30, 1985.

(b) Acquired pick, 1st round pick and 6th round pick in 1986 for first pick in supplemental draft, April 9, 1985.

(c) Acquired pick for cornerback Mario Clark, July 16, 1984.

(d) Traded pick for wide receiver Preston Dennard, August 1, 1984.

(e) Acquired pick and cornerback Rod Hill for 5th round pick and conditional 1986 pick, August 23, 1984.

(f) Traded pick for defensive back Brian Carpenter, September 19, 1984.

(g) Acquired pick for guard Reggie McKenzie, June 28, 1983.

BUFFALO BILLS
1985 ROOKIE AND FIRST-YEAR ROSTER

(1) Indicates player in previous NFL camp.
(2) Indicates player with USFL game experience.
(3) Indicates player in previous USFL camp.
(4) Indicates player with CFL game experience.
(5) Indicates player in previous CFL camp.
    All others classified as rookies.

Name	Pos.	Hgt.	Wgt.	Birth-date	College	How Acquired
Albright, Ira (2)	FB	5-11	253	1- 2-59	Northeastern State	FA
Alexander, Larry (1, 3)	DE	6-3	255	11-21-59	San Jose State	FA
Babyar, Chris	OG	6-4	264	6- 1-62	Illinois	D10
Bateson, Robert	LB	6-1	230	5-14-61	Cortland State	FA
Burkett, Chris	WR	6-4	202	8-23-62	Jackson State	D2a
Burroughs, Derrick	CB	6-1	176	5-18-62	Memphis State	D1a
Christy, Greg	OT	6-4	285	4-29-62	Pittsburgh	FA
Curry, Robert	NT	6-2	265	5-27-62	Missouri	FA
Davis, Russell (1)	TE	6-5	230	6-16-60	Maryland	FA
Devane, William (1)	NT	6-2	275	5-28-62	Clemson	FA
Emerson, Darryl (1)	WR	6-0	190	12-15-60	Maryland	FA
Everett, Emil	K	6-1	185	3- 2-62	Wittenberg	FA
Gallery, Jim (1)	K	6-1	193	9-15-61	Minnesota	FA
Garner, Hal	LB	6-4	219	1-18-62	Utah State	D3a
Gipson, Reggie (1)	RB	6-2	205	7-27-60	Alabama A&M	*FA '84
Gulley, Anthony	WR	6-1	200	1- 3-63	Texas Christian	FA
Hamby, Mike	DT	6-4	253	11- 2-62	Utah State	D6
Harbison, Charles (1, 2)	S	6-1	195	10-27-59	Gardner-Webb	FA
Haslett, Jon	LB	...	...	....	Clarion State	FA
Hellestrae, Dale	OT	6-5	261	7-11-62	Southern Methodist	D4a
Howard, Brian	G	6-1	275	....	Wyoming	FA
Howell, Leroy (1)	DE	6-4	260	11- 4-62	Appalachian State	*D9 '84
Johnson, Randy (2)	RB	5-11	210	4-11-62	Texas-Arlington	FA
Jones, Glenn	CB	5-10	170	12- 4-60	Norfolk State	D9
Johnston, Michael (1)	K	5-11	185	9-20-61	Notre Dame	FA
Lamar, Kevin	C	...	...	....		FA
Leavell, Mike	RB	6-0	220	....	Canisius	FA
Lowe, Kevin	RB	6-0	195	....	Wyoming	FA
Lyles, Rodney	LB	6-2	225	7-31-62	Michigan	FA
Norwood, Scott (1, 2)	K	6-0	207	7-17-60	James Madison	FA
Payne, Jimmy (1)	DE	6-4	265	2- 9-60	Georgia	*D4a '83
Perryman, James (2)	S	6-0	180	12-23-60	Millikin	FA
Phillips, Rudy (1, 4)	OL	6-3	240	2-25-58	North Texas State	FA
Pitts, Ron	CB	5-10	175	10-14-62	UCLA	D7
Potter, Richard	K	...	...	....		FA
Quinlivan, Gerry	LB	...	...	....	Buffalo	FA
Reed, Andre	WR	6-0	180	1-29-64	Kutztown State, Pa.	D4
Reich, Frank	QB	6-3	208	12- 4-61	Maryland	D3
Richardson, Eric (1)	WR	6-1	183	4-18-62	San Jose State	*D2 '84
Robinson, Jacque	RB	5-11	215	3- 5-63	Washington	D8
Sanchez, Emilio (1)	K	5-11	220	11- 8-59	Cal State-Fullerton	FA
Seawright, James	LB	6-2	219	3-30-62	South Carolina	D11
Smith, Bruce	DE	6-4	285	6-18-63	Virginia Tech	D1
Tate, Golden (1, 3)	WR	6-3	197	7- 5-60	Tennessee State	FA
Teal, Jimmy	WR	5-10	170	8-18-62	Texas A&M	D5
Thompson, Emmuel (1, 3)	CB	5-11	175	11-15-59	Texas A&I	FA
Tolliver, Mike (1)	WR	5-11	180	12-23-60	Stanford	FA
Traynowicz, Mark	OL	6-5	267	11-20-62	Nebraska	D2
Weiler, Mark	LB	...	...	....	Indiana	FA
Woodside, Paul	K	5-11	170	9- 2-63	West Virginia	D12

*Gipson and Richardson missed '84 season due to injury; Howell active for 1 game, did not play; Payne missed '83 and '84 seasons due to injury.

CHICAGO BEARS
(Central Division, National Conference)

Mike Ditka

Chairman of the Board—Edward McCaskey
President and Chief Executive Officer—Michael McCaskey
Vice-President, General Manager—Jerome Vainisi
Director of Player Personnel—Bill Tobin
Head Coach—Mike Ditka (3 years: 21-20)
Assistant Coaches:
    Research and Quality Control—Jim Dooley
    Defensive Line—Dale Haupt
    Offensive Coordinator—Ed Hughes
    Special Teams—Steve Kazor
    Defensive Backs—Jim LaRue
    Receivers—Ted Plumb
    Running Backs—Johnny Roland
    Defensive Coordinator—Buddy Ryan
    Offensive Line—Dick Stanfel
Coordinator of Media Relations—Ken Valdiserri
    (Office Phone 295-6600—Area Code 312)
Offices—55 East Jackson (Suite 1200), Chicago, Ill. 60604
Stadium—Soldier Field (Capacity: 65,793)
Team Colors—Orange, Navy Blue and White
Training Site—Halas Hall, Lake Forest, Ill.

1985 SCHEDULE
(All times local.
All games Sunday unless noted otherwise.)

Sept. 8	TAMPA BAY	12:00
Sept. 15	NEW ENGLAND	12:00
Sept. 19	at Minnesota (Thurs.)	7:00
Sept. 29	WASHINGTON	12:00
Oct. 6	at Tampa Bay	1:00
Oct. 13	at San Francisco	1:00
Oct. 21	GREEN BAY (Mon.)	8:00
Oct. 27	MINNESOTA	12:00
Nov. 3	at Green Bay	12:00
Nov. 10	DETROIT	12:00
Nov. 17	at Dallas	12:00
Nov. 24	ATLANTA	12:00
Dec. 2	at Miami (Mon.)	9:00
Dec. 8	INDIANAPOLIS	12:00
Dec. 14	at New York Jets (Sat.)	12:30
Dec. 22	at Detroit	1:00

1984 RESULTS—(Won 11, Lost 7)

Bears	Opp.		Att.
34 Tampa Bay	14	(H)	58,789
27 Denver	0	(H)	54,335
9 Green Bay	7	(A)	55,942
9 Seattle	38	(A)	61,520
14 Dallas	23	(H)	63,623
20 New Orleans	7	(H)	53,752
21 St. Louis	38	(A)	49,554
44 Tampa Bay	9	(A)	60,003
16 Minnesota	7	(H)	57,517
17 Los Angeles Raiders	6	(H)	59,858
13 Los Angeles Rams	29	(A)	62,021
16 Detroit	14	(H)	54,911
34 Minnesota	3	(A)	56,881
7 San Diego	20	(A)	45,470
14 Green Bay	20	(H)	59,374
30 Detroit	13	(A)	53,252

NFC SEMIFINAL GAME

23 Washington	19	(A)	55,431

NFC CHAMPIONSHIP GAME

0 San Francisco	23	(A)	61,040

1984 GAMES STARTED

16 games: Kurt Becker, Todd Bell, Jim Covert, Gary Fencik, Al Harris, Jay Hilgenberg, Steve McMichael, Walter Payton, Mike Singletary, Matt Suhey.

15 games: Mark Bortz, Willie Gault, Dan Hampton, Mike Richardson, Otis Wilson.

14 games: Mike Hartenstine, Keith Van Horne.

12 games: Dennis McKinnon.

11 games: Leslie Frazier.

10 games: Richard Dent.

9 games: Jim McMahon, Emery Moorehead.

7 games: Tyrone Keys, Jay Saldi.

6 games: Shaun Gayle.

4 games: Steve Fuller.

3 games: Brad Anderson.

2 games: Andy Frederick, Henry Waechter.

1 game: Bob Avellini, Brian Baschnagel, Jack Cameron, Rob Fada, Greg Landry, Rusty Lisch, Wilber Marshall.

CHICAGO BEARS 1985 VETERAN ROSTER

No.	Name	Pos.	Ht.	Wt.	NFL Exp.	Birth-date	College	Games in '84	How Acquired
86	Anderson, Brad	WR	6-2	196	2	1-21-61	Arizona	12	D8, '84
60	Andrews, Tom	C	6-4	261	2	1-11-62	Louisville	7	D4, '84
84	Baschnagel, Brian	WR	5-11	185	10	1-8-54	Ohio State	16	D3, '76
79	Becker, Kurt	G	6-5	270	4	12-22-58	Michigan	16	D6, '82
25	†Bell, Todd	S	6-1	205	5	11-28-58	Ohio State	16	D4, '81
62	Bortz, Mark	G	6-6	271	3	2-12-61	Iowa	15	D8a, '83
54	†Cabral, Brian	LB	6-1	227	7	6-23-56	Colorado	16	FA, '81
30	Cameron, Jack	WR	6-0	182	2	11-5-61	Winston-Salem State	16	OFA, '84
74	Covert, Jim	T	6-4	283	3	3-22-60	Pittsburgh	16	D1, '83
95	Dent, Richard	DE	6-5	253	3	12-13-60	Tennessee State	16	D8, '83
22	Duerson, Dave	S	6-1	205	3	11-28-60	Notre Dame	16	D3, '83
88	Dunsmore, Pat	TE	6-3	237	3	10-2-59	Drake	12	D4a, '83
64	Fada, Rob	G	6-2	272	3	5-7-61	Pittsburgh	13	D9, '83
45	Fencik, Gary	S	6-1	197	10	6-11-54	Yale	16	FA, '76
15	Finzer, Dave	P	6-0	195	2	2-3-59	DePauw	16	T-SD, '84
24	Fisher, Jeff	CB	5-10	195	5	2-25-58	Southern California	16	D7, '81
21	Frazier, Leslie	CB	6-0	189	5	4-3-59	Alcorn State	11	OFA, '81
71	Frederick, Andy	T	6-6	265	9	7-25-54	New Mexico	16	T-Cle, '83
4	Fuller, Steve	QB	6-4	195	7	1-5-57	Clemson	6	T-LA, '84
83	Gault, Willie	WR	6-0	178	3	9-5-60	Tennessee	16	D1a, '83
23	Gayle, Shaun	CB	5-11	191	2	3-8-62	Ohio State	15	D10, '84
29	Gentry, Dennis	RB	5-8	184	4	2-10-59	Baylor	16	D4, '82
	Gray, Kevin	S	5-11	179	2	9-11-57	Eastern Illinois	*0	FA, '85
99	Hampton, Dan	DT	6-5	266	7	9-19-57	Arkansas	15	D1, '79
90	†Harris, Al	LB	6-5	253	7	12-31-56	Arizona	16	D1a, '79
73	Hartenstine, Mike	DE	6-3	258	11	7-27-53	Penn State	16	D2, '75
63	Hilgenberg, Jay	C	6-3	255	5	3-21-59	Iowa	16	OFA, '81
75	Humphries, Stefan	G	6-3	265	2	1-20-62	Michigan	9	D3, '84
32	Hutchinson, Anthony	RB	5-10	186	3	2-4-61	Texas Tech	12	D10, '83
49	Jordan, Donald	RB	6-0	210	2	2-9-62	Houston	13	D12, '84
98	†Keys, Tyrone	DE	6-7	267	3	10-24-59	Mississippi State	15	T-NYJ, '83
89	Krenk, Mitch	TE	6-2	225	2	11-19-59	Nebraska	8	W-Dal, '84
12	Lisch, Rusty	QB	6-4	215	6	12-21-56	Notre Dame	7	FA, '84
82	†Margerum, Ken	WR	6-0	180	4	10-5-58	Stanford	*0	D3, '81
58	Marshall, Wilber	LB	6-1	225	2	4-18-62	Florida	15	D1, '84
85	McKinnon, Dennis	WR	6-1	185	3	8-22-61	Florida State	12	OFA, '83
9	McMahon, Jim	QB	6-1	185	4	8-21-59	Brigham Young	9	D1, '82
76	†McMichael, Steve	DT	6-2	263	6	10-17-57	Texas	16	FA, '81
87	†Moorehead, Emery	TE	6-2	225	9	3-22-54	Colorado	16	W-Den, '81
34	Payton, Walter	RB	5-10	202	11	7-25-54	Jackson State	16	D1, '75
	Potter, Kevin	S	5-10	188	2	12-19-59	Missouri	1	FA, '85
53	Rains, Dan	LB	6-1	222	3	4-26-56	Cincinnati	16	FA, '82
27	Richardson, Mike	CB	6-0	188	3	5-23-61	Arizona State	15	D2, '83
59	Rivera, Ron	LB	6-3	244	2	1-7-62	California	15	D2, '84
81	†Saldi, Jay	TE	6-3	227	10	10-8-54	South Carolina	15	T-Dal, '83
50	Singletary, Mike	LB	6-0	228	5	10-9-58	Baylor	16	D2, '81
26	Suhey, Matt	RB	5-11	216	6	7-7-58	Penn State	16	D2, '80
16	Thomas, Bob	K	5-10	177	10	8-7-52	Notre Dame	16	W-LA, '75
33	Thomas, Calvin	RB	5-11	235	4	1-7-60	Illinois	16	OFA '82
78	†Van Horne, Keith	T	6-6	265	5	11-6-57	Southern California	14	D1, '81
70	Waechter, Henry	DT	6-5	270	4	2-13-59	Nebraska	*3	FA, '84
55	Wilson, Otis	LB	6-2	231	6	9-15-57	Louisville	15	D1, '80

*Gray last active with New Orleans in '82 and Jacksonville (USFL) in '84; Margerum missed '84 season due to injury; Waechter played 1 game with Indianapolis, 2 with Chicago in '84.

†Option playout; subject to developments.

Retired—Jim Osborne, 13-year defensive tackle, 15 games in '84.

Also played with Bears in '84—QB Bob Avellini (4 games), QB Greg Landry (1), CB Terry Schmidt (15).

D—Draft; T—Trade; W—Waivers; FA—Free Agent; OFA—Original Free Agent.

CHICAGO BEARS
1985 DRAFT CHOICES

(Number following name designates order of selection among 336 players drafted.)

Round and Player		Position	College
1. PERRY, William	22	DT	Clemson
2. PHILLIPS, Reggie	49	DB	SMU
3. MANESS, James	78	WR	Texas Christian
4. BUTLER, Kevin	105	K	Georgia
5. Choice to New York Jets (a)			
6. Choice to Los Angeles Rams (b)			
7. BENNETT, Charles	190	DE	S.W. Louisiana
8. BUXTON, Steve	217	T	Indiana State
9. SANDERS, Thomas	250	RB	Texas A&M
10. CORYATT, Pat	273	DT	Baylor
11. MORRISSEY, James	302	LB	Michigan State
12. Choice to San Diego (c)			

(a) Traded pick for rights to defensive end Tyrone Keys, July 13, 1983.

(b) Traded pick and 11th round pick in 1984 for quarterback Steve Fuller, April 30, 1984.

(c) Traded pick for punter David Finzer, August 15, 1984.

CHICAGO BEARS
1985 ROOKIE AND FIRST-YEAR ROSTER

(1) Indicates player in previous NFL camp.
(2) Indicates player with USFL game experience.
(3) Indicates player in previous USFL camp.
(4) Indicates player with CFL game experience.
(5) Indicates player in previous CFL camp.
   All others classified as rookies.

Name	Pos.	Hgt.	Wgt.	Birth-date	College	How Acquired
Bennett, Charles	DT	6-5	250	2- 9-63	Southwestern Louisiana	D7
Butler, Kevin	K	6-1	190	7-24-62	Georgia	D4
Buxton, Steve	G/T	6-6	268	12-23-61	Indiana State	D8
Christopher, John (1, 3)	P	6-3	205	12-10-60	Moorehead State	FA
Clayton, Rozell	FB	6-1	217	7-24-62	Memphis State	FA
Coryatt, Pat	DT	6-2	287	6-18-61	Baylor	D10
Cruz, Ken	QB	6-1	190	12-13-61	Illinois	FA
Feldt, Mike	DB	6-1	200	9-11-62	Texas	FA
Foster, Deno	WR	6-3	185	1-16-62	Cincinnati	FA
Hanna, Barry	TE	6-2	232	11-24-62	Oklahoma State	FA
Heathcock, Bill	DT	6-5	260	9-21-62	Texas	FA
Hill, John	DB	5-10	180	7- 3-62	Duke	FA
Jackson, Jackie	RB	6-0	185	7-20-63	Southwestern	FA
Johnson, Stan	WR	6-3	200	9-16-63	Wisconsin/La Crosse	FA
Kallmeyer, Bruce (1)	PK	5-10	180	2- 8-62	Kansas	FA
Kindt, Don	TE	6-7	250	3- 9-61	Wisconsin/La Crosse	FA
Kingrey, Bill	DE	6-2	215	10-12-62	McNeese State	FA
Lombardi, Tony	FB	5-11	208	1-29-62	Arizona State	FA
Long, Matt (1)	C	6-3	265	3-16-61	San Diego State	FA
Maness, James	WR	6-1	174	5- 1-63	Texas Christian	D3
Miller, Ken (1, 4)	DB	5-11	180	6-24-58	Eastern Michigan	FA
Morrissey, Jim	LB	6-2	207	12-24-62	Michigan State	D11
Newell, Shaun (1)	DT/DE	6-3	257	2-26-62	Utah	*FA '84
Norman, Tim (1, 2)	G	6-6	270	7-10-59	Illinois	*FA '84
Ortego, Keith	WR	6-0	178	8-30-63	McNeese State	FA
Perry, William	DT	6-3	318	12-16-62	Clemson	D1
Phillips, Eddie (1, 3)	RB	5-11	208	2-23-61	Iowa	FA
Phillips, Reggie	DB	5-10	168	12-12-60	Southern Methodist	D2
Price, Jeff	WR	6-0	195	4-18-63	Purdue	FA
Ramunno, Joe	T	6-3	265	2- 1-62	Wyoming	FA
Riccio, Kevin (1)	TE	6-5	240	5-26-61	Virginia	FA
Robinson, Roger	CB	6-3	185	8- 6-62	Tennessee State	FA
Rowell, Eugene (1, 3)	OL/DT	6-3	265	2-15-58	Dubuque	D9
Sanders, Thomas	RB	5-11	195	1- 4-62	Texas A&M	D9
Spivak, Joe (3)	G	6-0	280	2-19-62	Illinois State	FA
Stewart, Ricky	FB	5-10	219	3- 1-62	McNeese State	FA
Stoops, Mike	DB	6-2	182	12-13-61	Iowa	FA
Storey, Kenneth	WR	6-2	185	11- 9-60	Cameron College, Okla.	FA
Taylor, Ken	CB	6-1	185	9- 2-63	Oregon State	FA
Thomas, Anthony	FB	5-10	195	11-15-62	Abilene Christian	FA
Tomczak, Mike	QB	6-1	192	10-23-62	Ohio State	FA
Viracola, Mike	P	5-11	180	6-28-62	Notre Dame	FA
Ward, Rick	K	6-2	210	4- 5-62	East Oregon State	FA
Wrightman, Tim (2)	TE	6-3	233	3-27-60	UCLA	D3 '82

*Newell and Norman missed '84 season due to injury.

CINCINNATI BENGALS
(Central Division, American Conference)

Sam Wyche

Chairman of the Board—Austin E. Knowlton
President—John Sawyer
Vice-President, General Manager—Paul E. Brown
Assistant General Manager—Michael Brown
Director of Player Personnel—Pete Brown
Assistant Director of Player Personnel—Frank Smouse
Head Coach—Sam Wyche (1 year: 8-8)
Assistant Coaches:
    Offensive Backfield—Jim Anderson
    Wide Receivers—Bruce Coslet
    Tight Ends—Bill Johnson
    Defensive Coord./Def. Backs—Dick LeBeau
    Offensive Line—Jim McNally
    Linebackers—Dick Selcer
    Defensive Line—Bill Urbanik
    Strength—Kim Wood
Director of Public Relations—Allan Heim
    (Office Phone: 621-3550—Area Code 513)
Offices—200 Riverfront Stadium, Cincinnati, O. 45202
Stadium—Riverfront Stadium (Capacity: 59,754)
Team Colors—Orange, Black and White
Training Site—Wilmington College, Wilmington, O.

1985 SCHEDULE
(All times local.
All games Sunday unless noted otherwise.)

Sept. 8	SEATTLE	1:00
Sept. 15	at St. Louis	12:00
Sept. 22	SAN DIEGO	1:00
Sept. 30	at Pittsburgh (Mon.)	9:00
Oct. 6	NEW YORK JETS	4:00
Oct. 13	NEW YORK GIANTS	1:00
Oct. 20	at Houston	12:00
Oct. 27	PITTSBURGH	4:00
Nov. 3	at Buffalo	1:00
Nov. 10	CLEVELAND	1:00
Nov. 17	at Los Angeles Raiders	1:00
Nov. 24	at Cleveland	1:00
Dec. 1	HOUSTON	1:00
Dec. 8	DALLAS	1:00
Dec. 15	at Washington	1:00
Dec. 22	at New England	1:00

1984 RESULTS—(Won 8, Lost 8)

Bengals		Opp.		Att.
17	Denver	20	(A)	74,178
22	Kansas City	27	(H)	47,111
23	New York Jets	43	(A)	64,193
14	Los Angeles Rams	24	(H)	45,406
17	Pittsburgh	38	(A)	57,098
13	Houston	3	(H)	43,637
14	New England	20	(A)	48,154
12	Cleveland	9	(H)	50,667
31	Houston	13	(A)	34,010
17	San Francisco	23	(A)	58,324
22	Pittsburgh	20	(H)	52,497
6	Seattle	26	(H)	50,280
35	Atlanta	14	(H)	44,678
20	Cleveland (OT)	17	(A)	51,774
24	New Orleans	21	(A)	40,855
52	Buffalo	21	(H)	55,771

1984 GAMES STARTED

16 games: Ross Browner, Eddie Edwards, M.L. Harris, Robert Jackson, Tim Krumrie, Anthony Munoz, Dave Rimington, Reggie Williams, Mike Wilson.

15 games: Louis Breeden, Max Montoya.

14 games: Brian Blados, Glenn Cameron, Cris Collinsworth.

13 games: Issac Curtis, Ray Horton.

12 games: Charles Alexander.

11 games: James Brooks, Jeff Schuh, Ron Simpkins.

9 games: Ken Anderson.

8 games: Bobby Kemp, Jim Turner.

5 games: Guy Frazier, Rick Razzano.

4 games: Boomer Esiason, Stanford Jennings, Larry Kinnebrew.

3 games: Steve Kreider, Turk Schonert.

2 games: Ray Griffin, Rodney Holman, Steve Maidlow, John Simmons, Gary Smith.

1 game: Bruce Kozerski, Gary Williams.

CINCINNATI BENGALS 1985 VETERAN ROSTER

No.	Name	Pos.	Ht.	Wt.	NFL Exp.	Birth-date	College	Games in '84	How Acquired
40	Alexander, Charles	RB	6-1	226	7	7-28-57	Louisiana State	16	D1a, '79
14	Anderson, Ken	QB	6-3	212	15	2-15-49	Augustana, Ill.	11	D3, '71
53	Barker, Leo	LB	6-1	221	2	11-7-59	New Mexico State	16	D7, '84
74	Blados, Brian	T	6-4	295	2	1-11-62	North Carolina	16	D1b, '84
	Bird, Steve	WR	5-11	176	3	10-20-60	Eastern Kentucky	*9	FA, '85
61	Boyarsky, Jerry	NT	6-3	290	5	5-15-59	Pittsburgh	15	FA, '82
3	Breech, Jim	K	5-6	161	7	4-11-56	California	16	FA, '80
34	Breeden, Louis	CB	5-11	185	8	10-26-53	North Carolina Central	16	D7, '77
21	Brooks, James	RB	5-10	182	5	12-28-58	Auburn	15	T-SD, '84
50	Cameron, Glenn	LB	6-2	228	11	2-21-53	Florida	16	D1, '75
76	Collins, Glen	DE	6-6	265	4	7-10-59	Mississippi State	16	D1, '82
80	Collinsworth, Cris	WR	6-5	192	5	1-27-59	Florida	15	D2, '81
85	Curtis, Isaac	WR	6-1	192	13	10-20-50	San Diego State	16	D1, '73
73	Edwards, Eddie	DE	6-5	256	9	4-25-54	Miami, Fla.	16	D1, '77
7	Esiason, Boomer	QB	6-4	220	2	4-17-61	Maryland	10	D2, '84
33	Farley, John	RB	5-10	202	2	8-11-61	Cal State-Sacramento	13	D4, '84
58	Frazier, Guy	LB	6-2	221	5	7-20-59	Wyoming	16	D4, '81
22	Griffin, James	S	6-2	197	3	9-7-61	Middle Tennessee State	16	D7, '83
83	Harris, M.L.	TE	6-5	238	6	1-16-54	Kansas State	16	FA, '80
27	Hicks, Bryan	S	6-0	192	4	1-24-57	McNeese State	*0	D5, '80
82	Holman, Rodney	TE	6-3	232	4	4-20-60	Tulane	16	D3, '82
20	Horton, Ray	CB	5-11	190	3	4-12-60	Washington	15	D2, '83
37	Jackson, Robert	S	5-10	186	4	10-10-58	Central Michigan	16	D11, '81
36	Jennings, Stanford	RB	6-1	205	2	3-12-62	Furman	15	D3, '84
26	Kemp, Bobby	S	6-0	191	5	5-29-59	Cal State-Fullerton	10	D8, '81
89	Kern, Don	TE	6-4	225	2	8-25-62	Arizona State	16	D6, '84
28	Kinnebrew, Larry	RB	6-1	252	2	6-11-59	Tennessee State	16	D6, '83
71	Koch, Pete	NT	6-6	265	2	1-23-62	Maryland	16	D1a, '84
64	Kozerski, Bruce	C	6-4	275	2	4-2-62	Holy Cross	16	D9, '84
86	Kreider, Steve	WR	6-3	192	7	5-12-58	Lehigh	16	D6, '79
69	Krumrie, Tim	NT	6-2	262	3	5-20-60	Wisconsin	16	D10, '83
55	Maidlow, Steve	LB	6-2	234	3	6-6-60	Michigan State	16	D4, '83
88	Martin, Mike	WR	5-10	186	3	11-18-60	Illinois	15	D8, '83
87	McInally, Pat	P	6-6	212	10	5-7-53	Harvard	16	D5, '75
65	Montoya, Max	G	6-5	275	7	5-12-56	UCLA	16	D7, '79
78	Munoz, Anthony	T	6-6	278	6	8-19-58	Southern California	16	D1, '80
68	Obrovac, Mike	G	6-6	275	4	10-11-55	Bowling Green	*0	FA, '81
42	Pickering, Clay	WR	6-5	215	2	6-2-61	Maine	3	OFA, '84
75	Reimers, Bruce	T	6-7	280	2	9-18-60	Iowa State	15	D8, '84
52	Rimington, Dave	C	6-3	288	3	8-13-62	Nebraska	16	D1, '83
15	Schonert, Turk	QB	6-1	190	6	1-15-57	Stanford	8	W-Chi, '80
59	Schuh, Jeff	LB	6-2	229	5	5-22-58	Minnesota	16	D7, '80
25	Simmons, John	CB	5-11	192	5	12-1-58	Southern Methodist	16	D3, '81
56	Simpkins, Ron	LB	6-1	235	5	4-2-58	Michigan	16	D7, '80
62	Smith, Gary	G	6-2	265	2	1-27-60	Virginia Tech	8	FA, '84
35	Turner, Jimmy	CB	6-0	187	3	6-15-59	UCLA	16	D3, '83
81	Verser, David	WR	6-1	202	5	3-1-58	Kansas	11	D1, '81
84	†Williams, Gary	WR	6-2	215	2	9-4-59	Ohio State	8	D11, '83
57	Williams, Reggie	LB	6-0	228	10	9-19-54	Dartmouth	16	D3a, '76
77	Wilson, Mike	T	6-5	271	8	5-28-55	Georgia	16	D4a, '77
32	Wilson, Stanley	RB	5-10	210	2	8-23-61	Oklahoma	1	D9, '83

*Hicks and Obrovac missed '84 season due to injury; Bird played 8 games with St. Louis, 1 with San Diego in '84.

†Option playout; subject to developments.

Also played with Bengals in '84—S Ralph Battle (3 games), DE Ross Browner (16), DE Ross Browner (16), QB Bryan Clark (1), CB Ray Griffin (12), LB Brian Pillman (6), LB Rick Razzano (10).

D—Draft; T—Trade; W—Waivers; FA—Free Agent; OFA—Original Free Agent.

CINCINNATI BENGALS
1985 DRAFT CHOICES

(Number following name designates order of selection among 336 players drafted.)

Round and Player		Position	College
1. BROWN, Eddie	13	WR	Miami, Fla.
1. KING, Emanuel from Seattle (a)	25	LB	Alabama
2. ZANDER, Carl	43	LB	Tennessee
3. THOMAS, Sean	70	DB	Texas Christian
4. TUGGLE, Anthony	97	DB	Nicholls State
5. DEGRATE, Tony	127	DT	Texas
5. DAVIS, Lee from New England (b)	129	DB	Mississippi
6. STOKES, Eric from Tampa Bay (c)	148	T	Northeastern
6. LESTER, Keith	154	TE	Murray State
7. LOCKLIN, Kim from Atlanta (d)	172	RB	New Mexico St.
7. WALTER, Joe	181	T	Texas Tech
8. STROBEL, Dave	211	LB	Iowa
9. CRUISE, Keith	238	DE	Northwestern
10. KING, Bernard	265	LB	Syracuse
11. STANFIELD, Harold	296	TE	Mississippi Col.
12. GARZA, Louis	322	T	New Mexico St.

(a) Acquired pick for center Blair Bush, June 29, 1983.
(b) Acquired pick, two 1st round picks in 1984 and 10th round pick in 1984 for 1st round pick in 1984, April 4, 1984.
(c) Acquired pick for tackle Don Swafford, July 24, 1984.
(d) Acquired pick for nose tackle Gary Burley, August 23, 1984.

CINCINNATI BENGALS
1985 ROOKIE AND FIRST-YEAR ROSTER

(1) Indicates player in previous NFL camp.
(2) Indicates player with USFL game experience.
(3) Indicates player in previous USFL camp.
(4) Indicates player with CFL game experience.
(5) Indicates player in previous CFL camp.
    All others classified as rookies.

Name	Pos.	Hgt.	Wgt.	Birth-date	College	How Acquired
Brown, Eddie	WR	6-0	185	12-18-62	Miami (Fla.)	D1
Collins, Larry	RB	6-1	220	10-30-63	Rice	FA
Cruise, Keith	DE	6-3	260	1-17-63	Northwestern	D9
Davis, Lee	CB	5-11	198	12-18-62	Mississippi	D5a
Degrate, Tony	NT	6-3	287	4-25-62	Texas	D5
Garza, Louis	T	6-3	300	11-17-62	New Mexico State	D12
King, Bernard	LB	6-0	228	7- 5-62	Syracuse	D10
King, Emanuel	LB	6-4	245	8-15-63	Alabama	D1a
Kinlaw, Rodney	NT	6-1	280	7-31-62	Fayetteville State	FA
Lester, Keith	TE	6-4	241	5-28-62	Murray State	D6a
Lewis, Mike (1)	WR	6-3	185	2- 2-61	Maryland	FA
Locklin, Kim	RB	5-11	200	11-21-63	New Mexico State	D7
Peace, Wayne (2)	QB	6-2	215	11- 3-61	Florida	SupD. '84
Rogers, Rick	RB	6-1	210	3-26-63	Michigan	FA
Simmons, Victor (1)	WR	6-3	194	11- 5-60	Oregon State	FA
Singleton, John (1, 3, 4)	DE	6-6	270	12-22-56	Texas-El Paso	FA
Smith, Darrell (1)	WR	6-2	195	11- 5-61	Central State-Ohio	FA
Stanfield, Harold	TE	6-3	238	1- 1-63	Mississippi College	D11
Stokes, Eric	T	6-3	285	1-13-62	Northeastern	D6
Strobel, Dave	LB	6-3	230	4- 3-62	Iowa	D8
Thomas, Sean	CB	6-0	290	4-12-62	Texas Christian	D3
Tuggle, Anthony	CB	6-0	211	9-16-63	Nicholls State	D4
Walter, Joe	T	6-5	290	6-18-63	Texas Tech	D7a
Zander, Carl	LB	6-2	235	3-23-63	Tennessee	D2

CLEVELAND BROWNS
(Central Division, American Conference)

Marty Schottenheimer

President—Arthur B. Modell
Executive Vice-President, Legal and Admin.—James Bailey
Executive Vice-President/Football Operations—Ernie Accorsi
Director of Player Relations—Paul Warfield
Vice President/Director of Personnel—Bill Davis
Vice President/Director of Finance—Mike Poplar
Vice President/Director of Public Relations—Kevin Byrne
  (Office Phone: 696-5555—Area Code 216)
Director of Pro Personnel—Chip Falivene
Director of Operations—Denny Lynch
Head Coach—Marty Schottenheimer (1 year: 4-4)
Assistant Coaches:
  Defensive Coordinator/Secondary—Tom Bettis
  Special Teams—Bill Cowher
  Asst. to Head Coach/Offense—Steve Crosby
  Quarterbacks—Greg Landry
  Receivers—Richard Mann
  Offensive Line—Howard Mudd
  Linebackers—Tom Olivadotti
  Offensive Coordinator—Joe Pendry
  Defensive Line—Tom Pratt
  Strength and Conditioning—Dave Redding
  Film Coordinator—Eddie Ulinski
  Special Assistant—Darvin Wallis
Offices—Cleveland Stadium, Cleveland, O. 44114
Stadium—Cleveland Stadium (Capacity: 80,098)
Team Colors—Brown, Orange and White
Training Site—Lakeland Community College, Mentor, O.

1985 SCHEDULE
(All times local.
All games Sunday unless noted otherwise.)

Sept. 8	ST. LOUIS	1:00
Sept. 16	PITTSBURGH (Mon.)	9:00
Sept. 22	at Dallas	12:00
Sept. 29	at San Diego	1:00
Oct. 6	NEW ENGLAND	1:00
Oct. 13	at Houston	12:00
Oct. 20	LOS ANGELES RAIDERS	1:00
Oct. 27	WASHINGTON	1:00
Nov. 3	at Pittsburgh	1:00
Nov. 10	at Cincinnati	1:00
Nov. 17	BUFFALO	1:00
Nov. 24	CINCINNATI	1:00
Dec. 1	at New York Giants	1:00
Dec. 8	at Seattle	1:00
Dec. 15	HOUSTON	1:00
Dec. 22	at New York Jets	1:00

1984 RESULTS—(Won 5, Lost 11)

Browns		Opp.		Att.
0	Seattle	33	(A)	59,540
17	Los Angeles Rams	20	(A)	43,043
14	Denver	24	(H)	61,980
20	Pittsburgh	10	(H)	77,312
6	Kansas City	10	(A)	40,785
16	New England	17	(H)	53,036
20	New York Jets	24	(H)	55,673
9	Cincinnati	12	(A)	50,667
14	New Orleans	16	(H)	52,489
13	Buffalo	10	(A)	33,343
7	San Francisco	41	(H)	60,092
23	Atlanta	7	(A)	28,280
27	Houston	10	(H)	46,077
17	Cincinnati (OT)	20	(H)	51,774
20	Pittsburgh	23	(A)	55,825
27	Houston	20	(A)	33,676

1984 GAMES STARTED

16 games: Mike Baab, Keith Baldwin, Chip Banks, Reggie Camp, Tom Cousineau, Joe DeLamielleure, Doug Dieken, Hanford Dixon, Al Gross, Robert Jackson, Eddie Johnson, Clay Matthews, Paul McDonald.

15 games: Bob Golic, Ozzie Newsome.

14 games: Don Rogers.

12 games: Frank Minnifield.

11 games: Duriel Harris.

10 games: Boyce Green.

9 games: Rickey Bolden, Bill Contz.

8 games: Harry Holt.

7 games: Mike Pruitt.

6 games: Paul Farren.

4 games: Brian Brennan, Johnny Davis.

3 games: Earnest Byner, Ricky Feacher, Lawrence Johnson.

2 games: Chris Rockins.

1 game: Willis Adams, Larry Braziel, Bruce Davis, George Lilja, Dave Puzzuoli, Tim Stracka, Dwight Walker, Charles White, Glen Young.

CLEVELAND BROWNS 1985 VETERAN ROSTER

No.	Name	Pos.	Ht.	Wt.	NFL Exp.	Birth-date	College	Games in '84	How Acquired
80	Adams, Willis	TE-WR	6-2	200	6	8-22-56	Houston	16	D1, '79
52	Ambrose, Dick	LB	6-0	228	10	1-17-53	Virginia	*0	D12, '75
53	†Anderson, Stuart	LB	6-1	225	4	12-25-59	Virginia	*6	FA, '84
61	Baab, Mike	C	6-4	270	4	12- 6-59	Texas	16	D5, '82
9	Bahr, Matt	K	5-10	175	7	7- 6-56	Penn State	16	T-SF, '81
99	Baldwin, Keith	DE	6-4	270	4	10-13-60	Texas A&M	16	D2, '82
56	Banks, Chip	LB	6-4	233	4	9-18-59	Southern California	16	D1, '82
24	Best, Greg	S	5-10	185	3	1-14-60	Kansas State	5	FA, '84
88	Bolden, Rickey	T-TE	6-6	250	2	9- 8-61	Southern Methodist	12	D4, '84
47	†Braziel, Larry	CB	6-0	184	7	9-25-54	Southern California	13	FA, '82
86	Brennan, Brian	WR	5-9	178	2	2-15-62	Boston College	15	D4a, '84
	Brown, Aaron	LB	6-2	235	4	1-13-56	Ohio State	*0	FA, '85
49	Burrell, Clinton	S	6-1	192	6	9- 4-56	Louisiana State	13	D6, '79
44	Byner, Earnest	RB	5-10	215	2	9-15-62	East Carolina	16	D10, '84
96	Camp, Reggie	DE	6-4	270	3	2-28-61	California	16	D3, '83
75	Contz, Bill	T	6-5	260	3	5-12-61	Penn State	15	D5, '83
50	Cousineau, Tom	LB	6-3	225	4	5- 6-57	Ohio State	16	T-Buf., '82
15	Cox, Steve	P-K	6-4	195	5	5-11-58	Arkansas	16	D5, '81
	Danielson, Gary	QB	6-2	196	9	9-10-51	Purdue	*15	T-Det., '85
85	Davis, Bruce	WR	5-8	160	2	2-25-63	Baylor	14	D2a, '84
38	Davis, Johnny	FB	6-1	235	8	7-17-56	Alabama	16	FA, '82
64	DeLamielleure, Joe	G	6-3	260	13	3-16-51	Michigan State	16	T-Buf., '80
29	†Dixon, Hanford	CB	5-11	182	5	12-25-58	Southern Mississippi	16	D1, '81
74	Farren, Paul	T	6-5	260	3	12-24-60	Boston University	15	D12, '83
83	Feacher, Ricky	WR	5-10	180	10	2-11-54	Mississippi Valley State	16	FA, '76
10	Flick, Tom	QB	6-3	190	4	8-30-58	Washington	1	FA, '84
94	Franks, Elvis	DE	6-4	265	6	7- 9-57	Morgan State	16	D5, '80
79	Golic, Bob	NT	6-2	260	6	10-26-57	Notre Dame	15	FA, '82
30	Green, Boyce	RB	5-11	215	3	6-24-60	Carson-Newman	16	D11, '83
27	Gross, Al	S	6-3	186	3	1- 4-61	Arizona	16	W-Dal., '83
78	Hairston, Carl	DE	6-4	260	10	12-15-52	Maryland (E. Shore)	16	T-Phi., '84
81	Holt, Harry	TE	6-4	230	3	12-29-57	Arizona	12	FA, '83
68	Jackson, Robert	G	6-5	260	11	4- 1-53	Duke	16	OFA, '75
51	Johnson, Eddie	LB	6-1	215	5	2- 3-59	Louisville	16	D7, '81
1	Johnson, Nate	WR-KR	6-0	195	2	5-12-57	Hillsdale, Mich.	*0	FA, '85
90	Jones, Willie	DE	6-4	257	4	11-22-57	Florida State	*0	FA, '85
77	Lewis, Darryl	TE	6-6	226	2	4-16-61	Texas-Arlington	2	FA, '84
62	Lilja, George	T	6-4	262	4	3- 3-58	Michigan	*7	FA, '84
59	Marshall, David	LB	6-3	220	2	1- 3-61	Eastern Michigan	16	FA, '85
57	Matthews, Clay	LB	6-2	235	8	3-15-56	Southern California	16	D1, '78
16	McDonald, Paul	QB	6-2	185	6	2-23-58	Southern California	16	D4a, '80
31	Minnifield, Frank	CB	5-9	180	2	1- 1-60	Louisville	15	FA, '84
82	Newsome, Ozzie	TE	6-2	232	8	3-16-56	Alabama	16	D1a, '78
58	Nicolas, Scott	LB	6-3	226	4	8- 7-60	Miami, Fla.	16	D12, '82
7	Nugent, Terry	QB	6-4	218	2	12- 5-61	Colorado State	*0	D6, '84
	Oatis, Victor	WR	6-0	184	2	1- 6-59	Northwestern (La.) St.	*0	FA, '85
43	Pruitt, Mike	FB	6-0	225	10	4- 3-54	Purdue	10	D1, '76
72	Puzzuoli, Dave	NT	6-3	260	3	1-12-61	Pittsburgh	16	D6a, '83
63	Risien, Cody	T	6-7	280	6	3-22-57	Texas A&M	*0	D7, '79
37	Rockins, Chris	S	6-0	195	2	5-18-62	Oklahoma State	16	D2, '84
20	Rogers, Don	S	6-1	206	2	9-17-62	UCLA	15	D1, '84
87	Stracka, Tim	TE	6-3	225	3	9-27-59	Wisconsin	6	D6, '83
12	Taylor, Jim Bob	QB	6-2	200	2	9- 9-59	Georgia Tech	*0	FA, '85
89	Walker, Dwight	WR	5-10	185	4	1-10-59	Nicholls State	11	D4, '82
	Watts, Rickey	WR	6-1	203	7	5-16-57	Tulsa	*0	FA, '85
55	Weathers, Curtis	LB	6-5	230	7	9-16-56	Mississippi	16	D9a, '79
21	Whitwell, Mike	S	6-0	175	3	11-14-58	Texas A&M	*0	D6, '82
84	Young, Glen	WR-KR	6-2	205	3	10-11-60	Mississippi State	2	FA, '84

*Ambrose was physically unable to perform in '84; Anderson played 2 games with Washington and 4 with Cleveland in '84; Brown last active with Tampa Bay in '80 and Winnipeg (CFL) in '84; Danielson played 15 games with Detroit in '84; N. Johnson last active with N.Y. Giants in '80 and Calgary (CFL) in '84; Jones last active with Oakland in '81 and Saskatchewan (CFL) in '84; Lilja played 3 games with N.Y. Jets and 4 with Cleveland in '84; Nugent active for 16 games, but did not play; Oatis missed '84 season due to injury with Indianapolis; Risien and Whitwell missed '84 season due to injury; Taylor last active with Baltimore in '83; Watts missed '84 season due to injury with Chicago.

†Option playout; subject to developments.

Retired—Tom DeLeone, 13-year center, 15 games in '84; Doug Dieken, 14-year tackle, 16 games in '84; Rod Perry, 10-year cornerback, 8 games in '84.

Also played with Browns in '84—RB James Black (2 games), KR Preston Brown (2), LB Jim Dumont (12), WR Duriel Harris (11), CB Lawrence Johnson (6), T Ted Petersen (4), RB Charles White (10).

D-Draft; T—Trade; W—Waivers; FA—Free Agent; OFA—Original Free Agent.

CLEVELAND BROWNS
1985 DRAFT CHOICES

(Number following name designates order of selection among 336 players drafted.)

Round and Player		Position	College
1. Choice to Green Bay thru Buffalo (a)			
2. ALLEN, Greg	35	RB	Florida State
3. Choice to Buffalo (b)			
4. Choice to Miami (c)			
5. Choice to Dallas through Buffalo (d)			
6. KREROWICZ, Mark	147	G	Ohio State
7. LANGHORNE, Reginald	175	WR	Elizabeth City St.
8. BANKS, Fred	203	WR	Liberty Baptist
9. Choice to Philadelphia (e)			
10. WILLIAMS, Larry	259	G	Notre Dame
11. TUCKER, Travis	287	TE	Southern Conn.
12. SWANSON, Shane	315	WR	Nebraska

(a) Browns traded pick, 3rd round pick and 6th round pick in 1986 to Bills for first pick in supplemental draft, April 9, 1985; Bills traded pick and 4th round pick in 1986 to Packers for 1st and 2nd round picks, April 30, 1985.

(b) See first part of (a).

(c) Traded pick for wide receiver Duriel Harris, March 27, 1984.

(d) Browns traded pick, 1st round pick in 1983 and 3rd round pick in 1984 to Bills for linebacker Tom Cousineau, April 23, 1982; Bills traded pick and conditional 1986 pick to Cowboys for cornerback Rod Hill and 5th round pick, August 23, 1984.

(e) Traded pick for defensive end Carl Hairston, February 9, 1984.

CLEVELAND BROWNS
1985 ROOKIE AND FIRST-YEAR ROSTER

(1) Indicates player in previous NFL camp.
(2) Indicates player with USFL game experience.
(3) Indicates player in previous USFL camp.
(4) Indicates player with CFL game experience.
(5) Indicates player in previous CFL camp.
  All others classified as rookies.

Name	Pos.	Hgt.	Wgt.	Birth-date	College	How Acquired
Addison, Chuck	WR-KR	6-3	200	8-31-60	Delaware State	FA
Allen, Greg	RB	6-0	200	6- 4-63	Florida State	D2
Banks, Fred	WR	5-10	177	5-26-62	Liberty Baptist	D8
Black, James (1)	RB	5-11	198	4- 3-62	Akron	FA
Blair, Anthony	WR	5-11	170	9- 9-57	Tennessee	FA
Bolzan, Scott (1, 3)	T	6-3	270	7-25-62	Northern Illinois	FA
Bond, John (4)	TE	6-4	210	3-19-61	Mississippi State	Supp. '84
Boone, Jamie (2)	CB-S	6-0	205	3- 6-59	Miami (Fla.)	FA
Brown, Greg (1, 3)	LB	6-2	225	12-27-61	Miami (Fla.)	FA
Brunot, Rick (1)	T	6-4	250	11- 6-61	Youngstown, Ohio	FA
Carpenter, Dean (1)	K	5-10	175	10- 6-59	Chicago	FA
Collier, Steve	DE	6-6	304	4-19-63	Bethune-Cookman	FA
Colson, Eddie	FB	5-10	228	9- 8-63	North Carolina	FA
Craver, Jon (1)	LB	6-3	240	3-24-61	James Madison	FA
Daly, Ray	CB-S	5-11	195	12- 9-62	Virginia	FA
Daum, Mark	LB	6-4	237	2-26-62	Nebraska	FA
Fontenot, Herman	WR	6-0	206	9-12-63	Louisiana State	FA
Gambrell, Michael (1)	C-G	6-3	262	7-24-62	Louisiana State	FA
Goedecker, Mike (2)	LB	6-1	225	8-25-59	Miami (Fla.)	FA
Hamilton, Waymon (2)	FB	6-0	227	5-31-61	Brigham Young	FA
Harrison, Marck (2)	RB	5-7	186	4-20-61	Wisconsin	FA
Hayes, Nat	LB	6-0	225	2-17-62	Wichita State	FA
Hicks, Randy	DE	6-3	235	12-10-61	Kent State	FA
Hill, Troy (2)	CB-S	5-11	174	2-18-62	Pittsburgh	FA
Hoggard, Dee Dee (1)	CB	6-0	188	5-20-61	North Carolina State	FA
Hunter, Keith	CB-S	5-11	199	5-16-61	Iowa	FA
Jefferson, Pernell	CB-S	5-9	190	6- 4-63	Guilford, N.C.	FA
Kenebrew, Len	WR	6-3	188	7-11-62	Indiana	FA
Krerowicz, Mark	G	6-4	285	3- 1-63	Ohio State	D6
Langhorne, Reginald	WR	6-1	203	4- 7-63	Elizabeth City State	D7
Lee, Tony (2)	K	6-1	180	10- 7-61	Toledo	FA
Lewis, Fred	LB	6-3	228	7-25-62	Louisiana State	FA
Mack, Kevin (2)	RB	6-0	212	8- 9-62	Clemson	Supp. '84
McCormick, Glenn (2)	C-G	6-5	257	1-28-60	Arizona	FA
Minor, Terry	CB-S	6-2	202	5-28-62	Knoxville College	FA
Moore, Glen	RB	5-11	203	3-20-61	Syracuse	FA
Morrill, David	NT	6-2	260	4-27-63	Ohio State	FA
Otte, Richard (1)	WR	5-11	185	8- 6-61	NE Missouri State	FA
Polenz, Mark (1)	C-G	6-5	270	6- 3-61	Central Michigan	FA
St. Louis, Todd (1)	RB-KR	5-10	195	7-18-62	Augustana (S.D.)	FA
Shakepeare, Stanley	WR	6-0	169	2- 5-63	Miami (Fla.)	FA
Siegrist, Ernest	TE	6-2	220	9- 5-62	East Stroudsburg	FA
Sikora, Robert (1)	T	6-8	285	6-14-62	Indiana	*FA '84
Simecka, Bennie	C	6-4	282	2-28-62	Kansas	FA
Simko, Jack	C	6-4	212	11-29-63	Syracuse	FA
Swanson, Shane	WR-KR	5-9	195	10- 4-62	Nebraska	D12
Taylor, Henry	LB	5-10	225	9-24-63	Florida State	FA
Tolle, Stewart	NT	6-3	265	2- 7-62	Bowling Green	FA
Tripoli, Paul	CB-S	6-0	197	12-14-61	Alabama	FA
Tucker, Travis	TE	6-3	227	9-19-63	South Connecticut State	D11
Vernasco, John (1)	QB	6-2	200	2- 8-61	Evansville	FA
White, James	T	6-3	245	7- 5-62	Louisiana State	FA
Williams, Larry	G	6-5	269	7- 3-63	Notre Dame	D10
Wright, Felix (1, 4)	S	6-2	190	6-22-59	Drake	FA

*Sikora active for 1 game in '84, did not play.

DALLAS COWBOYS
(Eastern Division, National Conference)

Tom Landry

General Partner—H.R. (Bum) Bright
President and General Manager—Texas E. Schramm
Vice-President, Personnel Development—Gil Brandt
Vice-President, Administration—Joe Bailey
Vice-President, Treasurer—Don Wilson
Head Coach—Tom Landry (25 years: 223-126-6)
Assistant Coaches:
   Research and Development—Neill Armstrong
   Running Backs—Al Lavan
   Special Teams—Alan Lowry
   Asst. Head Coach/Off. Line—Jim Myers
   Receivers—Dick Nolan
   Quarterbacks—Jim Shofner
   Defensive Backs—Gene Stallings
   Defensive Coordinator/Def. Line—Ernie Stautner
   Linebackers—Jerry Tubbs
   Conditioning—Bob Ward
Public Relations Director—Doug Todd
   (Office Phone: 369-8000—Area Code 214)
Offices—6116 North Central Expressway, Dallas, Tex. 75206
Stadium—Texas Stadium (Capacity: 65,101)
Team Colors—Royal Blue, Metallic Blue and White
Training Site—California Lutheran College, Thousand Oaks, Calif.

1985 SCHEDULE
(All times local.
All games Sunday unless noted otherwise.)

Sept. 9	WASHINGTON (Mon.)	8:00
Sept. 15	at Detroit	1:00
Sept. 22	CLEVELAND	12:00
Sept. 29	at Houston	12:00
Oct. 6	at New York Giants (night)	8:00
Oct. 13	PITTSBURGH	12:00
Oct. 20	at Philadelphia	1:00
Oct. 27	ATLANTA	12:00
Nov. 4	at St. Louis (Mon.)	8:00
Nov. 10	at Washington	4:00
Nov. 17	CHICAGO	12:00
Nov. 24	PHILADELPHIA	3:00
Nov. 28	ST. LOUIS (Thanksgiving)	3:00
Dec. 8	at Cincinnati	1:00
Dec. 15	NEW YORK GIANTS	12:00
Dec. 22	at San Francisco	1:00

1984 RESULTS—(Won 9, Lost 7)

Cowboys		Opp.		Att.
20	Los Angeles Rams	13	(A)	65,403
7	New York Giants	28	(A)	75,921
23	Philadelphia	17	(H)	64,521
20	Green Bay	6	(H)	64,222
23	Chicago	14	(A)	63,623
20	St. Louis	31	(H)	61,438
14	Washington	34	(A)	55,431
30	New Orleans (OT)	27	(H)	50,966
22	Indianapolis	3	(H)	58,724
7	New York Giants	19	(H)	60,235
24	St. Louis	17	(A)	48,721
3	Buffalo	14	(A)	74,391
20	New England	17	(H)	55,341
26	Philadelphia	10	(A)	66,322
28	Washington	30	(H)	64,286
21	Miami	28	(A)	74,139

1984 GAMES STARTED

16 games: Doug Cosbie, Tony Dorsett, Michael Downs, John Dutton, Ron Fellows, Mike Hegman, Jim Jeffcoat, Ed Jones, Tom Rafferty, Everson Walls, Randy White.

15 games: Dextor Clinkscale, Anthony Dickerson.

14 games: Phil Pozderac.

13 games: Kurt Petersen.

12 games: Ron Springs, Glen Titensor.

11 games: Tony Hill, Mike Renfro.

10 games: Gary Hogeboom.

9 games: Doug Donley, Herbert Scott.

8 games: Bob Breunig, Eugene Lockhart.

7 games: Jim Cooper.

6 games: Danny White.

4 games: Brian Baldinger, Tim Newsome, Howard Richards.

2 games: Bill Bates.

1 game: Fred Cornwell, John Hunt.

DALLAS COWBOYS 1985 VETERAN ROSTER

No.	Name	Pos.	Ht.	Wt.	NFL Exp.	Birth-date	College	Games in '84	How Acquired
36	Albritton, Vince	S	6-2	209	2	7-23-62	Washington	16	OFA, '84
31	Allen, Gary	RB	5-10	179	4	4-23-60	Hawaii	16	FA, '83
76	Aughtman, Dowe	G	6-3	258	2	1-28-61	Auburn	7	D11, '84
62	Baldinger, Brian	G-T	6-4	258	4	1- 7-59	Duke	16	OFA, '82
40	Bates, Bill	S	6-1	201	3	6- 6-61	Tennessee	12	OFA, '83
47	Clinkscale, Dextor	S	5-11	189	5	4-13-58	South Carolina St.	15	OFA, '80
61	Cooper, Jim	T	6-5	267	9	9-28-55	Temple	7	D6, '77
85	Cornwell, Fred	TE	6-6	237	2	8- 7-61	Southern California	14	D3, '84
84	Cosbie, Doug	TE	6-6	235	7	2-27-56	Santa Clara	16	D3, '79
55	DeOssie, Steve	LB	6-2	248	2	11-22-62	Boston College	16	D4, '84
51	Dickerson, Anthony	LB	6-2	222	6	6- 9-57	Southern Methodist	16	FA, '80
33	Dorsett, Tony	RB	5-11	185	9	4- 7-54	Pittsburgh	16	D1, '77
26	Downs, Michael	S	6-3	195	5	6- 9-59	Rice	16	OFA, '81
78	Dutton, John	DT	6-7	267	12	2- 6-51	Nebraska	16	T-Bal, '79
27	Fellows, Ron	CB	6-0	174	5	11- 7-58	Missouri	16	D7, '81
28	Granger, Norm	RB	5-9	220	2	9-14-61	Iowa	15	D5a, '84
86	Harris, Duriel	WR	5-11	176	10	11-27-54	New Mexico State	*16	FA, '84
58	Hegman, Mike	LB	6-1	231	10	1-17-53	Tennessee State	16	D7, '75
15	Hewko, Bob	QB	6-3	195	2	6- 8-60	Florida	*0	FA, '85
80	Hill, Tony	WR	6-2	198	9	6-23-56	Stanford	11	D3, '77
14	Hogeboom, Gary	QB	6-4	200	6	8-21-58	Central Michigan	16	D5, '80
97	Hopkins, Thomas	T	6-6	260	2	1-13-60	Alabama A&M	*0	FA, '85
21	Howard, Carl	CB	6-2	188	2	9-20-61	Rutgers	10	OFA, '84
79	Hunt, John	G	6-4	253	2	11- 6-62	Florida	2	D9, '84
77	Jeffcoat, Jim	DE	6-5	257	3	4- 1-61	Arizona State	16	D1, '83
72	Jones, Ed	DE	6-9	287	11	2-23-51	Tennessee State	16	D1, '74
23	Jones, James	RB	5-10	189	5	12- 6-58	Mississippi State	9	D3a, '80
73	Kitson, Syd	G	6-4	262	5	9-27-58	Wake Forest	*9	FA, '84
56	Lockhart, Eugene	LB	6-2	233	2	3- 8-61	Houston	15	D6, '84
35	McSwain, Chuck	RB	6-0	190	3	2-21-61	Clemson	15	D5, '83
30	Newsome, Timmy	RB	6-1	232	6	5-17-58	Winston-Salem State	15	D6, '80
16	Pelluer, Steve	QB	6-4	210	2	7-29-62	Washington	1	D5, '84
65	Petersen, Kurt	G	6-4	267	6	6-17-57	Missouri	13	D4, '80
81	Phillips, Kirk	WR	6-1	202	2	7-31-60	Tulsa	8	FA, '83
75	Pozderac, Phil	T	6-9	276	4	12-19-59	Notre Dame	15	D5, '82
64	Rafferty, Tom	C	6-3	254	10	8- 2-54	Penn State	16	D4, '76
82	Renfro, Mike	WR	6-0	188	8	6-19-55	Texas Christian	16	T-Hou, '84
70	Richards, Howard	T	6-6	260	5	8- 7-59	Missouri	11	D1, '81
50	Rohrer, Jeff	LB	6-3	225	4	12-25-58	Yale	16	D2, '82
89	Salonen, Brian	TE	6-2	227	2	7-29-61	Montana	16	D10, '84
66	Schultz, Chris	T	6-8	265	2	2-16-60	Arizona	*0	D7, '83
22	Scott, Victor	CB-S	5-11	196	2	6- 1-62	Colorado	16	D2, '84
1	Septien, Rafael	K	5-10	180	9	12-12-53	Southwest Louisiana	16	FA, '78
60	Smerek, Don	DT	6-7	255	4	12-20-57	Nevada-Reno	16	FA, '81
20	Springs, Ron	RB	6-1	224	7	11- 1-56	Ohio State	16	D5b, '79
32	Thurman, Dennis	CB	5-11	175	8	4-13-56	Southern California	16	D11, '78
63	Titensor, Glen	G	6-4	264	5	2-21-58	Brigham Young	15	D3, '81
71	Tuinei, Mark	DT	6-5	274	3	3-31-60	Hawaii	16	OFA, '83
57	Turner, Jimmie	LB	6-2	220	2	2-16-62	Presbyterian	5	FA, '84
24	Walls, Everson	CB	6-1	190	5	12-28-59	Grambling	16	OFA, '81
5	Warren, John	P	6-0	207	3	11- 8-60	Tennessee	3	OFA, '83
11	White, Danny	QB	6-2	197	10	2- 9-52	Arizona State	14	D3, '74
54	White, Randy	DT	6-4	260	11	1-15-53	Maryland	16	D1, '75

*Harris played 11 games with Cleveland, 5 with Dallas in '84; Hewko last active with Tampa Bay in '83; Hopkins last active with Cleveland in '84; Kitson played 8 games with Green Bay, 1 with Dallas in '84; Schultz missed '84 season due to injury.

†Option playout; subject to developments.

Retired—Bob Breunig, 10-year linebacker, 8 games in '84; Herb Scott, 10-year guard, 15 games in '84.

Also played with Cowboys in '84—LB Billy Cannon (8 games), WR Harold Carmichael (2), WR Doug Donley (15), P Jim Miller (1), WR Waddell Smith (2).

D—Draft; T—Trade; W—Waivers; FA—Free Agent; OFA—Original Free Agent.

DALLAS COWBOYS
1985 DRAFT CHOICES

(Number following name designates order of selection among 336 players drafted.)

Round and Player		Position	College
1. BROOKS, Kevin	17	DE	Michigan
2. PENN, Jesse	44	LB	Virginia Tech
3. KER, Crawford	76	G	Florida
4. LAVETTE, Robert	103	RB	Georgia Tech
5. WALKER, Herschel from Houston (a)	114	RB	Georgia
5. DARWIN, Matt from Cleveland through Buffalo (b)	119	C	Texas A&M
5. Choice to Buffalo (c)			
6. PLOEGER, Kurt from Indianapolis (d)	144	DE	Gustavus Adolphus
6. MORAN, Matt	157	G	Stanford
7. POWE, Karl from N.Y. Jets through Kansas City (e)	178	WR	Alabama State
7. HERRMANN, Jim	184	DE	Brigham Young
8. GONZALES, Leon	216	WR	Bethune-Cookman
9. STRASBURGER, Scott	243	LB	Nebraska
10. JONES, Joe	270	TE	Virginia Tech
11. DELLOCONO, Neal	297	LB	UCLA
12. JORDAN, Karl	324	LB	Vanderbilt

(a) Acquired pick, 2nd round pick in 1984 and wide receiver Mike Renfro for wide receiver Butch Johnson and 2nd round pick in 1984, April 13, 1984.

(b) Bills acquired pick, 1st round pick in 1983 and 3rd round pick in 1984 from Browns for linebacker Tom Cousineau, April 23, 1982; Cowboys acquired pick and conditional 1986 pick from Bills for cornerback Rod Hill and 5th round pick, August 23, 1984.

(c) See second part of (b).

(d) Acquired pick for tackle Steve Wright, August 27, 1983.

(e) Chiefs acquired pick from Jets for linebacker Charles Jackson, April 25, 1984; Cowboys acquired pick from Chiefs for running back Lawrence Ricks, August 24, 1983.

DALLAS COWBOYS
1985 ROOKIE AND FIRST-YEAR ROSTER

(1) Indicates player in previous NFL camp.
(2) Indicates player with USFL game experience.
(3) Indicates player in previous USFL camp.
(4) Indicates player with CFL game experience.
(5) Indicates player in previous CFL camp.
   All others classified as rookies.

Name	Pos.	Hgt.	Wgt.	Birth-date	College	How Acquired
Arendt, Chris (1, 3)	DE	6-5	239	5-31-61	Duke	*FA '84
Brooks, Kevin	DE	6-7	262	2- 9-63	Michigan	D1
Darwin, Matt	C/G	6-4	260	3-11-63	Texas A&M	D5b
Dellocono, Neal	LB	6-0	219	6- 1-63	UCLA	D11
Fitzpatrick, John (1)	OL	6-3	285	6- 6-61	Purdue	*FA '84
Fowler, Todd (2)	RB	6-3	212	6- 9-62	Stephen F. Austin	SupD '84
Gonzales, Leon	WR	5-10	158	9-21-63	Bethune-Cookman	D8
Herrman, Jim	DE	6-5	255	10-20-62	Brigham Young	D7b
Jenkins, Ron (1)	WR	5-11	166	2-28-61	Colorado State	*FA '84
Jones, Joe	TE	6-4	247	6-26-62	Virginia Tech	D10
Jordan, Karl	LB	6-1	244	1-12-63	Vanderbilt	D12
Ker, Crawford	G	6-4	293	5- 5-62	Florida	D3
Lavette, Robert	RB	5-11	192	9- 8-63	Georgia Tech	D4
Moore, Malcolm (2)	WR	6-3	199	6-24-61	Southern California	SupD '84
Moran, Matt	G	6-4	265	5-14-62	Stanford	D6b
Penn, Jesse	LB	6-2	222	9- 6-62	Virginia Tech	D2
Ploeger, Kurt	DT	6-5	265	12- 1-62	Gustavus Adolphus	D6a
Ponder, David (1)	DT	6-3	248	6-27-62	Florida State	FA
Powe, Karl	WR	6-2	177	1-17-62	Alabama State	D7a
Puzar, John (1)	C	6-6	255	6-27-62	Long Beach State	FA
Revell, Mike (1)	RB	5-11	197	1-23-62	Bethune-Cookman	FA
Strasburger, Scott	LB	6-2	204	2-14-63	Nebraska	D9

*Arendt, Fitzpatrick and Jenkins missed '84 season due to injury.
NOTE: 5th round pick Herschel Walker is with New Jersey Generals of the USFL.

DENVER BRONCOS
(Western Division, American Conference)

Dan Reeves

President and Chief Executive Officer—Patrick D. Bowlen
General Manager—John Beake
Vice-President/Head Coach—Dan Reeves (4 years: 34-23)
Assistant Coaches:
  Special Assistant—Marvin Bass
  Assistant Head Coach/Defense—Joe Collier
  Special Teams/Defensive Asst.—Chan Gailey
  Head Offensive Line—Alex Gibbs
  Defensive Line—Stan Jones
  Strength/Conditioning—Al Miller
  Linebackers—Myrel Moore
  Running Backs—Nick Nicolau
  Wide Receivers—Mike Shanahan
  Tight Ends/Asst. Offensive Line—Doc Urich
  Defensive Backs—Charlie West
Director of Media Relations—Jim Saccomano
  (Office Phone: 296-1982—Area Code 303)
Offices—5700 Logan St., Denver, Colo. 80216
Stadium—Mile High Stadium (Capacity: 75,100)
Team Colors—Orange, Blue and White
Training Site—University of Northern Colorado, Greeley, Colo.

1985 SCHEDULE
(All times local.
All games Sunday unless noted otherwise.)

Sept. 8	at Los Angeles Rams	1:00
Sept. 15	NEW ORLEANS	2:00
Sept. 22	at Atlanta	1:00
Sept. 29	MIAMI	2:00
Oct. 6	HOUSTON	2:00
Oct. 13	at Indianapolis	12:00
Oct. 20	SEATTLE	2:00
Oct. 27	at Kansas City	12:00
Nov. 3	at San Diego	1:00
Nov. 11	SAN FRANCISCO (Mon.)	7:00
Nov. 17	SAN DIEGO	2:00
Nov. 24	at Los Angeles Raiders	1:00
Dec. 1	at Pittsburgh	1:00
Dec. 8	LOS ANGELES RAIDERS	2:00
Dec. 14	KANSAS CITY (Sat.)	2:00
Dec. 20	at Seattle (Fri.)	5:00

1984 RESULTS—(Won 13, Lost 4)

Broncos		Opp.		Att.
20	Cincinnati	17	(H)	74,178
0	Chicago	27	(A)	54,335
24	Cleveland	14	(A)	61,980
21	Kansas City	0	(H)	74,263
16	Los Angeles Raiders	13	(H)	74,833
28	Detroit	7	(A)	55,836
17	Green Bay	14	(H)	62,546
37	Buffalo	7	(A)	31,204
22	Los Angeles Raiders (OT)	19	(A)	91,020
26	New England	19	(H)	74,908
16	San Diego	13	(A)	53,162
42	Minnesota	21	(H)	74,716
24	Seattle	27	(H)	74,922
13	Kansas City	16	(A)	38,494
16	San Diego	13	(H)	74,867
31	Seattle	14	(A)	64,411
	AFC SEMIFINAL GAME			
17	Pittsburgh	24	(H)	74,981

1984 GAMES STARTED

16 games: Bill Bryan, Steve Busick, Steve Foley, Mike Harden, Tom Jackson, Rulon Jones, Dave Studdard, Steve Watson.

15 games: Rubin Carter, Barney Chavous, Rick Dennison, Ken Lanier, Dennis Smith, Sammy Winder, Louis Wright.

14 games: Keith Bishop, John Elway, Paul Howard, Jim Ryan.

13 games: Clarence Kay.

10 games: Jim Wright.

9 games: Butch Johnson.

8 games: John Sawyer.

4 games: Mark Cooper.

3 games: Clint Sampson.

2 games: Winford Hood, Gary Kubiak, Rick Parros, Don Summers, Ken Woodard.

1 game: Walt Bowyer, Scott Garnett, Karl Mecklenburg, Randy Robbins, Gerald Willhite, Steve Wilson.

DENVER BRONCOS 1985 VETERAN ROSTER

No.	Name	Pos.	Ht.	Wt.	NFL Exp.	Birth-date	College	Games in '84	How Acquired
80	Alexander, Ray	WR	6-3	180	2	1-8-62	Florida A&M	8	OFA, '84
54	†Bishop, Keith	G-C	6-3	265	5	3-10-57	Baylor	16	D6, '80
65	Bowyer, Walt	DE	6-4	252	3	9-8-60	Arizona State	16	D10, '83
26	Brewer, Chris	RB	6-1	193	2	1-23-62	Arizona	13	D9, '84
64	Bryan, Bill	C	6-2	255	8	9-21-55	Duke	16	D4, '77
58	Busick, Steve	LB	6-4	227	5	12-10-58	Southern California	16	D7, '81
68	†Carter, Rubin	NT	6-0	256	11	12-12-52	Miami, Fla.	15	D5a, '75
79	Chavous, Barney	DE	6-3	258	13	3-22-51	South Carolina State	15	D2, '73
59	Comeaux, Darren	LB	6-1	227	4	4-15-60	Arizona State	16	OFA, '82
63	Cooper, Mark	G	6-5	267	3	2-14-60	Miami, Fla.	15	D2, '83
55	Dennison, Rick	LB	6-3	220	4	6-22-58	Colorado State	16	FA, '82
7	Elway, John	QB	6-3	202	3	6-28-60	Stanford	15	T-Bal, '83
43	Foley, Steve	S	6-2	190	9	11-11-53	Tulane	16	D8, '75
62	Freeman, Mike	G	6-3	256	2	10-13-61	Arizona	9	OFA, '84
66	Garnett, Scott	NT	6-2	271	2	13-3-62	Washington	16	D8a, '84
72	Graves, Marsharne	T	6-3	272	2	7-8-62	Arizona	1	OFA, '84
31	Harden, Mike	CB	6-1	192	6	2-16-58	Michigan	16	D5, '80
74	Hood, Winford	G	6-3	262	2	3-29-62	Georgia	16	D8, '84
60	Howard, Paul	G	6-3	260	12	9-12-50	Brigham Young	16	D3, '73
98	Hunley, Ricky	LB	6-2	238	2	11-11-61	Arizona	8	T-Cin, '84
66	Hyde, Glenn	G-C	6-3	255	9	3-14-51	Pittsburgh	*0	FA, '84
28	Jackson, Roger	S	6-0	186	4	2-28-59	Bethune-Cookman	16	OFA, '82
57	Jackson, Tom	LB	5-11	220	13	4-4-51	Louisville	16	D4, '73
86	Johnson, Butch	WR	6-1	187	10	5-28-54	Cal-Riverside	16	T-Hou, '84
75	Jones, Rulon	DE	6-6	260	6	3-25-58	Utah State	16	D2, '80
3	Karlis, Rich	K	6-0	180	4	5-23-59	Cincinnati	16	FA, '82
88	Kay, Clarence	TE	6-2	237	2	7-30-61	Georgia	16	D7, '84
8	Kubiak, Gary	QB	6-0	192	3	8-15-61	Texas A&M	7	D8, '83
33	Lang, Gene	RB	5-10	196	2	3-15-62	Louisiana State	16	D11, '84
76	Lanier, Ken	T	6-3	269	5	7-8-59	Florida State	16	D5, '81
22	Lilly, Tony	S	6-0	199	2	2-16-62	Florida	13	D3, '84
	Manning, Wade	CB	5-11	190	4	7-25-55	Ohio State	*0	FA, '85
69	Manor, Brison	DE	6-4	248	9	8-10-52	Arkansas	*11	FA, '76
77	Mecklenburg, Karl	DE-LB	6-3	250	3	9-1-60	Minnesota	16	D12, '83
29	Myers, Wilbur	S	5-11	195	2	8-17-61	Delta State	*0	OFA, '83
39	Myles, Jesse	RB	5-10	210	3	9-28-60	Louisiana State	7	OFA, '83
1	Norman, Chris	P	6-2	198	2	5-25-62	South Carolina	16	OFA, '84
24	Parros, Rick	RB	5-11	200	5	6-14-58	Utah State	15	D4, '80
48	Robbins, Randy	CB	6-2	189	2	9-14-62	Arizona	16	D4, '84
50	Ryan, Jim	LB	6-1	215	7	5-18-57	William & Mary	16	OFA, '79
84	Sampson, Clint	WR	5-11	183	3	1-4-61	San Diego State	12	D3, '83
83	Sawyer, John	TE	6-2	230	10	7-26-53	Southern Mississippi	10	FA, '83
	Scoggins, Eric	LB	6-2	235	2	1-23-59	Southern California	*0	FA, '85
	Shaffer, Craig	LB	6-1	227	4	3-31-59	Indiana State	*4	FA, '85
56	Smith, Aaron	LB	6-2	225	2	8-10-62	Utah State	10	D6, '84
49	Smith, Dennis	S	6-3	200	5	2-3-59	Southern California	15	D1, '81
	Stankavage, Scott	QB	6-1	194	2	7-5-62	North Carolina	1	OFA, '84
70	Studdard, Dave	T	6-4	260	7	11-22-55	Texas	16	FA, '79
85	Summers, Don	TE	6-4	226	2	2-2-61	Boise State	16	FA, '84
61	Townsend, Andre	DE-NT	6-3	265	2	10-8-62	Mississippi	16	D2, '84
81	Watson, Steve	WR	6-4	195	7	5-28-57	Temple	16	OFA, '79
47	Willhite, Gerald	RB	5-10	200	4	5-30-59	San Jose State	16	D1, '82
45	Wilson, Steve	CB	5-10	195	7	8-25-57	Howard	15	FA, '82
23	Winder, Sammy	RB	5-11	203	4	7-15-59	Southern Mississippi	16	D5, '82
52	†Woodard, Ken	LB	6-1	218	4	1-22-60	Tuskegee Institute	16	D10, '82
87	Wright, Jim	TE	6-3	240	6	9-1-56	Texas Christian	16	FA, '80
20	Wright, Louis	CB	6-2	200	11	1-31-53	San Jose State	16	D1, '75

*Myers missed '84 season due to injury; Manor played 6 games with Tampa Bay, 5 with Denver in '84; Shaffer played 4 games with St. Louis in '84; Hyde active for 1 game in '84, did not play; Manning last active with Denver in '82; Scoggins last active with San Francisco in '82 and Houston (USFL) in '84.

†Option playout; subject to developments.

Retired—Bob Swenson, 8-year linebacker, missed '84 season due to injury.

Also played with Broncos in '84—WR Dave Logan (4 games), WR Zack Thomas (12).

D—Draft; T—Trade; W—Waivers; FA—Free Agent; OFA—Original Free Agent.

DENVER BRONCOS
1985 DRAFT CHOICES

(Number following name designates order of selection among 336 players drafted.)

Round and Player		Position	College
1. SEWELL, Steve	26	RB	Oklahoma
2. JOHNSON, Vance from Houston (a)	31	WR	Arizona
2. FLETCHER, Simon	54	DE	Houston
3. Choice to Houston (b)			
4. McGREGOR, Keli	110	TE	Colorado State
5. Choice to Houston (a)			
5. HINSON, Billy from Miami (c)	139	G	Florida
6. Choice to N.Y. Jets (d)			
7. CAMERON, Dallas	194	NT	Miami, Fla.
8. RILEY, Eric	222	DB	Florida State
9. SMITH, Daryl	249	DB	North Alabama
10. FUNCK, Buddy from New England (e)	269	QB	New Mexico
10. ANDERSON, Ron	278	LB	SMU
11. ROLLE, Gary	306	WR	Florida
12. LYNCH, Dan	334	G	Washington St.

(a) Acquired pick for 2nd and 5th round picks, April 30, 1985.
(b) Traded pick for wide receiver Butch Johnson, August 20, 1984.
(c) Acquired pick for linebacker Larry Evans, August 15, 1983.
(d) Traded pick for linebacker Stan Blinka, February 15, 1984.
(e) Acquired pick for punter Luke Prestridge, August 20, 1984.

DENVER BRONCOS
1985 ROOKIE AND FIRST-YEAR ROSTER

(1) Indicates player in previous NFL camp.
(2) Indicates player with USFL game experience.
(3) Indicates player in previous USFL camp.
(4) Indicates player with CFL game experience.
(5) Indicates player in previous CFL camp.
    All others classified as rookies.

Name	Pos.	Hgt.	Wgt.	Birth-date	College	How Acquired
Anderson, Ron	LB	6-2	215	9-16-62	Southern Methodist	D10b
Baran, Dave	OL	6-5	275	6-28-63	UCLA	FA
Beasley, Victor	DB	6-0	190	9-30-62	Auburn	FA
Bednarek, Mike	OL	6-7	245	9 6-63	Moorhead State	FA
Blakeney, Lee	LB	6-0	230	9-18-61	Washington State	FA
Boadway, Steve	LB	6-3	230	6-20-63	Arizona	FA
Bomkamp, Gregg	DL	6-3	260	7-18-62	Baylor	FA
Booth, David	LB	6-3	220	12-20-62	Memphis State	FA
Bowdre, David	LB	6-3	230	12- 3-62	Texas Tech	FA
Bracken, Donald (1, 3)	P	6-1	214	2-16-62	Michigan	FA
Brown, Michael E.	RB	5-11	200	2-19-61	Texas	FA
Brown, Mike L.	LB	6-1	235	4-17-62	Ball State	FA
Brown, Rod	DB	6-0	180	10- 6-62	Oklahoma State	FA
Burns, Pat	NT	6-4	261	12- 2-63	Missouri	FA
Cameron, Dallas	NT	6-2	245	11- 6-62	Miami (Fla.)	D7

Name	Pos.	Hgt.	Wgt.	Birth-date	College	How Acquired
Ceasar, Nat	DB	6-3	196	1-28-61	Auburn	FA
Clark, Thomas (3)	DB	6-0	185	12-14-61	Troy State	FA
Comanche, Ron	LB	6-0	230	8-24-63	Southern University	FA
Cruce, Jeff	OL	6-6	246	4- 6-62	Clemson	FA
Dejarnette, Sam	RB	6-0	185	8- 5-62	Southern Mississippi	FA
Dillingham, Dave	OL	6-5	270	3- 2-62	Oklahoma	FA
Dirks, Rickey	RB	5-9	195	3-18-63	East Texas State	FA
Duncan, Bobby	QB	6-3	208	10-12-62	North Alabama	FA
Fletcher, Simon	DT	6-5	240	2-18-62	Houston	D2b
Funck, Buddy	QB	6-2	195	3-22-62	New Mexico	D10
Gallon, Russell (3)	DT	6-8	285	7-14-62	Florida	FA
Gray, Richard	TE	6-3	225	1- 8-62	Notre Dame	FA
Greene, Ricky	DB	5-9	185	8-25-61	Nebraska	FA
Groover, Richard	DB	5-11	185	8-21-62	Livingston (Ala.)	FA
Haina, John	LB	6-2	240	11-17-62	California	FA
Hinson, Billy	G	6-1	278	1- 8-63	Florida	D5
Hornfeck, Ray	DB	5-10	180	12-30-62	New Mexico	FA
James, Donald	NT	6-2	250	9-26-62	California	FA
Jarman, Murray	WR	6-5	210	1-26-61	Clemson	*D12 '84
Hunter, Daniel (1, 3)	CB	5-11	167	9- 1-62	Henderson State (Ala.)	FA
Johnson, Vance	WR	5-11	174	3-13-63	Arizona	D2
Jones, Demetrius (1, 3)	S	6-0	181	9-12-61	Western Michigan	*FA '84
Joyce, Jim (1)	DE	6-3	241	9-12-64	Maryland	*FA '84
Kelly, Clarence (3)	DR	6-0	170	11-29-62	Akron	FA
Kilgo, John	OL	6-3	275	10- 8-61	Boise State	FA
Kimball, Scott	WR	6-0	195	12-14-61	Nebraska	FA
Kragen, Greg (1)	DE	6-2	241	3- 4-62	Utah State	FA
Lewis, Robert	RB	6-0	185	10-13-62	Texas Tech	FA
Linderholm, Rick	OL	6-5	265	3-31-62	Montana	FA
Lobenstein, Bill	DL	6-3	260	5-11-61	Wisconsin-Whitewater	FA
Lynch, Dan	G	6-3	265	6-21-62	Washington State	D12
McGregor, Keli	TE	6-7	252	1-23-63	Colorado State	D4
McRae, Scott	LB	6-3	235	9- 1-62	Alabama	FA
Naran, Randy	QB	6-1	198	1-20-62	Nebraska-Omaha	FA
Niko, Maomao (1)	G	6-3	290	3-31-60	San Jose State	FA
Olton, Rob (1, 3)	K	5-10	197	2- 5-59	Wisconsin	FA
Pack, David (3)	WR	6-2	200	10-23-62	U. of the South (Tenn.)	FA
Powell, Kirk	P	6-1	200	8- 6-61	Colorado State	FA
Price, Steve (1)	WR	6-1	196	6- 5-61	Southwestern Oklahoma State	FA
Riley, Eric	CB	6-0	170	8-15-62	Florida State	D8
Raridon, Scott (1)	OT	6-3	275	2-22-61	Nebraska	T-Phi. '85
Roberts, Aaron	RB	6-0	190	12-26-62	Michigan State	FA
Rolle, Gary	WR	5-11	169	2-16-62	Florida	D11
Rutt, Thomas	OL	6-5	275	11-23-62	Montana	FA
Saffy, Randy	OL	6-4	265	10- 9-62	Tulane	FA
Schonert, Steven (1, 3)	K	5-8	175	4-30-60	Northern Iowa	FA
Schulter, Joe	RB	6-2	222	1-20-61	Azusa Pacific (Calif.)	FA
Sciaraffa, Anthony	DB	5-10	195	8- 5-61	Texas Christian	FA
Scissum, Willard	OL	6-4	270	10-28-62	Alabama	FA
Sewell, Steve	RB	6-3	210	4- 2-63	Oklahoma	D1
Shupe, Mark	OL	6-5	270	4-25-62	Arizona State	FA
Sims, Jack	OL	6-2	250	4-21-62	Hawaii	FA
Smith, Darryl	CB	6-0	180	5- 8-63	North Alabama	D9
Stanley, Dwayne	RB	6-0	185	10-24-62	Ouachita Baptist (Ark.)	FA
Swanke, Rob (1)	NT	6-2	253	11-17-61	Boston College	*FA '84
Swing, Dale	OL	6-3	248	11-23-62	Clemson	FA
Tatom, Buzz	TE	6-3	220	5-22-63	Texas Tech	FA
Taylor, Derrick	RB	5-9	185	7-21-61	Southern Illinois	FA
Thurson, Tommy (1, 3)	LB	6-2	230	11-16-62	Georgia	FA
Trahan, John	WR	5-9	165	4-19-61	Southern Colorado	FA
Travis, Clinton	WR	5-10	180	11-28-62	Adams State	FA
Whitehead, Derrick	DL	6-5	265	5-29-62	Eastern Michigan	FA
Wiley, Bryan	RB	6-1	205	12- 5-62	UCLA	FA
Willis, Larry	WR	5-10	170	7-13-63	Fresno State	FA
Woodson, Anthony	LB	6-2	220	7-12-62	Hawaii	FA
Wright, Will	LB	6-4	225	10-13-62	Eastern New Mexico	FA
Young, Joe	OL	6-2	270	4- 9-61	Texas Christian	FA
Younger, Robert	OL	6-3	255	12-14-61	East Tennessee State	FA

*Jarman tried out with Phoenix Suns of NBA in '84; Jones, Joyce and Swanke missed '84 season due to injury.

DETROIT LIONS
(Central Division, National Conference)

Darryl Rogers

Owner and President—William Clay Ford

Executive Vice-President and G.M.—Russ Thomas

Head Coach/Dir. of Football Operations—Darryl Rogers (First Year)

Assistant Coaches:
Offensive Coordinator/Quarterbacks—Bob Baker
Special Teams—Carl Battershell
Strength and Conditioning—Don Clemons
Administrative Assistant—Don Doll
Defensive Coordinator—Wayne Fontes
Receivers—Paul Lanham
Offensive Line—Bill Muir
Linebackers—Mike Murphy
Defensive Line—Rex Norris
Defensive Backfield—Willie Shaw
Offensive Backfield—Ivy Williams

Public Relations Director—George Heddleston
(Office Phone: 335-4131—Area Code 313)

Offices—1200 Featherstone Road, Box 4200, Pontiac, Mich. 48057

Stadium—Pontiac Silverdome (Capacity: 80,638)

Team Colors—Honolulu Blue and Silver

Training Site—Oakland University, Rochester, Mich.

1985 SCHEDULE
(All times local.
All games Sunday unless noted otherwise.)

Sept. 8	at Atlanta	1:00
Sept. 15	DALLAS	1:00
Sept. 22	at Indianapolis	12:00
Sept. 29	TAMPA BAY	1:00
Oct. 6	at Green Bay	12:00
Oct. 13	at Washington	1:00
Oct. 20	SAN FRANCISCO	1:00
Oct. 27	MIAMI	1:00
Nov. 3	at Minnesota	12:00
Nov. 10	at Chicago	12:00
Nov. 17	MINNESOTA	4:00
Nov. 24	at Tampa Bay	1:00
Nov. 28	N.Y JETS (Thanksgiving)	12:30
Dec. 8	at New England	1:00
Dec. 15	GREEN BAY	1:00
Dec. 22	CHICAGO	1:00

1984 RESULTS—(Won 4, Lost 11, Tied 1)

Lions		Opp.		Att.
27	San Francisco	30	(H)	56,782
27	Atlanta (OT)	24	(A)	49,878
17	Tampa Bay	21	(A)	44,560
28	Minnesota	29	(H)	57,511
24	San Diego	27	(A)	53,509
7	Denver	28	(H)	55,836
13	Tampa Bay (OT)	7	(H)	44,308
16	Minnesota	14	(A)	57,953
9	Green Bay	41	(A)	54,289
23	Philadelphia (OT)	23	(H)	59,141
14	Washington	28	(A)	50,212
14	Chicago	16	(A)	54,911
31	Green Bay	28	(H)	63,698
17	Seattle	38	(A)	62,441
3	Los Angeles Raiders	24	(H)	66,710
13	Chicago	30	(H)	53,252

1984 GAMES STARTED

16 games: Garry Cobb, Mike Cofer, Chris Dieterich, Keith Dorney, Doug English, William Gay, Don Greco, Alvin Hall, James Jones, Bruce McNorton, Bobby Watkins, Jimmy Williams.

15 games: Curtis Green, Leonard Thompson.

14 games: Gary Danielson.

13 games: Ken Fantetti, William Graham.

9 games: Mark Nichols, Rob Rubick.

8 games: Donald Laster, Billy Sims.

7 games: Amos Fowler, David Lewis.

6 games: Larry Lee, Steve Mott.

5 games: Reese McCall.

4 games: Homer Elias.

3 games: Dexter Bussey, Jeff Chadwick, Steve Doig, Ken Jenkins, Demetrious Johnson.

2 games: Dave D'Addio.

1 game: Eric Hipple, Rich Strenger, Eric Williams, John Witkowski.

DETROIT LIONS 1985 VETERAN ROSTER

No.	Name	Pos.	Ht.	Wt.	NFL Exp.	Birth-date	College	Games in '84	How Acquired
68	Baack, Steve	T	6-3	260	2	11-16-60	Oregon	16	D3b, '84
54	Barnes, Roosevelt	LB	6-2	228	4	8-3-58	Purdue	16	D10, '82
11	Black, Michael	P	6-1	197	3	1-18-61	Arizona State	16	D7, '83
80	Bland, Carl	WR	5-11	182	2	8-17-61	Virginia Union	3	OFA, '84
89	Chadwick, Jeff	WR	6-3	190	3	12-16-60	Grand Valley State	16	OFA, '83
53	†Cobb, Garry	LB	6-2	227	7	3-16-57	Southern California	16	FA, '79
66	Cofer, Michael	DE	6-4	245	3	4-7-60	Tennessee	16	D3, '83
50	Curley, August	LB	6-2	226	3	1-24-60	Southern California	8	D4, '83
44	D'Addio, Dave	FB	6-1	229	2	7-13-61	Maryland	16	D4, '84
72	Dieterich, Chris	G	6-3	260	6	7-27-58	North Carolina State	16	D6, '80
93	Dodge, Kirk	LB	6-1	231	2	6-4-62	Nevada-Las Vegas	11	FA, '84
58	†Doig, Steve	LB	6-2	245	4	3-28-60	New Hampshire	16	D3, '82
70	Dorney, Keith	T	6-5	265	7	12-3-57	Penn State	16	D1, '79
61	Elias, Homer	G	6-2	255	8	5-1-55	Tennessee State	12	D4a, '78
78	English, Doug	DT	6-5	258	10	8-25-53	Texas	16	D2, '75
57	Fantetti, Ken	LB	6-1	232	7	4-7-57	Wyoming	14	D2, '79
	Ferguson, Joe	QB	6-1	195	13	4-23-50	Arkansas	*12	T-Buf, '85
65	†Fowler, Amos	C	6-2	253	8	2-11-56	Southern Mississippi	15	D5, '78
26	Frizzell, William	CB	6-2	198	2	9-8-62	North Carolina Central	16	D10, '84
79	Gay, William	DE	6-4	257	8	5-28-55	Southern California	16	T-Den, '79
33	Graham, William	S	5-11	191	4	9-27-59	Texas	14	D5, '82
67	Greco, Don	G	6-2	265	4	4-1-59	Western Illinois	16	D3, '81
62	Green, Curtis	DT	6-3	258	5	6-3-57	Alabama State	16	D2, '81
35	Hall, Alvin	S	5-10	184	5	8-12-58	Miami, Ohio	16	FA, '81
17	Hipple, Eric	QB	6-2	198	6	9-16-57	Utah State	8	D4, '80
31	Jenkins, Kenneth	RB	5-8	185	3	5-8-59	Bucknell	14	FA, '83
21	Johnson, Demetrious	S	5-11	190	3	7-21-61	Missouri	16	D5, '83
51	Jones, David	C	6-2	257	2	10-25-61	Texas	10	D8, '84
30	Jones, James	FB	6-2	229	3	3-21-61	Florida	16	D1, '83
	Kane, Rick	RB	6-0	200	9	11-12-54	San Jose State	*12	FA, '85
92	†King, Angelo	LB	6-0	222	5	2-10-58	South Carolina State	16	T-Dal, '84
73	Laster, Don	T	6-4	278	3	12-13-58	Tennessee State	14	FA, '84
43	Latimer, Albert	S	5-11	181	5	10-14-57	Clemson	15	FA, '82
64	Lee, Larry	G	6-2	263	5	9-10-59	UCLA	15	D5, '81
87	Lewis, David	TE	6-3	235	2	6-8-61	California	16	D1, '84
14	Machurek, Mike	QB	6-0	205	4	7-22-60	Idaho State	4	D6, '82
82	Mandley, Pete	WR	5-9	191	2	7-29-61	Northern Arizona	15	D2, '84
83	Martin, Robbie	WR	5-8	178	5	12-3-58	Cal Poly-SLO	14	W-Pit, '81
81	McCall, Reese	TE	6-6	245	8	6-15-56	Auburn	16	W-TB, '83
29	McNorton, Bruce	S-CB	5-10	175	4	2-28-59	Georgetown Col., Ky.	16	D4, '82
36	Meade, Mike	FB	5-10	227	4	2-12-60	Penn State	15	W-GB, '84
	Morris, Thomas	DB	5-11	175	3	4-2-60	Michigan State	*0	FA, '85
63	Moss, Martin	DE	6-3	255	4	12-16-58	UCLA	16	D8, '82
52	Mott, Steve	C	6-2	265	3	3-24-61	Alabama	6	D5a, '83
3	Murray, Ed	K	5-9	175	6	8-29-56	Tulane	16	D7, '80
86	Nichols, Mark	WR	6-1	208	5	10-29-59	San Jose State	15	D1, '81
84	Rubick, Rob	TE	6-2	234	4	9-27-60	Grand Valley State	16	D12a, '82
20	Sims, Billy	RB	5-11	212	6	9-18-55	Oklahoma	8	D1, '80
71	Strenger, Rich	T	6-7	276	2	3-10-60	Michigan	1	D2, '83
39	Thompson, Leonard	WR	5-11	192	11	7-28-52	Oklahoma State	16	D8, '75
27	Watkins, Bobby	S-CB	5-10	184	4	5-31-60	Southwest Texas State	16	D2, '82
76	Williams, Eric	DT	6-4	260	2	2-24-62	Washington State	12	D3, '84
59	Williams, Jimmy	LB	6-2	230	4	11-15-60	Nebraska	16	D1, '82
18	Witkowski, John	QB	6-1	205	2	6-18-62	Columbia	3	D6, '84

*Ferguson played 12 games with Buffalo in '84; Kane played 12 games with Washington in '84; Morris last active with Tampa Bay in '83.

†Option playout; subject to developments.

Retired—Dexter Bussey, 11-year running back, 16 games in '84.

Also played with Lions in '84—QB Gary Danielson (15 games), LB Terry Tautolo (4), DB Danny Wagoner (1), DB Gardner Williams (3).

D—Draft; T—Trade; W—Waivers; FA—Free Agent; OFA—Original Free Agent.

DETROIT LIONS
1985 DRAFT CHOICES

(Number following name designates order of selection among 336 players drafted.)

Round and Player		Position	College
1. BROWN, Lomas	6	T	Florida
2. GLOVER, Kevin	34	C	Maryland
3. JOHNSON, James	62	LB	San Diego St.
4. HANCOCK, Kevin	90	LB	Baylor
5. McINTOSH, Joe	118	RB	No. Carolina St.
6. SHORT, Stan	146	G	Penn State
7. STATEN, Tony	174	DB	Angelo State
8. CALDWELL, Scotty	202	RB	Texas-Arlington
9. JAMES, June	230	LB	Texas
10. BEAUFORD, Clayton	258	WR	Auburn
11. HARRIS, Kevin	286	DB	Georgia
12. WEAVER, Mike	314	G	Georgia

DETROIT LIONS
1985 ROOKIE AND FIRST-YEAR ROSTER

(1) Indicates player in previous NFL camp.
(2) Indicates player with USFL game experience.
(3) Indicates player in previous USFL camp.
(4) Indicates player with CFL game experience.
(5) Indicates player in previous CFL camp.
    All others classified as rookies.

Name	Pos.	Hgt.	Wgt.	Birth-date	College	How Acquired
Alward, Scott	TE	6-5	237	10-31-62	Ferris State	FA
Barrows, Scott	G	6-2	278	3-31-63	West Virginia	FA
Beauford, Clayton	WR	5-10	173	3- 1-63	Auburn	D10
Brown, Lomas	T	6-4	282	3-30-63	Florida	D1
Caldwell, Scotty	RB	5-11	195	2- 8-63	Texas-Arlington	D8
Colvin, Jeff	TE	...	...	....	Colorado	FA
Cross, Ron	S	6-2	196	1- 3-63	Fresno State	FA
Dalton, William (1)	RB	5-10	200	2-26-61	West Virginia Tech	FA
Galloway, Duane (1, 3, 4)	CB	5-8	181	11- 7-61	Arizona State	FA
Glover, Kevin	C-G	6-2	267	6-17-63	Maryland	D2
Graeber, Ken	NT	6-2	265	10-30-61	Nebraska	FA
Hancock, Kevin	LB	6-2	223	1- 6-62	Baylor	D4
Harris, Kevin	S	6-0	196	9-27-63	Georgia	D11
Kanka, Thomas (1)	NT	...	...	....	Hillsdale	FA
Keslar, Jack	T	6-4	294	6- 5-62	West Virginia	FA
James, June	LB	6-1	218	12- 2-62	Texas	D9
Johnson, James	LB	6-2	236	6-21-62	San Diego State	D3
McIntosh, Joe	RB	5-10	189	12- 9-62	North Carolina State	D5
Pierzynski, Jeff	LB	6-1	222	7-27-62	Eastern Michigan	FA
Royster, Mark	CB	6-0	195	12-28-61	Wichita State	FA
Short, Stan	G	6-4	270	9-20-63	Penn State	D6
Spitzig, Kevin	LB	6-3	220	12-17-61	Iowa	FA
Staten, Tony	CB	5-9	178	2- 6-63	Angelo State	D7
Weaver, Mike	G	6-1	325	12-15-62	Georgia	D12

GREEN BAY PACKERS
(Central Division, National Conference)

Forrest Gregg

President—Hon. Robert J. Parins
Assistant to President—Bob Harlan
Assistant to President—Tom Miller
Head Coach—Forrest Gregg (8 years: 58-56)
Player Personnel Director—Dick Corrick
Director of Player Procurement—Chuck Hutchison
Assistant Coaches:
    Receivers—Lew Carpenter
    Strength and Conditioning—Virgil Knight
    Defensive Coordinator—Dick Modzelewski
    Linebackers—Herb Paterra
    Linebackers/Special Teams—Chuck Priefer
    Secondary—Ken Riley
    Offensive Coordinator—Bob Schnelker
    Offensive Backfield—George Sefcik
    Offensive Line—Jerry Wampfler
Public Relations Director—Lee Remmel
    (Office Phone: 494-2351—Area Code 414)
Offices—1265 Lombardi Ave., Green Bay, Wis. 54303
Mailing Address—P.O. Box 10628, Green Bay, Wis. 54307
Stadium—Lambeau Field, Green Bay (Capacity: 56,189); County Stadium, Milwaukee (Capacity: 55,958)
Team Colors—Green, Gold and White
Training Site—St. Norbert College, De Pere, Wis. (food and lodging only; workouts at Lambeau Field, Green Bay)

1985 SCHEDULE
(All times local.
All games Sunday unless noted otherwise.)

Sept. 8	at New England	1:00
Sept. 15	NEW YORK GIANTS	3:00
Sept. 22	NEW YORK JETS at Milwaukee	3:00
Sept. 29	at St. Louis	12:00
Oct. 6	DETROIT	12:00
Oct. 13	MINNESOTA at Milwaukee	12:00
Oct. 21	at Chicago (Mon.)	8:00
Oct. 27	at Indianapolis	1:00
Nov. 3	CHICAGO	12:00
Nov. 10	at Minnesota	12:00
Nov. 17	NEW ORLEANS at Milwaukee	12:00
Nov. 24	at Los Angeles Rams	1:00
Dec. 1	TAMPA BAY	12:00
Dec. 8	MIAMI	12:00
Dec. 15	at Detroit	1:00
Dec. 22	at Tampa Bay	1:00

1984 RESULTS—(Won 8, Lost 8)

Packers		Opp.		Att.
24	St. Louis	23	(H)	53,738
7	Los Angeles Raiders	28	(A)	46,269
7	Chicago	9	(H)	55,942
6	Dallas	20	(A)	64,222
27	Tampa Bay (OT)	30	(A)	47,487
28	San Diego	34	(H)	54,045
14	Denver	17	(A)	62,546
24	Seattle	30	(H)	52,286
41	Detroit	9	(H)	54,289
23	New Orleans	13	(A)	57,426
45	Minnesota	17	(H)	52,931
31	Los Angeles Rams	6	(H)	52,031
28	Detroit	31	(A)	63,698
27	Tampa Bay	14	(H)	46,800
20	Chicago	14	(A)	59,374
38	Minnesota	14	(A)	51,197

1984 GAMES STARTED

16 games: John Anderson, George Cumby, Mike Douglass, Gerry Ellis, Tom Flynn, Donnie Humphrey, Terry Jones, Mark Lee, Tim Lewis, James Lofton, Mark Murphy, Randy Scott.

15 games: Lynn Dickey, Tim Huffman.

14 games: Alphonso Carreker, Greg Koch, Karl Swanke.

13 games: Paul Coffman, Ron Hallstrom.

12 games: John Jefferson, Larry McCarren.

10 games: Jessie Clark.

5 games: Eddie Lee Ivery.

4 games: Phillip Epps, Blake Moore.

3 games: Dave Drechsler, Syd Kitson.

2 games: Henry Childs, Gary Lewis, Charles Martin, Keith Uecker.

1 game: Randy Wright.

GREEN BAY PACKERS 1985 VETERAN ROSTER

No.	Name	Pos.	Ht.	Wt.	NFL Exp.	Birth-date	College	Games in '84	How Acquired
59	Anderson, John	LB	6-3	229	8	2-14-56	Michigan	16	D1a, '78
93	†Brown, Robert	DE	6-2	250	4	5-21-60	Virginia Tech	16	D4, '82
	Brunner, Scott	QB	6-5	200	5	3-24-57	Delaware	*0	T-Den, '85
58	Cannon, Mark	C	6-3	258	2	6-14-52	Texas-Arlington	16	D11, '84
76	Carreker, Alphonso	DE	6-6	260	2	5-25-62	Florida State	14	D1, '84
88	†Cassidy, Ron	WR	6-0	180	6	7-23-57	Utah State	15	D8, '79
33	†Clark, Jessie	FB	6-0	233	3	1- 3-60	Arkansas	11	D7, '83
82	Coffman, Paul	TE	6-3	225	7	3-29-56	Kansas State	14	OFA, '78
21	Crouse, Ray	RB	5-11	214	2	3-16-59	Nevada-Las Vegas	16	FA, '84
52	Cumby, George	LB	6-0	224	6	7- 5-56	Oklahoma	16	D1a, '80
10	Del Greco, Al	K	5-10	195	2	3- 2-62	Auburn	9	FA, '84
12	Dickey, Lynn	QB	6-4	203	15	10-19-49	Kansas State	15	T-Hou, '76
99	Dorsey, John	LB	6-2	235	2	8-31-60	Connecticut	16	D4, '84
53	Douglass, Mike	LB	6-0	214	8	3-15-55	San Diego State	16	D5, '78
61	Drechsler, Dave	G	6-3	264	3	7-18-60	North Carolina	16	D2, '83
31	Ellis, Gerry	FB	5-11	225	6	11-12-57	Missouri	16	FA, '80
85	Epps, Phillip	WR	5-10	155	4	11-11-59	Texas Christian	16	D12, '82
41	Flynn, Tom	S	6-0	195	2	3-24-62	Pittsburgh	16	D5, '84
65	Hallstrom, Ron	T	6-6	283	4	6-11-59	Iowa	16	D1, '82
69	Harris, Leotis	G	6-1	265	7	6-28-55	Arkansas	*0	D6, '78
27	Hayes, Gary	CB	5-10	180	2	8-19-57	Fresno State	16	FA, '84
78	Hoffman, Gary	T	6-7	282	2	9-28-61	Santa Clara	1	D10, '84
38	Hood, Estus	CB	5-11	189	8	11-14-55	Illinois State	16	D3, '78
25	Huckleby, Harlan	RB	6-1	201	6	12-30-57	Michigan	16	FA, '80
74	Huffman, Tim	T	6-5	282	5	8-31-59	Notre Dame	16	D9, '81
79	Humphrey, Donnie	DE	6-3	275	2	4-20-61	Auburn	16	D3, '84
40	Ivery, Eddie Lee	RB	6-0	214	6	7-30-57	Georgia Tech	16	D1, '79
83	†Jefferson, John	WR	6-1	204	8	2- 3-56	Arizona State	13	T-SD, '81
90	Johnson, Ezra	DE	6-4	259	9	10- 2-55	Morris Brown	13	D1a, '77
43	Jones, Daryll	S	6-0	190	2	3-23-62	Georgia	16	D7, '84
63	Jones, Terry	DT	6-2	253	8	11- 8-56	Alabama	16	D11, '78
68	Koch, Greg	T	6-4	276	9	6-14-55	Arkansas	15	D2, '77
22	Lee, Mark	CB	5-11	188	6	3-20-58	Washington	16	D2, '80
56	Lewis, Cliff	LB	6-1	224	5	11- 9-59	Southern Mississippi	16	D12, '81
81	Lewis, Gary	TE	6-5	234	5	12-30-58	Texas-Arlington	3	D2, '81
26	Lewis, Tim	CB	5-11	191	3	12-18-61	Pittsburgh	16	D1, '83
80	Lofton, James	WR	6-3	197	8	7- 5-56	Stanford	16	D1, '78
94	Martin, Charles	DE	6-4	270	2	8-31-59	Livingston, Ala.	16	FA, '84
54	McCarren, Larry	C	6-3	251	13	11- 9-51	Illinois	12	D12, '73
29	McCoy, Mike	S	5-11	190	9	8-16-53	Colorado	*0	D3, '76
28	McLeod, Mike	S	6-0	180	2	5- 4-58	Montana State	12	FA, '84
60	Moore, Blake	C-G	6-5	272	6	5- 8-58	Wooster	11	FA, '84
37	Murphy, Mark	S	6-2	201	5	4-22-58	West Liberty State	16	OFA, '80
51	Prather, Guy	LB	6-2	229	5	3-28-58	Grambling	16	FA, '81
35	Rodgers, Del	RB	5-10	202	3	6-22-60	Utah	14	D3, '82
55	Scott, Randy	LB	6-1	222	5	1-31-59	Alabama	16	OFA, '81
13	†Scribner, Bucky	P	6-0	202	3	7-11-60	Kansas	16	D11, '83
67	Swanke, Karl	T	6-6	262	6	12-29-57	Boston College	15	D6, '80
84	Taylor, Lenny	WR	5-10	179	2	2-15-61	Tennessee	2	D12, '84
70	Uecker, Keith	G-T	6-5	270	4	6-29-60	Auburn	6	W-Den, '84
86	West, Ed	TE	6-1	242	2	8- 2-61	Auburn	16	OFA, '84
50	Wingo, Rich	LB	6-1	227	6	7-16-56	Alabama	16	D7a, '79
16	Wright, Randy	QB	6-2	194	2	1-12-61	Wisconsin	8	D6, '84

*Brunner missed '84 season due to injury with Denver; Harris and McCoy missed '84 season due to injury.

†Option playout; subject to developments.

Also played with Packers in '84—QB Rich Campbell (3 games); TE Henry Childs (3), K Eddie Garcia (7), T Boyd Jones (2), G Syd Kitson (8), NT Bill Neill (16), DB Dwayne O'Steen (4).

D—Draft; T—Trade; W—Waivers; FA—Free Agent; OFA—Original Free Agent.

GREEN BAY PACKERS
1985 DRAFT CHOICES

(Number following name designates order of selection among 336 players drafted.)

Round and Player		Position	College
1. RUETTGERS, Ken from Cleveland through Buffalo (a)	7	T	Southern Cal
1. Choice to Buffalo (b)			
2. Choice to Buffalo (b)			
3. MORAN, Rich	71	G	San Diego St.
4. STANLEY, Walter	98	WR	Mesa, Colo.
5. NOBLE, Brian	125	LB	Arizona State
6. LEWIS, Mark	155	TE	Texas A & M
7. WILSON, Eric from Minnesota (c)	171	LB	Maryland
7. ELLERSON, Gary	182	RB	Wisconsin
8. STILLS, Ken	209	DB	Wisconsin
9. JOHNSON, Morris	239	G	Alabama A & M
10. BURGESS, Ronnie	266	DB	Wake Forest
11. SHIELD, Joe	294	QB	Trinity, Conn.
12. MEYER, Jim	323	P	Arizona State

(a) Bills acquired pick, 3rd round pick and 6th round pick in 1986 from Browns for first pick in supplemental draft, April 9, 1985; Packers acquired pick and 4th round pick in 1986 from Bills for 1st and 2nd round picks, April 30, 1985.

(b) See second part of (a).

(c) Acquired pick for kicker Jan Stenerud, July 17, 1984.

GREEN BAY PACKERS
1985 ROOKIE AND FIRST-YEAR ROSTER

(1) Indicates player in previous NFL camp.
(2) Indicates player with USFL game experience.
(3) Indicates player in previous USFL camp.
(4) Indicates player with CFL game experience.
(5) Indicates player in previous CFL camp.
  All others classified as rookies.

Name	Pos.	Hgt.	Wgt.	Birth-date	College	How Acquired
Allen, Mark	CB-S	6-2	180	6-10-60	Brigham Young	FA
Bratel, Keith	WR	5-11	176	2-26-63	Carroll College	FA
Cole, Curt (1)	TE	6-4	230	1- 2-61	Texas Tech	FA
Edwards, Keith	RB	6-0	210	4- 4-62	Vanderbilt	FA
Ellerson, Gary	RB	5-11	220	7-17-63	Wisconsin	D7a
Fowler, Delbert (1, 4)	LB	6-3	220	5- 4-58	West Virginia	FA
Harris, George W. (1)	LB	6-3	228	12- 2-60	Houston	FA
Johnson, Morris	T-G	6-2	317	6-25-62	Alabama A&M	D9
Kapischke, Kurt (1, 3)	T-G	6-5	265	3-14-62	Augustana	FA
Lewis, Mark	TE	6-2	218	5-20-61	Texas A&M	D6
Martin, Dan (1)	OT	6-4	275	7- 4-61	Iowa State	FA
Mayo, Bill	T-G	6-4	288	4-26-63	Tennessee	FA
McDowell, Felix (1)	TE	6-4	238	11- 8-60	East Texas State	FA
Meyer, Jim	P	6-4	204	1- 3-62	Arizona State	D12
Moran, Rich	T-G	6-2	272	3-19-62	San Diego State	D3
Mosley, Andre (1)	CB	6-0	195	1-16-62	North Texas State	FA
Noble, Brian	LB	6-3	237	9- 6-62	Arizona State	D5
Quinlan, Peter (3)	DT-DE	6-2	275	2-26-62	Holy Cross	FA
Ruettgers, Ken	T-G	6-5	267	8-20-62	Southern California	D1
Shield, Joe	QB	6-1	185	6-26-62	Trinity College	D11
Stanley, Walter	WR-KR	5-9	180	11- 5-62	Mesa College (Colo.)	D4
Stills, Ken	DB	5-10	185	9- 6-63	Wisconsin	D8
Walter, Ken (1, 4)	C-G	6-4	260	3- 2-58	Texas Tech	*FA '84
White, Eddie	TE	6-3	240	12- 9-60	Arkansas	FA
Wilson, Eric	LB	6-1	247	10-17-62	Maryland	D7
Winckler, Bob (1, 3)	OT	6-3	290	4-16-61	Wisconsin	FA
Young, Andre (1, 4)	LB	6-2	225	4-16-60	Bowling Green	FA

  *Walter missed '84 season due to injury.
  NOTE: 10th round pick Ronnie Burgess signed with Ottawa of the Canadian Football League.

HOUSTON OILERS
(Central Division, American Conference)

Hugh Campbell

Owner-President—K. S. (Bud) Adams, Jr.
Executive Vice-President and G.M.—Ladd Herzeg
Vice-President, Player Personnel—Mike Holovak
Director of Administration—Rick Nichols
Head Coach—Hugh Campbell (1 year: 3-13)
Assistant Coaches:
   Linebackers—John Devlin
   Offensive Coordinator—Joe Faragalli
   Special Teams—Gene Gaines
   Defensive Coordinator—Jerry Glanville
   Defensive Backfield—Ken Houston
   Receivers—Bruce Lemmerman
   Defensive Line—Bob Padilla
   Offensive Backfield—Al Roberts
   Offensive Line—Bill Walsh
Media Relations Director—Bob Hyde
   (Office Phone: 797-1272—Area Code 713)
Offices—6910 Fannin, Houston, Tex. 77030
Mailing Address—P. O. Box 1516, Houston, Tex. 77251
Stadium—Astrodome (Capacity: 50,495)
Team Colors—Scarlet, Columbia Blue and White
Training Site—Angelo State University, San Angelo, Tex.

1985 SCHEDULE
(All times local.
All games Sunday unless noted otherwise.)

Sept. 8	MIAMI	12:00
Sept. 15	at Washington	1:00
Sept. 22	at Pittsburgh	1:00
Sept. 29	DALLAS	12:00
Oct. 6	at Denver	2:00
Oct. 13	CLEVELAND	12:00
Oct. 20	CINCINNATI	12:00
Oct. 27	at St. Louis	12:00
Nov. 3	KANSAS CITY	12:00
Nov. 10	at Buffalo	1:00
Nov. 17	PITTSBURGH	12:00
Nov. 24	SAN DIEGO	12:00
Dec. 1	at Cincinnati	1:00
Dec. 8	NEW YORK GIANTS	3:00
Dec. 15	at Cleveland	1:00
Dec. 22	at Indianapolis	4:00

1984 RESULTS—(Won 3, Lost 13)

Oilers		Opp.		Att.
14	Los Angeles Raiders	24	(H)	49,029
21	Indianapolis	35	(H)	43,820
14	San Diego	31	(A)	52,266
10	Atlanta	42	(A)	45,248
10	New Orleans	27	(H)	43,108
3	Cincinnati	13	(A)	43,637
10	Miami	28	(A)	54,080
21	San Francisco	34	(H)	39,900
13	Cincinnati	31	(H)	34,010
7	Pittsburgh	35	(A)	48,892
17	Kansas City	16	(A)	44,464
31	New York Jets	20	(H)	40,141
10	Cleveland	27	(A)	46,077
23	Pittsburgh (OT)	20	(H)	39,786
16	Los Angeles Rams	27	(A)	49,092
20	Cleveland	27	(H)	33,676

1984 GAMES STARTED

16 games: Robert Abraham, Jesse Baker, Gregg Bingham, Keith Bostic, Robert Brazile, Steve Brown, Chris Dressel, Bruce Matthews, Warren Moon, Mike Munchak, Avon Riley, Jamie Williams.

15 games: Harvey Salem, Willie Tullis.

14 games: Carter Hartwig, Tim Smith, Mike Stensrud.

12 games: Bob Hamm.

10 games: John Schuhmacher, Dean Steinkuhler, Herkie Walls.

9 games: Larry Moriarty.

7 games: Jim Romano.

6 games: Earl Campbell.

5 games: Pat Howell.

3 games: Steve Bryant, Jerome Foster, Michael Holston, Brian Sochia.

2 games: Jeff Donaldson, Eric Mullins.

1 game: Bo Eason, Stan Edwards, Eric Moran.

HOUSTON OILERS 1985 VETERAN ROSTER

No.	Name	Pos.	Ht.	Wt.	NFL Exp.	Birth-date	College	Games in '84	How Acquired
56	†Abraham, Robert	LB	6-1	230	4	7-13-60	North Carolina State	16	D3a, '82
29	Allen, Patrick	CB	5-10	173	2	8-26-61	Utah State	16	D4a, '84
75	†Baker, Jesse	DE	6-5	271	7	7-10-57	Jacksonville State	16	D2a, '79
54	†Bingham, Gregg	LB	6-1	232	13	3-13-51	Purdue	16	D4, '73
25	Bostic, Keith	S	6-1	210	3	1-17-61	Michigan	16	D2a, '73
52	Brazile, Robert	LB	6-4	253	11	2- 7-53	Jackson State	16	D1, '75
24	Brown, Steve	CB	5-11	189	3	5-20-60	Oregon	16	D3b, '83
81	Bryant, Steve	WR	6-2	197	4	10-10-59	Purdue	14	D4, '82
8	Cooper, Joe	K	5-10	175	2	10-30-60	California	7	FA, '84
31	Donaldson, Jeff	S	6-0	193	2	4-19-62	Colorado	16	D9, '84
88	Dressel, Chris	TE	6-4	238	3	2- 7-61	Stanford	16	D3a, '83
21	Eason, Bo	S	6-2	200	2	3-10-61	Cal-Davis	10	D2a, '84
32	Edwards, Stan	RB	6-0	210	4	5-20-60	Michigan	14	D3, '82
78	Foster, Jerome	DE	6-2	263	3	7-25-60	Ohio State	9	D5a, '83
77	France, Doug	T	6-5	278	10	4-26-53	Ohio State	*0	T-Ram, '83
59	Grimsley, John	LB	6-2	232	2	2-25-62	Kentucky	16	D6, '84
	Harris, Tim	RB	5-9	206	2	6-15-61	Washington State	*0	FA, '85
36	Hartwig, Carter	S	6-0	203	7	2- 2-56	Southern California	14	D8, '79
84	†Holston, Mike	WR	6-3	191	5	1- 8-58	Morgan State	16	D3, '81
66	Howell, Pat	G	6-6	265	7	3-12-57	Southern California	11	FA, '83
50	†Hunt, Daryl	LB	6-3	243	7	11- 3-56	Oklahoma	5	D6, '79
97	Johnson, Mike	DE	6-5	253	2	4-24-62	Illinois	16	D9a, '84
57	Joiner, Tim	LB	6-4	248	3	1- 7-61	Louisiana State	11	D3, '83
38	Joyner, Willie	RB	5-10	200	2	4- 2-62	Maryland	10	D7, '84
4	†Kempf, Florian	K	5-9	170	4	5-25-56	Pennsylvania	9	FA, '84
27	Kennedy, Mike	S	6-0	195	3	2-26-59	Toledo	11	FA, '84
	Klug, Dave	LB	6-4	230	4	5-17-58	Concordia, Minn.	*0	FA, '85
10	Luck, Oliver	QB	6-2	196	4	4- 5-60	West Virginia	4	D2, '82
28	Lyday, Allen	CB-S	5-10	186	2	9-16-60	Nebraska	4	FA, '84
93	Lyles, Robert	LB	6-1	223	2	3-21-61	Texas Christian	6	D5, '84
74	Matthews, Bruce	T	6-4	280	3	8- 8-61	Southern California	16	D1, '83
89	McCloskey, Mike	TE	6-5	246	3	2- 2-61	Penn State	15	D4a, '83
26	Meadows, Darryl	S	6-1	198	3	2-15-61	Toledo	13	OFA, '83
91	Meads, Johnny	LB	6-2	225	2	6-25-61	Nicholls State	16	D3, '84
1	Moon, Warren	QB	6-3	208	2	11-18-56	Washington	16	FA, '84
76	Moran, Eric	T	6-5	282	2	6-10-60	Washington	8	FA, '84
30	Moriarty, Larry	RB	6-1	240	3	4-24-58	Notre Dame	14	D5, '83
80	Mullins, Eric	WR	5-11	181	2	7-30-62	Stanford	14	D6a, '84
63	Munchak, Mike	G	6-3	286	4	3- 5-60	Penn State	16	D1, '82
12	Ransom, Brian	QB	6-3	202	3	7- 9-60	Tennessee State	*0	FA, '83
53	Riley, Avon	LB	6-3	236	5	2-10-58	UCLA	16	D9, '81
85	†Roaches, Carl	KR-WR	5-8	170	6	10- 2-53	Texas A&M	16	FA, '80
55	Romano, Jim	C	6-3	255	4	9- 7-59	Penn State	*14	T-Rai, '84
73	Salem, Harvey	T	6-6	285	3	1-15-61	California	16	D2, '83
62	†Schuhmacher, John	G	6-3	277	6	9-23-55	Southern California	16	D12, '78
83	Smith, Tim	WR	6-2	206	6	3-20-57	Nebraska	16	D3, '80
72	Sochia, Brian	NT	6-3	254	3	7-21-61	Northwest Oklahoma St.	16	OFA, '83
70	Steinkuhler, Dean	T	6-3	273	2	1-27-61	Nebraska	10	D1, '84
67	Stensrud, Mike	NT	6-5	280	7	2-19-56	Iowa State	16	D2, '79
98	Studaway, Mark	DE	6-3	269	2	9-20-60	Tennessee	6	D4, '84
51	†Thompson, Ted	LB	6-1	218	11	1-17-53	Southern Methodist	16	OFA, '75
20	Tullis, Willie	CB	6-0	195	5	4- 5-58	Troy State	16	D8, '81
82	Walls, Herkie	WR	5-8	160	3	7-18-61	Texas	14	D7, '83
	Whittington, Arthur	RB	5-11	185	6	9- 4-55	Southern Methodist	*0	FA, '85
87	Williams, Jamie	TE	6-4	232	3	2-25-60	Nebraska	16	W-TB, '84
33	Woolfolk, Butch	RB	6-1	207	4	3- 1-60	Michigan	*15	T-NYG, '85

*France missed '84 season due to injury; Harris last active with Pittsburgh in '83; Klug last active with Kansas City in '84; Ransom active for 16 games but did not play; Romano played 6 games with L.A. Raiders, 8 in Houston in '84; Whittington last active with Buffalo in '82 and Oakland (USFL) in '84; Woolfolk played 15 games with N.Y. Giants in '84.

†Option playout; subject to developments.

Also played with Oilers in '84—DE Bryan Caldwell (8 games), RB Earl Campbell (6), C David Carter (7), RB Donnie Craft (1), DE Bob Hamm (12), P John James (16), RB Richard Williams (7).

D—Draft; T—Trade; W—Waivers; FA—Free Agent; OFA—Original Free Agent.

HOUSTON OILERS
1985 DRAFT CHOICES

(Number following name designates order of selection among 336 players drafted.)

Round and Player		Position	College
1. Choice to Atlanta thru Minnesota (a)			
1. CHILDRESS, Ray from Minnesota (b)	3	DE	Texas A&M
1. JOHNSON, Richard from New Orleans (c)	11	DB	Wisconsin
2. Choice to Denver (d)			
2. BYRD, Richard from T.B. through Denver (e)	36	DE	So. Mississippi
3. Choice to N.Y. Giants (f)			
3. KELLEY, Mike from Denver (g)	82	C	Notre Dame
4. BRIEHL, Tom	87	LB	Stanford
5. Choice to Dallas (h)			
5. BUSH, Frank from L.A. Rams through K.C. (i)	133	LB	No. Carolina St.
5. JOHNSON, Lee from Denver (j)	138	K	Brigham Young
6. Choice to L.A. Raiders (k)			
6. KRAKOSKI, Joe from Kansas City (l)	153	LB	Washington
7. AKIU, Mike	170	WR	Hawaii
8. THOMAS, Chuck	199	C	Oklahoma
9. TASKER, Steve	226	KR	Northwestern
10. GOLIC, Mike	255	DE	Notre Dame
11. DREWREY, Willie	281	KR	West Virginia
12. VONDER HAAR, Mark	311	DT	Minnesota

(a) Oilers traded pick to Vikings in switch of first-round positions, April 9, 1985; Vikings traded pick to Falcons for 1st and 3rd round picks, April 30, 1985.

(b) See first part of (a).

(c) Acquired pick for running back Earl Campbell, October 9, 1984.

(d) Traded pick for 2nd and 5th round picks, April 30, 1985.

(e) Broncos acquired pick and 4th round pick in 1984 from Buccaneers for quarterback Steve DeBerg, April 24, 1984; Oilers acquired pick from Broncos, see (d).

(f) Traded pick for running back Butch Woolfolk, March 21, 1985.

(g) Acquired pick for wide receiver Butch Johnson, August 20, 1984.

(h) Traded pick, 2nd round pick in 1984 and wide receiver Mike Renfro for wide receiver Butch Johnson and 2nd round pick in 1984, April 13, 1984.

(i) Chiefs acquired pick and cornerback Lucious Smith from Rams for quarterback Steve Fuller, August 19, 1983; Oilers acquired pick and 6th round pick from Chiefs for defensive end Bob Hamm and 1986 pick, April 30, 1985.

(j) See (d).

(k) Traded pick and 3rd round pick for center Jim Romano, October 9, 1984.

(l) See second part of (i).

HOUSTON OILERS
1985 ROOKIE AND FIRST-YEAR ROSTER

(1) Indicates player in previous NFL camp.
(2) Indicates player with USFL game experience.
(3) Indicates player in previous USFL camp.
(4) Indicates player with CFL game experience.
(5) Indicates player in previous CFL camp.
    All others classified as rookies.

Name	Pos.	Hgt.	Wgt.	Birth-date	College	How Acquired
Akiu, Mike	WR	5-9	185	2-12-62	Hawaii	D7
Briehl, Tom	LB	6-3	247	9- 8-62	Stanford	D4
Bush, Frank	LB	6-1	218	1-10-63	North Carolina State	D5
Byrd, Richard	DE	6-3	255	3-20-62	Southern Mississippi	D2
Campbell, Donnie	QB	6-5	218	12-18-61	Kansas State	FA
Childress, Ray	DE	6-6	267	10-20-62	Texas A&M	D1
Drewrey, Willie	WR	5-7	158	4-28-63	West Virginia	D11
Fuller, Ardell	WR	6-1	182	12-13-62	Vanderbilt	FA
Golic, Mike	DL	6-5	265	12-12-62	Notre Dame	D10
Gordon, Scott (1)	OG	6-4	265	9-23-60	Santa Clara	FA
Hall, Brian	CB	6-2	200	10- 8-61	Oklahoma	FA
Hare, Frank	DT	6-2	244	2-13-63	Kentucky	FA
Harlien, Matt	OT	6-4	270	9-16-60	Texas Tech	FA
Harraka, Greg	OL	6-2	266	6- 1-62	Maryland	FA
Johnson, Lee	P-K	6-1	204	11- 2-61	Brigham Young	D5a
Johnson, Richard	CB	6-0	195	10-20-62	Wisconsin	D1a
Jordan, Kent (1)	TE	6-7	235	10-29-59	St. Mary's	FA
Kelley, Mike	C-OG	6-5	266	8-27-62	Notre Dame	D3
Kellermeyer, Doug (1, 3)	OT	6-2	265	6- 1-61	Brigham Young	FA
Krakoski, Joe	LB	6-1	224	11-11-62	Washington	D6
Schlecht, Mark (1)	P	6-2	200	6-17-59	Nebraska (Omaha)	FA
Tasker, Steve	PR-KR	5-9	185	4-10-62	Northwestern	D9
Thomas, Chuck	C	6-2	270	2-24-60	Oklahoma	D8
Thomas, John (3)	CB	6-2	190	1- 7-62	Texas Christian	FA
Turner, Greg	DB	5-11	192	6-12-62	Arizona	FA
Vernon, Derron	RB	6-0	188	3-22-62	Eastern Michigan	FA
VonderHaar, Mark	OT	6-5	255	2- 6-62	Minnesota	D12
Weil, Jack (1)	P	5-11	175	3-16-62	Wyoming	FA

INDIANAPOLIS COLTS
(Eastern Division, American Conference)

Rod Dowhower

President and Treasurer—Robert Irsay
General Manager—Jim Irsay
Assistant General Manager—Bob Terpening
Player Personnel Director—Jack Bushofsky
College Scout—Clyde Powers
Head Coach—Rod Dowhower (First Year)

Assistant Coaches:
   Quarterbacks—John Becker
   Secondary—George Catavolos
   Defensive Coordinator—George Hill
   Assistant Head Coach/Off. Line—Tom Lovat
   Offensive Coordinator/Backs—Billie Matthews
   Receivers—Chip Myers
   Special Teams/Asst. Off Line—Keith Rowen
   Defensive Line—Steve Sidwell
   Linebackers—Rick Venturi
   Strength—Tom Zupancic

Public Relations Director—Bob Eller
   (Office Phone: 252-2658—Area Code 317)
Mailing Address—P. O. Box 20000, Indianapolis, Ind. 46220
Stadium—Hoosier Dome (Capacity: 61,000)
Team Colors—Royal Blue, White and Silver
Training Site—Anderson College, Anderson, Ind.

1985 SCHEDULE
(All times local.
All games Sunday unless noted otherwise.)

Sept.	8	at Pittsburgh	1:00
Sept.	15	at Miami	4:00
Sept.	22	DETROIT	12:00
Sept.	29	at New York Jets	4:00
Oct.	6	BUFFALO	12:00
Oct.	13	DENVER	12:00
Oct.	20	at Buffalo	1:00
Oct.	27	GREEN BAY	1:00
Nov.	3	NEW YORK JETS	4:00
Nov.	10	at New England	1:00
Nov.	17	MIAMI	1:00
Nov.	24	at Kansas City	3:00
Dec.	1	NEW ENGLAND	1:00
Dec.	8	at Chicago	12:00
Dec.	15	at Tampa Bay	1:00
Dec.	22	HOUSTON	4:00

1984 RESULTS—(Won 4, Lost 12)

Colts		Opp.		Att.
14	New York Jets	23	(H)	60,500
35	Houston	21	(A)	43,820
33	St. Louis	34	(H)	60,274
7	Miami	44	(A)	55,415
31	Buffalo	17	(H)	60,032
7	Washington	35	(H)	60,012
7	Philadelphia	16	(A)	50,277
17	Pittsburgh	16	(H)	60,026
3	Dallas	22	(A)	58,724
10	San Diego	38	(H)	60,143
9	New York Jets	5	(A)	51,066
17	New England	50	(H)	60,009
7	Los Angeles Raiders	21	(A)	40,289
15	Buffalo	21	(A)	20,693
17	Miami	35	(H)	60,411
10	New England	16	(A)	22,383

1984 GAMES STARTED

16 games: Ray Donaldson, Nesby Glasgow, Barry Krauss, Randy McMillan, Ron Solt.
15 games: Ray Butler, Vernon Maxwell, Clifton Odom, Ben Utt, Blaise Winter.
14 games: Eugene Daniel, Mark Kafentzis, Leo Wisniewski.
13 games: Johnie Cooks, Jim Mills.
12 games: Tracy Porter.
10 games: Donnell Thompson.
9 games: Curtis Dickey, Mike Pagel, Steve Wright, Dave Young.
8 games: Preston Davis, Tim Sherwin.
7 games: Greg Bracelin.
6 games: Chris Hinton, Tate Randle.
5 games: James Burroughs, Frank Middleton, Art Schlichter.
4 games: Matt Bouza, Ted Petersen.
2 games: Mark Herrmann, Alvin Moore, Chris Scott, Brad White.
1 game: Steve Hathaway, Mike Humiston, Mark Kirchner, Steve Parker, Vaughn Williams.

INDIANAPOLIS COLTS 1985 VETERAN ROSTER

No.	Name	Pos.	Ht.	Wt.	NFL Exp.	Birth-date	College	Games in '84	How Acquired
2	Allegre, Raul	K	5-10	165	3	6-15-59	Texas	12	T-Dal, '83
30	†Anderson, Larry	S	5-11	194	8	9-25-56	Louisiana Tech	12	W-Pit, '82
	Baldischwiler, Karl	T	6-5	260	7	1-19-56	Oklahoma	*0	T-Det, '83
61	Bailey, Don	C	6-4	257	2	3-24-61	Miami, Fla.	10	FA, '84
97	Beach, Pat	TE	6-4	243	3	12-28-59	Washington State	*0	D6, '82
48	†Bell, Mark	TE	6-5	246	6	8-30-57	Colorado State	16	FA, '83
5	Biasucci, Dean	K	6-0	188	2	7-25-62	Western Carolina	15	FA, '84
85	Bouza, Matt	WR	6-3	209	4	4- 8-59	California	16	FA, '82
52	Bracelin, Greg	LB	6-1	216	6	4-16-57	California	16	FA, '82
45	†Burroughs, James	CB	6-1	187	4	1-21-58	Michigan State	6	D3, '82
80	Butler, Ray	WR	6-3	197	6	6-28-56	Southern California	16	D4, '80
72	Call, Kevin	T	6-7	289	2	11-13-61	Colorado State	15	D5a, '84
98	Cooks, Johnie	LB	6-4	243	4	11-23-58	Mississippi State	16	D1, '82
38	Daniel, Eugene	CB	5-11	179	2	5- 4-61	Louisiana State	15	D8, '84
27	Davis, Preston	CB	5-11	180	2	3-10-62	Baylor	12	FA, '84
33	Dickey, Curtis	RB	6-0	222	6	11-27-56	Texas A&M	10	D1, '80
53	Donaldson, Ray	C	6-4	273	6	5-17-58	Georgia	16	D2, '80
65	Gardner, Ellis	T-G	6-5	250	3	9-16-61	Georgia Tech	9	FA, '84
25	Glasgow, Nesby	S	5-10	180	7	4-15-57	Washington	16	D8a, '79
58	Hathaway, Steve	LB	6-4	238	2	4-26-62	West Virginia	6	D12, '84
	Henderson, Wyatt	WR	5-10	180	2	11-10-56	Fresno State	*0	FA, '85
88	Henry, Bernard	WR	6-1	180	4	4- 9-60	Arizona State	14	OFA, '82
75	Hinton, Chris	G	6-4	283	3	7-31-61	Northwestern	6	T-Den, '83
57	†Humiston, Mike	LB	6-3	240	5	1- 8-59	Weber State	16	FA, '84
29	†Kafentzis, Mark	S	5-10	200	4	6-30-58	Hawaii	16	FA, '83
63	Kirchner, Mark	T	6-3	261	3	10-19-59	Baylor	11	FA, '84
55	Krauss, Barry	LB	6-3	249	7	3-17-57	Alabama	16	D1, '79
56	Maxwell, Vernon	LB	6-2	238	3	10-25-61	Arizona State	16	D2, '83
32	McMillan, Randy	FB	6-0	212	5	12-17-58	Pittsburgh	16	D1, '81
43	Middleton, Frank	RB	5-11	201	2	10-28-60	Florida A&M	16	FA, '84
76	Mills, Jim	T	6-9	281	3	9-23-61	Hawaii	14	D9, '83
23	Moore, Alvin	RB	6-0	198	3	5-30-59	Arizona State	13	D7, '83
93	Odom, Cliff	LB	6-2	235	5	9-15-58	Texas-Arlington	16	FA, '82
90	Padjen, Gary	LB	6-2	241	4	7- 2-58	Arizona State	16	FA, '82
18	Pagel, Mike	QB	6-2	205	4	9-13-60	Arizona State	11	D4, '82
78	Parker, Steve	DE	6-3	262	3	9-21-59	Eastern Illinois	9	FA, '83
87	†Porter, Tracy	WR	6-2	202	5	6- 1-59	Louisiana State	16	T-Det, '83
21	Radachowsky, George	CB-S	5-11	178	2	9- 7-62	Boston College	16	T-Ram, '84
35	Randle, Tate	CB	6-0	196	4	8-15-59	Texas Tech	16	FA, '83
10	Schlichter, Art	QB	6-3	210	3	4-25-60	Ohio State	9	D1a, '82
95	Scott, Chris	DE	6-5	253	2	12-11-61	Purdue	14	D3, '84
83	Sherwin, Tim	TE	6-6	245	5	5- 4-58	Boston College	16	D4, '81
	Simmons, Cleo	TE	6-2	225	2	10-21-60	Jackson State	*0	FA, '85
91	Smith, Byron	DE	6-5	264	2	12-21-62	California	3	SupD, '84
86	Smith, Phil	WR	6-3	188	3	4-28-61	San Diego State	16	D4, '83
66	Solt, Ron	G	6-3	275	2	5-19-62	Maryland	16	D1a, '84
3	Stark, Rohn	P	6-3	203	4	6- 4-59	Florida State	16	D2a, '82
99	Thompson, Donnell	DE	6-5	263	5	10-27-58	North Carolina	10	D1a, '81
64	Utt, Ben	G	6-5	280	4	6-13-59	Georgia Tech	16	FA, '82
94	Virkus, Scott	DE	6-5	248	3	9- 7-59	San Francisco, C.C.	*8	FA, '84
92	White, Brad	NT	6-2	260	5	8-18-58	Tennessee	15	FA, '84
39	Williams, Newton	FB	5-10	219	8	5-19-59	Arizona State	*0	W-SF, '83
40	Williams, Vaughn	CB-S	6-2	193	2	12-14-61	Stanford	10	FA, '84
96	Winter, Blaise	DE	6-3	262	2	1-31-62	Syracuse	16	D2, '84
69	Wisniewski, Leo	NT	6-1	259	4	11- 6-59	Penn State	14	D2, '82
34	Wonsley, George	RB	6-0	212	2	11-23-60	Mississippi State	14	D4a, '84
81	Young, Dave	TE	6-5	243	4	2- 9-59	Purdue	13	FA, '83

*Baldischwiler, Beach, and N. Williams missed '84 season due to injury; Henderson last active with San Diego in '81 and Jacksonville (USFL) in '84; Simmons last active with Dallas in '83; Virkus played 2 games with Buffalo, 5 with New England and 1 with Indianapolis in '84.

†Option playout; subject to developments.

Also played with Colts in '84—S Kim Anderson (1 game), T Andy Ekern (2), C Grant Feasel (6), QB Mark Herrmann (3), DB Bo Scott Metcalf (1), T Ted Petersen (9), DE Henry Waechter (1), G Steve Wright (12).

D—Draft; T—Trade; W—Waivers; FA—Free Agent; OFA—Original Free Agent; SupD—Supplemental Draft.

INDIANAPOLIS COLTS
1985 DRAFT CHOICES

(Number following name designates order of selection among 336 players drafted.)

Round and Player		Position	College
1. BICKETT, Duane	5	LB	Southern Cal
2. ANDERSON, Don	32	DB	Purdue
3. YOUNG, Anthony	61	DB	Temple
4. BROUGHTON, Willie	88	DE	Miami, Fla.
5. CARON, Roger	117	T	Harvard
6. Choice to Dallas (a)			
7. HARBOUR, James	173	WR	Mississippi
8. NICHOLS, Ricky	200	WR	East Carolina
9. BOYER, Mark	229	TE	Southern California
10. PINESETT, Andre	256	DT	Cal. St.-Fullerton
11. Choice to L.A. Rams (b)			
12. BURNETTE, Dave	312	T	Central Arkansas

(a) Traded pick for tackle Steve Wright, August 27, 1983.
(b) Traded pick for defensive back George Radachowsky, August 27, 1984.

INDIANAPOLIS COLTS
1985 ROOKIE AND FIRST-YEAR ROSTER

(1) Indicates player in previous NFL camp.
(2) Indicates player with USFL game experience.
(3) Indicates player in previous USFL camp.
(4) Indicates player with CFL game experience.
(5) Indicates player in previous CFL camp.
   All others classified as rookies.

Name	Pos.	Hgt.	Wgt.	Birth-date	College	How Acquired
Aikens, Carl	WR	6-1	187	6- 5-62	Northern Illinois	FA
Anderson, Don	CB	5-10	185	7- 8-63	Purdue	D2
Basso, Phil	QB	6-1	175	4-27-61	Liberty Baptist	FA
Bickett, Duane	LB	6-5	232	12- 1-62	Southern California	D1
Blackburn, Drew	G	6-4	265	3-31-62	Mississippi College	FA
Boyer, Mark	TE	6-4	232	9-16-62	Southern California	D9
Bromley, Phil	C	6-2	255	11-18-62	Florida	FA
Brooks, Mark	FB	6-0	235	5-15-63	Notre Dame	FA
Broughton, Willie	DE	6-5	245	9- 9-64	Miami (Fla.)	D4
Brown, Orlando	RB	5-10	200	12-31-62	Indiana	FA
Brown, Ray (1, 3)	DE	6-4	260	8-28-61	Clemson	FA
Burnette, David	OT	6-6	278	3-24-61	Central Arkansas	D12
Caron, Roger	OT	6-5	270	6- 3-62	Harvard	D5
Crnkovich, Nick	TE	6-3	238	4- 7-63	Wabash	FA
Dwenger, Rick	FB	5-10	217	5-12-61	Indiana State	FA
Gandy, Geff (1)	LB	6-2	238	5- 1-60	Baylor	FA
Grant, Randy	WR	5-11	175	6- 2-63	Illinois	FA
Groom, Tracy	G	....	....	....	Stephen F. Austin	FA
Gross, James (1, 3)	LB	6-1	230	11- 7-61	Maryland	FA
Harbour, James	WR	6-0	190	11-10-62	Mississippi	D7
Harris, Neil (3)	DB	6-0	195	2-12-62	Nebraska	FA
Hunley, Lamonte	LB	6-1	225	1-31-63	Arizona	FA
Lowry, Orlando (1)	LB	6-4	230	8-14-61	Ohio State	FA
Merritts, James (1, 3)	NT	6-3	264	3-22-61	West Virginia	FA
Nichols, Ricky	WR	5-10	180	7-27-62	East Carolina	D8
O'Brien, Chuck	WR	5-10	178	....	Eastern New Mexico	FA
Peoples, Carlton (2)	CB	6-0	181	11- 9-60	Tennessee	FA
Pinesett, Andre	DE	6-2	245	7-25-61	Cal. St.-Fullerton	D10
Poles, Robert (1, 3)	DE	6-5	275	2-24-61	Boston College	FA
Richardson, Ed	LB	6-2	225	11- 9-61	Clemson	FA
Sinclair, Ian	C	6-4	253	7-22-60	Miami (Fla.)	FA
Smith, Eric	S	5-10	186	12-22-59	Southern Methodist	FA
Smith, Mark (1, 3)	WR	6-0	180	4- 4-62	North Carolina	FA
Taylor, Garfield (1)	RB	6-1	198	2- 3-61	Kansas	FA
Tootle, Jeff (1)	LB	6-2	230	8-29-62	Mesa College, Colo.	FA
Underwood, Gene	CB	5-11	175	1- 6-61	Cal Poly-SLO	FA
Washington, Tim (1, 3)	DB	5-11	187	11- 7-59	Fresno State	FA
Williams, Oliver (1, 3)	WR	6-3	195	10-17-60	Illinois	FA
Wray, Steve (1, 3)	QB	6-2	215	1-29-60	Franklin (Ind.)	FA
Young, Anthony	SS	6-0	187	10- 8-63	Temple	D3
Ziolkowski, Ron (1)	LB	6-1	230	4- 5-62	James Madison	FA

KANSAS CITY CHIEFS
(Western Division, American Conference)

John Mackovic

Owner—Lamar Hunt
President—Jack W. Steadman
General Manager and Vice-President—Jim Schaaf
Director of Player Personnel—Les Miller
Head Coach—John Mackovic (2 years: 14-18)
Assistant Coaches:
    Defensive Quality Control—Dave Brazil
    Defensive Line—Walt Corey
    Inside Linebackers—Dan Daniel
    Offensive Line—Marty Galbraith
    Defensive Backs—Doug Graber
    Offensive Assistant/Off. Quality Control—J.D. Helm
    Off./Def. Lines/Strength & Conditioning—C.T. Hewgley
    Quarterbacks—Pete McCulley
    Offensive Backs—Willie Peete
    Outside Linebackers/Special Teams—Jim Vechiarella
    Receivers—Richard Williamson
Public Relations Director—Bob Sprenger
    (Office Phone: 924-9300—Area Code 816)
Offices—One Arrowhead Drive, Kansas City, Mo. 64129
Stadium—Arrowhead Stadium (Capacity: 78,198)
Team Colors—Red, Gold and White
Training Site—William Jewell College, Liberty, Mo.

1985 SCHEDULE
(All times local.
All games Sunday unless noted otherwise.)

Sept. 8	at New Orleans	12:00
Sept. 12	L.A. RAIDERS (Thurs.)	7:00
Sept. 22	at Miami	4:00
Sept. 29	SEATTLE	12:00
Oct. 6	at Los Angeles Raiders	1:00
Oct. 13	at San Diego	1:00
Oct. 20	LOS ANGELES RAMS	12:00
Oct. 27	DENVER	12:00
Nov. 3	at Houston	12:00
Nov. 10	PITTSBURGH	12:00
Nov. 17	at San Francisco	1:00
Nov. 24	INDIANAPOLIS	3:00
Dec. 1	at Seattle	1:00
Dec. 8	ATLANTA	12:00
Dec. 14	at Denver (Sat.)	2:00
Dec. 22	SAN DIEGO	12:00

1984 RESULTS—(Won 8, Lost 8)

Chiefs		Opp.		Att.
37	Pittsburgh	27	(A)	56,709
27	Cincinnati	22	(A)	47,111
20	Los Angeles Raiders	22	(H)	75,111
0	Denver	21	(A)	74,263
10	Cleveland	6	(H)	40,785
16	New York Jets	17	(H)	51,843
31	San Diego	13	(H)	62,233
7	New York Jets	28	(A)	66,782
24	Tampa Bay	20	(A)	41,710
0	Seattle	45	(A)	61,396
16	Houston	17	(H)	44,464
7	Los Angeles Raiders	17	(A)	48,575
27	New York Giants	28	(A)	74,383
16	Denver	13	(H)	38,494
34	Seattle	7	(H)	34,855
42	San Diego	21	(A)	40,221

1984 GAMES STARTED

16 games: Brad Budde, Lloyd Burruss, Carlos Carson, Deron Cherry, Tom Condon, Calvin Daniels, Henry Marshall, Kevin Ross, Bob Rush, Art Still.

15 games: Matt Herkenhoff, Albert Lewis.

14 games: Mike Bell, Bill Maas, Gary Spani.

12 games: Willie Scott.

10 games: Jim Rourke.

9 games: Jerry Blanton, Herman Heard, Billy Jackson, Ken McAlister.

8 games: Todd Blackledge, Bill Kenney.

7 games: Theotis Brown, John Zamberlin.

6 games: Dave Lutz.

4 games: Walt Arnold, Charles Jackson, Ken Lacy.

3 games: Jeff Paine.

2 games: Dave Lindstrom, Scott Radecic.

1 game: John Alt, Ed Beckman, Greg Hill, Eric Holle, Ken Kremer, David Little, Stephone Paige.

KANSAS CITY CHIEFS 1985 VETERAN ROSTER

No.	Name	Pos.	Ht.	Wt.	NFL Exp.	Birth-date	College	Games in '84	How Acquired
76	Alt, John	T	6-7	278	2	5-30-62	Iowa	15	D1a, '84
6	Arnold, Jim	P	6-2	212	3	1-31-61	Vanderbilt	16	D5, '83
87	Arnold, Walt	TE	6-3	234	6	8-31-58	New Mexico	*14	FA, '84
68	Auer, Scott	G-T	6-4	255	2	10- 4-61	Michigan State	16	D9, '84
77	Baldinger, Rich	T-G	6-4	285	4	12-31-59	Wake Forest	14	FA, '83
99	Bell, Mike	DE	6-4	250	6	8-30-57	Colorado State	15	D1, '79
14	Blackledge, Todd	QB	6-3	225	3	2-25-61	Penn State	11	D1, '83
57	Blanton, Jerry	LB	6-1	236	7	12-10-56	Kentucky	10	FA, '78
27	Brown, Theotis	RB	6-2	225	7	4-20-57	UCLA	14	FA, '83
66	Budde, Brad	G	6-4	260	6	5- 9-58	Southern California	16	D1, '80
34	Burruss, Lloyd	S	6-0	202	5	10-31-57	Maryland	16	D3b, '81
88	Carson, Carlos	WR	5-11	180	6	12-28-58	Louisiana State	16	D5, '80
20	†Cherry, Deron	S	5-11	190	5	9-12-59	Rutgers	16	OFA, '81
65	Condon, Tom	G	6-3	275	12	12-26-52	Boston College	16	D10, '74
50	Daniels, Calvin	LB	6-3	236	4	12-26-58	North Carolina	16	D2, '82
73	Dawson, Mike	NT	6-3	245	10	10-16-53	Arizona	9	FA, '84
38	Gunter, Michael	RB	5-11	205	2	1-18-61	Tulsa	4	FA, '84
	Hamm, Bob	DE	6-4	263	3	4-24-59	Nevada-Reno	*12	T-Hou, '85
82	Hancock, Anthony	WR-KR	6-0	200	4	6-10-60	Tennessee	14	D1, '82
44	Heard, Herman	RB	5-10	184	2	11-24-61	Southern Colorado	16	D3, '84
60	Herkenhoff, Matt	T	6-4	275	10	4- 2-51	Minnesota	15	D4, '74
23	Hill, Greg	CB	6-1	189	3	2-12-61	Oklahoma State	15	W-Hou. '84
93	Holle, Eric	DE-NT	6-4	250	2	9- 5-60	Texas	16	D5, '84
43	Jackson, Billy	RB	5-10	215	5	9-13-59	Alabama	16	D7, '81
52	Jolly, Ken	LB	6-2	220	2	2-28-62	Mid-America Nazarene	16	OFA, '84
9	Kenney, Bill	QB	6-4	211	7	1-20-55	Northern Colorado	9	FA, '79
91	Kremer, Ken	NT	6-4	260	7	7-16-57	Ball State	16	D7, '79
40	Lacy, Ken	RB	6-0	222	2	11- 1-60	Tulsa	15	FA, '84
26	Lane, Skip	CB-S	6-1	208	2	1-30-60	Mississippi	*4	FA, '84
29	Lewis, Albert	CB	6-2	190	3	10- 6-60	Grambling	15	D3, '83
71	†Lindstrom, Dave	DE	6-6	255	8	11-16-54	Boston University	16	W-SD, '78
62	Lingner, Adam	C-G	6-4	250	3	11- 2-60	Illinois	16	D9, '83
84	Little, Dave	TE	6-2	239	2	4-18-61	Middle Tennessee State	10	FA, '84
8	Lowery, Nick	K	6-4	189	6	5-27-56	Dartmouth	16	FA, '80
72	Lutz, David	T	6-5	285	3	12-30-59	Georgia Tech	7	D2, '83
63	Maas, Bill	NT	6-4	265	2	3- 2-62	Pittsburgh	14	D1, '84
89	Marshall, Henry	WR	6-2	220	10	8- 9-54	Missouri	16	D3b, '76
94	McAlister, Ken	LB	6-5	220	4	4-15-60	San Francisco	15	FA, '84
11	Osiecki, Sandy	QB	6-5	202	2	5-18-60	Arizona State	4	FA, '84
83	Paige, Stephone	WR	6-1	180	3	10-15-61	Fresno State	16	OFA, '83
95	Paine, Jeff	LB	6-2	224	2	8-19-61	Texas A&M	14	D5a, '84
21	Parker, Kerry	CB	6-1	200	2	10- 3-55	Grambling	15	FA, '84
97	Radecic, Scott	LB	6-3	240	2	6-14-62	Penn State	16	D2, '84
30	Robinson, Mark	S	5-10	206	2	9-13-62	Penn State	16	D4, '84
31	Ross, Kevin	CB	5-9	180	2	1-16-62	Temple	16	D7, '84
70	†Rourke, Jim	T-G	6-5	263	6	2-10-57	Boston College	13	FA, '80
53	Rush, Bob	C	6-5	264	8	2-27-55	Memphis State	16	T-SD, '83
81	Scott, Willie	TE	6-4	245	5	2-13-59	South Carolina	15	D1, '81
86	Smith, J.T.	WR-KR	6-2	185	8	10-29-55	North Texas State	15	FA, '78
59	Spani, Gary	LB	6-2	228	8	1- 9-56	Kansas State	14	D3, '78
67	Still, Art	DE	6-7	257	8	12- 5-55	Kentucky	16	D1, '78
35	Thomas, Ken	RB	5-9	211	2	2-11-60	San Jose State	*0	D7, '83
56	Zamberlin, John	LB	6-2	226	7	2-13-56	Pacific Lutheran	8	W-NE, '83

*W. Arnold played 4 games with Washington, 10 with Kansas City in '84; Hamm played 12 games with Houston in '84; Lane played 3 games with New York Jets, 1 with Kansas City in '84; Thomas missed '84 season due to injury.

†Option playout; subject to developments.

Also played with Chiefs in '84—TE Ed Beckman (13 games), LB Charles Jackson (4), CB Van Jakes (8), RB Lawrence Ricks (5).

D—Draft; T—Trade; W—Waivers; FA—Free Agent; OFA—Original Free Agent.

KANSAS CITY CHIEFS
1985 DRAFT CHOICES

(Number following name designates order of selection among 336 players drafted.)

Round and Player		Position	College
1. HORTON, Ethan	15	RB	North Carolina
2. HAYES, Jonathan	41	TE	Iowa
3. Choice to San Diego (a)			
4. OLDERMAN, Bob	99	G	Virginia
5. KING, Bruce	126	RB	Purdue
6. BOSTIC, Jonathan from Philadelphia (b)	149	DB	Bethune-Cookman
6. Choice to Houston (c)			
7. THOMSON, Vince from San Diego (d)	180	DE	Missouri Western
7. HEFFERNAN, Dave	183	G	Miami, Fla.
8. HILLARY, Ira	210	WR	South Carolina
9. ARMENTROUT, Mike	237	DB	S.W. Missouri
10. SMITH, Jeff	267	RB	Nebraska
11. JACKSON, Chris	293	C	SMU
12. LeBEL, Harper	321	C	Colorado State

(a) Traded pick for offensive lineman Bob Rush, July 11, 1983.
(b) Acquired pick for tight end Al Dixon, August 30, 1983.
(c) Traded pick and 5th round pick for defensive end Bob Hamm and 1986 pick, April 30, 1984.
(d) Acquired pick for running back Jewerl Thomas, May 1, 1984.

KANSAS CITY CHIEFS
1985 ROOKIE AND FIRST-YEAR ROSTER

(1) Indicates player in previous NFL camp.
(2) Indicates player with USFL game experience.
(3) Indicates player in previous USFL camp.
(4) Indicates player with CFL game experience.
(5) Indicates player in previous CFL camp.
   All others classified as rookies.

Name	Pos.	Hgt.	Wgt.	Birth-date	College	How Acquired
Aldisert, Caesar	LB	6-3	220	12-13-62	Pittsburgh	FA
Armentrout, Mike	S	5-10	193	6- 9-63	Southwest Missouri	D9
Bostic, John	CB	5-9	175	10- 6-62	Bethune-Cookman	D6
Brandon, Mark	CB	5-8	173	9-23-63	Toledo	FA
Brown, Byron	RB	5-8	175	10-28-61	Nevada-Las Vegas	FA
Burse, William (3)	LB	6-2	232	9- 3-61	Kentucky State	FA
Byford, Bill	DE	6-3	247	12- 9-62	Northwest Oklahoma	FA
Cocroft, Sherman (1)	S	6-1	193	8-29-61	San Jose State	FA
Courtney, Matt (2)	S	5-11	188	12-21-61	Idaho State	FA
Daniels, Bob	DE	6-2	255	3-10-63	Kansas	FA
Dowdell, Mark	TE	6-2	220	10-18-62	Bowling Green	FA
Eisher, Doug	G	6-2	260	3-16-62	Nevada-Las Vegas	FA
Fiala, Dan	LB	6-3	220	2- 3-63	Colorado State	FA
Fojtik, Brad (1)	DE-NT	6-5	270	9-17-61	Florida State	FA
Glover, Clyde (1)	DE	6-6	280	7-26-60	Fresno State	FA
Goodell, Terry	T	6-3	258	2-12-62	Central Michigan	FA
Green, Willie	LB	6-2	228	6- 5-61	Arizona State	FA
Gwinn, Derek (1)	G	6-3	251	12-20-60	Georgia Tech	*FA '84
Hairston, Malcolm	LB	6-1	215	12-20-61	Wake Forest	FA
Harrington, Scott	NT	6-1	260	4- 2-63	Boston College	FA
Hayes, Jonathan	TE	6-5	233	8-11-62	Iowa	D2
Heffernan, Dave	OL	6-3	255	10-28-62	Miami (Fla.)	D7a
Hill, Andy	WR	5-8	169	1-26-62	Missouri	FA
Hillary, Ira	WR	5-10	186	11-13-62	South Carolina	D8
Horton, Ethan	RB	6-3	229	12-19-62	North Carolina	D1
Jackson, Chris	C	6-3	265	8-21-61	Southern Methodist	D11
Jones, E. J. (1)	RB	5-11	219	2- 1-62	Kansas	FA
King, Bruce	RB	6-1	219	1- 7-63	Purdue	D5
Lang, Mark	LB	6-2	235	6-27-61	Texas	*D12 '84
LaBel, Harper	C	6-4	251	7-14-63	Colorado State	D12
McCashland, Mike	S	6-0	194	6-15-61	Nebraska	FA
Marshall, John	WR	6-1	180	6-28-63	Washington State	FA
Merritt, Charlie	LB	6-1	229	1-13-63	Carson-Newman	FA
Nelson, Dirk	P	6-0	195	7-23-62	Kansas	FA
O'Brien, Joe	NT	6-1	258	11-17-61	Montana State	FA
Olderman, Robert	G	6-4	272	6- 5-62	Virginia	D4
Polk, Scott	LB	6-3	227	10-11-61	Texas A&M	FA
Porter, Rob (1)	S	6-2	195	5- 9-62	Holy Cross	*FA '84
Pryor, David (1, 3)	P	6-3	230	6-18-60	Southern California	FA
Robinson, Charles	T	6-3	263	2-25-63	Bethune-Cookman	FA
Robinson, Eric (2)	RB	5-8	183	12-12-60	Indiana State	FA
Robinson, Frank	RB	5-8	186	1-20-62	San Jose State	FA
Russell, Kevin	QB	6-0	180	6-12-62	California State	FA
Schwartzburg, Dodge	K	5-7	166	5- 6-62	Kansas	FA
Smith, Chris	RB	6-0	222	6- 1-63	Notre Dame	FA
Smith, Jeff	RB	5-9	201	3-22-62	Nebraska	D10
Stephenson, Larry	QB	6-2	194	4-23-61	Livingston U.	FA
Stevens, Rufus (1)	WR	6-3	182	1-13-61	Grambling	*D16 '84
Thompson, Bennie	S	6-0	197	2-10-63	Grambling	FA
Thomson, Vince	DE	6-4	265	9- 4-63	Missouri Western	D7
Tobin, Steve (1, 3)	K	6-2	220	4- 1-60	Wyoming	FA
Turner, Bill	C	6-5	272	3-24-63	Texas-El Paso	FA
Voelker, Randy	G	6-4	250	5-17-63	Kansas State	FA
Walter, John	TE	6-2	227	12-15-62	Penn State	FA
Williams, Jeff	WR	6-2	184	8-28-62	Hampton Institute	FA
Wood, David	WR	6-1	190	1-26-62	West Texas State	FA
Young, Renard (1, 3)	CB	5-10	178	7-31-61	Nevada-Las Vegas	FA

*Gwinn, Lang, Porter and Stevens missed '84 season due to injury.

LOS ANGELES RAIDERS
(Western Division, American Conference)

Tom Flores

Managing General Partner—Al Davis
Executive Assistant—Al LoCasale
Personnel Operations—Ron Wolf
Business Manager—Ken LaRue
Senior Administrators—Tom Grimes, Irv Kaze
Marketing/Promotions—Mike Ornstein
Marketing/Community Affairs—Gil Hernandez
Head Coach—Tom Flores (6 years: 58-31)
Assistant Coaches:
    Offensive Line—Sam Boghosian
    Defensive Backfield—Willie Brown
    Defensive Backfield—Chet Franklin
    Quarterbacks—Larry Kennan
    Defensive Line—Earl Leggett
    Tight Ends/Strength and Conditioning—Bob Mischak
    Football Operations/Special Teams—Steve Ortmayer
    Coaches Assistant—Terry Robiskie
    Offensive Line—Art Shell
    Receivers—Tom Walsh
    Offensive Backfield—Ray Willsey
    Linebackers—Bob Zeman
    (Office Phone: 322-3451—Area Code 213)
Offices—332 Center St., El Segundo, Calif. 90245
Stadium—Los Angeles Memorial Coliseum (Capacity: 92,516)
Team Colors—Silver and Black
Training Site—Oxnard Hilton Hotel, Oxnard, Calif.

1985 SCHEDULE
(All times local.
All games Sunday unless noted otherwise.)

Sept. 8	NEW YORK JETS	1:00
Sept. 12	at Kansas City (Thurs.)	7:00
Sept. 22	SAN FRANCISCO	1:00
Sept. 29	at New England	1:00
Oct. 6	KANSAS CITY	1:00
Oct. 13	NEW ORLEANS	1:00
Oct. 20	at Cleveland	1:00
Oct. 28	SAN DIEGO (Mon.)	6:00
Nov. 3	at Seattle	1:00
Nov. 10	at San Diego	1:00
Nov. 17	CINCINNATI	1:00
Nov. 24	DENVER	1:00
Dec. 1	at Atlanta	4:00
Dec. 8	at Denver	2:00
Dec. 15	SEATTLE	1:00
Dec. 23	at Los Angeles Rams (Mon.)	6:00

1984 RESULTS—(Won 11, Lost 6)

Raiders		Opp.		Att.
24	Houston	14	(A)	49,029
28	Green Bay	7	(H)	46,269
22	Kansas City	20	(A)	75,111
33	San Diego	30	(H)	76,131
13	Denver	16	(A)	74,833
28	Seattle	14	(H)	77,904
23	Minnesota	20	(H)	49,276
44	San Diego	37	(A)	57,442
19	Denver (OT)	22	(H)	91,020
6	Chicago	17	(A)	59,858
14	Seattle	17	(A)	64,001
17	Kansas City	7	(H)	48,575
21	Indianapolis	7	(H)	40,289
45	Miami	34	(A)	71,222
24	Detroit	3	(A)	66,710
7	Pittsburgh	13	(H)	83,056
AFC WILD-CARD GAME				
7	Seattle	13	(A)	62,049

1984 GAMES STARTED

16 games: Marcus Allen, Lyle Alzado, Todd Christensen, Mike Davis, Lester Hayes, Mike Haynes, Kenny King, Henry Lawrence, Howie Long, Rod Martin, Vann McElroy.

15 games: Malcolm Barnwell, Bruce Davis.

14 games: Cliff Branch, Dave Dalby.

13 games: Reggie Kinlaw.

12 games: Matt Millen.

11 games: Bob Nelson.

10 games: Don Mosebar, Marc Wilson.

9 games: Charley Hannah.

8 games: Brad Van Pelt.

7 games: Curt Marsh, Jack Squirek.

6 games: Mickey Marvin, Jim Plunkett.

5 games: Jeff Barnes.

3 games: Stanley Adams, Bill Pickel, Dokie Williams.

2 games: Jim Romano.

1 game: Darryl Byrd, Shelby Jordan, Odis McKinney.

LOS ANGELES RAIDERS 1985 VETERAN ROSTER

No.	Name	Pos.	Ht.	Wt.	NFL Exp.	Birth-date	College	Games in '84	How Acquired
97	Ackerman, Rick	NT	6-4	250	4	6-16-59	Memphis State	*15	FA, '84
59	Adams, Stanley	LB	6-2	215	2	5-22-60	Memphis State	4	FA, '82
32	Allen, Marcus	RB	6-2	205	4	3-22-60	Southern California	16	D1, '82
77	Alzado, Lyle	DE	6-3	260	14	4-3-49	Yankton, S.D.	16	T-Cle, '82
10	Bahr, Chris	K	5-10	170	10	2-3-53	Penn State	16	FA, '80
56	Barnes, Jeff	LB	6-2	230	9	3-1-55	California	16	D5a, '77
80	Barnwell, Malcolm	WR	5-11	185	5	6-28-58	Virginia Union	16	D7, '80
86	Belk, Rocky	WR	6-0	185	2	6-20-60	Miami, Fla.	*0	FA, '85
21	Branch, Cliff	WR	5-11	170	14	8-1-48	Colorado	14	D4, '77
66	Bryant, Warren	T	6-7	285	9	11-11-55	Kentucky	*9	FA, '84
54	Byrd, Darryl	LB	6-1	220	3	9-3-60	Illinois	16	OFA, '83
57	Caldwell, Tony	LB	6-1	225	3	4-1-61	Washington	16	D3, '83
	Campbell, Rich	QB	6-4	219	5	12-21-58	California	*3	T-GB '85
87	Casper, Dave	TE	6-4	240	12	2-2-52	Notre Dame	7	FA, '84
46	Christensen, Todd	TE	6-3	230	7	8-3-56	Brigham Young	16	FA, '79
50	†Dalby, Dave	C	6-3	255	14	8-19-50	UCLA	16	D4a, '72
79	Davis, Bruce	T	6-6	280	7	6-21-56	UCLA	16	D11, '79
45	Davis, James	CB	6-0	190	4	6-12-57	Southern University	15	D5, '81
36	Davis, Mike	S	6-3	205	8	4-15-56	Colorado	16	D2, '77
8	Guy, Ray	P	6-3	195	13	12-22-49	Southern Mississippi	16	D1, '73
73	Hannah, Charley	G	6-5	260	9	7-26-55	Alabama	15	T-NE, '83
27	Hawkins, Frank	RB	5-9	210	5	7-3-59	Nevada-Reno	16	D10, '81
37	Hayes, Lester	CB	6-0	200	9	1-22-55	Texas A&M	16	D5, '77
22	Haynes, Mike	CB	6-2	190	10	7-1-53	Arizona State	16	T-NE, '83
11	Humm, David	QB	6-2	190	11	4-2-52	Nebraska	3	FA, '83
31	Jensen, Derrick	TE-RB	6-1	215	7	4-27-56	Texas-Arlington	16	D3, '78
	Jones, Gordon	WR	6-0	190	6	7-25-57	Pittsburgh	*0	FA, '85
99	Jones, Sean	DE	6-7	265	2	12-19-62	Northeastern	16	D2, '84
74	Jordan, Shelby	T	6-7	280	10	1-23-52	Washington, Mo.	11	T-NE, '83
52	Junkin, Trey	LB	6-2	220	3	1-23-61	Louisiana Tech	*14	FA, '85
33	King, Kenny	RB	5-11	205	7	3-7-57	Oklahoma	16	T-Hou, '80
62	Kinlaw, Reggie	NT	6-2	245	6	1-9-57	Oklahoma	13	D12a, '79
	Krimm, John	S	6-1	190	2	5-30-60	Notre Dame	*0	FA, '85
70	Lawrence, Henry	T	6-4	270	12	9-26-51	Florida A&M	16	D1, '74
75	Long, Howie	DE	6-5	270	5	1-6-60	Villanova	16	D2, '81
60	Marsh, Curt	G	6-5	270	4	8-25-59	Washington	16	D1a, '81
53	Martin, Rod	LB	6-2	225	9	4-7-54	Southern California	16	FA, '77
65	Marvin, Mickey	G	6-4	265	9	10-5-55	Tennessee	9	D4, '77
43	McCall, Joe	RB	6-0	195	2	2-17-62	Pittsburgh	3	D3, '77
26	McElroy, Vann	S	6-2	190	4	1-13-60	Baylor	16	D3, '82
23	McKinney, Odis	S	6-2	190	8	5-19-57	Colorado	16	T-NYG, '80
55	Millen, Matt	LB	6-2	250	6	3-12-58	Penn State	16	D2, '80
28	†Montgomery, Cle	WR	5-8	180	5	7-1-56	Abilene Christian	16	FA, '81
72	Mosebar, Don	G	6-6	260	3	9-11-61	Southern California	10	D1, '83
51	†Nelson, Bob	LB	6-4	235	9	6-30-53	Nebraska	12	FA, '80
81	Parker, Andy	TE	6-5	240	2	9-8-61	Utah	9	D5, '84
71	Pickel, Bill	NT	6-5	260	3	11-5-59	Rutgers	16	D2, '83
16	Plunkett, Jim	QB	6-2	220	15	12-5-47	Stanford	8	FA, '78
34	Pruitt, Greg	RB	5-10	190	13	8-1-51	Oklahoma	15	T-Cle, '82
88	Seale, Sam	WR	5-9	175	2	10-6-62	Western State, Colo.	12	D8, '84
58	Squirek, Jack	LB	6-4	230	4	2-16-59	Illinois	12	D2, '82
	Teague, Matthew	LB	6-4	233	2	10-22-58	Prairie View A&M	*0	FA, '85
30	Toran, Stacey	S	6-2	200	2	11-10-61	Notre Dame	16	D6, '84
93	Townsend, Greg	DE	6-3	240	3	11-3-61	Texas Christian	16	D4, '83
91	Van Pelt, Brad	LB	6-5	235	13	4-5-51	Michigan State	9	T-Min, '84
20	Watts, Ted	CB	6-0	190	5	5-29-59	Texas Tech	16	D1, '81
67	Wheeler, Dwight	C-T	6-3	275	7	1-3-55	Tennessee State	4	FA, '84
85	Williams, Dokie	WR	5-11	180	3	8-25-60	UCLA	16	D5, '83
38	Willis, Chester	RB	5-11	200	5	5-2-58	Auburn	16	D11, '81
6	Wilson, Marc	QB	6-6	205	6	2-15-57	Brigham Young	16	D1, '80

*Ackerman played 9 games with San Diego, 6 with Raiders in '84; Belk last played with Cleveland in '83; Bryant played 4 games with Atlanta, 5 with Raiders in '84; Campbell played 3 games with Green Bay in '84; G. Jones active for 1 game with L.A. Rams in '84, did not play; Junkin played 2 games with Buffalo, 12 with Washington in '84; Krimm last played with New Orleans in '83; Teague last active with Atlanta in '81, played with Saskatchewan of CFL in '84.

†Option playout; subject to developments.

Also played with Raiders in '84—NT Greg Boyd (5 games), LB Larry McCoy (4), LB Mark Merrill (2), T Ed Muransky (3), C Jim Romano (6), RB Jimmy Smith (7).

D—Draft; T—Trade; W—Waivers; FA—Free Agent; OFA—Original Free Agent.

LOS ANGELES RAIDERS
1985 DRAFT CHOICES

(Number following name designates order of selection among 336 players drafted.)

Round and Player		Position	College
1. HESTER, Jessie	23	WR	Florida State
2. Choice to New England (a)			
3. MOFFETT, Tim	79	WR	Mississippi
3. ADAMS, Stefon from Washington through Houston (b)	80	DB	East Carolina
4. KIMMEL, Jamie from Washington (c)	107	LB	Syracuse
4. Choice to New England (d)			
5. REEDER, Dan	135	RB	Delaware
6. HILGER, Rusty from Houston (e)	143	QB	Oklahoma State
6. Choice to Minnesota (f)			
7. BELCHER, Kevin from N.Y. Giants (g)	186	T	Wisconsin
7. PATTISON, Mark from New England (h)	188	WR	Washington
7. CLARK, Bret	191	DB	Nebraska
7. HADEN, Nick from Washington through New England (i)	192	C	Penn State
8. WINGATE, Leonard	220	DT	S. C. State
9. SYDNOR, Chris	246	DB	Penn State
10. McKENZIE, Reggie from Washington (j)	275	LB	Tennessee
10. MYRES, Albert	276	DB	Tulsa
11. STRACHAN, Steve	303	RB	Boston College
12. POLK, Raymond	332	DB	Oklahoma State

(a) Traded pick and 1st round pick in 1984 for cornerback Mike Haynes and 7th round pick, November 10, 1983.

(b) Oilers acquired pick from Redskins for 4th round pick in 1984, May 1, 1984; Raiders acquired pick and 6th round pick from Oilers for center Jim Romano, October 9, 1984.

(c) Acquired pick for wide receiver Calvin Muhammad, October 3, 1984.

(d) Traded pick for tackle Shelby Jordan, September 16, 1983.

(e) See second part of (b).

(f) Traded pick and 2nd round pick in 1986 for linebacker Brad Van Pelt, October 9, 1984.

(g) Acquired pick for safety Kenny Hill, August 27, 1984.

(h) See (a).

(i) Patriots acquired pick from Redskins for defensive back Ricky Smith, September 11, 1984; Raiders acquired pick from Patriots as penalty for Patriots tampering with scout John Polonchek.

(j) Acquired pick for tackle Morris Towns, August 30, 1984.

LOS ANGELES RAIDERS
1985 ROOKIE AND FIRST-YEAR ROSTER

(1) Indicates player in previous NFL camp.
(2) Indicates player with USFL game experience.
(3) Indicates player in previous USFL camp.
(4) Indicates player with CFL game experience.
(5) Indicates player in previous CFL camp.
  All others classified as rookies.

Name	Pos.	Hgt.	Wgt.	Birth- date	College	How Acquired
Adams, Stefon	CB	5-10	190	8-11-63	East Carolina	D3a
Barksdale, Rod	DB	6-1	182	9- 8-62	Arizona	FA
Belcher, Kevin	T	6-5	310	11- 9-61	Wisconsin	D7
Bias, Moe (1)	LB	6-2	230	9- 1-61	Illinois	FA
Burningham, Rex (2)	OT	6-4	265	9- 1-59	Brigham Young	FA
Carter, Archie (1)	LB	6-3	220	9-15-60	Illinois	FA
Christmas, Ernie (4)	DB	5-11	182	10-28-60	San Francisco State	FA
Coppens, John	QB	6-2	210	10- 9-62	Illinois State	FA
Cummings, Elton	LB	6-3	230	8- 5-63	Houston	FA
Darnell, Ralph	DT	6-5	250	5- 3-62	Texas	FA
Forester, Scott	C	6-4	252	8- 7-61	Southwest Texas State	FA
Gazzaniga, Dan	OT	6-5	255	1-26-63	Cal-Davis	FA
Geonetta, Pat	WR	5-6	170	6-21-61	Colorado College	FA
Greene, Kevin	DB	5-11	185	4- 7-62	Pacific	FA
Griffin, George	OL	6-5	260	8-21-63	Cameron	FA
Haden, Nick	C	6-2	270	11- 7-62	Penn State	D7c
Hagood, Rickey (1)	NT	6-1	285	4-24-61	South Carolina	FA
Hester, Jessie	WR	5-11	170	1-21-63	Florida State	D1
Hilger, Rusty	QB	6-4	200	5- 9-62	Oklahoma State	D6
James, Ronnie (2)	RB	6-2	235	1- 2-61	Grambling	FA
Jensen, Russ (2)	QB	6-2	215	7-13-61	California Lutheran	FA
Johnson, Bobby (1)	RB	6-1	185	9-30-62	San Jose State	FA
Kimmel, Jamie	LB	6-3	240	3-29-62	Syracuse	D4
Linwood, Byron	S	6-2	198	3-31-63	Texas Christian	FA
Lubischer, Steve (1)	LB	6-2	220	6-29-62	Boston College	FA
Mannon, Mark	G	6-4	260	10-19-62	UCLA	FA
McCall, Jeff (1, 3)	TE	6-2	220	7- 4-60	Clemson	FA
McGee, Gert	LB	6-4	230	10-18-60	Kentfield J.C.	FA
McKenzie, Reggie	LB	6-1	235	2- 8-63	Tennessee	D10
Mendoza, Mike	QB	6-1	200	10-26-63	Northern Arizona	FA
Moffett, Tim	WR	6-1	180	2-28-62	Mississippi	D3
Myres, Albert	S	6-0	195	5- 5-63	Tulsa	D10a
Niualiku, George (1)	G	6-3	265	4-30-61	California	FA
Norvelle, Randy	G	6-5	270	7-25-63	Wyoming	FA
Palyo, Mark	OT	6-5	270	11-17-62	Richmond	FA
Pattison, Mark	WR	6-2	190	12-13-61	Washington	D7a
Polk, Raymond	CB	5-9	190	6-10-62	Oklahoma State	D12
Reeder, Dan	RB	5-11	225	3-18-61	Delaware	D5
Smith, Gene	CB	6-1	200	8-20-62	Georgetown	FA
Smith, Kevin	WR	6-3	220	7-30-61	Utah State	FA
Stinnett, Eddie (1)	FB	6-0	230	4-14-61	Brigham Young	FA
Strachan, Steve	RB	6-1	215	3-22-63	Boston College	D11
Sydnor, Chris	S	6-0	195	8-14-62	Penn State	D9
Wahl, Steve (1)	G	6-6	250	8-10-60	Cal Poly-SLO	FA
Williams, Quency (1)	DE	6-2	225	4-10-61	Auburn	*FA '84
Williams, Ricky (1)	CB	6-1	195	4-27-60	Langston	*FA '84
Willis, Mitch (1)	NT	6-8	280	3-16-62	Southern Methodist	*D7 '84
Wingate, Leonard	NT	6-3	265	11- 3-61	South Carolina State	D8
Young, Butch	DB	5-7	172	4-19-63	Rutgers	FA

*Q. Williams, R. Williams and Willis missed '84 season due to injury.
NOTE: 7th-round pick Bret Clark signed with Tampa Bay Bandits of the USFL.

LOS ANGELES RAMS
(Western Division, National Conference)

John Robinson

President—Georgia Frontiere
Vice-President, Finance—John Shaw
Administrator of Football Operations—Jack Faulkner
Director of Operations—Dick Beam
Director of Player Personnel—John Math
Legal Counsel—Jay Zygmunt
Head Coach—John Robinson (2 years: 19-13)
Assistant Coaches:
   Wide Receivers—Lew Erber
   Defensive Line—Marv Goux
   Special Teams—Gil Haskell
   Offensive Line—Hudson Houck
   Defensive Backfield—Steve Shafer
   Defensive Coordinator—Fritz Shurmur
   Running Backs—Bruce Snyder
   Tight Ends—Norval Turner
   Outside Linebackers—Fred Whittingham
Director of Public Relations—Pete Donovan
(Office Phones: 535-7267—Area Code 714; 585-5400—Area Code 213)
Offices—2327 W. Lincoln Ave., Anaheim, Calif. 92801
Stadium—Anaheim Stadium (Capacity: 69,007)
Team Colors—Royal Blue, Gold and White
Training Site—California St. University, Fullerton, Calif.

1985 SCHEDULE
(All times local.
All games Sunday unless noted otherwise.)

Sept. 8	DENVER	1:00
Sept. 15	at Philadelphia	1:00
Sept. 23	at Seattle (Mon.)	6:00
Sept. 29	ATLANTA	1:00
Oct. 6	MINNESOTA	1:00
Oct. 13	at Tampa Bay	1:00
Oct. 20	at Kansas City	12:00
Oct. 27	SAN FRANCISCO	1:00
Nov. 3	NEW ORLEANS	1:00
Nov. 10	at New York Giants	1:00
Nov. 17	at Atlanta	1:00
Nov. 24	GREEN BAY	1:00
Dec. 1	at New Orleans	12:00
Dec. 9	at San Francisco (Mon.)	6:00
Dec. 15	ST. LOUIS	1:00
Dec. 23	L.A. RAIDERS (Mon.)	6:00

1984 RESULTS—(Won 10, Lost 7)

Rams		Opp.		Att.
13	Dallas	20	(H)	65,403
20	Cleveland	17	(H)	43,043
14	Pittsburgh	24	(A)	58,104
24	Cincinnati	14	(A)	45,406
33	New York Giants	12	(H)	53,417
28	Atlanta	30	(H)	47,832
28	New Orleans	10	(A)	63,161
24	Atlanta	10	(A)	52,861
0	San Francisco	33	(H)	65,481
16	St. Louis	13	(A)	50,950
29	Chicago	13	(H)	62,021
6	Green Bay	31	(A)	52,031
34	Tampa Bay	33	(A)	42,242
34	New Orleans	21	(H)	49,348
27	Houston	16	(H)	49,092
16	San Francisco	19	(A)	59,743
	NFC WILD-CARD GAME			
13	New York Giants	16	(H)	67,037

1984 GAMES STARTED

16 games: Bill Bain, Jim Collins, Eric Dickerson, Reggie Doss, Carl Ekern, Henry Ellard, Gary Green, Dennis Harrah, David Hill, Drew Hill, Kent Hill, LeRoy Irvin, Greg Meisner, Mel Owens, Doug Smith.

15 games: Jack Youngblood.

13 games: Mike Guman, Jeff Kemp.

11 games: George Andrews, Nolan Cromwell.

9 games: Irv Pankey.

7 games: Eric Harris, Johnnie Johnson, Vince Newsome, Jackie Slater.

5 games: Mike Wilcher.

3 games: Vince Ferragamo.

2 games: Mike Barber.

1 game: James McDonald, Doug Reed.

LOS ANGELES RAMS 1985 VETERAN ROSTER

No.	Name	Pos.	Ht.	Wt.	NFL Exp.	Birth-date	College	Games in '84	How Acquired
52	†Andrews, George	LB	6-3	225	7	11-28-55	Nebraska	11	D1, '79
62	Bain, Bill	T	6-4	290	11	8-9-52	Southern California	16	FA, '79
86	Barber, Mike	TE	6-3	237	10	6-4-53	Louisiana Tech	11	T-Hou, '82
96	Barnett, Doug	LB	6-3	250	3	4-12-60	Azusa Pacific	*0	D5a, '82
90	Brady, Ed	LB	6-2	228	2	6-17-60	Illinois	16	D8, '84
89	Brown, Ron	WR	5-11	181	2	3-31-61	Arizona State	16	T-Cle, '84
50	Collins, Jim	LB	6-2	230	5	6-11-58	Syracuse	16	D2, '81
21	Cromwell, Nolan	S	6-1	200	9	1-30-55	Kansas	11	D2, '77
28	Croudip, David	CB	5-8	183	2	1-25-59	San Diego State	16	FA, '84
45	Crutchfield, Dwayne	RB	6-0	235	4	9-30-59	Iowa State	15	T-Hou, '84
70	DeJurnett, Charles	NT	6-4	260	9	6-17-52	San Jose State	16	FA, '82
29	Dickerson, Eric	RB	6-3	220	3	9-2-60	Southern Methodist	16	D1, '83
8	Dils, Steve	QB	6-1	191	7	12-8-55	Stanford	*10	T-Min, '84
71	Doss, Reggie	DE	6-4	263	8	12-7-56	Hampton Institute	16	D7, '78
55	Ekern, Carl	LB	6-3	222	9	5-27-54	San Jose State	16	D5, '76
80	Ellard, Henry	WR	5-11	170	3	7-21-61	Fresno State	16	D2, '83
	Erxleben, Russell	P	6-4	221	5	1-13-57	Texas	*0	FA, '85
84	Farmer, George	WR	5-10	175	4	12-5-58	Southern University	14	D9, '80
88	Faulkner, Chris	TE	6-4	260	2	4-13-60	Florida	8	FA, '84
15	Ferragamo, Vince	QB	6-3	212	8	4-24-54	Nebraska	3	D4, '77
82	Grant, Otis	WR	6-3	197	3	8-13-61	Michigan State	14	D5, '83
27	Green, Gary	CB	5-11	191	9	10-2-55	Baylor	16	T-KC, '84
44	Guman, Mike	RB	6-2	218	6	4-21-58	Penn State	16	D6, '80
60	Harrah, Dennis	G	6-5	265	11	3-9-53	Miami, Fla.	16	D1a, '75
26	Harris, Eric	CB	6-3	202	6	8-11-55	Memphis State	7	T-KC, '83
81	Hill, David	TE	6-2	228	10	1-1-54	Texas A&I	16	T-Det, '83
87	Hill, Drew	WR	5-9	170	7	10-5-56	Georgia Tech	16	D12, '79
72	Hill, Kent	G	6-5	260	7	3-7-57	Georgia Tech	16	D1a, '79
47	Irvin, LeRoy	CB	5-11	184	6	9-15-57	Kansas	16	D3a, '80
59	Jerue, Mark	LB	6-3	229	3	1-15-60	Washington	16	T-Bal, '83
77	Jeter, Gary	DE	6-4	260	9	3-24-55	Southern California	5	T-NYG, '83
20	Johnson, Johnnie	S	6-1	183	6	10-8-56	Texas	9	D1, '80
24	†Jones, A.J.	RB	6-1	202	4	5-30-59	Texas	13	D8, '82
46	Kamana, John	RB	6-2	215	2	12-3-61	Southern California	3	OFA, '84
9	Kemp, Jeff	QB	6-0	201	5	7-11-59	Dartmouth	14	OFA, '81
76	Kowalski, Gary	T	6-5	275	2	7-2-60	Boston College	*0	D6, '83
1	Lansford, Mike	K	6-0	183	4	7-20-58	Washington	16	FA, '82
57	Laughlin, Jim	LB	6-1	222	6	7-5-58	Ohio State	3	FA, '84
83	McDonald, James	TE	6-5	230	3	3-29-61	Southern California	16	OFA, '83
63	McDonald, Mike	LB	6-1	235	2	6-22-58	Southern California	16	OFA, '83
69	†Meisner, Greg	NT	6-3	253	5	4-23-59	Pittsburgh	16	D3, '81
98	Miller, Shawn	NT	6-4	255	2	3-14-61	Utah State	8	FA, '84
6	Misko, John	P	6-5	207	4	10-1-54	Oregon State	16	FA, '82
22	Newsome, Vince	S	6-1	179	3	1-22-61	Washington	16	D4a, '83
58	†Owens, Mel	LB	6-2	224	5	12-7-58	Michigan	16	D1, '81
75	Pankey, Irv	T	6-4	267	5	12-15-58	Penn State	16	D2, '80
43	Pleasant, Mike	CB	6-1	195	2	8-16-58	Oklahoma	5	FA, '84
30	Redden, Barry	RB	5-10	205	4	7-21-60	Richmond	14	D1, '82
93	Reed, Doug	DE	6-3	250	2	7-16-60	San Diego State	9	D4, '83
66	Reese, Booker	DE	6-6	260	4	9-20-59	Bethune-Cookman	*10	T-TB, '84
64	†Shearin, Joe	G	6-4	250	3	4-16-60	Texas	15	D7, '82
78	Slater, Jackie	T	6-4	271	10	5-27-54	Jackson State	7	D3, '76
61	Slaton, Tony	C	6-3	269	2	4-12-61	Southern California	*0	FA, '84
56	Smith, Doug	C	6-3	253	8	11-25-56	Bowling Green	16	OFA, '78
37	†Sully, Ivory	S	6-0	200	7	6-20-57	Delaware	16	OFA, '79
51	Vann, Norwood	LB	6-2	225	2	2-18-62	East Carolina	16	D10, '84
54	Wilcher, Mike	LB	6-3	235	3	3-20-60	North Carolina	15	D2a, '83
85	Youngblood, Jack	DE	6-4	242	15	1-26-50	Florida	15	D1a, '71

*Barnett and Kowalski missed '84 season due to injury; Erxleben last active with New Orleans in '83; Dils played 3 games with Minnesota, 7 games with Los Angeles Rams in '84; Reese played 1 game with Tampa Bay, 9 games with Los Angeles Rams in '84; Slaton active for 3 games in '84, did not play.
†Option playout; subject to developments.
Also played with Rams in '84—G Russ Bolinger (16 games), LB Jim Youngblood (5).
D—Draft; T—Trade; W—Waivers; FA—Free Agent; OFA—Original Free Agent.

LOS ANGELES RAMS
1985 DRAFT CHOICES

(Number following name designates order of selection among 336 players drafted.)

Round and Player		Position	College
1. GRAY, Jerry	21	DB	Texas
2. SCOTT, Chuck	50	WR	Vanderbilt
3. HATCHER, Dale	77	P	Clemson
4. Choice to Minnesota (a)			
5. GREENE, Kevin from Buffalo (b)	113	LB	Auburn
5. Choice to Houston through Kansas City (c)			
6. YOUNG, Mike from Chicago (d)	161	WR	UCLA
6. JOHNSON, Damone	162	TE	Cal Poly-Obispo
7. BRADLEY, Danny	189	RB	Oklahoma
8. McINTYRE, Marlon	218	RB	Pittsburgh
9. SWANSON, Gary	245	LB	Cal Poly-Obispo
10. LOVE, Duval	274	G	UCLA
11. FLUTIE, Doug from Indianapolis (e)	285	QB	Boston College
11. BROWN, Kevin	301	DB	Northwestern
12. Choice to Tampa Bay (f)			

(a) Traded pick for quarterback Steve Dils, September 18, 1984.

(b) Acquired pick for wide receiver Preston Dennard, August 1, 1984.

(c) Rams traded pick and cornerback Lucious Smith to Chiefs for quarterback Steve Fuller, August 19, 1983; Chiefs traded pick and 6th round pick to Oilers for defensive end Bob Hamm and 1986 pick, April 30, 1985.

(d) Acquired pick and 11th round pick in 1984 for quarterback Steve Fuller, April 30, 1984.

(e) Acquired pick for defensive back George Radachowsky, August 27, 1984.

(f) Traded pick for defensive end Booker Reese, September 4, 1984.

LOS ANGELES RAMS
1985 ROOKIE AND FIRST-YEAR ROSTER

(1) Indicates player in previous NFL camp.
(2) Indicates player with USFL game experience.
(3) Indicates player in previous USFL camp.
(4) Indicates player with CFL game experience.
(5) Indicates player in previous CFL camp.
    All others classified as rookies.

Name	Pos.	Hgt.	Wgt.	Birth-date	College	How Acquired
Bradley, Danny	RB	5-9	178	3- 2-63	Oklahoma	D7
Brock, Dieter (4)	QB	6-0	195	2-12-51	Jacksonville State	FA
Brown, Kevin	S	6-0	189	5-10-63	Northwestern	D11a
Fisher, Roderick (1)	CB	5-10	190	11-23-61	Oklahoma State	*D12 '84
Gibson, Steve	DE	6-3	260	5- 5-62	Cal Poly-SLO	FA
Gray, Jerry	CB	6-0	190	12- 2-62	Texas	D1
Greene, Kevin	LB	6-3	238	7-31-62	Auburn	D5
Hatcher, Dale	P	6-2	195	4- 5-63	Clemson	D3
Johnson, Damone	TE	6-4	230	3- 2-62	Cal Poly-SLO	D6a
Love, Duval	G	6-3	263	6-24-63	UCLA	D10
McIntyre, Marion	RB	5-11	230	8-28-62	Pittsburgh	D8
McQuaid, Dan (1)	T	6-7	255	10- 4-60	Nevada-Las Vegas	*FA '84
Meyer, John (1)	DE	6-6	256	5-28-59	Arizona State	FA
Scott, Chuck	WR	6-2	202	5-24-63	Vanderbilt	D2
Shiner, Mike	OT	6-8	285	1-27-61	Notre Dame	FA
Stephens, Hal (1)	T	6-4	252	4-14-61	East Carolina	*D5 '84
Swanson, Gary	LB	6-1	236	8-17-61	Cal Poly-SLO	D9
Tinsley, Scott (1)	QB	6-2	195	11-14-59	Southern California	*FA '84
Wise, Francois	TE	6-5	240	5-15-58	Long Beach State	FA
Young, Michael	WR	6-1	185	2- 2-62	UCLA	D6

*Fisher, McQuaid, Stephens and Tinsley missed '84 season due to injury.
NOTE: 11th-round pick Doug Flutie is with the New Jersey Generals of the USFL.

MIAMI DOLPHINS
(Eastern Division, American Conference)

Don Shula

President—Joseph Robbie
Executive Vice-President and G.M.—J. Michael Robbie
Vice-President/Public Affairs—Joe Abrell
Vice-President and Head Coach—Don Shula (22 years: 227-82-6)
Director, Pro Scouting—Charley Winner
Director, Player Personnel—Chuck Connor
Assistant Coaches:
    Special Teams—Tom Keane
    Linebackers—Bob Matheson
    Defensive Backfield—Mel Phillips
    Offense/Offensive Line—John Sandusky
    Defensive Line—Mike Scarry
    Quarterbacks and Receivers—David Shula
    Defense—Chuck Studley
    Offensive Backfield—Carl Taseff
    Strength and Conditioning—Junior Wade
Director of Publicity—Chip Namias
    (Office Phone: 576-1000—Area Code 305)
Offices—4770 Biscayne Blvd., (Suite 1440) Miami, Fla. 33137
Stadium—Orange Bowl (Capacity: 75,206)
Team Colors—Aqua and Orange
Training Site—St. Thomas University, Miami, Fla.

1985 SCHEDULE
(All times local.
All games Sunday unless noted otherwise.)

Sept. 8	at Houston	12:00
Sept. 15	INDIANAPOLIS	4:00
Sept. 22	KANSAS CITY	4:00
Sept. 29	at Denver	2:00
Oct. 6	PITTSBURGH	1:00
Oct. 14	at New York Jets (Mon.)	9:00
Oct. 20	TAMPA BAY	4:00
Oct. 27	at Detroit	1:00
Nov. 3	at New England	1:00
Nov. 10	NEW YORK JETS	4:00
Nov. 17	at Indianapolis	1:00
Nov. 24	at Buffalo	1:00
Dec. 2	CHICAGO (Mon.)	9:00
Dec. 8	at Green Bay	12:00
Dec. 16	NEW ENGLAND (Mon.)	9:00
Dec. 22	BUFFALO	1:00

1984 RESULTS—(Won 16, Lost 3)

Dolphins		Opp.		Att.
35	Washington	17	(A)	52,683
28	New England	7	(H)	66,083
21	Buffalo	17	(A)	65,455
44	Indianapolis	7	(H)	55,415
36	St. Louis	28	(A)	46,991
31	Pittsburgh	7	(A)	59,103
28	Houston	10	(H)	54,080
44	New England	24	(A)	60,711
38	Buffalo	7	(H)	58,824
31	New York Jets	17	(A)	72,655
24	Philadelphia	23	(H)	70,227
28	San Diego (OT)	34	(A)	53,041
28	New York Jets	17	(H)	74,884
34	Los Angeles Raiders	45	(H)	71,222
35	Indianapolis	17	(A)	60,411
28	Dallas	21	(H)	74,139
	AFC SEMIFINAL GAME			
31	Seattle	10	(H)	73,469
	AFC CHAMPIONSHIP GAME			
45	Pittsburgh	28	(H)	76,029
	NFL CHAMPIONSHIP GAME			
16	San Francisco	38	(*)	84,059

*Stanford Stadium, Palo Alto, Calif.

1984 GAMES STARTED

16 games: Doug Betters, Glenn Blackwood, Lyle Blackwood, Bob Brudzinski, Mark Duper, Roy Foster, Jon Giesler, Dan Johnson, William Judson, Dan Marino, Ed Newman, Dwight Stephenson.

15 games: Bob Baumhower, Charles Bowser, Mark Clayton.

12 games: Cleveland Green, Tony Nathan.

10 games: Kim Bokamper, Don McNeal, Earnest Rhone.

9 games: Woody Bennett, Mark Brown.

8 games: A.J. Duhe.

6 games: Mike Charles, Paul Lankford.

5 games: Jay Brophy, Bruce Hardy.

4 games: Eric Laakso.

2 games: Joe Carter, Andra Franklin, Jim Jensen.

1 game: Bill Barnett, Nat Moore, Rodell Thomas.

MIAMI DOLPHINS 1985 VETERAN ROSTER

No.	Name	Pos.	Ht.	Wt.	NFL Exp.	Birth-date	College	Games in '84	How Acquired
	Ballard, Quinton	NT	6-3	290	2	11-18-60	Elon, N.C.	*0	FA, '85
70	†Barnett, Bill	DE	6-4	260	6	5-10-56	Nebraska	16	D3, '80
73	Baumhower, Bob	NT	6-5	265	9	8- 4-55	Alabama	15	D2, '77
34	Bennett, Woody	FB	6-2	225	7	3-24-55	Miami, Fla.	16	W-NYJ, '80
78	Benson, Charles	DE	6-3	267	3	11-21-60	Baylor	16	D3, '83
75	Betters, Doug	DE	6-7	265	8	6-11-56	Nevada-Reno	16	D6, '78
47	†Blackwood, Glenn	S	6-0	190	7	2-23-57	Texas	16	D8a, '79
42	†Blackwood, Lyle	S	6-1	190	13	5-24-51	Texas Christian	16	FA, '81
58	Bokamper, Kim	DE	6-6	255	9	9-25-54	San Jose State	11	D1a, '76
56	Bowser, Charles	LB	6-3	235	4	10- 2-59	Duke	15	D4, '82
53	Brophy, Jay	LB	6-3	233	2	7-27-60	Miami, Fla.	11	D2, '84
43	Brown, Bud	S	6-0	194	2	4-19-61	Southern Mississippi	16	D11, '84
51	Brown, Mark	LB	6-2	225	3	7-18-61	Purdue	16	D9, '83
59	†Brudzinski, Bob	LB	6-4	223	9	1- 1-55	Ohio State	16	T-Ram, '81
23	Carter, Joe	RB	5-11	198	2	6-23-62	Alabama	13	D4, '84
71	Charles, Mike	NT	6-4	285	3	9-23-62	Syracuse	16	D2, '83
	Clark, Bryan	QB	6-2	196	3	7-27-60	Michigan State	*1	T-Cin, '85
76	Clark, Steve	G	6-4	255	4	8- 2-60	Utah	12	D9, '82
83	Clayton, Mark	WR	5-9	175	3	4- 8-61	Louisville	15	D8, '83
77	Duhe, A.J.	LB	6-4	235	9	11-27-55	Louisiana State	12	D1, '77
85	Duper, Mark	WR	5-9	187	4	1-25-59	Northwestern State, La.	16	D2, '82
61	Foster, Roy	G	6-4	275	4	5-24-60	Southern California	16	D1, '82
37	Franklin, Andra	FB	5-10	225	4	8-22-59	Nebraska	2	D2, '81
	Garcia, Eddie	K	5-8	178	2	4-15-60	Southern Methodist	*0	FA, '85
79	Giesler, Jon	T	6-5	260	7	12-23-56	Michigan	16	D1, '79
74	Green, Cleveland	T	6-3	262	7	9-11-57	Southern University	16	OFA, '79
84	Hardy, Bruce	TE	6-5	232	8	6- 1-56	Arizona State	16	D9, '78
88	Heflin, Vince	WR	6-0	185	4	7- 7-59	Central State, Ohio	16	OFA, '82
90	Hester, Ron	LB	6-2	222	2	5-26-59	Florida State	*0	D6a, '82
31	†Hill, Eddie	RB	6-2	210	7	5-13-57	Memphis State	16	T-Ram, '81
11	†Jensen, Jim	WR	6-4	215	5	11-14-58	Boston University	16	D11, '81
87	†Johnson, Dan	TE	6-3	240	3	5-17-60	Iowa State	16	D7, '82
46	†Johnson, Pete	FB	6-0	250	9	3-22-54	Ohio State	*16	T-SD, '84
49	Judson, William	CB	6-1	190	4	3-26-59	South Carolina State	16	D8, '81
40	Kozlowski, Mike	S	6-1	198	6	2-24-56	Colorado	16	D10a, '79
68	Laakso, Eric	T	6-4	260	8	11-29-56	Tulane	4	D4a, '78
44	†Lankford, Paul	CB	6-2	184	4	6-15-58	Penn State	16	D3, '82
72	Lee, Ronnie	G	6-4	265	7	12-24-56	Baylor	16	T-Atl, '84
13	Marino, Dan	QB	6-4	214	3	9-15-61	Pittsburgh	16	D1, '83
28	McNeal, Don	CB	5-11	192	5	5- 6-58	Alabama	11	D1, '80
89	†Moore, Nat	WR	5-9	188	12	9-19-51	Florida	16	D3, '74
22	Nathan, Tony	RB	6-0	206	7	12-14-56	Alabama	16	D3, '79
64	Newman, Ed	G	6-2	255	13	6- 4-51	Duke	16	D6, '73
55	Rhone, Earnie	LB	6-2	224	10	8-20-53	Henderson St., Ark.	15	OFA, '75
4	Roby, Reggie	P	6-2	243	3	7-30-61	Iowa	16	D6, '83
80	†Rose, Joe	TE	6-3	230	6	6-24-57	California	9	D7, '80
50	Shipp, Jackie	LB	6-2	236	2	3-19-62	Oklahoma	16	D1, '84
45	Sowell, Robert	CB	5-11	175	3	6-23-61	Howard	16	OFA, '83
	Stauch, Scott	RB	6-1	208	2	1-3-59	UCLA	*0	FA, '85
57	Stephenson, Dwight	C	6-2	255	6	11-20-57	Alabama	16	D2, '80
10	†Strock, Don	QB	6-5	220	12	11-27-50	Virginia Tech	16	D5, '73
60	Toews, Jeff	G-C	6-3	255	7	11- 4-57	Washington	16	D2, '79
32	Vigorito, Tom	RB	5-10	190	3	10-23-59	Virginia	*0	D5a, '81
5	Von Schamann, Uwe	K	6-1	185	7	4-23-56	Oklahoma	16	D7, '79
41	†Walker, Fulton	CB	5-11	196	5	4-30-58	West Virginia	12	D6, '81

*Hester and Vigorito missed entire '84 season due to injury; Ballard last active with Baltimore in '83; B. Clark played 1 game with Cincinnati in '84; Garcia last active with Green Bay in '83; P. Johnson played 3 games with San Diego, 13 with Miami; Stauch last active with New Orleans in '81.

†Option playout; subject to developments.

Retired—Jimmy Cefalo, 7-year wide receiver, 16 games in '84; Bob Kuechenberg, 14-year guard, missed '84 season due to injury.

Also played with Dolphins in '84—WR Fernanza Burgess (3 games), TE John Chesley (1), LB Ed Judie (2), LB Sanders Shiver (14), LB Rodell Thomas (14).

D—Draft; T—Trade; W—Waivers; FA—Free Agent; OFA—Original Free Agent.

MIAMI DOLPHINS
1985 DRAFT CHOICES

(Number following name designates order of selection among 336 players drafted.)

Round and Player		Position	College
1. HAMPTON, Lorenzo	27	RB	Florida
2. Choice to San Diego (a)			
3. LITTLE, George from Philadelphia (b)	65	DT	Iowa
3. MOYER, Alex	83	LB	Northeastern
4. SMITH, Mike from Cleveland (c)	91	DB	Texas-El Paso
4. DELLENBACH, Jeff	111	T	Wisconsin
5. Choice to Denver (d)			
6. SHORTHOSE, George from Atlanta (e)	145	WR	Missouri
6. DAVENPORT, Ron	167	RB	Louisville
7. REVEIZ, Fuad	195	K	Tennessee
8. SHARP, Dan	223	TE	Texas Christian
9. HINDS, Adam	251	DB	Oklahoma State
10. PENDLETON, Mike	279	DB	Indiana
11. JONES, Mike	307	RB	Tulane
12. NOBLE, Ray	335	DB	California

(a) Traded pick and rights to defensive tackle Dewey Forte for running back Pete Johnson, September 22, 1984.

(b) Acquired pick for center Mark Dennard, March 7, 1984.

(c) Acquired pick for wide receiver Duriel Harris, March 27, 1984.

(d) Traded pick for linebacker Larry Evans, August 15, 1983.

(e) Acquired pick and offensive lineman Ronnie Lee for cornerback Gerald Small, August 26, 1984.

MIAMI DOLPHINS
1985 ROOKIE AND FIRST-YEAR ROSTER

(1) Indicates player in previous NFL camp.
(2) Indicates player with USFL game experience.
(3) Indicates player in previous USFL camp.
(4) Indicates player with CFL game experience.
(5) Indicates player in previous CFL camp.
     All others classified as rookies.

Name	Pos.	Hgt.	Wgt.	Birth-date	College	How Acquired
Carson, Malcolm (1, 2)......	C/G	6-2	260	11- 1-59	Tennessee-Chattanooga	FA
Carvalho, Bernard (1)........	G/T	6-4	262	9-29-61	Hawaii	FA
Chesley, John (1)	TE	6-5	235	7- 2-62	Oklahoma State	FA
Davenport, Ron	FB	6-2	225	12-22-62	Louisville	D6a
Dellenbach, Jeff..................	OT	6-6	280	2-14-63	Wisconsin	D4a
Flores, Sam (1).....................	K	6-0	185	11- 8-61	C.W. Post	FA
Hampton, Lorenzo	RB	6-0	212	3-12-62	Florida	D1
Hanks, Duan (1, 3)..............	WR	6-0	180	7-28-61	Stephen F. Austin	FA
Harris, Johnny (1, 3)..........	DE	6-4	266	8- 3-60	Mississippi Valley	FA
Higgins, Robert..................	LB	6-1	220	11-19-59	Emporia State	FA
Hinds, Adam	S	6-3	201	7-21-61	Oklahoma State	D9
Jones, Mike	HB	5-11	187	8- 2-63	Tulane	D11
Landry, Ronnie (1).............	RB	6-1	221	7- 8-62	McNeese State	*D8 '84
Lavin, Pete.........................	S	6-1	195	4-17-61	Whittier College	FA
Little, George	DT	6-4	254	6-27-63	Iowa State	D3
Moyer, Alex	LB	6-2	223	10-25-63	Northwestern	D3a
Nelson, David (1, 3)	RB	6-1	235	11-23-63	Heidelberg College	*FA
Noble, Ray	CB	6-0	170	12-19-62	California	D12
Pendleton, Mike..................	DB	6-2	185	4-11-61	Indiana	D10
Radle, Thomas (1)	TE	6-5	240	5-27-61	Virginia Military	FA
Reveiz, Fuad.......................	K	6-0	228	2- 4-63	Tennessee	D7
Sharp, Dan..........................	TE	6-3	230	2- 5-62	Texas-Christian	D8
Shorthose, George.............	WR	6-0	200	12-22-61	Missouri	D6
Smith, Mike	DB	6-0	174	10-24-62	Texas-El Paso	D4
Smythe, Mark (1)	DE	6-3	265	12-12-59	Indiana	FA
Southerland, Ken................	OL	6-6	272	8-13-62	Georgia Tech	FA
Thaxton, James (1)............	DB	5-11	175	3-16-62	Louisiana Tech	FA
Thurman, Tony...................	CB	6-0	194	3-15-62	Boston College	FA
Vanderwende, Kyle...........	QB	6-2	215	9- 6-63	Miami (Fla.)	FA
Washington, Keith..............	WR	5-11	190	10- 8-59	None	FA
White, Mike........................	G/C	6-3	241	10-21-61	Alabama	FA
Weir, Robert.......................	DE	6-3	274	2- 4-61	Southern Methodist	FA

*Landry missed '84 season due to injury.

MINNESOTA VIKINGS
(Central Division, National Conference)

Bud Grant

President—Max Winter
Executive Vice-President and General Manager—Mike Lynn
Director of Football Operations—Jerry Reichow
Player Personnel Director—Frank Gilliam
Head Coach—Bud Grant (17 years: 151-87-5)
Assistant Coaches:
   Defensive Assistant—Tom Batta
   Asst. Head Coach/Off. Coord.—Jerry Burns
   Defensive Backs—Pete Carroll
   Defensive Coordinator—Bob Hollway
   Offensive Line—John Michels
   Linebackers—Floyd Reese
   Kicking Teams/Tight Ends—Dick Rehbein
   Running Backs—Marc Trestman
   Defensive Line—Paul Wiggin
Public Relations Director—Merrill Swanson
   (Office Phone: 828-6500—Area Code 612)
Offices—9520 Viking Drive, Eden Prairie, Minn. 55344
Stadium—Metrodome, Minneapolis, Minn. (Capacity: 62,212)
Team Colors—Purple, Gold and White
Training Site—Mankato State University, Mankato, Minn.

1985 SCHEDULE
(All times local.
All games Sunday unless noted otherwise.)

Date	Opponent	Time
Sept. 8	SAN FRANCISCO	12:00
Sept. 15	at Tampa Bay	4:00
Sept. 19	CHICAGO (Thurs.)	7:00
Sept. 29	at Buffalo	1:00
Oct. 6	at Los Angeles Rams	1:00
Oct. 13	vs. Green Bay at Milwaukee	12:00
Oct. 20	SAN DIEGO	12:00
Oct. 27	at Chicago	12:00
Nov. 3	DETROIT	12:00
Nov. 10	GREEN BAY	12:00
Nov. 17	at Detroit	4:00
Nov. 24	NEW ORLEANS	12:00
Dec. 1	at Philadelphia	1:00
Dec. 8	TAMPA BAY	3:00
Dec. 15	at Atlanta	1:00
Dec. 22	PHILADELPHIA	12:00

1984 RESULTS—(Won 3, Lost 13)

Vikings		Opp.		Att.
13	San Diego	42	(H)	57,276
17	Philadelphia	19	(A)	55,942
27	Atlanta	20	(H)	53,955
29	Detroit	28	(A)	57,511
12	Seattle	20	(H)	57,171
31	Tampa Bay	35	(A)	47,405
20	Los Angeles Raiders	23	(A)	49,276
14	Detroit	16	(H)	57,953
7	Chicago	16	(A)	57,517
27	Tampa Bay	24	(H)	54,949
17	Green Bay	45	(A)	52,931
21	Denver	42	(A)	74,716
3	Chicago	34	(H)	56,881
17	Washington	31	(H)	55,017
7	San Francisco	51	(A)	56,670
14	Green Bay	38	(H)	51,197

1984 GAMES STARTED

16 games: Tom Hannon, Tim Irwin, Steve Riley, Terry Tausch.
15 games: Charlie Johnson, Dennis Johnson, Curtis Rouse, Scott Studwell.
14 games: Alfred Anderson, Mike Jones, Steve Jordan, Carl Lee.
13 games: Rufus Bess, Fred McNeill.
11 games: Sammy White.
10 games: Neil Elshire, Ron Sams, John Swain.
9 games: Matt Blair, Ted Brown, Tommy Kramer.
8 games: Joey Browner, Darrin Nelson, Robin Sendlein.
6 games: Doug Martin, Mark Mullaney, Greg Smith.
5 games: Randy Holloway, Leo Lewis, Wade Wilson.
4 games: Willie Teal.
3 games: Grant Feasel, Jim Hough.
2 games: Archie Manning, Mike Mularkey.
1 game: Walker Ashley, Robert Cobb, Dwight Collins, Wes Hamilton, Terry LeCount, Chris Martin, Joe Senser.

MINNESOTA VIKINGS 1985 VETERAN ROSTER

No.	Name	Pos.	Ht.	Wt.	NFL Exp.	Birth-date	College	Games in '84	How Acquired
46	Anderson, Alfred	RB	6-1	213	2	8- 4-61	Baylor	16	D3, '84
69	Arbubakrr, Hasson	DE	6-4	250	3	12- 9-60	Texas Tech	4	FA, '84
58	Ashley, Walker Lee	LB	6-0	240	3	7-28-60	Penn State	15	D3, '83
21	Bess, Rufus	CB	5-9	185	7	3-13-56	South Carolina State	16	W-Buf, '82
59	Blair, Matt	LB	6-5	235	12	9-20-50	Iowa State	11	D2a, '74
62	Boyd, Brent	G	6-3	275	5	3-23-57	UCLA	*0	D3, '80
23	Brown, Ted	RB	5-10	210	7	2- 2-57	North Carolina State	13	D1, '79
47	Browner, Joey	S	6-2	205	3	5-15-60	Southern California	16	D1, '83
82	Bruer, Bob	TE	6-5	240	6	5-22-54	Mankato State	*0	FA, '80
8	†Coleman, Greg	P	6-0	185	9	9- 9-54	Florida A&M	16	FA, '78
84	Collins, Dwight	WR	6-1	208	2	8-23-61	Pittsburgh	16	D6, '84
43	Colter, Jeff	CB	5-10	171	2	4-23-61	Kansas	16	OFA, '84
73	†Elshire, Neil	DE	6-6	260	5	3- 8-58	Oregon	12	W-Was, '81
64	Feasel, Grant	C-T	6-8	278	3	6-28-60	Abilene Christian	*15	FA, '84
50	Fowlkes, Dennis	LB	6-2	230	3	3-11-61	West Virginia	14	FA, '83
25	Greene, Marcellus	CB	6-0	184	2	12-12-57	Arizona	14	W-Ram, '84
90	Haines, John	NT	6-6	260	2	12-16-61	Texas	8	D7, '84
61	Hamilton, Wes	G	6-3	270	10	4-24-53	Tulsa	4	D3, '76
45	Hannon, Tom	S	5-11	195	9	3- 5-55	Michigan State	16	D3, '77
60	Hernandez, Matt	T	6-6	262	3	10-16-61	Purdue	13	FA, '84
51	Hough, Jim	G	6-2	275	8	8- 4-56	Utah State	9	D4, '78
76	Irwin, Tim	T	6-6	285	5	12-13-58	Tennessee	16	D3, '81
65	Johnson, Charlie	NT	6-3	275	9	2-17-52	Colorado	16	T-Phi, '82
52	Johnson, Dennis	LB	6-3	235	6	6-19-58	Southern California	16	D4, '80
89	Jones, Mike	WR	5-11	176	3	4-14-60	Tennessee State	16	D6, '83
83	Jordan, Steve	TE	6-3	230	4	1-10-61	Brown	14	D7, '82
9	Kramer, Tommy	QB	6-2	205	9	3- 7-55	Rice	9	D1, '77
39	Lee, Carl	CB-S	5-11	185	3	4- 6-61	Marshall	16	D7, '83
87	†Lewis, Leo	WR	5-8	170	5	9-17-56	Missouri	16	FA, '81
4	Manning, Archie	QB	6-3	211	15	5- 9-49	Mississippi	6	T-Hou, '83
56	Martin, Chris	LB	6-2	230	3	12-19-60	Auburn	16	W-NO, '84
79	Martin, Doug	DE	6-3	255	6	5-22-57	Washington	13	D1, '80
54	McNeill, Fred	LB	6-2	230	12	5- 6-52	UCLA	13	D1, '74
86	Mularkey, Mike	TE	6-4	245	3	11-19-61	Florida	16	FA, '83
77	Mullaney, Mark	DE	6-6	245	11	4-30-53	Colorado State	7	D1, '75
20	†Nelson, Darrin	RB	5-9	180	4	1- 2-59	Stanford	15	D1, '82
49	Nord, Keith	S	6-0	195	6	3-13-57	St. Cloud St., Minn.	*0	OFA, '79
36	Rice, Allen	RB-S	5-10	198	2	4- 5-62	Baylor	14	D5a, '84
78	†Riley, Steve	T	6-6	260	12	11-23-52	Southern California	16	D1a, '74
68	†Rouse, Curtis	G	6-3	305	4	7-13-60	Tenn.-Chattanooga	16	D11, '82
67	†Sams, Ron	G	6-3	255	2	4-12-61	Pittsburgh	12	W-GB, '84
57	Sendlein, Robin	LB	6-3	225	5	12- 1-58	Texas	15	D2a, '81
81	†Senser, Joe	TE	6-4	235	6	8-18-56	West Chester St., Pa.	8	D6, '79
91	Smith, Gregory	NT	6-3	261	2	10-22-59	Kansas	16	OFA, '84
3	Stenerud, Jan	K	6-2	190	19	11-26-42	Montana State	16	T-GB, '84
55	Studwell, Scott	LB	6-2	230	9	8-27-54	Illinois	16	D9, '77
29	Swain, John	CB	6-1	195	5	9- 4-59	Miami, Fla.	15	D4, '81
	Swilley, Dennis	C	6-3	241	8	6-28-55	North Texas State	*0	D2, '77
66	Tausch, Terry	T	6-5	275	4	2- 5-59	Texas	16	D2, '82
37	Teal, Willie	CB	5-10	195	6	12-20-57	Louisiana State	11	D2, '80
24	Turner, Maurice	RB	5-11	199	2	9-10-60	Utah State	13	FA, '84
34	Wagoner, Dan	S	5-10	180	3	12-12-59	Kansas	*5	FA, '84
85	White, Sammy	WR	5-11	195	10	3-16-54	Grambling	13	D2, '76
11	Wilson, Wade	QB	6-3	210	5	2- 1-59	East Texas State	8	D8, '81
	Young, Rickey	RB	6-2	200	10	12- 7-53	Jackson State	*0	T-SD, '78

*Boyd, Bruer and Nord missed '84 season due to injury; Feasel played 6 games with Indianapolis, 9 with Minnesota in '84; Swilley last active with Minnesota in '83; Wagoner played 1 game with Detroit, 4 with Minnesota in '84; Young last active with Minnesota in '83.

†Option playout; subject to developments.

Also played with Vikings in '84—G Malcolm Carson (1 game), DE Robert Cobb (2), QB Steve Dils (3), G Bill Dugan (1), TE Don Hasselbeck (16), DE Randy Holloway (8), WR Terry LeCount (2), RB David Nelson (2), LB Mark Stewart (4), NT Paul Sverchek (3), DT Ruben Vaughan (5), WR Billy Waddy (4).

D—Draft; T—Trade; W—Waivers; FA—Free Agent; OFA—Original Free Agent.

MINNESOTA VIKINGS
1985 DRAFT CHOICES

(Number following name designates order of selection among 336 players drafted.)

Round and Player		Position	College
1. Choice to Houston (a)			
1. DOLEMAN, Chris from Atlanta (b)	4	LB	Pittsburgh
2. HOLT, Issiac	30	DB	Alcorn State
3. LOWDERMILK, Kirk	59	C	Ohio State
3. MEAMBER, Tim from Atlanta (c)	60	LB	Washington
3. LONG, Tim from San Diego (d)	66	T	Memphis State
4. RHYMES, Buster	85	WR	Oklahoma
4. MORRELL, Kyle from L.A. Rams (e)	106	DB	Brigham Young
5. MacDONALD, Mark	115	G	Boston College
6. BONO, Steve	142	QB	UCLA
6. NEWTON, Tim from L.A. Raiders (f)	164	NT	Florida
7. Choice to Green Bay (g)			
8. BLAIR, Nikita	198	LB	Texas-El Paso
9. COVINGTON, Jamie	227	RB	Syracuse
10. JOHNSON, Juan	254	WR	Langston, Okla.
11. WILLIAMS, Tim	283	DB	N. C. A&T
12. JONES, Byron	310	NT	Tulsa

(a) Traded pick in switch of first-round positions, April 9, 1985.

(b) Acquired pick and 3rd round pick for 1st round pick, April 30, 1985.

(c) see (b).

(d) Acquired pick for defensive back John Turner, August 10, 1984.

(e) Acquired pick for quarterback Steve Dils, September 18, 1984.

(f) Acquired pick and 2nd round pick in 1986 for linebacker Brad Van Pelt, October 9, 1984.

(g) Traded pick for kicker Jan Stenerud, July 17, 1984.

MINNESOTA VIKINGS
1985 ROOKIE AND FIRST-YEAR ROSTER

(1) Indicates player in previous NFL camp.
(2) Indicates player with USFL game experience.
(3) Indicates player in previous USFL camp.
(4) Indicates player with CFL game experience.
(5) Indicates player in previous CFL camp.
  All others classified as rookies.

Name	Pos.	Hgt.	Wgt.	Birth-date	College	How Acquired
Blair, Nikita	LB	6-2	224	11-19-62	Texas-El Paso	D8
Bono, Steve	QB	6-3	211	5-11-62	UCLA	D6
Borman, Dave	P	5-11	200	8-25-60	Northwest Missouri	FA
Brown, Melvin A. (1)	CB	5-11	187	10-25-58	Mississippi	*D10 '83
Brown, Melvin L. (1)	WR	6-4	198	11-29-59	Alabama	*FA '84
Covington, Jaime	RB	6-0	218	12-12-62	Syracuse	D9
Doleman, Chris	LB	6-5	250	10-16-61	Pittsburgh	D1
Gustafson, Jim (1)	WR	6-1	185	3-16-61	St. Thomas	FA
Hechinger, Rick	G	6-5	255	6-19-62	Memphis State	FA
Holt, Issiac	CB	6-1	197	10- 4-62	Alcorn State	D2
Johnson, Juan	WR	5-11	185	2-21-62	Langston	D10
Jones, Byron	NT	6-3	276	7- 5-62	Tulsa	D12
Kidd, Keith (1)	WR	6-1	198	9-10-62	Arkansas	*D9 '84
Lewis, David	RB	5-10	205	12-12-61	Northern Iowa	FA
Long, Tim	T	6-5	305	4-20-63	Memphis State	D3b
Lowdermilk, Kirk	C	6-3	265	4-10-63	Ohio State	D3
MacDonald, Mark	G	6-4	267	4-30-61	Boston College	D5
Meamber, Tim	LB	6-3	228	10-29-62	Washington	D3a
Morrell, Kyle	S	6-1	189	10- 9-63	Brigham Young	D4a
Newton, Tim	NT	6-0	302	3-23-63	Florida	D6a
Renn, Matt	C	6-1	267	4-30-63	Wisconsin-River Falls	FA
Rhymes, Buster	WR	6-1	212	1-27-62	Oklahoma	D4
Rosnagle, Ted (1, 2, 4)	CB-S	6-3	202	9-29-61	Portland State	FA
Rush, Mark (2)	RB	6-2	230	3-31-59	Miami, Fla.	FA
Smith, Allanda (2)	S	6-2	190	3- 7-62	Texas Christian	SupD '84
Smith, Robert (2)	DE	6-5	245	12- 3-62	Grambling	SupD '84
Spencer, James (1)	LB	6-2	236	11-22-61	Oklahoma State	*D10 '84
Williams, Tim	CB-S	6-1	200	2-21-63	North Carolina A&T	D11

*Melvin A. Brown missed '83 and '84 seasons due to injury; Melvin L. Brown, Kidd and Spencer missed '84 season due to injury.

NEW ENGLAND PATRIOTS
(Eastern Division, American Conference)

Raymond Berry

President—William H. Sullivan, Jr.
Executive Vice-President—Charles W. Sullivan
Vice-President—Francis (Bucko) Kilroy
General Manager—Patrick Sullivan
Director of Player Development—Dick Steinberg
Director of Pro Scouting—Bill McPeak
Head Coach—Raymond Berry (1 year: 4-4)
Assistant Coaches:
    Strength and Conditioning—Dean Brittenham
    Defensive Backfield—Jim Carr
    Offensive Backfield—Bobby Grier
    Asst. Head Coach-Offense/Off. Line—Rod Humenuik
    Asst. Receiver Coach—Harold Jackson
    Defensive Line—Ed Khayat
    Defensive Coordinator—Rod Rust
    Special Teams/Tight Ends—Dante Scarnecchia
    Linebackers—Don Shinnick
    Receivers/Quarterbacks—Les Steckel
Director of Publicity—Jim Greenidge
    (Office Phone: 543-7911 or 262-1776—Area Code 617)
Offices—Sullivan Stadium, Route 1, Foxboro, Mass. 02035
Stadium—Sullivan Stadium, Foxboro, Mass. (Capacity: 60,890)
Team Colors—Red, White and Blue
Training Site—Bryant College, Smithfield, R. I.

1985 SCHEDULE
(All times local.
All games Sunday unless noted otherwise.)

Sept. 8	GREEN BAY	1:00
Sept. 15	at Chicago	12:00
Sept. 22	at Buffalo	1:00
Sept. 29	LOS ANGELES RAIDERS	1:00
Oct. 6	at Cleveland	1:00
Oct. 13	BUFFALO	1:00
Oct. 20	NEW YORK JETS	4:00
Oct. 27	at Tampa Bay	1:00
Nov. 3	MIAMI	1:00
Nov. 10	INDIANAPOLIS	1:00
Nov. 17	at Seattle	1:00
Nov. 24	at New York Jets	1:00
Dec. 1	at Indianapolis	1:00
Dec. 8	DETROIT	1:00
Dec. 16	at Miami (Mon.)	9:00
Dec. 22	CINCINNATI	1:00

1984 RESULTS—(Won 9, Lost 7)

Patriots		Opp.		Att.
21	Buffalo	17	(A)	48,528
7	Miami	28	(A)	66,083
38	Seattle	23	(H)	43,140
10	Washington	26	(H)	60,503
28	New York Jets	21	(A)	68,978
17	Cleveland	16	(A)	53,036
20	Cincinnati	14	(H)	48,154
24	Miami	44	(H)	60,711
30	New York Jets	20	(H)	60,513
19	Denver	26	(A)	74,908
38	Buffalo	10	(H)	43,313
50	Indianapolis	17	(A)	60,009
17	Dallas	20	(A)	55,341
10	St. Louis	33	(H)	53,558
17	Philadelphia	27	(A)	41,581
16	Indianapolis	10	(H)	22,383

1984 GAMES STARTED

16 games: Don Blackmon, Ray Clayborn, Darryl Haley, Brian Holloway, Steve Nelson, Dennis Owens, Kenneth Sims, Stephen Starring, Andre Tippett, Ron Wooten.

15 games: Lin Dawson, John Hannah, Roland James, Larry McGrew, Toby Williams.

13 games: Tony Eason, Derrick Ramsey.

12 games: Pete Brock, Stanley Morgan.

10 games: Fred Marion.

8 games: Ernest Gibson, Ronnie Lippett.

7 games: Craig James, Rick Sanford.

5 games: Anthony Collins, Guy Morriss.

4 games: Mosi Tatupu.

3 games: Irving Fryar, Steve Grogan, Cedric Jones.

1 game: Julius Adams, Greg Hawthorne, Bo Robinson, Clayton Weishuhn.

NEW ENGLAND PATRIOTS 1985 VETERAN ROSTER

No.	Name	Pos.	Ht.	Wt.	NFL Exp.	Birth-date	College	Games in '84	How Acquired
85	Adams, Julius	DE	6-3	265	14	4-26-48	Texas Southern	16	D2, '71
55	Blackmon, Don	LB	6-2	230	5	3-14-58	Tulsa	16	D4, '81
58	Brock, Pete	C	6-3	225	10	7-14-54	Colorado	12	D1a, '76
3	Camarillo, Rich	P	5-11	191	5	11-29-59	Washington	7	OFA, '81
26	Clayborn, Ray	CB	6-0	186	9	1- 2-55	Texas	16	D1, '77
33	Collins, Tony	RB-KR	5-11	212	5	5-27-50	East Carolina	16	D2, '81
	Crump, George	DE	6-4	260	2	7-22-59	East Carolina	*0	D4, '82
87	Dawson, Lin	TE	6-3	240	5	6-24-59	North Carolina State	16	D8a, '81
47	†Dombroski, Paul	S	6-0	185	6	8- 8-56	Linfield College	14	W-KC, '81
11	Eason, Tony	QB	6-4	212	3	10- 8-59	Illinois	16	D1, '83
56	Fairchild, Paul	G	6-2	235	2	8-14-61	Kansas	7	D5, '84
1	†Franklin, Tony	K	5-8	182	7	11-18-56	Texas A&M	16	T-Phi, '84
80	Fryar, Irving	WR-PR	6-0	200	2	9-28-62	Nebraska	14	D1, '84
43	Gibson, Ernest	CB	5-10	185	2	10- 3-61	Furman	15	D6, '84
59	†Golden, Tim	LB	6-1	220	4	11-15-59	Florida	15	OFA, '81
14	Grogan, Steve	QB	6-4	210	11	7-24-53	Kansas State	3	D5, '75
68	Haley, Darryl	T	6-4	275	4	2-16-61	Utah	16	D2b, '82
73	Hannah, John	G	6-3	265	13	4- 4-51	Alabama	15	D1, '73
40	Hawthorne, Greg	WR-RB	6-3	225	7	9- 5-56	Baylor	14	T-Pit, '84
70	†Henson, Luther	NT	6-0	275	4	3-25-9	Ohio State	9	FA, '82
76	Holloway, Brian	T	6-7	285	5	7-25-59	Stanford	16	D1, '81
51	Ingram, Brian	LB	6-4	235	4	10-31-59	Tennessee	12	D4a, '82
32	James, Craig	RB	6-0	215	2	1- 2-61	Southern Methodist	15	D7, '83
38	James, Roland	S	6-2	191	6	2-18-58	Tennessee	15	D1, '80
83	Jones, Cedric	WR	6-0	184	4	6- 1-60	Duke	14	D3, '82
19	†Kerrigan, Mike	QB	6-3	205	3	4-27-60	Northwestern	1	FA, '82
22	†Lee, Keith	S	5-11	193	5	12-22-57	Colorado State	15	FA, '81
42	Lippett, Ronnie	CB	5-11	180	3	12-10-60	Miami, Fla.	16	D8, '83
31	Marion, Fred	S	6-2	191	4	8- 2-59	Miami, Fla.	16	D5, '82
50	McGrew, Larry	LB	6-5	233	5	7-23-57	Southern California	16	D2, '80
23	McSwain, Rod	CB	6-1	198	2	1-28-62	Clemson	15	T-Atl, '84
67	Moore, Steve	T	6-4	285	3	10- 1-60	Tennessee State	16	D3a, '83
86	Morgan, Stanley	WR	5-11	181	9	2-17-55	Tennessee	13	D1a, '77
75	†Morriss, Guy	C	6-4	270	13	5-13-51	Texas Christian	16	FA, '84
57	Nelson, Steve	LB	6-2	230	12	4-26-51	North Dakota State	16	D2a, '74
98	Owens, Dennis	NT	6-1	258	4	2-24-60	North Carolina State	16	OFA, '82
88	Ramsey, Derrick	TE	6-5	235	8	12-23-56	Kentucky	16	T-Rai, '83
52	Rembert, Johnny	LB	6-3	234	3	1-19-61	Clemson	7	D4, '83
95	Reynolds, Ed	LB	6-5	230	3	9-23-61	Virginia	16	OFA, '83
41	Robinson, Bo	RB	6-2	235	7	5-27-56	West Texas State	16	W-Atl, '84
65	Rogers, Doug	DE	6-5	270	4	6-23-60	Stanford	12	W-Atl, '83
25	Sanford, Rick	S	6-1	192	7	1- 9-57	South Carolina	16	D1, '79
77	Sims, Ken	DE	6-5	271	4	10-31-59	Texas	16	D1, '82
81	Starring, Stephen	WR-KR	5-10	172	3	7-30-61	McNeese State	16	D3, '83
30	Tatupu, Mosi	RB	6-0	227	8	4-26-55	Southern California	16	D8a, '78
56	Tippett, Andre	LB	6-3	241	4	12-27-59	Iowa	16	D2a, '82
82	Weathers, Clarence	WR	5-9	170	3	1-10-62	Delaware State	9	OFA, '83
24	Weathers, Robert	RB	6-2	222	4	9-13-60	Arizona State	2	D2, '82
53	Weishuhn, Clayton	LB	6-2	221	3	10- 9-59	Angelo State	1	D3a, '82
54	Williams, Ed	LB	6-4	244	2	8- 9-61	Texas	14	D2, '84
44	Williams, Jon	RB-KR	5-9	205	2	6- 1-61	Penn State	9	D3, '84
72	Williams, Lester	NT	6-3	272	4	1-19-59	Miami, Fla.	7	D1a, '82
90	Williams, Toby	DE	6-3	265	3	11-19-59	Nebraska	16	D10a, '83
	Wilson, Darryal	WR	6-0	182	2	9-19-60	Tennessee	*0	D2, '83
61	Wooten, Ron	G	6-4	273	4	6-28-59	North Carolina	16	D6, '81

*Crump and Wilson missed '84 season due to injury.

†Option playout; subject to developments.

Also played with Patriots in '84—P Luke Prestridge (9 games), DB Ricky Smith (1), DE Scott Virkus (5).

D—Draft; T—Trade; W—Waivers; FA—Free Agent; OFA—Original Free Agent.

NEW ENGLAND PATRIOTS
1985 DRAFT CHOICES

(Number following name designates order of selection among 336 players drafted.)

Round and Player		Position	College
1. Choice to San Francisco (a)			
1. MATICH, Trevor from San Francisco (a)	28	C	Brigham Young
2. VERIS, Garin	48	DE	Stanford
2. BOWMAN, Jim from L.A. Raiders (b)	52	DB	Cent. Michigan
2. THOMAS, Ben from San Francisco (a)	56	DE	Auburn
3. Choice to San Francisco (a)			
3. McMILLIAN, Audrey from San Francisco (a)	84	DB	Houston
4. TOTH, Tom	102	T	W'tern Michigan
4. PHELAN, Gerard from L.A. Raiders (c)	108	WR	Boston College
5. Choice to Cincinnati (d)			
6. Choice to Philadelphia (e)			
7. Choice to L.A. Raiders (f)			
8. Choice to Atlanta (g)			
8. HODGE, Milford from San Francisco (h)	224	DT	Washington St.
9. Choice to Pittsburgh (i)			
10. Choice to Denver (j)			
11. LEWIS, Paul	295	RB	Boston U.
12. MUMFORD, Tony	328	RB	Penn State

(a) Traded 1st and 3rd round picks for 1st, 2nd and 3rd round picks, April 30, 1985.
(b) Acquired pick and 1st round pick in 1984 for cornerback Mike Haynes and 7th round pick, November 10, 1983.
(c) Acquired pick for tackle Shelby Jordan, September 16, 1983.
(d) Traded pick, two 1st round picks in 1984 and 10th round pick in 1984 for 1st round pick in 1984, April 4, 1984.
(e) Traded pick for kicker Tony Franklin, February 21, 1984.
(f) See (b).
(g) Traded pick for cornerback Rod McSwain, August 27, 1984.
(h) Acquired pick, 7th round pick in 1984 and conditional 7th round pick in 1986 for quarterback Matt Cavanaugh, August 10, 1983.
(i) Traded pick for wide receiver Greg Hawthorne, August 21, 1984.
(j) Traded pick for punter Luke Prestridge, August 20, 1984.

NEW ENGLAND PATRIOTS
1985 ROOKIE AND FIRST-YEAR ROSTER

(1) Indicates player in previous NFL camp.
(2) Indicates player with USFL game experience.
(3) Indicates player in previous USFL camp.
(4) Indicates player with CFL game experience.
(5) Indicates player in previous CFL camp.
   All others classified as rookies.

Name	Pos.	Hgt.	Wgt.	Birth-date	College	How Acquired
Aamodt, Jay	DB	6-0	187	12-15-62	Winona State	FA
Anae, Robert	G	6-4	250	12-21-58	Brigham Young	FA
Andreoli, John (1)	LB	6-2	230	3-30-60	Holy Cross	*FA '84
Askew, Ricky (1)	TE	6-5	225	2-22-61	Rice	FA '84
Atkinson, Jess	K	5-9	175	12-11-61	Maryland	FA
Bodine, Troy	QB	6-1	210	6-21-63	Cincinnati	FA
Bonitati, Bill	LB	6-2	230	9-29-60	Rhode Island	FA
Bowman, Jim	S	6-2	210	10-26-63	Central Michigan	D2a
Brennan, Pat	QB	6-1	205	1- 4-63	Franklin	FA
Bromell, Rockie	DB	6-0	180	4-14-61	Rhode Island	FA
Bullen, Butch	WR	6-0	170	4- 7-62	Vanderbilt	FA
Creswell, Smiley (1)	DE	6-4	251	12-11-59	Michigan State	*D5 '83
Darby, Stephone	LB	6-2	240	9-24-61	Johnson C. Smith	FA
Donnelly, Rick	P	6-0	185	....	Wyoming	FA
Ferguson, Michael	RB	5-11	200	7-28-61	Winston-Salem State	FA
Garron, Arnold (1)	SS/FS	6-1	195	4-15-62	New Hampshire	FA
Hill, Daryl (3)	CB	5-10	175	8-30-62	Cal-Davis	FA
Hobby, Ron	DB	6-0	185	2- 6-63	Syracuse	FA
Hodge, Milford	DT	6-3	278	3-11-61	Washington State	D8
Hoffman, Jeff	OL	6-2	255	11-14-63	Sacramento State	FA
Larus, Steve	TE	6-4	234	2-16-61	Emory & Henry (Va.)	FA
LeBlanc, Michael	RB	5-11	199	5- 5-62	Stephen F. Austin	FA
Lewis, Charles (1)	FB	5-11	239	4-23-61	Albany State	FA
Lewis, Howard (1, 3)	CB	6-0	182	9-29-60	Virginia	FA
Lewis, Paul	RB	5-8	197	9-12-62	Boston University	D11
Matich, Trevor	C	6-4	270	10- 9-61	Brigham Young	D1
McMillian, Audrey	FS/CB	5-11	190	8-13-62	Houston	D3
Mocarski, Robert	OL	6-4	265	5- 9-63	Boston University	FA
Moore, Rodney (1)	DB	6-1	197	9- 8-60	North Texas State	FA
Mullahey, Nick (1)	OL	6-2	280	5-15-61	Boise State	FA
Mumford, Tony	RB	6-0	215	6-14-63	Penn State	D12
Nardone, David	P	6-0	195	2-27-62	Florida	FA
Norris, Jon	OL	6-3	265	11- 1-62	American International	FA
Pereira, Dave	DB	5-11	196	3-15-63	Boston College	FA
Perkins, Chris	K	6-3	200	9- 7-62	Florida	D4a
Phelan, Gerard	WR	6-0	190	1-20-63	Boston College	D4a
Ramsey, Tom (1, 2)	QB	6-0	189	7- 9-61	UCLA	*D10b '83
Richards, Fred	OL	6-3	265	7-14-62	Southern Mississippi	FA
Robinson, Melvin	WR	5-8	167	9- 4-62	Houston	FA
Sanders, William	DT	6-4	250	7-20-62	North Alabama	FA
Schubert, Eric (2)	K	5-8	193	5-28-62	Pittsburgh	FA
Sealby, Randall	LB	6-2	225	5-16-60	Missouri	FA
Starnes, John	P	6-3	182	12-25-62	North Texas State	FA
Steevens, John	C/OG	6-3	265	12-28-60	Fresno State	FA
Stinnett, Michael	K	5-11	175	4- 6-63	James Madison	FA
Stonewall, Ricke	RB	5-7	182	12-17-61	Millersville State	FA
Strang, Doug	QB	6-1	205	10- 5-62	Penn State	FA
Sutton, Frank	G	6-3	265	....	Jackson State	FA
Thomas, Ben	DE	6-4	280	7- 2-61	Auburn	D2b
Toth, Tom	OT	6-5	275	5-23-62	Western Michigan	D4
Veris, Garin	DE	6-4	255	2-27-63	Stanford	D2
White, Marc	RB	5-11	210	10-15-63	Utah State	FA
Williams, Craig (1)	RB	6-1	225	4- 4-62	Lafayette	*FA '84
Williams, Derwin (1)	WR	6-0	170	5- 6-61	New Mexico	*FA '84
Windham, David (1)	LB	6-2	240	3-14-61	Jackson State	*D9 '84
Youssef, Gehad	K	6-1	190	9-17-62	Bowling Green	FA

  *Andreoli, Ramsey, C. Williams, D. Williams and Windham missed '84 season due to injury; Creswell missed '83 and '84 seasons due to injury.

NEW ORLEANS SAINTS
(Western Division, National Conference)

Bum Phillips

Managing General Partner—Tom Benson Jr.
President—Eddie Jones
Director of Operations—Pat Peppler
Head Coach and G.M.—O. A. (Bum) Phillips (10 years: 78-69)
Assistant Coaches:
   Tight Ends—Andy Everest
   Offensive Coordinator—King Hill
   Offensive Backfield—John Levra
   Offensive Line—Carl Mauck
   Strength—Russell Paternostro
   Defensive Coordinator—Wade Phillips
   Special Teams—Harold Richardson
   Quality Control—Joe Spencer
   Linebackers—John Paul Young
   Defensive Line—Willie Zapalac
Director of Public Relations—Greg Suit
   (Office Phone: 733-6147—Area Code 504)
Offices—1500 Poydras St., New Orleans, La. 70112
Stadium—Louisiana Superdome (Capacity: 69,105)
Team Colors—Old Gold, Black and White
Training Site—Louisiana Tech, Ruston, La.

1985 SCHEDULE
(All times local.
All games Sunday unless noted otherwise.)

Sept. 8	KANSAS CITY	12:00
Sept. 15	at Denver	2:00
Sept. 22	TAMPA BAY	12:00
Sept. 29	at San Francisco	1:00
Oct. 6	PHILADELPHIA	12:00
Oct. 13	at Los Angeles Raiders	1:00
Oct. 20	at Atlanta	1:00
Oct. 27	NEW YORK GIANTS	3:00
Nov. 3	at Los Angeles Rams	1:00
Nov. 10	SEATTLE	12:00
Nov. 17	vs. Green Bay at Milwaukee	12:00
Nov. 24	at Minnesota	12:00
Dec. 1	LOS ANGELES RAMS	12:00
Dec. 8	at St. Louis	12:00
Dec. 15	SAN FRANCISCO	12:00
Dec. 22	ATLANTA	12:00

1984 RESULTS—(Won 7, Lost 9)

Saints		Opp.		Att.
28	Atlanta	36	(H)	66,652
17	Tampa Bay	13	(H)	54,686
20	San Francisco	30	(A)	57,611
34	St. Louis	24	(H)	58,723
27	Houston	10	(A)	43,108
7	Chicago	20	(A)	53,752
10	Los Angeles Rams	28	(H)	63,161
27	Dallas (OT)	30	(A)	50,966
16	Cleveland	14	(A)	52,489
13	Green Bay	23	(H)	57,426
17	Atlanta	13	(A)	40,590
27	Pittsburgh	24	(H)	66,005
3	San Francisco	35	(H)	65,177
21	Los Angeles Rams	34	(A)	49,348
21	Cincinnati	24	(H)	40,855
10	New York Giants	3	(A)	63,739

1984 GAMES STARTED

16 games: Hoby Brenner, Russell Gary, Rickey Jackson, Whitney Paul, Johnnie Poe, George Rogers, Frank Wattelet, Dave Waymer, Jim Wilks, Dennis Winston.

15 games: Bruce Clark, Kelvin Clark, Steve Korte, Jim Kovach.

14 games: Stan Brock, Hokie Gajan, Richard Todd.

13 games: Jeff Groth.

11 games: Brad Edelman, John Hill, Derland Moore.

8 games: Chris Ward, Tyrone Young.

6 games: Eugene Goodlow.

5 games: Louis Oubre, Lindsay Scott.

3 games: Tony Elliott, Frank Warren.

2 games: Dave Wilson, Wayne Wilson.

1 game: Dave Lafary, Glen Redd.

NEW ORLEANS SAINTS 1985 VETERAN ROSTER

No.	Name	Pos.	Ht.	Wt.	NFL Exp.	Birth-date	College	Games in '84	How Acquired
7	Andersen, Morten	K	6-2	205	4	8-19-60	Michigan State	16	D4, '82
22	Anthony, Tyrone	RB	5-11	212	2	3- 3-62	North Carolina	15	D3a, '84
85	Brenner, Hoby	TE	6-4	245	5	6- 2-59	Southern California	16	D3a, '81
67	†Brock, Stan	T	6-6	288	6	6- 8-58	Colorado	14	D1, '80
35	Campbell, Earl	RB	5-11	233	8	3-29-55	Texas	*14	T-Hou, '84
65	†Carter, David	C	6-2	275	9	11-27-53	Western Kentucky	*14	FA, '84
75	Clark, Bruce	DE	6-3	281	4	3-31-58	Penn State	15	T-GB, '82
68	Clark, Kelvin	G	6-3	273	7	1-30-56	Nebraska	16	T-Den, '82
83	Duckett, Kenny	WR	6-0	179	4	10- 1-59	Wake Forest	11	D3b, '82
63	Edelman, Brad	G	6-6	262	4	9- 3-60	Missouri	11	D2, '82
99	Elliott, Tony	NT	6-2	280	4	4-23-59	North Texas State	4	D5, '82
26	Fields, Jitter	CB	5-8	188	2	8-16-62	Texas	13	D5, '84
46	Gajan, Hokie	FB	5-11	226	4	9- 6-59	Louisiana State	14	D10, '81
20	Gary, Russell	S	5-11	196	5	7-31-59	Nebraska	16	D2, '81
97	Geathers, James	DE	6-7	267	2	6-26-60	Wichita State	16	D2, '84
88	Goodlow, Eugene	WR	6-2	181	3	12-19-58	Kansas State	10	D3, '82
86	Groth, Jeff	WR	5-10	181	7	7- 2-57	Bowling Green	16	FA, '81
10	Hansen, Brian	P	6-3	218	2	10-26-60	Sioux Falls, S.D.	16	D9, '84
28	Harding, Greg	S	6-2	197	2	7-31-60	Nicholls State	3	FA, '84
87	†Hardy, Larry	TE	6-3	246	8	7- 9-56	Jackson State	6	D12, '78
92	Haynes, James	LB	6-2	227	2	8- 9-60	Mississippi Valley State	10	FA, '84
61	Hilgenberg, Joel	C-G	6-3	253	2	7-10-62	Iowa	10	D4, '84
24	Hoage, Terry	S	6-3	199	2	4-11-62	Georgia	14	D3, '84
57	Jackson, Rickey	LB	6-2	239	5	3-20-58	Pittsburgh	16	D2a, '81
34	Johnson, Bobby	CB-S	6-0	187	3	9- 1-60	Texas	16	FA, '83
60	Korte, Steve	C	6-2	271	3	1-15-60	Arkansas	15	D2, '83
52	Kovach, Jim	LB	6-2	239	7	5- 1-56	Kentucky	15	D4, '79
64	Lafary, Dave	T	6-7	285	8	1-13-55	Purdue	1	D5, '77
93	Lewis, Gary	NT	6-3	261	2	1-14-61	Oklahoma State	*0	D4, '83
98	Lewis, Reggie	DE	6-2	251	4	1-20-54	San Diego State	13	FA, '82
29	†Lewis, Rodney	CB	5-11	186	3	4- 2-59	Nebraska	16	D3, '83
19	†Merkens, Guido	QB-WR	6-1	197	8	8-14-55	Sam Houston State	16	FA, '80
84	†Miller, Junior	TE	6-4	244	6	11-26-57	Nebraska	15	T-Atl, '84
74	Moore, Derland	NT	6-4	273	13	10- 7-51	Oklahoma	12	D2, '73
66	Oubre, Louis	G	6-4	272	4	5-15-58	Oklahoma	12	D5, '81
51	Paul, Whitney	LB	6-3	218	10	10- 8-55	Colorado	16	T-KC, '82
53	Pelluer, Scott	LB	6-2	227	5	4-28-59	Washington State	16	W-Dal, '81
25	†Poe, Johnnie	CB	6-1	194	5	8-29-59	Missouri	16	D6a, '81
58	†Redd, Glen	LB	6-1	231	4	6-17-58	Brigham Young	16	D6b, '81
41	†Rogers, Jimmy	RB	5-10	195	6	6-29-55	Oklahoma	16	FA, '80
80	Scott, Lindsay	WR	6-1	200	4	12- 6-60	Georgia	16	D1, '82
96	Thorp, Don	NT	6-4	260	2	7-10-62	Illinois	5	D6, '84
82	Tice, John	TE	6-5	243	3	6-22-60	Maryland	10	D3, '83
11	†Todd, Richard	QB	6-2	212	10	11-19-53	Alabama	15	T-NYJ, '84
72	Ward, Chris	T	6-3	269	8	12-16-55	Ohio State	13	FA, '84
73	Warren, Frank	DE	6-4	278	5	9-14-59	Auburn	16	D3, '81
49	†Wattelet, Frank	S	6-0	185	5	10-25-58	Kansas	16	OFA, '81
44	Waymer, Dave	CB	6-1	188	6	7- 1-58	Notre Dame	16	D2, '80
94	Wilks, Jim	DE	6-5	265	5	3-12-58	San Diego State	16	D12, '80
18	Wilson, Dave	QB	6-3	211	4	4-27-59	Illinois	5	SupD, '81
45	†Wilson, Tim	FB	6-3	237	9	1-14-55	Maryland	12	W-Rai, '83
30	Wilson, Wayne	RB	6-3	220	7	9- 4-57	Shepherd, W. Va.	14	FA, '79
56	Winston, Dennis	LB	6-0	244	9	10-25-55	Arkansas	16	T-Pit, '82
89	†Young, Tyrone	WR	6-6	192	3	4-29-60	Florida	16	FA, '83

*Campbell played 6 games with Houston, 8 with New Orleans in '84; Carter played 7 games with Houston, 7 with New Orleans in '84; G. Lewis missed '84 season due to injury.

†Option playout; subject to developments.

Also played with Saints in '84—C John Hill (11 games), C Jim Pietrzak (10), RB George Rogers (16), QB Ken Stabler (3).

D—Draft; T—Trade; W—Waivers; FA—Free Agent; OFA—Original Free Agent; SupD—Supplemental Draft.

NEW ORLEANS SAINTS
1985 DRAFT CHOICES

(Number following name designates order of selection among 336 players drafted.)

Round and Player	Position		College
1. Choice to Houston (a)			
1. TOLES, Alvin from Washington (b)	24	LB	Tennessee
2. GILBERT, Daren	38	T	Cal. St.-Full.
3. DEL RIO, Jack	68	LB	Southern Calif.
4. ALLEN, Billy	95	DB	Florida State
5. Choice to Washington (b)			
6. Choice to Atlanta (c)			
7. MARTIN, Eric	179	WR	Louisiana State
8. KOHLBRAND, Joe	206	DE	Miami, Fla.
9. JOHNSON, Earl	236	DB	South Carolina
10. Choice to Washington (b)			
11. Choice to Washington (b)			
12. SONGY, Treg	320	DB	Tulane

(a) Traded pick for running back Earl Campbell, October 9, 1984.

(b) Acquired pick for running back George Rogers and 5th, 10th and 11th round picks, April 26, 1985.

(c) Traded pick for tight end Junior Miller, August 26, 1984.

NEW ORLEANS SAINTS
1985 ROOKIE AND FIRST-YEAR ROSTER

(1) Indicates player in previous NFL camp.
(2) Indicates player with USFL game experience.
(3) Indicates player in previous USFL camp.
(4) Indicates player with CFL game experience.
(5) Indicates player in previous CFL camp.
　All others classified as rookies.

Name	Pos.	Hgt.	Wgt.	Birth-date	College	How Acquired
Allen, Billy	DB	5-11	210	9-25-58	Florida State	D4
Dellocono, Michael	WR	5-9	176	6-25-61	Louisiana Tech	*FA '84
Del Rio, Jack	LB	6-4	235	4- 4-63	Southern California	D3
Fowler, Bobby (1)	TE	6-2	230	9-11-60	Louisiana Tech	FA
Gilbert, Daren	T	6-6	285	10- 3-63	California State-Fullerton	D2
Johnson, Earl	CB	6-0	190	10-20-63	South Carolina	D9
Kohlbrand, Joe	DE	6-4	242	3-18-63	Miami (Fla.)	D8
Manuel, Henry Lee	WR	6-0	190	....	Southwestern Louisiana	FA
Martin, Eric	WR	6-1	195	11- 8-61	Louisiana State	D7
Peters, Ken (1)	TE	6-4	245	9-30-60	Houston	FA
Powell, Kelly (1, 3)	QB	6-4	204	10- 6-61	Mississippi	FA
Songy, Treg	DB	6-1	195	6-15-63	Tulane	D12
Toles, Alvin	LB	6-1	211	3-23-63	Tennessee	D1
Worsham, David (3)	QB	6-3	207	4-15-59	Arkansas Tech	FA

*Dellocono missed '84 season due to injury.

NEW YORK GIANTS
(Eastern Division, National Conference)

Bill Parcells

President—Wellington T. Mara
Vice-President and Treasurer—Timothy J. Mara
Vice-President and Secretary—Raymond J. Walsh
Vice-President and General Manager—George Young
Assistant General Manager—Harry Hulmes
Director of Player Personnel—Tom Boisture
Director of Pro Personnel—Tim Rooney
Head Coach—Bill Parcells (2 years: 12-19-1)
Assistant Coaches:
    Defensive Coordinator/Linebackers—Bill Belichick
    Special Teams—Romeo Crennel
    Offensive Coordinator—Ron Erhardt
    Defensive Backs—Len Fontes
    Running Backs—Ray Handley
    Offensive Line—Fred Hoaglin
    Receivers—Pat Hodgson
    Defensive Line—Lamar Leachman
    Strength and Conditioning—Johnny Parker
    Tight Ends—Mike Pope
    Defensive Assistant—Mike Sweatman
Director of Media Services—Ed Croke
    (Office Phone: 935-8111—Area Code 201)
Offices—Giants Stadium, East Rutherford, N. J. 07073
Stadium—Giants Stadium (Capacity: 76,891)
Team Colors—Royal Blue, Red and White
Training Site—Pace University, Pleasantville, N. Y.

1985 SCHEDULE
(All times local.
All games Sunday unless noted otherwise.)

Sept. 8	PHILADELPHIA	1:00
Sept. 15	at Green Bay	3:00
Sept. 22	ST. LOUIS	1:00
Sept. 29	at Philadelphia	1:00
Oct. 6	DALLAS (night)	8:00
Oct. 13	at Cincinnati	1:00
Oct. 20	WASHINGTON	1:00
Oct. 27	at New Orleans	3:00
Nov. 3	TAMPA BAY	1:00
Nov. 10	LOS ANGELES RAMS	1:00
Nov. 18	at Washington (Mon.)	9:00
Nov. 24	at St. Louis	3:00
Dec. 1	CLEVELAND	1:00
Dec. 8	at Houston	3:00
Dec. 15	at Dallas	12:00
Dec. 21	PITTSBURGH (Sat.)	12:30

1984 RESULTS—(Won 10, Lost 8)

Giants	Opp.		Att.
28 Philadelphia	27	(H)	71,520
28 Dallas	7	(H)	75,921
14 Washington	30	(A)	52,997
17 Tampa Bay	14	(H)	72,650
12 Los Angeles Rams	33	(A)	53,417
10 San Francisco	31	(H)	76,112
19 Atlanta	7	(A)	50,268
10 Philadelphia	24	(A)	64,677
37 Washington	13	(H)	76,192
19 Dallas	7	(A)	60,235
17 Tampa Bay	20	(A)	46,534
16 St. Louis	10	(H)	73,428
28 Kansas City	27	(H)	74,383
20 New York Jets	10	(A)	74,975
21 St. Louis	31	(A)	49,973
3 New Orleans	10	(H)	63,739
NFC WILD-CARD GAME			
16 Los Angeles Rams	13	(A)	67,037
NFC SEMIFINAL GAME			
10 San Francisco	21	(A)	60,303

1984 GAMES STARTED

16 games: Kevin Belcher, Brad Benson, Rob Carpenter, Harry Carson, Bob Johnson, Zeke Mowatt, Karl Nelson, Phil Simms, Lawrence Taylor, Perry Williams.

15 games: Bill Ard, Jim Burt, Mark Haynes, Terry Kinard.

14 games: Curtis McGriff.

11 games: Earnest Gray, Leonard Marshall, Gary Reasons.

8 games: Bill Currier, Chris Godfrey, Joe Morris, William Roberts, Butch Woolfolk.

7 games: Ken Hill.

6 games: Andy Headen, Byron Hunt.

5 games: Dee Hardison, Lionel Manuel, Joe McLaughlin.

4 games: Carl Banks.

2 games: George Martin, Pete Shaw.

1 game: Kenny Daniel, David Jordan, Jerome Sally.

NEW YORK GIANTS 1985 VETERAN ROSTER

No.	Name	Pos.	Ht.	Wt.	NFL Exp.	Birth-date	College	Games in '84	How Acquired
67	Ard, Bill	G	6-3	270	5	3-12-59	Wake Forest	15	D8b, '81
58	Banks, Carl	LB	6-4	235	2	8-29-62	Michigan State	16	D1, '84
	Battle, Ralph	S	6-2	205	2	6-15-61	Jacksonville State	*3	FA, '85
73	Belcher, Kevin	G	6-3	276	3	2-23-61	Texas-El Paso	16	D6, '83
60	Benson, Brad	T	6-3	270	8	11-25-55	Penn State	16	FA, '77
64	Burt, Jim	NT	6-1	260	5	6- 7-59	Miami, Fla.	16	OFA, '81
26	Carpenter, Rob	RB	6-1	226	9	4-20-55	Miami, Ohio	16	T-Hou, '81
53	Carson, Harry	LB	6-2	240	10	11-26-53	South Carolina State	16	D4a, '76
31	Cephous, Frank	RB	5-10	205	2	7- 4-61	UCLA	16	D11, '84
29	Currier, Bill	S	6-0	196	9	1- 5-55	South Carolina	9	T-NE, '81
24	Daniel, Kenny	CB	5-10	180	2	6- 1-60	San Jose State	15	FA, '84
37	Flowers, Larry	S	6-1	195	5	4-19-58	Texas Tech	16	W-TB, '80
30	Galbreath, Tony	RB	6-0	228	10	1-29-54	Missouri	16	T-Min, '84
61	Godfrey, Chris	G	6-3	265	3	5-17-58	Michigan	10	FA, '84
62	Goode, Conrad	T	6-6	285	2	1-19-62	Missouri	8	D4, '84
83	†Gray, Earnest	WR	6-3	191	7	3- 2-57	Memphis State	12	D2, '79
6	Haji-Sheikh, Ali	K	6-0	170	3	1-11-61	Michigan	16	D9, '83
79	Hardison, Dee	DE	6-4	274	8	5- 2-56	North Carolina	15	FA, '81
	Hasselbeck, Don	TE	6-7	240	9	4- 1-55	Colorado	*16	FA, '85
36	†Haynes, Mark	CB	5-11	195	6	11- 6-58	Colorado	15	D1, '80
54	Headen, Andy	LB	6-5	242	3	7- 8-60	Clemson	11	D8, '83
48	Hill, Kenny	S	6-0	195	5	7-25-58	Yale	12	T-Rai, '84
15	Hostetler, Jeff	QB	6-3	212	2	4-22-61	West Virginia	*0	D3, '84
57	Hunt, Byron	LB	6-5	242	5	12-17-58	Southern Methodist	13	D9, '81
13	Jennings, Dave	P	6-4	200	12	6- 8-52	St. Lawrence	16	FA, '74
88	Johnson, Bob	WR	5-11	171	2	12-14-61	Kansas	16	FA, '84
51	Jones, Robbie	LB	6-2	230	2	12-25-59	Alabama	16	D12, '83
69	Jordan, David	G	6-6	276	2	7-14-62	Auburn	14	D10, '84
43	Kinard, Terry	S	6-1	200	3	11-24-59	Clemson	15	D1, '83
72	King, Gordon	T	6-6	275	7	2- 3-56	Stanford	*0	D1, '78
86	Manuel, Lionel	WR	5-11	175	2	4-13-62	Pacific	16	D7, '84
70	Marshall, Leonard	DE	6-3	285	3	10-22-61	Louisiana State	16	D2, '83
75	Martin, George	DE	6-4	255	11	2-16-53	Oregon	16	D11, '75
80	McConkey, Phil	WR	5-10	170	2	2-24-57	Navy	13	FA, '83
45	McDaniel, LeCharls	CB	5-9	169	5	10-15-58	Cal Poly-SLO	*0	FA, '83
76	McGriff, Curtis	DE	6-5	276	6	5-17-58	Alabama	16	OFA, '80
52	†McLaughlin, Joe	LB	6-1	235	7	7- 1-57	Massachusetts	16	FA, '80
71	Merrill, Casey	DE	6-4	260	7	7-16-57	Cal-Davis	16	FA, '83
20	Morris, Joe	RB	5-7	195	4	9-15-60	Syracuse	16	D2, '82
84	Mowatt, Zeke	TE	6-3	240	3	3- 5-61	Florida State	16	OFA, '83
81	Mullady, Tom	TE	6-3	235	7	1-30-57	Southwestern	16	FA, '79
63	Nelson, Karl	T	6-6	285	2	6-14-60	Iowa State	16	D3, '83
34	Patterson, Elvis	CB	5-11	188	2	10-21-60	Kansas	15	OFA, '84
55	Reasons, Gary	LB	6-4	234	2	2-18-62	N.W. Louisiana State	16	D4a, '84
66	Roberts, Bill	T	6-5	280	2	8- 5-62	Ohio State	11	D1a, '84
17	Rutledge, Jeff	QB	6-1	195	7	1-22-57	Alabama	16	T-Ram, '82
78	Sally, Jerome	NT	6-3	270	4	2-24-59	Missouri	16	FA, '82
11	†Simms, Phil	QB	6-3	214	7	11- 3-56	Morehead State	16	D1, '79
56	Taylor, Lawrence	LB	6-3	243	5	2- 4-59	North Carolina	16	D1, '81
38	Tuggle, John	RB	6-1	210	2	1-31-61	California	*0	D12b, '83
59	Umphrey, Rich	C	6-3	270	4	12-13-58	Colorado	15	D5, '82
87	Williams, Byron	WR	6-2	183	3	10-31-60	Texas-Arlington	16	FA, '83
23	Williams, Perry	CB	6-2	203	2	5-12-61	North Carolina State	16	D7, '83

*Battle played 3 games with Cincinnati in '84; Hasselbeck played 16 games with Minnesota in '84; Hostetler active for 16 games, did not play; King and Tuggle missed '84 season due to injuries; McDaniel active for 2 games, did not play.

†Option playout; subject to developments.

Also played with Giants in '84—WR John Mistler (1 game), S Pete Shaw (16), RB Butch Woolfolk (15).

D—Draft; T—Trade; W—Waivers; FA—Free Agent; OFA—Original Free Agent.

NEW YORK GIANTS
1985 DRAFT CHOICES

(Number following name designates order of selection among 336 players drafted.)

Round and Player		Position	College
1. ADAMS, George	19	RB	Kentucky
2. ROBINSON, Stacy	46	WR	N. Dakota St.
3. DAVIS, Tyrone from Houston (a)	58	DB	Clemson
3. JOHNSTON, Brian	73	C	North Carolina
4. BAVARO, Mark	100	TE	Notre Dame
5. HENDERSON, Tracy	132	WR	Iowa State
6. OLIVER, Jack	159	G	Memphis State
6. PEMBROOK, Mark from Seattle (b)	165	DB	Cal. St.-Full.
7. Choice to L.A. Raiders (c)			
8. ROUSON, Lee	213	RB	Colorado
9. WRIGHT, Frank	240	NT	South Carolina
10. DUBROC, Gregg	272	LB	Louisiana State
11. YOUNG, Allen	299	DB	Virginia Tech
12. WELCH, Herb	326	DB	UCLA

(a) Acquired pick for running back Butch Woolfolk, March 21, 1985.

(b) Acquired pick and 5th round pick in 1984 for cornerback Terry Jackson, March 12, 1984.

(c) Traded pick for safety Kenny Hill, August 27, 1984.

NEW YORK GIANTS
1985 ROOKIE AND FIRST-YEAR ROSTER

(1) Indicates player in previous NFL camp.
(2) Indicates player with USFL game experience.
(3) Indicates player in previous USFL camp.
(4) Indicates player with CFL game experience.
(5) Indicates player in previous CFL camp.
All others classified as rookies.

Name	Pos.	Hgt.	Wgt.	Birth-date	College	How Acquired
Adams, George	RB	6-1	225	12-22-62	Kentucky	D1
Allen, Mark (1, 3)	TE	6-4	225	4-29-60	Montclair State	FA
Baker, Tony	RB	6-1	200	9- 9-63	Cornell	FA
Bavaro, Mark	TE	6-4	245	4-28-63	Notre Dame	D4
Belcher, Jack (1, 2)	C	6-4	278	4-17-61	Boston College	FA
Bell, Maurice (3)	LB	6-2	222	3-14-62	Stephen F. Austin	FA
Bond, David (1)	DT	6-4	250	4-14-62	Virginia	FA
Bouier, Lorenzo (1, 3)	RB	6-1	200	2-27-61	Maine	FA
Carthon, Maurice (2)	FB	6-1	225	4-24-61	Arkansas State	FA
Chambers, Lorenzo	RB	5-9	192	9-30-63	Dartmouth	FA
Chatman, Ricky	LB	6-2	230	1- 4-62	Louisiana State	FA
Colquitt, Jim	P	6-4	210	1-17-63	Tennessee	FA
Culpepper, Walt	LB	6-0	215	4-13-63	Georgia	FA
Davis, Tyrone	DB	6-1	190	11-17-61	Clemson	D3
Dubroc, Gregg	LB	6-3	230	1-15-62	Louisiana State	D10
Fourcade, John (3, 4)	QB	6-1	198	10-11-62	Mississippi	FA
Gordon, Leon	DB	6-1	197	4-11-62	Virginia Tech	FA
Goodman, Don (1)	RB	5-11	200	4-23-59	Cincinnati	FA
Green, Lawrence (1)	LB	6-2	230	5-15-62	Tennessee-Chattanooga	*D12 '84
Harmon, Mark	K	5-8	175	12-13-61	Stanford	FA
Harris, Clint (1)	S	6-0	205	8-19-62	East Carolina	*D5 '84
Henderson, Tracy	WR	6-0	185	6- 7-64	Iowa State	D5
Hill, Greg	WR	5-11	170	5- 7-61	Maryland	FA
Hooks, Mike	LB	6-3	235	5-21-62	Iowa	FA
James, Victor (1, 2)	WR	6-0	190	2- 6-61	Colorado	FA
Johnson, Damian	T	6-5	290	12-18-62	Kansas State	FA
Johnston, Brian	C	6-3	175	11-26-62	North Carolina	D3a
Kowgios, Nick	RB	5-11	218	11-19-62	Lafayette	FA
Mack, Phillip	DT	6-3	260	....	Lamar	FA
Magwood, Frank (1)	WR	6-0	188	7- 7-61	Clemson	*D12 '83
Marvin, Al	DT	6-4	297	5-20-59	Alabama State	FA
Oliver, Jack	G	6-4	285	2- 3-62	Memphis State	D6
Pembrook, Mark	DB	6-0	197	9-17-63	Cal. St.-Fullerton	D6a
Rasheed, Eric	WR	5-7	158	4-29-63	Western Carolina	FA
Robinson, Stacy	WR	5-11	186	2-19-62	North Dakota State	D2
Rouson, Lee	RB	6-1	210	10-18-62	Colorado	D8
Salter, Mark	G	6-4	260	10-16-63	Canisius	FA
Watson, Ron	DB	5-10	186	7-19-61	Clemson	FA
Welch, Herb	DB	5-11	180	1-12-61	UCLA	D12
Winters, Larry	DB	6-1	210	2-14-60	St. Paul's	FA
Wright, Frank	DT	6-3	276	11-25-61	South Carolina	D9
Young, Al	DB	6-0	190	8-30-62	Virginia Tech	D11

*Green and Harris missed '84 season due to injury; Magwood missed '83 and '84 seasons due to injury.

NEW YORK JETS
(Eastern Division, American Conference)

Joe Walton

Chairman of the Board—Leon Hess
President—Jim Kensil
Director of Player Personnel—Mike Hickey
Director of Pro Personnel—Jim Royer
Head Coach—Joe Walton (2 years: 14-18)
Assistant Coaches:
  Offensive Line—Bill Austin
  Quarterbacks—Zeke Bratkowski
  Defensive Line—Ray Callahan
  Defensive Coordinator/Def. Backs—Bud Carson
  Special Assistant to Head Coach—Mike Faulkiner
  Running Backs—Bobby Hammond
  Offensive Coordinator/Receivers—Rick Kotite
  Special Teams—Larry Pasquale
  Linebackers—Dan Radakovich
Director of Public Relations—Frank Ramos
  (Office Phone: 421-6600—Area Code 212)
Offices—598 Madison Ave., New York, N.Y. 10022
Stadium—Giants Stadium (Capacity: 76,891)
Team Colors—Kelly Green and White
Training Site—Hofstra University, Hempstead, N.Y.

1985 SCHEDULE
(All times local.
All games Sunday unless noted otherwise.)

Sept. 8	at Los Angeles Raiders	1:00
Sept. 15	BUFFALO	1:00
Sept. 22	vs. Green Bay at Milwaukee	3:00
Sept. 29	INDIANAPOLIS	4:00
Oct. 6	at Cincinnati	4:00
Oct. 14	MIAMI (Mon.)	9:00
Oct. 20	at New England	4:00
Oct. 27	SEATTLE	1:00
Nov. 3	at Indianapolis	4:00
Nov. 10	at Miami	4:00
Nov. 17	TAMPA BAY	1:00
Nov. 24	NEW ENGLAND	1:00
Nov. 28	at Detroit (Thanksgiving)	12:30
Dec. 8	at Buffalo	1:00
Dec. 14	CHICAGO (Sat.)	12:30
Dec. 22	CLEVELAND	1:00

1984 RESULTS—(Won 7, Lost 9)

Jets		Opp.		Att.
23	Indianapolis	14	(A)	60,500
17	Pittsburgh	23	(H)	70,564
43	Cincinnati	23	(H)	64,193
28	Buffalo	26	(A)	48,330
21	New England	28	(H)	68,978
17	Kansas City	16	(A)	51,843
24	Cleveland	20	(A)	55,673
28	Kansas City	7	(H)	66,782
20	New England	30	(A)	60,513
17	Miami	31	(H)	72,655
5	Indianapolis	9	(H)	51,066
20	Houston	31	(A)	40,141
17	Miami	28	(A)	74,884
10	New York Giants	20	(H)	74,975
21	Buffalo	17	(H)	45,378
21	Tampa Bay	41	(A)	43,817

1984 GAMES STARTED

16 games: Dan Alexander, Joe Fields, Mark Gastineau, Reggie McElroy, Marvin Powell, Mickey Shuler.

15 games: Lance Mehl.

14 games: Johnny Lynn, Stan Waldemore.

13 games: Barry Bennett, Greg Buttle.

12 games: Freeman McNeil, Darrol Ray.

11 games: Joe Klecko, Pat Ryan, Kirk Springs.

10 games: Marty Lyons, Wesley Walker.

9 games: Kyle Clifton, Glenn Dennison, Ron Faurot.

8 games: Russell Carter, Lam Jones.

7 games: Derrick Gaffney, Ken Schroy.

6 games: Davlin Mullen.

5 games: Marion Barber, Ken O'Brien, John Woodring.

4 games: Bobby Humphery.

3 games: Tony Paige, Ben Rudolph.

2 games: Tom Baldwin, Bobby Bell, Bob Crable, Mike Dennis, George Floyd, Rusty Guilbeau, Johnny Hector, Bobby Jackson, Rocky Klever, Cedric Minter, Jim Sweeney.

NEW YORK JETS 1985 VETERAN ROSTER

No.	Name	Pos.	Ht.	Wt.	NFL Exp.	Birth-date	College	Games in '84	How Acquired
60	Alexander, Dan	G	6-4	260	9	6-17-55	Louisiana State	16	D8, '77
35	Augustyniak, Mike	FB	5-11	226	4	7-17-56	Purdue	*0	FA, '81
17	Avellini, Bob	QB	6-2	209	11	8-28-53	Maryland	*4	FA, '84
95	Baldwin, Tom	DT	6-4	270	2	5-13-61	Tulsa	16	D9, '84
63	Banker, Ted	G-C	6-2	255	2	2-17-61	Southeast Missouri	4	FA, '83
31	†Barber, Marion	FB	6-2	224	4	12- 6-59	Minnesota	14	D2, '81
58	Bell, Bobby	LB	6-3	217	2	2- 7-62	Missouri	15	D4, '84
78	Bennett, Barry	DT	6-4	260	8	12-10-55	Concordia, Minn.	15	FA, '82
64	Bingham, Guy	C-G-T	6-3	255	6	2-25-58	Montana	16	D10, '80
23	Bligen, Dennis	RB	5-11	215	2	3- 3-62	St. John's	1	OFA, '84
83	Bruckner, Nick	WR	5-11	185	3	5-19-61	Syracuse	16	OFA, '83
51	Buttle, Greg	LB	6-3	232	10	6-20-54	Penn State	14	D3, '76
27	Carter, Russell	CB-S	6-2	195	2	2-10-62	Southern Methodist	11	D1, '84
59	Clifton, Kyle	LB	6-4	233	2	8-23-62	Texas Christian	16	D3, '84
50	Crable, Bob	LB	6-3	234	4	9-22-59	Notre Dame	5	D1, '82
88	Davidson, Chy	WR	5-11	175	2	5- 9-59	Rhode Island	3	FA, '84
22	†Dennis, Mike	S-CB	5-10	195	6	6- 6-58	Wyoming	*6	FA, '84
86	Dennison, Glenn	TE	6-3	225	2	11-17-61	Miami, Fla.	16	D2a, '84
52	†Eliopulos, Jim	LB	6-2	229	3	4-18-59	Wyoming	11	FA, '83
74	Faurot, Ron	DE-LB	6-7	262	2	1-27-62	Arkansas	15	D1a, '84
65	Fields, Joe	C	6-2	253	11	11-14-53	Widener	16	D14, '75
38	Floyd, George	S-CB	5-11	190	3	12-21-60	Eastern Kentucky	8	D4, '82
81	Gaffney, Derrick	WR	6-1	182	8	5-24-55	Florida	12	D8, '78
99	Gastineau, Mark	DE	6-5	265	7	11-20-56	East Central Oklahoma	16	D2, '79
94	Guilbeau, Rusty	LB	6-4	237	4	11-20-58	McNeese State	16	FA, '82
39	Hamilton, Harry	S	6-0	193	2	11-29-62	Penn State	8	D7, '84
42	Harper, Bruce	RB-KR	5-8	179	9	6-20-55	Kutztown State	4	OFA, '77
34	Hector, Johnny	RB	5-11	197	3	11-26-60	Texas A&M	13	D2, '83
84	Humphery, Bobby	WR-KR	5-10	170	2	8-23-61	New Mexico State	16	D9, '83
40	Jackson, Bobby	CB	5-10	180	9	12-23-56	Florida State	3	D6, '78
	Jackson, Charles	LB	6-2	222	8	3-22-55	Washington	*4	T-KC, '85
80	Jones, Johnny (Lam)	WR	5-11	180	6	4- 4-58	Texas	8	D1, '80
73	Klecko, Joe	DT-DE	6-3	263	9	10-15-53	Temple	12	D6, '77
89	Klever, Rocky	TE	6-3	225	3	7-10-59	Montana	16	D9, '82
5	Leahy, Pat	K	6-0	193	12	3-19-51	St. Louis University	16	FA, '74
29	Lynn, Johnny	CB-S	6-0	198	6	12-19-56	UCLA	14	D4a, '79
93	Lyons, Marty	DE-DT	6-5	269	7	1-15-57	Alabama	13	D1, '79
68	†McElroy, Reggie	T	6-6	270	3	3- 4-60	West Texas State	16	D2, '82
24	McNeil, Freeman	RB	5-11	212	5	4-22-59	UCLA	12	D1, '81
56	Mehl, Lance	LB	6-3	233	6	2-14-58	Penn State	16	D3, '80
25	Minter, Cedric	RB-KR	5-10	200	2	11-13-58	Boise State	8	FA, '84
20	Mullen, Davlin	CB-KR	6-1	177	3	2-17-60	Western Kentucky	15	D8, '83
7	O'Brien, Ken	QB	6-4	214	3	11-27-60	Cal-Davis	10	D1, '83
49	Paige, Tony	FB	5-10	230	2	10-14-62	Virginia Tech	16	D6, '84
	Parlavecchio, Chet	LB	6-2	225	2	2-14-60	Penn State	*0	FA, '85
79	Powell, Marvin	T	6-5	270	9	8-30-55	Southern California	16	D1, '77
28	Ray, Darrol	S	6-1	198	6	6-25-58	Oklahoma	15	D2, '80
10	Ryan, Pat	QB	6-3	210	8	9-16-55	Tennessee	16	D11, '78
48	Schroy, Ken	S	6-2	198	9	9-22-52	Maryland	12	FA, '76
82	Shuler, Mickey	TE	6-3	231	8	8-21-56	Penn State	16	D3, '78
87	†Sohn, Kurt	WR	5-11	180	4	6-26-57	Fordham	5	FA, '81
21	Springs, Kirk	S-KR	6-0	192	5	8-10-58	Miami, Ohio	16	FA, '81
53	Sweeney, Jim	G-C	6-4	260	2	8- 8-62	Pittsburgh	10	D2, '84
70	Waldemore, Stan	G-T	6-4	269	8	2-20-55	Nebraska	14	FA, '78
85	Walker, Wesley	WR	6-0	182	9	5-26-55	California	12	D2, '77
57	Woodring, John	LB	6-2	232	5	4- 4-59	Brown	15	D6, '81

*Augustyniak missed '84 season due to injury; Avellini played 4 games with Chicago and active for 5 with New York Jets, did not play in '84; Dennis played 2 games with San Diego, 4 with New York Jets in '84; C. Jackson played 4 games with Kansas City in '84; Parlavecchio last active with St. Louis in '83.

†Option playout; subject to developments.

Also played with Jets in '84—S Fernanza Burgess (11 games), CB-S Skip Lane (3), C George Lilja (3), P Chuck Ramsey (16), DT-DE Ben Rudolph (16).

D—Draft; T—Trade; W—Waivers; FA—Free Agent; OFA—Original Free Agent.

NEW YORK JETS
1985 DRAFT CHOICES

(Number following name designates order of selection among 336 players drafted.)

Round and Player		Position	College
1. TOON, Al	10	WR	Wisconsin
2. LYLES, Lester	40	DB	Virginia
3. ELDER, Donnie	67	DB	Memphis State
4. ALLEN, Doug	94	WR	Arizona State
5. BENSON, Troy from Tampa Bay (a)	120	LB	Pittsburgh
5. LUFT, Brian	124	DT	Southern Calif.
5. SMITH, Tony from Chicago (b)	134	WR	San Jose State
6. DEATON, Jeff	151	G	Stanford
6. MIANO, Rich from Denver (c)	166	DB	Hawaii
7. Choice to Dallas through Kansas City (d)			
8. MONGER, Matt	208	LB	Oklahoma State
9. WATERS, Mike	235	RB	San Diego St.
10. GLENN, Kerry	262	DB	Minnesota
11. WHITE, Brad	292	DE	Texas Tech
12. WALLACE, Bill	319	WR	Pittsburgh

(a) Acquired pick for running back Scott Dierking, April 17, 1984.
(b) Acquired pick for rights to defensive end Tyrone Keys, July 13, 1983.
(c) Acquired pick for linebacker Stan Blinka, February 15, 1984.
(d) Jets traded pick to Chiefs for linebacker Charles Jackson, April 25, 1985; Chiefs traded pick to Cowboys for running back Lawrence Ricks, August 24, 1983.

NEW YORK JETS
1985 ROOKIE AND FIRST-YEAR ROSTER

(1) Indicates player in previous NFL camp.
(2) Indicates player with USFL game experience.
(3) Indicates player in previous USFL camp.
(4) Indicates player with CFL game experience.
(5) Indicates player in previous CFL camp.
    All others classified as rookies.

Name	Pos.	Hgt.	Wgt.	Birth-date	College	How Acquired
Allen, Doug	WR	5-10	180	4-22-63	Arizona State	D4
Armstrong, Tron (1)	WR	6-2	200	8-18-61	Eastern Kentucky	*D5 '84
Barnes, Duane (1, 3)	T	6-5	268	8- 1-60	West Virginia	FA
Benson, Troy	LB	6-2	235	7-30-63	Pittsburgh	D5
Campbell, Todd (1, 3)	DT	6-1	265	1-28-61	West Virginia	FA
Collins, Scott (1)	LB	6-1	230	11-10-60	Oregon Tech	*FA '84
Cone, Ronny (1)	FB	6-2	225	4-27-61	Georgia Tech	*D10 '84
Crum, Stu (2)	K	5-7	165	11- 4-59	Tulsa	D12 '83
Deaton, Jeff	G-T	6-3	280	4-26-62	Stanford	D6
Durden, Mike (1, 4)	CB-S	6-1	185	5- 4-59	UCLA	FA
Elder, Donnie	CB	5-9	175	12-13-62	Memphis State	D3
Franklin, Derrick (1, 3)	CB	5-10	179	7-13-61	Fresno State	FA
Furnas, Mike (1)	RB	6-0	235	4-18-61	Tennessee	FA
Gardner, Kenneth (1, 3)	TE	6-4	220	1-25-60	Tennessee State	FA
Glenn, Kerry	CB	5-9	175	3-31-62	Minnesota	D10
Green, Darren (1)	WR	5-9	168	3-19-62	Kansas	FA
Griggs, Billy (1)	TE	6-3	230	8- 4-62	Virginia	*D8 '84
Gunter, Gregory	C	6-3	265	5-16-62	C.W. Post (N.Y.)	FA
Harris, Willie (1, 2)	CB-S	6-1	185	4- 4-60	North Carolina	FA
Howard, Doug (1, 3)	G	6-6	268	6-14-59	North Carolina State	FA
Hunter, Jimmy (1, 3)	LB	6-2	225	4-10-60	Indiana	FA
Kaifes, Eric (1, 3)	P	6-4	215	7-16-60	Southern Methodist	FA
Luft, Brian	DT	6-6	270	9- 5-63	Southern California	D5a
Lyles, Lester	S	6-3	215	12-27-62	Virginia	D2
McArthur, Kevin (1)	LB	6-1	223	5-11-62	Lamar	FA
McCarthy, John	QB	6-4	208	1-31-61	Williams (Mass.)	FA
Messemer, James	K	6-4	215	8- 3-59	Texas Tech	FA
Miano, Rich	S	6-0	200	9- 3-62	Hawaii	D6a
Monger, Matt	LB	6-1	235	11-15-61	Oklahoma State	D8
Newman, Donald (1, 4)	S	6-2	205	11-22-58	Idaho	FA
Nizolek, Scott (1, 2)	TE	6-2	225	2-23-61	Boston College	FA
Ogren, Mark (1)	LB	6-3	219	11-16-61	Minnesota-Duluth	*FA '84
Pendock, Bill	DT	6-2	269	3- 7-61	Syracuse	FA
Reda, Louis (1)	S	6-0	192	10-10-61	Delaware	*FA '84
Schuchts, Wayne (1)	QB-P	6-2	205	3-25-61	Virginia	FA
Shumate, Mark (1, 4)	DT	6-5	265	3-30-60	Wisconsin	FA
Smith, Tony	WR	5-11	170	6-28-62	San Jose State	D5b
Toon, Al	WR	6-4	200	4-30-63	Wisconsin	D1
Viaene, Jim (1)	DT	6-1	263	3-19-62	Wisconsin-Superior	FA
Wallace, Bill	WR	6-2	190	2-14-62	Pittsburgh	D12
Waters, Mike	FB	6-2	225	3- 5-62	San Diego State	D9
White, Brad	DE	6-6	245	9-26-61	Texas Tech	D11
Williams, James (1)	TE	6-1	223	4-18-61	Wyoming	FA
Woetzel, Keith (1, 3)	LB	6-1	222	11-15-60	Rutgers	FA
Wright, Bret (1)	P	6-4	205	1- 5-62	Southeast Louisiana	*D8a '84

*Armstrong, Collins, Cone, Griggs, Ogren, Reda and Wright missed '84 season due to injury.

PHILADELPHIA EAGLES
(Eastern Division, National Conference)

Marion Campbell

Owner—Norman Braman
Co-Owner—Edward Leibowitz
Head Coach—Marion Campbell (5 years: 17-39-1)
Executive Director of Player Personnel—Lynn Stiles
Vice President and G.M.—Harry Gamble
Assistant Coaches:
  Defensive Line—Tom Brasher
  Secondary—Fred Bruney
  Linebackers—Chuck Clausen
  Receivers—Tom Coughlin
  Tight Ends/Special Teams—Frank Gansz
  Offensive Line—Ken Iman
  Running Backs—Milt Jackson
  Offensive Coordinator—Ted Marchibroda
Director of Communications—Ed Wisneski
  (Office Phone: 463-2500—Area Code 215)
Offices—Veterans Stadium, Philadelphia, Pa. 19148
Stadium—Veterans Stadium (Capacity: 71,640)
Team Colors—Kelly Green, White and Silver
Training Site—West Chester University, West Chester, Pa.

1985 SCHEDULE
(All times local.
All games Sunday unless noted otherwise.)

Sept. 8	at New York Giants	1:00
Sept. 15	LOS ANGELES RAMS	1:00
Sept. 22	at Washington	1:00
Sept. 29	NEW YORK GIANTS	1:00
Oct. 6	at New Orleans	12:00
Oct. 13	at St. Louis	12:00
Oct. 20	DALLAS	1:00
Oct. 27	BUFFALO	1:00
Nov. 3	at San Francisco	1:00
Nov. 10	ATLANTA	1:00
Nov. 17	ST. LOUIS	1:00
Nov. 24	at Dallas	3:00
Dec. 1	MINNESOTA	1:00
Dec. 8	WASHINGTON	1:00
Dec. 15	at San Diego	1:00
Dec. 22	at Minnesota	12:00

1984 RESULTS—(Won 6, Lost 9, Tied 1)

Eagles		Opp.		Att.
27	New York Giants	28	(A)	71,520
19	Minnesota	17	(H)	55,942
17	Dallas	23	(A)	64,521
9	San Francisco	21	(H)	62,771
0	Washington	20	(A)	53,064
27	Buffalo	17	(A)	37,555
16	Indianapolis	7	(H)	50,277
24	New York Giants	10	(H)	64,677
14	St. Louis	34	(H)	54,310
23	Detroit (OT)	23	(A)	59,141
23	Miami	24	(A)	70,227
16	Washington	10	(H)	63,117
16	St. Louis	17	(A)	39,858
10	Dallas	26	(H)	66,322
27	New England	17	(H)	41,581
10	Atlanta	26	(A)	15,582

1984 GAMES STARTED

16 games: Ron Baker, Greg Brown, Ken Clarke, Mark Dennard, Herman Edwards, Ray Ellis, Anthony Griggs, Dennis Harrison, Dean Miraldi, John Spagnola, Joel Williams.

15 games: Wes Hopkins, Hubert Oliver, Jerry Robinson.

14 games: Leonard Mitchell, Wilbert Montgomery, Mike Quick, Reggie Wilkes.

13 games: Ron Jaworski.

12 games: Elbert Foules.

11 games: Steve Kenney.

9 games: Kenny Jackson.

5 games: Vyto Kab, Petey Perot, Brenard Wilson, Tony Woodruff.

3 games: Joe Pisarcik.

2 games: Jody Schulz, Jerry Sisemore.

1 game: Melvin Hoover, Mike Reichenbach, Mike Williams.

PHILADELPHIA EAGLES 1985 VETERAN ROSTER

No.	Name	Pos.	Ht.	Wt.	NFL Exp.	Birth-date	College	Games in '84	How Acquired
96	Armstrong, Harvey	NT	6-2	265	4	12-29-59	Southern Methodist	16	D7, '82
63	Baker, Ron	G	6-4	270	8	11-19-54	Oklahoma State	16	T-Bal, '80
98	Brown, Greg	DE	6-5	260	5	1- 5-57	Kansas State	16	OFA, '81
	Caldwell, Bryan	DE	6-4	248	2	5-6-60	Arizona State	*8	FA, '85
11	Christensen, Jeff	QB	6-3	200	3	1- 8-60	Eastern Illinois	*0	FA, '84
71	Clarke, Ken	NT	6-2	255	8	8-28-56	Syracuse	16	OFA, '78
21	Cooper, Evan	CB-KR	5-11	180	2	6-28-62	Michigan	16	D4, '84
94	Darby, Byron	DE	6-4	260	3	6- 4-60	Southern California	16	D5, '83
65	Dennard, Mark	C	6-1	252	7	11- 2-55	Texas A&M	16	T-Mia, '84
	DuPree, Myron	S	5-11	180	2	10-15-61	No. Carolina Central	*0	FA, '85
46	†Edwards, Herman	CB	6-0	190	9	4-27-54	San Diego State	16	OFA, '77
24	Ellis, Ray	S	6-1	192	5	4-27-59	Ohio State	16	D12, '81
39	Everett, Major	FB	5-11	215	3	1- 4-60	Mississippi College	16	FA, '83
67	Feehery, Gerry	C	6-2	268	3	3- 9-60	Syracuse	6	OFA, '83
29	Foules, Elbert	CB	5-11	185	3	7- 4-61	Alcorn State	16	OFA, '83
86	Garrity, Gregg	WR	5-10	171	3	11-24-60	Penn State	*10	FA, '84
58	Griggs, Anthony	LB	6-3	230	4	2-12-60	Ohio State	16	D4, '82
26	Haddix, Michael	FB	6-2	225	3	12-27-61	Mississippi State	14	D1, '83
47	Hardy, Andre	RB	6-1	233	2	11-28-61	St. Mary's, Calif.	6	D5, '84
68	Harrison, Dennis	DE	6-8	280	8	7-31-56	Vanderbilt	16	D4, '78
80	Hayes, Joe	WR-KR	5-9	185	2	9-15-60	Central State, Okla.	12	D7, '84
85	†Hoover, Melvin	WR	6-0	185	4	8-21-59	Arizona State	12	FA, '82
48	Hopkins, Wes	S	6-1	210	3	9-26-61	Southern Methodist	16	D2, '83
2	Horan, Michael	P	5-11	190	2	2- 1-59	Long Beach State	16	FA, '84
81	Jackson, Kenny	WR	6-0	180	2	2-15-62	Penn State	11	D1, '84
7	Jaworski, Ron	QB	6-2	196	12	3-23-51	Youngstown State	13	T-Ram, '77
84	Kab, Vyto	TE	6-5	240	4	12-23-59	Penn State	16	D3, '82
73	Kenney, Steve	G	6-4	270	6	12-26-55	Clemson	11	OFA, '79
52	Kraynak, Rich	LB	6-1	225	3	1-20-60	Pittsburgh	14	D8, '82
5	May, Dean	QB	6-5	220	2	5-26-62	Louisville	2	FA, '84
8	McFadden, Paul	K	5-11	155	2	9-24-61	Youngstown State	16	D12, '84
64	Miraldi, Dean	T	6-5	285	3	4- 8-58	Utah	16	D2, '81
74	†Mitchell, Leonard	T	6-7	285	5	10-12-58	Houston	16	D1, '81
31	Montgomery, Wilbert	RB	5-10	195	9	9-16-54	Abilene Christian	16	D6a, '77
34	Oliver, Hubie	FB	5-10	212	4	11-12-57	Arizona	16	D10, '81
9	Pisarcik, Joe	QB	6-4	217	9	7- 2-52	New Mexico State	7	T-NYG, '80
82	Quick, Mike	WR	6-2	190	4	5-14-59	North Carolina State	14	D1, '82
55	Reichenbach, Mike	LB	6-2	235	2	9-14-61	East Stroudsburg	12	OFA, '84
56	Robinson, Jerry	LB	6-2	225	7	12-18-56	UCLA	15	D1, '79
79	Russell, Rusty	T	6-5	295	2	8-16-63	South Carolina	1	D3, '84
87	Sampleton, Lawrence	TE	6-5	233	4	9-25-59	Texas	16	D2, '82
53	Schulz, Jody	LB	6-4	235	3	8-17-60	East Carolina	15	D2a, '83
88	Spagnola, John	TE	6-4	240	6	8- 1-57	Yale	16	FA, '79
93	†Strauthers, Thomas	DE	6-4	265	3	4- 6-61	Jackson State	16	D10, '83
20	Waters, Andre	CB-KR	5-11	182	2	3-10-62	Cheyney St., Pa.	16	OFA, '84
51	Wilkes, Reggie	LB	6-4	235	8	5-27-56	Georgia Tech	14	D3, '78
59	†Williams, Joel	LB	6-1	225	7	12-13-56	Wisconsin-La Crosse	16	T-Atl, '83
32	Williams, Michael	RB	6-2	225	3	7-16-61	Mississippi College	16	D4, '83
22	Wilson, Brenard	S-CB	6-0	180	7	8-15-55	Vanderbilt	16	OFA, '78
83	Woodruff, Tony	WR	6-0	185	4	11-12-58	Fresno State	16	D9, '82
43	Young, Roynell	CB	6-1	181	6	12- 1-57	Alcorn State	7	D1, '80

*Caldwell played 8 games with Houston in '84; Christensen active for 3 games, did not play; DuPree last active with Denver in '83; Garrity played 6 games with Pittsburgh, 4 with Philadelphia in '84.

†Option playout; subject to development.

Also played with Eagles in '84—LB Bill Cowher (4 games), OL Dave Pacella (16), G Petey Perot (12), CB-S Lou Rash (4), T Jerry Sisemore (2).

D—Draft; T—Trade; W—Waivers; FA—Free Agent; OFA—Original Free Agent.

PHILADELPHIA EAGLES
1985 DRAFT CHOICES

(Number following name designates order of selection among 336 players drafted.)

Round and Player	Position		College
1. ALLEN, Kevin	9	T	Indiana
2. CUNNINGHAM, Randall	37	QB	Nev.-Las Vegas
3. Choice to Miami (a)			
4. NARON, Greg	93	G	North Carolina
5. JILES, Dwayne	121	LB	Texas Tech
6. Choice to Kansas City (b)			
6. REEVES, Ken from New England (c)	156	T	Texas A&M
7. Choice to Washington (d)			
8. POLLEY, Tom	205	LB	Nev.-Las Vegas
9. TOUB, Dave from Cleveland (e)	231	C	Texas-El Paso
9. DRAKE, Joe	233	DT	Arizona
10. KELSO, Mark	261	DB	William & Mary
11. HUNTER, Herman	289	RB	Tennessee St.
12. RUSSELL, Todd	317	DB	Boston College

(a) Traded pick for center Mark Dennard, March 7, 1984.
(b) Traded pick for tight end Al Dixon, August 30, 1983.
(c) Acquired pick for kicker Tony Franklin, February 21, 1984.
(d) Traded pick for quarterback Bob Holly, August 14, 1984.
(e) Acquired pick for defensive end Carl Hairston, February 9, 1984.

PHILADELPHIA EAGLES
1985 ROOKIE AND FIRST-YEAR ROSTER

(1) Indicates player in previous NFL camp.
(2) Indicates player with USFL game experience.
(3) Indicates player in previous USFL camp.
(4) Indicates player with CFL game experience.
(5) Indicates player in previous CFL camp.
    All others classified as rookies.

Name	Pos.	Hgt.	Wgt.	Birth-date	College	How Acquired
Allen, Kevin	T	6-5	285	6-21-63	Indiana	D1
Brewster, Tim (1)	TE	6-3	242	10-13-60	Illinois	FA
Chambers, Tim	DB-PR	5-10	185	12- 5-62	Pennsylvania	FA
Cunningham, Randall	QB-P	6-4	195	3-27-63	Nevada-Las Vegas	D2
Drake, Joe	NT	6-2	295	5-28-63	Arizona	D9a
Evans, Leon (1)	DE	6-6	270	10-12-61	Miami (Fla.)	*FA '84
Flemons, Tommy	DL	6-3	257	7- 1-61	Oklahoma	FA
Guthrie, Kevin (1)	WR	5-11	170	6-28-62	Princeton	FA
Harris, Michael	CB	5-11	180	3-30-63	Delaware	FA
Hunter, Herman	RB-KR	6-1	190	2-14-61	Tennessee State	D11
Irving, Mike	RB-KR	5-8	183	11-27-62	West Chester (Pa.)	FA
Jelesky, Tom (1)	T	6-6	290	10- 4-60	Purdue	*FA '83
Jiles, Dwayne	LB	6-4	240	11-23-61	Texas Tech	D5
Kelso, Mark	S-PR	5-11	186	7-23-63	William & Mary	D10
Kimmel, Jon (2)	LB	6-4	247	7-21-60	Colgate	FA
Maune, Neil (1)	G	6-4	281	11- 4-60	Notre Dame	FA
Naron, Greg	G	6-4	270	10-21-63	North Carolina	D4
Pacifico, Ralph	WR	...	...	....		FA
Polley, Tom	LB	6-3	235	2-17-62	Nevada-Las Vegas	D8
Reeves, Ken	T-G	6-5	270	10- 4-61	Texas A&M	D6
Robertson, John (1)	OT	6-5	270	9-26-61	East Carolina	FA
Rogers, Steve (1, 2)	OT	6-4	265	1- 9-59	Brigham Young	FA
Russell, Todd	CB	6-1	190	9- 5-61	Boston College	D12
Slater, Sam (1)	T	6-9	290	6- 8-62	Weber State	*FA '84
Smith, Brad	DE	6-6	251	9- 6-62	Brigham Young	FA
Tatum, Rowland (1)	LB	6-2	240	11-20-62	Ohio State	FA
Toub, Dave	C	6-3	278	6- 1-62	Texas-El Paso	D9
Volpe, Pete	LB	5-11	220	5- 3-62	Upsala (N.J.)	FA
Yuknus, Albert	K	6-1	180	....	Bucknell	FA

*Evans, Jelesky and Slater missed '84 season due to injury.

PITTSBURGH STEELERS
(Central Division, American Conference)

Chuck Noll

Chairman of the Board—Arthur J. Rooney
President—Daniel M. Rooney
Vice-President—John R. McGinley
Vice-President—Arthur J. Rooney, Jr.
Director of Player Personnel—Dick Haley
Head Coach—Chuck Noll (16 years: 142-88-1)
Assistant Coaches:
    Offensive Line (Tackles/Tight Ends)—Ron Blackledge
    Defensive Coordinator—Tony Dungy
    Assistant Conditioning—Walt Evans
    Inside Linebackers—Dennis Fitzgerald
    Offensive Backfield—Dick Hoak
    Outside Linebackers—Jed Hughes
    Offensive Line (Centers/Guards)—Hal Hunter
    Defensive Line/Conditioning—Jon Kolb
    Offensive Coordinator—Tom Moore
Publicity Director—Joe Gordon
    (Office Phone: 323-1200—Area Code 412)
Offices—Three Rivers Stadium, 300 Stadium Circle, Pittsburgh, Pa. 15212
Stadium—Three Rivers Stadium (Capacity: 59,000)
Colors—Black and Gold
Training Site—St. Vincent's College, Latrobe, Pa.

1985 SCHEDULE
(All times local.)
All games Sunday unless noted otherwise.)

Sept. 8	INDIANAPOLIS	1:00
Sept. 16	at Cleveland (Mon.)	9:00
Sept. 22	HOUSTON	1:00
Sept. 30	CINCINNATI (Mon.)	9:00
Oct. 6	at Miami	1:00
Oct. 13	at Dallas	12:00
Oct. 20	ST. LOUIS	1:00
Oct. 27	at Cincinnati	4:00
Nov. 3	CLEVELAND	1:00
Nov. 10	at Kansas City	12:00
Nov. 17	at Houston	12:00
Nov. 24	WASHINGTON	1:00
Dec. 1	DENVER	1:00
Dec. 5	at San Diego (Thurs.)	5:00
Dec. 15	BUFFALO	1:00
Dec. 21	at New York Giants (Sat.)	12:30

1984 RESULTS—(Won 10, Lost 8)

Steelers		Opp.		Att.
27	Kansas City	37	(H)	56,709
23	New York Jets	17	(A)	70,564
24	Los Angeles Rams	14	(H)	58,104
10	Cleveland	20	(A)	77,312
38	Cincinnati	17	(H)	57,098
7	Miami	31	(H)	59,103
20	San Francisco	17	(A)	59,110
16	Indianapolis	17	(A)	60,026
35	Atlanta	10	(H)	55,971
35	Houston	7	(H)	48,892
20	Cincinnati	22	(A)	52,497
24	New Orleans	27	(A)	66,005
52	San Diego	24	(H)	55,856
20	Houston (OT)	23	(A)	39,786
23	Cleveland	20	(H)	55,825
13	Los Angeles Raiders	7	(A)	83,056
	AFC SEMIFINAL GAME			
24	Denver	17	(A)	74,981
	AFC CHAMPIONSHIP GAME			
28	Miami	45	(A)	76,029

1984 GAMES STARTED

16 games: Robin Cole, Gary Dunn, Tunch Ilkin, Mike Merriweather, Donnie Shell, John Stallworth, Mike Webster.

15 games: Bryan Hinkle, Frank Pollard.

14 games: John Goodman, Sam Washington, Dwayne Woodruff.

13 games: David Little.

12 games: Eric Williams.

11 games: Keith Gary.

10 games: Blake Wingle.

9 games: Rich Erenberg, Mark Malone, Darrell Nelson, Craig Wolfley.

8 games: Louis Lipps.

7 games: Walter Abercrombie, Larry Brown, Terry Long, Weegie Thompson, David Woodley.

6 games: Emil Boures, Ray Snell.

5 games: Edmund Nelson.

4 games: Chris Brown, Bennie Cunningham, Rick Woods.

3 games: Chris Kolodziejski, Jack Lambert.

2 games: Pete Rostosky, Keith Willis.

1 game: Steve August, Craig Bingham, Calvin Sweeney, Elton Veals.

PITTSBURGH STEELERS 1985 VETERAN ROSTER

No.	Name	Pos.	Ht.	Wt.	NFL Exp.	Birth-date	College	Games in '84	How Acquired
34	Abercrombie, Walter	RB	6-0	210	4	9-26-59	Baylor	14	D1, '82
1	Anderson, Gary	K	5-11	170	4	7-16-59	Syracuse	16	W-Buf, '82
77	August, Steve	T	6-5	258	9	9- 4-54	Tulsa	*11	T-Sea, '84
54	Bingham, Craig	LB	6-2	220	4	9-29-59	Syracuse	11	D6a, '82
71	Boures, Emil	G-T	6-1	261	4	1-29-60	Pittsburgh	8	D7a, '82
23	Brown, Chris	CB-S	6-0	195	2	4-11-62	Notre Dame	16	D6, '84
79	Brown, Larry	T	6-4	270	15	6-16-49	Kansas	7	D5, '71
10	Campbell, Scott	QB	6-0	201	2	4-15-62	Purdue	5	D7, '84
80	Capers, Wayne	WR	6-2	193	3	5-17-61	Kansas	16	D2, '83
78	Catano, Mark	DE	6-3	265	2	1-26-62	Valdosta State	16	OFA, '84
33	Clayton, Harvey	CB	5-9	180	3	4- 4-61	Florida State	14	OFA, '83
56	Cole, Robin	LB	6-2	225	9	9-11-55	New Mexico	16	D1, '77
5	Colquitt, Craig	P	6-1	182	7	6- 9-54	Tennessee	16	D3, '78
40	Corley, Anthony	RB	6-0	210	2	8-10-60	Nevada-Reno	14	FA, '84
89	Cunningham, Bennie	TE	6-5	255	10	12-23-54	Clemson	7	D1, '76
67	Dunn, Gary	NT	6-3	265	9	8-24-53	Miami, Fla.	16	D6, '76
	Echols, Terry	LB	6-0	220	2	1-10-62	Marshall	4	OFA, '84
24	Erenberg, Rich	RB-KR	5-10	200	2	4-17-62	Colgate	16	D9, '84
92	Gary, Keith	DE	6-3	260	3	9-14-59	Oklahoma	16	D1, '81
26	Gillespie, Fernandars	RB	5-10	185	2	2-26-62	William Jewell, Mo.	14	D12, '84
95	Goodman, John	DE	6-6	255	5	11-12-58	Oklahoma	14	D2a, '80
53	Hinkle, Bryan	LB	6-2	220	4	6- 4-59	Oregon	15	D6, '81
62	Ilkin, Tunch	T	6-3	255	6	9-23-57	Indiana State	16	D6, '80
29	Johnson, Ron	S	5-11	195	8	6- 8-56	Eastern Michigan	15	D1, '78
90	Kohrs, Bob	LB	6-3	235	5	11- 8-58	Arizona State	10	D2, '80
84	Kolodziejski, Chris	TE	6-3	231	2	1- 5-61	Wyoming	7	D2, '84
58	Lambert, Jack	LB	6-4	220	12	7- 8-52	Kent State	8	D2, '74
83	Lipps, Louis	WR-KR	5-10	190	2	8- 9-62	Southern Mississippi	14	D1, '84
50	Little, David	LB	6-1	230	5	1- 3-59	Florida	16	D7, '81
74	Long, Terry	G	5-11	272	2	7-21-59	East Carolina	12	D4a, '84
16	Malone, Mark	QB	6-4	218	6	11-22-58	Arizona State	13	D1, '80
57	Merriweather, Mike	LB	6-2	215	4	11-26-60	Pacific	16	D3, '82
81	Nelson, Darrell	TE	6-2	235	2	10-27-61	Memphis State	11	OFA, '84
64	Nelson, Edmund	NT-DE	6-3	270	4	4- 3-60	Auburn	16	D7, '82
30	Pollard, Frank	RB	6-0	218	6	6-15-57	Baylor	15	D11, '80
60	Rasmussen, Randy	C-G	6-1	253	2	9-27-60	Minnesota	16	D8, '84
88	Rodgers, John	TE	6-2	238	4	2- 7-60	Louisiana Tech	6	OFA, '82
63	Rostosky, Pete	T	6-4	255	2	7-29-61	Connecticut	8	FA, '83
59	Seabaugh, Todd	LB	6-4	225	2	3-16-61	San Diego State	16	D3, '83
31	Shell, Donnie	S	5-11	190	12	8-26-51	South Carolina State	16	OFA, '74
72	†Snell, Ray	T	6-4	265	6	2-24-58	Wisconsin	13	T-TB, '84
36	Spencer, Todd	RB	6-0	200	2	7-26-62	Southern California	7	OFA, '84
82	Stallworth, John	WR	6-2	191	12	7-15-52	Alabama A&M	16	D4, '74
85	Sweeney, Calvin	WR	6-2	190	6	1-12-55	Southern California	9	D4a, '79
87	Thompson, Weegie	WR	6-6	210	2	3-21-61	Florida State	16	D4, '84
38	Veals, Elton	RB	5-11	230	2	3-26-61	Tulane	15	D11, '84
41	Washington, Sam	CB	5-8	180	4	3- 7-60	Mississippi Valley State	14	OFA, '82
52	Webster, Mike	C	6-1	250	12	3-18-52	Wisconsin	16	D5, '74
21	Williams, Eric	S	6-1	183	3	2-21-60	North Carolina State	16	D6, '83
28	Williams, Robert	S	5-11	202	2	9-26-62	Eastern Illinois	2	OFA, '84
93	Willis, Keith	DE	6-1	260	4	7-29-59	Northeastern	12	OFA, '82
61	Wingle, Blake	G	6-1	267	3	4-17-60	UCLA	15	D9, '83
73	Wolfley, Craig	G	6-1	255	6	5-19-58	Syracuse	9	D5, '80
19	Woodley, David	QB	6-2	204	6	10-25-58	Louisiana State	7	T-Mia, '84
49	Woodruff, Dwayne	CB	6-0	198	7	2-18-57	Louisville	16	D6a, '79
22	Woods, Rick	S	6-0	191	4	11-16-59	Boise State	15	D4, '82

*August played 6 games with Seattle and 5 with Pittsburgh in '84.
†Option playout; subject to developments.
Also played with Steelers in '84—WR Gregg Garrity (6 games).
D—Draft; T—Trade; W—Waivers; FA—Free Agent; OFA—Original Free Agent.

PITTSBURGH STEELERS
1985 DRAFT CHOICES

(Number following name designates order of selection among 336 players drafted.)

Round and Player		Position	College
1. SIMS, Darryl	20	DE	Wisconsin
2. BEHNING, Mark	47	T	Nebraska
3. HOBLEY, Liffort	74	DB	Louisiana State
4. TURK, Dan	101	C	Wisconsin
5. Choice to Seattle (a)			
5. JACOBS, Cam from Washington (b)	136	LB	Kentucky
6. CARR, Gregg	160	LB	Auburn
7. ANDREWS, Alan	187	TE	Rutgers
8. NEWSOME, Harry	214	P	Wake Forest
9. SMALL, Fred	241	LB	Washington
9. HARRIS, Andre from New England (c)	242	DB	Minnesota
10. WHITE, Oliver	268	TE	Kentucky
11. MATICHAK, Terry	300	DB	Missouri
12. SANCHEZ, Jeff	327	DB	Georgia

(a) Traded pick for tackle Steve August, October 9, 1984.
(b) Acquired pick for offensive lineman Rick Donnalley, August 20, 1984.
(c) Acquired pick for wide receiver Greg Hawthorne, August 21, 1984.

PITTSBURGH STEELERS
1985 ROOKIE AND FIRST-YEAR ROSTER

(1) Indicates player in previous NFL camp.
(2) Indicates player with USFL game experience.
(3) Indicates player in previous USFL camp.
(4) Indicates player with CFL game experience.
(5) Indicates player in previous CFL camp.
　　All others classified as rookies.

Name	Pos.	Hgt.	Wgt.	Birth-date	College	How Acquired
Andrews, Alan	TE	6-5	235	2-15-62	Rutgers	D7
Andrews, Danny	RB	5-10	180	3- 2-63	UCLA	FA
Baker, Andrew	WR	6-2	185	....	Rutgers	FA
Behning, Mark	OT	6-6	291	9-26-61	Nebraska	D2
Bowens, Nate	DE	6-4	232	6- 9-62	Southwest Oklahoma State	FA
Brooks, Darryl	S	5-11	200	12-16-62	West Virginia State	FA
Carr, Gregg	LB	6-1	219	3-31-62	Auburn	D6
Clark, Randy (1)	S	6-0	197	2-18-62	Florida	FA
Cleveland, DeCarlos (1)	DE	6-3	268	7- 9-61	Kent State	*FA '84
Dickey, Charlie	G	6-2	268	12-31-62	Arizona	FA
Dixon, Tom (2)	C-G	6-1	252	8-21-61	Michigan	SupD '84
Edwards, Dave	S	6-0	195	3-31-62	Illinois	FA
Goode, Frank	LB	6-2	238	12-18-63	Youngstown State	FA
Gothard, Preston	TE	6-4	235	2-23-62	Alabama	FA
Gowdy, Cornell	CB	6-1	195	10- 2-63	Morgan State	FA
Graham, Russ (1)	OT	6-4	265	5- 5-61	Oklahoma State	*FA '84
Harris, Andre	CB	5-11	194	6-30-62	Minnesota	D9a
Hobley, Liffort	S	6-0	207	10-12-62	Louisiana State	D3
Holmes, Russell	LB	6-3	213	3- 1-63	Akron	FA
Howe, Glen (1)	OT	6-6	270	10-18-61	Southern Mississippi	FA
Huff, Alan	NT	6-3	255	10-20-63	Marshall	FA
Jacobs, Cam	LB	6-1	218	3-10-62	Kentucky	D5
Linebarger, Tom	DT	6-4	263	4-24-62	Southern Methodist	FA
Little, Steve	NT	6-3	260	10-27-61	Iowa State	FA
Madison, L.E. (1)	LB	6-1	225	7-15-62	Kansas State	*FA '84
Matichak, Terry	S	6-1	197	4- 6-62	Missouri	D11
McJunkin, Kirk (1)	G	6-3	250	3-15-61	Texas	*D10 '84
Moore, James	DE	6-4	255	7-29-62	Texas	FA
Moore, Roderick	RB	6-0	235	10-17-61	Temple	FA
Nesselt, Mike	C	6-4	240	5- 5-63	Wake Forest	FA
Newsome, Harry	P	6-0	186	1-25-63	Wake Forest	D8
Pippens, Woody	RB	6-0	220	2- 7-63	Thiel (Pa.)	FA
Pokorny, Frank	WR	6-0	198	5-13-63	Youngstown State	FA
Powell, Kevin	DL	6-4	260	3-17-63	Youngstown State	FA
Quinlivan, Mark	TE	6-6	210	....	Yale	FA
Rayburn, Sam	G	6-2	265	....	Texas-Arlington	FA
Sanchez, Jeff	S	5-11	180	5-11-62	Georgia	D12
Scarsella, Dave	NT	6-4	265	2-10-63	Mercyhurst (Pa.)	FA
Shaw, Bryan	WR	6-0	197	....	Northwest Missouri State	FA
Sims, Darryl	DE	6-3	265	7-23-61	Wisconsin	D1
Small, Fred	LB	5-11	231	7-15-63	Washington	D9
Smith, Torin	NT	6-4	278	....	Hampton Institute	FA
Sumpter, James	LB	6-1	220	7- 4-62	South Carolina	FA
Sutton, Mike (1)	S	6-0	190	9-27-61	William & Mary	FA
Turk, Dan	C	6-4	259	6-25-62	Wisconsin	D4
Walko, Robert	DL	6-4	260	5-27-62	Kent State	FA
White, Oliver	TE	6-1	237	5-28-63	Kentucky	D10

*Cleveland, Graham, Madison and McJunkin missed '84 season due to injury.

ST. LOUIS CARDINALS
(Eastern Division, National Conference)

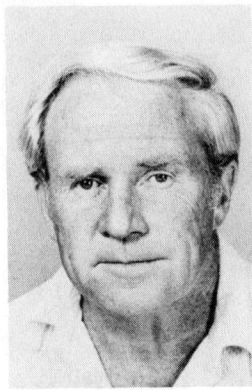

Jim Hanifan

Chairman—William V. Bidwill
President—Bing Devine
Vice-President, Administration—Curt Mosher
Director of Pro Personnel—Larry Wilson
Director of Player Personnel—George Boone
Head Coach—Jim Hanifan (5 years: 34-38-1)
Assistant Coaches:
    Offensive Backfield—Chuck Banker
    Linebackers—Rudy Feldman
    Flexibility/Strength—Pete Hoener
    Offensive Coordinator—Dick Jamieson
    Special Assistant to Head Coach—Leon McLaughlin
    Offensive Line—Ernie McMillan
    Assistant Head Coach/Defense—Floyd Peters
    Special Teams—Jerry Smith
    Receivers—Emmitt Thomas
    Defensive Backfield—Lance Van Zandt
Director of Public Relations—Michael Menchel
    (Office Phone: 421-0777—Area Code 314)
Offices—Busch Stadium, 200 Stadium Plaza, St. Louis, Mo. 63102
Stadium—Busch Stadium (Capacity: 51,392)
Team Colors—Cardinal Red, Black and White
Training Site—Eastern Illinois University, Charleston, Ill.

1985 SCHEDULE
(All times local.
All games Sunday unless noted otherwise.)

Sept. 8	at Cleveland	1:00
Sept. 15	CINCINNATI	12:00
Sept. 22	at New York Giants	1:00
Sept. 29	GREEN BAY	12:00
Oct. 7	at Washington (Mon.)	9:00
Oct. 13	PHILADELPHIA	12:00
Oct. 20	at Pittsburgh	1:00
Oct. 27	HOUSTON	12:00
Nov. 4	DALLAS (Mon.)	8:00
Nov. 10	at Tampa Bay	1:00
Nov. 17	at Philadelphia	1:00
Nov. 24	NEW YORK GIANTS	3:00
Nov. 28	at Dallas (Thanksgiving)	3:00
Dec. 8	NEW ORLEANS	12:00
Dec. 15	at Los Angeles Rams	1:00
Dec. 21	WASHINGTON (Sat.)	3:00

1984 RESULTS—(Won 9, Lost 7)

Cardinals		Opp.		Att.
23	Green Bay	24	(A)	53,738
37	Buffalo	7	(H)	35,785
34	Indianapolis	33	(A)	60,274
24	New Orleans	34	(A)	58,723
28	Miami	36	(H)	46,991
31	Dallas	20	(A)	61,438
38	Chicago	21	(H)	49,554
26	Washington	24	(H)	50,262
34	Philadelphia	14	(A)	54,310
13	Los Angeles Rams	16	(H)	50,950
17	Dallas	24	(H)	48,721
10	New York Giants	16	(A)	73,428
17	Philadelphia	16	(H)	39,858
33	New England	10	(A)	53,558
31	New York Giants	21	(H)	49,973
27	Washington	29	(A)	54,299

1984 GAMES STARTED

16 games: Joe Bostic, Randy Clark, Roy Green, Curtis Greer, E.J. Junior, Neil Lomax, Doug Marsh, Benny Perrin, Tootie Robbins, Luis Sharpe, Pat Tilley.

15 games: Ottis Anderson, Al Baker, Wayne Smith, Lionel Washington.

14 games: David Galloway, Terry Stieve.

13 games: Thomas Howard.

11 games: Leonard Smith.

10 games: Kurt Allerman.

9 games: Earl Ferrell.

6 games: Charlie Baker, Ramsey Dardar, Mark Duda, Elois Grooms, Lee Nelson.

5 games: Greg LaFleur.

3 games: Bob Harris.

1 game: Dan Audick, Doug Dawson, John Goode, Jeff Griffin, Randy Holloway, Randy Love, Stump Mitchell.

ST. LOUIS CARDINALS 1985 VETERAN ROSTER

No.	Name	Pos.	Ht.	Wt.	NFL Exp.	Birth-date	College	Games in '84	How Acquired
58	Ahrens, Dave	LB	6-3	230	5	12- 5-58	Wisconsin	16	D6, '81
51	Allerman, Kurt	LB	6-2	232	9	8-30-50	Penn State	16	W-GB, '82
32	Anderson, Ottis	RB	6-2	220	7	1-19-57	Miami, Fla.	15	D1, '79
60	Baker, Al	DE	6-6	270	8	12- 9-56	Colorado State	15	T-Det, '83
52	Baker, Charlie	LB	6-2	234	6	9-26-57	New Mexico	9	D3a, '80
18	Birdsong, Carl	P	6-0	192	5	1- 1-59	S.W. Oklahoma State	16	W-Buf, '81
71	Bostic, Joe	G	6-3	268	7	4-20-57	Clemson	16	D3, '79
64	Clark, Randy	C	6-3	254	6	7-27-57	Northern Illinois	16	FA, '80
62	Dardar, Ramsey	DT	6-2	264	2	10- 3-59	Louisiana State	16	D3, '83
66	Dawson, Doug	G	6-3	267	2	12-27-61	Texas	15	D2, '84
73	Duda, Mark	DT	6-3	263	3	2- 4-61	Maryland	8	D4, '83
86	Duncan, Clyde	WR	6-1	192	2	2- 5-61	Tennessee	8	D1, '84
31	Ferrell, Earl	RB	6-0	215	4	3-27-58	East Tennessee State	16	D5a, '82
65	Galloway, David	DT	6-3	277	4	2-16-59	Florida	14	D2, '82
84	Goode, John	TE	6-2	222	2	11- 5-62	Youngstown State	16	D5a, '84
81	Green, Roy	WR	6-0	195	7	6-30-57	Henderson St., Ark.	16	D4, '79
75	Greer, Curtis	DE	6-4	258	6	11-10-57	Michigan	16	D1, '80
35	†Griffin, Jeff	CB	6-0	185	5	7-19-58	Utah	8	D3, '81
78	Grooms, Elois	DT	6-4	250	11	5-20-53	Tennessee Tech	11	T-NO, '82
39	Harrell, Willard	RB	5-9	190	11	9-16-52	Pacific	16	FA, '78
36	Harrington, Perry	RB	5-11	210	6	3-13-58	Jackson State	6	FA, '84
50	Harris, Bob	LB	6-2	215	3	11-11-60	Auburn	16	D8, '83
46	Heflin, Victor	CB	6-0	184	3	7- 7-60	Delaware State	16	FA, '83
59	Howard, Thomas	LB	6-2	220	9	8-18-54	Texas Tech	15	T-KC, '84
54	Junior, E. J.	LB	6-3	235	5	12- 8-59	Alabama	16	D1, '81
89	†LaFleur, Greg	TE	6-4	236	5	9-16-58	Louisiana State	16	W-Phi, '81
15	Lomax, Neil	QB	6-3	214	5	2-17-59	Portland State	16	D2, '81
40	Love, Randy	RB	6-1	205	7	9-30-56	Houston	16	FA, '79
82	Mack, Cedric	WR-CB	6-0	190	3	9-14-60	Baylor	12	D2, '83
12	Mackey, Kyle	QB	6-2	220	2	3- 2-62	East Texas State	*0	D11, '84
80	†Marsh, Doug	TE	6-3	238	6	6-18-58	Michigan	16	D2, '80
76	Mays, Stafford	DE	6-2	250	6	3-13-58	Washington	16	D9, '80
87	McGill, Eddie	TE	6-6	225	3	7- 5-60	Western Carolina	*0	D10, '82
14	McIvor, Rick	QB	6-4	210	2	9-26-60	Texas	4	D3, '84
30	Mitchell, Stump	RB	5-9	188	5	3-15-59	The Citadel	16	D9, '81
38	Nelson, Lee	S	5-10	185	10	1-30-54	Florida State	16	D15, '76
57	Noga, Niko	LB	6-1	230	2	3- 2-62	Hawaii	16	D8, '84
11	O'Donoghue, Neil	K	6-6	210	9	6-18-53	Auburn	16	FA, '80
23	Perrin, Benny	S	6-2	178	4	10-20-59	Alabama	16	D3, '82
85	†Pittman, Danny	WR	6-2	205	6	4- 3-58	Wyoming	10	W-NYG, '83
70	Plunkett, Art	T	6-7	270	5	3- 8-59	Nevada-Las Vegas	16	W-Ram, '81
72	Ralph, Dan	DT	6-4	260	2	3- 9-61	Oregon	6	FA, '84
63	Robbins, Tootie	T	6-4	278	4	6- 2-58	East Carolina	16	D4, '83
56	†Scott, Carlos	C	6-4	300	3	7- 2-60	Texas-El Paso	16	D7, '83
45	Smith, Leonard	S	5-11	190	3	9- 2-60	McNeese State	12	D1, '83
44	Smith, Wayne	CB	6-0	175	6	5- 9-57	Purdue	16	W-Det, '82
68	Stieve, Terry	G	6-2	265	9	3-10-54	Wisconsin	14	T-NO, '78
83	†Tilley, Pat	WR	5-10	178	10	2-15-53	Louisiana Tech	16	D4, '76
33	Walker, Quentin	RB	6-1	200	2	8-27-61	Virginia	3	D7, '84
48	Washington, Lionel	CB	6-0	184	3	10-21-60	Tulane	15	D4a, '83
42	Whitaker, Bill	S	6-0	182	5	11-18-59	Missouri	7	FA, '83

*Mackey active for 16 games, did not play; McGill missed '84 season due to injury.

†Option playout; subject to developments.

Also played with Cardinals in '84—G Dan Audick (7 games); S Martin Bayless (3), WR Steve Bird (8), LB Bill Davis (1), DE Randy Holloway (6), S Bill Kay (10), LB Craig Shaffer (4), T Luis Sharpe (16). D—Draft; T—Trade; W—Waivers; FA—Free Agent; OFA—Original Free Agent.

ST. LOUIS CARDINALS
1985 DRAFT CHOICES

(Number following name designates order of selection among 336 players drafted.)

Round and Player		Position	College
1. NUNN, Freddie Joe	18	LB	Mississippi
2. Choice to Atlanta (a)			
2. BERGOLD, Scott from Washington through Atlanta (b)	51	T	Wisconsin
3. SMITH, Lance	72	T	Louisiana State
4. WOLFLEY, Ron	104	RB	West Virginia
5. DUNN, K.D. from Atlanta (c)	116	TE	Clemson
5. WONG, Louis	131	G	Brigham Young
6. NOVACEK, Jay	158	WR	Wyoming
7. Choice to Washington through Kansas City (d)			
8. MONACO, Rob	212	G	Vanderbilt
9. WILLIAMS, Scott	244	TE	Georgia
10. WILLIAMS, Dennis	271	RB	Furman
11. ANDERSON, Ricky	298	K	Vanderbilt
12. YOUNG, Lonnie	325	DB	Michigan State

(a) Traded pick for 2nd and 5th round picks, April 30, 1985.

(b) Falcons acquired pick, 1st round pick in 1986 and running back Joe Washington from Redskins for 2nd round pick and 2nd and 6th round picks in 1986, April 30, 1985; Cardinals acquired pick from Falcons, see (a).

(c) See (a).

(d) Cardinals traded pick to Chiefs for linebacker Thomas Howard, September 1, 1984; Chiefs traded pick to Redskins for 6th round pick in 1986, April 30, 1985.

ST. LOUIS CARDINALS
1985 ROOKIE AND FIRST-YEAR ROSTER

(1) Indicates player in previous NFL camp.
(2) Indicates player with USFL game experience.
(3) Indicates player in previous USFL camp.
(4) Indicates player with CFL game experience.
(5) Indicates player in previous CFL camp.
    All others classified as rookies.

Name	Pos.	Hgt.	Wgt.	Birth-date	College	How Acquired
Alston, Wilford	RB	5-10	205	2-28-60	The Citadel	FA
Anderson, Ricky	K	6-2	190	1-24-63	Vanderbilt	D11
Bergold, Scott	OT	6-7	255	11-19-61	Wisconsin	D2
Bowers, Alan (1)	RB	6-0	206	....	Illinois State	*FA '84
Calhoun, Paul	DB	6-2	199	10-28-63	Kentucky	FA
Clark, Ralph	OT	6-4	259	12- 7-62	Northern Iowa	FA
Davis, Billy (1)	LB	6-4	200	12- 6-61	Clemson	*FA '84
Dunn, K.D.	TE	6-3	220	4-28-63	Clemson	D5
Ferrell, David	LB	6-1	210	7-14-60	East Tennessee State	FA
Holloway, Herman	RB	6-1	204	11-30-61	Arkansas-Pine Bluff	FA
Jones, Ed	DE	6-4	236	7-22-62	Virginia State	FA
Miller, Bob	C	6-2	248	3- 2-62	Illinois	FA
Monaco, Rob	OT	6-3	270	9- 5-61	Vanderbilt	D8
Novacek, Jay	WR	6-4	211	10-24-62	Wyoming	D6
Nunn, Freddie Joe	LB	6-4	233	4- 9-62	Mississippi	D1
Patterson, Reno	DT	6-2	255	4-22-61	Bethune-Cookman	FA
Smith, Lance	G	6-2	273	1- 1-63	Louisiana State	D3
Thomas, Curtland (1, 3)	WR	5-11	182	2-19-62	Missouri	FA
Walker, John (1)	RB	6-0	205	8-31-61	Texas	*D9 '84
West, James (1, 4)	LB	6-2	220	12-19-57	Texas Southern	FA
Williams, Dennis	RB	6-1	227	1- 1-62	Furman	D10
Williams, Scott	TE	6-1	234	7-21-62	Georgia	D9
Wolfley, Ron	FB	6-0	222	10-14-62	West Virginia	D4
Wong, Louis	OT	6-4	259	1- 5-63	Brigham Young	D5a
Young, Lonnie	DB	6-1	182	7-18-63	Michigan State	D12

*Bowers and Walker missed '84 season due to injury; Davis played 1 game with St. Louis in '84.

SAN DIEGO CHARGERS
(Western Division, American Conference)

Don Coryell

President—Alex G. Spanos
General Manager—John R. Sanders
Assistant General Manager—Paul (Tank) Younger
Assistant to President—Jack Teele
Assistant to President—Warren Jones
Head Coach—Don Coryell (12 years: 102-68-1)
Assistant Coaches:
    Defensive Coordinator—Tom Bass
    Special Offensive Assistant—Hank Bauer
    Special Offensive Assistant—Marv Braden
    Defensive Line—Gunther Cunningham
    Offensive Backs—Earnel Durden
    Offensive Coordinator—Dave Levy
    Receivers—Al Saunders
    Defensive Backs—Jim Wagstaff
    Linebackers—Chuck Weber
    Assistant Head Coach—Ernie Zampese
Public Relations Director—Rick Smith
    (Office Phone: 280-2111—Area Code 619)
Offices—San Diego Jack Murphy Stadium, P. O. Box 20666, San
    Diego, Calif. 92120
Stadium—San Diego Jack Murphy Stadium (Capacity: 60,100)
Team Colors—Blue and Gold
Training Site—University of California, San Diego

1985 SCHEDULE
(All times local.
All games Sunday unless noted otherwise.)

Sept. 8	at Buffalo	4:00
Sept. 15	SEATTLE	1:00
Sept. 22	at Cincinnati	1:00
Sept. 29	CLEVELAND	1:00
Oct. 6	at Seattle	1:00
Oct. 13	KANSAS CITY	1:00
Oct. 20	at Minnesota	12:00
Oct. 28	at Los Angeles Raiders (Mon.)	6:00
Nov. 3	DENVER	1:00
Nov. 10	LOS ANGELES RAIDERS	1:00
Nov. 17	at Denver	2:00
Nov. 24	at Houston	12:00
Dec. 1	BUFFALO	1:00
Dec. 5	PITTSBURGH (Thurs.)	5:00
Dec. 15	PHILADELPHIA	1:00
Dec. 22	at Kansas City	12:00

1984 RESULTS—(Won 7, Lost 9)

Chargers		Opp.		Att.
42	Minnesota	13	(A)	57,276
17	Seattle	31	(A)	61,314
31	Houston	14	(H)	52,266
30	Los Angeles Raiders	33	(A)	76,131
27	Detroit	24	(H)	53,509
34	Green Bay	28	(A)	54,045
13	Kansas City	31	(A)	62,233
37	Los Angeles Raiders	44	(H)	57,442
0	Seattle	24	(H)	53,974
38	Indianapolis	10	(A)	60,143
13	Denver	16	(H)	53,162
34	Miami (OT)	28	(H)	53,041
24	Pittsburgh	52	(A)	55,856
20	Chicago	7	(H)	45,470
13	Denver	16	(A)	74,867
21	Kansas City	42	(H)	40,221

1984 GAMES STARTED

16 games: Sam Claphan, Keith Ferguson, Mike Green, Charlie Joiner, Linden King, Dennis McKnight, Billy Ray Smith, Doug Wilkerson.

15 games: Wes Chandler, Chuck Ehin, Woodrow Lowe.

14 games: Earnest Jackson.

13 games: Gill Byrd, Dan Fouts, Ken Greene, Don Macek, Eric Sievers, Ed White.

12 games: Bill Elko.

10 games: Tim Fox.

7 games: Danny Walters, Kellen Winslow.

6 games: John Turner.

4 games: Ron Egloff, Andy Gissinger, Pete Holohan, Miles McPherson.

3 games: Bill Kay, Ed Luther, Wayne Morris, Lucious Smith, Andre Young.

2 games: Rick Ackerman, Derrel Gofourth, Bob Gregor, Keith Guthrie, Lionel James.

1 game: Carlos Bradley, Bobby Duckworth, Gary Johnson, Chuck Muncie.

SAN DIEGO CHARGERS 1985 VETERAN ROSTER

No.	Name	Pos.	Ht.	Wt.	NFL Exp.	Birth-date	College	Games in '84	How Acquired
86	Bendross, Jesse	WR	6-0	197	2	5-19-61	Alabama	16	D7, '84
6	Benirschke, Rolf	K	6-1	184	9	2- 7-55	Cal-Davis	14	W-Oak, '79
50	Bradley, Carlos	LB	6-0	226	5	4-27-60	Wake Forest	8	D11a, '81
	Brown, Don	T	6-6	262	2	4- 2-59	Santa Clara	*0	FA, '82
7	Buford, Maury	P	6-1	191	4	2-18-60	Texas Tech	16	D8, '82
22	Byrd, Gill	CB	5-10	201	3	2-20-61	San Jose State	13	D1b, '83
89	Chandler, Wes	WR	6-0	182	8	8-22-56	Florida	15	T-NO, '81
91	Chickillo, Tony	NT	6-3	259	2	7- 8-60	Miami, Fla.	1	FA, '84
77	Claphan, Sam	T	6-6	282	5	10-10-56	Oklahoma	16	FA, '81
82	Duckworth, Bobby	WR	6-3	196	4	11-27-58	Arkansas	16	D6, '81
84	Egloff, Ron	TE	6-5	227	9	10- 2-55	Wisconsin	12	FA, '84
78	Ehin, Chuck	DE	6-4	260	3	7- 1-61	Brigham Young	16	D12a, '83
68	Elko, Bill	NT	6-5	280	3	12-28-59	Louisiana State	15	D7, '83
76	Ferguson, Keith	DE	6-5	255	5	4- 3-59	Ohio State	16	D5, '81
14	Fouts, Dan	QB	6-3	203	13	6-10-51	Oregon	13	D3, '73
48	Fox, Tim	S	5-11	186	10	11- 1-53	Ohio State	11	T-NE, '82
75	†Gissinger, Andrew	C-T	6-5	282	4	7- 4-59	Syracuse	16	D6, '81
69	Gofourth, Derrel	G-C	6-3	250	9	3-20-55	Oklahoma State	16	T-GB, '83
58	Green, Mike	LB	6-0	239	3	6-29-61	Oklahoma State	16	D9, '83
28	Greene, Ken	S	6-2	196	8	5- 8-56	Washington State	15	T-StL, '83
43	Gregor, Bob	S	6-2	191	5	2-10-57	Washington State	7	D4a, '80
73	Guthrie, Keith	NT	6-3	267	2	8-17-62	Texas A&M	11	D6, '84
20	Henderson, Reuben	CB	6-0	196	5	10- 3-58	San Diego State	12	T-Chi, '83
	Herrmann, Mark	QB	6-5	199	4	1- 8-59	Purdue	*3	T-Ind, '85
88	Holohan, Pete	TE	6-4	249	5	7-25-59	Notre Dame	15	D7, '81
41	Jackson, Earnest	RB	5-10	206	3	12-18-59	Texas A&M	16	D8, '83
26	James, Lionel	KR-RB	5-6	172	2	5-25-62	Auburn	16	D5, '84
18	Joiner, Charlie	WR	5-11	180	17	10-14-47	Grambling	16	T-Cin, '76
31	Kay, Bill	CB	6-1	190	5	1-10-60	Purdue	*15	FA, '84
57	†King, Linden	LB	6-4	250	8	6-28-55	Colorado State	16	D3, '77
64	†Loewen, Chuck	G-T	6-4	268	5	1-23-57	South Dakota State	13	D7, '80
51	Lowe, Woodrow	LB	6-0	219	10	6- 9-54	Alabama	15	D5, '76
62	Macek, Don	C	6-2	260	10	7- 2-54	Boston College	13	D2, '76
12	Mathison, Bruce	QB	6-3	203	3	4-25-59	Nebraska	2	D10, '83
21	McGee, Buford	RB	6-0	206	2	8-16-60	Mississippi	16	D11, '84
60	McKnight, Dennis	C-G	6-3	272	4	9-12-59	Drake	16	FA, '82
24	McPherson, Miles	CB-S	5-11	191	4	3-30-60	New Haven University	9	FA, '82
83	Micho, Bob	TE	6-3	227	2	3- 7-62	Texas	6	W-Den, '84
25	†Morris, Wayne	RB	6-0	208	10	5- 3-54	Southern Methodist	10	FA, '84
46	Muncie, Chuck	RB	6-2	230	9	3-17-53	California	1	T-NO, '80
55	Nelson, Derrie	LB	6-1	238	3	2- 8-58	Nebraska	6	FA, '82
93	Nelson, Shane	LB	6-1	232	8	5-25-55	Baylor	*0	FA, '85
56	Osby, Vince	LB	6-0	222	2	7- 8-61	Illinois	16	OFA, '84
52	Preston, Ray	LB	6-0	221	10	1-25-54	Syracuse	10	D11, '76
	Ricardo, Benny	K	5-10	170	8	1- 4-54	San Diego State	2	FA, '85
90	Robinson, Fred	DE	6-4	240	2	10-22-61	Miami, Fla.	16	FA, '84
85	Sievers, Eric	TE	6-3	236	5	11- 9-58	Maryland	14	D4a, '81
54	Smith, Billy Ray	LB	6-3	231	3	8-10-61	Arkansas	16	D1, '83
45	Smith, Johnny Ray	CB	5-9	190	4	9- 7-57	Lamar	1	W-TB, '84
33	Smith, Lucious	CB	5-10	190	6	1-17-57	Cal State-Fullerton	*13	FA, '84
32	Thomas, Jewerl	RB	5-10	230	6	9-10-57	San Jose State	7	T-KC, '84
59	Thrift, Cliff	LB	6-1	237	7	5- 3-56	East Central Oklahoma	16	D3, '79
27	Turner, John	CB-S	6-0	193	8	2-22-56	Miami, Fla.	15	T-Min, '84
23	Walters, Danny	CB	6-1	180	3	11- 4-60	Arkansas	8	D4, '83
67	White, Ed	T	6-2	284	17	4- 4-47	California	15	T-Min, '78
63	Wilkerson, Doug	G	6-3	253	16	3-27-47	North Carolina Central	16	T-Hou, '70
99	Williams, Lee	DE	6-6	270	2	10-15-62	Bethune-Cookman	8	SupD, '84
80	Winslow, Kellen	TE	6-5	242	7	11- 5-57	Missouri	7	D1, '79
49	Young, Andre	S	6-0	190	4	11-22-60	Louisiana Tech	13	D10, '82

*Brown last active with San Diego in '83; Herrmann played 3 games with Indianapolis in '84; Kay played 10 games with St. Louis, 5 with San Diego in '84; S. Nelson last active with Buffalo in '82; L. Smith played 4 games with Buffalo, 9 with San Diego in '84.

†Option playout; subject to developments.

Also played with Chargers in '84—NT Rick Ackerman (9 games), WR Steve Bird (1), CB-S Scott Byers (6), CB-S Mike Dennis (2), DT Rickey Hagood (2), DT Gary Johnson (4), RB Pete Johnson (3), QB Ed Luther (15), LB Eric Williams (13).

D—Draft; T—Trade; W—Waivers; FA—Free Agent; OFA—Original Free Agent; SupD—Supplemental Draft.

SAN DIEGO CHARGERS
1985 DRAFT CHOICES

(Number following name designates order of selection among 336 players drafted.)

Round and Player	Position		College
1. LACHEY, Jim	12	G	Ohio State
2. DAVIS, Wayne	39	DB	Indiana State
2. DALE, Jeffery from Miami (a)	55	DB	Louisiana State
3. Choice to Minnesota (b)			
3. HENDY, John from Kansas City (c)	69	DB	Cal. St.-L.B.
4. MOJSIEJENKO, Ralf	96	K	Michigan State
5. Choice to Seattle (d)			
6. LEWIS, Terry	150	DB	Michigan State
7. Choice to Kansas City (e)			
7. FELLOWS, Mark from San Francisco (f)	196	LB	Montana State
8. ADAMS, Curtis	207	RB	Cent. Michigan
9. BERNER, Paul	234	QB	Pacific
9. REMSBERG, Dan from San Francisco (g)	252	T	Abilene Christ.
10. KING, David	264	DB	Auburn
11. SMITH, Jeff	291	NT	Kentucky
12. SIMMONS, Tony	318	DE	Tennessee
12. PEARSON, Bret from Chicago (h)	329	TE	Wisconsin

(a) Acquired pick and rights to defensive tackle Dewey Forte for running back Pete Johnson, September 22, 1984.

(b) Traded pick for defensive back John Turner, August 10, 1984.

(c) Acquired pick for offensive lineman Bob Rush, July 11, 1983.

(d) Traded pick and 5th round pick in 1984 for wide receiver Roger Carr and running back Sherman Smith, August 24, 1983.

(e) Traded pick for running back Jewerl Thomas, May 1, 1984.

(f) Acquired pick and 8th round pick in 1983 for linebacker Bob Horn, June 9, 1982.

(g) Acquired pick and 8th and 12th round picks in 1984 for defensive lineman Louie Kelcher, March 28, 1984.

(h) Acquired pick for punter David Finzer, August 15, 1984.

SAN DIEGO CHARGERS
1985 ROOKIE AND FIRST-YEAR ROSTER

(1) Indicates player in previous NFL camp.
(2) Indicates player with USFL game experience.
(3) Indicates player in previous USFL camp.
(4) Indicates player with CFL game experience.
(5) Indicates player in previous CFL camp.
　All others classified as rookies.

Name	Pos.	Hgt.	Wgt.	Birth-date	College	How Acquired
Adams, Curtis	RB	6-0	185	4-30-62	Central Michigan	D8
Barnes, Zach (1)	DE	6-5	267	11- 9-60	Alabama State	*D9 '84
Berner, Paul	QB	6-2	210	12-18-60	Pacific	D9
Breske, Todd	WR	....	......	..	....	FA
Calip, Neal	TE	....	....	..	....	FA
Casarino, Dario (1, 2)	P	6-7	240	9-30-57	Washington	FA
Costello, Rocky (1)	K	5-10	165	10-31-61	Fresno State	FA
Craighead, Bobby (1)	RB	6-1	201	6- 7-61	Northeast Louisiana	*D8 '84
Crawford, Larry (4)	S	6-0	187	12-18-59	Iowa State	FA
Dale, Jeff	S	6-3	210	10- 6-62	Louisiana State	D2a
Davis, Jeff (1)	S	6-1	190	4-20-61	South Dakota	FA
Davis, Wayne	CB	5-11	175	7-17-63	Indiana State	D2
Fellows, Mark	LB	6-0	220	2-26-63	Montana State	D7
Forte, Dewey (2)	NT	6-5	290	8-31-61	Bethune-Cookman	T-Mia '84
Guendling, Mike (1)	OLB	6-3	241	6-18-62	Northwestern	*D2 '84
Hawn, Jim (1)	G	6-4	274	5- 6-61	Arizona State	*FA '84
Hendy, John	CB	5-10	187	10- 9-62	Long Beach State	D3
Jackson, Terry	DT	6-4	265	7- 7-63	Stanford	FA
Jefferson, Doug	RB	....	....	..	Stephen F. Austin	FA
Kearse, Tim (4)	WR	5-11	190	10-24-59	San Jose State	D11 '83
Kelly, Joe	WR	6-0	175	12- 9-62	Vanderbilt	FA
Knight, Steve (1, 3)	G-T	6-4	277	3-13-62	Tennessee	FA
Korff, Mark	LB	6-1	230	4- 5-63	Florida	FA
Lachey, Jim	OT	6-6	278	6- 4-63	Ohio State	D1
Lewis, Terry	CB	5-11	190	12- 9-62	Michigan State	D6
McDougald, Rance	WR	5-10	175	..	California	FA
Mojsiejenko, Ralf	P/K	6-3	198	1-28-63	Michigan State	D4
Nobles, Joe	WR	....	....	..	....	FA
O'Bard, Ronnie (1, 3)	CB	5-10	185	6-11-58	Brigham Young	FA
Olson, Ken (2)	K	5-11	190	9-15-59	Salisbury State (Md.)	FA
Passmore, Don	WR	5-8	155	12-19-61	Illinois	FA
Pearson, Bret	TE	6-4	230	3-31-62	Wisconsin	D12a
Pickett, Edgar (1, 3)	OLB	6-1	235	1-30-62	Clemson	FA
Rackley, Dave (2)	CB	5-9	170	2- 2-61	Texas Southern	FA
Remsberg, Dan	T	6-4	275	4- 7-62	Abilene Christian	D9a
Searcey, Bill (1, 2)	OL	6-2	265	3- 3-58	Alabama	FA
Simmons, Tony	DE	6-4	256	12-18-62	Tennessee	D12
Simpson, Michael	NT	....	....	..	....	FA
Smith, Jeff	NT	6-2	265	1-19-63	Kentucky	D11
Smith, Linzey	WR	6-2	197	2-23-63	Florida	FA
Steels, Anthony (1, 2)	RB-KR	5-9	195	1- 8-59	Nebraska	FA
Stevenson, Mark (1, 2)	C-G	6-3	277	2-24-56	Western Illinois	FA
Trimble, Scott	OL	6-5	290	5-10-63	Florida	FA
White, Bill (1, 2)	RB	5-11	190	1- 3-59	Missouri	FA
Wilson, Earl (4)	DE	6-4	268	9-13-58	Kentucky	FA
Wilson, Mark (1)	S	5-11	198	10- 8-60	Abilene Christian	FA
Woodard, Ray (1)	DE	6-6	274	10-20-61	Texas	*D8a '84
Yancy, Billy (1, 2)	CB	5-10	175	6-16-58	Fresno State	FA

*Barnes, Craighead, Guendling, Hawn and Woodard missed '84 season due to injury.

SAN FRANCISCO 49ers
(Western Division, National Conference)

Bill Walsh

Owner—Edward J. DeBartolo, Jr.
President and Head Coach—Bill Walsh (6 years: 49-40)
Vice President and General Manager—John McVay
Director of College Scouting—Tony Razzano
Director of Pro Personnel—Allen Webb
Assistant Coaches:
    Strength and Conditioning—Jerry Attaway
    Quarterbacks and Receivers—Paul Hackett
    Linebackers—Norb Hecker
    Running Backs—Sherm Lewis
    Offensive Line—Bobb McKittrick
    Defensive Line—Bill McPherson
    Secondary—Ray Rhodes
    Defensive Coordinator—George Seifert
    Special Teams—Fred vonAppen
Public Relations Director—Jerry Walker
    (Office Phone: 365-3420—Area Code 415)
Offices—711 Nevada Street, Redwood City, Calif. 94061
Stadium—Candlestick Park (Capacity: 61,413)
Team Colors—49er Gold and Scarlet
Training Site—Sierra Community College, Rocklin, Calif.

1985 SCHEDULE
(All times local.
All games Sunday unless noted otherwise.)

Date	Opponent	Time
Sept. 8	at Minnesota	12:00
Sept. 15	ATLANTA	1:00
Sept. 22	at Los Angeles Raiders	1:00
Sept. 29	NEW ORLEANS	1:00
Oct. 6	at Atlanta	1:00
Oct. 13	CHICAGO	1:00
Oct. 20	at Detroit	1:00
Oct. 27	at Los Angeles Rams	1:00
Nov. 3	PHILADELPHIA	1:00
Nov. 11	at Denver (Mon.)	7:00
Nov. 17	KANSAS CITY	1:00
Nov. 25	SEATTLE (Mon.)	6:00
Dec. 1	at Washington	4:00
Dec. 9	LOS ANGELES RAMS (Mon.)	6:00
Dec. 15	at New Orleans	12:00
Dec. 22	DALLAS	1:00

1984 RESULTS—(Won 18, Lost 1)

49ers	Opp.		Att.
30 Detroit	27	(A)	56,782
37 Washington	31	(H)	59,707
30 New Orleans	20	(H)	57,611
21 Philadelphia	9	(A)	62,771
14 Atlanta	5	(H)	57,990
31 New York Giants	10	(A)	76,112
17 Pittsburgh	20	(H)	59,110
34 Houston	21	(A)	39,900
33 Los Angeles Rams	0	(A)	65,481
23 Cincinnati	17	(H)	58,324
41 Cleveland	7	(A)	60,092
24 Tampa Bay	17	(H)	57,704
35 New Orleans	3	(A)	65,177
35 Atlanta	17	(A)	29,644
51 Minnesota	7	(H)	56,670
19 Los Angeles Rams	16	(H)	59,743
NFC SEMIFINAL GAME			
21 New York Giants	10	(H)	60,303
NFC CHAMPIONSHIP GAME			
23 Chicago	0	(H)	61,040
NFL CHAMPIONSHIP GAME			
38 Miami	16	(*)	84,059

*Stanford Stadium, Palo Alto, Calif.

1984 GAMES STARTED

16 games: John Ayers, Dwaine Board, Dan Bunz, Roger Craig, Randy Cross, Riki Ellison, Dwight Hicks, Fred Quillan, Manu Tuiasosopo, Keena Turner.

15 games: Keith Fahnhorst, Joe Montana, Bubba Paris, Wendell Tyler, Carlton Williamson.

14 games: Dwight Clark, Jack Reynolds, Eric Wright.

13 games: Freddie Solomon.

11 games: Ronnie Lott.

8 games: Earl Cooper, Russ Francis.

7 games: Lawrence Pillers, Jim Stuckey.

6 games: Mario Clark.

3 games: Mike Wilson.

2 games: Jim Fahnhorst, John Frank, Jeff Stover.

1 game: Matt Cavanaugh, Jeff Fuller, Tom Holmoe, Allan Kennedy, Bill Ring, Billy Shields.

SAN FRANCISCO 49ers 1985 VETERAN ROSTER

No.	Name	Pos.	Ht.	Wt.	NFL Exp.	Birth-date	College	Games in '84	How Acquired
68	Ayers, John	G	6-5	265	9	4-14-53	West Texas State	16	D8, '76
76	Board, Dwaine	DE	6-5	248	6	11-29-56	North Carolina A&T	16	W-Pit, '79
57	Bunz, Dan	LB	6-4	225	7	10- 7-55	Cal St.-Long Beach	16	D1a, '78
95	Carter, Michael	NT	6-2	281	2	10-29-60	Southern Methodist	16	D5, '84
6	†Cavanaugh, Matt	QB	6-2	212	8	10-27-56	Pittsburgh	8	T-NE, '83
87	Clark, Dwight	WR	6-4	215	7	1- 8-57	Clemson	16	D10, '79
29	Clark, Mario	CB	6-2	195	10	3-29-54	Oregon	11	T-Buf, '84
47	Collier, Tim	CB	6-0	176	9	5-31-54	East Texas State	*0	FA, '82
89	Cooper, Earl	TE	6-2	227	6	9-17-57	Rice	16	D1, '80
33	Craig, Roger	FB	6-0	222	3	7-10-60	Nebraska	16	D2, '83
51	Cross, Randy	G	6-3	265	10	4-25-54	UCLA	16	D2, '76
74	Dean, Fred	DE	6-2	232	11	2-24-52	Louisiana Tech	5	T-SD, '81
50	Ellison, Riki	LB	6-2	220	3	8-15-60	Southern California	16	D5, '83
55	Fahnhorst, Jim	LB	6-4	230	2	11- 8-58	Minnesota	14	FA, '84
71	Fahnhorst, Keith	T	6-6	273	12	2- 6-52	Minnesota	15	D2, '74
54	Ferrari, Ron	LB	6-0	212	4	7-30-59	Illinois	11	D7, '82
81	Francis, Russ	TE	6-6	242	10	4- 3-53	Oregon	10	T-NE, '82
86	Frank, John	TE	6-3	225	2	4-17-62	Ohio State	15	D2, '84
49	Fuller, Jeff	S	6-2	216	2	8- 8-62	Texas A&M	13	D5a, '84
24	Harmon, Derrick	RB	5-10	202	2	4-26-63	Cornell	16	D9a, '84
75	Harty, John	NT	6-4	263	4	12-17-58	Iowa	*0	D2, '81
22	Hicks, Dwight	S	6-1	192	7	4- 5-56	Michigan	16	FA, '79
28	†Holmoe, Tom	CB-S	6-2	180	3	3- 7-60	Brigham Young	16	D4, '83
97	Johnson, Gary	NT	6-2	261	11	8-31-53	Grambling	*16	T-SD, '84
66	Kennedy, Allan	T	6-7	275	4	1- 8-58	Washington State	15	FA, '81
42	Lott, Ronnie	S-CB	6-0	199	5	5- 8-59	Southern California	12	D1, '81
	Lumpkin, Joey	LB	6-2	230	3	2-19-60	Arizona State	*0	FA, '85
53	†McColl, Milt	LB	6-6	230	5	8-28-59	Stanford	16	OFA, '81
62	McIntyre, Guy	G	6-3	271	2	2-17-61	Georgia	15	D3, '84
43	McLemore, Dana	KR-CB	5-10	183	4	7- 1-60	Hawaii	16	D10, '82
32	Monroe, Carl	RB-KR	5-8	166	3	2-20-60	Utah	16	OFA, '83
16	Montana, Joe	QB	6-2	195	7	6-11-56	Notre Dame	16	D3, '79
52	Montgomery, Blanchard	LB	6-2	236	3	2-17-61	UCLA	16	D3, '83
83	Nehemiah, Renaldo	WR	6-1	183	4	3-24-59	Maryland	16	OFA, '82
77	Paris, Bubba	T	6-6	295	3	10- 6-60	Michigan	16	D2, '82
65	Pillers, Lawrence	NT-DE	6-4	250	10	11- 4-52	Alcorn State	16	W-NYJ, '80
56	Quillan, Fred	C	6-5	266	8	1-27-56	Oregon	16	D7, '78
64	Reynolds, Jack	LB	6-1	232	16	11-22-47	Tennessee	15	FA, '81
30	Ring, Bill	RB	5-10	205	5	12-13-56	Brigham Young	16	FA, '81
4	Runager, Max	P	6-1	189	7	3-24-56	South Carolina	14	FA, '84
61	Sapolu, Jesse	G	6-4	260	2	3-10-61	Hawaii	1	D11, '83
90	Shell, Todd	LB	6-4	225	2	6-24-62	Brigham Young	16	D1, '84
67	Shields, Billy	T	6-8	279	11	8-23-53	Georgia Tech	10	FA, '84
88	Solomon, Freddie	WR	5-11	188	11	1-11-53	Tampa	14	T-Mia, '78
72	Stover, Jeff	NT	6-5	275	4	5-22-58	Oregon	6	OFA, '82
79	†Stuckey, Jim	DE	6-4	253	6	6-21-58	Clemson	16	D1a, '80
	Thompson, Gary	CB	6-0	180	2	2-23-59	San Jose State	*0	FA, '85
78	Tuiasosopo, Manu	NT	6-3	252	7	8-30-57	UCLA	16	T-Sea, '84
58	Turner, Keena	LB	6-2	219	6	10-22-58	Purdue	16	D2, '80
26	Tyler, Wendell	RB	5-10	200	8	5-20-55	UCLA	16	T-Ram, '83
99	Walter, Mike	LB	6-3	238	3	11-30-60	Oregon	16	W-Dal, '84
14	Wersching, Ray	K	5-11	210	13	8-21-50	California	16	FA, '77
	Williams, Gardner	CB	6-2	190	2	12-11-61	St. Mary's	*3	FA, '85
27	Williamson, Carlton	S	6-0	204	5	6-12-58	Pittsburgh	15	D3, '81
85	Wilson, Mike	WR	6-3	210	5	12-19-58	Washington State	13	FA, '81
21	Wright, Eric	CB	6-1	180	5	4-18-59	Missouri	16	D2a, '81

*Collier and Harty missed '84 season due to injury; Johnson played 4 games with San Diego, 12 with San Francisco in '84; Lumpkin last active with Buffalo in '83; Thompson last active with Buffalo in '83; Williams played 3 games with Detroit.

†Option playout; subject to developments.

Also played with 49ers in '84—DE Greg Boyd (2 games), TE Al Dixon (2), NT Louie Kelcher (16), C John Macaulay (3), P Tom Orosz (2).

D—Draft; T—Trade; W—Waivers; FA—Free Agent; OFA—Original Free Agent.

SAN FRANCISCO 49ers
1985 DRAFT CHOICES

(Number following name designates order of selection among 336 players drafted.)

Round and Player		Position	College
1. RICE, Jerry from New England (a)	16	WR	Mississippi Valley
1. Choice to New England (a)			
2. Choice to New England (a)			
3. MOORE, Ricky from New England (a)	75	RB	Alabama
3. Choice to New England (a)			
4. Choice to Buffalo (b)			
5. COLLIE, Bruce	140	T	Texas-Arlington
6. BARRY, Scott	168	QB	Cal.-Davis
7. Choice to San Diego (c)			
8. Choice to New England (d)			
9. Choice to San Diego (e)			
10. Choice to Seattle (f)			
11. WOOD, David	308	DE	Arizona
12. CHUMLEY, Donald	336	DT	Georgia

(a) Acquired 1st and 3rd round picks for 1st, 2nd and 3rd round picks, April 30, 1985.
(b) Traded pick for cornerback Mario Clark, July 16, 1984.
(c) Traded pick and 8th round pick in 1983 for linebacker Bob Horn, June 9, 1982.
(d) Traded pick, 7th round pick in 1984 and conditional 7th round pick in 1986 for quarterback Matt Cavanaugh, August 10, 1983.
(e) Traded pick and 8th and 12th round picks in 1984 for defensive lineman Louie Kelcher, March 28, 1984.
(f) Traded pick and 4th round pick in 1984 for nose tackle Manu Tuiasosopo, April 4, 1984.

SAN FRANCISCO 49ers
1985 ROOKIE AND FIRST-YEAR ROSTER

(1) Indicates player in previous NFL camp.
(2) Indicates player with USFL game experience.
(3) Indicates player in previous USFL camp.
(4) Indicates player with CFL game experience.
(5) Indicates player in previous CFL camp.
   All others classified as rookies.

Name	Pos.	Hgt.	Wgt.	Birth-date	College	How Acquired
Aboulhosn, Hassan (1)	P	6-2	210	5-15-59	North Virginia C.C.	FA
Baker, Keith (4)	WR	5-10	187	6- 4-57	Texas Southern	FA
Barry, Scott	QB	6-2	190	10-17-62	Cal-Davis	D6
Bonner, Mark (1, 3)	OT	6-5	250	10-19-59	Oregon St.	*FA '84
Brafford, Todd (1)	G	6-5	270	9- 2-60	Utah State	FA
Brown, James	NT	6-3	270	5- 9-60	Savannah State	FA
Chumley, Donald	NT	6-4	259	3-14-62	Georgia	D12
Collie, Bruce	T	6-6	275	6-27-62	Texas-Arlington	D5
Dow, Don (1, 3)	OT	6-6	280	8-15-60	Washington	*FA '84
Fleming, Allen (1)	WR	5-11	175	9-10-62	Cal-Davis	*FA '84
Freeman, Reese (1, 2)	NT	6-3	265	4- 5-62	Northern Colorado	FA
Goodman, Vyn	LB	6-2	230	2-22-61	San Jose State	FA
Huff, Charles	CB-S	5-11	195	2-24-63	Presbyterian State	FA
Jones, Don (1)	WR	6-2	200	10-13-60	Texas A&M	FA
McCann, Douglas	S	6-3	205	10-26-62	Santa Clara	FA
Metter, Jeff (1)	LB	6-3	220	3- 8-60	Eastern Washington	FA
Moore, Brian	C	6-3	280	10- 1-61	Cal Poly-SLO	FA
Moore, Dana (2)	P	5-10	185	9- 7-61	Mississippi State	FA
Moore, Ricky	FB	5-11	236	4- 7-63	Alabama	D3
Morris, Raymond (1)	LB	5-11	240	6- 8-61	Texas-El Paso	FA
Nelson, Byron (1)	T	6-5	280	5- 8-62	Arizona	FA
Price, Eric	CB-S	5-10	185	2-13-63	Stanford	FA
Rice, Jerry	WR	6-2	200	10-13-62	Mississippi Valley St.	D1
Rogers, Shawn (1, 3)	RB	5-11	195	1- 2-61	Cal-Davis	FA
Selden, William	LB	6-2	220	8-28-62	Santa Clara	FA
Smith, Steve	T	6-7	280	1- 2-62	Pacific	FA
Villa, Steven	QB	6-2	200	11-14-61	Santa Clara	FA
Wood, David	DE	6-4	255	5-12-62	Arizona	D11
Wyman, Mike	NT	6-6	245	3-22-62	Stanford	FA

Bonner, Dow and Fleming missed '84 season due to injury.

SEATTLE SEAHAWKS
(Western Division, American Conference)

Chuck Knox

President/General Manager—Mike McCormack
Assistant General Manager—Chuck Allen
Director of Player Personnel—Mike Allman
Head Coach—Chuck Knox (12 years: 112-62-1)
Assistant Coaches:
  Asst. Head Coach/Def. Coord./Linebackers—Tom Catlin
  Defensive Line—George Dyer
  Offensive Backs—Chick Harris
  Defensive Backs—Ralph Hawkins
  Quarterbacks—Ken Meyer
  Receivers—Steve Moore
  Offensive Coordinator—Ray Prochaska
  Offensive Line—Kent Stephenson
  Special Teams/Tight Ends—Rusty Tillman
  Special Assignments—Joe Vitt
Director of Public Relations—Gary Wright
  (Office Phone: 827-9777—Area Code 206)
Offices—5305 Lake Washington Blvd., Kirkland, Wash. 98033
Stadium—The Kingdome (Capacity: 64,752)
Team Colors—Blue, Green and Silver
Training Site—Eastern Washington University, Cheney, Wash.

1985 SCHEDULE
(All times local.
All games Sunday unless noted otherwise.)

Sept. 8	at Cincinnati	1:00
Sept. 15	at San Diego	1:00
Sept. 23	LOS ANGELES RAMS (Mon.)	6:00
Sept. 29	at Kansas City	12:00
Oct. 6	SAN DIEGO	1:00
Oct. 13	ATLANTA	1:00
Oct. 20	at Denver	2:00
Oct. 27	at New York Jets	1:00
Nov. 3	LOS ANGELES RAIDERS	1:00
Nov. 10	at New Orleans	12:00
Nov. 17	NEW ENGLAND	1:00
Nov. 25	at San Francisco (Mon.)	6:00
Dec. 1	KANSAS CITY	1:00
Dec. 8	CLEVELAND	1:00
Dec. 15	at Los Angeles Raiders	1:00
Dec. 20	DENVER (Fri.)	5:00

1984 RESULTS—(Won 13, Lost 5)

Seahawks		Opp.		Att.
33	Cleveland	0	(H)	59,540
31	San Diego	17	(H)	61,314
23	New England	38	(A)	43,140
38	Chicago	9	(H)	61,520
20	Minnesota	12	(A)	57,171
14	Los Angeles Raiders	28	(A)	77,904
31	Buffalo	28	(H)	59,034
30	Green Bay	24	(A)	52,286
24	San Diego	0	(A)	53,974
45	Kansas City	0	(H)	61,396
17	Los Angeles Raiders	14	(H)	64,001
26	Cincinnati	6	(A)	50,280
27	Denver	24	(A)	74,922
38	Detroit	17	(H)	62,441
7	Kansas City	34	(A)	34,855
14	Denver	31	(H)	64,411
	AFC WILD-CARD GAME			
13	Los Angeles Raiders	7	(H)	62,049
	AFC SEMIFINAL GAME			
10	Miami	31	(A)	73,469

1984 GAMES STARTED

16 games: Dave Brown, Jeff Bryant, Blair Bush, Keith Butler, Kenny Easley, Ron Essink, Jacob Green, John Harris, Dave Krieg, Steve Largent, Joe Nash, Bob Pratt, Shelton Robinson, Bruce Scholtz.
15 games: Keith Simpson.
13 games: Charle Young.
11 games: Greg Gaines.
10 games: Bob Cryder.
8 games: Edwin Bailey, Reggie McKenzie, Mike Tice, Daryl Turner.
7 games: Eric Lane.
6 games: Steve August, Franco Harris, David Hughes.
5 games: Michael Jackson.
4 games: Pete Metzelaars.
3 games: Dan Doornink.
2 games: Cullen Bryant, Zachary Dixon, Paul Johns, Randall Morris.
1 game: Terry Taylor, Curt Warner.

SEATTLE SEAHAWKS 1985 VETERAN ROSTER

No.	Name	Pos.	Ht.	Wt.	NFL Exp.	Birth- date	College	Games in '84	How Acquired
69	Abramowitz, Sid	T	6-6	280	3	5-21-60	Tulsa	4	FA, '84
65	Bailey, Edwin	G	6-4	265	5	5-15-59	South Carolina State	12	D5, '81
	Borchardt, Jon	G	6-5	255	7	8-13-57	Montana State	*16	T-Buf, '85
22	†Brown, Dave	CB	6-2	190	11	1-16-53	Michigan	16	VA, '76
77	Bryant, Jeff	DE	6-5	270	4	5-22-60	Clemson	16	D1, '82
59	Bush, Blair	C	6-3	252	8	11-25-56	Washington	16	T-Cin, '83
96	Butler, Chuck	LB	6-0	220	2	12-18-61	Boise State	8	OFA, '84
53	†Butler, Keith	LB	6-4	238	8	5-16-56	Memphis State	16	D2, '78
83	Castor, Chris	WR	6-0	170	3	8-13-60	Duke	15	D5, '83
78	Cryder, Bob	T	6-4	282	8	9- 7-56	Alabama	16	T-NE, '84
31	†Dixon, Zachary	RB	6-1	204	7	3- 5-57	Temple	13	FA, '83
33	Doornink, Dan	FB	6-3	210	8	2- 1-56	Washington State	16	T-NYG, '79
45	Easley, Kenny	S	6-3	206	5	1-15-59	UCLA	16	D1, '81
68	Edwards, Randy	DE	6-4	255	2	3- 9-61	Alabama	13	OFA, '84
64	Essink, Ron	T	6-6	275	6	7-30-58	Grand Valley State	16	D10, '80
74	†Fanning, Mike	DE	6-6	255	11	2- 2-53	Notre Dame	16	FA, '84
56	Gaines, Greg	LB	6-3	220	4	10-16-58	Tennessee	16	OFA, '81
79	Green, Jacob	DE	6-3	255	6	1-21-57	Texas A&M	16	D1, '80
	Griffin, Ray	DB	5-10	186	8	6-29-56	Ohio State	*12	FA, '85
44	Harris, John	S	6-2	200	8	6-13-56	Arizona State	16	D7, '78
63	Hicks, Mark	LB	6-2	225	2	11- 7-60	Arizona State	*0	OFA, '83
46	†Hughes, David	FB	6-0	220	5	6- 1-59	Boise State	16	D2, '81
55	Jackson, Michael	LB	6-1	220	7	7-15-57	Washington	8	D3, '79
24	Jackson, Terry	CB	5-11	197	8	12- 9-55	San Diego State	16	T-NYG, '84
9	Johnson, Norm	K	6-2	193	4	5-31-60	UCLA	16	OFA, '82
60	Kaiser, John	LB	6-3	221	2	6- 6-62	Arizona	16	D6, '84
62	†Kauahi, Kani	C	6-2	260	4	9- 6-59	Hawaii	16	OFA, '82
	Komlo, Jeff	QB	6-2	200	6	7-30-56	Delaware	*0	FA, '85
17	Krieg, Dave	QB	6-1	185	6	10-20-58	Milton, Wis.	16	OFA, '80
37	Lane, Eric	RB	6-0	195	5	1- 6-59	Brigham Young	15	D8, '81
80	Largent, Steve	WR	5-11	184	10	9-28-54	Tulsa	16	T-Hou, '76
73	Mangiero, Dino	NT	6-2	270	6	12-19-58	Rutgers	15	W-KC, '84
67	†McKenzie, Reggie	G	6-5	255	14	7-27-50	Michigan	10	T-Buf, '83
51	Merriman, Sam	LB	6-3	225	3	5- 5-61	Idaho	16	D7, '83
88	Metzelaars, Pete	TE	6-7	240	4	5-24-60	Wabash, Ind.	9	D3, '82
71	Millard, Bryan	T	6-5	284	2	12- 2-60	Texas	14	FA, '84
43	Morris, Randall	RB	6-0	190	2	4-22-61	Tennessee	10	D10, '84
21	Moyer, Paul	S	6-1	201	3	7-26-61	Arizona State	16	OFA, '83
72	Nash, Joe	NT	6-2	250	4	10-11-60	Boston College	16	OFA, '82
	Poole, Nathan	RB	5-9	212	5	12-17-56	Louisville	*0	FA, '85
61	Pratt, Robert	G	6-4	250	12	5-25-51	North Carolina	16	T-Bal, '82
	Prestridge, Luke	P	6-4	235	7	9-17-56	Baylor	*9	FA, '85
57	Robinson, Shelton	LB	6-2	233	4	9-14-60	North Carolina	16	OFA, '82
58	Scholtz, Bruce	LB	6-6	240	4	9-26-58	Texas	16	D2, '82
75	Schreiber, Adam	G	6-4	284	4	2-20-62	Texas	6	D9, '84
42	Simpson, Keith	CB	6-1	195	8	3- 9-56	Memphis State	15	D1, '78
82	Skansi, Paul	WR	5-11	190	3	1-11-61	Washington	7	FA, '84
20	Taylor, Terry	CB	5-10	175	2	7-18-61	Southern Illinois	16	D1, '84
86	†Tice, Mike	TE	6-7	250	5	2- 2-59	Maryland	16	OFA, '81
81	Turner, Daryl	WR	6-3	198	2	12-15-61	Michigan State	16	D2, '84
89	Walker, Byron	WR	6-0	190	4	7-28-60	The Citadel	16	OFA, '82
28	Warner, Curt	RB	5-11	205	2	3-18-61	Penn State	1	D1, '83
8	†West, Jeff	P	6-2	205	10	4- 6-53	Cincinnati	16	FA, '81
54	Williams, Eugene	LB	6-1	220	3	6-15-60	Tulsa	*0	D7, '82
87	†Young, Charle	TE	6-4	234	13	2- 5-51	Southern California	15	FA, '83
50	Young, Fredd	LB	6-1	225	2	11-14-61	New Mexico State	16	D3, '84
10	Zorn, Jim	QB	6-2	200	10	5-10-53	Cal Poly-Pomona	16	FA, '76

*Hicks and Williams missed '84 season due to injury; Borchardt played 16 games with Buffalo in '84; Griffin played 12 games with Cincinnati in '84; Komlo missed '84 season due to injury with Tampa Bay; Poole last active with Denver in '83; Prestridge played 9 games with New England in '84.

†Option playout; subject to developments.

Also played with Seahawks in '84—T Steve August (6 games), FB Cullen Bryant (9), S Don Dufek (9), FB Franco Harris (8), WR Paul Johns (4), WR Dwight Scales (4), S Ray Wilmer (3).

D—Draft; T—Trade; W—Waivers; FA—Free Agent; OFA—Original Free Agent; VA—Veteran Allocation.

SEATTLE SEAHAWKS
1985 DRAFT CHOICES

(Number following name designates order of selection among 336 players drafted.)

Round and Player		Position	College
1. Choice to Cincinnati (a)			
2. GILL, Owen	53	RB	Iowa
3. GREENE, Danny	81	WR	Washington
4. DAVIS, Tony	109	TE	Missouri
5. NAPOLITAN, Mark from San Diego (b)	123	C	Michigan State
5. BROWN, Arnold from Pittsburgh (c)	128	DB	N. C. Central
5. JONES, Johnnie	137	RB	Tennessee
6. Choice to N.Y. Giants (d)			
7. MATTES, Ron	193	T	Virginia
8. LEWIS, Judious	221	WR	Arkansas State
9. OTTO, Bob	248	DE	Idaho State
10. CONNER, John	277	QB	Arizona
10. BOWERS, James from San Francisco (e)	280	DB	Memphis State
11. COOPER, Louis	305	LB	Western Carolina
12. Choice to Buffalo (f)			

(a) Traded pick for center Blair Bush, June 29, 1983.

(b) Acquired pick and 5th round pick in 1984 for wide receiver Roger Carr and running back Sherman Smith, August 24, 1983.

(c) Acquired pick for tackle Steve August, October 9, 1984.

(d) Traded pick and 5th round pick in 1984 for cornerback Terry Jackson, March 12, 1984.

(e) Acquired pick and 4th round pick in 1984 for nose tackle Manu Tuiasosopo, April 4, 1984.

(f) Traded pick for guard Reggie McKenzie, June 28, 1983.

SEATTLE SEAHAWKS
1985 ROOKIE AND FIRST-YEAR ROSTER

(1) Indicates player in previous NFL camp.
(2) Indicates player with USFL game experience.
(3) Indicates player in previous USFL camp.
(4) Indicates player with CFL game experience.
(5) Indicates player in previous CFL camp.
  All others classified as rookies.

Name	Pos.	Hgt.	Wgt.	Birth-date	College	How Acquired
Babka, Beau	G	6-2	290	10- 5-62	Hawaii	FA
Beverley, Anthony	LB	6-1	220	1- 7-63	Southern Methodist	FA
Blazek, Pete	T	6-6	270	8- 6-61	Georgia Tech	FA
Bowers, James	S	6-2	195	8- 8-62	Memphis State	D10a
Brown, Arnold	CB	5-11	185	8-27-62	North Carolina Central	D5a
Conner, John	QB	6-2	200	5- 9-61	Arizona	D10
Cooper, Louis	LB	6-2	235	8- 5-63	Western Carolina	D11
Cortes, Julio	LB	6-1	217	8-13-62	Miami (Fla.)	FA
Davis, Tony	TE	6-5	248	2-11-62	Missouri	D4
Dorning, Dale	DE	6-5	237	2- 7-62	Oregon	FA
Gargus, James	P	6-3	226	2-13-61	Texas Christian	FA
Gilbert, Gale	QB	6-3	215	12-20-61	California	FA
Gill, Owen	FB	6-1	230	2-19-62	Iowa	D2
Greene, Danny	WR	5-11	195	12-26-61	Washington	D3
Grimminger, Harry	G	6-3	272	4-11-62	Nebraska	FA
Haeusler, Greg	LB	6-1	223	8-12-62	Southern Mississippi	FA
Haysbert, Adam	WR	6-0	182	2-16-62	Brigham Young	FA
Hines, Ernest	T	6-5	285	9- 7-62	Norfolk State	FA
Hudetz, Bob	LB	6-1	238	6-13-62	Oregon	FA
Jones, Johnnie	RB	5-10	192	6-30-62	Tennessee	D5a
La Bomme, Don	RB	6-0	216	10-23-62	Washington State	FA
Latham, Matt	S	6-0	175	1- 6-62	Connecticut	FA
Lewis, Judious	WR	5-9	175	9-11-62	Arkansas State	D8
Manley, Bruce	S	6-1	180	2-12-61	Norfolk State	FA
Marshall, Kurt	TE	6-4	248	5- 5-62	Murray State	FA
Mattes, Ron	T	6-6	285	8- 8-63	Virginia	D7
Mergenhagen, Paul	NT	6-4	260	7-20-62	Baylor	FA
Morgan, Steve	RB	5-10	200	7-27-61	Toledo	FA
Murray, T.J.	P	6-2	235	9-17-62	Catholic University (D.C.)	FA
Napolitan, Mark	C	6-3	265	2- 4-62	Michigan State	D5
Neville, Thomas	T	6-5	290	9- 4-61	Fresno State	FA
Otto, Bob	DE	6-6	250	12-16-62	Idaho State	D9
Robinson, Eugene	CB	6-0	180	5-28-63	Colgate	FA
Scott, Michael	WR	6-0	190	3-19-63	Pacific	FA
Staples, Lenson	LB	6-2	245	5- 8-63	Missouri	FA
Tushar, John	G	6-3	260	2-23-62	Cincinnati	FA
Walker, Carlton	G	6-3	280	1-17-62	Utah	FA
Winfrey, Leon	WR	5-9	170	10- 6-60	Morris Brown	FA
Wood, Barry	T	6-6	265	4-26-63	Connecticut	FA
Wood, Tony	K	5-9	195	3-20-63	Tulane	FA
Wrice, Tony	CB	5-11	179	7- 8-63	Northwestern (Ia.)	FA
Wynter, Gino	WR	6-0	190	11-22-59	Vanderbilt	FA

TAMPA BAY BUCCANEERS
(Central Division, National Conference)

Leeman Bennett

Chairman of the Board—Hugh F. Culverhouse
President—John H. McKay
Vice President/Head Coach—Leeman Bennett (6 years: 46-41)
Vice-President—Joy Culverhouse
Assistant to the Chairman of the Board—Phil Krueger
Director of Player Personnel—Jim Gruden
Personnel Scouts—Gary Horton, Erik Widmark, Leland Kendall
Assistant Coaches:
    Special Assignments—Greg Brown
    Strength—Joe Diange
    Offensive Line—Kim Helton
    Defensive Line—Don Lawrence
    Running Backs—Vic Rapp
    Offensive Coord./Quarterbacks—Jimmy Raye
    Defensive Backs—Dick Roach
    Receivers—Larry Seiple
    Defensive Coord./Linebackers—Doug Shively
    Special Teams/Linebackers—Howard Tippett
Director of Public Relations—Rick Odioso
    (Office Phone: 870-2700—Area Code 813)
Offices—One Buccaneer Place, Tampa, Fla. 33607
Stadium—Tampa Stadium (Capacity: 74,317)
Team Colors—Florida Orange, White and Red
Training Site—Tampa, Fla.

1985 SCHEDULE
(All times local.
All games Sunday unless noted otherwise.)

Sept. 8	at Chicago	12:00
Sept. 15	MINNESOTA	4:00
Sept. 22	at New Orleans	12:00
Sept. 29	at Detroit	1:00
Oct. 6	CHICAGO	1:00
Oct. 13	LOS ANGELES RAMS	1:00
Oct. 20	at Miami	4:00
Oct. 27	NEW ENGLAND	1:00
Nov. 3	at New York Giants	1:00
Nov. 10	ST. LOUIS	1:00
Nov. 17	at New York Jets	1:00
Nov. 24	DETROIT	1:00
Dec. 1	at Green Bay	12:00
Dec. 8	at Minnesota	3:00
Dec. 15	INDIANAPOLIS	1:00
Dec. 22	GREEN BAY	1:00

1984 RESULTS—(Won 6, Lost 10)

Buccaneers		Opp.		Att.
14	Chicago	34	(A)	58,789
13	New Orleans	17	(A)	54,686
21	Detroit	17	(H)	44,560
14	New York Giants	17	(A)	72,650
30	Green Bay (OT)	27	(H)	47,487
35	Minnesota	31	(H)	47,405
7	Detroit (OT)	13	(A)	44,308
9	Chicago	44	(H)	60,003
20	Kansas City	24	(A)	41,710
24	Minnesota	27	(A)	54,949
20	New York Giants	17	(H)	46,534
17	San Francisco	24	(A)	57,704
33	Los Angeles Rams	34	(H)	42,242
14	Green Bay	27	(A)	46,800
23	Atlanta	6	(H)	33,808
41	New York Jets	21	(H)	43,817

1984 GAMES STARTED

16 games: Scot Brantley, John Cannon, Jeremiah Castille, Jeff Davis, Kevin House, Dave Logan, Lee Roy Selmon, James Wilder.

15 games: John Holt.

14 games: Sean Farrell, Jimmie Giles, Ron Heller, Beasley Reece, Eugene Sanders.

13 games: Steve DeBerg, Steve Wilson.

12 games: Steve Courson.

11 games: Jerry Bell.

10 games: Keith Browner.

9 games: Adger Armstrong, Cedric Brown, Gerald Carter, Mark Cotney.

8 games: Hugh Green.

7 games: Chris Washington.

6 games: Cecil Johnson.

3 games: Glenn Bujnoch, Randy Grimes, Noah Jackson, Jack Thompson.

2 games: Jay Carroll, Scott Dierking, Ken Kaplan, Kelly Thomas.

1 game: Fred Acorn, Melvin Carver, Robert Thompson.

TAMPA BAY BUCCANEERS 1985 VETERAN ROSTER

No.	Name	Pos.	Ht.	Wt.	NFL Exp.	Birth-date	College	Games in '84	How Acquired
27	Acorn, Fred	CB	5-10	180	2	3-17-61	Texas	16	D3, '84
2	Ariri, Obed	K	5-8	170	2	4- 7-56	Clemson	16	FA, '84
46	†Armstrong, Adger	RB	6-0	225	6	6-21-57	Texas A&M	15	FA, '83
82	Bell, Jerry	TE	6-5	230	4	3- 7-59	Arizona State	16	D3, '82
83	Bell, Theo	WR	6-0	195	9	12-21-53	Arizona	15	FA, '81
71	Braggs, Byron	DE	6-4	270	5	10-10-59	Alabama	14	W-GB, '84
52	Brantley, Scot	LB	6-1	230	6	3- 7-59	Florida	16	D3, '80
29	†Bright, Leon	RB	5-9	190	5	5-19-55	Florida State	12	FA, '84
34	†Brown, Cedric	S	6-2	200	9	5- 6-54	Kent State	9	FA, '77
57	Browner, Keith	LB	6-5	240	2	1-24-62	Southern California	16	D2, '84
77	†Bujnoch, Glenn	G	6-6	265	10	12-20-53	Texas A&M	8	FA, '83
78	Cannon, John	DE	6-5	260	4	7-30-60	William & Mary	16	D3a, '82
86	Carroll, Jay	TE	6-4	230	2	11- 8-61	Minnesota	16	D7, '84
87	Carter, Gerald	WR	6-1	190	6	6-19-57	Texas A&M	16	FA, '80
28	Carver, Melvin	RB	5-11	225	4	7-14-59	Nevada-Las Vegas	5	OFA, '82
23	Castille, Jeremiah	CB	5-10	175	3	1-15-61	Alabama	16	D3, '83
33	Cotney, Mark	S	6-0	205	10	6-26-52	Cameron St., Okla.	16	VA, '76
72	Courson, Steve	G	6-1	270	8	10- 1-55	South Carolina	14	T-Pit, '84
31	Curry, Craig	S	6-0	190	2	7-20-61	Texas	5	FA, '84
75	Darns, Phil	DE	6-3	245	2	7-27-59	Mississippi Valley	2	FA, '84
58	Davis, Jeff	LB	6-0	230	4	1-26-60	Clemson	16	D5, '82
17	DeBerg, Steve	QB	6-3	205	9	1-19-54	San Jose State	16	T-Den, '84
25	Dierking, Scott	RB	5-11	225	9	5-24-55	Purdue	8	T-NYJ, '84
81	Dixon, Dwayne	WR	6-1	205	2	8- 2-62	Florida	10	FA, '84
62	Farrell, Sean	G	6-3	260	4	5-25-60	Penn State	15	D1, '82
44	Ferguson, Vagas	RB	6-0	205	4	3- 6-57	Notre Dame	*0	FA, '85
5	Garcia, Frank	P	6-0	205	3	6- 5-57	Arizona	16	FA, '83
88	Giles, Jimmie	TE	6-3	240	9	11- 8-54	Alcorn State	14	T-Hou, '78
53	Green, Hugh	LB	6-2	225	5	7-27-59	Pittsburgh	8	D1, '81
60	Grimes, Randy	C-G	6-4	265	3	7-20-60	Baylor	10	D2, '83
73	Heller, Ron	T	6-6	270	2	8-25-62	Penn State	14	D4, '84
21	Holt, John	CB	5-11	180	5	5-14-59	West Texas State	15	D4, '81
89	House, Kevin	WR	6-1	185	6	12-20-57	Southern Illinois	16	D2, '80
91	Janata, John	T	6-7	275	2	4-10-61	Illinois	*0	FA, '85
56	Johnson, Cecil	LB	6-2	235	9	8- 9-55	Pittsburgh	8	OFA, '77
79	Kaplan, Ken	T	6-4	270	2	1-12-60	New Hampshire	16	D6, '83
16	Kiel, Blair	QB	6-0	200	2	11-29-61	Notre Dame	10	D11, '84
76	Logan, David	NT	6-2	250	7	10-25-56	Pittsburgh	16	D12, '79
67	Morgan, Karl	NT	6-1	255	2	2-23-61	UCLA	13	FA, '84
20	†Morton, Michael	RB	5-8	180	4	2- 6-60	Nevada-Las Vegas	16	D12, '82
26	Owens, James	RB	5-11	200	7	7- 5-55	UCLA	4	T-SF, '81
38	Peoples, George	RB	6-0	215	4	8-25-60	Auburn	6	FA, '84
43	Reece, Beasley	S	6-1	195	10	3-18-54	North Texas State	16	W-NYG, '83
74	Sanders, Gene	T	6-3	285	7	11-10-56	Texas A&M	16	D8, '79
63	Selmon, Lee Roy	DE	6-3	250	10	10-20-54	Oklahoma	16	D1, '76
55	Spradlin, Danny	LB	6-1	235	5	3- 3-59	Tennessee	15	T-Dal, '83
70	Thomas, Kelly	T	6-6	270	3	9- 9-60	Southern California	10	D4, '83
84	Thomas, Zack	WR	6-0	185	3	9- 8-60	South Carolina State	*14	FA, '84
14	Thompson, Jack	QB	6-3	220	6	5-18-56	Washington State	5	T-Cin, '83
59	Thompson, Robert	LB	6-3	230	3	2- 4-60	Michigan	9	FA, '83
51	Washington, Chris	LB	6-4	225	2	3- 6-62	Iowa State	16	D6, '84
32	Wilder, James	RB	6-3	220	5	5-12-58	Missouri	16	D2, '81
50	Wilson, Steve	C	6-4	270	10	5-19-54	Georgia	16	D5a, '76
85	Witte, Mark	TE	6-3	235	3	12- 3-59	North Texas State	16	D11, '83

*Ferguson last active with Cleveland in '83 and Chicago (USFL) in '84; Janata last active with Chicago in '83; Z. Thomas played 12 games with Denver, 2 with Tampa Bay in '84.

†Option playout; subject to developments.

Also played with Buccaneers in '84—DB Randy Clark (2 games), S Maurice Harvey (15), G. Noah Jackson (6), DE Brison Manor (6), DE Booker Reese (1), CB Norris Thomas (15), WR Perry Tuttle (3), CB Mike Washington (1), LB Richard Wood (16).

D—Draft; T—Trade; W—Waivers; FA—Free Agent; OFA—Original Free Agent; VA—Veteran Allocation.

TAMPA BAY BUCCANEERS
1985 DRAFT CHOICES

(Number following name designates order of selection among 336 players drafted.)

Round and Player		Position	College
1. HOLMES, Ron	8	DE	Washington
2. Choice to Houston through Denver (a)			
3. RANDLE, Ervin	64	LB	Baylor
4. HEAVEN, Mike	92	DB	Illinois
5. Choice to N.Y. Jets (b)			
6. Choice to Cincinnati (c)			
7. PRIOR, Mike	176	DB	Illinois State
8. FREEMAN, Phil	204	WR	Arizona
9. CALABRIA, Steve	232	QB	Colgate
10. IGWEBUIKE, Donald	260	K	Clemson
11. WILLIAMS, James	288	RB	Memphis State
12. ROCKFORD, Jim	316	DB	Oklahoma
12. MELKA, Jim from L.A. Rams (d)	330	LB	Wisconsin

(a) Traded pick and 4th round pick in 1984 to Broncos for quarterback Steve DeBerg, April 24, 1984; Broncos traded pick and 5th round pick to Oilers for 2nd round pick, April 30, 1985.

(b) Traded pick for running back Scott Dierking, April 17, 1984.

(c) Traded pick for tackle Don Swafford, July 24, 1984.

(d) Acquired pick for defensive end Booker Reese, September 4, 1984.

TAMPA BAY BUCCANEERS
1985 ROOKIE AND FIRST-YEAR ROSTER

(1) Indicates player in previous NFL camp.
(2) Indicates player with USFL game experience.
(3) Indicates player in previous USFL camp.
(4) Indicates player with CFL game experience.
(5) Indicates player in previous CFL camp.
   All others classified as rookies.

Name	Pos.	Hgt.	Wgt.	Birth-date	College	How Acquired
Abbott, Vince (1, 2)	PK	5-11	200	5-31-58	Cal. State-Fullerton	FA
Aldredge, Corwyn	TE	6-5	225	9- 6-63	Mississippi State	FA
Branton, Gene (1)	WR	6-4	235	11-23-60	Texas Southern	*D6 '83
Burke, Dave	DB	5-11	195	11-23-61	Nebraska	FA
Calabria, Steve	QB	6-3	215	6-20-63	Colgate	D9
Calhoun, Ken	CB	6-1	195	4- 2-63	Miami (Fla.)	FA
Campbell, Allen Dale (3)	LB	6-5	235	....	Salem	FA
Delegal, Lucious	DB	6-2	205	2- 2-62	Miami (Fla.)	FA
Emerson, Brad	OT	6-5	260	....	Wheaton	FA
Epps, Kelvin	WR	5-10	170	7-24-63	Texas	FA
Freeman, Phil	WR	5-11	180	12- 9-62	Arizona	D8
Gilliard, Bryant	DB	6-0	190	11-26-61	South Carolina	FA
Gunn, Carlton (2)	NT	6-2	305	8-12-60	Carson-Newman (Tenn.)	FA
Harrell, John	OT	6-4	265	12-22-63	Louisiana State	FA
Heaven, Mike	DB	5-11	180	12-20-63	Illinois	D4
Hines, Joe (1, 2)	LB	6-0	225	2-14-60	Texas Christian	FA
Holmes, Ron	DE	6-4	255	8-26-63	Washington	D1
Howard, Joe	WR	5-9	170	12-21-62	Notre Dame	FA
Igwebuike, Donald	PK	5-9	170	12-27-60	Clemson	D10
Jostes, Randy (2)	NT	6-4	270	8-15-61	Missouri	FA
Kennell, Lonnie (1, 3)	NT	6-2	270	12- 8-61	Wichita State	FA
Magee, Calvin	TE	6-3	235	4-23-63	Southern University	FA
Mallory, Rick (1)	OG	6-2	265	10-25-56	Washington	*D9 '84
Melka, Jim	LB	6-1	230	1-15-62	Wisconsin	D12a
Miles, Freddie	RB	...	...	....	Florida	FA
Moore, Willie	LB	6-1	235	4-21-62	Southern Mississippi	FA
Nelson, Sim	TE	6-3	230	6- 9-63	Michigan	FA
Newton, Kelvin (1, 2)	LB	6-1	235	4-20-59	Texas Christian	FA
Prior, Mike	DB	6-0	200	11-14-63	Illinois State	D7
Pritchett, Doug	DB	5-11	190	7-31-62	Louisville	FA
Randle, Ervin	LB	6-3	250	10-12-62	Baylor	D3
Retherford, David (5)	WR	6-0	180	4-19-61	Purdue	FA
Risher, Alan (2)	QB	6-2	190	5- 6-61	Louisiana State	FA
Rockford, Jim	DB	5-10	180	9- 5-61	Oklahoma	D12
Rodgers, Jim	DB	6-1	195	1-25-62	Washington	FA
Rowe, Steve	P	6-5	230	....	Eastern Kentucky	FA
Schulte, Rick	OG	6-3	260	11-24-63	Illinois	FA
Scott, Ed (3)	WR	6-0	190	12-29-62	Idaho State	FA
Sommerfield, Mike (2)	DE	6-4	240	2- 1-59	Central Florida	FA
Swafford, Don (1)	OT	6-7	280	3-22-57	Florida	*T-Cin '84
Vogel, Paul	LB	6-1	215	2-22-61	South Carolina	FA
Wilkes, Del	G	6-3	255	12-21-61	South Carolina	FA
Williams, Carl	WR	6-2	175	1-21-63	Louisville	FA
Williams, James	RB	5-10	205	2-27-62	Memphis State	D11
Wright, Jerry	WR	5-11	170	12- 9-62	Eastern Illinois	FA
Wroten, Tony	TE	6-3	225	10- 8-62	Washington	FA

*Branton, Mallory and Swafford missed '84 season due to injury.

WASHINGTON REDSKINS
(Eastern Division, National Conference)

Joe Gibbs

Chairman, Chief Operating Executive—Jack Kent Cooke
President—Edward Bennett Williams
Executive Vice President—John Kent Cooke
Senior Vice-President—Gerard T. Gabrys
General Manager—Bobby Beathard
Director of Player Personnel—Mike Allman
Director of Pro Scouting—Kirk Mee
Head Coach—Joe Gibbs (4 years: 41-16)
Assistant Coaches:
    Offensive Backfield—Don Breaux
    Assistant Head Coach-Offense—Joe Bugel
    Defensive Coordinator—Larry Peccatiello
    Assistant Head Coach-Defense—Richie Petitbon
    Quarterbacks—Jerry Rhome
    Strength and Conditioning—Dan Riley
    Special Teams—Wayne Sevier
    Tight Ends—Warren Simmons
    Receivers—Charley Taylor
    Defensive Line—LaVern Torgeson
Public Relations—Charlie Taylor
    (Office Phone: 471-9100—Area Code 703)
Offices—Redskin Park, 13832 Redskin Drive, Herndon, Va.; P. O. Box 17247, Dulles International Airport, Washington, D. C. 20041
Stadium—RFK Memorial Stadium (Capacity: 55,431)
Team Colors—Burgundy and Gold
Training Site—Dickinson College, Carlisle, Pa.

1985 SCHEDULE
(All times local.
All games Sunday unless noted otherwise.)

Sept. 9	at Dallas (Mon.)	8:00
Sept. 15	HOUSTON	1:00
Sept. 22	PHILADELPHIA	1:00
Sept. 29	at Chicago	12:00
Oct. 7	ST. LOUIS (Mon.)	9:00
Oct. 13	DETROIT	1:00
Oct. 20	at New York Giants	1:00
Oct. 27	at Cleveland	1:00
Nov. 3	at Atlanta	1:00
Nov. 10	DALLAS	4:00
Nov. 18	NEW YORK GIANTS (Mon.)	9:00
Nov. 24	at Pittsburgh	1:00
Dec. 1	SAN FRANCISCO	4:00
Dec. 8	at Philadelphia	1:00
Dec. 15	CINCINNATI	1:00
Dec. 21	at St. Louis (Sat.)	3:00

1984 RESULTS—(Won 11, Lost 6)

Redskins		Opp.		Att.
17	Miami	35	(H)	52,683
31	San Francisco	37	(A)	59,707
30	New York Giants	14	(H)	52,997
26	New England	10	(A)	60,503
20	Philadelphia	0	(H)	53,064
35	Indianapolis	7	(A)	60,012
34	Dallas	14	(H)	55,431
24	St. Louis	26	(A)	50,262
13	New York Giants	37	(A)	76,192
27	Atlanta	14	(H)	51,301
28	Detroit	14	(H)	50,212
10	Philadelphia	16	(A)	63,117
41	Buffalo	14	(H)	51,513
31	Minnesota	17	(A)	55,017
30	Dallas	28	(A)	64,286
29	St. Louis	27	(H)	54,299
	NFC SEMIFINAL GAME			
19	Chicago	23	(H)	55,431

1984 GAMES STARTED

16 games: Darrell Green, Russ Grimm, Joe Jacoby, Mark May, Art Monk, Neal Olkewicz, Joe Theismann, Don Warren.

15 games: Dave Butz, Darryl Grant, Mel Kaufman, Charles Mann.

14 games: Vernon Dean, Curtis Jordan, Dexter Manley, John Riggins, Rick Walker.

12 games: Rich Milot.

10 games: Ken Coffey.

9 games: Ken Huff.

8 games: Jeff Bostic, Rick Donnalley, Calvin Muhammad.

7 games: George Starke.

6 games: Tony Peters.

5 games: Monte Coleman.

4 games: Charlie Brown.

3 games: Tom Beasley.

2 games: Clint Didier, Keith Griffin, Mark McGrath, Mark Murphy, Virgil Seay, Anthony Washington.

1 game: Perry Brooks, Todd Liebenstein.

WASHINGTON REDSKINS 1985 VETERAN ROSTER

No.	Name	Pos.	Ht.	Wt.	NFL Exp.	Birth-date	College	Games in '84	How Acquired
67	†Beasley, Tom	DE	6-5	248	8	8-11-54	Virginia Tech	13	FA, '84
53	Bostic, Jeff	C	6-2	258	6	9-18-58	Clemson	8	FA, '80
69	Brooks, Perry	DT	6-3	270	8	12- 4-54	Southern University	16	FA, '77
87	Brown, Charlie	WR	5-10	179	4	10-29-58	South Carolina State	9	D8, '81
65	†Butz, Dave	DT	6-7	295	13	6-23-50	Purdue	15	VFA, '75
48	Coffey, Ken	S	6-0	190	3	11- 7-60	Southwest Texas State	12	D9, '82
51	Coleman, Monte	LB	6-2	230	7	11- 4-57	Central Arkansas	16	D11, '79
54	†Cronan, Peter	LB	6-2	238	8	1-13-55	Boston College	3	FA, '81
32	Dean, Vernon	CB	5-11	178	4	5- 5-59	San Diego State	16	D2, '82
86	Didier, Clint	TE	6-5	240	4	4- 4-59	Portland State	11	D12, '81
76	Donnalley, Rick	C-G	6-2	257	4	12-11-58	North Carolina	15	T-Pit, '84
77	Grant, Darryl	DT	6-1	275	5	11-22-59	Rice	15	D9, '81
28	Green, Darrell	CB	5-8	170	3	2-15-60	Texas A&I	16	D1, '83
35	Griffin, Keith	RB	5-8	185	2	10-26-61	Miami, Fla.	16	D10, '84
68	Grimm, Russ	G	6-3	275	5	5- 2-59	Pittsburgh	16	D3, '81
5	Hayes, Jeff	P	5-11	175	4	8-19-59	North Carolina	16	OFA, '82
	Haynes, Louis	LB	6-0	227	3	1- 1-60	North Texas State	*0	FA, '85
61	Huff, Ken	G	6-4	265	11	2-21-53	North Carolina	15	FA, '83
66	Jacoby, Joe	T	6-7	305	5	7- 6-59	Louisville	16	OFA, '81
82	Jones, Anthony	TE	6-3	248	2	5-16-60	Wichita State	16	D11, '84
22	†Jordan, Curtis	S	6-2	205	9	1-25-54	Texas Tech	16	W-TB, '81
55	Kaufman, Mel	LB	6-2	218	5	2-24-58	Cal Poly-SLO	15	OFA, '81
63	Kimball, Bruce	G	6-2	260	3	8-19-56	Massachusetts	8	FA, '83
50	Kubin, Larry	LB	6-2	234	4	2-26-59	Penn State	16	D6, '81
12	Laufenberg, Babe	QB	6-2	195	2	12- 5-59	Indiana	*0	D6, '83
79	Liebenstein, Todd	DE	6-6	255	3	1- 9-60	Nevada-Las Vegas	1	D4, '82
72	Manley, Dexter	DE	6-3	250	5	2- 2-59	Oklahoma State	15	D5, '81
71	Mann, Charles	DE	6-6	260	3	4-12-61	Nevada-Reno	16	D3, '83
84	†Mauti, Rich	WR	6-0	195	8	5-24-54	Penn State	16	FA, '84
73	May, Mark	T	6-6	295	5	11- 2-59	Pittsburgh	16	D1, '81
78	McGee, Tony	DE	6-3	249	15	1-18-49	Bishop, Tex.	16	T-NE, '82
83	†McGrath, Mark	WR	5-11	175	4	12-17-57	Montana State	13	FA, '83
57	Milot, Rich	LB	6-4	237	7	5-28-57	Penn State	14	D7, '79
81	Monk, Art	WR	6-3	209	6	12- 5-57	Syracuse	16	D1, '80
30	Moore, Jeff	RB	6-0	196	6	8-20-56	Jackson State	7	FA, '84
3	†Moseley, Mark	K	6-0	204	14	3-12-48	Stephen F. Austin	16	FA, '74
89	Muhammad, Calvin	WR	6-0	190	4	12-10-58	Texas Southern	10	T-Rai, '84
29	Murphy, Mark	S	6-4	210	9	7-13-55	Colgate	7	OFA, '77
21	Nelms, Mike	KR-WR	6-1	202	6	4- 8-55	Baylor	16	FA, '80
52	Olkewicz, Neal	LB	6-0	233	7	1-30-57	Maryland	16	OFA, '79
23	Peters, Tony	S	6-1	190	10	4-28-53	Oklahoma	8	T-Cle, '79
44	†Riggins, John	RB	6-2	240	14	8- 4-49	Kansas	14	VFA, '76
	Rogers, George	RB	6-2	224	5	12- 8-58	South Carolina	*16	T-NO, '85
10	Schroeder, Jay	QB	6-4	215	2	6-28-61	UCLA	*0	D3, '84
26	Smith, Ricky	CB	6-0	182	4	7-20-60	Alabama State	*12	T-NE, '84
74	Starke, George	T	6-5	260	13	7-18-48	Columbia	9	W-Dal, '72
	Sverchek, Paul	DT	6-3	256	2	5- 9-61	Cal Poly-SLO	*3	FA, '85
7	Theismann, Joe	QB	6-0	198	12	9- 9-49	Notre Dame	16	T-Mia, '74
62	Towns, Morris	T	6-4	263	9	1-10-54	Missouri	4	T-Rai, '84
88	Walker, Rick	TE	6-4	235	9	5-28-55	UCLA	16	FA, '80
85	Warren, Don	TE	6-4	242	7	5- 5-56	San Diego State	16	D4, '79
24	Washington, Anthony	CB	6-1	204	5	2- 4-58	Fresno State	16	T-Pit, '83
47	Williams, Greg	S	5-11	185	4	8- 1-59	Mississippi State	16	OFA, '82
	Williams, Mike	TE	6-4	251	3	8-27-59	Alabama A&M	1	D5, '82
39	Wonsley, Otis	RB	5-10	214	5	8-13-57	Alcorn State	16	FA, '81

*Haynes last active with Kansas City in '83; Laufenberg missed '84 season due to injury; Rogers played 16 games with New Orleans in '84; Schroeder active with Washington for 16 games in '84, did not play; Smith played 1 game with New England, 11 with Washington in '84; Sverchek played 3 games with Minnesota in '84.

†Option playout; subject to development.

Retired—Jim Hart, 19-year quarterback, 2 games in '84.

Also played with Redskins in '84—LB Stuart Anderson (2 games), TE Walt Arnold (4), CB Brian Carpenter (3), WR Alvin Garrett (3), LB Trey Junkin (12), RB Rick Kane (12), WR Virgil Seay (11), RB Jimmy Smith (1), G-T J.T. Turner (1), RB Joe Washington (7), LB Jim Youngblood (1).

D—Draft; T—Trade; W—Waivers; FA—Free Agent; OFA—Original Free Agent; VFA—Veteran Free Agent.

WASHINGTON REDSKINS
1985 DRAFT CHOICES

(Number following name designates order of selection among 336 players drafted.)

Round and Player		Position	College
1. Choice to New Orleans (a)			
2. NIXON, Tory from Atlanta (b)	33	DB	San Diego St.
2. Choice to St.Louis through Atlanta (c)			
3. Choice to L.A. Raiders through Houston (d)			
4. Choice to L.A. Raiders (e)			
5. CHERRY, Raphel from New Orleans (a)	122	RB	Hawaii
5. Choice to Pittsburgh (f)			
6. LEE, Danzell	163	TE	Lamar
7. HARRIS, Jamie from Philadelphia (g)	177	KR	Oklahoma State
7. VITAL, Lionel from St. Louis through Kansas City (h)	185	RB	Nicholls State
7. Choice to L.A. Raiders through New England (i)			
8. WILBURN, Barry	219	DB	Mississippi
9. GEIER, Mitch	247	G	Troy State
10. ORR, Terry from New Orleans (a)	263	RB	Texas
10. Choice to L.A. Raiders (j)			
11. McKENZIE, Raleigh from New Orleans (a)	290	G	Tennessee
11. KIMBLE, Garry	304	DB	Sam Houston St.
12. HAMEL, Dean from Buffalo (k)	309	DT	Tulsa
12. WINN, Bryant	331	LB	Houston

(a) Traded pick for running back George Rogers and 5th, 10th and 11th round picks, April 26, 1985.

(b) Acquired pick and 2nd and 6th round picks in 1986 for running back Joe Washington, 2nd round pick and 1st round pick in 1986, April 30, 1985.

(c) Redskins traded pick to Falcons, see (b); Falcons traded pick and 5th round pick to Cardinals for 2nd round pick, April 30, 1985.

(d) Redskins traded pick to Oilers for 4th round pick in 1984, May 1, 1984; Oilers traded pick and 6th round pick to Raiders for center Jim Romano, October 9, 1984.

(e) Traded pick for wide receiver Calvin Muhammad, October 3, 1984.

(f) Traded pick for offensive lineman Rick Donnalley, August 20, 1984.

(g) Acquired pick for quarterback Bob Holly, August 14, 1984.

(h) Chiefs acquired pick from Cardinals for linebacker Thomas Howard, September 1, 1984; Redskins acquired pick from Chiefs for 6th round pick in 1986, April 30, 1985.

(i) Redskins traded pick to Patriots for defensive back Ricky Smith, September 11, 1984; Patriots forfeited pick to Raiders as penalty for tampering with scout John Polonchek.

(j) Traded pick for tackle Morris Towns, August 30, 1984.

(k) Acquired pick for defensive back Brian Carpenter, September 19, 1984.

WASHINGTON REDSKINS
1985 ROOKIE AND FIRST-YEAR ROSTER

(1) Indicates player in previous NFL camp.
(2) Indicates player with USFL game experience.
(3) Indicates player in previous USFL camp.

(4) Indicates player with CFL game experience.
(5) Indicates player in previous CFL camp.

All others classified as rookies.

Name	Pos.	Hgt.	Wgt.	Birth-date	College	How Acquired
Allen, Brian (1)	WR	6-1	183	8- 6-62	Idaho	*FA '84
Allen, Marv	LB	6-3	230	4- 7-60	Brigham Young	FA
Anderson, Tony	WR	5-10	175	10- 4-63	Southern Illinois	FA
Auer, Jim	OT	6-1	260	1- 4-62	Georgia	FA
Biggers, Keith	LB	6-2	215	....	Southern California	FA
Branch, Reggie	RB	5-11	227	10-22-62	East Carolina	FA
Branion, Joby	CB	5-11	190	3-12-63	Duke	FA
Cherry, Raphel	CB	6-0	194	12-19-61	Hawaii	D5
Clark, Gary (2)	WR	5-10	175	5- 1-62	James Madison	SupD '84
Coleman, Dan	DT	6-4	265	8-14-62	Murray State	FA
Dailey, Darnell (1, 2)	LB	6-3	250	9- 8-59	Maryland	FA
DuBois, Napoleon	S	6-1	183	2- 6-63	Richmond	FA
Eernissee, Dan	C	6-3	247	9-25-61	Washington	FA
Falter, Rod	S	5-11	195	5-10-63	Kearney State College (Neb.)	FA
Ford, Kenny	LB	6-3	215	11-23-62	Texas A&M	FA
Gary, Andre	WR	6-0	200	8-14-63	Texas-Arlington	FA
Geier, Mitch	G	6-4	283	3-15-62	Troy State	D9
Hall, Vincent	RB	5-9	174	4- 8-63	Middle Tennessee	FA
Hamel, Dean	DT	6-3	275	7- 7-61	Tulsa	D12
Hamilton, Steve (1)	DE	6-4	253	9-28-61	East Carolina	*D2a '84
Harris, Jamie	WR/KR	5-9	170	3-23-62	Oklahoma State	D7
Hartman, Tom	T	6-6	280	5- 8-62	Virginia Tech	FA
Hunter, Tony	RB	5-10	205	2-24-63	Minnesota	FA
Jackson, Ron	RB	5-11	189	2-26-62	Washington	FA
Jones, Greg (1)	RB	5-11	184	7- 1-60	Alcorn State	*FA '84
Kafentzis, Kurt	S	6-1	189	12-31-62	Hawaii	FA
Kenealy, Mike	S	6-0	187	4- 3-63	Central Michigan	FA
Kepano, Tony	G	6-1	258	5-24-63	Georgia Tech	FA
Kimble, Gary	CB	5-11	184	4- 5-63	Sam Houston	D11
Knapton, Bob (1, 2)	LB	6-2	225	5-22-60	Northern Colorado	FA
Lake, Gene	RB	5-10	220	12- 1-58	Delaware State	FA
Layher, Floyd	T	6-7	285	7-30-62	Pacific	FA
Lee, Danzell	TE	6-2	232	3-16-63	Lamar	D6
Legg, Bill	C	6-3	265	4- 9-62	West Virginia	FA
Lonergan, Dan	QB	6-3	210	9-19-62	Penn State	FA
McClearn, Mike (1, 2)	T	6-4	273	1- 7-61	Temple	FA
McKenzie, Raleigh	G	6-2	262	2- 8-63	Tennessee	D11
Mills, David	TE	6-2	225	11-17-61	Brigham Young	FA
Moog, Aaron	DE	6-4	260	2- 3-62	Nevada-Las Vegas	FA
Newton, Mike	RB	5-11	227	5-14-62	Southern Connecticut	FA
Nixon, Tory	CB	5-10	186	2-24-62	San Diego State	D2
Orr, Terry	RB	6-3	227	9-27-61	Texas	D10
Osswald, Chris	C	6-4	260	11-13-62	Wisconsin	FA
Pearson, J.C.	CB	5-10	185	....	Washington	FA
Pegues, Jeff (1)	LB	6-2	236	1-19-62	East Carolina	*D5 '84
Pendergrass, Boris	WR	6-0	175	12-22-63	Rutgers	FA
Pendleton, Kirk (1)	WR	6-3	195	4- 4-62	Brigham Young	FA
Peterson, Ron	T	6-10	300	10- 8-63	Nebraska-Omaha	FA
Phillips, Joe	WR	5-9	188	4-12-63	Kentucky	FA
Pope, Bobby	G	6-3	271	8-19-62	North Carolina	FA
Rogers, Gregory	CB	5-8	177	4-19-63	Towson State	FA
Rosborough, Willie (2)	DE	6-4	243	1- 9-61	Washington	FA
Satele, Alvis	LB	6-0	228	4-30-63	Hawaii	FA
Singer, Curt (1)	T	6-5	264	11- 4-61	Tennessee	*D6 '84
Slater, Bob (1)	DT	6-4	265	11-14-60	Oklahoma	*D2 '84
Smith, Keith	TE	6-4	240	6-14-61	Texas-El Paso	FA
Suelter, Roger	RB	6-0	205	11-14-62	Kearney State College (Neb.)	FA
Vital, Lionel	RB	5-9	195	7-15-63	Nicholls State	D7a
Wilburn, Barry	S	6-3	186	12- 9-63	Mississippi	D8
Williams, Kevin	CB	5-10	175	11-28-61	Iowa State	FA
Winn, Bryant	LB	6-3	231	11- 7-62	Houston	D12a
Wooten, Mike	C	6-3	253	10-23-62	Virginia Military Institute	FA
Zalenski, Scott	G	6-5	265	6-12-62	Ohio State	FA

*B. Allen, Hamilton, Jones, Pegues, Singer and Slater missed '84 season due to injury.

NFL Stars Shine Bright

By LARRY FELSER

One of the relentlessly used sports cliches of the 1980s is "on a roll." And it could not be avoided during the 1984 National Football League season, which was a story of consistency and excellence for one team and two individuals.

The team was the San Francisco 49ers.

The 49ers began the season prosaicly. There was a three-point victory over Detroit the first week, followed by a six-point success against Washington and a 10-point decision over New Orleans.

The team was bothered by injuries and various malfunctions, much like any other NFL squad. A month into the season, Bill Walsh, the San Francisco coach, was overcome by a sense of melodrama.

"We're existing from day to day, from practice to practice, from game to game," said Walsh, borrowing from Winston Churchill. "We have to play at our best every week. At some point we're going to have to put our best team on the field."

San Francisco, a team viewed by its coach as a figurative mountain climber, inching its way from crisis to crisis, looked surprisingly robust to its opposition. The 49ers almost never lost. It was the other guys who lost their footing and plunged into the NFL abyss.

It wasn't until the seventh game of the season that San Francisco lost for the first—and last—time.

It took a smashing comeback in the last four minutes by the Pittsburgh Steelers, playing in hostile Candlestick Park, to pull it off. Mark Malone threw a six-yard touchdown pass to John Stallworth with just over three minutes left to tie the game and then Bryan Hinkle, a linebacker, made a spectacular, one-handed interception to set up Gary Anderson's game-winning, 21-yard field goal with less than a minute and a half remaining. The final: Steelers 20, 49ers 17.

"Super Bowl victories are great," said Pittsburgh Coach Chuck Noll, "but I've never been associated with a better victory than this one."

By November, San Francisco was no longer winning prosaically. The Rams were shut out, 33-0, as Dwaine Board led a savage pass rush. Cleveland, boasting the second-ranked defense in the league, was smashed, 41-7. New Orleans went down, 35-3.

After the 49ers had pulverized Minnesota, 51-7, Walsh said that his quarterback, the nerveless Joe Montana, had played his greatest game yet.

Montana's statistics were somewhat modest for quarterbacks in this passing era: 15 completions in 21 attempts for 246 yards and three touchdowns.

But San Francisco standards are different. Being a great passer does not equate to being a great quarterback in Walsh's perspective. Montana supervises an offense that produces a running play when the percentages say pass and passing plays when the expectation is run. It is a drama without a script, a hit that is virtually improvised.

Montana's poise, good judgement, grace under fire and instinct proved to be the perfect complement to Walsh's creation.

By the time the playoffs arrived, the San Francisco offense was virtually choreographed and the defense was a study in disciplined violence. The New York Giants' offense was held without a touchdown in a 21-10 victory and Chicago was shut out, 23-0. Bears' Coach Mike Ditka admitted, "we got a lesson."

The season's masterpiece, however, was the carving, serving and consumption of Miami's American Conference champions, 38-16, before a predominantly home crowd at Stanford Stadium in Super Bowl XIX.

The individuals who made the 1984 season something special were Miami quarterback Dan Marino and Los Angeles Rams running back Eric Dickerson.

Marino did not start prosaically. On opening day, the Dolphins played in Washington and the second-year quarterback treated RFK Stadium as if it were his home field. Marino completed 21 of 38 passes for 311 yards and five touchdowns as Miami scored a 35-17 victory.

To confront Marino without a defense functioning in full capacity was like signing a death warrant. The St. Louis Cardinals played Miami while three of their cornerbacks were ailing and Marino went for the jugular. He completed 24 passes on 36 attempts for 429 yards and three touchdowns in a 36-28 Dolphins victory.

At the end of October, after he had dissected Buffalo, 38-7, Marino's efficiency prompted Bills nose tackle Fred Smerlas to observe, "if he continues like that, he'll be in the Hall of Fame by his third year."

Miami finally lost in its 12th game of the season, falling to San Diego, 34-28, in overtime. Marino made up for that loss when he threw four touchdown passes the next week against the New York Jets.

The NFL record book's section on passing was shredded by the time the regular season had ended. Marino passed for 48 touchdowns, smashing the record (36) held jointly by Y.A. Tittle and George Blanda, a pair of Hall of Famers. Marino's 362 completions, 5,084 yards and nine 300-yard passing games also were records.

San Francisco Coach Bill Walsh got a victory ride after his 49ers dismantled the Miami Dolphins, 38-16, in Super Bowl XIX.

Eric Dickerson also made a major assault on the record book in 1984. The Rams' premier running back almost slipped through the first half of the season unnoticed. But a 164-yard game against New Orleans at midseason attracted more than routine attention. Routine, that is, for Dickerson. A few weeks later, he exploded for 208 yards against St. Louis. Chicago was playing as tough a defense as anybody in the NFL when Dickerson met the Bears. He ran for 149 yards that day.

When Dickerson first came into the professional ranks in 1983, O.J. Simpson predicted that Eric would be the one to break his single-season rushing record of 2,003 yards, set in 14 games during the 1973 season with Buffalo.

Dickerson broke the record with his greatest day ever, a 215-yard performance against Houston in Game 15. He finished the season with 2,105 yards and a per-carry average of 5.6.

The development of Marino and other young strong-armed quarterbacks over the last few years has led the NFL's defensive coordinators to look for an antidote. Their answer: A fierce

pass rush. It was no coincidence in 1984 that the teams with the best pass-rush records made the playoffs. Conversely, the worst pass-rush records belonged to the bottom teams.

The Bears helped propel themselves to the championship of the NFC's Central Division with a nine-sack day against the defending Super Bowl champion Los Angeles Raiders. End Richard Dent accounted for 4½ sacks in that game and finished the season as the NFC sack leader.

Linebacker Lawrence Taylor started the New York Giants on their playoff march by causing two fumbles as he sacked Gary Hogeboom of Dallas. The Giants sacked Hogeboom three other times in recording a 28-7 triumph in Week 2.

The Rams sacked Giants quarterback Phil Simms five times and also recorded three safeties. The worst beating of the year, however, was absorbed by Cleveland quarterback Paul McDonald when the Kansas City Chiefs sent him to the turf 11 times.

San Francisco complemented its versatile

Washington receiver Art Monk shattered the single-season record by catching 106 passes in 1984.

injury that also threatened his career.

The Detroit Lions won a courtroom battle against the United States Football League's Houston Gamblers for the services of star running back Billy Sims. But Sims suffered a knee injury that cut short his season.

The Seattle Seahawks qualified for their first playoffs in 1983, primarily because of the running of rookie star Curt Warner. But 10 plays into the '84 season, Warner suffered a knee injury that made him a spectator for the remainder of the year.

Warner's injury, ironically, set the stage for the Seahawks to become one of the biggest surprises of the '84 season. With Warner in the lineup, the Seahawks offense was dubbed "Ground Chuck," a reference to the offensive philosophy of the team's conservative coach, Chuck Knox. With Warner out of the lineup, the Seahawks went completely out of character. Knox went with Dave Krieg, who hadn't spent a full year as a starter, and the Seahawks played high-risk offense. Krieg had one of the highest interception rates in the NFL, but he also passed for 32 touchdowns, a figure surpassed only by Marino. Seattle won a dozen regular-season games, a figure topped only by San Francisco, Miami and Denver, the team that nosed out the Seahawks for the championship of the AFC's rugged Western Division.

Pittsburgh, with its blitz-happy defense and rebuilt offense, was another surprise, but no more so than its closest pursuer in the AFC Central—the Cincinnati Bengals.

The Bengals were 0-5 starting the second week of October. When they defeated Houston, 13-3, for the first victory of rookie Coach Sam Wyche's career, Wyche cracked, "did Reagan call?"

Cincinnati returned to its losing ways the following week, but then the Bengals put on a furious rally and won seven of their last nine games, including the last four. They were not eliminated from the playoff picture until the Steelers upset the Raiders just a few hours after Cincinnati finished its season by beating the Bills, 52-21.

Denver, an underachiever in '83, put its emphasis on defense and won 10 of its first 11 games. The Broncos never looked back, winning the hotly-contested West title.

Even though Marino and Dickerson dominated most of the headlines, there were other memorable individual achievements.

When Chicago's Walter Payton ran for 154 yards against New Orleans in the sixth week, he succeeded Jim Brown as the NFL's all-time career ground gainer. By the time the day had ended, Payton's career total was 12,400 yards, 88 more than Brown.

Payton's 1,684 yards for the season was second only to Dickerson in the NFL, but his year went beyond statistics. In one game he played quarterback for a brief time as the result of injuries. In a 23-19 playoff victory over Wash-

offense with a pass rush that featured waves of fresh linemen. In the 23-0 playoff shutout against Chicago, the 49ers had nine sacks. In the Super Bowl, the 49ers became the first team to seriously penetrate Marino's usually-tight protection.

It was a season of lost stars, as well as active ones.

Atlanta's William Andrews, considered the most underrated back in the NFL, went down with a career-threatening knee injury before the season even started.

Kellen Winslow, San Diego's peerless tight end, had a bizarre season. He actually "retired" after the first game of the season following a contract renegotiation squabble. Shortly after he returned, he suffered a severe knee

Pittsburgh receiver John Stallworth (82), the NFL's comeback player of the year, joined forces with rookie receiver Louis Lipps to help the Steelers capture the AFC Central Division crown.

Franco Harris, in position to become the most prolific rusher in football history, played only briefly in Seattle after being released by Pittsburgh.

ington, Payton faked a reverse handoff, then threw a 19-yard touchdown pass to tight end Pat Dunsmore for the game's first touchdown, giving the Bears a lead they never lost.

Washington's Art Monk shattered a record that had stood since 1964, catching 106 passes. Charley Hennigan of the American Football League's Houston Oilers held the previous record of 101. Monk smashed Hennigan's record in style, catching 11 passes for 136 yards and two touchdowns in the Redskins' final regular-season game, a 29-27 victory that eliminated St. Louis from the playoff picture.

Another record-setter was Miami's Mark Clayton, who caught a record 18 touchdown passes in his first season as a starter. Another receiver, John Stallworth, was the comeback player of the year. The Pittsburgh veteran, after suffering through several injury-plagued seasons, caught 80 passes for 1,395 yards, a 17.4-yard average and 11 touchdowns. He was helped by the emergence of another Steeler receiver, NFL Rookie of the Year Louis Lipps.

While Stallworth provided one of the year's happiest stories, the saga of another onetime Pittsburgh star, Franco Harris, was one of the saddest.

Harris, along with Payton, was in position to break Brown's career rushing record on the eve of the season opener. But after a salary wrangle with his old team and a long holdout, Harris was released. The Seattle Seahawks signed him after Warner's injury, but he lasted only until midseason and was put on waivers.

Another sad story was the decline of the Dallas Cowboys. Not only did the Cowboys fail to make the playoffs, but they suffered the year's most ignominious defeat. They visited Buffalo in November to play the Bills, who had lost 14 straight games. Rookie Greg Bell burst 85 yards for a touchdown on the game's first play from scrimmage. It was the longest run ever against the Cowboys and sparked a 14-3 upset.

"It was total humiliation," said Dallas running back Tony Dorsett.

There were the inevitable coaching changes during and after the season.

Sam Rutigliano was fired by Cleveland, despite having signed a long-term extension in training camp. Defensive coordinator Marty Schottenheimer was named to replace him. New England had a winning record (5-3) at midseason when Ron Meyer was fired. That was triggered by Meyer's attempt to fire defensive coordinator Rod Rust against the wishes of the front office. Hall of Fame receiver Raymond Berry, out of football for three years and never a head coach, was named to replace him.

Frank Kush, Indianapolis' authoritarian coach, quit before the final game to become coach of the USFL's Arizona Wranglers. After the season, St. Louis' offensive coordinator, Rod Dowhower, was named to replace Kush.

John McKay of Tampa Bay announced his retirement a month early, but he still went out in controversy. Late in the final game McKay ordered his defense to allow the New York Jets to score in order to give running back James Wilder of the Buccaneers an opportunity to pass Dickerson as the NFL record-holder in combined rushing and receiving yardage. His defense complied, but Wilder still finished 15 yards behind Dickerson.

"That was a disgrace," fumed Jets' Coach Joe Walton, as annoyed at McKay's action as much as the 41-21 defeat his team suffered.

"I leave as I came," said McKay, "a controversial man." Leeman Bennett, a former Atlanta coach (1977-82), replaced McKay.

Les Steckel, Minnesota's rookie coach, was fired the day after a 3-13 season came to a merciful end. A short time later, Bud Grant, the most successful coach in the team's history, was coaxed out of retirement.

The Detroit Lions bounced longtime coach Monte Clark and replaced him with Darryl Rogers of Arizona State. The Lions fell to 4-11-1 in '84 after winning the NFC Central the year before.

'84 REGULAR SEASON GAMES
FIRST WEEK

RESULTS OF WEEK 1
Sunday, September 2

Atlanta 36, New Orleans 28 at N.O.
Chicago 34, Tampa Bay 14 at Chi.
Denver 20, Cincinnati 17 at Den.
Green Bay 24, St. Louis 23 at G.B.
Kansas City 37, Pittsburgh 27 at Pitts.
L.A. Raiders 24, Houston 14 at Hous.
Miami 35, Washington 17 at Wash.
New England 21, Buffalo 17 at Buff.
N.Y. Giants 28, Philadelphia 27 at N.Y.
N.Y. Jets 23, Indianapolis 14 at Ind.
San Diego 42, Minnesota 13 at Minn.
San Francisco 30, Detroit 27 at Det.

Monday, September 3

Seattle 33, Cleveland 0 at Sea.
Dallas 20, L.A. Rams 13 at L.A.

The 65th National Football League season opened on September 2 with Miami Dolphins quarterback Dan Marino giving fans a sneak preview. Marino, who in 1983 became the first rookie quarterback to earn a starting berth in the Pro Bowl, shredded the Washington secondary for five touchdown passes in the Dolphins' 35-17 opening-day rout of the Redskins at RFK Stadium. The five scoring tosses were the first of 48 that Marino would throw during the 1984 season. That total shattered the league record of 36 and helped the second-year pro from the University of Pittsburgh earn NFL Most Valuable Player honors.

"They give you the chance to make the big play," Marino said of the Washington secondary. "They play a lot of man-to-man. I'm glad to have thrown five touchdown passes, but I would have been just as glad if we had run it in five times." Two of Marino's scoring passes went to wide receiver Mark Duper, two to Jim Jensen, a converted quarterback, and another to Mark Clayton.

"We went into the game with the idea of throwing the ball because Washington has such a big, tough run defense," said Miami Coach Don Shula. "We wanted to get the good matchups on our pass plays. When you get Marino and Duper matched up against anyone, you're in a great position."

The opening-day victory was Miami's fourth straight.

Another quarterback who jumped off to a fast start was the New York Giants' Phil Simms, a former No. 1 draft choice who had been plagued by injuries for much of his NFL career. Simms, starting his first game since 1981, threw for four touchdowns and 409 yards in the Giants' 28-27 win against NFC Eastern

Division-rival Philadelphia. Two of Simms' TD throws went to rookie free-agent receiver Bobby Johnson. His 409 yards enabled him to join Y.A. Tittle as the only quarterbacks in Giants history to pass for more than 400 yards in one game.

Kansas City's second-year quarterback Todd Blackledge was forced into action after the Chiefs' regular signal-caller, Pro Bowler Bill Kenney, was injured in the final preseason game. The former Penn State All-America, who was making his first NFL start, responded in fine fashion, running for one touchdown and throwing for another in the Chiefs' 37-27 victory over Pittsburgh. The Steelers didn't help themselves by committing four turnovers that led to two K.C. touchdowns and two field goals.

Another player who filled in for an injured Pro Bowler on opening day was Atlanta's Gerald Riggs, who rushed for a club-record 202 yards and scored twice in the Falcons' 36-28 triumph over New Orleans. Riggs was filling in for William Andrews, the Falcons' fine all-purpose back who suffered a season-ending knee injury in a preseason non-contact drill. Riggs, who had backed up Andrews for the previous three seasons, was making his first start during that span. Ironically, Andrews had set the record (167 yards) exactly five years earlier to the day in his first NFL game, also against the Saints in the New Orleans Superdome.

The Super Bowl champion Los Angeles Raiders began defense of their title with a 24-14 triumph over the Houston Oilers. The game marked the NFL debut of Oilers quarterback Warren Moon, a six-year Canadian Football League veteran who signed a five-year, $6 million contract with Houston in the off-season. Moon had a respectable debut, completing 12 of 29 passes for 201 yards and two touchdowns. But the Raiders got the Oilers into a physical, rough-and-tumble type game—Los Angeles was penalized 11 times, Houston nine—and the Raiders' superior talent won out in the end. Minor scuffles and skirmishes broke out between the two teams throughout the game.

San Diego wide receiver Charlie Joiner became only the fourth player in NFL history to go over the 10,000-yard mark in receiving yardage in the Chargers' 42-13 shellacking of Minnesota. Joiner caught three passes good for 52 yards to join Don Maynard, Harold Jackson and Lance Alworth in the 10,000-yard club. Joiner finished the day with 10,033 career yards.

The Chargers, however, really didn't need much help from Joiner to win this game. Quarterback Dan Fouts connected with Wes Chan-

Miami quarterback Dan Marino was never better than he was in Week 1, throwing five touchdown passes in the Dolphins' 35-17 victory over Washington.

dler for a pair of touchdowns and running back Pete Johnson scored on a pair of one-yard runs as San Diego built a 21-3 halftime lead and then scored three touchdowns in 7:28 of the third period to put the Vikes away. The game was the first of Les Steckel's Minnesota head coaching career.

Forrest Gregg had better luck in his first game as Green Bay coach as the Packers beat St. Louis, 24-23. James Lofton ravaged the St. Louis secondary for seven catches and 134 yards as the Pack won its fifth straight season opener. The Cardinals had a chance to win with 2:10 remaining in the game, but place-kicker Neil O'Donoghue, who earlier in the quarter hit a 48-yard field goal, missed from 45 yards out. O'Donoghue also missed a critical extra point in the third quarter.

In their first game in Indianapolis, the Colts showed the hometown fans how not to play football. They dropped numerous passes and committed five turnovers that led to 17 New York Jets points in a 23-14 loss to their AFC Eastern Division rivals. Seven-year veteran Pat Ryan, who was elevated to the Jets' No. 1 quarterback slot after the off-season trade of Richard Todd to New Orleans, threw two touchdown passes to Mickey Shuler in his first NFL start.

The Chicago Bears were even more fortunate than the Jets, benefitting from eight Tampa Bay turnovers in a 34-14 rout. The Bears, who more than doubled Tampa Bay's time of possession, won a season opener for the first time since 1979—the last year in which they made the playoffs.

New England jumped on Buffalo for three touchdowns in slightly more than 18 minutes and then held off the Bills to win their AFC Eastern Division game, 21-17. Steve Grogan threw two touchdown passes in the game's first eight minutes, including a 65-yarder to Stephen Starring on the second play from scrimmage.

Gary Kubiak came off the bench after regular quarterback John Elway dislocated his shoulder and led the Broncos to victory over the Cincinnati Bengals, 20-17. Elway was injured with Denver leading, 13-3, but the Bengals took a 17-13 lead early in the final period. Kubiak, however, drove the Broncos 75 yards in 13 plays, completing six of eight passes in the march, before hooking up with rookie tight end Clarence Kay for the game-winner from eight yards out with 5:26 to play.

The San Francisco 49ers returned to the site of their Super Bowl XVI triumph—the Pontiac Silverdome—and edged the Detroit Lions, 30-27. The winning points came off the foot of placekicker Ray Wersching, who booted a 22-yarder with four seconds left. The game-winning drive started at the 49ers' 24-yard line with 5:01 left to play.

In a Monday game, the Seattle Seahawks crushed Cleveland, 33-0, in the Kingdome. The Seahawks' defense held the Browns to 120 yards total offense, forced five turnovers and was credited with seven quarterback sacks. It was the first time Cleveland had been shut out since 1977.

Seattle quarterback Dave Krieg threw three touchdown passes to lead the way. But the Seahawks paid dearly for the win, their first-ever on opening day, as running back Curt Warner, who had led the AFC in rushing his rookie season (1983), injured his right knee while making a cut near the Cleveland goal line and was lost for the season.

In the Monday night game, Dallas overcame a 13-0 deficit after the first quarter to upend the Los Angeles Rams, 20-13. Tony Dorsett fumbled four times but scored the game-winning touchdown from seven yards out with 3:56 left.

The real story of the game, however, was Cowboys quarterback Gary Hogeboom, who was making his first NFL start after winning a well-publicized duel with incumbent Danny White. Hogeboom proved Coach Tom Landry was right—at least in this game—by completing a club-record 33 passes for 343 yards to help Dallas avenge a 24-17 loss to the Rams at Texas Stadium in the 1983 playoffs.

Falcons-Saints
SUNDAY, SEPTEMBER 2
SCORE BY PERIODS

Atlanta	5	14	7	10—36
New Orleans	7	14	0	7—28

SCORING
Atlanta—Field goal Luckhurst 38, 4:07 1st.
Atlanta—Safety, Todd tackled in end zone, 4:47 1st.
New Orleans—G. Rogers 3 run (Andersen kick), 11:01 1st.
Atlanta—Jackson 50 pass from Bartkowski (Luckhurst kick), 2:19 2nd.
New Orleans—Young 18 pass from Todd (Andersen kick), 5:30 2nd.
Atlanta—Riggs 3 run (Luckhurst kick), 10:20 2nd.
New Orleans—G. Rogers 4 run (Andersen kick), 14:19 2nd.
Atlanta—Bailey 5 pass from Bartkowski (Luckhurst kick), 9:10 3rd.
Atlanta—Riggs 1 run (Luckhurst kick), 1:49 4th.
New Orleans—Tice 3 pass from Todd (Andersen kick), 10:17 4th.
Atlanta—Field goal Luckhurst 48, 13:14 4th.

TEAM STATISTICS

	Atlanta	New Orleans
First downs	22	23
Rushes-Yards	46-249	31-120
Passing yards	173	148
Sacked-Yards lost	3-24	4-37
Return yards	95	172
Passes	14-21-2	16-32-3
Punts	3-45.3	3-37.7
Fumbles-Lost	2-1	2-1
Penalties-Yards	14-143	9-75
Time of possession	29:11	30:49
Attendance—66,652. No-shows—4,401.		

INDIVIDUAL STATISTICS
Rushing—Atlanta, Riggs 35-202, Cain 10-49, Bartkowski 1-minus 2; New Orleans, G. Rogers 20-102, W. Wilson 8-29, Gajan 2-4, Hansen 1-minus 15.

Passing—Atlanta, Bartkowski 14-21-2-197; New Orleans, Todd 16-32-3-185.

Receiving—Atlanta, Bailey 5-53, B. Johnson 4-58, Jackson 3-59, Benson 1-20, Cox 1-6; New Orleans, Goodlow 5-72, Gajan 3-22, G. Rogers 2-16, Wilson 2-4, Groth 1-31, Scott 1-19, Young 1-18, Tice 1-3.

Kickoff Returns—Atlanta, Matthews 1-3, B. Johnson 1-21, Williams 1-20; New Orleans, Duckett 4-103, Fields 1-31.

Punt Returns—Atlanta, B. Johnson 2-54; New Orleans, Fields 2-15.

Interceptions—Atlanta, K. Johnson 1-2, Butler 2-25; New Orleans, Waymer 1-9, Jackson 1-14.

Punting—Atlanta, Giacomarro 3-45.3; New Orleans, Hansen 3-37.7.

Field Goals—Atlanta, Luckhurst 2-2; New Orleans, none attempted.

Sacks—Atlanta, Burley 1½, Bryan 1½, Smith; New Orleans, B. Clark, Jackson, Paul.

Buccaneers-Bears
SUNDAY, SEPTEMBER 2
SCORE BY PERIODS

Tampa Bay	0	7	0	7	—14
Chicago	3	10	14	7	—34

SCORING

Chicago—Field goal B. Thomas 29, 3:45 1st.
Tampa Bay—Carter 74 pass from Thompson (Ariri kick), 2:45 2nd.
Chicago—Field goal B. Thomas 32, 9:15 2nd.
Chicago—McMahon 9 run (B. Thomas kick), 12:10 2nd.
Chicago—Gault 21 pass from McMahon (B. Thomas kick), 6:29 3rd.
Chicago—Suhey 1 run (B. Thomas kick), 8:23 3rd.
Chicago—Hutchinson 1 run (B. Thomas kick), 9:58 4th.
Tampa Bay—Owens 4 pass from DeBerg (Ariri kick), 11:44 4th.

TEAM STATISTICS

	Tampa Bay	Chicago
First downs	11	20
Rushes-Yards	18-89	49-183
Passing yards	165	144
Sacked-Yards lost	4-36	2-11
Return yards	135	115
Passes	9-27-6	17-23-1
Punts	5-46.0	5-42.0
Fumbles-Lost	2-2	2-1
Penalties-Yards	7-44	10-69
Time of possession	19:16	40:44

Attendance—58,789. No-shows—1,460.

INDIVIDUAL STATISTICS

Rushing—Tampa Bay, Armstrong 1-3, Wilder 16-73, Thompson 1-13; Chicago, Suhey 14-57, Payton 16-61, McMahon 3-21, Gentry 7-5, C. Thomas 4-25, Hutchinson 2-minus 4, Jordan 3-18.

Passing—Tampa Bay, Thompson 4-17-4—105, DeBerg 5-10-2—96; Chicago, McMahon 16-22-1—138, Avellini 1-1-0—17.

Receiving—Tampa Bay, Carter 2-86, Giles 2-41, Armstrong 1-2, House 1-12, Wilder 2-56, Owens 1-4; Chicago, Payton 6-18, Suhey 4-30, McKinnon 2-23, Gentry 1-7, Gault 2-40, Saldi 1-20, Baschnagel 1-17.

Kickoff Returns—Tampa Bay, Owens 4-61, Morton 2-54, Wood 1-6.

Punt Returns—Tampa Bay, Bell 1-0; Chicago, Fisher 2-13.

Interceptions—Tampa Bay, Brown 1-14; Chicago, Fencik 2-64, Singletary 1-4, Richardson 1-0, Harris 1-34, Schmidt 1-0.

Punting—Tampa Bay, Garcia 5-46.0; Chicago, Finzer 5-42.0.

Field Goals—Tampa Bay, none attempted; Chicago, B. Thomas 2-3 (missed: 34).

Sacks—Tampa Bay, C. Washington, Green; Chicago, Singletary, Hartenstine, Keys, Hampton.

Bengals-Broncos
SUNDAY, SEPTEMBER 2
SCORE BY PERIODS

Cincinnati	0	3	7	7	—17
Denver	0	13	0	7	—20

SCORING

Cincinnati—Field goal Breech 46, 5:27 2nd.
Denver—Johnson 25 pass from Elway (kick failed), 10:15 2nd.
Denver—Lang 1 run (Karlis kick), 13:03 2nd.
Cincinnati—Brooks 1 run (Breech kick), 7:51 3rd.
Cincinnati—Kinnebrew 1 run (Breech kick), 3:18 4th.
Denver—Kay 8 pass from Kubiak (Karlis kick), 9:34 4th.

TEAM STATISTICS

	Cincinnati	Denver
First downs	29	19
Rushes-Yards	38-111	30-121
Passing yards	322	202
Sacked-Yards lost	4-35	1-4
Return yards	31	97
Passes	26-50-1	18-29-1
Punts	3-51.3	5-42.6
Fumbles-Lost	2-1	1-1
Penalties-Yards	2-14	8-55
Time of possession	35:35	24:25

Attendance—74,178. No-shows—922.

INDIVIDUAL STATISTICS

Rushing—Cincinnati, Brooks 17-45, Alexander 10-29, Kinnebrew 8-12, Anderson 1-9, Jennings 2-16; Denver, Winder 17-94, Elway 3-13, Myles 1-2, Willhite 3-8, Lang 3-18, Kubiak 3-minus 14.

Passing—Cincinnati, Anderson 25-49-1—323, McInally 1-1-0—34; Denver, Elway 8-13-1—127, Kubiak 10-16-0—79.

Receiving—Cincinnati, Collinsworth 10-141, Harris 4-62, Alexander 4-35, Brooks 3-15, Verser 2-39, Kinnebrew 1-4, Holman 1-27, Jennings 1-34; Denver, Johnson 4-56, Winder 4-38, Sampson 3-34, Sawyer 3-15, Myles 1-10, Watson 1-40, Lang 1-5, Kay 1-8.

Kickoff Returns—Cincinnati, Verser 1-11, Simmons 1-5; Denver, Lang 2-36, Thomas 1-22.

Punt Returns—Cincinnati, Simmons 1-0; Denver, Thomas 2-17.

Interceptions—Cincinnati, Cameron 1-15; Denver, Wilson 1-22.

Punting—Cincinnati, McInally 3-51.3; Denver, Norman 5-42.6.

Field Goals—Cincinnati, Breech 1-3 (missed: 50, 22); Denver, none attempted.

Sacks—Cincinnati, Browner; Denver, Carter, Jones, Mecklenburg, Woodard.

Cardinals-Packers
SUNDAY, SEPTEMBER 2
SCORE BY PERIODS

St. Louis	7	0	6	10	—23
Green Bay	0	14	10	0	—24

SCORING

St. Louis—Tilley 14 pass from Lomax (O'Donoghue kick), 11:41 1st.
Green Bay—Clark 1 run (Garcia kick), 7:40 2nd.
Green Bay—Coffman 3 pass from Dickey (Garcia kick), 13:03 2nd.
Green Bay—Dickey 1 run (Garcia kick), 2:15 3rd.
St. Louis—Anderson 3 run (kick failed), 6:28 3rd.
Green Bay—Field goal Garcia 38, 9:58 3rd.
St. Louis—Green 19 pass from Lomax (O'Donoghue kick), 3:11 4th.
St. Louis—Field goal O'Donoghue 48, 6:52 4th.

TEAM STATISTICS

	St. Louis	Green Bay
First downs	19	21
Rushes-Yards	29-157	32-102
Passing yards	260	164
Sacked-Yards lost	2-10	3-24
Return yards	137	188
Passes	25-35-1	16-22-1
Punts	5-42.8	5-49.0
Fumbles-Lost	0-0	0-0
Penalties-Yards	10-79	2-11
Time of possession	33:20	26:40

Attendance—53,738. No-shows—2,294.

INDIVIDUAL STATISTICS

Rushing—St. Louis, Mitchell 4-88, Anderson 18-51, Love 1-10, Lomax 2-9, Ferrell 3-9, Green 1-minus 10; Green Bay, Clark 11-53, Huckleby 7-34, Ellis 10-17, Rodgers 1-3, Dickey 3-minus 5.

Passing—St. Louis, Lomax 25-35-1—270; Green Bay, Dickey 16-22-1—188.

Receiving—St. Louis, Tilley 6-60, Mitchell 4-36, LaFleur 3-26, Marsh 3-37, Green 3-67, Anderson 3-12, Ferrell 2-22, Goode 1-10; Green Bay, Lofton 7-134, Coffman 3-25, Ellis 3-14, Clark 2-4, Jefferson 1-11.

Kickoff Returns—St. Louis, Bird 5-103; Green Bay, Huckleby 3-80, D. Rogers 1-20.

Punt Returns—St. Louis, Bird 3-34; Green Bay, Epps 4-66.

Interceptions—St. Louis, Perrin 1-0; Green Bay, Flynn 1-22.

Punting—St. Louis, Birdsong 5-42.8; Green Bay, Scribner 5-49.0.

Field Goals—St. Louis, O'Donoghue 1-2 (missed: 45); Green Bay, Garcia 1-2 (missed: 29).

Sacks—St. Louis, Duda 1½, Junior, Harris ½; Green Bay, Carreker, Douglass.

Chiefs-Steelers
SUNDAY, SEPTEMBER 2
SCORE BY PERIODS

Kansas City	7	17	13	0—37
Pittsburgh	3	14	3	7—27

SCORING

Kansas City—Blackledge 1 run (Lowery kick), 5:16 1st.
Pittsburgh—Field goal Anderson 30, 10:38 1st.
Kansas City—Field goal Lowery 37, 1:11 2nd.
Kansas City—Brown 3 run (Lowery kick), 4:55 2nd.
Pittsburgh—Lipps 80 pass from Woodley (Anderson kick), 6:53 2nd.
Kansas City—Brown 6 run (Lowery kick), 10:14 2nd.
Pittsburgh—Stallworth 29 pass from Woodley (Anderson kick), 14:27 2nd.
Pittsburgh—Field goal Anderson 47, 2:04 3rd.
Kansas City—Paige 22 pass from Blackledge (Lowery kick), 7:03 3rd.
Kansas City—Field goal Lowery 47, 8:13 3rd.
Kansas City—Field goal Lowery 37, 10:24 3rd.
Pittsburgh—Lipps 21 pass from Malone (Anderson kick), 14:37 4th.

TEAM STATISTICS

	Kansas City	Pittsburgh
First downs	18	20
Rushes-Yards	31-94	24-46
Passing yards	170	419
Sacked-Yards lost	0-0	5-39
Return yards	70	210
Passes	19-37-0	22-41-2
Punts	6-48.0	2-39.5
Fumbles-Lost	1-1	3-2
Penalties-Yards	4-32	7-69
Time of possession	30:39	29:21

Attendance—56,709. No-shows—2,291.

INDIVIDUAL STATISTICS

Rushing—Kansas City, Blackledge 2-5, Brown 17-58, B. Jackson 1-2, Heard 8-30, Ricks 2-1, Osiecki 1-minus 2; Pittsburgh, Woodley 2-minus 6, Abercrombie 7-13, Pollard 11-28, Erenberg 2-5, Malone 2-6.

Passing—Kansas City, Blackledge 19-36-0—170, Osiecki 0-1-0—0; Pittsburgh, Woodley 11-17-1—225, Malone 11-24-1—233.

Receiving—Kansas City, B. Jackson 1-9, Carson 4-37, Hancock 3-34, Brown 4-17, Marshall 2-28, Heard 1-4, Paige 2-29, Smith 2-12; Pittsburgh, Sweeney 2-25, Erenberg 3-33, Lipps 6-183, Stallworth 8-167, Pollard 2-36, Thompson 1-14.

Kickoff Returns—Kansas City, Paige 1-21, Cherry 1-0; Pittsburgh, Erenberg 7-174.

Punt Returns—Kansas City, Smith 1-7; Pittsburgh, Lipps 4-36.

Interceptions—Kansas City, Cherry 1-26, C. Jackson 1-16.

Punting—Kansas City, Arnold 6-48.0; Pittsburgh, Colquitt 2-39.5.

Field Goals—Kansas City, Lowery 3-3; Pittsburgh, Anderson 2-3 (missed: 48).

Sacks—Kansas City, Daniels, Bell, Still, Maas, Kremer.

Raiders-Oilers
SUNDAY, SEPTEMBER 2
SCORE BY PERIODS

Los Angeles Raiders	0	0	13	11—24
Houston	0	7	0	7—14

SCORING

Houston—Holston 10 pass from Moon (Kempf kick), 11:38 2nd.
Los Angeles—Allen 1 run (kick failed), 4:40 3rd.
Los Angeles—Hawkins 1 run (Bahr kick), 9:28 3rd.
Los Angeles—Plunkett 1 run (pass failed), 4:07 4th.
Los Angeles—Field goal Bahr 28, 10:45 4th.
Los Angeles—Safety, offensive holding in end zone, 11:15 4th.
Houston—McCloskey 5 pass from Moon (Kempf kick), 14:17 4th.

TEAM STATISTICS

	Los Angeles	Houston
First downs	20	18
Rushes-Yards	35-142	36-120
Passing yards	174	156
Sacked-Yards lost	3-24	5-45
Return yards	125	61
Passes	15-37-0	12-29-0
Punts	7-40.9	10-37.7
Fumbles-Lost	3-1	3-0
Penalties-Yards	11-92	9-117
Time of possession	31:45	28:15

Attendance—49,029. No-shows—3,649.

INDIVIDUAL STATISTICS

Rushing—Los Angeles, Allen 22-83, Hawkins 5-17, Plunkett 5-16, King 2-23, McCall 1-3; Houston, Campbell 25-92, Moriarty 6-18, Moon 4-1, Joyner 1-9.

Passing—Los Angeles, Plunkett 15-36-0—198, Allen 0-1-0—0; Houston, Moon 12-29-0—201.

Receiving—Los Angeles, Branch 4-61, Allen 5-38, Christensen 4-56, King 1-minus 3, Williams 1-46; Houston, Bryant 4-66, Moriarty 1-24, Dressel 2-17, Holston 1-10, Williams 1-8, Smith 1-20, McCloskey 2-56.

Kickoff Returns—Los Angeles, Montgomery 3-59, Pruitt 1-0; Houston, Brown 3-17, Allen 2-41.

Punt Returns—Los Angeles, Pruitt 6-66.

Punting—Los Angeles, Guy 7-40.9; Houston, James 10-37.7.

Field Goals—Los Angeles, Bahr 1-2 (missed: 40); Houston, none attempted.

Sacks—Los Angeles, Pickel 3, Alzado, Long; Houston, Stensrud 1½, Baker 1½.

Dolphins-Redskins
SUNDAY, SEPTEMBER 2
SCORE BY PERIODS

Miami	7	7	21	0—35
Washington	0	10	0	7—17

SCORING
Miami—Duper 26 pass from Marino (von Schamann kick), 13:16 1st.
Washington—Riggins 1 run (Moseley kick), 3:48 2nd.
Washington—Field goal Moseley 33, 11:47 2nd.
Miami—Duper 74 pass from Marino (von Schamann kick), 12:54 2nd.
Miami—Jensen 6 pass from Marino (von Schamann kick), 3:47 3rd.
Miami—Clayton 9 pass from Marino (von Schamann kick), 9:08 3rd.
Miami—Jensen 4 pass from Marino (von Schamann kick), 11:50 3rd.
Washington—J. Washington 4 run (Moseley kick), 7:44 4th.

TEAM STATISTICS

	Miami	Washington
First downs	18	23
Rushes-Yards	30-86	29-156
Passing yards	311	193
Sacked-Yards lost	0-0	2-11
Return yards	152	148
Passes	21-28-0	21-36-2
Punts	5-45.8	4-43.8
Fumbles-Lost	0-0	1-1
Penalties-Yards	4-45	3-20
Time of possession	28:48	31:12

Attendance—52,683. No-shows—2,748.

INDIVIDUAL STATISTICS
Rushing—Miami, Nathan 10-26, Franklin 13-48, Bennett 4-19, Marino 3-minus 7; Washington, Riggins 15-98, Washington 12-38, Theismann 2-20.

Passing—Miami, Marino 21-28-0—311; Washington, Theismann 21-36-2—204.

Receiving—Miami, Duper 6-178, Jensen 5-40, Clayton 3-31, Johnson 3-17, Moore 1-8, Cefalo 1-2, Rose 2-35; Washington, Brown 6-60, Riggins 2-18, Monk 3-54, Walker 2-15, Warren 2-29, Garrett 1-5, J. Washington 5-23.

Kickoff Returns—Miami, Clayton 1-14; Washington, Nelms 3-86, Smith 2-38.

Punt Returns—Miami, Clayton 3-18, Heflin 3-53; Washington, Nelms 3-24.

Interceptions—Miami, G. Blackwood 1-27, Judson 1-40.

Punting—Miami, Roby 5-45.8; Washington, Hayes 4-43.8.

Field Goals—Miami, none attempted; Washington, Moseley 1-2 (missed: 48).

Sacks—Miami, Brudzinski, Baumhower.

Patriots-Bills
SUNDAY, SEPTEMBER 2
SCORE BY PERIODS

New England	14	7	0	0—21
Buffalo	0	3	7	7—17

SCORING
New England—Starring 65 pass from Grogan (Franklin kick), 0:51 1st.
New England—Ramsey 3 pass from Grogan (Franklin kick), 7:53 1st.
New England—Collins 4 run (Franklin kick), 3:04 2nd.
Buffalo—Field goal Danelo 27, 11:40 2nd.
Buffalo—Dennard 8 pass from Ferguson (Danelo kick), 9:39 3rd.
Buffalo—Hunter 9 pass from Ferguson (Danelo kick), 10:54 4th.

TEAM STATISTICS

	New England	Buffalo
First downs	16	24
Rushes-Yards	29-102	29-94
Passing yards	213	232
Sacked-Yards lost	2-14	3-31
Return yards	107	109
Passes	12-22-1	27-40-0
Punts	4-42.3	3-44.7
Fumbles-Lost	1-1	3-1
Penalties-Yards	7-43	4-35
Time of possession	25:52	34:08

Attendance—48,528. No-shows—1,121.

INDIVIDUAL STATISTICS
Rushing—New England, Collins 21-83, Grogan 3-minus 4, Tatupu 5-23; Buffalo, Bell 12-29, Moore 4-26, Ferguson 3-15, Neal 2-2, V. Williams 7-16, Hunter 1-6.

Passing—New England, Grogan 12-22-1—227; Buffalo, Ferguson 27-40-0—263.

Receiving—New England, Starring 3-105, Jones 4-71, D. Ramsey 2-13, Collins 2-24, Dawson 1-14; Buffalo, Franklin 10-96, Hunter 5-58, Neal 3-35, Moore 2-13, Brookins 3-30, Dawkins 2-16, Dennard 2-15.

Kickoff Returns—New England, Smith 1-22, J. Williams 3-72; Buffalo, Wilson 4-66.

Punt Returns—New England, Starring 2-13; Buffalo, Wilson 3-30.

Interceptions—Buffalo, Romes 1-13.

Punting—New England, Prestridge 4-42.3; Buffalo, Kidd 3-44.7.

Field Goals—New England, none attempted; Buffalo, Danelo 1-2 (missed: 45).

Sacks—New England, Tippert 2½, L. Williams ½; Buffalo, Kush, Talley.

Eagles-Giants
SUNDAY, SEPTEMBER 2
SCORE BY PERIODS

Philadelphia	3	3	14	7—27
New York Giants	7	14	0	7—28

SCORING
Philadelphia—Field goal McFadden 47, 4:15 1st.
New York—Mowatt 24 pass from Simms (Haji-Sheikh kick), 6:39 1st.
Philadelphia—Field goal McFadden 41, 2:39 2nd.
New York—B. Williams 65 pass from Simms (Haji-Sheikh kick), 3:05 2nd.
New York—Johnson 35 pass from Simms (Haji-Sheikh kick), 12:13 2nd.
Philadelphia—Montgomery 4 run (McFadden kick), 4:17 3rd.
Philadelphia—Quick 14 pass from Jaworski (McFadden kick), 14:12 3rd.
New York—Johnson 16 pass from Simms (Haji-Sheikh kick), 0:58 4th.
Philadelphia—Kraynak 8 blocked punt return (McFadden kick), 9:15 4th.

TEAM STATISTICS

	Philadelphia	New York
First downs	17	23
Rushes-Yards	21-62	41-109
Passing yards	252	388
Sacked-Yards lost	3-14	2-21
Return yards	62	37
Passes	19-33-0	23-30-0
Punts	5-50.2	6-31.8
Fumbles-Lost	1-0	1-1
Penalties-Yards	5-37	7-95
Time of possession	25:24	34:36

Attendance—71,520. No-shows—4,830.

INDIVIDUAL STATISTICS
Rushing—Philadelphia, Oliver 2-7, Montgomery 7-20, Haddix 5-15, Hardy 6-25, Quick 1-minus 5; New York,

Carpenter 16-25, Woolfolk 9-39, Simms 6-20, Morris 8-22, Galbreath 2-3.

Passing—Philadelphia, Jaworski 19-33-0—266; New York, Simms 23-30-0—409.

Receiving—Philadelphia, Quick 8-147, Jackson 2-15, Oliver 1-3, Montgomery 4-47, Haddix 2-14, Woodruff 1-30, Spagnola 1-10; New York, Gray 2-33, B. Williams 5-167, Mowatt 2-30, Galbreath 1-8, Morris 1-4, Johnson 8-137, Carpenter 3-19, Woolfolk 1-11.

Kickoff Returns—Philadelphia, Hayes 2-31, Hardy 1-20; New York, Woolfolk 2-27.

Punt Returns—Philadelphia, Cooper 2-11; New York, McConkey 1-10.

Punting—Philadelphia, Horan 5-50.2; New York, Jennings 5-38.2.

Field Goals—Philadelphia, McFadden 2-3 (missed: 37); New York, none attempted.

Sacks—Philadelphia, J. Williams, Brown ½, Armstrong ½; New York, Merrill 2, Taylor.

Jets-Colts
SUNDAY, SEPTEMBER 2
SCORE BY PERIODS

New York Jets	0	7	9	7—23
Indianapolis	0	7	0	7—14

SCORING

Indianapolis—Dickey 3 run (Allegre kick), 4:11 2nd.
New York—Shuler 13 pass from Ryan (Leahy kick), 14:53 2nd.
New York—Field goal Leahy 29, 5:45 3rd.
New York—Shuler 8 pass from Ryan (kick failed), 13:09 3rd.
Indianapolis—Middleton 3 run (Allegre kick), 4:54 4th.
New York—Buttle 4 fumble return (Leahy kick), 13:25 4th.

TEAM STATISTICS

	New York	Indianapolis
First downs	23	19
Rushes-Yards	43-155	30-122
Passing yards	153	172
Sacked-Yards lost	1-10	4-27
Return yards	135	91
Passes	14-29-2	17-26-1
Punts	3-47.0	5-47.0
Fumbles-Lost	2-1	4-4
Penalties-Yards	6-55	6-58
Time of possession	35:14	24:16

Attendance—60,500 (est.). No-shows—NA.

INDIVIDUAL STATISTICS

Rushing—New York, McNeil 29-112, Hector 6-23, Walker 1-1, Paige 3-6, Ryan 1-1, Minter 1-10, Harper 1-2, Barber 1-0; Indianapolis, Dickey 12-40, McMillan 8-32, Pagel 4-43, Moore 4-2, Middleton 2-5.

Passing—New York, Ryan 14-29-2—163; Indianapolis, Pagel 17-26-1—199.

Receiving—New York, Gaffney 5-73, Walker 3-39, Shuler 3-30, Harper 1-9, Hector 1-7, McNeil 1-5; Indianapolis, Porter 4-51, Butler 3-34, Sherwin 2-33, McMillan 2-39, Wonsley 2-3, Dickey 1-4, Moore 1-5, Bouza 1-20, Middleton 1-10.

Kickoff Returns—New York, Humphrey 2-78, Springs 1-8; Indianapolis, L. Anderson 2-51, Smith 1-26.

Punt Returns—New York, Springs 3-49; Indianapolis, L. Anderson 2-7.

Interceptions—New York, Lynn 1-0; Indianapolis, Daniel 2-7.

Punting—New York, Ramsey 3-47.0; Indianapolis, Stark 5-47.0.

Field Goals—New York, Leahy 1-2 (missed: 43); Indianapolis, none attempted.

Sacks—New York, Gastineau 3, Bennett; Indianapolis, Winter.

Chargers-Vikings
SUNDAY, SEPTEMBER 2
SCORE BY PERIODS

San Diego	14	7	21	0—42
Minnesota	3	0	7	3—13

SCORING

San Diego—Chandler 20 pass from Fouts (Benirschke kick), 3:21 1st.
Minnesota—Field goal Stenerud 41, 7:14 1st.
San Diego—Chandler 17 pass from Fouts (Benirschke kick), 12:55 1st.
San Diego—Johnson 1 run (Benirschke kick), 14:30 2nd.
San Diego—Johnson 1 run (Benirschke kick), 2:33 3rd.
San Diego—Joiner 25 pass from Holohan (Benirschke kick), 5:41 3rd.
San Diego—Byrd 18 interception return (Benirschke kick), 7:28 3rd.
Minnesota—Browner 63 fumble recovery (Stenerud kick), 14:11 3rd.
Minnesota—Field goal Stenerud 52, 10:44 4th.

TEAM STATISTICS

	San Diego	Minnesota
First downs	27	12
Rushes-Yards	36-130	26-115
Passing yards	396	91
Sacked-Yards lost	0-0	4-13
Return yards	71	137
Passes	27-35-0	11-30-3
Punts	3-37.3	4-42.5
Fumbles-Lost	3-2	4-1
Penalties-Yards	10-118	4-38
Time of possession	32:11	27:49

Attendance—57,276. No-shows—4,645.

INDIVIDUAL STATISTICS

Rushing—San Diego, Muncie 14-51, Jackson 6-24, Johnson 9-25, McGee 2-8, Thomas 5-22; Minnesota, Brown 12-53, Darrin Nelson 4-16, Jones 2-2, Coleman 1-minus 2, Rice 4-29, Dave Nelson 1-3, Anderson 2-14.

Passing—San Diego, Fouts 21-28-0—292, Holohan 1-1-0—25, Luther 5-6-0—79; Minnesota, Kramer 11-30-3—104.

Receiving—San Diego, Winslow 4-33, Chandler 5-89, Sievers 4-33, Holohan 2-36, Joiner 3-52, Muncie 4-38, Duckworth 4-115, Johnson 1-0; Minnesota, Jordan 3-33, Darrin Nelson 1-7, LeCount 1-14, Rice 2-33, Brown 3-10, Anderson 1-7.

Kickoff Returns—San Diego, Jackson 1-10; Minnesota, Darrin Nelson 2-39, Anderson 3-66, Rice 2-21.

Punt Returns—San Diego, James 1-12; Minnesota, Darrin Nelson 1-11, Teal 1-0.

Interceptions—San Diego, Young 2-31, Byrd 1-18.

Punting—San Diego, Buford 3-37.3; Minnesota, Coleman 4-42.5.

Field Goals—San Diego, Benirschke 0-1 (missed: 28); Minnesota, Stenerud 2-2.

Sacks—San Diego, Ferguson 2, Ackerman, Robinson.

49ers-Lions
SUNDAY, SEPTEMBER 2
SCORE BY PERIODS

San Francisco	7	7	3	13—30
Detroit	7	6	7	7—27

SCORING

Detroit—Sims 2 run (Murray kick), 10:10 1st.
San Francisco—Monroe 5 pass from Montana (Wersching kick), 15:00 1st.
Detroit—Field goal Murray 39, 3:53 2nd.
San Francisco—Tyler 2 run (Wersching kick), 9:59 2nd.

Detroit—Field goal Murray 43, 14:57 2nd.
Detroit—J. Jones 2 pass from Danielson (Murray kick), 8:24 3rd.
San Francisco—Field goal Wersching 42, 14:10 3rd.
San Francisco—Field goal Wersching 53, 4:31 4th.
San Francisco—Tyler 9 run (Wersching kick), 6:35 4th.
Detroit—Thompson 49 pass from Danielson (Murray kick), 9:59 4th.
San Francisco—Field goal Wersching 22, 14:56 4th.

TEAM STATISTICS

	San Francisco	Detroit
First downs	24	19
Rushes-Yards	32-124	28-132
Passing yards	174	166
Sacked-Yards lost	2-14	2-11
Return yards	198	98
Passes	16-25-0	17-24-0
Punts	2-45.5	4-44.0
Fumbles-Lost	2-1	0-0
Penalties-Yards	2-32	6-45
Time of possession	30:44	29:16

Attendance—56,782. No-shows—3,352.

INDIVIDUAL STATISTICS

Rushing—San Francisco, Tyler 16-87, Craig 8-15, Ring 5-16, Monroe 2-6, Cooper 1-0; Detroit, Sims 17-69, J. Jones 8-31, Danielson 1-16, Nichols 1-13, Jenkins 1-3.

Passing—San Francisco, Montana 16-25-0—188; Detroit, Danielson 17-24-0—177.

Receiving—San Francisco, Solomon 4-61, Craig 3-32, Francis 2-33, Clark 2-19, Nehemiah 2-18, Cooper 1-11, Tyler 1-9; Detroit, J. Jones 5-25, Thompson 3-58, Chadwick 3-33, Nichols 2-34, Lewis 2-22, Sims 2-5.

Kickoff Returns—San Francisco, Monroe 4-93, McLemore 1-16, Ring 1-27; Detroit, Martin 3-57, Jenkins 2-33.

Punt Returns—San Francisco, McLemore 3-62; Detroit, Martin 1-8.

Punting—San Francisco, Orosz 2-45.5; Detroit, Black 4-44.0.

Field Goals—San Francisco, Wersching 3-3; Detroit, Murray 2-2.

Sacks—San Francisco, Tuiasosopo, Board; Detroit, Cofer, Green.

Browns-Seahawks
MONDAY, SEPTEMBER 3
SCORE BY PERIODS

Cleveland	0	0	0	0—	0
Seattle	7	13	13	0—	33

SCORING

Seattle—Tice 5 pass from Krieg (N. Johnson kick), 7:12 1st.
Seattle—Field goal N. Johnson 22, 8:35 2nd.
Seattle—Johns 7 pass from Krieg (N. Johnson kick), 11:47 2nd.
Seattle—Field goal N. Johnson 50, 14:36 2nd.
Seattle—Field goal N. Johnson 41, 8:48 3rd.
Seattle—Field goal N. Johnson 24, 9:25 3rd.
Seattle—Turner 34 pass from Krieg (N. Johnson kick), 12:41 3rd.

TEAM STATISTICS

	Cleveland	Seattle
First downs	10	20
Rushes-Yards	18-52	46-145
Passing yards	68	162
Sacked-Yards lost	7-48	2-17
Return yards	139	115
Passes	9-28-2	14-28-1
Punts	8-34.1	4-35.8
Fumbles-Lost	4-3	3-2
Penalties-Yards	6-39	5-67
Time of possession	23:57	36:03

Attendance—59,540. No-shows—5,366.

INDIVIDUAL STATISTICS

Rushing—Cleveland, Pruitt 15-43, Green 3-9; Seattle, Warner 10-40, Hughes 11-38, Dixon 15-36, Lane 1-15, Krieg 3-9, Bryant 2-4, Zorn 4-3.

Passing—Cleveland, McDonald 8-27-2—114, Flick 1-1-0—2; Seattle, Krieg 14-28-1—179.

Receiving—Cleveland, Feacher 3-35, Harris 2-45, Newsome 2-22, Holt 1-12, Green 1-2; Seattle, Johns 3-49, Metzelaars 3-46, Largent 2-17, Turner 1-34, Warner 1-19, Bryant 1-9, Tice 1-5, Dixon 1-0, Doornink 1-0.

Kickoff Returns—Cleveland, White 1-10, B. Davis 5-88, Byner 2-32; Seattle, Dixon 1-18.

Punt Returns—Cleveland, Brennan 1-9; Seattle, Johns 3-26, Easley 2-59.

Interceptions—Cleveland, L. Johnson 1-0; Seattle, Harris 1-12, Brown 1-0.

Punting—Cleveland, Cox 7-39.0; Seattle, West 4-35.8.

Field Goals—Cleveland, Bahr 0-1 (missed: 44); Seattle, N. Johnson 4-4.

Sacks—Cleveland, Puzzuoli, Hairston; Seattle, Green 3, Nash 2, J. Bryant, Fanning.

Cowboys-Rams
MONDAY, SEPTEMBER 3
SCORE BY PERIODS

Dallas	0	7	3	10—	20
Los Angeles Rams	13	0	0	0—	13

SCORING

Los Angeles—Dickerson 2 run (Lansford kick), 3:01 1st.
Los Angeles—Field goal Lansford 31, 9:35 1st.
Los Angeles—Field goal Lansford 36, 12:32 1st.
Dallas—Cosbie 19 pass from Hogeboom (Septien kick), 9:09 2nd.
Dallas—Field goal Septien 31, 8:59 3rd.
Dallas—Field goal Septien 52, 1:16 4th.
Dallas—Dorsett 7 run (Septien kick), 11:04 4th.

TEAM STATISTICS

	Dallas	Los Angeles
First downs	26	11
Rushes-Yards	34-115	24-137
Passing yards	321	67
Sacked-Yards lost	2-22	3-17
Return yards	60	134
Passes	33-47-1	11-34-5
Punts	5-34.6	5-40.0
Fumbles-Lost	6-4	0-0
Penalties-Yards	5-46	6-45
Time of possession	37:53	22:07

Attendance—65,403. No-shows—3,442.

INDIVIDUAL STATISTICS

Rushing—Dallas, Dorsett 25-81, Newsome 4-16, Springs 3-5, Hogeboom 2-13; Los Angeles, Dickerson 21-138, Ferragamo 3-minus 1.

Passing—Dallas, Hogeboom 33-47-1—343; Los Angeles, Ferragamo 11-33-4—84, Dickerson 0-1-1—0.

Receiving—Dallas, Dorsett 10-66, Donley 9-137, Cosbie 8-99, Hill 2-30, Springs 2-2, Phillips 1-6, Newsome 1-3; Los Angeles, Ellard 3-22, Grant 2-24, Dickerson 2-20, Farmer 2-10, David Hill 1-5, Guman 1-3.

Kickoff Returns—Dallas, Fellows 4-55; Los Angeles, Redden 2-44, Drew Hill 2-40.

Punt Returns—Dallas, Allen 3-3; Los Angeles, Ellard 4-27.

Interceptions—Dallas, Clinkscale 2-23, Hegman 1-0, Walls 1-12, Downs 1-22; Los Angeles, Green 1-23.

Punting—Dallas, Miller 5-34.6; Los Angeles, Misko 5-40.0.

Field Goals—Dallas, Septien 2-2; Los Angeles, Lansford 2-2.

Sacks—Dallas, Hegman, Jeffcoat, Jones; Los Angeles, Andrews, Meisner.

SECOND WEEK

RESULTS OF WEEK 2

Thursday, September 6

Pittsburgh 23, N.Y. Jets 17 at N.Y.

Sunday, September 9

Chicago 27, Denver 0 at Chi.
Detroit 27, Atlanta 24 (OT) at Atl.
Indianapolis 35, Houston 21 at Hous.
Kansas City 27, Cincinnati 22 at Cin.
L.A. Raiders 28, Green Bay 7 at L.A.
L.A. Rams 20, Cleveland 17 at L.A.
Miami 28, New England 7 at Mia.
New Orleans 17, Tampa Bay 13 at N.O.
N.Y. Giants 28, Dallas 7 at N.Y.
Philadelphia 19, Minnesota 17 at Phila.
St. Louis 37, Buffalo 7 at St. L.
Seattle 31, San Diego 17 at Sea.

Monday, September 10

San Francisco 37, Washington 31 at S.F.

Playing on a losing team year after year will wear down the patience of any NFL player.

Since New York Giants linebacker Harry Carson broke into the league as a fourth-round draft pick in 1976, the Giants had compiled a 40-76-1 record in eight seasons (prior to 1984). Finally, during the team's August training camp, Carson said enough is enough. He left camp without an explanation but returned three days later and explained that he simply was tired of losing. After the first two games of the 1984 season, Carson was singing a much different tune.

"They made me feel very proud of being next to them," said Carson of his Giants teammates after they had shocked the Dallas Cowboys, 28-7, enabling them to win their first two games at the start of the season for the first time since 1968. "We put it to them and this has to be one of the highlights of my Giants' career. They've been beating us ever since I've been here." For the record, the Cowboys had beaten the Giants in 12 of their 14 meetings since 1976.

But none of that mattered when the two teams took the field for this NFC Eastern Division clash. Phil Simms threw three touchdown passes and the New York defense, particularly linebacker Lawrence Taylor, forced the Cowboys into numerous turnovers and mistakes. Two of Simms' TD passes came 75 seconds apart late in the first quarter to give New York a 14-0 lead. But the game's biggest play occurred early in the second quarter.

With the Cowboys facing a third-and-three situation at the Giants' 6-yard line and trailing, 14-0, Dallas running backs Timmy Newsome and Ron Springs messed up their assignments, allowing Taylor to get an open shot at Cowboys quarterback Gary Hogeboom. The ball popped loose and Giants linebacker Andy Headen

Giants quarterback Phil Simms threw for three touchdowns in a surprisingly easy 28-7 triumph over Dallas in Week 2.

picked it up and rambled 81 yards for another New York touchdown.

"They (Newsome and Springs) got messed up," said Dallas Coach Tom Landry. "We interchanged them during the timeout, and Springs thought he was the fullback. He wasn't, tried to adjust and got caught in motion. But I don't think it mattered. It was a pretty good play by Lawrence Taylor."

Taylor made another good play later in the second quarter, sacking Hogeboom again and forcing another fumble. This time, Giants safety Terry Kinard recovered at the New York 5. The Cowboys turned the ball over four times.

But that total paled in comparison to the San Diego Chargers, who turned the ball over eight times in a 31-17 loss to Seattle. A 10-0 Chargers lead after one quarter was quickly erased by the turnovers and Seahawks quarterback Dave Krieg, who ran for two touchdowns and threw for another.

The game marked the Seattle debut of Franco Harris, who was signed as a free agent the preceding week. Harris, the NFL's No. 2 all-time leading rusher and an integral part of the Pittsburgh Steelers' four Super Bowl championship teams of the 1970s, became embroiled in a contract dispute with the Steelers and finally was waived. Seattle signed him when star running back Curt Warner was lost for the season in the Seahawks' opener against Cleveland. Harris rushed for 46 yards on 14 carries.

Another debut of sorts took place in the New Jersey Meadowlands when the New York Jets took on Pittsburgh in a Thursday night game. The game marked the Jets' first appearance at Giants Stadium as the host team after spending the previous 20 seasons at Shea Stadium in New York City. But the debut was not a happy one for the Jets or their fans as the Steelers won, 23-17, behind David Woodley's two touchdown passes and Gary Anderson's three field goals. The victory was Pittsburgh's eighth in as many games with the Jets.

In a game billed as a matchup of the two best cornerbacks and the two best wide receiver in the game, corners Mike Haynes and Lester Hayes of the Los Angeles Raiders came out on top in their duel with James Lofton and John Jefferson of the Packers. Jefferson caught only three passes and Lofton was shut out for only the third time in his seven-year NFL career as the Raiders rolled to an easy 28-7 triumph.

The Pack's slim chance to win disappeared on the game's sixth play from scrimmage as quarterback Lynn Dickey suffered a bruised back and was forced from the contest. His replacement, rookie Randy Wright from Wisconsin, had all kinds of trouble trying to move his club against the L.A. defense and was replaced in the final quarter by four-year man Rich Campbell.

The Denver Broncos also employed three quarterbacks in their game with the Chicago Bears and did even worse than Green Bay—the Broncos didn't score. Gary Kubiak, John Elway and Scott Stankavage all took their best shots against a tough Chicago defense and came up empty. The Bears cruised to a 27-0 victory as Walter Payton rushed for 179 yards and broke loose for the longest touchdown run of his career, a 72-yard jaunt, in the second quarter. Ironically, Payton's longest non-scoring run—76 yards—came against Denver in 1978. Payton also surpassed Jim Brown's NFL career combined yardage mark (rushing and receiving) and Bob Thomas' nine points enabled him to surpass George Blanda as the Bears' all-time leading scorer.

Mick Luckhurst became the Atlanta Falcons' all-time leader in points scored, but it was the points he didn't score that proved decisive in the Falcons' 27-24 overtime loss to the Detroit Lions. Luckhurst missed a 47-yard field goal attempt that could have won the game with 1:56 remaining in regulation. Given a reprieve, the Lions took the opening kickoff in the extra period and marched the length of the field. Eddie Murray's 48-yarder 5:06 into overtime gave Detroit the victory.

The Philadelphia Eagles' game with Minnesota didn't require an overtime, but it did come down to the final play of the game. On fourth down and goal from the Vikings' 1-yard line with seven seconds left, it appeared that Philadelphia running back Wilbert Montgomery was stopped behind the line of scrimmage. But crew chief John Grier flagged Vikings linebacker Robin Sendlein for a facemasking penalty. Given another chance, Eagles quarterback Ron Jaworski hit tight end John Spagnola for a game-winning touchdown. The 19-17 victory was only the Eagles' third in their last 14 games at Veterans Stadium.

One NFL club that never seems to have trouble winning at home is Miami. The Dolphins beat AFC Eastern Division-rival New England for the 17th straight time at the Orange Bowl, 28-7. The victory ran the Dolphins' record in regular-season games at the Orange Bowl to 83-17-1 in the 101 games since Don Shula took the reigns as Miami coach in 1970.

Dan Marino again was the key for the Dolphins, hooking up on touchdown passes with second-year receiver Mark Clayton on Miami's first two second-half possessions. Before the explosion, the Patriots had managed to hold the Dolphins to a 7-7 deadlock. The pivotal play came after Clayton's first TD catch when Pats wide receiver Cedric Jones fumbled at his own 16-yard line and his college roommate, linebacker Charles Bowser, recovered for Miami. Clayton scored again two plays after the fumble.

The Colts won their first NFL regular-season game as an Indianapolis-based franchise with a 35-21 triumph over the Houston Oilers at the Astrodome. Quarterback Mike Pagel led the assault with three touchdown passes and ran for a fourth. Houston's Earl Campbell ran for three touchdowns.

The Kansas City Chiefs captured their second straight road victory, beating Cincinnati, 27-22. Todd Blackledge threw for two touchdowns as the Chiefs topped their 1983 mark of one road victory.

The St. Louis Cardinals crushed Buffalo, 37-7, in the most lopsided game of the NFL's second weekend. Ottis Anderson's two touchdowns and Neil Lomax's two TD passes led the way as the Cardinals put the Bills away early by scoring on each of their first three possessions. Buffalo didn't penetrate into St. Louis territory until the second half.

In Los Angeles, the Rams' Eric Dickerson rushed six times for 48 yards in a game-winning drive that resulted in Mike Lansford's 27-yard field goal and a 20-17 L.A. victory over Cleveland. Dickerson finished with 102 yards on 27 carries. Ironically, the game was tied by the Rams earlier in the period when wide receiver Ron Brown, a member of the 1984 gold-medal U.S. Olympic 400-meter relay team, caught a five-yard pass from Vince Ferragamo for his first NFL touchdown. Brown had been drafted originally by the Browns in '83 and then traded to Los Angeles.

In New Orleans, the Saints' Hokie Gajan accounted for 64 yards of an 88-yard drive that led to his team's 17-13 triumph over Tampa Bay. Gajan took a seven-yard swing pass from quarterback Richard Todd and turned it upfield for a 51-yard gain. Gajan then ran for five yards on first down before taking it the final eight yards with 1:53 left to play.

In the Monday night game, San Francisco quarterback Joe Montana completed 24 of 40 passes for 381 yards and two touchdowns and ran for another as the 49ers upended Washington, 37-31. The Redskins were held to just four first downs in the opening half as San Francisco built a 27-3 lead at intermission.

Washington rebounded by scoring on four of its first six possessions of the second half, but could pull no closer than six points.

Steelers-Jets
THURSDAY, SEPTEMBER 6
SCORE BY PERIODS

Pittsburgh	7	6	7	3—23
New York Jets	0	7	10	0—17

SCORING

Pittsburgh—Lipps 6 pass from Woodley (Anderson kick), 13:00 1st.
New York—Walker 14 pass from Ryan (Leahy kick), 4:09 2nd.
Pittsburgh—Field goal Anderson 32, 8:32 2nd.
Pittsburgh—Field goal Anderson 43, 14:08 2nd.
New York—Humphrey 97 kickoff return (Leahy kick), 0:15 3rd.
Pittsburgh—Thompson 3 pass from Woodley (Anderson kick), 2:26 3rd.
New York—Field goal Leahy 52, 9:58 3rd.
Pittsburgh—Field goal Anderson 37, 1:46 4th.

TEAM STATISTICS

	Pittsburgh	New York
First downs	19	11
Rushes-Yards	40-121	21-77
Passing yards	172	99
Sacked-Yards lost	2-15	4-27
Return yards	139	209
Passes	14-25-1	11-27-3
Punts	3-37.3	6-37.0
Fumbles-Lost	2-1	2-1
Penalties-Yards	5-50	10-115
Time of possession	37:43	22:17
Attendance—70,564. No-shows—6,327.		

INDIVIDUAL STATISTICS

Rushing—Pittsburgh, Erenberg 15-60, Pollard 17-36, Abercrombie 7-18, Woodley 1-7; New York, McNeil 12-30, Barber 4-24, Hector 3-17, Ryan 2-6.

Passing—Pittsburgh, Woodley 14-25-1—187; New York, Ryan 11-27-3—126.
Receiving—Pittsburgh, Lipps 4-77, Stallworth 3-30, Pollard 3-18, Thompson 2-16, Cunningham 1-29, Erenberg 1-17; New York, Shuler 3-31, Minter 2-14, Walker 2-33, Sohn 1-12, Gaffney 2-31, Hector 1-5.
Kickoff Returns—Pittsburgh, Erenberg 4-66; New York, Humphery 4-153, Springs 1-19, Minter 1-17.
Punt Returns—Pittsburgh, Lipps 4-48, Long 1-0; New York, Bruckner 1-20.
Interceptions—Pittsburgh, Washington 2-55, Woods 1-0; New York, Buttle 1-0.
Punting—Pittsburgh, Colquitt 3-37.3; New York, Ramsey 6-37.0.
Field Goals—Pittsburgh, Anderson 3-6 (missed: 32, 43, 27); New York, Leahy 1-1.
Sacks—Pittsburgh, Little, Merriweather, Nelson, Willis; New York, Gastineau 2.

Broncos-Bears
SUNDAY, SEPTEMBER 9
SCORE BY PERIODS

Denver	0	0	0	0— 0
Chicago	10	17	0	0—27

SCORING

Chicago—Field goal B. Thomas 38, 4:55 1st.
Chicago—Gault 61 pass from McMahon (B. Thomas kick), 11:47 1st.
Chicago—Payton 72 run (B. Thomas kick), 5:11 2nd.
Chicago—Field goal B. Thomas 26, 12:17 2nd.
Chicago—Suhey 4 run (B. Thomas kick), 14:36 2nd.

TEAM STATISTICS

	Denver	Chicago
First downs	8	15
Rushes-Yards	22-53	50-302
Passing yards	77	104
Sacked-Yards lost	3-32	1-8
Return yards	126	127
Passes	9-27-2	10-17-1
Punts	9-39.6	5-39.6
Fumbles-Lost	5-2	2-2
Penalties-Yards	3-17	9-65
Time of possession	23:54	36:06
Attendance—54,335. No-shows—7,023.		

INDIVIDUAL STATISTICS

Rushing—Denver, Willhite 12-32, Winder 7-16, Lang 1-6, Elway 1-0, Parros 1-minus 1; Chicago, Suhey 12-59, Payton 20-179, McMahon 2-8, Gentry 3-8, C. Thomas 4-21, Hutchinson 7-25, Jordan 2-2.
Passing—Denver, Kubiak 3-6-1—40, Elway 2-3-0—53, Stankavage 4-18-1—16; Chicago, MaMahon 5-8-0—93, Avellini 5-9-1—19.
Receiving—Denver, Sawyer 1-17, Johnson 1-16, Watson 2-21, Lang 1-4, Sampson 1-7, Willhite 1-14, Summers 2-30; Chicago, McKinnon 1-17, Payton 2-7, Gault 1-61, Suhey 2-9, Moorehead 1-6, Baschnagel 2-minus 1, Gentry 1-13.
Kickoff Returns—Denver, Thomas 3-65, Lang 3-34; Chicago, Gentry 1-20.
Punt Returns—Denver, Thomas 4-27; Chicago, Fisher 4-65.
Interceptions—Denver, Foley 1-0; Chicago, Frazier 2-42.
Punting—Denver, Norman 9-39.0; Chicago, Finzer 5-39.6.
Field Goals—Denver, Karlis 0-1 (missed: 50); Chicago, B. Thomas 2-2.
Sacks—Denver, Ryan; Chicago, Bell, Keys, Wilson.

Lions-Falcons
SUNDAY, SEPTEMBER 9
SCORE BY PERIODS

Detroit	10	7	7	3—27
Atlanta	0	10	7	7	0—24

SCORING

Detroit—Sims 9 run (Murray kick), 5:14 1st.

Detroit—Field goal Murray 46, 9:52 1st.

Detroit—Lewis 11 pass from Danielson (Murray kick), 4:13 2nd.

Atlanta—Riggs 1 run (Luckhurst kick), 10:32 2nd.

Atlanta—Field goal Luckhurst 51, 15:00 2nd.

Atlanta—B. Johnson 45 pass from Bartkowski (Luckhurst kick), 5:08 3rd.

Detroit—Thompson 11 pass from Danielson (Murray kick), 10:50 3rd.

Atlanta—Bailey 29 pass from Bartkowski (Luckhurst kick), 0:05 4th.

Detroit—Field goal Murray 48, 5:06 OT.

TEAM STATISTICS

	Detroit	Atlanta
First downs	28	22
Rushes-Yards	42-208	25-91
Passing yards	241	289
Sacked-Yards lost	1-9	1-10
Return yards	67	100
Passes	21-32-0	24-28-0
Punts	3-50.0	4-40.0
Fumbles-Lost	1-0	0-0
Penalties-Yards	10-74	10-71
Time of possession	39:50	25:16

Attendance—49,878. No-shows—5,851.

INDIVIDUAL STATISTICS

Rushing—Detroit, Sims 23-140, Jones 15-50, Jenkins 3-11, Nichols 1-7; Atlanta, Riggs 19-78, Cain 5-15, Bartkowski 1-minus 2.

Passing—Detroit, Danielson 21-32-0—250; Atlanta, Bartkowski 24-28-0—299.

Receiving—Detroit, Jones 5-44, Lewis 4-68, Nichols 3-51, Chadwick 3-35, Thompson 2-30, Jenkins 1-6, Rubick 1-6, Sims 1-5, Martin 1-5; Atlanta, B. Johnson 8-116, A. Jackson 6-63, Cox 5-58, Bailey 3-43, Riggs 1-11, Benson 1-8.

Kickoff Returns—Detroit, Jenkins 2-56; Atlanta, Curran 5-98.

Punt Returns—Detroit, Martin 2-11; Atlanta, B. Johnson 1-2.

Punting—Detroit, Black 3-50.0; Atlanta, Giacomarro 4-40.0.

Field Goals—Detroit, Murray 2-4 (missed: 46, 55); Atlanta, Luckhurst 1-2 (missed: 47).

Sacks—Detroit, Gay; Atlanta, Frye.

Colts-Oilers
SUNDAY, SEPTEMBER 9
SCORE BY PERIODS

Indianapolis	0	21	7	7—35
Houston	7	7	0	7—21

SCORING

Houston—Campbell 2 run (Kempf kick), 7:19 1st.

Indianapolis—Pagel 1 run (Biasucci kick), 2:07 2nd.

Houston—Campbell 15 run (Kempf kick), 6:20 2nd.

Indianapolis—Dickey 9 run (Biasucci kick), 9:05 2nd.

Indianapolis—Butler 31 pass from Pagel (Biasucci kick), 13:48 2nd.

Indianapolis—Butler 14 pass from Pagel (Biasucci kick), 9:13 3rd.

Houston—Campbell 1 run (Kempf kick), 4:08 4th.

Indianapolis—Porter 33 pass from Pagel (Biasucci kick), 9:02 4th.

TEAM STATISTICS

	Indianapolis	Houston
First downs	24	24
Rushes-Yards	48-168	20-72
Passing yards	215	343
Sacked-Yards lost	0-0	4-22
Return yards	79	75

	Indianapolis	Houston
Passes	15-20-0	23-43-0
Punts	5-38.8	6-37.2
Fumbles-Lost	0-0	2-1
Penalties-Yards	6-58	7-77
Time of possession	31:47	28:13

Attendance—43,820. No-shows—3,508.

INDIVIDUAL STATISTICS

Rushing—Indianapolis, Dickey 22-84, McMillan 14-46, Pagel 7-26, Moore 2-6, Wonsley 3-6; Houston, Campbell 15-44, Moon 2-8, Moriarty 3-20.

Passing—Indianapolis, Pagel 15-20-0—215; Houston, Moon 23-43-0—365.

Receiving—Indianapolis, Porter 6-91, Butler 5-74, Dickey 2-27, Wonsley 1-17, McMillan 1-6; Houston, Holston 7-98, Smith 6-102, Williams 3-63, Bryant 3-51, Dressel 2-18, McCloskey 2-33.

Kickoff Returns—Indianapolis, Anderson 2-30, Hathaway 1-2, Middleton 1-11; Houston, Allen 2-43, Roaches 1-25.

Punt Returns—Indianapolis, Anderson 4-36; Houston, Roaches 2-7.

Punting—Indianapolis, Stark 5-38.8; Houston, James 6-37.2.

Field Goals—Indianapolis, none attempted; Houston, none attempted.

Sacks—Indianapolis, Winter, Cooks, Bracelin, Maxwell.

Chiefs-Bengals
SUNDAY, SEPTEMBER 9
SCORE BY PERIODS

Kansas City	7	7	10	3—27
Cincinnati	0	14	3	5—22

SCORING

Kansas City—Brown 5 run (Lowery kick), 4:20 1st.

Kansas City—Hancock 46 pass from Blackledge (Lowery kick), 2:04 2nd.

Cincinnati—Horton 48 interception return (Breech kick), 3:58 2nd.

Cincinnati—Alexander 2 run (Breech kick), 8:38 2nd.

Cincinnati—Field goal Breech 48, 5:55 3rd.

Kansas City—Carson 19 pass from Blackledge (Lowery kick), 9:29 3rd.

Kansas City—Field goal Lowery 52, 10:05 3rd.

Cincinnati—Safety, Blackledge fumbled out of end zone, 4:07 4th.

Cincinnati—Field goal Breech 29, 9:50 4th.

Kansas City—Field goal Lowery 40, 13:10 4th.

TEAM STATISTICS

	Kansas City	Cincinnati
First downs	17	22
Rushes-Yards	22-74	32-127
Passing yards	249	275
Sacked-Yards lost	3-31	5-35
Return yards	119	165
Passes	18-35-1	24-37-0
Punts	5-46.6	6-44.8
Fumbles-Lost	3-1	2-2
Penalties-Yards	7-60	5-45
Time of possession	26:27	33:33

Attendance—47,111. No-shows—3,695.

INDIVIDUAL STATISTICS

Rushing—Kansas City, Brown 14-48, B. Jackson 4-12, Heard 1-2, Blackledge 3-12; Cincinnati, Brooks 5-11, Alexander 11-46, Kinnebrew 3-15, Jennings 8-43, Farley 4-7, Anderson 1-5.

Passing—Kansas City, Blackledge 18-35-1—280; Cincinnati, Anderson 24-37-0—310.

Receiving—Kansas City, Brown 3-14, Paige 3-60, Hancock 3-109, Scott 5-42, Carson 2-26, Marshall 1-23, B. Jackson 1-6; Cincinnati, Collinsworth 5-96, Alexander 3-48, Brooks 3-28, Harris 2-40, Jennings 4-17, Kinnebrew

1-4, Farley 1-10, Kreider 4-54, Curtis 1-13.

Kickoff Returns—Kansas City, Paige 3-60, Ricks 2-39; Cincinnati, Verser 2-35, Martin 2-33, Jennings 2-33.

Punt Returns—Kansas City, Smith 3-20; Cincinnati, Simmons 3-13, Martin 1-3.

Interceptions—Cincinnati, Horton 1-48.

Punting—Kansas City, Arnold 5-46.6; Cincinnati, McInally 6-44.8.

Field Goals—Kansas City, Lowery 2-2; Cincinnati, Breech 2-3 (missed: 55).

Sacks—Kansas City, Bell 2½, Still 2½; Cincinnati, R. Williams, Edwards, Frazier.

Packers-Raiders
SUNDAY, SEPTEMBER 9
SCORE BY PERIODS

Green Bay	0	7	0	0— 7
Los Angeles Raiders	7	0	7	14—28

SCORING

Los Angeles—Christensen 3 pass from Plunkett (Bahr kick), 11:47 1st.

Green Bay—West 7 pass from Wright (Garcia kick), 14:03 2nd.

Los Angeles—Hawkins 1 run (Bahr kick), 4:09 3rd.

Los Angeles—Allen 7 run (Bahr kick), 1:38 4th.

Los Angeles—Jensen 1 run (Bahr kick), 14:19 4th.

TEAM STATISTICS

	Green Bay	Los Angeles
First downs	15	18
Rushes-Yards	24-115	32-121
Passing yards	94	112
Sacked-Yards lost	5-41	5-42
Return yards	98	136
Passes	17-38-2	14-22-1
Punts	9-45.6	8-47.0
Fumbles-Lost	0-0	2-1
Penalties-Yards	9-68	8-48
Time of possession	30:00	30:00

Attendance—46,269. No-shows—7,788.

INDIVIDUAL STATISTICS

Rushing—Green Bay, Ellis 11-54, Clark 9-33, Lofton 1-17, Huckleby 2-8, Crouse 1-3; Los Angeles, Allen 20-81, King 3-22, Hawkins 5-8, Plunkett 1-7, Jensen 3-3.

Passing—Green Bay, Wright 10-24-0—67, Campbell 4-8-2—37, Dickey 2-5-0—14, Ellis 1-1-0—17; Los Angeles, Plunkett 14-22-1—154.

Receiving—Green Bay, Childs 4-32, Ellis 3-21, Jefferson 3-19, Huckleby 2-23, Rodgers 2-19, Clark 2-14, West 1-7; Los Angeles, Branch 5-60, Barnwell 3-54, Christensen 3-27, Allen 3-13.

Kickoff Returns—Green Bay, Huckleby 3-46, Rodgers 2-36; Los Angeles, Williams 2-51.

Punt Returns—Green Bay, Epps 3-16; Los Angeles, Pruitt 6-59.

Interceptions—Green Bay, T. Lewis 1-0; Los Angeles, McElroy 1-11, Barnes 1-15.

Punting—Green Bay, Scribner 9-45.6; Los Angeles, Guy 8-47.0.

Field Goals—Green Bay, none attempted; Los Angeles, none attempted.

Sacks—Green Bay, Carreker, Douglass, Anderson, T. Jones, Brown; Los Angeles, Alzado 1½, Martin, Pickel, Long, M. Davis ½.

Browns-Rams
SUNDAY, SEPTEMBER 9
SCORE BY PERIODS

Cleveland	7	3	7	0—17
Los Angeles Rams	7	3	0	10—20

SCORING

Los Angeles—Irvin 81 interception return (Lansford kick), 9:29 1st.

Cleveland—Pruitt 6 run (Bahr kick), 12:07 1st.

Los Angeles—Field goal Lansford 37, 3:31 2nd.

Cleveland—Field goal Bahr 25, 14:32 2nd.

Cleveland—Newsome 4 pass from McDonald (Bahr kick), 13:54 3rd.

Los Angeles—Brown 5 pass from Ferragamo (Lansford kick), 4:14 4th.

Los Angeles—Field goal Lansford 27, 13:35 4th.

TEAM STATISTICS

	Cleveland	Los Angeles
First downs	16	14
Rushes-Yards	30-82	33-136
Passing yards	251	90
Sacked-Yards lost	2-12	2-11
Return yards	99	217
Passes	18-35-1	12-20-2
Punts	6-42.5	4-42.5
Fumbles-Lost	1-1	1-1
Penalties-Yards	8-55	6-44
Time of possession	31:30	28:30

Attendance—43,043. No-shows—9,459.

INDIVIDUAL STATISTICS

Rushing—Cleveland, Pruitt 27-78, Green 2-2, McDonald 1-2; Los Angeles, Dickerson 27-102, Crutchfield 5-30, Ellard 1-4.

Passing—Cleveland, McDonald 18-35-1—263; Los Angeles, Ferragamo 12-20-2—101.

Receiving—Cleveland, Newsome 8-65, Brennan 5-75, Feacher 1-64, Harris 2-50, Pruitt 2-9; Los Angeles, David Hill 2-23, Ellard 2-21, Brown 2-11, Dickerson 2-9, Drew Hill 1-11, Guman 1-11, J. McDonald 1-8, Farmer 1-7.

Kickoff Returns—Cleveland, Brown 5-74; Los Angeles, Drew Hill 3-77.

Punt Returns—Cleveland, Brennan 3-15; Los Angeles, Ellard 4-59.

Interceptions—Cleveland, Dixon 1-1, Cousineau 1-9; Los Angeles, Irvin 1-81.

Punting—Cleveland, Cox 6-42.5; Los Angeles, Misko 4-42.5.

Field Goals—Cleveland, Bahr 1-2 (missed: 46); Los Angeles, Lansford 2-2.

Sacks—Cleveland, Baldwin, Camp; Los Angeles, Youngblood 2.

Patriots-Dolphins
SUNDAY, SEPTEMBER 9
SCORE BY PERIODS

New England	0	7	0	0— 7
Miami	0	7	14	7—28

SCORING

Miami—Duper 35 pass from Jensen (von Schamann kick), 8:23 2nd.

New England—Dawson 9 pass from Grogan (Franklin kick), 14:04 2nd.

Miami—Clayton 38 pass from Marino (von Schamann kick), 2:22 3rd.

Miami—Clayton 15 pass from Marino (von Schamann kick), 3:58 3rd.

Miami—Judson 60 run with lateraled interception (von Schamann kick), 12:07 4th.

TEAM STATISTICS

	New England	Miami
First downs	18	17
Rushes-Yards	28-127	30-74
Passing yards	205	269
Sacked-Yards lost	2-12	0-0
Return yards	66	158
Passes	20-42-4	17-28-2
Punts	8-39.6	5-41.6
Fumbles-Lost	2-1	0-0
Penalties-Yards	6-53	6-46
Time of possession	30:46	29:14

Attendance—66,083. No-shows—1,760.

INDIVIDUAL STATISTICS

Rushing—New England, Collins 20-87, Tatupu 3-17, Grogan 3-16, C. James 2-7; Miami, Nathan 10-36, Franklin 7-26, Bennett 10-13, Marino 3-minus 1.

Passing—New England, Grogan 20-42-4—217; Miami, Marino 16-27-2—234, Jensen 1-1-0—35.

Receiving—New England, Ramsey 5-70, Dawson 4-35, Jones 3-39, Collins 3-13, Starring 2-29, Fryar 1-22, Tatupu 1-2, C. James 1-7; Miami, Clayton 5-75, Duper 4-66, Johnson 3-47, Nathan 2-24, Rose 1-22, Hardy 1-18, Moore 1-17.

Kickoff Returns—New England, J. Williams 3-49; Miami, Heflin 2-15.

Punt Returns—New England, Fryar 2-14; Miami, Clayton 3-23.

Interceptions—New England, Blackmon 1-3, R. James 1-0; Miami, Blackwood 2-27, Judson (with lateral) 0-60, Kozlowski 1-26, McNeal 1-7.

Punting—New England, Prestridge 8-39.6; Miami, Roby 5-41.6.

Field Goals—New England, none attempted; Miami, von Schamann 0-2 (missed: 39, 42).

Sacks—Miami, Rhone, Betters.

Buccaneers-Saints
SUNDAY, SEPTEMBER 9
SCORE BY PERIODS

Tampa Bay	7	3	3	0—13	
New Orleans	0	7	3	7—17	

SCORING

Tampa Bay—Armstrong 2 pass from Thompson (Ariri kick), 13:29 1st.
New Orleans—Anthony 2 run (Andersen kick), 9:28 2nd.
Tampa Bay—Field goal Ariri 48, 14:50 2nd.
Tampa Bay—Field goal Ariri 40, 3:16 3rd.
New Orleans—Field goal Andersen 23, 14:11 3rd.
New Orleans—Gajan 8 run (Andersen kick), 13:07 4th.

TEAM STATISTICS

	Tampa Bay	New Orleans
First downs	20	17
Rushes-Yards	37-130	29-130
Passing yards	134	203
Sacked-Yards lost	7-41	1-10
Return yards	95	116
Passes	15-22-0	13-23-0
Punts	4-43.8	3-41.0
Fumbles-Lost	3-0	0-0
Penalties-Yards	7-56	10-89
Time of possession	34:22	25:38

Attendance—54,686. No-shows—5,305.

INDIVIDUAL STATISTICS

Rushing—Tampa Bay, Wilder 21-75, Thompson 4-22, Carver 6-20, Armstrong 3-11, Owens 1-1, Morton 1-minus 2, DeBerg 1-3; New Orleans, G. Rogers 18-56, Gajan 6-42, Anthony 2-21, Todd 3-11.

Passing—Tampa Bay, Thompson 15-22-0—175; New Orleans, Todd 13-23-0—213.

Receiving—Tampa Bay, T. Bell 3-52, Armstrong 4-41, House 3-34, Giles 2-18, Wilder 2-17, Carter 1-13; New Orleans, Gajan 4-75, Groth 3-46, Scott 2-39, Young 2-36, Brenner 1-12, Duckett 1-5.

Kickoff Returns—Tampa Bay, Owens 1-33, Morton 2-54; New Orleans, Duckett 2-34, Fields 2-68.

Punt Returns—Tampa Bay, T. Bell 1-8; New Orleans, Fields 1-14.

Punting—Tampa Bay, Garcia 4-43.8; New Orleans, Hansen 3-41.0.

Field Goals—Tampa Bay, Ariri 2-2; New Orleans, Andersen 1-1.

Sacks—Tampa Bay, Green; New Orleans, Clark 3, Jackson 2, Paul, Geathers.

Cowboys-Giants
SUNDAY, SEPTEMBER 9
SCORE BY PERIODS

Dallas	0	0	7	0— 7	
New York Giants	14	7	7	0—28	

SCORING

New York—B. Williams 62 pass from Simms (Haji-Sheikh kick), 13:27 1st.
New York—Manuel 16 pass from Simms (Haji-Sheikh kick), 14:42 1st.
New York—Headen 81 fumble return (Haji-Sheikh kick), 5:45 2nd.
New York—Mowatt 18 pass from Simms (Haji-Sheikh kick), 0:16 3rd.
Dallas—Cosbie 2 pass from Hogeboom (Septien kick), 6:12 3rd.

TEAM STATISTICS

	Dallas	New York
First downs	23	15
Rushes-Yards	24-138	37-120
Passing yards	206	164
Sacked-Yards lost	5-36	2-21
Return yards	127	59
Passes	21-43-1	10-20-0
Punts	8-39.3	9-41.0
Fumbles-Lost	3-3	2-1
Penalties-Yards	7-61	5-44
Time of possession	27:36	32:24

Attendance—75,921. No-shows—917.

INDIVIDUAL STATISTICS

Rushing—Dallas, Dorsett 15-95, Springs 5-14, Newsome 4-29; New York, Woolfolk 2-minus 1, Carpenter 22-87, Simms 1-0, Morris 10-15, Manuel 1-11, Galbreath 1-8.

Passing—Dallas, Hogeboom 21-43-1—242; New York, Simms 10-20-0—185.

Receiving—Dallas, Dorsett 2-12, Cosbie 2-13, Springs 7-59, Newsome 3-50, Renfro 4-78, Donley 3-30; New York, Woolfolk 1-3, Gray 2-20, Mowatt 3-47, B. Williams 2-72, Manuel 1-16, Johnson 1-27.

Kickoff Returns—Dallas, Fellows 2-39, Allen 2-29; New York, Woolfolk 1-21.

Punt Returns—Dallas, Allen 7-59; New York, McConkey, 5-9.

Interceptions—New York, Kinard 1-29.

Punting—Dallas, D. White 8-39.3; New York, Jennings 9-41.0.

Field Goals—Dallas, none attempted; New York, none attempted.

Sacks—Dallas, R. White, Jeffcoat; New York, Taylor 3, Merrill ½, Burt ½, Martin ½, Marshall ½.

Vikings-Eagles
SUNDAY, SEPTEMBER 9
SCORE BY PERIODS

Minnesota	3	0	0	14—17	
Philadelphia	3	6	3	7—19	

SCORING

Minnesota—Field goal Stenerud 38, 7:01 1st.
Philadelphia—Field goal McFadden 27, 11:03 1st.
Philadelphia—Field goal McFadden 37, 13:14 2nd.
Philadelphia—Field goal McFadden 49, 14:59 2nd.
Philadelphia—Field goal McFadden 37, 12:28 3rd.
Minnesota—Kramer 20 pass from Anderson (Stenerud kick), 1:28 4th.
Minnesota—Anderson 1 run (Stenerud kick), 3:11 4th.
Philadelphia—Spagnola 1 pass from Jaworski (McFadden kick), 14:58 4th.

TEAM STATISTICS

	Minnesota	Philadelphia
First downs	14	21

	Minnesota	Philadelphia
Rushes-Yards	28-118	33-152
Passing yards	113	224
Sacked-Yards lost	1-8	2-16
Return yards	56	102
Passes	12-21-1	27-37-0
Punts	6-41.8	4-36.0
Fumbles-Lost	2-0	2-2
Penalties-Yards	10-90	6-58
Time of possession	24:52	35:08

Attendance—55,942. No-shows—4,225.

INDIVIDUAL STATISTICS

Rushing—Minnesota, Anderson 20-105, Rice 3-13, Brown 3-10, Kramer 1-0, Collins 1-minus 10; Philadelphia, Montgomery 19-98, Oliver 6-26, Haddix 3-10, Hardy 4-10, Jaworski 1-8.

Passing—Minnesota, Kramer 11-20-1—101, Anderson 1-1-0—20; Philadelphia, Jaworski 27-37-0—240.

Receiving—Minnesota, Jordan 2-27, Lewis 2-26, Rice 2-17, Kramer 1-20, White 1-17, Brown 1-5, Anderson 2-2, Jones 1-7; Philadelphia, Spagnola, 8-62, Haddix 5-45, Jackson 4-36, Montgomery 4-31, Hardy 2-22, Oliver 2-15, Woodruff 1-12, Hoover 1-17.

Kickoff Returns—Minnesota, Nelson 1-0, Bess 3-47; Philadelphia, Hayes 2-43, Waters 1-17.

Punt Returns—Minnesota, Bess 2-9; Philadelphia, Cooper 2-14.

Interceptions—Philadelphia, Wilson 1-28.

Punting—Minnesota, Coleman 6-41.8; Philadelphia, Horan 4-36.0.

Field Goals—Minnesota, Stenerud 1-1; Philadelphia, McFadden 4-4.

Sacks—Minnesota, Mullaney, Cobb; Philadelphia, Clarke ½, Brown ½.

Bills-Cardinals
SUNDAY, SEPTEMBER 9
SCORE BY PERIODS

Buffalo	0	0	7	0—	7
St. Louis	17	7	7	6—	37

SCORING

St. Louis—Field goal O'Donoghue 23, 4:50 1st.
St. Louis—Green 4 pass from Lomax (O'Donoghue kick), 7:37 1st.
St. Louis—Anderson 4 pass from Lomax (O'Donoghue kick), 13:26 1st.
St. Louis—Anderson 2 run (O'Donoghue kick), 14:11 2nd.
St. Louis—Mitchell 1 run (O'Donoghue kick), 7:04 3rd.
Buffalo—Dennard 22 pass from Ferguson (Danelo kick), 12:08 3rd.
St. Louis—Field goal O'Donoghue 21, 2:32 4th.
St. Louis—Field goal O'Donoghue 52, 12:08 4th.

TEAM STATISTICS

	Buffalo	St. Louis
First downs	9	28
Rushes-Yards	8-54	46-221
Passing yards	117	265
Sacked-Yards lost	4-31	0-0
Return yards	141	137
Passes	13-32-3	21-33-0
Punts	6-35.8	1-36.0
Fumbles-Lost	0-0	0-0
Penalties-Yards	7-42	7-55
Time of possession	17:17	42:43

Attendance—35,785. No-shows—2,727.

INDIVIDUAL STATISTICS

Rushing—Buffalo, Kofler 2-30, Ferguson 1-15, V. Williams 1-6, Bell 4-3; St. Louis, Anderson 20-83, Mitchell 11-62, Love 6-34, Ferrell 5-31, Lomax 1-6, McIvor 3-5.

Passing—Buffalo, Ferguson 12-21-2—144, Kofler 1-11-1—4; St. Louis, Lomax 21-29-0—265, McIvor 0-4-0—0.

Receiving—Buffalo, Hunter 4-50, Dawkins 2-47, Dennard 1-22, Franklin 2-9, Brookins 2-8, Moore 1-6, V. Wil-

liams 1-6; St. Louis, Tilley 5-79, Marsh 3-72, Green 3-51, Mack 2-31, Anderson 5-15, Harrell 1-9, Ferrell 2-8.

Kickoff Returns—Buffalo, Wilson 5-87, V. Williams 3-54; St. Louis, Mitchell 1-39, Harrell 1-17.

Punt Returns—St. Louis, Mitchell 4-63.

Interceptions—St. Louis, W. Smith 1-0, Washington 2-18.

Punting—Buffalo, Kidd 6-35.8; St. Louis, Birdsong 1-36.0.

Field Goals—Buffalo, Danelo 0-1 (missed: 52); St. Louis, O'Donoghue 3-6 (missed: 47, 47, 53).

Sacks—St. Louis, A. Baker, Duda, Greer, Mays.

Chargers-Seahawks
SUNDAY, SEPTEMBER 9
SCORE BY PERIODS

San Diego	10	0	0	7—	17
Seattle	0	10	7	14—	31

SCORING

San Diego—Field goal Benirschke 43, 4:04 1st.
San Diego—Duckworth 61 pass from Fouts (Benirschke kick), 10:30 1st.
Seattle—Lane 1 run (N. Johnson kick), 3:26 2nd.
Seattle—Field goal N. Johnson 41, 14:58 2nd.
Seattle—Krieg 37 run (N. Johnson kick), 6:43 3rd.
Seattle—Krieg 3 run (N. Johnson kick), 0:50 4th.
Seattle—Turner 22 pass from Krieg (N. Johnson kick), 10:26 4th.
San Diego—Sievers 4 pass from Fouts (Benirschke kick), 14:36 4th.

TEAM STATISTICS

	San Diego	Seattle
First downs	21	21
Rushes-Yards	21-97	43-173
Passing yards	318	257
Sacked-Yards lost	2-14	1-6
Return yards	104	105
Passes	23-40-4	18-38-1
Punts	4-34.8	8-39.9
Fumbles-Lost	4-4	1-1
Penalties-Yards	4-16	11-80
Time of possession	24:01	35:59

Attendance—61,314. No-shows—3,592.

INDIVIDUAL STATISTICS

Rushing—San Diego, Jackson 16-89, P. Johnson 4-6, Fouts 1-2; Seattle, Krieg 6-61, F. Harris 14-46, Lane 10-36, Hughes 10-23, C. Bryant 2-6, Doornink 1-1.

Passing—San Diego, Fouts 23-40-4—332; Seattle, Krieg 18-38-1—263.

Receiving—San Diego, Chandler 7-55, Holohan 6-133, Joiner 4-43, Sievers 3-29, Duckworth 1-61, P. Johnson 1-7, Jackson 1-4; Seattle, C. Young 5-51, Johns 5-48, Turner 3-97, Tice 2-35, Largent 2-27, Doornink 1-5.

Kickoff Returns—San Diego, James 4-78, Gofourth 1-0; Seattle, Hughes 2-41, C. Bryant 1-20.

Punt Returns—San Diego, James 3-11; Seattle, Johns 1-13.

Interceptions—San Diego, King 1-15; Seattle, J. Harris 2-26, Brown 1-4, J. Bryant 1-1.

Punting—San Diego, Buford 4-34.8; Seattle, West 8-39.9.

Field Goals—San Diego, Benirschke 1-1; Seattle, N. Johnson 1-2 (missed: 53).

Sacks—San Diego, Ferguson; Seattle, J. Bryant, Nash.

Redskins-49ers
MONDAY, SEPTEMBER 10
SCORE BY PERIODS

Washington	0	3	14	14—	31
San Francisco	14	13	0	10—	37

SCORING

San Francisco—Tyler 7 run (Wersching kick), 2:59 1st.

Running back Wendell Tyler accounted for San Francisco's first two touchdowns in a 37-31 victory over Washington in Week 2's Monday night game.

San Francisco—Tyler 5 pass from Montana (Wersching kick), 4:18 1st.
San Francisco—Field goal Wersching 19, 3:52 2nd.
San Francisco—Field goal Wersching 46, 10:55 2nd.
San Francisco—D. Clark 15 pass from Montana (Wersching kick), 11:36 2nd.
Washington—Field goal Moseley 38, 13:49 2nd.
Washington—Brown 14 pass from Theismann (Moseley kick), 3:16 3rd.
Washington—Riggins 1 run (Moseley kick), 13:58 3rd.
San Francisco—Montana 7 run (Wersching kick), 9:45 4th.
Washington—Riggins 1 run (Moseley kick), 11:51 4th.
San Francisco—Field goal Wersching 38, 13:07 4th.
Washington—Seay 12 pass from Theismann (Moseley kick), 14:45 4th.

TEAM STATISTICS

	Washington	San Francisco
First downs	20	30
Rushes-Yards	21-62	40-167
Passing yards	309	367
Sacked-Yards lost	4-22	2-14
Return yards	126	66
Passes	24-43-0	24-40-0
Punts	7-36.6	3-34.7
Fumbles-Lost	3-0	3-2

	Washington	San Francisco
Penalties-Yards	6-60	6-50
Time of possession	25:15	34:45

Attendance—59,707. No-shows—1,678.

INDIVIDUAL STATISTICS

Rushing—Washington, Theismann 7-35, J. Washington 3-15, Riggins 10-12, Monk 1-0; San Francisco, Tyler 20-96, Craig 17-57, Montana 3-14.

Passing—Washington, Theismann 24-43-0—331; San Francisco, Montana 24-40-0—381.

Receiving—Washington, Monk 10-200, J. Washington 5-30, Seay 3-44, Warren 3-37, Brown 2-20, Riggins 1-0; San Francisco, D. Clark 5-105, Solomon 5-27, Francis 5-55, Cooper 3-44, Craig 3-37, Wilson 2-58, Tyler 1-50.

Kickoff Returns—Washington, Nelms 6-116, Griffin 1-10; San Francisco, Monroe 2-5, McLemore 1-14, Harmon 2-47.

Punt Returns—Washington, Nelms 2-8, Seay 1-minus 2; San Francisco, McLemore 2-8.

Punting—Washington, Hayes 7-36.6; San Francisco, Orosz 3-34.7.

Field Goals—Washington, Moseley 1-1; San Francisco, Wersching 3-3.

Sacks—Washington, Kaufman, Manley; San Francisco, McColl 3, Board.

THIRD WEEK

RESULTS OF WEEK 3
Sunday, September 16

Chicago 9, Green Bay 7 at G.B.
Dallas 23, Philadelphia 17 at Dall.
Denver 24, Cleveland 14 at Cleve.
L.A. Raiders 22, Kansas City 20 at K.C.
Minnesota 27, Atlanta 20 at Minn.
New England 38, Seattle 23 at N.E.
N.Y. Jets 43, Cincinnati 23 at N.Y.
Pittsburgh 24, L.A. Rams 14 at Pitts.
St. Louis 34, Indianapolis 33 at Ind.
San Diego 31, Houston 14 at S.D.
San Francisco 30, New Orleans 20 at S.F.
Tampa Bay 21, Detroit 17 at T.B.
Washington 30, N.Y. Giants 14 at Wash.

Monday, September 17

Miami 21, Buffalo 17 at Buff.

Winning in the National Football League is difficult enough without having your quarterback throw four interceptions. Unless, of course, you're the defending Super Bowl champion Los Angeles Raiders.

Jim Plunkett, who had guided the Raiders to the league championship nine months earlier, threw four interceptions in an AFC Western Division clash with the Kansas City Chiefs. The first two were picked off by safety Deron Cherry and killed L.A. drives deep in Kansas City territory in the second period. The third was grabbed by Chiefs rookie Kevin Ross and returned 71 yards for a touchdown to give the Chiefs a 10-0 second-quarter lead. The final one, by safety Lloyd Burruss, set up a five-yard TD jaunt by Herman Heard that gave Kansas City a 20-19 lead with 4:44 left in the game.

But it still wasn't enough for the Chiefs.

"When you intercept someone like Plunkett four times, it's hard to imagine that you'll get beat," Cherry said. "You have to play the Raiders the whole 60 minutes."

The Chiefs came close, but Chris Bahr's 19-yard field goal with 1 minute to play gave the Raiders a 22-20 victory. The winning kick came after a six-play, 73-yard drive, the biggest gain coming on a 42-yard Plunkett pass to Malcolm Barnwell.

"It was a must situation," Barnwell said. "We had to get the job done. The line gave Jim time, and Jim picked it up and found me open."

The Chiefs had built a 13-0 lead as 75,111 fans looked on. But Bahr kicked a 43-yard field goal on the final play of the first half to put the Raiders on the board. The Raiders dominated the second half, allowing only Heard's touchdown run.

"We're a second-half team," said L.A. Coach Tom Flores. "We're physically strong and that normally shows in the second half. But the important thing is that we're 3-0."

Another team that improved its record to 3-0 was Chicago. The surprising Bears thus led the NFC Central Division by two full games three weeks into the season. Although the Chicago offense managed only three field goals in a 9-7 victory over division-rival Green Bay, it controlled the ball most of the game, doubling Green Bay's time of possession. When the Packers did have possession, they couldn't get moving. Their initial first down of the game came on their lone touchdown drive late in the second quarter and the Packers managed just 154 yards for the afternoon. Still, Green Bay had a chance to win until Eddie Garcia missed a 47-yard field goal attempt in the final quarter.

The San Diego Chargers, known for their quick-strike air attack, clubbed winless Houston, 31-14, by controlling the ball nearly 41 minutes behind the running of second-year man Earnest Jackson, who was making his first NFL start after Chuck Muncie was traded to Miami (in a deal that subsequently was cancelled). Jackson scored three touchdowns, his first in the pros, as Coach Don Coryell won his 100th NFL game, including playoffs.

Minnesota rookie Coach Les Steckel, meanwhile, picked up his first NFL win in a 27-20 triumph over visiting Atlanta. The Vikes broke a 6-6 halftime tie with three third-period touchdowns. Two of the touchdowns came on passes from quarterback Tommy Kramer and the third was thrown by rookie running back Alfred Anderson, who hooked up with fellow rookie Dwight Collins on a 43-yard pass play. It was Anderson's second TD pass in as many games; he hooked up with Kramer against Philadelphia the previous week.

Dallas, a team known for its intricate, complicated and computerized offensive and defensive formations, used a gimmick play to edge the Eagles, 23-17, in a NFC Eastern Division game. Leading 16-10 late in the third quarter and facing a first down at the Philadelphia 49-yard line, quarterback Gary Hogeboom threw a backward pass to wide receiver Mike Renfro in the flat. Renfro then threw a high pass that floated over the head of Eagles safety Wes Hopkins and into the hands of fellow receiver Doug Donley in the Philly end zone. The touchdown proved decisive. The Eagles scored once more early in the final period, but were then held without a first down in the final 10 minutes.

Two clubs pulled their starting quarterbacks after poor starts and were led to victory by their backups.

At Foxboro, Mass., Tony Eason replaced Steve Grogan with the Pats trailing Seattle, 23-0, in the second quarter and led New England to its greatest comeback win in franchise history. The Pats had not managed a first down or completed a pass before Eason's entrance. The second-year pro from Illinois responded with two touchdown passes and ran for a third as New England held the Seahawks scoreless the rest of the game in a 38-23 victory.

At Tampa Bay, Steve DeBerg replaced Jack Thompson with the Buccaneers trailing Detroit, 14-0, in the second period. On his first series, DeBerg drove the club 67 yards in 11 plays before hitting Gerald Carter with a 5-yard touchdown pass. James Wilder's 2-yard TD run in the third period and the ensuing conversion tied the score, but the Lions regained the advantage on an Eddie Murray field goal.

DeBerg, however, wasn't finished. He drove the Bucs 81 yards in seven plays before hitting tight end Jimmie Giles with a 5-yard TD pass with 3:11 remaining, lifting Tampa Bay to a 21-17 victory.

One quarterback replacement wasn't quite as fortunate as Eason and DeBerg.

In a game at San Francisco, the Saints' Ken Stabler came off the bench when starter Richard Todd got off to a disastrous start against the 49ers. Of his seven passing attempts, Todd completed two to his teammates and three to San Francisco. The three interceptions helped stake the 49ers to a 17-0 lead in the second period.

Stabler, a 15-year NFL veteran, threw a pair of touchdown passes and Morten Andersen kicked a pair of field goals to pull the Saints into a 20-17 lead. But the 49ers prevailed in the end as Matt Cavanaugh, subbing for injured quarterback Joe Montana, connected with Earl Cooper for a 23-yard game-winning touchdown pass and the 49ers went on to record a 30-20 victory.

After falling behind Cincinnati, 16-13, on Ken Anderson's 80-yard TD pass to tight end M.L. Harris 18 seconds into the third period, the New York Jets responded with 30 unanswered points to rout the Bengals, 43-23. New York scored on six straight second-half possessions as the Bengals committed four costly turnovers in that span. Anderson was intercepted four times by the Jets and New York kicker Pat Leahy booted a career-high five field goals.

St. Louis' Neil O'Donoghue kicked only two field goals for the Cardinals, but one of those came with seven seconds left in regulation as the Cardinals edged the Indianapolis Colts, 34-33. Neil Lomax and Roy Green combined on 47- and 56-yard touchdown plays in the final period to pull St. Louis within two points of the Colts after trailing the entire second half. A 96-yard kickoff return by Indianapolis' Phil Smith on the final play of the third quarter had given the Colts a 26-17 lead before the Cardinals' rally.

The Denver Broncos also had to rally after falling behind the Cleveland Browns, 14-0. Running back Mike Pruitt scored on two short touchdown plunges to give the Browns an early lead. But the Broncos scored 17 points in the final five minutes of the first half and went on to win the nationally-televised Sunday night game, 24-14. Safety Dennis Smith intercepted a pass by Browns quarterback Paul McDonald to set up the first score, a 23-yard pass from John Elway to Clint Sampson. Then Elway connected with Butch Johnson on another touchdown to cap an eight-play, 83-yard drive, and Rich Karlis added a 25-yard field goal with four seconds left in the half to give Denver a lead it never relinquished. It was the Broncos' seventh straight victory over Cleveland since 1975.

Washington's Vernon Dean made his first start of the season and responded with three interceptions of Giants quarterback Phil Simms in a 30-14 Redskins triumph. Dean, who started as a rookie in Washington's Super Bowl season of 1982, got the cornerback job back after Anthony Washington struggled in the Skins' first two games of 1984, both losses. Dean returned one of the interceptions 36 yards for a touchdown to give the Redskins a 23-14 lead. The interception came just two plays after Mark Moseley's 21-yard field goal had given Washington a 16-14 lead and seemed to take the steam out of the previously undefeated Giants.

Pittsburgh's Sam Washington picked off two Vince Ferragamo passes that proved critical in the Steelers' 24-14 victory over the Rams. Washington returned one interception 12 yards for a touchdown and the other came in his own end zone, stopping a Rams drive. The Pittsburgh defense held Rams running back Eric Dickerson to 49 yards (71 below his average), sacked Ferragamo and Jeff Kemp five times (all credited to nose tackle Edmund Nelson) and picked off three passes.

Pittsburgh rookie receiver Louis Lipps, the Steelers' No. 1 draft choice in 1984, continued to impress. Lipps caught a touchdown pass from David Woodley, his fourth TD in three NFL games.

In the Monday night game, the Miami Dolphins traveled to Buffalo and escaped with a 21-17 win over the Bills in an AFC Eastern Division matchup. The Dolphins dominated the first half and stretched their lead to 21-3 early in the third quarter on Dan Marino's third touchdown pass of the game. Ironically, Marino had thrown three TD passes the last time he faced Buffalo, in 1983, in his first NFL start.

Wide receivers Mark Duper, Mark Clayton and Nat Moore each caught a TD pass.

The Bills scored two touchdowns in the second half to cut the deficit to four points. They were driving again when wide receiver Byron Franklin fumbled at the Miami 38 with five minutes remaining to end the Bills' last chance.

Bears-Packers
SUNDAY, SEPTEMBER 16
SCORE BY PERIODS

Chicago	3	3	0	3—9
Green Bay	0	7	0	0—7

SCORING
Chicago—Field goal B. Thomas 18, 10:37 1st.
Chicago—Field goal B. Thomas 49, 2:06 2nd.
Green Bay—Clark 1 run (Garcia kick), 10:39 2nd.
Chicago—Field goal B. Thomas 29, 3:49 4th.

TEAM STATISTICS

	Chicago	Green Bay
First downs	15	10
Rushes-Yards	47-180	19-32
Passing yards	165	122
Sacked-Yards lost	1-7	3-20
Return yards	88	75
Passes	15-24-1	11-23-1
Punts	6-39.8	8-42.6
Fumbles-Lost	1-0	0-0
Penalties-Yards	11-94	3-24
Time of possession	40:50	19:10

Attendance—55,942. No-shows—213.

INDIVIDUAL STATISTICS
Rushing—Chicago, Payton 27-110, Suhey 11-25, McMahon 4-44, C. Thomas 2-11, Avellini 2-minus 5, Finzer 1-minus 5; Green Bay, Ellis 7-18, Huckleby 6-5, Clark 4-11, Crouse 1-0, Dickey 1-minus 2.

Passing—Chicago, McMahon 4-7-0—39, Avellini 11-17-1—133; Green Bay, Dickey 11-23-1—142.

Receiving—Chicago, Suhey 4-23, Payton 3-29, McKinnon 3-29, Moorehead 2-65, Saldi 2-19, Gault 1-7; Green Bay, Lofton 4-89, Clark 4-29, G. Lewis 2-14, Ellis 1-10.

Kickoff Returns—Chicago, Gentry 1-14, Cameron 1-15; Green Bay, Rodgers 3-61.

Punt Returns—Chicago, Fisher 6-59; Green Bay, Epps 3-14.

Interceptions—Chicago, Frazier 1-0; Green Bay, T. Lewis 1-0.

Punting—Chicago, Finzer 6-39.8; Green Bay, Scribner 8-42.6.

Field Goals—Chicago, B. Thomas 3-3; Green Bay, Garcia 0-1 (missed: 47).

Sacks—Chicago, McMichael 1½, Hampton 1½; Green Bay, Humphrey.

Eagles-Cowboys
SUNDAY, SEPTEMBER 16
SCORE BY PERIODS

Philadelphia	0	10	0	7—17
Dallas	3	10	10	0—23

SCORING
Dallas—Field goal Septien 47, 13:13 1st.
Dallas—Field goal Septien 51, 6:12 2nd.
Philadelphia—Quick 16 pass from Jaworski (McFadden kick), 12:32 2nd.
Dallas—Springs 25 pass from Hogeboom (Septien kick), 13:49 2nd.
Philadelphia—Field goal McFadden 39, 14:46 2nd.
Dallas—Field goal Septien 30, 10:32 3rd.
Dallas—Donley 49 pass from Renfro (Septien kick), 12:53 3rd.
Philadelphia—Quick 9 pass from Jaworski (McFadden kick), 4:32 4th.

TEAM STATISTICS

	Philadelphia	Dallas
First downs	20	21
Rushes-Yards	20-56	34-95
Passing yards	243	352
Sacked-Yards lost	1-9	2-17
Return yards	151	165

	Philadelphia	Dallas
Passes	22-48-3	23-41-0
Punts	7-45.7	7-38.7
Fumbles-Lost	0-0	0-1
Penalties-Yards	4-30	8-49
Time of possession	29:00	31:00

Attendance—64,521. No-shows—152.

INDIVIDUAL STATISTICS
Rushing—Philadelphia, Montgomery 14-47, Oliver 1-minus 2, Haddix 4-8, Hardy 1-3; Dallas, Dorsett 22-66, Hogeboom 1-0, Springs 7-30, Donley 1-minus 1, Newsome 2-5, Smith 1-minus 5.

Passing—Philadelphia, Jaworski 22-48-3—252; Dallas, Hogeboom 22-40-0—320, Renfro 1-1-0—49.

Receiving—Philadelphia, Quick 5-62, Montgomery 1-14, Oliver 2-11, Jackson 1-10, Haddix 1-3, Spagnola 8-80, Woodruff 3-59, Kab 1-13; Dallas, Dorsett 3-29, Renfro 4-68, Springs 5-84, Donley 5-122, Cosbie 4-40, Newsome 1-19, Smith 1-7.

Kickoff Returns—Philadelphia, Hayes 3-71, Waters 1-32, Everett 2-32; Dallas, Allen 4-95.

Punt Returns—Philadelphia, Cooper 2-16; Dallas, Allen 4-15.

Interceptions—Dallas, Hegman 1-0, Downs 1-12, Thurman 1-43.

Punting—Philadelphia, Horan 7-45.6; Dallas, D. White 7-38.7.

Field Goals—Philadelphia, McFadden 1-2 (missed: 39); Dallas, Septien 3-4 (missed: 28).

Sacks—Philadelphia, Brown, Schulz; Dallas, Hegman.

Broncos-Browns
SUNDAY, SEPTEMBER 16
SCORE BY PERIODS

Denver	0	17	0	7—24
Cleveland	7	7	0	0—14

SCORING
Cleveland—Pruitt 1 run (Bahr kick), 13:23 1st.
Cleveland—Pruitt 2 run (Bahr kick), 6:28 2nd.
Denver—Sampson 23 pass from Elway (Karlis kick), 10:10 2nd.
Denver—Johnson 18 pass from Elway (Karlis kick), 13:41 2nd.
Denver—Field goal Karlis 25, 14:56 2nd.
Denver—Robbins 62 interception return (Karlis kick), 14:23 4th.

TEAM STATISTICS

	Denver	Cleveland
First downs	18	21
Rushes-Yards	26-136	29-79
Passing yards	161	231
Sacked-Yards lost	2-9	7-51
Return yards	204	101
Passes	15-35-1	22-42-3
Punts	8-36.4	6-42.8
Fumbles-Lost	2-1	2-1
Penalties-Yards	10-78	8-62
Time of possession	23:29	36:31

Attendance—61,980. No-shows—1,871.

INDIVIDUAL STATISTICS
Rushing—Denver, Winder 17-76, Elway 5-45, Lang 1-6, Parros 1-1, Willhite 2-8; Cleveland, Pruitt 24-67, Green 3-9, McDonald 2-3.

Passing—Denver, Elway 15-35-1—170; Cleveland, McDonald 22-42-3—282.

Receiving—Denver, Kay 2-7, Winder 7-56, Sampson 1-23, Johnson 4-64, Watson 1-20; Cleveland, Brennan 7-84, Harris 5-104, Winn 1-1, Holt 5-59, Green 1-4, Newsome 2-12, Feacher 1-18.

Kickoff Returns—Denver, Thomas 3-85; Cleveland, Brown 3-62, Contz 1-10, Byner 1-20.

Punt Returns—Denver, Thomas 2-13, Willhite 1-21; Cleveland, Brennan 3-9.

Interceptions—Denver, D. Smith 1-3, Robbins 1-62, Wilson 1-20; Cleveland, Cousineau 1-0.

Punting—Denver, Norman 8-36.4; Cleveland, Cox 6-42.8.

Field Goals—Denver, Karlis 1-1; Cleveland, Bahr 0-1 (missed: 36).

Sacks—Denver, Bowyer 2, Chavous, Jones, Robbins, Jackson, Busick; Cleveland, Matthews 2.

Raiders-Chiefs
SUNDAY, SEPTEMBER 16
SCORE BY PERIODS

Los Angeles Raiders	0	3	6	13—22
Kansas City	3	10	0	7—20

SCORING

Kansas City—Field goal Lowery 29, 7:49 1st.
Kansas City—Ross 71 interception return (Lowery kick), 9:44 2nd.
Kansas City—Field goal Lowery 27, 13:13 2nd.
Los Angeles—Field goal Bahr 43, 15:00 2nd.
Los Angeles—Christensen 3 pass from Plunkett (kick blocked), 11:07 3rd.
Los Angeles—Hawkins 1 run (Bahr kick), 0:56 4th.
Los Angeles—Field goal Bahr 24, 6:53 4th.
Kansas City—Heard 5 run (Lowery kick), 10:16 4th.
Los Angeles—Field goal Bahr 19, 14:00 4th.

TEAM STATISTICS

	Los Angeles	Kansas City
First downs	27	19
Rushes-Yards	32-81	22-92
Passing yards	302	187
Sacked-Yards lost	2-11	0-0
Return yards	180	138
Passes	28-48-4	17-37-2
Punts	5-37.4	6-40.0
Fumbles-Lost	0-0	1-1
Penalties-Yards	12-132	12-126
Time of possession	32:40	27:20

Attendance—75,111. No-shows—2,149.

INDIVIDUAL STATISTICS

Rushing—Los Angeles, Allen 22-69, King 4-6, Plunkett 2-3, Hawkins 4-3; Kansas City, Brown 12-44, Heard 6-32, B. Jackson 3-14, Lacy 1-2.

Passing—Los Angeles, Plunkett 28-47-4—313, Allen 0-1-0—0; Kansas City, Blackledge 17-37-2—187.

Receiving—Los Angeles, Barnwell 8-129, Christensen 9-93, Allen 6-46, King 3-22, Branch 1-18, Hawkins 1-5; Kansas City, Carson 5-66, Paige 3-58, Brown 5-30, Marshall 2-19, Smith 1-18, Hancock 1-6.

Kickoff Returns—Los Angeles, D. Williams 3-75, Montgomery 2-43; Kansas City, Paige 1-14, Ricks 3-44.

Punt Returns—Los Angeles, Pruitt 5-34.

Interceptions—Los Angeles, Martin 1-17, M. Davis 1-11; Kansas City, Burruss 1-0, Ross 1-71, Cherry 2-9.

Punting—Los Angeles, Guy 5-37.4; Kansas City, Arnold 6-40.0.

Field Goals—Los Angeles, Bahr 3-3; Kansas City, Lowery 2-3 (missed: 30).

Sacks—Kansas City, Bell, Still.

Falcons-Vikings
SUNDAY, SEPTEMBER 16
SCORE BY PERIODS

Atlanta	3	3	7	7—20
Minnesota	3	3	21	0—27

SCORING

Atlanta—Field goal Luckhurst 33, 6:28 1st.
Minnesota—Field goal Stenerud 22, 11:21 1st.
Minnesota—Field goal Stenerud 54, 0:31 2nd.
Atlanta—Field goal Luckhurst 43, 8:56 2nd.

Minnesota—Lewis 42 pass from Kramer (Stenerud kick), 2:50 3rd.
Atlanta—Bailey 57 pass from Bartkowski (Luckhurst kick), 5:02 3rd.
Minnesota—Jordan 21 pass from Kramer (Stenerud kick), 9:10 3rd.
Minnesota—Collins 43 pass from Anderson (Stenerud kick), 13:01 3rd.
Atlanta—B. Johnson 32 pass from Bartkowski (Luckhurst kick), 9:17 4th.

TEAM STATISTICS

	Atlanta	Minnesota
First downs	13	23
Rushes-Yards	25-111	37-180
Passing yards	147	234
Sacked-Yards lost	7-48	2-12
Return yards	146	125
Passes	14-24-1	16-32-0
Punts	5-44.0	4-33.0
Fumbles-Lost	3-1	4-1
Penalties-Yards	10-85	4-25
Time of possession	28:24	31:36

Attendance—53,955. No-shows—7,371.

INDIVIDUAL STATISTICS

Rushing—Atlanta, Riggs 17-83, Bartkowski 4-19, B. Johnson 1-minus 3, Cain 3-12; Minnesota, Anderson 17-79, Nelson 15-96, Kramer 4-minus 6, Waddy 1-11.

Passing—Atlanta, Bartkowski 14-24-1—195; Minnesota, Kramer 15-30-0—203, Anderson 1-2-0—43.

Receiving—Atlanta, B. Johnson 4-50, Benson 3-19, Riggs 3-24, Bailey 4-102; Minnesota, Jordan 4-60, White 2-23, Nelson 2-5, Lewis 3-69, Collins 1-43, Jones 2-32, Anderson 1-0, Mularkey 1-14.

Kickoff Returns—Atlanta, Curran 1-9, Tate 1-19, Stamps 3-88; Minnesota, Nelson 1-19, Anderson 3-81.

Punt Returns—Atlanta, B. Johnson 3-30; Minnesota, Nelson 3-25.

Interceptions—Minnesota, Lee 1-0.

Punting—Atlanta, Giacomarro 5-44.0; Minnesota, Coleman 3-44.0.

Field Goals—Atlanta, Luckhurst 2-2; Minnesota, Stenerud 2-3 (missed: 53).

Sacks—Atlanta, Frye, K. Johnson; Minnesota, Holloway 4½, C. Johnson, McNeill, Vaughan ½.

Seahawks-Patriots
SUNDAY, SEPTEMBER 16
SCORE BY PERIODS

Seattle	9	14	0	0—23
New England	0	7	14	17—38

SCORING

Seattle—Field goal N. Johnson 42, 6:43 1st.
Seattle—Turner 41 pass from Krieg (kick failed), 10:15 1st.
Seattle—Johns 47 punt return (N. Johnson kick), 4:44 2nd.
Seattle—Easley 25 interception return (N. Johnson kick), 5:44 2nd.
New England—Eason 25 run (Franklin kick), 14:25 2nd.
New England—Ramsey 2 pass from Eason (Franklin kick), 2:26 3rd.
New England—Tatupu 1 run (Franklin kick), 10:26 3rd.
New England—Field goal Franklin 32, 8:29 4th.
New England—Tatupu 10 run (Franklin kick), 9:30 4th.
New England—Fryar 15 pass from Eason (Franklin kick), 13:01 4th.

TEAM STATISTICS

	Seattle	New England
First downs	16	22
Rushes-Yards	28-37	45-189
Passing yards	215	102
Sacked-Yards lost	5-50	4-24
Return yards	216	141

	Seattle	New England
Passes	17-35-2	12-26-1
Punts	9-38.6	8-42.4
Fumbles-Lost	4-1	5-1
Penalties-Yards	7-107	6-60
Time of possession	26:54	33:06

Attendance—43,140. No-shows—2,352.

INDIVIDUAL STATISTICS

Rushing—Seattle, Hughes 8-18, F. Harris 10-13, Lane 7-5, Krieg 3-1; New England, Collins 20-107, Tatupu 9-35, C. James 10-33, Eason 4-25, Grogan 1-0, Fryar 1-minus 11.

Passing—Seattle, Krieg 17-35-2—265; New England, Eason 12-22-0—126, Grogan 0-4-1—0.

Receiving—Seattle, Johns 8-105, Turner 2-50, Largent 3-38, Tice 2-37, Walker 1-24, Young 1-11; New England, Starring 4-46, Dawson 2-30, Ramsey 3-24, Fryar 2-24, Collins 1-2.

Kickoff Returns—Seattle, Hughes 7-134; New England, Fryar 3-56.

Punt Returns—Seattle, Johns 3-79, Easley 1-1; New England, Fryar 3-62.

Interceptions—Seattle, Easley 1-25; New England, Dombrowski 1-23, Sanford 1-0.

Punting—Seattle, West 9-38.6; New England, Prestridge 8-42.4.

Field Goals—Seattle, N. Johnson 1-1; New England, Franklin 1-1.

Sacks—Seattle, J. Bryant 2½, Gaines, Nash ½; New England, Nelson, Owens, Tippett, Rogers, Blackmon ½, Sims ½.

Bengals-Jets
SUNDAY, SEPTEMBER 16
SCORE BY PERIODS

Cincinnati	9	0	7	7—23
New York Jets	6	7	10	20—43

SCORING

New York—Field goal Leahy 22, 5:03 1st.
Cincinnati—Field goal Breech 21, 10:36 1st.
New York—Field goal Leahy 39, 11:51 1st.
Cincinnati—Brooks 3 pass from Anderson (pass failed), 14:56 1st.
New York—McNeil 15 run (Leahy kick), 7:15 2nd.
Cincinnati—Harris 80 pass from Anderson (Breech kick), 0:18 3rd.
New York—Field goal Leahy 32, 8:18 3rd.
New York—Shuler 9 pass from Ryan (Leahy kick), 10:50 3rd.
New York—Field goal Leahy 36, 0:13 4th.
New York—McNeil 33 run (Leahy kick), 1:48 4th.
New York—Field goal Leahy 29, 9:31 4th.
New York—Harper 9 run (Leahy kick), 11:38 4th.
Cincinnati—Esiason 1 run (Breech kick), 14:39 4th.

TEAM STATISTICS

	Cincinnati	New York
First downs	20	25
Rushes-Yards	22-85	36-178
Passing yards	339	219
Sacked-Yards lost	2-8	4-32
Return yards	170	250
Passes	20-31-4	20-33-0
Punts	2-53.5	2-33.5
Fumbles-Lost	3-2	0-0
Penalties-Yards	5-40	5-51
Time of possession	23:01	36:59

Attendance—64,193. No-shows—12,698.

INDIVIDUAL STATISTICS

Rushing—Cincinnati, Kinnebrew 6-55, Alexander 8-14, Anderson 1-13, Brooks 4-minus 6, Esiason 3-9; New York, McNeil 26-150, Harper 5-26, Hector 2-1, Paige 1-2, Barber 1-0, O'Brien 1-minus 1.

Passing—Cincinnati, Anderson 16-22-4—316, Schonert

0-2-0—0, Esiason 4-7-0—31; New York, Ryan 20-33-0 —251.

Receiving—Cincinnati, Harris 4-148, Collinsworth 4-97, Holman 3-28, Brooks 3-10, Jennings 1-21, Curtis 1-12, Kinnebrew 4-31; New York, Walker 5-73, Gaffney 4-55, Humphrey 2-32, McNeil 2-32, Harper 2-21, Shuler 3-25, Barber 1-8, Dennison 1-5.

Kickoff Returns—Cincinnati, Martin 4-100, Jennings 3-65; New York, Humphrey 1-46, Springs 3-110, Gaffney 1-6.

Punt Returns—Cincinnati, Simmons 1-5; New York, Springs 2-26.

Interceptions—New York, Schroy 1-13, Ray 1-28, Lynn 1-16, Buttle 1-5.

Punting—Cincinnati, McInally 2-53.5; New York, Ramsey 2-33.5.

Field Goals—Cincinnati, Breech 1-1; New York, Leahy 5-5.

Sacks—Cincinnati, Edwards 2, Williams, Schuh; New York, Gastineau 2.

Rams-Steelers
SUNDAY, SEPTEMBER 16
SCORE BY PERIODS

Los Angeles	7	0	7	0—14
Pittsburgh	0	14	3	7—24

SCORING

Los Angeles—Crutchfield 4 pass from Ferragamo (Lansford kick), 11:38 1st.
Pittsburgh—Cunningham 1 pass from Woodley (Anderson kick), 7:13 2nd.
Pittsburgh—Washington 12 interception return (Anderson kick), 8:28 2nd.
Pittsburgh—Field goal Anderson 41, 2:56 3rd.
Los Angeles—Drew Hill 57 pass from Kemp (Lansford kick), 9:05 3rd.
Pittsburgh—Lipps 11 pass from Woodley (Anderson kick), 1:28 4th.

TEAM STATISTICS

	Los Angeles	Pittsburgh
First downs	15	20
Rushes-Yards	27-83	35-119
Passing yards	213	226
Sacked-Yards lost	5-46	3-18
Return yards	64	136
Passes	15-30-3	20-30-0
Punts	7-44.3	5-40.8
Fumbles-Lost	2-0	7-2
Penalties-Yards	6-76	9-73
Time of possession	26:58	33:02

Attendance—58,104. No-shows—896.

INDIVIDUAL STATISTICS

Rushing—Los Angeles, Dickerson 23-49, Ferragamo 1-1, Kemp 3-33; Pittsburgh, Erenberg 20-83, Pollard 3-11, Woodley 3-5, Veals 4-6, Corley 5-14.

Passing—Los Angeles, Ferragamo 6-13-2—132, Kemp 9-17-1—127; Pittsburgh, Woodley 20-30-0—244.

Receiving—Los Angeles, Drew Hill 4-152, Dickerson 3-16, Guman 2-36, Crutchfield 1-4, Ellard 3-36, David Hill 1-6, Grant 1-9; Pittsburgh, Lipps 5-77, Stallworth 6-100, Pollard 1-5, Erenberg 5-39, Cunningham 2-14, Thompson 1-9.

Kickoff Returns—Los Angeles, Redden 1-21, Drew Hill 2-32; Pittsburgh, Spencer 3-23.

Punt Returns—Los Angeles, Ellard 2-11; Pittsburgh, Lipps 5-69.

Interceptions—Pittsburgh, Washington 2-44, Woods 1-0.

Punting—Los Angeles, Misko 7-44.3; Pittsburgh, Colquitt 5-40.8.

Field Goals—Los Angeles, Lansford 0-1 (missed: 35); Pittsburgh, Anderson 1-2 (missed: 37).

Sacks—Los Angeles, Andrews, Doss, Owens; Pittsburgh, Nelson 5.

Cardinals-Colts
SUNDAY, SEPTEMBER 16
SCORE BY PERIODS

St. Louis	0	14	3	17—34
Indianapolis	7	10	9	7—33

SCORING
Indianapolis—Dickey 10 run (Biasucci kick), 13:30 1st.
St. Louis—Anderson 10 run (O'Donoghue kick), 2:49 2nd.
St. Louis—L. Smith 25 interception return (O'Donoghue kick), 7:48 2nd.
Indianapolis—Porter 63 pass from Dickey (Biasucci kick), 9:37 2nd.
Indianapolis—Field goal Biasucci 21, 14:54 2nd.
Indianapolis—Field goal Biasucci 50, 11:23 3rd.
St. Louis—Field goal O'Donoghue 47, 14:55 3rd.
Indianapolis—Smith 96 kickoff return (kick failed), 15:00 3rd.
St. Louis—Green 47 pass from Lomax (O'Donoghue kick), 1:22 4th.
Indianapolis—Young 5 pass from Pagel (Biasucci kick), 7:39 4th.
St. Louis—Green 56 pass from Lomax (O'Donoghue kick), 11:32 4th.
St. Louis—Field goal O'Donoghue 46, 14:53 4th.

TEAM STATISTICS

	St. Louis	Indianapolis
First downs	19	22
Rushes-Yards	26-132	38-189
Passing yards	265	209
Sacked-Yards lost	1-5	4-27
Return yards	233	250
Passes	16-39-3	12-26-2
Punts	6-42.8	6-44.7
Fumbles-Lost	3-0	2-1
Penalties-Yards	8-60	7-50
Time of possession	28:05	31:55
Attendance—60,274. No-shows—463.		

INDIVIDUAL STATISTICS
Rushing—St. Louis, Anderson 23-119, Ferrell 3-13; Indianapolis, Dickey 23-121, McMillan 11-40, Pagel 2-21, Moore 2-7.
Passing—St. Louis, Lomax 16-39-3—270; Indianapolis, Pagel 11-25-2—173, Dickey 1-1-0—63.
Receiving—St. Louis, Marsh 2-22, Anderson 4-32, Green 8-183, Tilley 2-33; Indianapolis, Young 3-40, Bouza 2-43, Porter 4-120, Butler 1-15, Moore 1-9, Dickey 1-9.
Kickoff Returns—St. Louis, Mitchell 5-117, Harrell 1-14; Indianapolis, Smith 6-162, L. Anderson 1-17.
Punt Returns—St. Louis, Bird 1-17, Mitchell 3-37; Indianapolis, Anderson 2-8.
Interceptions—St. Louis, L. Smith 1-25, W. Smith 1-23; Indianapolis, Randle 1-54, Burroughs 2-9.
Punting—St. Louis, Birdsong 6-42.8; Indianapolis, Stark 6-44.7.
Field Goals—St. Louis, O'Donoghue 2-2; Indianapolis, Biasucci 2-2.
Sacks—St. Louis, Greer, Harris, A. Baker, Galloway; Indianapolis, Maxwell.

Oilers-Chargers
SUNDAY, SEPTEMBER 16
SCORE BY PERIODS

Houston	0	7	0	7—14
San Diego	14	14	0	3—31

SCORING
San Diego—Jackson 3 run (Benirschke kick), 5:06 1st.
San Diego—Jackson 1 run (Benirschke kick), 14:41 1st.
San Diego—P. Johnson 1 run (Benirschke kick), 9:31 2nd.
Houston—Smith 75 pass from Moon (Kempf kick), 9:51 2nd.
San Diego—Jackson 6 run (Benirschke kick), 11:43 2nd.

San Diego—Field goal Benirschke 23, 5:00 4th.
Houston—Mullins 7 pass from Luck (Kempf kick), 13:55 4th.

TEAM STATISTICS

	Houston	San Diego
First downs	14	29
Rushes-Yards	12-27	39-147
Passing yards	257	330
Sacked-Yards lost	3-25	2-15
Return yards	104	28
Passes	15-35-0	27-40-1
Punts	9-38.8	5-36.6
Fumbles-Lost	1-1	1-0
Penalties-Yards	6-35	10-74
Time of possession	19:08	40:52
Attendance—52,266. No-shows—6,923.		

INDIVIDUAL STATISTICS
Rushing—Houston, Campbell 7-8, Moriarty 3-11, Joyner 1-minus 1, Luck 1-9; San Diego, Jackson 21-97, P. Johnson 6-15, Thomas 5-15, McGee 7-20.
Passing—Houston, Moon 11-31-0—212, Luck 4-4-0—70; San Diego, Fouts 26-37-1—336, Luther 1-3-0—9.
Receiving—Houston, Smith 5-159, Williams 2-24, Bryant 1-11, Mullins 3-50, Holston 1-15, Moriarty 2-16, Dressel 1-7; San Diego, Winslow 10-146, Chandler 5-89, Holohan 3-27, Duckworth 3-44, Joiner 1-13, Jackson 2-14, Fouts 1-0, Sievers 2-12.
Kickoff Returns—Houston, Allen 2-39, Roaches 2-41; San Diego, James 1-0.
Punt Returns—Houston, Roaches 4-22; San Diego, James 5-28.
Interceptions—Houston, Hartwig 1-2.
Punting—Houston, James 9-38.8; San Diego, Buford 5-36.6.
Field Goals—Houston, none attempted; San Diego, Benirschke 1-1.
Sacks—Houston, Baker, Riley ½, Sochia ½; San Diego, Greene, Smith, King.

Saints-49ers
SUNDAY, SEPTEMBER 16
SCORE BY PERIODS

New Orleans	0	10	10	0—20
San Francisco	7	10	0	13—30

SCORING
San Francisco—Solomon 32 pass from Montana (Wersching kick), 2:52 1st.
San Francisco—Field goal Wersching 31, 3:38 2nd.
San Francisco—Tyler 3 run (Wersching kick), 1:48 2nd.
New Orleans—Goodlow 7 pass from Stabler (Andersen kick), 5:24 2nd.
New Orleans—Field goal Andersen 32, 0:59 2nd.
New Orleans—Brenner 26 pass from Stabler (Andersen kick), 3:49 3rd.
New Orleans—Field goal Andersen 41, 5:42 3rd.
San Francisco—Cooper 23 pass from Cavanaugh (Wersching kick), 3:36 4th.
San Francisco—Field goal Wersching 22, 0:56 4th.
San Francisco—Field goal Wersching 40, 1:36 4th.

TEAM STATISTICS

	New Orleans	San Francisco
First downs	20	19
Rushes-Yards	31-119	32-148
Passing yards	149	159
Sacked-Yards lost	2-13	3-20
Return yards	166	160
Passes	16-34-5	13-26-1
Punts	3-46.0	5-40.8
Fumbles-Lost	0-0	1-0
Penalties-Yards	4-47	6-54
Time of possession	31:38	28:22
Attendance—57,611. No-shows—3,771.		

Tony Eason came off the bench in the second quarter to rally New England from a 23-point deficit to a 38-23 victory over Seattle in Week 3.

INDIVIDUAL STATISTICS

Rushing—New Orleans, G. Rogers 23-88, W. Wilson 7-25, Todd 1-6; San Francisco, Tyler 18-82, Craig 10-47, Montana 1-14, Harmon 2-9, Cavanaugh 1-minus 4.

Passing—New Orleans, Stabler 14-27-2—157, Todd 2-7-3—5; San Francisco, Montana 10-17-1—128, Cavanaugh 3-8-0—51, D. Clark 0-1-0—0.

Receiving—New Orleans, Goodlow 6-62, Young 2-35, Brenner 2-33, Groth 2-16, Gajan 2-4, Scott 1-7, G. Rogers 1-5; San Francisco, Solomon 3-72, Craig 3-22, Cooper 2-37, Tyler 2-19, Francis 1-14, D. Clark 1-12, Monroe 1-3.

Kickoff Returns—New Orleans, Duckett 5-88, J. Fields 2-36; San Francisco, Monroe 2-31, Harmon 1-24.

Punt Returns—New Orleans, J. Fields 4-26; San Francisco, McLemore 2-7.

Interceptions—New Orleans, Poe 1-16; San Francisco, Bunz 1-2, Fuller 1-38, Hicks 1-29, Lott 1-15, Shell 1-14.

Punting—New Orleans, Hansen 3-46.0; San Francisco, Runager 5-40.8.

Field Goals—New Orleans, Andersen 2-3 (missed: 42); San Francisco, Wersching 3-4 (missed: 42).

Sacks—New Orleans, B. Clark, Jackson, Wilks; San Francisco, Board, Stuckey.

Lions-Buccaneers

SUNDAY, SEPTEMBER 16

SCORE BY PERIODS

Detroit	7	7	3	0—17
Tampa Bay	0	7	7	7—21

SCORING

Detroit—Nichols 77 pass from Danielson (Murray kick), 1:36 1st.

Detroit—Danielson 4 run (Murray kick), 7:14 2nd.
Tampa Bay—Carter 5 pass from DeBerg (Ariri kick), 13:06 2nd.
Tampa Bay—Wilder 2 run (Ariri kick), 8:50 3rd.
Detroit—Field goal Murray 28, 11:10 3rd.
Tampa Bay—Giles 5 pass from DeBerg (Ariri kick), 11:49 4th.

TEAM STATISTICS

	Detroit	Tampa Bay
First downs	13	23
Rushes-Yards	26-102	26-89
Passing yards	168	236
Sacked-Yards lost	2-8	2-16
Return yards	56	107
Passes	15-36-0	24-40-1
Punts	6-42.0	5-39.2
Fumbles-Lost	2-0	3-1
Penalties-Yards	8-49	9-70
Time of possession	25:55	34:05

Attendance—44,560. No-shows—8,327.

INDIVIDUAL STATISTICS

Rushing—Detroit, Sims 11-39, Jones 10-34, Danielson 3-14, Jenkins 1-8, Nichols 1-7; Tampa Bay, Wilder 22-89, Morton 1-2, Carver 1-0, DeBerg 2-minus 2.

Passing—Detroit, Danielson 15-36-0—176; Tampa Bay, DeBerg 18-27-0—195, Thompson 6-13-1—57.

Receiving—Detroit, Nichols 1-77, Jones 5-40, Sims 5-28, Chadwick 2-16, Thompson 2-15; Tampa Bay, House 4-79, Wilder 8-56, Carter 6-45, T. Bell 2-28, J. Bell 1-25, Owens 1-9, Giles 1-5, Carver 1-5.

Kickoff Returns—Detroit, Jenkins 2-39, Martin 1-5; Tampa Bay, Owens 2-70, Morton 2-36.

Punt Returns—Detroit, Martin 2-12; Tampa Bay, T. Bell 1-0, Holt 3-1.

Interceptions—Detroit, Watkins 1-0.

Punting—Detroit, Black 6-42.0; Tampa Bay, Garcia 5-39.2.

Field Goals—Detroit, Murray 1-2 (missed: 52); Tampa Bay, Ariri 0-1 (missed: 43).

Sacks—Detroit, English 2; Tampa Bay, Selmon, Cotney.

Giants-Redskins
SUNDAY, SEPTEMBER 16
SCORE BY PERIODS

New York Giants	7	0	7	0—14
Washington	7	6	0	17—30

SCORING

Washington—Riggins 1 run (Moseley kick), 7:46 1st.
New York—Carpenter 1 run (Haji-Sheikh kick), 11:58 1st.
Washington—Riggins 1 run (kick failed), 3:18 2nd.
New York—Johnson 27 pass from Simms (Haji-Sheikh kick), 3:47 3rd.
Washington—Field goal Moseley 21, 0:49 4th.
Washington—Dean 36 interception return (Moseley kick), 1:11 4th.
Washington—Jordan 29 fumble return (Moseley kick), 6:57 4th.

TEAM STATISTICS

	New York	Washington
First downs	20	20
Rushes-Yards	21-47	40-131
Passing yards	302	129
Sacked-Yards lost	5-45	2-16
Return yards	135	147
Passes	22-45-3	15-31-2
Punts	5-43.2	7-40.9
Fumbles-Lost	3-2	1-1
Penalties-Yards	7-87	5-47
Time of possession	25:26	34:34

Attendance—52,997. No-shows—2,434.

INDIVIDUAL STATISTICS

Rushing—New York, Carpenter 14-41, Morris 3-5, Woolfolk 2-minus 1, Manuel 1-minus 1, Simms 1-3; Washington, Riggins 30-92, J. Washington 5-20, Theismann 4-17, Walker 1-2.

Passing—New York, Simms 22-45-3—347; Washington, Theismann 15-30-2—145, J. Washington 0-1-0—0.

Receiving—New York, Johnson 6-117, Gray 2-31, McConkey 3-67, Galbreath 6-68, B. Williams 5-64; Washington, Monk 8-78, Warren 3-23, J. Washington 1-12, Seay 2-21, Walker 1-11.

Kickoff Returns—New York, McConkey 5-102; Washington, Nelms 3-42.

Punt Returns—New York, McConkey 3-11; Washington, Nelms 5-44.

Interceptions—New York, Haynes 1-8; Hunt 1-14; Washington, Dean 3-61.

Punting—New York, Jennings 5-43.2; Washington, Hayes 7-40.9.

Field Goals—New York, Haji-Sheikh 0-2 (missed: 55, 37); Washington, Moseley 1-1.

Sacks—New York, Burt, Martin; Washington, Coleman 2, Manley 1½, Mann ½, Brooks ½, McGee ½.

Dolphins-Bills
MONDAY, SEPTEMBER 17
SCORE BY PERIODS

Miami	7	7	7	0—21
Buffalo	0	3	7	7—17

SCORING

Miami—Duper 11 pass from Marino (von Schamann kick), 12:51 1st.
Miami—Clayton 12 pass from Marino (von Schamann kick), 9:56 2nd.
Buffalo—Field goal Danelo 33, 14:55 2nd.
Miami—Moore 1 pass from Marino (von Schamann kick), 4:33 3rd.
Buffalo—Neal 1 run (Danelo kick), 11:03 3rd.
Buffalo—Dawkins 37 pass from Ferguson (Danelo kick), 5:40 4th.

TEAM STATISTICS

	Miami	Buffalo
First downs	23	16
Rushes-Yards	33-79	19-68
Passing yards	289	228
Sacked-Yards lost	1-7	3-31
Return yards	87	117
Passes	26-35-1	23-38-0
Punts	2-38.5	4-40.0
Fumbles-Lost	4-2	4-2
Penalties-Yards	5-43	9-70
Time of possession	32:58	27:02

Attendance—65,455. No-shows—862.

INDIVIDUAL STATISTICS

Rushing—Miami, Nathan 12-27, Bennett 16-56, Marino 5-minus 4; Buffalo, Neal 12-34, V. Williams 4-5, Ferguson 2-28, Moore 1-1.

Passing—Miami, Marino 26-35-1—296; Buffalo, Ferguson 23-38-0—259.

Receiving—Miami, Jensen 2-18, Rose 1-18, Johnson 3-44, Duper 5-68, Clayton 2-34, Cefalo 4-52, Nathan 4-24, Moore 4-29, Hardy 1-9; Buffalo, Bell 1-8, Neal 3-21, Dennard 1-6, Franklin 7-92, V. Williams 3-39, Barnett 2-26, Moore 2-10, White 1-6, Dawkins 3-51.

Kickoff Returns—Miami, Heflin 4-54; Buffalo, Wilson 2-38, V. Williams 1-20.

Punt Returns—Miami, Clayton 2-23; Buffalo, Wilson 2-14.

Interceptions—Buffalo, Freeman 1-45.

Punting—Miami, Roby 2-38.5; Buffalo, Kidd 4-40.0.

Field Goals—Miami, von Schamann 0-1 (missed: 36); Buffalo, Danelo 1-2 (missed: 47).

Sacks—Miami, Bowser 2, Betters; Buffalo, B. Williams.

FOURTH WEEK

RESULTS OF WEEK 4
Sunday, September 23

Atlanta 42, Houston 10 at Atl.
Cleveland 20, Pittsburgh 10 at Cleve.
Dallas 20, Green Bay 6 at Dall.
Denver 21, Kansas City 0 at Den.
L.A. Rams 24, Cincinnati 14 at Cin.
Miami 44, Indianapolis 7 at Mia.
Minnesota 29, Detroit 28 at Det.
New Orleans 34, St. Louis 24 at N.O.
N.Y. Giants 17, Tampa Bay 14 at N.Y.
N.Y. Jets 28, Buffalo 26 at Buff.
San Francisco 21, Philadelphia 9 at Phila.
Seattle 38, Chicago 9 at Sea.
Washington 26, New England 10 at N.E.

Monday, September 24

L.A. Raiders 33, San Diego 30 at L.A.

When the New York Jets selected Alabama's Richard Todd in the first round of the 1976 NFL draft, more than a few eyebrows were raised. Not that the Jets didn't need a quarterback. Joe Namath was near the end of his illustrious career and the Jets had not yet groomed a successor. But Todd was so similar to Namath—big, strong, good-looking and from Alabama—that New Yorkers were bound to expect immediate Namath-like results.

But things never worked out for Todd in New York. When he didn't live up to their expectations, the fans took to booing and vented their frustrations on the young quarterback— something they had never done to Namath. In his eight seasons with the Jets, Todd could advance his club no farther than the AFC title game (after the '82 season). That game probably was Todd's worst as a pro. He threw five interceptions as the Jets were shut out by Miami. That game, more than any other, convinced Jets officials that they could never win a Super Bowl with Todd at quarterback.

Prior to the 1984 season, the Jets traded him to New Orleans for a No. 1 draft choice. But Todd's debut was not smooth and the Saints lost two of their first three games. Against San Francisco in the third game of the year, Todd completed just two of seven passes and threw three interceptions before being yanked by Coach Bum Phillips and replaced by yet another Alabama quarterback, Ken Stabler.

Despite being greeted by boos from the hometown fans at the beginning of the Saints' next game (against St. Louis), Todd responded with a 14-of-29 passing day for 264 yards as New Orleans won, 34-24. After the Cardinals had increased their lead to 24-20 with 9:21 left in the game on a Neil O'Donoghue field goal, Todd responded by driving the Saints 76 yards in six plays for the game-winning touchdown— a 30-yard pass to Wayne Wilson with 6:07 left.

Richard Todd broke into the NFL with the Jets in 1976 (above) before joining the Saints in 1984.

"It's nothing," Todd said after the victory when asked if the fans' booing upset him. "Hey, you should be up in New York. It's worse."

Todd's replacement with the Jets, Pat Ryan, enjoyed the best game of his seven-year NFL career as New York edged division-rival Buffalo, 28-26. Ryan, who served as Todd's backup before inheriting the No. 1 job when Todd was traded, threw three touchdown passes to Wesley Walker as the Jets overcame an early 10-0 Buffalo lead. Walker caught seven passes for 128 yards.

Another veteran quarterback enjoyed a rare start. San Francisco's Matt Cavanaugh, who got the call because Joe Montana was sidelined with bruised ribs, made his first start with the 49ers and completed half of his 34 passes for 252 yards and three touchdowns in a 21-9 victory over Philadelphia. Eagles Owner Leonard Tose had "guaranteed" a victory over San Francisco early in the week.

The Rams' Jeff Kemp, who stepped in when regular quarterback Vince Ferragamo couldn't play because of injury, led Los Angeles to a 24-14 interconference victory over Cincinnati. In the first start of Kemp's four-year pro career, he responded with a 13-of-23 passing performance, including a key 52-yard TD pass to wide receiver Ron Brown late in the third quarter that broke a 7-7 deadlock. But the Bengals rallied for a touchdown with 1:49 remaining to cut the Rams' lead to 17-14 before L.A.'s Mike Guman startled everybody by picking up the ensuing onside kickoff and returning it 43 yards for the game's final score.

The Washington-New England game at Foxboro, Mass., could have been called The John Riggins Milestone Day as the Redskins' 35-year-old fullback rushed for 140 yards in a 26-10 romp over the Pats. Riggins' big day gave him an NFL-career total of 9,778 yards, moving him past Joe Perry (9,723) into fifth place on the all-time rushing list. It also gave Riggins 5,898 yards in his seven-plus years with Washington, breaking Larry Brown's team mark. And when Riggins scored the Redskins' first TD late in the opening period, he became the fifth player in league history to score 100 career touchdowns. (Jim Brown, Lenny Moore, Don Hutson and Franco Harris are the others.) The Redskins rolled up 235 yards on the ground and held the ball for 43:12—against a defense that entered the contest ranked second in the league in defending against the run.

Atlanta's Gerald Riggs, meanwhile, came into the Falcons' home game with Houston as the NFL's leading rusher after the season's first three weeks and embellished his rushing total with a 120-yard performance against the lowly Oilers. Riggs also scored two touchdowns and Steve Bartkowski threw for three other TDs in a 42-10 rout. Ironically, the Falcons had gone 13 straight games without scoring a touchdown in the first quarter before scoring three against Houston. Two of the TDs were set up by Earl Campbell fumbles.

The Chicago Bears' offense was plagued by six turnovers, and the opportunistic Seattle Seahawks made them pay in a 38-9 victory. The Seahawks defense converted three of the turnovers into touchdowns, giving the unit a total of five in its last two games.

After the Bears had taken a 7-0 lead with a seven-play, 80-yard drive that was capped by Walter Payton's scoring toss to Matt Suhey, Seahawks cornerback Keith Simpson intercepted a Bob Avellini pass and returned it 39 yards for the tying touchdown. It was all downhill from there for Seattle, which added a second-quarter field goal before scoring three touchdowns in the third quarter. Payton, with 116 yards, surpassed Seattle's Franco Harris to move into second place on the NFL's all-time rushing list behind Jim Brown.

The Dallas Cowboys intercepted four Green Bay passes and sacked Packer quarterbacks six times in a 20-6 triumph. Cornerback Everson Walls, who led the league in interceptions his first two NFL seasons (1981-82), picked off two against Green Bay. The six points allowed by the Cowboys—which came on an interception return—was the lowest total in a regular-season game in five seasons.

The New York Giants also used a tough defense in winning their game against Tampa Bay, 17-14. The Giants defense forced two turnovers and had five sacks—including four by linebacker Lawrence Taylor—as the New York offense began each of its three scoring drives in Tampa Bay territory. Phil Simms threw for two touchdowns to lead the Giants attack, but the losing Buccaneers actually led in both rushing and passing yardage. James Wilder ran for 112 yards for Tampa Bay.

Denver's Sammy Winder rolled up 139 yards for the Broncos as they won their AFC Western Division clash with Kansas City, 21-0. K.C. offense came up with just two first downs in the game's first 18 minutes as the Chiefs suffered their first shutout in five years. The Bronco defense harrassed quarterback Todd Blackledge most of the afternoon, sacking him once, picking off two passes and holding him to 23 completions in 48 attempts. Safety Mike Harden returned one of the interceptions 45 yards for a touchdown.

Pittsburgh cornerback Sam Washington picked off a Paul McDonald pass and returned it 69 yards for a touchdown late in the first half of the Steelers' game with the Cleveland Browns. It was the second interception return for Washington in as many weeks and the third against McDonald in four games.

But the Browns came back with 20 second-half points and held the Steelers to just one field goal in winning this AFC Central Division game, 20-10. McDonald passed for 222 yards and two touchdowns in the second half as the Browns won their first game of 1984.

Detroit quarterback Gary Danielson and

wide receiver Leonard Thompson hooked up for three touchdowns, but it still wasn't enough as the Lions lost to Minnesota, 29-28. Placekicker Jan Stenerud, an 18-year NFL veteran acquired in a preseason trade from Green Bay, kicked five field goals for Minnesota. The Lions, who entered the contest as the only team without a turnover in the season's first three weeks, fumbled the ball away three times in the second half.

The Miami Dolphins' 44-7 blowout of division-rival Indianapolis was the week's most one-sided game. After the Colts had tied the score at 7-7 early in the second quarter, Dan Marino hooked up with Mark Duper for an 80-yard scoring play just 24 seconds later. Marino and Duper combined for another touchdown later in the quarter as Miami moved out to a 23-7 halftime lead. The Dolphins then added 21 unanswered points in the second half to improve their season record to 4-0.

In the Monday night game, the Los Angeles Raiders came from behind to defeat San Diego, 33-30. Marcus Allen scored four touchdowns to lead the Raiders' attack, including the game-winner from a yard out with 45 seconds remaining in regulation time. Allen's third TD with 8:20 left had cut the Chargers' 30-20 advantage to four points.

The victory improved L.A.'s remarkable record in Monday night games to 21-2-1. The last Raider loss on a Monday night was to San Diego, 23-10, on the final weekend of the 1981 season.

Oilers-Falcons
SUNDAY, SEPTEMBER 23
SCORE BY PERIODS

Houston	0	10	0	0—10
Atlanta	21	0	14	7—42

SCORING

Atlanta—Cox 23 pass from Bartkowski (Luckhurst kick), 4:58 1st.
Atlanta—Riggs 2 run (Luckhurst kick), 9:07 1st.
Atlanta—Riggs 4 run (Luckhurst kick), 14:41 1st.
Houston—Field goal Kempf 22, 9:41 2nd.
Houston—Moriarty 2 pass from Moon (Kempf kick), 14:59 2nd.
Atlanta—B. Johnson 25 pass from Bartkowski (Luckhurst kick), 6:08 3rd.
Atlanta—Cox 16 pass from Bartkowski (Luckhurst kick), 13:46 3rd.
Atlanta—J. Jackson 35 interception return (Luckhurst kick), 13:56 4th.

TEAM STATISTICS

	Houston	Atlanta
First downs	20	18
Rushes-Yards	34-90	31-138
Passing yards	187	193
Sacked-Yards lost	4-21	3-18
Return yards	80	119
Passes	17-28-1	13-17-0
Punts	3-47.7	3-43.7
Fumbles-Lost	6-3	3-1
Penalties-Yards	5-27	10-62
Time of possession	30:45	29:15

Attendance—45,248. No-shows—8,792.

INDIVIDUAL STATISTICS

Rushing—Houston, Campbell 17-49, Moon 7-22, Moriarty 7-13, Edwards 2-6, Mullins 1-0; Atlanta, Riggs 25-120, Stamps 2-14, Austin 2-4, Bartkowski 1-0, Moroski 1-0.

Passing—Houston, Moon 17-28-1—208; Atlanta, Bartkowski 11-13-0—195, Moroski 2-4-0—16.

Receiving—Houston, Smith 5-52, Williams 3-42, Bryant 2-42, McCloskey 2-34, Campbell 2-20, Dressel 2-16, Moriarty 1-2; Atlanta, Cox 3-47, B. Johnson 2-65, Bailey 2-19, C. Benson 2-5, A. Jackson 1-48, Riggs 1-11, Hodge 1-9, Matthews 1-7.

Kickoff Returns—Houston, Allen 2-39, Roaches 3-39; Atlanta, Tate 2-48, Malancon 1-0.

Punt Returns—Houston, Roaches 1-2; Atlanta, B. Johnson 3-36.

Interceptions—Atlanta, J. Jackson 1-35.

Punting—Houston, James 3-47.3; Atlanta, Giacomarro 3-43.7.

Field Goals—Houston, Kempf 1-2 (missed: 43); Atlanta, none attempted.

Sacks—Houston, Baker 2, Sochia; Atlanta, Yeates 2, Smith, Pitts.

Steelers-Browns
SUNDAY, SEPTEMBER 23
SCORE BY PERIODS

Pittsburgh	0	7	3	0—10
Cleveland	0	0	10	10—20

SCORING

Pittsburgh—Washington 69 interception return (Anderson kick), 10:56 2nd.
Cleveland—Field goal Bahr 18, 4:12 3rd.
Cleveland—Green 44 pass from McDonald (Bahr kick), 6:14 3rd.
Pittsburgh—Field goal Anderson 46, 11:56 3rd.
Cleveland—Harris 3 pass from McDonald (Bahr kick), 0:11 4th.
Cleveland—Field goal Bahr 48, 3:48 4th.

TEAM STATISTICS

	Pittsburgh	Cleveland
First downs	12	17
Rushes-Yards	28-71	45-128
Passing yards	148	285
Sacked-Yards lost	1-5	1-8
Return yards	147	78
Passes	9-25-1	15-28-1
Punts	7-40.4	6-41.2
Fumbles-Lost	5-2	2-0
Penalties-Yards	10-63	9-95
Time of possession	24:06	35:54

Attendance—77,312. No-shows—2,229.

INDIVIDUAL STATISTICS

Rushing—Pittsburgh, Veals 12-35, Erenberg 12-23, Woodley 2-1, Gillespie 2-12; Cleveland, Green 16-41, Pruitt 26-83, McDonald 3-4.

Passing—Pittsburgh, Woodley 9-25-1—153; Cleveland, McDonald 15-28-1—293.

Receiving—Pittsburgh, Stallworth 3-68, Erenberg 1-5, Lipps 3-43, Thompson 1-25, Gillespie 1-12; Cleveland, Green 3-76, Holt 3-89, Newsome 6-99, Brennan 1-19, Pruitt 1-7, Harris 1-3.

Kickoff Returns—Pittsburgh, Spencer 3-72; Cleveland, White 2-33.

Punt Returns—Pittsburgh, Lipps 3-6; Cleveland, Harris 4-43.

Interceptions—Pittsburgh, Washington 1-69; Cleveland, Gross 1-2.

Punting—Pittsburgh, Colquitt 7-40.4; Cleveland, Cox 6-41.2.

Field Goals—Pittsburgh, Anderson 1-1; Cleveland, Bahr 2-3 (missed: 42).

Sacks—Pittsburgh, Cole; Cleveland, Baldwin.

Packers-Cowboys

SUNDAY, SEPTEMBER 23

SCORE BY PERIODS

Green Bay	0	0	6	0— 6
Dallas	7	6	0	7—20

SCORING

Dallas—Newsome 1 run (Septien kick), 13:50 1st.
Dallas—Field goal Septien 32, 3:31 2nd.
Dallas—Field goal Septien 42, 14:48 2nd.
Green Bay—Brown 5 interception return (kick failed), 3:30 3rd.
Dallas—Dorsett 7 run (Septien kick), 14:14 4th.

TEAM STATISTICS

	Green Bay	Dallas
First downs	16	19
Rushes-Yards	28-125	37-100
Passing yards	82	200
Sacked-Yards lost	6-39	4-30
Return yards	125	87
Passes	11-35-4	17-35-1
Punts	9-49.4	11-38.1
Fumbles-Lost	2-0	2-0
Penalties-Yards	7-53	11-95
Time of possession	27:02	32:58

Attendance—64,222. No-shows—879.

INDIVIDUAL STATISTICS

Rushing—Green Bay, Clark 10-55, Crouse 6-26, Ellis 7-23, Huckleby 2-10, Lofton 1-8, Wright 2-3; Dallas, Dorsett 20-44, Newsome 7-30, Springs 9-25, Hogeboom 1-1.

Passing—Green Bay, Dickey 5-16-1—64, Wright 6-18-3—57, Ellis 0-1-0—0; Dallas, Hogeboom 17-35-1—230.

Receiving—Green Bay, Ellis 3-35, Epps 2-34, Jefferson 2-31, Lofton 1-8, West 1-9, Cassidy 1-6, Huckleby 1-minus 2; Dallas, Cosbie 7-103, Dorsett 3-35, Donley 2-30, Springs 2-27, Renfro 2-24, Newsome 1-11.

Kickoff Returns—Green Bay, Huckleby 5-98; Dallas, Allen 1-21.

Punt Returns—Green Bay, Epps 7-22; Dallas, Allen 5-66.

Interceptions—Green Bay, Brown 1-5; Dallas, Dickerson 1-0, Thurman 1-0, Walls 2-0.

Punting—Green Bay, Scribner 9-49.4; Dallas, D. White 11-38.1.

Field Goals—Green Bay, Garcia 0-1 (missed: 37); Dallas, Septien 2-2.

Sacks—Green Bay, Cumby 2, Douglass, Johnson; Dallas, Downs 2, R. White 1½, Dutton 1½, Jeffcoat.

Chiefs-Broncos

SUNDAY, SEPTEMBER 23

SCORE BY PERIODS

Kansas City	0	0	0	0— 0
Denver	0	14	7	0—21

SCORING

Denver—Winder 6 run (Karlis kick), 4:27 2nd.
Denver—Parros 3 run (Karlis kick), 12:37 2nd.
Denver—Harden 45 interception return (Karlis kick), 10:13 3rd.

TEAM STATISTICS

	Kansas City	Denver
First downs	16	21
Rushes-Yards	16-50	36-210
Passing yards	287	157
Sacked-Yards lost	1-8	4-15
Return yards	85	67
Passes	23-48-2	17-29-2
Punts	9-45.9	7-44.7
Fumbles-Lost	2-0	0-0
Penalties-Yards	7-46	4-22
Time of possession	27:38	32:22

Attendance—74,263. No-shows—837.

INDIVIDUAL STATISTICS

Rushing—Kansas City, Brown 10-36, Blackledge 2-5, Heard 3-2, Lacy 1-7; Denver, Winder 31-139, Willhite 4-68, Parros 1-3.

Passing—Kansas City, Blackledge 23-48-2—295; Denver, Elway 17-29-2—172.

Receiving—Kansas City, Scott 5-48, Brown 6-46, Carson 3-46, Marshall 8-148, Heard 1-7; Denver, Watson 7-93, Winder 3-14, Logan 1-3, Sawyer 6-62.

Kickoff Returns—Kansas City, Paige 1-19, Scott 1-9.

Punt Returns—Kansas City, Smith 2-6; Denver, Thomas 4-22.

Interceptions—Kansas City, Burruss 1-16, Radecic 1-35; Denver, Foley 1-0, Harden 1-45.

Punting—Kansas City, Arnold 9-45.9; Denver, Norman 7-44.7.

Field Goals—Kansas City, Lowery 0-2 (missed: 38, 38); Denver, Karlis 0-1 (missed: 46).

Sacks—Kansas City, Still 2, Lindstrom, McAlister; Denver, T. Jackson.

Rams-Bengals

SUNDAY, SEPTEMBER 23

SCORE BY PERIODS

Los Angeles Rams	0	7	7	10—24
Cincinnati	0	0	7	7—14

SCORING

Los Angeles—Dickerson 6 run (Lansford kick), 8:07 2nd.
Cincinnati—Kinnebrew 2 run (Breech kick), 7:33 3rd.
Los Angeles—Brown 52 pass from Kemp (Lansford kick), 12:59 3rd.
Los Angeles—Field goal Lansford 29, 10:45 4th.
Cincinnati—Collinsworth 10 pass from Anderson (Breech kick), 13:11 4th.
Los Angeles—Guman 43 kickoff return (Lansford kick), 13:17 4th.

TEAM STATISTICS

	Los Angeles	Cincinnati
First downs	17	19
Rushes-Yards	38-136	34-129
Passing yards	185	186
Sacked-Yards lost	2-20	2-0
Return yards	145	85
Passes	13-23-0	18-32-2
Punts	4-39.0	6-45.8
Fumbles-Lost	4-3	3-2
Penalties-Yards	2-23	5-36
Time of possession	30:29	29:31

Attendance—45,406. No-shows—10,436..

INDIVIDUAL STATISTICS

Rushing—Los Angeles, Dickerson 22-89, Crutchfield 8-21, Redden 7-28, Kemp 1-minus 2; Cincinnati, S. Wilson 17-74, Jennings 1-3, Brooks 3-minus 1, Kinnebrew 6-21, Alexander 4-23, Anderson 2-2, Collinsworth 1-7.

Passing—Los Angeles, Kemp 13-23-0—205; Cincinnati, Anderson 17-31-2—143, McInally 1-1-0—43.

Receiving—Los Angeles, David Hill 5-60, Guman 3-21, Grant 1-8, Ellard 1-22, Brown 2-87, Crutchfield 1-7; Cincinnati, Brooks 1-3, S. Wilson 2-15, Collinsworth 4-26, Holman 2-21, Curtis 1-6, Alexander 3-19, Jennings 2-54, Harris 3-42.

Kickoff Returns—Los Angeles, Redden 1-31, Guman 1-43, Crutchfield 1-20; Cincinnati, Martin 3-52, Brooks 2-34.

Punt Returns—Los Angeles, Ellard 4-32; Cincinnati, Martin 1-0, Horton 2-minus 1.

Interceptions—Los Angeles, Green 1-5, Irvin 1-14.

Punting—Los Angeles, Misko 4-39.0; Cincinnati, McInally 6-45.8.

Field Goals—Los Angeles, Lansford 1-3 (missed: 46, 45); Cincinnati, none attempted.

Sacks—Los Angeles, Youngblood, Owens; Cincinnati, Williams, Browner.

Colts-Dolphins
SUNDAY, SEPTEMBER 23
SCORE BY PERIODS

Indianapolis	0	7	0	0— 7
Miami	7	16	14	7—44

SCORING

Miami—P. Johnson 1 run (von Schamann kick), 12:02 1st.
Indianapolis—Young 5 pass from Pagel (Biasucci kick), 2:17 2nd.
Miami—Duper 80 pass from Marino (kick failed), 2:41 2nd.
Miami—Field goal von Schamann 27, 7:39 2nd.
Miami—Duper 5 pass from Marino (von Schamann kick), 14:01 2nd.
Miami—McNeal 11 interception return (von Schamann kick), 5:07 3rd.
Miami—Bennett 4 run (von Schamann kick), 14:12 3rd.
Miami—Bennett 1 run (von Schamann kick), 5:03 4th.

TEAM STATISTICS

	Indianapolis	Miami
First downs	15	23
Rushes-Yards	30-152	40-139
Passing yards	71	260
Sacked-Yards lost	6-43	0-0
Return yards	69	167
Passes	11-24-3	15-30-0
Punts	8-50.0	3-53.0
Fumbles-Lost	1-1	3-1
Penalties-Yards	5-49	1-5
Time of possession	26:54	33:06

Attendance—55,415. No-shows—2,398..

INDIVIDUAL STATISTICS

Rushing—Indianapolis, Dickey 15-77, McMillan 13-67, Schlichter 1-7, Middleton 1-1; Miami, Carter 16-68, Bennett 7-36, P. Johnson 11-20, Nathan 3-13, Moore 1-3, Strock 1-0.
Passing—Indianapolis, Pagel 8-15-2—104, Schlichter 3-9-1—10; Miami, Marino 14-29-0—257, Strock 1-1-0—3.
Receiving—Indianapolis, Young 4-46, Butler 3-36, Porter 2-26, Dickey 2-6; Miami, Duper 7-173, Cefalo 2-23, Nathan 2-17, Rose 2-13, Bennett 1-20, Jensen 1-14.
Kickoff Returns—Indianapolis, L. Anderson 4-69.
Punt Returns—Miami, Heflin 6-76.
Interceptions—Miami, G. Blackwood 2-80, McNeal 1-11.
Punting—Indianapolis, Stark 8-50.0; Miami, Roby 3-53.0.
Field Goals—Indianapolis, Biasucci 0-1 (missed: 55); Miami, von Schamann 1-2 (missed: 27).
Sacks—Miami, Betters 3, Baumhower, Brudzinski, Barnett.

Vikings-Lions
SUNDAY, SEPTEMBER 23
SCORE BY PERIODS

Minnesota	7	9	10	3—29
Detroit	7	7	7	7—28

SCORING

Minnesota—White 26 pass from Kramer (Stenerud kick), 3:42 1st.
Detroit—Thompson 1 pass from Danielson (Murray kick), 8:51 1st.
Minnesota—Field goal Stenerud 35, 2:55 2nd.
Detroit—Thompson 66 pass from Danielson (Murray kick), 3:56 2nd.
Minnesota—Field goal Stenerud 32, 10:07 2nd.
Minnesota—Field goal Stenerud 37, 14:39 2nd.
Minnesota—C. Martin 8 fumble return (Stenerud kick), 3:42 3rd.

Detroit—Jones 10 pass from Danielson (Murray kick), 6:29 3rd.
Minnesota—Field goal Stenerud 34, 13:29 3rd.
Minnesota—Field goal Stenerud 19, 12:53 4th.
Detroit—Thompson 15 pass from Danielson (Murray kick), 14:34 4th.

TEAM STATISTICS

	Minnesota	Detroit
First downs	23	17
Rushes-Yards	42-205	21-114
Passing yards	215	222
Sacked-Yards lost	2-10	1-9
Return yards	110	191
Passes	15-26-0	25-31-0
Punts	4-33.0	4-41.0
Fumbles-Lost	0-0	3-3
Penalties-Yards	12-122	10-104
Time of possession	35:30	24:30

Attendance—57,511. No-shows—4,141.

INDIVIDUAL STATISTICS

Rushing—Minnesota, Anderson 19-120, Nelson 11-36, Brown 6-36, Kramer 4-16, Rice 2-minus 3; Detroit, Sims 12-66, Danielson 5-49, Jones 3-12, Thompson 1-minus 13.
Passing—Minnesota, Kramer 15-25-0—225, Anderson 0-1-0—0; Detroit, Danielson 24-30-0—218, Jones 1-1-0—13.
Receiving—Minnesota, Lewis 5-101, White 5-89, Nelson 2-21, Brown 2-20, Anderson 1-minus 6; Detroit, Jones 10-70, Thompson 7-98, Sims 6-46, Nichols 2-17.
Kickoff Returns—Minnesota, Nelson 1-38, Anderson 3-59; Detroit, Jenkins 5-115, Mandley 3-73.
Punt Returns—Minnesota, Nelson 2-13; Detroit, Martin 2-3.
Punting—Minnesota, Coleman 4-33.0; Detroit, Black 4-41.0.
Field Goals—Minnesota, Stenerud 5-5; Detroit, none attempted.
Sacks—Minnesota, C. Johnson; Detroit, Cofer, Green.

Cardinals-Saints
SUNDAY, SEPTEMBER 23
SCORE BY PERIODS

St. Louis	0	7	7	10—24
New Orleans	10	3	7	14—34

SCORING

New Orleans—Field goal Andersen 25, 4:02 1st.
New Orleans—W. Wilson 34 pass from Gajan (Andersen kick), 8:03 1st.
St. Louis—Ferrell 11 pass from Lomax (O'Donoghue kick), 4:24 2nd.
New Orleans—Field goal Andersen 29, 14:59 2nd.
St. Louis—Mitchell 7 run (O'Donoghue kick), 6:15 3rd.
New Orleans—Brenner 15 pass from Todd (Andersen kick), 10:13 3rd.
St. Louis—Mitchell 22 run (O'Donoghue kick), 0:06 4th.
St. Louis—Field goal O'Donoghue 39, 5:39 4th.
New Orleans—W. Wilson 30 pass from Todd (Andersen kick), 8:53 4th.
New Orleans—Wattelet 22 fumble return (Andersen kick), 15:00 4th.

TEAM STATISTICS

	St. Louis	New Orleans
First downs	22	25
Rushes-Yards	20-113	36-152
Passing-Yards	224	298
Sacked-Yards lost	5-45	0-0
Return yards	144	148
Passes	23-33-0	15-30-1
Punts	5-46.0	4-36.8
Fumbles-Lost	4-3	2-1

	St. Louis	New Orleans
Penalties-Yards	10-79	5-38
Time of possession	29:58	30:02
Attendance—58,723. No-shows—5,162.		

INDIVIDUAL STATISTICS

Rushing—St. Louis, Mitchell 10-77, Anderson 5-22, Ferrell 4-14, Lomax 1-0; New Orleans, G. Rogers 18-63, Gajan 6-45, W. Wilson 8-29, Anthony 4-15.

Passing—St. Louis, Lomax 23-33-0—269; New Orleans, Todd 14-29-1—264, Gajan 1-1-0—34.

Receiving—St. Louis, Mitchell 6-75, Tilley 4-62, LaFleur 3-52, Green 2-25, Ferrell 2-21, Harrell 2-13, Marsh 1-11, Anderson 2-3, Love 1-7; New Orleans, Brenner 6-131, W. Wilson 3-69, Goodlow 3-57, Young 2-24, Groth 1-17.

Kickoff Returns—St. Louis, Mitchell 3-74, Harrell 2-25; New Orleans, Duckett 2-33, Fields 3-51.

Punt Returns—St. Louis, Bird 1-5, Mitchell 2-21; New Orleans, Fields 2-64.

Interceptions—St. Louis, Heflin 1-19.

Punting—St. Louis, Birdsong 5-46.0; New Orleans, Hansen 4-36.8.

Field Goals—St. Louis, O'Donoghue 1-1; New Orleans, Andersen 2-2.

Sacks—New Orleans, Reggie Lewis 2, Geathers 2, Jackson.

Buccaneers-Giants
SUNDAY, SEPTEMBER 23
SCORE BY PERIODS

Tampa Bay	0	0	7	7—14
New York Giants	0	10	0	7—17

SCORING

New York—Field goal Haji-Sheikh 34, 3:55 2nd.

New York—Johnson 20 pass from Simms (Haji-Sheikh kick), 9:00 2nd.

Tampa Bay—Wilder 1 run (Ariri kick), 4:54 3rd.

New York—Mowatt 21 pass from Simms (Haji-Sheikh kick), 8:47 4th.

Tampa Bay—Armstrong 1 run (Ariri kick), 10:58 4th.

TEAM STATISTICS

	Tampa Bay	New York
First downs	22	17
Rushes-Yards	29-137	33-119
Passing yards	189	161
Sacked-Yards lost	5-40	3-25
Return yards	84	128
Passes	18-31-1	17-34-0
Punts	6-43.2	6-46.7
Fumbles-Lost	1-1	1-0
Penalties-Yards	7-47	6-40
Time of possession	29:14	30:46
Attendance—72,650. No-shows—4,165.		

INDIVIDUAL STATISTICS

Rushing—Tampa Bay, Wilder 24-112, Carver 4-24, Armstrong 1-1; New York, Carpenter 20-70, Simms 5-30, Woolfolk 6-7, Galbreath 1-8, Morris 1-4.

Passing—Tampa Bay, DeBerg 18-31-1—229; New York, Simms 17-34-0—186.

Receiving—Tampa Bay, Wilder 4-65, House 5-45, Carver 1-10, Giles 2-24, Carter 2-57, J. Bell 2-18, T. Bell 1-8, Armstrong 1-2; New York, B. Williams 4-42, Mowatt 4-42, Woolfolk 4-28, Galbreath 3-20, Johnson 2-54.

Kickoff Returns—Tampa Bay, Owens 1-4, Morton 3-64; New York, McConkey 1-18, Morris 1-13, Hill 1-27.

Punt Returns—Tampa Bay, Holt 3-16; New York, McConkey 4-66.

Interceptions—New York, Headen 1-4.

Punting—Tampa Bay, Garcia 6-43.2; New York, Jennings 6-46.7.

Field Goals—Tampa Bay, Ariri 0-1 (missed: 53); New York, Haji-Sheikh 1-2 (missed: 39).

Sacks—Tampa Bay, L. Selmon, Logan, Cannon; New York, Taylor 4, Merrill.

Jets-Bills
SUNDAY, SEPTEMBER 23
SCORE BY PERIODS

New York Jets	0	21	0	7—28
Buffalo	10	0	9	7—26

SCORING

Buffalo—Field goal Danelo 52, 6:20 1st.

Buffalo—V. Williams 1 pass from Ferguson (Danelo kick), 10:21 1st.

New York—Paige 2 run (Leahy kick), 1:31 2nd.

New York—Walker 12 pass from Ryan (Leahy kick), 5:15 2nd.

New York—Walker 44 pass from Ryan (Leahy kick), 8:23 2nd.

Buffalo—Field goal Danelo 36, 2:35 3rd.

Buffalo—Field goal Danelo 27, 7:57 3rd.

Buffalo—Field goal Danelo 20, 14:14 3rd.

New York—Walker 35 pass from Ryan (Leahy kick), 8:56 4th.

Buffalo—Dawkins 31 pass from Ferguson (Danelo kick), 11:02 4th.

TEAM STATISTICS

	New York	Buffalo
First downs	23	24
Rushes-Yards	33-143	21-87
Passing yards	248	304
Sacked-Yards lost	0-0	4-36
Return yards	15	86
Passes	17-26-1	31-51-1
Punts	4-30.8	4-40.0
Fumbles-Lost	3-2	2-0
Penalties-Yards	4-25	10-83
Time of possession	29:03	30:57
Attendance—48,330. No-shows—1,426.		

INDIVIDUAL STATISTICS

Rushing—New York, McNeil 24-112, Harper 2-0, Paige 5-31, Ryan 2-0; Buffalo, Bell 11-45, Moore 4-10, Ferguson 1-2, V. Williams 3-11, Brookins 1-16, Kofler 1-3.

Passing—New York, Ryan 17-26-1—248; Buffalo, Ferguson 31-46-0—340, Kofler 0-5-1—0.

Receiving—New York, McNeil 2-17, Gaffney 3-50, Shuler 2-26, Walker 7-128, Dennison 2-14, Harper 1-13; Buffalo, Dawkins 3-56, Franklin 5-55, Moore 9-41, Brookins 3-64, V. Williams 1-1, Barnett 4-32, Riddick 3-67, Neal 1-4, Bell 1-10, Dennard 1-10.

Kickoff Returns—New York, Paige 1-0; Buffalo, Wilson 1-29, V. Williams 2-25, Bell 1-15.

Punt Returns—New York, Springs 3-15; Buffalo, Wilson 2-10.

Interceptions—New York, Schroy 1-0; Buffalo, Smith 1-7.

Punting—New York, Ramsey 4-30.8; Buffalo, Kidd 4-40.0.

Field Goals—New York, Leahy 0-1 (missed: 52); Buffalo, Danelo 4-5 (missed: 40).

Sacks—New York, Mehl 2, Gastineau, Rudolph.

49ers-Eagles
SUNDAY, SEPTEMBER 23
SCORE BY PERIODS

San Francisco	7	7	0	7—21
Philadelphia	0	6	3	0— 9

SCORING

San Francisco—Craig 35 pass from Cavanaugh (Wersching kick), 13:30 1st.

Philadelphia—Field goal McFadden 35, 3:08 2nd.

Philadelphia—Field goal McFadden 32, 14:05 2nd.

San Francisco—Solomon 2 pass from Cavanaugh (Wersching kick), 14:48 2nd.

Philadelphia—Field goal McFadden 33, 8:47 3rd.

Washington fullback John Riggins had a big day against New England in Week 4, rushing for 140 yards and one touchdown in a 26-10 Redskins' triumph.

San Francisco—D. Clark 51 pass from Cavanaugh (Wersching kick), 4:11 4th.

TEAM STATISTICS

	San Francisco	Philadelphia
First downs	23	15
Rushes-Yards	37-177	20-72
Passing yards	221	169
Sacked-Yards lost	4-31	2-18
Return yards	173	51
Passes	17-34-0	16-41-1
Punts	7-39.1	7-40.0
Fumbles-Lost	2-0	0-0
Penalties-Yards	12-141	4-30
Time of possession	34:31	25:29

Attendance—62,771. No-shows—1,178.

INDIVIDUAL STATISTICS

Rushing—San Francisco, Tyler 21-113, Craig 10-39, Ring 3-18, Monroe 1-7, Harmon 1-3, Cavanaugh 1-minus 3; Philadelphia, Montgomery 12-51, Oliver 5-13, Haddix 3-8.

Passing—San Francisco, Cavanaugh 17-34-0—252; Philadelphia, Jaworski 16-40-1—187, Montgomery 0-1-0—0.

Receiving—San Francisco, Craig 4-58, D. Clark 3-84, Monroe 3-24, Nehemiah 2-32, Tyler 2-28, Francis 2-24, Solomon 1-2; Philadelphia, Montgomery 7-46, Jackson 4-87, Quick 2-36, Haddix 2-9, Woodruff 1-9.

Kickoff Returns—San Francisco, Monroe 2-63, Harmon 2-67; Philadelphia, Hayes 1-20, Strauthers 1-12.

Punt Returns—San Francisco, McLemore 4-34; Philadelphia, Cooper 3-19.

Interceptions—San Francisco, J. Fahnhorst 1-9.

Punting—San Francisco, Runager 7-39.1; Philadelphia, Horan 7-40.0.

Field Goals—Wersching 0-2 (missed: 30,44); Philadelphia, McFadden 3-3.

Sacks—San Francisco, Pillers, Tuiasosopo; Philadelphia, Brown, Clarke, Strauthers, Griggs.

Bears-Seahawks

SUNDAY, SEPTEMBER 23

SCORE BY PERIODS

Chicago	7	0	0	2— 9
Seattle	7	3	21	7—38

SCORING

Chicago—Suhey 3 pass from Payton (B. Thomas kick), 3:46 1st.

Seattle—Simpson 39 interception return (N. Johnson kick), 7:11 1st.

Seattle—Field goal N. Johnson 27, 1:44 2nd.

Seattle—Krieg 3 run (N. Johnson kick), 4:23 3rd.

Seattle—Lane 55 pass from Krieg (N. Johnson kick), 10:15 3rd.

Seattle—Nash recovered fumble in end zone (N. Johnson kick), 11:14 3rd.

Chicago—Safety, Seattle penalized for holding in end zone, 3:37 4th.

Seattle—T. Jackson 62 interception return (N. Johnson kick), 14:49 4th.

TEAM STATISTICS

	Chicago	Seattle
First downs	20	12
Rushes-Yards	35-136	35-93
Passing yards	165	110
Sacked-Yards lost	4-34	4-36
Return yards	95	156
Passes	20-39-3	6-16-0
Punts	7-36.4	9-40.6
Fumbles-Lost	4-3	2-1
Penalties-Yards	11-76	11-105
Time of possession	32:18	27:42

Attendance—61,520. No-shows—3,386.

INDIVIDUAL STATISTICS

Rushing—Chicago, Payton 24-116, Lisch 2-13, Suhey 6-11, Avellini 1-0, C. Thomas 2-minus 4; Seattle, Lane 17-50, F. Harris 14-23, Krieg 3-18, Doornink 1-2.

Passing—Chicago, Avellini 13-26-1—119, Lisch 6-12-2—77, Payton 1-1-0—3; Seattle, Krieg 6-16-0—146.

Receiving—Chicago, Gault 6-73, McKinnon 4-35, Suhey 3-11, Moorehead 2-33, Payton 2-12, Saldi 1-19, Baschnagel 1-10, C. Thomas 1-6; Seattle, Lane 1-55, Pratt 1-30, Largent 1-29, Doornink 1-25, Johns 1-5, Turner 1-2.

Kickoff Returns—Chicago, Gentry 1-23, Cameron 4-63; Seattle, C. Bryant 2-33.

Punt Returns—Chicago, Fisher 6-9; Seattle, Johns 4-22.

Interceptions—Seattle, Simpson 1-39, Brown 1-0, T. Jackson 1-62.

Punting—Chicago, Finzer 6-42.5; Seattle, West 9-40.6.

Field Goals—Chicago, B. Thomas 0-1 (missed: 46); Seattle, N. Johnson 1-1.

Sacks—Chicago, Keys, McMichael, Dent, Osborne; Seattle, Green, M. Jackson, Simpson, Fanning.

Redskins-Patriots
SUNDAY, SEPTEMBER 23
SCORE BY PERIODS

Washington	7	3	13	3—26
New England	0	0	7	3—10

SCORING

Washington—Riggins 13 run (Moseley kick), 12:56 1st.
Washington—Field goal Moseley 19, 8:26 2nd.
Washington—Field goal Moseley 42, 6:24 3rd.
Washington—Brown 15 pass from Theismann (Moseley kick), 6:53 3rd.
New England—Starring 38 pass from Eason (Franklin kick), 9:34 3rd.
Washington—Field goal Moseley 22, 14:59 3rd.
New England—Field goal Franklin 22, 2:52 4th.
Washington—Field goal Moseley 27, 13:03 4th.

TEAM STATISTICS

	Washington	New England
First downs	23	13
Rushes-Yards	54-235	11-17
Passing yards	97	225
Sacked-Yards lost	2-13	4-29
Return yards	43	42
Passes	11-19-0	21-31-0
Punts	3-34.3	4-36.3
Fumbles-Lost	0-0	2-2
Penalties-Yards	9-67	6-71
Time of possession	43:12	16:48

Attendance—60,503. No-shows—453.

INDIVIDUAL STATISTICS

Rushing—Washington, Riggins 33-140, J. Washington 17-61, Theismann 4-34; New England, Collins 5-10, Tatupu 4-minus 5, C. James 2-12.

Passing—Washington, Theismann 11-19-0—110; New England, Eason 21-31-0—254.

Receiving—Washington, Monk 5-37, Brown 4-36, Walker 1-19, Warren 1-18; New England, Ramsey 5-48, Fryar 3-43, Starring 7-98, Tatupu 1-6, Collins 1-5, Dawson 3-40, C. James 1-14.

Kickoff Returns—Washington, Nelms 2-25; New England, Tatupu 1-9, Jones 1-20.

Punt Returns—Washington, Nelms 3-18; New England, Fryar 2-13.

Punting—Washington, Hayes 3-34.3; New England, Prestridge 4-36.3.

Field Goals—Washington, Moseley 4-4; New England, Franklin 1-2 (missed: 44).

Sacks—Washington, Manley, Coleman, Mann, McGee; New England, Owens, L. Williams.

Chargers-Raiders
MONDAY, SEPTEMBER 24
SCORE BY PERIODS

San Diego	7	3	3	17—30
Los Angeles Raiders	6	7	7	13—33

SCORING

Los Angeles—Field goal Bahr 42, 3:43 1st.
San Diego—Winslow 11 pass from Fouts (Benirschke kick), 8:16 1st.
Los Angeles—Field goal Bahr 36, 12:09 1st.
San Diego—Field goal Benirschke 51, 7:54 2nd.
Los Angeles—Allen 1 run (Bahr kick), 14:54 2nd.
Los Angeles—Allen 30 pass from Plunkett (Bahr kick), 3:50 3rd.
San Diego—Field goal Benirschke 33, 7:46 3rd.
San Diego—Jackson 1 run (Benirschke kick), 1:18 4th.
San Diego—Field goal Benirschke 48, 3:58 4th.
San Diego—Lowe 32 interception return (Benirschke kick), 4:39 4th.
Los Angeles—Allen 2 run (kick failed), 6:40 4th.
Los Angeles—Allen 1 run (Bahr kick), 14:15 4th.

TEAM STATISTICS

	San Diego	Los Angeles
First downs	23	26
Rushes-Yards	32-147	27-49
Passing yards	196	348
Sacked-Yards lost	4-31	2-15
Return yards	66	47
Passes	19-37-1	24-33-1
Punts	4-45.3	3-37.3
Fumbles-Lost	2-0	1-1
Penalties-Yards	8-62	4-30
Time of possession	32:04	27:56

Attendance—76,131. No-shows—4,543.

INDIVIDUAL STATISTICS

Rushing—San Diego, Jackson 29-155, Fouts 1-minus 3, McGee 2-minus 5; Los Angeles, Allen 18-47, Hawkins 4-3, King 2-1, Pruitt 2-0, Plunkett 1-minus 2.

Passing—San Diego, Fouts 19-37-1—227; Los Angeles, Plunkett 24-33-1—363.

Receiving—San Diego, Winslow 9-119, Holohan 4-71, Jackson 3-21, Chandler 2-7, Sievers 1-9; Los Angeles, Christensen 8-120, Branch 4-92, Allen 6-62, Barnwell 3-62, Hawkins 2-19, Pruitt 1-8.

Kickoff Returns—San Diego, James 5-90, Egloff 1-11, McGee 1-19; Los Angeles, Williams 4-118, Montgomery 3-62.

Punt Returns—San Diego, James 1-4; Los Angeles, Pruitt 4-44.

Interceptions—San Diego, Lowe 1-32; Los Angeles, Haynes 1-3.

Punting—San Diego, Buford 4-45.3; Los Angeles, Guy 3-37.3.

Field Goals—San Diego, Benirschke 3-3; Los Angeles, Bahr 2-2.

Sacks—San Diego, Ferguson, Lowe; Los Angeles, Martin 2, Barnes, Pickel.

FIFTH WEEK

RESULTS OF WEEK 5

Sunday, September 30

Dallas 23, Chicago 14 at Chi.
Denver 16, L.A. Raiders 13 at Den.
Indianapolis 31, Buffalo 17 at Ind.
Kansas City 10, Cleveland 6 at K.C.
L.A. Rams 33, N.Y. Giants 12 at L.A.
Miami 36, St. Louis 28 at St. L.
New England 28, N.Y. Jets 21 at N.Y.
New Orleans 27, Houston 10 at Hous.
San Diego 27, Detroit 24 at S.D.
San Francisco 14, Atlanta 5 at S.F.
Seattle 20, Minnesota 12 at Minn.
Tampa Bay 30, Green Bay 27 (OT) at T.B.
Washington 20, Philadelphia 0 at Wash.

Monday, October 1

Pittsburgh 38, Cincinnati 17 at Pitts.

"We were lucky to win," said Tampa Bay Coach John McKay after the Buccaneers defeated Green Bay, 30-27 in overtime, in a matchup of NFC Central Division teams. "But then again, we've been unlucky to lose so many times."

McKay, a highly successful coach during his college coaching days at Southern California, learned all about losing during his days as coach of the expansion Tampa Bay franchise. In its first season (1976), the club lost all 14 of its regular-season games, a pair of three-point defeats representing the closest thing to victory. The Bucs opened the 1977 season by losing their first 12 contests, thereby establishing an NFL record for consecutive losses—26. But Tampa Bay won its first game against New Orleans in Week 13, and then closed the 1977 campaign with another victory—its first ever at home—against St. Louis.

Tampa Bay's best season came in 1979, when the club finished the regular season at 10-6 and advanced all the way to the NFC title game, where its season ended with a 9-0 loss to the Rams. The Bucs also made the playoffs in 1981 and '82, the latter being the strike-shortened nine-game season.

But the bottom fell out in 1983, when the Bucs tied Houston for the worst record in the league at 2-14. To make matters worse, starting quarterback Doug Williams had abandoned the team before the '83 season for the greener pastures of the USFL, painting a bleak picture for the team's immediate future.

But five games into the '84 season, Tampa Bay had a 2-3 record, good enough for a second-place tie with Minnesota, one game behind division-leading Chicago. It was Obed Ariri's 48-yard field goal with 4:22 left in overtime that clinched the victory over the Packers.

"I knew it was good from the start," said the Nigerian-born kicker. "I didn't even look at it. When I hit the ball I could tell it would make it all the way."

Trailing, 27-20, with 1:52 left in regulation, Green Bay forced the overtime with a 75-yard drive. The tying touchdown came when wide receiver James Lofton caught a pass from Lynn Dickey at the Tampa Bay 12 and then lateraled to running back Gerry Ellis, who took it in from the 15 with eight seconds left in regulation.

The San Diego Chargers pulled out a three-point win over Detroit, 27-24, but the Lions' inability to execute two plays late in the game cost them a victory.

After the Chargers jumped out to a 24-7 half-time lead by scoring on four of their first five possessions, the Lions rallied in the second half to trail by only six, 27-21, with five minutes remaining. With the ball on the San Diego 3-yard line, a motion penalty on Detroit fullback James Jones nullified a touchdown run by Leonard Thompson. Then, on the next play, a touchdown pass to Jones was called back on an offensive pass interference call against wide receiver Mark Nichols. For the game, the Lions were flagged for 13 penalties and 161 yards.

The Miami Dolphins' offense was near perfect in a 36-28 triumph over St. Louis. Quarterback Dan Marino threw for a club-record 429 yards on 24-of-36 passing as the Miami offense didn't commit a turnover and punted only once. Marino passed for 318 yards in the first half, with receivers Mark Duper and Mark Clayton both going over the 100-yard mark. They finished the day with 164 and 143 yards, respectively, with Clayton catching one of Marino's three touchdown passes. Uwe von Schamann kicked three field goals as the Dolphins won their fifth game without a defeat.

The San Francisco 49ers joined the Dolphins as the NFL's only unbeaten teams by stopping Atlanta, 14-5. The Falcons entered the contest with a 30.5 points-per-game average, best in the NFC, and led the 49ers in total yards—418 to 310—in the game. But the Falcons were held without a touchdown by a stingy 49er defense that stretched to nine the number of quarters without allowing a touchdown. Atlanta had to settle for a field goal after a first-quarter goal-line stand; were stopped at the San Francisco 1-yard line on a fourth-down play in the final period, and fumbled another time at the 49ers' 9-yard line.

The Denver Broncos handed the defending Super Bowl champion Los Angeles Raiders their first loss of the season, 16-13. The L.A. offense was held to 12 first downs, 70 yards rushing and one touchdown as both defenses dominated. Fights and scuffles occurred throughout the game between the long-time AFC Western Division rivals.

The Broncos' game-winning touchdown

Indianapolis fullback Randy McMillan exploded for 108 yards and two touchdowns in the second half of a 31-17 victory over Buffalo in Week 5.

capped an 11-play, 82-yard march and came on a four-yard run by Gerald Willhite. The final eight plays of the drive were runs and Denver used a solid ground attack to eat up time and prevent the Raiders from making a comeback in the final 4:34 of the game.

Defense also played a big part in Kansas City's 10-6 victory over the Cleveland Browns. The Chiefs' defense sacked Browns' quarter-back Paul McDonald 11 times and picked off four of his passes. Linebacker Ken McAlister, who played basketball but did not compete in football during his college days at San Francis-co, led the charge with three sacks, four solo tackles, three assists and one interception. McAlister was making the first start of his NFL career. Chiefs rookie lineman Bill Maas also had three sacks.

Ironically, Kansas City's defense ranked last in the league overall and next-to-last in pass defense prior to the Cleveland game. The unit's 11 sacks missed by one the NFL record of 12 set by Dallas in 1966 and equalled by St. Louis in 1980.

Defense also was the name of the game in Los Angeles, where the Rams set an NFL record by recording three safeties in a 33-12 victory over the New York Giants. Two of the safeties came off blocked punts and the third occurred when quarterback Phil Simms was tackled in his own end zone. All three safeties came in the third quarter.

The L.A. defense dominated throughout the game. The Giants' first score came when the Rams' special teams failed to cover the opening kickoff in their own end zone and the other came with four minutes to play and the outcome long decided. The Giants were held to eight rushing yards while Rams' star Eric Dickerson ran for 120.

Chicago's Walter Payton piled up 130 first-half yards, but Dallas slowed him down in the second and stopped the Bears, 23-14. The All-Pro running back accounted for all 57 yards in a six-play first-half drive that put the Bears on top, 14-10, after the Cowboys had taken a 10-7 lead on a 68-yard pass from Gary Hogeboom to Tony Dorsett. Dallas scored again after Payton's 20-yard touchdown run to take a 17-14 halftime lead.

The second half, however, was a complete reversal from the first. Payton rushed only five times for 25 yards as Chicago Coach Mike Ditka relied on his passing attack. It didn't work and the Bears were held scoreless as the Cowboys rolled to their sixth straight victory over Chicago.

Indianapolis' Randy McMillan's performance was a direct opposite of Payton's. McMillan managed just six yards in the first half of the Colts' 31-17 triumph over Buffalo. The teams battled to a 10-10 halftime tie as the Bills twice botched excellent scoring chances late in the half, once settling for a field goal after enjoying a first down at the Indianapolis 5-yard line. Later, the Bills messed up a field-goal attempt with a high snap.

In the second half, the tide changed. McMillan exploded for 108 yards and scored two touchdowns as the Colts took command. Indianapolis quarterback Mike Pagel attempted only one pass on 67- and 96-yard scoring drives.

The New England Patriots went to the air and were rewarded with a 28-21 victory over the Jets. Quarterback Tony Eason threw for 354 yards and three touchdowns and ran for a fourth. The touchdown drives covered 83, 78, 72 and 92 yards as Eason became the first New England quarterback in four seasons to pass for more than 300 yards. New York quarterback Pat Ryan threw for 297 yards, but was sacked six times and intercepted once by the Pats defense.

Houston Coach Hugh Campbell benched million-dollar quarterback Warren Moon after the Oilers fell behind New Orleans, 17-0, at halftime, but third-year man Oliver Luck fared only a little better. Luck pulled his team to within 17-10 early in the final period, but the Saints proceeded to run off 10 more points to win easily, 27-10. Regardless of whether Moon or Luck was calling the signals, the Oiler offense was anemic. It totalled just 133 yards in total offense—2.8 yards per play—and eight first downs. And the offense gave the Saints a 14-0 first-quarter lead when a Moon pass was intercepted by safety Frank Wattelet and returned 35 yards for a score.

The Minnesota offense wasn't much better in a 20-12 loss to Seattle. Placekicker Jan Stenerud, who kicked five field goals the previous Sunday against Detroit, booted four this time to account for all the Vikings' points. The Seahawks defense, however, had a lot to do with Minnesota's problems, forcing four turnovers and sacking quarterback Tommy Kramer five times.

Eric Lane was the Seahawks' offensive star, rushing for 113 yards on just 14 carries and scoring on a 40-yard run after the Vikings had pulled to within 13-12 on a Stenerud field goal with 3:59 left in the game.

The Washington Redskins had little trouble with NFC Eastern Division rival Philadelphia in winning their third straight game, 20-0. The Eagles were held without a touchdown for the second straight week and didn't advance as far as the Skins' 45-yard line until late in the third quarter. John Riggins' 104 yards and one touchdown paced the offense as Washington won for the sixth time in a row against the Eagles.

The Pittsburgh Steelers disposed of division-rival Cincinnati, 38-17, in the Monday night game. The Steeler defense led the way with six sacks and five interceptions to set up two Pittsburgh touchdowns while scoring two others. Donnie Shell and Dwayne Woodruff each picked off two Turk Schonert passes and returned one for a score. Shell's third-quarter interception set up a 23-yard David Woodley-to-Weegie Thompson touchdown while Woodruff's fourth-period interception set up Walter Abercrombie's five-yard scoring run.

Ironically, the Steelers had beaten the Bengals in a Monday night game during the 1983 season with the defense scoring three touchdowns.

Cowboys-Bears

SUNDAY, SEPTEMBER 30

SCORE BY PERIODS

Dallas	10	7	3	3—23
Chicago	7	7	0	0—14

SCORING

Dallas—Field goal Septien 44, 2:49 1st.

Chicago—McMahon 16 run (B. Thomas kick), 11:03 1st.

Dallas—Dorsett 68 pass from Hogeboom (Septien kick), 12:01 1st.
Chicago—Payton 20 run (B. Thomas kick), 0:51 2nd.
Dallas—Newsome 2 run (Septien kick), 4:05 2nd.
Dallas—Field goal Septien 32, 11:29 3rd.
Dallas—Field goal Septien 23, 10:49 4th.

TEAM STATISTICS

	Dallas	Chicago
First downs	17	26
Rushes-Yards	25-59	47-283
Passing yards	254	117
Sacked-Yards lost	1-11	2-5
Return yards	68	130
Passes	18-29-0	11-23-1
Punts	5-42.6	3-39.3
Fumbles-Lost	1-0	4-1
Penalties-Yards	8-115	8-55
Time of possession	24:37	35:23

Attendance—63,623. No-shows—2,167.

INDIVIDUAL STATISTICS

Rushing—Dallas, Dorsett 18-51, Newsome 5-8, Hogeboom 2-0; Chicago, Suhey 15-48, Payton 25-155, McMahon 5-45, C. Thomas 1-4, Lisch 1-31.

Passing—Dallas, Hogeboom 18-29-0—265; Chicago, McMahon 6-14-0—79, Lisch 5-8-1—43.

Receiving—Dallas, Donley 2-11, Dorsett 4-80, Cosbie 4-48, Renfro 4-72, Newsome 4-54; Chicago, McKinnon 4-53, Moorehead 1-22, Suhey 2-24, Gault 2-7, Payton 2-16.

Kickoff Returns—Dallas, Allen 3-50; Chicago, Cameron 1-40, Gentry 4-58, Duerson 1-26.

Punt Returns—Dallas, Allen 2-9; Chicago, Fisher 2-6.

Interceptions—Dallas, Clinkscale 1-9.

Punting—Dallas, D. White 5-42.6; Chicago, Finzer 3-39.3.

Field Goals—Dallas, Septien 3-3; Chicago, B. Thomas, 0-2 (missed: 41, 43).

Sacks—Dallas, Jeffcoat, Clinkscale; Chicago, McMichael.

Raiders-Broncos
SUNDAY, SEPTEMBER 30
SCORE BY PERIODS

Los Angeles Raiders	0	7	3	3—13
Denver	0	6	10	0—16

SCORING

Denver—Field goal Karlis 27, 1:35 2nd.
Los Angeles—Christensen 19 pass from Plunkett (Bahr kick), 4:54 2nd.
Denver—Field goal Karlis 32, 14:46 2nd.
Denver—Field goal Karlis 19, 4:17 3rd.
Los Angeles—Field goal Bahr 27, 7:47 3rd.
Denver—Willhite 4 run (Karlis kick), 12:41 3rd.
Los Angeles—Field goal Bahr 50, 1:41 4th.

TEAM STATISTICS

	Los Angeles	Denver
First downs	12	26
Rushes-Yards	19-70	48-233
Passing yards	211	119
Sacked-Yards lost	2-9	3-20
Return yards	26	77
Passes	15-32-2	14-26-1
Punts	6-46.2	6-45.5
Fumbles-Lost	1-0	0-0
Penalties-Yards	7-45	1-9
Time of possession	24:43	35:17

Attendance—74,833. No-shows—267.

INDIVIDUAL STATISTICS

Rushing—Los Angeles, Allen 13-66, King 1-minus 1, Plunkett 3-minus 4, Hawkins 3-9; Denver, Winder 16-91, Elway 4-15, Willhite 21-82, Parros 7-45.

Passing—Los Angeles, Plunkett 15-32-2—220; Denver, Elway 14-26-1—139.

Receiving—Los Angeles, King 2-14, Christensen 5-76, Allen 4-44, Branch 3-38, Barnwell 1-48; Denver, Johnson 3-38, Watson 6-79, Sawyer 3-15, Winder 1-6, Parros 1-1.

Kickoff Returns—Denver, Lang 1-20.

Punt Returns—Los Angeles, Pruitt 3-14; Denver, Willhite 3-57.

Interceptions—Los Angeles, Haynes 1-12; Denver, Harden 2-0.

Punting—Los Angeles, Guy 6-46.2; Denver, Norman 6-45.5.

Field Goals—Los Angeles, Bahr 2-2; Denver, Karlis 3-3.

Sacks—Los Angeles, Martin 2, Haynes; Denver, T. Jackson, Dennison.

Bills-Colts
SUNDAY, SEPTEMBER 30
SCORE BY PERIODS

Buffalo	0	10	7	0—17
Indianapolis	7	3	7	14—31

SCORING

Indianapolis—Butler 7 pass from Pagel (Biasucci kick), 8:19 1st.
Buffalo—Field goal Danelo 23, 2:02 2nd.
Buffalo—Dufek 11 run (Danelo kick), 7:05 2nd.
Indianapolis—Field goal Biasucci 43, 14:57 2nd.
Buffalo—Dennard 4 pass from Dufek (Danelo kick), 6:07 3rd.
Indianapolis—McMillan 10 run (Biasucci kick), 13:37 3rd.
Indianapolis—McMillan 31 run (Biasucci kick), 5:24 4th.
Indianapolis—Kafentzis 59 interception return (Biasucci kick), 8:22 4th.

TEAM STATISTICS

	Buffalo	Indianapolis
First downs	23	21
Rushes-Yards	39-179	34-188
Passing yards	169	142
Sacked-Yards lost	5-35	1-10
Return yards	68	148
Passes	15-35-3	14-23-0
Punts	5-50.0	5-46.6
Fumbles-Lost	0-0	1-1
Penalties-Yards	7-55	7-45
Time of possession	34:32	25:28

Attendance—60,032. No-shows—621.

INDIVIDUAL STATISTICS

Rushing—Buffalo, Bell 29-144, Neal 9-24, Dufek 1-11; Indianapolis, McMillan 16-114, Dickey 14-72, Pagel 3-9, Smith 1-minus 7.

Passing—Buffalo, Dufek 15-35-3—204; Indianapolis, Pagel 14-23-0—152.

Receiving—Buffalo, Franklin 5-91, Dennard 3-37, Brookins 2-32, Brammer 3-17, Dawkins 2-27; Indianapolis, Butler 6-60, Porter 4-47, McMillan 2-28, Young 1-9, Dickey 1-8.

Kickoff Returns—Buffalo, Wilson 2-35; Indianapolis, Wonsley 2-29.

Punt Returns—Buffalo, Wilson 4-33; Indianapolis, Glasgow 2-49, Anderson 3-11.

Interceptions—Indianapolis, Daniel 1-0, Burroughs 1-0, Kafentzis 1-59.

Punting—Buffalo, Kidd 5-50.0; Indianapolis, Stark 5-46.6.

Field Goals—Buffalo, Danelo 1-1; Indianapolis, Biasucci 1-2 (missed: 53).

Sacks—Buffalo, B. Williams; Indianapolis, Maxwell 2, Bracelin, Krauss, Odom.

Browns-Chiefs
SUNDAY, SEPTEMBER 30
SCORE BY PERIODS

Cleveland	0	3	3	0— 6
Kansas City	0	3	0	7—10

SCORING

Cleveland—Field goal Bahr 34, 10:31 2nd.
Kansas City—Field goal Lowery 42, 14:57 2nd.
Cleveland—Field goal Bahr 23, 10:27 3rd.
Kansas City—B. Jackson 9 pass from Blackledge (Lowery kick), 3:58 4th.

TEAM STATISTICS

	Cleveland	Kansas City
First downs	16	17
Rushes-Yards	26-78	31-95
Passing yards	108	139
Sacked-Yards lost	11-78	2-16
Return yards	160	184
Passes	17-38-4	15-33-2
Punts	7-43.7	6-45.1
Fumbles-Lost	1-0	3-2
Penalties-Yards	7-55	8-45
Time of possession	33:14	26:46
Attendance—40,785. No-shows—1,296.		

INDIVIDUAL STATISTICS

Rushing—Cleveland, Pruitt 20-67, Holt 1-12, Green 5-minus 1; Kansas City, Brown 13-35, Lacy 6-24, B. Jackson 4-22, Heard 4-11, Blackledge 4-3.

Passing—Cleveland, McDonald 17-38-4—186; Kansas City, Blackledge 15-33-2—155.

Receiving—Cleveland, Newsome 7-74, Walker 4-44, Harris 2-26, Feacher 1-22, Holt 1-8, Adams 1-8, Pruitt 1-4; Kansas City, Brown 4-29, B. Jackson 4-29, Marshall 4-63, Paige 1-15, Carson 1-13, Scott 1-6.

Kickoff Returns—Cleveland, White 2-37, Byner 1-28; Kansas City, Paige 1-45, Smith 1-12.

Punt Returns—Cleveland, Harris 5-30; Kansas City, Smith 4-38.

Interceptions—Cleveland, Minnifield 1-26, Rogers 1-39; Kansas City, Ross 1-1, Daniels 1-0, McAlister 1-22, Cherry 1-67.

Punting—Cleveland, Cox 7-43.7; Kansas City, Arnold 6-45.1.

Field Goals—Cleveland, Bahr 2-2; Kansas City, Lowery 1-1.

Sacks—Cleveland, Camp, Baldwin; Kansas City, McAlister 3, Maas 3, Still 2, Bell, Kremer, Spani.

Giants-Rams

SUNDAY, SEPTEMBER 30
SCORE BY PERIODS

New York Giants	6	0	0	6—12
Los Angeles Rams	0	17	16	0—33

SCORING

New York—McConkey recovered kickoff in end zone (kick failed), 0:09 1st.
Los Angeles—Crutchfield 1 run (Lansford kick), 0:03 2nd.
Los Angeles—Ellard 83 punt return (Lansford kick), 9:28 2nd.
Los Angeles—Field goal Lansford 33, 11:51 2nd.
Los Angeles—Safety, blocked punt out of end zone, 1:00 3rd.
Los Angeles—Safety, Simms tackled in end zone, 3:20 3rd.
Los Angeles—David Hill 2 pass from Kemp (Lansford kick), 4:25 3rd.
Los Angeles—Field goal Lansford 35, 10:55 3rd.
Los Angeles—Safety, blocked punt out of end zone, 12:24 3rd.
New York—Gray 15 pass from Simms (kick failed), 11:06 4th.

TEAM STATISTICS

	New York	Los Angeles
First downs	19	19
Rushes-Yards	13-8	41-204
Passing yards	244	105

	New York	Los Angeles
Sacked-Yards lost	5-41	2-8
Return yards	109	168
Passes	25-49-0	8-17-0
Punts	8-33.0	7-40.4
Fumbles-Lost	1-1	1-0
Penalties-Yards	12-95	5-39
Time of possession	27:20	32:40
Attendance—53,417. No-shows—5,160.		

INDIVIDUAL STATISTICS

Rushing—New York, Carpenter 9-6, Woolfolk 3-2, Cephous 1-0; Los Angeles, Dickerson 22-120, Crutchfield 10-30, Redden 8-50, Kemp 1-4.

Passing—New York, Simms 24-48-0—276, Rutledge 1-1-0—9; Los Angeles, Kemp 8-17-0—113.

Receiving—New York, Gray 9-112, Johnson 4-46, Mowatt 4-41, Mullady 2-35, Carpenter 2-21, Galbreath 2-20, McConkey 1-9, Woolfolk 1-1; Los Angeles, Dickerson 3-27, Ellard 2-69, David Hill 2-11, Faulkner 1-6.

Kickoff Returns—New York, McConkey 4-65, Cephous 2-35; Los Angeles, Drew Hill 2-40, Ellard 1-12, Irvin 2-33.

Punt Returns—New York, McConkey 2-9; Los Angeles, Ellard 1-83, Irvin 1-0.

Punting—New York, Jennings 6-44.0; Los Angeles, Misko 7-40.4.

Field Goals—New York, Haji-Sheikh 0-1 (missed: 44); Los Angeles, Lansford 2-3 (missed: 38).

Sacks—New York, Martin, Hill; Los Angeles, Youngblood 2, Doss, DeJurnett, Ekern.

Dolphins-Cardinals

SUNDAY, SEPTEMBER 30
SCORE BY PERIODS

Miami	6	20	0	10—36
St. Louis	0	14	7	7—28

SCORING

Miami—Field goal von Schamann 27, 4:52 1st.
Miami—Field goal von Schamann 26, 11:53 1st.
Miami—Rose 26 pass from Marino (kick failed), 1:05 2nd.
St. Louis—Mitchell 2 run (O'Donoghue kick), 5:58 2nd.
Miami—Johnson 1 run (von Schamann kick), 9:34 2nd.
St. Louis—Marsh 22 pass from Lomax (O'Donoghue kick), 13:49 2nd.
Miami—Clayton 29 pass from Marino (von Schamann kick), 14:40 2nd.
St. Louis—Ferrell 11 run (O'Donoghue kick), 14:20 3rd.
Miami—Nathan 23 pass from Marino (von Schamann kick), 3:19 4th.
Miami—Field goal von Schamann 27, 7:12 4th.
St. Louis—Mitchell 4 run (O'Donoghue kick), 11:14 4th.

TEAM STATISTICS

	Miami	St. Louis
First downs	26	24
Rushes-Yards	29-132	26-137
Passing yards	429	308
Sacked-Yards lost	1-9	0-0
Return yards	52	137
Passes	24-37-0	22-37-0
Punts	1-44.0	4-31.8
Fumbles-Lost	0-0	1-1
Penalties-Yards	4-35	4-30
Time of possession	30:33	29:27
Attendance—46,991. No-shows—1,614.		

INDIVIDUAL STATISTICS

Rushing—Miami, Bennett 11-45, Carter 6-28, P. Johnson 3-6, Nathan 7-40, Clayton 1-15, Marino 1-minus 2; St. Louis, Mitchell 20-109, Ferrell 5-24, Harrell 1-4.

Passing—Miami, Marino 24-36-0—429, Strock 0-1-0—0; St. Louis, Lomax 22-37-0—308.

Receiving—Miami, D. Johnson 2-40, Nathan 5-39, Duper 8-164, Clayton 5-143, Rose 2-34, Cefalo 2-9; St.

Louis, Tilley 5-69, LaFleur 2-45, Mitchell 3-23, Green 4-48, Marsh 5-97, Harrell 1-8, Ferrell 2-18.

Kickoff Returns—Miami, Kozlowski 1-12, Walker 3-40, Duhe 1-0; St. Louis, Bird 4-87, Harrell 3-50.

Punting—Miami, Roby 1-44.0; St. Louis, Birdsong 4-31.8.

Field Goals—Miami, von Schamann 3-4 (missed: 35); St. Louis, none attempted.

Sacks—St. Louis, Mays.

Patriots-Jets
SUNDAY, SEPTEMBER 30
SCORE BY PERIODS

New England	7	7	14	0—28
New York Jets	7	7	0	7—21

SCORING

New York—Walker 12 pass from Ryan (Leahy kick), 7:45 1st.

New England—Dawson 2 pass from Eason (Franklin kick), 12:50 1st.

New York—Paige 1 run (Leahy kick), 10:39 2nd.

New England—Eason 4 run (Franklin kick), 14:02 2nd.

New England—Robinson 4 pass from Eason (Franklin kick), 5:46 3rd.

New England—Morgan 43 pass from Eason (Franklin kick), 12:19 3rd.

New York—Shuler 7 pass from Ryan (Leahy kick), 5:29 4th.

TEAM STATISTICS

	New England	New York
First downs	29	19
Rushes-Yards	30-122	26-115
Passing yards	354	258
Sacked-Yards lost	0-0	6-39
Return yards	104	110
Passes	28-42-0	20-31-1
Punts	2-51.0	4-46.3
Fumbles-Lost	2-1	5-0
Penalties-Yards	4-40	4-32
Time of possession	32:29	27:31
Attendance—68,978. No-shows—7,913.		

INDIVIDUAL STATISTICS

Rushing—New England, Collins 16-69, Eason 8-11, Ta-tupu 4-37, C. James 2-5; New York, Ryan 4-41, McNeil 13-36, Barber 2-12, Harper 2-20, Hector 3-5, Paige 2-1.

Passing—New England, Eason 28-42-0—354; New York, Ryan 20-31-1—297.

Receiving—New England, Dawson 6-84, Ramsey 5-81, Starring 6-49, Hawthorne 1-25, Jones 2-27, C. James 1-6, Collins 4-19, Morgan 1-43, Fryar 1-16, Robinson 1-4; New York, Walker 4-76, Paige 2-14, Harper 1-28, Shuler 4-65, Gaffney 3-54, Dennison 2-19, Humphrey 2-29, McNeil 2-12.

Kickoff Returns—New England, J. Williams 3-48, Fryar 1-21; New York, Humphrey 4-102, Springs 1-4.

Punt Returns—New England, Fryar 2-6, Gibson 1-3; New York, Springs 1-4.

Interceptions—New England, Marion 1-26.

Punting—New England, Prestridge 2-51.0; New York, Ramsey 4-46.3.

Field Goals—New England, Franklin 0-2 (missed: 33, 49); New York, none attempted.

Sacks—New England, Tippett 2, Rogers, Marion, Sims, T. Williams ½, Blackmon ½.

Saints-Oilers
SUNDAY, SEPTEMBER 30
SCORE BY PERIODS

New Orleans	14	3	0	10—27
Houston	0	0	3	7—10

SCORING

New Orleans—Gajan 15 run (Andersen kick), 5:35 1st.

New Orleans—Wattelet 35 interception return (Andersen kick), 11:40 1st.

New Orleans—Field goal Andersen 23, 14:37 2nd.

Houston—Field goal Kempf 25, 13:16 3rd.

Houston—Campbell 1 run (Kempf kick), 0:42 4th.

New Orleans—Field goal Andersen 27, 5:13 4th.

New Orleans—Gajan 37 run (Andersen kick), 9:38 4th.

TEAM STATISTICS

	New Orleans	Houston
First downs	20	8
Rushes-Yards	46-197	25-84
Passing yards	160	49
Sacked-Yards lost	3-28	4-34
Return yards	108	96
Passes	14-22-1	7-18-1
Punts	3-46.7	6-40.7
Fumbles-Lost	2-1	1-0
Penalties-Yards	4-25	4-21
Time of possession	36:24	23:36
Attendance—43,108. No-shows—8,424.		

INDIVIDUAL STATISTICS

Rushing—New Orleans, G. Rogers 19-72, Gajan 11-90, W. Wilson 9-6, Anthony 4-21, Todd 1-0, T. Wilson 2-8; Houston, Campbell 15-38, Moriarty 7-31, Moon 2-13, Luck 1-2.

Passing—New Orleans, Todd 14-22-1—188; Houston, Moon 3-8-2—36, Luck 4-10-0—47.

Receiving—New Orleans, G. Rogers 2-18, Goodlow 1-9, W. Wilson 4-23, Groth 2-42, Brenner 1-28, Scott 3-36, Young 1-32; Houston, Smith 3-59, Williams 1-7, Holston 1-8, Edwards 1-4, Dressel 1-5.

Kickoff Returns—New Orleans, Anthony 2-35, T. Wilson 1-16; Houston, Roaches 2-54, Walls 2-57.

Punt Returns—New Orleans, Groth 4-22; Houston, Roaches 2-4.

Interceptions—New Orleans, Waymer 1-0, Wattelet 1-35; Houston, Abraham 1-1.

Punting—New Orleans, Hansen 3-46.7; Houston, James 6-40.7.

Field Goals—New Orleans, Andersen 2-3 (missed: 40); Houston, Kempf 1-1.

Sacks—New Orleans, Paul 2, Wilks, Moore; Houston, Brazile 2, Baker.

Lions-Chargers
SUNDAY, SEPTEMBER 30
SCORE BY PERIODS

Detroit	0	7	14	3—24
San Diego	7	17	0	3—27

SCORING

San Diego—Thomas 1 run (Benirschke kick), 9:43 1st.

San Diego—Thomas 1 run (Benirschke kick), 2:57 2nd.

San Diego—McGee 3 run (Benirschke kick), 10:17 2nd.

Detroit—Sims 1 run (Murray kick), 13:49 2nd.

San Diego—Field goal Benirschke 18, 14:56 2nd.

Detroit—Sims 1 run (Murray kick), 1:41 3rd.

Detroit—Chadwick 12 run (Murray kick), 8:53 3rd.

San Diego—Field goal Benirschke 41, 6:43 4th.

Detroit—Field goal Murray 44, 11:04 4th.

TEAM STATISTICS

	Detroit	San Diego
First downs	21	30
Rushes-Yards	23-147	39-114
Passing yards	236	261
Sacked-Yards lost	4-33	1-7
Return yards	86	67
Passes	20-25-0	22-35-0

	Detroit	San Diego
Punts	3-38.0	2-55.5
Fumbles-Lost	1-0	1-1
Penalties-Yards	13-161	9-109
Time of possession	27:30	32:30

Attendance—53,509. No-shows—6,340.

INDIVIDUAL STATISTICS

Rushing—Detroit, Sims 14-119, Jones 6-9, Chadwick 1-12, Jenkins 2-7; San Diego, Jackson 6-18, Fouts 4-minus 6, McGee 16-40, Thomas 3-4, James 10-58.

Passing—Detroit, Danielson 20-25-0—269; San Diego, Fouts 22-34-0—268, James 0-1-0—0.

Receiving—Detroit, Sims 2-14, Nichols 3-74, Thompson 4-80, Lewis 1-5, Chadwick 2-27, Rubick 1-24; San Diego, Joiner 7-87, Sievers 1-21, Holohan 3-50, McGee 2-4, Winslow 6-80, James 2-15, Chandler 1-11.

Kickoff Returns—Detroit, Jenkins 2-42, Mandley 2-30, D'Addio 1-0; San Diego, James 2-47, Egloff 1-9.

Punt Returns—Detroit, Martin 1-14; San Diego, James 1-11.

Punting—Detroit, Black 3-38.0; San Diego, Buford 2-55.5.

Field Goals—Detroit, Murray 1-2 (missed: 34); San Diego, Benirschke 2-2.

Sacks—Detroit, Gay; San Diego, King 1½, Smith, Ferguson ½, Bradley ½, Robinson ½.

Falcons-49ers
SUNDAY, SEPTEMBER 30
SCORE BY PERIODS

Atlanta	3	0	0	2—	5
San Francisco	0	14	0	0—	14

SCORING

Atlanta—Field goal Luckhurst 22, 7:55 1st.

San Francisco—Francis 5 pass from Montana (Wersching kick), 10:53 2nd.

San Francisco—Wilson 21 pass from Montana (Wersching kick), 14:33 2nd.

Atlanta—Safety, Runager forced out of end zone by Case, 13:15 4th.

TEAM STATISTICS

	Atlanta	San Francisco
First downs	22	17
Rushes-Yards	35-161	32-161
Passing yards	257	149
Sacked-Yards lost	2-10	0-0
Return yards	48	62
Passes	22-41-2	13-25-0
Punts	4-38.8	6-36.5
Fumbles-Lost	3-1	3-2
Penalties-Yards	5-45	5-56
Time of possession	34:57	25:43

Attendance—57,990. No-shows—NA.

INDIVIDUAL STATISTICS

Rushing—Atlanta, Riggs 28-136, Cain 4-14, B. Johnson 2-11, Giacomarro 1-0; San Francisco, Tyler 12-99, Craig 10-44, Montana 4-14, Cooper 1-7, Ring 2-3, Harmon 2-minus 1, Runager 1-minus 5.

Passing—Atlanta, Bartkowski 22-41-2—267; San Francisco, Montana 13-25-0—149.

Receiving—Atlanta, A. Jackson 6-51, B. Johnson 5-73, Bailey 4-97, Riggs 3-15, Cox 2-20, Cain 2-11; San Francisco, Francis 5-44, Wilson 3-47, Clark 1-22, Solomon 1-18, Tyler 1-7, Craig 1-6, Cooper 1-5.

Kickoff Returns—Atlanta, Stamps 1-6, B. Johnson 1-18; San Francisco, Monroe 1-29.

Punt Returns—Atlanta, B. Johnson 2-14; San Francisco, McLemore 2-17.

Interceptions—San Francisco, Lott 1-0, Williamson 1-16.

Punting—Atlanta, Giacomarro 4-38.8; San Francisco, Runager 5-43.8.

Field Goals—Atlanta, Luckhurst 1-1; San Francisco, none attempted.

Sacks—San Francisco, Bunz, Board.

Seahawks-Vikings
SUNDAY, SEPTEMBER 30
SCORE BY PERIODS

Seattle	7	3	0	10—20	
Minnesota	3	3	3	3—12	

SCORING

Minnesota—Field goal Stenerud 43, 4:42 1st.

Seattle—Largent 20 pass from Krieg (N. Johnson kick), 8:23 1st.

Minnesota—Field goal Stenerud 44, 13:59 2nd.

Seattle—Field goal N. Johnson 41, 14:57 2nd.

Minnesota—Field goal Stenerud 28, 6:48 3rd.

Seattle—Field goal N. Johnson 31, 0:03 4th.

Minnesota—Field goal Stenerud 34, 11:01 4th.

Seattle—Lane 40 run (N. Johnson kick), 13:52 4th.

TEAM STATISTICS

	Seattle	Minnesota
First downs	19	20
Rushes-Yards	30-192	35-138
Passing yards	217	196
Sacked-Yards lost	1-5	5-31
Return yards	131	66
Passes	17-27-3	16-31-1
Punts	4-39.2	3-48.0
Fumbles-Lost	2-1	3-3
Penalties-Yards	12-126	5-45
Time of possession	27:18	32:42

Attendance—57,171. No-shows—4,836.

INDIVIDUAL STATISTICS

Rushing—Seattle, Lane 14-113, F. Harris 9-52, Krieg 4-23, Morris 3-4; Minnesota, Anderson 21-69, Brown 6-54, Nelson 7-15, Kramer 1-0.

Passing—Seattle, Krieg 17-27-3—222; Minnesota, Kramer 16-31-1—227.

Receiving—Seattle, Largent 8-130, Young 2-15, Doornink 1-9, Turner 2-26, Morris 2-25, Castor 2-17; Minnesota, Lewis 4-75, White 1-47, Nelson 2-14, Brown 2-8, Jordan 2-13, Jones 5-70.

Kickoff Returns—Seattle, Dixon 4-80, Hughes 1-22; Minnesota, Nelson 2-35.

Punt Returns—Seattle, Easley 2-11; Minnesota, Nelson 1-0.

Interceptions—Seattle, Gaines 1-18; Minnesota, Studwell 1-20, Bess 1-0, Swain 1-11.

Punting—Seattle, West 4-39.2; Minnesota, Coleman 3-48.0.

Field Goals—Seattle, N. Johnson 2-2; Minnesota, Stenerud 4-4.

Sacks—Seattle, Bryant 2, Green 1½, Nash ½, Gaines ½, Edwards ½; Minnesota, Sendlein.

Packers-Buccaneers
SUNDAY, SEPTEMBER 30
SCORE BY PERIODS

Green Bay	10	3	7	7	0—27
Tampa Bay	7	10	0	10	3—30

SCORING

Tampa Bay—Wilder 33 run (Ariri kick), 7:41 1st.

Green Bay—Clark 43 run (Garcia kick), 8:20 1st.

Green Bay—Field goal Garcia 41, 10:00 1st.

Tampa Bay—Field goal Ariri 46, 8:48 2nd.

Tampa Bay—DeBerg 6 run (Ariri kick), 14:30 2nd.

Green Bay—Field goal Garcia 51, 15:00 2nd.

Green Bay—Coffman 4 pass from Dickey (Garcia kick), 13:27 3rd.

Tampa Bay—Field goal Ariri 49, 2:56 4th.

Tampa Bay—Logan 27 interception return (Ariri kick), 8:25 4th.

Green Bay—Ellis 15 run with lateral from Lofton (Garcia kick), 14:52 4th.
Tampa Bay—Field goal Ariri 48, 10:38 OT.

TEAM STATISTICS

	Green Bay	Tampa Bay
First downs	18	25
Rushes-Yards	39-167	47-180
Passing yards	216	226
Sacked-Yards lost	2-16	3-20
Return yards	210	149
Passes	16-31-3	21-41-3
Punts	8-44-4	5-41.2
Fumbles-Lost	2-2	1-1
Penalties-Yards	11-86	9-65
Time of possession	29:50	40:48

Attendance—47,487. No-shows—7,837.

INDIVIDUAL STATISTICS

Rushing—Green Bay, Clark 6-63, Ellis 14-58, Huckleby 5-29, Crouse 14-17; Tampa Bay, Wilder 43-172, DeBerg 3-7, Morton 1-1.

Passing—Green Bay, Dickey 16-31-3—232; Tampa Bay, DeBerg 21-40-3—246, Garcia 0-1-0—0.

Receiving—Green Bay, Lofton 3-70, Ellis 3-41, Jefferson 3-37, Epps 2-37, Huckleby 3-28, Clark 1-15, Coffman 1-4; Tampa Bay, Carter 8-75, House 4-48, Wilder 4-44, J. Bell 2-28, Giles 1-23, Armstrong 1-16, Carver 1-12.

Kickoff Returns—Green Bay, Epps 6-122, Prather 1-7; Tampa Bay, Morton 2-45, Wood 1-16, Bright 2-33.

Punt Returns—Green Bay, Epps 3-19; Tampa Bay, Bright 2-24.

Interceptions—Green Bay, T. Lewis 2-40, Anderson 1-22; Tampa Bay, Brantley 1-4, Castille 1-0, Logan 1-27.

Punting—Green Bay, Scribner 8-44.4; Tampa Bay, Garcia 5-41.2.

Field Goals—Green Bay, Garcia 2-3 (missed: 49); Tampa Bay, Ariri 3-4 (missed: 50).

Sacks—Green Bay, Murphy, Scott, Johnson; Tampa Bay, Selmon, Browner.

Eagles-Redskins
SUNDAY, SEPTEMBER 30
SCORE BY PERIODS

Philadelphia	0	0	0	0— 0
Washington	0	10	7	3—20

SCORING

Washington—Monk 51 pass from Theismann (Moseley kick), 1:21 2nd.
Washington—Field goal Moseley 35, 13:17 2nd.
Washington—Riggins 1 run (Moseley kick), 11:35 3rd.
Washington—Field goal Moseley 29, 7:23 4th.

TEAM STATISTICS

	Philadelphia	Washington
First downs	14	19
Rushes-Yards	19-76	45-232
Passing yards	136	86
Sacked-Yards lost	4-34	3-28
Return yards	105	131
Passes	18-35-1	9-20-1
Punts	7-36.7	3-36.7
Fumbles-Lost	2-1	0-0
Penalties-Yards	2-19	1-5
Time of possession	25:36	34:24

Attendance—53,064. No-shows—2,367.

INDIVIDUAL STATISTICS

Rushing—Philadelphia, Montgomery 12-54, Oliver 4-7, Hardy 2-5, Jaworski 1-10; Washington, Riggins 28-104, Griffin 7-57, Wonsley 4-15, Theismann 6-56.

Passing—Philadelphia, Jaworski 18-35-1—170; Washington, Theismann 9-20-1—114.

Receiving—Philadelphia, Jackson 1-12, Spagnola 2-20, Montgomery 5-31, Oliver 3-2, Quick 2-47, Wood-

ruff 1-17, Haddix 4-41; Washington, Monk 5-80, Warren 1-20, Riggins 2-12, Seay 1-2.

Kickoff Returns—Philadelphia, Hayes 4-74, Waters 1-10; Washington, Kane 1-12.

Punt Returns—Washington, Nelms 6-99.

Interceptions—Philadelphia, Hopkins 1-21; Washington, Dean 1-20.

Punting—Philadelphia, Horan 7-36.7; Washington, Hayes 3-36.7.

Field Goals—Philadelphia, none attempted; Washington, Moseley 2-3 (missed: 45).

Sacks—Philadelphia, Brown 2, Harrison; Washington, Manley 2½, McGee, Mann ½.

Bengals-Steelers
MONDAY, OCTOBER 1
SCORE BY PERIODS

Cincinnati	0	10	0	7—17
Pittsburgh	0	14	10	14—38

SCORING

Pittsburgh—Erenberg 31 run (Anderson kick), 1:50 2nd.
Pittsburgh—Woodruff 42 interception return (Anderson kick), 2:58 2nd.
Cincinnati—Jennings 38 pass from Schonert (Breech kick), 7:53 2nd.
Cincinnati—Field goal Breech 32, 14:54 2nd.
Pittsburgh—Field goal Anderson 31, 10:44 3rd.
Pittsburgh—Thompson 23 pass from Woodley (Anderson kick), 13:26 3rd.
Cincinnati—Schonert 1 run (Breech kick), 1:33 4th.
Pittsburgh—Abercrombie 5 run (Anderson kick), 10:12 4th.
Pittsburgh—Shell 52 interception return (Anderson kick), 10:37 4th.

TEAM STATISTICS

	Cincinnati	Pittsburgh
First downs	15	22
Rushes-Yards	26-125	36-151
Passing yards	155	241
Sacked-Yards lost	6-37	1-11
Return yards	116	179
Passes	19-32-5	19-30-3
Punts	6-40.7	3-46.7
Fumbles-Lost	1-0	4-1
Penalties-Yards	4-40	4-35
Time of possession	28:04	31:56

Attendance—57,098. No-shows—1,902.

INDIVIDUAL STATISTICS

Rushing—Cincinnati, Alexander 9-54, Brooks 3-5, Jennings 6-10, Kinnebrew 1-0, Schonert 7-56; Pittsburgh, Erenberg 16-55, Pollard 8-52, Woodley 1-0, Abercrombie 5-37, Corley 2-5, Spencer 1-0, Gillespie 1-2, Veals 1-2, Malone 1-minus 2.

Passing—Cincinnati, Anderson 6-9-1—50, Schonert 12-20-4—133, Esiason 1-3-0—9; Pittsburgh, Woodley 19-30-3—252.

Receiving—Cincinnati, Harris 5-57, Brooks 2-9, Kinnebrew 1-9, Collinsworth 3-32, Kreider 1-10, Jennings 2-36, Alexander 2-4, Curtis 2-26, Holman 1-9; Pittsburgh, Erenberg 5-34, Lipps 2-21, Stallworth 6-119, Kolodziejski 2-17, Pollard 1-8, Capers 2-30, Thompson 1-23.

Kickoff Returns—Cincinnati, Jennings 3-54, Farley 1-32, Martin 1-24; Pittsburgh, Spencer 3-48, Catano 1-0.

Punt Returns—Cincinnati, Martin 1-2; Pittsburgh, Lipps 2-5, Woods 2-22.

Interceptions—Cincinnati, Jackson 1-4, Breeden 1-0, R. Griffin 1-0; Pittsburgh, Washington 1-0, Woodruff 2-48, Shell 2-56.

Punting—Cincinnati, McInally 6-40.7; Pittsburgh, Colquitt 3-46.7.

Field Goals—Cincinnati, Breech 1-1; Pittsburgh, Anderson 1-1.

Sacks—Cincinnati, R. Williams; Pittsburgh, Merriweather 3, Hinkle 2, Gary.

SIXTH WEEK

RESULTS OF WEEK 6
Sunday, October 7

Atlanta 30, L.A. Rams 28 at L.A.
Chicago 20, New Orleans 7 at Chi.
Cincinnati 13, Houston 3 at Cin.
Denver 28, Detroit 7 at Det.
L.A. Raiders 28, Seattle 14 at L.A.
Miami 31, Pittsburgh 7 at Pitts.
New England 17, Cleveland 16 at Cleve.
N.Y. Jets 17, Kansas City 16 at K.C.
Philadelphia 27, Buffalo 17 at Buff.
St. Louis 31, Dallas 20 at Dall.
San Diego 34, Green Bay 28 at G.B.
Tampa Bay 35, Minnesota 31 at T.B.
Washington 35, Indianapolis 7 at Ind.

Monday, October 8

San Francisco 31, N.Y. Giants 10 at N.Y.

THE record had stood for 19 years as the most illustrious individual achievement in the history of pro football.

When Jim Brown walked away from the game after the 1965 season, he left an indelible mark on the National Football League. In nine seasons with the Cleveland Browns, Brown rushed for 12,312 yards in 118 games—an incredible average of 104.3 yards per game. The Browns won 67 percent of their games with Brown as their fullback, including an NFL championship in 1964. The man generally accepted as the greatest ever at his position decided to give up the glories of the gridiron for the glories of acting at the tender age of 29. The all-time rushing record was his, and the No. 2 man on the list, former San Francisco great Joe Perry, was 2,589 yards behind—and retired.

But all good things must end some day and, like Babe Ruth's home run record and Wilt Chamberlain's National Basketball Association points record, Brown's mark also fell.

Walter Jerry Payton was only 11 years old when the record was set, but 12,313 yards later, at age 30, the record was his, thanks to a 154-yard performance that helped his team, the Chicago Bears, defeat New Orleans, 20-7. Payton, who finished the day with 12,400 career yards, scored the go-ahead touchdown on the final play of the first half as the Bears won for the fourth time in six starts in 1984.

"For the past three weeks, I've tried to conceal it, but there's been a lot of pressure," said Payton, who broke the mark with a six-yard carry 57 seconds into the second half. The record-breaker came on the 2,795th rushing attempt of his 136-game, 10-year NFL career. Ironically, Payton broke another of Brown's records with his 59th career 100-yard game. "I was so nervous, so very nervous, that I was shaking. I'm just glad this whole thing with the cameras and mikes is over with. I'm also glad

that we won the game."

Chicago actually had little trouble defeating the Saints. In addition to Payton's touchdown, quarterback Jim McMahon connected with Dennis McKinnon for another and Bob Thomas booted two field goals. The Bears defense hounded Saints quarterback Richard Todd most of the afternoon, holding him to just seven completions in 26 pass attempts.

Another defensive unit that had a big day was Denver's. The Broncos intercepted seven passes, recovered three fumbles, recorded six sacks and scored two touchdowns in a 28-7 triumph over the Detroit Lions. After the Broncos offense scored midway through the first period on an 11-play, 69-yard touchdown march, Lions running back Billy Sims fumbled on Detroit's next possession after taking a solid hit from cornerback Louis Wright. Rulon Jones plucked the fumble out of the air and rambled five yards for another touchdown and the extra point gave Denver a 14-0 lead.

Denver's final touchdown came when linebacker Ken Woodard picked off a Mike Machurek pass and returned it 27 yards. Machurek was intercepted three times after replacing Lions' starter Gary Danielson, who suffered four interceptions. Danielson had not thrown an interception in Detroit's first five games.

Cleveland quarterback Paul McDonald threw only one interception in the Browns' game with New England, but it came at the worst possible time. With the Browns trailing by one point and seven seconds left in the game, McDonald threw a pass intended for Duriel Harris near the Patriots' goal line. But New England cornerback Raymond Clayborn picked it off and returned it 85 yards into Browns' territory. The interception was Clayborn's first in 31 games. The New England star made the Pro Bowl in 1983 without making a single interception.

The Browns, who once led in the game, 16-3, before losing 17-16, had missed another chance to win two minutes earlier. Placekicker Matt Bahr, who had kicked field goals from 24, 48 and 27 yards, missed a 36-yarder, setting up Clayborn's late heroics.

Atlanta's Mick Luckhurst didn't miss his opportunity, kicking a 37-yard field goal as time expired to give his team a 30-28 verdict over the Los Angeles Rams. Luckhurst, who already had kicked field goals from 52 and 51 yards out, connected on the game-winner after Atlanta drove 66 yards in 12 plays after taking over at its own 15-yard line with 5:01 remaining. The Falcons had to convert two fourth-down plays on the march.

The win was Atlanta's first in Los Angeles against the Rams, whose record had stood at 14-0-2 when hosting their NFC Western Division rivals. Atlanta's Lynn Cain had the best day of his six-year NFL career, rushing for 145 yards and three touchdowns while subbing for the injured Gerald Riggs. Riggs had been filling in capably for William Andrews, the Falcons' All-Pro running back who was injured in the preseason and lost for the season.

Rookie Bengals quarterback Boomer Esiason made his first NFL start (because of injuries to Ken Anderson and Turk Schonert) and led Cincinnati to its first victory of the season, a 13-3 decision over the Houston Oilers. The Oilers, who were also looking for their first victory of 1984, dropped to 0-6 and lost for the 21st straight time on the road, an NFL record.

Esiason, the first quarterback taken in the 1984 draft, completed just 13 passes for 159 yards but scored the game's only touchdown, a three-yard sneak in the third quarter, to put the Bengals ahead for good, 10-3. The victory gave Bengals Coach Sam Wyche his first NFL win while leaving his Houston counterpart, Hugh Campbell, still searching for his.

Raiders quarterback Marc Wilson saw his first game action of 1984 when Jim Plunkett was hurt early in the first quarter and led Los Angeles to a 28-14 triumph over Seattle. Wilson connected with Marcus Allen on a 58-yard scoring play for the go-ahead touchdown with 5:32 left in a 14-14 game. Allen caught the pass at the Seahawks' 30-yard line and sped untouched into the Seattle end zone. The Raiders added an insurance touchdown 19 seconds later when linebacker Rod Martin picked off a Dave Krieg pass and returned it 14 yards for a score.

The Washington Redskins made short work of Indianapolis en route to a 35-7 victory. Washington quarterback Joe Theismann, who had struggled through his first five games, threw for 267 yards and four touchdowns while completing 17 of 20 passes in one of his best NFL performances. Three of Theismann's scoring tosses were to wide receiver Art Monk as the Skins blew open a 7-7 game with a 21-point second-quarter explosion. Defensively, two Vernon Dean interceptions set up two Redskin touchdowns and five quarterback sacks helped to hold the Colts' ground game, ranked second in the league before the game, to only 71 yards.

In a battle of quarterbacks, San Diego beat Green Bay, 34-28, in an interconference game. The Chargers' Dan Fouts completed 31 of 50 passes for 376 yards and three touchdowns while the Packers' Lynn Dickey connected on 25 of 39 attempts for 384 yards and three touchdowns. On the receiving end of the aerial circus were the Chargers' Kellen Winslow, who caught 15 balls for 157 yards, and the Packers' Paul Coffman and James Lofton, who were 8-for-104 and 5-for-158, respectively. Ironically, in a game with so much passing, Earnest Jackson set a San Diego team record with 32 rushing attempts.

The St. Louis Cardinals won their first game at Texas Stadium since 1977 and their second in history, beating the Cowboys, 31-20. The Cards used a balanced offensive attack with quarterback Neil Lomax throwing for 354 yards and three touchdowns and running back Ottis Anderson rushing for 110 yards on 25 carries. St. Louis averaged better than six yards per offensive play.

The Cards led by only one point at halftime, 14-13, before scoring 17 unanswered points in the third quarter to coast to victory, their second in their last 12 meetings with the Cowboys. Lomax completed touchdown passes of 70 and 45 yards to wide receiver Roy Green.

Miami quarterback Dan Marino made his first appearance in Pittsburgh since his collegiate days there and led the Dolphins to a 31-7 triumph over the Steelers. The loss was the Steelers' worst at Three Rivers Stadium since the facility opened in 1970.

The game was billed as a matchup between Marino and Pittsburgh quarterback David Woodley, who had been the Dolphins' starting quarterback before being beaten out of the job by Marino in 1983 and subsequently traded to the Steelers. But the matchup never unfolded as Woodley suffered a concussion on Pittsburgh's second possession of the day and was replaced by Mark Malone. It really didn't matter, however, as the Dolphins, behind two Marino touchdown passes, exploded for 21 points in the second quarter to put the game away. A 21-yard fumble return by nose tackle Bob Baumhower with 1:14 left in the half was the crushing blow.

A fumble by Kansas City running back Theotis Brown late in the first half proved to be the pivotal play in the Chiefs' 17-16 loss to the New York Jets. With K.C. leading, 9-3, on the strength of three Nick Lowery field goals, Brown fumbled at his own 20-yard line. Ron Faurot recovered for the Jets and, five plays later, Tony Paige scored from a yard out for a 10-9 New York advantage. The Jets increased their lead to eight points with another touchdown early in the second half before holding off a late Kansas City rally that included the Chiefs' lone touchdown of the day.

The Minnesota Vikings scored touchdowns on each of their first two possessions and Tommy Kramer threw for 386 yards, but it still wasn't enough as the Vikes lost an NFC Central Division contest to Tampa Bay, 35-31. Steve DeBerg threw two touchdown passes and James Wilder ran for two other scores to lead the comeback against the error-prone Vikings, who fumbled seven times, threw two interceptions and were flagged 13 times for 101 yards in penalties.

Buffalo continued to flounder, losing its sixth game in as many tries. Rookie running back Greg Bell scored two touchdowns for the Bills,

Walter Payton became the NFL's all-time rushing leader with a 154-yard performance against New Orleans in a 20-7 Bears victory in Week 6.

but Philadelphia quarterback Ron Jaworski threw for two scores and ran for a third in a 27-17 Eagles triumph. The Bills joined the Houston Oilers as the only NFL teams without a victory after six weeks.

At the other end of the spectrum, the San Francisco 49ers joined Miami in the undefeated ranks by crushing the New York Giants, 31-10, in the Monday night game. The 49ers scored on their sixth play of the game, a 59-yard pass from Joe Montana to Renaldo Nehemiah, and never looked back, scoring two more touchdowns before the first quarter was half over. Dana McLemore's 79-yard punt return 75 seconds after the 49ers' second TD

gave San Francisco a 21-0 lead.

The 49ers defense, which had not allowed a touchdown in its previous two games, saw that streak snapped when the Giants' Butch Woolfolk scored from two yards out with 1:17 remaining in the game.

Falcons-Rams
SUNDAY, OCTOBER 7
SCORE BY PERIODS

Atlanta	0	10	7	13—30
Los Angeles Rams	0	7	14	7—28

SCORING
Atlanta—Cain 31 run (Luckhurst kick), 1:44 2nd.

Atlanta—Field goal Luckhurst 52, 11:55 2nd.
Los Angeles—Ellard 14 pass from Dils (Lansford kick),
14:57 2nd.
Los Angeles—Dickerson 2 run (Lansford kick), 5:01 3rd.
Atlanta—Cain 1 run (Luckhurst kick), 9:00 3rd.
Los Angeles—Drew Hill 63 pass from Kemp (Lansford
kick), 9:54 3rd.
Atlanta—Cain 9 run (Luckhurst kick), 2:54 4th.
Atlanta—Field goal Luckhurst 51, 4:43 4th.
Los Angeles—Dickerson 47 run (Lansford kick), 7:26 4th.
Atlanta—Field goal Luckhurst 37, 15:00 4th.

TEAM STATISTICS

	Atlanta	Los Angeles
First downs	18	17
Rushes-Yards	37-147	29-156
Passing yards	209	167
Sacked-Yards lost	3-14	2-23
Return yards	81	143
Passes	14-19-0	13-23-0
Punts	3-51.3	4-42.0
Fumbles-Lost	2-1	3-1
Penalties-Yards	7-55	6-47
Time of possession	34:47	25:13

Attendance—47,832. No-shows—6,486.

INDIVIDUAL STATISTICS

Rushing—Atlanta, Cain 35-145, Bartkowski 1-2, Austin
1-0; Los Angeles, Dickerson 19-107, Crutchfield 7-21,
Kemp 2-26, Guman 1-2.

Passing—Atlanta, Bartkowski 14-19-0—223; Los Angeles, Kemp 11-19-0—168, Dils 2-4-0—22.

Receiving—Atlanta, Bailey 7-158, Cain 3-18, Hodge 2-
31, B. Johnson 1-9, Cox 1-7; Los Angeles, Drew Hill 3-89,
David Hill 3-32, Farmer 2-28, Guman 2-4, Dickerson 1-17,
Ellard 1-14, Redden 1-6.

Kickoff Returns—Atlanta, Tate 4-50, Gaison 1-15; Los
Angeles, Redden 3-73, Ellard 1-12, Drew Hill 1-26.

Punt Returns—Atlanta, B. Johnson 4-16; Los Angeles,
Ellard 2-20, Irvin 1-12.

Punting—Atlanta, Giacomarro 3-51.3; Los Angeles,
Misko 4-42.0.

Field Goals—Atlanta, Luckhurst 3-3; Los Angeles, none
attempted.

Sacks—Atlanta, Kuykendall, Harris; Los Angeles,
Youngblood, Andrews, Owens.

Saints-Bears

SUNDAY, OCTOBER 7
SCORE BY PERIODS

New Orleans	0	7	0	0— 7
Chicago	6	7	0	7—20

SCORING

Chicago—Field goal B. Thomas 48, 5:17 1st.
Chicago—Field goal B. Thomas 46, 14:32 1st.
New Orleans—W. Wilson 15 pass from Todd (Andersen
kick), 12:15 2nd.
Chicago—Payton 1 run (B. Thomas kick), 14:57 2nd.
Chicago—McKinnon 16 pass from McMahon (B. Thomas
kick), 5:40 4th.

TEAM STATISTICS

	New Orleans	Chicago
First downs	14	25
Rushes-Yards	31-176	49-246
Passing yards	145	97
Sacked-Yards lost	1-13	4-31
Return yards	60	62
Passes	7-26-0	10-14-0
Punts	7-45.7	7-40.1
Fumbles-Lost	1-1	0-0
Penalties-Yards	10-68	5-35
Time of possession	24:50	35:10

Attendance—53,752. No-shows—12,038.

INDIVIDUAL STATISTICS

Rushing—New Orleans, G. Rogers 16-99, Gajan 7-51,
W. Wilson 6-19, Todd 2-7; Chicago, Suhey 11-44, Payton
32-154, McMahon 4-25, McKinnon 1-21, Gentry 1-2.

Passing—New Orleans, Todd 7-26-0—158; Chicago,
McMahon 10-14-0—128.

Receiving—New Orleans, Gajan 1-2, Brenner 1-19, W.
Wilson 2-27, Tice 1-17, Young 2-93; Chicago, Suhey 3-45,
Gault 2-33, Moorehead 1-18, Payton 2-11, Saldi 1-5,
McKinnon 1-16.

Kickoff Returns—New Orleans, Duckett 2-33, Fields 1-
22.

Punt Returns—New Orleans, Fields 1-5; Chicago,
McKinnon 5-62.

Punting—New Orleans, Hansen 7-45.7; Chicago, Finzer
7-40.1.

Field Goals—New Orleans, none attempted; Chicago, B.
Thomas 2-2.

Sacks—New Orleans, Jackson, Geathers, Paul, Warren;
Chicago, Hampton ½, McMichael ½.

Oilers-Bengals

SUNDAY, OCTOBER 7
SCORE BY PERIODS

Houston	0	0	3	0— 3
Cincinnati	0	3	7	3—13

SCORING

Cincinnati—Field goal Breech 33, 14:57 2nd.
Houston—Field goal Kempf 24, 4:48 3rd.
Cincinnati—Esiason 3 run (Breech kick), 11:59 3rd.
Cincinnati—Field goal Breech 22, 13:00 4th.

TEAM STATISTICS

	Houston	Cincinnati
First downs	13	20
Rushes-Yards	25-85	38-169
Passing yards	150	159
Sacked-Yards lost	4-31	0-0
Return yards	108	116
Passes	15-33-0	13-24-2
Punts	8-41.8	4-44.0
Fumbles-Lost	2-1	1-1
Penalties-Yards	8-59	4-33
Time of possession	28:33	31:27

Attendance—43,637. No-shows—9,950.

INDIVIDUAL STATISTICS

Rushing—Houston, Campbell 17-47, Edwards 3-8, Moon
5-30; Cincinnati, Alexander 10-34, Jennings 12-68, Kinnebrew 12-59, Esiason 4-8.

Passing—Houston, Moon 15-33-0—181; Cincinnati,
Esiason 13-24-2—159.

Receiving—Houston, Williams 5-68, Dressel 3-26, Walls
3-43, Campbell 1-7, Smith 2-22, Edwards 1-15; Cincinnati, Alexander 5-23, Jennings 2-38, Collinsworth 4-75,
Harris 2-23.

Kickoff Returns—Houston, Roaches 1-49, Walls 1-11,
Williams 1-0; Cincinnati, Martin 1-20, Harris 1-12.

Punt Returns—Houston, Roaches 3-13; Cincinnati, Simmons 1-2, Martin 3-82.

Interceptions—Houston, Hartwig 1-19, Tullis 1-16.

Punting—Houston, James 8-41.8; Cincinnati, McInally
4-44.0.

Field Goals—Houston, Kempf 1-1; Cincinnati, Breech 2-
3 (missed: 51).

Sacks—Cincinnati, Browner 2, R. Williams, Collins.

Broncos-Lions

SUNDAY, OCTOBER 7
SCORE BY PERIODS

Denver	14	7	0	7—28
Detroit	0	7	0	0— 7

SCORING

Denver—Winder 1 run (Karlis kick), 7:40 1st.
Denver—Jones 5 fumble return (Karlis kick), 8:34 1st.
Detroit—Danielson 2 run (Murray kick), 0:35 2nd.
Denver—Watson 42 pass from Elway (Karlis kick), 14:26 2nd.
Denver—Woodard 27 interception return (Karlis kick), 9:29 4th.

TEAM STATISTICS

	Denver	Detroit
First downs	19	20
Rushes-Yards	32-108	23-92
Passing yards	179	256
Sacked-Yards lost	3-31	6-59
Return yards	147	69
Passes	16-22-1	23-50-7
Punts	5-36.0	2-43.5
Fumbles-Lost	3-2	4-3
Penalties-Yards	7-104	9-67
Time of possession	27:50	32:10

Attendance—55,836. No-shows—4,958.

INDIVIDUAL STATISTICS

Rushing—Denver, Willhite 15-81, Winder 7-17, Elway 4-8, Parros 3-3, Brewer 3-minus 1; Detroit, Sims 15-51, Jones 4-28, Danielson 3-9, Thompson 1-4.

Passing—Denver, Elway 16-22-1—210; Detroit, Danielson 17-29-4—244, Machurek 6-21-3—71.

Receiving—Denver, Watson 7-111, Winder 2-24, Sampson 1-25, Willhite 1-13, Johnson 1-13, Kay 1-11, Parros 1-9, J. Wright 1-8, Studdard 1-minus 4; Detroit, Sims 9-80, Thompson 4-67, Nichols 4-62, Chadwick 2-20, Jones 2-13, Lewis 1-58, Jenkins 1-15.

Kickoff Returns—Denver, Thomas 1-19, Long 1-17; Detroit, Jenkins 2-34, Mandley 3-35.

Interceptions—Denver, Wilson 2-11, Mecklenburg 1-63, Woodard 1-27, Lilly 1-5, Busick 1-5, D. Smith 1-0; Detroit, McNorton 1-0.

Punting—Denver, Norman 5-36.0; Detroit, Black 2-43.5.

Field Goals—Denver, Karlis 0-1 (missed: 51); Detroit, none attempted.

Sacks—Denver, Mecklenburg, T. Jackson, D. Smith, Comeaux, Chavous, Garnett; Detroit, English, Gay, Fantetti.

Seahawks-Raiders

SUNDAY, OCTOBER 7

SCORE BY PERIODS

Seattle	0	7	0	7—14
Los Angeles Raiders	0	14	0	14—28

SCORING

Los Angeles—Allen 1 run (Bahr kick), 4:29 2nd.
Los Angeles—Christensen 24 pass from Wilson (Bahr kick), 7:04 2nd.
Seattle—Largent 27 pass from Krieg (Johnson kick), 12:22 2nd.
Seattle—Hughes 2 run (Johnson kick), 1:03 4th.
Los Angeles—Allen 58 pass from Wilson (Bahr kick), 9:28 4th.
Los Angeles—Martin 14 interception return (Bahr kick), 9:47 4th.

TEAM STATISTICS

	Seattle	Los Angeles
First downs	17	13
Rushes-Yards	40-131	31-79
Passing yards	61	296
Sacked-Yards lost	6-49	3-13
Return yards	63	70
Passes	8-19-2	12-23-1
Punts	10-37.6	7-39.6
Fumbles-Lost	1-1	2-1
Penalties-Yards	5-45	14-85
Time of possession	33:53	26:07

Attendance—77,904. No-shows—3,025.

INDIVIDUAL STATISTICS

Rushing—Seattle, Morris 15-87, Hughes 6-18, F. Harris 9-13, Krieg 2-7, Lane 8-6; Los Angeles, Allen 15-40, Hawkins 6-21, King 4-13, Pruitt 3-4, Montgomery 1-1, Willis 1-0, Wilson 1-0.

Passing—Seattle, Krieg 5-12-1—74, Zorn 3-7-1—36; Los Angeles, Wilson 12-19-0—309, Plunkett 0-4-1—0.

Receiving—Seattle, Largent 4-66, Scales 2-22, Doornink 1-13, Metzelaars 1-9; Los Angeles, Allen 4-173, Christensen 4-70, Barnwell 4-66.

Kickoff Returns—Seattle, Dixon 2-37; Los Angeles, Williams 2-56.

Punt Returns—Seattle, Easley 1-11; Los Angeles, Pruitt 1-0.

Interceptions—Seattle, Scholtz 1-15; Los Angeles, Martin 1-14, McElroy 1-0.

Punting—Seattle, West 10-37.6; Los Angeles, Guy 7-39.6.

Field Goals—Seattle, none attempted; Los Angeles, Bahr 0-1 (missed: 30).

Sacks—Seattle, J. Bryant, Green, Nash; Los Angeles, Pickel, Martin, Long, Townsend, M. Davis, Millen.

Dolphins-Steelers

SUNDAY, OCTOBER 7

SCORE BY PERIODS

Miami	0	21	3	7—31
Pittsburgh	0	0	7	0— 7

SCORING

Miami—Hardy 3 pass from Marino (von Schamann kick), 7:11 2nd.
Miami—Rose 34 pass from Marino (von Schamann kick), 12:39 2nd.
Miami—Baumhower 21 fumble return (von Schamann kick), 13:46 2nd.
Miami—Field goal von Schamann 37, 8:15 3rd.
Pittsburgh—Pollard 1 run (Anderson kick), 15:00 3rd.
Miami—Bennett 1 run (von Schamann kick), 3:50 4th.

TEAM STATISTICS

	Miami	Pittsburgh
First downs	20	17
Rushes-Yards	35-116	26-79
Passing yards	226	208
Sacked-Yards lost	0-0	3-20
Return yards	112	148
Passes	16-24-1	19-44-2
Punts	5-38.4	5-39.4
Fumbles-Lost	1-0	4-1
Penalties-Yards	4-24	9-84
Time of possession	32:00	28:00

Attendance—59,103. No-shows—None.

INDIVIDUAL STATISTICS

Rushing—Miami, Nathan 13-58, Bennett 13-35, Carter 2-4, P. Johnson 6-24, Strock 1-minus 5; Pittsburgh, Pollard 8-35, Erenberg 7-17, Woodley 1-0, Abercrombie 8-32, Veals 1-2, Malone 1-minus 7.

Passing—Miami, Marino 16-24-1—226; Pittsburgh, Woodley 0-2-0—0, Malone 19-42-2—228.

Receiving—Miami, Rose 2-48, Nathan 4-37, Cefalo 2-8, Clayton 5-110, Hardy 1-3, Duper 2-20; Pittsburgh, Kolodziejski 2-20, Stallworth 6-94, Abercrombie 4-17, Capers 3-30, Thompson 3-46, Erenberg 1-21.

Kickoff Returns—Miami, Walker 2-39; Pittsburgh, Spencer 5-120.

Punt Returns—Miami, Walker 4-31; Pittsburgh, Woods 3-15.

Interceptions—Miami, B. Brown 1-53, Judson 1-minus 11; Pittsburgh, Hinkle 1-13.

Punting—Miami, Roby 5-38.4; Pittsburgh, Colquitt 5-39.4.

Field Goals—Miami, von Schamann 1-1; Pittsburgh, Anderson 0-1 (missed: 49).

Sacks—Miami, Bowser, Charles, Duhe.

Patriots-Browns
SUNDAY, OCTOBER 7
SCORE BY PERIODS

New England	3	0	7	7—17
Cleveland	0	9	7	0—16

SCORING

New England—Field goal Franklin 45, 10:59 1st.
Cleveland—Field goal Bahr 24, 2:23 2nd.
Cleveland—Field goal Bahr 48, 5:31 2nd.
Cleveland—Field goal Bahr 27, 14:22 2nd.
Cleveland—Harris 16 pass from McDonald (Bahr kick), 5:46 3rd.
New England—Starring 42 pass from Eason (Franklin kick), 8:56 3rd.
New England—Collins 2 run (Franklin kick), 0:50 4th.

TEAM STATISTICS

	New England	Cleveland
First downs	14	23
Rushes-Yards	26-109	24-44
Passing yards	145	305
Sacked-Yards lost	5-33	4-15
Return yards	128	72
Passes	14-21-0	23-37-1
Punts	6-40.2	2-42.5
Fumbles-Lost	0-0	3-1
Penalties-Yards	11-63	7-55
Time of possession	28:09	31:51

Attendance—53,036. No-shows—1,053.

INDIVIDUAL STATISTICS

Rushing—New England, Tatupu 20-83, Collins 2-6, Fryar 1-0, Eason 3-20; Cleveland, Green 19-33, Byner 5-11.

Passing—New England, Eason 14-21-0—178; Cleveland, McDonald 23-37-1—320.

Receiving—New England, Ramsey 6-65, Fryar 1-10, Tatupu 2-14, Starring 3-77, Dawson 2-12; Cleveland, Newsome 6-55, Walker 3-42, Harris 7-120, Stracka 1-15, Brennan 1-29, Byner 2-14, Feacher 3-45.

Kickoff Returns—New England, J. Williams 2-45; Cleveland, Byner 4-55.

Punt Returns—New England, Fryar 1-minus 2; Cleveland, Walker 2-17.

Interceptions—New England, Clayborn 1-85.

Punting—New England, Prestridge 6-40.2; Cleveland, Cox 2-42.5.

Field Goals—New England, Franklin 1-1; Cleveland, Bahr 3-4 (missed: 36).

Sacks—New England, Tippett, Sims, Nelson, Owens ½, T. Williams ½; Cleveland, Camp 2½, Matthews, Golic, Banks ½.

Jets-Chiefs
SUNDAY, OCTOBER 7
SCORE BY PERIODS

New York Jets	0	10	7	0—17
Kansas City	6	3	0	7—16

SCORING

Kansas City—Field goal Lowery 31, 4:52 1st.
Kansas City—Field goal Lowery 42, 13:48 1st.
Kansas City—Field goal Lowery 21, 8:03 2nd.
New York—Field goal Leahy 37, 12:37 2nd.
New York—Paige 1 run (Leahy kick), 14:29 2nd.
New York—Shuler 15 pass from Ryan (Leahy kick), 3:59 3rd.
Kansas City—Scott 1 pass from Blackledge (Lowery kick), 10:18 4th.

TEAM STATISTICS

	New York	Kansas City
First downs	21	20
Rushes-Yards	40-172	32-205
Passing yards	158	125
Sacked-Yards lost	0-0	2-25
Return yards	91	25
Passes	13-23-1	15-25-0
Punts	3-46.7	2-48.5
Fumbles-Lost	0-0	2-1
Penalties-Yards	7-37	4-45
Time of possession	30:12	29:48

Attendance—51,843. No-shows—1,324.

INDIVIDUAL STATISTICS

Rushing—New York, McNeil 19-107, Hector 14-56, Paige 4-7, Ryan 2-2, Barber 1-0; Kansas City, Brown 13-90, Jackson 3-24, Heard 6-23, Lacy 6-18, Blackledge 3-41, Paige 1-9.

Passing—New York, Ryan 13-23-1—158; Kansas City, Blackledge 15-25-0—150.

Receiving—New York, Walker 5-66, Shuler 4-45, McNeil 2-20, Hector 1-19, Barber 1-8; Kansas City, Scott 4-25, Brown 4-25, Heard 3-19, Paige 2-46, Carson 1-22, Little 1-13.

Kickoff Returns—New York, Springs 2-44, Humphery 1-20, Bruckner 1-17; Kansas City, Smith 1-23.

Punt Returns—New York, Springs 1-10; Kansas City, Smith 1-2.

Interceptions—Kansas City, Ross 1-0.

Punting—New York, Ramsey 3-46.7; Kansas City, Arnold 2-48.5.

Field Goals—New York, Leahy 1-1; Kansas City, Lowrey 3-3.

Sacks—New York, Gastineau, Klecko.

Eagles-Bills
SUNDAY, OCTOBER 7
SCORE BY PERIODS

Philadelphia	7	10	3	7—27
Buffalo	7	3	0	7—17

SCORING

Buffalo—Bell 12 run (Danelo kick), 4:22 1st.
Philadelphia—Woodruff 15 pass from Jaworski (McFadden kick), 13:33 1st.
Buffalo—Field goal Danelo 27, 5:50 2nd.
Philadelphia—Kab 4 pass from Jaworski (McFadden kick), 14:11 2nd.
Philadelphia—Field goal McFadden 36, 14:53 2nd.
Philadelphia—Field goal McFadden 22, 13:27 3rd.
Buffalo—Bell 3 run (Danelo kick), 2:42 4th.
Philadelphia—Jaworski 1 run (McFadden kick), 10:59 4th.

TEAM STATISTICS

	Philadelphia	Buffalo
First downs	23	20
Rushes-Yards	30-111	29-118
Passing Yards	228	160
Sacked-Yards lost	1-6	3-23
Return yards	102	113
Passes	24-38-0	14-38-1
Punts	6-37.0	4-48.8
Fumbles-Lost	1-0	3-1
Penalties-Yards	9-92	7-61
Time of possession	33:09	26:51

Attendance—37,555. No-shows—1,514.

INDIVIDUAL STATISTICS

Rushing—Philadelphia, Montgomery 13-67, Jaworski 2-1, Oliver 7-26, M. Williams 8-17; Buffalo, Bell 20-77, Dufek 4-18, Moore 2-11, Kofler 3-12.

Passing—Philadelphia, Jaworski 24-38-0—234; Buffalo, Dufek 4-12-0—49, Kofler 10-26-1—134.

Receiving—Philadelphia, Montgomery 6-45, Oliver 2-4, Woodruff 4-39, Jackson 5-65, Spagnola 5-68, Kab 1-4, M. Williams 1-9; Buffalo, Dennard 3-36, Franklin 4-71,

Brookins 1-14, Bell 4-49, Brammer 1-6, Dawkins 1-7.

Kickoff Returns—Philadelphia, Hayes 3-63; Buffalo, Wilson 3-49, White 1-5, V. Williams 1-17.

Punt Returns—Philadelphia, Cooper 2-8; Buffalo, Wilson 5-42.

Interceptions—Philadelphia, Ellis 1-31.

Punting—Philadelphia, Horan 6-37.0; Buffalo, Kidd 4-48.8.

Field Goals—Philadelphia, McFadden 2-2; Buffalo, Danelo 1-3 (missed: 52, 36).

Sacks—Philadelphia, Brown, Wilkes, Armstrong ½, Harrison ½; Buffalo, Haslett.

Cardinals-Cowboys
SUNDAY, OCTOBER 7
SCORE BY PERIODS

St. Louis	7	7	17	0—31
Dallas	7	6	0	7—20

SCORING

St. Louis—Marsh 20 pass from Lomax (O'Donoghue kick), 5:20 1st.

Dallas—Dorsett 31 run (Septien kick), 10:29 1st.

Dallas—Field goal Septien 35, 12:34 2nd.

St. Louis—Mitchell 3 run (O'Donoghue kick), 14:08 2nd.

Dallas—Field goal Septien 36, 14:59 2nd.

St. Louis—Field goal O'Donoghue 22, 5:13 3rd.

St. Louis—Green 70 pass from Lomax (O'Donoghue kick), 7:40 3rd.

St. Louis—Green 45 pass from Lomax (O'Donoghue kick), 13:21 3rd.

Dallas—Cornwell 10 pass from D. White (Septien kick), 4th.

TEAM STATISTICS

	St. Louis	Dallas
First downs	23	19
Rushes-Yards	41-152	20-121
Passing yards	325	177
Sacked-Yards lost	4-29	2-21
Return yards	119	108
Passes	19-29-0	18-36-2
Punts	3-45.3	4-41.3
Fumbles-Lost	2-0	2-1
Penalties-Yards	7-75	6-35
Time of possession	39:15	20:45

Attendance—61,438. No-shows—3,663.

INDIVIDUAL STATISTICS

Rushing—St. Louis, Anderson 25-110, Mitchell 5-17, Ferrell 4-15, Love 2-5, Lomax 4-5, LaFleur 1-0; Dallas, Dorsett 14-96, Newsome 3-17, Springs 3-8.

Passing—St. Louis, Lomax 19-29-0—354; Dallas, Hogeboom 13-28-2—143, D. White 5-8-0—55.

Receiving—St. Louis, Green 8-189, Tilley 4-82, LaFleur 2-30, Ferrell 3-22, Marsh 1-20, Mitchell 1-11; Dallas, Donley 5-54, Renfro 3-58, Dorsett 3-25, Springs 3-16, Cornwell 2-23, Cosbie 1-13, Newsome 1-9.

Kickoff Returns—St. Louis, Mitchell 3-53, Harrell 1-23, Ferrell 1-0; Dallas, McSwain 5-102, Granger 1-1.

Punt Returns—St. Louis, Mitchell 3-25; Dallas, Allen 1-5.

Interceptions—St. Louis, Junior 1-18, Perrin 1-0.

Punting—St. Louis, Birdsong 3-45.3; Dallas, D. White 4-41.3.

Field Goals—St. Louis, O'Donoghue 1-2 (missed: 46); Dallas, Septien 2-3 (missed: 42).

Sacks—St. Louis, Greer, Mays ½, Harris ½; Dallas, Jones, Dickerson, Hegman, Jeffcoat.

Chargers-Packers
SUNDAY, OCTOBER 7
SCORE BY PERIODS

San Diego	7	7	10	10—34
Green Bay	7	7	7	7—28

SCORING

San Diego—Duckworth 27 pass from Fouts (Benirschke kick), 1:59 1st.

Green Bay—Coffman 3 pass from Dickey (Garcia kick), 4:34 1st.

San Diego—Holohan 3 pass from Fouts (Benirschke kick), 0:02 2nd.

Green Bay—West 29 pass from Dickey (Garcia kick), 14:14 2nd.

San Diego—Jackson 9 pass from Fouts (Benirschke kick), 1:04 3rd.

Green Bay—Ellis 4 run (Garcia kick), 8:16 3rd.

San Diego—Field goal Benirschke 31, 12:46 3rd.

San Diego—Jackson 1 run (Benirschke kick), 3:39 4th.

Green Bay—Lofton 25 pass from Dickey (Garcia kick), 8:09 4th.

San Diego—Field goal Benirschke 39, 13:28 4th.

TEAM STATISTICS

	San Diego	Green Bay
First downs	28	18
Rushes-Yards	37-101	12-47
Passing yards	352	368
Sacked-Yards lost	3-24	3-16
Return yards	149	124
Passes	31-50-0	25-39-2
Punts	4-43.5	6-39.2
Fumbles-Lost	1-0	1-0
Penalties-Yards	9-84	9-83
Time of possession	41:36	18:24

Attendance—54,045. No-shows—2,110.

INDIVIDUAL STATISTICS

Rushing—San Diego, Jackson 32-93, James 1-12, McGee 1-4, Fouts 3-minus 8; Green Bay, Huckleby 3-25, Clark 4-10, Ellis 3-11, Lofton 1-1, Dickey 1-0.

Passing—San Diego, Fouts 31-50-0—376; Green Bay, Dickey 25-39-2—384.

Receiving—San Diego, Winslow 15-157, Holohan 7-68, Joiner 4-47, Duckworth 2-71, Sievers 2-24, Jackson 1-9; Green Bay, Coffman 8-104, Lofton 5-158, Jefferson 3-35, Ellis 3-12, Clark 3-29, West 2-33, Epps 1-13.

Kickoff Returns—San Diego, James 3-93, McGee, 1-17; Green Bay, Epps 3-51, Rodgers 2-40, Huckleby 1-7.

Punt Returns—San Diego, James 2-13; Green Bay, Epps 3-26.

Interceptions—San Diego, Byrd 1-13, Smith 1-13.

Punting—San Diego, Buford 4-43.5; Green Bay, Scribner 6-39.2.

Field Goals—San Diego, Benirschke 2-4 (missed: 58, 25); Green Bay, none attempted.

Sacks—San Diego, Ferguson, Fox, Lowe; Green Bay, Douglass, Martin, Johnson.

Vikings-Buccaneers
SUNDAY, OCTOBER 7
SCORE BY PERIODS

Minnesota	14	7	0	10—31
Tampa Bay	7	14	7	7—35

SCORING

Minnesota—Brown 1 run (Stenerud kick), 4:38 1st.

Minnesota—Brown 13 pass from Kramer (Stenerud kick), 8:45 1st.

Tampa Bay—Armstrong 1 run (Ariri kick), 14:20 1st.

Tampa Bay—House 7 pass from DeBerg (Ariri kick), 2:36 2nd.

Minnesota—Mularkey 1 pass from Kramer (Stenerud kick), 5:07 2nd.

Tampa Bay—Wilder 1 run (Ariri kick), 9:45 2nd.

Tampa Bay—Carter 6 pass from DeBerg (Ariri kick), 9:31 3rd.

Minnesota—Field goal Stenerud 20, 6:33 4th.

Tampa Bay—Wilder 10 run (Ariri kick), 9:10 4th.
Minnesota—Anderson 5 run (Stenerud kick), 13:50 4th.

TEAM STATISTICS

	Minnesota	Tampa Bay
First downs	30	18
Rushes-Yards	32-169	31-102
Passing yards	374	212
Sacked-Yards lost	3-19	0-0
Return yards	127	137
Passes	28-49-2	16-29-0
Punts	2-41.0	7-40.6
Fumbles-Lost	7-3	1-0
Penalties-Yards	13-101	2-15
Time of possession	32:59	27:01

Attendance—47,405. No-shows—6,147.

INDIVIDUAL STATISTICS

Rushing—Minnesota, Brown 9-80, Anderson 18-78, Waddy 2-13, Manning 1-0, Kramer 2-minus 2; Tampa Bay, Wilder 25-89, Morton 3-16, Armstrong 1-1, DeBerg 2-minus 4.

Passing—Minnesota, Kramer 27-47-2—386, Manning 1-2-0—7; Tampa Bay, DeBerg 16-29-0—212.

Receiving—Minnesota, Jones 6-110, Lewis 4-72, Brown 8-71, White 3-71, Jordan 4-54, Nelson 2-14, Mularkey 1-1; Tampa Bay, House 7-126, Wilder 6-40, Giles 1-22, J. Bell 1-18, Carter 1-6.

Kickoff Returns—Minnesota, Anderson 3-48, Waddy 3-64; Tampa Bay, Morton 4-79, Wood 1-14.

Punt Returns—Minnesota, Lewis 2-18, Waddy 1-minus 3; Tampa Bay, Bright 1-6.

Interceptions—Tampa Bay, Brantley 1-13, Holt 1-25.

Punting—Minnesota, Coleman 2-41.0; Tampa Bay, Garcia 7-40.6.

Field Goals—Minnesota, Stenerud 1-1; Tampa Bay, none attempted.

Sacks—Tampa Bay, Logan 2, Selmon.

Redskins-Colts
SUNDAY, OCTOBER 7
SCORE BY PERIODS

Washington	7	21	7	0—35
Indianapolis	7	0	0	0— 7

SCORING

Washington—Monk 10 pass from Theismann (Moseley kick), 5:59 1st.

Indianapolis—Moore 2 run (Allegre kick), 11:40 1st.

Washington—Monk 48 pass from Theismann (Moseley kick), 5:28 2nd.

Washington—Riggins 1 run (Moseley kick), 13:06 2nd.

Washington—Monk 16 pass from Theismann (Moseley kick), 14:23 2nd.

Washington—McGrath 11 pass from Theismann (Moseley kick), 11:10 3rd.

TEAM STATISTICS

	Washington	Indianapolis
First downs	25	12
Rushes-Yards	39-178	20-71
Passing yards	268	115
Sacked-Yards lost	1-6	5-39
Return yards	108	97
Passes	18-22-1	11-29-2
Punts	3-33.7	7-47.9
Fumbles-Lost	3-1	0-0
Penalties-Yards	7-48	1-8
Time of possession	39:16	20:44

Attendance—60,012. No-shows—681.

INDIVIDUAL STATISTICS

Rushing—Washington, Riggins 19-94, Griffin 14-44, Kane 3-40, Theismann 1-4, Hart 2-minus 4; Indianapolis, Moore 9-31, McMillan 7-19, Schlichter 1-minus 10, Dickey 2-3, Wonsley 1-8.

Passing—Washington, Theismann 17-20-1—267, Hart

1-2-0—7; Indianapolis, Pagel 10-23-2—140, Schlichter 1-6-0—14.

Receiving—Washington, Monk 8-141, McGrath 7-82, Didier 1-37, Warren 1-7, Kane 1-7; Indianapolis, Butler 4-56, Porter 2-44, McMillan 2-14, Young 2-36, Moore 1-4.

Kickoff Returns—Washington, Nelms 2-66; Indianapolis, Smith 6-85.

Punt Returns—Washington, Nelms 2-20, Mauti 1-2.

Interceptions—Washington, Dean 2-22; Indianapolis, Randle 1-12.

Punting—Washington, Hayes 3-33.7; Indianapolis, Stark 7-47.9.

Field Goals—Washington, none attempted; Indianapolis, none attempted.

Sacks—Washington, Coleman 2, Grant 2, Beasley; Indianapolis, Parker.

49ers-Giants
MONDAY, OCTOBER 8
SCORE BY PERIODS

San Francisco	21	7	3	0—31
New York Giants	3	0	0	7—10

SCORING

San Francisco—Nehemiah 59 pass from Montana (Wersching kick), 2:32 1st.

San Francisco—Frank 1 pass from Montana (Wersching kick), 6:18 1st.

San Francisco—McLemore 79 punt return (Wersching kick), 7:33 1st.

New York—Field goal Haji-Sheikh 20, 13:11 1st.

San Francisco—Craig 8 pass from Montana (Wersching kick), 5:54 2nd.

San Francisco—Field goal Wersching 37, 5:46 3rd.

New York—Woolfolk 2 run (Haji-Sheikh kick), 13:43 4th.

TEAM STATISTICS

	San Francisco	New York
First downs	18	23
Rushes-Yards	32-167	23-113
Passing yards	217	276
Sacked-Yards lost	1-1	4-27
Return yards	123	142
Passes	16-27-0	25-44-2
Punts	5-39.0	5-42.4
Fumbles-Lost	1-0	0-0
Penalties-Yards	7-40	3-20
Time of possession	28:08	31:52

Attendance—76,112. No-shows—NA.

INDIVIDUAL STATISTICS

Rushing—San Francisco, Tyler 14-101, Craig 9-33, Ring 3-6, Montana 2-7, Harmon 3-23 Cavanaugh 1-minus 3; New York, Woolfolk 7-21, Carpenter 11-45, Simms 3-22, Morris 2-25.

Passing—San Francisco, Montana 15-24-0—207, Cavanaugh 1-3-0—11; New York, Simms 24-43-2—290, Galbreath 1-1-0—13.

Receiving—San Francisco, Nehemiah 1-59, Craig 7-95, Wilson 2-23, Frank 1-1, D. Clark 3-27, Tyler 1-7, Francis 1-6; New York, Manuel 5-78, Mowatt 3-44, Simms 1-13, Gray 4-51, Johnson 3-34, Galbreath 2-18, Woolfolk 2-10, Carpenter 1-10, B. Williams 1-6, Morris 3-39.

Kickoff Returns—San Francisco, Monroe 1-20, Cooper 1-0; New York, McConkey 3-67, Cephous 1-30, Morris 1-10.

Punt Returns—San Francisco, McLemore 4-103; New York, McConkey 3-35.

Interceptions—San Francisco, Hicks 1-0, J. Fahnhorst 1-0.

Punting—San Francisco, Runager 5-39.0; New York, Jennings 5-42.4.

Field Goals—San Francisco, Wersching 1-1; New York, Haij-Sheikh 1-2 (missed: 30).

Sacks—San Francisco, Ellison, Turner, Carter, McColl; New York, Headen.

SEVENTH WEEK

RESULTS OF WEEK 7
Sunday, October 14

Detroit 13, Tampa Bay 7 (OT) at Det.
Kansas City 31, San Diego 13 at K.C.
L.A. Raiders 23, Minnesota 20 at L.A.
L.A. Rams 28, New Orleans 10 at N.O.
Miami 28, Houston 10 at Mia.
New England 20, Cincinnati 14 at N.E.
N.Y. Giants 19, Atlanta 7 at Atl.
N.Y. Jets 24, Cleveland 20 at Cleve.
Philadelphia 16, Indianapolis 7 at Phila.
Pittsburgh 20, San Francisco 17 at S.F.
St. Louis 38, Chicago 21 at St. L.
Seattle 31, Buffalo 28 at Sea.
Washington 34, Dallas 14 at Wash.

Monday, October 15

Denver 17, Green Bay 14 at Den.

When the San Francisco 49ers played host to the Pittsburgh Steelers on the seventh weekend of the 1984 season, they were listed as solid favorites. Their 6-0 record was one of the two unbeaten marks in the NFL and they were coming off a 31-10 thrashing of the New York Giants in the Meadowlands just six days earlier. The Steelers, on the other hand, were 3-3 after suffering a 31-7 drubbing at the hands of the Miami Dolphins the week before. It was Pittsburgh's worst defeat in the NFL since a 41-7 loss to Baltimore in 1968.

But nobody's perfect. The 49ers lost the game, 20-17, and, in the process, their shot at a perfect season. The loss to Pittsburgh proved to be San Francisco's only blemish in a Super Bowl championship season, a season in which the 49ers won 18 of 19 contests, including the playoffs. The 1972 Miami Dolphins (17-0) were the only team in NFL history to go through an entire season and postseason without losing a game. The 49ers came within four points of being the second.

The normally disciplined 49ers made at least four critical mistakes that cost them their chance at immortality.

Mistake No. 1 came in the first quarter, when a 51-yard field goal by Ray Wersching was called back because of an illegal formation. No. 2 came late in the game, with San Francisco leading, 17-10. Pittsburgh was held to just one yard on three successive plays from the 49ers' 7-yard line, but on fourth down, cornerback Eric Wright was called for pass interference against the Steelers' John Stallworth, giving Pittsburgh a first down. Mark Malone then hit Stallworth with a game-tying touchdown pass from six yards out with 3:21 to play.

Mistake No. 3 followed quickly when, on San Francisco's ensuing possession, quarterback Joe Montana threw a poor sideline pass that was picked off by Steelers linebacker Bryan Hinkle and returned to the San Francisco 3.

The interception, only the second thrown by Montana in the season, set up Gary Anderson's 21-yard game-winning field goal moments later.

After Anderson's field goal, the 49ers had one last chance. They drove to the Pittsburgh 20-yard line in seven plays, setting up a possible game-tying field goal. But Wersching, who earlier had hit a 30-yarder and the nullified 51-yarder, was wide to the left from 37 yards out.

"I just hope we don't have many games like this one," said 49ers Coach Bill Walsh. They didn't.

The Dolphins, who would go on to be the league's second-best regular-season record and a date with the 49ers in Super Bowl XIX, remained the NFL's only unbeaten team through seven weeks. The Dolphins crushed winless Houston, 28-10, extending the Oilers' league-record road losing streak to 22 games. Dan Marino's three touchdown passes gave him 20 for the season, equalling his Pro Bowl output during his 1983 rookie season. Rookie Joe Carter scored the first touchdown of his NFL career and his 105 rushing yards marked the first time since 1982 that a Miami running back had gone over the 100-yard barrier.

Rams running back Eric Dickerson continued his 100-yard assaults with a 164-yard effort in Los Angeles' 28-10 victory over NFC Western Division rival New Orleans. Quarterback Jeff Kemp passed for three touchdowns as the Rams exploded for 21 second-quarter points to blow open a close game.

Saints Coach Bum Phillips tried a platoon system with running backs George Rogers and Earl Campbell and quarterbacks Richard Todd and Ken Stabler. The results were dismal as the Saints running game totaled just 95 yards—Rogers and Campbell had just 30 between them—and the quarterbacks threw three interceptions. The game was Campbell's first with New Orleans after being acquired from Houston in a trade the previous week.

For the second week in a row, the New England Patriots rallied to pull out a victory. A week earlier, the Pats trailed Cleveland, 16-3, before edging the Browns, 17-16. Against Cincinnati, the Pats trailed, 14-3, at halftime before scoring 17 unanswered points in the second half to win, 20-14. New England managed 93 yards in total offense in the first half but came back with 255 in the second. Quarterback Tony Eason led the comeback with 13- and 25-yard scoring runs in the final two quarters. The Pats marched 72 yards in six plays for a touchdown on their first possession of the third period.

The San Diego Chargers' high-powered offense failed to score a touchdown in a 31-13 loss to Kansas City. San Diego's only points came on two Benny Ricardo field goals and a 99-yard interception return by cornerback Gill Byrd.

The Chiefs were boosted by the return of Bill Kenney at quarterback. Kenney, a Pro Bowler in '83 when he threw for a club-record 4,348 yards, broke the thumb on his passing hand in the final 1984 preseason game and missed the Chiefs' first six contests. His replacement, second-year man Todd Blackledge, led the Chiefs to a 3-3 record and a 10-6 halftime lead in the San Diego game. Chiefs Coach John Mackovic, however, played Kenney at quarterback in the second half and the six-year veteran responded with 238 yards passing and a pair of touchdowns.

The New York Giants rolled over the Atlanta Falcons, 19-7, for their fourth victory in seven games. The Giants grabbed a commanding 16-0 halftime lead on two Rob Carpenter touchdowns and a field goal as the Falcons' offense sputtered at inopportune times. Atlanta came away empty when one drive stalled at the New York 1-yard line after a first-and-goal situation. Quarterback Steve Bartkowski did not complete a pass in the final 21 minutes of the opening half.

Giants placekicker Ali Haji-Sheikh booted two field goals in the contest, but missed three other attempts to drop his season record to 4 for 12. Haji-Sheikh, the NFC Pro Bowl kicker in 1983 as a rookie, also missed his third extra-point attempt of 1984.

One kicker not struggling in the early portion of the '84 season was Philadelphia rookie Paul McFadden, who won the vacant place-kicking job when Tony Franklin was traded to New England in the offseason. McFadden booted three field goals in the Eagles' 16-7 triumph over the visiting Indianapolis Colts to run his season record to 15 for 17. Two of McFadden's kicks came in the second quarter as Philadelphia took a 13-0 halftime lead. The Philly defense held the Colts to no pass completions, two first downs and only 45 total yards in the opening 30 minutes.

The smallest Silverdome crowd in seven years (44,308) saw the Lions improve their season record to 2-5 with a 13-7 overtime victory against division-rival Tampa Bay. Quarterback Gary Danielson, who was replaced by Eric Hipple as the Lions' starting signal-caller the week before the game, came off the bench to replace an injured Hipple early in the second period with Detroit trailing, 7-0. He responded by running 18 yards for the tying touchdown late in the first half and then hooked up with wide receiver Leonard Thompson 4:34 into the extra period for the game-winner.

Bucs placekicker Obed Ariri could have won the game for Tampa Bay, but his 42-yard field goal attempt missed badly at the end of regulation time. The Bucs lost another chance to win when, after getting the ball first in overtime, James Wilder fumbled and William Gay recovered for Detroit at his own 41. The Lions then drove 59 yards in four plays for the winning touchdown.

The L.A. Raiders needed all 60 minutes to pull out a 23-20 triumph over visiting Minnesota. In a sloppily-played game that saw 26 penalties handed out between the two teams, the Raiders prevailed on Chris Bahr's third field goal as time expired. The Raiders started their game-winning drive at the Vikings' 36-yard line with 3:15 left after forcing the Vikes to punt from their own end zone. Los Angeles trailed, 13-7, after one quarter and 20-13 after three periods before pulling out the decision.

The New York Jets pulled out a 24-20 win against Cleveland with a big assist from the Browns' defense. Leading 20-17 with 8:30 remaining in the game, Browns safety Al Gross kicked Jets tight end Mickey Shuler in a pileup. The penalty gave New York a first down at the Cleveland 42 and, six plays later, rookie running back Tony Paige scored the game-winner for the Jets with 5:39 left. Browns tight end Ozzie Newsome set Cleveland team records for receptions with 14 and yards with 191 in the losing effort.

The first Dallas-Washington game of 1984, traditionally a tense, hotly contested matchup, turned into a blowout as the Redskins scored 34 consecutive points in a 34-14 rout. The Cowboys grabbed the early advantage when Tony Dorsett scampered 29 yards on Dallas' first possession for a 7-0 lead. But Washington linebacker Monte Coleman picked off a Gary Hogeboom pass later in the first quarter and returned it 49 yards to tie the game. From that point, the Redskins were never headed, scoring 27 more unanswered points before Dorsett's second TD early in the final period. Joe Theismann's three touchdown passes and John Riggins' 165 yards rushing led the Redskins' offense. Riggins, who was held without a touchdown for the first time in eight games, went over the 10,000-yard mark in career rushing yardage. Riggins joined Walter Payton, Jim Brown, Franco Harris and O.J. Simpson as the only NFL players to accomplish that feat.

St. Louis scored a pair of fourth-quarter touchdowns to break open a tight game and defeat Chicago, 38-21. Both the Cardinals and Bears scored on their first possessions of the game and the lead changed hands six times in the first three periods.

St. Louis led, 17-14, at halftime before the Bears scored on their first possession of the third quarter to regain the lead at 21-17. But from that point on, the Chicago offense was held to just 29 total yards and the Bears defense, which had sacked Cards' quarterback Neil Lomax five times in the first half, was neutralized.

Buffalo and Seattle also struggled through a seesaw affair. The Seahawks jumped to a 17-0 first-quarter lead despite managing only 17 yards in total offense. Both Seattle touchdowns were set up by blocks of John Kidd punts.

The Bills rebounded, however, to take a 28-24 lead early in the final period on two Joe Ferguson touchdown passes, a punt return and a fumble return. But the Seahawks eventually prevailed, 31-28, as Dave Krieg and Steve Largent hooked up for a 51-yard touchdown midway through the period. The win came in Coach Chuck Knox's first meeting against the club he coached for five seasons before leaving for Seattle in 1983.

The Denver Broncos defeated the Green Bay Packers, 17-14, in a Monday night game with an unusual twist. With a snowstorm raging in Denver at the game's outset, the Broncos won the opening coin toss and elected to give the Packers the ball first. It was a wise decision. On the first play from scrimmage, Green Bay's Gerry Ellis fumbled the ball and Broncos safety Steve Foley returned it 22 yards for a score. Then, when the Pack got the ball back, Jessie Clark fumbled on the first play from scrimmage. This time, cornerback Louie Wright recovered and returned it 27 yards for a touchdown. Denver led, 14-0, after the first 37 seconds without their offense even having taken the field.

As things turned out, that was just as well. The Broncos managed only 10 first downs and 193 total yards as it struggled against the elements. The Green Bay offense, under the direction of quarterback Lynn Dickey, was superb considering the conditions. Dickey threw for 371 yards—206 to wide receiver James Lofton—as the Packers offense moved the ball well but had difficulty getting it over the goal line. Denver placekicker Rich Karlis booted a 30-yard field goal early in the second quarter as Green Bay suffered its sixth straight loss.

Detroit quarterback Gary Danielson came off the bench to lead the Lions to a 13-7 overtime victory against Tampa Bay. Danielson ran 18 yards for the tying score and passed 37 yards to Leonard Thompson for the game-winner.

Buccaneers-Lions
SUNDAY, OCTOBER 14
SCORE BY PERIODS

Tampa Bay	7	0	0	0	0— 7
Detroit	0	7	0	0	6—13

SCORING
Tampa Bay—House 25 pass from DeBerg (Ariri kick), 14:00 1st.
Detroit—Danielson 18 run (Murray kick), 14:31 2nd.
Detroit—Thompson 37 pass from Danielson, 4:34 OT.

TEAM STATISTICS

	Tampa Bay	Detroit
First downs	19	16
Rushes-Yards	38-90	31-176
Passing yards	259	137
Sacked-Yards lost	1-13	1-13
Return yards	59	56
Passes	25-29-0	11-23-0
Punts	4-44.0	6-38.0
Fumbles-Lost	4-3	1-1
Penalties-Yards	9-65	10-89
Time of possession	37:51	26:43

Attendance—44,308. No-shows—12,261.

INDIVIDUAL STATISTICS
Rushing—Tampa Bay, Wilder 31-67, DeBerg 4-21, Dierking 1-3, Morton 2-minus 1; Detroit, Sims 16-100, Danielson 5-39, J. Jones 8-34, Hipple 2-3.

Passing—Tampa Bay, DeBerg 25-29-0—272; Detroit, Hipple 5-11-0—59, Danielson 6-12-0—91.

Receiving—Tampa Bay, Wilder 9-60, House 4-67, Carter 4-50, J. Bell 3-36, Giles 2-33, Armstrong 2-8, T. Bell 1-18; Detroit, Thompson 5-82, Sims 2-29, J. Jones 2-26, Lewis 2-13.

Kickoff Returns—Tampa Bay, Morton 2-38; Detroit, Martin 1-15, Hall 1-23.

Punt Returns—Tampa Bay, Bright 4-21; Detroit, Martin 2-18.

Punting—Tampa Bay, Garcia 4-43.8; Detroit, Black 6-38.3.

Field Goals—Tampa Bay, Ariri 0-1 (missed: 42); Detroit, Murray 0-1 (missed: 32).

Sacks—Tampa Bay, Manor; Detroit, Green.

Chargers-Chiefs
SUNDAY, OCTOBER 14
SCORE BY PERIODS

San Diego	3	3	7	0—13
Kansas City	10	0	7	14—31

SCORING
Kansas City—Lacy 24 run (Lowery kick), 1:46 1st.
San Diego—Field goal Ricardo 38, 5:03 1st.
Kansas City—Field goal Lowery 22, 12:47 1st.
San Diego—Field goal Ricardo 42, 4:02 2nd.
San Diego—Byrd 99 interception return (Ricardo kick), 9:04 3rd.
Kansas City—Paige 18 pass from Kenney (Lowery kick), 10:40 3rd.
Kansas City—Beckman 5 pass from Kenney (Lowery kick), 7:59 4th.
Kansas City—Heard 69 run (Lowery kick), 10:23 4th.

TEAM STATISTICS

	San Diego	Kansas City
First downs	17	24
Rushes-Yards	19-77	22-146
Passing yards	243	360
Sacked-Yards lost	3-33	1-11
Return yards	286	148
Passes	32-48-2	23-41-3
Punts	6-46.3	4-46.5
Fumbles-Lost	3-3	3-1
Penalties-Yards	11-127	10-73
Time of possession	32:44	27:16

Attendance—62,233. No-shows—5,232.

INDIVIDUAL STATISTICS
Rushing—San Diego, Jackson 16-68, McGee 2-6, Moore 1-3; Kansas City, Lacy 7-40, Brown 4-15, Blackledge 1-4, Heard 7-84, Jackson 2-5, Kenney 1-minus 2.

Passing—San Diego, Fouts 30-46-2—270, Luther 2-2-0—6; Kansas City, Blackledge 10-19-1—133, Kenney 13-22-2—238.

Receiving—San Diego, Chandler 8-93, Holohan 3-38, Joiner 6-66, Duckworth 1-10, Sievers 3-22, Jackson 6-20, Winslow 3-21, Morris 1-2, James 1-4; Kansas City, Marshall 5-64, Brown 1-11, Carson 7-165, Scott 3-47, Lacy 3-18, Heard 1-16, Paige 2-45, Beckman 1-5.

Kickoff Returns—San Diego, James 3-78, McGee 2-61; Kansas City, Paige 2-42, Smith 2-46.

Punt Returns—San Diego, James 2-16; Kansas City, Smith 4-42.

Interceptions—San Diego, Byrd 1-99, Lowe 1-20, Gregor 1-12; Kansas City, Cherry 1-18, Lewis 1-0.

Punting—San Diego, Buford 6-46.3; Kansas City, J. Arnold 4-46.5.

Field Goals—San Diego, Ricardo 2-2; Kansas City, Lowery 1-1.

Sacks—San Diego, Green; Kansas City, Daniels 2, Bell ½, Still ½.

Vikings-Raiders
SUNDAY, OCTOBER 14
SCORE BY PERIODS

Minnesota	13	0	7	0—20
Los Angeles Raiders	7	3	3	10—23

SCORING
Los Angeles—Christensen 34 pass from Wilson (Bahr kick), 3:23 1st.
Minnesota—Jones 70 pass from Kramer (Stenerud kick), 5:02 1st.
Minnesota—Rice 3 run (kick failed), 9:09 1st.
Los Angeles—Field goal Bahr 22, 7:39 2nd.
Los Angeles—Field goal Bahr 24, 7:13 3rd.
Minnesota—Mularkey 2 pass from Kramer (Stenerud kick), 13:14 3rd.
Los Angeles—Allen 1 run (Bahr kick), 2:08 4th.
Los Angeles—Field goal Bahr 20, 15:00 4th.

TEAM STATISTICS

	Minnesota	Los Angeles
First downs	16	24
Rushes-Yards	31-104	32-142
Passing yards	122	251
Sacked-Yards lost	5-46	2-17
Return yards	149	157
Passes	11-19-0	21-37-1
Punts	7-42.7	5-46.6
Fumbles-Lost	4-2	1-1
Penalties-Yards	10-96	16-140
Time of possession	25:45	34:15

Attendance—49,276. No-shows—5,047.

INDIVIDUAL STATISTICS
Rushing—Minnesota, Anderson 15-53, Brown 12-38, Nelson 1-10, Rice 1-3, Kramer 2-0; Los Angeles, Hawkins 11-65, Allen 17-54, Wilson 2-16, King 2-7.

Passing—Minnesota, Kramer 11-19-0—168; Los Angeles, Wilson 21-37-1—268.

Receiving—Minnesota, Jones 5-132, Brown 2-13, Jordan 1-13, White 1-8, Mularkey 1-2, Anderson 1-0; Los Angeles, Barnwell 6-86, Christensen 4-73, Allen 6-42, Branch 2-31, Williams 1-26, King 2-10.

Kickoff Returns—Minnesota, Nelson 5-103; Los Angeles, Williams 3-72, Montgomery 1-22.

Punt Returns—Minnesota, Nelson 2-37; Los Angeles, Pruitt 5-63.

Interceptions—Minnesota, Swain 1-9.

Punting—Minnesota, Coleman 7-42.7; Los Angeles, Guy 5-46.6.

Field Goals—Minnesota, none attempted; Los Angeles, Bahr 3-4 (missed: 44).

Sacks—Minnesota, Mullaney, Elshire; Los Angeles, Jones, Martin, Long, Millen, Townsend.

Rams-Saints
SUNDAY, OCTOBER 14
SCORE BY PERIODS

Los Angeles Rams	0	21	7	0—28
New Orleans	3	0	0	7—10

SCORING
New Orleans—Field goal Andersen 47, 11:17 1st.
Los Angeles—Drew Hill 25 pass from Kemp (Lansford kick), 0:08 2nd.
Los Angeles—Ellard 13 pass from Kemp (Lansford kick), 6:24 2nd.
Los Angeles—Cromwell 33 interception return (Lansford kick), 8:06 2nd.
Los Angeles—Brown 21 pass from Kemp (Lansford kick), 11:18 3rd.
New Orleans—Gajan 1 run (Andersen kick), 1:16 4th.

TEAM STATISTICS

	Los Angeles	New Orleans
First downs	17	22
Rushes-Yards	34-204	30-95
Passing yards	138	204
Sacked-Yards lost	1-4	2-19
Return yards	119	89
Passes	8-19-0	25-47-3
Punts	5-38.6	3-48.7
Fumbles-Lost	3-1	1-0
Penalties-Yards	7-72	10-65
Time of possession	25:34	34:26

Attendance—63,161. No-shows—7,913.

INDIVIDUAL STATISTICS
Rushing—Los Angeles, Dickerson 21-164, Crutchfield 7-27, Redden 4-7, Kemp 2-6; New Orleans, Gajan 13-54, Campbell 5-19, G. Rogers 5-11, W. Wilson 5-10, Anthony 1-3, Todd 1-minus 2.

Passing—Los Angeles, Kemp 8-19-0—142; New Orleans, Stabler 17-34-1—148; Todd 8-13-2—75.

Receiving—Los Angeles, Ellard 2-42, Guman 2-28, Brown 2-41, Drew Hill 1-25, Barber 1-6; New Orleans, G. Rogers 2-13, W. Wilson 3-37, Young 2-24, Gajan 3-15,

Groth 3-27, Tice 3-24, Brenner 1-13, Miller 3-15, Duckett 2-19, Scott 2-30, Anthony 1-6.

Kickoff Returns—Los Angeles, Drew Hill 1-13; New Orleans, Duckett 5-89.

Punt Returns—Los Angeles, Irvin 2-32.

Interceptions—Los Angeles, Irvin 1-20, Cromwell 2-54.

Punting—Los Angeles, Misko 5-38.6; New Orleans, Hansen 3-48.7.

Field Goals—Los Angeles, none attempted; New Orleans, Andersen 1-1.

Sacks—Los Angeles, Andrews 2; New Orleans, Paul.

Oilers-Dolphins
SUNDAY, OCTOBER 14
SCORE BY PERIODS

Houston	0	0	3	7—10
Miami	0	7	7	14—28

SCORING

Miami—Clayton 27 pass from Marino (von Schamann kick), 13:06 2nd.
Miami—Duper 17 pass from Marino (von Schamann kick), 6:40 3rd.
Houston—Field goal Kempf 49, 13:00 3rd.
Miami—Moore 32 pass from Marino (von Schamann kick), 3:49 4th.
Miami—Carter 25 run (von Schamann kick), 9:43 4th.
Houston—Dressel 9 pass from Moon (Kempf kick), 12:22 4th.

TEAM STATISTICS

	Houston	Miami
First downs	16	28
Rushes-Yards	26-83	34-208
Passing yards	156	307
Sacked-Yards lost	1-14	2-14
Return yards	45	73
Passes	19-28-1	25-32-0
Punts	5-41.4	1-53.0
Fumbles-Lost	0-0	2-1
Penalties-Yards	3-15	7-71
Time of possession	26:58	33:02

Attendance—54,080. No-shows—5,026.

INDIVIDUAL STATISTICS

Rushing—Houston, Joyner 4-3, Moriarty 16-66, Moon 3-0, Edwards 3-14; Miami, Nathan 5-27, Bennett 5-36, Carter 13-105, P. Johnson 10-36, Marino 1-4.

Passing—Houston, Moon 19-28-1—170; Miami, Marino 25-32-0—321.

Receiving—Houston, Walls 1-11, Dressel 7-47, Bryant 3-34, Moriarty 2-6, Roaches 1-12, Williams 4-51, Edwards 1-9; Miami, Duper 6-83, Clayton 4-61, Jensen 1-15, Moore 4-87, Nathan 2-14, D. Johnson 2-19, Hardy 3-26, Carter 3-16.

Kickoff Returns—Houston, Walls 2-45; Miami, Walker 2-49, Clayton 1-1.

Punt Returns—Miami, Walker 3-17.

Interceptions—Miami, L. Blackwood 1-4, Judson (with lateral) 0-2.

Punting—Houston, James 5-41.4; Miami, Roby 1-53.0.

Field Goals—Houston, Kempf 1-1; Miami, von Schamann 0-3 (missed: 58, 54, 53).

Sacks—Houston, Baker, Stensrud; Miami, Betters.

Bengals-Patriots
SUNDAY, OCTOBER 14
SCORE BY PERIODS

Cincinnati	7	7	0	0—14
New England	3	0	7	10—20

SCORING

New England—Field goal Franklin 20, 6:17 1st.
Cincinnati—Harris 34 pass from Esiason (Breech kick), 14:05 1st.

Cincinnati—Collinsworth 7 pass from Esiason (Breech kick), 11:30 2nd.
New England—Eason 13 run (Franklin kick), 4:07 3rd.
New England—Eason 25 run (Franklin kick), 3:52 4th.
New England—Field goal Franklin 27, 13:10 4th.

TEAM STATISTICS

	Cincinnati	New England
First downs	20	17
Rushes-Yards	43-155	37-175
Passing yards	154	173
Sacked-Yards lost	2-20	2-14
Return yards	106	81
Passes	13-26-0	11-22-1
Punts	5-39.0	4-42.0
Fumbles-Lost	3-1	4-2
Penalties-Yards	6-52	7-53
Time of possession	31:48	28:12

Attendance—48,154. No-shows—267.

INDIVIDUAL STATISTICS

Rushing—Cincinnati, Jennings 11-44, Alexander 11-41, Kinnebrew 13-34, Esiason 5-25, Brooks 3-11; New England, Tatupu 22-93, Eason 6-39, Collins 5-22, C. James 4-21.

Passing—Cincinnati, Esiason 13-26-0—174; New England, Eason 11-22-1—187.

Receiving—Cincinnati, Collinsworth 6-91, Harris 3-58, Holman 1-11, Jennings 2-10, Brooks 1-4; New England, Morgan 3-102, Fryar 1-26, Ramsey 2-20, Tatupu 3-16, Starring 1-15, Robinson 1-8.

Kickoff Returns—Cincinnati, Jennings 3-70, Farley 1-18, Martin 1-0; New England, J. Williams 2-48, Lee 1-12.

Punt Returns—Cincinnati, Martin 1-18; New England, Fryar 3-21.

Interceptions—Cincinnati, Jackson 1-0.

Punting—Cincinnati, McInally 5-39.0; New England, Prestridge 4-42.0.

Field Goals—Cincinnati, Breech 0-2 (missed: 37, 35); New England, Franklin 2-2.

Sacks—Cincinnati, R. Williams, Edwards; New England, Blackmon 2.

Giants-Falcons
SUNDAY, OCTOBER 14
SCORE BY PERIODS

New York Giants	6	10	3	0—19
Atlanta	0	0	7	0— 7

SCORING

New York—Carpenter 1 run (kick failed), 5:36 1st.
New York—Carpenter 9 pass from Simms (Haji-Sheikh kick), 5:04 2nd.
New York—Field goal Haji-Sheikh 41, 14:51 2nd.
Atlanta—Riggs 1 run (Luckhurst kick), 8:01 3rd.
New York—Field goal Haji-Sheikh 34, 13:28 3rd.

TEAM STATISTICS

	New York	Atlanta
First downs	16	16
Rushes-Yards	38-94	28-102
Passing yards	243	180
Sacked-Yards lost	1-4	3-31
Return yards	97	64
Passes	16-25-0	19-31-3
Punts	4-40.3	5-38.2
Fumbles-Lost	1-1	2-1
Penalties-Yards	3-25	7-40
Time of possession	33:20	26:40

Attendance—50,268. No-shows—8,288.

INDIVIDUAL STATISTICS

Rushing—New York, Carpenter 23-50, Morris 7-18, Woolfolk 6-16, Simms 1-6, Galbreath 1-4; Atlanta, Riggs 10-63, Cain 15-29, Bartkowski 2-7, Austin 1-3.

Passing—New York, Simms 16-25-0—247; Atlanta, Bartkowski 19-31-3—211.

Receiving—New York, Manuel 4-120, Carpenter 4-36, Gray 3-34, Mowatt 2-41, Morris 1-7, Galbreath 1-5, Johnson 1-4; Atlanta, A. Jackson 4-47, Bailey 3-76, Hodge 3-38, Riggs 3-18, Cox 3-9, Benson 1-17, Cain 1-3, Landrum 1-3.

Kickoff Returns—New York, McConkey 2-27; Atlanta, Tate 2-31, Johnson 1-24.

Punt Returns—New York, McConkey 5-22; Atlanta, Curran 2-9.

Interceptions—New York, Haynes 1-22, Reasons 1-26, P. Williams 1-0.

Punting—New York, Jennings 4-40.3; Atlanta, Giacomarro 5-38.2.

Field Goals—New York, Haji-Sheikh 2-5 (missed: 42, 47, 49); Atlanta, none attempted.

Sacks—New York, Banks, Burt, Martin; Atlanta, Benish.

Jets - Browns
SUNDAY, OCTOBER 14
SCORE BY PERIODS

New York Jets	7	10	0	7	24
Cleveland	7	7	3	3	20

SCORING

New York—McNeil 3 run (Leahy kick), 2:04 1st.
Cleveland—Pruitt 1 run (Bahr kick), 11:07 1st.
New York—Field goal Leahy 30, 9:12 2nd.
New York—McNeil 8 run (Leahy kick), 10:20 2nd.
Cleveland—Pruitt 1 run (Bahr kick), 13:01 2nd.
Cleveland—Field goal Bahr 49, 9:26 3rd.
Cleveland—Field goal Bahr 18, 2:26 4th.
New York—Paige 1 run (Leahy kick), 9:21 4th.

TEAM STATISTICS

	New York	Cleveland
First downs	19	26
Rushes-Yards	33-192	32-117
Passing yards	144	267
Sacked-Yards lost	1-1	4-32
Return yards	107	90
Passes	11-26-3	25-37-0
Punts	4-43.3	3-41.3
Fumbles-Lost	1-0	1-1
Penalties-Yards	5-25	4-39
Time of possession	25:21	34:39
Attendance—55,673. No-shows—1,350.		

INDIVIDUAL STATISTICS

Rushing—New York, Hector 10-97, McNeil 11-54, Ryan 7-13, Paige 2-8, Barber 3-20; Cleveland, White 11-30, Pruitt 20-79, McDonald 1-8.

Passing—New York, Ryan 11-26-3—145; Cleveland, McDonald 25-37-0—299.

Receiving—New York, Dennison 1-8, McNeil 2-10, Humphery 2-30, Gaffney 1-14, Shuler 2-41, Hector 3-42; Cleveland, Newsome 14-191, Brennan 1-9, Pruitt 1-9, Adams 1-24, McDonald 1-minus 4, Feacher 3-22, White 2-13, Harris 2-26, Walker 0-9.

Kickoff Returns—New York, Humphery 1-38, Springs 2-43; Cleveland, Byner 3-71.

Punt Returns—New York, Springs 2-26; Cleveland, Walker 2-16.

Interceptions—Cleveland, Puzzuoli 1-0, Johnson 2-3.

Punting—New York, Ramsey 4-43.3; Cleveland, Cox 3-41.3.

Field Goals—New York, Leahy 1-1; Cleveland, Bahr 2-3 (missed: 31).

Sacks—New York, Gastineau 2, Lyons, Rudolph ½, Baldwin ½; Cleveland, Matthews.

Colts - Eagles
SUNDAY, OCTOBER 14
SCORE BY PERIODS

Indianapolis	0	0	0	7	7
Philadelphia	7	6	0	3	16

SCORING

Philadelphia—Quick 6 pass from Jaworski (McFadden kick), 13:31 1st.
Philadelphia—Field goal McFadden 34, 4:51 2nd.
Philadelphia—Field goal McFadden 32, 14:50 2nd.
Indianapolis—McMillan 1 run (Allegre kick), 2:33 4th.
Philadelphia—Field goal McFadden 33, 12:45 4th.

TEAM STATISTICS

	Indianapolis	Philadelphia
First downs	13	19
Rushes-Yards	33-127	27-49
Passing yards	72	252
Sacked-Yards lost	5-30	2-17
Return yards	90	77
Passes	11-22-1	29-43-1
Punts	7-43.1	5-43.0
Fumbles-Lost	4-1	3-2
Penalties-Yards	5-44	5-29
Time of possession	23:58	36:02
Attendance—50,277. No-shows—12,025.		

INDIVIDUAL STATISTICS

Rushing—Indianapolis, McMillan 16-75, Moore 6-20, Pagel 4-18, Middleton 7-14; Philadelphia, Montgomery 10-19, Oliver 6-16, M. Williams 10-15, Pisarcik 1-minus 1.

Passing—Indianapolis, Pagel 8-18-0—89, Schlichter 3-4-1—13; Philadelphia, Jaworski 21-29-1—194, Pisarcik 8-14-0—75.

Receiving—Indianapolis, Middleton 3-25, Bouza 3-23, Butler 2-27, Porter 1-16, McMillan 1-9, Moore 1-2; Philadelphia, Quick 7-86, Spagnola 7-46, Montgomery 4-47, Oliver 4-39, Jackson 4-35, M. Williams 3-16.

Kickoff Returns—Indianapolis, Smith 2-52, Moore 2-19, Radachowsky 1-0; Philadelphia, Hayes 2-28.

Punt Returns—Indianapolis, Bouza 3-17; Philadelphia, Cooper 5-49.

Interceptions—Indianapolis, Krauss 1-2; Philadelphia, Foules 1-0.

Punting—Indianapolis, Stark 7-43.1; Philadelphia, Horan 5-43.0.

Field Goals—Indianapolis, Allegre 0-1 (missed: 52); Philadelphia, McFadden 3-3.

Sacks—Indianapolis, Thompson, Wisniewski; Philadelphia, Harrison 2, Clarke 2, Strauthers.

Steelers - 49ers
SUNDAY, OCTOBER 14
SCORE BY PERIODS

Pittsburgh	7	3	0	10	20
San Francisco	0	7	0	10	17

SCORING

Pittsburgh—Erenberg 2 run (Anderson kick), 6:21 1st.
Pittsburgh—Field goal Anderson 48, 7:00 2nd.
San Francisco—Montana 7 run (Wersching kick), 13:57 2nd.
San Francisco—Field goal Wersching 30, 2:12 4th.
San Francisco—Tyler 7 run (Wersching kick), 4:12 4th.
Pittsburgh—Stallworth 6 pass from Malone (Anderson kick), 11:39 4th.
Pittsburgh—Field goal Anderson 21, 13:18 4th.

TEAM STATISTICS

	Pittsburgh	San Francisco
First downs	23	22
Rushes-Yards	47-175	20-117
Passing yards	149	241
Sacked-Yards lost	1-7	0-0
Return yards	106	131
Passes	11-18-1	24-34-1
Punts	2-41.0	3-30.7
Fumbles-Lost	1-0	1-0
Penalties-Yards	11-68	8-57
Time of possession	34:45	25:15
Attendance—59,110. No-shows—2,256.		

INDIVIDUAL STATISTICS

Rushing—Pittsburgh, Pollard 24-105, Erenberg 11-44, Abercrombie 8-23, Malone 3-2, Veals 1-1; San Francisco, Tyler 11-59, Craig 6-29, Montana 3-29.

Passing—Pittsburgh, Malone 11-18-1—156; San Francisco, Montana 24-33-1—241, Harmon 0-1-0—0.

Receiving—Pittsburgh, Stallworth 6-78, Thompson 1-23, Kolodziejski 1-22, Erenberg 1-12, Capers 1-11, Garrity 1-10; San Francisco, Craig 7-43, Cooper 6-50, D. Clark 5-67, Francis 2-50, Tyler 2-13, Wilson 1-14, Monroe 1-4.

Kickoff Returns—Pittsburgh, Spencer 4-60; San Francisco, Harmon 3-85, Monroe 1-22.

Punt Returns—Pittsburgh, Woods 1-3; San Francisco, McLemore 1-5.

Interceptions—Pittsburgh, Hinkle 1-43; San Francisco, Turner 1-19.

Punting—Pittsburgh, Colquitt 2-41.0; San Francisco, Runager 3-30.7.

Field Goals—Pittsburgh, Anderson 2-2; San Francisco, Wersching 1-2 (missed: 37).

Sacks—San Francisco, Board.

Bears-Cardinals
SUNDAY, OCTOBER 14
SCORE BY PERIODS

Chicago	7	7	7	0—21
St. Louis	10	7	7	14—38

SCORING

St. Louis—Field goal O'Donoghue 44, 4:32 1st.

Chicago—Gault 28 pass from McMahon (B. Thomas kick), 6:32 1st.

St. Louis—Love 5 run (O'Donoghue kick), 11:04 1st.

Chicago—Payton 1 run (B. Thomas kick), 7:44 2nd.

St. Louis—Anderson 9 run (O'Donoghue kick), 9:37 2nd.

Chicago—Suhey 1 run (B. Thomas kick), 9:17 3rd.

St. Louis—Anderson 1 pass from Lomax (O'Donoghue kick), 12:50 3rd.

St. Louis—Lomax 9 run (O'Donoghue kick), 10:22 4th.

St. Louis—Harrell 1 run (O'Donoghue kick), 14:22 4th.

TEAM STATISTICS

	Chicago	St. Louis
First downs	20	23
Rushes-Yards	37-178	28-124
Passing yards	192	230
Sacked-Yards lost	2-10	5-41
Return yards	126	122
Passes	13-26-1	14-24-1
Punts	4-34.4	3-35.3
Fumbles-Lost	2-2	0-0
Penalties-Yards	10-74	4-30
Time of possession	31:05	28:55

Attendance—49,554. No-shows—1,963.

INDIVIDUAL STATISTICS

Rushing—Chicago, Payton 23-100, McMahon 6-60, Suhey 8-18; St. Louis, Anderson 19-82, Ferrell 2-2, Love 2-6, Lomax 2-29, Mitchell 1-5, Harrell 2-0.

Passing—Chicago, McMahon 13-23-0—202, Payton 0-1-0—0, Lisch 0-2-1—0; St. Louis, Lomax 14-24-1—271.

Receiving—Chicago, McKinnon 3-65, Gault 3-84, Suhey 5-42, Saldi 2-11; St. Louis, Marsh 1-7, Green 6-166, Anderson 2-10, Tilley 2-57, Mitchell 3-31.

Kickoff Returns—Chicago, Cameron 4-86, Gentry 1-33; St. Louis, Mitchell 3-80.

Punt Returns—Chicago, Fisher 1-8; St. Louis, Mitchell 3-32.

Interceptions—Chicago, Gayle 1-minus 1; St. Louis, Washington 1-10.

Punting—Chicago, Finzer 3-45.6; St. Louis, Birdsong 3-35.3.

Field Goals—Chicago, none attempted; St. Louis, O'Donoghue 1-2 (missed: 31).

Sacks—Chicago, Hampton 2, Bell, Wilson, Dent; St. Louis, Greer, Galloway.

Washington quarterback Joe Theismann threw three touchdown passes as the Redskins rolled to a 34-14 victory over Dallas in Week 7.

Bills-Seahawks
SUNDAY, OCTOBER 14
SCORE BY PERIODS

Buffalo	0	14	7	7—28
Seattle	17	0	7	7—31

SCORING

Seattle—Turner 4 pass from Krieg (Johnson kick), 10:54 1st.

Seattle—Largent 10 pass from Krieg (Johnson kick), 13:00 1st.

Seattle—Field goal Johnson 25, 15:00 1st.

Buffalo—Sanford 46 fumble return (Danelo kick), 12:11 2nd.

Buffalo—Wilson 65 punt return (Danelo kick), 13:33 2nd.
Seattle—Lane 1 run (Johnson kick), 3:18 3rd.
Buffalo—Franklin 50 pass from Ferguson (Danelo kick), 8:50 3rd.
Buffalo—Dennard 3 pass from Ferguson (Danelo kick), 3:40 4th.
Seattle—Largent 51 pass from Krieg (Johnson kick), 6:53 4th.

TEAM STATISTICS

	Buffalo	Seattle
First downs	19	15
Rushes-Yards	35-142	22-41
Passing yards	214	197
Sacked-Yards lost	1-13	3-34
Return yards	184	139
Passes	14-32-2	17-29-2
Punts	4-17.3	6-39.0
Fumbles-Lost	3-2	2-1
Penalties-Yards	13-99	7-60
Time of possession	35:13	24:47

Attendance—59,034. No-shows—5,876.

INDIVIDUAL STATISTICS

Rushing—Buffalo, Bell 28-113, Neal 3-25, Moore 2-7, Ferguson 2-minus 3; Seattle, Lane 6-21, Morris 8-12, F. Harris 3-4, Krieg 3-3, Hughes 2-1.

Passing—Buffalo, Ferguson 14-32-2—227; Seattle, Krieg 17-29-2—231.

Receiving—Buffalo, Bell 6-66, Franklin 3-73, Dennard 3-69, White 1-11, Neal 1-8; Seattle, Largent 5-106, Turner 4-50, Lane 4-22, Metzelaars 1-25, Doornink 1-15, Hughes 1-10, Morris 1-3.

Kickoff Returns—Buffalo, Wilson 3-51, V. Williams 3-43; Seattle, Dixon 5-103.

Punt Returns—Buffalo, Wilson 3-65; Seattle, Easley 2-20.

Interceptions—Buffalo, Romes 1-0, Smerlas 1-25; Seattle, Jackson 1-16, Brown 1-0.

Punting—Buffalo, Kidd 2-34.5; Seattle, West 6-39.0.

Field Goals—Buffalo, Danelo 0-1 (missed: 33); Seattle, Johnson 1-1.

Sacks—Buffalo, Smerlas, Freeman, Talley; Seattle, Fanning.

Cowboys-Redskins
SUNDAY, OCTOBER 14
SCORE BY PERIODS

Dallas	7	0	0	7	14
Washington	7	10	10	7	34

SCORING

Dallas—Dorsett 29 run (Septien kick), 2:32 1st.
Washington—Coleman 49 interception return (Moseley kick), 10:10 1st.
Washington—Didier 8 pass from Theismann (Moseley kick), 2:51 2nd.
Washington—Field goal Moseley 20, 12:34 2nd.
Washington—Muhammad 80 pass from Theismann (Moseley kick), 0:18 3rd.
Washington—Field goal Moseley 22, 9:46 3rd.
Washington—Didier 3 pass from Theismann (Moseley kick), 0:06 4th.
Dallas—Dorsett 6 run (Septien kick), 4:08 4th.

TEAM STATISTICS

	Dallas	Washington
First downs	21	19
Rushes-Yards	24-90	45-241
Passing yards	269	182
Sacked-Yards lost	3-25	0-0
Return yards	123	124
Passes	26-44-3	11-17-0
Punts	6-40.2	3-42.3
Fumbles-Lost	2-1	3-2
Penalties-Yards	4-66	4-20
Time of possession	29:59	30:01

Attendance—55,431. No-shows—None.

INDIVIDUAL STATISTICS

Rushing—Dallas, Dorsett 18-81, Hogeboom 1-0, Springs 4-8, Newsome 1-1; Washington, Riggins 32-165, Griffin 6-41, Theismann 4-33, Kane 3-2.

Passing—Dallas, Hogeboom 13-24-2—169, D. White 13-20-1—125; Washington, Theismann 11-17-0—182.

Receiving—Dallas, Cosbie 5-73, Hill 9-134, Springs 5-25, Renfro 2-42, Newsome 2-17, Dorsett 2-2, Pozderac 1-1; Washington, Monk 4-67, Muhammad 5-104, Didier 2-11.

Kickoff Returns—Dallas, Allen 6-117; Washington, Nelms 2-44.

Punt Returns—Dallas, Allen 2-6; Washington, Nelms 3-16.

Interceptions—Washington, Coleman 1-49, Milot 2-15.

Punting—Dallas, D. White 6-40.2; Washington, Hayes 3-42.3.

Field Goals—Dallas, none attempted; Washington, Moseley 2-3 (missed: 47).

Sacks—Washington, Butz 1½, McGee, Coleman ½.

Packers-Broncos
MONDAY, OCTOBER 15
SCORE BY PERIODS

Green Bay	0	0	7	7	14
Denver	14	3	0	0	17

SCORING

Denver—Foley 22 fumble return (Karlis kick), 0:16 1st.
Denver—L. Wright 27 fumble return (Karlis kick), 0:37 1st.
Denver—Field goal Karlis 30, 0:50 2nd.
Green Bay—Ellis 5 run (Garcia kick), 13:45 3rd.
Green Bay—Lofton 54 pass from Dickey (Garcia kick), 7:29 4th.

TEAM STATISTICS

	Green Bay	Denver
First downs	25	10
Rushes-Yards	26-74	31-92
Passing yards	349	101
Sacked-Yards lost	3-22	0-0
Return yards	159	55
Passes	27-39-1	11-20-1
Punts	3-32.3	8-38.0
Fumbles-Lost	7-4	2-0
Penalties-Yards	6-40	10-80
Time of possession	33:36	26:24

Attendance—62,546. No-shows—12,554.

INDIVIDUAL STATISTICS

Rushing—Green Bay, Ellis 9-27, Clark 11-37, Huckleby 4-9, Dickey 2-1; Denver, Winder 29-86, Parros 1-6, Elway 1-0.

Passing—Green Bay, Dickey 27-37-1—371, Ellis 0-1-0—0, Wright 0-1-0—0; Denver, Elway 11-20-1—101.

Receiving—Green Bay, Coffman 5-49, Huckleby 1-12, Jefferson 3-33, Lofton 11-206, Ellis 4-42, Clark 3-29; Denver, Watson 4-42, Willhite 3-31, Winder 3-17, Kay 1-11.

Kickoff Returns—Green Bay, Rodgers 5-130; Denver, Dennison 1-16, Willhite 1-19.

Punt Returns—Green Bay, Epps 4-21; Denver, Thomas 1-0.

Interceptions—Green Bay, Murphy 1-8; Denver, Foley 1-20.

Punting—Green Bay, Scribner 3-32.3; Denver, Norman 8-38.0.

Field Goals—Green Bay, Garcia 0-2 (missed: 29, 30); Denver, Karlis 1-1.

Sacks—Denver, Jones 2, Chavous.

EIGHTH WEEK

RESULTS OF WEEK 8
Sunday, October 21

Chicago 44, Tampa Bay 9 at T.B.
Cincinnati 12, Cleveland 9 at Cin.
Dallas 30, New Orleans 27 (OT) at Dall.
Denver 37, Buffalo 7 at Buff.
Detroit 16, Minnesota 14 at Minn.
Indianapolis 17, Pittsburgh 16 at Ind.
L.A. Raiders 44, San Diego 37 at S.D.
Miami 44, New England 24 at N.E.
N.Y. Jets 28, Kansas City 7 at N.Y.
Philadelphia 24, N.Y. Giants 10 at Phila.
St. Louis 26, Washington 24 at St.L.
San Francisco 34, Houston 21 at Hous.
Seattle 30, Green Bay 24 at G.B.

Monday, October 22

L.A. Rams 24, Atlanta 10 at Atl.

An old adage says that lightning never strikes twice in the same spot. But the New Orleans Saints know different.

On September 25, 1983, the Saints paid a visit to Texas Stadium for a game against the Dallas Cowboys. New Orleans held a 20-13 lead midway through the fourth quarter and appeared headed to victory before lightning struck. When Cowboys defensive end Ed Jones broke through the Saints front-line and blocked a field goal attempt by Morten Andersen, defensive back Ron Fellows scooped up the loose football and sprinted 62 yards for a Dallas touchdown. The Saints, however, remained in control by blocking the Cowboys' extra-point attempt. The biggest lightning bolt hit with two minutes to play when Cowboys linebacker Anthony Dickerson sacked Saints quarterback Ken Stabler in the New Orleans end zone. The safety gave Dallas a 21-20 victory.

A year later, on October 21, 1984, the Saints made a return visit to Texas Stadium. Another bolt of lightning was just waiting to strike. New Orleans enjoyed a 27-6 lead after three quarters, but the Cowboys struck for 21 fourth-quarter points, setting up overtime. The tying touchdown was scored when Dallas defensive tackle Randy White sacked Stabler in the Saints' end zone, the ball popped loose and Jim Jeffcoat recovered with 2:53 remaining in regulation time. A 41-yard Rafael Septien field goal in overtime gave Dallas a 30-27 victory.

"Can you recall a tougher loss?" asked stunned Saints Coach Bum Phillips before answering his own question. "Yes, last year right here and the game with the Rams last year. We are a victim of our own mistakes."

The Saints had lost a heartbreaker to the Rams on the final weekend of the 1983 season when, needing a victory to clinch a spot in the playoffs, L.A.'s Mike Lansford kicked a 42-yard field goal with two seconds left for a 26-24 L.A. victory. New Orleans, the only club in the 28-member National Football League that has never made the playoffs, knows all too well about tough losses.

The San Diego Chargers also were becoming familiar with tough losses. The latest, a wild, 44-37 loss to the Los Angeles Raiders, came just four weeks after losing a 33-30 decision to the Raiders. L.A.'s Marc Wilson threw five scoring passes in the second game between the teams, but it was the Chargers' own mistakes that cost them a victory. The Chargers turned the ball over four times inside their own 20-yard line, leading to 24 Raider points. L.A. outscored San Diego, 20-0, in the third period, with 17 of those points coming within a 2:10 span.

Dan Fouts threw for 410 yards and three touchdowns for San Diego, but it was his third interception of the day that proved pivotal. After the Chargers blew apparent touchdowns on the preceding two plays—one on a fumble at the 3-yard line and the other because of a holding penalty—Fouts' final pass in the Raiders' end zone was picked off by L.A. cornerback Ted Watts.

A record crowd of 57,442 turned out at Jack Murphy Stadium to see the Raiders-Chargers shootout, but only 31,204 fans—the smallest crowd at Rich Stadium in six years—turned out to see the 0-7 Bills battle Denver. The game was no contest as the Broncos, employing a stout defense, rolled to a 37-7 triumph. The Denver defense, which had scored six touchdowns in its previous seven games, set up the Broncos' first two touchdowns of the afternoon, both second-period passes by John Elway. The Buffalo offense didn't reach the Denver 41-yard line until midway through the final period on its only touchdown drive.

The league's other winless team, the Houston Oilers, had surprising success moving the ball against 6-1 San Francisco. The Oilers' offense scored 21 points and racked up 432 total yards against one of the NFL's top defenses. Quarterback Warren Moon, a former Canadian Football League standout, had the best game of his young NFL career, passing for 356 yards and two touchdowns.

But Houston's defense was no match for the 49ers' offense. Joe Montana threw for 353 yards and three touchdowns and the 49ers scored 10 points on their first two possessions in cruising to a 34-21 victory.

The Chicago Bears had no trouble in routing division-rival Tampa Bay, 44-9, in a mistake-filled game. The clubs were flagged for a combined 31 penalties, just six short of the league record. The Bears scored on a six-play, 57-yard drive on their first possession of the game and never looked back. Three Tampa Bay penalties were called on the drive. Walter Payton's second touchdown on Chicago's next possession gave the Bears a 14-0 first-quarter lead. Jim McMahon threw three scoring passes for Chicago.

Miami quarterback Dan Marino did McMahon one better, throwing four scoring tosses in the Dolphins' 44-24 triumph over New England. Marino's four TD passes gave him 24 at the halfway point of the season.

The Miami offensive machine, ranked first in the league the entire season, was at its best against the Patriots. The Dolphins scored on seven of their nine possessions, with the scoring drives averaging 72 yards apiece. The 552 total net yards were the most ever surrendered by a New England team.

The Minnesota Vikings' offense collapsed in the second half of a 16-14 loss to Detroit. Holding a 14-0 lead late in the first half—thanks in part to 10 penalties for 89 yards against the Lions—the bottom fell out on the Vikes. Quarterback Tommy Kramer was forced from the contest after a hit from Detroit linebacker Mike Cofer. Kramer's replacement, Archie Manning, was ineffective. In the second half, Minnesota did not record a first down and managed just six yards in total offense as Manning, who was sacked twice, completed one of his nine passes for 13 yards.

The Lions, meanwhile, rallied in the final two quarters. They scored on their first second-half possession (Billy Sims' 1-yard run) to cut the deficit to 14-7 and placekicker Eddie Murray added three field goals, including the game-winner with 49 seconds left, as the Lions won at Minnesota for the first time since 1974.

The Philadelphia Eagles won their third straight game, the team's longest winning streak in three seasons, with a 24-10 verdict over NFC Eastern Division-rival New York. Quarterback Ron Jaworski led the offense with three touchdown passes, including two in the pivotal fourth period, but the Philly defense was the story of the game.

With the score tied at 10-10 late in the final period, Eagles defensive end Greg Brown sacked Giants quarterback Phil Simms deep in New York territory. The ball popped loose and linebacker Jerry Robinson recovered for Philadelphia on the 8-yard line. Three plays later, Jaworski hit Melvin Hoover with an 11-yard scoring pass and the extra-point gave the Eagles a 17-10 lead. Then, on the Giants' next possession, a Simms pass was picked off by safety Ray Ellis. Jaworski hit Tony Woodruff for another Eagles' touchdown moments later.

The Indianapolis Colts came up with their biggest win of the '84 season by scoring 17 points in the final quarter and defeating Pittsburgh, 17-16. The Colts trailed, 13-0, heading into the final quarter and had not crossed the Steelers' 30-yard line. But then the Indianapolis offense started to roll.

The Steelers still were clinging to a 16-10 lead when the Colts began the game-winning rally at their own 20-yard line with 1:35 remaining. After moving the ball to his own 46, Colts quarterback Mike Pagel lofted a pass for wide receiver Ray Butler at the Pittsburgh 30. Steelers cornerback Sam Washington, who was tied for the NFL lead in interceptions with six, went high in the air to try for his seventh. But Washington succeeded only in tipping the ball twice, and it fell into Butler's outstretched hands. Butler ran the remaining distance untouched for the game-winning score with 34 seconds left.

Another game that wasn't decided until the final minute was St. Louis' 26-24 victory over division-rival Washington. Cards placekicker Neil O'Donoghue, who earlier in the game had missed a crucial extra-point and field-goal attempts of 34 and 40 yards, hit a game-winning 21-yard field goal with 3 seconds left. The Cardinals, who trailed 21-10 at one point in the third period, pulled to within 24-23 early in the fourth quarter when Neil Lomax hit wide receiver Roy Green with an 83-yard touchdown pass. O'Donoghue missed the point after.

The Cards' game-winning drive started at their own 33-yard line with 2:24 to play. Lomax hit Stump Mitchell for a 16-yard gain on a third-and-eight play and later connected with Pat Tilley on a 21-yard gain. That set the stage for O'Donoghue's last-second heroics that ended the Redskins' five-game winning streak.

The New York Jets defeated Kansas City for the second time in three weeks with a 28-7 decision at the Meadowlands. Pat Ryan threw for three touchdowns to lead the offense, but the Jets' defense and special teams were outstanding. On the Chiefs' first nine possessions, their best field position was their own 23-yard line. K.C. quarterback Bill Kenney was held to 84 net passing yards and sacked four times. Mark Gastineau, who led the league in quarterback sacks, was credited with 1½ sacks and also recovered a Kenney fumble in the Kansas City end zone for a touchdown.

The Green Bay Packers lost their seventh straight game after an opening-day victory with a 30-24 loss to Seattle. Three Seahawk touchdowns were called back because of penalties in a sloppy game marred by 28 infractions. Still, the Packers, who scored on a 79-yard Lynn Dickey-to-James Lofton touchdown pass on the game's first play, had a chance to win it in the final minute. But a Dickey pass intended for John Jefferson at the Seattle 10-yard line with 24 seconds left was intercepted by cornerback Terry Jackson.

The Cleveland Browns also dropped to 1-7 with a 12-9 loss to division-rival Cincinnati. No touchdowns were scored as the game boiled down to a battle of field goals. Cleveland's Steve Cox hit the longest—a 60-yarder in the second period, the second-longest in league history—but Cincinnati's Jim Breech hit the most, four. Breech's final field goal, a 33-yarder

St. Louis' Roy Green hauled in two Neil Lomax touchdown passes in Week 8 as the Cardinals edged Washington, 26-24.

as time expired, won the game for the Bengals.

In the Monday night game, the Los Angeles Rams scored three second-quarter touchdowns in winning an NFC Western Division game with Atlanta, 24-10. Eric Dickerson rushed for 142 yards, 108 in the first half, as Los Angeles avenged a two-point loss to the Falcons two weeks earlier in Los Angeles. L.A.'s Henry Ellard scored two touchdowns, one on a 9-yard pass from Jeff Kemp and the other on a 69-yard punt return.

Bears-Buccaneers

SUNDAY, OCTOBER 21

SCORE BY PERIODS

Chicago	14	6	7	17—44
Tampa Bay	0	3	0	6— 9

SCORING

Chicago—Payton 8 run (B. Thomas kick), 4:30 1st.
Chicago—Payton 3 run (B. Thomas kick), 12:32 1st.
Tampa Bay—Field goal Ariri 46, 4:05 2nd.
Chicago—McKinnon 32 pass from McMahon (kick failed), 7:45 2nd.
Chicago—Gault 10 pass from McMahon (B. Thomas kick), 7:13 3rd.
Chicago—Field goal B. Thomas 49, 0:25 4th.
Tampa Bay—Carter 3 pass from DeBerg (kick failed), 9:00 4th.
Chicago—Anderson 49 pass from McMahon (B. Thomas kick), 10:23 4th.
Chicago—Gentry 5 run (B. Thomas kick), 13:02 4th.

TEAM STATISTICS

	Chicago	Tampa Bay
First downs	23	17
Rushes-Yards	39-169	15-45
Passing yards	258	247
Sacked-Yards lost	1-3	6-41
Returns yards	88	185
Passes	13-19-0	24-39-1
Punts	2-40.5	3-47.7
Fumbles-Lost	0-0	4-1
Penalties-Yards	16-114	15-104
Time of possession	31:21	28:39

Attendance—60,003. No-shows—5,954.

INDIVIDUAL STATISTICS

Rushing—Chicago, Suhey 5-24, McMahon 6-24, Payton 20-72, C. Thomas 2-9, Jordan 2-25, Gentry 2-8, Hutchison 2-7; Tampa Bay, Wilder 13-44, DeBerg 2-1.

Passing—Chicago, McMahon 12-18-0—219, Payton 1-1-0-1—42; Tampa Bay, DeBerg 24-39-1—288.

Receiving—Chicago, Moorehead 2-40, McKinnon 2-51, Dunsmore 1-20, Payton 3-25, McMahon 1-42, Gault 2-27, Saldi 1-7, Anderson 1-49; Tampa Bay, House 5-61, Carter 10-109, Wilder 2-12, J. Bell 2-26, Giles 4-63, Dixon 1-17.

Kickoff Returns—Chicago, Cameron 1-22, Bell 1-17; Tampa Bay, Bright 3-53, Morton 5-108.

Punt Returns—Chicago, Fisher 3-35; Tampa Bay, Bright 2-24.

Interceptions—Chicago, Frazier 1-14.

Punting—Chicago, Finzer 2-40.5; Tampa Bay, Garcia 3-47.7.

Field Goals—Chicago, B. Thomas 1-2 (missed: 29); Tampa Bay, Ariri 1-1.

Sacks—Chicago, Dent 3, Hartenstine 2, Fencik; Tampa Bay, Cotney.

Browns-Bengals
SUNDAY, OCTOBER 21
SCORE BY PERIODS

Cleveland	3	3	0	3— 9
Cincinnati	3	3	0	6—12

SCORING

Cincinnati—Field goal Breech 24, 5:24 1st.
Cleveland—Field goal Bahr 50, 13:50 1st.
Cincinnati—Field goal Breech 23, 6:05 2nd.
Cleveland—Field goal Cox 60, 14:32 2nd.
Cincinnati—Field goal Breech 25, 0:46 4th.
Cleveland—Field goal Bahr 47, 12:58 4th.
Cincinnati—Field goal Breech 33, 15:00 4th.

TEAM STATISTICS

	Cleveland	Cincinnati
First downs	24	18
Rushes-Yards	19-56	33-124
Passing yards	268	176
Sacked-Yards lost	5-32	3-26
Return yards	112	168
Passes	27-47-2	18-34-1
Punts	5-47.0	7-42.0
Fumbles-Lost	2-2	2-1
Penalties-Yards	9-78	6-40
Time of possession	29:44	30:16

Attendance—50,667. No-shows—8,912.

INDIVIDUAL STATISTICS

Rushing—Cleveland, Pruitt 4-11, White 12-28, Byner 3-17; Cincinnati, Esiason 4-11, Jennings 8-38, Alexander 12-29, Brooks 6-24, Anderson 2-17, Kinnebrew 1-5.

Passing—Cleveland, McDonald 27-47-2—300; Cincinnati, Esiason 1-7-0—4, Anderson 8-12-1—68, Schonert 9-15-0—130.

Receiving—Cleveland, Newsome 4-20, Walker 3-34, Bolden 1-19, Byner 3-36, Harris 5-71, Adams 8-94, Feacher 1-11, White 2-15; Cincinnati, Alexander 3-26, Collinsworth 3-24, Holman 2-39, Curtis 2-19, Brooks 1-5, Jennings 4-26, Harris 1-4, Verser 1-17, Martin 1-42.

Kickoff Returns—Cleveland, B. Davis 3-51, Nicolas 1-12; Cincinnati, Jennings 2-65, Farley 2-12.

Punt Returns—Cleveland, Walker 2-17; Cincinnati, Martin 2-52.

Interceptions—Cleveland, Gross 1-32; Cincinnati, Breeden 1-26, Kemp 1-13.

Punting—Cleveland, Cox 5-47.0; Cincinnati, McInally 7-42.0.

Field Goals—Cleveland, Bahr 2-2, Cox 1-2 (missed 52); Cincinnati, Breech 4-4.

Sacks—Cleveland, Matthews 2, Golic; Cincinnati, Browner, Collins, Edwards, Horton, Krumrie.

Saints-Cowboys
SUNDAY, OCTOBER 21
SCORE BY PERIODS

New Orleans	0	17	10	0	0—27
Dallas	3	3	0	21	3—30

SCORING

Dallas—Field goal Septien 37, 5:12 1st.
New Orleans—Young 36 pass from Todd (Andersen kick), 1:01 2nd.
Dallas—Field goal Septien 27, 10:25 2nd.
New Orleans—Gajan 62 run (Andersen kick), 2:54 2nd.
New Orleans—Field goal Andersen 49, 14:58 2nd.
New Orleans—Field goal Andersen 50, 3:25 3rd.
New Orleans—Winston 43 interception return (Andersen kick), 5:38 3rd.
Dallas—Dorsett 3 run (Septien kick), 1:39 4th.
Dallas—Renfro 12 pass from D. White (Septien kick), 11:01 4th.
Dallas—Jeffcoat recovered fumble in end zone (Septien kick), 12:07 4th.
Dallas—Field goal Septien 41, 3:42 OT.

TEAM STATISTICS

	New Orleans	Dallas
First downs	17	22
Rushes-Yards	44-235	29-98
Passing yards	106	194
Sacked-Yards lost	1-9	6-45
Return yards	44	27
Passes	7-25-3	26-43-2
Punts	3-45.3	8-37.8
Fumbles-Lost	2-2	1-0
Penalties-Yards	13-113	8-58
Time of possession	30:49	32:53

Attendance—50,966. No-shows—14,135.

INDIVIDUAL STATISTICS

Rushing—New Orleans, G. Rogers 12-52, Gajan 9-78, W. Wilson 6-13, Todd 4-26, Campbell 12-67, Stabler 1-minus 1; Dallas, Dorsett 21-80, Hogeboom 2-2, Springs 4-11, White 1-5.

Passing—New Orleans, Todd 5-16-1—81, Stabler 2-9-2—34; Dallas, Hogeboom 11-18-1—107, D. White 15-25-1—132.

Receiving—New Orleans, Gajan 1-5, Groth 2-41, Young 2-49, Scott 2-20; Dallas, Dorsett 2-1, Hill 7-90, Springs 5-29, Cosbie 4-40, Renfro 6-79, J. Jones 2-0.

Kickoff Returns—New Orleans, Anthony 4-143, Duckett 2-34; Dallas, McSwain 3-64, Allen 3-66, Granger 1-5.

Punt Returns—New Orleans, Groth 1-1; Dallas, Allen 2-13.

Interceptions—New Orleans, Waymer 1-0, Winston 1-43; Dallas, Downs 2-14, Fellows 1-0.

Punting—New Orleans, Hansen 3-45.3; Dallas, D. White 8-37.9.

Field Goals—New Orleans, Andersen 2-3 (missed: 45); Dallas, Septien 3-3.

Sacks—New Orleans, B. Clark 2, Jackson 1½, Wilks 1½, Geathers; Dallas, R. White.

Broncos-Bills
SUNDAY, OCTOBER 21
SCORE BY PERIODS

Denver	3	20	7	7—37
Buffalo	0	0	0	7— 7

SCORING

Denver—Field goal Karlis 45, 6:15 1st.
Denver—Kay 3 pass from Elway (Karlis kick), 0:32 2nd.
Denver—Watson 52 pass from Elway (Karlis kick), 2:30 2nd.
Denver—Field goal Karlis 45, 14:29 2nd.
Denver—Field goal Karlis 40, 14:56 2nd.
Denver—Kubiak 3 run (Karlis kick), 9:39 3rd.
Denver—Winder 14 pass from Kubiak (Karlis kick), 6:23 4th.
Buffalo—Brookins 70 pass from Kofler (Danelo kick), 7:42 4th.

TEAM STATISTICS

	Denver	Buffalo
First downs	24	10
Rushes-Yards	27-107	19-71
Passing yards	231	155
Sacked-Yards lost	4-31	6-54
Return yards	80	174
Passes	21-40-0	17-32-4
Punts	8-37.1	9-44.8
Fumbles-Lost	3-0	1-1
Penalties-Yards	2-15	10-95
Time of possession	33:03	26:57

Attendance—31,204. No-shows—2,857.

INDIVIDUAL STATISTICS

Rushing—Denver, Winder 15-65, Elway 1-0, Kubiak 4-19, Willhite 1-4, Parros 6-19; Buffalo, Neal 4-16, Bell 9-28, V. Williams 1-4, Ferguson 1-1, Franklin 1-minus 7, Kofler 3-28.

Passing—Denver, Elway 12-23-0—148, Kubiak

8-16-0—97, Willhite 1-1-0—17; Buffalo, Ferguson 9-19-2—77, Kofler 8-13-2—132.

Receiving—Denver, Johnson 4-47, Winder 4-32, Watson 5-89, Kay 3-29, Willhite 1-4, J. Wright 3-41, Kubiak 1-20; Buffalo, Franklin 5-64, Barnett 2-9, Bell 7-54, Dennard 1-4, Neal 1-8, Brookins 1-70.

Kickoff Returns—Denver, Harden 1-4; Buffalo, Wilson 4-54, V. Williams 2-75, David 1-6.

Punt Returns—Denver, Thomas 3-16, Willhite 1-9; Buffalo, Wilson 4-37.

Interceptions—Denver, Foley 1-24, Busick 1-16, Comeaux 1-4, L. Wright 1-1, Wilson 0-6.

Punting—Denver, Norman 8-37.1; Buffalo, Kidd 9-44.8.

Field Goals—Denver, Karlis 3-3; Buffalo, none attempted.

Sacks—Denver, Mecklenburg 2, Chavous, Jones, Ryan, Woodard; Buffalo, McNanie 2, David, K. Johnson.

Lions-Vikings
SUNDAY, OCTOBER 21
SCORE BY PERIODS

Detroit	0	0	10	6—16
Minnesota	7	7	0	0—14

SCORING

Minnesota—Nelson 7 pass from Kramer (Stenerud kick), 14:30 1st.
Minnesota—Brown 2 run (Stenerud kick), 1:55 2nd.
Detroit—Sims 1 run (Murray kick), 5:27 3rd.
Detroit—Field goal Murray 44, 13:26 3rd.
Detroit—Field goal Murray 41, 10:28 4th.
Detroit—Field goal Murray 41, 14:11 4th.

TEAM STATISTICS

	Detroit	Minnesota
First downs	20	14
Rushes-Yards	42-185	22-33
Passing yards	250	157
Sacked-Yards lost	1-10	4-25
Return yards	172	123
Passes	19-28-1	12-29-2
Punts	5-38.8	8-45.9
Fumbles-Lost	6-2	1-0
Penalties-Yards	14-119	7-45
Time of possession	36:57	23:03
Attendance—57,953. No-shows—4,216.		

INDIVIDUAL STATISTICS

Rushing—Detroit, Sims 22-103, Danielson 5-24, Bussey 14-44, Martin 1-14; Minnesota, Anderson 6-16, Brown 11-6, Kramer 1-1, Manning 2-10, Nelson 1-5, Collins 1-minus 5.

Passing—Detroit, Danielson 19-28-1—260; Minnesota, Kramer 7-15-1—142, Manning 5-14-1—40.

Receiving—Detroit, Nichols 5-117, Sims 4-32, Thompson 5-62, Bussey 1-25, Chadwick 1-10, J. Jones 3-14; Minnesota, Jordan 3-48, White 2-34, Lewis 2-65, Nelson 1-7, Jones 1-4, Brown 3-24.

Kickoff Returns—Detroit, Mandley 2-42, Martin 1-23; Minnesota, Anderson 3-64, Nelson 1-34, Rouse 1-7.

Punt Returns—Detroit, Martin 7-71; Minnesota, Nelson 2-18.

Interceptions—Detroit, Hall 1-36, Watkins 1-0; Minnesota, Hannon 1-0.

Punting—Detroit, Black 5-38.8; Minnesota, Coleman 8-45.9.

Field Goals—Detroit, Murray 3-3; Minnesota, none attempted.

Sacks—Detroit, Cofer 2½, Gay, Green ½; Minnesota, Elshire.

Steelers-Colts
SUNDAY, OCTOBER 21
SCORE BY PERIODS

Pittsburgh	3	10	0	3—16
Indianapolis	0	0	0	17—17

SCORING

Pittsburgh—Field goal Anderson 53, 5:40 1st.
Pittsburgh—Lipps 62 pass from Woodley (Anderson kick), 4:16 2nd.
Pittsburgh—Field goal Anderson 25, 14:46 2nd.
Indianapolis—Field goal Allegre 41, 2:38 4th.
Indianapolis—Moore 8 run (Allegre kick), 9:20 4th.
Pittsburgh—Field goal Anderson 43, 13:25 4th.
Indianapolis—Butler 54 pass from Pagel (Allegre kick), 14:26 4th.

TEAM STATISTICS

	Pittsburgh	Indianapolis
First downs	18	21
Rushes-Yards	32-127	32-127
Passing yards	278	174
Sacked-Yards lost	1-5	6-61
Return yards	66	11
Passes	14-30-1	18-31-1
Punts	6-43.7	7-47.4
Fumbles-Lost	0-0	1-0
Penalties-Yards	11-106	7-54
Time of possession	27:22	32:38
Attendance—60,026. No-shows—657.		

INDIVIDUAL STATISTICS

Rushing—Pittsburgh, Pollard 20-81, Erenberg 8-30, Abercrombie 2-7, Veals 1-2, Woodley 1-7; Indianapolis, Middleton 13-62, Dickey 9-30, Moore 3-13, Wonsley 3-6, McMillan 3-6, Pagel 1-10.

Passing—Pittsburgh, Woodley 12-27-1—212, Malone 2-3-0—71; Indianapolis, Herrmann 5-13-1—57, Pagel 13-17-0—178, Moore 0-1-0—0.

Receiving—Pittsburgh, Stallworth 5-101, Lipps 1-62, Erenberg 3-24, Pollard 2-12, Thompson 2-72, Garrity 1-12; Indianapolis, Middleton 5-30, Butler 3-79, Young 3-39, Bouza 2-26, Henry 2-35, Porter 1-13, Sherwin 1-9, Moore 1-4.

Punt Returns—Pittsburgh, Lipps 6-56; Indianapolis, Glasgow 2-11.

Interceptions—Pittsburgh, Washington 1-5; Indianapolis, Randle 1-0.

Punting—Pittsburgh, Colquitt 6-43.7; Indianapolis, Stark 7-47.4.

Field Goals—Pittsburgh, Anderson 3-3; Indianapolis, Allegre 1-1.

Sacks—Pittsburgh, Merriweather 3, Dunn, Gary, Goodman ½, E. Nelson ½; Indianapolis, Maxwell.

Raiders-Chargers
SUNDAY, OCTOBER 21
SCORE BY PERIODS

Los Angeles Raiders	7	7	20	10—44
San Diego	7	13	0	17—37

SCORING

San Diego—Jackson 5 run (Ricardo kick), 5:04 1st.
Los Angeles—Allen 10 pass from Wilson (Bahr kick), 8:41 1st.
San Diego—Chandler 22 pass from Fouts (kick failed), 9:49 2nd.
San Diego—Jackson 32 run (Ricardo kick), 13:07 2nd.
Los Angeles—Barnwell 45 pass from Wilson (Bahr kick), 14:32 2nd.
Los Angeles—Field goal Bahr 42, 3:26 3rd.
Los Angeles—Jensen 1 pass from Wilson (Bahr kick), 8:35 3rd.
Los Angeles—Field goal Bahr 33, 10:18 3rd.
Los Angeles—Williams 20 pass from Wilson (Bahr kick), 10:45 3rd.
San Diego—Field goal Ricardo 29, 1:40 4th.
Los Angeles—Barnwell 51 pass from Wilson (Bahr kick), 2:47 4th.
San Diego—Winslow 5 pass from Fouts (Ricardo kick), 4:49 4th.
Los Angeles—Field goal Bahr 32, 11:06 4th.

San Diego—Duckworth 50 pass from Fouts (Ricardo kick), 12:24 4th.

TEAM STATISTICS

	Los Angeles	San Diego
First downs	23	30
Rushes-Yards	34-170	23-85
Passing yards	328	379
Sacked-Yards lost	2-4	4-31
Return yards	151	131
Passes	24-37-1	24-45-3
Punts	2-30.5	3-44.7
Fumbles-Lost	4-2	4-2
Penalties-Yards	10-113	7-56
Time of possession	29:32	30:28

Attendance—57,442. No-shows—2,741.

INDIVIDUAL STATISTICS

Rushing—Los Angeles, Allen 19-107, Wilson 5-6, King 6-33, Hawkins 4-24; San Diego, Jackson 20-98, Fouts 2-minus 14, McGee 1-1.

Passing—Los Angeles, Wilson 24-37-1—332; San Diego, Fouts 24-45-3—410.

Receiving—Los Angeles, Christensen 4-42, Allen 5-40, Branch 4-64, Williams 2-37, King 5-48, Hawkins 1-4, Barnwell 2-96, Jensen 1-1; San Diego, Bendross 2-47, Winslow 8-107, Sievers 2-30, Holohan 6-86, Chandler 1-22, Jackson 1-12, Joiner 2-25, Duckworth 1-50, James 1-31.

Kickoff Returns—Los Angeles, Montgomery 5-110, Willis 1-13; San Diego, James 4-72, McGee 2-52.

Punt Returns—Los Angeles, Pruitt 2-19.

Interceptions—Los Angeles, Van Pelt 1-9, M. Davis 1-0, Watts 1-0; San Diego, Smith 1-7.

Punting—Los Angeles, Guy 2-30.5; San Diego, Buford 3-44.7.

Field Goals—Los Angeles, Bahr 3-4 (missed: 38); San Diego, Ricardo 1-1.

Sacks—Los Angeles, Alzado, Martin, McKinney, Townsend; San Diego, Robinson, Elko ½, Ferguson ½.

Dolphins-Patriots
SUNDAY, OCTOBER 21
SCORE BY PERIODS

Miami	3	13	14	14—44
New England	3	7	7	7—24

SCORING

Miami—Field goal von Schamann 28, 6:27 1st.
New England—Field goal Franklin 48, 12:27 1st.
Miami—P. Johnson 1 run (von Schamann kick), 0:28 2nd.
New England—Weathers 14 pass from Eason (Franklin kick), 13:07 2nd.
Miami—Moore 19 pass from Marino (kick failed), 14:54 2nd.
Miami—D. Johnson 5 pass from Marino (von Schamann kick), 8:20 3rd.
New England—Morgan 76 pass from Eason (Franklin kick), 8:39 3rd.
Miami—Clayton 15 pass from Marino (von Schamann kick), 12:29 3rd.
New England—Ramsey 5 pass from Eason (Franklin kick), 3:33 4th.
Miami—Moore 15 pass from Marino (von Schamann kick), 6:36 4th.
Miami—P. Johnson 3 run (von Schamann kick), 14:39 4th.

TEAM STATISTICS

	Miami	New England
First downs	32	18
Rushes-Yards	37-236	27-102
Passing yards	316	306
Sacked-Yards lost	0-0	1-7
Return yards	58	113
Passes	24-39-1	19-29-0
Punts	1-38.0	3-57.0
Fumbles-Lost	0-0	1-1
Penalties-Yards	6-36	6-36
Time of possession	31:59	28:01

Attendance—60,711. No-shows—179.

INDIVIDUAL STATISTICS

Rushing—Miami, Carter 14-92, Bennett 14-80, Clayton 1-30, P. Johnson 6-16, Marino 1-9, Nathan 1-9; New England, Tatupu 20-90, Collins 4-10, Eason 2-2, Starring 1-0.

Passing—Miami, Marino 24-39-1—316; New England, Eason 19-29-0—313.

Receiving—Miami, Clayton 7-99, D. Johnson 5-73, Moore 5-61, Nathan 1-24, Cefalo 1-19, Duper 1-15, Jensen 1-12, Carter 2-11, Hardy 1-2; New England, Morgan 3-114, Starring 4-64, Weathers 3-53, Ramsey 5-32, Tatupu 2-30, Robinson 1-17, Dawson 1-3.

Kickoff Returns—Miami, Walker 3-58; New England, J. Williams 5-86, Robinson 1-14.

Punt Returns—Miami, Walker 1-0; New England, Starring 1-13.

Interceptions—New England, Gibson 1-0.

Punting—Miami, Roby 1-38.0; New England, Prestridge 3-57.0.

Field Goals—Miami, von Schamann 1-1; New England, Franklin 1-1.

Sacks—Miami, Betters.

Chiefs-Jets
SUNDAY, OCTOBER 21
SCORE BY PERIODS

Kansas City	0	0	0	7— 7
New York Jets	7	7	7	7—28

SCORING

New York—Humphery 44 pass from Ryan (Leahy kick), 3:46 1st.
New York—Shuler 16 pass from Ryan (Leahy kick), 14:06 2nd.
New York—Gastineau recovered fumble in end zone (Ryan run), 3:38 3rd.
Kansas City—Lacy 7 pass from Kenney (Lowery kick), 1:05 4th.
New York—Minter 39 pass from Ryan (Leahy kick), 8:23 4th.

TEAM STATISTICS

	Kansas City	New York
First downs	16	23
Rushes-Yards	24-121	38-115
Passing yards	84	258
Sacked-Yards lost	4-40	2-11
Return yards	121	86
Passes	12-25-1	22-32-0
Punts	6-47.7	6-45.0
Fumbles-Lost	2-1	1-0
Penalties-Yards	4-30	8-65
Time of possession	22:06	37:54

Attendance—66,782. No-shows—10,109.

INDIVIDUAL STATISTICS

Rushing—Kansas City, Heard 13-69, Jackson 7-46, Lacy 3-5, Paige 1-1; New York, Hector 23-58, Ryan 3-13, T. Paige 3-9, Minter 3-4, Barber 5-35, O'Brien 1-minus 4.

Passing—Kansas City, Kenney 12-25-1—124; New York, Ryan 21-31-0—260, O'Brien 1-1-0—9.

Receiving—Kansas City, Marshall 2-33, Heard 2-20, Carson 2-17, Jackson 2-14, W. Arnold 1-14, Scott 1-11, Paige 1-8, Lacy 1-7; New York, Shuler 7-58, Hector 5-53, Minter 3-51, Humphery 2-53, Barber 2-24, Sohn 1-16, Gaffney 1-8, Dennison 1-6.

Kickoff Returns—Kansas City, Paige 4-91; New York, Springs 2-31.

Punt Returns—Kansas City, Smith 4-30; New York, Springs 5-55.

Interceptions—New York, Carter 1-0.

Punting—Kansas City, J. Arnold 6-47.7; New York, Ramsey 6-45.0.

Field Goals—Kansas City, Lowery 0-1 (missed: 54); New York, none attempted.

Sacks—Kansas City, Bell 1½, Still ½; New York, Gastineau 1½, Baldwin, Bennett, Klecko ½.

Giants-Eagles
SUNDAY, OCTOBER 21
SCORE BY PERIODS

New York Giants	0	7	3	0—10
Philadelphia	7	3	0	14—24

SCORING

Philadelphia—Jackson 83 pass from Jaworski (McFadden kick), 10:34 1st.
New York—Carpenter 1 run (Haji-Sheikh kick), 13:38 2nd.
Philadelphia—Field goal McFadden 45, 14:43 2nd.
New York—Field goal Haji-Sheikh 31, 9:36 3rd.
Philadelphia—Hoover 11 pass from Jaworski (McFadden kick), 8:47 4th.
Philadelphia—Woodruff 37 pass from Jaworski (McFadden kick), 13:56 4th.

TEAM STATISTICS

	New York	Philadelphia
First downs	16	17
Rushes-Yards	30-59	24-86
Passing yards	216	239
Sacked-Yards lost	5-32	5-48
Return yards	151	53
Passes	16-33-1	17-37-0
Punts	6-39.2	7-44.0
Fumbles-Lost	1-1	0-0
Penalties-Yards	6-55	10-75
Time of possession	29:38	30:22

Attendance—64,677. No-shows—3,360.

INDIVIDUAL STATISTICS

Rushing—New York, Carpenter 18-47, Galbreath 5-12, Woolfolk 4-8, Simms 1-4, Morris 1-minus 4, Manuel 1-minus 8; Philadelphia, Montgomery 16-61, Oliver 7-23, M. Williams 1-2.

Passing—New York, Simms 16-33-1—248, Philadelphia, Jaworski 17-37-0—287.

Receiving—New York, Johnson 4-83, Gray 4-57, Galbreath 4-31, Manuel 2-54, Carpenter 2-23; Philadelphia, Woodruff 3-65, Quick 3-41, Spagnola 3-36, Oliver 3-14, Hoover 2-26, Montgomery 2-22, Jackson 1-83.

Kickoff Returns—New York, McConkey 3-77, Morris 1-8, McLaughlin 1-7; Philadelphia, Cooper 2-38.

Punt Returns—New York, McConkey 6-59; Philadelphia, Cooper 2-1.

Interceptions—Philadelphia, Ellis 1-14.

Punting—New York, Jennings 6-39.2; Philadelphia, Horan 7-44.0.

Field Goals—New York, Haji-Sheikh 1-3 (missed: 48, 52); Philadelphia, McFadden 1-2 (missed: 52).

Sacks—New York, Merrill 2½, Burt, Sally, Marshall ½; Philadelphia, Harrison 2, Brown 1½, Robinson, J. Williams ½.

Redskins-Cardinals
SUNDAY, OCTOBER 21
SCORE BY PERIODS

Washington	7	0	14	3—24
St. Louis	7	3	7	9—26

SCORING

St. Louis—Green 38 pass from Lomax (O'Donoghue kick), 2:25 1st.
Washington—Didier 3 pass from Theismann (Moseley kick), 13:41 1st.
St. Louis—Field goal O'Donoghue 29, 4:43 2nd.
Washington—Riggins 2 run (Moseley kick), 6:36 3rd.
Washington—Walker 7 pass from Theismann (Moseley kick), 10:37 3rd.
St. Louis—Marsh 19 pass from Lomax (O'Donoghue kick), 13:42 3rd.
Washington—Field goal Moseley 39, 3:09 4th.
St. Louis—Green 83 pass from Lomax (kick failed), 3:29 4th.
St. Louis—Field goal O'Donoghue 21, 14:57 4th.

TEAM STATISTICS

	Washington	St. Louis
First downs	21	22
Rushes-Yards	35-103	24-120
Passing yards	193	336
Sacked-Yards lost	4-31	3-25
Return yards	91	130
Passes	15-29-0	20-38-0
Punts	6-36.5	2-37.0
Fumbles-Lost	2-1	3-2
Penalties-Yards	5-45	5-40
Time of possession	31:40	28:20

Attendance—50,262. No-shows—1,255.

INDIVIDUAL STATISTICS

Rushing—Washington, Riggins 32-98, Theismann 2-3, Griffin 1-2; St. Louis, Anderson 16-76, Mitchell 4-21, Lomax 3-28, Marsh 1 minus-5.

Passing—Washington, Theismann 15-29-0—224; St. Louis, Lomax 20-38-0—361.

Receiving—Washington, Muhammad 5-86, Monk 6-87, Didier 2-39, Moore 1-5, Walker 1-7; St. Louis, Anderson 3-16, Green 6-163, Marsh 6-99, Ferrell 1-5, Tilley 2-46, Pittman 1-16, Mitchell 1-16.

Kickoff Returns—Washington, Nelms 4-73, Mauti 1-16, Kane 1-0; St. Louis, Pittman 3-98, Mitchell 2-22.

Punt Returns—Washington, Nelms 1-2; St. Louis, Mitchell 3-10.

Punting—Washington, Hayes 6-36.5; St. Louis, Birdsong 2-37.0.

Field Goals—Washington, Moseley 1-1; St. Louis, O'Donoghue 2-4 (missed: 34, 40).

Sacks—Washington, Milot, Grant, McGee; St. Louis, Greer, Baker, Junior, Nelson.

49ers-Oilers
SUNDAY, OCTOBER 21
SCORE BY PERIODS

San Francisco	10	7	3	14—34
Houston	0	7	7	7—21

SCORING

San Francisco—Francis 11 pass from Montana (Wersching kick), 5:04 1st.
San Francisco—Field goal Wersching 26, 11:43 1st.
Houston—Moriarty 1 run (Kempf kick), 0:11 2nd.
San Francisco—Tyler 26 pass from Montana (Wersching kick), 14:31 2nd.
San Francisco—Field goal Wersching 22, 2:38 3rd.
Houston—Smith 45 pass from Moon (Kempf kick), 9:22 3rd.
San Francisco—Craig 5 run (Wersching kick), 7:10 4th.
Houston—J. Williams 29 pass from Moon (Kempf kick), 9:42 4th.
San Francisco—D. Clark 80 pass from Montana (Wersching kick), 10:00 4th.

TEAM STATISTICS

	San Francisco	Houston
First downs	25	22
Rushes-Yards	38-164	18-82
Passing yards	353	350
Sacked-Yards lost	1-0	2-6
Return yards	85	105
Passes	25-35-1	25-33-2
Punts	3-49.3	3-46.3
Fumbles-Lost	2-0	3-1
Penalties-Yards	8-70	7-75
Time of possession	34:13	25:47

Attendance—39,900. No-shows—8,905.

INDIVIDUAL STATISTICS

Rushing—San Francisco, Tyler 23-108, Craig 8-31, Montana 5-13, Cooper 1-6, Harmon 1-6; Houston, Moriarty 9-36, Walls 2-5, Moon 5-31, Edwards 2-10.

Passing—San Francisco, Montana 25-35-1—353; Houston, Moon 25-33-2—356.

Receiving—San Francisco, Craig 7-61, Wilson 3-36, Francis 2-27, Monroe 1-22, D. Clark 5-127, Cooper 2-10, Tyler 2-33, Frank 2-17, Nehemiah 1-20; Houston, Smith 6-101, Edwards 2-21, Moriarty 5-50, Walls 3-29, J. Williams 3-62, Roaches 1-12, Mullins 2-28, Dressel 2-48, Bryant 1-5.

Kickoff Returns—San Francisco, Harmon 1-25, Monroe 1-13, McIntyre 1-0; Houston, Walls 3-49, Roaches 1-7.

Punt Returns—San Francisco, McLemore 3-47; Houston, Roaches 2-23.

Interceptions—San Francisco, McLemore 1-0, Wright 1-0; Houston, Brown 1-26.

Punting—San Francisco, Runager 3-49.3; Houston, James 3-46.3.

Field Goals—San Francisco, Wersching 2-2; Houston, Kempf 0-1 (missed: 33).

Sacks—San Francisco, Ellison, Stuckey; Houston, Eason.

Seahawks-Packers
SUNDAY, OCTOBER 21
SCORE BY PERIODS

Seattle	7	13	7	3—30
Green Bay	17	0	7	0—24

SCORING

Green Bay—Lofton 79 pass from Dickey (Del Greco kick), 0:19 1st.

Seattle—Largent 31 pass from Krieg (Johnson kick), 3:36 1st.

Green Bay—Lofton 20 pass from Dickey (Del Greco kick), 7:34 1st.

Green Bay—Field goal Del Greco 42, 14:04 1st.

Seattle—Field goal Johnson 29, 2:46 2nd.

Seattle—Field goal Johnson 39, 12:49 2nd.

Seattle—Doornink 2 run (Johnson kick), 14:05 2nd.

Seattle—Turner 25 pass from Krieg (Johnson kick), 3:43 3rd.

Green Bay—Ellis 8 pass from Dickey (Del Greco kick), 13:50 3rd.

Seattle—Field goal Johnson 45, 6:24 4th.

TEAM STATISTICS

	Seattle	Green Bay
First downs	22	22
Rushes-Yards	29-97	21-92
Passing yards	281	312
Sacked-Yards lost	5-29	6-52
Return yards	124	151
Passes	22-35-2	24-38-3
Punts	2-40.0	3-39.0
Fumbles-Lost	0-0	1-0
Penalties-Yards	17-128	11-107
Time of possession	31:42	28:18

Attendance—52,286. No-shows—3,817.

INDIVIDUAL STATISTICS

Rushing—Seattle, Lane 9-32, Morris 6-18, F. Harris 6-16, Krieg 5-18, Hughes 3-13; Green Bay, Clark 11-69, Huckleby 2-6, Ellis 4-3, Lofton 1-5, Dickey 3-9.

Passing—Seattle, Krieg 22-35-2—310; Green Bay, Dickey 24-38-3—364.

Receiving—Seattle, Largent 7-129, Doornink 2-35, C. Young 4-37, F. Harris 1-3, Castor 1-11, Lane 3-14, Walker 3-56, Turner 1-25; Green Bay, Lofton 5-162, Coffman 3-29, Ellis 5-54, Epps 4-65, Huckleby 1-4, Jefferson 2-27, Clark 4-23.

Kickoff Returns—Seattle, Dixon 5-69; Green Bay, Rodgers 6-88.

Punt Returns—Seattle, Easley 2-35; Green Bay, Epps 1-5.

Interceptions—Seattle, Taylor 1-20, J. Harris 1-0, Jackson 1-0; Green Bay, Lee 1-11, Cumby 1-7.

Punting—Seattle, West 2-40.0; Green Bay, Scribner 3-39.0.

Field Goals—Seattle, Johnson 3-3; Green Bay, Del Greco 1-1.

Sacks—Seattle, K. Butler, Fanning, Gaines, Green, J. Harris, Simpson; Green Bay, Anderson, Brown, Douglass, Johnson, Neill.

Rams-Falcons
MONDAY, OCTOBER 22
SCORE BY PERIODS

Los Angeles Rams	0	21	0	3—24
Atlanta	0	3	0	7—10

SCORING

Los Angeles—Dickerson 10 run (Lansford kick), 1:03 2nd.

Los Angeles—Ellard 9 pass from Kemp (Lansford kick), 2:11 2nd.

Atlanta—Field goal Luckhurst 39, 6:54 2nd.

Los Angeles—Ellard 69 punt return (Lansford kick), 14:21 2nd.

Los Angeles—Field goal Lansford 18, 7:33 4th.

Atlanta—Bailey 18 pass from Bartkowski (Luckhurst kick), 13:52 4th.

TEAM STATISTICS

	Los Angeles	Atlanta
First downs	16	11
Rushes-Yards	41-186	25-79
Passing yards	113	138
Sacked-Yards lost	3-16	1-6
Return yards	150	67
Passes	14-19-0	20-31-0
Punts	5-37.0	6-48.5
Fumbles-Lost	3-3	6-3
Penalties-Yards	9-97	8-60
Time of possession	31:39	28:21

Attendance—52,861. No-shows—7,876.

INDIVIDUAL STATISTICS

Rushing—Los Angeles, Dickerson 25-142, Crutchfield 7-27, Redden 7-21, Kemp 2-minus 4; Atlanta, Riggs 20-66, Bartkowski 3-11, Hodge 1-9, Stamps 1-minus 7.

Passing—Los Angeles, Kemp 14-19-0—129; Atlanta, Bartkowski 20-31-0—144.

Receiving—Los Angeles, Grant 4-18, Brown 3-74, David Hill 2-13, Guman 2-8, Ellard 1-9, Drew Hill 1-5, Dickerson 1-2; Atlanta, Hodge 6-55, Riggs 6-24, Bailey 2-32, Landrum 1-9, A. Jackson 1-8, Cox 1-7, Curran 1-7, Stamps 1-4, Benson 1-minus 2.

Kickoff Returns—Los Angeles, Redden 1-40; Atlanta, Stamps 1-21, Johnson 3-43.

Punt Returns—Los Angeles, Ellard 3-104, Johnson 1-3, Irvin 1-3; Atlanta, Curran 3-3.

Punting—Los Angeles, Misko 5-37.0; Atlanta, Giacomarro 6-48.5.

Field Goals—Los Angeles, Lansford 1-2 (missed: 48); Atlanta, Luckhurst 1-3 (missed: 42, 49).

Sacks—Los Angeles, Doss; Atlanta, Pitts 1½, Benish, Smith ½.

NINTH WEEK

RESULTS OF WEEK 9

Sunday, October 28

Chicago 16, Minnesota 7 at Chi.
Cincinnati 31, Houston 13 at Hous.
Dallas 22, Indianapolis 3 at Dal.
Denver 22, L.A. Raiders 19 (OT) at L.A.
Green Bay 41, Detroit 9 at G.B.
Kansas City 24, Tampa Bay 20 at K.C.
Miami 38, Buffalo 7 at Mia.
New England 30, N.Y. Jets 20 at N.E.
New Orleans 16, Cleveland 14 at Cleve.
N.Y. Giants 37, Washington 13 at N.Y.
Pittsburgh 35, Atlanta 10 at Pitts.
St. Louis 34, Philadelphia 14 at Phila.
San Francisco 33, L.A. Rams 0 at L.A.

Monday, October 29

Seattle 24, San Diego 0 at S.D.

Defense wins championships.

That simple notion long has been the guiding force in building top football teams, regardless of whether it's at the high school, college or professional level. Explosive, high-powered offenses are nice, but sooner or later they will have an off day. A strong defense is always there.

One of the surprise clubs of the 1984 season was Denver, a strong defensive team that was being compared to the Orange Crush unit of 1977, the Broncos' Super Bowl year. Through nine weeks, the Denver defense was leading the league in fewest points allowed with 118, or slightly more than 13 points per game. In an era where playing rules are structured to help the offense score points, such points-per-game averages are unusual. The Bronco defense also boasted 40 takeaways and a plus-22 turnover ratio, both figures by far the best in the NFL.

The Broncos' latest game, a 22-19 overtime triumph against the defending Super Bowl champion Raiders, was a case in point. The defense forced seven L.A. turnovers, including three in the final minutes of regulation and overtime, that led to the victory. First, with the Raiders protecting a 19-12 lead late in the contest, running back Marcus Allen carried for an 11-yard gain deep in Denver territory. Linebacker Ken Woodard hit Allen hard, forcing him to fumble, and Rulon Jones recovered for the Broncos. The offense then moved 84 yards in 11 plays to tie the score with 24 seconds remaining, Gary Kubiak throwing 12 yards to Steve Watson for the equalizer.

In the overtime, L.A. quarterback Marc Wilson threw 41 yards to Malcolm Barnwell at the Denver 11. Instead of going for a field goal on first down, L.A. tried another running play. Frank Hawkins carried and was stripped of the ball by safety Mike Harden, with Steve Foley recovering for Denver at the 7. Then, on the Raiders' next possession, Wilson overthrew

Dokie Williams, and Roger Jackson intercepted for Denver, returning the ball 23 yards to the Raiders' 22-yard line with 38 seconds left. Two plays later, Denver's Rich Karlis kicked a game-winning field goal as time expired in overtime.

"Denver's been winning on big turnovers and big-play defense," said Raiders defensive tackle Howie Long. "Today was no exception. You can't downplay that, but I'm a firm believer that you can't do it for a whole year."

Maybe not. But 8-1 is not a bad start.

Another defense that was winning games belonged to Chicago. The Bears were ranked No. 1 in the league in yardage surrendered. They showed division-rival Minnesota just how good a defense they had in a deceptively close 16-7 victory. Chicago had a team-record 11 sacks, just one shy of the league mark, as they harrassed Vikings quarterback Archie Manning all afternoon. Manning, subbing for the injured Tommy Kramer, was sacked three times in succession and five times in six offensive plays at one point. The defense came within 1:54 of recording a shutout.

Offensively, the Bears were just as potent. They scored touchdowns on their first two possessions in rolling to a 16-0 halftime advantage. It was the second week in succession that the Bears scored touchdowns on their first two possessions. Although he didn't score, Walter Payton's 54 yards rushing put him over 1,000 for the season, the eighth time in his career he reached that figure. That tied Payton with Franco Harris for the NFL record for most 1,000-yard seasons.

Green Bay's Eddie Lee Ivery, who had not carried the ball in over a year because of drug problems, rushed for 116 yards on only nine carries and became the first Packer to rush for 100 yards in a game in 1984. Ivery, quarterback Lynn Dickey, who threw for four touchdowns, and rookie safety Tom Flynn, who intercepted three passes, sparked the Packers' 41-9 victory over Detroit that snapped Green Bay's seven-game losing streak.

Two other streaks remained intact when Miami trounced AFC Eastern Division-rival Buffalo, 38-7. The Dolphins moved to 9-0 on the year while Buffalo remained winless. Dan Marino, who had broken Bob Griese's club record for most touchdown passes in a season the previous week against New England, snapped Griese's Miami record for passing yards in one season and threw three touchdown passes against the Bills. The Dolphins jumped to a commanding 24-0 lead at halftime and held the Bills scoreless until the final two minutes of the game.

The high-rolling San Francisco 49ers crushed division-rival Los Angeles, 33-0, handing the Rams their first shutout since 1981. Joe

Montana led the 49ers' charge with 365 passing yards and three touchdowns. One of the TD passes went to Roger Craig, who also scored on a six-yard run in the third period, the first touchdown scored by the 49ers in the third quarter in 1984.

The Rams moved the ball to the San Francisco 1-yard line in the second quarter and 4-yard line in the fourth. But Eric Dickerson, who played with a sprained toe, fumbled the ball through the end zone for a touchback on the first opportunity and quarterback Jeff Kemp threw three straight incompletions on the second.

In a game that matched clubs with three-game winning streaks, St. Louis upended Philadelphia, 34-14. Ironically, the Eagles had yielded but 34 points in their three previous wins before giving up that many against the Cardinals. Neil Lomax completed 20 of 26 passes for 286 yards and two touchdowns while Stump Mitchell ran for two other scores to lead the attack. The Cards defense harrassed Philly quarterback Ron Jaworski most of the day, sacking him six times and picking off three of his passes, including one by safety Benny Perrin in the St. Louis end zone late in the opening half with the Cardinals clinging to a 17-14 lead.

In an interconference game that got off to a crazy start, Pittsburgh won easily over Atlanta, 35-10. On the first play from scrimmage, Steelers quarterback Mark Malone, starting his second game of the season in place of the injured David Woodley, threw a pass that cornerback Kenny Johnson intercepted. But on the Falcons' first offensive play, fullback Gerald Riggs fumbled and Steelers' corner Dwayne Woodruff returned it 65 yards for a touchdown. Malone later threw three touchdown passes in the Pittsburgh rout.

Strangely, Atlanta's only points of the day came on a field goal as time expired in the first half and a touchdown as the game ended.

Danny White made his first 1984 start at quarterback as Dallas crushed the Indianapolis Colts, 22-3. White, who had previously come off the bench in relief of Gary Hogeboom, completed 13 of 14 passes for 170 yards and two touchdowns in the first half as the Cowboys took a 13-0 lead. Tony Dorsett rushed for 104 yards on 24 carries for his first 100-yard performance in Dallas' last 11 games and also went over the 9,000 mark for his career.

The Cowboys defense had its best game of the '84 season, holding the Colts to eight first downs, forcing four turnovers and getting three sacks. The 155 total yards allowed were the fewest surrendered by Dallas in six years.

The Tampa Bay Buccaneers and Kansas City Chiefs took to the air in a battle at K.C.'s Arrowhead Stadium. The clubs combined for just 159 rushing yards and set an NFL record for most pass attempts by both teams in one game with 100. The Bucs' Steve DeBerg threw 54 passes, completing 24 for 280 yards and two touchdowns. The Chiefs' Bill Kenney heaved the ball 46 times, completing 26 for 332 yards and two scores in Kansas City's 24-20 victory. The 100 passes eclipsed the old record of 98 set in a Baltimore-Minnesota game in 1969.

Two head coaches made their NFL debuts in Week 9, but only one came away a winner.

Raymond Berry replaced Ron Meyer at New England and saw his team fall behind the New York Jets, 20-6, at the half. The Jets scored on each of their last four possessions of the half while holding the Patriots to just two field goals.

But the Patriots turned things around in the second half. Sparked by the running of Craig James, who, ironically, played college ball for Meyer at Southern Methodist, the Pats scored 24 unanswered points to win, 30-20. James rushed for 79 yards and his 25-yard scoring run late in the third period, New England's first touchdown, cut the deficit to four points.

Defensive coordinator Marty Schottenheimer took over at Cleveland for Sam Rutigliano, but the Browns lost again. A 16-14 loss to New Orleans was the Browns' eighth in nine games and their fifth straight by less than five points. Saints placekicker Morten Andersen kicked three field goals, one with 3:05 left in the game and another from 53 yards out as time expired. New Orleans started its game-winning drive from its own 23 with 59 seconds remaining.

At Houston, the Bengals' Larry Kinnebrew, who scored just three touchdowns in his 1983 rookie season, scored four in Cincinnati's 31-13 AFC Central Division win against Houston. It marked the seventh straight time that Cincinnati had beat the Oilers and it was Houston's 31st loss in its last 34 games.

At New York, the Giants' Joe Morris, a third-year pro, enjoyed his best professional game by scoring three touchdowns in a 37-13 triumph over Washington. The TDs were Morris' first of the season and gave him five in his NFL career. Prior to this game, New York had scored only four rushing touchdowns in its previous eight games. It also was the Giants' first victory against the Redskins after six straight losses.

The Seattle Seahawks handed the San Diego Chargers their first shutout since 1979 with a 24-0 victory in the Monday night game. Dave Krieg and Steve Largent accounted for the Seahawks' offense, teaming for 11-, 13- and 16-yard touchdown passes. A swarming Seattle defense, which sacked Chargers quarterback Dan Fouts six times and held him to 153 net passing yards, was led by safety Kenny Easley, who intercepted three passes, including one at the Seattle 5-yard line to foil San Diego's best scoring opportunity.

The loss was the Chargers' fifth straight against an AFC Western Division team.

Vikings-Bears
SUNDAY, OCTOBER 28
SCORE BY PERIODS

Minnesota	0	0	0	7—	7
Chicago	6	10	0	0—16	

SCORING
Chicago—Suhey 2 run (kick failed), 12:02 1st.
Chicago—McKinnon 18 pass from McMahon (B. Thomas kick), 4:32 2nd.
Chicago—Field goal B. Thomas 19, 14:57 2nd.
Minnesota—Lewis 22 pass from Wilson (Stenerud kick), 13:06 4th.

TEAM STATISTICS
	Minnesota	Chicago
First downs	16	18
Rushes-Yards	16-41	40-129
Passing yards	126	178
Sacked-Yards lost	11-101	1-2
Return yards	74	72
Passes	20-36-2	16-27-0
Punts	8-36.9	6-36.2
Fumbles-Lost	4-0	1-1
Penalties-Yards	1-10	4-53
Time of possession	26:16	33:44

Attendance—57,517. No-shows—8,273.

INDIVIDUAL STATISTICS
Rushing—Minnesota, Manning 4-20, Anderson 5-19, Brown 3-17, Nelson 4-minus 15; Chicago, Payton 22-54, McMahon 6-39, Suhey 9-31, Finzer 1-5, C. Thomas 1-2, Moorehead 1-minus 2.

Passing—Minnesota, Manning 14-24-1—138, Wilson 6-12-1—89; Chicago, McMahon 16-26-0—180, Payton 0-1-0—0.

Receiving—Minnesota, Lewis 3-71, White 3-51, Jordan 5-43, Senser 3-28, Nelson 3-16, Jones 2-9, Brown 1-9; Chicago, Moorehead 3-64, Gault 3-36, McKinnon 2-23, Suhey 3-21, Payton 3-18, Dunsmore 1-16, C. Thomas 1-2.

Kickoff Returns—Minnesota, Anderson 1-31, Nelson 1-26, Rice 1-13; Chicago, Cameron 1-20.

Punt Returns—Minnesota, Nelson 1-4; Chicago, Fisher 6-38.

Interceptions—Chicago, Richardson 1-7, Bell 1-7.

Punting—Minnesota, Coleman 8-36.9; Chicago, Finzer 6-36.2.

Field Goals—Minnesota, Stenerud 0-1 (missed: 46); Chicago, B. Thomas 1-2 (missed: 53).

Sacks—Minnesota, C. Johnson; Chicago, Wilson 2½, Dent 2, Bell 1½, Hampton 1½, McMichael 1½, Harris, Hartenstine.

Bengals-Oilers
SUNDAY, OCTOBER 28
SCORE BY PERIODS

Cincinnati	0	17	7	7—31	
Houston	7	0	0	6—13	

SCORING
Houston—Moriarty 1 run (Kempt kick), 12:59 1st.
Cincinnati—Kinnebrew 1 run (Breech kick), 3:41 2nd.
Cincinnati—Kinnebrew 3 run (Breech kick), 7:32 2nd.
Cincinnati—Field goal Breech 34, 14:59 2nd.
Cincinnati—Kinnebrew 11 pass from Anderson (Breech kick), 9:25 3rd.
Cincinnati—Kinnebrew 1 run (Breech kick), 2:14 4th.
Houston—Luck 4 run (pass failed), 7:42 4th.

TEAM STATISTICS
	Cincinnati	Houston
First downs	26	20
Rushes-Yards	47-219	22-98
Passing yards	154	218
Sacked-Yards lost	0-0	3-26
Return yards	112	122
Passes	18-24-1	17-28-3

	Cincinnati	Houston
Punts	2-41.0	2-41.5
Fumbles-Lost	1-1	1-1
Penalties-Yards	4-32	3-30
Time of possession	35:46	24:14

Attendance—34,010. No-shows—12,255.

INDIVIDUAL STATISTICS
Rushing—Cincinnati, Jennings 8-31, Kinnebrew 19-80, Anderson 1-12, Alexander 6-18, Brooks 12-76, Verser 1-2; Houston, Moriarty 13-32, Moon 3-13, Edwards 2-20, Walls 1-minus 5, Luck 3-38.

Passing—Cincinnati, Anderson 18-24-1—154; Houston, Moon 11-18-2—196, Luck 6-10-1—48.

Receiving—Cincinnati, Kinnebrew 2-23, Collinsworth 4-43, Curtis 1-12, Brooks 3-15, Jennings 4-14, Martin 1-18, Holman 1-13, Harris 1-16; Houston, Walls 2-93, Moriarty 3-20, Bryant 1-13, Smith 4-51, J. Williams 2-16, Dressel 2-22, McCloskey 1-7, Edwards 2-22.

Kickoff Returns—Cincinnati, Jennings 2-44, Farley 1-23; Houston, Roaches 5-122.

Punt Returns—Cincinnati, Martin 2-41.

Interceptions—Cincinnati, Turner 1-4, Simmons 1-0, R. Williams 1-0; Houston, Tullis 1-0.

Punting—Cincinnati, McInally 2-41.0; Houston, James 2-41.5.

Field Goals—Cincinnati, Breech 1-1; Houston, none attempted.

Sacks—Cincinnati, Browner, Cameron, R. Williams.

Colts-Cowboys
SUNDAY, OCTOBER 28
SCORE BY PERIODS

Indianapolis	0	0	0	3—	3
Dallas	0	13	3	6—22	

SCORING
Dallas—Hill 38 pass from D. White (Septien kick), 5:07 2nd.
Dallas—Cosbie 5 pass from D. White (kick failed), 14:51 2nd.
Dallas—Field goal Septien 19, 11:34 3rd.
Dallas—Field goal Septien 19, 0:33 4th.
Dallas—Field goal Septien 24, 2:51 4th.
Indianapolis—Field goal Allegre 52, 4:31 4th.

TEAM STATISTICS
	Indianapolis	Dallas
First downs	8	27
Rushes-Yards	24-73	39-135
Passing yards	82	262
Sacked-Yards lost	3-20	0-0
Return yards	87	77
Passes	9-22-2	21-32-0
Punts	6-47.5	4-37.3
Fumbles-Lost	3-2	2-2
Penalties-Yards	9-106	6-63
Time of possession	22:33	37:27

Attendance—58,724. No-shows—3,530.

INDIVIDUAL STATISTICS
Rushing—Indianapolis, McMillan 12-43, Dickey 9-22, Pagel 2-4, Middleton 1-4; Dallas, Dorsett 24-104, Newsome 8-21, Springs 5-5, J. Jones 2-5.

Passing—Indianapolis, Pagel 3-10-0—29, Herrmann 6-11-1—73, Stark 0-1-1—0; Dallas, D. White 21-32-0—262.

Receiving—Indianapolis, Bouza 5-47, McMillan 3-55, Dickey 1-0; Dallas, Hill 8-125, Cosbie 4-49, Renfro 3-35, Newsome 2-20, Dorsett 1-11, Donley 1-9, Carmichael 1-7, Springs 1-6.

Kickoff Returns—Indianapolis, Kafentzis 3-50, Smith 1-35, Sherwin 1-2; Dallas, Allen 1-18, Salonen 1-8.

Punt Returns—Indianapolis, Glasgow 1-0; Dallas, Allen 5-45.

Interceptions—Dallas, Bates 1-3, Hegman 1-3.

Punting—Indianapolis, Stark 6-47.5; Dallas, Warren 4-37.3.

Field Goals—Indianapolis, Allegre 1-1; Dallas, Septien 3-3.

Sacks—Dallas, Bates, E. Jones, Hegman ½, Lockhart ½.

Broncos-Raiders
SUNDAY, OCTOBER 28
SCORE BY PERIODS

Denver	0	6	0	13	3—22
L.A. Raiders	9	3	7	0	0—19

SCORING

Los Angeles—Safety, Martin tackled Kubiak in end zone, 7:55 1st.
Los Angeles—Allen 36 pass from Wilson (Bahr kick), 13:15 1st.
Los Angeles—Field goal Bahr 44, 6:32 2nd.
Denver—Field goal Karlis 41, 11:51 2nd.
Denver—Field goal Karlis 24, 14:36 2nd.
Los Angeles—Allen 1 run (Bahr kick), 10:07 3rd.
Denver—Kay 4 pass from Kubiak (pass failed), 1:45 4th.
Denver—Watson 12 pass from Kubiak (Karlis kick), 14:36 4th.
Denver—Field goal Karlis 35, 15:00 OT.

TEAM STATISTICS

	Denver	Los Angeles
First downs	24	20
Rushes-Yards	46-182	38-122
Passing yards	178	234
Sacked-Yards lost	4-28	3-18
Return yards	159	58
Passes	21-34-0	19-36-3
Punts	6-246	4-170
Fumbles-Lost	4-3	6-4
Penalties-Yards	7-48	5-55
Time of possession	37:39	37:21

Attendance—91,020. No-shows—1,449.

INDIVIDUAL STATISTICS

Rushing—Denver, Winder 34-126, Willhite 10-34, Kubiak 2-22; Los Angeles, Allen 16-70, Hawkins 10-26, King 8-20, Humm 1-9, Wilson 3-minus 3.

Passing—Denver, Kubiak 21-34-0—206; Los Angeles, Wilson 19-36-3—252.

Receiving—Denver, Watson 5-82, Johnson 5-49, Winder 5-29, Willhite 2-24, Sawyer 2-18, Kay 1-4, J. Wright 1-0; Los Angeles, Allen 6-63, Barnwell 4-77, Christensen 4-55, Williams 4-53, Pruitt 1-4.

Kickoff Returns—Denver, Thomas 3-53, Lang 1-23; Los Angeles, Williams 4-123, Montgomery 2-41, Pruitt 1-13.

Punt Returns—Denver, Thomas 2-16; Los Angeles, Pruitt 4-32.

Interceptions—Denver, Harden 1-34, R. Jackson 1-23, D. Smith 1-10.

Punting—Denver, Norman 6-41.0; Los Angeles, Guy 4-42.5.

Field Goals—Denver, Karlis 3-4 (missed: .42); Los Angeles, Bahr 1-2 (missed: 47).

Sacks—Denver, T. Jackson 2, Townsend; Los Angeles, Martin 2, M. Davis, Long.

Lions-Packers
SUNDAY, OCTOBER 28
SCORE BY PERIODS

Detroit	3	6	0	0—	9
Green Bay	14	14	10	3—41	

SCORING

Green Bay—Clark 1 run (Del Greco kick), 4:38 1st.
Green Bay—Coffman 20 pass from Dickey (Del Greco kick), 10:46 1st.
Detroit—Field goal Murray 46, 14:40 1st.
Detroit—Field goal Murray 37, 7:33 2nd.

Green Bay—Coffman 3 pass from Dickey (Del Greco kick), 10:46 2nd.
Detroit—Field goal Murray 41, 13:24 2nd.
Green Bay—Moore 3 pass from Dickey (Del Greco kick), 14:55 2nd.
Green Bay—Lofton 6 pass from Dickey (Del Greco kick), 3:47 3rd.
Green Bay—Field goal Del Greco 45, 11:36 3rd.
Green Bay—Field goal Del Greco 34, 7:36 4th.

TEAM STATISTICS

	Detroit	Green Bay
First downs	20	30
Rushes-Yards	14-65	38-195
Passing yards	243	244
Sacked-Yards lost	3-21	1-10
Return yards	68	126
Passes	25-48-3	18-26-0
Punts	3-36.7	4-35.8
Fumbles-Lost	3-0	0-0
Penalties-Yards	12-83	8-90
Time of possession	26:43	33:17

Attendance—54,289. No-shows—1,866.

INDIVIDUAL STATISTICS

Rushing—Detroit, J. Jones 5-20, Danielson 3-16, Jenkins 3-12, Machurek 1-9, Bussey 2-8; Green Bay, Ivery 9-116, Ellis 8-33, Clark 8-19, Huckleby 1-10, Crouse 6-8, Wright 1-5, Rodgers 4-4, Dickey 1-0.

Passing—Detroit, Danielson 21-36-1—234, Machurek 4-12-2—30; Green Bay, Dickey 17-25-0—248, Wright 1-1-0—6.

Receiving—Detroit, Chadwick 4-64, J. Jones 4-43, Rubick 2-34, Jenkins 4-30, Thompson 3-32, Lewis 2-23, Mandley 2-19, Martin 1-9, D'Addio 1-12, McCall 1-5, Bussey 1-minus 7; Green Bay, Lofton 5-80, Coffman 5-69, Clark 4-51, Jefferson 3-51, Moore 1-3.

Kickoff Returns—Detroit, Mandley 3-23, Martin 3-23, Meade 2-17; Green Bay, Rodgers 3-57, Huckleby 1-18.

Punt Returns—Detroit, Martin 1-4, Jenkins 1-1; Green Bay, Flynn 2-18.

Interceptions—Green Bay, Flynn 3-23.

Punting—Detroit, Black 3-36.7; Green Bay, Scribner 4-35.8.

Field Goals—Detroit, Murray 3-3; Green Bay, Del Greco 2-2.

Sacks—Detroit, Cobb; Green Bay, Johnson, T. Jones, Scott.

Buccaneers-Chiefs
SUNDAY, OCTOBER 28
SCORE BY PERIODS

Tampa Bay	0	7	6	7—20	
Kansas City	0	7	7	10—24	

SCORING

Kansas City—Lacy 2 run (Lowery kick), 4:02 2nd.
Tampa Bay—House 7 pass from DeBerg (Ariri kick), 12:39 2nd.
Kansas City—Lacy 5 pass from Kenney (Lowery kick), 3:56 3rd.
Tampa Bay—Field goal Ariri 34, 8:27 3rd.
Tampa Bay—Field goal Ariri 25, 14:39 3rd.
Kansas City—Marshall 27 pass from Kenney (Lowery kick), 5:31 4th.
Kansas City—Field goal Lowery 47, 7:49 4th.
Tampa Bay—Dierking 5 pass from DeBerg (Ariri kick), 10:53 4th.

TEAM STATISTICS

	Tampa Bay	Kansas City
First downs	23	21
Rushes-Yards	29-106	23-53
Passing yards	244	313
Sacked-Yards lost	4-36	2-19
Return yards	127	127
Passes	29-54-3	26-46-2

	Tampa Bay	Kansas City
Punts	6-34.8	5-36.4
Fumbles-Lost	0-0	3-2
Penalties-Yards	6-40	7-45
Time of possession	34:11	25:49

Attendance—41,710. No-shows—2,586.

INDIVIDUAL STATISTICS

Rushing—Tampa Bay, Wilder 25-91, Dierking 2-11, De-Berg 2-4; Kansas City, Jackson 5-31, Heard 12-12, Lacy 4-12, Kenney 2-minus 2.

Passing—Tampa Bay, DeBerg 24-54-3—280; Kansas City, Kenney 26-46-2—332.

Receiving—Tampa Bay, House 10-100, Wilder 7-44, T. Bell 3-38, J. Bell 3-33, Carroll 3-29, Carter 2-31, Dierking 1-5; Kansas City, Carson 7-131, Marshall 4-43, Beckman 4-28, Heard 3-25, Hancock 2-51, Jackson 2-16, Lacy 2-8, Paige 1-28, W. Arnold 1-2.

Kickoff Returns—Tampa Bay, Bright 3-73, Morton 1-26, Wood 1-0; Kansas City, Smith 3-49, Paige 1-17, Hancock 1-15.

Punt Returns—Tampa Bay, Bright 2-2; Kansas City, Smith 2-15.

Interceptions—Tampa Bay, Cotney 1-26, Davis 1-0; Kansas City, Ross 1-21, McAlister 1-11, Hill 1-minus 1.

Punting—Tampa Bay, Garcia 6-34.8; Kansas City, J. Arnold 5-36.4.

Field Goals—Tampa Bay, Ariri 2-3 (missed: 46); Kansas City, Lowery 1-3 (missed: 37, 50).

Sacks—Tampa Bay, Brantley, Washington; Kansas City, Still 2, Dawson, Bell ½, Daniels ½.

Bills-Dolphins
SUNDAY, OCTOBER 28
SCORE BY PERIODS

Buffalo	0	0	0	7— 7
Miami	7	17	0	14—38

SCORING

Miami—Clayton 7 pass from Marino (von Schamann kick), 11:42 1st.

Miami—D. Johnson 10 pass from Marino (von Schamann kick), 0:07 2nd.

Miami—Field goal von Schamann 22, 7:05 2nd.

Miami—Clayton 65 pass from Marino (von Schamann kick), 12:27 2nd.

Miami—Bennett 1 run (von Schamann kick), 0:41 4th.

Miami—P. Johnson 1 run (von Schamann kick), 11:34 4th.

Buffalo—Dennard 5 pass from Kofler (Danelo kick), 13:38 4th.

TEAM STATISTICS

	Buffalo	Miami
First downs	15	28
Rushes-Yards	16-103	31-191
Passing yards	170	302
Sacked-Yards lost	5-41	1-4
Return yards	155	94
Passes	27-40-1	22-32-3
Punts	6-43.2	2-39.5
Fumbles-Lost	4-3	0-0
Penalties-Yards	7-55	2-20
Time of possession	27:23	32:37

Attendance—58,824. No-shows—3,073.

INDIVIDUAL STATISTICS

Rushing—Buffalo, Bell 10-62, Ferguson 1-20, Neal 3-12, Riddick 1-6, Moore 1-3; Miami, Carter 12-93, Nathan 3-40, P. Johnson 9-30, Bennett 6-21, Marino 1-7.

Passing—Buffalo, Ferguson 20-30-1—136, Kofler 7-10-0—75; Miami, Marino 19-28-3—282, Strock 3-4-0—24.

Receiving—Buffalo, Dennard 8-72, Riddick 6-61, Hunter 4-27, Franklin 4-23, Moore 4-15, Brookins 1-13; Miami, Clayton 3-106, Duper 5-74, Moore 5-38, Nathan 3-35, Hardy 2-31, D. Johnson 2-10, Cefalo 1-8, Carter 1-4.

Kickoff Returns—Buffalo, Wilson 4-75, V. Williams 1-25.

Punt Returns—Miami, Walker 2-45, Kozlowski 1-20.

Interceptions—Buffalo, Romes 1-55, Bellinger 1-0, Freeman 1-0; Miami, Sowell 1-7, Langford 0-22.

Punting—Buffalo, Kidd 6-43.2; Miami, Roby 2-39.5.

Field Goals—Buffalo, Danelo 0-1 (missed: 42); Miami, von Schamann 1-1.

Sacks—Buffalo, McNanie; Miami, Bowser 2, Charles 2, Benson.

Jets-Patriots
SUNDAY, OCTOBER 28
SCORE BY PERIODS

New York Jets	10	10	0	0—20
New England	0	6	10	14—30

SCORING

New York—Field goal Leahy 46, 10:57 1st.

New York—Klever 7 pass from O'Brien (Leahy kick), 15:00 1st.

New England—Field goal Franklin 20, 5:10 2nd.

New York—Field goal Leahy 18, 9:19 2nd.

New York—Barber 2 run (Leahy kick), 13:39 2nd.

New England—Field goal Franklin 27, 15:00 2nd.

New England—Field goal Franklin 47, 9:21 3rd.

New England—C. James 25 run (Franklin kick), 13:34 3rd.

New England—Starring 5 pass from Eason (Franklin kick), 4:07 4th.

New England—Collins 4 run (Franklin kick), 12:07 4th.

TEAM STATISTICS

	New York	New England
First downs	19	23
Rushes-Yards	30-166	28-122
Passing yards	132	244
Sacked-Yards lost	4-38	4-29
Return yards	124	138
Passes	15-25-2	23-35-1
Punts	5-34.6	5-46.6
Fumbles-Lost	0-0	0-0
Penalties-Yards	6-43	6-47
Time of possession	28:58	31:02

Attendance—60,513. No-shows—377.

INDIVIDUAL STATISTICS

Rushing—New York, McNeil 17-110, Hector 7-40, Barber 2-8, Paige 3-4, O'Brien 1-4; New England, C. James 10-79, Collins 6-19, Tatupu 9-18, Eason 3-6.

Passing—New York, Ryan 9-16-2—89, O'Brien 6-9-0—81; New England, Eason 23-35-1—273.

Receiving—New York, Jones 7-95, Shuler 2-20, Walker 2-11, Hector 2-9, McNeil 1-28, Klever 1-7; New England, Dawson 5-56, Starring 4-35, Ramsey 4-31, Morgan 3-60, Tatupu 2-30, C. James 2-18, Weathers 1-17, Collins 1-8, Hawthorne 1-18.

Kickoff Returns—New York, Springs 4-82, Paige 1-0; New England, J. Williams 5-105.

Punt Returns—New York, Springs 3-23; New England, Starring 3-19.

Interceptions—New York, Carter 1-19; New England, R. James 1-14, Nelson 1-0.

Punting—New York, Ramsey 5-34.6; New England, Prestridge 5-46.6.

Field Goals—New York, Leahy 2-2; New England, Franklin 3-3.

Sacks—New York, Gastineau 3, Faurot; New England, Owens 2, Adams, Blackmon.

Saints-Browns
SUNDAY, OCTOBER 28
SCORE BY PERIODS

New Orleans	0	10	0	6—16
Cleveland	0	7	7	0—14

SCORING

New Orleans—Gajan 2 pass from Todd (Andersen kick), 5:53 2nd.
Cleveland—Newsome 5 pass from McDonald (Bahr kick), 11:47 2nd.
New Orleans—Field goal Andersen 26, 15:00 2nd.
Cleveland—Newsome 6 pass from McDonald (Bahr kick), 8:38 3rd.
New Orleans—Field goal Andersen 21, 11:55 4th.
New Orleans—Field goal Andersen 53, 15:00 4th.

TEAM STATISTICS

	New Orleans	Cleveland
First downs	18	17
Rushes-Yards	31-111	31-83
Passing yards	262	179
Sacked-Yards lost	3-32	2-14
Return yards	71	109
Passes	21-27-0	16-23-0
Punts	4-44.5	5-42.0
Fumbles-Lost	1-1	1-0
Penalties-Yards	6-50	9-75
Time of possession	30:05	29:55

Attendance—52,489. No-shows—1,172.

INDIVIDUAL STATISTICS

Rushing—New Orleans, Gajan 7-52, G. Rogers 11-26, W. Wilson 3-19, Campbell 6-9, Todd 3-8, Duckett 1-minus 3; Cleveland, Green 23-74, Pruitt 5-11, B. Davis 1-6, McDonald 1-0, Walker 1-minus 8.

Passing—New Orleans, Todd 21-27-0—294; Cleveland, McDonald 16-23-0—193.

Receiving—New Orleans, Gajan 6-29, Young 4-101, W. Wilson 4-47, Groth 3-33, Scott 1-36, Brenner 1-27, Anthony 1-11, Miller 1-10; Cleveland, Adams 4-62, Newsome 4-42, Harris 3-31, Brennan 2-26, Byner 1-21, B. Davis 1-6, Green 1-5.

Kickoff Returns—New Orleans, Duckett 2-59; Cleveland, B. Davis 1-25, Byner 1-21.

Punt Returns—New Orleans, Fields 3-12; Cleveland, Brennan 4-43.

Punting—New Orleans, Hansen 4-44.5; Cleveland, Cox 5-42.0.

Field Goals—New Orleans, Andersen 3-3; Cleveland, Bahr 0-2 (missed: 34, 37).

Sacks—New Orleans, B. Clark, Wilks; Cleveland, Camp 1½, Baldwin, Franks ½.

Redskins-Giants
SUNDAY, OCTOBER 28
SCORE BY PERIODS

Washington	0	6	0	7—13
New York Giants	14	9	7	7—37

SCORING

New York—Gray 23 pass from Simms (Haji-Sheikh kick), 10:49 1st.
New York—Morris 2 run (Haji-Sheikh kick), 13:56 1st.
New York—Morris 1 run (kick failed), 7:23 2nd.
New York—Field goal Haji-Sheikh 19, 9:29 2nd.
Washington—Field goal Moseley 23, 12:00 2nd.
Washington—Field goal Moseley 33, 14:36 2nd.
New York—Morris 5 run (Haji-Sheikh kick), 9:37 3rd.
New York—Johnson 8 pass from Simms (Haji-Sheikh kick), 0:04 4th.
Washington—Moore 4 pass from Theismann (Moseley kick), 7:16 4th.

TEAM STATISTICS

	Washington	New York
First downs	15	25
Rushes-Yards	23-79	34-130
Passing yards	248	294
Sacked-Yards lost	3-26	7-45
Return yards	110	79
Passes	23-46-1	18-29-0
Punts	7-37.2	7-38.0
Fumbles-Lost	1-1	2-1
Penalties-Yards	4-24	5-40
Time of possession	26:36	33:24

Attendance—76,192. No-shows—688.

INDIVIDUAL STATISTICS

Rushing—Washington, Riggins 16-51, Theismann 3-25, Griffin 2-4, Kane 1-1, Hart 1-minus 2; New York, Morris 15-68, Carpenter 11-41, Galbreath 3-18, Cephous 2-2, Simms 3-1.

Passing—Washington, Theismann 21-41-1—255, Hart 2-5-0—19; New York, Simms 18-29-0—339.

Receiving—Washington, Moore 9-75, Monk 4-104, Seay 3-44, Griffin 3-19, Didier 2-8, McGrath 1-18, Jones 1-6; New York, Gray 7-128, B. Williams 3-51, Manuel 3-45, McConkey 2-62, Johnson 2-19, Mowatt 1-34.

Kickoff Returns—Washington, Nelms 4-70; New York, McConkey 2-38, McLaughlin 1-11.

Punt Returns—Washington, Nelms 6-40; New York, McConkey 5-23.

Interceptions—New York, P. Williams 1-7.

Punting—Washington, Hayes 7-37.2; New York, Jennings 7-38.0.

Field Goals—Washington, Moseley 2-3 (missed: 40); New York, Haji-Sheikh 1-1.

Sacks—Washington, Coleman 2½, Manley 2, Butz, Kaufman, Brooks ½; New York, Merrill, Reasons, Taylor.

Falcons-Steelers
SUNDAY, OCTOBER 28
SCORE BY PERIODS

Atlanta	0	3	0	7—10
Pittsburgh	7	7	14	7—35

SCORING

Pittsburgh—Woodruff 65 fumble return (Anderson kick), 0:33 1st.
Pittsburgh—Stallworth 20 pass from Malone (Anderson kick), 12:36 2nd.
Atlanta—Field goal Luckhurst 40, 15:00 2nd.
Pittsburgh—Pollard 5 run (Anderson kick), 8:53 3rd.
Pittsburgh—Stallworth 31 pass from Malone (Anderson kick), 12:16 3rd.
Pittsburgh—Erenberg 7 pass from Malone (Anderson kick), 6:47 4th.
Atlanta—Bailey 9 pass from Moroski (Luckhurst kick), 15:00 4th.

TEAM STATISTICS

	Atlanta	Pittsburgh
First downs	15	17
Rushes-Yards	31-103	35-169
Passing yards	193	145
Sacked-Yards lost	4-32	2-17
Return yards	195	85
Passes	22-28-1	11-22-2
Punts	8-41.0	5-38.2
Fumbles-Lost	3-2	1-1
Penalties-Yards	10-92	4-30
Time of possession	32:52	27:08

Attendance—55,971. No-shows—3,029.

INDIVIDUAL STATISTICS

Rushing—Atlanta, Riggs 25-80, Moroski 3-16, Hodge 1-8, Stamps 1-1, Bartkowski 1-minus 2; Pittsburgh, Pollard 14-111, Abercrombie 12-35, Corley 2-10, Erenberg 3-9, Veals 2-6, Gillespie 1-2, Malone 1-minus 4.

Passing—Atlanta, Bartkowski 19-23-1—167, Moroski 3-5-0—58; Pittsburgh, Malone 11-21-2—162, Campbell 0-1-0—0.

Receiving—Atlanta, Riggs 6-42, Bailey 4-61, Stamps 3-44, C. Benson 3-34, Hodge 3-28, Cox 3-16; Pittsburgh,

— 192 —

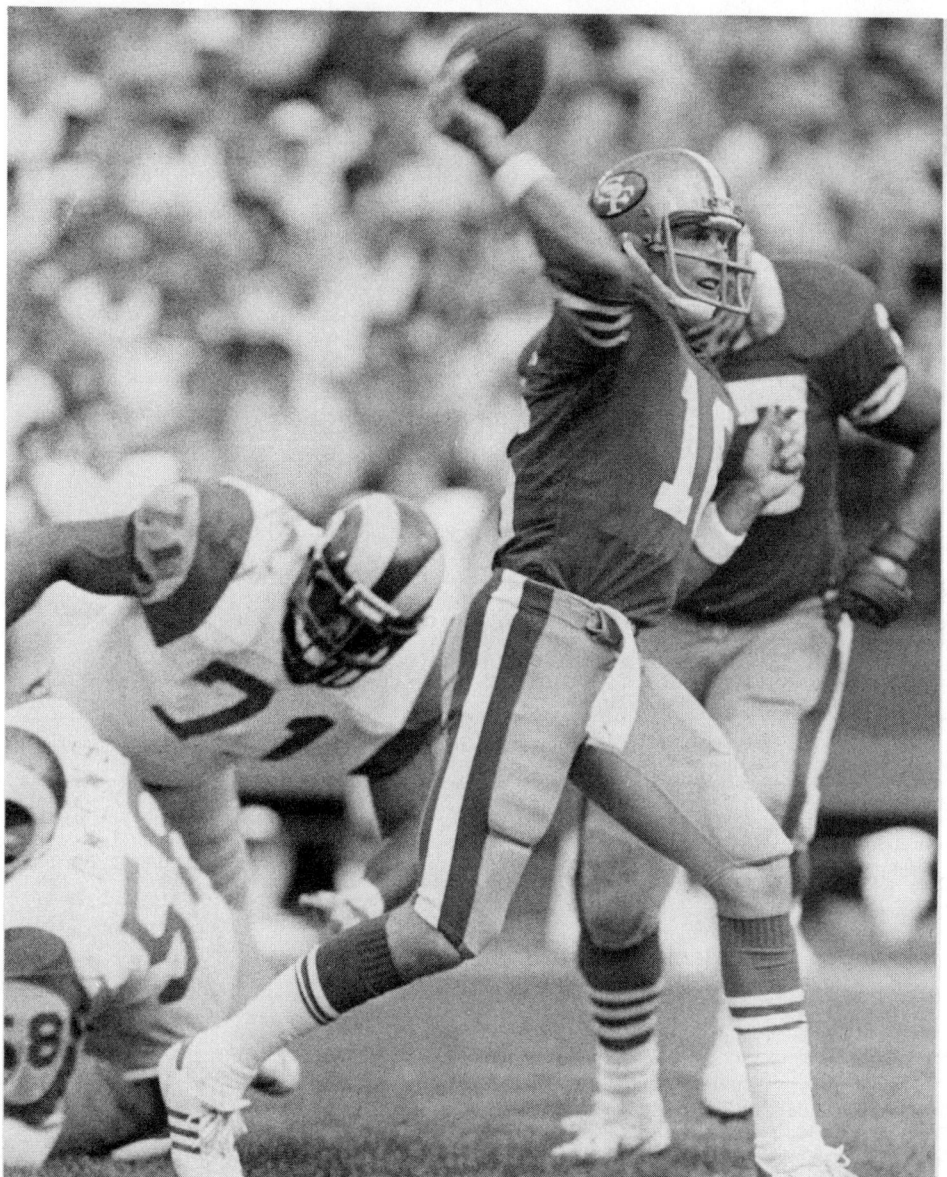

Joe Montana's three touchdown passes led the 49ers in their 33-0 rout of the Los Angeles Rams in Week 9.

Stallworth 3-62, Erenberg 3-24, Thompson 2-37, D. Nelson 1-19, Pollard 1-18, Abercrombie 1-2.

Kickoff Returns—Atlanta, Stamps 5-149.

Punt Returns—Atlanta, Curran 4-9; Pittsburgh, Lipps 5-85.

Interceptions—Atlanta, Johnson 2-37; Pittsburgh, Woodruff 1-0.

Punting—Atlanta, Giacomarro 8-41.0; Pittsburgh, Colquitt 5-38.2.

Field Goals—Atlanta, Luckhurst 1-2 (missed: 54); Pittsburgh, none attempted.

Sacks—Atlanta, J. Jackson, Pitts; Pittsburgh, Goodman, Hinkle, Merriweather, E. Nelson.

Cardinals-Eagles

SUNDAY, OCTOBER 28

SCORE BY PERIODS

St. Louis	0	17	7	10—34
Philadelphia	7	7	0	0—14

SCORING

Philadelphia—Kab 2 pass from Jaworski (McFadden kick), 12:12 1st.

St. Louis—Mitchell 1 run (O'Donoghue kick), 2:09 2nd.

Philadelphia—Quick 90 pass from Jaworski (McFadden kick), 3:19 2nd.

St. Louis—Field goal O'Donoghue 28, 8:50 2nd.
St. Louis—Tilley 8 pass from Lomax (O'Donoghue kick), 9:59 2nd.
St. Louis—Marsh 24 pass from Lomax (O'Donoghue kick), 5:22 3rd.
St. Louis—Mitchell 1 run (O'Donoghue kick), 4:32 4th.
St. Louis—Field goal O'Donoghue 47, 11:22 4th.

TEAM STATISTICS

	St. Louis	Philadelphia
First downs	23	15
Rushes-Yards	40-156	13-47
Passing yards	271	290
Sacked-Yards lost	2-15	6-56
Return yards	106	139
Passes	20-26-1	23-42-3
Punts	4-27.8	3-49.3
Fumbles-Lost	0-0	2-1
Penalties-Yards	5-35	4-45
Time of possession	36:03	23:57

Attendance—54,310. No-shows—7,872.

INDIVIDUAL STATISTICS

Rushing—St. Louis, Anderson 18-75, Ferrell 3-33, Lomax 4-25, Mitchell 9-21, Harrell 2-2, Love 4-0; Philadelphia, Montgomery 10-43, Oliver 2-2, Haddix 1-2.

Passing—St. Louis, Lomax 20-26-1—286. Philadelphia, Jaworski 22-38-3—340. Pisarcik 1-4-0—6.

Receiving—St. Louis, Anderson 7-75, Green 3-64, Marsh 3-85, Tilley 3-32, Mitchell 1-16, Ferrell 1-9, Harrell 1-3, LaFleur 1-2; Philadelphia, Quick 6-170, Montgomery 3-43, Haddix 6-33, Spagnola 2-26, Hoover 1-44, Kab 1-2, Woodruff 1-14, Oliver 3-14.

Kickoff Returns—St. Louis, Harrell 2-46, Mitchell 1-25; Philadelphia, Cooper 4-101, Everett 1-8.

Punt Returns—St. Louis, Mitchell 2-21; Philadelphia, Cooper 1-7.

Interceptions—St. Louis, Washington 1-14, Perrin 1-0, W. Smith 1-0; Philadelphia, Hopkins 1-33.

Punting—St. Louis, Birdsong 4-27.8; Philadelphia, Horan 3-49.3.

Field Goals—St. Louis, O'Donoghue 2-2; Philadelphia, none attempted.

Sacks—St. Louis, Greer 2, Galloway 1½, Mays, Nelson, Duda ½; Philadelphia, Clarke, Harrison.

49ers-Rams
SUNDAY, OCTOBER 28
SCORE BY PERIODS

San Francisco	3	16	7	7—33
Los Angeles Rams	0	0	0	0— 0

SCORING

San Francisco—Field goal Wersching 46, 4:38 1st.
San Francisco—Field goal Wersching 46, 7:43 2nd.
San Francisco—Craig 64 pass from Montana (pass failed), 10:30 2nd.
San Francisco—Solomon 6 pass from Montana (Wersching kick), 12:22 2nd.
San Francisco—Craig 6 run (Wersching kick), 11:49 3rd.
San Francisco—D. Clark 44 pass from Montana (Wersching kick), 7:58 4th.

TEAM STATISTICS

	San Francisco	Los Angeles
First downs	23	12
Rushes-Yards	39-111	19-72
Passing yards	361	134
Sacked-Yards lost	2-15	5-46
Return yards	35	123
Passes	22-32-0	14-30-2
Punts	3-38.0	6-39.8
Fumbles-Lost	2-2	5-3
Penalties-Yards	6-41	3-25
Time of possession	35:26	24:34

Attendance—65,481. No-shows—3,459.

INDIVIDUAL STATISTICS

Rushing—San Francisco, Tyler 13-27, Harmon 5-25, Craig 10-24, Ring 4-16, Montana 6-11, Solomon 1-8; Los Angeles, Dickerson 13-38, Kemp 4-27, Ellard 1-5, Redden 1-2.

Passing—San Francisco, Montana 21-31-0—365, Cavanaugh 1-1-0—11; Los Angeles, Kemp 14-30-2—180.

Receiving—San Francisco, Solomon 6-94, D. Clark 4-90, Nehemiah 3-48, Cooper 3-29, Craig 2-83, Tyler 2-17, Frank 2-15; Los Angeles, Ellard 4-94, Drew Hill 4-31, Brown 2-26, Dickerson 3-19, Guman 1-10.

Kickoff Returns—San Francisco, Harmon 1-13; Los Angeles, Drew Hill 3-66, Redden 3-51.

Punt Returns—San Francisco, McLemore 1-22; Los Angeles, Ellard 1-6.

Interceptions—San Francisco, Lott 1-0, Wright 1-0.

Punting—San Francisco, Runager 3-38.0; Los Angeles, Misko 6-39.8.

Field Goals—San Francisco, Wersching 2-2; Los Angeles, none attempted.

Sacks—San Francisco, Board 2, Carter 2, Stuckey; Los Angeles, Green, Harris ½, Youngblood ½.

Seahawks-Chargers
MONDAY, OCTOBER 29
SCORE BY PERIODS

Seattle	7	10	7	0—24
San Diego	0	0	0	0— 0

SCORING

Seattle—Largent 11 pass from Krieg (Johnson kick), 11:44 1st.
Seattle—Field goal Johnson 42, 5:52 2nd.
Seattle—Largent 13 pass from Krieg (Johnson kick), 14:23 2nd.
Seattle—Largent 16 pass from Krieg (Johnson kick), 3:48 3nd.

TEAM STATISTICS

	Seattle	San Diego
First downs	18	16
Rushes-Yards	33-81	23-48
Passing yards	274	153
Sacked-Yards lost	1-8	6-47
Return yards	111	105
Passes	23-29-1	24-40-3
Punts	5-37.6	6-43.3
Fumbles-Lost	2-2	4-1
Penalties-Yards	8-59	2-10
Time of possession	29:41	30:19

Attendance—53,974. No-shows—5,805.

INDIVIDUAL STATISTICS

Rushing—Seattle, F. Harris 3-3, Morris 9-22, Hughes 10-36, Dixon 9-23, Krieg 2-minus 3; San Diego, Jackson 18-38, James 4-10, Fouts 1-0.

Passing—Seattle, Krieg 23-29-1—282; San Diego, Fouts 24-39-2—200, James 0-1-1—0.

Receiving—Seattle, Morris 2-8, Turner 6-92, Walker 4-73, Largent 4-51, Hughes 4-10, Castor 2-15, Doornink 1-32; San Diego, Sievers 1-7, Egloff 2-26, James 7-46, Joiner 3-33, Jackson 4-13, Bendross 4-48, Duckworth 2-18, Morris 1-9.

Kickoff Returns—Seattle, Hughes 1-38; San Diego, James 5-80.

Punt Returns—Seattle, Easley 4-40; San Diego, James 1-4.

Interceptions—Seattle, Easley 3-33; San Diego, Smith 1-21.

Punting—Seattle, West 5-37.6; San Diego, Buford 6-43.3.

Field Goals—Seattle, Johnson 1-1; San Diego, none attempted.

Sacks—Seattle, Green 2, Nash, Moyer, Fanning, F. Young; San Diego, Ferguson.

TENTH WEEK

Sunday, November 4

Chicago 17, L.A. Raiders 6 at Chi.
Cleveland 13, Buffalo 10 at Buff.
Denver 26, New England 19 at Den.
Green Bay 23, New Orleans 13 at N.O.
L.A. Rams 16, St. Louis 13 at St. L.
Miami 31, N.Y. Jets 17 at N.Y.
Minnesota 27, Tampa Bay 24 at Minn.
N.Y. Giants 19, Dallas 7 at Dall.
Philadelphia 23, Detroit 23 (OT) at Det.
Pittsburgh 35, Houston 7 at Pitts.
San Diego 38, Indianapolis 10 at Ind.
San Francisco 23, Cincinnati 17 at S.F.
Seattle 45, Kansas City 0 at Sea.

Monday, November 5

Washington 27, Atlanta 14 at Wash.

Like a fine wine, placekicker Jan Stenerud seems to get better with age. The latest proof came when Stenerud booted a 53-yard field goal with two seconds left to give the Minnesota Vikings a 27-24 victory over division-rival Tampa Bay. And Stenerud, the oldest player in the National Football League, didn't just barely eke his game-winning kick over the crossbar.

"He would have made it from 60 yards," said holder Greg Coleman, the Vikings' punter. Tampa Bay nose tackle David Logan was even more impressed. "How old is that guy anyway, 43?" wondered Logan. "I didn't know he had 53 yards in him."

Stenerud actually was 40 years old, three weeks away from his 41st birthday. Logan is not the only person in the NFL to underestimate the strength of Stenerud's leg. His two previous NFL employers also made that mistake.

Stenerud broke into pro football with the Kansas City Chiefs of the old American Football League in 1967. In his first season, he led that league in both field goals made and field goals attempted. Stenerud spent 13 years with the Chiefs and helped Kansas City to two Super Bowl appearances. But prior to the 1980 season, the Chiefs figured the 36-year-old Stenerud was washed up in pro ball. They released him and handed the job to a free-agent kicker, Nick Lowery, who already had been cut by four other NFL clubs.

Green Bay signed Stenerud with four games left in the '80 season, and he spent the next three years with the Packers. Late in the 1983 season, Stenerud kicked the 336th field goal of his career to break George Blanda's NFL record. Stenerud finished the '83 season with 1,523 points in his 17-year professional career, good for third place on the all-time list. Still, after the season the Packers gave up on Stenerud—trading him to Minnesota for a seventh-round draft pick—and decided to go with Eddie Garcia as their placekicker. Garcia had played only 12 games in a two-year NFL career.

Stenerud brought consistency to Minnesota, hitting on 17 of 19 field goal attempts with five- and four-field goal performances through the season's first 10 weeks.

"Hey, let's go for it now," Stenerud recalled telling 38-year-old Minnesota Coach Les Steckel when the coach wanted to run one more play at the Bucs' 36-yard line before trying a field goal. Steckel complied and benefited from listening to an elder.

Week 10 was not so enjoyable for some other placekickers, however.

Detroit's Eddie Murray, who had hit successfully on three attempts during regulation, missed a 21-yard attempt in overtime and the Lions had to settle for a 23-23 tie with Philadelphia. Murray, who had hit nine in a row before the miss, bounced his kick off the right goal post after the Lions, taking possession of the ball at the start of overtime, drove from their own 41-yard line to the Eagles' 3. Philadelphia rookie placekicker Paul McFadden also had three field goals in the game, including a 40-yarder with three seconds left that sent the game into overtime.

The tie game was the only one played in the NFL during the '84 season and the eighth since the league instituted overtime play in 1974.

In St. Louis, defensive end Jack Youngblood, who played one of the best games of his 14-year NFL career, blocked a 48-yard field goal attempt by Cardinal kicker Neil O'Donoghue on the final play of the game to give Los Angeles a 16-13 victory. Before the block, Youngblood had three of the Rams' six quarterback sacks and numerous tackles as St. Louis saw its four-game winning streak snapped. The Cardinals, featuring the NFC's top-rated offense, managed just 69 yards rushing against Los Angeles.

The Rams' rushing attack, on the other hand, was devastating. Eric Dickerson carried for 49 yards on the game's second play, had 107 yards after the first quarter, 152 at the half and finished with 208 yards on 21 carries. Jeff Kemp threw for only 90 net passing yards, but 52 came on a touchdown pass to Ron Brown for the only L.A. touchdown.

The New York Giants also managed only one touchdown, but still escaped with a 19-7 victory over Dallas. Ali Haji-Sheikh, who had struggled for much of the season, booted four field goals for the Giants' other points. The triumph was the Giants' second against the Cowboys in the '84 season, marking the first time they had swept their NFC Eastern Division rival in a season series since 1963. It also was the Giants' first win at Texas Stadium in 10 years.

Another game in which both teams scored

only one touchdown was Cleveland's 13-10 win over Buffalo. Ironically, fumble returns accounted for both scores, with linebacker Chris Keating returning one 34 yards in the second period for the Bills and Earnest Byner going 55 yards in the final quarter for the Browns. Byner's return, his first NFL touchdown, came after Willis Adams fumbled a pass from Browns' quarterback Paul McDonald after being hit by linebacker Lawrence Johnson. The ball popped up in the air and Byner, a running back, picked it off while at full speed and scored the game-winning touchdown. The hard-luck Bills dropped to 0-10 for the season.

The Houston Oilers also remained winless through 10 games after dropping a 35-7 game at Pittsburgh. Steelers quarterback Mark Malone, starting his third game in place of the injured David Woodley, threw for three touchdowns and ran for another as Pittsburgh won for the third time with him as the starter. Wide receiver John Stallworth was on the receiving end of each of Malone's scoring tosses, the first time in his 11-year career he had caught three touchdown passes in a game. Linebacker Bryan Hinkle recovered two fumbles, setting up a Steeler touchdown with the first and scoring himself with the second, as the Oilers went down to their NFL-record 23rd straight road loss.

Chicago, Denver and Seattle all continued their winning ways, thanks to great defense.

The Bears upended the Los Angeles Raiders, 17-6, by forcing five Raider turnovers and getting nine quarterback sacks. Defensive end Richard Dent, the NFC leader in sacks, had half of the Bears' total. Incredibly, the nine sacks gave Chicago 20 in its last two games. The six Raider points marked the sixth time in 10 games that the Bear defense had held its opponent to fewer than 10 points.

At Denver, linebacker Steve Busick stripped New England's Mosi Tatupu of the ball and safety Dennis Smith returned the fumble 64 yards for the winning touchdown with 1:45 left in the Broncos' 26-19 come-from-behind win over the Patriots. The touchdown was the seventh scored by the Denver defense in 10 games.

The Patriots, who had been making a habit of coming from behind to win in earlier games, had the tables turned as the Broncos scored two touchdowns in the final four minutes, the other coming on a five-yard pass from John Elway to Butch Johnson. New England almost got the tying touchdown late in the game but Tony Eason's pass with 21 seconds remaining was intercepted by Steve Foley at the Broncos' 5-yard line.

At Seattle, the opportunistic Seahawks' defense put on a memorable performance in a 45-0 drubbing of division-rival Kansas City. Seahawk defenders intercepted six passes and returned an NFL-record four for touchdowns.

Dave Brown returned two interceptions for touchdowns to tie a record while Seattle's 330 yards in interception return yardage set another NFL mark. Keith Simpson and Kenny Easley also returned interceptions for scores. The four touchdowns gave Seattle's defense a total of eight in its first 10 games.

The shutout—Seattle's largest margin of victory ever—was the Seahawks' second in a row and third in 10 games. The Chiefs' offense ran 76 offensive plays compared to Seattle's 56, but a 28-point second-quarter explosion blew the game open.

The Miami Dolphins found themselves trailing at halftime for the first time all season, but rallied in the second half to defeat the New York Jets, 31-17, and remain unbeaten. The Dolphins scored the game's final 17 points to run their record to 10-0.

The Jets' defense harrassed quarterback Dan Marino throughout the first half, holding him to just nine completions in 21 attempts for 150 yards as New York grabbed a 10-7 lead at the intermission. The Jets still held the lead, 17-14, midway through the final quarter before the Dolphins rallied. Marino capped a four-play, 80-yard drive with a 47-yard scoring pass to Mark Clayton with 7:45 left for a 21-17 lead. Miami then scored 10 more points to open up a four-game lead over the Jets and Patriots in the AFC Eastern Division.

San Francisco remained the dominant team in the National Conference after a 23-17 verdict over Cincinnati. Quarterback Joe Montana, who was intercepted four times, threw a four-yard scoring pass to Freddie Solomon with 1:39 left to clinch the victory. The Bengals' offense was held to just five first downs and no points in the second half after Cincinnati held a 17-7 lead at the half.

The game was the first between the teams since their 1982 meeting in Super Bowl XVI, a game San Francisco won, 26-21. Ironically, the 49ers compiled 26 first downs to 21 for the Bengals in their 1984 encounter.

Dan Fouts threw three touchdown passes and Charlie Joiner caught nine passes for 119 yards and one touchdown as San Diego defeated Indianapolis, 38-10. The Chargers' defense intercepted Colts quarterback Mark Herrmann four times as Don Coryell won the 100th regular-season game of his 12-year NFL coaching career. Coryell is the only coach to have won 100 games in both college and pro football.

The Green Bay Packers won for the second straight week after losing seven in a row earlier in the season with a 23-13 victory at New Orleans. Tight end Paul Coffman hauled in two touchdown passes from Lynn Dickey and Al Del Greco kicked three field goals to lead the Pack. Green Bay scored 10 unanswered points in the third period to snap a 10-10 halftime tie.

The Washington Redskins had little trouble in disposing of Atlanta, 27-14, in the Monday

	Los Angeles	Chicago
First downs	12	11
Rushes-Yards	23-75	47-175
Passing yards	106	84
Sacked-Yards lost	9-58	1-11
Return yards	116	130
Passes	12-28-3	7-16-1
Punts	5-44.4	7-41.1
Fumbles-Lost	4-2	2-0
Penalties-Yards	1-5	4-40
Time of possession	26:07	33:53

Attendance—59,858. No-shows—5,932.

INDIVIDUAL STATISTICS

Rushing—Los Angeles, Wilson 1-3, Allen 15-42, King 3-20, Humm 1-minus 2, Hawkins 3-12; Chicago, Suhey 8-17, Payton 27-111, McMahon 3-10, C. Thomas 5-23, Fuller 4-14.

Passing—Los Angeles, Wilson 7-19-2—70, Humm 4-7-1—56, Allen 1-2-0—38; Chicago, McMahon 3-11-1—68, Fuller 4-5-0—27.

Receiving—Los Angeles, Allen 4-53, Christensen 5-61, Williams 3-50; Chicago, Gault 1-50, Suhey 1-11, Payton 3-15, Moorehead 2-19.

Kickoff Returns—Los Angeles, Williams 1-33, Montgomery 1-16, Pruitt 1-3; Chicago, Gentry 2-36.

Punt Returns—Los Angeles, Pruitt 3-34; Chicago, Fisher 4-42.

Interceptions—Los Angeles, McElroy 1-31; Chicago, Fencik 2-19, Frazier 1-33.

Punting—Los Angeles, Guy 5-44.4; Chicago, Finzer 7-41.1.

Field Goals—Los Angeles, Bahr 2-2; Chicago, B. Thomas 1-1.

Sacks—Los Angeles, Long ½, Nelson ½; Chicago, Dent 4½, Wilson 1½, Harris, Hartenstine, Singletary.

Veteran Pittsburgh wide receiver John Stallworth caught three touchdown passes from Mark Malone in the Steelers' 35-7 triumph over Houston in Week 10.

night game at RFK Stadium. John Riggins rushed for 100 yards and two touchdowns while quarterback Joe Theismann threw one scoring pass and ran for another touchdown. The Falcons tied the game at 14-14 midway through the third quarter on Gerald Riggs' second touchdown of the night before two more Washington touchdowns put the game away. The win moved the Redskins into a four-way tie for first place in the NFC Eastern Division while the Falcons fell to the cellar of the NFC West.

Raiders-Bears

SUNDAY, NOVEMBER 4

SCORE BY PERIODS

Los Angeles Raiders	0	3	3	0— 6
Chicago	7	7	0	3—17

SCORING

Chicago—Payton 18 run (B. Thomas kick), 8:21 1st.
Chicago—Payton 8 run (B. Thomas kick), 2:28 2nd.
Los Angeles—Field goal Bahr 44, 14:31 2nd.
Los Angeles—Field goal Bahr 40, 5:57 3rd.
Chicago—Field goal B. Thomas 29, 13:39 4th.

Browns-Bills

SUNDAY, NOVEMBER 4

SCORE BY PERIODS

Cleveland	3	3	0	7—13
Buffalo	0	7	3	0—10

SCORING

Cleveland—Field goal Bahr 28, 11:10 1st.
Buffalo—Keating 34 fumble return (Nelson kick), 13:13 2nd.
Cleveland—Field goal Bahr 36, 14:55 2nd.
Buffalo—Field goal Nelson 42, 7:18 3rd.
Cleveland—Byner 55 fumble return (Bahr kick), 7:27 4th.

TEAM STATISTICS

	Cleveland	Buffalo
First downs	16	13
Rushes-Yards	43-211	29-106
Passing yards	73	77
Sacked-Yards lost	2-13	3-33
Return yards	76	83
Passes	7-18-1	16-24-2
Punts	3-40.3	4-40.5
Fumbles-Lost	4-2	1-0
Penalties-Yards	8-95	7-58
Time of possession	28:39	31:21

Attendance—33,343. No-shows—2,517.

INDIVIDUAL STATISTICS

Rushing—Cleveland, Green 29-156, McDonald 5-minus 3, Byner 9-58; Buffalo, Moore 1-1, Bell 20-82, Neal 5-17, V. Williams 2-8, Ferguson 1-minus 2.

Passing—Cleveland, McDonald 7-18-1—86; Buffalo, Ferguson 16-24-2—110.

Receiving—Cleveland, Newsome 4-53, Harris 2-20, Adams 1-13; Buffalo, Moore 1-7, Bell 6-27, White 1-8, Franklin 1-9, Hunter 3-14, Dawkins 3-38, Riddick 1-7.

Kickoff Returns—Cleveland, Byner 1-25, B. Davis 1-20; Buffalo, V. Williams 3-56, Wilson 1-0.

Punt Returns—Cleveland, Brennan 2-15; Buffalo, Wilson 1-27.

Interceptions—Cleveland, Gross 1-16, Rockins 1-0; Buffalo, Carpenter 1-0.

Punting—Cleveland, Cox 3-40.3; Buffalo, Kidd 4-40.5.

Field Goals—Cleveland, Bahr 2-2; Buffalo, Nelson 1-2 (missed: 37).

Sacks—Cleveland, Hairston 2, Matthews; Buffalo, Smerlas, Talley.

Patriots-Broncos
SUNDAY, NOVEMBER 4
SCORE BY PERIODS

New England	3	3	7	6—19
Denver	0	6	6	14—26

SCORING

New England—Field goal Franklin 30, 14:09 1st.
New England—Field goal Franklin 40, 7:33 2nd.
Denver—Watson 35 pass from Elway (kick failed), 12:01 2nd.
New England—Weathers 15 pass from Eason (Franklin kick), 6:04 3rd.
Denver—Johnson 17 pass from Elway (kick failed), 13:36 3rd.
New England—Field goal Franklin 47, 2:04 4th.
New England—Field goal Franklin 19, 6:36 4th.
Denver—Johnson 5 pass from Elway (Karlis kick), 10:57 4th.
Denver—D. Smith 64 fumble return (Karlis kick), 13:15 4th.

TEAM STATISTICS

	New England	Denver
First downs	25	18
Rushes-Yards	36-195	18-28
Passing yards	289	291
Sacked-Yards lost	4-24	3-24
Return yards	139	134
Passes	21-38-1	26-40-1
Punts	4-43.0	7-44.7
Fumbles-Lost	2-2	2-0
Penalties-Yards	4-35	4-48
Time of possession	31:25	28:35

Attendance—74,908. No-shows—192.

INDIVIDUAL STATISTICS

Rushing—New England, C. James 20-120, Tatupu 8-37, Collins 6-20, Eason 2-18; Denver, Winder 14-25, Elway 4-3.

Passing—New England, Eason 21-38-1—313; Denver, Elway 26-40-1—315.

Receiving—New England, Morgan 8-122, Hawthorne 2-45, Ramsey 2-42, Starring 1-25, Weathers 2-26, Jones 2-24, C. James 3-15, Dawson 1-14; Denver, Johnson 9-156, Watson 8-134, Kay 1-21, Winder 5-7, Summers 1-2, Sawyer 2-minus 5.

Kickoff Returns—New England, Collins 3-104; Denver, Thomas 3-57, Lang 2-45, A. Smith 1-2.

Punt Returns—New England, Starring 4-28, Weathers 1-7; Denver, Thomas 2-7.

Interceptions—New England, Clayborn 1-0; Denver, Foley 1-13.

Punting—New England, Camarillo 4-43.0; Denver, Norman 7-44.7.

Field Goals—New England, Franklin 4-5 (missed: 36); Denver, none attempted.

Sacks—New England, Blackmon, Rembert, Tippett; Denver, Townsend 2, Carter, Jones ½, Ryan ½.

Packers-Saints
SUNDAY, NOVEMBER 4
SCORE BY PERIODS

Green Bay	0	10	10	3—23
New Orleans	7	3	0	3—13

SCORING

New Orleans—W. Wilson 1 run (Andersen kick), 12:51 1st.
Green Bay—Field goal Del Greco 41, 1:45 2nd.
Green Bay—Coffman 33 pass from Dickey (Del Greco kick), 7:16 2nd.
New Orleans—Field goal Andersen 35, 14:56 2nd.
Green Bay—Coffman 5 pass from Dickey (Del Greco kick), 6:33 3rd.
Green Bay—Field goal Del Greco 34, 13:06 3rd.
New Orleans—Field goal Andersen 46, 6:26 4th.
Green Bay—Field goal Del Greco 41, 13:04 4th.

TEAM STATISTICS

	Green Bay	New Orleans
First downs	20	23
Rushes-Yards	36-207	34-181
Passing yards	166	141
Sacked-Yards lost	1-7	2-22
Return yards	101	115
Passes	15-28-0	18-32-2
Punts	5-39.8	4-49.3
Fumbles-Lost	1-0	1-1
Penalties-Yards	12-98	6-31
Time of possession	29:05	30:55

Attendance—57,426. No-shows—8,054.

INDIVIDUAL STATISTICS

Rushing—Green Bay, Ellis 10-86, Ivery 16-78, Lofton 1-26, Clark 8-19, Dickey 1-minus 2; New Orleans, Gajan 9-54, W. Wilson 5-53, G. Rogers 10-44, Campbell 7-21, Todd 2-8, Anthony 1-1.

Passing—Green Bay, Dickey 15-28-0—173; New Orleans, Todd 18-32-2—163.

Receiving—Green Bay, Coffman 4-51, Lofton 3-63, Ellis 3-15, Clark 2-12, Epps 1-16, Jefferson 1-9, Ivery 1-7; New Orleans, Scott 3-28, Groth 3-26, Gajan 3-19, Anthony 2-37, Young 2-16, W. Wilson 2-12, Tice 1-11, Brenner 1-9, G. Rogers 1-5.

Kickoff Returns—Green Bay, Epps 2-42, Rodgers 1-13; New Orleans, Anthony 4-49, Duckett 2-41.

Punt Returns—Green Bay, Flynn 3-30; New Orleans, Fields 3-25.

Interceptions—Green Bay, Flynn 1-16, McCoy 1-0.

Punting—Green Bay, Scribner 5-39.8; New Orleans, Hansen 4-49.3.

Field Goals—Green Bay, Del Greco 3-3; New Orleans, Andersen 2-2.

Sacks—Green Bay, Brown, T. Jones; New Orleans, Jackson.

Rams-Cardinals
SUNDAY, NOVEMBER 4
SCORE BY PERIODS

Los Angeles Rams	3	0	10	3—16
St. Louis	3	10	0	0—13

SCORING

Los Angeles—Field goal Lansford 33, 2:43 1st.
St. Louis—Field goal O'Donoghue 49, 13:36 1st.
St. Louis—Green 53 pass from Lomax (O'Donoghue kick), 1:09 2nd.
St. Louis—Field goal O'Donoghue 43, 13:13 2nd.
Los Angeles—Brown 52 pass from Kemp (Lansford kick), 2:43 3rd.
Los Angeles—Field goal Lansford 27, 13:47 3rd.
Los Angeles—Field goal Lansford 32, 6:06 4th.

TEAM STATISTICS

	Los Angeles	St. Louis
First downs	11	20
Rushes-Yards	28-201	22-69
Passing yards	115	293
Sacked-Yards lost	3-30	6-48
Return yards	115	130
Passes	5-14-0	34-52-2
Punts	6-33.8	3-47.3
Fumbles-Lost	1-1	3-2

— 198 —

	Los Angeles	St. Louis
Penalties-Yards	4-35	12-92
Time of possession	22:10	37:50
Attendance—50,950. No-shows—567.		

INDIVIDUAL STATISTICS

Rushing—Los Angeles, Dickerson 21-208, Redden 2-7, Kemp 2-minus 4, Ellard 1-minus 14, Crutchfield 2-4; St. Louis, Love 1-5, Anderson 16-33, Ferrell 2-8, Mitchell 1-5, Lomax 2-18.

Passing—Los Angeles, Kemp 5-14-0—90; St. Louis, Lomax 34-52-2—341.

Receiving—Los Angeles, Ellard 2-28, Brown 2-57, Guman 1-5; St. Louis, Mitchell 2-14, Ferrell 5-33, Anderson 11-74, Green 5-105, Harrell 3-16, Marsh 3-24, Tilley 2-41, Mack 2-24, Love 1-10.

Kickoff Returns—Los Angeles, Redden 2-45, Drew Hill 2-33; St. Louis, Mitchell 4-103, Pittman 1-24.

Punt Returns—Los Angeles, Ellard 1-minus 3; St. Louis, Mitchell 3-3.

Interceptions—Los Angeles, Collins 1-40, Cromwell 1-0.

Punting—Los Angeles, Misko 6-33.8; St. Louis, Birdsong 3-47.3.

Field Goals—Los Angeles, Lansford 3-4 (missed: 51); St. Louis, O'Donoghue 2-3 (missed: 48).

Sacks—Los Angeles, Youngblood 3, Andrews, DeJurnett, Doss; St. Louis, Greer, Holloway, Junior.

Dolphins-Jets
SUNDAY, NOVEMBER 4
SCORE BY PERIODS

Miami	7	0	7	17—31
New York Jets	7	3	0	7—17

SCORING

Miami—Moore 37 pass from Marino (von Schamann kick), 7:22 1st.

New York—Walker 33 pass from Ryan (Leahy kick), 9:57 1st.

New York—Field goal Leahy 32, 13:46 2nd.

Miami—Bennett 3 run (von Schamann kick), 10:39 3rd.

New York—McNeil 6 run (Leahy kick), 5:29 4th.

Miami—Clayton 47 pass from Marino (von Schamann kick), 7:15 4th.

Miami—Field goal von Schamann 30, 11:04 4th.

Miami—P. Johnson 2 run (von Schamann kick), 13:03 4th.

TEAM STATISTICS

	Miami	New York
First downs	24	14
Rushes-Yards	28-100	29-200
Passing yards	407	86
Sacked-Yards lost	2-15	5-39
Return yards	54	133
Passes	23-42-2	12-28-2
Punts	3-48.3	8-39.3
Fumbles-Lost	3-2	0-0
Penalties-Yards	8-60	8-80
Time of possession	30:46	29:14
Attendance—72,655. No-shows—4,236.		

INDIVIDUAL STATISTICS

Rushing—Miami, Nathan 8-43, Bennett 9-45, Marino 4-4, Carter 3-5, P. Johnson 4-3; New York, McNeil 20-132, Hector 7-28, Paige 1-24, Ryan 1-16.

Passing—Miami, Marino 23-42-2—422; New York, Ryan 12-28-2—125.

Receiving—Miami, Duper 7-155, Moore 5-105, Nathan 5-60, Clayton 2-61, D. Johnson 2-27, Hardy 2-14; New York, Walker 4-60, McNeil 4-29, Shuler 2-18, Jones 1-11, Dennison 1-7.

Kickoff Returns—Miami, Walker 2-37; New York, Springs 3-61, Humphery 2-37.

Punt Returns—Miami, Walker 2-4, Kozlowski 1-6; New York, Springs 1-2.

Interceptions—Miami, Duhe 1-7, Lankford 1-0; New York, Ray 1-26, Carter 1-7.

Punting—Miami, Roby 3-48.3; New York, Ramsey 8-39.3.

Field Goals—Miami, von Schamann 1-2 (missed: 44); New York, Leahy 1-2 (missed: 25).

Sacks—Miami, Bowser 2, Betters, Bokamper, Thomas; New York, Bennett, Gastineau.

Buccaneers-Vikings
SUNDAY, NOVEMBER 4
SCORE BY PERIODS

Tampa Bay	7	7	0	10—24
Minnesota	3	7	7	10—27

SCORING

Tampa Bay—Wilder 6 run (Ariri kick), 5:29 1st.

Minnesota—Field goal Stenerud 30, 11:45 1st.

Tampa Bay—Wilder 2 run (Ariri kick), 2:29 2nd.

Minnesota—Jordan 4 run (Stenerud kick), 9:59 2nd.

Minnesota—Nelson 5 run (Stenerud kick), 5:10 3rd.

Tampa Bay—Field goal Ariri 29, 3:19 4th.

Minnesota—Brown 3 pass from Wilson (Stenerud kick), 8:53 4th.

Tampa Bay—House 11 pass from DeBerg (Ariri kick), 13:57 4th.

Minnesota—Field goal Stenerud 53, 14:58 4th.

TEAM STATISTICS

	Tampa Bay	Minnesota
First downs	23	24
Rushes-Yards	32-153	34-144
Passing yards	183	218
Sacked-Yards lost	2-15	2-18
Return yards	166	132
Passes	17-36-1	24-36-2
Punts	4-44.5	2-42.0
Fumbles-Lost	3-1	0-0
Penalties-Yards	7-51	5-40
Time of possession	31:02	28:58
Attendance—54,949. No-shows—7,048.		

INDIVIDUAL STATISTICS

Rushing—Tampa Bay, Wilder 30-146, DeBerg 2-7; Minnesota, Brown 10-32, Wilson 3-6, Lewis 1-5, Nelson 5-32, Anderson 13-52, Jordan 1-4, Coleman 1-13.

Passing—Tampa Bay, DeBerg 17-36-1—198; Minnesota, Wilson 24-36-2—236.

Receiving—Tampa Bay, Dixon 3-45, Carter 2-25, Giles 2-16, J. Bell 1-26, Wilder 4-46, Armstrong 1-10, House 4-30; Minnesota, Brown 9-86, Anderson 1-5, Jones 4-50, Nelson 2-10, Jordan 5-43, White 1-23, Lewis 2-19.

Kickoff Returns—Tampa Bay, Morton 4-91, Bright 2-33; Minnesota, Nelson 5-112.

Punt Returns—Tampa Bay, Bright 1-12; Minnesota, Nelson 2-20.

Interceptions—Tampa Bay, Cotney 1-22, Castille 1-8; Minnesota, McNeill 1-0.

Punting—Tampa Bay, Garcia 4-44.5; Minnesota, Coleman 2-42.0.

Field Goals—Tampa Bay, Ariri 1-1; Minnesota, Stenerud 2-2.

Sacks—Tampa Bay, Selmon, Washington; Minnesota, Bess, Browner.

Giants-Cowboys
SUNDAY, NOVEMBER 4
SCORE BY PERIODS

New York Giants	6	0	7	6—19
Dallas	0	7	0	0— 7

SCORING

New York—Field goal Haji-Sheikh 40, 4:35 1st.

New York—Field goal Haji-Sheikh 38, 10:48 1st.

Dallas—Hill 30 pass from Hogeboom (Septien kick), 9:49 2nd.

New York—Manuel 9 pass from Simms (Haji-Sheikh kick), 11:48 3rd.
New York—Field goal Haji-Sheikh 23, 4:02 4th.
New York—Field goal Haji-Sheikh 27, 13:22 4th.

TEAM STATISTICS

	New York	Dallas
First downs	18	13
Rushes-Yards	37-122	28-116
Passing yards	227	140
Sacked-Yards lost	2-17	5-38
Return yards	108	143
Passes	16-37-1	14-31-2
Punts	7-38.6	10-40.1
Fumbles-Lost	1-1	2-1
Penalties-Yards	1-10	7-59
Time of possession	33:23	26:37

Attendance—60,235. No-shows—4,866.

INDIVIDUAL STATISTICS

Rushing—New York, Carpenter 24-77, Morris 12-47, Simms 1-minus 2; Dallas, Dorsett 13-78, Springs 9-23, Newsome 3-8, Donley 1-6, Hogeboom 2-1.

Passing—New York, Simms 16-37-1—244; Dallas, D. White 1-6-0—20, Hogeboom 13-25-2—158.

Receiving—New York, Manuel 5-102, Mowatt 5-80, Gray 3-39, Carpenter 2-18, Johnson 1-5; Dallas, Springs 7-71, Dorsett 4-48, Hill 1-30, Cosbie 1-23, Newsome 1-6.

Kickoff Returns—New York, McConkey 2-55; Dallas, McSwain 4-101, Allen 1-15.

Punt Returns—New York, McConkey 8-38; Dallas, Allen 2-27.

Interceptions—New York, Haynes 1-15, Kinard 1-0; Dallas, Thurman 1-0.

Punting—New York, Jennings 7-38.6; Dallas, Warren 10-40.1.

Field Goals—New York, Haji-Sheikh 4-4; Dallas, none attempted.

Sacks—New York, Marshall 2½, Martin, Merrill, Taylor ½; Dallas, R. White 1½, Bates ½.

Eagles-Lions
SUNDAY, NOVEMBER 4
SCORE BY PERIODS

Philadelphia	3	3	7	10	0—23
Detroit	7	10	0	6	0—23

SCORING

Detroit—J. Jones 4 pass from Danielson (Murray kick), 4:58 1st.
Philadelphia—Field goal McFadden 52, 12:43 1st.
Detroit—Danielson 22 pass from J. Jones (Murray kick), 2:55 2nd.
Detroit—Field goal Murray 32, 13:04 2nd.
Philadelphia—Field goal McFadden 51, 15:00 2nd.
Philadelphia—Quick 68 pass from Jaworski (McFadden kick), 2:57 3rd.
Detroit—Field goal Murray 33, 0:04 4th.
Philadelphia—Haddix 2 run (McFadden kick), 6:27 4th.
Detroit—Field goal Murray 18, 13:57 4th.
Philadelphia—Field goal McFadden 40, 14:57 4th.

TEAM STATISTICS

	Philadelphia	Detroit
First downs	18	25
Rushes-Yards	23-64	38-164
Passing yards	230	258
Sacked-Yards lost	4-24	8-66
Return yards	208	183
Passes	20-39-2	25-40-2
Punts	6-42.8	6-46.2
Fumbles-Lost	2-1	3-0
Penalties-Yards	5-45	4-20
Time of possession	32:44	42:16

Attendance—59,141. No-shows—8,342.

INDIVIDUAL STATISTICS

Rushing—Philadelphia, Montgomery 13-28, Oliver 7-28,

Haddix 3-8; Detroit, J. Jones 16-80, Jenkins 17-76, Black 1-4, Bussey 2-2, Danielson 2-2.

Passing—Philadelphia, Jaworski 20-39-2—254; Detroit, Danielson 23-38-2—275, J. Jones 2-2-0—49.

Receiving—Philadelphia, Montgomery 6-39, Quick 5-110, Spagnola 4-63, Oliver 2-7, Woodruff 1-14, Kab 1-13, Haddix 1-8; Detroit, Jenkins 8-128, Thompson 5-62, J. Jones 5-38, Chadwick 3-58, Danielson 1-22, Rubick 1-9, Nichols 1-7, Bussey 1-0.

Kickoff Returns—Philadelphia, Hayes 3-70, Waters 2-38, Cooper 1-28; Detroit, Jenkins 3-77, Hall 2-58, Martin 1-22.

Punt Returns—Philadelphia, Cooper 6-34; Detroit, Martin 2-15, Hall 1-11.

Interceptions—Philadelphia, Ellis 1-31, Foules 1-7; Detroit, Watkins 2-0.

Punting—Philadelphia, Horan 6-42.8; Detroit, Black 6-46.2.

Field Goals—Philadelphia, McFadden 3-3; Detroit, Murray 3-4 (missed: 21).

Sacks—Philadelphia, Darby 2, Harrison 2, Brown, Clarke, Griggs, Hopkins; Detroit, Gay, Green, J. Williams, Cofer ½, Fantetti ½.

Oilers-Steelers
SUNDAY, NOVEMBER 4
SCORE BY PERIODS

Houston	0	0	7	0— 7
Pittsburgh	7	14	14	0—35

SCORING

Pittsburgh—Stallworth 43 pass from Malone (Anderson kick), 3:17 1st.
Pittsburgh—Malone 13 run (Anderson kick), 4:29 2nd.
Pittsburgh—Stallworth 18 pass from Malone (Anderson kick), 9:58 2nd.
Pittsburgh—Stallworth 39 pass from Malone (Anderson kick), 6:05 3rd.
Pittsburgh—Hinkle 21 fumble return (Anderson kick), 6:25 3rd.
Houston—J. Williams 5 pass from Luck (Cooper kick), 14:34 3rd.

TEAM STATISTICS

	Houston	Pittsburgh
First downs	17	17
Rushes-Yards	26-97	46-191
Passing yards	176	131
Sacked-Yards lost	5-48	1-8
Return yards	148	83
Passes	18-32-0	9-15-2
Punts	4-38.5	4-37.5
Fumbles-Lost	7-4	3-1
Penalties-Yards	5-30	5-47
Time of possession	28:04	31:56

Attendance—48,892. No-shows—10,108.

INDIVIDUAL STATISTICS

Rushing—Houston, Moriarty 12-30, Edwards 4-32, Moon 5-9, Luck 5-26; Pittsburgh, Erenberg 6-26, Pollard 13-33, Abercrombie 7-41, Lipps 1-4, Corley 7-47, Malone 2-23, Gillespie 3-2, Veals 5-21, Capers 1-minus 3, Campbell 1-minus 3.

Passing—Houston, Moon 10-20-0—133, Luck 8-12-0—91; Pittsburgh, Malone 9-14-1—139, Campbell 0-1-1-0.

Receiving—Houston, Dressel 4-34, Walls 1-12, J. Williams 3-24, Smith 5-78, Roaches 1-24, Moriarty 1-5, Moon 1-28, Edwards 1-8, Bryant 1-11; Pittsburgh, Erenberg 2-5, Stallworth 4-109, Abercrombie 1-7, Lipps 1-8, Capers 1-10.

Kickoff Returns—Houston, Roaches 5-134; Pittsburgh, Erenberg 2-31.

Punt Returns—Houston, Roaches 1-0; Pittsburgh, Lipps 4-52.

Interceptions—Houston, Lyday 1-12, Hartwig 1-2.

Punting—Houston, James 4-38.5; Pittsburgh, Colquitt 4-37.5.

Chicago's Walter Payton accounted for the game's only two touchdowns as the Bears upended the Los Angeles Raiders, 17-6, in Week 10.

Field Goals—Houston, Cooper 0-1 (missed: 43); Pittsburgh, none attempted.

Sacks—Houston, Stensrud; Pittsburgh, Hinkle 1½, Merriweather 1½, Cole, Willis.

Chargers-Colts
SUNDAY, NOVEMBER 4
SCORE BY PERIODS

San Diego	7	10	7	14—38
Indianapolis	0	7	3	0—10

SCORING

San Diego—Jackson 2 run (Benirschke kick), 13:11 1st.

San Diego—Field goal Benirschke 23, 0:03 2nd.

Indianapolis—Butler 74 pass from Herrmann (Allegre kick), 1:43 2nd.

San Diego—Joiner 7 pass from Fouts (Benirschke kick), 7:24 2nd.

San Diego—Morris 1 run (Benirschke kick), 5:07 3rd.

Indianapolis—Field goal Allegre 54, 11:17 3rd.

San Diego—Chandler 20 pass from Fouts (Benirschke kick), 2:48 4th.

San Diego—McGee 2 pass from Fouts (Benirschke kick), 13:04 4th.

TEAM STATISTICS

	San Diego	Indianapolis
First downs	24	13
Rushes-Yards	33-119	22-90
Passing yards	283	205
Sacked-Yards lost	0-0	2-17
Return yards	184	139
Passes	27-38-2	18-32-4
Punts	2-54.5	3-45.7
Fumbles-Lost	1-0	4-1
Penalties-Yards	8-50	5-35
Time of possession	35:28	24:32

Attendance—60,143. No-shows—527.

Rushing—San Diego, Jackson 23-71, Morris 2-0, McGee 6-45, James 1-1, Thomas 1-2; Indianapolis, McMillan 11-52, Dickey 8-26, Wonsley 2-15, Smith 1-minus 3.

Passing—San Diego, Fouts 27-38-2—283; Indianapolis, Herrmann 18-32-4—222.

Receiving—San Diego, Joiner 9-119, Bendross 3-44, Egloff 5-36, Chandler 4-42, Jackson 3-35, James 1-4, McGee 2-3; Indianapolis, Butler 3-94, Dickey 5-48, Porter 2-29, Wonsley 3-10, Young 1-minus 6, Bouza 2-38, Henry 1-7, McMillan 1-2.

Kickoff Returns—San Diego, Bird 2-15, McGee 1-22; Indianapolis, Smith 5-88, Kafentzis 2-19.

Punt Returns—San Diego, Bird 1-4; Indianapolis, Glasgow 1-11.

Interceptions—San Diego, Turner 1-43, King 1-37, Fox 1-36, Byrd 1-27; Indianapolis, Krauss 1-18, Davis 1-3.

Punting—San Diego, Buford 2-54.5; Indianapolis, Stark 3-45.7.

Field Goals—San Diego, Benirschke 1-1; Indianapolis, Allegre 1-2 (missed: 34).

Sacks—San Diego, Ehin, King.

Bengals-49ers
SUNDAY, NOVEMBER 4
SCORE BY PERIODS

Cincinnati	3	14	0	0—17
San Francisco	0	7	3	13—23

SCORING

Cincinnati—Field goal Breech 39, 13:55 1st.

San Francisco—Cooper 12 pass from Montana (Wersching kick), 2:53 2nd.

Cincinnati—Kinnebrew 6 run (Breech kick), 7:58 2nd.

Cincinnati—Collinsworth 7 pass from Anderson (Breech kick), 11:50 2nd.

San Francisco—Field goal Wersching 29, 6:06 3rd.

San Francisco—Field goal Wersching 35, 5:14 4th.

San Francisco—Field goal Wersching 24, 9:14 4th.
San Francisco—Solomon 4 pass from Montana (Wersching kick), 13:21 4th.

TEAM STATISTICS

	Cincinnati	San Francisco
First downs	21	26
Rushes-Yards	25-116	31-91
Passing yards	230	294
Sacked-Yards lost	6-39	1-7
Return yards	144	190
Passes	21-34-2	27-42-4
Punts	6-38.2	2-47.0
Fumbles-Lost	0-0	0-0
Penalties-Yards	6-46	5-30
Time of possession	29:24	30:36

Attendance—58,324. No-shows—3,042.

INDIVIDUAL STATISTICS

Rushing—Cincinnati, Alexander 8-48, Kinnebrew 11-41, Brooks 6-27; San Francisco, Tyler 14-52, Craig 12-34, Harmon 2-10, Montana 3-minus 5.

Passing—Cincinnati, Anderson 21-34-2—269; San Francisco, Montana 27-42-4—301.

Receiving—Cincinnati, Harris 5-59, Collinsworth 4-71, Curtis 3-40, Brooks 3-33, Kinnebrew 2-33, Alexander 2-12, Verser 1-20, Holman 1-1; San Francisco, D. Clark 7-124, Craig 7-44, Tyler 4-29, Solomon 3-38, Cooper 3-33, Ring 1-15, Nehemiah 1-10, Monroe 1-8.

Kickoff Returns—Cincinnati, Brooks 4-73; San Francisco, Monroe 4-99.

Punt Returns—Cincinnati, Simmons 1-25; San Francisco, McLemore 4-54.

Interceptions—Cincinnati, Kemp 2-0, R. Williams 1-33, R. Griffin 1-13; San Francisco, Williamson 1-26, Lott 1-11.

Punting—Cincinnati, McInally 6-38.2; San Francisco, Runager 2-47.0.

Field Goals—Cincinnati, Breech 1-1; San Francisco, Wersching 3-3.

Sacks—Cincinnati, Krumrie; San Francisco, G. Johnson 2, Ferrari, Lott, Pillers, Tuiasosopo.

Chiefs-Seahawks

SUNDAY, NOVEMBER 4
SCORE BY PERIODS

Kansas City	0	0	0	0— 0
Seattle	3	28	7	7—45

SCORING

Seattle—Field goal Johnson 29, 8:32 1st.
Seattle—Brown 95 interception return (Johnson kick), 1:31 2nd.
Seattle—Simpson 76 interception return (Johnson kick), 3:42 2nd.
Seattle—Doornink 11 pass from Krieg (Johnson kick), 7:13 2nd.
Seattle—Tice 2 pass from Krieg (Johnson kick), 14:18 2nd.
Seattle—Brown 58 interception return (Johnson kick), 2:20 3rd.
Seattle—Easley 58 interception return (Johnson kick), 13:25 4th.

TEAM STATISTICS

	Kansas City	Seattle
First downs	17	17
Rushes-Yards	21-78	34-132
Passing yards	162	129
Sacked-Yards lost	4-42	1-9
Return yards	171	370
Passes	23-51-6	12-21-1
Punts	8-46.6	5-37.2
Fumbles-Lost	2-0	0-0
Penalties-Yards	6-54	7-54
Time of possession	32:23	27:37

Attendance—61,396. No-shows—3,519.

INDIVIDUAL STATISTICS

Rushing—Kansas City, Heard 13-53, Jackson 3-11, Blackledge 1-6, Brown 1-3, Lacy 2-3, Gunter 1-2; Seattle, Dixon 9-54, Doornink 13-51, Hughes 9-32, Zorn 1-minus 2, C. Bryant 1-minus 3, Krieg 1-0.

Passing—Kansas City, Kenney 8-18-2—86, Osiecki 7-16-1—64, Blackledge 8-17-3—54; Seattle, Krieg 12-20-1—138, Zorn 0-1-0—0.

Receiving—Kansas City, Smith 5-49, Marshall 4-39, Brown 3-15, Carson 2-30, Paige 2-28, W. Arnold 2-17, Jackson 2-7, Scott 1-13, Beckman 1-5, Lacy 1-1; Seattle, Turner 3-37, Doornink 3-36, Young 2-15, Walker 1-27, Largent 1-11, Hughes 1-10, Tice 1-2.

Kickoff Returns—Kansas City, Paige 5-77, Smith 3-55; Seattle, Dixon 1-8.

Punt Returns—Kansas City, Smith 1-8; Seattle, Easley 2-17, Skansi 2-15.

Interceptions—Kansas City, Lewis 1-31; Seattle, Brown 2-153, Taylor 2-43, Simpson 1-76, Easley 1-58.

Punting—Kansas City, J. Arnold 8-46.6; Seattle, West 5-37.2.

Field Goals—Kansas City, none attempted; Seattle, Johnson 1-2 (missed: 51).

Sacks—Kansas City, Maas; Seattle, J. Bryant, Green, Jackson, Nash.

Falcons-Redskins

MONDAY, NOVEMBER 5
SCORE BY PERIODS

Atlanta	0	7	7	0—14
Washington	0	14	6	7—27

SCORING

Washington—Riggins 1 run (Moseley kick), 2:25 2nd.
Washington—Theismann 1 run (Moseley kick), 7:38 2nd.
Atlanta—Riggs 1 run (Luckhurst kick), 4:18 2nd.
Atlanta—Riggs 10 run (Luckhurst kick), 6:19 3rd.
Washington—Riggins 1 run (kick failed), 13:18 3rd.
Washington—Muhammad 7 pass from Theismann (Moseley kick), 6:01 4th.

TEAM STATISTICS

	Atlanta	Washington
First downs	16	24
Rushes-Yards	29-148	40-126
Passing yards	124	129
Sacked-Yards lost	7-44	4-41
Return yards	35	81
Passes	13-25-1	19-25-1
Punts	5-41.6	4-50.8
Fumbles-Lost	4-2	3-1
Penalties-Yards	5-68	3-25
Time of possession	28:09	31:51

Attendance—51,301. No-shows—4,130.

INDIVIDUAL STATISTICS

Rushing—Atlanta, Riggs 27-134, Cain 1-4, Moroski 1-10; Washington, Riggins 32-100, Theismann 8-26.

Passing—Atlanta, Bartkowski 5-10-0—69, Moroski 8-15-1—99; Washington, Theismann 19-25-1—170.

Receiving—Atlanta, Bailey 7-94, C. Benson 2-22, Landrum 2-19, A. Jackson 1-25, Riggs 1-8; Washington, Monk 5-45, Muhammad 6-57, Warren 2-21, Didier 4-34, Moore 1-2, Riggins 1-11.

Kickoff Returns—Atlanta, Stamps 3-53, Johnson 1-12, Tyrrell 1-0; Washington, Nelms 3-77.

Punt Returns—Atlanta, Johnson 4-25; Washington, Nelms 2-31, Green 1-0.

Interceptions—Atlanta, Britt 1-10; Washington, Green 1-50.

Punting—Atlanta, Giacomarro 5-41.6; Washington, Hayes 4-50.8.

Field Goals—Atlanta, none attempted; Washington, none attempted.

Sacks—Atlanta, Smith 2, Richardson, Burley; Washington, Mann 2, Kaufman 2, Grant, Butz, Beasley.

ELEVENTH WEEK

RESULTS OF WEEK 11

Sunday, November 11

Cincinnati 22, Pittsburgh 20 at Cin.
Dallas 24, St. Louis 17 at St. L.
Denver 16, San Diego 13 at S.D.
Green Bay 45, Minnesota 17 at G.B.
Houston 17, Kansas City 16 at K.C.
Indianapolis 9, N.Y. Jets 5 at N.Y.
L.A. Rams 29, Chicago 13 at L.A.
Miami 24, Philadelphia 23 at Mia.
New England 38, Buffalo 10 at N.E.
New Orleans 17, Atlanta 13 at Atl.
San Francisco 41, Cleveland 7 at Cleve.
Tampa Bay 20, N.Y. Giants 17 at T.B.
Washington 28, Detroit 14 at Wash.

Monday, November 12

Seattle 17, L.A. Raiders 14 at Sea.

After playing the first 10 games on their 1984 schedule, the Houston Oilers stood at 0-10 and hadn't come within 10 points of beating anybody. They had lost games by as many as 32 points and as few as 10. At least the league's other 0-10 team, the Buffalo Bills, were coming close. The Bills had lost by two points once, three points twice and four points on two other occasions.

The Oilers also were facing the possibility of becoming the first NFL team to lose 16 games in one season and had not won a game on the road since the second week of the 1981 season —a league-record 23 straight road losses.

But the Oilers finally got the taste of victory in Week 11, and they did it on the road, recording a 17-16 triumph over the Chiefs in Kansas City. Trailing 9-7 entering the final quarter, Houston scored 10 points before withstanding a late K.C. rally.

"This win will help us more than it would most teams," said quarterback Warren Moon, who scored the go-ahead touchdown from a yard out in the fourth period. "It's a confidence-builder for a very young football team." Moon's touchdown came eight plays after Chiefs quarterback Todd Blackledge fumbled at the Houston 45-yard line and Mike Stensrud recovered for the Oilers. That was the only turnover committed by either club in the game.

Before the touchdown, it looked like Kansas City might escape with a win despite scoring only nine points on three Nick Lowery field goals against the worst defense in the league. But fate, for a change, was smiling favorably on the Oilers.

"We knew they were bound to win a game," said Blackledge afterward. "But we didn't want it to be today." K.C. defensive end Mike Bell was even more stunned. "Man, I just can't believe this. It hurts to lose. But to become the first victim of a team that was 0-10 is embar-

rassing."

The New England Patriots avoided Kansas City's fate by dropping Buffalo to 0-11 with a 38-10 triumph at Foxboro, Mass. Tony Eason's three touchdown passes and Tony Collins' two scoring runs led the way as the Pats scored 28 points in the final 18 minutes to blow open a 10-10 game. The victory was New England's fifth straight against its AFC Eastern Division rival.

The Patriots defense held Buffalo quarterbacks Joe Ferguson and Matt Kofler to a combined 13 completions in 48 attempts and sacked them eight times. The Bills' offense was held to 189 total yards.

St. Louis' defense held Dallas to 59 total yards, quarterback Gary Hogeboom to three completions in 16 attempts and Tony Dorsett to 15 yards on nine carries in the second half, but still lost to the Cowboys, 24-17, in a NFC Eastern Division matchup. Mistakes proved costly as Dallas scored two of its touchdowns after St. Louis turnovers and the third after blocking a field-goal attempt. Rookie cornerback Victor Scott of the Cowboys picked off a Neil Lomax pass in the fourth period at the Cardinal 37-yard line. Three plays later, Hogeboom hit Ron Springs with a 26-yard touchdown pass for what proved to be the winning points.

Mistakes also cost the 2-8 Cleveland Browns any chance they might have had to upset 9-1 San Francisco in an interconference game. The Browns fumbled the opening kickoff and committed four first-half turnovers as the 49ers grabbed a 13-0 lead. The 49ers proceeded to pile it on in the second half, scoring 28 more points before Cleveland's lone touchdown with less than four minutes to play made the final score 41-7. The Browns defense entered the contest ranked No. 2 in the league behind Chicago—having given up only 13 touchdowns in 10 games—but San Francisco scorched it for 468 total yards and five touchdowns. Joe Montana threw a pair of scoring passes to Freddie Solomon and Roger Craig scored two touchdowns as the 49er offense began seven of its first nine possessions in Cleveland territory.

The Denver Broncos crossed midfield only two times in the first half of their game with division-rival San Diego. But the Broncos, trailing 13-6 early in the final period, rallied for 10 points in the fourth quarter to defeat the Chargers, 16-13. The game-winning touchdown came on a one-yard plunge by Sammy Winder with 38 seconds left to play after a 10-play, 77-yard drive. It marked the third straight week the 10-1 Broncos had rallied late to win and the victory was Denver's ninth in a row. Rolf Benirschke missed a 46-yard field goal attempt with two seconds left to end the Chargers' last chance.

The Cincinnati Bengals also rallied for a touchdown in the final minute of play to upend AFC Central Division-rival Pittsburgh, 22-20. Bengals running back Larry Kinnebrew's three-yard scoring run with 35 seconds left was the game-winner after quarterback Turk Schonert, who replaced the injured Ken Anderson earlier in the contest, completed three key passes in the final drive, including a 23-yarder to Cris Collinsworth. The Stanford product completed seven of his 10 attempts after replacing Anderson in the third quarter.

Keith Griffin, a rookie running back who helped the University of Miami (Fla.) win a national championship in 1983, subbed for injured John Riggins in the Washington backfield and rushed for 114 yards on 32 carries as the Redskins beat the Detroit Lions, 28-14. The win was the Redskins' 12th straight over the Lions in Washington dating back to 1939.

Although Griffin got the yardage, teammate Otis Wonsley got the touchdowns. Wonsley scored on three short runs as Washington built up a commanding 28-0 lead early in the second half. The Lions scored twice late in the third period to cut the deficit in half, but could come no closer as penalties and turnovers late in the game killed drives.

A rainstorm at Giants Stadium in New Jersey prevented either team from scoring a touchdown in Indianapolis' 9-5 win over the New York Jets. Three field goals by Raul Allegre accounted for all the Colts' scoring in a game that saw both clubs combine for only 18 first downs. The Jets' points came on a safety and Pat Leahy's 27-yard field goal early in the second half. Ironically, the Jets marched 63 yards to set up Leahy's field goal but had just 37 total yards and two first downs the entire first half.

The Los Angeles Rams also had trouble in the first half of their home game with the Chicago Bears. The Bears led, 13-6, at the intermission before the Rams exploded for 23 unanswered points in the final two quarters to win, 29-13. The game's biggest play came in the third quarter when Jeff Kemp hit Henry Ellard for a 63-yard touchdown to cut the deficit to one point. On the Rams' next possession, Kemp directed a 95-yard drive that ended with a one-yard Eric Dickerson touchdown run and gave L.A. a 19-13 lead.

Dickerson, who scored another touchdown later in the game, rushed for 149 yards, becoming the first back to hit the century mark against the league's top-rated defense in 1984. Chicago led the NFL in quarterback sacks with 47—including 20 in its last two games—but had none against Los Angeles.

While Dickerson maintained his position at the top of the league's rushing charts after 11 weeks with 1,309 yards, Tampa Bay's James Wilder continued to lead the NFL in total offense (combined rushing, receiving and returns) as the Buccaneers edged the New York Giants, 20-17. Wilder rushed for 99 yards and scored one touchdown as Tampa Bay avenged a 17-14 loss to New York seven weeks earlier. Wilder, who finished the game with 1,062 rushing yards for the season, went over the 1,000-yard mark for the first time in his four-year pro career.

Wide receiver Kevin House, who caught a 10-yard touchdown pass from Steve DeBerg to tie the game at 10-10 late in the third period, made two critical fourth-quarter receptions for the Bucs. A 42-yarder from DeBerg set up Wilder's touchdown and a 26-yard catch set up Obed Ariri's game-winning field goal with 4:52 to play.

Atlanta's Gerald Riggs rushed for 90 yards to go over the 1,000-yard mark for the season and scored the Falcons' only touchdown, but it wasn't enough as New Orleans prevailed, 17-13, in a NFC Western Division game. Saints tight end Hoby Brenner caught a pair of scoring tosses from Richard Todd to send the Falcons to their fifth straight defeat. Brenner's second TD came early in the final quarter to erase a 13-10 Atlanta lead, the first time in 19 quarters the Falcons had led in a game.

The Miami Dolphins needed a blocked extra-point attempt by defensive end Doug Betters with 1:52 remaining to defeat Philadelphia, 24-23, in an interconference game. Eagles quarterback Ron Jaworski had connected with Melvin Hoover on a 38-yard touchdown pass moments earlier as Philly, the last-place team in the NFC Eastern Division, nearly forced the unbeaten Dolphins into overtime. Instead, Betters' block gave Miami an 11-0 regular-season mark, the second-best start in NFL history (the 1972 Dolphins recorded a perfect 14-0 regular-season mark).

The game also was noteworthy because quarterback Dan Marino's one touchdown pass—his 30th of the '84 season—gave him 50 in his first two years in the NFL. No other signal-caller in league history had reached that milestone as quickly as Marino.

Green Bay quarterback Lynn Dickey threw four touchdown passes as the Packers pounded division-rival Minnesota, 45-17. Two of Dickey's TD passes came in the third period, both to running back Jessie Clark, as Green Bay broke open a 17-17 game. The Packers then added two more touchdowns in the final quarter to win their third straight game while handing the Vikings their sixth loss in seven outings.

The Los Angeles Raiders suffered a rare Monday night defeat in a 17-14 loss to AFC Western Division-rival Seattle. The loss was only the Raiders' third in 25 Monday night games, by far the best record of any NFL team in the weekly, nationally-televised game.

Seahawks quarterback Dave Krieg threw two third-quarter touchdown passes as Seattle scored all its points in the quarter to overcome

Green Bay quarterback Lynn Dickey threw four touchdown passes to lead the Packers to a 45-17 rout of Minnesota in Week 11.

a 7-0 L.A. halftime lead. The Raiders' first-half touchdown by Marcus Allen was the first yielded by the Seahawks' defense in 10 quarters. Allen scored another one-yard TD early in the final period, but it wasn't enough to prevent the 9-2 Seahawks from winning their fifth straight game.

Steelers-Bengals
SUNDAY, NOVEMBER 11
SCORE BY PERIODS

Pittsburgh	0	13	0	7	20
Cincinnati	3	0	12	7	22

SCORING

Cincinnati—Field goal Breech 21, 8:22 1st.
Pittsburgh—Field goal Anderson 47, 3:04 2nd.
Pittsburgh—Malone 1 run (Anderson kick), 12:07 2nd.
Pittsburgh—Field goal Anderson 21, 15:00 2nd.
Cincinnati—Brooks 24 run (kick failed), 1:48 3rd.
Cincinnati—Field goal Breech 42, 6:05 3rd.
Cincinnati—Field goal Breech 28, 11:42 3rd.
Pittsburgh—Lipps 36 run (Anderson kick), 3:00 4th.
Cincinnati—Kinnebrew 3 run (Breech kick), 14:25 4th.

TEAM STATISTICS

	Pittsburgh	Cincinnati
First downs	20	15
Rushes-Yards	38-160	30-116
Passing yards	150	192
Sacked-Yards lost	3-26	3-17
Return yards	104	172
Passes	16-31-3	12-18-0
Punts	4-40.5	4-46.3
Fumbles-Lost	0-0	1-1
Penalties-Yards	6-57	6-52
Time of possession	31:47	28:13
Attendance—52,497. No-shows—7,097.		

INDIVIDUAL STATISTICS

Rushing—Pittsburgh, Erenberg 10-29, Abercrombie 6-8, Pollard 17-68, Corley 2-13, Malone 2-6, Lipps 1-36; Cincinnati, Kinnebrew 13-60, Brooks 13-54, Alexander 3-5, Schonert 1-minus 3.

Passing—Pittsburgh, Malone 16-31-3—150; Cincinnati, Anderson 5-8-0—77, Schonert 7-10-0—115.

Receiving—Pittsburgh, Stallworth 7-76, Lipps 2-18, Erenberg 5-38, Pollard 2-18; Cincinnati, Collinsworth 4-66, Holman 2-42, Harris 2-56, Kinnebrew 2-10, Brooks 2-18.

Kickoff Returns—Pittsburgh, Veals 3-22, Erenberg 2-35; Cincinnati, Martin 3-55, Farley 1-8.

Punt Returns—Pittsburgh, Lipps 4-47; Cincinnati, Martin 3-28, Simmons 1-11.

Interceptions—Cincinnati, Breeden 2-70, Horton 1-0.

Punting—Pittsburgh, Colquitt 4-40.5; Cincinnati, McInally 4-46.3.

Field Goals—Pittsburgh, Anderson 2-2; Cincinnati, Breech 3-3.

Sacks—Pittsburgh, Clayton, Goodman, Gary ½, E. Nelson ½; Cincinnati, Collins, Edwards, R. Williams.

Cowboys-Cardinals
SUNDAY, NOVEMBER 11
SCORE BY PERIODS

Dallas	7	10	0	7	24
St. Louis	0	7	10	0	17

SCORING

Dallas—Springs 1 run (Septien kick), 6:47 1st.
St. Louis—Tilley 15 pass from Lomax (O'Donoghue kick), 0:15 2nd.
Dallas—J. Jones 8 pass from Hogeboom (Septien kick), 6:54 2nd.
Dallas—Field goal Septien 35, 14:51 2nd.
St. Louis—Love 1 pass from Lomax (O'Donoghue kick), 1:56 3rd.
St. Louis—Field goal O'Donoghue 30, 7:38 3rd.
Dallas—Springs 26 pass from Hogeboom (Septien kick), 5:57 4th.

TEAM STATISTICS

	Dallas	St. Louis
First downs	16	25
Rushes-Yards	30-116	26-78
Passing yards	134	357
Sacked-Yards lost	2-13	5-31
Return yards	81	106
Passes	12-33-2	27-52-2
Punts	7-35.6	4-32.8
Fumbles-Lost	2-0	5-4
Penalties-Yards	5-53	9-85
Time of possession	25:56	34:04
Attendance—48,721. No-shows—2,796.		

INDIVIDUAL STATISTICS

Rushing—Dallas, Dorsett 19-84, Springs 8-29, Hogeboom 3-3; St. Louis, Anderson 19-69, Ferrell 3-5, Love 1-2, Mitchell 2-4, Lomax 1-minus 3.

Passing—Dallas, Hogeboom 12-33-2—147; St. Louis, Lomax 27-52-2—388.

Receiving—Dallas, Dorsett 1-21, Springs 4-44, Cosbie 3-38, J. Jones 1-8, Hill 3-36; St. Louis, Green 8-99, Tilley 5-76, Anderson 4-55, Marsh 3-80, LaFleur 2-30, Ferrell 1-21, Harrell 2-20, Love 1-1, Mitchell 1-6.

Kickoff Returns—Dallas, Allen 2-47, McSwain 2-29; St. Louis, Mitchell 4-83, Pittman 1-14.

Punt Returns—St. Louis, Mitchell 4-9.

Interceptions—Dallas, Scott 1-5, Thurman 1-0; St. Louis, Griffin 1-0, Washington 1-0.

Punting—Dallas, Warren 7-35.6; St. Louis, Birdsong 4-32.8.

Field Goals—Dallas, Septien 1-4 (missed: 42, 48, 45); St. Louis, O'Donoghue 1-2 (missed: 49).

Sacks—Dallas, Albritton, Jeffcoat, E. Jones, Smerek, R. White; St. Louis, Galloway 2.

Broncos-Chargers
SUNDAY, NOVEMBER 11
SCORE BY PERIODS

Denver	3	3	0	10	16
San Diego	7	3	0	3	13

SCORING

Denver—Field goal Karlis 44, 4:07 1st.
San Diego—Joiner 25 pass from Fouts (Benirschke kick), 9:23 1st.
Denver—Field goal Karlis 45, 5:45 2nd.
San Diego—Field goal Benirschke 49, 12:16 2nd.
San Diego—Field goal Benirschke 43, 0:56 4th.
Denver—Field goal Karlis 37, 6:19 4th.
Denver—Winder 1 run (Karlis kick), 14:22 4th.

TEAM STATISTICS

	Denver	San Diego
First downs	17	20
Rushes-Yards	28-62	25-112
Passing yards	177	254
Sacked-Yards lost	3-11	1-7
Return yards	112	24
Passes	19-35-0	22-38-0
Punts	4-35.0	5-36.0
Fumbles-Lost	2-0	3-1
Penalties-Yards	5-33	13-112
Time of possession	30:08	29:52
Attendance—53,162. No-shows—7,002.		

INDIVIDUAL STATISTICS

Rushing—Denver, Winder 22-37, Elway 6-25; San

Diego, McGee 5-18, Jackson 14-69, James 4-16, Morris 2-9.

Passing—Denver, Elway 19-35-0—188; San Diego, Fouts 22-38-0—261.

Receiving—Denver, Kay 2-9, Johnson 3-38, Winder 2-15, Watson 5-49, J. Wright 2-21, Alexander 3-46, Willhite 2-10; San Diego, Egloff 3-27, Jackson 2-26, Joiner 6-85, Duckworth 1-17, James 3-20, Bendross 1-9, Chandler 3-60, Gissinger 1-3, Holohan 1-9, Morris 1-5.

Kickoff Returns—Denver, Thomas 3-48, Lang 1-33; San Diego, James 1-17, McGee 1-7.

Punt Returns—Denver, Willhite 3-31; San Diego, James 1-0, L. Smith 1-0.

Punting—Denver, Norman 4-35.0; San Diego, Buford 5-36.0.

Field Goals—Denver, Karlis 3-4 (missed: 34); San Diego, Benirschke 2-3 (missed: 46).

Sacks—Denver, Jones; San Diego, Elko, Ferguson, King.

Vikings-Packers
SUNDAY, NOVEMBER 11
SCORE BY PERIODS

Minnesota	0	10	7	0—17
Green Bay	7	10	14	14—45

SCORING

Green Bay—Coffman 7 pass from Dickey (Del Greco kick), 8:56 1st.

Green Bay—Field goal Del Greco 24, 1:33 2nd.

Minnesota—Field goal Stenerud 39, 6:48 2nd.

Minnesota—Jordan 14 pass from Wilson (Stenerud kick), 13:03 2nd.

Green Bay—West 2 run (Del Greco kick), 14:37 2nd.

Minnesota—Anderson 28 pass from Wilson (Stenerud kick), 2:49 3rd.

Green Bay—Clark 18 pass from Dickey (Del Greco kick), 6:43 3rd.

Green Bay—Clark 2 pass from Dickey (Del Greco kick), 14:06 3rd.

Green Bay—Lofton 63 pass from Dickey (Del Greco kick), 1:53 4th.

Green Bay—Ellis 6 run (Del Greco kick), 4:51 4th.

TEAM STATISTICS

	Minnesota	Green Bay
First downs	14	26
Rushes-Yards	28-110	37-208
Passing yards	162	305
Sacked-Yards lost	3-21	1-8
Return yards	166	98
Passes	19-37-1	23-41-1
Punts	8-35.0	5-45.0
Fumbles-Lost	2-1	1-0
Penalties-Yards	1-5	2-10
Time of possession	27:03	32:57

Attendance—52,931. No-shows—3,020.

INDIVIDUAL STATISTICS

Rushing—Minnesota, Brown 14-72, Anderson 12-26, Wilson 2-12; Green Bay, Ellis 10-107, Ivery 11-55, Rodgers 4-23, Crouse 4-14, Clark 5-6, West 1-2, Wright 2-1.

Passing—Minnesota, Wilson 19-37-1—183; Green Bay, Dickey 22-40-1—303, Wright 1-1-0—10.

Receiving—Minnesota, Jordan 2-19, Brown 8-29, Jones 3-46, Lewis 4-28, Anderson 1-28, Collins 1-33; Green Bay, Clark 6-43, Jefferson 4-77, Coffman 4-40, Ivery 1-0, Lofton 4-119, Ellis 2-3, Epps 1-21, Cassidy 1-10.

Kickoff Returns—Minnesota, Nelson 4-81, Anderson 3-44, Rouse 1-15; Green Bay, Rodgers 3-61, Epps 1-17.

Punt Returns—Minnesota, Nelson 3-6; Green Bay, Flynn 3-24.

Interceptions—Minnesota, Browner 1-20; Green Bay, T. Lewis 1-0, Murphy (with lateral) 0-minus 4.

Punting—Minnesota, Coleman 8-35.0; Green Bay, Scribner 5-45.0.

Field Goals—Minnesota, Stenerud 1-2 (missed: 46); Green Bay, Del Greco 1-1.

Sacks—Minnesota, Haines; Green Bay, Johnson 2, Anderson ½, Cumby ½.

Oilers-Chiefs
SUNDAY, NOVEMBER 11
SCORE BY PERIODS

Houston	0	7	0	10—17
Kansas City	3	3	3	7—16

SCORING

Kansas City—Field goal Lowery 31, 9:11 1st.

Houston—J. Williams 2 pass from Moon (Cooper kick), 1:37 2nd.

Kansas City—Field goal Lowery 38, 14:58 2nd.

Kansas City—Field goal Lowery 33, 8:42 3rd.

Houston—Moon 1 run (Cooper kick), 2:31 4th.

Houston—Field goal Cooper 44, 13:26 4th.

Kansas City—Marshall 4 pass from Blackledge (Lowery kick), 14:34 4th.

TEAM STATISTICS

	Houston	Kansas City
First downs	18	21
Rushes-Yards	38-157	23-131
Passing yards	140	191
Sacked-Yards lost	5-40	5-45
Return yards	115	150
Passes	19-26-0	20-41-0
Punts	10-41.2	9-44.2
Fumbles-Lost	0-0	1-1
Penalties-Yards	6-68	4-30
Time of possession	32:22	27:38

Attendance—44,464. No-shows—4,070.

INDIVIDUAL STATISTICS

Rushing—Houston, Moriarty 29-117, Edwards 4-28, Moon 5-12; Kansas City, Heard 14-73, Blackledge 2-26, Jackson 6-23, Paige 1-9.

Passing—Houston, Moon 19-26-0—180; Kansas City, Blackledge 20-41-0—236.

Receiving—Houston, Smith 8-107, Moriarty 6-36, J. Williams 3-14, Dressel 1-16, Mullins 1-7; Kansas City, Marshall 6-79, Heard 4-35, W. Arnold 2-25, Paige 2-10, Carson 1-30, Lacy 1-20, Hancock 1-17, Jackson 1-11, Beckman 1-6, Scott 1-3.

Kickoff Returns—Houston, Roaches 3-68, Thompson 1-16; Kansas City, Paige 4-86.

Punt Returns—Houston, Roaches 3-31; Kansas City, Smith 6-64.

Punting—Houston, James 10-41.2; Kansas City, J. Arnold 9-44.2.

Field Goals—Houston, Cooper 1-1; Kansas City, Lowery 3-3.

Sacks—Houston, Bingham 2, Baker, Hamm, Riley; Kansas City, Bell 2, Daniels, Lewis, Lindstrom ½, Still ½.

Bears-Rams
SUNDAY, NOVEMBER 11
SCORE BY PERIODS

Chicago	7	6	0	0—13
Los Angeles Rams	0	6	6	17—29

SCORING

Chicago—Fuller 1 run (B. Thomas kick), 10:56 1st.

Chicago—Field goal B. Thomas 20, 2:21 2nd.

Los Angeles—Field goal Lansford 21, 7:33 2nd.

Los Angeles—Field goal Lansford 45, 12:46 2nd.

Chicago—Field goal B. Thomas 52, 15:00 2nd.

Los Angeles—Ellard 63 pass from Kemp (kick failed), 5:06 3rd.

Los Angeles—Dickerson 1 run (Lansford kick), 1:40 4th.

Los Angeles—Dickerson 4 run (Lansford kick), 2:59 4th.
Los Angeles—Field goal Lansford 29, 6:44 4th.

TEAM STATISTICS

	Chicago	Los Angeles
First downs	15	17
Rushes-Yards	25-94	35-195
Passing yards	227	175
Sacked-Yards lost	2-13	0-0
Return yards	107	40
Passes	21-27-0	7-15-0
Punts	3-39.7	2-44.5
Fumbles-Lost	3-1	0-0
Penalties-Yards	8-63	3-10
Time of possession	30:38	29:22

Attendance—62,021. No-shows—5,799.

INDIVIDUAL STATISTICS

Rushing—Chicago, Payton 13-60, Fuller 6-29, Suhey 3-11, C. Thomas 1-3, Baschnagel 1-0, McKinnon 1-minus 9; Los Angeles, Dickerson 28-149, Crutchfield 5-44, Kemp 1-2, Redden 1-0.

Passing—Chicago, Fuller 21-27-0—240; Los Angeles, Kemp 7-15-0—175.

Receiving—Chicago, Payton 7-78, Moorehead 3-44, McKinnon 3-39, Suhey 3-14, C. Thomas 2-14, Dunsmore 2-33, Gault 1-18; Los Angeles, Ellard 3-93, Brown 3-71, Farmer 1-11.

Kickoff Returns—Chicago, Jordan 5-62, Cameron 2-36; Los Angeles, Redden 2-33, Drew Hill 1-7.

Punt Returns—Chicago, Fisher 2-19; Los Angeles, Ellard 1-0.

Punting—Chicago, Finzer 3-39.7; Los Angeles, Misko 2-44.5.

Field Goals—Chicago, B. Thomas 2-2; Los Angeles, Lansford 3-3.

Sacks—Los Angeles, Wilcher, Collins ½, Owens ½.

Colts-Jets
SUNDAY, NOVEMBER 11
SCORE BY PERIODS

Indianapolis	3	3	0	3—9
New York Jets	0	2	3	0—5

SCORING

Indianapolis—Field goal Allegre 44, 7:49 1st.
New York—Safety, ball snapped out of end zone, 6:02 2nd.
Indianapolis—Field goal Allegre 46, 14:46 2nd.
New York—Field goal Leahy 27, 6:46 3rd.
Indianapolis—Field goal Allegre 25, 4:47 4th.

TEAM STATISTICS

	Indianapolis	New York
First downs	11	7
Rushes-Yards	57-153	24-78
Passing yards	50	65
Sacked-Yards lost	1-8	6-51
Return yards	87	101
Passes	6-15-0	12-28-1
Punts	7-39.7	9-39.4
Fumbles-Lost	3-0	1-1
Penalties-Yards	2-15	2-15
Time of possession	36:02	23:58

Attendance—51,066. No-shows—25,825.

INDIVIDUAL STATISTICS

Rushing—Indianapolis, Middleton 31-73, McMillan 7-16, Wonsley 14-41, Schlichter 3-23, Stark 2-0; New York, Hector 15-71, Barber 5-5, Ryan 2-0, O'Brien 2-2.

Passing—Indianapolis, Pagel 4-12-0—37, Schlichter 2-3-0—21; New York, Ryan 7-15-0—66, O'Brien 5-13-1—50.

Receiving—Indianapolis, Sherwin 2-29, Butler 2-19, Porter 2-10; New York, Shuler 6-58, Walker 2-26, Barber 2-12, Jones 1-17, Dennison 1-3.

Kickoff Returns—Indianapolis, Smith 1-25; New York, Springs 2-54, Humphery 1-14, Banker 1-5.

Punt Returns—Indianapolis, Anderson 6-54; New York, Springs 4-28.

Interceptions—Indianapolis, Glasgow 1-8.

Punting—Indianapolis, Stark 7-39.7; New York, Ramsey 9-39.4.

Field Goals—Indianapolis, Allegre 3-5 (missed: 47, 45); New York, Leahy 1-1.

Sacks—Indianapolis, Wisniewski 3, Thompson 2, Cooks; New York, Mehl.

Eagles-Dolphins
SUNDAY, NOVEMBER 11
SCORE BY PERIODS

Philadelphia	14	0	3	6—23
Miami	0	7	7	10—24

SCORING

Philadelphia—Quick 19 pass from Jaworski (McFadden kick), 4:25 1st.
Philadelphia—Woodruff 13 pass from Jaworski (McFadden kick), 12:26 1st.
Miami—Nathan 11 pass from Marino (von Schamann kick), 13:48 2nd.
Philadelphia—Field goal McFadden 45, 7:17 3rd.
Miami—Bennett 2 run (von Schamann kick), 12:53 3rd.
Miami—P. Johnson 1 run (von Schamann kick), 1:37 4th.
Miami—Field goal von Schamann 27, 10:33 4th.
Philadelphia—Hoover 38 pass from Jaworski (kick blocked), 13:08 4th.

TEAM STATISTICS

	Philadelphia	Miami
First downs	19	21
Rushes-Yards	35-177	33-97
Passing yards	187	234
Sacked-Yards lost	2-16	1-12
Return yards	66	129
Passes	14-25-2	20-34-1
Punts	4-46.5	3-46.3
Fumbles-Lost	0-0	2-0
Penalties-Yards	7-36	2-10
Time of possession	31:01	28:59

Attendance—70,227. No-shows—578.

INDIVIDUAL STATISTICS

Rushing—Philadelphia, Montgomery 10-56, Haddix 9-55, M. Williams 7-27, Oliver 9-39; Miami, Nathan 8-50, Bennett 11-36, Carter 7-6, P. Johnson 5-5, Marino 2-0.

Passing—Philadelphia, Jaworski 14-25-2—203; Miami, Marino 20-34-1—246.

Receiving—Philadelphia, Quick 2-27, Woodruff 5-93, Spagnola 4-39, Haddix 2-6, Hoover 1-38; Miami, Duper 2-26, Clayton 4-75, Nathan 6-72, Hardy 1-7, Moore 3-35, Bennett 1-1, Jensen 1-14, D. Johnson 2-16.

Kickoff Returns—Philadelphia, Hayes 2-33, Waters 1-18; Miami, Walker 3-52, Hill 1-14.

Punt Returns—Philadelphia, Cooper 1-9; Miami, Walker 3-23, Kozlowski 1-12.

Interceptions—Philadelphia, Ellis 1-6; Miami, L. Blackwood 1-15, Lankford 1-3.

Punting—Philadelphia, Horan 4-46.5; Miami, Roby 3-46.3.

Field Goals—Philadelphia, McFadden 1-1; Miami, von Schamann 1-1.

Sacks—Philadelphia, Harrison; Miami, Bokamper 2.

Bills-Patriots
SUNDAY, NOVEMBER 11
SCORE BY PERIODS

Buffalo	7	0	3	0—10
New England	0	10	14	14—38

SCORING

Buffalo—Dennard 68 pass from Ferguson (Nelson kick), 9:11 1st.

New England—Jones 17 pass from Eason (Franklin kick), 3:03 2nd.

New England—Field goal Franklin 21, 14:23 2nd.

Buffalo—Field goal Nelson 34, 3:23 3rd.

New England—Collins 1 run (Franklin kick), 12:10 3rd.

New England—Collins 1 run (Franklin kick), 15:00 3rd.

New England—Morgan 24 pass from Eason (Franklin kick), 5:45 4th.

New England—Jones 7 pass from Eason (Franklin kick), 12:51 4th.

TEAM STATISTICS

	Buffalo	New England
First downs	12	21
Rushes-Yards	18-77	33-68
Passing yards	112	210
Sacked-Yards lost	8-94	3-17
Return yards	182	149
Passes	13-48-3	23-34-2
Punts	6-46.2	7-40.7
Fumbles-Lost	3-1	1-1
Penalties-Yards	4-60	3-20
Time of possession	25:06	34:54

Attendance—43,313. No-shows—2,743.

INDIVIDUAL STATISTICS

Rushing—Buffalo, Bell 15-63, Ferguson 2-10, Kofler 1-4; New England, C. James 23-55, Eason 6-12, Collins 4-1.

Passing—Buffalo, Ferguson 9-29-3—142, Kofler 4-19-0—64; New England, Eason 23-34-2—227.

Receiving—Buffalo, Dennard 2-73, Hunter 3-47, Brammer 2-14, Riddick 2-28, White 1-3, Franklin 2-36, Moore 1-5; New England, Morgan 5-68, C. James 6-30, Jones 5-49, Ramsey 3-33, Robinson 1-3, Starring 1-11, Dawson 1-18, Hawthorne 1-15.

Kickoff Returns—Buffalo, V. Williams 7-179; New England, Collins 3-60.

Punt Returns—Buffalo, Wilson 1-3; New England, Fryar 4-66.

Interceptions—Buffalo, Carpenter 1-0, Freeman 1-0; New England, Lippett 2-10, Marion 1-13.

Punting—Buffalo, Kidd 6-46.2; New England, Camarillo 7-40.7.

Field Goals—Buffalo, Nelson 1-2 (missed: 43); New England, Franklin 1-1.

Sacks—Buffalo, K. Johnson 2, Freeman; New England, Henson 2, Tippett 2, Adams, Nelson, Sims, T. Williams.

Saints-Falcons

SUNDAY, NOVEMBER 11

SCORE BY PERIODS

New Orleans	10	0	0	7—17
Atlanta	0	10	3	0—13

SCORING

New Orleans—Brenner 36 pass from Todd (Andersen kick), 3:22 1st.

New Orleans—Field goal Andersen 47, 13:45 1st.

Atlanta—Riggs 1 run (Luckhurst kick), 4:38 2nd.

Atlanta—Field goal Luckhurst 39, 12:56 2nd.

Atlanta—Field goal Luckhurst 24, 14:14 3rd.

New Orleans—Brenner 17 pass from Todd (Andersen kick), 2:49 4th.

TEAM STATISTICS

	New Orleans	Atlanta
First downs	17	20
Rushes-Yards	31-87	35-120
Passing yards	235	160
Sacked-Yards lost	0-0	5-47
Return yards	102	77
Passes	15-31-1	20-33-0
Punts	3-42.3	5-39.8

	New Orleans	Atlanta
Fumbles-Lost	1-0	2-1
Penalties-Yards	7-86	9-76
Time of possession	26:19	33:41

Attendance—40,590. No-shows—20,159.

INDIVIDUAL STATISTICS

Rushing—New Orleans, G. Rogers 19-61, Gajan 6-27, Todd 1-9, W. Wilson 4-2, Hansen 1-minus 12; Atlanta, Riggs 29-90, Moroski 4-17, Pridemore 1-7, C. Benson 1-6.

Passing—New Orleans, Todd 15-31-1—235; Atlanta, Moroski 20-33-0—207.

Receiving—New Orleans, Brenner 4-96, Gajan 3-20, Groth 2-31, W. Wilson 2-27, G. Rogers 2-20, Miller 1-22, Young 1-19; Atlanta, C. Benson 5-50, Bailey 4-64, A. Jackson 3-25, Cox 2-27, Cain 2-24, Hodge 2-14, Riggs 2-3.

Kickoff Returns—New Orleans, Duckett 3-44, Anthony 1-27; Atlanta, Stamps 2-40, Johnson 1-17.

Punt Returns—New Orleans, Fields 3-31; Atlanta, Johnson 2-20.

Interceptions—Atlanta, Pridemore 1-0.

Punting—New Orleans, Hansen 3-42.3; Atlanta, Giacomarro 5-39.8.

Field Goals—New Orleans, Andersen 1-3 (missed: 49, 45); Atlanta, Luckhurst 2-3 (missed: 47).

Sacks—New Orleans, Wilks 2½, Jackson, Paul, B. Clark ½.

49ers-Browns

SUNDAY, NOVEMBER 11

SCORE BY PERIODS

San Francisco	6	7	14	14—41
Cleveland	0	0	0	7— 7

SCORING

San Francisco—Field goal Wersching 47, 1:34 1st.

San Francisco—Field goal Wersching 26, 7:44 1st.

San Francisco—Craig 20 run (Wersching kick), 4:04 2nd.

San Francisco—Craig 2 run (Wersching kick), 10:26 3rd.

San Francisco—Solomon 60 pass from Montana (Wersching kick), 15:00 3rd.

San Francisco—Solomon 2 pass from Montana (Wersching kick), 4:17 4th.

San Francisco—Ring 5 run (Wersching kick), 8:04 4th.

Cleveland—B. Davis 18 pass from McDonald (Bahr kick), 11:22 4th.

TEAM STATISTICS

	San Francisco	Cleveland
First downs	23	10
Rushes-Yards	39-213	20-43
Passing yards	255	208
Sacked-Yards lost	1-8	2-12
Return yards	90	125
Passes	24-30-1	13-33-1
Punts	2-38.5	6-37.0
Fumbles-Lost	1-1	5-3
Penalties-Yards	7-45	5-32
Time of possession	35:27	24:33

Attendance—60,092. No-shows—3,472.

INDIVIDUAL STATISTICS

Rushing—San Francisco, Craig 9-45, Montana 2-4, Tyler 17-87, Ring 6-48, Harmon 5-29; Cleveland, Green 13-38, Byner 5-5, McDonald 2-0.

Passing—San Francisco, Montana 24-30-1—263; Cleveland, McDonald 13-33-1—220.

Receiving—San Francisco, Tyler 4-12, Craig 8-49, D. Clark 2-19, Ring 1-minus 1, Cooper 2-35, Frank 1-21, Solomon 5-105, Nehemiah 1-23; Cleveland, Green 2-11, Adams 3-30, Newsome 2-56, B. Davis 4-64, Byner 1-7, Brennan 1-52.

Kickoff Returns—San Francisco, Monroe 1-44; Cleveland, Byner 3-59, B. Davis 3-58.

Punt Returns—San Francisco, McLemore 4-25.

Interceptions—San Francisco, Turner 1-21; Cleveland, Banks 1-8.

Punting—San Francisco, Runager 2-38.5; Cleveland, Cox 6-37.0.

Field Goals—San Francisco, Wersching 2-3 (missed: 37); Cleveland, none attempted.

Sacks—San Francisco, Board, Carter; Cleveland, Camp.

Lions-Redskins
SUNDAY, NOVEMBER 11
SCORE BY PERIODS

Detroit	0	0	14	0—14
Washington	14	7	7	0—28

SCORING

Washington—Moore 7 pass from Theismann (Moseley kick), 12:25 1st.
Washington—Wonsley 1 run (Moseley kick), 14:01 1st.
Washington—Wonsley 1 run (Moseley kick), 10:05 2nd.
Washington—Wonsley 3 run (Moseley kick), 3:01 3rd.
Detroit—J. Jones 1 run (Murray kick), 6:14 3rd.
Detroit—Rubick 19 pass from Danielson (Murray kick), 14:15 3rd.

TEAM STATISTICS

	Detroit	Washington
First downs	21	24
Rushes-Yards	22-169	41-122
Passing yards	189	168
Sacked-Yards lost	4-37	5-35
Return yards	81	142
Passes	18-42-3	17-36-0
Punts	4-40.8	8-31.1
Fumbles-Lost	2-2	1-1
Penalties-Yards	10-85	9-80
Time of possession	26:45	33:15

Attendance—50,212. No-shows—5,219.

INDIVIDUAL STATISTICS

Rushing—Detroit, J. Jones 9-83, Jenkins 6-33, Danielson 3-44, Bussey 4-9; Washington, Griffin 32-114, Wonsley 6-16, Moore 1-5, Hayes 1-minus 11, Theismann 1-minus 2.

Passing—Detroit, Danielson 18-41-3—226; Jenkins 0-1-0—0; Washington, Theismann 17-36-0—203.

Receiving—Detroit, Chadwick 1-2, J. Jones 6-71, Jenkins 2-11, McCall 1-3, Bussey 3-24, Mandley 1-19, Lewis 1-7, Thompson 1-47, Rubick 2-42; Washington, Monk 5-34, Muhammad 7-105, Moore 1-7, Griffin 1-8, Didier 3-49.

Kickoff Returns—Detroit, Hall 3-62; Washington, Seay 3-53.

Punt Returns—Detroit, Hall 6-19, Johnson 1-0; Washington, Nelms 3-23, Coleman 0-27.

Interceptions—Washington, Smith 1-37, Jordan 1-2, Green 1-0.

Punting—Detroit, Black 4-40.8; Washington, Hayes 7-35.7.

Field Goals—Detroit, none attempted; Washington, none attempted.

Sacks—Detroit, Green 2, English 1½, Gay 1½; Washington, Manley 3, Grant ½, Mann ½.

Giants-Buccaneers
SUNDAY, NOVEMBER 11
SCORE BY PERIODS

New York Giants	3	0	7	7—17
Tampa Bay	0	3	7	10—20

SCORING

New York—Field goal Haji-Sheikh 41, 8:46 1st.
Tampa Bay—Field goal Ariri 37, 2:57 2nd.
New York—Mowatt 23 pass from Simms (Haji-Sheikh kick), 2:16 3rd.

Tampa Bay—House 10 pass from DeBerg (Ariri kick), 10:14 3rd.
Tampa Bay—Wilder 1 run (Ariri kick), 4:42 4th.
Tampa Bay—Field goal Ariri 20, 10:08 4th.
New York—Johnson 11 pass from Simms (Haji-Sheikh kick), 13:58 4th.

TEAM STATISTICS

	New York	Tampa Bay
First downs	14	24
Rushes-Yards	20-65	41-116
Passing yards	173	223
Sacked-Yards lost	2-25	2-15
Return yards	76	88
Passes	21-33-1	16-28-2
Punts	6-40.0	3-39.0
Fumbles-Lost	2-0	1-1
Penalties-Yards	6-43	4-35
Time of possession	24:53	35:07

Attendance—46,534. No-shows—11,374.

INDIVIDUAL STATISTICS

Rushing—New York, Carpenter 10-46, Morris 4-10, Simms 6-9; Tampa Bay, Wilder 34-99, Carter 1-16, Morton 3-3, Armstrong 1-0, DeBerg 2-minus 2.

Passing—New York, Simms 21-33-1—198; Tampa Bay, DeBerg 16-28-2—238.

Receiving—New York, Johnson 5-62, Mowatt 5-47, Galbreath 4-27, Gray 2-24, Manuel 2-16, Morris 2-13, Carpenter 1-9; Tampa Bay, House 4-89, Carter 4-49, J. Bell 2-38, Giles 3-36, Armstrong 3-26.

Kickoff Returns—New York, McConkey 4-55, Morris 1-14; Tampa Bay, Morton 1-28, Bright 1-11.

Punt Returns—New York, McConkey 1-1; Tampa Bay, Bright 4-27.

Interceptions—New York, Carson 1-6, Haynes 1-0; Tampa Bay, Cotney 1-22.

Punting—New York, Jennings 6-40.0; Tampa Bay, Garcia 3-39.0.

Field Goals—New York, Haji-Skeikh 1-1; Tampa Bay, Ariri 2-2.

Sacks—New York, Burt, Martin; Tampa Bay, Logan, Washington.

Raiders-Seahawks
MONDAY, NOVEMBER 12
SCORE BY PERIODS

Los Angeles Raiders	0	7	0	7—14
Seattle	0	0	17	0—17

SCORING

Los Angeles—Allen 1 run (Bahr kick), 5:11 2nd.
Seattle—Field goal Johnson 27, 2:39 3rd.
Seattle—Walker 8 pass from Krieg (Johnson kick), 7:43 3rd.
Seattle—Turner 20 pass from Krieg (Johnson kick), 10:58 3rd.
Los Angeles—Allen 1 run (Bahr kick), 1:22 4th.

TEAM STATISTICS

	Los Angeles	Seattle
First downs	19	11
Rushes-Yards	36-141	27-85
Passing yards	169	122
Sacked-Yards lost	4-22	6-34
Return yards	58	77
Passes	16-34-3	11-25-1
Punts	6-42.0	10-41.6
Fumbles-Lost	4-3	1-1
Penalties-Yards	7-73	10-80
Time of possession	29:46	30:14

Attendance—64,001. No-shows—930.

INDIVIDUAL STATISTICS

Rushing—Los Angeles, Hawkins 14-65, Allen 15-57, Wilson 2-12, King 5-7; Seattle, Doornink 10-41, Krieg 2-14, Hughes 5-13, Dixon 7-11, Morris 3-6.

Tampa Bay's James Wilder maintained his position as the NFL's total offense leader through 11 weeks as he rushed for 99 yards and scored one touchdown in the Bucs' 20-17 victory over the New York Giants.

Passing—Los Angeles, Wilson 16-34-3—191; Seattle, Krieg 11-25-1—156.

Receiving—Los Angeles, Christensen 6-71, Allen 5-37, Barnwell 2-57, Branch 2-12, Hawkins 1-14; Seattle, Turner 3-67, Young 2-45, Doornink 2-20, Hughes 2-10, Walker 1-8, Largent 1-6.

Kickoff Returns—Los Angeles, Montgomery 3-41; Seattle, Hughes 2-29, Morris 1-7.

Punt Returns—Los Angeles, Pruitt 4-17; Seattle, Skan-si 3-28.

Interceptions—Los Angeles, McElroy 1-0; Seattle, Easley 2-1, Harris 1-12.

Punting—Los Angeles, Guy 6-42.0; Seattle, West 10-41.6.

Field Goals—Los Angeles, Bahr 0-1 (missed: 45); Seattle, Johnson 1-1.

Sacks—Los Angeles, Pickel 2, Squirek, Long, Nelson, Townsend; Seattle, Green 2, J. Bryant, Fanning.

TWELFTH WEEK

RESULTS OF WEEK 12

Sunday, November 18

Buffalo 14, Dallas 3 at Buff.
Chicago 16, Detroit 14 at Chi.
Cleveland 23, Atlanta 7 at Atl.
Denver 42, Minnesota 21 at Den.
Green Bay 31, L.A. Rams 6 at G.B.
Houston 31, N.Y. Jets 20 at Hous.
L.A. Raiders 17, Kansas City 7 at L.A.
New England 50, Indianapolis 17 at Ind.
N.Y. Giants 16, St. Louis 10 at N.Y.
Philadelphia 16, Washington 10 at Phila.
San Diego 34, Miami 28 (OT) at S.D.
San Francisco 24, Tampa Bay 17 at S.F.
Seattle 26, Cincinnati 6 at Cin.

Monday, November 19

New Orleans 27, Pittsburgh 24 at N.O.

As the Miami Dolphins piled up victory after victory during the early part of the 1984 season, observers began comparing them to the 1972 Miami club, the only team in NFL history to go through an entire season and postseason undefeated. One observer who refused to fall into that trap was Coach Don Shula, who guided the '72 Dolphins to 14 regular-season victories and two playoff wins before a 14-7 victory over the Washington Redskins in Super Bowl VII. "Ask me to compare them after we go undefeated," Shula said.

All talk of an undefeated season ended in Week 12 when the Dolphins lost a 34-28 overtime decision to the San Diego Chargers. Rookie running back Buford McGee, an 11th-round draft pick out of Mississippi, ran 25 yards for the winning score after the Chargers won the coin flip to start the overtime. Kick returner Lionel James, another rookie from Auburn, returned the ball 25 yards to the 31-yard line to get the drive started. Quarterback Dan Fouts, who threw four touchdown passes in regulation time, completed key 15-yard passes to tight end Eric Sievers and wide receiver Pete Holohan to put the Chargers deep in Miami territory. McGee's run around right end 3:17 into the extra period sent the 53,041 Charger partisans at Jack Murphy Stadium into hysteria.

"It's tough going into that situation being a rookie," said McGee, who came in for Earnest Jackson a few plays earlier after Jackson left the game with cramps. "I was kind of scared. I was supposed to stay behind (guard) Doug Wilkerson and cut off his hip. After I got inside Doug, I looked for pursuit, but our receivers must have thrown some pretty good blocks because I didn't see anybody."

The Chargers had tied the game on Fouts' three-yard touchdown toss to Sievers with 51 seconds left in regulation after a 19-play, 91-yard march. Miami's Uwe von Schamann then missed a 44-yard field goal attempt as time expired.

"We let this one get away and all of us are upset about it," said Shula, whose team saw a fourth-quarter 28-14 lead evaporate. The loss snapped a streak of 16 consecutive wins in regular-season games for the Dolphins, one shy of the 1933-34 Chicago Bears' league mark. "I thought we were ready to play a good game. We haven't played a good one in three weeks."

The Buffalo Bills also reversed their fortunes in Week 12, winning their first game of the season and shocking the Dallas Cowboys, 14-3. The Cowboys were 7-4 and tied for the top spot in the NFC Eastern Division before the game. But the Bills, with one of the largest crowds in recent years at Rich Stadium looking on, pulled off the upset behind the running of rookie Greg Bell.

Bell, the Bills' No. 1 draft choice in 1984 despite missing much of his final year at Notre Dame with a broken leg, rushed for more yards against Dallas (206) than he did in his final year with the Irish (169). Bell's biggest gainer came on the Bills' first play from scrimmage, when he went 85 yards for a touchdown 21 seconds into the game. It was the longest run from scrimmage ever against the Cowboys. Bell scored the Bills' other touchdown on a three-yard pass from Joe Ferguson early in the final period as the Bills snapped their 14-game losing streak.

While Bell was putting on his one-man offensive show against Dallas, Raiders linebacker Rod Martin was conducting a defensive clinic in Los Angeles' 17-7 victory over division-rival Kansas City. Martin, an eight-year veteran from Southern Cal, returned a fumble by Chiefs quarterback Bill Kenney 77 yards for a touchdown in the first period and sacked Kenney, forcing him to fumble again, in the second. Howie Long recovered the second fumble and, six plays later, Raiders quarterback Marc Wilson connected with Dokie Williams for a 12-yard touchdown pass and a 14-0 halftime lead. The L.A. defense, which held Kansas City to 182 yards in total offense, lost a shutout when the Chiefs scored a touchdown with 1:41 left to play. The victory was the first in four games for the defending Super Bowl champions.

The Seattle defense, which led the league in opponents turnovers, forced Cincinnati into five, including three on the Bengals' first five possessions, and went on to record a 26-6 victory. The Bengals took the opening kickoff and ran the ball 13 straight times, reaching the Seattle 8-yard line. The Seahawks forced running back Larry Kinnebrew to fumble on the next play, however. Then, on the Bengals' next possession, James Brooks fumbled at his own 49 and the Seahawks recovered. Six plays later, Zachary Dixon scored the first of his two touchdowns, giving Seattle a lead it never re-

Denver quarterback John Elway threw five touchdown passes in the first three periods as the Broncos cruised to an easy 42-21 victory over Minnesota in Week 12.

linquished. Seattle's defense did not yield a touchdown as the Seahawks won for the sixth straight week.

Green Bay won its fourth game in a row after losing seven straight early in the year, beating the Los Angeles Rams, 31-6. The Packers' defense, which allowed only three touchdowns during the team's four-game win streak, limited the Rams to two field goals. Defensive back Tim Lewis, a former No. 1 draft pick out of Pittsburgh, capped the scoring with a 99-yard interception return with 5:24 to play—the longest interception return in Green Bay history.

One week after getting burned for five touchdowns in a loss to San Francisco, the Cleveland Browns' defense returned to form in a 23-7 victory over Atlanta. The Browns set a club record for quarterback sacks with 11 while winning for just the third time in 1984. The loss was the Falcons' sixth straight. One of the sacks, by nose tackle Dave Puzzuoli, knocked Falcons quarterback Steve Bartkowski out for the remainder of the season. Cleveland was led offensively by Paul McDonald's two touchdown passes and Matt Bahr's three field goals.

Chicago's Bob Thomas also kicked three field goals, including the game-winner from 19 yards out with three seconds left, as the Bears won against NFC Central Division-rival Detroit, 16-14. It was Chicago's seventh consecutive victory over a division opponent.

The Bears' only touchdown came on their first possession of the game—the ninth time in 12 games they scored the first time they had the ball.

Fred Dean played his first game of the season after a contract holdout and came up with two key defensive plays in San Francisco's 24-17 win over Tampa Bay. In the second period with the game scoreless, Dean hit Tampa Bay quarterback Steve DeBerg, forcing a poorly thrown ball that was intercepted by linebacker Keena Turner at the Buccaneer 44-yard line. The 49ers scored their first touchdown of the game minutes later. With 4:49 left in the contest and the 49ers protecting a seven-point lead, Dean sacked DeBerg on a third-down play at the San Francisco 38.

DeBerg, who broke into the NFL with the 49ers in 1978, fired two touchdown passes and compiled 316 passing yards. But the 49ers improved their season record to 11-1 and clinched at least a wild-card berth in the playoffs.

The Denver Broncos also improved their record to 11-1 with their 10th straight triumph, a 42-21 rout of the Minnesota Vikings. It was the offense, for a change, that led the way as John Elway tied a club record with five touchdown passes. Elway's chance to break the mark ended late in the third quarter when Coach Dan Reeves replaced him with Gary Kubiak after the Broncos took a commanding 42-7 lead.

The woeful Vikings fell behind, 21-0, before getting their initial first down early in the second period in losing for the ninth time in 12 games. Minnesota turned the ball over five times, with Denver scoring touchdowns after four of them. For the second straight week, the Vikings' defense gave up more than 40 points.

The Indianapolis Colts' defense was burned for 48 points by New England in a 50-17 loss to the Patriots. Pats quarterback Tony Eason threw four touchdown passes, including three in the first half to tight end Derrick Ramsey. The 50 points were the most scored by New England since a 50-21 win over the Baltimore Colts exactly five years earlier.

The game was also noteworthy because it marked the first NFL starting assignment for Indianapolis quarterback Art Schlichter, one of the Colts' first-round picks in the 1982 draft. Schlichter, who was suspended for the entire 1983 season by Commissioner Pete Rozelle for gambling activities, accounted for both Indianapolis touchdowns, running 13 yards for one and passing 13 yards for the other.

In two games that were remarkably similiar, the New York Giants and Philadelphia Eagles won NFC Eastern Division games. The Giants upended St. Louis, 16-10, behind six Cardinal turnovers and three field goals by Ali Haji-Sheikh. The Cards, who lost for the third straight week after an earlier four-game win streak, led the Giants in rushing yardage, passing yardage and first downs.

The Eagles defeated Washington, also by a 16-10 score, thanks in large part to six Redskin turnovers and three field goals by Paul McFad-den. The Redskins, who lost for the first time in three weeks, led the Eagles in rushing, passing and first downs.

Washington's John Riggins rushed for 92 yards in the losing effort, going over the 1,000-yard mark for the fifth time in his 13-year NFL career. Riggins became the oldest player—at 35 years, 3½ months—to rush for 1,000 yards. John Henry Johnson of the Pittsburgh Steelers was 35 years, 1 month when he rushed for 1,048 yards in 1964.

At the Houston Astrodome, the Oilers' Warren Moon had the best game of his rookie NFL season on his 28th birthday as his three touchdown passes led the Oilers to a 31-20 victory over the New York Jets. After the Jets had scored on their first three possessions of the game for a 13-0 lead, Moon and the Oilers rolled up 31 unanswered points to win their second straight game. It was the first time since 1981 that the Oilers had won two games in succession.

At the New Orleans Superdome in the Monday night game, Richard Todd celebrated his 31st birthday by leading the Saints to a 27-24 decision over Pittsburgh. Todd threw scoring passes to seldom-used tight ends Larry Hardy and Junior Miller as New Orleans broke a Monday night jinx with its first victory in seven games.

Defensively, New Orleans' Bruce Clark recovered two fumbles and had one interception while linebacker Dennis Winston, a former Steeler, came back to haunt his former teammates with a 47-yard interception return in the final period for the game-winning points. It was New Orleans' first triumph over Pittsburgh since 1969, when the Steelers were 1-13 under first-year Coach Chuck Noll.

Cowboys - Bills
SUNDAY, NOVEMBER 18
SCORE BY PERIODS

Dallas	0	3	0	0— 3
Buffalo	7	0	0	7—14

SCORING
Buffalo—Bell 85 run (Nelson kick), 0:21 1st.
Dallas—Field goal Septien 20, 0:27 2nd.
Buffalo—Bell 3 pass from Ferguson (Nelson kick), 3:12 4th.

TEAM STATISTICS

	Dallas	Buffalo
First downs	19	14
Rushes-Yards	24-78	33-203
Passing yards	219	104
Sacked-Yards lost	3-23	2-13
Return yards	113	80
Passes	22-46-2	13-30-2
Punts	6-32.5	8-43.5
Fumbles-Lost	2-1	1-0
Penalties-Yards	5-55	4-58
Time of possession	30:38	29:22

Attendance—74,391. No-shows—5,066.

INDIVIDUAL STATISTICS
Rushing—Dallas, Newsome 3-10, Dorsett 17-70, Springs 2-minus 3, J. Jones 1-2, Hogeboom 1-minus 1;

Buffalo, Bell 27-206, Moore 3-3, Riddick 1-minus 2, Ferguson 2-minus 4.

Passing—Dallas, Hogeboom 22-45-2—242, Renfro 0-1-0—0; Buffalo, Ferguson 13-29-2—117, Kofler 0-1-0—0.

Receiving—Dallas, Hill 4-35, Renfro 2-28, Dorsett 5-29, Cosbie 6-92, Springs 2-15, J. Jones 1-9, Newsome 2-34; Buffalo, Brookins 1-11, Franklin 6-55, Brammer 1-12, Bell 2-12, Moore 2-14, Riddick 1-13.

Kickoff Returns—Dallas, Allen 3-59; Buffalo, Wilson 1-17, V. Williams 1-13.

Punt Returns—Dallas, Allen 3-22; Buffalo, Wilson 3-24.

Interceptions—Dallas, Lockhart 1-32, Fellows 1-0; Buffalo, Kush 1-15, Carpenter 1-11.

Punting—Dallas, D. White 6-32.5; Buffalo, Kidd 8-43.5.

Field Goals—Dallas, Septien 1-2 (missed: 47); Buffalo, none attempted.

Sacks—Dallas, Downs, Jeffcoat; Buffalo, K. Johnson, Keating, B. Williams.

Lions-Bears
SUNDAY, NOVEMBER 18
SCORE BY PERIODS

Detroit	0	7	7	0—14
Chicago	7	3	0	6—16

SCORING

Chicago—Dunsmore 1 pass from Fuller (Thomas kick), 10:12 1st.
Chicago—Field goal B. Thomas 24, 0:04 2nd.
Detroit—J. Jones 1 run (Murray kick), 5:20 2nd.
Detroit—Chadwick 7 pass from Danielson (Murray kick), 8:54 3rd.
Chicago—Field goal B. Thomas 52, 3:29 4th.
Chicago—Field goal B. Thomas 19, 14:57 4th.

TEAM STATISTICS

	Detroit	Chicago
First downs	11	11
Rushes-Yards	26-71	41-175
Passing yards	96	156
Sacked-Yards lost	3-19	3-15
Return yards	66	41
Passes	10-16-0	14-25-0
Punts	5-26.8	3-33.7
Fumbles-Lost	2-1	2-0
Penalties-Yards	4-25	1-12
Time of possession	23:16	36:44
Attendance—54,911. No-shows—10,879.		

INDIVIDUAL STATISTICS

Rushing—Detroit, J. Jones 17-42, Jenkins 5-16, D'Addio 3-11, Thompson 1-2; Chicago, Payton 29-66, C. Thomas 5-52, Fuller 3-37, Suhey 4-20.

Passing—Detroit, Danielson 10-16-0—115; Chicago, Fuller 13-23-0—164, Baschnagel 1-2-0—7.

Receiving—Detroit, J. Jones 2-13, Thompson 1-35, Rubick 1-13, Chadwick 3-32, Nichols 2-21, Jenkins 1-1; Chicago, McKinnon 5-83, Dunsmore 1-1, C. Thomas 1-minus 2, Payton 4-43, Gault 1-12, Cabral 1-7, Moorehead 1-27.

Kickoff Returns—Detroit, Hall 3-66, Meade 1-0; Chicago, Cameron 2-25, Duerson 1-14.

Punt Returns—Detroit, Mandley 1-0; Chicago, Fisher 2-2.

Punting—Detroit, Black 5-26.8; Chicago, Finzer 3-33.7.

Field Goals—Detroit, none attempted; Chicago, B. Thomas 3-3.

Sacks—Detroit, Cofer 1½, Gay, Cobb ½; Chicago, Dent 2, Hampton.

Browns-Falcons
SUNDAY, NOVEMBER 18
SCORE BY PERIODS

Cleveland	10	3	0	10—23
Atlanta	7	0	0	0— 7

SCORING

Atlanta—Bailey 20 pass from Bartkowski (Luckhurst kick), 4:13 1st.
Cleveland—B. Davis 43 pass from McDonald (Bahr kick), 11:35 1st.
Cleveland—Field goal Bahr 27, 14:26 1st.
Cleveland—Field goal Bahr 46, 6:51 2nd.
Cleveland—Newsome 16 pass from McDonald (Bahr kick), 1:49 4th.
Cleveland—Field goal Bahr 20, 9:26 4th.

TEAM STATISTICS

	Cleveland	Atlanta
First downs	17	18
Rushes-Yards	34-113	22-71
Passing yards	217	139
Sacked-Yards lost	1-4	11-95
Return yards	37	148
Passes	14-24-1	23-38-2
Punts	3-46.0	5-41.0
Fumbles-Lost	1-1	4-2
Penalties-Yards	5-35	2-20
Time of possession	28:56	31:04
Attendance—28,280. No-shows—21,490.		

INDIVIDUAL STATISTICS

Rushing—Cleveland, Green 30-121, Byner 2-0, McDonald 2-minus 8; Atlanta, Riggs 21-71, Bartkowski 1-0.

Passing—Cleveland, McDonald 13-23-1—205, Cox 1-1-0—16; Atlanta, Bartkowski 19-28-2—191, Moroski 4-10-1—43.

Receiving—Cleveland, Newsome 5-97, Brennan 3-37, B. Davis 2-49, Holt 2-13, Feacher 1-16, Green 1-9; Atlanta, Riggs 6-41, Bailey 4-55, Cox 4-44, A. Jackson 3-38, Hodge 2-29, C. Benson 1-8, Cain 1-7, Tuttle 1-7, Landrum 1-5.

Kickoff Returns—Cleveland, Byner 1-17; Atlanta, Austin 4-77, Johnson 1-26, Stamps 1-20.

Punt Returns—Atlanta, Johnson 2-23.

Interceptions—Cleveland, Perry 1-17, Dixon 1-3; Atlanta, Small 1-2.

Punting—Cleveland, Cox 3-46.0; Atlanta, Giacomarro 5-41.0.

Field Goals—Cleveland, Bahr 3-3; Atlanta, none attempted.

Sacks—Cleveland, Matthews 3½, Banks 2, Baldwin, Camp, Franks, Hairston, Puzzuoli, Johnson ½; Atlanta, Pitts.

Vikings-Broncos
SUNDAY, NOVEMBER 18
SCORE BY PERIODS

Minnesota	0	7	0	14—21
Denver	21	14	7	0—42

SCORING

Denver—Willhite 13 run (Karlis kick), 13:31 1st.
Denver—Winder 8 pass from Elway (Karlis kick), 10:13 1st.
Denver—Watson 26 pass from Elway (Karlis kick), 14:52 1st.
Minnesota—Brown 21 pass from Kramer (Stenerud kick), 1:19 2nd.
Denver—Johnson 19 pass from Elway (Karlis kick), 6:28 2nd.
Denver—Alexander 12 pass from Elway (Karlis kick), 14:42 2nd.
Denver—Watson 13 pass from Elway (Karlis kick), 6:44 3rd.
Minnesota—Brown 1 run (Stenerud kick), 2:56 4th.
Minnesota—Rice 15 lateral from Senser on pass from Wilson (Stenerud kick), 15:00 4th.

TEAM STATISTICS

	Minnesota	Denver
First downs	19	22

	Minnesota	Denver
Rushes-Yards	21-67	36-206
Passing yards	247	229
Sacked-Yards lost	5-27	1-9
Return yards	179	94
Passes	23-41-3	18-23-0
Punts	4-37.0	5-39.4
Fumbles-Lost	3-2	3-2
Penalties-Yards	1-5	4-42
Time of possession	28:22	31:38

Attendance—74,716. No-shows—384.

INDIVIDUAL STATISTICS

Rushing—Minnesota, Kramer 1-0, Anderson 7-11, Brown 7-24, Nelson 6-32; Denver, Elway 1-0, Winder 12-75, Willhite 3-22, Parros 7-65, Lang 2-10, Myles 4-5, Brewer 7-29.

Passing—Minnesota, Kramer 11-19-2—122, Anderson 1-2-0—32, Wilson 11-20-1—120; Denver, Elway 16-19-0—218, Willhite 0-1-0—0, Kubiak 2-3-0—20.

Receiving—Minnesota, Anderson 2-15, Brown 6-68, Lewis 3-64, Collins 4-33, Jordan 3-35, Jones 1-22, Senser 3-24, Rice 0-9, Nelson 1-4; Denver, Johnson 3-47, Winder 3-8, Watson 5-123, Parros 1-4, Kay 1-11, J. Wright 1-5, Willhite 1-8, Brewer 2-20, Alexander 1-12.

Kickoff Returns—Minnesota, Anderson 3-74, Nelson 2-74, Turner 1-14; Denver, Lang 2-60, Thomas 1-2.

Punt Returns—Minnesota, Nelson 2-17; Denver, Willhite 3-19, Wilson 1-0.

Interceptions—Denver, Ryan 1-13, Harden 1-0, Robbins 1-0.

Punting—Minnesota, Coleman 4-37.0; Denver, Norman 5-39.4.

Field Goals—Minnesota, none attempted; Denver, none attempted.

Sacks—Minnesota, Elshire; Denver, Mecklenburg 2, Bowyer, Townsend, Woodard.

Rams-Packers
SUNDAY, NOVEMBER 18
SCORE BY PERIODS

Los Angeles Rams	3	3	0	0—	6
Green Bay	0	14	10	7—	31

SCORING

Los Angeles—Field goal Lansford 21, 5:41 1st.
Green Bay—Ivery 1 run (Del Greco kick), 7:17 2nd.
Los Angeles—Field goal Lansford 50, 12:46 2nd.
Green Bay—Ivery 1 run (Del Greco kick), 14:31 2nd.
Green Bay—Field goal Del Greco 21, 2:39 3rd.
Green Bay—Ivery 2 run (Del Greco kick), 10:40 3rd.
Green Bay—T. Lewis 99 interception return (Del Greco kick), 9:36 4th.

TEAM STATISTICS

	Los Angeles	Green Bay
First downs	16	18
Rushes-Yards	31-166	29-122
Passing yards	131	192
Sacked-Yards lost	1-9	1-2
Return yards	143	181
Passes	16-35-3	15-27-2
Punts	6-34.0	3-34.0
Fumbles-Lost	2-1	0-0
Penalties-Yards	13-109	5-35
Time of possession	32:01	27:59

Attendance—52,031. No-shows—3,839.

INDIVIDUAL STATISTICS

Rushing—Los Angeles, Dickerson 25-132, Redden 3-25, Kemp 3-9; Green Bay, Ellis 7-32, Ivery 15-77, Crouse 5-6, Lofton 1-6, Rodgers 1-1.

Passing—Los Angeles, Kemp 14-32-2—118, Dils 2-3-1—22; Green Bay, Dickey 15-27-2—194.

Receiving—Los Angeles, David Hill 5-38, Ellard 2-28, Guman 2-19, Barber 2-11, Drew Hill 1-8, Dickerson 3-14, Brown 1-22; Green Bay, Ellis 2-8, Ivery 3-22, Crouse 1-0, Lofton 6-129, Jefferson 1-9, Epps 1-21, Coffman 1-5.

Kickoff Returns—Los Angeles, Redden 3-87, Drew Hill 2-31; Green Bay, Rodgers 3-63.

Punt Returns—Los Angeles, Irvin 1-4; Green Bay, Epps 1-5.

Interceptions—Los Angeles, Johnson 2-21; Green Bay, T. Lewis 1-99, Lee 1-14, Anderson 1-0.

Punting—Los Angeles, Misko 6-34.0; Green Bay, Scribner 3-34.0.

Field Goals—Los Angeles, Lansford 2-2; Green Bay, Del Greco 1-3 (missed: 54, 36).

Sacks—Los Angeles, DeJurnett; Green Bay, Scott.

Jets-Oilers
SUNDAY, NOVEMBER 18
SCORE BY PERIODS

New York Jets	10	3	0	7—	20
Houston	0	10	14	7—	31

SCORING

New York—Barber 12 run (Leahy kick), 5:38 1st.
New York—Field goal Leahy 19, 13:01 1st.
New York—Field goal Leahy 27, 2:54 2nd.
Houston—Smith 5 pass from Moon (Cooper kick), 9:24 2nd.
Houston—Field goal Cooper 43, 15:00 2nd.
Houston—Smith 14 pass from Moon (Cooper kick), 3:03 3rd.
Houston—Walls 10 pass from Moon (Cooper kick), 10:52 3rd.
Houston—Moriarty 51 run (Cooper kick), 4:54 4th.
New York—Paige 3 run (Leahy kick), 10:09 4th.

TEAM STATISTICS

	New York	Houston
First downs	19	20
Rushes-Yards	33-138	32-187
Passing yards	203	215
Sacked-Yards lost	3-23	1-8
Return yards	136	100
Passes	19-36-1	21-29-0
Punts	4-37.0	4-37.5
Fumbles-Lost	2-1	3-2
Penalties-Yards	6-60	11-80
Time of possession	31:47	28:13

Attendance—40,141. No-shows—9,335.

INDIVIDUAL STATISTICS

Rushing—New York, McNeil 20-69, Barber 4-31, O'Brien 3-14, Hector 5-21, Paige 1-3; Houston, Moriarty 23-138, Edwards 2-24, Moon 6-5, Walls 1-20.

Passing—New York, O'Brien 19-36-1—226; Houston, Moon 20-28-0—207, Moriarty 1-1-0—16.

Receiving—New York, Shuler 4-47, Jones 6-75, McNeil 3-43, Walker 3-38, Hector 1-6, Humphery 1-10, Paige 1-7; Houston, Moriarty 4-27, J. Williams 3-37, Edwards 4-22, Dressel 3-43, Smith 4-46, Walls 3-48.

Kickoff Returns—New York, Humphery 3-61, Springs 2-65; Houston, Walls 3-53, Roaches 1-21.

Punt Returns—New York, Springs 3-10; Houston, Roaches 2-4.

Interceptions—Houston, Tullis 1-22.

Punting—New York, Ramsey 4-37.0; Houston, James 4-37.5.

Field Goals—New York, Leahy 2-3 (missed: 43); Houston, Cooper 1-1.

Sacks—New York, Gastineau; Houston, Baker, Foster, Hamm.

Chiefs-Raiders
SUNDAY, NOVEMBER 18
SCORE BY PERIODS

Kansas City	0	0	0	7—	7
Los Angeles Raiders	7	7	0	3—	17

SCORING

Los Angeles—Martin 77 fumble return (Bahr kick), 10:16 1st.

Los Angeles—Williams 12 pass from Wilson (Bahr kick), 14:47 2nd.
Los Angeles—Field goal Bahr 22, 9:53 4th.
Kansas City—Scott 3 pass from Kenney (Lowery kick), 13:19 4th.

TEAM STATISTICS

	Kansas City	Los Angeles
First downs	14	20
Rushes-Yards	16-20	49-219
Passing yards	162	80
Sacked-Yards lost	4-32	3-23
Return yards	96	73
Passes	19-37-1	12-21-1
Punts	8-50.9	6-41.7
Fumbles-Lost	2-2	5-3
Penalties-Yards	6-45	12-90
Time of possession	24:11	35:49

Attendance—48,575. No-shows—12,440.

INDIVIDUAL STATISTICS

Rushing—Kansas City, Heard 7-22, Lacy 1-4, Brown 7-2, Carson 1-minus 8; Los Angeles, Allen 16-95, King 15-72, Hawkins 12-45, Wilson 5-5, Pruitt 1-2.

Passing—Kansas City, Kenney 19-37-1—194; Los Angeles, Wilson 12-21-1—103.

Receiving—Kansas City, Carson 3-58, Marshall 4-35, Scott 4-29, Brown 2-22, Lacy 2-19, Paige 2-18, W. Arnold 1-7, Jackson 1-6; Los Angeles, Williams 1-54, Christensen 3-23, Allen 3-21, Hawkins 1-5.

Kickoff Returns—Kansas City, Smith 2-36, Paige 1-21; Los Angeles, Montgomery 1-23.

Punt Returns—Kansas City, Smith 4-39; Los Angeles, Pruitt 5-42.

Interceptions—Kansas City, Lewis 1-0; Los Angeles, J. Davis 1-8.

Punting—Kansas City, J. Arnold 8-50.9; Los Angeles, Guy 6-41.7.

Field Goals—Kansas City, Lowery 0-1 (missed: 47); Los Angeles, Bahr 1-2 (missed: 47).

Sacks—Kansas City, Still 2, Bell; Los Angeles, M. Davis, Long, Martin, Townsend.

Patriots-Colts
SUNDAY, NOVEMBER 18
SCORE BY PERIODS

New England	16	10	7	17—50
Indianapolis	0	10	0	7—17

SCORING

New England—Ramsey 4 pass from Eason (Franklin kick), 7:41 1st.
New England—Safety, Middleton tackled in end zone by R. James, 10:54 1st.
New England—Ramsey 25 pass from Eason (Franklin kick), 14:07 1st.
Indianapolis—Schlichter 13 run (Allegre kick), 5:17 2nd.
New England—Ramsey 26 pass from Eason (Franklin kick), 11:56 2nd.
Indianapolis—Field goal Allegre 35, 13:45 2nd.
New England—Field goal Franklin 28, 14:57 2nd.
New England—Morgan 12 pass from Eason (Franklin kick), 6:56 3rd.
New England—Field goal Franklin 40, 0:51 4th.
New England—Tatupu 1 run (Franklin kick), 9:50 4th.
Indianapolis—Henry 13 pass from Schlichter (Allegre kick), 12:45 4th.
New England—Tatupu 20 run (Franklin kick), 14:14 4th.

TEAM STATISTICS

	New England	Indianapolis
First downs	26	17
Rushes-Yards	27-117	28-137
Passing yards	260	129
Sacked-Yards lost	6-44	7-59
Return yards	155	183
Passes	30-43-0	16-32-1

	New England	Indianapolis
Punts	6-47.2	6-35.7
Fumbles-Lost	0-0	4-0
Penalties-Yards	4-35	7-83
Time of possession	33:39	26:21

Attendance—60,009. No-shows—647.

INDIVIDUAL STATISTICS

Rushing—New England, C. James 11-38, Collins 7-36, Tatupu 8-40, Eason 1-3; Indianapolis, Schlichter 4-59, McMillan 12-52, Middleton 8-14, Moore 2-11, Wonsley 2-1.

Passing—New England, Eason 29-42-0—291, Kerrigan 1-1-0—13; Indianapolis, Schlichter 16-32-1—188.

Receiving—New England, Ramsey 8-104, Dawson 5-53, Collins 3-16, C. James 3-17, Hawthorne 2-24, Starring 1-8, Morgan 4-50, Weathers 1-13, Tatupu 1-4, Jones 1-6, Fryar 1-9; Indianapolis, Porter 4-63, Moore 3-22, Wonsley 3-17, Henry 2-26, Sherwin 1-21, Butler 1-25.

Kickoff Returns—New England, Collins 3-83, Fryar 1-18; Indianapolis, Smith 4-66, Anderson 2-84, Wonsley 1-10.

Punt Returns—New England, Fryar 3-52; Indianapolis, Anderson 2-23.

Interceptions—New England, Sanford 1-2.

Punting—New England, Camarillo 6-47.2; Indianapolis, Stark 6-35.7.

Field Goals—New England, Franklin 2-2; Indianapolis, Allegre 1-2 (missed: 61).

Sacks—New England, T. Williams 3, Tippett 2, Adams, Nelson; Indianapolis, Cooks 3, Wisniewski 2, Maxwell.

Cardinals-Giants
SUNDAY, NOVEMBER 18
SCORE BY PERIODS

St. Louis	0	7	0	3—10
New York Giants	0	0	9	7—16

SCORING

St. Louis—Lomax 1 run (O'Donoghue kick), 3:38 2nd.
New York—Field goal Haji-Sheikh 34, 8:04 3rd.
New York—Field goal Haji-Sheikh 39, 8:40 3rd.
New York—Field goal Haji-Sheikh 45, 14:26 3rd.
New York—Manuel 11 pass from Simms (Haji-Sheikh kick), 9:07 4th.
St. Louis—Field goal O'Donoghue 20, 13:03 4th.

TEAM STATISTICS

	St. Louis	New York
First downs	20	14
Rushes-Yards	34-133	32-102
Passing yards	203	165
Sacked-Yards lost	2-27	2-13
Return yards	127	99
Passes	19-38-4	12-30-2
Punts	5-34.6	6-35.7
Fumbles-Lost	3-2	0-0
Penalties-Yards	3-26	4-35
Time of possession	31:01	28:59

Attendance—73,428. No-shows—3,451.

INDIVIDUAL STATISTICS

Rushing—St. Louis, Anderson 24-111, Love 6-18, Mitchell 3-3, Lomax 1-1; New York, Carpenter 21-71, Morris 11-31.

Passing—St. Louis, Lomax 19-38-4—230; New York, Simms 12-30-2—178.

Receiving—St. Louis, Anderson 6-112, Love 4-15, Mitchell 1-10, Tilley 2-20, Green 1-23, LaFleur 1-2, Marsh 3-23, Harrell 1-15; New York, Manuel 3-80, Carpenter 3-19, Johnson 2-45, B. Williams 1-7, McConkey 2-16, Galbreath 1-11.

Kickoff Returns—St. Louis, Pittman 5-89; New York, McConkey 2-37, Morris 1-13.

Punt Returns—St. Louis, Pittman 3-10; New York, McConkey 3-12.

Interceptions—St. Louis, Perrin 1-22, L. Smith 1-6;

New York, Haynes 2-38, Reasons 1-0, Taylor 1-minus 1.

Punting—St. Louis, Birdsong 5-34.6; New York, Jennings 6-35.7.

Field Goals—St. Louis, O'Donoghue 1-1; New York, Haji-Sheikh 3-5 (missed: 52, 34).

Sacks—St. Louis, A. Baker, Junior; New York, Marshall, Taylor.

Redskins-Eagles
SUNDAY, NOVEMBER 18
SCORE BY PERIODS

Washington	0	7	3	0—10
Philadelphia	3	3	10	0—16

SCORING

Philadelphia—Field goal McFadden 43, 4:35 1st.

Washington—Didier 3 pass from Theismann (Moseley kick), 12:44 2nd.

Philadelphia—Field goal McFadden 34, 14:59 2nd.

Philadelphia—Field goal McFadden 41, 3:03 3rd.

Washington—Field goal Moseley 33, 9:34 3rd.

Philadelphia—Waters 89 kickoff return (McFadden kick), 9:52 3rd.

TEAM STATISTICS

	Washington	Philadelphia
First downs	16	13
Rushes-Yards	31-117	27-64
Passing yards	144	101
Sacked-Yards lost	1-5	3-26
Return yards	161	128
Passes	21-38-3	14-28-1
Punts	4-41.3	6-34.5
Fumbles-Lost	4-3	1-1
Penalties-Yards	10-124	2-13
Time of possession	31:50	28:10

Attendance—63,117. No-shows—9,555.

INDIVIDUAL STATISTICS

Rushing—Washington, Riggins 26-92, Theismann 4-23, Griffin 1-2; Philadelphia, Montgomery 9-20, M. Williams 6-19, Oliver 6-18, Haddix 5-8, Jaworski 1-minus 1.

Passing—Washington, Theismann 21-38-3—149; Philadelphia, Jaworski 14-28-1—127.

Receiving—Washington, Monk 8-80, Didier 5-30, Moore 3-13, Muhammad 2-12, Griffin 2-10, Warren 1-4; Philadelphia, Kab 3-42, Montgomery 3-7, Spagnola 2-26, Haddix 2-18, Woodruff 2-17, M. Williams 1-15, Oliver 1-2.

Kickoff Returns—Washington, Nelms 4-84, Griffin 1-8; Philadelphia, Cooper 2-31, Waters 1-89.

Punt Returns—Washington, Nelms 4-21, Green 1-13.

Interceptions—Washington, A. Washington 1-25; Philadelphia, Ellis 1-8, Edwards 1-0, Foules 1-0.

Punting—Washington, Hayes 4-41.3; Philadelphia, Horan 6-34.5.

Field Goals—Washington, Moseley 1-2 (missed: 35); Philadelphia, McFadden 3-4 (missed: 44).

Sacks—Washington, Butz 1½, Grant, Kaufman, ½; Philadelphia, Harrison ½, Schulz ½.

Dolphins-Chargers
SUNDAY, NOVEMBER 18
SCORE BY PERIODS

Miami	0	21	7	0	0—28
San Diego	7	7	0	14	6—34

SCORING

San Diego—Sievers 3 pass from Fouts (Benirschke kick), 14:27 1st.

Miami—Clayton 12 pass from Marino (von Schamann kick), 3:01 2nd.

Miami—P. Johnson 1 run (von Schamann kick), 7:30 2nd.

San Diego—Joiner 4 pass from Fouts (Benirschke kick), 12:33 2nd.

Miami—Bennett 4 pass from Marino (von Schamann kick), 14:13 2nd.

Miami—P. Johnson 3 run (von Schamann kick), 12:10 3rd.

San Diego—Joiner 19 pass from Fouts (Benirschke kick), 1:31 4th.

San Diego—Sievers 3 pass from Fouts (Benirschke kick), 14:09 4th.

San Diego—McGee 25 run (no kick), 3:17 OT.

TEAM STATISTICS

	Miami	San Diego
First downs	24	34
Rushes-Yards	22-96	36-166
Passing yards	338	371
Sacked-Yards lost	0-0	1-9
Return yards	200	97
Passes	28-41-1	37-56-1
Punts	2-42.0	4-44.3
Fumbles-Lost	2-2	0-0
Penalties-Yards	1-5	3-20
Time of possession	23:26	39:51

Attendance—53,041. No-shows—7,193.

INDIVIDUAL STATISTICS

Rushing—Miami, Nathan 11-66, Bennett 7-24, P. Johnson 4-6; San Diego, Jackson 28-124, McGee 8-42.

Passing—Miami, Marino 28-41-1—338; San Diego, Fouts 37-56-1—380.

Receiving—Miami, Clayton 6-71, Duper 5-99, Cefalo 1-10, D. Johnson 3-30, Moore 2-21, Hardy 4-50, Nathan 6-53, Bennett 1-4; San Diego, Chandler 5-55, Jackson 6-19, Duckworth 2-60, Holohan 5-58, Sievers 12-119, Joiner 4-59, James 2-10, Morris 1-0.

Kickoff Returns—Miami, Walker 5-146; San Diego, James 4-97.

Punt Returns—Miami, Walker 3-35.

Interceptions—Miami, L. Blackwood 1-12, Judson (with lateral) 0-7; San Diego, Turner 1-0.

Punting—Miami, Roby 2-42.0; San Diego, Buford 4-44.3.

Field Goals—Miami, von Schamann 0-1 (missed: 44); San Diego, Benirschke 0-1 (missed: 46).

Sacks—Miami, Betters.

Buccaneers-49ers
SUNDAY, NOVEMBER 18
SCORE BY PERIODS

Tampa Bay	0	10	0	7—17
San Francisco	0	14	7	3—24

SCORING

San Francisco—Craig 2 run (Wersching kick), 4:16 2nd.

Tampa Bay—Field goal Ariri 27, 7:47 2nd.

San Francisco—Solomon 3 run (Wersching kick), 11:54 2nd.

Tampa Bay—Giles 9 pass from DeBerg (Ariri kick), 14:11 2nd.

San Francisco—Tyler 1 run (Wersching kick), 10:54 3rd.

Tampa Bay—Carter 9 pass from DeBerg (Ariri kick), 1:21 4th.

San Francisco—Field goal Wersching 39, 6:21 4th.

TEAM STATISTICS

	Tampa Bay	San Francisco
First downs	23	25
Rushes-Yards	20-89	38-190
Passing yards	308	238
Sacked-Yards lost	1-8	2-9
Return yards	61	99
Passes	26-41-2	19-23-0
Punts	3-41.0	2-48.0
Fumbles-Lost	2-1	3-3
Penalties-Yards	7-38	3-35
Time of possession	28:17	31:43

Attendance—57,704. No-shows—3,660.

INDIVIDUAL STATISTICS

Rushing—Tampa Bay, Wilder 18-89, DeBerg 2-0; San

Francisco, Tyler 16-97, Craig 16-86, Solomon 1-3, Montana 4-2, Harmon 1-2.

Passing—Tampa Bay, DeBerg 26-41-2—316; San Francisco, Montana 19-23-0—247.

Receiving—Tampa Bay, Carter 9-166, Wilder 5-35, House 4-50, Giles 3-25, J. Bell 2-24, Armstrong 2-11, T. Bell 1-5; San Francisco, D. Clark 5-56, Craig 4-22, Cooper 3-32, Monroe 2-73, Solomon 2-24, Nehemiah 1-22, Tyler 1-11, Wilson 1-7.

Kickoff Returns—Tampa Bay, Morton 2-35, Bright 1-19; San Francisco, Monroe 2-42, Harmon 1-35.

Punt Returns—Tampa Bay, Bright 1-7; San Francisco, McLemore 1-6.

Interceptions—San Francisco, Hicks 1-13, Turner 1-3.

Punting—Tampa Bay, Garcia 3-41.0; San Francisco, Runager 2-48.0.

Field Goals—Tampa Bay, Ariri 1-2 (missed: 48); San Francisco, Wersching 1-1.

Sacks—Tampa Bay, Logan, Washington; San Francisco, Dean.

Seahawks-Bengals
SUNDAY, NOVEMBER 18
SCORE BY PERIODS

Seattle	7	10	0	9—26
Cincinnati	0	3	3	0— 6

SCORING

Seattle—Dixon 2 run (Johnson kick), 13:22 1st.

Seattle—Largent 12 pass from Krieg (Johnson kick), 5:33 2nd.

Cincinnati—Field goal Breech 30, 11:06 2nd.

Seattle—Field goal Johnson 25, 14:52 2nd.

Cincinnati—Field goal Breech 33, 14:22 3rd.

Seattle—Safety, Schonert tackled in end zone by J. Bryant, 1:16 4th.

Seattle—Dixon 1 run (Johnson kick), 5:11 4th.

TEAM STATISTICS

	Seattle	Cincinnati
First downs	15	20
Rushes-Yards	34-120	32-162
Passing yards	104	115
Sacked-Yards lost	1-4	4-40
Return yards	97	49
Passes	10-16-1	15-28-2
Punts	5-30.0	1-40.0
Fumbles-Lost	1-0	5-3
Penalties-Yards	3-30	12-103
Time of possession	28:32	31:28

Attendance—50,280. No-shows—8,864.

INDIVIDUAL STATISTICS

Rushing—Seattle, C. Bryant 12-41, Doornink 17-67, Dixon 2-3, Krieg 3-9; Cincinnati, Kinnebrew 22-119, Brooks 6-25, Schonert 2-5, Alexander 2-13.

Passing—Seattle, Krieg 10-16-1—108; Cincinnati, Schonert 14-26-1—141, Esiason 1-2-1—14.

Receiving—Seattle, Largent 5-65, C. Young 2-15, Turner 1-2, Doornink 1-26, C. Bryant 1-0; Cincinnati, Collinsworth 3-35, Harris 4-31, Kinnebrew 1-15, Brooks 1-50, Martin 1-10, Alexander 1-14.

Kickoff Returns—Seattle, Hughes 2-37, Dixon 1-22, Harris 1-7; Cincinnati, Jennings 3-37, Kinnebrew 1-7, G. Williams 1-0.

Punt Returns—Seattle, Skansi 1-4; Cincinnati, Martin 2-5, Simmons 1-0.

Interceptions—Seattle, Brown 1-27, Easley 1-0; Cincinnati, Horton 1-0.

Punting—Seattle, West 5-30.0; Cincinnati, McInally 1-40.0.

Field Goals—Seattle, Johnson 1-1; Cincinnati, Breech 2-2.

Sacks—Seattle, J. Bryant 2, Fanning, Gaines; Cincinnati, Browner.

Steelers-Saints
MONDAY, NOVEMBER 19
SCORE BY PERIODS

Pittsburgh	0	14	0	10—24
New Orleans	3	10	0	14—27

SCORING

New Orleans—Field goal Andersen 27, 14:16 1st.

Pittsburgh—Lipps 76 punt return (Anderson kick), 5:52 2nd.

Pittsburgh—Stallworth 14 pass from Malone (Anderson kick), 9:52 2nd.

New Orleans—Field goal Andersen 32, 13:10 2nd.

New Orleans—Hardy 28 pass from Todd (Andersen kick), 14:43 2nd.

Pittsburgh—Field goal Anderson 21, 0:22 4th.

New Orleans—Miller 21 pass from Todd (Andersen kick), 7:02 4th.

New Orleans—Winston 47 interception return (Andersen kick), 8:36 4th.

Pittsburgh—Lipps 25 pass from Campbell (Anderson kick), 13:43 4th.

TEAM STATISTICS

	Pittsburgh	New Orleans
First downs	18	16
Rushes-Yards	32-115	32-89
Passing yards	217	176
Sacked-Yards lost	3-24	6-47
Return yards	239	157
Passes	16-28-2	18-31-2
Punts	5-44.6	6-47.7
Fumbles-Lost	4-2	2-1
Penalties-Yards	5-49	3-20
Time of possession	27:16	32:44

Attendance—66,005. No-shows—5,111.

INDIVIDUAL STATISTICS

Rushing—Pittsburgh, Abercrombie 11-63, Pollard 16-40, Erenberg 3-13, Malone 2-minus 1; New Orleans, G. Rogers 17-43, Campbell 5-13, Anthony 2-13, W. Wilson 4-9, Todd 4-11.

Passing—Pittsburgh, Malone 10-19-2—158, Campbell 6-9-0—83; New Orleans, Todd 18-31-2—223.

Receiving—Pittsburgh, Stallworth 4-86, Lipps 4-81, Erenberg 4-49, Thompson 1-15, Pollard 2-5, Abercrombie 1-5; New Orleans, W. Wilson 8-39, Groth 3-44, Young 2-69, Scott 2-19, Anthony 1-3, Hardy 1-28, Miller 1-21.

Kickoff Returns—Pittsburgh, Erenberg 5-103; New Orleans, W. Wilson 1-23, Anthony 3-66.

Punt Returns—Pittsburgh, Lipps 4-128; New Orleans, Fields 2-12.

Interceptions—Pittsburgh, Woodruff 2-8; New Orleans, B. Clark 1-9, Winston 1-47.

Punting—Pittsburgh, Colquitt 5-44.6; New Orleans, Hansen 6-47.7.

Field Goals—Pittsburgh, Anderson 1-2 (missed: 43); New Orleans, Andersen 2-2.

Sacks—Pittsburgh, Merriweather 3, Gary, Williams, Willis; New Orleans, B. Clark, Warren, Winston ½, Paul ½.

THIRTEENTH WEEK

RESULTS OF WEEK 13

Thursday, November 22

Dallas 20, New England 17 at Dall.
Detroit 31, Green Bay 28 at Det.

Sunday, November 25

Chicago 34, Minnesota 3 at Minn.
Cincinnati 35, Atlanta 14 at Cin.
Cleveland 27, Houston 10 at Cleve.
L.A. Raiders 21, Indianapolis 7 at L.A.
L.A. Rams 34, Tampa Bay 33 at T.B.
N.Y. Giants 28, Kansas City 27 at N.Y.
Pittsburgh 52, San Diego 24 at Pitts.
St. Louis 17, Philadelphia 16 at St. L.
San Francisco 35, New Orleans 3 at N.O.
Seattle 27, Denver 24 at Den.
Washington 41, Buffalo 14 at Wash.

Monday, November 26

Miami 28, N.Y. Jets 17 at Mia.

The matchup had all the makings of a classic defensive struggle. The Denver Broncos, 11-1 and winners of 10 straight games, were leading the American Football Conference Western Division with a defense that ranked first in the league in fewest points allowed (171) and second in opponents turnovers (49). The Seattle Seahawks, 10-2 and winners of six straight, were second in the division with a defense that ranked second in the NFL in points allowed (176) and first in opponents turnovers (55).

So what happened when two of the best teams in football met for the first time in 1984? On the first play from scrimmage, Seattle's Dave Krieg hooked up with rookie wide receiver Daryl Turner on an 80-yard touchdown pass. The Seahawks went on to win the game, 27-24, in an offensive outburst that saw Krieg throw for three touchdowns and 406 yards and his counterpart, Denver's John Elway, throw for two scores and 275 yards. Although neither club rushed for 100 yards, Steve Largent, the Seahawks' Pro Bowl receiver, caught 12 passes for 191 yards, both Seattle club records, and one touchdown.

"There are good vibes between Krieg and Largent," said Broncos cornerback Louis Wright. "We made some mistakes today, and he (Largent) took advantage of them."

The Seattle offense also took advantage of a fumble by Denver tight end Clarence Kay midway through the final period. Norm Johnson kicked a 28-yard field goal minutes later that expanded the Seahawks' lead to 27-17.

Elway brought the Broncos back, however, hitting rookie running back Gene Lang with a nine-yard scoring pass just two minutes later. And on Denver's next possession, Elway drove the team within range for a possible game-tying field goal in the final minute. But Rich Karlis, who had hit a 27-yarder in the first period, shanked a 25-yarder with 39 seconds left.

"I hit the ball well," said Karlis. "It just went straight into the upright. The bottom line is that I just missed it. There was no excuse for it."

"We were hoping for a big play on that field goal attempt," said Seahawks Coach Chuck Knox, whose club had made many big plays in the franchise's most successful season ever. "The ball just bounced right for us. That's football."

Football is also Thanksgiving Day games in Detroit, and the Lions celebrated the 50th anniversary of their first Thanksgiving Day game with a 31-28 triumph over long-time rival Green Bay. The Packers-Lions matchup was the 14th between the two clubs in the Thanksgiving Day series, but the first since 1963.

The Lions proved to be a rude holiday host, holding the ball for nearly three-quarters of the game and piling up 33 first downs and 518 total yards. Quarterback Gary Danielson led the assault with three touchdown passes as the Lions ended Green Bay's four-game winning streak and avenged a 41-9 shellacking at the hands of the Packers four weeks earlier. Detroit improved its record 22-21-2 when hosting games on Thanksgiving Day.

The Dallas Cowboys played Thanksgiving host to New England and carved up the Patriots, 20-17. The Cowboys entered the contest still aching from a 14-3 upset loss to previously winless Buffalo four days earlier. The winning points came off the foot of placekicker Rafael Septien, whose 23-yard field goal with four seconds left clinched the Cowboys' fifth win over New England in as many tries.

Tony Eason's one-yard sneak with 1:58 remaining had tied the game, 17-17, but the Pats' second-year quarterback had an otherwise rough day. He was held to 19 completions in 38 attempts and sacked 10 times by a swarming Dallas defense. Eason's second pass of the day was intercepted by safety Michael Downs and returned 27 yards for a touchdown. The Cowboys improved their Thanksgiving Day record to 13-3-1.

Cleveland Browns rookie wide receiver Brian Brennan watched Boston College quarterback Doug Flutie throw a miracle 48-yard touchdown pass on the final play of the game in the Eagles' 47-45 victory over Miami (Fla.) on the Friday after Thanksgiving. Brennan, one of Flutie's primary targets for three seasons at BC, came out two days later and caught his first two NFL scoring passes in the Browns' 27-10 win over Houston. Paul McDonald threw three touchdown passes as Cleveland won for the third time in five games under new Coach Marty Schottenheimer.

Steve Largent hauled in 12 passes for 191 yards and a touchdown as the Seahawks edged Denver, 27-24, in a showdown between AFC Western Division powers in Week 13.

The Washington Redskins scored on their first four possessions, rolling up 24 points in the game's first 16 minutes, and coasted to an easy 41-14 victory over the Buffalo Bills. Joe Theismann completed 26 of 33 passes for 311 yards to supplant Sonny Jurgensen as the Redskins' all-time leading passer. Theismann finished the game with 22,706 yards to Jurgensen's 22,585. The Bills could muster only one first down in the time it took Washington to build its 24-0 lead.

Mark Malone broke Terry Bradshaw's club record for completion percentage in Pittsburgh's 52-24 rout of San Diego. Malone completed 18 of 22 passes for an 81.82 success rate while throwing four touchdown passes, three to veteran wide receiver John Stallworth. Malone also ran for one touchdown while Walter Abercrombie—one of the few Pittsburgh offensive weapons who didn't score—came up with the first 100-yard rushing game of his three-year career. The Steelers scored on seven of their first nine possessions in amassing the largest point total in Chuck Noll's 16 years as Pittsburgh coach.

For the Chargers, who were outrushed 202 yards to 31 and forced to pass, Charlie Joiner caught six passes to break the NFL record for career pass receptions. Joiner, in his 16th professional season, finished the game with 651 catches to surpass by two Charley Taylor's former record.

While Malone set the Pittsburgh team record for completion percentage, Cincinnati's Turk Schonert, subbing for the injured Ken Anderson, came up with the fourth-best single-day performance in league history. Schonert completed 20 of 23 passes for an 86.96 completion rate in the Bengals' 35-14 triumph over Atlanta. Ironically, Schonert's performance didn't even set the Cincinnati club record because Anderson holds the league mark with a 90.91 game against Pittsburgh in 1974.

The Bengals built a 21-0 halftime lead in handing the Falcons their seventh straight defeat. Schonert and wide receiver Cris Collinsworth hooked up for a pair of touchdowns, the first coming on a 57-yard completion on the game's fourth play.

Philadelphia quarterback Ron Jaworski, whose 116 consecutive starts was tops among all active NFL signal-callers, suffered a broken leg on the third play of the Eagles' 17-16 loss at St. Louis. His replacement, Joe Pisarcik, outdueled the Cards' Neil Lomax, but the Eagles lost when Neil O'Donoghue hit a 44-yard field goal for St. Louis with eight seconds left. The Cards drove 72 yards in the final 1:49 to set up O'Donoghue's winning kick.

The Cardinals had a 14-6 lead with nine minutes left, but turnovers on three straight possessions helped the Eagles score 10 points to take the lead. But the Eagles missed a chance to go up by five points when placekicker Paul McFadden, whose 32-yard field goal with 1:10 left to play had given Philly a two-point lead, missed on a 26-yarder with 4:18 remaining. That left the door open for O'Donoghue's winning kick.

The Kansas City Chiefs held a 13-point lead over the New York Giants with nine minutes left but ended up dropping a one-point decision, 28-27. Quarterback Phil Simms, whose three first-half interceptions were largely responsible for New York scoring only seven points, led the Giants on 90- and 80-yard scoring marches in the final minutes. Simms hit Bobby Johnson with a 22-yard scoring pass with 7:30 left and Zeke Mowatt on a three-yarder with 2:22 remaining. Rob Carpenter scored New York's other touchdowns as Kansas City, despite three touchdown passes by Bill Kenney, lost for the fourth week in a row.

Eric Dickerson scored three touchdowns and set up another with a 51-yard run as the Los Angeles Rams upended NFC Central Division rival Tampa Bay, 34-33. Dickerson was too much for the Bucs to handle, rushing for 191 yards, including 142 in the second half, as L.A. scored 17 fourth-quarter points to pull out the victory.

Steve DeBerg threw two touchdown passes and James Wilder scored on two one-yard runs for Tampa Bay, but the Bucs' inability to convert the extra point after their first touchdown proved costly. Obed Ariri's kick sailed through the uprights but was called back on a holding penalty. On his next attempt, the Rams' Gary Jeter broke through the line and blocked the kick.

The Los Angeles Raiders had little difficulty in disposing of Indianapolis, 21-7. The L.A. defense held the opposition to fewer than 200 yards in total offense for the second straight week—the Colts had 158—and kept Indianapolis penned up on its own end of the field until late in the third quarter, when a fumble by punt returner Greg Pruitt gave the Colts the ball at the 1-yard line, setting up Indianapolis' only touchdown. Marc Wilson's two touchdown passes and one scoring run accounted for all the Raiders points.

The San Francisco 49ers and Chicago Bears each clinched their division title with wins in Week 13.

The 49ers crushed New Orleans, 35-3, with a 28-point second-half explosion to take the NFC Western Division crown. Joe Montana, who struggled in the opening half, threw for two touchdowns in the third period while rookie linebacker Todd Shell, the 49ers' No. 1 draft pick out of Brigham Young, returned an interception 53 yards for a touchdown. Shell also had two of the San Francisco defense's eight quarterback sacks.

The Bears clinched the NFC Central, the franchise's first title of any kind since winning the NFL championship in 1963, with a 34-3 rout of division-rival Minnesota. The Bears' league-leading defense came up with one of its strongest performances of the season, holding the Vikings to just nine first downs and fewer than

100 yards rushing and passing. The Bears ran off 34 straight points after an early Minnesota field goal to improve to 9-4 on the season.

The playoff appearance would be only Chicago's third since winning the '63 title. The Bears made it as a wild-card entry in both 1977 and 1979, losing their first postseason game each time.

One club familiar with postseason play was the Miami Dolphins, who ran their season record to 12-1 with a 28-17 decision over the New York Jets in the Monday night game. The Dolphins, who already had clinched the AFC Eastern Division title, would be making their 11th appearance in the playoffs since Don Shula took over as coach in 1970.

In the victory over New York, Dan Marino's four touchdown passes accounted for all of Miami's points as the second-year quarterback tied the NFL record for touchdown passes in a single season with 36. Ironically, Marino was born during the 1961 season in which George Blanda established the record with the Houston Oilers of the old American Football League.

Patriots-Cowboys
THURSDAY, NOVEMBER 22
SCORE BY PERIODS

New England	3	0	0	14—17
Dallas	7	3	7	3—20

SCORING

Dallas—Downs 27 interception return (Septien kick), 2:04 1st.

New England—Field goal Franklin 29, 5:52 1st.

Dallas—Field goal Septien 28, 0:07 2nd.

Dallas—Hill 9 pass from D. White (Septien kick), 11:57 3rd.

New England—Ramsey 1 pass from Eason (Franklin kick), 0:05 4th.

New England—Eason 1 run (Franklin kick), 13:02 4th.

Dallas—Field goal Septien 23, 14:56 4th.

TEAM STATISTICS

	New England	Dallas
First downs	19	18
Rushes-Yards	25-150	30-67
Passing yards	147	275
Sacked-Yards lost	10-57	2-13
Return yards	127	157
Passes	19-38-1	21-41-1
Punts	11-43.5	10-38.0
Fumbles-Lost	2-0	2-1
Penalties-Yards	4-30	5-25
Time of possession	30:36	29:24

Attendance—55,341. No-shows—9,760.

INDIVIDUAL STATISTICS

Rushing—New England, C. James 19-112, Tatupu 2-15, Eason 2-14, Collins 2-9; Dallas, Dorsett 19-49, Newsome 6-18, D. White 2-1, J. Jones 2-0, Springs 1-minus 1.

Passing—New England, Eason 19-38-1—204; Dallas, D. White 21-41-1—288.

Receiving—New England, Starring 6-61, Ramsey 5-71, C. James 2-22, Dawson 3-32, Jones 1-7, Weathers 1-6, Morgan 1-5; Dallas, Hill 8-125, Donley 4-74, Dorsett 3-40, Newsome 3-4, Cosbie 2-36, Harris 1-9.

Kickoff Returns—New England, Robinson 1-14, Hawthorne 1-14, Collins 3-64; Dallas, Allen 3-60, Salonen 1-22.

Punt Returns—New England, Fryar 7-18; Dallas, Allen 5-48.

Interceptions—New England, Clayborn 1-17; Dallas, Downs 1-27.

Punting—New England, Camarillo 11-43.5; Dallas, D. White 10-38.0.

Field Goals—New England, Franklin 1-2 (missed: 52); Dallas, Septien 2-2.

Sacks—New England, McGrew, Tippett; Dallas, R. White 3, E. Jones 2, Bates 2, Dickerson, Downs, Tuinei.

Packers-Lions
THURSDAY, NOVEMBER 22
SCORE BY PERIODS

Green Bay	14	7	0	7—28
Detroit	0	17	7	7—31

SCORING

Green Bay—Ellis 40 run (Del Greco kick), 1:33 1st.

Green Bay—Coffman 44 pass from Dickey (Del Greco kick), 8:04 1st.

Detroit—Lewis 10 pass from Danielson (Murray kick), 3:38 2nd.

Green Bay—Ivery 7 pass from Dickey (Del Greco kick), 8:15 2nd.

Detroit—Lewis 21 pass from Danielson (Murray kick), 13:46 2nd.

Detroit—Field goal Murray 32, 15:00 2nd.

Detroit—J. Jones 1 run (Murray kick), 13:52 3rd.

Detroit—Chadwick 21 pass from Danielson (Murray kick), 7:45 4th.

Green Bay—Epps 4 pass from Wright (Del Greco kick), 14:05 4th.

TEAM STATISTICS

	Green Bay	Detroit
First downs	14	33
Rushes-Yards	16-109	45-171
Passing yards	197	347
Sacked-Yards lost	2-18	1-6
Return yards	130	64
Passes	13-24-2	25-34-1
Punts	4-42.8	2-40.5
Fumbles-Lost	0-0	4-1
Penalties-Yards	5-35	9-71
Time of possession	15:13	44:27

Attendance—63,698. No-shows—7,103.

INDIVIDUAL STATISTICS

Rushing—Green Bay, Ellis 4-45, Ivery 10-44, Crouse 2-20; Detroit, Jenkins 13-71, J. Jones 18-59, D'Addio 4-35, Danielson 5-14, Bussey 4-13, Nichols 1-minus 21.

Passing—Green Bay, Dickey 8-17-1—115, Wright 5-7-1—100; Detroit, Danielson 24-33-1—305, Machurek 1-1-0—48.

Receiving—Green Bay, Ivery 5-46, Epps 3-70, Crouse 2-30, Coffman 1-44, Lofton 1-24, Ellis 1-1; Detroit, J. Jones 7-75, Nichols 4-108, Lewis 3-40, Thompson 3-24, Chadwick 2-42, Jenkins 2-26, Rubick 2-23, Bussey 1-8, McCall 1-7.

Kickoff Returns—Green Bay, Rodgers 4-87, Huckleby 1-12; Detroit, Hall 4-49.

Punt Returns—Detroit, Mandley 1-10.

Interceptions—Green Bay, Flynn 1-31; Detroit, Graham 1-15, Watkins 1-0.

Punting—Green Bay, Scribner 4-42.8; Detroit, Black 2-40.5.

Field Goals—Green Bay, none attempted; Detroit, Murray 1-2 (missed: 54).

Sacks—Green Bay, Anderson; Detroit, Cofer, Gay.

Bears-Vikings
SUNDAY, NOVEMBER 25
SCORE BY PERIODS

Chicago	7	10	17	0—34
Minnesota	3	0	0	0— 3

SCORING

Minnesota—Field goal Stenerud 19, 10:41 1st.

Chicago—Gault 30 pass from Fuller (B. Thomas kick), 13:28 1st.

Chicago—Field goal B. Thomas 45, 7:48 2nd.

Chicago—Moorehead 13 pass from Fuller (B. Thomas kick), 14:36 2nd.

Chicago—Field goal B. Thomas 37, 5:01 3rd.

Chicago—Bell 36 interception return (B. Thomas kick), 5:32 3rd.

Chicago—Payton 2 run (B. Thomas kick), 12:19 3rd.

TEAM STATISTICS

	Chicago	Minnesota
First downs	20	9
Rushes-Yards	42-229	19-90
Passing yards	170	71
Sacked-Yards lost	1-8	3-19
Return yards	137	188
Passes	16-25-0	12-31-2
Punts	5-41.2	8-48.3
Fumbles-Lost	0-0	0-0
Penalties-Yards	2-10	2-15
Time of possession	36:41	23:19

Attendance—56,881. No-shows—5,352.

INDIVIDUAL STATISTICS

Rushing—Chicago, Payton 23-117, Suhey 4-23, Fuller 2-9, Jordan 4-25, Gentry 3-17, Hutchison 3-11, C. Thomas 2-20, Lisch 1-7; Minnesota, Brown 5-20, Anderson 10-39, Nelson 4-31.

Passing—Chicago, Fuller 12-19-0—143, Lisch 4-6-0—35; Minnesota, Wilson 12-31-2—90.

Receiving—Chicago, Suhey 2-9, Gault 3-53, Payton 2-33, Anderson 1-17, Baschnagel 1-13, Moorehead 1-13, Dunsmore 1-2, Jordan 1-6, Cameron 1-13, Saldi 1-9, Hutchison 1-7, C. Thomas 1-3; Minnesota, Brown 1-6, White 1-15, Jordan 2-15, Jones 1-16, Collins 1-6, Anderson 2-13, Nelson 1-0, Lewis 2-14, Senser 1-5.

Kickoff Returns—Chicago, Cameron 2-55; Minnesota, Nelson 7-168.

Punt Returns—Chicago, Fisher 4-43; Minnesota, Nelson 3-20.

Interceptions—Chicago, Bell 2-39.

Punting—Chicago, Finzer 5-41.2; Minnesota, Coleman 8-48.3.

Field Goals—Chicago, B. Thomas 2-2; Minnesota, Stenerud 1-1.

Sacks—Chicago, Hartenstine, Bell ½, Hampton ½, Singletary ½, Wilson ½; Minnesota, C. Martin.

Falcons-Bengals
SUNDAY, NOVEMBER 25
SCORE BY PERIODS

Atlanta	0	0	14	0—14
Cincinnati	14	7	7	7—35

SCORING

Cincinnati—Collinsworth 57 pass from Schonert (Breech kick), 1:46 1st.

Cincinnati—Kinnebrew 1 run (Breech kick), 14:45 1st.

Cincinnati—Jackson 28 interception return (Breech kick), 0:09 2nd.

Cincinnati—Alexander 1 run (Breech kick), 1:46 3rd.

Atlanta—Riggs 6 run (Luckhurst kick), 5:59 3rd.

Atlanta—Riggs 2 run (Luckhurst kick), 12:24 3rd.

Cincinnati—Collinsworth 20 pass from Schonert (Breech kick), 12:05 4th.

TEAM STATISTICS

	Atlanta	Cincinnati
First downs	19	26
Rushes-Yards	28-117	35-121
Passing yards	197	273
Sacked-Yards lost	1-9	3-26
Return yards	153	139

	Atlanta	Cincinnati
Passes	17-34-2	22-25-1
Punts	3-41.3	3-36.0
Fumbles-Lost	1-1	2-0
Penalties-Yards	5-28	3-25
Time of possession	26:09	33:51

Attendance—44,678. No-shows—7,199.

INDIVIDUAL STATISTICS

Rushing—Atlanta, Riggs 21-89, Moroski 5-26, C. Benson 2-2; Cincinnati, Kinnebrew 16-44, Brooks 7-22, Schonert 1-1, Jennings 6-47, Alexander 2-6, Harris 1-minus 2, Farley 2-3.

Passing—Atlanta, Moroski 17-34-2—206; Cincinnati, Schonert 20-23-1—288, Esiason 2-2-0—9.

Receiving—Atlanta, Riggs 1-3, A. Jackson 7-94, Cox 1-9, C. Benson 2-18, Bailey 3-61, Cain 1-7, Hodge 2-14; Cincinnati, Kinnebrew 2-14, Collinsworth 6-134, Harris 5-90, Brooks 2-14, Jennings 2-13, Holman 1-3, Kreider 1-14, Kern 1-9, Alexander 1-5, Farley 1-1.

Kickoff Returns—Atlanta, Johnson 4-68, Curran 2-61; Cincinnati, Martin 2-45, Jennings 1-21.

Punt Returns—Atlanta, Johnson 1-4; Cincinnati, Martin 1-26, Simmons 1-5.

Interceptions—Atlanta, Johnson 1-20; Cincinnati, Jackson 1-28, Kemp 1-14.

Punting—Atlanta, Giacomarro 3-41.3; Cincinnati, McInally 3-36.0.

Field Goals—Atlanta, Luckhurst 0-1 (missed: 35); Cincinnati, Breech 0-1 (missed: 51).

Sacks—Atlanta, T. Benson, Pitts, Richardson; Cincinnati, Krumrie.

Oilers-Browns
SUNDAY, NOVEMBER 25
SCORE BY PERIODS

Houston	7	0	0	3—10
Cleveland	7	13	0	7—27

SCORING

Cleveland—Brennan 14 pass from McDonald (Bahr kick), 7:31 1st.
Houston—Bostic 22 fumble return (Cooper kick), 12:04 1st.
Cleveland—Field goal Bahr 18, 4:23 2nd.
Cleveland—Newsome 12 pass from McDonald (Bahr kick), 8:32 2nd.
Cleveland—Field goal Bahr 29, 13:09 2nd.
Houston—Field goal Cooper 39, 3:04 4th.
Cleveland—Brennan 7 pass from McDonald (Bahr kick), 10:40 4th.

TEAM STATISTICS

	Houston	Cleveland
First downs	11	18
Rushes-Yards	25-109	38-120
Passing yards	38	142
Sacked-Yards lost	4-46	1-9
Return yards	97	175
Passes	9-20-2	16-26-1
Punts	6-41.2	2-43.0
Fumbles-Lost	3-0	1-1
Penalties-Yards	7-44	3-20
Time of possession	26:35	33:25

Attendance—46,077. No-shows—1,275.

INDIVIDUAL STATISTICS

Rushing—Houston, Moriarty 16-81, Edwards 3-20, Moon 3-4, Joyner 3-4; Cleveland, Green 26-74, Byner 9-41, White 1-4, J. Davis 1-5, McDonald 1-minus 4.

Passing—Houston, Moon 9-20-2—84; Cleveland, McDonald 16-26-1—151.

Receiving—Houston, Bryant 1-14, J. Williams 2-22, Dressel 1-15, McCloskey 1-11, Walls 1-9, Moriarty 1-minus 4, Holston 1-11, Edwards 1-6; Cleveland, Newsome 10-102, Brennan 4-34, Holt 1-6, Walker 1-9.

Kickoff Returns—Houston, Allen 3-48, Roaches 1-25, Walls 1-22; Cleveland, B. Davis 2-50, Byner 1-15.

Punt Returns—Houston, Roaches 1-0; Cleveland, Brennan 5-54.

Interceptions—Houston, Brazile 1-2; Cleveland, Gross 1-47, Dixon 1-9.

Punting—Houston, James 6-41.2; Cleveland, Cox 2-43.0.

Field Goals— Houston, Cooper 1-1; Cleveland, Bahr 2-2.

Sacks—Houston, Bostic; Cleveland, Camp 3, Matthews.

Colts-Raiders
SUNDAY, NOVEMBER 25
SCORE BY PERIODS

Indianapolis	0	0	7	0— 7
Los Angeles Raiders	7	7	0	7—21

SCORING

Los Angeles—Christensen 7 pass from Wilson (Bahr kick), 5:02 1st.
Los Angeles—Casper 1 pass from Wilson (Bahr kick), 8:42 2nd.
Indianapolis—McMillan 1 run (Allegre kick), 9:18 3rd.
Los Angeles—Wilson 14 run (Bahr kick), 1:42 4th.

TEAM STATISTICS

	Indianapolis	Los Angeles
First downs	10	21
Rushes-Yards	29-77	42-177
Passing yards	81	106
Sacked-Yards lost	6-44	6-40
Return yards	119	111
Passes	10-27-1	13-23-2
Punts	10-44.4	8-39.8
Fumbles-Lost	2-1	1-1
Penalties-Yards	7-41	10-102
Time of possession	26:08	33:52

Attendance—40,289. No-shows—9,134.

INDIVIDUAL STATISTICS

Rushing—Indianapolis, Dickey 16-41, Schlichter 4-20, McMillan 9-16; Los Angeles, Allen 18-110, Hawkins 12-45, Wilson 4-13, King 5-11, Willis 2-2, Pruitt 1-minus 4.

Passing—Indianapolis, Schlichter 10-27-1—125; Los Angeles, Wilson 13-23-2—146.

Receiving—Indianapolis, Porter 4-43, Dickey 1-33, Butler 1-16, Sherwin 2-14, Bouza 1-12, McMillan 1-7; Los Angeles, Christensen 6-77, Barnwell 4-46, Casper 2-14, Allen 1-9.

Kickoff Returns—Indianapolis, Anderson 2-52, Smith 2-27; Los Angeles, Williams 2-32.

Punt Returns—Indianapolis, Anderson 5-20; Los Angeles, Pruitt 5-49, Montgomery 1-5.

Interceptions—Indianapolis, Daniel 1-0, Krauss 1-0; Los Angeles, Haynes 1-25.

Punting—Indianapolis, Stark 10-44.4; Los Angeles, Guy 8-39.8.

Field Goals—Indianapolis, none attempted; Los Angeles, none attempted.

Sacks—Indianapolis, Cooks 4½, Wisniewski, Maxwell ½; Los Angeles, M. Davis 2, Long 2, Ackerman, Squirek.

Rams-Buccaneers
SUNDAY, NOVEMBER 25
SCORE BY PERIODS

Los Angeles Rams	0	10	7	17—34
Tampa Bay	9	7	10	7—33

SCORING

Tampa Bay—Field goal Ariri 26, 4:54 1st.
Tampa Bay—Wilder 1 run (kick failed), 13:40 1st.
Los Angeles—Dickerson 2 run (Lansford kick), 4:32 2nd.
Tampa Bay—J. Bell 16 pass from DeBerg (Ariri kick), 9:18 2nd.
Los Angeles—Field goal Lansford 35, 13:16 2nd.
Los Angeles—Dickerson 1 run (Lansford kick), 3:49 3rd.
Tampa Bay—Field goal Ariri 24, 10:02 3rd.

Tampa Bay—Armstrong 6 pass from DeBerg (Ariri kick), 15:00 3rd.
Los Angeles—Kemp 1 run (Lansford kick), 2:37 4th.
Los Angeles—Dickerson 33 run (Lansford kick), 4:42 4th.
Los Angeles—Field goal Lansford 27, 9:25 4th.
Tampa Bay—Wilder 1 run (Ariri kick), 12:09 4th.

TEAM STATISTICS

	Los Angeles	Tampa Bay
First downs	19	28
Rushes-Yards	43-299	22-84
Passing yards	68	322
Sacked-Yards lost	0-0	0-0
Return yards	152	129
Passes	7-10-0	27-44-1
Punts	3-32.3	2-40.0
Fumbles-Lost	1-1	2-1
Penalties-Yards	7-57	7-45
Time of possession	29:53	30:07

Attendance—42,242. No-shows—10,556.

INDIVIDUAL STATISTICS

Rushing—Los Angeles, Dickerson 28-191, Redden 3-48, Crutchfield 8-43, Brown 1-16, Kemp 3-1; Tampa Bay, Wilder 20-77, DeBerg 2-7.

Passing—Los Angeles, Kemp 7-10-0—68; Tampa Bay, DeBerg 27-44-1—322.

Receiving—Los Angeles, Ellard 1-23, Farmer 1-19, Guman 1-10, David Hill 1-9, Grant 1-5, Dickerson 1-3, Barber 1-minus 1; Tampa Bay, T. Bell 4-88, Wilder 10-80, House 4-50, J. Bell 3-47, Carter 3-33, Armstrong 2-17, Dixon 1-7.

Kickoff Returns—Los Angeles, Drew Hill 4-101, Redden 1-20; Tampa Bay, Bright 3-49, Morton 2-69.

Punt Returns—Los Angeles, Ellard 2-31; Tampa Bay, Bright 1-11.

Interceptions—Los Angeles, Irvin 1-0.

Punting—Los Angeles, Misko 3-32.3; Tampa Bay, Garcia 2-40.0.

Field Goals—Los Angeles, Lansford 2-2; Tampa Bay, Ariri 2-2.

Chiefs-Giants
SUNDAY, NOVEMBER 25
SCORE BY PERIODS

Kansas City	0	17	0	10—27
New York Giants	0	7	7	14—28

SCORING

Kansas City—Paige 26 pass from Kenney (Lowery kick), 3:39 2nd.
New York—Carpenter 1 run (Haji-Sheikh kick), 9:36 2nd.
Kansas City—Field goal Lowery 41, 14:13 2nd.
Kansas City—Scott 8 pass from Kenney (Lowery kick), 14:46 2nd.
New York—Carpenter 1 run (Haji-Sheikh kick), 6:30 3rd.
Kansas City—Field goal Lowery 52, 2:24 4th.
Kansas City—Carson 34 pass from Kenney (Lowery kick), 5:42 4th.
New York—Johnson 22 pass from Simms (Haji-Sheikh kick), 7:30 4th.
New York—Mowatt 3 pass from Simms (Haji-Sheikh kick), 12:38 4th.

TEAM STATISTICS

	Kansas City	New York
First downs	15	29
Rushes-Yards	22-64	38-147
Passing yards	276	324
Sacked-Yards lost	1-10	2-19
Return yards	219	142
Passes	18-36-1	24-41-3
Punts	7-42.3	5-38.6
Fumbles-Lost	2-1	1-0
Penalties-Yards	5-25	1-10
Time of possession	23:05	36:55

Attendance—74,383. No-shows—2,467.

INDIVIDUAL STATISTICS

Rushing—Kansas City, Heard 10-30, Jackson 5-24, Lacy 4-8, Kenney 1-1, Brown 1-1, J. Arnold 1-0; New York, Carpenter 22-86, Morris 12-50, Simms 2-11, Galbreath 2-0.

Passing—Kansas City, Kenney 18-36-1—286; New York, Simms 24-41-3—343.

Receiving—Kansas City, Carson 5-153, Marshall 5-59, Paige 2-37, Scott 2-17, Brown 2-11, Lacy 1-5, Heard 1-4; New York, Mowatt 7-126, Johnson 4-81, Morris 4-56, Carpenter 4-19, Galbreath 3-24, B. Williams 2-37.

Kickoff Returns—Kansas City, Smith 4-117, Paige 1-13; New York, Woolfolk 4-66, Morris 1-11.

Punt Returns—Kansas City, Smith 3-22; New York, Manuel 3-47, McConkey 1-11.

Interceptions—Kansas City, Ross 1-31, Lewis 1-26, Cherry 1-20; New York, Currier 1-3.

Punting—Kansas City, J. Arnold 7-42.3; New York, Jennings 5-38.6.

Field Goals—Kansas City, Lowery 2-2; New York, Haji-Sheikh 0-1 (missed: 52).

Sacks—Kansas City, Daniels, Still; New York, Banks.

Chargers-Steelers
SUNDAY, NOVEMBER 25
SCORE BY PERIODS

San Diego	0	10	7	7—24
Pittsburgh	3	21	21	7—52

SCORING

Pittsburgh—Field goal Anderson 55, 6:25 1st.
Pittsburgh—Lipps 15 pass from Malone (Anderson kick), 1:25 2nd.
Pittsburgh—Pollard 2 run (Anderson kick), 3:48 2nd.
San Diego—Field goal Benirschke 29, 8:29 2nd.
Pittsburgh—Stallworth 30 pass from Malone (Anderson kick), 12:39 2nd.
San Diego—James 58 punt return (Benirschke kick), 14:45 2nd.
San Diego—Chandler 63 pass from Luther (Benirschke kick), 1:12 3rd.
Pittsburgh—Pollard 2 run (Anderson kick), 11:18 3rd.
Pittsburgh—Stallworth 5 pass from Malone (Anderson kick), 11:45 3rd.
Pittsburgh—Stallworth 45 pass from Malone (Anderson kick), 14:18 3rd.
Pittsburgh—Malone 1 run (Anderson kick), 8:43 4th.
San Diego—Joiner 25 pass from Luther (Benirschke kick), 9:49 4th.

TEAM STATISTICS

	San Diego	Pittsburgh
First downs	23	28
Rushes-Yards	15-31	46-202
Passing yards	391	243
Sacked-Yards lost	1-10	1-10
Return yards	213	134
Passes	32-51-4	18-22-0
Punts	2-58.0	3-41.0
Fumbles-Lost	2-1	1-0
Penalties-Yards	5-71	7-56
Time of possession	26:06	33:54

Attendance—55,856. No-shows—3,144.

INDIVIDUAL STATISTICS

Rushing—San Diego, Jackson 10-23, McGee 4-8, James 1-0; Pittsburgh, Pollard 19-79, Abercrombie 19-109, Erenberg 1-5, Malone 2-minus 1, Veals 4-12, Campbell 1-minus 2.

Passing—San Diego, Fouts 11-19-1—105, Luther 21-32-3—296; Pittsburgh, Malone 18-22-0—253.

Receiving—San Diego, Bendross 2-13, Holohan 6-59, Chandler 4-105, Duckworth 4-74, Sievers 3-31, James 4-28, Jackson 1-3, Joiner 6-70, McGee 2-18; Pittsburgh, Abercrombie 1-3, Pollard 2-4, Lipps 7-118, Stallworth 7-116, D. Nelson 1-12.

Kickoff Returns—San Diego, James 5-106, McGee 2-38; Pittsburgh, Erenberg 3-59, Corley 1-15.

Punt Returns—San Diego, James 2-69; Pittsburgh, Lipps 2-16.

Interceptions—Pittsburgh, Brown 1-31, Cole 1-12, Merriweather 1-1, Williams 1-0.

Punting—San Diego, Buford 2-58.0; Pittsburgh, Colquitt 3-41.0.

Field Goals—San Diego, Benirschke 1-2 (missed: 49); Pittsburgh, Anderson 1-1.

Sacks—San Diego, Lowe; Pittsburgh, Merriweather.

Eagles-Cardinals
SUNDAY, NOVEMBER 25
SCORE BY PERIODS

Philadelphia	0	6	0	10—16
St. Louis	7	0	7	3—17

SCORING

St. Louis—Mitchell 24 pass from Lomax (O'Donoghue kick), 5:04 1st.

Philadelphia—Field goal McFadden 31, 1:30 2nd.

Philadelphia—Field goal McFadden 43, 14:53 2nd.

St. Louis—Tilley 19 pass from Lomax (O'Donoghue kick), 11:21 3rd.

Philadelphia—Quick 16 pass from Pisarcik (McFadden kick), 8:02 4th.

Philadelphia—Field goal McFadden 32, 13:50 4th.

St. Louis—Field goal O'Donoghue 44, 14:52 4th.

TEAM STATISTICS

	Philadelphia	St. Louis
First downs	17	12
Rushes-Yards	30-95	26-119
Passing yards	197	100
Sacked-Yards lost	5-30	5-41
Return yards	75	96
Passes	24-39-0	16-34-1
Punts	8-39.8	9-43.1
Fumbles-Lost	2-2	3-2
Penalties-Yards	3-20	4-46
Time of possession	35:07	24:53

Attendance—39,858. No-shows—2,739.

INDIVIDUAL STATISTICS

Rushing—Philadelphia, Oliver 5-19, Montgomery 16-60, Haddix 8-13, M. Williams 1-3; St. Louis, Anderson 21-92, Ferrell 2-9, Lomax 3-18.

Passing—Philadelphia, Pisarcik 24-39-0—226; St. Louis, Lomax 16-34-1—141.

Receiving—Philadelphia, Oliver 2-4, Montgomery 5-31, Haddix 2-12, Spagnola 3-29, Quick 8-107, Woodruff 3-41, M. Williams 1-2; St. Louis, Mitchell 1-24, Ferrell 1-3, Anderson 3-4, Marsh 2-17, Tilley 3-30, Pittman 1-8, Green 5-55.

Kickoff Returns—Philadelphia, Cooper 3-29, Ellis 1-10; St. Louis, Pittman 3-49, Harrell 2-28.

Punt Returns—Philadelphia, Cooper 4-16; St. Louis, Mitchell 3-19, Pittman 1-0.

Interceptions—Philadelphia, Foules 1-20.

Punting—Philadelphia, Horan 8-39.8; St. Louis, Birdsong 9-43.1.

Field Goals—Philadelphia, McFadden 3-4 (missed 26); St. Louis, O'Donoghue 1-1.

Sacks—Philadelphia, Armstrong, Brown, Clarke, Darby, Harrison; St. Louis, Greer 2, A. Baker, Grooms, Junior.

49ers-Saints
SUNDAY, NOVEMBER 25
SCORE BY PERIODS

San Francisco	0	7	14	14—35
New Orleans	0	3	0	0— 3

SCORING

San Francisco—Craig 1 run (Wersching kick), 9:17 2nd.

New Orleans—Field goal Andersen 27, 12:42 2nd.

San Francisco—Cooper 19 pass from Montana (Wersching kick), 6:24 3rd.

San Francisco—Solomon 28 pass from Montana (Wersching kick), 8:08 3rd.

San Francisco—Shell 53 interception return (Wersching kick), 3:25 4th.

San Francisco—Ring 1 run (Wersching kick), 10:39 4th.

TEAM STATISTICS

	San Francisco	New Orleans
First downs	22	12
Rushes-Yards	33-219	28-131
Passing yards	188	70
Sacked-Yards lost	1-13	8-48
Return yards	107	133
Passes	15-32-0	14-26-1
Punts	6-44.3	8-45.5
Fumbles-Lost	1-0	1-0
Penalties-Yards	4-60	3-20
Time of possession	27:48	32:12

Attendance—65,177. No-shows—5,815.

INDIVIDUAL STATISTICS

Rushing—San Francisco, Tyler 15-117, Solomon 1-47, Harmon 5-26, Craig 7-25, Ring 4-3, Montana 1-1; New Orleans, G. Rogers 21-88, Todd 3-17, Anthony 2-15, W. Wilson 1-6, Campbell 1-5.

Passing—San Francisco, Montana 14-30-0—177, Harmon 0-1-0—0, Cavanaugh 1-1-0—24; New Orleans, Todd 9-18-1—72, Wilson 5-8-0—46.

Receiving—San Francisco, Solomon 3-63, Wilson 3-44, Cooper 3-36, Craig 2-24, Tyler 2-17, D. Clark 1-11, Frank 1-6; New Orleans, Anthony 4-31, Groth 1-31, Brenner 3-28, Young 2-17, Hardy 2-14, Scott 1-4, G. Rogers 1-minus 7.

Kickoff Returns—New Orleans, Fields 4-92, Anthony 2-41.

Punt Returns—San Francisco, McLemore 7-54.

Interceptions—San Francisco, Shell 1-53.

Punting—San Francisco, Runager 6-44.3; New Orleans, Hansen 8-45.5.

Field Goals—San Francisco, Wersching 0-2 (missed: 48, 53); New Orleans, Andersen 1-2 (missed: 54).

Sacks—San Francisco, Dean 2, Shell 2, M. Clark, Johnson, Stover, Tuiasosopo; New Orleans, Kovach.

Seahawks-Broncos
SUNDAY, NOVEMBER 25
SCORE BY PERIODS

Seattle	7	3	7	10—27
Denver	3	7	7	7—24

SCORING

Seattle—Turner 80 pass from Krieg (Johnson kick), 0:15 1st.

Denver—Field goal Karlis 27, 7:07 1st.

Seattle—Field goal Johnson 33, 0:18 2nd.

Denver—Johnson 19 pass from Elway (Karlis kick), 10:07 2nd.

Seattle—Hughes 6 pass from Krieg (Johnson kick), 5:36 3rd.

Denver—Lang 2 run (Karlis kick), 7:44 3rd.

Seattle—Largent 3 pass from Krieg (Johnson kick), 2:30 4th.

Seattle—Field goal Johnson 28, 8:28 4th.

Denver—Lang 9 pass from Elway (Karlis kick), 10:35 4th.

TEAM STATISTICS

	Seattle	Denver
First downs	20	18
Rushes-Yards	25-60	21-93
Passing yards	406	258
Sacked-Yards lost	0-0	2-17
Return yards	48	41
Passes	30-44-0	15-27-1
Punts	6-33.0	5-56.6

	Seattle	Denver
Fumbles-Lost	2-0	2-1
Penalties-Yards	9-81	3-20
Time of possession	37:36	22:24

Attendance—74,922. No-shows—178.

INDIVIDUAL STATISTICS

Rushing—Seattle, Doornink 9-32, Hughes 7-19, Morris 1-0, Dixon 4-6, Largent 1-4, Krieg 3-minus 1; Denver, Parros 5-8, Winder 10-40, Elway 5-43, Lang 1-2.

Passing—Seattle, Krieg 30-44-0—406; Denver, Elway 15-27-1—275.

Receiving—Seattle, Turner 1-80, Hughes 6-24, Doornink 7-55, Largent 12-191, Walker 1-16, C. Young 3-40; Denver, Watson 4-74, Sampson 1-11, Alexander 1-41, Johnson 1-19, Lang 2-15, Willhite 3-94, Kay 2-9, Myles 1-12.

Kickoff Returns—Denver, Lang 2-36.

Punt Returns—Seattle, Skansi 4-48; Denver, Willhite 1-5.

Interceptions—Seattle, Brown 1-0.

Punting—Seattle, West 6-33.0; Denver, Norman 5-56.6.

Field Goals—Seattle, Johnson 2-3 (missed: 29); Denver, Karlis 1-2 (missed: 25).

Sacks—Seattle, Green 1½, Robinson ½.

Bills-Redskins
SUNDAY, NOVEMBER 25
SCORE BY PERIODS

Buffalo	0	7	7	0—14
Washington	17	10	7	7—41

SCORING

Washington—Monk 11 pass from Theismann (Moseley kick), 3:28 1st.

Washington—Field goal Moseley 38, 7:31 1st.

Washington—Riggins 2 run (Moseley kick), 11:31 1st.

Washington—Brown 18 pass from Theismann (Moseley kick), 0:57 2nd.

Buffalo—Franklin 8 pass from Ferguson (Nelson kick), 9:14 2nd.

Washington—Field goal Moseley 51, 15:00 2nd.

Buffalo—Dennard 36 pass from Ferguson (Nelson kick), 1:55 3rd.

Washington—Dean 11 interception return (Moseley kick), 9:35 3rd.

Washington—Wonsley 3 run (Moseley kick), 9:57 4th.

TEAM STATISTICS

	Buffalo	Washington
First downs	13	27
Rushes-Yards	20-85	39-116
Passing yards	86	305
Sacked-Yards lost	7-61	1-6
Return yards	115	141
Passes	14-34-2	26-33-1
Punts	5-44.0	1-49.0
Fumbles-Lost	2-1	4-2
Penalties-Yards	7-45	3-25
Time of possession	23:37	36:23

Attendance—51,513. No-shows—3,918.

INDIVIDUAL STATISTICS

Rushing—Buffalo, Bell 13-53, Moore 2-6, Neal 3-13, Ferguson 2-13; Washington, Riggins 3-6, Griffin 25-92, Theismann 4-3, Wonsley 5-7, Moore 2-8.

Passing—Buffalo, Ferguson 11-26-2—124, Kofler 3-8-0—23; Washington, Theismann 26-33-1—311.

Receiving—Buffalo, Dennard 3-45, Franklin 3-20,

Moore 2-8, Riddick 3-41, Mosley 3-33; Washington, Monk 11-104, Muhammad 4-97, Riggins 1-2, Griffin 1-8, Didier 4-26, Brown 4-68, Moore 1-6.

Kickoff Returns—Buffalo, V. Williams 5-100, Wilson 1-15; Washington, Griffin 2-44, Kane 1-31.

Punt Returns—Washington, Nelms 4-39.

Interceptions—Buffalo, Talley 1-0; Washington, Jordan 1-16, Dean 1-11.

Punting—Buffalo, Kidd 5-44.0; Washington, Hayes 1-49.0.

Field Goals—Buffalo, none attempted; Washington, Moseley 2-3 (missed: 50).

Sacks—Buffalo, Talley; Washington, Brooks 2, Milot 2, Coleman, Grant, Mann.

Jets-Dolphins
MONDAY, NOVEMBER 26
SCORE BY PERIODS

New York Jets	7	3	7	0—17
Miami	0	14	14	0—28

SCORING

New York—McNeil 28 pass from O'Brien (Leahy kick), 12:08 1st.

Miami—Clayton 5 pass from Marino (von Schamann kick), 0:19 2nd.

New York—Field goal Leahy 30, 3:27 2nd.

Miami—Hardy 1 pass from Marino (von Schamann kick), 14:45 2nd.

Miami—D. Johnson 7 pass from Marino (von Schamann kick), 1:13 3rd.

New York—Paige 1 run (Leahy kick), 7:56 3rd.

Miami—Hardy 12 pass from Marino (von Schamann kick), 10:49 3rd.

TEAM STATISTICS

	New York	Miami
First downs	26	25
Rushes-Yards	38-166	24-154
Passing yards	235	183
Sacked-Yards lost	3-32	1-9
Return yards	66	26
Passes	21-39-1	19-32-1
Punts	5-34.8	5-50.6
Fumbles-Lost	0-0	1-0
Penalties-Yards	5-41	4-20
Time of possession	36:53	23:07

Attendance—74,884. No-shows—118.

INDIVIDUAL STATISTICS

Rushing—New York, McNeil 24-116, Minter 6-20, Dennison 1-4, Paige 6-26, Barber 1-0; Miami, Bennett 10-66, Carter 4-37, Nathan 7-53, P. Johnson 1-0, Marino 2-minus 2.

Passing—New York, O'Brien 21-39-1—267; Miami, Marino 19-31-0—192, Clayton 0-1-1—0.

Receiving—New York, Shuler 6-67, Jones 4-41, McNeil 3-64, Humphery 2-23, Klever 2-22, Dennison 2-30, Minter 1-9, Bruckner 1-11; Miami, Duper 1-11, Clayton 5-69, Nathan 3-26, Hardy 6-51, D. Johnson 2-22, Bennett 1-6, Moore 1-7.

Kickoff Returns—New York, Paige 1-7, Mullen 2-34; Miami, Walker 1-26.

Interceptions—New York, Mullen 1-25; Miami, Lankford 1-0.

Punting—New York, Ramsey 5-34.8; Miami, Roby 5-50.6.

Field Goals—New York, Leahy 1-1; Miami, none attempted.

Sacks—New York, Bennett; Miami, Duhe, Betters, Bowser.

FOURTEENTH WEEK

RESULTS OF WEEK 14

Thursday, November 29

Washington 31, Minnesota 17 at Minn.

Sunday, December 2

Buffalo 21, Indianapolis 15 at Buff.
Cincinnati 20, Cleveland 17 (OT) at Cleve.
Dallas 26, Philadelphia 10 at Phila.
Green Bay 27, Tampa Bay 14 at G.B.
Houston 23, Pittsburgh 20 (OT) at Hous.
Kansas City 16, Denver 13 at K.C.
L.A. Raiders 45, Miami 34 at Mia.
L.A. Rams 34, New Orleans 21 at L.A.
N.Y. Giants 20, N.Y. Jets 10
St. Louis 33, New England 10 at N.E.
San Francisco 35, Atlanta 17 at Atl.
Seattle 38, Detroit 17 at Sea.

Monday, December 3

San Diego 20, Chicago 7 at S.D.

When the Cincinnati Bengals and Cleveland Browns met in Week 8, their game was unusual—at least by current pro football standards. In an age when teams are putting points on the board in rapid succession and breaking offensive records by the bushelful, the Bengals and Browns dueled for 60 minutes without either side scoring a touchdown. Cincinnati eventually prevailed, 12-9, with placekicker Jim Breech booting four field goals for the Bengals and Steve Cox hitting a 60-yarder, the second-longest in league history, for the Browns.

Some offense.

But when the two AFC Central Division rivals met again in Week 14 to renew their battle of Ohio, the Bengals won again, 20-17 in overtime, with the help of a freak play. Trailing, 17-10, with the ball at the Cleveland 1-yard line, Cincinnati rookie quarterback Boomer Esiason rolled to his right on the last play of the game and lobbed a pass to 6-foot-6, 278-pound Anthony Munoz, the Bengals' All-Pro offensive lineman. Munoz, an eligible receiver on the tackle-eligible play, caught the pass with one tick left on the clock to send the game into overtime. In the extra period, Breech solidified the Bengals' state bragging rights with a 35-yard field goal on Cincinnati's first overtime possession after the Browns had failed to score.

"I really didn't have much of a chance to think about it," Munoz said of the touchdown pass, his first pass reception since high school. "Boomer looks at me and says, 'It's coming to you.' I'm glad Coach (Sam) Wyche has that much confidence in me."

"That was going to be the play if we were down there in a tough, short-yardage, go-for-guts kind of a play," said Wyche, in his first year as the Cincinnati coach. "Cleveland didn't give us anything. We had to work for every damn point."

Actually, two critical Cleveland mistakes led to the Munoz touchdown. First, the Bengals' Rodney Holman was left uncovered and blocked a Cox punt with one minute left in regulation. John Simmons recovered for the Bengals on the Browns' 28. Then, on the play preceding the touchdown, cornerback Hanford Dixon was called for pass interference at the Cleveland 11. The penalty put the ball on the 1.

"We didn't anticipate this sort of scenario," said Breech, "but what a great ending."

The Washington Redskins got off to a great start when they took on Minnesota in a Thursday night game. Joe Theismann hooked up with newly acquired wide receiver Calvin Muhammad on the first play of the game for a 68-yard touchdown and the Redskins proceeded to roll up 31 first-half points. Muhammad, obtained in a trade from the Los Angeles Raiders earlier in the season, caught five passes for 115 yards as the Redskins won, 31-17. Theismann threw one other scoring pass in the first half and had 13 straight completions at one point.

The Vikings, stunned by Washington's fast start—including fumble recoveries for touchdowns by Joe Jacoby and Darryl Grant—rallied for 17 points behind reserve quarterback Archie Manning in the second half. Manning threw two touchdown passes to Leo Lewis, the last with 9:05 left to play. But the Vikes could draw no closer, despite having the ball on the Washington 3-yard line with three minutes left.

The defending Super Bowl champion Los Angeles Raiders also got off to a fast start in their showdown game with the Miami Dolphins in the Orange Bowl. Pro Bowl cornerback Mike Haynes picked off a Dan Marino pass on the Dolphins' first possession and returned it 97 yards for a 7-0 L.A. lead. Haynes intercepted another Marino pass later in the game to set up a Raider touchdown in a 45-34 victory.

Marino did throw four touchdown passes to establish a league record of 40 scoring passes in one season. But Marino's efforts were not enough as Marcus Allen carried 20 times for 155 yards and three touchdowns and Raiders Coach Tom Flores ran his record to 5-0 in games against Miami Coach Don Shula.

The bragging rights to New York City were won by the Giants, who scored points on four consecutive possessions in the second and third periods to upend the Jets, 20-10. The Jets, who committed all three of their turnovers in Giants' territory, lost their sixth straight game, the club's longest losing streak since 1977.

Ironically, the game was played at Giants Stadium and the Giants, the stadium's sole NFL tenant its first eight years, were considered the "road" team for this game. The Jets

Raiders cornerback Mike Haynes picked off two Dan Marino passes, returning one 97 yards for a touchdown, in L.A.'s 45-34 victory over Miami in Week 14.

were in their first season of using Giants Stadium as their home park after 20 years at Shea Stadium.

Denver placekicker Rich Karlis probably felt like finding a new profession after missing a game-tying field goal for the second straight week. Karlis, who banged a 25-yard attempt off the right goal post in the Broncos' 27-24 loss to Seattle in Week 13, banged a 42-yarder off the left post in the waning moments of the Broncos' 16-13 loss at Kansas City. Denver's second straight loss, on the heels of a 10-game winning streak, dropped the Broncos one game behind Seattle in the AFC Western Division.

Karlis' counterpart, Nick Lowery, had an excellent day for the Chiefs, hitting on three field goals in the fourth period as K.C. overcame a 13-7 Denver lead after three quarters. Lowery's final kick was a 42-yarder with 1:56 remaining.

Houston rookie placekicker Joe Cooper booted his third field goal of the day, at 5:53 of overtime, to give the Oilers a 23-20 triumph over AFC Central Division-rival Pittsburgh. The Oilers, who were victorious for the third time in four weeks, won the coin flip to start the extra period and drove 63 yards in 13 plays to set up Cooper's 30-yard kick.

The Steelers, who had tied the game on Mark Malone's seven-yard scoring strike to rookie Louis Lipps, suffered their first overtime loss ever. It also was the 100th overtime game played in the NFL since the rule took effect in 1974.

The Dallas Cowboys clinched their 19th consecutive winning season with a 26-10 verdict over division-rival Philadelphia. The Cowboys' streak is the longest ever in the NFL and the third-longest in pro sports history. Only the New York Yankees, with 39 straight winning seasons between 1926-64 and the Montreal Canadiens, with 32 straight between 1952-83, have compiled longer streaks.

But the 9-5 Cowboys were far from dominant in their record-setting game. They turned the ball over six times—including a team-record five interceptions—and combined with the Eagles for 10 turnovers in a sloppily played game. Tony Dorsett's 110 yards rushing led the Dallas attack, pushing the eight-year pro over the 1,000-yard mark for the seventh time in his career. No NFL running back rushed for 1,000 yards in the nine-game, strike-shortened 1982 season.

On the opposite end of the spectrum, the New Orleans Saints clinched their 18th consecutive season without a winning record in a 34-21 loss to the Los Angeles Rams. The Saints, whose best seasons came in 1979 and 1983 with 8-8 marks, could only shoot for another break-even season after dropping to 6-8 with two games left.

New Orleans trailed, 24-0 and 27-7, before rallying to within six points behind backup quarterback Dave Wilson's three touchdown passes. But Henry Ellard, who caught two scoring passes for the Rams, caught a 34-yarder from Jeff Kemp midway through the final period for a 13-point L.A. lead. Eric Dickerson, in hot pursuit of O.J. Simpson's single-season rushing record, rushed for 149 yards to pull within 211 yards of Simpson's 1973-record 2,003.

Quarterback Dave Krieg set a Seattle club record with five touchdown passes in the Seahawks' 38-17 victory over the Detroit Lions. Krieg threw two scoring passes each to veteran Steve Largent and rookie Daryl Turner as Seattle took over sole possession of first place in the AFC Western Division with its eighth straight win. Largent's two TD catches ran his season total to 12, also a Seahawk record.

The St. Louis Cardinals opted for a strong running attack to defeat New England 33-10. Cardinals quarterback Neil Lomax attempted just 15 passes as the Cards rolled up 220 yards rushing on 54 attempts. Ottis Anderson led the ground assault with 136 yards on 30 carries to go over the 1,000-yard mark for the fifth time in his career. The strategy also kept the ball away from the Patriots; they ran just 19 first-half plays (St. Louis ran 41) as the Cardinals grabbed a commanding 27-3 halftime lead. The Pats' offense had run only five plays when the Cards took a 14-0 first-quarter lead on linebacker Thomas Howard's 29-yard fumble return.

The Green Bay Packers trailed Tampa Bay, 14-0, late in the third period before rallying for 27 straight points to win against their NFC Central Division rival, 27-14. Quarterback Lynn Dickey and running back Eddie Lee Ivery led the comeback, Dickey throwing for one touchdown and running for another and Ivery running for two scores.

Tampa Bay grabbed a 7-0 lead early in the second quarter when James Wilder, the NFL's total offense leader, completed the first pass of his four-year pro career for a touchdown to fellow running back Adger Armstrong. Wilder also rushed for 88 yards in miserable weather conditions to break Ricky Bell's team record for rushing yardage in one season. Wilder finished the game with 1,316 to Bell's 1,263 in the 1979 season. Bell, the NFL's top draft pick in 1977, died four days before the game from cardiac arrest at age 29.

The San Francisco 49ers ran their record to 13-1 and clinched home-field advantage for the NFC playoffs with a 35-17 victory over Atlanta. Joe Montana threw two touchdown passes and the 49ers' defense scored two touchdowns and set up a third as the 49ers won their ninth straight road game. Defensive tackle Gary Johnson returned a fumble 33 yards for a touchdown late in the first half and cornerback Dana McLemore returned a Mike Moroski pass 54 yards for a score late in the third period. Keena Turner's fourth-quarter interception set up San Francisco's final touchdown.

A crowd of only 29,644 in Atlanta turned out to see the Falcons drop their eighth straight game. Although the game was played in the rain, it was the third straight Atlanta home game with more than 20,000 no-shows.

A crowd of just 20,693 turned out in Buffalo to watch the 1-12 Bills battle the 4-9 Indianapolis Colts. The people who stayed away missed a first-quarter explosion by Buffalo, including touchdowns on each of its first three possessions. Joe Dufek, a second-year free agent out of Yale, replaced veteran Joe Ferguson at quarterback and threw first-quarter scoring passes to Tony Hunter and Byron Franklin as Buffalo grabbed an early 21-0 lead. The Bills scored no more points after the opening period, but held on to defeat the Colts, 21-15, for their second victory of the year.

In the Monday night contest, San Diego scored 14 points in the final quarter to defeat Chicago, 20-7. The winning touchdown was scored by wide receiver Bobby Duckworth on an 88-yard pass play from backup quarterback Ed Luther. Duckworth had blown a touchdown in the third quarter when he dropped the ball at the Chicago 2-yard line after lifting his arms in the air to celebrate.

The Chargers' much-maligned defense harassed quarterbacks Rusty Lisch and Steve Fuller most of the evening. The Bears were held scoreless in the first period for the first time in the '84 season. Rookie defensive end Lee Williams, a former United States Football League player, returned an interception 66 yards for the Chargers' final score.

Redskins-Vikings
THURSDAY, NOVEMBER 29
SCORE BY PERIODS

Washington	17	14	0	0—31
Minnesota	0	0	10	7—17

SCORING

Washington—Muhammad 68 pass from Theismann (Moseley kick), 0:18 1st.

Washington—Field goal Moseley 30, 11:17 1st.

Washington—Didier 4 pass from Theismann (Moseley kick), 14:47 1st.

Washington—Jacoby fumble recovery in end zone (Moseley kick), 4:14 2nd.

Washington—Grant 22 fumble return (Moseley kick), 7:26 2nd.

Minnesota—Field goal Stenerud 31, 3:23 3rd.

Minnesota—Lewis 14 pass from Manning (Stenerud kick), 9:45 3rd.

Minnesota—Lewis 8 pass from Manning (Stenerud kick), 5:55 4th.

TEAM STATISTICS

	Washington	Minnesota
First downs	19	21
Rushes-Yards	29-129	29-170
Passing yards	217	200
Sacked-Yards lost	2-6	3-27
Return yards	175	109
Passes	19-24-0	19-39-2
Punts	2-39.5	3-51.7
Fumbles-Lost	3-1	2-2
Penalties-Yards	4-45	4-30
Time of possession	29:37	30:23

Attendance—55,017. No-shows—6,882.

INDIVIDUAL STATISTICS

Rushing—Washington, Griffin 9-52, Hayes 1-24, Wonsley 2-minus 2, J. Washington 16-56, Theismann 1-minus 1; Minnesota, Wilson 2-6, Nelson 7-53, Anderson 13-45, Manning 2-13, Rice 3-10, Jones 2-43.

Passing—Washington, Theismann 19-24-0—223; Minnesota, Wilson 8-17-2—63, Manning 11-22-0—164.

Receiving—Washington, Muhammad 5-115, Monk 6-45, Brown 1-7, Griffin 1-minus 2, Didier 3-33, Moore 1-7, McGrath 2-18; Minnesota, Nelson 2-5, Lewis 7-130, Jordan 2-11, Jones 3-29, Hasselbeck 1-10, Senser 2-17, Anderson 1-16, Mularkey 1-9.

Kickoff Returns—Washington, Nelms 1-29, Griffin 3-70; Minnesota, Nelson 4-77, Anderson 1-27.

Punt Returns—Washington, Nelms 2-34; Minnesota, Lewis 1-5.

Interceptions—Washington, Milot 1-27, Coffey 1-15.

Punting—Washington, Hayes 2-39.5; Minnesota, Coleman 3-51.7.

Field Goals—Washington, Moseley 1-2 (missed: 27); Minnesota, Stenerud 1-1.

Sacks—Washington, Mann, Grant, Olkewicz; Minnesota, Elshire 1½, Arbubakrr ½.

Colts-Bills
SCORE BY PERIODS

Indianapolis	0	9	3	3—15
Buffalo	21	0	0	0—21

SCORING
Buffalo—Bell 7 run (Nelson kick), 4:11 1st.

Buffalo—Hunter 18 pass from Dufek (Nelson kick), 12:21 1st.

Buffalo—Franklin 64 pass from Dufek (Nelson kick), 15:00 1st.

Indianapolis—Safety, Wilson tackled in end zone, 1:07 2nd.

Indianapolis—Middleton 14 pass from Schlichter (Allegre kick), 13:14 2nd.

Indianapolis—Field goal Allegre 28, 5:51 3rd.

Indianapolis—Field goal Allegre 21, 5:12 4th.

TEAM STATISTICS

	Indianapolis	Buffalo
First downs	13	15
Rushes-Yards	31-116	41-104
Passing yards	125	155
Sacked-Yards lost	2-10	1-9
Return yards	131	83
Passes	11-28-1	11-22-1
Punts	8-47.4	7-38.6
Fumbles-Lost	3-3	2-1
Penalties-Yards	9-69	9-65
Time of possession	26:53	33:07

Attendance—20,693. No-shows—3,169.

INDIVIDUAL STATISTICS
Rushing—Indianapolis, Moore 7-35, McMillan 7-30, Schlichter 5-21, Middleton 5-9, Wonsley 7-21; Buffalo, Bell 30-83, Neal 6-25, Riddick 1-minus 1, Dufek 2-minus 7, Brookins 1-11, Kofler 1-minus 7.

Passing—Indianapolis, Schlichter 11-28-1—135; Buffalo, Dufek 11-22-1—164.

Receiving—Indianapolis, Butler 2-28, Porter 2-16, Bouza 2-20, Middleton 2-26, Sherwin 1-25, Henry 2-20; Buffalo, Dennard 1-15, Hunter 4-51, Franklin 3-82, Bell 2-11, Mosley 1-5.

Kickoff Returns—Indianapolis, Anderson 3-72, Smith 2-36; Buffalo, V. Williams 4-46.

Punt Returns—Indianapolis, Anderson 3-23; Buffalo, Wilson 5-12.

Interceptions—Indianapolis, Daniel 1-0; Buffalo, Romes 1-35.

Punting—Indianapolis, Stark 8-47.4; Buffalo, Kidd 7-38.6.

Field Goals—Indianapolis, Allegre 2-2; Buffalo, none attempted.

Sacks—Indianapolis, Maxwell; Buffalo, Haslett, Talley.

Bengals-Browns
SCORE BY PERIODS

Cincinnati	7	0	0	10	3—20
Cleveland	0	10	0	7	0—17

SCORING
Cincinnati—Jennings 15 pass from Schonert (Breech kick), 9:40 1st.

Cleveland—Field goal Bahr 24, 0:39 2nd.

Cleveland—Brennan 21 pass from McDonald (Bahr kick), 10:08 2nd.

Cleveland—Pruitt 1 run (Bahr kick), 4:50 4th.

Cincinnati—Field goal Breech 22, 9:28 4th.

Cincinnati—Munoz 1 pass from Esiason (Breech kick), 14:59 4th.

Cincinnati—Field goal Breech 35, 4:34 OT.

TEAM STATISTICS

	Cincinnati	Cleveland
First downs	21	20
Rushes-Yards	33-119	32-96
Passing yards	229	183
Sacked-Yards lost	2-17	1-8
Return yards	108	66
Passes	28-41-1	18-24-0
Punts	3-28.0	4-48.3
Fumbles-Lost	2-0	1-0
Penalties-Yards	3-13	2-24
Time of possession	35:16	29:18

Attendance—51,774. No-shows—1,615.

INDIVIDUAL STATISTICS
Rushing—Cincinnati, Kinnebrew 5-7, Jennings 9-38, Schonert 2-18, Alexander 13-37, Brooks 3-16, Martin 1-3; Cleveland, Green 12-35, Byner 3-3, Pruitt 17-58.

Passing—Cincinnati, Schonert 16-21-1—138, Esiason 12-20-0—108; Cleveland, McDonald 18-24-0—191.

Receiving—Cincinnati, Collinsworth 1-7, Kinnebrew 2-10, Harris 5-53, Kreider 6-85, Jennings 5-29, Alexander 3-12, Kern 1-5, Verser 1-22, Holman 1-8, Martin 1-4, Brooks 1-3, Munoz 1-1; Cleveland, Brennan 5-55, Newsome 8-62, Feacher 3-54, Adams 1-11, Byner 1-9.

Kickoff Returns—Cincinnati, Jennings 2-46, Martin 1-16; Cleveland, B. Davis 3-37, Byner 1-19.

Punt Returns—Cincinnati, Martin 2-16, Simmons 1-30; Cleveland, Brennan 1-4.

Interceptions—Cleveland, Gross 1-6.

Punting—Cincinnati, McInally 3-28.0; Cleveland, Cox 4-48.3.

Field Goals—Cincinnati, Breech 2-3 (missed: 43); Cleveland, Bahr 1-1, Cox 0-1 (missed: 64).

Sacks—Cincinnati, Edwards; Cleveland, Camp, Matthews.

Cowboys-Eagles
SCORE BY PERIODS

Dallas	7	0	16	3—26
Philadelphia	0	3	0	7—10

SCORING
Dallas—Thurman 38 interception return (Septien kick), 6:46 1st.

Philadelphia—Field goal McFadden 23, 3:18 2nd.

Dallas—Springs 57 pass from D. White (Septien kick), 4:26 3rd.

Dallas—Safety, Dutton sacked Pisarcik in end zone, 4:39 3rd.

Dallas—Newsome 8 run (Septien kick), 12:47 3rd.

Philadelphia—Kab 2 pass from Pisarcik (McFadden kick), 10:58 4th.

Dallas—Field goal Septien 32, 13:09 4th.

TEAM STATISTICS

	Dallas	Philadelphia
First downs	16	13
Rushes-Yards	39-190	19-38
Passing yards	96	135
Sacked-Yards lost	3-29	6-55
Return yards	170	102
Passes	8-26-5	23-45-2
Punts	6-32.7	8-46.6
Fumbles-Lost	2-1	2-2
Penalties-Yards	5-61	3-27
Time of possession	29:08	30:52

Attendance—66,322. No-shows—6,003.

INDIVIDUAL STATISTICS
Rushing—Dallas, Dorsett 22-110, Newsome 8-37, Springs 5-30, D. White 1-7, J. Jones 3-6; Philadelphia, Montgomery 11-29, Oliver 1-6, Haddix 7-3.

Passing—Dallas, D. White 8-25-4—125, Dorsett 0-1-1—0; Philadelphia, Pisarcik 23-44-2—190, Montgomery 0-1-0—0.

Receiving—Dallas, Hill 3-25, J. Jones 2-30, Springs 1-57, Renfro 1-12, Newsome 1-1; Philadelphia, Spagnola 11-114, Haddix 6-42, Oliver 2-minus 1, Hoover 1-18, Woodruff 1-10, M. Williams 1-5, Kab 1-2.

Kickoff Returns—Dallas, McSwain 2-24, Allen 1-23; Philadelphia, Cooper 3-40, Waters 1-20.

Punt Returns—Dallas, Allen 6-59; Philadelphia, Cooper 1-7.

Interceptions—Dallas, Thurman 1-38, Downs 1-26; Philadelphia, Hopkins 2-26, Ellis 1-29, Wilkes 1-6, Edwards 1-0.

Punting—Dallas, D. White 6-32.7; Philadelphia, Horan 8-46.6.

Field Goals—Dallas, Septien 1-1; Philadelphia, McFadden 1-1.

Sacks—Dallas, Jeffcoat 2, R. White 2, Dutton, E. Jones; Philadelphia, Brown 1½, Griggs, Hopkins ½.

Buccaneers-Packers
SUNDAY, DECEMBER 2
SCORE BY PERIODS

Tampa Bay	0	7	7	0—14
Green Bay	0	0	7	20—27

SCORING

Tampa Bay—Armstrong 16 pass from Wilder (Ariri kick), 5:43 2nd.

Tampa Bay—J. Bell 13 pass from DeBerg (Ariri kick), 8:07 3rd.

Green Bay—Ivery 4 run (Del Greco kick), 10:49 3rd.

Green Bay—Dickey 1 run (Del Greco kick), 0:46 4th.

Green Bay—Crouse 10 pass from Dickey (kick failed), 4:25 4th.

Green Bay—Ivery 2 run (Del Greco kick), 10:49 4th.

TEAM STATISTICS

	Tampa Bay	Green Bay
First downs	19	20
Rushes-Yards	30-100	33-106
Passing yards	175	205
Sacked-Yards lost	3-31	0-0
Return yards	109	98
Passes	23-39-2	18-32-3
Punts	6-39.8	5-40.6
Fumbles-Lost	4-4	1-1
Penalties-Yards	10-80	7-65
Time of possession	33:48	26:12

Attendance—46,800. No-shows—9,173.

INDIVIDUAL STATISTICS

Rushing—Tampa Bay, Wilder 27-88, Armstrong 2-12, DeBerg 1-0; Green Bay, Ivery 16-73, Ellis 4-12, Crouse 6-31, Dickey 3-minus 3, Huckleby 2-minus 1, Rodgers 2-minus 6.

Passing—Tampa Bay, DeBerg 22-38-2—190, Wilder 1-1-0—16; Green Bay, Dickey 18-32-3—205.

Receiving—Tampa Bay, House 6-105, Carter 2-14, J. Bell 2-17, Armstrong 2-22, Wilder 11-48; Green Bay, Ivery 5-29, Coffman 4-63, Crouse 4-36, Epps 3-38, Ellis 2-39.

Kickoff Returns—Tampa Bay, Morton 2-25, Bright 1-10, Wood 1-7, Spradlin 1-5; Green Bay, Rodgers 2-41, D. Jones 1-19.

Punt Returns—Tampa Bay, Bright 3-10, T. Bell 1-2; Green Bay, Flynn 4-24.

Interceptions—Tampa Bay, Brantley 1-38, Reece 1-12, Cannon 1-0; Green Bay, T. Lewis 1-12, Anderson 1-2.

Punting—Tampa Bay, Garcia 6-39.8; Green Bay, Scribner 5-40.6.

Field Goals—Tampa Bay, Ariri 0-1 (missed: 31); Green Bay, none attempted.

Sacks—Green Bay, Brown, T. Jones, Martin.

Steelers-Oilers
SUNDAY, DECEMBER 2
SCORE BY PERIODS

Pittsburgh	3	0	10	7	0—20
Houston	3	10	0	7	3—23

SCORING

Pittsburgh—Field goal Anderson 32, 6:10 1st.

Houston—Field goal Cooper 19, 13:59 1st.

Houston—Field goal Cooper 38, 10:28 2nd.

Houston—Dressel 5 pass from Moon (Cooper kick), 14:39 2nd.

Pittsburgh—Thompson 5 pass from Malone (Anderson kick), 7:48 3rd.

Pittsburgh—Field goal Anderson 24, 12:15 3rd.

Houston—Edwards 5 run (Cooper kick), 3:26 4th.

Pittsburgh—Lipps 7 pass from Malone (Anderson kick), 9:56 4th.

Houston—Field goal Cooper 30, 5:53 OT.

TEAM STATISTICS

	Pittsburgh	Houston
First downs	14	23
Rushes-Yards	30-127	33-121
Passing yards	145	303
Sacked-Yards lost	3-48	0-0
Return yards	150	142
Passes	16-33-2	27-45-3
Punts	6-40.5	7-36.7
Fumbles-Lost	2-1	1-0
Penalties-Yards	4-29	7-70
Time of possession	29:44	35:59

Attendance—39,786. No-shows—9,303.

INDIVIDUAL STATISTICS

Rushing—Pittsburgh, Pollard 15-57, Abercrombie 10-39, Lipps 1-31, Malone 3-2, Colquitt 1-0; Houston, Edwards 25-79, Moon 3-35, Joyner 5-7.

Passing—Pittsburgh, Malone 16-33-2—193; Houston, Moon 27-45-3—303.

Receiving—Pittsburgh, Stallworth 6-113, Lipps 4-43, Abercrombie 4-18, Erenberg 1-14, Thompson 1-5; Houston, Smith 7-108, Holston 7-61, Edwards 5-35, Walls 3-32, Bryant 2-31, J. Williams 1-20, McCloskey 1-11, Dressel 1-5.

Kickoff Returns—Pittsburgh, Erenberg 2-50, Veals 1-18; Houston, R. Williams 3-57, Roaches 1-24.

Punt Returns—Pittsburgh, Lipps 5-35; Houston, Roaches 2-26.

Interceptions—Pittsburgh, Williams 1-44, Shell 1-3, Clayton 1-0; Houston, Eason 1-20, Tullis 1-10, Thompson (with lateral) 0-5.

Punting—Pittsburgh, Colquitt 6-40.5; Houston, James 7-36.7.

Field Goals—Pittsburgh, Anderson 2-2; Houston, Cooper 3-3.

Sacks—Houston, Baker 1½, Stensrud, Johnson ½.

Broncos-Chiefs
SUNDAY, DECEMBER 2
SCORE BY PERIODS

Denver	7	3	3	0—13
Kansas City	0	7	0	9—16

SCORING

Denver—Watson 48 pass from Elway (Karlis kick), 14:12 1st.

Denver—Field goal Karlis 22, 10:00 2nd.

Kansas City—Carson 24 pass from Kenney (Lowery kick), 14:52 2nd.

Denver—Field goal Karlis 37, 1:12 3rd.

Kansas City—Field goal Lowery 46, 3:19 4th.

Kansas City—Field goal Lowery 28, 7:59 4th.

Kansas City—Field goal Lowery 42, 13:04 4th.

TEAM STATISTICS

	Denver	Kansas City
First downs	17	17
Rushes-Yards	34-145	27-93
Passing yards	164	225
Sacked-Yards lost	3-19	6-56
Return yards	131	96
Passes	16-36-1	20-38-1
Punts	8-31.0	7-40.9
Fumbles-Lost	2-2	5-2
Penalties-Yards	2-10	3-61
Time of possession	32:27	27:33

Attendance—38,494. No-shows—6,454.

INDIVIDUAL STATISTICS

Rushing—Denver, Winder 25-96, Willhite 4-23, Elway 3-24, Parros 2-2; Kansas City, Heard 22-84, Lacy 3-10, Gunter 1-1, Kenney 1-minus 2.

Passing—Denver, Elway 16-36-1—183; Kansas City, Kenney 20-38-1—281.

Receiving—Denver, Willhite 6-50, Watson 4-89, Winder 2-8, J. Wright 1-17, Sampson 1-9, Alexander 1-5, Johnson 1-5; Kansas City, Carson 7-126, Heard 4-49, Brown 4-16, Paige 2-46, Marshall 1-29, W. Arnold 1-11, Lacy 1-4.

Kickoff Returns—Denver, Willhite 2-65, Lang 1-27, Dennison 1-11; Kansas City, Smith 2-38, Paige 1-22.

Punt Returns—Denver, Willhite 5-28; Kansas City, Smith 3-36.

Interceptions—Denver, Harden 1-0; Kansas City, Lewis 1-0.

Punting—Denver, Norman 8-31.0; Kansas City, J. Arnold 7-40.9.

Field Goals—Denver, Karlis 2-3 (missed: 42); Kansas City, Lowery 3-4 (missed: 55).

Sacks—Denver, Chavous 2, Dennison, Jones, Mecklenburg, Townsend; Kansas City, Blanton 2, Still.

Raiders-Dolphins
SUNDAY, DECEMBER 2
SCORE BY PERIODS

Los Angeles Raiders	7	10	7	21—45
Miami	7	6	14	7—34

SCORING

Los Angeles—Haynes 97 interception return (Bahr kick), 7:03 1st.

Miami—Cefalo 4 pass from Marino (von Schamann kick), 13:19 1st.

Miami—Nathan 6 run (kick blocked), 2:08 2nd.

Los Angeles—Allen 11 run (Bahr kick), 10:52 2nd.

Los Angeles—Field goal Bahr 44, 11:36 2nd.

Los Angeles—Casper 7 pass from Wilson (Bahr kick), 5:25 3rd.

Miami—Clayton 64 pass from Marino (von Schamann kick), 10:03 3rd.

Miami—Clayton 11 pass from Marino (von Schamann kick), 11:22 3rd.

Los Angeles—Williams 75 pass from Wilson (Bahr kick), 6:07 4th.

Los Angeles—Allen 6 run (Bahr kick), 8:01 4th.

Miami—Duper 10 pass from Marino (von Schamann kick), 12:51 4th.

Los Angeles—Allen 52 run (Bahr kick), 13:17 4th.

TEAM STATISTICS

	Los Angeles	Miami
First downs	18	30
Rushes-Yards	32-179	24-81
Passing yards	225	434
Sacked-Yards lost	2-16	3-36
Return yards	234	97
asses	13-24-1	35-57-2
Punts	5-40.0	6-46.0
Fumbles-Lost	1-1	1-0
Penalties-Yards	8-77	7-60
Time of possession	24:59	35:01

Attendance—71,222. No-shows—3,929.

INDIVIDUAL STATISTICS

Rushing—Los Angeles, King 3-15, Allen 20-155, Hawkins 6-17, Wilson 3-minus 8; Miami, Nathan 6-27, Bennett 6-36, P. Johnson 5-6, Carter 6-16, Marino 1-minus 4.

Passing—Los Angeles, Wilson 13-24-1—241; Miami, Marino 35-57-2—470.

Receiving—Los Angeles, Allen 1-10, Christensen 6-70, Barnwell 2-24, King 1-8, Williams 2-122, Casper 1-7; Miami, Duper 5-76, Clayton 9-177, Nathan 6-75, Moore 4-31, Bennett 1-9, Cefalo 1-4, D. Johnson 4-39, Rose 2-25, Carter 2-22, Jensen 1-12.

Kickoff Returns—Los Angeles, Montgomery 1-42, Williams 1-26, McKinney 1-0; Miami, Walker 4-72.

Punt Returns—Los Angeles, Montgomery 2-15; Miami, Walker 1-2.

Interceptions—Los Angeles, Haynes 2-151; Miami, Judson 1-23.

Punting—Los Angeles, Guy 5-40.0; Miami, Roby 6-46.0.

Field Goals—Los Angeles, Bahr 1-1; Miami, none attempted.

Sacks—Los Angeles, Long, Pickel, Townsend; Miami, Betters, Brudzinski.

Saints-Rams
SUNDAY, DECEMBER 2
SCORE BY PERIODS

New Orleans	0	7	0	14—21
Los Angeles Rams	14	10	3	7—34

SCORING

Los Angeles—Irvin 51 interception return (Lansford kick), 4:52 1st.

Los Angeles—Dickerson 7 run (Lansford kick), 10:59 1st.

Los Angeles—Ellard 16 pass from Kemp (Lansford kick), 0:11 2nd.

Los Angeles—Field goal Lansford 25, 5:49 2nd.

New Orleans—Scott 14 pass from D. Wilson (Andersen kick), 11:39 2nd.

Los Angeles—Field goal Lansford 30, 13:00 3rd.

New Orleans—Young 3 pass from D. Wilson (Andersen kick), 0:44 4th.

New Orleans—Goodlow 8 pass from D. Wilson (Andersen kick), 5:54 4th.

Los Angeles—Ellard 34 pass from Kemp (Lansford kick), 7:36 4th.

TEAM STATISTICS

	New. Orleans	Los Angeles
First downs	15	17
Rushes-Yards	21-96	47-214
Passing yards	128	127
Sacked-Yards lost	5-33	0-0
Return yards	122	183
Passes	15-34-4	10-24-2
Punts	6-43.0	4-36.5
Fumbles-Lost	2-1	3-2
Penalties-Yards	1-10	4-40
Time of possession	25:10	34:50

Attendance—49,348. No-shows—8,060.

INDIVIDUAL STATISTICS

Rushing—New Orleans, Gajan 7-49, G. Rogers 9-22, Anthony 3-15, Todd 2-10; Los Angeles, Dickerson 33-149, Kemp 6-42, Redden 4-5, Crutchfield 3-9, Brown 1-9.

Passing—New Orleans, Todd 1-5-2—22, D. Wilson 14-29-2—139; Los Angeles, Kemp 10-24-2—127.

Receiving—New Orleans, Scott 3-40, Brenner 3-38, Groth 2-29, Goodlow 2-22, Young 2-14, Miller 2-13, Gajan 1-5; Los Angeles, Ellard 2-50, Redden 3-33, Brown 2-27, Barber 1-8, Dickerson 1-6, David Hill 1-3.

Kickoff Returns—New Orleans, Fields 4-55, Anthony 2-43; Los Angeles, Drew Hill 1-35.

Punt Returns—New Orleans, Fields 1-8; Los Angeles, Ellard 4-38.

Interceptions—New Orleans, Kovach 1-16, Waymer 1-0; Los Angeles, Green 1-60, Irvin 1-51, Collins 1-3, Owens 1-minus 4.

Punting—New Orleans, Hansen 6-43.0; Los Angeles, Misko 4-36.5.

Field Goals—New Orleans, none attempted; Los Angeles, Lansford 2-2.

Sacks—Los Angeles, Doss 2½, Meisner 1½, Jeter.

Giants-Jets
SUNDAY, DECEMBER 2
SCORE BY PERIODS

New York Giants	0	10	7	3—20
New York Jets	0	0	3	7—10

SCORING

Giants—Carpenter 1 run (Haji-Sheikh kick), 11:16 2nd.
Giants—Field goal Haji-Sheikh 48, 14:56 2nd.
Giants—Morris 8 run (Haji-Sheikh kick), 8:00 3rd.
Jets—Field goal Leahy 43, 11:08 3rd.
Giants—Field goal Haji-Sheikh 30, 0:03 4th.
Jets—Jones 32 pass from O'Brien (Leahy kick), 1:17 4th.

TEAM STATISTICS

	Giants	Jets
First downs	26	20
Rushes-Yards	40-169	20-67
Passing yards	216	341
Sacked-Yards lost	4-36	3-21
Return yards	54	85
Passes	18-28-1	29-42-1
Punts	5-29.8	2-41.5
Fumbles-Lost	0-0	2-2
Penalties-Yards	3-30	7-42
Time of possession	34:24	25:36

Attendance—74,975. No-shows—1,916.

INDIVIDUAL STATISTICS

Rushing—Giants, Morris 17-83, Galbreath 6-36, Carpenter 12-28, Simms 4-21, Woolfolk 1-1; Jets, McNeil 14-42, Barber 2-13, O'Brien 3-12, Paige 1-0.

Passing—Giants, Simms 18-28-1—252; Jets, O'Brien 28-41-1—351, Ryan 1-1-0—11.

Receiving—Giants, Galbreath 6-81, Mowatt 4-45, Manuel 3-45, Carpenter 3-35, B. Williams 1-25, Johnson 1-21; Jets, Shuler 11-127, Jones 4-103, Humphery 3-29, Minter 2-21, Dennison 2-21, McNeil 3-34, Barber 4-27.

Kickoff Returns—Giants, Cephous 2-47; Jets, Minter 2-29, Humphery 1-52.

Punt Returns—Giants, Manuel 1-0; Jets, Springs 1-4.

Interceptions—Giants, Haynes 1-7; Jets, Clifton 1-0.

Punting—Giants, Jennings 4-37.3; Jets, Ramsey 2-41.5.

Field Goals—Giants, Haji-Sheikh 2-2; Jets, Leahy 1-3 (missed: 54, 36).

Sacks—Giants, Marshall 2, Burt ½, Merrill ½; Jets, Klecko 1½, Lyons, Mehl, Gastineau ½.

Cardinals-Patriots
SUNDAY, DECEMBER 2
SCORE BY PERIODS

St. Louis	14	13	0	6—33
New England	3	0	7	0—10

SCORING

St. Louis—Marsh 1 pass from Lomax (O'Donoghue kick), 9:00 1st.

St. Louis—Howard 29 fumble return (O'Donoghue kick), 11:24 1st.

New England—Field goal Franklin 19, 14:19 1st.
St. Louis—Field goal O'Donoghue 36, 4:56 2nd.
St. Louis—Field goal O'Donoghue 33, 9:19 2nd.

St. Louis—Anderson 2 run (O'Donoghue kick), 14:46 2nd.

New England—Dawson 11 pass from Eason (Franklin kick) 4:34 3rd.

St. Louis—Mitchell 3 run (kick blocked), 5:21 4th.

TEAM STATISTICS

	St. Louis	New England
First downs	20	14
Rushes-Yards	54-220	15-87
Passing yards	85	136
Sacked-Yards lost	1-7	8-55
Return yards	108	138
Passes	9-15-0	16-32-1
Punts	6-38.2	7-42.1
Fumbles-Lost	2-1	2-2
Penalties-Yards	3-20	5-35
Time of possession	37:27	22:33

Attendance—53,558. No-shows—207.

INDIVIDUAL STATISTICS

Rushing—St. Louis, Anderson 30-136, Ferrell 5-19, Lomax 6-39, Mitchell 9-19, Love 1-1, Harrington 3-6; New England, C. James 8-78, Collins 3-1, Eason 1-2, Tatupu 3-6.

Passing—St. Louis, Lomax 9-15-0—92; New England, Eason 16-32-1—191.

Receiving—St. Louis, Green 2-32, Anderson 3-35, Mack 1-6, Marsh 1-1, Mitchell 1-12, Tilley 1-6; New England, C. James 2-18, Dawson 3-27, Ramsey 4-59, Morgan 3-24, Starring 2-31, Tatupu 1-18, Fryar 1-14.

Kickoff Returns—St. Louis, Mitchell 2-40, Love 1-1; New England, Collins 6-74, Lee 1-17.

Punt Returns—St. Louis, Mitchell 5-67; New England, Fryar 4-47.

Interceptions—St. Louis, Griffin 1-0.

Punting—St. Louis, Birdsong 6-38.2; New England, Camarillo 7-42.1.

Field Goals—St. Louis, O'Donoghue 2-2; New England, Franklin 1-1.

Sacks—St. Louis, Junior 2½, A. Baker 2, Greer 2, L. Smith, Holloway ½; New England, Tippett.

49ers-Falcons
SUNDAY, DECEMBER 2
SCORE BY PERIODS

San Francisco	7	14	7	7—35
Atlanta	3	7	7	0—17

SCORING

Atlanta—Field goal Luckhurst 32, 3:26 1st.
San Francisco—Solomon 64 pass from Montana (Wersching kick), 5:11 1st.
San Francisco—D. Clark 6 pass from Montana (Wersching kick), 0:10 2nd.
Atlanta—Riggs 2 run (Luckhurst kick), 11:56 2nd.
San Francisco—Johnson 33 fumble return (Wersching kick), 13:39 2nd.
Atlanta—A. Jackson 48 pass from Moroski (Luckhurst kick), 7:19 3rd.
San Francisco—McLemore 54 interception return (Wersching kick), 13:29 3rd.
San Francisco—Craig 5 run (Wersching kick), 5:59 4th.

TEAM STATISTICS

	San Francisco	Atlanta
First downs	15	23
Rushes-Yards	31-143	36-153
Passing yards	147	261
Sacked-Yards lost	2-18	3-28
Return yards	188	112
Passes	12-24-2	22-43-3
Punts	5-39.6	5-32.6
Fumbles-Lost	1-1	3-3
Penalties-Yards	9-73	8-50
Time of possession	24:33	35:27

Attendance—29,644. No-shows—26,492.

INDIVIDUAL STATISTICS

Rushing—San Francisco, Tyler 15-69, Craig 8-36, Solomon 2-20, Ring 4-8, Montana 1-6, Harmon 1-4; Atlanta, Riggs 30-133, Moroski 4-19, Cain 2-1.

Passing—San Francisco, Montana 12-24-2—165; Atlanta, Moroski 22-43-3—289.

Receiving—San Francisco, Cooper 4-51, Craig 4-42, D. Clark 2-12, Solomon 1-64, Ring 1-minus 4; Atlanta, A. Jackson 11-193, Riggs 3-35, Bailey 3-28, Cox 3-22, C. Benson 1-7, Hodge 1-4.

Kickoff Returns—San Francisco, Monroe 2-26, McLemore 1-50, Harmon 1-18; Atlanta, Curran 3-51, Johnson 2-46.

Punt Returns—San Francisco, McLemore 3-32; Atlanta, Seay 4-minus 1.

Interceptions—San Francisco, McLemore 1-54, Turner 1-8, M. Clark 1-0; Atlanta, Johnson 1-16, Pridemore 1-0.

Punting—San Francisco, Runager 5-39.6; Atlanta, Giacomarro 4-40.8.

Field Goals—San Francisco, Wersching 0-2 (missed: 46, 48); Atlanta, Luckhurst 1-1.

Sacks—San Francisco, Dean, Johnson, Turner; Atlanta, Provence, Smith.

Lions-Seahawks
SUNDAY, DECEMBER 2
SCORE BY PERIODS

Detroit	3	14	0	0—17
Seattle	7	14	0	17—38

SCORING

Seattle—Largent 7 pass from Krieg (Johnson kick), 10:44 1st.

Detroit—Field goal Murray 45, 14:51 1st.

Detroit—Jenkins 25 run (Murray kick), 1:59 2nd.

Seattle—Largent 13 pass from Krieg (Johnson kick), 5:24 2nd.

Detroit—J. Jones 15 pass from Danielson (Murray kick), 11:51 2nd.

Seattle—Turner 4 pass from Krieg (Johnson kick), 14:24 2nd.

Seattle—Turner 51 pass from Krieg (Johnson kick), 1:43 4th.

Seattle—Field goal Johnson 36, 5:06 4th.

Seattle—Tice 5 pass from Krieg (Johnson kick), 8:03 4th.

TEAM STATISTICS

	Detroit	Seattle
First downs	16	23
Rushes-Yards	28-108	28-113
Passing yards	139	275
Sacked-Yards lost	5-35	2-19
Return yards	126	85
Passes	14-25-2	27-38-1
Punts	4-36.5	3-33.7
Fumbles-Lost	1-0	1-1
Penalties-Yards	2-10	3-20
Time of possession	26:47	33:13
Attendance—62,441. No-shows—2,480.		

INDIVIDUAL STATISTICS

Rushing—Detroit, Jenkins 12-73, J. Jones 9-27, Witkowski 1-10, Bussey 2-6, Danielson 3-2, Black 1-minus 10; Seattle, Hughes 7-46, Morris 11-39, Doornink 6-21, Largent 1-6, Young 1-5, Zorn 2-minus 4.

Passing—Detroit, Danielson 11-20-2—117, Witkowski 3-5-0—57; Seattle, Krieg 27-38-1—294.

Receiving—Detroit, J. Jones 6-42, Thompson 2-38, Chadwick 2-26, Rubick 2-21, Jenkins 1-25, Nichols 1-22;

Seattle, Largent 8-104, Hughes 5-40, C. Young 4-20, Doornink 3-22, Turner 2-55, Castor 2-25, Skansi 1-16, Morris 1-7, Tice 1-5.

Kickoff Returns—Detroit, Hall 2-58, Mandley 2-40; Seattle, Dixon 3-57.

Punt Returns—Seattle, Skansi 2-19.

Interceptions—Detroit, Hall 1-28; Seattle, Easley 1-9, T. Jackson 1-0.

Punting—Detroit, Black 4-36.5; Seattle, West 3-33.7.

Field Goals—Detroit, Murray 1-1; Seattle, Johnson 1-1.

Sacks—Detroit, Cobb, Green; Seattle, J. Bryant 3, Edwards, Mangiero.

Bears-Chargers
MONDAY, DECEMBER 3
SCORE BY PERIODS

Chicago	0	0	7	0— 7
San Diego	0	6	0	14—20

SCORING

San Diego—Field goal Benirschke 48, 0:14 2nd.

San Diego—Field goal Benirschke 27, 14:38 2nd.

Chicago—Payton 10 run (B. Thomas kick), 8:22 3rd.

San Diego—Duckworth 88 pass from Luther (Benirschke kick), 5:23 4th.

San Diego—L. Williams 66 interception return (Benirschke kick), 13:45 4th.

TEAM STATISTICS

	Chicago	San Diego
First downs	18	9
Rushes-Yards	33-164	21-77
Passing yards	148	242
Sacked-Yards lost	5-37	4-33
Return yards	116	171
Passes	21-37-1	12-29-0
Punts	11-37.5	8-38.0
Fumbles-Lost	3-2	5-2
Penalties-Yards	7-46	2-10
Time of possession	37:09	22:51
Attendance—45,470. No-shows—14,519.		

INDIVIDUAL STATISTICS

Rushing—Chicago, Payton 23-92, Lisch 5-51, C. Thomas 3-14, Suhey 2-7; San Diego, Jackson 18-59, McGee 1-11, Luther 2-7.

Passing—Chicago, Lisch 18-33-1—164, Fuller 3-4-0—21; San Diego, Luther 12-29-0—275.

Receiving—Chicago, Payton 4-38, Suhey 4-36, Gault 4-28, Dunsmore 1-20, C. Thomas 3-16, Baschnagel 1-14, Anderson 1-11, Saldi 1-8, Krenk 1-7, Moorehead 1-7; San Diego, Duckworth 3-185, Chandler 3-47, Sievers 3-18, Joiner 1-12, Holohan 1-10, Jackson 1-3.

Kickoff Returns—Chicago, Duerson 2-44, Cameron 1-17, Bell 1-16; San Diego, James 2-88.

Punt Returns—Chicago, Fisher 4-36; San Diego, James 6-117.

Interceptions—San Diego, L. Williams 1-66.

Punting—Chicago, Finzer 11-37.5; San Diego, Buford 8-38.0.

Field Goals—Chicago, none attempted; San Diego, Benirschke 2-3 (missed: 52).

Sacks—Chicago, Hampton 1½, Duerson, McMichael ½; San Diego, Robinson 2, Smith, Ehin, L. Williams.

FIFTEENTH WEEK

RESULTS OF WEEK 15

Saturday, December 8

N.Y. Jets 21, Buffalo 17 at N.Y.
San Francisco 51, Minnesota 7 at S.F.

Sunday, December 9

Cincinnati 24, New Orleans 21 at N.O.
Denver 16, San Diego 13 at Den.
Green Bay 20, Chicago 14 at Chi.
Kansas City 34, Seattle 7 at K.C.
L.A. Rams 27, Houston 16 at L.A.
Miami 35, Indianapolis 17 at Ind.
Philadelphia 27, New England 17 at Phila.
Pittsburgh 23, Cleveland 20 at Pitts.
St. Louis 31, N.Y. Giants 21 at St. L.
Tampa Bay 23, Atlanta 6 at T.B.
Washington 30, Dallas 28 at Dall.

Monday, December 10

L.A. Raiders 24, Detroit 3 at Det.

The 1984 season was becoming more and more like a broken record.

First Walter Payton broke Jim Brown's all-time career rushing record in Week 6. Then Charlie Joiner eclipsed Charley Taylor's career pass receptions mark in Week 13. Next Dan Marino tied the record shared by George Blanda and Y.A. Tittle for single-season touchdown passes in Week 13 before breaking the mark in Week 14. And Eric Dickerson capped the assault in Week 15 by breaking a record that many NFL observers believed would stand for years to come.

Dickerson, the Los Angeles Rams' fabulous second-year running back, entered the contest against the Houston Oilers needing 212 yards to break O.J. Simpson's single-season rushing record of 2,003 yards, set by the Juice with the Buffalo Bills in 1973. Dickerson got 215.

"It feels fantastic. It feels great," said Dickerson, who finished the game with 2,007 yards on 353 carries. Simpson, who set the mark in a 14-game season, got his 2,003 yards on 332 carries. "I'm glad to get it behind me. I was getting tired of people asking me about it. It was getting hard to sleep."

If Dickerson was having a difficult time sleeping, think about the poor Houston defense, the league's worst at defending the run. Dickerson ravaged the Oilers for his 215 yards on just 27 carries—an incredible 8-yard average per rush. He rushed for 106 yards in the first half, 41 in the third period and 68 in the final quarter in the best game of his NFL career. Dickerson also set a league record by recording his 12th 100-yard game of the season and he scored two touchdowns in the 27-16 Rams' win. Simpson (in 1973) and Earl Campbell (1979) had shared the record for most 100-yard games with 11.

"I don't know when I've seen anyone more determined than Eric Dickerson," said Rams Coach John Robinson. "The look in his eyes was something absolutely fierce."

Dickerson, who set the record on his last carry of the game, a nine-yard gain with 3:12 remaining, said that a number of Houston players were using unfair tactics in an effort to keep him from getting the record.

"They were taking some cheap shots," said Dickerson, whose longest run of the day was 33 yards. "They got me a little riled up. They twisted my legs and twisted my knees after some plays. It was unnecessary."

The 3-11 Minnesota Vikings were no match for the 13-1 San Francisco 49ers in a Saturday afternoon game. The 49ers, having already clinched the home-field advantage in the playoffs with the NFC's best record, destroyed the woeful Vikes, 51-7, to tie the league record for most wins in one season. The 1972 Miami Dolphins set the mark en route to a perfect 17-0 campaign that included three playoff victories.

San Francisco jumped to a 31-7 halftime lead behind three touchdown passes by quarterback Joe Montana, who completed 15 of 21 passes for 246 yards in the half before being replaced by backup Matt Cavanaugh. Wendell Tyler, Derrick Harmon and Bill Ring each ran for touchdowns as the 49ers racked up the franchise's highest point total in 19 years.

In the other Saturday game, the New York Jets snapped a six-game losing streak with a 21-17 triumph over division-rival Buffalo. Jets rookie Russell Carter, who previously had played only at cornerback, made his first start at free safety and came up with two sacks, one fumble recovery and one interception as New York rebounded with 14 second-half points to lift its season record to 7-8.

For the Bills, who dropped to 2-13, rookie running back Greg Bell scored one touchdown and went over the 1,000-yard rushing mark for the year. Bell finished the day with 1,042 yards, the only rookie to rush for 1,000 yards in 1984.

Tampa Bay running back James Wilder, meanwhile, went over 2,000 total yards in the Buccaneers' 23-6 win over Atlanta. Wilder had 147 total yards against the Falcons to run his season total to 2,066 and he also broke Eric Dickerson's NFL record (442) for combined (rushing and receiving) attempts in one season with 452. A crowd of only 33,808—the smallest in Tampa Bay history—turned out to see the Bucs hand Atlanta its ninth straight defeat.

The Cleveland Browns kept intact their dubious record of never having won at Pittsburgh's Three Rivers Stadium when Gary Anderson booted a 34-yard field goal with five seconds left for a 23-20 Steelers victory. The Browns have lost 15 consecutive times at Three Rivers Stadium, which opened in 1970.

Anderson's game-winning kick, his third

Rams running back Eric Dickerson eclipsed O.J. Simpson's single-season rushing record by exploding for a career-high 215 yards in a 27-16 triumph over Houston in Week 15.

field goal of the game, came after the Steelers took over at their own 44-yard line with 3:09 remaining in the game. Pittsburgh then drove 39 yards in eight plays to run its season record to 8-7, one game ahead of Cincinnati in the AFC Central Division.

The Bengals kept pace with the Steelers by winning their game against New Orleans, 24-21. Veteran quarterback Ken Anderson came off the bench early in the second period to replace struggling rookie Boomer Esiason and led Cincinnati to touchdowns on three of its next four possessions, including scoring passes to James Brooks and Stanford Jennings.

Another division championship that wouldn't be decided until the final Sunday was the NFC East, where Dallas, the New York Giants and St. Louis were tied with 9-6 records, one game behind Washington.

The Redskins led the division after 15 weeks by rebounding from a 21-6 halftime deficit against the Cowboys to win, 30-28. Washington's victory, despite being outgained in total yards and giving up eight quarterback sacks, gave the Redskins their first series sweep ever against their longtime nemesis.

The Cowboys, who dominated the first half behind three Danny White touchdown passes, committed three costly third-period turnovers that gave the Redskins 17 unanswered points. First, Washington cornerback Darrell Green intercepted a White pass and returned it 32 yards for a touchdown. Then, on the ensuing kickoff, the Cowboys' Chuck McSwain fumbled and Anthony Washington recovered at the Dallas 31. Joe Theismann hit Calvin Muhammad for a 22-yard touchdown moments later. Later in the quarter, Timmy Newsome fumbled at the Dallas 23 with Mel Kaufman recovering for the Redskins. Mark Moseley's 21-yard field goal gave Washington its first lead, 23-21, and the teams swapped fourth-quarter touchdowns.

The Cardinals stayed in the thick of the division race with a 31-21 victory over the Giants. Quarterback Neil Lomax threw three scoring passes for the Cards while Ottis Anderson's 12-yard scoring run and Neil O'Donoghue's 34-yard field goal in the fourth period provided the margin of victory. Lomax's 305 passing yards put him over 4,000 for the season, the only quarterback besides Miami's Dan Marino and the Giants' Phil Simms to reach that plateau in 1984.

Heading into the final weekend, neither the Redskins, Cowboys, Giants nor Cardinals had clinched a playoff spot or been mathematically eliminated from postseason play.

The Denver Broncos and Seattle Seahawks remained neck-and-neck for the AFC Western Division title after the Broncos' victory over San Diego and the Seahawks' upset loss at Kansas City.

Denver beat San Diego, 16-13, when placekicker Rich Karlis booted a 28-yard field goal with 2:08 remaining in the game. It was the third field goal of the day for Karlis, who had hit the uprights with game-tying field-goal attempts in the Broncos' previous two games, both three-point losses. All 13 Charger points came after Denver turnovers that gave San Diego possession deep in Bronco territory.

Seattle's record also was 12-3 after a surprising 34-7 loss to the Chiefs snapped its eight-game winning streak. Just five weeks earlier, the Seahawks had crushed the Chiefs, 45-0, in the Kingdome by intercepting six passes and returning an NFL-record four for touchdowns. This time, it was Kansas City's turn to pick off six passes, with rookie linebacker Scott Radecic's 19-yard return for a touchdown giving the Chiefs a 17-7 second-quarter lead.

For the first time in 1984, the Seahawks' defense—which led the NFL in opponents turnovers—failed to come up with a single turnover.

The New England Patriots saw their slim hopes for an AFC wild-card berth disappear with a 27-17 loss to Philadelphia. Eagles quarterback Joe Pisarcik ran for two touchdowns and Wilbert Montgomery ran for another as Philadelphia's three rushing touchdowns matched its total of the previous 14 games. Montgomery's 100 yards rushing, in fact, marked the first time a Philly player rushed for 100 yards in one game since Montgomery got 147 against Houston on December 19, 1982. The Eagles had come into the game with the NFL's worst running attack, averaging 82 yards per game.

In what turned out to be Frank Kush's final game as coach of the Colts, Indianapolis lost an AFC Eastern Division game to Miami, 35-17. Kush, who was 11-28-1 since taking over as coach of the Colts in 1982, resigned with one game remaining in the season to become coach of the United States Football League's Arizona Outlaws.

For the first 30 minutes, it looked like the Colts might pull off a major upset. They led Miami, 17-7, at the half after controlling the ball for better than 20 minutes. But the Dolphins' offense got rolling in the second half. Quarterback Dan Marino threw four touchdown passes in the final two periods and the Dolphins' defense, which had yielded 233 yards and 18 first downs in the first half, held Indianapolis to only 27 total yards and two first downs in the second. Marino's four TD passes extended his NFL single-season record to 44 and his fourth 400-yard passing performance extended another record.

The Green Bay Packers upset division-rival Chicago, 20-14, when third-string quarterback Rich Campbell threw a 43-yard touchdown pass to Phillip Epps with 34 seconds left in the game. Campbell, who played because of injuries to Lynn Dickey and rookie Randy Wright, also threw a three-yard scoring pass to tight end Ed West in the second period. The touchdown passes were the first of Campbell's four-year pro career after being the Packers' No. 1 draft choice in 1981.

The loss put a damper on a fabulous performance by the Bears' Walter Payton. The All-Pro running back rushed 35 times for 175 yards, scored one touchdown and threw a halfback option pass for another. He also played one series at quarterback late in the first half when Rusty Lisch was having trouble moving the Chicago offense. Payton played six downs at quarterback in the shotgun formation but didn't complete a pass as two fell incomplete and another was intercepted by Packers rookie Tom Flynn.

The Los Angeles Raiders won for the 22nd time in 26 appearances on Monday night with a 24-3 trouncing of interconference rival Detroit. Marc Wilson and Jim Plunkett each threw a scoring pass while Cle Montgomery returned a punt 69 yards for another score early in the final period. The Raiders defense held Detroit to 10 first downs and had eight quarterback sacks as L.A. improved its record to 11-4 with one game remaining. The Lions, winners of the NFC Central Division in 1983, dropped to 4-10-1 in their worst season in five years.

Bills - Jets
SATURDAY, DECEMBER 8
SCORE BY PERIODS

Buffalo	7	10	0	0—17
New York Jets	7	0	7	7—21

SCORING
Buffalo—David 36 blocked punt return (Nelson kick), 9:57 1st.
New York—Minter 6 run (Leahy kick), 14:39 1st.
Buffalo—Bell 3 run (Nelson kick), 8:11 2nd.
Buffalo—Field goal Nelson 47, 13:52 2nd.
New York—Walker 39 pass from O'Brien (Leahy kick), 14:21 3rd.
New York—Paige 3 run (Leahy kick), 4:13 4th.

TEAM STATISTICS

	Buffalo	New York
First downs	11	21
Rushes-Yards	24-82	39-140
Passing yards	140	203
Sacked-Yards lost	3-22	2-14
Return yards	105	187
Passes	14-34-2	17-30-1
Punts	9-36.4	6-34.3
Fumbles-Lost	2-1	3-3
Penalties-Yards	6-41	4-20
Time of possession	27:34	32:26

Attendance—45,378. No-shows—31,513.

INDIVIDUAL STATISTICS
Rushing—Buffalo, Bell 18-54, Moore 3-17, Neal 2-7, Dufek 1-4; New York, Hector 20-73, Minter 14-58, O'Brien 2-0, Paige 3-9.
Passing—Buffalo, Dufek 14-34-2—162; New York, O'Brien 17-30-1—217.
Receiving—Buffalo, Hunter 7-39, Dawkins 1-28, Brookins 2-60, Bell 1-9, Franklin 2-18, Riddick 1-8; New York, Shuler 1-55, Jones 5-85, Dennison 2-23, Walker 2-47, Minter 1-11, Paige 1-minus 1.
Kickoff Returns—Buffalo, V. Williams 1-54, Wilson 1-

24; New York, Minter 2-71, Humphery 1-59, Shuler 1-0.
Punt Returns—New York, Minter 3-36, Mullen 1-8.
Interceptions—Buffalo, Romes 1-27; New York, Springs 1-13, Carter 1-0.
Punting—Buffalo, Kidd 9-36.4; New York, Ramsey 5-41.2.
Field Goals—Buffalo, Nelson 1-1; New York, none attempted.
Sacks—Buffalo, Haslett, Kush; New York, Carter 2, Gastineau.

Vikings - 49ers
SATURDAY, DECEMBER 8
SCORE BY PERIODS

Minnesota	0	7	0	0— 7
San Francisco	14	17	6	14—51

SCORING
San Francisco—D. Clark 44 pass from Montana (Wersching kick), 8:16 1st.
San Francisco—Solomon 3 pass from Montana (Wersching kick), 13:19 1st.
Minnesota—Nelson 5 run (Stenerud kick), 1:44 2nd.
San Francisco—Tyler 5 run (Wersching kick), 5:48 2nd.
San Francisco—Nehemiah 59 pass from Montana (Wersching kick), 8:06 2nd.
San Francisco—Field goal Wersching 41, 14:57 2nd.
San Francisco—Field goal Wersching 25, 5:12 3rd.
San Francisco—Field goal Wersching 38, 14:16 3rd.
San Francisco—Harmon 3 run (Wersching kick), 4:52 4th.
San Francisco—Ring 15 run (Wersching kick), 11:58 4th.

TEAM STATISTICS

	Minnesota	San Francisco
First downs	18	29
Rushes-Yards	24-90	40-184
Passing yards	175	337
Sacked-Yards lost	6-58	1-9
Return yards	193	102
Passes	21-39-1	25-35-0
Punts	7-44.3	2-48.5
Fumbles-Lost	0-0	1-0
Penalties-Yards	7-65	4-25
Time of possession	26:41	33:19

Attendance—56,670. No-shows—4,714.

INDIVIDUAL STATISTICS
Rushing—Minnesota, Nelson 7-38, Anderson 12-33, Lewis 1-6, Wilson 2-6, Rice 1-6, Manning 1-1; San Francisco, Harmon 11-56, Craig 7-45, Ring 7-44, Tyler 13-36, Montana 1-4, Cavanaugh 1-minus 1.
Passing—Minnesota, Wilson 18-32-1—212, Manning 3-7-0—21; San Francisco, Montana 15-21-0—246, Cavanaugh 10-14-0—100.
Receiving—Minnesota, Senser 6-36, Lewis 3-55, Jones 3-53, Mularkey 3-50, Nelson 3-26, Anderson 2-7, Collins 1-6; San Francisco, Nehemiah 6-125, Craig 4-31, D. Clark 3-73, Cooper 3-46, Solomon 3-32, Francis 2-21, Wilson 2-16, Harmon 1-2, Monroe 1-0.
Kickoff Returns—Minnesota, Anderson 4-96, Nelson 3-67, Lewis 1-21; San Francisco, Harmon 1-43, Wilson 1-14.
Punt Returns—Minnesota, Nelson 1-9; San Francisco, McLemore 2-31.
Interceptions—San Francisco, Shell 1-14.
Punting—Minnesota, Coleman 7-44.3; San Francisco, Runager 2-48.5.
Field Goals—Minnesota, none attempted; San Francisco, Wersching 3-3.
Sacks—Minnesota, D. Martin; San Francisco, Board 2, Fuller 1½, Williams, Walter, Stover ½.

Bengals - Saints
SUNDAY, DECEMBER 9
SCORE BY PERIODS

Cincinnati	0	3	14	7—24
New Orleans	0	7	7	7—21

SCORING

Cincinnati—Field goal Breech 35, 14:36 2nd.
New Orleans—Brenner 54 pass from D. Wilson (Andersen kick), 15:00 2nd.
Cincinnati—Brooks 27 pass from Anderson (Breech kick), 4:49 3rd.
Cincinnati—Jennings 15 pass from Anderson (Breech kick), 9:53 3rd.
New Orleans—Brenner 35 pass from D. Wilson (Andersen kick), 14:13 3rd.
Cincinnati—Jennings 1 run (Breech kick), 4:34 4th.
New Orleans—Goodlow 5 pass from D. Wilson (Andersen kick), 14:11 4th.

TEAM STATISTICS

	Cincinnati	New Orleans
First downs	20	23
Rushes-Yards	35-107	31-146
Passing yards	172	254
Sacked-Yards lost	2-20	6-51
Return yards	31	108
Passes	19-32-0	20-32-1
Punts	6-47.2	4-43.2
Fumbles-Lost	0-0	3-3
Penalties-Yards	9-70	6-55
Time of possession	27:39	32:21

Attendance—40,855. No-shows—15,430.

INDIVIDUAL STATISTICS

Rushing—Cincinnati, Alexander 17-58, Brooks 7-34, Kinnebrew 4-10, Esiason 2-10, Jennings 3-1, Anderson 2-minus 6; New Orleans, Gajan 12-47, G. Rogers 7-33, W. Wilson 4-33, Campbell 7-32, Anthony 1-1.
Passing—Cincinnati, Esiason 1-6-0—1, Anderson 18-26-0—191; New Orleans, D. Wilson 20-32-1—325.
Receiving—Cincinnati, Martin 4-43, Kreider 3-31, Jennings 4-41, Brooks 1-27, Holman 3-24, Verser 1-15, Harris 1-6, Alexander 2-5; New Orleans, Brenner 3-101, Gajan 7-90, Anthony 3-25, Goodlow 5-59, Young 2-50.
Kickoff Returns—Cincinnati, Jennings 1-17; New Orleans, Anthony 3-69, Fields 1-15.
Punt Returns—Cincinnati, Martin 1-14; New Orleans, Fields 4-24.
Interceptions—Cincinnati, Schuh 1-0.
Punting—Cincinnati, McInally 6-47.2; New Orleans, Hansen 4-43.2.
Field Goals—Cincinnati, Breech 1-2 (missed: 50); New Orleans, none attempted.
Sacks—Cincinnati, Edwards 2, Browner, Frazier, Krumrie, Schuh; New Orleans, Jackson 2.

Chargers-Broncos
SUNDAY, DECEMBER 9
SCORE BY PERIODS

San Diego	6	0	0	7	13
Denver	0	6	7	3	16

SCORING

San Diego—Field goal Benirschke 42, 10:33 1st.
San Diego—Field goal Benirschke 41, 11:39 1st.
Denver—Field goal Karlis 30, 12:10 2nd.
Denver—Field goal Karlis 50, 15:00 2nd.
Denver—Winder 4 run (Karlis kick), 7:14 3rd.
San Diego—McGee 4 pass from Luther (Benirschke kick), 1:19 4th.
Denver—Field goal Karlis 28, 12:52 4th.

TEAM STATISTICS

	San Diego	Denver
First downs	16	22
Rushes-Yards	25-87	38-162
Passing yards	147	181
Sacked-Yards lost	3-24	1-12
Return yards	37	98
Passes	18-35-0	18-31-1
Punts	4-43.0	2-44.5
Fumbles-Lost	1-0	4-3
Penalties-Yards	4-25	4-20
Time of possession	26:57	33:03

Attendance—74,867. No-shows—233.

INDIVIDUAL STATISTICS

Rushing—San Diego, McGee 5-17, Jackson 19-68, Luther 1-2; Denver, Winder 22-90, Willhite 2-9, Elway 7-23, Johnson 1-3, Parros 6-37.
Passing—San Diego, Luther 18-35-0—171; Denver, Elway 18-31-1—193.
Receiving—San Diego, Jackson 5-24, Holohan 4-51, Chandler 1-1, Bendross 3-44, McGee 2-8, Joiner 2-27, Duckworth 1-16; Denver, Johnson 3-39, Watson 3-40, Winder 2-21, Parros 2-7, Alexander 2-28, Willhite 4-32, J. Wright 1-12, Sampson 1-14.
Kickoff Returns—San Diego, James 1-18; Denver, Lang 2-43, Willhite 1-25.
Punt Returns—San Diego, James 2-10; Denver, Willhite 3-30.
Interceptions—San Diego, Lowe 1-9.
Punting—San Diego, Buford 4-43.0; Denver, Norman 2-44.5.
Field Goals—San Diego, Benirschke 2-3 (missed: 53); Denver, Karlis 3-3.
Sacks—San Diego, Young; Denver, Jones 2, Dennison.

Packers-Bears
SUNDAY, DECEMBER 9
SCORE BY PERIODS

Green Bay	0	7	6	7	20
Chicago	0	0	7	7	14

SCORING

Green Bay—West 3 pass from Campbell (Del Greco kick), 13:05 2nd.
Chicago—Suhey 2 pass from Payton (B. Thomas kick), 9:15 3rd.
Green Bay—Rodgers 97 kickoff return (kick failed), 9:37 3rd.
Chicago—Payton 7 run (B. Thomas kick), 2:38 4th.
Green Bay—Epps 43 pass from Campbell (Del Greco kick), 14:26 4th.

TEAM STATISTICS

	Green Bay	Chicago
First downs	17	25
Rushes-Yards	30-110	51-228
Passing yards	177	73
Sacked-Yards lost	3-23	5-28
Return yards	155	98
Passes	13-31-2	11-27-2
Punts	6-42.5	6-41.8
Fumbles-Lost	0-0	4-3
Penalties-Yards	6-59	5-30
Time of possession	24:25	35:35

Attendance—59,374. No-shows—6,416.

INDIVIDUAL STATISTICS

Rushing—Green Bay, Ivery 12-50, Ellis 9-28, Wright 3-0, Lofton 1-19, Crouse 2-1, Campbell 2-2, Huckleby 1-10; Chicago, Payton 35-175, Lisch 6-23, Gentry 1-2, C. Thomas 2-2, Suhey 7-26.
Passing—Green Bay, Wright 4-10-0—75, Ellis 0-1-0—0, Scribner 0-1-0—0, Campbell 9-19-2—125; Chicago, Lisch 10-23-1—99, Payton 1-4-1—2.
Receiving—Green Bay, Crouse 2-27, Coffman 2-33, Lofton 2-28, Epps 3-65, Ellis 1-17, West 1-3, Ivery 2-27; Chicago, Suhey 5-34, Moorehead 4-53, Dunsmore 2-14.
Kickoff Returns—Green Bay, Rodgers 3-130; Chicago, Cameron 3-29, Gault 1-12, Duerson (with lateral) 0-11.
Punt Returns—Green Bay, Flynn 3-22; Chicago, Fisher 3-14, Duerson 1-4.
Interceptions—Green Bay, Flynn 2-3; Chicago, Fencik 1-19, Duerson 1-9.
Punting—Green Bay, Scribner 6-42.5; Chicago, Finzer 6-41.8.

Field Goals—Green Bay, Del Greco 0-1 (missed: 46); Chicago, none attempted.

Sacks—Green Bay, Douglass 3, Carreker, Martin; Chicago, Dent 2, Hampton.

Seahawks-Chiefs
SUNDAY, DECEMBER 9
SCORE BY PERIODS

Seattle	7	0	0	0— 7
Kansas City	7	17	7	3—34

SCORING

Kansas City—Heard 2 run (Lowery kick), 6:34 1st.
Seattle—Turner 49 pass from Krieg (Johnson kick), 14:06 1st.
Kansas City—Field goal Lowery 29, 3:39 2nd.
Kansas City—Radecic 19 interception return (Lowery kick), 4:36 2nd.
Kansas City—Marshall 26 pass from Kenney (Lowery kick), 9:38 2nd.
Kansas City—Carson 25 pass from Kenney (Lowery kick), 12:28 3rd.
Kansas City—Field goal Lowery 22, 2:43 4th.

TEAM STATISTICS

	Seattle	Kansas City
First downs	18	20
Rushes-Yards	22-66	38-91
Passing yards	307	325
Sacked-Yards lost	0-0	0-0
Return yards	135	82
Passes	21-46-6	19-38-0
Punts	5-33.4	6-45.2
Fumbles-Lost	1-0	2-0
Penalties-Yards	6-54	8-51
Time of possession	28:44	31:16

Attendance—34,855. No-shows—3,966.

INDIVIDUAL STATISTICS

Rushing—Seattle, Hughes 8-32, Dixon 6-16, C. Bryant 3-10, Lane 2-7, Morris 2-1, Krieg 1-0; Kansas City, Heard 24-73, Lacy 5-24. Jackson 2-1, Brown 1-minus 2, Kenney 1-minus 2, Gunter 5-minus 3.

Passing—Seattle, Krieg 17-38-5—263, Zorn 4-8-1—44; Kansas City, Kenney 18-37-0—312, Blackledge 1-1-0 —13.

Receiving—Seattle, Largent 4-98, Skansi 3-44, Morris 3-18, Turner 2-58, C. Young 2-32, Lane 2-9, Castor 1-21, C. Bryant 1-11, Tice 1-6, Dixon 1-6, Hughes 1-4; Kansas City, Marshall 8-166, Carson 4-80, Heard 3-39, Paige 3-31, W. Arnold 1-9.

Kickoff Returns—Seattle, Morris 4-83, Dixon 2-16; Kansas City, Hancock 1-17, Smith 1-15.

Punt Returns—Seattle, Skanski 3-31, Dixon 1-5; Kansas City, Hancock 1-5.

Interceptions—Kansas City, Radecic 1-19, Blanton 1-14, Daniels 1-11, Kremer 1-1, Cherry 1-0, Ross 1-0.

Punting—Seattle, West 5-33.4; Kansas City, J. Arnold 6-45.2.

Field Goals—Seattle, none attempted; Kansas City, Lowery 2-4 (missed: 41, 36).

Oilers-Rams
SUNDAY, DECEMBER 9
SCORE BY PERIODS

Houston	3	10	3	0—16
Los Angeles Rams	17	3	0	7—27

SCORING

Los Angeles—Drew Hill 57 pass from Kemp (Lansford kick), 1:52 1st.
Houston—Field goal Cooper 21, 7:38 1st.
Los Angeles—Dickerson 7 run (Lansford kick), 10:32 1st.
Los Angeles—Field goal Lansford 35, 13:18 1st.
Houston—Field goal Cooper 42, 1:41 2nd.

Houston—Moriarty 4 run (Cooper kick), 8:47 2nd.
Los Angeles—Field goal Lansford 19, 12:34 2nd.
Houston—Field goal Cooper 18, 7:10 3rd.
Los Angeles—Dickerson 6 run (Lansford kick), 9:11 4th.

TEAM STATISTICS

	Houston	Los Angeles
First downs	23	21
Rushes-Yards	33-154	34-276
Passing yards	184	177
Sacked-Yards lost	3-16	2-22
Return yards	91	138
Passes	19-29-1	12-23-0
Punts	3-32.0	2-36.0
Fumbles-Lost	1-1	0-0
Penalties-Yards	4-25	6-54
Time of possession	35:01	24:59

Attendance—49,092. No-shows—7,828.

INDIVIDUAL STATISTICS

Rushing—Houston, Moriarty 24-102, Edwards 6-28, Moon 3-24; Los Angeles, Dickerson 27-215, Crutchfield .7-61.

Passing—Houston, Moon 19-29-1—200; Los Angeles, Kemp 12-23-0—199.

Receiving—Houston, Smith 6-69, Dressel 4-27, J. Williams 2-28, Moriarty 2-18, Edwards 2-9, Roaches 1-21, Walls 1-14, Holston 1-14; Los Angeles, Ellard 3-49, David Hill 3-43, J. McDonald 2-25, Barber 2-18, Drew Hill 1-57, Brown 1-7.

Kickoff Returns—Houston, Walls 3-52, J. Williams 2-27, Roaches 1-12; Los Angeles, Pleasant 2-48, Drew Hill 2-42.

Punt Returns—Los Angeles, Irvin 1-17.

Interceptions—Los Angeles, Newsome 1-31.

Punting—Houston, James 3-32.0; Los Angeles, Misko 2-36.0.

Field Goals—Houston, Cooper 3-3; Los Angeles, Lansford 2-3 (missed: 41).

Sacks—Houston, Baker, Sochia; Los Angeles, Doss, Meisner, Newsome.

Dolphins-Colts
SUNDAY, DECEMBER 9
SCORE BY PERIODS

Miami	7	0	14	14—35
Indianapolis	7	10	0	0—17

SCORING

Indianapolis—Butler 5 pass from Pagel (Allegre kick), 9:01 1st.
Miami—Bennett 2 run (von Schamann kick), 13:03 1st.
Indianapolis—Field goal Allegre 52, 1:39 2nd.
Indianapolis—McMillan 6 run (Allegre kick), 13:03 2nd.
Miami—Moore 2 pass from Marino (von Schamann kick), 3:57 3rd.
Miami—Hardy 2 pass from Marino (von Schamann kick), 12:46 3rd.
Miami—Cefalo 25 pass from Marino (von Schamann kick), 10:19 4th.
Miami—Clayton 7 pass from Marino (von Schamann kick), 14:36 4th.

TEAM STATISTICS

	Miami	Indianapolis
First downs	29	20
Rushes-Yards	27-75	33-170
Passing yards	387	90
Sacked-Yards lost	2-17	3-28
Return yards	98	135
Passes	29-41-1	12-26-2
Punts	2-39.0	3-44.3
Fumbles-Lost	4-1	2-0
Penalties-Yards	3-15	6-45
Time of possession	30:44	29:16

Attendance—60,411. No-shows—284.

INDIVIDUAL STATISTICS

Rushing—Miami, Bennett 9-34, Carter 14-32, Nathan 1-4, P. Johnson 3-5; Indianapolis, McMillan 11-73, Middleton 16-74, Wonsley 3-5, Pagel 3-18.

Passing—Miami, Marino 29-41-1—404; Indianapolis, Pagel 11-23-1—110, Schlichter 1-3-1—8.

Receiving—Miami, Clayton 9-127, Nathan 5-33, Moore 5-87, Duper 3-41, Hardy 3-21, Cefalo 2-39, D. Johnson 1-42, Jensen 1-14; Indianapolis, Butler 4-33, McMillan 3-28, Bouza 2-18, Porter 1-21, Middleton 1-6, Sherwin 1-12.

Kickoff Returns—Miami, Walker 2-56; Indianapolis, Anderson 2-68, P. Smith 2-49.

Punt Returns—Miami, Walker 1-6, Kozlowski 1-3.

Interceptions—Miami, G. Blackwood 1-35, L. Blackwood 0-minus 2, Brudzinski 1-0; Indianapolis, Daniel 1-18.

Punting—Miami, Roby 2-39.0; Indianapolis, Stark 3-44.3.

Field Goals—Miami, none attempted; Indianapolis, Allegre 1-2 (missed: 54).

Sacks—Miami, Bowser 2, Barnett; Indianapolis, Thompson, White.

Patriots-Eagles
SUNDAY, DECEMBER 9
SCORE BY PERIODS

New England	10	0	7	0—17
Philadelphia	7	10	3	7—27

SCORING

New England—Field goal Franklin 24, 3:41 1st.

Philadelphia—Pisarcik 1 run (McFadden kick), 7:49 1st.

New England—Morgan 9 pass from Eason (Franklin kick), 14:10 1st.

Philadelphia—Field goal McFadden 50, 5:42 2nd.

Philadelphia—Montgomery 10 run (McFadden kick), 14:06 2nd.

Philadelphia—Field goal McFadden 46, 3:39 3rd.

New England—Jones recovered fumble in end zone (Franklin kick), 12:04 3rd.

Philadelphia—Pisarcik 3 run (McFadden kick), 9:15 4th.

TEAM STATISTICS

	New England	Philadelphia
First downs	21	19
Rushes-Yards	36-175	28-136
Passing yards	162	170
Sacked-Yards lost	4-32	5-35
Return yards	123	160
Passes	12-28-1	16-29-1
Punts	8-39.1	6-42.0
Fumbles-Lost	3-0	1-0
Penalties-Yards	3-20	3-26
Time of possession	31:08	28:52

Attendance—41,581. No-shows—17,653.

INDIVIDUAL STATISTICS

Rushing—New England, C. James 19-92, Collins 12-60, Tatupu 4-20, Eason 1-3; Philadelphia, Montgomery 19-100, Pisarcik 5-20, Oliver 3-18, Hardy 1-minus 2.

Passing—New England, Eason 12-28-1—194; Philadelphia, Pisarcik 16-29-1—205.

Receiving—New England, Morgan 5-101, Ramsey 5-68, Collins 1-13, C. James 1-12; Philadelphia, Quick 6-84, Montgomery 4-21, Woodruff 2-51, Jackson 2-26, Spagnola 1-16, Oliver 1-7.

Kickoff Returns—New England, Collins 5-105, Lee 1-14; Philadelphia, Waters 3-60, Ellis 1-15.

Punt Returns—Philadelphia, Cooper 7-58.

Interceptions—New England, Gibson 1-4; Philadelphia, Hopkins 1-27.

Punting—New England, Camarillo 8-39.1; Philadelphia, Horan 6-42.0.

Field Goals—New England, Franklin 1-2 (missed: 38); Philadelphia, McFadden 2-3 (missed: 48).

Sacks—New England, Tippett 2, Adams, Owens, T. Williams; Philadelphia, Darby 1½, Harrison 1½, Brown.

Browns-Steelers
SUNDAY, DECEMBER 9
SCORE BY PERIODS

Cleveland	3	10	0	7—20
Pittsburgh	7	10	3	3—23

SCORING

Cleveland—Field goal Bahr 29, 7:56 1st.

Pittsburgh—Lipps 61 pass from Malone (Anderson kick), 12:36 1st.

Pittsburgh—Field goal Anderson 40, 2:24 2nd.

Cleveland—Field goal Bahr 49, 6:42 2nd.

Pittsburgh—Pollard 1 run (Anderson kick), 13:03 2nd.

Cleveland—Feacher 16 pass from McDonald (Bahr kick), 14:33 2nd.

Pittsburgh—Field goal Anderson 22, 10:59 3rd.

Cleveland—McDonald 3 run (Bahr kick), 6:11 4th.

Pittsburgh—Field goal Anderson 34, 14:55 4th.

TEAM STATISTICS

	Cleveland	Pittsburgh
First downs	21	16
Rushes-Yards	32-140	30-125
Passing yards	202	222
Sacked-Yards lost	2-9	1-7
Return yards	115	141
Passes	19-33-4	13-26-2
Punts	5-49.8	5-43.2
Fumbles-Lost	2-0	2-0
Penalties-Yards	8-50	8-70
Time of possession	33:55	26:05

Attendance—55,825. No-shows—3,175.

INDIVIDUAL STATISTICS

Rushing—Cleveland, Byner 15-103, Green 11-25, Pruitt 5-9, McDonald 1-3; Pittsburgh, Abercrombie 15-74, Pollard 9-37, Malone 4-8, Campbell 1-0, Erenberg 1-6.

Passing—Cleveland, McDonald 19-33-4—211; Pittsburgh, Malone 11-22-2—203, Campbell 2-4-0—26.

Receiving—Cleveland, Young 1-47, Holt 3-31, Brennan 3-16, Feacher 3-56, Newsome 5-33, Green 2-9, Adams 2-19; Pittsburgh, Abercrombie 2-11, Pollard 5-62, Lipps 3-97, Erenberg 1-22, Stallworth 2-37.

Kickoff Returns—Cleveland, Byner 2-32, Young 1-23, Holt 1-1; Pittsburgh, Erenberg 2-50, Gillespie 1-12, Brown 1-11.

Punt Returns—Cleveland, Brennan 4-41; Pittsburgh, Lipps 3-38.

Interceptions—Cleveland, Dixon 2-18; Pittsburgh, Shell 2-1, Hinkle 1-21, Merriweather 1-8.

Punting—Cleveland, Cox 5-49.8; Pittsburgh, Colquitt 5-43.2.

Field Goals—Cleveland, Bahr 2-2; Pittsburgh, Anderson 3-3.

Sacks—Cleveland, Camp; Pittsburgh, Merriweather, Willis.

Giants-Cardinals
SUNDAY, DECEMBER 9
SCORE BY PERIODS

New York Giants	7	0	14	0—21
St. Louis	0	14	7	10—31

SCORING

New York—Manuel 5 pass from Simms (Haji-Sheikh kick), 10:58 1st.

St. Louis—Tilley 4 pass from Lomax (O'Donoghue kick), 6:14 2nd.

St. Louis—Mitchell 44 pass from Lomax (O'Donoghue kick), 10:03 2nd.

New York—Mowatt 18 pass from Simms (Haji-Sheikh kick), 5:03 3rd.

St. Louis—Green 35 pass from Lomax (O'Donoghue kick), 6:19 3rd.

New York—Carpenter 1 run (Haji-Sheikh kick), 11:01 3rd.

St. Louis—Anderson 12 run (O'Donoghue kick), 2:43 4th.

St. Louis—Field goal O'Donoghue 34, 10:06 4th.

Pittsburgh placekicker Gary Anderson pinned Cleveland with its 15th loss in 15 games at Three Rivers Stadium by booting a 34-yard field goal with five seconds left for a 23-20 Steelers victory.

TEAM STATISTICS

	New York	St. Louis
First downs	20	22
Rushes-Yards	27-148	31-114
Passing yards	159	296
Sacked-Yards lost	3-16	5-29
Return yards	134	113
Passes	13-31-2	24-34-0
Punts	4-34.5	3-31.7
Fumbles-Lost	0-0	2-2
Penalties-Yards	4-35	7-50
Time of possession	25:33	34:27

Attendance—49,973. No-shows—1,544.

INDIVIDUAL STATISTICS

Rushing—New York, Morris 16-107, Carpenter 10-43, Simms 1-minus 2; St. Louis, Anderson 23-91, Mitchell 2-3, Ferrell 3-21, Lomax 3-minus 1.

Passing—New York, Simms 13-31-2—175; St. Louis, Lomax 23-33-0—305, Mitchell 1-1-0—20.

Receiving—New York, Johnson 3-51, Manuel 3-37, Mowatt 5-77, Belcher 1-4, Galbreath 1-6; St. Louis, Green 6-89, Marsh 2-15, Pittman 3-67, Anderson 5-44, Ferrell 3-30, Tilley 2-20, LaFleur 2-16, Mitchell 1-44.

Kickoff Returns—New York, Woolfolk 5-84, Daniel 1-52; St. Louis Mitchell 3-103.

Punt Returns—New York, Manuel 1-minus 2; St. Louis, Mitchell 2-14.

Interceptions—St. Louis, Howard 2-minus 4.

Punting—New York, Jennings 4-34.5; St. Louis, Birdsong 3-31.7.

Field Goals—New York, Haji-Sheikh 0-2 (missed: 33, 47); St. Louis, O'Donoghue 1-2 (missed: 40).

Sacks—New York, Burt 2, Hunt, Sally, Taylor; St. Louis, A. Baker 2, Greer.

Falcons-Buccaneers

SUNDAY, DECEMBER 9
SCORE BY PERIODS

Atlanta	0	6	0	0— 6
Tampa Bay	3	10	7	3—23

SCORING

Tampa Bay—Field goal Ariri 30, 5:00 1st.
Tampa Bay—DeBerg 2 run (Ariri kick), 3:29 2nd.
Atlanta—Field goal Luckhurst 33, 7:08 2nd.
Atlanta—Field goal Luckhurst 49, 12:35 2nd.

Tampa Bay—Field goal Ariri 36, 14:51 2nd.
Tampa Bay—Wilder 1 run (Ariri kick), 4:10 3rd.
Tampa Bay—Field goal Ariri 28, 6:01 4th.

TEAM STATISTICS

	Atlanta	Tampa Bay
First downs	15	21
Rushes-Yards	19-70	36-143
Passing yards	204	192
Sacked-Yards lost	4-23	0-0
Return yards	132	134
Passes	22-38-2	18-29-0
Punts	3-37.0	3-46.3
Fumbles-Lost	0-0	0-0
Penalties-Yards	9-83	6-60
Time of possession	28:10	31:50

Attendance—33,808. No-shows—18,201.

INDIVIDUAL STATISTICS

Rushing—Atlanta, Riggs 15-53, Moroski 2-7, Cain 1-3, Archer 1-7; Tampa Bay, Wilder 28-125, DeBerg 1-2, Armstrong 1-6, Morton 5-8, Peoples 1-2.

Passing—Atlanta, Moroski 22-37-1—227, Archer 0-1-1—0; Tampa Bay, DeBerg 18-29-0—192.

Receiving—Atlanta, A. Jackson 5-70, Cox 2-13, Bailey 4-54, Landrum 1-30, Riggs 5-21, C. Benson 2-19, Cain 1-8, Hodge 2-12; Tampa Bay, J. Bell 4-40, House 5-39, Armstrong 2-7, Wilder 2-22, T. Bell 4-80, Giles 1-4.

Kickoff Returns—Atlanta, Johnson 3-64, Seay 2-55; Tampa Bay, Morton 3-83.

Punt Returns—Atlanta, Seay 3-13; Tampa Bay, Bright 1-8.

Interceptions—Tampa Bay, Cotney 1-29, Acorn 1-14.

Punting—Atlanta, Giacomarro 3-37.0; Tampa Bay, Garcia 3-46.3.

Field Goals—Atlanta, Luckhurst 2-2; Tampa Bay, Ariri 3-3.

Sacks—Tampa Bay, Logan 1½, Browner, Selmon, Cannon ½.

Redskins-Cowboys
SUNDAY, DECEMBER 9
SCORE BY PERIODS

Washington	0	6	17	7—30
Dallas	7	14	0	7—28

SCORING

Dallas—Donley 6 pass from D. White (Septien kick), 5:22 1st.
Washington—Field goal Moseley 31, 6:27 2nd.
Dallas—Cosbie 2 pass from D. White (Septien kick), 7:52 2nd.
Washington—Field goal Moseley 34, 11:10 2nd.
Dallas—Renfro 60 pass from D. White (Septien kick), 13:10 2nd.
Washington—Green 32 interception return (Moseley kick), 2:03 3rd.
Washington—Muhammad 22 pass from Theismann (Moseley kick), 3:41 3rd.
Washington—Field goal Moseley 21, 13:40 3rd.
Dallas—Hill 43 pass from D. White (Septien kick), 0:06 4th.
Washington—Riggins 1 run (Moseley kick), 8:17 4th.

TEAM STATISTICS

	Washington	Dallas
First downs	22	25
Rushes-Yards	35-151	24-106
Passing yards	148	281
Sacked-Yards lost	8-57	5-46
Return yards	124	100
Passes	17-31-0	22-42-2
Punts	7-42.7	4-37.3
Fumbles-Lost	3-0	3-2
Penalties-Yards	6-71	6-49
Time of possession	33:21	26:39

Attendance—64,286. No-shows—815.

INDIVIDUAL STATISTICS

Rushing—Washington, Theismann 6-18, Riggins 24-111, Monk 1-18, J. Washington 3-2, Wonsley 1-2; Dallas, D. White 1-8, Dorsett 15-42, Newsome 6-48, Springs 2-8.

Passing—Washington, Theismann 17-31-0—205; Dallas, D. White 22-42-2—327.

Receiving—Washington, Didier 3-39, Monk 7-80, Muhammad 3-43, Brown 1-9, J. Washington 1-7, Warren 2-27; Dallas, Dorsett 2-32, Hill 7-119, Newsome 2-22, Donley 1-6, Cosbie 4-39, Renfro 3-80, Springs 2-19, J. Jones 1-10.

Kickoff Returns—Washington, Nelms 4-77; Dallas, McSwain 3-63.

Punt Returns—Washington, Coffey 1-6, Nelms 2-0; Dallas, Allen 5-37.

Interceptions—Washington, Green 2-41.

Punting—Washington, Hayes 7-42.7; Dallas, D. White 4-37.3.

Field Goals—Washington, Moseley 3-3; Dallas, none attempted.

Sacks—Washington, Manley 2, Brooks, Kaufman, Milot; Dallas, Jeffcoat 2½, Lockhart 2, Bates 1½, E. Jones, Thurman.

Raiders-Lions
MONDAY, DECEMBER 10
SCORE BY PERIODS

Los Angeles Raiders	0	7	3	14—24
Detroit	0	3	0	0— 3

SCORING

Los Angeles—Christensen 12 pass from Wilson (Bahr kick), 7:42 2nd.
Detroit—Field goal Murray 48, 14:19 2nd.
Los Angeles—Field goal Bahr 37, 9:12 3rd.
Los Angeles—Montgomery 69 punt return (Bahr kick), 4:16 4th.
Los Angeles—Allen 73 pass from Plunkett (Bahr kick), 9:32 4th.

TEAM STATISTICS

	Los Angeles	Detroit
First downs	14	10
Rushes-Yards	34-66	20-61
Passing yards	281	196
Sacked-Yards lost	3-15	8-58
Return yards	206	114
Passes	14-23-2	16-39-2
Punts	6-45.3	10-48.0
Fumbles-Lost	7-0	0-0
Penalties-Yards	8-55	12-106
Time of possession	31:03	28:57

Attendance—66,710. No-shows—4,032.

INDIVIDUAL STATISTICS

Rushing—Los Angeles, Allen 17-56, Wilson 4-4, Hawkins 4-3, King 4-3, Willis 2-2, Plunkett 3-minus 2; Detroit, Jenkins 10-37, Witkowski 4-10, J. Jones 4-7, Danielson 1-5, Bussey 1-2.

Passing—Los Angeles, Wilson 11-19-2—194, Plunkett 3-4-0—102; Detroit, Witkowski 7-19-0—91, Danielson 6-10-1—119, Machurek 3-9-1—44, J. Jones 0-1-0—0.

Receiving—Los Angeles, Christensen 5-61, Allen 3-93, Barnwell 3-54, Williams 1-72, Casper 1-8, Branch 1-8; Detroit, J. Jones 6-85, Chadwick 4-78, Nichols 2-62, Rubick 2-16, Bussey 1-9, Jenkins 1-4.

Kickoff Returns—Los Angeles, Montgomery 2-54; Detroit, Manley 3-56, Hall 2-22.

Punt Returns—Los Angeles, Montgomery 9-152; Detroit, Martin 2-35.

Interceptions—Los Angeles, McKinney 1-0, Hayes 1-0; Detroit, Fantetti 1-1, McNorton 1-0.

Punting—Los Angeles, Guy 6-45.3; Detroit, Black 10-48.0.

Field Goals—Los Angeles, Bahr 1-2 (missed: 36); Detroit, Murray 1-1.

Sacks—Los Angeles, Pickel 3½, Alzado 2½, Townsend, Millen ½, Long ½; Detroit, Cobb, J. Williams, English.

SIXTEENTH WEEK

RESULTS OF WEEK 16

Friday, December 14
San Francisco 19, L.A. Rams 16 at S.F.

Saturday, December 15
Denver 31, Seattle 14 at Sea.
New Orleans 10, N.Y. Giants 3 at N.Y.

Sunday, December 16
Atlanta 26, Philadelphia 10 at Atl.
Chicago 30, Detroit 13 at Det.
Cincinnati 52, Buffalo 21 at Cin.
Cleveland 27, Houston 20 at Hous.
Green Bay 38, Minnesota 14 at Minn.
Kansas City 42, San Diego 21 at S.D.
New England 16, Indianapolis 10 at N.E.
Pittsburgh 13, L.A. Raiders 7 at L.A.
Tampa Bay 41, N.Y. Jets 21 at T.B.
Washington 29, St. Louis 27 at Wash.

Monday, December 17
Miami 28, Dallas 21 at Mia.

Washington's RFK Stadium has become a house of horrors. Since Joe Gibbs took over as Redskins coach in 1981, the team had won 26 of 32 home games as it prepared to meet St. Louis in its 1984 season-ending game. Considering that the Redskins had lost their first three home games in an 0-5 start in 1981, Washington's 26-3 record in games at RFK since that time is even more amazing. No other NFL club could boast such home success during this same period.

RFK Stadium had been especially cruel to the Cardinals. Washington had beaten their NFC East counterparts by scores of 23-0, 42-21, 28-0 and 45-7 in the nation's capital since Jim Hanifan's 1980 arrival as Cardinals head coach.

With that dismal past as the backdrop, St. Louis came to RFK with a mission. Much more than pride was at stake. The Cards trailed the Redskins by one game in the Eastern Division standings and a St. Louis victory would give the Cardinals the division title and a spot in the playoffs. A loss would send them home. Because the Cardinals, Cowboys and Giants all had 9-6 records, winning one of the NFC's two wild-card playoff berths was not possible. For St. Louis in Week 16, it was a do-or-die situation.

After the Redskins grabbed a commanding 23-7 halftime lead on two Joe Theismann-to-Art Monk touchdown passes and a John Riggins scoring run, it looked like just another typical St. Louis at Washington game; a blowout. But looks can be deceiving.

"At halftime, we said that anybody who didn't think we could win the game shouldn't go back out," said Cardinals safety Benny Perrin. All the Cardinals came out, and they nearly pulled it off. With quarterback Neil Lomax completing all but three of his 28 second-half pass attempts, St. Louis rallied to take a 27-26 lead—its first of the game—with 6:15 left in regulation time. The go-ahead score came when Lomax hit wide receiver Roy Green with his second scoring pass of the half to culminate a six-play, 94-yard drive. Lomax's 468 yards passing—314 in the second half—was the most ever recorded by a St. Louis quarterback.

But Washington battled back. Mark Moseley finally gave the Redskins a 29-27 victory by kicking a 37-yard field goal with 1:33 left. "I prepared myself all week for this," said Moseley, who had hit 21- and 37-yard field goals earlier but missed the extra point after the Redskins' first touchdown. "Somehow, I thought it would come down to this."

A last-gasp 50-yard field goal try by the Cardinals' Neil O'Donoghue on the final play of the game fell short and, with it, so did St. Louis' postseason aspirations. "You can look back on a couple of plays and say you could have or should have, but we didn't and that's it," said Cardinals running back Ottis Anderson.

It also took the full 16 weeks of the regular season to determine a champion in the AFC Western Division, the NFL's best division in 1984. Both Denver and Seattle entered their Saturday afternoon showdown with 12-3 records, the winner to claim the division title and a week's rest before its first playoff game and the loser to take on the defending Super Bowl champion Los Angeles Raiders in the AFC wild-card game the following weekend.

Although the contest was played in the Seattle Kingdome, the Broncos won, 31-14, to capture the AFC West crown for the first time since 1978. In a game three weeks earlier between the teams at Denver, the Seahawks burned the Broncos for a touchdown on the game's first play from scrimmage en route to a 27-24 triumph. In their rematch, Denver turned the tables, scoring on a five-play, 80-yard drive on its first possession. Quarterback John Elway scored the touchdown from a yard out after throwing a 73-yard pass to Steve Watson to set it up.

Denver led, 10-7, at the half but turned two Seattle turnovers into touchdowns in the third period. First, the Seahawks' Randall Morris fumbled the second-half kickoff to set up a 14-yard Elway-to-Jim Wright touchdown. Later in the quarter, safety Steve Foley picked off a pass from Seattle's Dave Krieg and returned it 40 yards for another score. The Seahawks, who led the AFC West by a game before losing their final two contests, scored only one more touchdown the remainder of the game.

The New Orleans Saints upended the New York Giants, 10-3, in the other Saturday afternoon game. Ironically, even though the Giants entered the game tied with St. Louis and Dallas in a battle for the NFC's final wild-card berth, it didn't matter whether or not the Giants beat the Saints in their final regular-season game. For the Giants to claim the wild-card spot, they needed for both the Cardinals and Cowboys to lose their final games of 1984. Luckily for the Giants, that's exactly what happened.

The Saints, who concluded a disappointing 7-9 season, scored the game's only touchdown on their first possession, a two-yard pass from David Wilson to Hokie Gajan. But that lone touchdown proved to be more than enough as the Giants, with their worst offensive showing of 1984, scored only on a 37-yard Ali Haji-Sheikh field goal. New York mustered 189 yards in total offense and scored only one field goal despite having the ball inside the New Orleans 20-yard line on four occasions. Giants quarterback Phil Simms was sacked seven times.

In a Friday night game that meant more for historical reasons than it did in the NFC Western Division standings, San Francisco defeated the Los Angeles Rams, 19-16. The 49ers, who had wrapped up the division title weeks earlier, won for the 15th time in 16 regular-season games, breaking the 1972 Miami Dolphins' league record for most wins in one regular season. The Dolphins had won 14 regular-season games en route to a perfect 17-0 Super Bowl season.

Although Rams running back Eric Dickerson missed rushing for 100 or more yards for only the fourth time in 1984, his 98 yards extended his league record for most yards rushing in one season to 2,105. Dickerson, who set a rookie rushing record of 1,808 yards in 1983, finished his second professional season only 87 yards shy of the 4,000 mark. Despite the loss, the 10-6 Rams ended up with one of the NFC's two wild-card playoff berths.

Pittsburgh had to defeat or tie the Raiders in Los Angeles in its final game to clinch the AFC Central Division title. The Steelers did just that, upsetting the defending league champions, 13-7, to win the division by one game over the Cincinnati Bengals. The young Steelers, who had 15 rookies on their roster at season's end, used the formula for success made famous by their Super Bowl predecessors—defense. Pittsburgh held Los Angeles to 54 total yards in the first half and 188 in the game. The Raiders didn't score until wide receiver Dokie Williams hauled in a two-yard scoring pass from Jim Plunkett with 3:10 left.

The Steelers, who led only 3-0 entering the final period, scored 10 fourth-quarter points to put the game away. A 59-yard run by Walter Abercrombie to the L.A. 1-yard line set up a Frank Pollard scoring run for the Steelers' only touchdown.

Until Pittsburgh's victory, it looked like Cincinnati might win the AFC Central. The Bengals, despite finishing the regular season with an 8-8 record, would have taken the crown

with a better divisional record had the Steelers lost their final game. The Bengals routed Buffalo, 52-21, behind three first-half touchdown passes by Ken Anderson. Anderson completed 16 of 20 passes in the half as Cincinnati jumped out to a 28-7 lead. The Bengals, who lost their first five games under rookie Coach Sam Wyche, finished the season strong, winning eight of their final 11 games. The Bills, in their first season under Coach Kay Stephenson, finished the '84 season at 2-14—the league's worst record.

In a game remarkably similar to the Buffalo-Cincinnati contest, the Green Bay Packers defeated Minnesota, 38-14. The Pack, under first-year Coach Forrest Gregg, lost seven of its first eight games before rallying to a 7-1 record in the second half and finishing at the .500 mark. Quarterback Lynn Dickey led the Green Bay assault against the Vikings, completing 16 of 20 first-half passes for two touchdowns while running for a third. The Packers led at the half, 31-0—the third consecutive game Minnesota surrendered 31 points before the intermission.

The final game for Minnesota was a mirror image of the entire season—disaster. Under rookie Coach Les Steckel, the Vikes finished the season at 3-13, the worst record in the franchise's 24-year history. Steckel was fired the following day and replaced by Bud Grant, who coached the Vikes for 17 seasons before retiring after the 1983 campaign.

John McKay, the only coach in Tampa Bay's nine-year NFL existence, saw his Bucs score a team-record 41 points in his final game, a 41-21 triumph over the New York Jets. Steve DeBerg threw for three touchdowns and James Wilder scored two others as Tampa Bay finished the '84 season with a 6-10 record. The club was 44-88-1 in nine years under McKay, who earlier in the season had announced his retirement, effective at the end of the season.

McKay's NFL coaching career ended with a storm of controversy.

After Wilder's four-yard touchdown run with 1:21 remaining had given the Bucs a 41-14 lead, McKay ordered an onside kick to get the ball back. Wilder, one of the league's premier running backs, was 16 yards short of breaking the NFL record for combined yardage (rushing and receiving) in one season, a record set by Eric Dickerson two days earlier. After three onside kick attempts failed and New York got the ball, McKay ordered his team to allow the Jets to score—thereby giving the Bucs and Wilder more time on the clock to set the record. Bucs linebacker Keith Browner actually backpedaled into the end zone when Jets running back Johnny Hector scored on a one-yard touchdown run in the final minute. When Tampa Bay did get the ball back, Wilder was gang-tackled by the Jets on three carries for no additional yards.

Cincinnati cruised to a 52-21 triumph over Buffalo behind Ken Anderson's three touchdown passes to finish the season at 8-8.

Although Dickerson (2,244 yards) and Wilder (2,229) both finished ahead of him in 1984, Chicago's Walter Payton contributed 62 yards rushing and 25 receiving in the Bears' 30-13 win over Detroit. The 87 combined yards gave the NFL's all-time leading rusher a total of 2,052 combined yards for the season—making Payton the first player in league history to reach 2,000 yards in consecutive seasons. In '83, Payton had 2,028 combined yards.

Payton, reserve quarterback Greg Landry (making his first NFL start in three seasons) and the rest of the Chicago offense had to take a back seat to the Bears' defense on this day, however. The league's top-rated defense put together one of its best performances of the year, holding the Lions to 196 total yards. The Bears also sacked Detroit quarterbacks John Witkowski and Eric Hipple 12 times to tie the league record for most sacks in a game. Chicago's 72 sacks in 1984 set a league record in that category, eclipsing the mark of 67 set in 1967 by the Oakland Raiders in 14 games.

The Kansas City Chiefs closed out an 8-8 season with their third consecutive triumph, a 42-21 rout of division-rival San Diego. The Chiefs, behind three Bill Kenney touchdown passes, jumped to a 28-0 halftime lead and increased the margin to 42 points late in the third period. The Chargers, who finished a disappointing 7-9 and in the cellar of the AFC West, scored three late touchdowns to make the final score respectable. San Diego did not win a game within its division all season.

In the season finale for two AFC Central Division clubs going nowhere, Cleveland upended Houston, 27-20. Rookie running back Earnest Byner, a 10th-round draft pick from East Carolina, rushed for 188 yards and scored two touchdowns to lead the Browns. Byner, who rushed for 103 yards in a losing effort against Pittsburgh the previous week, had rushed for only 135 yards in Cleveland's first 14 games.

The Browns, who won four of their final eight games after Marty Schottenheimer took over as coach at midseason, finished the year at 5-11. The Oilers, who tied for the league's worst record at 2-14 in 1983, finished the '84 season at 3-13.

The smallest crowd in the 14-year history of Sullivan Stadium (22,383) turned out for the Patriots' season-ending encounter with Indianapolis. The Pats won the game, 16-10, as Tony Franklin hit three field goals and Craig James rushed for 138 yards in the best game of his NFL rookie year. New England finished the year 9-7 while Indianapolis, coached by Hal Hunter in the season's final game after Frank Kush's resignation, finished at 4-12.

An even smaller crowd (15,582) turned out in Atlanta as the Falcons closed a disastrous season with a 26-10 decision over Philadelphia. The Falcons won for only the fourth time in 16 games and snapped a nine-game losing streak.

Quarterback David Archer, a rookie free agent from Iowa State, led the Falcons, completing 12 of 18 passes after relieving starter Mike Moroski. Archer's first NFL pass completion came on a 16-yard touchdown toss to tight end Arthur Cox late in the first half. Mick Luckhurst also kicked four field goals for Atlanta.

There was anything but a small crowd at the Orange Bowl for the Monday night game between the Dolphins and Dallas Cowboys. A crowd of 74,139 came out to see the 13-2 Dolphins battle for home-field advantage in the AFC playoffs and the Cowboys fight for their playoff lives. The Miami fans didn't go home unhappy.

Behind four touchdown passes by Dan Marino—three to wide receiver Mark Clayton—the Dolphins won the NFL's final regular-season game, 28-21. Marino's four TD passes extended his NFL record to 48 and Clayton's three scoring catches gave him 18 for the season, breaking the league mark of 17 shared by Don Hutson, Elroy Hirsch and Bill Groman. Two of the Marino-to-Clayton scores came on 39- and 63-yard bombs in the final 2:31 to put Marino over the 5,000-yard passing mark for the season. Marino became the first quarterback in league history to pass for more than 5,000 yards, finishing the year at 5,084.

The Cowboys, who entered the game with a 9-6 record and had to win to qualify for a NFC wild-card spot, tied the game at 21-21 with 1:47 left on a 66-yard touchdown pass from Danny White to Tony Hill. But Marino and Clayton hooked up for the game-winner just 56 seconds later and Dallas, a team embroiled in controversy for much of the '84 season, failed to make the playoffs for the first time in 10 years.

Rams-49ers
FRIDAY, DECEMBER 14
SCORE BY PERIODS

Los Angeles Rams	3	10	0	3—16
San Francisco	14	3	0	2—19

SCORING
Los Angeles—Field goal Lansford 41, 4:25 1st.
San Francisco—Solomon 47 pass from Montana (Wersching kick), 6:46 1st.
San Francisco—Cooper 1 pass from Montana (Wersching kick), 14:02 1st.
San Francisco—Field goal Wersching 38, 0:55 2nd.
Los Angeles—Dickerson 4 run (Lansford kick), 3:38 2nd.
Los Angeles—Field goal Lansford 28, 15:00 2nd.
Los Angeles—Field goal Lansford 42, 11:17 4th.
San Francisco—Safety, Johnson tackled Kemp in end zone, 13:54 4th.

TEAM STATISTICS

	Los Angeles	San Francisco
First downs	19	15
Rushes-Yards	37-185	20-89
Passing yards	170	200
Sacked-Yards lost	1-10	4-19
Return yards	95	84
Passes	11-22-0	20-31-0
Punts	4-37.8	6-44.5
Fumbles	2-1	2-0
Penalties-Yards	6-57	8-75
Time of possession	32:52	27:08

Attendance—59,743. No-shows—1,633.

INDIVIDUAL STATISTICS
Rushing—Los Angeles, Dickerson 26-98, Redden 5-54, Crutchfield 4-20, Kemp 2-13; San Francisco, Craig 8-59, Tyler 8-32, Montana 3-4, Solomon 1-minus 6.

Passing—Los Angeles, Kemp 11-22-0—180; San Francisco, Montana 20-31-0—219.

Receiving—Los Angeles, Brown 3-55, Drew Hill 2-43, Ellard 2-22, David Hill 1-26, J. McDonald 1-22, Guman 1-6, Dickerson 1-6; San Francisco, Cooper 5-40, Craig 5-26, Solomon 3-87, D. Clark 3-32, Tyler 3-23, Francis 1-11.

Kickoff Returns—Los Angeles, Redden 4-85; San Francisco, Monroe 4-74.

Punt Returns—Los Angeles, Irvin 2-15, Ellard 1-minus 5; San Francisco, McLemore 2-14.

Punting—Los Angeles, Misko 4-37.8; San Francisco, Runager 6-44.5.

Field Goals—Los Angeles, Lansford 3-4 (missed: 30); San Francisco, Wersching 1-2 (missed: 48).

Sacks—Los Angeles, Doss, Green, Reed, Wilcher; San Francisco, Johnson.

Broncos-Seahawks
SATURDAY, DECEMBER 15
SCORE BY PERIODS

Denver	10	0	14	7—31
Seattle	0	7	7	0—14

SCORING
Denver—Elway 1 run (Karlis kick), 2:25 1st.
Denver—Field goal Karlis 34, 9:54 1st.
Seattle—Doornink 4 pass from Krieg (Johnson kick), 4:32 2nd.
Denver—J. Wright 14 pass from Elway (Karlis kick), 2:34 3rd.
Denver—Foley 40 interception return (Karlis kick), 10:35 3rd.
Seattle—C. Young 14 pass from Krieg (Johnson kick), 14:09 3rd.
Denver—Parros 4 run (Karlis kick), 0:46 4th.

TEAM STATISTICS

	Denver	Seattle
First downs	15	23
Rushes-Yards	33-143	19-79
Passing yards	148	306
Sacked-Yards lost	0-0	4-28
Return yards	112	188
Passes	9-21-4	30-51-2
Punts	3-35.7	4-37.3
Fumbles-Lost	1-0	1-1
Penalties-Yards	4-35	7-83
Time of possession	27:32	32:28

Attendance—64,411. No-shows—601.

INDIVIDUAL STATISTICS
Rushing—Denver, Winder 18-80, Elway 9-43, Parros 6-20; Seattle, Hughes 8-38, Lane 6-14, Krieg 5-27.

Passing—Denver, Elway 9-21-4—148; Seattle, Krieg 30-50-2—334, Zorn 0-1-0—0.

Receiving—Denver, Willhite 3-18, Watson 2-84, Kay 1-15, J. Wright 1-14, Winder 1-13, Parros 1-4; Seattle,

— 248 —

Largent 7-96, Doornink 6-72, C. Young 6-56, Turner 3-40, Skansi 3-25, Walker 2-31, Hughes 2-13, Lane 1-1.

Kickoff Returns—Denver, Lang 1-30; Seattle, Morris 3-53, Hughes 2-47, Dixon 1-36.

Punt Returns—Seattle, Skansi 1-0.

Interceptions—Denver, Mecklenburg 1-42, Foley 1-40; Seattle, Simpson 2-23, Harris 1-29, Easley 1-0.

Punting—Denver, Norman 3-35.7; Seattle, West 4-37.3.

Field Goals—Denver, Karlis 1-1; Seattle, Johnson 0-1 (missed: 42).

Sacks—Denver, Chavous 2, Carter, Jones.

Saints-Giants
SATURDAY, DECEMBER 15
SCORE BY PERIODS

New Orleans	7	0	0	3	10
New York Giants	0	3	0	0	3

SCORING

New Orleans—Gajan 2 pass from D. Wilson (Andersen kick), 7:06 1st.
New York—Field goal Haji-Sheikh 37, 0:29 2nd.
New Orleans—Field goal Andersen 37, 1:05 4th.

TEAM STATISTICS

	New Orleans	New York
First downs	15	15
Rushes-Yards	37-101	28-113
Passing yards	137	76
Sacked-Yards lost	0-0	7-51
Return yards	58	51
Passes	12-24-1	12-26-2
Punts	5-33.0	5-40.0
Fumbles-Lost	1-0	1-0
Penalties-Yards	4-57	6-39
Time of possession	31:02	28:58

Attendance—63,739. No-shows—13,128.

INDIVIDUAL STATISTICS

Rushing—New Orleans, G. Rogers 15-49, Campbell 7-24, Gajan 7-22, W. Wilson 4-8, Goodlow 1-5, D. Wilson 3-minus 7; New York, Simms 6-43, Carpenter 7-33, Morris 14-29, Galbreath 1-8.

Passing—New Orleans, D. Wilson 12-24-1—137; New York, Simms 12-26-2—127.

Receiving—New Orleans, Groth 5-73, W. Wilson 3-29, Brenner 1-19, Hardy 1-8, G. Rogers 1-6, Gajan 1-2; New York, Mowatt 3-44, Galbreath 3-38, Manuel 2-26, Johnson 1-9, Morris 1-5, Mistler 1-5, Carpenter 1-0.

Kickoff Returns—New Orleans, Fields 2-25; New York, Woolfolk 2-34.

Punt Returns—New Orleans, Groth 1-9, Fields 1-0; New York, Manuel 3-17.

Interceptions—New Orleans, Wattelet 1-17, Johnson 1-7; New York, P. Williams 1-0.

Punting—New Orleans, Hansen 5-33.0; New York, Jennings 5-40.0.

Field Goals—New Orleans, Andersen 1-2 (missed: 41); New York, Haji-Sheikh 1-2 (missed: 40).

Sacks—New Orleans, Paul 2, Warren 2, B. Clark, Geathers, R. Jackson.

Eagles-Falcons
SUNDAY, DECEMBER 16
SCORE BY PERIODS

Philadelphia	3	0	7	0	10
Atlanta	3	10	7	6	26

SCORING

Philadelphia—Field goal McFadden 20, 7:36 1st.
Atlanta—Field goal Luckhurst 38, 11:44 1st.
Atlanta—Field goal Luckhurst 29, 2:24 2nd.
Atlanta—Cox 16 pass from Archer (Luckhurst kick), 12:15 2nd.

Atlanta—Riggs 2 run (Luckhurst kick), 2:34 3rd.
Philadelphia—Quick 15 pass from Pisarcik (McFadden kick), 6:36 3rd.
Atlanta—Field goal Luckhurst 27, 4:13 4th.
Atlanta—Field goal Luckhurst 34, 13:56 4th.

TEAM STATISTICS

	Philadelphia	Atlanta
First downs	20	24
Rushes-Yards	12-53	38-126
Passing yards	308	203
Sacked-Yards lost	8-59	9-56
Return yards	68	66
Passes	25-47-0	16-28-1
Punts	3-47.7	23-3
Fumbles-Lost	4-4	1-1
Penalties-Yards	5-60	5-33
Time of possession	26:11	33:49

Attendance—15,582. No-shows—29,137.

INDIVIDUAL STATISTICS

Rushing—Philadelphia, Montgomery 11-53, Pisarcik 1-0; Atlanta, Riggs 31-88, Archer 5-31, Cain 1-4, Moroski 1-3.

Passing—Philadelphia, Pisarcik 24-46-0—334, May 1-1-0—33; Atlanta, Moroski 4-10-1—62, Archer 12-18-0—197.

Receiving—Philadelphia, Quick 7-135, Montgomery 6-77, Spagnola 4-66, Oliver 4-21, Jackson 2-29, Kab 1-26, Woodruff 1-13; Atlanta, Bailey 8-110, Cox 3-44, A. Jackson 2-26, Riggs 1-21, C. Benson 1-19, Cain 1-9.

Kickoff Returns—Philadelphia, Waters 2-35, Cooper 2-32; Atlanta, Johnson 3-59.

Punt Returns—Philadelphia, Cooper 2-1; Atlanta, Johnson 1-7.

Interceptions—Philadelphia, Ellis 1-0.

Punting—Philadelphia, Horan 3-47.7; Atlanta, Giacomarro 2-39.5.

Field Goals—Philadelphia, McFadden 1-2 (missed: 37); Atlanta, Luckhurst 4-5 (missed: 45).

Sacks—Philadelphia, Brown 3½, Clark 2, Darby 2, Armstrong 1½; Atlanta, Provence 1½, Richardson 1½, T. Benson, Burley, J. Jackson, Smith, Bryan ½, Curry ½.

Bears-Lions
SUNDAY, DECEMBER 16
SCORE BY PERIODS

Chicago	0	14	3	13	30
Detroit	3	3	0	7	13

SCORING

Detroit—Field goal Murray 52, 4:12 1st.
Chicago—C. Thomas 1 run (B. Thomas kick), 2:08 2nd.
Detroit—Field goal Murray 45, 6:28 2nd.
Chicago—Landry 1 run (B. Thomas kick), 14:21 2nd.
Chicago—Field goal B. Thomas 30, 12:31 3rd.
Chicago—Field goal B. Thomas 35, 4:46 4th.
Chicago—Gault 55 pass from Landry (B. Thomas kick), 6:37 4th.
Chicago—Field goal B. Thomas 42, 10:29 4th.
Detroit—Jones 4 pass from Hipple (Murray kick), 13:41 4th.

TEAM STATISTICS

	Chicago	Detroit
First downs	13	13
Rushes-Yards	43-94	15-47
Passing yards	199	149
Sacked-Yards lost	0-0	12-100
Return yards	168	179
Passes	11-21-3	14-38-1
Punts	5-42.8	9-41.8
Fumbles-Lost	1-0	3-1
Penalties-Yards	3-15	5-57
Time of possession	34:48	25:12

Attendance—53,252. No-shows—12,221.

INDIVIDUAL STATISTICS

Rushing—Chicago, Payton 22-62, Gentry 4-37, C. Thomas 6-4, Landry 2-1, Lisch 3-minus 4, Suhey 6-minus 6; Detroit, Jones 4-16, Witkowski 2-13, Jenkins 5-11, Bussey 3-7, Black 1-0.

Passing—Chicago, Landry 11-20-3—199, Lisch 0-1-0 —0; Detroit, Hipple 11-27-1—187, Witkowski 3-10-0— 62, Jones 0-1-0—0.

Receiving—Chicago, Moorehead 5-86, Payton 2-25, Gentry 2-9, Gault 1-55, Krenk 1-24; Detroit, Chadwick 5-82, Nichols 4-92, Thompson 2-38, Jones 2-18, Bussey 1-19.

Kickoff Returns—Chicago, Cameron 2-40, Gentry 1-25; Detroit, Mandley 4-91, Hall 2-47, Meade 1-15.

Punt Returns—Chicago, Fisher 8-103; Detroit, Martin 3-19.

Interceptions—Chicago, Bell 1-0; Detroit, Graham 2-7, Watkins 1-0.

Punting—Chicago, Finzer 5-42.8; Detroit, Black 9-41.8.

Field Goals—Chicago, B. Thomas 3-3; Detroit, Murray 2-2.

Sacks—Chicago, McMichael 2½, Hampton 2, Waechter 2, Wilson 2, Dent 1½, Duerson, Singletary.

Bills-Bengals
SUNDAY, DECEMBER 16
SCORE BY PERIODS

Buffalo	7	0	7	7—21
Cincinnati	7	21	3	21—52

SCORING

Buffalo—Bell 5 run (Nelson kick), 4:06 1st.
Cincinnati—Collinsworth 12 pass from Anderson (Breech kick), 8:06 1st.
Cincinnati—Kinnebrew 1 run (Breech kick), 0:54 2nd.
Cincinnati—Holman 11 pass from Anderson (Breech kick), 7:36 2nd.
Cincinnati—Kreider 11 pass from Anderson (Breech kick), 14:22 2nd.
Cincinnati—Field goal Breech 36, 5:20 3rd.
Buffalo—Franklin 16 pass from Dufek (Nelson kick), 12:57 3rd.
Cincinnati—Jennings 20 run (Breech kick), 3:26 4th.
Cincinnati—Simmons 43 interception return (Breech kick), 9:10 4th.
Cincinnati—Griffin 57 interception return (Breech kick), 11:46 4th.
Buffalo—Bell 1 run (Nelson kick), 14:46 4th.

TEAM STATISTICS

	Buffalo	Cincinnati
First downs	25	27
Rushes-Yards	18-64	36-201
Passing yards	281	218
Sacked-Yards lost	2-21	1-9
Return yards	149	274
Passes	36-58-3	20-28-0
Punts	6-41.0	3-35.7
Fumbles-Lost	0-0	4-2
Penalties-Yards	10-75	5-52
Time of possession	29:05	30:55

Attendance—55,771. No-shows—3,703.

INDIVIDUAL STATISTICS

Rushing—Buffalo, Bell 16-58, Moore 1-minus 1, Ferguson 1-7; Cincinnati, Brooks 7-52, Alexander 6-26, Verser 1-3, Jennings 5-42, Kinnebrew 14-65, Anderson 1-12, Farley 1-1, Esiason 1-0.

Passing—Buffalo, Dufek 30-47-3—250, Mosley 0-1-0 —0, Ferguson 6-10-0—52; Cincinnati, Anderson 17-23-0 —206, Esiason 3-5-0—21.

Receiving—Buffalo, Hunter 3-45, Bell 4-31, Dawkins 4-25, Dennard 1-13, Riddick 6-51, Moore 9-53, Franklin 7-68, Brookins 2-16; Cincinnati, Brooks 2-23, Collinsworth 3-62, Jennings 2-13, Harris 1-14, Martin 3-40, Holman 2-13, Kreider 5-49, Curtis 1-7, Kinnebrew 1-6.

Kickoff Returns—Buffalo, V. Williams 5-113, Wilson 2-36; Cincinnati, Martin 1-41, Brooks 1-37.

Punt Returns—Cincinnati, Martin 4-89, Simmons 1-7.

Interceptions—Cincinnati, J. Griffin 1-57, Simmons 1-43, Jackson 1-0.

Punting—Buffalo, Kidd 6-41.0; Cincinnati, McInally 3-35.7.

Field Goals—Buffalo, none attempted; Cincinnati, Breech 1-1.

Sacks—Buffalo, Keating; Cincinnati, Krumrie, R. Williams.

Browns-Oilers
SUNDAY, DECEMBER 16
SCORE BY PERIODS

Cleveland	7	3	7	10—27
Houston	0	7	10	3—20

SCORING

Cleveland—Byner 2 run (Bahr kick), 7:35 1st.
Cleveland—Field goal Bahr 29, 2:19 2nd.
Houston—Moriarty 4 run (Cooper kick), 7:12 2nd.
Houston—Field goal Cooper 33, 7:45 3rd.
Cleveland—Byner 15 run (Bahr kick), 10:05 3rd.
Houston—Moriarty 4 run (Cooper kick), 14:03 3rd.
Cleveland—J. Davis 3 run (Bahr kick), 4:19 4th.
Houston—Field goal Cooper 26, 8:37 4th.
Cleveland—Field goal Bahr 29, 12:17 4th.

TEAM STATISTICS

	Cleveland	Houston
First downs	23	18
Rushes-Yards	36-254	27-90
Passing yards	145	306
Sacked-Yards lost	2-13	0-0
Return yards	141	157
Passes	14-22-1	19-31-0
Punts	4-53.0	2-44.0
Fumbles-Lost	0-0	2-1
Penalties-Yards	13-119	7-40
Time of possession	30:26	29:34

Attendance—33,676. No-shows—14,894.

INDIVIDUAL STATISTICS

Rushing—Cleveland, Byner 21-188, Green 10-57, J. Davis 2-10, McDonald 3-minus 1; Houston, Moriarty 21-90, Moon 1-4, Edwards 4-minus 2, Cooper 1-minus 2.

Passing—Cleveland, McDonald 14-22-1—158; Houston, Moon 19-31-0—306.

Receiving—Cleveland, Holt 4-43, Feacher 2-39, Byner 3-31, Brennan 2-19, Newsome 2-18, Green 1-8; Houston, Smith 7-167, J. Williams 3-59, Holston 2-42, Dressel 4-32, Moriarty 3-6.

Kickoff Returns—Cleveland, Young 4-111, Byner 1-21; Houston, Roaches 3-78, Joyner 3-57.

Punt Returns—Cleveland, Brennan 2-9; Houston Roaches 2-20.

Interceptions—Houston, Allen 1-2.

Punting—Cleveland, Cox 4-53.0; Houston, James 2-44.0.

Field Goals—Cleveland, Bahr 2-2; Houston, Cooper 2-3 (missed: 42).

Sacks—Houston, Bostic, Sochia.

Packers-Vikings
SUNDAY, DECEMBER 16
SCORE BY PERIODS

Green Bay	10	21	7	0—38
Minnesota	0	0	7	7—14

SCORING

Green Bay—Epps 21 pass from Dickey (Del Greco kick), 5:17 1st.
Green Bay—Field goal Del Greco 30, 11:31 1st.
Green Bay—Ivery 5 run (Del Greco kick), 6:27 2nd.

Green Bay—West 2 pass from Dickey (Del Greco kick), 9:23 2nd.
Green Bay—Dickey 1 run (Del Greco kick), 14:08 2nd.
Minnesota—Nelson 4 run (Stenerud kick), 10:14 3rd.
Green Bay—Lofton 27 pass from Campbell (Del Greco kick), 11:42 3rd.
Minnesota—Teal 53 interception return (Stenerud kick), 9:06 4th.

TEAM STATISTICS

	Green Bay	Minnesota
First downs	26	16
Rushes-Yards	41-214	21-70
Passing yards	234	171
Sacked-Yards lost	2-20	4-30
Return yards	67	168
Passes	19-31-3	22-37-4
Punts	2-39.5	5-47.6
Fumbles-Lost	2-1	3-1
Penalties-Yards	6-46	3-30
Time of possession	31:30	28:30

Attendance—51,197. No-shows—11,058.

INDIVIDUAL STATISTICS

Rushing—Green Bay, Ivery 10-59, Ellis 7-24, Lofton 2-11, Crouse 6-43, Dickey 3-8, Rodgers 13-69; Minnesota, Anderson 11-14, Nelson 8-57, Collins 1-1, Manning 1-minus 2.

Passing—Green Bay, Dickey 16-20-0—198, Campbell 3-11-3—56; Minnesota, Wilson 4-10-2—26, Manning 18-25-1—175, Anderson 0-1-1—0, Coleman 0-1-0—0.

Receiving—Green Bay, Epps 5-60, Ivery 2-10, Coffman 2-46, Lofton 5-91, West 1-2, Rodgers 3-37, Taylor 1-8; Minnesota, Mularkey 7-58, Collins 3-22, Nelson 5-33, Anderson 2-15, Lewis 3-41, White 1-21, Jones 1-11.

Kickoff Returns—Green Bay, Rodgers 1-16; Minnesota, Anderson 3-49, Smith 2-26, Nelson 1-18, Turner 1-7.

Punt Returns—Green Bay, Hayes 4-24; Minnesota, Lewis 1-8.

Interceptions—Green Bay, Flynn 1-11, Hood 1-8, Lee 1-8; Minnesota, Bess 2-7, Teal 1-53.

Punting—Green Bay, Scribner 2-39.5; Minnesota, Coleman 5-47.6.

Field Goals—Green Bay, Del Greco 1-1; Minnesota, none attempted.

Sacks—Green Bay, Anderson, Brown, Douglass, Humphrey; Minnesota, Haines, C. Johnson.

Chiefs-Chargers
SUNDAY, DECEMBER 16
SCORE BY PERIODS

Kansas City	14	14	14	0—42
San Diego	0	0	7	14—21

SCORING

Kansas City—Jackson 3 run (Lowery kick), 4:07 1st.
Kansas City—W. Arnold 4 pass from Kenney (Lowery kick), 10:40 1st.
Kansas City—Marshall 8 pass from Kenney (Lowery kick), 1:41 2nd.
Kansas City—Paige 65 pass from Kenney (Lowery kick), 13:50 2nd.
Kansas City—Heard 3 run (Lowery kick), 2:48 3rd.
Kansas City—Brown 1 run (Lowery kick), 10:16 3rd.
San Diego—Chandler 15 pass from Luther (Benirschke kick), 14:29 3rd.
San Diego—McGee 2 run (Benirschke kick), 8:59 4th.
San Diego—McGee 3 run (Benirschke kick), 14:05 4th.

TEAM STATISTICS

	Kansas City	San Diego
First downs	23	26
Rushes-Yards	36-120	31-110
Passing yards	279	333
Sacked-Yards lost	0-0	0-0
Return yards	27	165

	Kansas City	San Diego
Passes	18-25-0	24-45-0
Punts	4-42.5	4-35.8
Fumbles-Lost	0-0	0-0
Penalties-Yards	4-38	7-73
Time of possession	28:43	31:17

Attendance—40,221. No-shows—18,965.

INDIVIDUAL STATISTICS

Rushing—Kansas City, Heard 15-84, Jackson 5-10, Lacy 3-8, Kenney 1-minus 1, Brown 4-7, Gunter 8-12; San Diego, Jackson 19-79, Luther 1-2, McGee 7-11, James 4-18.

Passing—Kansas City, Kenney 17-23-0—245, Blackledge 1-2-0—34; San Diego, Luther 24-44-0—333, Holohan 0-1-0—0.

Receiving—Kansas City, Marshall 6-84, W. Arnold 2-10, Heard 2-5, Carson 3-78, Scott 1-12, Jackson 1-3, Paige 2-82, Lacy 1-5; San Diego, Joiner 3-55, Jackson 3-19, Bendross 1-8, Egloff 1-3, Holohan 5-38, James 3-52, Sievers 4-83, Chandler 3-32, McGee 1-43.

Kickoff Returns—Kansas City, Paige 1-16, Carson 1-2; San Diego, McGee 4-99, James 2-53.

Punt Returns—Kansas City, Hancock 2-9; San Diego, James 3-13.

Punting—Kansas City, J. Arnold 4-42.5; San Diego, Buford 4-35.8.

Field Goals—Kansas City, none attempted; San Diego, Benirschke 0-1 (missed: 39).

Colts-Patriots
SUNDAY, DECEMBER 16
SCORE BY PERIODS

Indianapolis	0	0	10	0—10
New England	3	10	0	3—16

SCORING

New England—Field goal Franklin 21, 14:02 1st.
New England—Dawson 3 pass from Eason (Franklin kick), 6:16 2nd.
New England—Field goal Franklin 34, 13:58 2nd.
Indianapolis—Field goal Allegre 25, 9:58 3rd.
Indianapolis—Henry 19 pass from Schlichter (Allegre kick), 11:30 3rd.
New England—Field goal Franklin 36, 14:10 4th.

TEAM STATISTICS

	Indianapolis	New England
First downs	13	19
Rushes-Yards	21-65	49-175
Passing yards	174	60
Sacked-Yards lost	3-14	7-63
Return yards	103	127
Passes	15-28-1	11-17-0
Punts	5-44.8	5-38.6
Fumbles-Lost	1-1	2-1
Penalties-Yards	6-38	4-33
Time of possession	21:11	38:49

Attendance—22,383. No-shows—8,388.

INDIVIDUAL STATISTICS

Rushing—Indianapolis, McMillan 7-31, Middleton 8-19, Wonsley 2-8, Schlichter 1-5, Moore 3-2; New England, C. James 30-138, Tatupu 12-44, Collins 5-10, Starring 1-minus 16, Eason 1-minus 1.

Passing—Indianapolis, Schlichter 15-28-1—188; New England, Eason 11-17-0—123.

Receiving—Indianapolis, Butler 3-68, Henry 4-51, Sherwin 1-26, Bouza 2-23, McMillan 2-11, Moore 1-6, Middleton 2-3; New England, Tatupu 3-39, Ramsey 2-31, Jones 1-21, Morgan 2-20, Dawson 2-9, Starring 1-3.

Kickoff Returns—Indianapolis, Anderson 4-82, Wonsley 1-13; New England, Collins 2-54, Robinson 1-10.

Punt Returns—Indianapolis, Glasgow 1-8, Padjen 1-0; New England, Fryar 3-50.

Interceptions—New England, Lippett 1-13.

Punting—Indianapolis, Stark 5-44.8; New England, Camarillo 5-38.6.

Field Goals—Indianapolis, Allegre 1-2 (missed: 42); New England, Franklin 3-3.

Sacks—Indianapolis, Cooks 2, Odom 2, Krauss, White, Winter; New England, Tippett 2, Owens.

Steelers-Raiders

SUNDAY, DECEMBER 16
SCORE BY PERIODS

Pittsburgh	3	0	0	10	13
Los Angeles Raiders	0	0	0	7	7

SCORING
Pittsburgh—Field goal Anderson 26, 12:04 1st.
Pittsburgh—Pollard 1 run (Anderson kick), 0:04 4th.
Pittsburgh—Field goal Anderson 37, 9:25 4th.
Los Angeles—Williams 2 pass from Plunkett (Bahr kick), 11:50 4th.

TEAM STATISTICS

	Pittsburgh	Los Angeles
First downs	21	14
Rushes-Yards	50-197	20-57
Passing yards	168	131
Sacked-Yards lost	2-23	3-37
Return yards	56	131
Passes	13-23-1	14-33-2
Punts	5-44.8	8-39.5
Fumbles-Lost	1-1	1-0
Penalties-Yards	7-62	10-67
Time of possession	37:43	22:17

Attendance—83,056. No-shows—4,245.

INDIVIDUAL STATISTICS
Rushing—Pittsburgh, Abercrombie 28-111, Pollard 19-78, Malone 3-8; Los Angeles, Allen 13-38, Hawkins 5-13, Wilson 1-8, Pruitt 1-minus 2.

Passing—Pittsburgh, Malone 13-23-1—191; Los Angeles, Wilson 5-13-1—45, Plunkett 9-20-1—123.

Receiving—Pittsburgh, Abercrombie 2-72, Stallworth 4-39, Lipps 3-32, Erenberg 2-21, Cunningham 1-21, Thompson 1-6; Los Angeles, Barnwell 3-52, Williams 3-49, Christensen 4-32, Branch 1-17, Allen 2-14, Hawkins 1-4.

Kickoff Returns—Pittsburgh, Erenberg 1-17; Los Angeles, Montgomery 3-57, Williams 1-20.

Punt Returns—Pittsburgh, Lipps 2-38, Clayton 1-0; Los Angeles, Montgomery 2-22.

Interceptions—Pittsburgh, Shell 2-1; Los Angeles, Haynes 1-32.

Punting—Pittsburgh, Colquitt 5-44.8; Los Angeles, Guy 8-39.5.

Field Goals—Pittsburgh, Anderson 2-3 (missed: 39); Los Angeles, none attempted.

Sacks—Pittsburgh, Hinkle, E. Williams, Gary ½, Merriweather ½; Los Angeles, Long, Martin.

Jets-Buccaneers

SUNDAY, DECEMBER 16
SCORE BY PERIODS

New York Jets	0	7	0	14	21
Tampa Bay	10	7	3	21	41

SCORING
Tampa Bay—Field goal Ariri 37, 6:06 1st.
Tampa Bay—Wilder 6 run (Ariri kick), 7:53 1st.
Tampa Bay—J. Bell 3 pass from DeBerg (Ariri kick), 3:05 2nd.
New York—Dennison 5 pass from O'Brien (Leahy kick), 13:39 2nd.
Tampa Bay—Field goal Ariri 35, 6:15 3rd.
Tampa Bay—J. Bell 18 pass from DeBerg (Ariri kick), 0:05 4th.
Tampa Bay—Carroll 4 pass from DeBerg (Ariri kick), 2:50 4th.

New York—Paige 3 pass from O'Brien (Leahy kick), 11:38 4th.
Tampa Bay—Wilder 4 run (Ariri kick), 13:39 4th.
New York—Hector 1 run (Leahy kick), 14:06 4th.

TEAM STATISTICS

	New York	Tampa Bay
First downs	19	28
Rushes-Yards	23-91	32-116
Passing yards	161	230
Sacked-Yards lost	6-40	5-50
Return yards	146	119
Passes	19-34-2	26-34-0
Punts	4-40.3	2-48.0
Fumbles-Lost	3-1	4-2
Penalties-Yards	8-73	5-45
Time of possession	27:12	32:48

Attendance—43,817. No-shows—13,231.

INDIVIDUAL STATISTICS
Rushing—New York, Hector 10-45, Minter 10-44, O'Brien 3-2; Tampa Bay, Wilder 31-103, DeBerg 1-13.

Passing—New York, O'Brien 19-34-2—201; Tampa Bay, DeBerg 26-34-0—280.

Receiving—New York, Shuler 3-70, Jones 4-43, Hector 6-41, Walker 2-26, Paige 2-13, Dennison 1-5, Minter 1-3; Tampa Bay, House 6-70, Wilder 9-60, Carter 4-57, J. Bell 3-47, Carroll 2-21, Armstrong 1-18, T. Bell 1-7.

Kickoff Returns—New York, Minter 5-107, Humphery 1-22, Davidson 1-9; Tampa Bay, Bright 1-17.

Punt Returns—New York, Minter 1-8; Tampa Bay, Bright 1-21, Z. Thomas 1-7.

Interceptions—Tampa Bay, Castille 1-30, Cotney 1-24.

Punting—New York, Ramsey 4-40.3; Tampa Bay, Garcia 2-48.0.

Field Goals—New York, Leahy 0-1 (missed: 45); Tampa Bay, Ariri 2-2.

Sacks—New York, Gastineau 2, Bennett, Carter, Faurot; Tampa Bay, Cannon 2, Green 2, Selmon 2.

Cardinals-Redskins

SUNDAY, DECEMBER 16
SCORE BY PERIODS

St. Louis	0	7	10	10	27
Washington	6	17	3	3	29

SCORING
Washington—Monk 23 pass from Theismann (kick failed), 5:41 1st.
Washington—Monk 12 pass from Theismann (Moseley kick), 3:06 2nd.
St. Louis—Lomax 1 run (O'Donoghue kick), 9:25 2nd.
Washington—Riggins 5 run (Moseley kick), 10:26 2nd.
Washington—Field goal Moseley 21, 13:03 2nd.
St. Louis—Field goal O'Donoghue 30, 3:17 3rd.
St. Louis—Green 75 pass from Lomax (O'Donoghue kick), 6:45 3rd.
Washington—Field goal Moseley 37, 11:06 3rd.
St. Louis—Field goal O'Donoghue 34, 1:40 4th.
St. Louis—Green 18 pass from Lomax (O'Donoghue kick), 8:45 4th.
Washington—Field goal Moseley 37, 13:27 4th.

TEAM STATISTICS

	St. Louis	Washington
First downs	23	22
Rushes-Yards	16-43	32-96
Passing yards	444	260
Sacked-Yards lost	3-24	6-38
Return yards	180	112
Passes	37-46-1	20-35-1
Punts	5-29.0	4-38.0
Fumbles-Lost	1-1	1-0
Penalties-Yards	10-87	1-5
Time of possession	27:27	32:33

Attendance—54,299. No-shows—1,162.

Washington's Mark Moseley kicks a 37-yard field goal late in the game to clinch a 29-27 victory against St. Louis in Week 16, giving the Redskins the NFC Eastern Division crown.

INDIVIDUAL STATISTICS

Rushing—St. Louis, Anderson 12-24, Ferrell 1-1, Lomax 3-18; Washington, Riggins 27-76, Theismann 5-20.

Passing—St. Louis, Lomax 37-46-1—468; Washington, Theismann 20-35-1—298.

Receiving—St. Louis, Green 8-196, Tilley 4-35, Anderson 12-124, Ferrell 3-26, Goode 2-13, Marsh 1-5, Pittman 5-54, Harrell 2-15; Washington, Monk 11-136, Warren 2-6, Muhammad 5-110, Didier 1-44, J. Washington 1-2.

Kickoff Returns—St. Louis, Pittman 4-94, Harrell 1-28, Green 1-18, Mitchell 1-16; Washington, Nelms 4-71, Griffin 2-32.

Punt Returns—St. Louis, Mitchell 1-12; Washington, Nelms 1-9, Williams 1-0.

Interceptions—St. Louis, W. Smith 1-12; Washington, Green 1-0.

Punting—St. Louis, Birdsong 4-36.3; Washington, Hayes 4-38.0.

Field Goals—St. Louis, O'Donoghue 2-3 (missed: 50); Washington, Moseley 3-3.

Sacks—St. Louis, Junior 2, A. Baker, Greer, Grooms, Nelson; Washington, Brooks, Coleman, Manley.

Cowboys-Dolphins

MONDAY, DECEMBER 17

SCORE BY PERIODS

Dallas	0	0	7	14	21
Miami	0	7	7	14	28

SCORING

Miami—Clayton 41 pass from Marino (von Schamann kick), 6:01 2nd.

Miami—Hardy 3 pass from Marino (von Schamann kick), 4:17 3rd.

Dallas—Newsome 1 run (Septien kick), 13:13 3rd.

Dallas—Newsome 4 run (Septien kick), 7:32 4th.

Miami—Clayton 39 pass from Marino (von Schamann kick), 12:29 4th.

Dallas—Hill 66 pass from D. White (Septien kick), 13:13 4th.

Miami—Clayton 63 pass from Marino (von Schamann kick), 14:09 4th.

TEAM STATISTICS

	Dallas	Miami
First downs	21	17
Rushes-Yards	28-90	26-61
Passing yards	226	328
Sacked-Yards lost	3-20	1-12
Return yards	146	89
Passes	20-35-2	23-40-2
Punts	7-39.9	5-45.4
Fumbles-Lost	2-0	3-1
Penalties-Yards	4-61	3-32
Time of possession	29:47	30:13

Attendance—74,139. No-shows—966.

INDIVIDUAL STATISTICS

Rushing—Dallas, Dorsett 19-58, Springs 1-5, Newsome 6-20, Hill 1-7, D. White 1-0; Miami, Bennett 7-14, Nathan 13-39, Carter 3-9, P. Johnson 2-2, Marino 1-minus 3.

Passing—Dallas, D. White 20-34-2—246, Springs 0-1-0—0; Miami, Marino 23-40-2—340.

Receiving—Dallas, Hill 6-115, Cosbie 5-83, Dorsett 6-28, Newsome 2-13, Renfro 1-7; Miami, Duper 4-57, Clayton 4-150, Nathan 7-46, Moore 3-47, Hardy 3-25, Cefalo 1-11, Bennett 1-4.

Kickoff Returns—Dallas, Allen 3-66, McSwain 1-20; Miami, Walker 2-42, Kozlowski 1-11.

Punt Returns—Dallas, Allen 2-32; Miami, Walker 1-6.

Interceptions—Dallas, Fellows 1-3, Downs 1-25; Miami, Judson 1-0, McNeal 1-30.

Punting—Dallas, D. White 7-39.9; Miami, Roby 5-45.4.

Field Goals—Dallas, none attempted; Miami, none attempted.

Sacks—Dallas, R. White; Miami, Betters 2, M. Brown.

DIVISIONAL PLAYOFFS AND CONFERENCE CHAMPIONSHIP GAMES

WILD-CARD GAMES

SEAHAWKS 13, RAIDERS 7

SEATTLE—The Los Angeles Raiders' defense of their Super Bowl XVIII championship ended early as the Raiders lost to Seattle in the American Football Conference wild-card game. Los Angeles, whose 11-5 regular-season mark was good only for third place in the tough AFC West, failed in its attempt to become the first NFL team to win back-to-back Super Bowls since the 1978-79 Pittsburgh Steelers.

"I thought we were ready," said Raiders Coach Tom Flores, who led his club to Super Bowl triumphs in 1981 against Philadelphia and 1984 against Washington. "It's a disappointing loss because we don't get to come back. We just haven't been very productive offensively all season."

L.A.'s offensive problems were never more evident than against the Seahawks. The Raiders' only touchdown came on a Jim Plunkett pass to Marcus Allen in the final five minutes, and the deepest penetration the Raiders had before the touchdown was the Seattle 41-yard line in the second period. Plunkett, who hadn't started at quarterback in 10 weeks because of hip and stomach injuries, was sacked six times—five in the opening half—by the Seahawks defense. Seattle's defensive line dominated the war in the trenches.

"We blitzed early. We wanted them to know we were going to put pressure on them," said Seahawks linebacker Keith Butler, who had one sack. "After that, our defensive line just did a heck of a job." The entire Seattle defense did a heck of a job, holding L.A. to just seven points after yielding 34 and 31 points in Seattle's final two regular-season games. Those two games, both losses, enabled Denver to capture the AFC West title.

The Seattle offense did a great job, too, against one of the NFL's most aggressive defenses. Pro Bowl quarterback Dave Krieg, who had 32 regular-season touchdown passes, threw the ball just 10 times against the Raiders, completing four for 70 yards. Krieg had attempted 38 and 50 passes, respectively, in those season-ending losses to Kansas City and Denver. And Pro Bowl wide receiver Steve Largent, who had caught at least one pass in 107 consecutive regular-season games, didn't catch a single pass against Los Angeles.

Instead, Seattle relied on unheralded running back Dan Doornink, who rushed for only 215 yards during the regular season. Doornink ravaged the Raiders defense for 126 yards on 29 carries in the best game of his seven-year

pro career. Known primarily for his receiving skills out of the backfield, Doornink helped the Seahawks to their most productive rushing day (205 yards) all season.

"Dan Doornink has been making big plays for us all season," said Seattle Coach Chuck Knox, who saw his club avenge a 30-14 loss to the Raiders in the 1983 AFC championship game. "Whatever we've asked him to do, he's done, whether it's running the ball or catching passes coming out of the backfield."

Although the Seahawks dominated with the run, their only touchdown came via the pass—a 26-yard strike from Krieg to rookie Daryl Turner in the second quarter. That score came after a nine-play, 93-yard drive and, combined with two second-half Norm Johnson field goals, sent the Seahawks on their way to Miami for an AFC semifinal playoff game against the Dolphins the following weekend.

"It's just great to beat the Raiders," said Doornink after the Seahawks had done so for the second time in three meetings in 1984. "Anytime you beat the Raiders, it's sweet. They're such a good team."

SATURDAY, DECEMBER 22
SCORE BY PERIODS

Los Angeles Raiders	0	0	0	7— 7
Seattle	0	7	3	3—13

SCORING

Seattle—Turner 26 pass from Krieg (Johnson kick), 10:41 2nd. Drive: 93 yards, 9 plays.

Seattle—Field goal Johnson 35, 13:31 3rd. Drive: 21 yards, 7 plays.

Seattle—Field goal Johnson 44, 4:10 4th. Drive: 23 yards, 5 plays.

Los Angeles—Allen 46 pass from Plunkett (Bahr kick), 9:55 4th. Drive: 78 yards, 6 plays.

TEAM STATISTICS

	Los Angeles	Seattle
FIRST DOWNS	14	17
By rushing	5	12
By passing	8	4
By penalty	1	1
THIRD DOWN EFFICIENCY	4-13	2-13
TOTAL NET YARDS	240	251
Offensive plays	58	61
Average gain per play	4.1	4.1
NET YARDS RUSHING	105	205
Total rushes	25	51
Average gain per rush	4.2	4.1
NET YARDS PASSING	135	46
Sacked-Yards lost	6-49	2-24
Gross yards passing	184	70
PASSES	14-27-2	4-10-0
Average gain per pass	4.1	3.8
PUNTS	8-41.9	8-37.8
Had blocked	0	0
TOTAL RETURN YARDAGE	33	111
Punt returns	3-5	5-52
Kickoff returns	2-28	2-38
Interception returns	0-0	2-21

Seattle fullback Dan Doornink proved to be nearly unstoppable in the AFC wild-card game, rushing for 126 yards in the Seahawks' 13-7 victory over the Los Angeles Raiders.

	Los Angeles	Seattle
PENALTIES-YARDS	8-68	7-55
FUMBLES-LOST	2-1	0-0
TIME OF POSSESSION	25:41	34:19

Attendance—62,049. No-shows—2,861.

INDIVIDUAL STATISTICS

Rushing—Los Angeles, Allen 17-61, Hawkins 6-34, Pruitt 1-6, King 1-4; Seattle, Doornink 29-126, Hughes 14-54, Lane 4-17, Krieg 3-10, Largent 1-minus 2.

Passing—Los Angeles, Plunkett 14-27-2—184; Seattle, Krieg 4-10-0—70.

Receiving—Los Angeles, Allen 5-90, Hawkins 4-27, Barnwell 3-34, Christensen 1-21, King 1-12; Seattle, Turner 1-26, Tice 1-20, Doornink 1-14, Hughes 1-10.

Kickoff Returns—Los Angeles, Pruitt 2-28; Seattle, Hughes 2-38.

Punt Returns—Los Angeles, Montgomery 3-5; Seattle, Easley 5-52.

Interceptions—Seattle, Easley 1-21, Harris 1-0.

Punting—Los Angeles, Guy 8-41.9; Seattle, West 8-37.8.

Field Goals—Los Angeles, none attempted; Seattle, Johnson 2-2.

Sacks—Los Angeles, Alzado 2; Seattle, Green 2½, Butler, Fanning, Mangiero, J. Bryant ½.

GIANTS 16, RAMS 13

ANAHEIM—The New York Giants were a team in 1984 that got little respect. Despite finishing the regular season with a 9-7 record—including two victories over division-rival Dallas—and capturing one of the NFC's two wild-card berths, most observers didn't feel the Giants were a playoff-caliber club. After all, New York finished the previous season with a horrid 3-12-1 ledger, hardly the mark of a playoff club. And their nine wins in '84 had come against a sub-par Cowboys team, and NFL weak sisters Philadelphia, Tampa Bay, Atlanta, Kansas City and the New York Jets. Only victories over Washington and St. Louis, the critics said, were impressive.

And the fact that the Giants stumbled in their final two regular-season games against the Cardinals and Saints before "backing" into the NFC's final playoff spot only added fuel to the skeptics' fire.

"It seems like we're a team that nobody expects anything from," said Giants Coach Bill Parcells after his club beat the Los Angeles Rams in the NFC wild-card game. "We kind of had our backs to the wall several times during the season and every time we got them to the wall, we just seemed to be able to muster up enough energy to get it done."

Such was the case in the wild-card victory over the Rams. Few observers gave the Giants much hope of defeating the Rams at Anaheim Stadium before a sellout crowd of 67,037. On that same field in Week 5 of the regular season, L.A. crushed the Giants, 33-12. In that game, the Rams recorded an NFL-record three safeties, five quarterback sacks and blocked two punts while New York placekicker Ali Haji-Sheikh missed two extra points.

But the playoff game was different.

"They played really flawless football today," said Rams running back Eric Dickerson. "That's why they beat us. They didn't make any mistakes and we did."

Dickerson made one of the biggest mistakes of all. Although he rushed for 107 yards and scored the only Los Angeles touchdown, it was Dickerson's first-quarter fumble that turned the tide in New York's favor. With the Giants holding a 3-0 lead, Dickerson fumbled at his own 23-yard line with Bill Currier recovering for the Giants. Nine plays later, Rob Carpenter scored from a yard out for a 10-0 New York lead.

"We knew we would see them play at their best and they did," said Rams Coach John Robinson. "They played an excellent defensive game and we could never get back the touchdown we gave away on that fumble."

Actually, the Rams did recover that touchdown, scoring four plays after Giants safety Terry Kinard was called for interfering with tight end James McDonald at the New York 29-yard line. Dickerson scored the Rams'

Fullback Rob Carpenter scored the only New York touchdown in the Giants' 16-13 NFC wild-card triumph over the Los Angeles Rams.

touchdown from 14 yards out to cut the Giants' lead to 13-10.

After Haji-Sheikh's third field goal of the game gave New York a 16-10 lead entering the final quarter, the Rams let a golden opportunity to take the lead slip through their fingers. After driving 75 yards for a first-and-goal at the New York 7 midway through the period, the Rams were forced to settle for a Mike Lansford field goal instead of a go-ahead touchdown. Dickerson gained three yards on first down, but reserve running back Dwayne Crutchfield lost those three yards on the following play. A pass from Jeff Kemp to Henry Ellard netted only two more yards before Lansford booted a 22-yarder. The Rams never came close to scoring again.

"We should have come away from that 17-16," said Robinson. "That was just a complete failure."

The victory put the Giants into the NFC

semifinals the following week against the 49ers at San Francisco. The 49ers, winners of 15 of 16 regular-season games—including a 21-point win over the Giants—would be heavily favored. But then again, so were the Rams.

"After this win, next Saturday's game will give us a chance to show what we can do," said Carpenter. "I don't think anyone will give us a chance against the 49ers."

SUNDAY, DECEMBER 23
SCORE BY PERIODS

New York Giants	10	0	6	0	—16
Los Angeles Rams	0	3	7	3	—13

SCORING

New York—Field goal Haji-Sheikh 37, 6:32 1st. Drive: 33 yards, 9 plays.

New York—Carpenter 1 run (Haji-Sheikh kick), 13:50 1st. Drive: 23 yards, 9 plays.

Los Angeles—Field goal Lansford 38, 14:00 2nd. Drive: 38 yards, 6 plays.

New York—Field goal Haji-Sheikh 39, 5:10 3rd. Drive: 49 yards, 8 plays.

Los Angeles—Dickerson 14 run (Lansford kick), 8:35 3rd. Drive: 78 yards, 6 plays.

New York—Field goal Haji-Sheikh 36, 14:20 3rd. Drive: 61 yards, 11 plays.

Los Angeles—Field goal Lansford 22, 7:58 4th. Drive: 77 yards, 12 plays.

TEAM STATISTICS

	New York	Los Angeles
FIRST DOWNS	16	12
By rushing	5	5
By passing	8	5
By penalty	3	2
THIRD DOWN EFFICIENCY	8-16	2-7

	New York	Los Angeles
TOTAL NET YARDS	192	214
Offensive plays	62	43
Average gain per play	3.1	5.0
NET YARDS RUSHING	40	107
Total rushes	27	26
Average gain per rush	1.5	4.1
NET YARDS PASSING	152	107
Sacked-Yards lost	4-27	2-2
Gross yards passing	179	109
PASSES	22-31-0	11-15-0
Average gain per pass	4.3	6.3
PUNTS	4-38.8	4-37.8
Had blocked	0	0
TOTAL RETURN YARDAGE	94	109
Punt returns	3-25	2-17
Kickoff returns	4-69	5-92
Interception returns	0-0	0-0
PENALTIES-YARDS	5-81	10-75
FUMBLES LOST	3-0	2-2
TIME OF POSSESSION	34:03	25:57

Attendance—67,037. No-shows—1,053.

INDIVIDUAL STATISTICS

Rushing—New York, Morris 10-21, Carpenter 13-20, Simms 4-minus 1; Los Angeles, Dickerson 23-107, Kemp 1-2, Crutchfield 2-minus 2.

Passing—New York, Simms 22-31-0—179; Los Angeles, Kemp 11-15-0—109.

Receiving—New York, Mowatt 7-73, Manuel 3-52, Carpenter 7-23, Gray 2-20, Johnson 1-6, Galbreath 1-3, Morris 1-2; Los Angeles, Brown 3-32, Barber 3-31, Ellard 2-22, J. McDonald 2-18, David Hill 1-6.

Kickoff Returns—New York, Hill 3-49, Cephous 1-20; Los Angeles, Redden 5-92.

Punt Returns—New York, Manuel 3-25; Los Angeles, Ellard 2-17.

Punting—New York, Jennings 4-38.8; Los Angeles, Misko 4-37.8.

Field Goals—New York, Haji-Sheikh 3-3; Los Angeles, Lansford 1-1.

Sacks—New York, Taylor, Martin; Los Angeles, Collins, Wilcher, Ekern, DeJurnett.

DIVISIONAL PLAYOFF GAMES

DOLPHINS 31, SEAHAWKS 10

MIAMI—Two days before Miami met Seattle in the National Football League playoffs, Dolphins nose tackle Bob Baumhower thought back to past seasons, when Bill Arnsparger was defensive coordinator of the Killer Bees.

"It was Arnsparger's defense," Baumhower said. "We played together for awhile, and there was this feeling that you knew what the guy next to you was going to do."

He paused for a moment. "You know, we still have the same players, and we can play the same across the board," he said. "But one guy can't break down when the other 10 are doing the job. If we cut out the mistakes, we're still a good defense."

Baumhower's words proved prophetic when the Dolphins romped past Seattle to advance to the AFC title game. During the last half of the regular season, the Killer Bees hardly were buzzing. But against the Seahawks, the breakdowns disappeared, and they were at their stinging best.

The Seahawks were stymied by the Dolphins, who refused to be pushed around the way the Los Angeles Raiders were in the AFC wild-card game the week before.

The Seahawks ran 51 times and gained a season-high 205 yards against Los Angeles. Against the Dolphins, who sported the NFL's No. 22 rushing defense, they gained a mere 51 yards—the best performance of the season for Miami's defense—on 18 attempts. All this, even though Miami employed rookie Jay Brophy and second-year man Mark Brown at inside linebacker.

Brown and Brophy, who had suffered two broken thumbs in 1984, had fine games against the Seahawks, who also were confronted at times by a four-man Miami line on obvious rushing downs. No question the Dolphins had been well prepared. The linebackers and defensive backs worked an hour overtime earlier in the week to review fundamentals.

Take away Steve Largent's 56-yard touchdown catch in the second quarter, and Seattle had just 73 yards in the opening half. "We worked all week on making sure they didn't cut back on us," said Baumhower. "That's how they really hurt the Raiders. They'd get to the point of attack, and then they'd change direction and make yards. That didn't happen against us."

To win, the Seahawks had to be able to control the ball and force Dolphins quarterback Dan Marino to throw into their talented, seven-man secondary. Instead, it was the Dolphins who dominated the clock with a surprisingly capable rushing attack (143 yards), which they used frequently when Seattle inserted those extra defensive backs. Tony Nath-

an had 76 yards and a 14-yard touchdown run for Miami.

"We've got a good feeling again about ourselves," said Dolphins safety Lyle Blackwood. It certainly was a better feeling than Miami had in 1983, when Seattle rallied in the closing moments to pull off a stunning, 27-20 upset. The Miami players used that loss as a rallying cry in their pregame preparations.

Of course, the Seahawks had a healthy Curt Warner at running back for that game. Without Warner, who was lost for the season after suffering a serious knee injury in the Seahawks' first game, Seattle just didn't have the ability to neutralize the relentless pressure of Marino and the Dolphins. Fullback Dan Doornink, who rushed for 126 yards against the Raiders, had only 35 against Miami.

Marino was facing the league's most opportunistic defense, which led both in interceptions (38) and fumble recoveries (25). He struggled at times trying to find holes in that talented secondary, but even two interceptions couldn't discourage him from eventually throwing three touchdown passes.

One of those touchdowns resulted from a sensational 33-yard catch by wide receiver Mark Clayton, who leaped over cornerback Keith Simpson at the end-zone flag, tipped the ball and then caught it.

Miami also got a break when a third first-half Seattle interception, by Kenny Easley, was nullified by an offsides penalty. On the next play, Marino lofted a 34-yard scoring pass to Jimmy Cefalo for a 14-3 lead.

In all, it was an average day on the job for Marino, who wound up with 21 of 34 completions for 262 yards and wasn't dumped by a defense that had 55 sacks during the regular season. But, then again, the Dolphins allowed Marino to be sacked only 13 times all season.

SATURDAY, DECEMBER 29
SCORE BY PERIODS

Seattle	0	10	0	0—	10
Miami	7	7	14	3—	31

SCORING

Miami—Nathan 14 run (von Schamann kick), 10:51 1st. Drive: 68 yards, 8 plays.

Seattle—Field goal Johnson 27, 1:23 2nd. Drive: 29 yards, 7 plays.

Miami—Cefalo 34 pass from Marino (von Schamann kick), 4:07 2nd. Drive: 60 yards, 4 plays.

Seattle—Largent 56 pass from Krieg (Johnson kick), 11:37 2nd. Drive: 70 yards, 4 plays.

Miami—Hardy 3 pass from Marino (von Schamann kick), 10:35 3rd. Drive: 76 yards, 13 plays.

Miami—Clayton 33 pass from Marino (von Schamann kick), 12:35 3rd. Drive: 34 yards, 2 plays.

Miami—Field goal von Schamann 37, 3:32 4th. Drive: 69 yards, 8 plays.

TEAM STATISTICS

	Seattle	Miami
FIRST DOWNS	8	22

49ers 21, GIANTS 10

SAN FRANCISCO—After they had stumbled past the New York Giants in a NFC divisional playoff game, the San Francisco 49ers were something less than elated to learn that the Chicago Bears would be their opponent in the NFC championship game.

It's not that the 49ers wanted a return engagement against the Washington Redskins, to whom they lost the 1983 conference championship. It's that the 49ers lost to the Bears, 13-3, in 1983, when Coach Bill Walsh's famous offense endured one of its most frustrating days. The three points were the fewest scored by a Walsh-coached 49ers team.

After the way quarterback Joe Montana and the rest of his crew performed against the Giants, the offense wasn't exactly bubbling with anticipation at the prospect of facing Chicago's unusual and potent league-leading defense.

The 49ers were brilliant against New York for all of about 15 minutes. They jumped out to a 14-0 lead on their first two possessions, which ended with Montana touchdown passes of 21 yards to Dwight Clark and nine yards to Russ Francis.

After that, the offense and special teams were nearly as helpless as the 60,303 fans at Candlestick Park.

Montana threw three interceptions, one of which was returned for a touchdown and another of which set up a field goal. That accounted for all of the Giants' scoring.

Montana did complete 25 of 39 passes for 309 yards and three touchdowns, and he even took off on an unforgettable 53-yard run, after lulling Giants defenders into thinking he was heading out of bounds. But he also committed enough mistakes to keep the 49ers from blowing the Giants into the Bay.

Montana made amends almost as soon as the 49ers regained the ball after Harry Carson's second-quarter interception return had cut San Francisco's lead to 14-10. They moved 73 yards in five plays and one controversial penalty (a late hit by defensive back Bill Currier), scoring on a 29-yard touchdown pass from Montana to wide receiver Freddie Solomon.

The payoff came on a play-action fake that pulled safety Terry Kinard so close to the line of scrimmage that Solomon needed to sneak past only cornerback Perry Williams. But the completion still wasn't an easy one.

"I saw Freddie try to make a move to the outside, so that's where I was throwing when, all of a sudden, he went back inside," Montana said. "At the last second I sort of guided the ball that way and luckily it got to him."

When Wersching connected on the coversion with 4:09 left, it marked the end of the scoring for the day.

The 49ers did manage to drive to New York's 17-, 13- and 21-yard lines in the second half, but they collected only frustration. There was an interception by Gary Reasons, a 39-yard field goal attempt blocked by Elvis Patterson and an errant 34-yard field goal attempt by Ray Wersching.

Reasons' interception arrived two plays after Montana had scrambled 53 yards. It was the longest run by a 49er in 1984, but it came at a price. Montana, wearied by the long run, hadn't quite caught his breath before throwing his next pass.

"I didn't throw it with much oomph. I probably was still a little tired," Montana said. "That really bugged me, because Solomon was open for the touchdown. I just didn't get it there."

One of the 49ers' biggest frustrations on offense was an inability to run. Running back Wendell Tyler gained only 35 yards on 14 carries and fullback Roger Craig added 34 yards on 10 carries. The 49ers totalled 131 yards on the ground, including Montana's long gainer.

All-Pro linebacker Lawrence Taylor enjoyed his best game in four encounters with the

49ers—five tackles, one assist and two sacks. But his efficiency was noticeably reduced—he had only one more tackle—after he suffered a knee injury on the fifth play of the second half.

The 49ers' defense, meanwhile, held the Giants to 260 total yards, intercepted two passes and sacked quarterback Phil Simms six times, including two by Fred Dean.

"We knew our offense was having some problems," said strong safety Carlton Williamson. "We knew we would have to carry the team until they got on track. We escaped with a win. Now I hope we can put it all together next week."

New York Giants	0	10	0	0—10
San Francisco	14	7	0	0—21

SCORING

San Francisco—Clark 21 pass from Montana (Wersching kick), 3:05 1st. Drive: 71 yards, 8 plays.
San Francisco—Francis 9 pass from Montana (Wersching kick), 6:48 1st. Drive: 12 yards, 2 plays.
New York—Field goal Haji-Sheikh 46, 3:26 2nd. Drive: 37 yards, 11 plays.
New York—Carson 14 interception return (Haji-Sheikh kick), 8:19 2nd.
San Francisco—Solomon 29 pass from Montana (Wersching kick), 10:51 2nd. Drive: 73 yards, 5 plays.

TEAM STATISTICS

	New York	San Francisco
FIRST DOWNS	18	22
By rushing	7	5
By passing	10	16
By penalty	1	1
THIRD DOWN EFFICIENCY	7-17	8-15
TOTAL NET YARDS	260	412
Offensive plays	75	71
Average gain per play	3.50	5.80
NET YARDS RUSHING	87	131
Total rushes	25	28
Average gain per rush	3.5	4.7
NET YARDS PASSING	173	281
Sacked-Yards lost	6-45	4-28
Gross yards passing	218	309
PASSES	25-44-2	25-39-3
Average gain per pass	3.5	6.5
PUNTS	6-37.7	5-42.0
Had blocked	0	0
TOTAL RETURN YARDAGE	190	97
Punt returns	3-22	2-7
Kickoff returns	4-109	3-40
Interception returns	3-47	2-50
PENALTIES-YARDS	2-25	5-29
FUMBLES-LOST	2-1	0-0
TIME OF POSSESSION	31:29	28:31

Attendance—60,303. No-shows—1,021.

INDIVIDUAL STATISTICS

Rushing—New York, Morris 17-46, Galbreath 4-34, Carpenter 3-4, Simms 1-3; San Francisco, Montana 3-63, Tyler 14-35, Craig 10-34, Harmon 1-minus 1.

Passing—New York, Simms 25-44-2—218; San Francisco, Montana 25-39-3—309.

Receiving—New York, Mowatt 5-49, Morris 4-45, Manuel 2-32, Galbreath 4-25, Johnson 3-23, Carpenter 5-22, Mullady 2-22; San Francisco, D. Clark 9-112, Solomon 4-94, Wilson 3-37, Craig 4-31, Tyler 2-26, Francis 1-9, Cooper 2-0.

Interceptions—New York, Reasons 2-33, Carson 1-14; San Francisco, Lott 1-38, Ellison 1-12.

Punting—New York, Jennings 6-37.7; San Francisco, Runager 5-42.0.

Punt Returns—New York, Manuel 3-22; San Francisco, McLemore 2-7.

Kickoff Returns—New York, Hill 4-109; San Francisco, Monroe 2-26, Harmon 1-14.

Field Goals—New York, Haji-Sheikh 1-2 (missed: 33); San Francisco, Wersching 0-2 (missed: 39, 34).

Sacks—New York, Taylor 2, Merrill, Burt; San Francisco, Dean 2, Board 1½, Stover 1½, McColl.

BEARS 23, REDSKINS 19

WASHINGTON—It wasn't 73-0, the way the old man used to win in Washington, but it was still his kind of a game. It was obvious that the Chicago Bears had the initials GSH etched on their hearts as well as on their sleeves.

The Bears still live by the legacy left by their founding father, the late George S. Halas, who died during the 1983 National Football League season. And his indomitable spirit was never more present than when Coach Mike Ditka led the 1984 Chicago team into RFK Stadium for a NFC divisional playoff game.

The Bears forced three fumbles, sacked quarterback Joe Theismann seven times and stopped the Washington Redskins in scoring territory three times in the fourth quarter to pound their way to victory before a startled Washington crowd. Halas would have loved it. This was old-fashioned, bone-crushing George Halas football.

Theismann, who would be counting Bears in his sleep, said, "It was kind of like being on the freeway at rush hour—without a car."

It was the Bears' first playoff victory in 21 years—or since Halas coached them to their last championship in 1963. The fiery-eyed tight end on that team was a guy named Mike Ditka. And this victory came in the same city where Halas' Bears posted one of the most famous scores in history—the 73-0 drubbing of the Redskins in the 1940 championship game.

The prize for their 1984 triumph was a berth opposite the 49ers in the NFC title game in San Francisco the following week.

For the Redskins, the frustrating loss ended their bid for a third straight trip to the Super Bowl. Only Miami, which succeeded after the 1971, '72 and '73 seasons, had played in three straight Super Bowls.

What made Chicago's victory all the more impressive was the absence of No. 1 quarterback Jim McMahon, who was lost for the season with a lacerated kidney after 10 games.

All the Bears asked of backup Steve Fuller, who was playing his first game in a month, was modest production. That's what he gave them. He passed for 211 yards, but that was a misleading figure. Receiver Willie Gault, a world class sprinter, accounted for 75 of those when he broke a tackle by Darrell Green and ran for a touchdown. Another 33 yards came on a shuttle pass to fullback Matt Suhey. Fuller's ledger for the day also included a fumbled snap in the third quarter, after the Bears had pulled away to a 23-10 lead.

Put it all together—along with one of Walter Payton's specialities, a touchdown pass on a halfback option play—and the Bears didn't need much more offense. The defense did the rest.

Chicago's unrelenting pass rush seemed to rattle Theismann, who looked confused on occasion. Bears linebacker Al Harris said as much. "Al Harris can say that because he won," Theismann said. "I disagree with him, but he can say that."

The Redskins' offensive line suffered a blow on the next-to-last play of the first quarter, when guard Ken Huff fell beneath fullback John Riggins and left the game with a broken ankle. That left the Redskins without three of their top six linemen. Center Jeff Bostic and tackle George Starke had been injured earlier in the season. Morris Towns, who had missed the regular season with a broken ankle and had been activated just before the game, had to be rushed into duty. The Redskins were never the same. After controlling the ball 12 of the first 15 minutes, they had it only 17 of the final 45.

The Redskins' offensive linemen were huffing and puffing by game's end. "They sounded like Hoover vacuum cleaners out there," said Bears defensive tackle Dan Hampton.

With their offensive line in disarray, the Redskins virtually ignored the running game. They had five first downs in Chicago territory in the fourth quarter, and ran Riggins on just one of them. He picked up two yards on the play.

Ditka had so much confidence in his defense by the fourth quarter that he traded an intentional safety for field position. That cut the margin from six to four points. The Redskins had three fourth-quarter chances—at the Bears' 37 with 13:27 left, at the Bears' 40 with 9:52 left and at the Bears' 45 with 8:08 left—after the safety. They were foiled each time.

The Bears came up with the best offensive play of the day. That was Payton's nifty TD pass, which came after he'd swept to his right, faked a reverse handoff to Dennis McKinnon and then threw a 19-yard spiral to tight end Pat Dunsmore. Redskins safety Curtis Jordan went for the fake reverse and let Dunsmore get free.

It was a day when a lot of things went right for the Bears. "They just played relentless football and when you play that relentless, some good things have to happen to you," Ditka said.

George Halas couldn't have put it any better.

Veteran tackle Dan Hampton had two of the Bears' seven sacks in Chicago's 23-19 playoff win over Washington.

Chicago—Dunsmore 19 pass from Payton (B. Thomas kick), 13:00 2nd. Drive: 65 yards, 6 plays.

Chicago—Gault 75 pass from Fuller (kick failed), 0:26 3rd. Drive: 80 yards, 2 plays.

Washington—Riggins 1 run (Moseley kick), 5:25 3rd. Drive: 74 yards, 10 plays.

Chicago—McKinnon 16 pass from Fuller (B. Thomas kick), 10:55 3rd. Drive: 77 yards, 9 plays.

Washington—Riggins 2 run (Moseley kick), 14:55 3rd. Drive: 36 yards, 5 plays.

Washington—Safety, Finzer stepped out of end zone, 6:52 4th.

TEAM STATISTICS

	Chicago	Washington
FIRST DOWNS	13	22
By rushing	5	6
By passing	7	14
By penalty	1	2
THIRD DOWN EFFICIENCY	3-13	6-16
TOTAL NET YARDS	310	336
Offensive plays	57	76
Average gain per play	5.4	4.4
NET YARDS RUSHING	114	93
Total rushes	35	27
Average gain per rush	3.3	3.4
NET YARDS PASSING	196	243
Sacked-Yards lost	5-34	7-49
Gross yards passing	230	292
PASSES	10-17-0	22-42-1
Average gain per pass	8.9	5.0
PUNTS	5-39.4	5-36.8
Had blocked	0	0
TOTAL RETURN YARDAGE	91	141
Punt returns	2-74	3-29
Kickoff returns	3-74	6-112
Interception returns	1-0	0-0
PENALTIES-YARDS	6-34	7-55
FUMBLES-LOST	2-1	3-2
TIME OF POSSESSION	30:24	29:36

Attendance—55,431. No-shows—None.

INDIVIDUAL STATISTICS

Rushing—Chicago, Payton 24-104, Suhey 7-7, Fuller 2-

SUNDAY, DECEMBER 30
SCORE BY PERIODS

Chicago	0	10	13	0—23
Washington	3	0	14	2—19

SCORING

Washington—Field goal Moseley 25, 7:03 1st. Drive: 56 yards, 13 plays.

Chicago—Field goal B. Thomas 34, 3:31 2nd.

5, Finzer 1-minus 7, C. Thomas 1-5; Washington, Riggins 21-50, J. Washington 1-5, Theismann 5-38.

Passing—Chicago, Fuller 9-15-0—211, Payton 1-2-0 —10; Washington, Theismann 22-42-1—292.

Receiving—Chicago, McKinnon 4-72, Moorehead 1-6, C. Thomas 1-13, Dunsmore 1-19, Gault 1-75, Suhey 1-33, Payton 1-12; Washington, Monk 10-122, J. Washington 2-12, Muhammad 5-62, Didier 4-85, Warren 1-11.

Interceptions—Chicago, Richardson 1-0.

Punting—Chicago, Finzer 5-39.4; Washington, Hayes 5-36.8.

Punt Returns—Chicago, Fisher 2-17; Washington, Nelms 3-29.

Kickoff Returns—Chicago, Gault 3-74; Washington, Nelms 4-77, Kane 1-10, Coleman (with lateral) 0-25, Griffin 1-0.

Field Goals—Chicago, B. Thomas 1-1; Washington, Moseley 1-2 (missed: 41).

Sacks—Chicago, Dent 3, Hampton 2, McMichael, Waechter; Washington, Milot 3½, Manley, Grant ½.

STEELERS 24, BRONCOS 17

DENVER—In the sudden-death playoffs, death came suddenly for the AFC West champion Denver Broncos. But the Pittsburgh Steelers, who didn't capture the AFC Central title until the final day of the regular season, walked out of Mile High Stadium with new life and a shot at the AFC championship the following week against the Dolphins in Miami.

Orange Magic, which had been Denver's trademark through 13 regular-season victories, turned to Orange Tragic against Pittsburgh. And John Elway's dream of a Super Bowl appearance at his alma mater in Stanford Stadium ended abruptly when his fourth-quarter pass intended for Ray Alexander was intercepted by Pittsburgh free safety Eric Williams at the 31-yard line and returned all the way to the 2.

Frank Pollard's touchdown from there with 1:59 to play broke a 17-17 tie and gave the Steelers their trip to Miami.

"The dream is over now," Elway said. "But, heck, I'm still young. I said it before: It would have been a great fantasy to go back there and play a Super Bowl game. But as long as we get to a Super Bowl, I don't care where it's played."

"I guess we all pulled together today," said Williams, a second-year free safety from North Carolina State. "People talk about you, and you get mad. Everybody said we didn't belong here, but I guess we showed them we did.

"I don't think Elway ever saw me (on the interception). He looked at me just as the play was starting, but then he just looked at his receiver."

Williams was right.

"I never saw him," said Elway, who finished the game limping badly from a groin pull and a banged up left knee.

Elway's interception, however, was only the final blunder in Denver's offensive tragedy of errors. Twice in the first half, the Broncos were inside Pittsburgh's 25-yard line and didn't

score. Rich Karlis missed a 39-yard first-quarter field-goal attempt to foil the first scoring opportunity, and Elway threw an interception to nose tackle Gary Dunn from the 6-yard line to frustrate the second.

"The key to the game was our inability to score when we got the ball down in plus territory," said Broncos Coach Dan Reeves.

Pittsburgh, the best team in the AFC against the rush, made the Broncos look awful trying to rush. Sammy Winder carried 15 times and gained only 37 yards, and he was the only Denver running back with more than one carry.

The rest of what little offense the Broncos mustered came from Steve Watson, who caught 11 passes for 177 yards, including a 52-yard gain on a halfback pass from Gerald Willhite. Watson, too, had a 20-yard touchdown reception for Denver's final score and a short-lived 17-10 lead.

But Watson wasn't enough to counter Pittsburgh's mix-and match offense, which ran and passed with equal success against Denver. Steeler running backs Pollard and Walter Abercrombie found enough soft spots in the defense to gain 174 yards between them, and quarterback Mark Malone threw 17 completions for 224 yards and a touchdown.

"I knew we could handle them up front," said Pollard, who also scored the Steelers' first touchdown from the 1-yard line. "I wasn't surprised. I know what kind of offensive line we have, and I knew we could run on them. I knew it was going to be my day."

And Malone was reading the defense right. The Broncos were so conscious of the deep-threat capabilities of John Stallworth and Louis Lipps that they left themselves vulnerable underneath.

"Those guys were so scared of us going deep, they gave us what seemed like a 25-yard cushion," Malone said. "They were scared to death of the long pass, so we hit them underneath all day. We wanted to get the high percentage first-down passes, and I wanted not to throw the ball where they could intercept it. By far this was the best offensive and team effort we've had all year. This game shouldn't have been as close as it was, score-wise. Doesn't matter, though."

It might have, however. Steelers' placekicker Gary Anderson might have given Pittsburgh some breathing room, but he missed field goal attempts from 39, 26, and 40 yards.

Anderson's miss from the 16-yard line came with 3:35 left and the score still 17-17.

"It's hard to join in the excitement of such a big win, because, personally, I had such a tough day," he said. "But I'll tell you: It would be a thousand times tougher for me if we were going to be sitting at home next week. It's a big relief when somebody pulls it out for you. There have been some times when I've pulled our guys out, and today they pulled me out."

Fullback Frank Pollard's 2-yard touchdown run with two minutes left to play gave Pittsburgh its 24-17 upset win at Denver.

SUNDAY, DECEMBER 30
SCORE BY PERIODS

Pittsburgh	0	10	7	7—24
Denver	7	0	10	0—17

SCORING

Denver—J. Wright 9 pass from Elway (Karlis kick), 8:30 1st. Drive: 22 yards, 5 plays.

Pittsburgh—Field goal Anderson 28, 0:04 2nd. Drive: 62 yards, 12 plays.

Pittsburgh—Pollard 1 run (Anderson kick), 13:46 2nd. Drive: 78 yards, 8 plays.

Denver—Field goal Karlis 21, 2:50 3rd. Drive: 0 yards, 4 plays.

Denver—Watson 20 pass from Elway (Karlis kick), 7:45 3rd. Drive: 46 yards, 6 plays.

Pittsburgh—Lipps 10 pass from Malone (Anderson kick), 11:41 3rd. Drive: 66 yards, 7 plays.

Pittsburgh—Pollard 2 run (Anderson kick), 13:01 4th. Drive: 2 yards, 3 plays.

TEAM STATISTICS

	Pittsburgh	Denver
FIRST DOWNS	25	15
By rushing	12	4
By passing	13	11
By penalty	0	0
THIRD DOWN EFFICIENCY	5-13	4-13
TOTAL NET YARDS	381	250
Offensive plays	70	64
Average gain per play	5.4	3.9
NET YARDS RUSHING	169	51
Total rushes	40	22
Average gain per rush	4.2	2.3
NET YARDS PASSING	212	199
Sacked-Yards lost	2-12	4-37
Gross yards passing	224	236

	Pittsburgh	Denver
PASSES	17-28-0	20-38-2
Average gain per pass	7.1	4.7
PUNTS	3-28.3	4-42.3
Had blocked	1	0
TOTAL RETURN YARDAGE	145	73
Punt returns	3-9	2-17
Kickoff returns	4-102	2-56
Interception returns	2-34	0-0
PENALTIES-YARDS	4-30	1-5
FUMBLES-LOST	3-2	2-0
TIME OF POSSESSION	32:52	27:08

Attendance—74,981. No-shows—96.

INDIVIDUAL STATISTICS

Rushing—Pittsburgh, Pollard 16-99, Abercrombie 17-75, Malone 5-minus 6, Lipps 1-0, Veals 1-1; Denver, Elway 4-16, Winder 15-37, Watson 1-minus 3, Willhite 1-1, Parros 1-0.

Passing—Pittsburgh, Malone 17-28-0—224; Denver, Elway 19-37-2—184, Willhite 1-1-0—52.

Receiving—Pittsburgh, Abercrombie 3-18, Pollard 4-48, Lipps 5-86, Stallworth 3-38, Cunningham 1-19, Thompson 1-15; Denver, Winder 4-22, Watson 11-177, J. Wright 2-16, Willhite 2-12, Alexander 1-9.

Interceptions—Pittsburgh, Dunn 1-5, E. Williams 1-29.

Punting—Pittsburgh, Colquitt 2-42.5; Denver, Norman 4-42.3

Punt Returns—Pittsburgh, Lipps 3-9; Denver, Willhite 2-17.

Kickoff Returns—Pittsburgh, Erenberg 1-29, Lipps 3-73; Denver, Willhite 2-56.

Field Goals—Pittsburgh, Anderson 1-4 (missed: 40, 26, 39); Denver, Karlis 1-3 (missed: 39, 57).

Sacks—Pittsburgh, Little 2, Merriweather, Gary; Denver, Ryan, Jones.

DOLPHINS 45, STEELERS 28

MIAMI—The Pittsburgh Steelers were determined to live by the blitz in the American Football Conference championship game against the Miami Dolphins' Dan Marino, the young quarterback whom Coach Don Shula calls "the fastest gun in football."

But the Steelers died by the blitz, as defensive backs Dwayne Woodruff, Donnie Shell, Eric Williams, Sam Washington and Chris Brown constantly found themselves in single coverage against the likes of speedsters Mark Duper and Mark Clayton and the venerable Nat Moore.

It was a mismatch. Marino directed a 569-yard offense against Pittsburgh as he passed for AFC title game records of 421 yards (he was 21-for-32) and four touchdowns.

The victory put the Dolphins in Super Bowl XIX two weeks later at Palo Alto, Calif. It would be Miami's second appearance in the NFL championship game in three years.

Because the Steelers' defensive line failed to register a single sack, the Pittsburgh-born Marino had an easy time against the club he idolized in his youth.

And he did it even though Clayton, his top receiver (who had an NFL record 18 touchdown catches during the regular season) went out of the game with a bruised shoulder two minutes before halftime, when the Dolphins were four points behind.

Marino, who set regular-season records of 48 touchdown passes and 5,084 yards, easily could have broken Dan Fouts' all-time playoff passing record of 433 yards (accomplished in San Diego's double-overtime victory over Miami following the 1981 season), except that he was not permitted to throw a pass in the last 11 minutes. Shula wasn't going to be accused of running up the score.

The Steelers, who had the worst regular-season record (9-7) of any finalist in an NFL conference title game, were generous in their praise of the record-breaking quarterback.

"The Dolphins have a helluva passing game," said Shell. "It's well-designed, but it's not the design that makes it go—it's No. 13 (Marino)."

"We played the right kind of defense today (the blitz)," said Woodruff. "But even if you play the right defense, a good offense still can beat it."

Three Miami touchdowns came on passes of 36 yards or longer. Two other touchdowns were set up by 28-yard passes. All five of the long ones came against the blitz—when there was single coverage on Duper, Clayton, Moore and tight end Joe Rose.

Most of those completions were variations of the same play.

"When we knew they'd be blitzing, we just sent everybody (three wide receivers and the tight end) on a 'take-off' pattern," said Marino. "We knew we had the speed to beat their safeties."

"When Pittsburgh was in a blitz," said Duper, "their cornerbacks would drop back three steps and stop. So we'd send two guys deep on each side of the field—and each of their safetymen would have to cover one or the other guy coming down his side. All Danny had to do was figure out who'd be open, and he did."

The Steelers had the first chance on offense and drove to the Miami 30 before coming up empty, as cornerback William Judson intercepted Mark Malone in the end zone and brought the ball out to the Dolphins' 33.

Four plays later, with the ball at the Steelers' 40, Marino sent Clayton on a fly pattern down the right sideline.

When Miami clubbed Pittsburgh, 31-7, in the teams' regular-season encounter in Week 6, the Steelers sent two defenders in pursuit of the more-heralded Duper. "But when I lined up (for the touchdown catch), I saw they were doubling on me," said Clayton. "I didn't expect that. I wanted to tell them: 'Hey, guys, Duper is on the other side of the field.'"

The double coverage of Clayton, though, quickly became lack of coverage. "Danny did a couple of pump fakes and that froze the cornerback (Woodruff) long enough for Clayton to get past him," said Shula. The 40-yard reception gave Miami a 7-0 lead.

Moments later, Doug Betters recovered a Frank Pollard fumble at the Steelers' 31. But Washington broke up two Marino passes in the next series, Uwe von Schamann was short on a 52-yard field goal try and the Steelers eventually forged a 7-7 tie on a 66-yard drive capped by Rich Erenberg's seven-yard run late in the opening period.

Pittsburgh took a 14-10 lead with 2:52 left in the half as perennial All-Pro receiver John Stallworth broke free on a 65-yard pass play from Malone. "We did get burned a couple of times on defense," Shula allowed. "But each time, our offense was able to answer the challenge."

The answer came with 90 seconds remaining until intermission. Duper beat Steelers nickel back Brown on a 41-yard fly pattern and the Dolphins were in front to stay. Two plays later, Lyle Blackwood intercepted Malone at the Pittsburgh 35 and Marino had 1:09 left in which to drive the Dolphins to the end zone. He needed only 33 seconds. A 28-yard completion to Rose put Miami on the Pittsburgh one-yard line and Tony Nathan scored from two yards out on third down. It was 24-14, Miami.

The Dolphins got their third touchdown

Dolphins running back Tony Nathan receives congratulations from quarterback Dan Marino (left) after his 2-yard scoring run just before halftime gave Miami a 24-14 lead over Pittsburgh in the AFC title game.

Miami Coach Don Shula talks with star quarterback Dan Marino in the closing seconds of the AFC title game.

within the span of three minutes, 18 seconds when Marino pitched 36 yards to Duper on a fly pattern, four plays into the second half. The victim this time was Washington, who knew he was beaten and tried to take an interference penalty by diving at Duper's legs before the ball came down. Washington drew the yellow flag, but failed to knock Duper off stride, and Miami had a 31-14 lead. Duper was truly super in this game, catching five passes for 148 yards and two touchdowns.

The Steelers didn't fold, responding with a 72-yard drive that ended when Malone tossed 19 yards to Stallworth for a score that cut the Dolphins' lead to 31-21 with 23 minutes to play. The catch gave Stallworth his second TD of the game and a record 12 touchdown receptions in postseason play.

But Marino stole a page from the Steelers' ball-control book, driving the Dolphins 80 yards in 10 plays. The march consumed 6:15 and when Woody Bennett took a one-yard swan dive into the end zone for a 38-21 Miami lead, just before the end of the third quarter, the outcome no longer was in doubt.

In the final period, Marino (six yards to Moore) and Malone (29 yards to Wayne Capers) swapped scoring passes to put the final numbers on the board.

"What more can you say about Danny?" asked Shula. "He continues to rise to the occasion. He continually picked up the fact the Steelers would be blitzing and he made the adjustments. When you catch their defense in a situation where the blitzes can be picked up, you can really hurt them. And he did."

SCORE BY PERIODS

Pittsburgh	7	7	7	7—28
Miami	7	17	14	7—45

SCORING

Miami—Clayton 40 pass from Marino (von Schamann kick), 7:15 1st. Drive: 67 yards, 4 plays.

Pittsburgh—Erenberg 7 run (Anderson kick), 11:30 1st. Drive: 66 yards, 7 plays.

Miami—Field goal von Schamann 26, 5:56 2nd. Drive: 55 yards, 8 plays.

Pittsburgh—Stallworth 65 pass from Malone (Anderson kick), 12:08 2nd. Drive: 71 yards, 3 plays.

Miami—Duper 41 pass from Marino (von Schamann kick), 13:30 2nd. Drive: 77 yards, 5 plays.

Miami—Nathan 2 run (von Schamann kick), 14:24 2nd. Drive: 35 yards, 3 plays.

Miami—Duper 36 pass from Marino (von Schamann kick), 1:48 3rd. Drive: 78 yards, 4 plays.

Pittsburgh—Stallworth 19 pass from Malone (Anderson kick), 7:05 3rd. Drive: 72 yards, 9 plays.

Miami—Bennett 1 run (von Schamann kick), 13:20 3rd. Drive: 80 yards, 10 plays.

Miami—Moore 6 pass from Marino (von Schamann kick), 3:55 4th. Drive: 66 yards, 9 plays.

Pittsburgh—Capers 29 pass from Malone (Anderson kick), 14:35 4th. Drive: 84 yards, 5 plays.

TEAM STATISTICS

	Pittsburgh	Miami
FIRST DOWNS	22	28
By rushing	8	10
By passing	14	18
By penalty	0	0
THIRD DOWN EFFICIENCY	6-11	4-11
TOTAL NET YARDS	455	569
Offensive plays	68	71
Average gain per play	6.7	8.0
NET YARDS RUSHING	143	134
Total rushes	32	38
Average gain per rush	4.5	3.5
NET YARDS PASSING	312	435
Sacked-Yards lost	0-0	0-0
Gross yards passing	312	435
PASSES	20-36-3	22-33-1
Average gain per pass	8.7	13.2
PUNTS	3-43.7	2-42.5
Had blocked	0	0
TOTAL RETURN YARDAGE	131	116
Punt returns	1-7	3-12
Kickoff returns	5-106	3-62
Interception returns	1-18	3-42
PENALTIES-YARDS	3-30	3-25
FUMBLES-LOST	2-1	1-1
TIME OF POSSESSION	27:27	32:33

Attendance—76,029. No-shows—0.

INDIVIDUAL STATISTICS

Rushing—Pittsburgh, Abercrombie 15-68, Pollard 11-48, Erenberg 6-27; Miami, Nathan 19-64, P. Johnson 10-39, Bennett 8-33, Strock 1-minus 2.

Passing—Pittsburgh, Malone 20-36-3—312; Miami, Marino 21-32-1—421, Nathan 1-1-0—14.

Receiving—Pittsburgh, Stallworth 4-111, Lipps 3-45, Sweeney 3-42, Pollard 3-13, Erenberg 5-59, Capers 1-29, Abercrombie 1-13; Miami, Nathan 8-114, Duper 5-148, Clayton 4-95, Moore 2-34, Hardy 2-16, Rose 1-28.

Interceptions—Pittsburgh, Shell 1-18; Miami, Judson 1-34, G. Blackwood 1-4, L. Blackwood 1-4.

Punting—Pittsburgh, Colquitt 3-43.7; Miami, Roby 2-42.5.

Punt Returns—Pittsburgh, Lipps 1-7; Miami, Walker 2-10, Kozlowski 1-2.

Kickoff Returns—Pittsburgh, Erenberg 5-106; Miami, Walker 3-62.

Field Goals—Pittsburgh, Anderson 0-1 (missed: 53); Miami, von Schamann 1-2 (missed: 52).

Miami cornerback William Judson (top) intercepts a Mark Malone pass in the end zone while teammate Lyle Blackwood blocks out Steelers receiver John Stallworth in first period action. Below, Nat Moore scores Miami's final touchdown in the Dolphins' 45-28 victory.

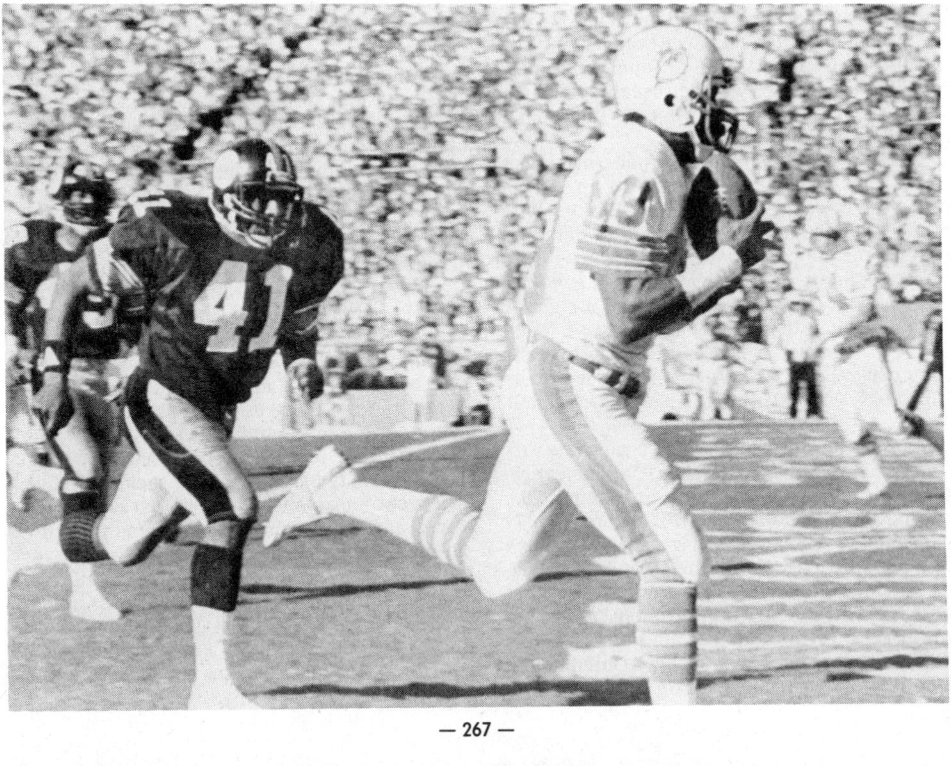

NFC CHAMPIONSHIP GAME

49ers 23, BEARS 0

SAN FRANCISCO—When it was over, the San Francisco 49ers won the National Football Conference title with the kind of balanced team performance that had made them such a formidable, and almost unbeatable, foe during the 1984 season.

But in the days before their triumph over the Chicago Bears, life was not so joyous in Camp Walsh.

There were two problems. First, the Bears' growling defense had been so frightening in beating the Washington Redskins the previous week that the 49ers suddenly became uptight.

"Early in the week, we had some concern about the atmosphere," said offensive right tackle Keith Fahnhorst. "It was real uptight after what we saw them do against Washington. We had to tell ourselves, 'We are the team that's 15-1 (in the National Football League's regular season); they've got to beat us.' We told each other not to let our confidence erode, because we are the better team. Things finally got back to normal."

At the same time, the 49ers' offense, especially the line, was trying to absorb some radical changes developed by Coach Bill Walsh, who viewed the Bears' league-leading defense as a personal challenge to his ability as a tactician.

"It was like learning a new offense in a few days," Fahnhorst said. "We fought it at first, because some of the protections violated your basic fundamentals, such as never leaving the middle unprotected. We all found ourselves blocking on people we never usually block on. As late as Saturday night, we were still talking and adjusting."

But if the 49ers were overly concerned about the Bears, Chicago should have been just as concerned about San Francisco. Besides winning all but one of their 17 games to date and playing for the conference title at home, 49ers offensive line coach Bobb McKittrick gave the Bears a warning a few days before the game: "We do a lot of things they haven't seen. Much of the offense is new plays and new formations they can't possibly be practicing. If our protection holds up, then the advantage swings our way."

As it turned out, the 49ers' offensive line protection, new schemes and just about everything else was superb in the title game. The raging Bears, who set an NFL record with 72 sacks in the regular season, got to quarterback Joe Montana only three times—and he actually fell down on two of those sacks. In the first half, when the Bears utilized their "46" alignment—the formation that had worried San Francisco the most—center Fred Quillan did a splendid job controlling tackle Dan Hampton, who becomes both a nose tackle and the key to Chicago's effectiveness. Left tackle Bubba Paris and left guard John Ayers shut out Chicago defensive end Richard Dent, the NFC's leading sacker. And right guard Randy Cross had the key block on a 39-yard run by Roger Craig in the fourth quarter that set up San Francisco's second touchdown.

The 49ers wound up gaining 387 yards, the most the Bears had surrendered all season after dominating league defensive statistics—they were first in total defense and were first against the rush, second against the pass. Chicago was yielding just 86 yards a game on the ground, but San Francisco rushed for 159 yards.

All this came on a day when Montana made some uncharacteristic bad plays. Two of those errors—a poorly thrown pass that was intercepted in the end zone by Gary Fencik, and a fumble of a third-down snap at the two-yard line—doused two first-half threats inside the Bears' 5 and kept the 49ers' lead to a mere 6-0 at halftime. Luckily for the 49ers, they wouldn't need to score any more points.

"With all this talking about how good the Chicago defense is, we got overlooked," said 49ers defensive end Dwaine Board. "Everyone forgot we played defense, too."

Chicago quarterback Steve Fuller never had a chance once the 49ers shut off the Bears' running game with aggressive play by jamming linebackers. With the linebackers charging hard and gambling, Chicago's league-best rushing attack couldn't move on first down. By the time they trailed, 20-0, the Bears had only seven rushing yards on first-down plays, which forced Fuller to throw into the 49ers' effective nickle coverage and four-man pass rush.

"This was the most pressure I've faced all season," Fuller said of the rush. "They just kept coming and coming. We weren't able to make the yardage on first down; that was our downfall." Another downfall was getting only 37 net yards passing—and none in the first half.

"We disguised our coverages differently and it confused Fuller, I think," said 49ers defensive back Dwight Hicks. The 49ers' secondary, one of the most aggressive in the NFL, did its usual job of manhandling receivers, which slowed up the Bears' patterns a half-step or so and contributed greatly to nine sacks of Fuller.

Except for an opening drive that covered 54 yards and ended when Bob Thomas missed a 41-yard field-goal attempt, the Bears never could run effectively. Walter Payton and Matt Suhey had runs of 15, 20 and eight yards in that possession, all against the 49ers' 4-3 pass rush alignment. But once San Francisco adjusted, the Bears were shut down, finishing with one total yard in the second quarter.

The 49ers' swarming defense got to Chicago quarterback Steve Fuller nine times in the NFC title game. Tackle Gary Johnson got him this time.

Meanwhile, the 49ers offense was also having problems. The game plan, which included lots of quick drops, short passes and roll-outs to cut off the Bears' pass rush, was working beautifully until the 49ers neared the end zone. Then it was comedy hour.

San Francisco reached the Chicago 2-yard line on its first possession, with Montana hitting on five of his six passes. But he dropped the third-down snap pulling away from center and Ray Wersching had to come on and kick a 21-yard field goal.

Fuller immediately threw an interception that Hicks may have caught on a short bounce. No matter, it gave the 49ers the ball on the Bears' 39. On second down from the 27, running back Wendell Tyler, who had been benched in a 1983 loss to Chicago because of fumbles, took a quick handoff from Montana off the 49ers' veer set and raced 25 yards to the 2.

But the run was wasted when Montana threw a lob pass off his back foot and failed to reach a wide-open Freddie Solomon in the back of the end zone. Instead, Fencik intercepted the pass.

Later, the 49ers tried Solomon at quarterback for one play (with Montana lining up at wide receiver), but the Bears stopped the option run for no gain. Then, two Montana passes of 14 yards each against Bear blitzes gave San Francisco a first down at the Chicago 4. But

Hampton knocked down a third-down pass and Wersching booted a 22-yard field goal.

The Bears couldn't believe their good fortune. At halftime, said guard Mark Bortz, "I thought the game was ours. All we had to do was get ahead and then we could start controlling things."

The 49ers' coaches were telling their players not to get discouraged, that they had prevented Montana from taking even one heavy shot, so it was just a matter of time before they would break loose.

"And we were telling the coaches that we could block them one-on-one, so we should run the ball," said Cross, one of three Pro Bowl players on the 49ers' line.

Even though Montana was sacked twice on the opening possession of the second half, the 49ers' persistence paid off. The Bears stopped using their "46" alignment so often and San Francisco jumped on Chicago's regular formations, finally scoring 6:33 into the third quarter on Tyler's nine-yard run. Tyler burst through three tacklers, with fullback Guy McIntyre (normally a guard) providing the lead block.

Trailing 13-0, Chicago finally crossed into San Francisco territory for the second time in the game, thanks to three straight completions by Fuller. But on a second and two from the 49ers' 21, he was sacked by Board for an eight-yard loss. On third down, despite plenty of time, he was dumped by Gary Johnson and

Despite the best efforts of Chicago's Al Harris, Wendell Tyler scores from nine yards out in the third period for a 13-0 San Francisco lead.

Chicago had to punt from the 40. Moments later, the 49ers used the 39-yard scamper by Craig to set up a 10-yard pass from Montana to Solomon for the touchdown that put the game out of Chicago's reach.

"We didn't want to get into too many predictable passing situations," said Chicago Coach Mike Ditka. "But the field seemed so long for us and so short for them. They were stuffing everything inside on our runs and we couldn't move them off the ball. We weren't going to win by throwing 50 times."

With the victory, San Francisco advanced to the Super Bowl for the second time in four years. With the game being played just down the road in Palo Alto, 49er fans certainly wouldn't have to travel very far to see their team battle for NFL bragging rights. "With the game in Palo Alto and all, people have been putting us in the Super Bowl since September," said linebacker Keena Turner. "I don't think there is any question now that we belong in that game."

SCORE BY PERIODS

Chicago	0	0	0	0— 0
San Francisco	3	3	7	10—23

SCORING

San Francisco—Field goal Wersching 21, 10:39 1st. Drive: 73 yards, 10 plays.

San Francisco—Field goal Wersching 22, 7:03 2nd. Drive: 65 yards, 13 plays.

San Francisco—Tyler 9 run (Wersching kick), 6:33 3rd. Drive: 35 yards, 5 plays.

San Francisco—Solomon 10 pass from Montana (Wersching kick), 3:45 4th. Drive: 88 yards, 8 plays.

San Francisco—Field goal Wersching 34, 13:03 4th. Drive: 36 yards, 8 plays.

TEAM STATISTICS

	Chicago	San Francisco
FIRST DOWNS	13	25
By rushing	9	9
By passing	3	14
By penalty	1	2
THIRD DOWN EFFICIENCY	5-16	4-11
TOTAL NET YARDS	186	387
Offensive plays	63	67
Average gain per play	3.0	5.8
NET YARDS RUSHING	149	159
Total rushes	32	29
Average gain per rush	4.7	5.5
NET YARDS PASSING	37	228
Sacked-Yards lost	9-50	3-8
Gross yards passing	87	236
PASSES	13-22-1	19-35-2
Average gain per pass	1.2	6.0
PUNTS	7-43.1	3-39.0
Had blocked	0	0
TOTAL RETURN YARDAGE	84	84
Punt returns	2-12	4-69
Kickoff returns	4-67	1-15
Interception returns	2-5	1-0
PENALTIES-YARDS	7-50	3-20
FUMBLES-LOST	1-0	1-0
TIME OF POSSESSION	31:53	28:07

Attendance—61,040. No-shows—296.

INDIVIDUAL STATISTICS

Rushing—Chicago, Payton 22-92, Fuller 6-39, Suhey 3-16, C. Thomas 1-2; San Francisco, Tyler 10-68, Craig 8-44, Montana 5-22, Harmon 3-18, Ring 2-5, Cavanaugh 1-2.

Passing—Chicago, Fuller 13-22-1—87; San Francisco, Montana 18-34-2—233, Cavanaugh 1-1-0—3.

Receiving—Chicago, McKinnon 3-48, Moorehead 2-14, Suhey 4-11, Payton 3-11, Dunsmore 1-3; San Francisco, D. Clark 4-83, Solomon 7-73, Wilson 2-25, Tyler 2-22, Francis 2-20, Nehemiah 1-10, Harmon 1-3.

The Bears' 23-0 NFC title game loss was a crushing blow for star running back Walter Payton, and the sign behind him tells the story.

Interceptions—Chicago, Fencik 2-5; San Francisco, Hicks 1-0.

Punting—Chicago, Finzer 7-43.1; San Francisco, Runager 3-39.0.

Punt Returns—Chicago, Fisher 2-12; San Francisco, McLemore 4-69.

Kickoff Returns—Chicago, Gentry 3-49, Gault 1-18; San Francisco, Harmon 1-15.

Field Goals—Chicago, B. Thomas 0-1 (missed: 41); San Francisco, Wersching 3-3.

Sacks—Chicago, Wilson, Keys, McMichael ½, Hampton ½; San Francisco, Johnson 3, Carter 2, Board, Dean, Stuckey, Pillers ½, Williamson ½.

The 49ers Strike Gold

By PAUL ATTNER
National Correspondent

PALO ALTO, Calif.—Don't mar the magnificent achievements of the San Francisco 49ers with talk about dynasties and future domination. Let the memories of the 1984 season be enough for now.

It is enough to remember that perhaps no team ever has put together a more impressive and more stunning Super Bowl performance than the 49ers, who so overwhelmed Miami, 38-16, in Stanford Stadium that it became difficult to recall how well the Dolphins had played in the weeks before the game.

It is enough to remember that no National Football League team ever has equaled San Francisco's 18 victories in a single season. Only a 20-17 loss to Pittsburgh in the season's seventh week stood in the way of San Francisco and a perfect 19-0 record.

"The loss was the best thing for us," said linebacker Dan Bunz after the ecstasy of Super Bowl XIX. "It took care of our big heads. I don't know if we would have come this far if we hadn't been taught a lesson."

The 49ers had taught us all a lesson: Don't ever expect these ever-so-promising Super Bowl games to live up to expectations. Even this ballyhooed matchup between the balance of the 49ers and Dan Marino's record-breaking skills turned into just another championship mismatch. It was the second straight Super Bowl where the winning team scored 38 points and the losers were held to only one touchdown.

The 49ers' offense gained a Super Bowl-record 537 total yards and tied the mark for points scored while the 49ers' defense limited the second highest scoring offense in league history to one touchdown, no second-half points and a horrid 25 rushing yards in only nine attempts.

Granted, San Francisco was favored going into the game, usually by three points and mostly because the game was being played only minutes from the 49ers' training site. But what happened couldn't have been predicted by even the most die hard of 49er fans.

"They came in here thinking they could do anything they wanted to anybody," said 49ers center Fred Quillan about the Dolphins. "I think we popped their bubble."

It was easy to get caught up in the Marino hysteria in the days preceding Super Bowl XIX. After all, pro football had never seen anything quite like this second-year phenom with the truckload of passing records and the cockiness of a Hall of Famer. Interest in the game became so intense that some fans spent $1,500 or more for a $60 seat.

"You heard and read so much about Marino that you wondered if we had an offense, too," said San Francisco guard Randy Cross. "I think it made everyone on our offense want to prove that we could play, too."

Unfortunately for Marino and the Dolphins, the Super Bowl would be unlike any other game he played all year. Marino showed every sign of falling prey to the mounting pressure. This was not the cool, calm Dan of earlier games. Instead, he performed much like, well, a second-year quarterback playing in his first Super Bowl.

Of course, the San Francisco defense contributed greatly to his troubles. Marino had not faced any defense in 1984, including that of the defending Super Bowl champion Los Angeles Raiders, that could use as many people and as many formations. The 49ers also had allowed the fewest points in the league, and then had given up just a field goal in the first two playoff games.

San Francisco had hoped it could handle Marino with its normal three-man defensive line. But by early in the second period, after Miami had used a no-huddle offense to score its only touchdown, the 49ers went almost entirely to their nickel personnel, which meant a four-man rush up front and reserve safeties Jeff Fuller and Tom Holmoe serving as combination defensive backs and linebackers.

"It all started from up front, with the line," said Keena Turner, the only starting linebacker to remain in the game. "Once they got pressure on Marino, he couldn't wait as long to throw and we could do a better job of coverage."

Marino had been sacked only 13 times in the regular season and not once in the playoffs. Given enough time, he hardly seemed bothered by defensive sets that featured six and seven defensive backs. But that all changed in this game. Marino was dropped a career-high four times even though the 49ers blitzed him on just a handful of occasions.

Instead, the defensive front wore down Miami's fine offensive line. Fred Dean, one of the league's premier pass rushers, usually is a spot player for the 49ers, but he was used much more than usual as part of the nickel personnel. He combined with tackle Gary Johnson to torment Marino.

Defensive coordinator George Seifert helped by putting in some new line stunts for the game. They were designed to put pressure on Miami's All-Pro center, Dwight Stephenson. "We had to tie him up on every play, so we could go right up the middle on Marino," said Johnson, who acknowledged that the 49ers weren't concerned with any scrambling from

San Francisco quarterback Joe Montana played perhaps the finest game of his six-year NFL career in Super Bowl XIX, leading the 49ers to a 38-16 conquest of Miami.

the weak-kneed quarterback.

"You could see him getting rattled out there," said Johnson, a former All-Pro who benefited greatly from the late-season return of Dean, who had been a contract holdout for 11 weeks. "Marino would throw away passes or he would talk more than usual to his lineman. We could see we were getting to him but you'd be upset, too, if you were getting hit a lot."

"Sometimes I didn't throw the ball well, sometimes I didn't have time and sometimes guys didn't get open," said a disgusted Marino. "They played the best any team has played against us defensively. They took us out of our scheme, I think. We knew what we had to do; we had to throw the ball against a four-man line."

Instead, the four-man line stymied him while also shutting off the Dolphins' feeble running game, which had its lowest output of the year. Marino threw 50 passes, completing 29—both Super Bowl records—but his 318 yards was his second lowest total in six games. And only one other time in 1984 had he been limited to just one touchdown pass. He had a record 48 during the regular season.

Mark Clayton caught six passes for 92 yards and said after the game that he was ill. Mark Duper was limited to one early catch. Otherwise, Marino was having problems dissecting the 49ers' ever-changing blend of defensive coverages. He completed only four passes for more than 20 yards, one for 30.

"He didn't have time to look us off his receiver," said safety Dwight Hicks. "He was getting too much pressure from our line. If he tried to go to another receiver, he would have to unload it in a hurry. We told the line that we'd cover just tight enough to give them extra time to get in on him. We didn't care if he completed anything short. We weren't going to be beat with short passes."

A glum Coach Don Shula, after his sixth Super Bowl and fourth loss, admitted, "This is going to be tough to live with during the off-season. Offensively, it was our poorest game of the year. We were stopped today."

But there was no stopping Joe Montana and the Niners' offense on this day. "After looking at the films (of Miami), we said, 'This is a Super Bowl defense?'" 49ers offensive line coach Bobb McKittrick said. "It's unusual for a

Running back Wendell Tyler, who rushed for 65 yards and caught four passes for 70 more in Super Bowl XIX, finds another gaping hole in the Miami defense.

one-dimensional team to make it to the Super Bowl, but Miami was unusual."

The Dolphins had the league's worst defense against the run (4.7 yards an attempt). "We could see in the films we could run against them," said McKittrick.

The films also showed the 49ers that Miami had a soft pass rush, going with its three-man front while the other eight players dropped back in zones. Often times, they wouldn't even look back at the quarterback to see if he was running. And running backs coming out of the backfield often were wide open.

"Bill (Walsh, the Niners' head coach) had his game plan in surprisingly early," said wide receiver Dwight Clark, who had five catches. "We just had a lot of time to perfect it. Everything that was open on film was open in the game, especially out patterns and stuff underneath for the backs."

And the San Francisco running backs, Wendell Tyler and Roger Craig, feasted on the weak Miami defense. Tyler rushed for 65 yards on 13 carries and caught four passes for 70 yards. And Craig, who was overshadowed for much of his college career at Nebraska and never given proper credit for being a fine, all-purpose running back, rushed for 58 yards and caught eight passes for 82 yards. Craig set a Super Bowl record with his three touchdowns, including two via the pass.

Aided by the impressive running game—the 49ers picked up 211 yards on the ground—Montana used action fakes that had the Dolphins off-balance all day. It became a textbook display, almost as easy as working against the scout team in practice.

"Joe will never say it, but it's understandable that with all the talk last week about Marino, he would like to do well," said Clark, Montana's best friend. "The talk pushed him. I know I am prejudiced, but he is the best quarterback around today, no question."

Walsh agreed. "He is clearly the best quarterback in football today and maybe the best in many years. He is No. 1 in leadership, assertiveness and he has those quick feet."

Montana merely is the NFL career leader in completion and interception percentage and overall rating. But he had thrown five interceptions in the first two playoff games, a statistic that clearly had San Francisco coaches worried.

They needn't have been concerned. Against Miami, not only was he extremely accurate (24-for-35) but he also scrambled away from trouble enough times to pick up a Super Bowl quarterback record for rushing with 59 yards. His feel for pressure and his ability to pick out receivers on the run left the Dolphins drained and frustrated.

"We knew we had to contain him but we

couldn't," said cornerback Don McNeal. "You'd look up and he would be running around. They dictated to us, we never could dictate to them."

Only in the early minutes did anything go Miami's way. After the most elaborate coin toss in history, with President Ronald Reagan flipping the silver over television from the White House (the 49ers even won the toss), San Francisco had to punt on its first possession.

Marino immediately drove the Dolphins to a 37-yard Uwe von Schamann field goal by completing four of his first five passes. A 33-yard pass to halfback Carl Monroe on a Montana rollout put San Francisco ahead, 7-3, but Miami used a no-huddle offense to respond immediately with a six-play, 70-yard march that ended on a two-yard scoring pass to tight end Dan Johnson.

That would be Miami's last proud moment in the game. Beginning with a possession early in the second period, the 49ers' defense put on a splendid display for the next 30 minutes, marred only by an end-of-the-half Miami drive that set up a 31-yard von Schamann field goal. Guard Guy McIntyre then fumbled the ensuing kickoff and von Schamann came on quickly to boot a 30-yarder as time ran out.

But otherwise, Marino and the Dolphins' offense was neutralized. On one possession, Marino missed two passes and usually reliable Reggie Roby got off the first of three short punts in a fourth-and-14 situation. Montana then connected with the versatile Craig for an eight-yard touchdown play and a 14-10 lead.

Then Marino underthrew a third-down pass to Nat Moore and Roby punted again on fourth and two. A 28-yard punt return by Dana McLemore put San Francisco at its 45, and the Niners were in the end zone six plays later, with Montana scrambling off left tackle from six yards out for the touchdown.

Two more Marino incompletions and Roby punted on fourth and 13. San Francisco began at its 48, but Miami recovered an apparent Freddie Solomon fumble after a reception at the Dolphins' 15. However, the officials ruled the play an incompletion and Craig soon ran in from the two behind a fine Tyler block for a 28-10 lead.

On his first two possessions of the second half, Marino was sacked three times and Miami was held to minus 10 yards. By then, Ray Wersching had booted a 27-yard field goal and Craig had his third touchdown, this one on a 16-yard pass over the middle, and San Francisco was ahead, 38-16.

For Miami, that meant five possessions with no first downs, minus nine yards and Marino 2-for-8 with three sacks. Hardly the Dolphins offense that averaged three touchdown passes a game in the regular season.

"This is truly the greatest moment of my career," said Walsh, who took the San Francisco

Roger Craig scores the game's final touchdown and his third of the day after catching a 16-yard Joe Montana pass in the third quarter.

job in 1979 and finished 2-14 his first season. "And this was the best game we ever played since I joined the 49ers.

"Maybe this will prove the merits of playing with a two-dimensional offense rather than relying on a one-dimensional attack."

After the brilliance of the 49ers in Super Bowl XIX, who could argue?

STANFORD STADIUM, PALO ALTO, CALIF.
SUNDAY, JANUARY 20
SCORE BY PERIODS

Miami...............................	10	6	0	0—16
San Francisco....................	7	21	10	0—38

SCORING

Miami—Field goal von Schamann 37, 7:36 1st. Drive: 45 yards, 7 plays.

San Francisco—Monroe 33 pass from Montana (Wersching kick), 11:48 1st. Drive: 78 yards, 8 plays.

Miami—D. Johnson 2 pass from Marino (von Schamann kick), 14:15 1st. Drive: 70 yards, 6 plays.

San Francisco—Craig 8 pass from Montana (Wersching kick), 3:26 2nd. Drive: 47 yards, 4 plays.

San Francisco—Montana 6 run (Wersching kick), 8:02 2nd. Drive: 55 yards, 6 plays.

Dolphins quarterback Dan Marino saw his fabulous 1984 season come to a horrible end in Super Bowl XIX, going down four times under the San Francisco defense's unrelenting pressure.

San Francisco—Craig 2 run (Wersching kick), 12:55 2nd. Drive: 52 yards, 9 plays.

Miami—Field goal von Schamann 31, 14:48 2nd. Drive: 73 yards, 12 plays.

Miami—Field goal von Schamann 30, 15:00 2nd. Drive: no yards, one play.

San Francisco—Field goal Wersching 27, 4:48 3rd. Drive: 43 yards, 10 plays.

San Francisco—Craig 16 pass from Montana (Wersching kick), 8:42 3rd. Drive: 70 yards, 5 plays.

TEAM STATISTICS

	Miami	San Francisco
FIRST DOWNS	19	31
By rushing	2	16
By passing	17	15
By penalty	0	0
THIRD-DOWN EFFICIENCY	4-12	6-11
TOTAL NET YARDS	314	537
Offensive plays	63	76
Average gain per play	5.0	7.1
NET YARDS RUSHING	25	211
Total rushes	9	40
Average gain per rush	2.8	5.3
NET YARDS PASSING	289	326
Sacked-Yards lost	4-29	1-5
Gross yards passing	318	331
PASSES	29-50-2	24-35-0
Average gain per pass	5.4	9.0
PUNTS	6-39.3	3-32.7
Had blocked	0	0
RETURN YARDAGE	155	91
Punt returns	2-15	5-51

	Miami	San Francisco
Kickoff returns	7-140	4-40
Interception returns	0-0	2-0
PENALTIES-YARDS	1-10	2-10
FUMBLES-LOST	1-0	2-2
TIME OF POSSESSION	22:49	37:11

Attendance—84,059. No-shows—0.

INDIVIDUAL STATISTICS

Rushing—Miami, Bennett 3-7, Nathan 5-18, Marino 1-0; San Francisco, Tyler 13-65, Craig 15-58, Montana 5-59, Harmon 5-20, Cooper 1-4, Solomon 1-5.

Passing—Miami, Marino 29-50-2—318; San Francisco, Montana 24-35-0—331.

Receiving—Miami, Nathan 10-83, D. Johnson 3-28, Clayton 6-92, Duper 1-11, Rose 6-73, Moore 2-17, Cefalo 1-14; San Francisco, Tyler 4-70, D. Clark 5-72, Craig 8-82, Monroe 1-33, Francis 5-60, Solomon 1-14.

Interceptions—San Francisco, Wright 1-0, Williamson 1-0.

Punting—Miami, Roby 6-39.3; San Francisco, Runager 3-32.7.

Punt Returns—Miami, Walker 2-15; San Francisco, McLemore 5-51.

Kickoff Returns—Miami, Walker 4-93, Hardy 2-31, Hill 1-16; San Francisco, Harmon 2-24, Monroe 1-16, McIntyre 1-0.

Field Goals—Miami, von Schamann 3-3; San Francisco, Wersching 1-1.

Sacks—Miami, Betters; San Francisco, Board 2, Tuiasosopo, Johnson.

San Francisco Coach Bill Walsh, Joe Montana and club owner Edward DeBartolo Jr. (top) are all smiles after Super Bowl XIX, but Miami Coach Don Shula (left) can only think of how things might have been.

SUPER BOWL SUMMARIES

SUPER BOWL I

January 15, 1967 at Los Angeles

Attendance—61,946

Kansas City (AFL) ...	0	10	0	0 — 10
Green Bay (NFL)	7	7	14	7 — 35

Winning coach—Vince Lombardi.
Most Valuable Player—Bart Starr.

SUPER BOWL II

January 14, 1968 at Miami

Attendance—75,546

Green Bay (NFL)	3	13	10	7 — 33
Oakland (AFL)	0	7	0	7 — 14

Winning coach—Vince Lombardi.
Most Valuable Player—Bart Starr.

SUPER BOWL III

January 12, 1969 at Miami

Attendance—75,389

New York (AFL).......	0	7	6	3 — 16
Baltimore (NFL)	0	0	0	7 — 7

Winning coach—Weeb Ewbank.
Most Valuable Player—Joe Namath.

SUPER BOWL IV

January 11, 1970 at New Orleans

Attendance—80,562

Minnesota (NFL)	0	0	7	0 — 7
Kansas City (AFL) ...	3	13	7	0 — 23

Winning coach—Hank Stram.
Most Valuable Player—Len Dawson.

SUPER BOWL V

January 17, 1971 at Miami

Attendance—79,204

Baltimore (AFC)......	0	6	0	10 — 16
Dallas (NFC)	3	10	0	0 — 13

Winning coach—Don McCafferty.
Most Valuable Player—Chuck Howley.

SUPER BOWL VI

January 16, 1972 at New Orleans

Attendance—81,023

Dallas (NFC)	3	7	7	7 — 24
Miami (AFC)	0	3	0	0 — 3

Winning coach—Tom Landry.
Most Valuable Player—Roger Staubach.

SUPER BOWL VII

January 14, 1973 at Los Angeles

Attendance—90,182

Miami (AFC)	7	7	0	0 — 14
Washington (NFC) ...	0	0	0	7 — 7

Winning coach—Don Shula.
Most Valuable Player—Jake Scott.

SUPER BOWL VIII

January 13, 1974 at Houston

Attendance—71,882

Minnesota (NFC).....	0	0	0	7 — 7
Miami (AFC)	14	3	7	0 — 24

Winning coach—Don Shula.
Most Valuable Player—Larry Csonka.

SUPER BOWL IX

January 12, 1975 at New Orleans

Attendance—80,997

Pittsburgh (AFC)	0	2	7	7 — 16
Minnesota (NFC).....	0	0	0	6 — 6

Winning coach—Chuck Noll.
Most Valuable Player—Franco Harris.

SUPER BOWL X

January 18, 1976 at Miami

Attendance—80,187

Dallas (NFC)	7	3	0	7 — 17
Pittsburgh (AFC)	7	0	0	14 — 21

Winning coach—Chuck Noll.
Most Valuable Player—Lynn Swann.

SUPER BOWL XI

January 9, 1977 at Pasadena

Attendance—103,428

Oakland (AFC)	0	16	3	13 — 32
Minnesota (NFC).....	0	0	7	7 — 14

Winning coach—John Madden.
Most Valuable Player—Fred Biletnikoff.

SUPER BOWL XII

January 15, 1978 at New Orleans

Attendance—75,804

Dallas (NFC)	10	3	7	7 — 27
Denver (AFC)...........	0	0	10	0 — 10

Winning coach—Tom Landry.
Most Valuable Players—Harvey Martin and Randy White.

SUPER BOWL XIII

January 21, 1979 at Miami

Attendance—78,656

Pittsburgh (AFC)	7	14	0	14 — 35
Dallas (NFC)	7	7	3	14 — 31

Winning coach—Chuck Noll.
Most Valuable Player—Terry Bradshaw.

The Louisiana Superdome will host Super Bowl XX on January 26, 1986.

SUPER BOWL XIV

January 20, 1980 at Pasadena

Attendance—103,985

Los Angeles (NFC)..	7	6	6	0 —	19
Pittsburgh (AFC).....	3	7	7	14 —	31

Winning coach—Chuck Noll.
Most Valuable Player—Terry Bradshaw.

SUPER BOWL XV

January 25, 1981 at New Orleans

Attendance—75,500

Oakland (AFC)	14	0	10	3 —	27
Philadelphia (NFC)..	0	3	0	7 —	10

Winning coach—Tom Flores.
Most Valuable Player—Jim Plunkett.

SUPER BOWL XVI

January 24, 1982 at Pontiac

Attendance—81,270

San Fran. (NFC)	7	13	0	6 —	26
Cincinnati (AFC)	0	0	7	14 —	21

Winning coach—Bill Walsh.
Most Valuable Player—Joe Montana.

SUPER BOWL XVII

January 30, 1983 at Pasadena

Attendance—103,667

Miami (AFC)	7	10	0	0 —	17
Washington (NFC)...	0	10	3	14 —	27

Winning coach—Joe Gibbs.
Most Valuable Player—John Riggins.

SUPER BOWL XVIII

January 22, 1984 at Tampa

Attendance—72,920

Washington (NFC)...	0	3	6	0 —	9
Los Angeles (AFC)..	7	14	14	3 —	38

Winning coach—Tom Flores.
Most Valuable Player—Marcus Allen.

SUPER BOWL XIX

January 20, 1985 at Palo Alto

Attendance—84,059

Miami (AFC)	10	6	0	0 —	16
San Fran. (NFC)	7	21	10	0 —	38

Winning coach—Bill Walsh.
Most Valuable Player—Joe Montana.

1984 NFL Statistics

1984 RUSHING

MOST YARDS, SEASON
> NFC: 2105—Eric Dickerson, L.A. Rams.
> AFC: 1179—Earnest Jackson, San Diego.

MOST YARDS, GAME
> NFC: 215—Eric Dickerson, L.A. Rams vs. Houston, December 9 (27 attempts).
> AFC: 206—Greg Bell, Buffalo vs. Dallas, November 18 (27 attempts).

LONGEST GAIN
> AFC: 85—Greg Bell, Buffalo vs. Dallas, November 18 (TD).
> NFC: 81—Billy Sims, Detroit at San Diego, September 30.

MOST ATTEMPTS, SEASON
> NFC: 407—James Wilder, Tampa Bay.
> AFC: 296—Earnest Jackson, San Diego.
> Sammy Winder, Denver.

MOST ATTEMPTS, GAME
> NFC: 43—James Wilder, Tampa Bay vs. Green Bay, September 30 (172 yards).
> AFC: 34—Sammy Winder, Denver at L.A. Raiders, October 28 (126 yards).

AVERAGE YARDS PER ATTEMPT
> NFC: 6.0—Hokie Gajan, New Orleans.
> AFC: 5.0—Joe Carter, Miami.

MOST TOUCHDOWNS
> NFC: 14—Eric Dickerson, L.A. Rams.
> John Riggins, Washington.
> AFC: 13—Marcus Allen, L.A. Raiders.

TEAM LEADERS
> NFC: ATLANTA: 1486, Gerald Riggs; CHICAGO: 1684, Walter Payton; DALLAS: 1189, Tony Dorsett; DETROIT: 687, Billy Sims; GREEN BAY: 581, Gerry Ellis; L.A. RAMS: 2105, Eric Dickerson; MINNESOTA: 773, Alfred Anderson; NEW ORLEANS: 914, George Rogers; N.Y. GIANTS: 795, Rob Carpenter; PHILADELPHIA: 789, Wilbert Montgomery; ST. LOUIS: 1174, Ottis Anderson; SAN FRANCISCO: 1262, Wendell Tyler; TAMPA BAY: 1544, James Wilder; WASHINGTON: 1239, John Riggins.
> AFC: BUFFALO: 1100, Greg Bell; CINCINNATI: 623, Larry Kinnebrew; CLEVELAND: 673, Boyce Green; DENVER: 1153, Sammy Winder; HOUSTON: 785, Larry Moriarty; INDIANAPOLIS: 705, Randy McMillan; KANSAS CITY: 684, Herman Heard; L.A. RAIDERS: 1168, Marcus Allen; MIAMI: 606, Woody Bennett; NEW ENGLAND: 790, Craig James; N.Y. JETS: 1070, Freeman McNeil; PITTSBURGH: 851, Frank Pollard; SAN DIEGO: 1179, Earnest Jackson; SEATTLE: 327, David Hughes.

TEAM CHAMPION
> NFC: 2974—Chicago.
> AFC: 2189—N.Y. Jets.

RUSHING—TEAM

NATIONAL FOOTBALL CONFERENCE

	Att.	Yards	Avg.	Long	TDs.
Chicago	674	2974	4.4	t72	22
L.A. Rams	541	2864	5.3	66	16
San Francisco	534	2465	4.6	47	21
Washington	588	2274	3.9	31	20
New Orleans	523	2171	4.2	t62	9
St. Louis	488	2088	4.3	39	21
Green Bay	461	2019	4.4	50	18
Detroit	446	2017	4.5	81	13
Atlanta	489	1994	4.1	57	16
Minnesota	444	1844	4.2	39	10
Tampa Bay	483	1776	3.7	37	17
Dallas	469	1714	3.7	t31	12
N.Y. Giants	493	1660	3.4	28	12
Philadelphia	381	1338	3.5	27	6
Conference Total	7014	29198	.....	81	213
Conference Average	501.0	2085.6	4.2	.....	15.2

AMERICAN FOOTBALL CONFERENCE

	Att.	Yards	Avg.	Long	TDs.
N.Y. Jets	504	2189	4.3	64	17
Cincinnati	540	2179	4.0	33	18
Pittsburgh	574	2179	3.8	52	13
Denver	508	2076	4.1	52	12
New England	482	2032	4.2	73	15
Indianapolis	510	2025	4.0	t31	13
Miami	484	1918	4.0	35	18
L.A. Raiders	516	1886	3.7	t52	19
Cleveland	489	1696	3.5	54	10
Houston	433	1656	3.8	t51	13
San Diego	456	1654	3.6	t32	18
Seattle	495	1645	3.3	t40	10
Buffalo	398	1643	4.1	t85	9
Kansas City	408	1527	3.7	t69	12
Conference Total	6797	26305	.....	t85	197
Conference Average	485.5	1878.9	3.9	.....	14.1
League Total	13811	55503	.....	t85	410
League Average	493.3	1982.3	4.0	.....	14.6

TOP TEN RUSHERS

	Att.	Yards	Avg.	Long	TDs.
DICKERSON, ERIC, L.A. Rams	379	2105	5.6	66	14
Payton, Walter, Chicago	381	1684	4.4	t72	11
Wilder, James, Tampa Bay	407	1544	3.8	37	13
Riggs, Gerald, Atlanta	353	1486	4.2	57	13
Tyler, Wendell, San Francisco	246	1262	5.1	40	7
Riggins, John, Washington	327	1239	3.8	24	14
Dorsett, Tony, Dallas	302	1189	3.9	t31	6
Jackson, Earnest, San Diego	296	1179	4.0	t32	8
Anderson, Ottis, St. Louis	289	1174	4.1	24	6
Allen, Marcus, L.A. Raiders	275	1168	4.2	t52	13

AFC—INDIVIDUALS

Player—Team	Att.	Yds.	Avg.	Lng.	TD
JACKSON, S.D.	296	1179	4.0	t32	8
Allen, L.A. Raiders	275	1168	4.2	t52	13
Winder, Den.	296	1153	3.9	24	4
Bell, Buff.	262	1100	4.2	t85	7
McNeil, N.Y. Jets	229	1070	4.7	53	5
Pollard, Pitt.	213	851	4.0	52	6
C. James, N.E.	160	790	4.9	73	1
Moriarty, Hou.	189	785	4.2	t51	6
McMillan, Ind.	163	705	4.3	t31	5
Heard, K.C.	165	684	4.1	t69	4
Green, Clev.	202	673	3.3	29	0
Kinnebrew, Cin.	154	623	4.0	23	9
Abercrombie, Pitt.	145	610	4.2	31	1
Bennett, Mia.	144	606	4.2	23	7
Nathan, Mia.	118	558	4.7	22	1
Tatupu, N.E.	133	553	4.2	t20	4
Collins, N.E.	138	550	4.0	21	5
Hector, N.Y. Jets	124	531	4.3	64	1
Dickey, Ind.	131	523	4.0	30	3
Pruitt, Clev.	163	506	3.1	14	6
Carter, Mia.	100	495	5.0	35	1
Alexander, Cin.	132	479	3.6	22	2
Byner, Clev.	72	426	5.9	54	2
Erenberg, Pitt.	115	405	3.5	t31	2
Brooks, Cin.	103	396	3.8	33	2
Jennings, Cin.	79	379	4.8	t20	2
Hawkins, L.A. Raiders.	108	376	3.5	17	3
Willhite, Den.	77	371	4.8	52	2
Brown, K.C.	97	337	3.5	25	4
Hughes, Sea.	94	327	3.5	14	1
Lane, Sea.	80	299	3.7	t40	4
Middleton, Ind.	92	275	3.0	20	1
Edwards, Hou.	60	267	4.5	20	1
King, L.A. Raiders	67	254	3.8	18	0
Elway, Den.	56	237	4.2	21	1
McGee, S.D.	67	226	3.4	30	4
B. Jackson, K.C.	50	225	4.5	16	1
Doornink, Sea.	57	215	3.8	25	0
Moon, Hou.	58	211	3.6	31	1
Parros, Den.	46	208	4.5	25	2
P. Johnson, S.D.-Mia.	87	205	2.4	9	12
Morris, Sea.	58	189	3.3	16	0

Player—Team	Att.	Yds.	Avg.	Lng.	TD
Krieg, Sea.	46	186	4.0	t37	3
Neal, Buff.	49	175	3.6	10	1
F. Harris, Sea.	68	170	2.5	16	0
Lacy, K.C.	46	165	3.6	t24	2
Eason, N.E.	40	154	3.9	t25	5
Dixon, Sea.	52	149	2.9	17	2
Pagel, Ind.	26	149	5.7	23	1
Barber, N.Y. Jets	31	148	4.8	18	2
Schlichter, Ind.	19	145	7.6	22	1
Minter, N.Y. Jets	34	136	4.0	14	1
Paige, N.Y. Jets	35	130	3.7	24	7
Moore, Ind.	38	127	3.3	18	2
James, S.D.	25	115	4.6	20	0
Wonsley, Ind.	37	111	3.0	13	0
Blackledge, K.C.	18	102	5.7	26	1
Ferguson, Buff.	19	102	5.4	20	0
Ryan, N.Y. Jets	23	92	4.0	16	0
Corley, Pitt.	18	89	4.9	23	0
Veals, Pitt.	31	87	2.8	9	0
Moore, Buff.	24	84	3.5	21	0
Kofler, Buff.	10	80	8.0	19	0
Schonert, Cin.	13	77	5.9	17	1
Luck, Hou.	10	75	7.5	18	1
Franklin, Mia.	20	74	3.7	12	0
S. Wilson, Cin.	17	74	4.4	9	0
Lipps, Pitt.	3	71	23.7	t36	1
Anderson, Cin.	11	64	5.8	14	0
Esiason, Cin.	19	63	3.3	9	2
White, Clev.	24	62	2.6	8	0
C. Bryant, Sea.	20	58	2.9	8	0
Wilson, L.A. Raiders	30	56	1.9	t14	1
Muncie, S.D.	14	51	3.6	11	0
Va. Williams, Buff.	18	51	2.8	7	0
Harper, N.Y. Jets	10	48	4.8	16	1
Thomas, S.D.	14	43	3.1	9	2
Lang, Den.	8	42	5.3	15	2
Malone, Pitt.	25	42	1.7	t13	3
Warner, Sea.	10	40	4.0	9	0
Clayton, Mia.	3	35	11.7	30	0
O'Brien, N.Y. Jets	16	29	1.8	7	0
Brewer, Den.	10	28	2.8	8	0
Brookins, Buff.	2	27	13.5	16	0
Kubiak, Den.	9	27	3.0	17	1
Dufek, Buff.	9	22	2.4	13	1
Joyner, Hou.	14	22	1.6	9	0
Walls, Hou.	4	20	5.0	20	0
Paige, K.C.	3	19	6.3	9	0
Gillespie, Pitt.	7	18	2.6	9	0
J. Davis, Clev.	3	15	5.0	8	1
Plunkett, L.A. Raiders	16	14	0.9	9	1
Woodley, Pitt.	11	14	1.3	7	0
Grogan, N.E.	7	12	1.7	1	0
Gunter, K.C.	15	12	0.8	4	0
Holt, Clev.	1	12	12.0	12	0
Morris, S.D.	5	12	2.4	5	1
Farley, Cin.	7	11	1.6	5	0
Luther, S.D.	4	11	2.8	7	0
Largent, Sea.	2	10	5.0	6	0
Collinsworth, Cin.	1	7	7.0	7	0
Humm, L.A. Raiders	2	7	3.5	9	0
Myles, Den.	5	7	1.4	2	0
B. Davis, Clev.	1	6	6.0	6	0
Hunter, Buff.	1	6	6.0	6	0
Verser, Cin.	2	5	2.5	3	0
C. Young, Sea.	1	5	5.0	5	0
Dennison, N.Y. Jets	1	4	4.0	4	0
McDonald, Clev.	22	4	0.2	10	1
Willis, L.A. Raiders	5	4	0.8	2	0
Jensen, L.A. Raiders	3	3	1.0	2	1
Johnson, Den.	1	3	3.0	3	0
Martin, Cin.	1	3	3.0	3	0
McCall, L.A. Raiders	1	3	3.0	3	0
Moore, Mia.	1	3	3.0	3	0
Riddick, Buff.	3	3	1.0	6	0
Montgomery, L.A.	1	1	1.0	1	0
Ricks, K.C.	2	1	0.5	1	0
Walker, N.Y. Jets	1	1	1.0	1	0
J. Arnold, K.C.	1	0	0.0	0	0
Colquitt, Pitt.	1	0	0.0	0	0
Mullins, Hou.	1	0	0.0	0	0
Pruitt, L.A. Raiders	8	0	0.0	3	0
Spencer, Pitt.	1	0	0.0	0	0
Stark, Ind.	2	0	0.0	0	0
Cooper, Hou.	1	−2	−2.0	−2	0
Harris, Cin.	1	−2	−2.0	−2	0
Osiecki, K.C.	1	−2	−2.0	−2	0
Capers, Pitt.	1	−3	−3.0	−3	0
Zorn, Sea.	7	−3	−0.4	7	0
Avellini, Chi.-N.Y. Jets	3	−5	−1.7	0	0
Campbell, Pitt.	3	−5	−1.7	0	0
Strock, Mia.	2	−5	−2.5	0	0
Franklin, Buff.	1	−7	−7.0	−7	0
Marino, Mia.	28	−7	−0.3	10	0
Carson, K.C.	1	−8	−8.0	−8	0
Kenney, K.C.	9	−8	−0.9	1	0
Walker, Clev.	1	−8	−8.0	−8	0
P. Smith, Ind.	2	−10	−5.0	−3	0
Fryar, N.E.	2	−11	−5.5	0	0
Starring, N.E.	2	−16	−8.0	0	0
Fouts, S.D.	12	−29	−2.4	3	0

NFC—INDIVIDUALS

Player—Team	Att.	Yds.	Avg.	Lng.	TD
DICKERSON, Rams	379	2105	5.6	66	14
Payton, Chi.	381	1684	4.4	t72	11
Wilder, T.B.	407	1544	3.8	37	13
Riggs, Atl.	353	1486	4.2	57	13
Tyler, S.F.	246	1262	5.1	40	7
Riggins, Wash.	327	1239	3.8	24	14
Dorsett, Dall.	302	1189	3.9	t31	6
Anderson, St.L.	289	1174	4.1	24	6
G. Rogers, N.O.	239	914	3.8	28	2
Carpenter, N.Y. Giants	250	795	3.2	22	7
Montgomery, Phila.	201	789	3.9	27	2
Anderson, Minn.	201	773	3.8	23	2
Sims, Det.	130	687	5.3	81	5
Craig, S.F.	155	649	4.2	28	7
Gajan, N.O.	102	615	6.0	t62	5
Ellis, G.B.	123	581	4.7	50	4
Ivery, G.B.	99	552	5.6	49	6
Jones, Det.	137	532	3.9	34	3
Morris, N.Y. Giants	133	510	3.8	28	4
Campbell, Hou.-N.O.	146	468	3.2	22	4
T. Brown, Minn.	98	442	4.5	19	3
Mitchell, St.L.	81	434	5.4	39	9
Suhey, Chi.	124	424	3.4	21	4
Griffin, Wash.	97	408	4.2	31	0
Nelson, Minn.	80	406	5.1	39	3
Clark, G.B.	87	375	4.3	t43	4
Jenkins, Det.	78	358	4.6	t25	1
Crutchfield, L.A. Rams	73	337	4.6	36	1
Theismann, Wash.	62	314	5.1	27	1
Cain, Atl.	77	276	3.6	t31	3
McMahon, Chi.	39	276	7.1	30	2
Newsome, Dall.	66	268	4.1	30	5
Oliver, Phila.	72	263	3.7	17	0
W. Wilson, N.O.	74	261	3.5	36	1
Redden, L.A. Rams	45	247	5.5	35	0
Danielson, Det.	41	218	5.3	40	3
Springs, Dall.	68	197	2.9	16	1
Harmon, S.F.	39	192	4.9	19	1
J. Washington, Wash.	56	192	3.4	12	1
Ferrell, St.L.	41	190	4.6	25	1
C. Thomas, Chi.	40	186	4.7	37	1
Lomax, St.L.	35	184	5.3	20	3
Crouse, G.B.	53	169	3.2	14	0
Ring, S.F.	38	162	4.3	34	3
Simms, N.Y. Giants	42	162	3.9	21	0
Kemp, L.A. Rams	34	153	4.5	23	1
Huckleby, G.B.	35	145	4.1	23	0
Haddix, Phila.	48	130	2.7	21	0
Lisch, Chi.	18	121	6.7	31	0
Montana, S.F.	39	118	3.0	15	2

Player—Team	Att.	Yds.	Avg.	Lng.	TD
Todd, N.O.	28	111	4.0	15	0
Anthony, N.O.	20	105	5.3	19	1
Moroski, Atl.	21	98	4.7	17	0
Galbreath, N.Y.Giants.	22	97	4.4	11	0
Rodgers, G.B.	25	94	3.8	15	0
Woolfolk, N.Y. Giants..	40	92	2.3	17	1
Bussey, Det.	32	91	2.8	18	0
Love, St.L.	25	90	3.6	13	1
Fuller, Chi.	15	89	5.9	26	1
M. Williams, Phila.	33	83	2.5	8	0
Lofton, G.B.	10	82	8.2	26	0
Gentry, Chi.	21	79	3.8	28	1
Solomon, S.F.	6	72	12.0	47	1
Jordan, Chi.	11	70	6.4	29	0
DeBerg, T.B.	28	59	2.1	14	2
Rice, Minn.	14	58	4.1	16	1
D'Addio, Det.	7	46	6.6	14	0
Jones, Minn.	4	45	11.3	36	0
Carver, T.B.	11	44	4.0	12	0
Kane, Wash.	17	43	2.5	10	0
Manning, Minn.	11	42	3.8	16	0
Hardy, Phila.	14	41	2.9	10	0
Hutchison, Chi.	14	39	2.8	6	1
Archer, Atl.	6	38	6.3	12	0
Wonsley, Wash.	18	38	2.1	7	4
J. Thompson, T.B.	5	35	7.0	13	0
Armstrong, T.B.	10	34	3.4	9	2
Bartkowski, Atl.	15	34	2.3	8	0
Witkowski, Det.	7	33	4.7	10	0
Wilson, Minn.	9	30	3.3	12	0
Morton, T.B.	16	27	1.7	8	0
Nichols, Det.	3	27	9.0	13	0
Brown, L.A. Rams	2	25	12.5	16	0
Waddy, Minn.	3	24	8.0	11	0
D. White, Dall.	6	21	3.5	8	0
Harrell, St.L.	9	20	2.2	7	1
Hogeboom, Dall.	15	19	1.3	11	0
Pisarcik, Phila.	7	19	2.7	16	2
Jaworski, Phila.	5	18	3.6	10	1
Monk, Wash.	2	18	9.0	18	0
Hodge, Atl.	2	17	8.5	9	0
Carter, T.B.	1	16	16.0	16	0
Stamps, Atl.	3	15	5.0	8	0
Dierking, T.B.	3	14	4.7	9	0
Martin, Det.	1	14	14.0	14	0
Cooper, S.F.	3	13	4.3	7	0
Hayes, Wash.	2	13	6.5	24	0
J. Jones, Dall.	8	13	1.6	6	0
Monroe, S.F.	3	13	4.3	7	0
Moore, Wash.	3	13	4.3	5	0
Chadwick, Det.	1	12	12.0	t12	1
McKinnon, Chi.	2	12	6.0	21	0
Coleman, Minn.	2	11	5.5	13	0
Lewis, Minn.	2	11	5.5	6	0
Wright, G.B.	8	11	1.4	5	0
Kramer, Minn.	15	9	0.6	14	0
Machurek, Det.	1	9	9.0	9	0
Benson, Atl.	3	8	2.7	6	0
B. Johnson, Atl.	3	8	2.7	11	0
T. Wilson, N.O.	2	8	4.0	5	0
Austin, Atl.	4	7	1.8	3	0
Hill, Dall.	1	7	7.0	7	0
Pridemore, Atl.	1	7	7.0	7	0
Dickey, G.B.	18	6	0.3	9	3
Harrington, St.L.	3	6	2.0	5	0
Donley, Dall.	2	5	2.5	6	0
Goodlow, N.O.	1	5	5.0	5	0
McIvor, St.L.	3	5	1.7	6	0
Jordan, Minn.	1	4	4.0	t4	1
Hipple, Det.	2	3	1.5	2	0
Nelson, Minn.	1	3	3.0	3	0
Campbell, G.B.	2	2	1.0	5	0
Cephous, N.Y. Giants	3	2	0.7	2	0
Guman, L.A. Rams	1	2	2.0	2	0
Manuel, N.Y. Giants	3	2	0.7	11	0
Peoples, T.B.	1	2	2.0	2	0
Walker, Wash.	1	2	2.0	2	0
West, G.B.	1	2	2.0	t2	1
Landry, Chi.	2	1	0.5	t1	1
Owens, T.B.	1	1	1.0	1	0
Baschnagel, Chi.	1	0	0.0	0	0
Ferragamo, L.A. Rams	4	0	0.0	2	0
Finzer, Chi.	2	0	0.0	5	0
Giacomarro, Atl.	1	0	0.0	0	0
Stabler, N.O.	1	−1	−1.0	−1	0
Moorehead, Chi.	1	−2	−2.0	−2	0
Duckett, N.O.	1	−3	−3.0	−3	0
Ellard, L.A. Rams	3	−5	−1.7	5	0
Marsh, St.L.	1	−5	−5.0	−5	0
Quick, Phila.	1	−5	−5.0	−5	0
Runager, S.F.	1	−5	−5.0	−5	0
Smith, Dall.	1	−5	−5.0	−5	0
Black, Det.	3	−6	−2.0	4	0
Hart, Wash.	3	−6	−2.0	−2	0
L. Thompson, Det.	3	−7	−2.3	4	0
D. Wilson, N.O.	3	−7	−2.3	−2	0
Green, St.L.	1	−10	−10.0	−10	0
Cavanaugh, S.F.	4	−11	−2.8	−1	0
Collins, Minn.	3	−14	−4.7	1	0
Hansen, N.O.	2	−27	−13.5	−12	0

t-Touchdown
Leader based on most yards gained

1984 PASSING

HIGHEST RATING
    AFC: 108.9—Dan Marino, Miami.
    NFC: 102.9—Joe Montana, San Francisco.

HIGHEST COMPLETION PERCENTAGE
    NFC: 67.3—Steve Bartkowski, Atlanta (269 attempts, 181 completions).
    AFC: 64.2—Dan Marino, Miami (564 attempts, 362 completions).

MOST ATTEMPTS, SEASON
    AFC: 564—Dan Marino, Miami.
    NFC: 560—Neil Lomax, St. Louis.

MOT COMPLETIONS, SEASON
    AFC: 362—Dan Marino, Miami.
    NFC: 345—Neil Lomax, St. Louis.

MOST YARDS, SEASON
    AFC: 5084—Dan Marino, Miami.
    NFC: 4614—Neil Lomax, St. Louis.

MOST YARDS, GAME
    AFC: 470—Dan Marino, Miami vs. L.A. Raiders, December 2 (57 attempts, 35
            completions).
    NFC: 468—Neil Lomax, St. Louis at Washington, December 16 (46 attempts, 37
            completions).

LONGEST GAIN
    AFC: 92—Marc Wilson (to Marcus Allen), L.A. Raiders vs. Seattle, October 7.
    NFC: 90—Ron Jaworski (to Mike Quick), Philadelphia vs. St. Louis, October 28
            (TD).

AVERAGE YARDS PER ATTEMPT
    AFC: 9.01—Dan Marino, Miami (564 attempts, 5084 yards).
    NFC: 8.40—Joe Montana, San Francisco (432 attempts, 3630 yards).

MOST TOUCHDOWN PASSES, SEASON
    AFC: 48—Dan Marino, Miami.
    NFC: 28—Neil Lomax, St. Louis.
            Joe Montana, San Francisco.

MOST TOUCHDOWN PASSES, GAME
    AFC: 5—John Elway, Denver vs. Minnesota, November 18.
           Dave Krieg, Seattle vs. Detroit, December 2.
           Dan Marino, Miami at Washington, September 2.
           Marc Wilson, L.A. Raiders at San Diego, October 21.
    NFC: 4—Gary Danielson, Detroit vs. Minnesota, September 23.
           Lynn Dickey, Green Bay vs. Detroit, October 28.
           Lynn Dickey, Green Bay vs. Minnesota, November 11.
           Phil Simms, N.Y. Giants vs. Philadelphia, September 2.
           Joe Theismann, Washington at Indianapolis, October 7.
           Danny White, Dallas vs. Washington, December 9.

LOWEST INTERCEPTION PERCENTAGE
    AFC: 1.9—Tony Eason, New England (431 attempts, 8 intercepted).
    NFC: 2.3—Joe Montana, San Francisco (432 attempts, 10 intercepted).

TEAM CHAMPION (Net Yards)
    AFC: 5018—Miami.
    NFC: 4257—St. Louis.

PASSING—TEAM

AMERICAN FOOTBALL CONFERENCE

	Atts.	Com.	Pct. Com.	Gross Yards	Tkd.- Yds. Lost	Net Yards	Avg. Yds. Att.	Avg. Yds. Com.	TD	Lng.	Had Int.
Miami	572	367	64.2	5146	14-128	5018	9.00	14.02	49	t80	18
San Diego	662	401	60.6	4928	36-285	4643	7.44	12.29	25	t88	21
Kansas City	593	305	51.4	3869	33-301	3568	6.52	12.69	21	t65	22
Seattle	497	283	56.9	3751	42-328	3423	7.55	13.25	32	t80	26
L.A. Raiders	491	266	54.2	3718	54-360	3358	7.57	13.98	21	92	28
Cincinnati	496	306	61.7	3659	45-358	3301	7.38	11.96	17	t80	22
Pittsburgh	443	240	54.2	3519	35-278	3241	7.94	14.66	25	t80	25
New England	500	292	58.4	3685	66-454	3231	7.37	12.62	26	t76	14
Houston	487	282	57.9	3610	49-382	3228	7.41	12.80	14	76	15
Cleveland	495	273	55.2	3490	55-358	3132	7.05	12.78	14	64	23
N.Y. Jets	488	272	55.7	3341	52-382	2959	6.85	12.28	20	49	21
Denver	475	263	55.4	3116	35-257	2859	6.56	11.85	22	73	17
Buffalo	588	298	50.7	3252	60-554	2698	5.53	10.91	18	t70	30
Indianapolis	411	206	50.1	2543	58-436	2107	6.19	12.34	13	t74	22
Conf. Total	7198	4054	---	51627	634-4861	46766	----	-----	317	t88	304
Conf. Average	514.1	289.6	56.3	3687.6	45.3-347.2	3340.4	7.17	12.73	22.6	--	21.7

NATIONAL FOOTBALL CONFERENCE

	Atts.	Com.	Pct. Com.	Gross Yards	Tkd.- Yds. Lost	Net Yards	Avg. Yds. Att.	Avg. Yds. Com.	TD	Lng.	Had Int.
St. Louis	566	347	61.3	4634	49-377	4257	8.19	13.35	28	t83	16
San Francisco	496	312	62.9	4079	27-178	3901	8.22	13.07	32	t80	10
N.Y. Giants	535	288	53.8	4066	55-434	3632	7.60	14.12	22	t65	18
Dallas	604	322	53.3	3995	48-389	3606	6.61	12.41	19	t68	26
Tampa Bay	563	334	59.3	3907	45-362	3545	6.94	11.70	22	t74	23
Green Bay	506	281	55.5	3740	42-310	3430	7.39	13.31	30	t79	30
Philadelphia	606	331	54.6	3823	60-463	3360	6.31	11.55	19	t90	17
Detroit	531	298	56.1	3787	61-486	3301	7.13	12.71	19	t77	22
Washington	485	286	59.0	3417	48-341	3076	7.05	11.95	24	t80	13
Atlanta	478	294	61.5	3546	67-496	3050	7.42	12.06	14	61	20
Minnesota	533	281	52.7	3337	64-465	2872	6.26	11.88	18	t70	25
New Orleans	476	246	51.7	3198	45-361	2837	6.72	13.00	21	74	28
Chicago	390	226	57.9	2695	36-232	2463	6.91	11.92	14	t61	15
L.A. Rams	358	176	49.2	2382	32-240	2142	6.65	13.53	16	68	17
Conf. Total	7127	4022	----	50606	679-5134	45472	----	-----	298	t90	280
Conf. Average	509.1	287.3	56.4	3614.7	48.5-366.7	3248.0	7.10	12.58	21.3	--	20.0
League Total	14325	8076	----	102233	1313-9995	92238	----	-----	615	t90	584
League Avg.	511.6	288.4	56.4	3651.2	46.9-357.0	3294.2	7.14	12.66	22.0	--	20.9

Leader based on net yards

TOP TEN PASSING QUALIFIERS

Player—Team	Att.	Cmp.	Pct. Cmp.	Yds.	Avg. Gain	TD	Pct. TD	Lg.	Int.	Pct. Int.	Rating Pts.
MARINO, DAN, Miami	564	362	64.2	5084	9.01	48	8.5	t80	17	3.0	108.9
Montana, Joe, S.F.	432	279	64.6	3630	8.40	28	6.5	t80	10	2.3	102.9
Eason, Tony, N.E.	431	259	60.1	3228	7.49	23	5.3	t76	8	1.9	93.4
Lomax, Neil, St.L.	560	345	61.6	4614	8.24	28	5.0	t83	16	2.9	92.5
Bartkowski, Steve, Atl.	269	181	67.3	2158	8.02	11	4.1	61	10	3.7	89.7
Theismann, Joe, Wash.	477	283	59.3	3391	7.11	24	5.0	t80	13	2.7	86.6
Dickey, Lynn, G.B.	401	237	59.1	3195	7.97	25	6.2	t79	19	4.7	85.6
Fouts, Dan, S.D.	507	317	62.5	3740	7.38	19	3.7	t61	17	3.4	83.4
Krieg, Dave, Sea.	480	276	57.5	3671	7.65	32	6.7	t80	24	5.0	83.3
Danielson, Gary, Det.	410	252	61.5	3076	7.50	17	4.1	t77	15	3.7	83.1

AFC INDIVIDUAL QUALIFIERS

Player—Team	Att.	Cmp.	Pct. Cmp.	Yds.	Avg. Gain	TD	Pct. TD	Lg.	Int.	Pct. Int.	Rating Pts.
MARINO, Mia.	564	362	64.2	5084	9.01	48	8.5	t80	17	3.0	108.9
Eason, N.E.	431	259	60.1	3228	7.49	23	5.3	t76	8	1.9	93.4
Fouts, S.D.	507	317	62.5	3740	7.38	19	3.7	t61	17	3.4	83.4
Krieg, Sea.	480	276	57.5	3671	7.65	32	6.7	t80	24	5.0	83.3
Anderson, Cin.	275	175	63.6	2107	7.66	10	3.6	t80	12	4.4	81.0
Kenney, K.C.	282	151	53.5	2098	7.44	15	5.3	t65	10	3.5	80.7
Moon, Hou.	450	259	57.6	3338	7.42	12	2.7	76	14	3.1	76.9
Elway, Den.	380	214	56.3	2598	6.84	18	4.7	73	15	3.9	76.8
Malone, Pitt.	272	147	54.0	2137	7.86	16	5.9	t61	17	6.3	73.4
Ryan, N.Y. Jets	285	156	54.7	1939	6.80	14	4.9	t44	14	4.9	72.0
Wilson, L.A. Raiders	282	153	54.3	2151	7.63	15	5.3	92	17	6.0	71.7
McDonald, Clev.	493	271	55.0	3472	7.04	14	2.8	64	23	4.7	67.3
Ferguson, Buff.	344	191	55.5	1991	5.79	12	3.5	t68	17	4.9	63.5
Blackledge, K.C.	294	147	50.0	1707	5.81	6	2.0	t46	11	3.7	59.2

AFC NON-QUALIFIERS

Player—Team	Att.	Cmp.	Pct. Cmp.	Yds.	Avg. Gain	TD	Pct. TD	Lg.	Int.	Pct. Int.	Rating Pts.
Luck, Hou.	36	22	61.1	256	7.11	2	5.6	37	1	2.8	89.6
Kubiak, Den.	75	44	58.7	440	5.87	4	5.3	41	1	1.3	87.6
Luther, S.D.	151	83	55.0	1163	7.70	5	3.3	t88	3	2.0	82.7
Woodley, Pitt.	156	85	54.5	1273	8.16	8	5.1	t80	7	4.5	79.9
Schonert, Cin.	117	78	66.7	945	8.08	4	3.4	t57	7	6.0	77.8
O'Brien, N.Y. Jets	203	116	57.1	1402	6.91	6	3.0	49	7	3.4	74.0
Pagel, Ind.	212	114	53.8	1426	6.73	8	3.8	t54	8	3.8	71.8
Campbell, Pitt.	15	8	53.3	109	7.27	1	6.7	t25	1	6.7	71.3
Plunkett, L.A. Raiders	198	108	54.5	1473	7.44	6	3.0	t73	10	5.1	67.6
Esiason, Cin.	102	51	50.0	530	5.20	3	2.9	36	3	2.9	62.9
Dufek, Buff.	150	74	49.3	829	5.53	4	2.7	t64	8	5.3	52.9
Avellini, Chi.-N.Y. Jets	53	30	56.6	288	5.43	0	0.0	50	3	5.7	48.3
Grogan, N.E.	68	32	47.1	444	6.53	3	4.4	t65	6	8.8	46.4
Schlichter, Ind.	140	62	44.3	702	5.01	3	2.1	54	7	5.0	46.2
Herrmann, Ind.	56	29	51.8	352	6.29	1	1.8	t74	6	10.7	37.8
Kofler, Buff.	93	33	35.5	432	4.65	2	2.2	t70	5	5.4	35.8
Osiecki, K.C.	17	7	41.2	64	3.76	0	0.0	19	1	5.9	27.6
Stankavage, Den.	18	4	22.2	58	3.22	0	0.0	16	1	5.6	17.4
Zorn, Sea.	17	7	41.2	80	4.71	0	0.0	21	2	11.8	16.4
(Less than 10 attempts)											
Allen, L.A. Raiders	4	1	25.0	38	9.50	0	0.0	38	0	0.0	66.7
Clayton, Mia.	1	0	0.0	0	0.00	0	0.0	0	1	100.0	0.0
Cox, Clev.	1	1	100.0	16	16.00	0	0.0	16	0	0.0	118.8
Dickey, Ind.	1	1	100.0	63	63.00	1	100.0	t63	0	0.0	158.3
Flick, Clev.	1	1	100.0	2	2.00	0	0.0	2	0	0.0	79.2
Holohan, S.D.	2	1	50.0	25	12.50	1	50.0	t25	0	0.0	135.4
Humm, L.A. Raiders	7	4	57.1	56	8.00	0	0.0	21	1	14.3	43.5
James, S.D.	2	0	0.0	0	0.00	0	0.0	0	1	50.0	0.0
Jensen, Mia.	1	1	100.0	35	35.00	1	100.0	t35	0	0.0	158.3
Kerrigan, N.E.	1	1	100.0	13	13.00	0	0.0	13	0	0.0	118.8
McInally, Cin.	2	2	100.0	77	38.50	0	0.0	43	0	0.0	118.8
Moore, Ind.	1	0	0.0	0	0.00	0	0.0	0	0	0.0	39.6
Moriarty, Hou.	1	1	100.0	16	16.00	0	0.0	16	0	0.0	118.8
Morris, Sea.	0	0	...	0	...	0	...	0	0	...	0.0
Mosley, Buff.	1	0	0.0	0	0.00	0	0.0	0	0	0.0	39.6
Stark, Ind.	1	0	0.0	0	0.00	0	0.0	0	1	100.0	0.0
Strock, Mia.	6	4	66.7	27	4.50	0	0.0	12	0	0.0	76.4
Willhite, Den.	2	1	50.0	20	10.00	0	0.0	20	0	0.0	85.4

NFC INDIVIDUAL QUALIFIERS

Player—Team	Att.	Cmp.	Pct. Cmp.	Yds.	Avg. Gain	TD	Pct. TD	Lg.	Int.	Pct. Int.	Rating Pts.
MONTANA, S.F.	432	279	64.6	3630	8.40	28	6.5	t80	10	2.3	102.9
Lomax, St.L.	560	345	61.6	4614	8.24	28	5.0	t83	16	2.9	92.5
Bartkowski, Atl.	269	181	67.3	2158	8.02	11	4.1	61	10	3.7	89.7
Theismann, Wash.	477	283	59.3	3391	7.11	24	5.0	t80	13	2.7	86.6
Dickey, G.B.	401	237	59.1	3195	7.97	25	6.2	t79	19	4.7	85.6
Danielson, Det.	410	252	61.5	3076	7.50	17	4.1	t77	15	3.7	83.1
DeBerg, T.B.	509	308	60.5	3554	6.98	19	3.7	55	18	3.5	79.3
Kemp, L.A. Rams	284	143	50.4	2021	7.12	13	4.6	t63	7	2.5	78.7
Simms, N.Y. Giants	533	286	53.7	4044	7.59	22	4.1	t65	18	3.4	78.1
Jaworski, Phil.	427	234	54.8	2754	6.45	16	3.7	t90	14	3.3	73.5
D. White, Dall.	233	126	54.1	1580	6.78	11	4.7	t66	11	4.7	71.5
Kramer, Minn.	236	124	52.5	1678	7.11	9	3.8	t70	10	4.2	70.6
Hogeboom, Dall.	367	195	53.1	2366	6.45	7	1.9	t68	14	3.8	63.7
Todd, N.O.	312	161	51.6	2178	6.98	11	3.5	74	19	6.1	60.6

NFC NON-QUALIFIERS

Player—Team	Att.	Cmp.	Pct. Cmp.	Yds.	Avg. Gain	TD	Pct. TD	Lg.	Int.	Pct. Int.	Rating Pts.
Fuller, Chi.	78	53	67.9	595	7.63	3	3.8	31	0	0.0	103.3
Cavanaugh, S.F.	61	33	54.1	449	7.36	4	6.6	t51	0	0.0	99.7
McMahon, Chi.	143	85	59.4	1146	8.01	8	5.6	t61	2	1.4	97.8
Archer, Atl.	18	11	61.1	181	10.06	1	5.6	34	1	5.6	90.3
D. Wilson, N.O.	93	51	54.8	647	6.96	7	7.5	t54	4	4.3	83.9
Pisarcik, Phil.	176	96	54.5	1036	5.89	3	1.7	40	3	1.7	70.6
Landry, Chi.	20	11	55.0	199	9.95	1	5.0	t55	3	15.0	66.5
Manning, Minn.	94	52	55.3	545	5.80	2	2.1	56	3	3.2	66.1
Hipple, Det.	38	16	42.1	246	6.47	1	2.6	40	1	2.6	62.0
Witkowski, Det.	34	13	38.2	210	6.18	0	0.0	39	0	0.0	59.7
Moroski, Atl.	191	102	53.4	1207	6.32	2	1.0	t48	9	4.7	56.8
Wilson, Minn.	195	102	52.3	1019	5.23	5	2.6	38	11	5.6	52.5
Campbell, G.B.	38	16	42.1	218	5.74	3	7.9	t43	5	13.2	47.8
J. Thompson, T.B.	52	25	48.1	337	6.48	2	3.8	t74	5	9.6	42.4
Stabler, N.O.	70	33	47.1	339	4.84	2	2.9	29	5	7.1	41.3
Lisch, Chi.	85	43	50.6	413	4.86	0	0.0	23	6	7.1	35.1
Wright, G.B.	62	27	43.5	310	5.00	2	3.2	56	6	9.7	30.4
Ferragamo, L.A. Rams	66	29	43.9	317	4.80	2	3.0	68	8	12.1	29.2
Machurek, Det.	43	14	32.6	193	4.49	0	0.0	48	6	14.0	8.3

St. Louis quarterback Neil Lomax had a terrific season in 1984, completing 61.6 percent of his passes for 4,614 yards and 28 touchdowns.

(Less than 10 attempts)

Anderson, Minn.	7	3	42.9	95	13.57	2	28.6	t43	1	14.3	89.9
Baschnagel, Chi.	2	1	50.0	7	3.50	0	0.0	7	0	0.0	58.3
D. Clark, S.F.	1	0	0.0	0	0.00	0	0.0	0	0	0.0	39.6
Coleman, Minn.	1	0	0.0	0	0.00	0	0.0	0	0	0.0	39.6
Dickerson, L.A. Rams	1	0	0.0	0	0.00	0	0.0	0	1	100.0	0.0
Dils, Minn.-L.A. Rams	7	4	57.1	44	6.29	1	14.3	t14	1	14.3	75.9
Dorsett, Dall.	1	0	0.0	0	0.00	0	0.0	0	1	100.0	0.0
Ellis, G.B.	4	1	25.0	17	4.25	0	0.0	17	0	0.0	44.8
Gajan, N.O.	1	1	100.0	34	34.00	1	100.0	t34	0	0.0	158.3
Galbreath, N.Y. Giants	1	1	100.0	13	13.00	0	0.0	13	0	0.0	118.8
Garcia, T.B.	1	0	0.0	0	0.00	0	0.0	0	0	0.0	39.6
Harmon, S.F.	2	0	0.0	0	0.00	0	0.0	0	0	0.0	39.6
Hart, Wash.	7	3	42.9	26	3.71	0	0.0	13	0	00	53.3
Jenkins, Det.	1	0	0.0	0	0.00	0	0.0	0	0	0.0	39.6
Jones, Det.	5	3	60.0	62	12.40	1	20.0	27	0	0.0	143.3
May, Phil.	1	1	100.0	33	33.00	0	0.0	33	0	0.0	118.8
McIvor, St.L.	4	0	0.0	0	0.00	0	0.0	0	0	0.0	39.6
Mitchell, St.L.	1	1	100.0	20	20.00	0	0.0	20	0	0.0	118.8
Montgomery, Phil.	2	0	0.0	0	0.00	0	0.0	0	0	0.0	39.6
Payton, Chi.	8	3	37.5	47	5.88	2	25.0	42	1	12.5	57.8
Perrin, St.L.	1	1	100.0	0	0.00	0	0.0	0	0	0.0	79.2
Renfro, Dall.	2	1	50.0	49	24.50	1	50.0	t49	0	0.0	135.4
Rutledge, N.Y. Giants	1	1	100.0	9	9.00	0	0.0	9	0	0.0	104.2
Scribner, G.B.	1	0	0.0	0	0.00	0	0.0	0	0	0.0	39.6
Springs, Dall.	1	0	0.0	0	0.00	0	0.0	0	0	0.0	39.6
Suhey, Chi.	1	0	0.0	0	0.00	0	0.0	0	0	0.0	39.6
J. Washington, Wash.	1	0	0.0	0	0.00	0	0.0	0	0	0.0	39.6
Wilder, T.B.	1	1	100.0	16	16.00	1	100.0	t16	0	0.0	158.3

t—Touchdown.

1984 PASS RECEIVING

MOST RECEPTIONS, SEASON
  NFC: 106—Art Monk, Washington.
  AFC: 89—Ozzie Newsome, Cleveland.

MOST RECEPTIONS, GAME
  AFC: 15—Kellen Winslow, San Diego at Green Bay, October 7 (157 yards).
  NFC: 12—Ottis Anderson, St. Louis at Washington, December 16 (124 yards).

MOST YARDS, SEASON
  NFC: 1555—Roy Green, St. Louis.
  AFC: 1395—John Stallworth, Pittsburgh.

MOST YARDS, GAME
  NFC: 206—James Lofton, Green Bay at Denver, October 15 (11 receptions).
  AFC: 191—Steve Largent, Seattle at Denver, November 25 (12 receptions).
      Ozzie Newsome, Cleveland at N.Y. Jets, October 14 (14 receptions).

LONGEST GAIN
  AFC: 92—Marcus Allen (from Marc Wilson), L.A. Raiders vs. Seattle, Oct. 7
  NFC: 90—Mike Quick (from Ron Jaworski), Phila. Vs. St. Louis, Oct. 28 (TD).

AVERAGE YARDS PER RECEPTION
  NFC: 22.0—James Lofton, Green Bay (62 receptions, 1361 yards).
  AFC: 20.4—Daryl Turner, Seattle (35 receptions, 715 yards).

MOST TOUCHDOWNS
  AFC: 18—Mark Clayton, Miami.
  NFC: 12—Roy Green, St. Louis.

TEAM LEADERS
  NFC: ATLANTA: 67, Stacey Bailey; CHICAGO: 45, Walter Payton; DALLAS:
      60, Doug Cosbie; DETROIT: 77, James Jones; GREEN BAY: 62,
      James Lofton; L.A. RAMS: 34, Henry Ellard; MINNESOTA: 47,
      Leo Lewis; NEW ORLEANS: 35, Hokie Gajan; N.Y. GIANTS: 48,
      Bob Johnson & Zeke Mowatt; PHILADELPHIA: 65, John Spag-
      nola; ST. LOUIS: 78, Roy Green; SAN FRANCISCO: 71, Roger
      Craig; TAMPA BAY: 85, James Wilder; WASHINGTON: 106, Art
      Monk.
  AFC: BUFFALO: 69, Byron Franklin; CINCINNATI: 65, Cris Collinsworth;
      CLEVELAND: 89, Ozzie Newsome; DENVER: 69, Steve Watson;
      HOUSTON: 69, Tim Smith; INDIANAPOLIS: 43, Raymond But-
      ler; KANSAS CITY: 62, Henry Marshall; L.A. RAIDERS: 80, Todd
      Christensen; MIAMI: 73, Mark Clayton; NEW ENGLAND: 66,
      Derrick Ramsey; N.Y. JETS: 68, Mickey Shuler; PITTSBURGH:
      80, John Stallworth; SAN DIEGO: 61, Charlie Joiner; SEATTLE:
      74, Steve Largent.

TOP TEN PASS RECEIVERS

Player—Team	No.	Yards	Avg.	Long	TDs.
MONK, ART, Washington	106	1372	12.9	72	7
Newsome, Ozzie, Cleveland	89	1001	11.2	52	5
Wilder, James, Tampa Bay	85	685	8.1	50	0
Stallworth, John, Pittsburgh	80	1395	17.4	51	11
Christensen, Todd, L.A. Raiders	80	1007	12.6	38	7
Green, Roy, St. Louis	78	1555	19.9	t83	12
Jones, James, Detroit	77	662	8.6	39	5
House, Kevin, Tampa Bay	76	1005	13.2	55	5
Largent, Steve, Seattle	74	1164	15.7	65	12
Clayton, Mark, Miami	73	1389	19.0	t65	18

TOP TEN PASS RECEIVERS BY YARDS

Player—Team	Yards	No.	Avg.	Long	TDs.
GREEN, ROY, St. Louis	1555	78	19.9	t83	12
Stallworth, John, Pittsburgh	1395	80	17.4	51	11
Clayton, Mark, Miami	1389	73	19.0	t65	18
Monk, Art, Washington	1372	106	12.9	72	7
Lofton, James, Green Bay	1361	62	22.0	t79	7
Duper, Mark, Miami	1306	71	18.4	t80	8
Watson, Steve, Denver	1170	69	17.0	73	7
Largent, Steve, Seattle	1164	74	15.7	65	12
Smith, Tim, Houston	1141	69	16.5	t75	4
Bailey, Stacey, Atlanta	1138	67	17.0	61	6

AFC—INDIVIDUALS

Player—Team	No.	Yds.	Avg.	Lng.	TD
Newsome, Clev.	89	1001	11.2	52	5
Stallworth, Pitt.	80	1395	17.4	51	11
Christensen, L.A. Raid.	80	1007	12.6	38	7
Largent, Sea.	74	1164	15.7	65	12
Clayton, Mia.	73	1389	19.0	t65	18
Duper, Mia.	71	1306	18.4	t80	8
Watson, Den.	69	1170	17.0	73	7
Smith, Hou.	69	1141	16.5	t75	4
Franklin, Buff.	69	862	12.5	t64	4
Shuler, N.Y. Jets	68	782	11.5	49	6
Ramsey, N.E.	66	792	12.0	34	7
Collinsworth, Cin.	64	989	15.5	t57	6
Allen, L.A. Raiders	64	758	11.8	92	5
Marshall, K.C.	62	912	14.7	37	4
Joiner, S.D.	61	793	13.0	41	6
Nathan, Mia.	61	579	9.5	26	2
Carson, K.C.	57	1078	18.9	57	4
Holohan, S.D.	56	734	13.1	51	1
Winslow, S.D.	55	663	12.1	33	2
Chandler, S.D.	52	708	13.6	t63	6
Harris, Cin.	48	759	15.8	t80	2
Starring, N.E.	46	657	14.3	t65	4
Lipps, Pitt.	45	860	19.1	t80	9
Barnwell, L.A. Raiders	45	851	18.9	t51	2
Winder, Den.	44	288	6.5	21	2
Butler, Ind.	43	664	15.4	t74	6
Moore, Mia.	43	573	13.3	t37	6
Johnson, Den.	42	587	14.0	49	6
Walker, N.Y. Jets	41	623	15.2	t44	7
J. Williams, Hou.	41	545	13.3	32	3
Sievers, S.D.	41	438	10.7	32	3
Dressel, Hou.	40	378	9.5	42	2
T. Porter, Ind.	39	590	15.1	t63	2
Dawson, N.E.	39	427	10.9	27	4
Jackson, S.D.	39	222	5.7	21	1
Morgan, N.E.	38	709	18.7	t76	5
Erenberg, Pitt.	38	358	9.4	25	1
Brown, K.C.	38	236	6.2	17	0
Turner, Sea.	35	715	20.4	t80	10
Brennan, Clev.	35	455	13.0	52	3
Jennings, Cin.	35	346	9.9	43	3
D. Johnson, Mia.	34	426	12.5	42	3
Bell, Buff.	34	277	8.1	37	1
Brooks, Cin.	34	268	7.9	t27	2
C. Young, Sea.	33	337	10.2	31	1
Hunter, Buff.	33	331	10.0	30	2
Moore, Buff.	33	172	5.2	14	0
Jones, N.Y. Jets	32	470	14.7	37	1
Doornink, Sea.	31	365	11.8	32	2
Moriarty, Hou.	31	206	6.6	24	1
Paige, K.C.	30	541	18.0	t65	4
Dennard, Buff.	30	417	13.9	t68	7
Alexander, Cin.	29	203	7.0	22	0
Hardy, Mia.	28	257	9.2	19	5
Scott, K.C.	28	253	9.0	27	3
Branch, L.A. Raiders	27	401	14.9	47	0
Willhite, Den.	27	298	11.0	63	0
Duckworth, S.D.	25	715	28.6	t88	4
McNeil, N.Y. Jets	25	294	11.8	32	1
Heard, K.C.	25	223	8.9	17	0
Riddick, Buff.	23	276	12.0	38	0
James, S.D.	23	206	9.0	31	0
Williams, L.A. Raiders	22	509	23.1	t75	4
Feacher, Clev.	22	382	17.4	64	1
Holston, Hou.	22	287	13.0	28	1
Bouza, Ind.	22	270	12.3	22	0
C. James, N.E.	22	159	7.2	16	0
Hughes, Sea.	22	121	5.5	25	1
Dawkins, Buff.	21	295	14.0	t37	2
Adams, Clev.	21	261	12.4	24	0
Holman, Cin.	21	239	11.4	27	1
Pollard, Pitt.	21	186	8.9	18	0
Holt, Clev.	20	261	13.1	36	0
Kreider, Cin.	20	243	12.2	27	1
Hector, N.Y. Jets	20	182	9.1	26	0
Edwards, Hou.	20	151	7.6	20	0
Gaffney, N.Y. Jets	19	285	15.0	29	0
Bryant, Hou.	19	278	14.6	28	0
Jones, N.E.	19	244	12.8	22	2
McMillan, Ind.	19	201	10.6	44	0
Kinnebrew, Cin.	19	159	8.4	22	1

Player—Team	No.	Yds.	Avg.	Lng.	TD
Brookins, Buff.	18	318	17.7	t70	1
Walls, Hou.	18	291	16.2	76	1
Cefalo, Mia.	18	185	10.3	t25	2
Thompson, Pitt.	17	291	17.1	59	3
Johns, Sea.	17	207	12.2	32	1
Sawyer, Den.	17	122	7.2	25	0
Bendross, S.D.	16	213	13.3	29	0
Tatupu, N.E.	16	159	9.9	24	0
Dennison, N.Y. Jets	16	141	8.8	20	1
Kay, Den.	16	136	8.5	21	3
Abercrombie, Pitt.	16	135	8.4	59	0
Collins, N.E.	16	100	6.3	19	0
Middleton, Ind.	15	112	7.5	16	1
B. Jackson, K.C.	15	101	6.7	11	1
Humphery, N.Y. Jets	14	206	14.7	t44	1
Young, Ind.	14	164	11.7	28	2
Dickey, Ind.	14	135	9.6	33	0
King, L.A. Raiders	14	99	7.1	15	0
Walker, Sea.	13	236	18.2	41	1
Jensen, Mia.	13	139	10.7	20	2
Lacy, K.C.	13	87	6.7	20	2
Rose, Mia.	12	195	16.3	t34	2
Curtis, Cin.	12	135	11.3	22	0
Green, Clev.	12	124	10.3	t44	1
Sherwin, Ind.	11	169	15.4	26	0
Fryar, N.E.	11	164	14.9	26	1
Martin, Cin.	11	164	14.9	42	0
Henry, Ind.	11	139	12.6	t19	2
Byner, Clev.	11	118	10.7	26	0
J. Wright, Den.	11	118	10.7	21	1
Lane, Sea.	11	101	9.2	t55	1
W. Arnold, Wash.-K.C.	11	95	8.6	15	1
Egloff, S.D.	11	92	8.4	17	0
Hancock, K.C.	10	217	21.7	t46	1
Walker, Clev.	10	122	12.2	25	0
Minter, N.Y. Jets	10	109	10.9	t39	1
Barber, N.Y. Jets	10	79	7.9	17	0
McCloskey, Hou.	9	152	16.9	51	1
Sampson, Den.	9	123	13.7	25	1
McGee, S.D.	9	76	8.4	43	2
Neal, Buff.	9	76	8.4	18	0
Morris, Sea.	9	61	6.8	18	0
Moore, Ind.	9	52	5.8	12	0
Wonsley, Ind.	9	47	5.2	17	0
Alexander, Den.	8	132	16.5	41	1
C. Weathers, N.E.	8	115	14.4	29	2
Tice, Sea.	8	90	11.3	30	3
Castor, Sea.	8	89	11.1	21	0
J.T. Smith, K.C.	8	69	8.6	16	0
Barnett, Buff.	8	67	8.4	18	0
Carter, Mia.	8	53	6.6	15	0
Hawthorne, N.E.	7	127	18.1	26	0
B. Davis, Clev.	7	119	17.0	t43	2
Skansi, Sea.	7	85	12.1	27	0
Capers, Pitt.	7	81	11.6	19	0
Hawkins, L.A. Raiders	7	51	7.3	15	0
Brammer, Buff.	7	49	7.0	12	0
Beckman, K.C.	7	44	6.3	9	1
Verser, Cin.	6	113	18.8	28	0
Mullins, Hou.	6	85	14.2	25	1
Bennett, Mia.	6	44	7.3	20	1
Paige, N.Y. Jets	6	31	5.2	10	1
Parros, Den.	6	25	4.2	9	0
Metzelaars, Sea.	5	80	16.0	25	0
Harper, N.Y. Jets	5	71	14.2	28	0
Kolodziejski, Pitt.	5	59	11.8	22	0
Va. Williams, Buff.	5	46	9.2	32	1
Pruitt, Clev.	5	29	5.8	9	0
White, Clev.	5	29	5.8	17	0
Morris, S.D.	5	20	4.0	9	0
Roaches, Hou.	4	69	17.3	24	0
Cunningham, Pitt.	4	64	16.0	29	1
Mosley, Buff.	4	38	9.5	17	0
Muncie, S.D.	4	38	9.5	20	0
Robinson, N.E.	4	32	8.0	17	1
Casper, L.A. Raiders	4	29	7.3	13	2
White, Buff.	4	28	7.0	11	0
Lang, Den.	4	24	6.0	t9	1
Summers, Den.	3	32	10.7	16	0
Klever, N.Y. Jets	3	29	9.7	13	1
C. Bryant, Sea.	3	20	6.7	11	0

Player—Team	No.	Yds.	Avg.	Lng.	TD
Nelson, Pitt.	2	31	15.5	19	0
Sohn, N.Y. Jets	2	28	14.0	16	0
Sweeney, Pitt.	2	25	12.5	16	0
Myles, Den.	2	22	11.0	12	0
Scales, Sea.	2	22	11.0	11	0
Brewer, Den.	2	20	10.0	16	0
S. Wilson, Cin.	2	15	7.5	11	0
Kern, Cin.	2	14	7.0	9	0
Pruitt, L.A. Raiders	2	12	6.0	8	0
Farley, Cin.	2	11	5.5	10	0
P. Johnson, S.D.	2	7	3.5	7	0
Dixon, Sea.	2	6	3.0	6	0
Young, Clev.	1	47	47.0	47	0
Pratt, Sea.	1	30	30.0	30	0
Kubiak, Den.	1	20	20.0	20	0
Bolden, Clev.	1	19	19.0	19	0
Warner, Sea.	1	19	19.0	19	0
Stracka, Clev.	1	15	15.0	15	0
Little, K.C.	1	13	13.0	13	0
Gillespie, Pitt.	1	12	12.0	12	0
Bruckner, N.Y. Jets	1	11	11.0	11	0
Gissinger, S.D.	1	3	3.0	3	0
F. Harris, Sea.	1	3	3.0	3	0
Logan, Den.	1	3	3.0	3	0
Jensen, L.A. Raiders	1	1	1.0	t1	1
Munoz, Cin.	1	1	1.0	t1	1
Fouts, S.D.	1	0	0.0	0	0
McDonald, Clev.	1	—4	—4.0	—4	0
Studdard, Den.	1	—4	—4.0	—4	0

AFC—TOP 25 PASS RECEIVERS BY YARDS

Player—Team	Yds.	No.	Avg.	Lng.	TD
Stallworth, Pitt.	1395	80	17.4	51	11
Clayton, Mia.	1389	73	19.0	t65	18
Duper, Mia.	1306	71	18.4	t80	8
Watson, Den.	1170	69	17.0	73	7
Largent, Sea.	1164	74	15.7	65	12
Smith, Hou.	1141	69	16.5	t75	4
Carson, K.C.	1078	57	18.9	57	4
Christensen, L.A. Raid.	1007	80	12.6	38	7
Newsome, Clev.	1001	89	11.2	52	5
Collinsworth, Cin.	989	64	15.5	t57	6
Marshall, K.C.	912	62	14.7	37	4
Franklin, Buff.	862	69	12.5	t64	4
Lipps, Pitt.	860	45	19.1	t80	9
Barnwell, L.A. Raiders.	851	45	18.9	t51	2
Joiner, S.D.	793	61	13.0	41	6
Ramsey, N.E.	792	66	12.0	34	7
Shuler, N.Y. Jets	782	68	11.5	49	6
Harris, Cin.	759	48	15.8	t80	2
Allen, L.A. Raiders	758	64	11.8	92	5
Holohan, S.D.	734	56	13.1	51	1
Duckworth, S.D.	715	25	28.6	t88	4
Turner, Sea.	715	35	20.4	t80	10
Morgan, N.E.	709	38	18.7	t76	5
Chandler, S.D.	708	52	13.6	t63	6
Butler, Ind.	664	43	15.4	t74	6

NFC—INDIVIDUALS

Player—Team	No.	Yds.	Avg.	Lng.	TD
MONK, Wash.	106	1372	12.9	72	7
Wilder, T.B.	85	685	8.1	50	0
Green, St.L.	78	1555	19.9	t83	12
Jones, Det.	77	662	8.6	39	5
House, T.B.	76	1005	13.2	55	5
Craig, S.F.	71	675	9.5	t64	3
Anderson, St.L.	70	611	8.7	57	2
Bailey, Atl.	67	1138	17.0	61	6
Spagnola, Phila.	65	701	10.8	34	1
Lofton, G.B.	62	1361	22.0	t79	7
Quick, Phila.	61	1052	17.2	t90	9
Carter, T.B.	60	816	13.6	t74	5
Cosbie, Dall.	60	789	13.2	36	4
Montgomery, Phila.	60	501	8.4	28	0
Hill, Dall.	58	864	14.9	t66	5
D. Clark, S.F.	52	880	16.9	t80	6
Tilley, St.L.	52	758	14.6	42	5
A. Jackson, Atl.	52	731	14.1	t50	2
Dorsett, Dall.	51	459	9.0	t68	1
L. Thompson, Det.	50	773	15.5	t66	6
Johnson, N.Y. Giants	48	795	16.6	45	7
Mowatt, N.Y. Giants	48	698	14.5	34	6
Lewis, Minn.	47	830	17.7	56	4
Springs, Dall.	46	454	9.9	t57	3
T. Brown, Minn.	46	349	7.6	35	3
Payton, Chi.	45	368	8.2	31	0
Coffman, G.B.	43	562	13.1	t44	9
Muhammad, Wash.	42	729	17.4	t80	4
Suhey, Chi.	42	312	7.4	23	2
Riggs, Atl.	42	277	6.6	21	0
Cooper, S.F.	41	459	11.2	26	4
Solomon, S.F.	40	737	18.4	t64	10
Marsh, St.L.	39	608	15.6	47	5
Jones, Minn.	38	591	15.6	t70	1
Jordan, Minn.	38	414	10.9	26	2
Chadwick, Det.	37	540	14.6	46	2
Galbreath, N.Y. Giants.	37	357	9.6	37	0
Ellis, G.B.	36	312	8.7	22	2
Renfro, Dall.	35	583	16.7	t60	2
Gajan, N.O.	35	288	8.2	51	2
Nichols, Det.	34	744	21.9	t77	1
Ellard, L.A. Rams	34	622	18.3	t63	6
Gault, Chi.	34	587	17.3	t61	6
Cox, Atl.	34	329	9.7	t23	3
Manuel, N.Y. Giants	33	619	18.8	53	4
Harris, Clev.-Dall.	33	521	15.8	43	2
Groth, N.O.	33	487	14.8	31	0
W. Wilson, N.O.	33	314	9.5	t34	3
Haddix, Phila.	33	231	7.0	22	0
Donley, Dall.	32	473	14.8	t49	2
Oliver, Phila.	32	142	4.4	21	0
Da. Hill, L.A. Rams	31	300	9.7	26	1
Sims, Det.	31	239	7.7	20	0
Woodruff, Phila.	30	484	16.1	38	3
Didier, Wash.	30	350	11.7	44	5
Young, S.F.	29	597	20.6	74	3
Moorehead, Chi.	29	497	17.1	50	1
McKinnon, Chi.	29	431	14.9	t32	3
J. Bell, T.B.	29	397	13.7	27	4
Clark, G.B.	29	234	8.1	20	2
Brenner, N.O.	28	554	19.8	57	6
Tyler, S.F.	28	230	8.2	t26	2
Nelson, Minn.	27	162	6.0	17	1
Epps, G.B.	26	435	16.7	56	3
Jackson, Phila.	26	398	15.3	t83	1
Jefferson, G.B.	26	339	13.0	33	0
Mitchell, St.L.	26	318	12.2	t44	3
Newsome, Dall.	26	263	10.1	29	0
C. Benson, Atl.	26	244	9.4	30	0
Ferrell, St.L.	26	218	8.4	21	1
Carpenter, N.Y. Giants.	26	209	8.0	19	1
B. Williams, N.Y.G.	24	471	19.6	t65	3
B. Johnson, Atl.	24	371	15.5	t45	3
Giles, T.B.	24	310	12.9	38	2
Hodge, Atl.	24	234	9.8	26	0
Brown, L.A. Rams	23	478	20.8	54	4
Francis, S.F.	23	285	12.4	32	2
T. Bell, T.B.	22	350	15.9	29	0
Goodlow, N.O.	22	281	12.8	23	3
Armstrong, T.B.	22	180	8.2	18	3
White, Minn.	21	399	19.0	47	3
Scott, N.O.	21	278	13.2	37	1
Jenkins, Det.	21	246	11.7	68	0
Dickerson, L.A. Rams	21	139	6.6	19	0
Guman, L.A. Rams	19	161	8.5	29	0
Ivery, G.B.	19	141	7.4	18	1
Nehemiah, S.F.	18	357	19.8	t59	2
Brown, Wash.	18	200	11.1	36	3
Warren, Wash.	18	192	10.7	26	0

Player—Team	No.	Yds.	Avg.	Lng.	TD	Player—Team	No.	Yds.	Avg.	Lng.	TD
Wilson, S.F.	17	245	14.4	44	1	Hardy, N.O.	4	50	12.5	t28	1
LaFleur, St.L.	17	198	11.6	23	0	Stamps, Atl.	4	48	12.0	31	0
Moore, Wash.	17	115	6.8	18	2	Redden, L.A. Rams	4	39	9.8	6	0
Anderson, Minn.	17	102	6.0	t28	1	Childs, G.B.	4	32	8.0	17	0
Lewis, Det.	16	236	14.8	58	3	Gentry, Chi.	4	29	7.3	13	0
Senser, Minn.	15	110	7.3	26	0	G. Lewis, G.B.	4	29	7.3	15	0
Dr. Hill, L.A. Rams	14	390	27.9	68	4	Anderson, Chi.	3	77	25.7	t49	1
Rubick, Det.	14	188	13.4	29	1	Mandley, Det.	3	38	12.7	19	0
Mularkey, Minn.	14	134	9.6	26	2	Campbell, Hou.-N.O.	3	27	9.0	15	0
Harrell, St.L.	14	106	7.6	15	0	Carver, T.B.	3	27	9.0	12	0
J. Washington, Wash.	13	74	5.7	12	0	Duckett, N.O.	3	24	8.0	11	0
Morris, N.Y. Giants	12	124	10.3	26	0	Goode, St.L.	3	23	7.7	10	0
Anthony, N.O.	12	113	9.4	32	0	McCall, Det.	3	15	5.0	7	0
Cain, Atl.	12	87	7.3	18	0	Ring, S.F.	3	10	3.3	15	0
G. Rogers, N.O.	12	76	6.3	15	0	Mullady, N.Y. Giants	2	35	17.5	22	0
Collins, Minn.	11	143	13.0	t43	1	Krenk, Chi.	2	31	15.5	24	0
Monroe, S.F.	11	139	12.6	47	1	Cornwell, Dall.	2	23	11.5	13	1
Pittman, St.L.	10	145	14.5	50	0	Garrity, Pitt.-Phila.	2	22	11.0	12	0
McGrath, Wash.	10	118	11.8	24	1	Hardy, Phila.	2	22	11.0	13	0
Seay, Wash.	9	111	12.3	19	1	Cassidy, G.B.	2	16	8.0	10	0
Dunsmore, Chi.	9	106	11.8	25	1	Owens, T.B.	2	13	6.5	9	1
Kab, Phila.	9	102	11.3	26	3	Crutchfield, L.A. Rams	2	11	5.5	7	1
Crouse, G.B.	9	93	10.3	25	1	McMahon, Chi.	1	42	42.0	42	0
Saldi, Chi.	9	90	10.0	20	0	Danielson, Det.	1	22	22.0	t22	1
Grant, L.A. Rams	9	64	7.1	15	0	Kramer, Minn.	1	20	20.0	t20	1
Bussey, Det.	9	63	7.0	19	0	LeCount, Minn.	1	14	14.0	14	0
Woolfolk, N.Y. Giants	9	53	5.9	13	0	Cameron, Chi.	1	13	13.0	13	0
C. Thomas, Chi.	9	39	4.3	9	0	Simms, N.Y. Giants	1	13	13.0	13	0
McConkey, N.Y. Giants	8	154	19.3	39	0	D'Addio, Det.	1	12	12.0	12	0
Miller, N.O.	8	81	10.1	22	1	Hasselbeck, Minn.	1	10	10.0	10	0
Huckleby, G.B.	8	65	8.1	13	0	Martin, Det.	1	9	9.0	9	0
Griffin, Wash.	8	43	5.4	8	0	Taylor, G.B.	1	8	8.0	8	0
Farmer, L.A. Rams	7	75	10.7	23	0	Cabral, Chi.	1	7	7.0	7	0
Frank, S.F.	7	60	8.6	21	1	Carmichael, Dall.	1	7	7.0	7	0
J. Jones, Dall.	7	57	8.1	19	1	Curran, Atl.	1	7	7.0	7	0
M. Williams, Phila.	7	47	6.7	15	0	Hutchison, Chi.	1	7	7.0	7	0
Riggins, Wash.	7	43	6.1	11	0	Kane, Wash.	1	7	7.0	7	0
Barber, L.A. Rams	7	42	6.0	11	0	Matthews, Atl.	1	7	7.0	7	0
Love, St.L.	7	33	4.7	16	1	Smith, Dall.	1	7	7.0	7	0
Hoover, Phila.	6	143	23.8	44	2	Tuttle, T.B.-Atl.	1	7	7.0	7	0
Landrum, Atl.	6	66	11.0	30	0	Faulkner, L.A. Rams	1	6	6.0	6	0
Tice, N.O.	6	55	9.2	17	1	Jones, Wash.	1	6	6.0	6	0
West, G.B.	6	54	9.0	t29	4	Jordan, Chi.	1	6	6.0	6	0
Baschnagel, Chi.	6	53	8.8	17	0	Phillips, Dall.	1	6	6.0	6	0
Dixon, T.B.	5	69	13.8	21	0	Dierking, T.B.	1	5	5.0	t5	1
Mack, St.L.	5	61	12.2	22	0	Garrett, Wash.	1	5	5.0	5	0
Rodgers, G.B.	5	56	11.2	22	0	Mistler, Buff.-N.Y.G.	1	5	5.0	5	0
Walker, Wash.	5	52	10.4	19	1	Belcher, N.Y. Giants	1	4	4.0	4	0
Carroll, T.B.	5	50	10.0	17	1	Moore, G.B.	1	3	3.0	t3	1
Rice, Minn.	4	59	14.8	24	1	Harmon, S.F.	1	2	2.0	2	0
J. McDonald, Rams	4	55	13.8	22	0	Pozderac, Dall.	1	1	1.0	1	0

NFC—TOP 25 PASS RECEIVERS BY YARDS

Player—Team	Yds.	No.	Avg.	Lng.	TD	Player—Team	Yds.	No.	Avg.	Lng.	TD
GREEN, St.L.	1555	78	19.9	t83	12	Tilley, St.L.	758	52	14.6	42	5
Monk, Wash.	1372	106	12.9	72	7	Nichols, Det.	744	34	21.9	t77	1
Lofton, G.B.	1361	62	22.0	t79	7	Solomon, S.F.	737	40	18.4	t64	10
Bailey, Atl.	1138	67	17.0	61	6	A. Jackson, Atl.	731	52	14.1	t50	2
Quick, Phila.	1052	61	17.2	t90	9	Muhammad, Wash.	729	42	17.4	t80	4
House, T.B.	1005	76	13.2	55	5	Spagnola, Phila.	701	65	10.8	34	1
D. Clark, S.F.	880	52	16.9	t80	6	Mowatt, N.Y. Giants	698	48	14.5	34	6
Hill, Dall.	864	58	14.9	t66	5	Wilder, T.B.	685	85	8.1	50	0
Lewis, Minn.	830	47	17.7	56	4	Craig, S.F.	675	71	9.5	t64	3
Carter, T.B.	816	60	13.6	t74	5	Jones, Det.	662	77	8.6	39	5
Johnson, N.Y. Giants	795	48	16.6	45	7	Ellard, L.A. Rams	622	34	18.3	t63	6
Cosbie, Dall.	789	60	13.2	36	4	Manuel, N.Y. Giants	619	33	18.8	53	4
L. Thompson, Det.	773	50	15.5	t66	6						

t-Touchdown
Leader based on most passes caught

1984 INTERCEPTIONS

MOST INTERCEPTIONS, SEASON
 AFC: 10—Kenny Easley, Seattle.
 NFC: 9—Tom Flynn, Green Bay.

MOST INTERCEPTIONS, GAME
 NFC: 3—Vernon Dean, Washington vs. N.Y. Giants, September 16 (61 yards).
   Tom Flynn, Green Bay vs. Detroit, October 28 (23 yards).
 AFC: 3—Kenny Easley, Seattle at San Diego, October 29 (33 yards).

MOST YARDS RETURNING INTERCEPTIONS
 AFC: 220—Mike Haynes, L.A. Raiders (6 interceptions).
 NFC: 166—LeRoy Irvin, L.A. Rams (5 interceptions).

LONGEST INTERCEPTION RETURN
 AFC: 99—Gill Byrd, San Diego at Kansas City, October 14 (TD).
 NFC: 99—Tim Lewis, Green Bay vs. L.A. Rams, November 18 (TD).

MOST TOUCHDOWNS, SEASON
 AFC: 2—Dave Brown, Seattle.
   Gill Byrd, San Diego.
   Kenny Easley, Seattle.
   Keith Simpson, Seattle.
   Sam Washington, Pittsburgh.
 NFC: 2—Vernon Dean, Washington.
   LeRoy Irvin, L.A. Rams.
   Dennis Winston, New Orleans.

MOST TOUCHDOWNS, GAME
 AFC: 2—Dave Brown, Seattle vs. Kansas City, November 4.
 NFC: 1—By 18 players.

TEAM LEADERS
 NFC: ATLANTA: 5, Kenny Johnson; CHICAGO: 5, Gary Fencik & Leslie Frazier; DALLAS: 7, Michael Downs; DETROIT: 6, Bobby Watkins; GREEN BAY: 9, Tom Flynn; L.A. RAMS: 5, LeRoy Irvin; MINNESOTA: 3, Rufus Bess; NEW ORLEANS: 4, Dave Waymer; N.Y. GIANTS: 7, Mark Haynes; PHILADELPHIA: 7, Ray Ellis; ST. LOUIS: 5, Lionel Washington; SAN FRANCISCO: 4, Ronnie Lott & Keena Turner; TAMPA BAY: 5, Mark Cotney; WASHINGTON: 7, Vernon Dean.
 AFC: BUFFALO: 5, Charles Romes; CINCINNATI: 4, Louis Breeden, Robert Jackson & Bobby Kemp; CLEVELAND: 5, Hanford Dixon & Al Gross; DENVER: 6, Steve Foley & Mike Harden; HOUSTON: 4, Willie Tullis; INDIANAPOLIS: 6, Eugene Daniel; KANSAS CITY: 7, Deron Cherry; L.A. RAIDERS: 6, Mike Haynes; MIAMI: 6, Glenn Blackwood; NEW ENGLAND: 3, Ray Clayborn & Ronnie Lippett; N.Y. JETS: 4, Russell Carter; PITTSBURGH: 7, Donnie Shell; SAN DIEGO: 4, Gill Byrd; SEATTLE: 10, Kenny Easley.

TEAM CHAMPION:
 AFC: 38—Seattle.
 NFC: 28—Dallas.

INTERCEPTIONS—TEAM

AMERICAN FOOTBALL CONFERENCE

Team	No.	Yards	Avg.	Long	TDs.
Seattle	38	697	18.3	t90	7
Denver	31	510	16.5	63	4
Pittsburgh	31	433	14.0	t69	4
Kansas City	30	465	15.5	t71	2
Cincinnati	25	368	14.7	70	4
Miami	24	478	19.9	t86	2
L.A. Raiders	20	339	17.0	t97	2
Cleveland	20	236	11.8	47	0
San Diego	19	499	26.3	t99	4
Indianapolis	18	190	10.6	t59	1
New England	17	210	12.4	85	0
Buffalo	16	233	14.6	55	0
N.Y. Jets	15	152	10.1	28	0
Houston	13	139	10.7	26	0
Conference Total	317	4949	----	t99	30
Conference Average	22.6	353.5	15.6	--	2.1

NATIONAL FOOTBALL CONFERENCE

Team	No.	Yards	Avg.	Long	TDs.
Dallas	28	297	10.6	43	2
Green Bay	27	338	12.5	t99	2
San Francisco	25	345	13.8	t54	2
Washington	21	391	18.6	50	4
Chicago	21	290	13.8	61	1
St. Louis	21	163	7.8	t25	1
Philadelphia	20	287	14.4	33	0
N.Y. Giants	19	182	9.6	29	0
Tampa Bay	18	308	17.1	38	1
L.A. Rams	17	399	23.5	t81	3
Detroit	14	87	6.2	36	0
New Orleans	13	213	16.4	t47	3
Atlanta	12	147	12.3	t35	1
Minnesota	11	120	10.9	t53	1
Conference Total	267	3567	----	t99	21
Conference Average	19.1	254.8	13.4	--	1.5
League Total	584	8516	----	t99	51
League Average	20.9	304.1	14.6	--	1.8

TOP TEN INTERCEPTORS

Player—Team	No.	Yards	Avg.	Long	TDs.
EASLEY, KENNY, Seattle	10	126	12.6	t58	2
Flynn, Tom, Green Bay	9	106	11.8	31	0
Brown, Dave, Seattle	8	179	22.4	t90	2
Lewis, Tim, Green Bay	7	151	21.6	t99	1
Downs, Michael, Dallas	7	126	18.0	t27	1
Ellis, Ray, Philadelphia	7	119	17.0	31	0
Dean, Vernon, Washington	7	114	16.3	t36	2
Haynes, Mark, N.Y. Giants	7	90	12.9	22	0
Cherry, Deron, Kansas City	7	140	20.0	67	0
Shell, Donnie, Pittsburgh	7	61	8.7	t52	1

AFC—INDIVIDUALS

Player—Team	No.	Yds.	Avg.	Lng.	TD
EASLEY, Seattle	10	126	12.6	t58	2
Brown, Sea.	8	179	22.4	t90	2
Cherry, K.C.	7	140	20.0	67	0
Shell, Pitt.	7	61	8.7	t52	1
Haynes, L.A. Raiders	6	220	36.7	t97	1
G. Blackwood, Mia.	6	169	28.2	50	0
Washington, Pitt.	6	138	23.0	t69	2
Ross, K.C.	6	124	20.7	t71	1
Foley, Den.	6	97	16.2	t40	1
Harden, Den.	6	79	13.2	t45	1
J. Harris, Sea.	6	79	13.2	29	0
Daniel, Ind.	6	25	4.2	18	0
Romes, Buff.	5	130	26.0	55	0
Gross, Clev.	5	103	20.6	47	0
Woodruff, Pitt.	5	56	11.2	t42	1
Dixon, Clev.	5	31	6.2	18	0
Byrd, S.D.	4	157	39.3	t99	2
Simpson, Sea.	4	138	34.5	t76	2
Judson, Mia.	4	121	30.3	t60	1
Breeden, Cin.	4	96	24.0	70	0
T. Jackson, Sea.	4	78	19.5	t62	1
Wilson, Den.	4	59	14.8	22	0
Lewis, K.C.	4	57	14.3	31	0
Tullis, Hou.	4	48	12.0	22	0
McElroy, L.A. Raiders	4	42	10.5	31	0
Jackson, Cin.	4	32	8.0	t28	1
Kemp, Cin.	4	27	6.8	14	0
Carter, N.Y. Jets	4	26	6.5	19	0
Clayborn, N.E.	3	102	34.0	85	0
Hinkle, Pitt.	3	77	25.7	43	0
Randle, Ind.	3	66	22.0	54	0
Taylor, Sea.	3	63	21.0	37	0
Lowe, S.D.	3	61	20.3	t32	1
Williams, Pitt.	3	49	16.3	44	0
Horton, Cin.	3	48	16.0	t48	1
Freeman, Buff.	3	45	15.0	45	0
McNeal, Mia.	3	41	13.7	30	1
B.R. Smith, S.D.	3	41	13.7	21	0
L. Blackwood, Mia.	3	29	9.7	15	0
Lankford, Mia.	3	25	8.3	22	0

Player—Team	No.	Yds.	Avg.	Lng.	TD	Player—Team	No.	Yds.	Avg.	Lng.	TD
Hartwig, Hou.	3	23	7.7	19	0	Dombroski, N.E.	1	23	23.0	23	0
Lippett, N.E.	3	23	7.7	13	0	R. Jackson, Den.	1	23	23.0	23	0
Krauss, Ind.	3	20	6.7	18	0	Eason, Hou.	1	20	20.0	20	0
D. Smith, Den.	3	13	4.3	10	0	Gaines, Sea.	1	18	18.0	18	0
Carpenter, Wash.-Buff.	3	11	3.7	11	0	Perry, Clev.	1	17	17.0	17	0
Burroughs, Ind.	3	9	3.0	6	0	C. Jackson, K.C.	1	16	16.0	16	0
Mecklenburg, Den.	2	105	52.5	63	0	Barnes, L.A. Raiders	1	15	15.0	15	0
Robbins, Den.	2	62	31.0	t62	1	Cameron, Cin.	1	15	15.0	15	0
Radecic, K.C.	2	54	27.0	35	1	Kush, Buff.	1	15	15.0	15	0
Ray, N.Y. Jets	2	54	27.0	28	0	Scholtz, Sea.	1	15	15.0	15	0
King, S.D.	2	52	26.0	37	0	Blanton, K.C.	1	14	14.0	14	0
Simmons, Cin.	2	43	21.5	t43	1	Ryan, Den.	1	13	13.0	13	0
Turner, S.D.	2	43	21.5	43	0	Springs, N.Y. Jets	1	13	13.0	13	0
Marion, N.E.	2	39	19.5	26	0	Cole, Pitt.	1	12	12.0	12	0
McAlister, K.C.	2	33	16.5	22	0	Gregor, S.D.	1	12	12.0	12	0
Williams, Cin.	2	33	16.5	33	0	Lyday, Hou.	1	12	12.0	12	0
Martin, L.A. Raiders	2	31	15.5	17	1	Van Pelt, L.A. Raiders	1	9	9.0	9	0
Young, S.D.	2	31	15.5	31	0	Banks, Clev.	1	8	8.0	8	0
Busick, Den.	2	21	10.5	16	0	J. Davis, L.A. Raiders	1	8	8.0	8	0
Burruss, K.C.	2	16	8.0	16	0	Glasgow, Ind.	1	8	8.0	8	0
Lynn, N.Y. Jets	2	16	8.0	16	0	Duhe, Mia.	1	7	7.0	7	0
R. James, N.E.	2	14	7.0	14	0	Smith, Buff.	1	7	7.0	7	0
R. Griffin, Cin.	2	13	6.5	13	0	Sowell, Mia.	1	7	7.0	7	0
Schroy, N.Y. Jets	2	13	6.5	13	0	Comeaux, Den.	1	5	5.0	5	0
Daniels, K.C.	2	11	5.5	11	0	Lilly, Den.	1	5	5.0	5	0
M. Davis, L.A. Raiders	2	11	5.5	11	0	Turner, Cin.	1	4	4.0	4	0
Cousineau, Clev.	2	9	4.5	9	0	Blackmon, N.E.	1	3	3.0	3	0
Merriweather, Pitt.	2	9	4.5	8	0	Davis, Ind.	1	3	3.0	3	0
Buttle, N.Y. Jets	2	5	2.5	5	0	Hayes, L.A. Raiders	1	3	3.0	3	0
Gibson, N.E.	2	4	2.0	4	0	Allen, Hou.	1	2	2.0	2	0
E. Johnson, Clev.	2	3	1.5	3	0	Brazile, Hou.	1	2	2.0	2	0
Sanford, N.E.	2	2	1.0	2	0	Abraham, Hou.	1	1	1.0	1	0
Woods, Pitt.	2	0	0.0	0	0	J. Bryant, Sea.	1	1	1.0	1	0
Hill, K.C.	2	—1	—0.5	0	0	Kremer, K.C.	1	1	1.0	1	0
L. Williams, S.D.	1	66	66.0	t66	1	L. Wright, Den.	1	1	1.0	1	0
Kafentzis, Ind.	1	59	59.0	t59	1	Bellinger, Buffalo	1	0	0.0	0	0
J. Griffin, Cin.	1	57	57.0	t57	1	Brudzinski, Mia.	1	0	0.0	0	0
B. Brown, Mia.	1	53	53.0	53	0	Clayton, Pitt.	1	0	0.0	0	0
Rogers, Clev.	1	39	39.0	39	0	Clifton, N.Y. Jets	1	0	0.0	0	0
Fox, S.D.	1	36	36.0	36	0	L. Johnson, Clev.	1	0	0.0	0	0
C. Brown, Pitt.	1	31	31.0	31	0	McKinney, LA Raiders	1	0	0.0	0	0
Woodard, Den.	1	27	27.0	t27	1	Nelson, N.E.	1	0	0.0	0	0
Brown, Hou.	1	26	26.0	26	0	Rockins, Clev.	1	0	0.0	0	0
Kozlowski, Mia.	1	26	26.0	26	0	Schuh, Cin.	1	0	0.0	0	0
Minnifield, Clev.	1	26	26.0	26	0	Talley, Buff.	1	0	0.0	0	0
Mullen, N.Y. Jets	1	25	25.0	25	0	Watts, L.A. Raiders	1	0	0.0	0	0
Smerlas, Buff.	1	25	25.0	25	0	Thompson, Hou.	0	5	.....	5	0

NFC—INDIVIDUALS

Player—Team	No.	Yds.	Avg.	Lng.	TD	Player—Team	No.	Yds.	Avg.	Lng.	TD
FLYNN, G.B.	9	106	11.8	31	0	Lee, G.B.	3	33	11.0	14	0
T. Lewis, G.B.	7	151	21.6	t99	1	Clinkscale, Dall.	3	32	10.7	23	0
Downs, Dall.	7	126	18.0	t27	1	Anderson, G.B.	3	24	8.0	22	0
Ellis, Phila.	7	119	17.0	31	0	Graham, Det.	3	22	7.3	15	0
Dean, Wash.	7	114	16.3	t36	2	Walls, Dall.	3	12	4.0	12	0
Haynes, N.Y. Giants	7	90	12.9	22	0	Bess, Minn.	3	7	2.3	7	0
Watkins, Det.	6	0	0.0	0	0	P. Williams, N.Y.G.	3	7	2.3	7	0
Irvin, L.A. Rams	5	166	33.2	t81	2	Fellows, Dall.	3	3	1.0	3	0
Cotney, T.B.	5	123	24.6	29	0	Hegman, Dall.	3	3	1.0	3	0
Hopkins, Phila.	5	107	21.4	33	0	Winston, N.O.	2	90	45.0	t47	2
Fencik, Chi.	5	102	20.4	61	0	Hall, Det.	2	64	32.0	36	0
Green, Wash.	5	91	18.2	50	1	McLemore, S.F.	2	54	27.0	t54	1
Frazier, Chi.	5	89	17.8	33	0	Wattel, N.O.	2	52	26.0	t35	1
Thurman, Dall.	5	81	16.2	43	1	Collins, L.A. Rams	2	43	21.5	40	0
K. Johnson, Atl.	5	75	15.0	28	0	Williamson, S.F.	2	42	21.0	26	0
Washington, St.L.	5	42	8.4	18	0	L. Smith, St.L.	2	31	15.5	t25	1
Turner, S.F.	4	51	12.8	21	0	Kinard, N.Y. Giants	2	29	14.5	29	0
Bell, Chi.	4	46	11.5	t36	1	Reasons, N.Y. Giants	2	26	13.0	26	0
W. Smith, St.L.	4	35	8.8	23	0	Butler, Atl.	2	25	12.5	25	0
Foules, Phila.	4	27	6.8	20	0	Johnson, L.A. Rams	2	21	10.5	21	0
Lott, S.F.	4	26	6.5	15	0	Swain, Minn.	2	20	10.0	11	0
Perrin, St.L.	4	22	5.5	22	0	Jordan, Wash.	2	18	9.0	16	0
Waymer, N.O.	4	9	2.3	9	0	Fahnhorst, S.F.	2	9	4.5	9	0
Green, L.A. Rams	3	88	29.3	60	0	Richardson, Chi.	2	7	3.5	7	0
Shell, S.F.	3	81	27.0	t53	1	Edwards, Phila.	2	0	0.0	0	0
Brantley, T.B.	3	55	18.3	38	0	Griffin, St.L.	2	0	0.0	0	0
Cromwell, L.A. Rams	3	54	18.0	t33	1	McNorton, Det.	2	0	0.0	0	0
Hicks, S.F.	3	42	14.0	29	0	Pridemore, Atl.	2	0	0.0	0	0
Milot, Wash.	3	42	14.0	27	0	Wright, S.F.	2	0	0.0	0	0
Castille, T.B.	3	38	12.7	30	0	Howard, St.L.	2	—4	—2.0	1	0

Green Bay's Tim Lewis makes one of his seven interceptions during 1984, this one against Tampa Bay. Lewis, who finished tied for second behind teammate Tom Flynn in most interceptions among NFC players, also had a club record 99-yard interception return against the Rams.

Player—Team	No.	Yds.	Avg.	Lng.	TD	Player—Team	No.	Yds.	Avg.	Lng.	TD
Teal, Minn.	1	53	53.0	t53	1	Hood, G.B.	1	8	8.0	8	0
Coleman, Wash.	1	49	49.0	t49	1	Cumby, G.B.	1	7	7.0	7	0
Fuller, S.F.	1	38	38.0	38	0	Currier, N.Y. Giants	1	7	7.0	7	0
R. Smith, N.E.-Wash.	1	37	37.0	37	0	Johnson, N.O.	1	7	7.0	7	0
J. Jackson, Atl.	1	35	35.0	t35	1	Carson, N.Y. Giants	1	6	6.0	6	0
Harris, Chi.	1	34	34.0	34	0	Wilkes, Phila.	1	6	6.0	6	0
Lockhart, Dall.	1	32	32.0	32	0	Brown, G.B.	1	5	5.0	t5	1
Newsome, L.A. Rams	1	31	31.0	31	0	V. Scott, Dall.	1	5	5.0	5	0
Wilson, Phila.	1	28	28.0	28	0	Headen, N.Y. Giants	1	4	4.0	4	0
Logan, T.B.	1	27	27.0	t27	1	Murphy, G.B.	1	4	4.0	8	0
Holt, T.B.	1	25	25.0	25	0	Singletary, Chi.	1	4	4.0	4	0
Washington, Wash.	1	25	25.0	25	0	Bates, Dall.	1	3	3.0	3	0
Browner, Minn.	1	20	20.0	20	0	Bunz, S.F.	1	2	2.0	2	0
Studwell, Minn.	1	20	20.0	20	0	Small, Atl.	1	2	2.0	2	0
Heflin, St.L.	1	19	19.0	19	0	Fantetti, Det.	1	1	1.0	1	0
Junior, St.L.	1	18	18.0	18	0	Cannon, T.B.	1	0	0.0	0	0
Kovach, N.O.	1	16	16.0	16	0	M. Clark, S.F.	1	0	0.0	0	0
Poe, N.O.	1	16	16.0	16	0	Davis, T.B.	1	0	0.0	0	0
Coffey, Wash.	1	15	15.0	15	0	Dickerson, Dall.	1	0	0.0	0	0
Acorn, T.B.	1	14	14.0	14	0	Hannon, Minn.	1	0	0.0	0	0
Brown, T.B.	1	14	14.0	14	0	Lee, Minn.	1	0	0.0	0	0
Hunt, N.Y. Giants	1	14	14.0	14	0	McLeod, G.B.	1	0	0.0	0	0
Jackson, N.O.	1	14	14.0	14	0	McNeill, Minn.	1	0	0.0	0	0
Reece, T.B.	1	12	12.0	12	0	Schmidt, Chi.	1	0	0.0	0	0
Britt, Atl.	1	10	10.0	10	0	Gayle, Chi.	1	−1	−1.0	−1	0
B. Clark, N.O.	1	9	9.0	9	0	Taylor, N.Y. Giants	1	−1	−1.0	−1	0
Duerson, Chi.	1	9	9.0	9	0	Owens, L.A. Rams	1	−4	−4.0	−4	0

t-Touchdown
Leader based on most interceptions.

1984 SCORING

MOST POINTS, SEASON

      Non-Kickers
AFC: 108—Marcus Allen, L.A. Raiders.
         Mark Clayton, Miami.
NFC: 84—Eric Dickerson, L.A. Rams.
         John Riggins, Washington.
      Kickers
NFC: 131—Ray Wersching, San Francisco.
AFC: 117—Gary Anderson, Pittsburgh.

MOST TOUCHDOWNS

AFC: 18—Marcus Allen, L.A. Raiders (13-rush, 5-pass).
         Mark Clayton, Miami (18-pass).
NFC: 14—Eric Dickerson, L.A. Rams (14-rush).
         John Riggins, Washington (14-rush).

MOST EXTRA POINTS

AFC: 66—Uwe von Schamann, Miami (70 attempts).
NFC: 56—Ray Wersching, San Francisco (56 attempts).

MOST FIELD GOALS

NFC: 30—Paul McFadden, Philadelphia (37 attempts).
AFC: 24—Gary Anderson, Pittsburgh (32 attempts).
         Matt Bahr, Cleveland (32 attempts).

MOST FIELD GOALS ATTEMPTED

NFC: 37—Paul McFadden, Philadelphia (30 field goals).
AFC: 33—Nick Lowery, Kansas City (23 field goals).

LONGEST FIELD GOAL

AFC: 60—Steve Cox, Cleveland at Cincinnati, October 21.
NFC: 54—Jan Stenerud, Minnesota vs. Atlanta, September 16.

MOST POINTS, GAME

AFC: 24—Marcus Allen, L.A. Raiders vs. San Diego, September 24 (4 TD, 3-rush, 1-pass).
         Larry Kinnebrew, Cincinnati at Houston, October 28 (4 TD, 3-rush, 1-pass).
NFC: 18—Lynn Cain, Atlanta at L.A. Rams, October 7 (3 TD, rush).
         Eric Dickerson, L.A. Rams at Tampa Bay, November 25 (3 TD, rush).
         Eddie Lee Ivery, Green Bay vs. L.A. Rams, November 18 (3 TD, rush).
         Art Monk, Washington at Indianapolis, October 7 (3 TD, pass).
         Joe Morris, N.Y. Giants vs. Washington, October 28 (3 TD, rush).
         Leonard Thompson, Detroit vs. Minnesota, September 23 (3 TD, pass).

TEAM LEADERS

NFC: ATLANTA: 91, Mick Luckhurst; CHICAGO: 101, Bob Thomas; DALLAS: 102, Rafael Septien; DETROIT: 91, Ed Murray; GREEN BAY: 61, Al Del Greco; L.A. RAMS: 112, Mike Lansford; MINNESOTA: 90, Jan Stenerud; NEW ORLEANS: 94, Morten Andersen; N.Y. GIANTS: 83, Ali Haji-Sheikh; PHILADELPHIA: 116, Paul McFadden; ST. LOUIS: 117, Neil O'Donoghue; SAN FRANCISCO: 131, Ray Wersching; TAMPA BAY: 95, Obed Ariri; WASHINGTON: 120, Mark Moseley.
AFC: BUFFALO: 48, Greg Bell; CINCINNATI: 103, Jim Breech; CLEVELAND: 97, Matt Bahr; DENVER: 101, Rich Karlis; HOUSTON: 46, Joe Cooper; INDIANAPOLIS: 47, Raul Allegre; KANSAS CITY: 104, Nick Lowery; L.A. RAIDERS: 108, Marcus Allen; MIAMI: 108, Mark Clayton; NEW ENGLAND: 108, Tony Franklin; N.Y. JETS: 89, Pat Leahy; PITTSBURGH: 117, Gary Anderson; SAN DIEGO: 92, Rolf Benirschke; SEATTLE: 110, Norm Johnson.

TEAM CHAMPION

AFC: 513—Miami.
NFC: 475—San Francisco.

SCORING—TEAM

AMERICAN FOOTBALL CONFERENCE

	Tot. Tds.	Tds. R.	Tds. P.	Tds. Misc.	XP	XPA	FG	FGA	Saf.	Tot. Pts.
Miami	70	18	49	3	66	70	9	19	0	513
Seattle	51	10	32	9	50	51	20	24	1	418
San Diego	48	18	25	5	46	47	20	29	0	394
Pittsburgh	45	13	25	7	45	45	24	32	0	387
L.A. Raiders	44	19	21	4	40	44	20	27	2	368
New England	42	15	26	1	42	42	22	28	1	362
Denver	42	12	22	8	38	42	21	28	0	353
Cincinnati	39	18	17	4	37	39	22	31	1	339
N.Y. Jets	40	17	20	3	39	40	17	24	1	332
Kansas City	35	12	21	2	35	35	23	33	0	314
Buffalo	31	9	18	4	31	31	11	21	0	250
Cleveland	25	10	14	1	25	25	25	35	0	250
Houston	28	13	14	1	27	28	15	19	0	240
Indianapolis	28	13	13	2	27	28	14	23	1	239
Conference Total	568	197	317	54	548	567	263	373	7	4759
Conf. Average	40.6	14.1	22.6	3.9	39.1	40.5	18.8	26.6	0.5	339.9

NATIONAL FOOTBALL CONFERENCE

	Tot. Tds.	Tds. R.	Tds. P.	Tds. Misc.	XP	XPA	FG	FGA	Saf.	Tot. Pts.
San Francisco	57	21	32	4	56	57	25	35	1	475
Washington	51	20	24	7	48	51	24	31	0	426
St. Louis	51	21	28	2	48	51	23	35	0	423
Green Bay	51	18	30	3	48	51	12	21	0	390
L.A. Rams	38	16	16	6	37	38	25	33	3	346
Tampa Bay	40	17	22	1	38	40	19	26	0	335
Chicago	37	22	14	1	35	37	22	28	1	325
Dallas	34	12	19	3	33	34	23	29	1	308
N.Y. Giants	36	12	22	2	32	36	17	33	0	299
New Orleans	34	9	21	4	34	34	20	27	0	298
Detroit	32	13	19	0	31	31	20	27	0	283
Atlanta	31	16	14	1	31	31	20	27	2	281
Philadelphia	27	6	19	2	26	27	30	37	0	278
Minnesota	31	10	18	3	30	31	20	23	0	276
Conference Total	550	213	298	39	527	549	300	412	8	4743
Conf. Average	39.3	15.2	21.3	2.8	37.6	39.2	21.4	29.4	0.6	338.8
League Total	1118	410	615	93	1075	1116	563	785	15	9502
League Average	39.9	14.6	22.0	3.3	38.4	39.9	20.1	28.0	0.5	339.4

TOP TEN SCORERS

NON-KICKERS

Player—Team	Total TDs.	Rush TDs.	Pass TDs.	Misc. TDs.	Tot. Pts.
ALLEN, L.A. Raiders	18	13	5	0	108
Clayton, Miami	18	0	18	0	108
Dickerson, L.A. Rams	14	14	0	0	84
Riggins, Wash.	14	14	0	0	84
Riggs, Atl.	13	13	0	0	78
Wilder, T.B.	13	13	0	0	78
Green, St.L.	12	0	12	0	72
P. Johnson, S.D.-Mia.	12	12	0	0	72
Largent, Sea.	12	0	12	0	72
5 players tied with	11				66

KICKERS

Player—Team	XP Made	XP Att.	FG Made	FG Att.	Tot. Pts.
WERSCHING, S.F	56	56	25	35	131
Moseley, Wash.	48	51	24	31	120
Anderson, Pitt.	45	45	24	32	117
O'Donoghue, St.L.	48	51	23	35	117
McFadden, Phila.	26	27	30	37	116
Lansford, L.A. Rams	37	38	25	33	112
N. Johnson, Sea.	50	51	20	24	110
Franklin, N.E.	42	42	22	28	108
Lowery, K.C.	35	35	23	33	104
Breech, Cin.	37	37	22	31	103

AFC—INDIVIDUALS

KICKERS

Player—Team	XP Made	XP Att.	FG Made	FG Att.	Tot. Pts.	Player—Team	XP Made	XP Att.	FG Made	FG Att.	Tot. Pts.
ANDERSON, Pitt.	45	45	24	32	117	Leahy, N.Y. Jets	38	39	17	24	89
N. Johnson, Sea.	50	51	20	24	110	Allegre, Ind.	14	14	11	18	47
Franklin, N.E.	42	42	22	28	108	Cooper, Hou.	13	13	11	13	46
Lowery, K.C.	35	35	23	33	104	Danelo, Buff.	17	17	8	16	41
Breech, Cin.	37	37	22	31	103	Kempf, Hou.	14	14	4	6	26
Karlis, Den.	38	41	21	28	101	Nelson, Buff.	14	14	3	5	23
Bahr, L.A. Raiders	40	42	20	27	100	Biasucci, Ind.	13	14	3	5	22
Bahr, Clev.	25	25	24	32	97	Ricardo, S.D.	5	6	3	3	14
von Schamann, Mia.	66	70	9	19	93	Cox, Clev.	0	0	1	3	3
Benirschke, S.D.	41	41	17	26	92						

NON-KICKERS

Player—Team	Total TDs.	Rush TDs.	Pass TDs.	Misc. TDs.	Tot. Pts.
ALLEN, L.A. Raiders	18	13	5	0	108
Clayton, Mia.	18	0	18	0	108
P. Johnson, S.D.-Mia.	12	12	0	0	72
Largent, Sea.	12	0	12	0	72
Lipps, Pitt.	11	1	9	1	66
Stallworth, Pitt.	11	0	11	0	66
Kinnebrew, Cin.	10	9	1	0	60
Turner, Sea.	10	0	10	0	60
Jackson, S.D.	9	8	1	0	54
Bell, Buff.	8	7	1	0	48
Bennett, Mia.	8	7	1	0	48
Duper, Mia.	8	0	8	0	48
Paige, N.Y. Jets	8	7	1	0	48
Christensen, Raiders	7	0	7	0	42
Dennard, Buff.	7	0	7	0	42
Moriarty, Hou.	7	6	1	0	42
Ramsey, N.E.	7	0	7	0	42
Walker, N.Y. Jets	7	0	7	0	42
Watson, Den.	7	0	7	0	42
Butler, Ind.	6	0	6	0	36
Chandler, S.D.	6	0	6	0	36
Collinsworth, Cin.	6	0	6	0	36
Johnson, Den.	6	0	6	0	36
Joiner, S.D.	6	0	6	0	36
McGee, S.D.	6	4	2	0	36
McNeil, N.Y. Jets	6	5	1	0	36
Moore, Mia.	6	0	6	0	36
Pollard, Pitt.	6	6	0	0	36
Pruitt, Clev.	6	6	0	0	36
Shuler, N.Y. Jets	6	0	6	0	36
Winder, Den.	6	4	2	0	36
Collins, N.E.	5	5	0	0	30
Eason, N.E.	5	5	0	0	30
Hardy, Mia.	5	0	5	0	30
Jennings, Cin.	5	2	3	0	30
Lane, Sea.	5	4	1	0	30
McMillan, Ind.	5	5	0	0	30
Morgan, N.E.	5	0	5	0	30
Newsome, Clev.	5	0	5	0	30
Brooks, Cin.	4	2	2	0	24
Brown, K.C.	4	4	0	0	24
Carson, K.C.	4	0	4	0	24
Dawson, N.E.	4	0	4	0	24
Duckworth, S.D.	4	0	4	0	24
Franklin, Buff.	4	0	4	0	24
Heard, K.C.	4	4	0	0	24
Lacy, K.C.	4	2	2	0	24
Marshall, K.C.	4	0	4	0	24
Paige, K.C.	4	0	4	0	24
Smith, Hou.	4	0	4	0	24
Starring, N.E.	4	0	4	0	24
Tatupu, N.E.	4	4	0	0	24
Williams, L.A. Raiders	4	0	4	0	24
Brennan, Clev.	3	0	3	0	18
Byner, Clev.	3	2	0	1	18
Dickey, Ind.	3	3	0	0	18
Erenberg, Pitt.	3	2	1	0	18
Hawkins, L.A. Raiders	3	3	0	0	18
D. Johnson, Mia.	3	0	3	0	18
Jones, N.E.	3	0	2	1	18
Kay, Den.	3	0	3	0	18
Krieg, Sea.	3	3	0	0	18
Lang, Den.	3	2	1	0	18
Malone, Pitt.	3	3	0	0	18
Nathan, Mia.	3	1	2	0	18
Scott, K.C.	3	0	3	0	18
Sievers, S.D.	3	0	3	0	18
Thompson, Pitt.	3	0	3	0	18
Tice, Sea.	3	0	3	0	18
J. Williams, Hou.	3	0	3	0	18
Martin, L.A. Raiders	2	0	0	2	*14
Alexander, Cin.	2	2	0	0	12
Barber, N.Y. Jets	2	2	0	0	12
Barnwell, L.A. Raiders	2	0	2	0	12
Brown, Sea.	2	0	0	2	12
Byrd, S.D.	2	0	0	2	12
Casper, L.A. Raiders	2	0	2	0	12
Cefalo, Mia.	2	0	2	0	12
B. Davis, Clev.	2	0	2	0	12
Dawkins, Buff.	2	0	2	0	12
Dixon, Sea.	2	2	0	0	12
Doornink, Sea.	2	0	2	0	12
Dressel, Hou.	2	0	2	0	12
Easley, Sea.	2	0	0	2	12
Esiason, Cin.	2	2	0	0	12
Foley, Den.	2	0	0	2	12
Harris, Cin.	2	0	2	0	12
Henry, Ind.	2	0	2	0	12
Hughes, Sea.	2	1	1	0	12
Humphery, N.Y. Jets	2	0	1	1	12
Hunter, Buff.	2	0	2	0	12
B. Jackson, K.C.	2	1	1	0	12
Jensen, L.A. Raiders	2	1	1	0	12
Jensen, Mia.	2	0	2	0	12
Johns, Sea.	2	0	1	1	12
Middleton, Ind.	2	1	1	0	12
Minter, N.Y. Jets	2	1	1	0	12
Moore, Ind.	2	2	0	0	12
Parros, Den.	2	2	0	0	12
Porter, Ind.	2	0	2	0	12
Rose, Mia.	2	0	2	0	12
Simpson, Sea.	2	0	0	2	12
Thomas, S.D.	2	2	0	0	12
Washington, Pitt.	2	0	0	2	12
C. Weathers, N.E.	2	0	2	0	12
Willhite, Den.	2	2	0	0	12
Winslow, S.D.	2	0	2	0	12
Woodruff, Pitt.	2	0	0	2	12
Young, Ind.	2	2	0	0	12
Abercrombie, Pitt.	1	1	0	0	6
Alexander, Den.	1	0	1	0	6
W. Arnold, Wash.-K.C.	1	0	1	0	6
Baumhower, Mia.	1	0	0	1	6
Beckman, K.C.	1	0	1	0	6
Blackledge, K.C.	1	1	0	0	6
Bostic, Hou.	1	0	0	1	6
Brookins, Buff.	1	0	1	0	6
Buttle, N.Y. Jets	1	0	0	1	6
Carter, Mia.	1	1	0	0	6
Cunningham, Pitt.	1	0	1	0	6
David, Buff.	1	0	0	1	6
J. Davis, Clev.	1	1	0	0	6
Dennison, N.Y. Jets	1	0	1	0	6
Dufek, Buff.	1	0	0	1	6
Edwards, Hou.	1	1	0	0	6
Elway, Den.	1	1	0	0	6
Feacher, Clev.	1	0	1	0	6
Fryar, N.E.	1	0	1	0	6
Gastineau, N.Y. Jets	1	0	0	1	6
Green, Clev.	1	0	1	0	6
J. Griffin, Cin.	1	0	0	1	6
Hancock, K.C.	1	0	1	0	6
Harden, Den.	1	0	0	1	6
Harper, N.Y. Jets	1	1	0	0	6
Haynes, L.A. Raiders	1	0	0	1	6
Hector, N.Y. Jets	1	1	0	0	6
Hinkle, Pitt.	1	0	0	1	6
Holman, Cin.	1	0	1	0	6
Holohan, S.D.	1	0	1	0	6
Holston, Hou.	1	0	1	0	6
Horton, Cin.	1	0	0	1	6
Jackson, Cin.	1	0	0	1	6
T. Jackson, Sea.	1	0	0	1	6
C. James, N.E.	1	1	0	0	6
James, S.D.	1	0	0	1	6
Jones, N.Y. Jets	1	0	1	0	6
R. Jones, Den.	1	0	0	1	6
Judson, Mia.	1	0	0	1	6
Kafentzis, Ind.	1	0	0	1	6
Keating, Buff.	1	0	0	1	6
Klever, N.Y. Jets	1	0	1	0	6
Kreider, Cin.	1	1	0	0	6
Kubiak, Den.	1	1	0	0	6
Lowe, S.D.	1	0	0	1	6
Luck, Hou.	1	0	1	0	6
McCloskey, Hou.	1	0	1	0	6
McDonald, Clev.	1	1	0	0	6
McNeal, Mia.	1	0	0	1	6

Player—Team	Total TDs.	Rush TDs.	Pass TDs.	Misc. TDs.	Tot. Pts.	Player—Team	Total TDs.	Rush TDs.	Pass TDs.	Misc. TDs.	Tot. Pts.
Montgomery, Raiders...	1	0	0	1	6	Simmons, Cin.	1	0	0	1	6
Moon, Hou.	1	1	0	0	6	D. Smith, Den.	1	0	0	1	6
Morris, S.D.	1	1	0	0	6	P. Smith, Ind.	1	0	0	1	6
Mullins, Hou.	1	0	1	0	6	Walker, Sea.	1	0	1	0	6
Munoz, Cin.	1	0	1	0	6	Walls, Hou.	1	0	1	0	6
Nash, Sea.	1	0	0	1	6	L. Williams, S.D.	1	0	0	1	6
Neal, Buff.	1	1	0	0	6	Va. Williams, Buff.	1	0	1	0	6
Pagel, Ind.	1	1	0	0	6	Wilson, Buff.	1	0	0	1	6
Plunkett, L.A. Raiders..	1	1	0	0	6	Wilson, L.A. Raiders	1	1	0	0	6
Radecic, K.C.	1	0	0	1	6	Woodard, Den.	1	0	0	1	6
Robbins, Den.	1	0	0	1	6	J. Wright, Den.	1	0	1	0	6
Robinson, N.E.	1	0	1	0	6	L. Wright, Den.	1	0	0	1	6
Ross, K.C.	1	0	0	1	6	C. Young, Sea.	1	0	1	0	6
Sampson, Den.	1	0	1	0	6	J. Bryant, Sea.	0	0	0	0	*2
Sanford, Buff.	1	0	0	1	6	Humiston, Ind.	0	0	0	0	*2
Schlichter, Ind.	1	1	0	0	6	R. James, N.E.	0	0	0	0	*2
Schonert, Cin.	1	1	0	0	6	Ryan, N.Y. Jets	0	0	0	0	†1
Shell, Pitt.	1	0	0	1	6						

NFC—INDIVIDUALS

KICKERS

Player—Team	XP Made	XP Att.	FG Made	FG Att.	Tot. Pts.
WERSCHING, S.F.	56	56	25	35	131
Moseley, Wash.	48	51	24	31	120
O'Donoghue, St.L.	48	51	23	35	117
McFadden, Phila.	26	27	30	37	116
Lansford, L.A. Rams	37	38	25	33	112
Septien, Dall.	33	34	23	29	102
B. Thomas, Chi.	35	37	22	28	101
Ariri, T.B.	38	40	19	26	95
Andersen, N.O.	34	34	20	27	94
Luckhurst, Atl.	31	31	20	27	91
Murray, Det.	31	31	20	27	91
Stenerud, Minn.	30	31	20	23	90
Haji-Sheikh, N.Y.G.	32	35	17	33	83
Del Greco, G.B.	34	34	9	12	61
Garcia, G.B.	14	15	3	9	23

NON-KICKERS

Player—Team	Total TDs.	Rush TDs.	Pass TDs.	Misc. TDs.	Tot. Pts.	Player—Team	Total TDs.	Rush TDs.	Pass TDs.	Misc. TDs.	Tot. Pts.
DICKERSON, Rams	14	14	0	0	84	Marsh, St.L.	5	0	5	0	30
Riggins, Wash.	14	14	0	0	84	Newsome, Dall.	5	5	0	0	30
Riggs, Atl.	13	13	0	0	78	Sims, Det.	5	5	0	0	30
Wilder, T.B.	13	13	0	0	78	Tilley, St.L.	5	0	5	0	30
Green, St.L.	12	0	12	0	72	West, G.B.	5	1	4	0	30
Mitchell, St.L.	11	9	2	0	66	J. Bell, T.B.	4	0	4	0	24
Payton, Chi.	11	11	0	0	66	Brown, L.A. Rams	4	0	4	0	24
Solomon, S.F.	11	1	10	0	66	Campbell, Hou.-N.O.	4	4	0	0	24
Craig, S.F.	10	7	3	0	60	Cooper, S.F.	4	0	4	0	24
Coffman, G.B.	9	0	9	0	54	Cosbie, Dall.	4	0	4	0	24
Quick, Phila.	9	0	9	0	54	Danielson, Det.	4	3	1	0	24
Tyler, S.F.	9	7	2	0	54	Dr. Hill, L.A. Rams	4	0	4	0	24
Anderson, St.L.	8	6	2	0	48	Lewis, Minn.	4	0	4	0	24
Carpenter, N.Y. Giants.	8	7	1	0	48	Manuel, N.Y. Giants	4	0	4	0	24
Ellard, L.A. Rams	8	0	6	2	48	Morris, N.Y. Giants	4	4	0	0	24
Jones, Det.	8	3	5	0	48	Muhammad, Wash.	4	0	4	0	24
Dorsett, Dall.	7	6	1	0	42	Nelson, Minn.	4	3	1	0	24
Gajan, N.O.	7	5	2	0	42	Springs, Dall.	4	1	3	0	24
Ivery, G.B.	7	6	1	0	42	W. Wilson, N.O.	4	1	3	0	24
Johnson, N.Y. Giants	7	0	7	0	42	Wonsley, Wash.	4	4	0	0	24
Lofton, G.B.	7	0	7	0	42	Anderson, Minn.	3	2	1	0	18
Monk, Wash.	7	0	7	0	42	Brown, Wash.	3	0	3	0	18
Bailey, Atl.	6	0	6	0	36	Cain, Atl.	3	0	3	0	18
Brenner, N.O.	6	0	6	0	36	Chadwick, Det.	3	1	2	0	18
T. Brown, Minn.	6	3	3	0	36	Cox, Atl.	3	0	3	0	18
D. Clark, S.F.	6	0	6	0	36	Dickey, G.B.	3	3	0	0	18
Clark, G.B.	6	4	2	0	36	Epps, G.B.	3	0	3	0	18
Ellis, G.B.	6	4	2	0	36	Goodlow, N.O.	3	0	3	0	18
Gault, Chi.	6	0	6	0	36	B. Johnson, Atl.	3	0	3	0	18
Mowatt, N.Y. Giants	6	0	6	0	36	Jordan, Minn.	3	1	2	0	18
Suhey, Chi.	6	4	2	0	36	Kab, Phila.	3	0	3	0	18
L. Thompson, Det.	6	0	6	0	36	Lewis, Det.	3	0	3	0	18
Armstrong, T.B.	5	2	3	0	30	Lomax, St.L.	3	3	0	0	18
Carter, T.B.	5	0	5	0	30	McKinnon, Chi.	3	0	3	0	18
Didier, Wash.	5	0	5	0	30	Ring, S.F.	3	0	3	0	18
Hill, Dall.	5	0	5	0	30	Woodruff, Phila.	3	0	3	0	18
House, T.B.	5	0	5	0	30	Young, N.O.	3	0	3	0	18
						Crutchfield, L.A. Rams.	2	1	1	0	12
						DeBerg, T.B.	2	2	0	0	12
						Dean, Wash.	2	0	0	2	12
						Donley, Dall.	2	0	2	0	12
						Ferrell, St.L.	2	1	1	0	12
						Francis, S.F.	2	0	2	0	12
						Giles, T.B.	2	0	2	0	12
						Gray, N.Y. Giants	2	0	2	0	12
						Harris, Clev.-Dall.	2	0	2	0	12
						Hoover, Phila.	2	0	2	0	12
						Irvin, L.A. Rams	2	0	0	2	12
						A. Jackson, Atl.	2	0	2	0	12
						Love, St.L.	2	1	1	0	12
						McLemore, S.F.	2	0	0	2	12
						McMahon, Chi.	2	2	0	0	12
						Montana, S.F.	2	2	0	0	12
						Montgomery, Phila.	2	2	0	0	12
						Moore, Wash.	2	0	2	0	12
						Mularkey, Minn.	2	0	2	0	12
						Nehemiah, S.F.	2	0	2	0	12

San Francisco placekicker Ray Wersching, who was a perfect 56-of-56 on extra point attempts last season, led the NFL in scoring with 131 points

Player—Team	Total TDs.	Rush TDs.	Pass TDs.	Misc. TDs.	Tot. Pts.
Pisarcik, Phila.	2	2	0	0	12
Renfro, Dall.	2	0	2	0	12
Rice, Minn.	2	1	1	0	12
G. Rogers, N.O.	2	2	0	0	12
Wattelet, N.O.	2	0	0	2	12
B. Williams, N.Y.G.	2	0	2	0	12
Winston, N.O.	2	0	0	2	12
G. Johnson, S.D.-S.F.	1	0	0	1	*8
Anderson, Chi.	1	0	1	0	6
Anthony, N.O.	1	1	0	0	6
Bell, Chi.	1	0	0	1	6
Brown, G.B.	1	0	0	1	6
Browner, Minn.	1	0	0	1	6
Carroll, T.B.	1	0	1	0	6
Coleman, Wash.	1	0	0	1	6
Collins, Minn.	1	0	1	0	6
Cornwell, Dall.	1	0	1	0	6
Cromwell, L.A. Rams	1	0	0	1	6
Crouse, G.B.	1	0	1	0	6
Dierking, T.B.	1	0	1	0	6
Downs, Dall.	1	0	0	1	6
Dunsmore, Chi.	1	0	1	0	6
Frank, S.F.	1	0	1	0	6
Fuller, Chi.	1	1	0	0	6
Gentry, Chi.	1	1	0	0	6
Grant, Wash.	1	0	0	1	6
Green, Wash.	1	0	0	1	6
Guman, L.A. Rams	1	0	0	1	6
Haddix, Phila.	1	1	0	0	6
Hardy, N.O.	1	0	1	0	6
Harmon, S.F.	1	1	0	0	6
Harrell, St.L.	1	1	0	0	6
Headen, N.Y. Giants	1	0	0	1	6
Da. Hill, L.A. Rams	1	0	1	0	6
Howard, St.L.	1	0	0	1	6
Hutchison, Chi.	1	1	0	0	6
J. Jackson, Atl.	1	0	0	1	6
Jackson, Phila.	1	0	1	0	6
Jacoby, Wash.	1	0	0	1	6
Jaworski, Phila.	1	1	0	0	6
Jeffcoat, Dall.	1	0	0	1	6
Jenkins, Det.	1	1	0	0	6
J. Jones, Dall.	1	0	1	0	6
Jones, Minn.	1	0	1	0	6
Jordan, Wash.	1	0	0	1	6
Kemp, L.A. Rams	1	1	0	0	6
Kramer, Minn.	1	0	1	0	6
Kraynak, Phila.	1	0	0	1	6
Landry, Chi.	1	1	0	0	6
T. Lewis, G.B.	1	0	0	1	6
Logan, T.B.	1	0	0	1	6
C. Martin, Minn.	1	0	0	1	6
McConkey, N.Y. Giants	1	0	0	1	6
McGrath, Wash.	1	0	1	0	6
Miller, N.O.	1	0	1	0	6
Monroe, S.F.	1	0	1	0	6
Moore, G.B.	1	0	1	0	6
Moorehead, Chi.	1	0	1	0	6
Nichols, Det.	1	0	1	0	6
Owens, T.B.	1	0	1	0	6
Rodgers, G.B.	1	0	0	1	6
Rubick, Det.	1	0	1	0	6
Scott, N.O.	1	0	1	0	6
Seay, Wash.	1	0	1	0	6
Shell, S.F.	1	0	0	1	6
L. Smith, St.L.	1	0	0	1	6
Spagnola, Phila.	1	0	1	0	6
Teal, Minn.	1	0	0	1	6
Theismann, Wash.	1	1	0	0	6
C. Thomas, Chi.	1	1	0	0	6
Thurman, Dall.	1	0	0	1	6
Tice, N.O.	1	0	1	0	6
Walker, Wash.	1	0	1	0	6
J. Washington, Wash.	1	1	0	0	6
Waters, Phila.	1	0	0	1	6
White, Minn.	1	0	1	0	6
Wilson, S.F.	1	0	1	0	6
Woolfolk, N.Y. Giants	1	1	0	0	6
Bryan, Atl.	0	0	0	0	*2
Case, Atl.	0	0	0	0	*2
Dutton, Dall.	0	0	0	0	*2
Sully, L.A. Rams	0	0	0	0	*2
Vann, L.A. Rams	0	0	0	0	*2

1984 PUNTING

AVERAGE YARDS PER PUNT
AFC: 44.9—Jim Arnold, Kansas City (98 punts, 4397 yards).
NFC: 43.8—Brian Hansen, New Orleans (63 punts, 3020 yards).

NET AVERAGE YARDS PER PUNT
AFC: 38.1—Reggie Roby, Miami (51 punts, 1943 net yards).
NFC: 36.6—Greg Coleman, Minnesota (82 punts, 2998 net yards).

LONGEST PUNT
AFC: 89—Luke Prestridge, New England vs. Miami, October 21.
NFC: 87—Dave Finzer, Chicago vs. New Orleans, October 7.

MOST PUNTS, SEASON
AFC: 98—Jim Arnold, Kansas City.
　　　Rohn Stark, Indianapolis.
NFC: 92—Mike Horan, Philadelphia.

MOST PUNTS, GAME
AFC: 11—Rich Camarillo, New England at Dallas, November 22.
NFC: 11—Dave Finzer, Chicago at San Diego, December 3.
　　　Danny White, Dallas vs. Green Bay, September 23.

TEAM CHAMPION
AFC: 44.9—Kansas City.
NFC: 43.1—New Orleans.

PUNTING—TEAM

NATIONAL FOOTBALL CONFERENCE

	Total Punts	Yards	Long	Avg.	TB.	Blk.	Opp. Ret.	Ret. Yds.	In 20	Net Avg.
New Orleans	70	3020	66	43.1	7	1	47	550	9	33.3
Minnesota	82	3473	62	42.4	2	0	49	435	16	36.6
Green Bay	85	3596	61	42.3	12	0	46	368	18	35.2
Philadelphia	92	3880	69	42.2	6	0	58	486	21	35.6
Tampa Bay	68	2849	60	41.9	9	0	36	310	12	34.7
Detroit	76	3164	63	41.6	8	0	49	516	13	32.7
San Francisco	62	2536	59	40.9	12	1	30	190	19	34.0
Atlanta	70	2855	58	40.8	6	2	42	450	12	32.6
Chicago	85	3328	87	39.2	4	2	41	249	26	35.3
Washington	73	2834	59	38.8	5	1	38	187	11	34.9
L.A. Rams	74	2866	58	38.7	9	0	35	196	21	33.6
N.Y. Giants	94	3598	54	38.3	10	4	50	479	22	31.1
Dallas	108	4123	54	38.2	11	0	55	230	25	34.0
St. Louis	68	2594	59	38.1	8	1	27	239	19	32.3
Conference Total	1107	44716	87	......	109	12	603	4885	244	......
Conference Avg.	79.1	3194.0	......	40.4	7.8	0.9	43.1	348.9	17.4	34.0

AMERICAN FOOTBALL CONFERENCE

	Total Punts	Yards	Long	Avg.	TB.	Blk.	Opp. Ret.	Ret. Yds.	In 20	Net Avg.
Kansas City	98	4397	63	44.9	13	0	60	461	22	37.5
Miami	51	2281	69	44.7	10	0	17	138	15	38.1
Indianapolis	98	4383	72	44.7	7	0	62	600	21	37.2
New England	92	3904	89	42.4	12	0	45	442	20	35.0
Cleveland	76	3213	69	42.3	8	2	43	489	16	33.7
Cincinnati	67	2832	61	42.3	8	0	38	310	19	35.3
San Diego	66	2773	60	42.0	3	0	43	399	11	35.1
L.A. Raiders	91	3809	63	41.9	12	0	34	345	25	35.4
Pittsburgh	70	2883	62	41.2	5	0	37	351	21	34.7
Buffalo	90	3696	63	41.1	8	2	52	597	16	32.7
Denver	96	3850	83	40.1	6	0	44	335	16	35.4
Houston	88	3482	55	39.6	5	0	60	618	20	31.4
N.Y. Jets	75	2935	64	39.1	8	1	37	242	19	33.8
Seattle	95	3567	60	37.5	10	0	32	205	24	33.3
Conference Total	1153	48005	89	......	115	5	604	5532	265	......
Conference Avg.	82.4	3428.9	......	41.6	8.2	0.4	43.1	395.1	18.9	34.8
League Total	2260	92721	89	......	224	17	1207	10417	509	......
League Average	80.7	3311.5	......	41.0	8.0	0.6	43.1	372.0	18.2	34.4

TOP TEN PUNTERS

Player—Team	Net Punts	Yards	Long	Avg.	Total Punts	TB.	Blk.	Opp. Ret.	Ret. Yds.	In 20	Net Avg.
ARNOLD, JIM, K.C.	98	4397	63	44.9	98	13	0	60	461	22	37.5
Roby, Reggie, Mia.	51	2281	69	44.7	51	10	0	17	138	15	38.1
Stark, Rohn, Ind.	98	4383	72	44.7	98	7	0	62	600	21	37.2
Hansen, Brian, N.O.	69	3020	66	43.8	70	7	1	47	550	9	33.3
Cox, Steve, Clev.	74	3213	69	43.4	76	8	2	43	489	16	33.7
Prestridge, Luke, N.E.	44	1884	89	42.8	44	5	0	21	228	8	35.4
Coleman, Greg, Minn.	82	3473	62	42.4	82	2	0	49	435	16	36.6
Scribner, Bucky, G.B.	85	3596	61	42.3	85	12	0	46	368	18	35.2
McInally, Pat, Cin.	67	2832	61	42.3	67	8	0	38	310	19	35.3
Horan, Mike, Phila.	92	3880	69	42.2	92	6	0	58	486	21	35.6

NFC—INDIVIDUALS

Player—Team	Net Punts	Yards	Long	Avg.	Total Punts	TB.	Blk.	Opp. Ret.	Ret. Yds.	In 20	Net Avg.
HANSEN, N.O.	69	3020	66	43.8	70	7	1	47	550	9	33.3
Coleman, Minn.	82	3473	62	42.4	82	2	0	49	435	16	36.6
Scribner, G.B.	85	3596	61	42.3	85	12	0	46	368	18	35.2
Horan, Phila.	92	3880	69	42.2	92	6	0	58	486	21	35.6
Giacomarro, Atl.	68	2855	58	42.0	70	6	2	42	450	12	32.6
Garcia, T.B.	68	2849	60	41.9	68	9	0	36	310	12	34.7
Runager, S.F.	56	2341	59	41.8	57	12	1	26	176	18	33.8
Black, Det.	76	3164	63	41.6	76	8	0	49	516	13	32.7
Finzer, Chi.	83	3328	87	40.1	85	4	2	41	249	26	35.3
Jennings, N.Y. Giants	90	3598	54	40.0	93	10	3	50	479	22	31.4
Hayes, Wash.	72	2834	59	39.4	73	5	1	38	187	11	34.9
Misko, L.A. Rams	74	2866	58	38.7	74	9	0	35	196	21	33.6
Birdsong, St.L.	67	2594	59	38.7	68	8	1	27	239	19	32.3
D. White, Dall.	82	3151	54	38.4	82	8	0	38	156	21	34.6
(Non-Qualifiers)											
Warren, Dall.	21	799	48	38.0	21	3	0	13	47	3	33.0
Miller, Dall.	5	173	41	34.6	5	0	0	4	27	1	29.2
Orosz, S.F.	5	195	55	39.0	5	0	0	4	14	1	36.2
Haji-Sheikh, N.Y. Giants	0	0	0	.....	1	0	1	0	0	0	0.0

AFC—INDIVIDUALS

Player—Team	Net Punts	Yards	Long	Avg.	Total Punts	TB.	Blk.	Opp. Ret.	Ret. Yds.	In 20	Net Avg.
J. ARNOLD, K.C.	98	4397	63	44.9	98	13	0	60	461	22	37.5
Roby, Mia.	51	2281	69	44.7	51	10	0	17	138	15	38.1
Stark, Ind.	98	4383	72	44.7	98	7	0	62	600	21	37.2
Cox, Clev.	74	3213	69	43.4	76	8	2	43	489	16	33.7
Prestridge, N.E.	44	1884	89	42.8	44	5	0	21	228	8	35.4
McInally, Cin.	67	2832	61	42.3	67	8	0	38	310	19	35.3
Camarillo, N.E.	48	2020	61	42.1	48	7	0	24	214	12	34.7
Buford, S.D.	66	2773	60	42.0	66	3	0	43	399	11	35.1
Kidd, Buff.	88	3696	63	42.0	90	8	2	52	597	16	32.7
Guy, L.A. Raiders	91	3809	63	41.9	91	12	0	34	345	25	35.4
Colquitt, Pitt.	70	2883	62	41.2	70	5	0	37	351	21	34.7
Norman, Den.	96	3850	83	40.1	96	6	0	44	335	16	35.4
Ramsey, N.Y. Jets	74	2935	64	39.7	75	8	1	37	242	19	33.8
James, Hou.	88	3482	55	39.6	88	5	0	60	618	20	31.4
West, Sea.	95	3567	60	37.5	95	10	0	32	205	24	33.3

Leader based on gross average, minimum 40 punts

1984 PUNT RETURNS

AVERAGE YARDS PER RETURN
   AFC: 15.7—Mike Martin, Cincinnati.
   NFC: 13.4—Henry Ellard, L.A. Rams.

MOST YARDS, SEASON
   AFC: 656—Louis Lipps, Pittsburgh.
   NFC: 521—Dana McLemore, San Francisco.

MOST YARDS, GAME
   AFC: 152—Cle Montgomery, L.A. Raiders at Detroit, December 10 (9 returns).
   NFC: 104—Henry Ellard, L.A. Rams at Atlanta, October 22 (3 returns).

LONGEST PUNT RETURN
   NFC: 83—Henry Ellard, L.A. Rams vs. N.Y. Giants, September 30.
   AFC: 76—Louis Lipps, Pittsburgh at New Orleans, November 19.

MOST RETURNS, SEASON
   NFC: 57—Jeff Fisher, Chicago.
   AFC: 53—Louis Lipps, Pittsburgh.
          Greg Pruitt, L.A. Raiders.

MOST RETURNS, GAME
   AFC: 9—Cle Montgomery, L.A. Raiders at Detroit, December 10 (152 yards).
   NFC: 8—Jeff Fisher, Chicago at Detroit, December 16 (103 yards).
          Phil McConkey, N.Y. Giants at Dallas, November 4 (38 yards).

MOST FAIR CATCHES
   NFC: 19—Evan Cooper, Philadelphia.
   AFC: 16—Greg Pruitt, L.A. Raiders.

TOUCHDOWNS
   NFC: 2—Henry Ellard, L.A. Rams vs. N.Y. Giants, September 30 (83 yards);
          L.A. Rams at Atlanta, October 22 (69 yards).
   AFC: 1—Lionel James, San Diego at Pittsburgh, November 25 (58 yards).
          Paul Johns, Seattle at New England, September 16 (47 yards).
          Louis Lipps, Pittsburgh at New Orleans, November 19 (76 yards).
          Cle Montgomery, L.A. Raiders at Detroit, December 10 (69 yards).
          Don Wilson, Buffalo at Seattle, October 14 (65 yards).

TEAM CHAMPION
   AFC: 12.4—Cincinnati.
   NFC: 12.2—L.A. Rams.

PUNT RETURNS—TEAM

AMERICAN FOOTBALL CONFERENCE

	No.	FC	Yards	Avg.	Long	TDs
L.A. Raiders	67	17	667	10.0	t69	1
Pittsburgh	61	2	696	11.4	t76	1
New England	48	15	430	9.0	55	0
Seattle	44	11	484	11.0	t47	1
Kansas City	42	15	346	8.2	27	0
Denver	41	12	318	7.8	35	0
Cleveland	40	13	322	8.1	19	0
Miami	39	27	365	9.4	37	0
Cincinnati	38	11	473	12.4	55	0
Indianapolis	38	12	278	7.3	35	0
N.Y. Jets	35	12	324	9.3	33	0
Buffalo	33	8	297	9.0	t65	1
San Diego	33	12	212	6.4	t58	1
Houston	26	8	152	5.8	18	0
Conference Total	585	175	5364	---	t76	5
Conference Average	41.8	12.5	383.1	9.2	--	0.4

NATIONAL FOOTBALL CONFERENCE

	No.	FC	Yards	Avg.	Long	TDs
Chicago	63	11	558	8.9	28	0
Washington	55	2	474	8.6	46	0
N.Y. Giants	55	18	368	6.7	31	0
Dallas	54	15	446	8.3	18	0
Green Bay	48	16	351	7.3	39	0

	No.	FC	Yards	Avg.	Long	TDs
St. Louis	47	5	399	8.5	39	0
San Francisco	45	11	521	11.6	t79	1
Atlanta	41	4	264	6.4	37	0
L.A. Rams	40	4	489	12.2	t83	2
Philadelphia	40	19	250	6.3	16	0
Detroit	36	11	241	6.7	23	0
Tampa Bay	34	5	207	6.1	21	0
New Orleans	33	18	268	8.1	61	0
Minnesota	31	10	217	7.0	21	0
Conference Total	622	149	5053	---	t83	3
Conference Average	44.4	10.6	360.9	8.1	--	0.2
League Total	1207	324	10417	---	t83	8
League Average	43.1	11.6	372.0	8.6	--	0.3

TOP TEN PUNT RETURNERS

	No.	FC	Yards	Avg.	Long	TDs
MARTIN, MIKE, Cincinnati	24	5	376	15.7	55	0
Ellard, Henry, L.A. Rams	30	3	403	13.4	t83	2
Lipps, Louis, Pittsburgh	53	2	656	12.4	t76	1
McLemore, Dana, San Francisco	45	11	521	11.6	t79	1
Willhite, Gerald, Denver	20	9	200	10.0	35	0
Fryar, Irving, New England	36	10	347	9.6	55	0
Wilson, Don, Buffalo	33	8	297	9.0	t65	1
Pruitt, Greg, L.A. Raiders	53	16	473	8.9	38	0
Springs, Kirk, N.Y. Jets	28	10	247	8.8	33	0
Mitchell, Stump, St. Louis	38	3	333	8.8	39	0

AFC—INDIVIDUALS

Player—Team	No.	FC	Yds.	Avg.	Lng.	TD
MARTIN, Cin.	24	5	376	15.7	55	0
Lipps, Pitt.	53	2	656	12.4	t76	1
Willhite, Den.	20	9	200	10.0	35	0
Fryar, N.E.	36	10	347	9.6	55	0
Wilson, Buff.	33	8	297	9.0	t65	1
Pruitt, L.A. Raiders	53	16	473	8.9	38	0
Springs, N.Y. Jets	28	10	247	8.8	33	0
J.T. Smith, K.C.	39	14	332	8.5	27	0
Walker, Mia.	21	14	169	8.0	33	0
Brennan, Clev.	25	10	199	8.0	19	0
James, S.D.	30	9	208	6.9	t58	1
L. Anderson, Ind.	27	7	182	6.7	19	0
Roaches, Hou.	26	8	152	5.8	18	0

(Non-Qualifiers)

Player—Team	No.	FC	Yds.	Avg.	Lng.	TD
Skansi, Sea.	16	2	145	9.1	16	0
Easley, Sea.	16	5	194	12.1	42	0
Montgomery, L.A.	14	1	194	13.9	t69	1
Simmons, Cin.	12	6	98	8.2	30	0
Johns, Sea.	11	4	140	12.7	t47	1
Starring, N.E.	10	1	73	7.3	16	0
Clayton, Mia.	8	2	79	9.9	22	0
Glasgow, Ind.	7	2	79	11.3	35	0
Woods, Pitt.	6	0	40	6.7	14	0
Walker, Clev.	6	3	50	8.3	13	0
Bird, St.L.-S.D.	6	0	60	10.0	17	0
Heflin, Mia.	6	1	76	12.7	37	0
Kozlowski, Mia.	4	4	41	10.3	20	0
Minter, N.Y. Jets	4	2	44	11.0	18	0
Hancock, K.C.	3	1	14	4.7	7	0
Bouza, Ind.	3	3	17	5.7	11	0
Horton, Cin.	2	0	−1	−0.5	1	0
Bruckner, N.Y. Jets	2	0	25	12.5	20	0
Clayton, Pitt.	1	0	0	0.0	0	0
Henderson, S.D.	1	2	0	0.0	0	0
Long, Pitt.	1	0	0	0.0	0	0
Padjen, Ind.	1	0	0	0.0	0	0
L. Smith, Buff.-S.D.	1	0	0	0.0	0	0
Wilson, Den.	1	0	0	0.0	0	0
Gibson, N.E.	1	0	3	3.0	3	0
Dixon, Sea.	1	0	5	5.0	5	0
C. Weathers, N.E.	1	0	7	7.0	7	0
Mullen, N.Y. Jets	1	0	8	8.0	8	0
G. Blackwood, Mia.	0	4	0	---	0	0
L. Blackwood, Mia.	0	2	0	---	0	0
Chandler, S.D.	0	1	0	---	0	0
R. James, N.E.	0	2	0	---	0	0
Sanford, N.E.	0	2	0	---	0	0

NFC—INDIVIDUALS

Player—Team	No.	FC	Yds.	Avg.	Lng.	TD
ELLARD, Rams	30	3	403	13.4	t83	2
McLemore, S.F.	45	11	521	11.6	t79	1
Mitchell, St.L.	38	3	333	8.8	39	0
Fields, N.O.	27	6	236	8.7	61	0
Nelms, Wash.	49	1	428	8.7	46	0
Fisher, Chi.	57	11	492	8.6	28	0
Martin, Det.	25	8	210	8.4	23	0
Allen, Dall.	54	15	446	8.3	18	0
Nelson, Minn.	23	9	180	7.8	21	0
Bright, T.B.	23	1	173	7.5	21	0
Epps, G.B.	29	10	199	6.9	39	0
McConkey, Giants	46	15	306	6.7	31	0
Cooper, Phila.	40	19	250	6.3	16	0
Z. Th'ms, Den.-T.B.	21	3	125	6.0	15	0

(Non-Qualifiers)

Player—Team	No.	FC	Yds.	Avg.	Lng.	TD
Flynn, G.B.	15	4	128	8.5	20	0
B. Johnson, Atl.	15	1	152	10.1	37	0
K. Johnson, Atl.	10	1	79	7.9	14	0
Curran, Atl.	9	1	21	2.3	10	0
Harris, Clev.-Dall.	9	0	73	8.1	13	0
Irvin, L.A. Rams	9	0	83	9.2	22	0
Seay, Wash.-Atl.	8	1	10	1.3	7	0
Manuel, Giants	8	3	62	7.8	22	0
Hall, Detroit	7	1	30	4.3	11	0
Holt, T.B.	6	3	17	2.8	8	0
Groth, N.O.	6	12	32	5.3	9	0
McKinnon, Chi.	5	0	62	12.4	18	0
T. Bell, T.B.	4	1	10	2.5	8	0
Pittman, St.L.	4	1	10	2.5	5	0
Hayes, G.B.	4	0	24	6.0	10	0
Lewis, Minn.	4	1	31	7.8	13	0
Mandley, Det.	2	2	0	0.0	0	0
Bess, Minn.	2	0	9	4.5	7	0
Green, Wash.	2	0	13	6.5	13	0
Waddy, Minn.	1	0	−3	−3.0	−3	0
Johnson, Det.	1	0	0	0.0	0	0
Kinard, Giants	1	0	0	0.0	0	0
Teal, Minn.	1	0	0	0.0	0	0
G. Williams, Wash.	1	0	0	0.0	0	0
Jenkins, Det.	1	0	1	1.0	1	0
Mauti, Wash.	1	1	2	2.0	2	0
Johnson, Rams	1	1	3	3.0	3	0
Duerson, Chi.	1	0	4	4.0	4	0
Coffey, Wash.	1	0	6	6.0	6	0
Green, St.L.	0	1	0	---	0	0
Murphy, G.B.	0	2	0	---	0	0
Coleman, Wash.	0	0	27	---	27	0

t-Touchdown
Leader based on average return, minimum 20 returns.

1984 KICKOFF RETURNS

YARDS PER RETURN
  AFC: 30.7—Bobby Humphery, N.Y. Jets.
  NFC: 23.0—Barry Redden, L.A. Rams.

MOST YARDS, SEASON
  AFC: 959—Lionel James, San Diego.
  NFC: 891—Darrin Nelson, Minnesota.

MOST YARDS, GAME
  AFC: 179—Van Williams, Buffalo at New England, November 11 (7 returns).
  NFC: 168—Darrin Nelson, Minnesota vs. Chicago, November 25 (7 returns).

LONGEST KICKOFF RETURN
  NFC: 97—Del Rodgers, Green Bay at Chicago, December 9 (TD).
  AFC: 97—Bobby Humphery, N.Y. Jets vs. Pittsburgh, September 6 (TD).

MOST RETURNS, SEASON
  AFC: 43—Lionel James, San Diego.
  NFC: 42—Mike Nelms, Washington.

MOST RETURNS, GAME
  AFC: 7—Rich Erenberg, Pittsburgh vs. Kansas City, September 2 (174 yards).
        David Hughes, Seattle at New England, September 16 (134 yards).
        Van Williams, Buffalo at New England, November 11 (179 yards).
  NFC: 7—Darrin Nelson, Minnesota vs. Chicago, November 25 (168 yards).

TOUCHDOWNS
  AFC: 1—Bobby Humphery, N.Y. Jets vs. Pittsburgh, September 2 (97 yards).
        Phil Smith, Indianapolis vs. St. Louis, September 16 (96 yards).
  NFC: 1—Mike Guman, L.A. Rams at Cincinnati, September 23 (43 yards).
        Del Rodgers, Green Bay at Chicago, December 9 (97 yards).
        Andre Waters, Philadelphia vs. Washington, November 18 (89 yards).

TEAM CHAMPION
  NFC: 22.1—San Francisco.
  AFC: 23.0—N.Y. Jets.

TOP TEN KICKOFF RETURNERS

Player—Team	No.	Yards	Avg.	Long	TDs.
HUMPHERY, BOBBY, N.Y. Jets	22	675	30.7	t97	1
Williams, Dokie, L.A. Raiders	24	621	25.9	62	0
Anderson, Larry, Ind.	22	525	23.9	69	0
Redden, Barry, L.A. Rams	23	530	23.0	40	0
Mitchell, Stump, St.L.	35	804	23.0	56	0
Nelson, Darrin, Minn.	39	891	22.8	47	0
Springs, Kirk, N.Y. Jets	23	521	22.7	73	0
Roaches, Carl, Hou.	30	679	22.6	49	0
James, Lionel, S.D.	43	959	22.3	55	0
Anthony, Tyrone, N.O.	22	490	22.3	64	0

KICKOFF RETURNS—TEAM

AMERICAN FOOTBALL CONFERENCE

Team	No.	Yards	Avg.	Long	TDs.
N.Y. Jets	65	1498	23.0	t97	1
Buffalo	76	1422	18.7	65	0
Houston	69	1352	19.6	49	0
Indianapolis	69	1331	19.3	t96	1
San Diego	63	1319	20.9	55	0
New England	63	1246	19.8	46	0
L.A. Raiders	56	1216	21.7	62	0
Cleveland	61	1157	19.0	40	0
Cincinnati	61	1155	18.9	46	0
Kansas City	56	1061	18.9	45	0
Pittsburgh	54	1026	19.0	47	0
Seattle	54	1007	18.6	38	0
Denver	45	897	19.9	40	0
Miami	44	799	18.2	41	0
Conference Total	836	16486	....	t97	2
Conference Average	59.7	1177.6	19.7	..	0.1

NATIONAL FOOTBALL CONFERENCE

Team	No.	Yards	Avg.	Long	TDs.
Minnesota	86	1775	20.6	47	0
St. Louis	74	1563	21.1	56	0
New Orleans	72	1465	20.3	64	0
Atlanta	70	1367	19.5	50	0
Green Bay	67	1362	20.3	t97	1
Tampa Bay	68	1354	19.9	43	0
Detroit	74	1347	18.2	46	0
L.A. Rams	58	1244	21.4	t43	1
Dallas	63	1199	19.0	34	0
Washington	60	1174	19.6	36	0
Philadelphia	59	1156	19.6	t89	1
N.Y. Giants	61	1117	18.3	52	0
San Francisco	47	1039	22.1	51	0
Chicago	49	896	18.3	40	0
Conference Total	908	18058	....	t97	3
Conference Average	64.9	1289.9	19.9	..	0.2
League Total	1744	34544	....	t97	5
League Average	62.3	1233.7	19.8	..	0.2

AFC—INDIVIDUALS

Player—Team	No.	Yds.	Avg.	Lng.	TD	Player—Team	No.	Yds.	Avg.	Lng.	TD
Humphery, N.Y. Jets	22	675	30.7	t97	1	Pruitt, L.A. Raiders	3	16	5.3	13	0
Williams, L.A. Raiders	24	621	25.9	62	0	Paige, N.Y. Jets	3	7	2.3	7	0
L. Anderson, Ind.	22	525	23.9	69	0	Mullen, N.Y. Jets	2	34	17.0	23	0
Springs, N.Y. Jets	23	521	22.7	73	0	Hancock, K.C.	2	32	16.0	17	0
Roaches, Hou.	30	679	22.6	49	0	Dennison, Den.	2	27	13.5	16	0
James, S.D.	43	959	22.3	55	0	Kozlowski, Mia.	2	23	11.5	12	0
Collins, N.E.	25	544	21.8	46	0	Egloff, S.D.	2	20	10.0	11	0
Montgomery, L.A.	26	555	21.3	42	0	Moore, Ind.	2	19	9.5	10	0
Walker, Mia.	29	617	21.3	41	0	Clayton, Mia.	2	15	7.5	14	0
Va. Williams, Buff.	39	820	21.0	65	0	Jones, N.E.	1	20	20.0	20	0
Jennings, Cin.	22	452	20.5	46	0	Bruckner, N.Y. Jets	1	17	17.0	17	0
Erenberg, Pitt.	28	575	20.5	47	0	Thompson, Hou.	1	16	16.0	16	0
P. Smith, Ind.	32	651	20.3	t96	1	Bell, Buff.	1	15	15.0	15	0
Paige, K.C.	27	544	20.1	45	0	Corley, Pitt.	1	15	15.0	15	0
J. Williams, N.E.	23	461	20.0	29	0	Simmons, Cin.	1	15	15.0	15	0
Byner, Clev.	22	415	18.9	28	0	Hawthorne, N.E.	1	14	14.0	14	0
Dixon, Sea.	25	446	17.8	36	0	Hill, Mia.	1	14	14.0	14	0
Wilson, Buff.	34	576	16.9	36	0	Willis, L.A. Raiders	1	13	13.0	13	0
(Non-Qualifiers)						Gillespie, Pitt.	1	12	12.0	12	0
Lang, Den.	19	404	21.3	38	0	Harris, Cin.	1	12	12.0	12	0
J.T. Smith, K.C.	19	391	20.6	39	0	Nicolas, Clev.	1	12	12.0	12	0
Martin, Cin.	19	386	20.3	44	0	C. Brown, Pitt.	1	11	11.0	11	0
Spencer, Pitt.	18	373	20.7	40	0	Jensen, L.A. Raiders	1	11	11.0	11	0
B. Davis, Clev.	18	369	20.5	40	0	Middleton, Ind.	1	11	11.0	11	0
Hughes, Sea.	17	348	20.5	38	0	Contz, Clev.	1	10	10.0	10	0
Walls, Hou.	15	289	19.3	29	0	Jackson, S.D.	1	10	10.0	10	0
McGee, S.D.	14	315	22.5	35	0	Davidson, N.Y. Jets	1	9	9.0	9	0
Allen, Hou.	11	210	19.1	23	0	Scott, K.C.	1	9	9.0	9	0
Bird, St.L-S.D.	11	205	18.6	28	0	Tatupu, N.E.	1	9	9.0	9	0
Minter, N.Y. Jets	10	224	22.4	52	0	J. Harris, Sea.	1	7	7.0	7	0
Heflin, Mia.	9	130	14.4	26	0	Kinnebrew, Cin.	1	7	7.0	7	0
Morris, Sea.	8	153	19.1	34	0	David, Buff.	1	6	6.0	6	0
Brown, Clev.	8	136	17.0	27	0	Gaffney, N.Y. Jets	1	6	6.0	6	0
Brooks, Cin.	7	144	20.6	37	0	Banker, N.Y. Jets	1	5	5.0	5	0
Farley, Cin.	6	93	15.5	32	0	White, Buff.	1	5	5.0	5	0
Young, Clev.	5	134	26.8	36	0	Harden, Den.	1	4	4.0	4	0
Fryar, N.E.	5	95	19.0	22	0	Carson, K.C.	1	2	2.0	2	0
R. Williams, Atl.-Hou.	5	84	16.8	21	0	Hathaway, Ind.	1	2	2.0	2	0
Ricks, K.C.	5	83	16.6	21	0	Sherwin, Ind.	1	2	2.0	2	0
White, Clev.	5	80	16.0	23	0	A. Smith, Den.	1	2	2.0	2	0
Kafentzis, Ind.	5	69	13.8	22	0	Holt, Clev.	1	1	1.0	1	0
Willhite, Den.	4	109	27.3	40	0	Catano, Pitt.	1	0	0.0	0	0
Wonsley, Ind.	4	52	13.0	20	0	Cherry, K.C.	1	0	0.0	0	0
Veals, Pitt.	4	40	10.0	18	0	Duhe, Mia.	1	0	0.0	0	0
Joyner, Hou.	3	57	19.0	24	0	Gofourth, S.D.	1	0	0.0	0	0
C. Bryant, Sea.	3	53	17.7	21	0	McKinney, Raiders	1	0	0.0	0	0
Verser, Cin.	3	46	15.3	23	0	Radachovsky, Ind.	1	0	0.0	0	0
K.L. Lee, N.E.	3	43	14.3	17	0	Shuler, N.Y. Jets	1	0	0.0	0	0
Robinson, N.E.	3	38	12.7	14	0	G. Williams, Cin.	1	0	0.0	0	0
Brown, Hou.	3	17	5.7	17	0	J. Williams, Hou.	1	0	0.0	0	0

NFC—INDIVIDUALS

Player—Team	No.	Yds.	Avg.	Lng.	TD
REDDEN, L.A. Rams...	23	530	23.0	40	0
Mitchell, St.L.	35	804	23.0	56	0
Dar. Nelson, Minn.	39	891	22.8	47	0
Anthony, N.O.	22	490	22.3	64	0
Morton, T.B.	38	835	22.0	43	0
Rodgers, G.B.	39	843	21.6	t97	1
Anderson, Minn.	30	639	21.3	41	0
Dr. Hill, L.A. Rams	26	543	20.9	40	0
Monroe, S.F.	27	561	20.8	44	0
Nelms, Wash.	42	860	20.5	36	0
Allen, Dall.	33	666	20.2	34	0
McSwain, Dall.	20	403	20.2	32	0
Hayes, Phila.	22	441	20.0	44	0
Duckett, N.O.	29	580	20.0	39	0
McConkey, N.Y. Giants	28	541	19.3	33	0
Cameron, Chi.	26	485	18.7	40	0
Mandley, Det.	22	390	17.7	32	0

(Non-Qualifiers)

Player—Team	No.	Yds.	Avg.	Lng.	TD
Stamps, Atl.	19	452	23.8	50	0
Hall, Det.	19	385	20.3	46	0
K. Johnson, Atl.	19	359	18.9	27	0
Fields, N.O.	19	356	18.7	31	0
Jenkins, Det.	18	396	22.0	32	0
Z. Thomas, Den.-T.B.	18	351	19.5	33	0
Cooper, Phila.	17	299	17.6	48	0
Bright, T.B.	16	303	18.9	33	0
Pittman, St.L.	14	319	22.8	43	0
Huckleby, G.B.	14	261	18.6	54	0
Woolfolk, N.Y. Giants	14	232	16.6	27	0
Harmon, S.F.	13	357	27.5	51	0
Waters, Phila.	13	319	24.5	t89	1
Harrell, St.L.	13	231	17.8	28	0
Epps, G.B.	12	232	19.3	47	0
Curran, Atl.	11	219	19.9	42	0
Gentry, Chi.	11	209	19.0	33	0
Martin, Det.	10	144	14.4	23	0
Cephous, N.Y. Giants	9	178	19.8	30	0
Griffin, Wash.	9	164	18.2	31	0
Tate, Atl.	9	148	16.4	31	0
Owens, T.B.	8	168	21.0	36	0
Fellows, Dall.	6	94	15.7	23	0
Morris, N.Y. Giants	6	69	11.5	14	0
Seay, Wash.-Atl.	5	108	21.6	28	0
Jordan, Chi.	5	62	12.4	22	0
Wood, T.B.	5	43	8.6	16	0
Duerson, Chi.	4	95	23.8	26	0
Austin, Atl.	4	77	19.3	23	0
Meade, Det.	4	32	8.0	15	0

Player—Team	No.	Yds.	Avg.	Lng.	TD
McLemore, S.F.	3	80	26.7	50	0
Waddy, Minn.	3	64	21.3	31	0
Bess, Minn.	3	47	15.7	19	0
Kane, Wash.	3	43	14.3	31	0
Everett, Phila.	3	40	13.3	18	0
Rice, Minn.	3	34	11.3	13	0
Pleasant, L.A. Rams	2	48	24.0	29	0
B. Johnson, Atl.	2	39	19.5	21	0
Smith, Wash.	2	38	19.0	22	0
Bell, Chi.	2	33	16.5	17	0
Irvin, L.A. Rams	2	33	16.5	22	0
Salonen, Dall.	2	30	15.0	22	0
Smith, Minn.	2	26	13.0	15	0
Ellis, Phila.	2	25	12.5	15	0
Ellard, L.A. Rams	2	24	12.0	12	0
Rouse, Minn.	2	22	11.0	15	0
Turner, Minn.	2	21	10.5	14	0
McLaughlin, Giants	2	18	9.0	11	0
Granger, Dall.	2	6	3.0	5	0
Daniel, N.Y. Giants	1	52	52.0	52	0
Guman, L.A. Rams	1	43	43.0	t43	1
Lewis, Minn.	1	31	31.0	31	0
Hill, N.Y. Giants	1	27	27.0	27	0
Ring, S.F.	1	27	27.0	27	0
W. Wilson, N.O.	1	23	23.0	23	0
R. Smith, N.E.-Wash.	1	22	22.0	22	0
Crutchfield, L.A. Rams.	1	20	20.0	20	0
Hardy, Phila.	1	20	20.0	20	0
D. Jones, G.B.	1	19	19.0	19	0
Green, St.L.	1	18	18.0	18	0
Mauti, Wash.	1	16	16.0	16	0
T. Wilson, N.O.	1	16	16.0	16	0
Gaison, Atl.	1	15	15.0	15	0
Wilson, S.F.	1	14	14.0	14	0
Gault, Chi.	1	12	12.0	12	0
Strauthers, Phila.	1	12	12.0	12	0
Prather, G.B.	1	7	7.0	7	0
Spradlin, T.B.	1	5	5.0	5	0
Matthews, Atl.	1	3	3.0	3	0
Sully, L.A. Rams	1	3	3.0	3	0
Love, St.L.	1	1	1.0	1	0
Cooper, S.F.	1	0	0.0	0	0
D'Addio, Det.	1	0	0.0	0	0
Ferrell, St.L.	1	0	0.0	0	0
Malancon, Atl.	1	0	0.0	0	0
McIntyre, S.F.	1	0	0.0	0	0
Dav. Nelson, Minn.	1	0	0.0	0	0
Tyrrell, Atl.	1	0	0.0	0	0

t—Touchdown.
Leader based on average return, minimum 20 returns

1984 AFC FIELD GOALS—INDIVIDUAL

Kicker and Club	1-19	20-29	30-39	40-49	50 & over	Totals	Avg. Yds. Att.	Avg. Yds. Made	Avg. Yds. Miss	Lg.
Johnson, Norm	0-0	9-10	4-4	6-7	1-3	20-24	35.5	33.9	43.8	50
Seattle	......	.900	1.000	.857	.333	.833				
Franklin, Tony	2-2	10-10	4-7	6-8	0-1	22-28	33.1	30.7	42.0	48
New England	1.000	1.000	.571	.750	.000	.786				
Anderson, Gary	0-0	8-9	6-9	8-11	2-3	24-32	36.7	35.3	41.0	55
Pittsburgh	......	.889	.667	.727	.667	.750				
Bahr, Matt	3-3	12-12	2-7	6-9	1-1	24-32	33.8	32.3	38.3	50
Cleveland	1.000	1.000	.286	.667	1.000	.750				
Karlis, Rich	1-1	6-7	7-8	6-9	1-3	21-28	36.0	34.1	41.4	50
Denver	1.000	.857	.875	.667	.333	.750				
Bahr, Chris	1-1	7-7	4-7	7-11	1-1	20-27	35.3	33.7	40.0	50
L.A. Raiders	1.000	1.000	.571	.636	1.000	.741				
Breech, Jim	0-0	9-10	10-12	3-4	0-5	22-31	35.0	31.4	43.8	48
Cincinnati	......	.900	.833	.750	.000	.710				
Leahy, Pat	2-2	5-6	7-8	2-5	1-3	17-24	35.3	32.2	42.6	52
N.Y. Jets	1.000	.833	.875	.400	.333	.708				
Lowery, Nick	0-0	7-7	6-11	8-10	2-5	23-33	38.2	36.3	42.6	52
Kansas City	......	1.000	.545	.800	.400	.697				
Benirschke, Rolf	1-1	4-6	3-4	8-11	1-4	17-26	39.4	37.0	44.0	51
San Diego	1.000	.667	.750	.727	.250	.654				
Allegre, Raul	0-0	4-4	1-2	3-6	3-6	11-18	42.1	38.5	47.9	54
Indianapolis	......	1.000	.500	.500	.500	.611				
Danelo, Joe	0-0	5-5	2-4	0-4	1-3	8-16	36.6	30.6	42.6	52
Buffalo	......	1.000	.500	.000	.333	.500				
von Schamann, Uwe	0-0	7-7	2-5	0-4	0-3	9-19	36.8	27.9	44.9	37
Miami	......	1.000	.400	.000	.000	.474				

Non-Qualifiers (Fewer than 16 attempts)

Kicker and Club	1-19	20-29	30-39	40-49	50 & over	Totals	Avg. Yds. Att.	Avg. Yds. Made	Avg. Yds. Miss	Lg.
Ricardo, Benny	0-0	1-1	1-1	1-1	0-0	3-3	36.3	36.3	0-0	42
San Diego	......	1.000	1.000	1.000	......	1.000				
Cooper, Joe	2-2	2-2	4-4	3-5	0-0	11-13	33.7	32.1	42.5	44
Houston	1.000	1.000	1.000	.600	......	.846				
Kempf, Florian	0-0	3-3	0-1	1-2	0-0	4-6	32.7	30.0	38.0	49
Houston	......	1.000	.000	.500	......	.667				
Biasucci, Dean	0-0	1-1	0-0	1-1	1-3	3-5	44.2	38.0	53.5	50
Indianapolis	......	1.000	......	1.000	.333	.600				
Nelson, Chuck	0-0	0-0	1-2	2-3	0-0	3-5	40.6	41.0	40.0	47
Buffalo	......	......	.500	.667	......	.600				
Cox, Steve	0-0	0-0	0-0	0-0	1-3	1-3	58.7	60.0	58.0	60
Cleveland	......	......	......	......	.333	.333				
Conference Totals	12-12	100-107	64-96	71-111	16-47	263-373	36.5	33.7	43.0	60
	1.000	.935	.667	.640	.340	.750				
League Totals	25-25	178-192	173-231	150-248	37-89	563-785	36.8	34.4	43.0	60
	1.000	.927	.749	.605	.416	.717				

1984 NFC FIELD GOALS—INDIVIDUAL

Kicker and Club	1-19	20-29	30-39	40-49	50 & over	Totals	Avg. Yds. Att.	Avg. Yds. Made	Avg. Yds. Miss	Lg.
Stenerud, Jan	2-2	3-3	9-9	3-5	3-4	20-23	37.0	35.3	48.3	54
Minnesota	1.000	1.000	1.000	.600	.750	.870				
McFadden, Paul	0-0	4-5	13-16	10-12	3-4	30-37	38.2	37.7	40.4	52
Philadelphia	......	.800	.813	.833	.750	.811				
Septien, Rafael	2-2	6-7	9-9	4-8	2-3	23-29	35.2	33.0	43.7	52
Dallas	1.000	.857	1.000	.500	.667	.793				
Thomas, Bob	3-3	6-7	5-6	6-9	2-3	22-28	36.2	34.9	41.0	52
Chicago	1.000	.857	.833	.667	.667	.786				
Moseley, Mark	1-1	9-10	12-13	1-5	1-2	24-31	33.1	30.6	41.7	51
Washington	1.000	.900	.923	.200	.500	.774				
Lansford, Mike	2-2	9-9	10-13	3-7	1-2	25-33	33.9	31.4	41.8	50
L.A. Rams	1.000	1.000	.769	.429	.500	.758				
Andersen, Morten	0-0	9-9	4-5	5-10	2-3	20-27	37.1	34.9	43.7	53
New Orleans	......	1.000	.800	.500	.667	.741				
Luckhurst, Mick	0-0	4-4	9-10	4-9	3-4	20-27	39.9	37.9	45.6	52
Atlanta	......	1.000	.900	.444	.750	.741				
Murray, Ed	1-1	1-2	5-7	12-13	1-4	20-27	40.6	40.2	42.0	52
Detroit	1.000	.500	.714	.923	.250	.741				
Ariri, Obed	0-0	7-7	6-7	6-10	0-2	19-26	37.6	35.0	44.7	49
Tampa Bay	......	1.000	.857	.600	.000	.731				
Wersching, Ray	1-1	8-8	8-11	7-13	1-2	25-35	37.0	34.5	43.3	53
San Francisco	1.000	1.000	.727	.538	.500	.714				
O'Donoghue, Neil	0-0	7-7	7-9	8-16	1-3	23-35	38.6	35.7	44.2	52
St. Louis	......	1.000	.778	.500	.333	.657				
Haji-Sheikh, Ali	1-1	3-3	8-13	5-12	0-4	17-33	38.8	34.2	43.8	48
N.Y. Giants	1.000	1.000	.615	.417	.000	.515				
Non-Qualifiers (Fewer than 16 attempts)										
Del Greco, Al	0-0	2-2	3-4	4-5	0-1	9-12	37.3	34.7	45.3	45
Green Bay	......	1.000	.750	.800	.000	.750				
Garcia, Eddie	0-0	0-2	1-3	1-3	1-1	3-9	39.0	43.3	36.8	51
Green Bay	......	.000	.333	.333	1.000	.333				
Conference Totals	13-13	78-85	109-135	79-137	21-42	300-412	37.2	35.0	43.0	54
	1.000	.918	.807	.577	.500	.728				

1984 FUMBLES—TEAM

NATIONAL FOOTBALL CONFERENCE

	Fum.	Own Rec.	Fum. *O.B.	TDs.	Opp. Rec.	Yds.	TDs.	Tot. Rec.
N.Y. Giants	17	8	0	0	16	88	1	24
Green Bay	17	10	0	0	15	—5	0	25
New Orleans	22	9	0	0	10	20	1	19
Philadelphia	23	7	0	0	11	0	0	18
San Francisco	26	13	1	0	12	45	1	25
Chicago	31	11	4	0	13	—2	0	24
L.A. Rams	31	11	2	0	22	36	0	33
St. Louis	32	10	2	0	12	56	1	22
Washington	33	16	2	1	21	62	2	37
Dallas	35	14	4	0	16	18	1	30
Detroit	36	21	1	0	11	—20	0	32
Tampa Bay	36	16	0	0	14	11	0	30
Atlanta	39	18	0	0	20	12	0	38
Minnesota	39	22	1	0	17	57	2	39
Conference Totals	417	186	17	1	210	378	9	396
Conference Average	29.8	13.3	1.2	0.1	15.0	27.0	0.6	28.3

AMERICAN FOOTBALL CONFERENCE

	Fum.	Own Rec.	Fum. *O.B.	TDs.	Opp. Rec.	Yds.	TDs.	Tot. Rec.
Seattle	24	8	3	0	25	—21	1	33
N.Y. Jets	26	12	1	0	18	68	2	30
Miami	26	16	0	0	12	60	1	28
New England	29	12	2	1	8	0	0	20
Buffalo	31	11	6	0	21	104	2	32
Cleveland	31	14	1	1	15	112	0	29
Cincinnati	32	13	2	0	15	0	0	28
Kansas City	34	16	3	0	11	—41	0	27
Indianapolis	35	14	5	0	13	—28	0	27
San Diego	35	14	4	0	17	19	0	31
Denver	36	18	1	0	24	117	4	42
Houston	36	19	1	0	11	18	1	30
Pittsburgh	40	23	2	0	10	104	2	33
L.A. Raiders	42	20	2	0	14	84	1	34
Conference Totals	457	210	33	2	214	596	14	424
Conference Average	32.6	15.0	2.4	0.1	15.3	42.6	1.0	30.3
League Totals	874	396	50	3	424	974	23	820
League Average	31.2	14.1	1.8	0.1	15.1	34.8	0.8	29.3

*Fumbled out of bounds.

Total yards include all fumble yardage (aborted plays, own & opponents recoveries). Fumbled through the end zone, ball awarded to opponents: Cincinnati (awarded to Pittsburgh), Detroit (awarded to Minnesota), Indianapolis (awarded to N.Y. Jets), Minnesota (awarded to Washington), L.A. Rams (awarded to San Francisco).

AFC—INDIVIDUALS

Player—Team	Fum.	Own Rec.	Opp. Rec.	Yds.	Tot. Rec.	Player—Team	Fum.	Own Rec.	Opp. Rec.	Yds.	Tot. Rec.
Adams, Clev.	1	0	0	0	0	Bingham, Hou.	0	0	1	7	1
Alexander, Cin.	2	0	0	0	0	Bingham, N.Y. Jets	0	0	1	0	1
Allen, L.A. Raiders	8	2	1	0	3	Bird, St.L.-S.D.	1	0	0	0	0
Alzado, L.A. Raiders	0	0	1	0	1	Blackledge, K.C.	8	4	0	—3	4
Anderson, Cin.	1	0	0	0	0	G. Blackwood, Mia.	0	0	1	0	1
L. Anderson, Ind.	4	0	0	0	0	L. Blackwood, Mia.	0	0	2	0	2
J. Arnold, K.C.	1	2	0	—9	2	Blanton, K.C.	0	0	1	0	1
Avellini, Chi.-N.Y. Jets.	2	0	0	0	0	Bolden, Clev.	1	0	0	0	0
Azelby, Buff.	0	0	1	0	1	Bostic, Hou.	0	0	2	25	2
Baab, Clev.	1	0	0	—11	0	Bouza, Ind.	1	0	0	0	0
Bailey, Ind.	2	0	1	—27	1	Bowser, Mia.	0	0	1	0	1
Baker, Hou.	0	0	1	0	1	Bowyer, Den.	0	0	1	0	1
Banks, Clev.	0	0	3	17	3	Branch, L.A. Raiders	0	2	0	2	2
Barber, N.Y. Jets	3	1	0	0	1	Brazile, Hou.	0	0	1	0	1
Barnes, L.A. Raiders	0	0	1	0	1	Breeden, Cin.	1	0	0	0	0
Barnett, Buff.	0	1	0	0	1	Brennan, Clev.	1	0	0	0	0
Barnwell, L.A. Raiders.	1	1	0	0	1	Brewer, Den.	0	0	1	0	1
Baumhower, Mia.	0	0	2	23	2	Brooks, Cin.	4	0	0	0	0
Bell, Buff.	5	3	0	0	3	C. Brown, Pitt.	0	0	1	0	1
Bell, Ind.	0	1	0	0	1	Brown, Sea.	1	0	0	0	0
Bell, K.C.	1	0	2	0	2	Brown, Hou.	1	0	1	0	1
Bendross, S.D.	1	0	0	0	0	Brown, K.C.	2	0	0	0	0
Bennett, N.Y. Jets	0	0	4	6	4	Browner, Cin.	0	0	1	0	1
Bennett, Mia.	4	2	0	0	2	Bruckner, N.Y. Jets	0	1	0	0	1
Betters, Mia.	0	0	1	0	1	Bryan, Den.	1	0	0	0	0
Bingham, Pitt.	0	0	1	0	1	C. Bryant, Sea.	0	1	0	0	1

Player—Team	Fum.	Own Rec.	Opp. Rec.	Yds.	Tot. Rec.
J. Bryant, Sea.	0	0	2	0	2
Bryant, Hou.	1	0	0	0	0
Burruss, K.C.	0	0	1	0	1
Busick, Den.	0	0	1	0	1
Buttle, N.Y. Jets	0	0	0	4	2
Byner, Clev.	3	2	0	55	2
Camp, Clev.	0	0	1	0	1
Campbell, Pitt.	1	1	0	0	1
Capers, Pitt.	1	2	0	2	2
Carpenter, Wash.-Buff.	0	0	2	0	2
Carson, K.C.	0	1	1	0	2
Carter, Mia.	3	2	0	0	2
Carter, Den.	0	0	2	0	2
Cefalo, Mia.	1	0	0	0	0
Christensen, L.A.	1	0	1	0	1
Clayton, Pitt.	0	0	1	0	1
Clayton, Mia.	2	1	0	0	1
Clifton, N.Y. Jets	0	0	1	0	1
Cole, Pitt.	0	0	1	8	1
Collins, N.E.	3	0	0	0	0
Collins, Cin.	0	0	1	0	1
Collinsworth, Cin.	0	1	0	0	1
Comeaux, Den.	0	0	1	0	1
Condon, K.C.	0	1	0	0	1
Corley, Pitt.	0	2	0	0	2
Cousineau, Clev.	0	0	2	0	2
Curtis, Cin.	1	0	0	0	0
Dalby, L.A. Raiders	0	1	0	0	1
Daniels, K.C.	0	0	2	0	2
B. Davis, Clev.	2	0	0	0	0
J. Davis, L.A. Raiders	0	1	1	0	2
M. Davis, L.A. Raiders	0	0	1	0	1
Dawkins, Buff.	0	1	0	0	1
Dawson, N.E.	0	1	0	0	1
DeLamielleure, Clev.	0	1	0	0	1
Dennard, Buff.	1	0	0	0	0
Dennison, Den.	0	1	0	0	1
Dickey, Ind.	6	1	0	0	1
Dieken, Clev.	0	1	0	0	1
Dixon, Clev.	0	0	1	0	1
Dixon, Sea.	1	0	0	0	0
Dressel, Hou.	1	0	0	0	0
Duckworth, S.D.	1	0	0	0	0
Dufek, Sea.	0	0	1	0	1
Dufek, Buff.	1	0	0	0	0
Duper, Mia.	0	1	0	0	1
Easley, Sea.	0	0	1	0	1
Eason, Hou.	0	0	1	0	1
Eason, N.E.	7	2	0	-5	2
Edwards, Cin.	0	0	3	-2	3
Edwards, Hou.	2	0	0	0	0
Ehin, S.D.	0	0	1	0	1
Elway, Den.	14	5	0	-10	5
Erenberg, Pitt.	3	3	0	0	3
Esiason, Cin.	4	2	0	-2	2
Farley, Cin.	1	1	0	0	1
Farren, Clev.	0	1	0	0	1
Faurot, N.Y. Jets	0	0	1	0	1
Ferguson, Buff.	8	2	0	-26	2
Ferguson, S.D.	0	0	1	0	1
Fields, N.Y. Jets	0	1	0	0	1
Flick, Clev.	1	0	0	0	0
Foley, Den.	0	0	2	22	2
Foster, Mia.	0	1	0	0	1
Fouts, S.D.	8	1	0	0	1
Fox, S.D.	0	0	1	0	1
Franklin, Buff.	4	0	0	0	0
Freeman, Buff.	0	0	1	0	1
Fryar, N.E.	4	1	0	0	1
Gaffney, N.Y. Jets	0	1	0	0	1
Garnett, Den.	0	0	1	0	1
Gary, Pitt.	0	0	1	6	1
Gastineau, N.Y. Jets	0	0	1	0	1
Gibson, N.E.	0	0	1	0	1
Gillespie, Pitt.	1	2	0	0	2
Glasgow, Ind.	1	0	1	3	1
Golden, N.E.	0	1	0	0	1
Golic, Clev.	0	0	1	18	1
Green, Clev.	3	2	0	0	2
Green, Sea.	0	0	4	0	4
Green, S.D.	0	0	1	0	1
Greene, S.D.	0	0	2	0	2
J. Griffin, Cin.	0	2	0	0	2
R. Griffin, Cin.	0	0	1	0	1
Grogan, N.E.	4	2	0	-3	2
Gross, Clev.	0	0	2	28	2
Hamm, Hou.	0	0	1	0	1
Hancock, K.C.	1	1	0	0	1
Harden, Den.	1	0	2	0	2
J. Harris, Sea.	0	0	1	0	1
Harris, Cin.	2	1	0	0	1
Hartwig, Hou.	0	0	1	0	1
Haslett, Buff.	0	0	3	10	3
Hathaway, Ind.	0	0	1	0	1
Hawkins, L.A. Raiders	3	1	0	0	1
Heard, K.C.	5	3	0	0	3
Hector, N.Y. Jets	2	0	0	0	0
Heflin, Mia.	1	0	0	0	0
Henderson, S.D.	1	0	0	0	0
Hill, K.C.	1	0	0	0	0
Hinkle, Pitt.	0	0	2	21	2
Holle, K.C.	0	0	1	2	1
Holman, Cin.	1	0	1	0	1
Holohan, S.D.	0	1	1	19	2
Holston, Hou.	0	1	0	0	1
Horton, Cin.	0	0	1	0	1
Hughes, Sea.	4	2	1	0	3
Humiston, Ind.	0	0	2	0	2
Humm, L.A. Raiders	2	1	0	0	1
Humphery, N.Y. Jets	2	2	0	0	2
Hunter, Buff.	1	1	0	0	1
B. Jackson, K.C.	2	0	1	0	1
Jackson, S.D.	3	2	0	0	2
Jackson, Clev.	0	1	0	0	1
Jackson, Cin.	0	1	2	0	3
T. Jackson, Den.	0	0	1	0	1
C. James, N.E.	4	0	0	0	0
James, S.D.	9	4	0	0	4
R. James, N.E.	0	0	1	0	1
Jennings, Cin.	3	2	0	-4	2
Johns, Sea.	2	0	0	0	0
Johnson, Den.	1	0	0	0	0
K. Johnson, Buff.	0	0	1	0	1
Johnson, Hou.	0	0	1	0	1
P. Johnson, S.D.-Mia.	1	2	0	0	2
Joiner, Hou.	0	1	0	0	1
Jones, N.E.	1	1	0	0	1
Jones, N.Y. Jets	1	0	0	0	0
R. Jones, Den.	0	0	2	5	2
Judie, Mia.	0	1	0	0	1
Judson, Mia.	0	0	2	37	2
Kafentzis, Ind.	1	0	0	0	0
Kauahi, Sea.	0	0	2	0	2
Kay, Den.	1	0	0	0	0
Keating, Buff.	0	0	1	34	1
Kemp, Cin.	1	0	1	0	1
Kenney, K.C.	8	3	0	-34	3
King, L.A. Raiders	3	1	0	0	1
King, S.D.	1	0	2	0	2
Kinnebrew, Cin.	4	0	0	0	0
Klecko, N.Y. Jets	0	0	2	0	2
Kofler, Buff.	1	1	0	0	1
Krauss, Ind.	1	0	2	-5	2
Kreider, Cin.	1	0	0	0	0
Krieg, Sea.	11	3	0	-24	3
Krumrie, Cin.	0	0	1	8	1
Kubiak, Den.	1	0	0	0	0
Kush, Buff.	1	0	1	0	1
Lacy, K.C.	2	0	0	0	0
Lane, Sea.	1	1	2	0	3
Lang, Den.	0	1	0	6	1
Lanier, Den.	0	1	0	0	1
Lankford, Mia.	0	0	1	0	1
Largent, Sea.	1	0	0	0	0
Lilly, Den.	1	0	1	3	1
Lippett, N.E.	1	0	1	0	1
Lipps, Pitt.	8	2	0	0	2
Long, L.A. Raiders	0	0	2	4	2
Long, Pitt.	1	0	0	0	0
Lowe, S.D.	1	0	0	0	0
Luck, Hou.	2	2	0	0	2
Luther, S.D.	2	0	0	0	0

Player—Team	Fum.	Own Rec.	Opp. Rec.	Yds.	Tot. Rec.
Lynn, N.Y. Jets	0	0	0	2	0
Malone, Pitt.	4	2	0	0	2
Marino, Mia.	6	2	0	-3	2
Marion, N.E.	0	1	0	0	1
Marshall, K.C.	2	0	0	0	0
Martin, Cin.	4	2	0	0	2
Martin, L.A. Raiders	0	0	1	77	1
Marve, Buff.	0	0	3	0	3
Marvin, L.A. Raiders	0	1	0	0	1
Matthews, Clev.	0	0	1	0	1
Maxwell, Ind.	0	0	2	0	2
McAlister, K.C.	0	1	0	0	1
McDonald, Clev.	16	5	0	-5	5
McElroy, L.A. Raiders	0	1	3	12	4
McGee, S.D.	1	1	0	0	1
McKinney, Raiders	1	1	0	0	1
McKnight, S.D.	0	2	0	0	2
McMillan, Ind.	1	0	0	0	0
McNeal, Mia.	0	0	2	5	2
McNeil, N.Y. Jets	4	1	0	0	1
McPherson, S.D.	0	0	1	0	1
McSwain, N.E.	0	0	1	0	1
Mecklenburg, Den.	0	0	1	0	1
Mehl, N.Y. Jets	0	0	1	0	1
Merriweather, Pitt.	0	0	1	0	1
Metzelaars, Sea.	1	0	0	0	0
Middleton, Ind.	2	2	0	0	2
Minnifield, Clev.	0	0	2	10	2
Minter, N.Y. Jets	1	0	0	0	0
Montgomery, Raiders	1	1	0	0	1
Moon, Hou.	17	7	0	-1	7
Moore, Ind.	3	0	0	0	0
Moore, Buff.	4	1	0	0	1
Moore, Mia.	2	0	0	0	0
Moriarty, Hou.	5	2	0	-3	2
Morris, Sea.	2	1	0	0	1
Morris, S.D.	0	1	0	0	1
Muncie, S.D.	1	0	0	0	0
Munoz, Cin.	0	1	0	0	1
Nash, Sea.	0	0	3	0	3
Nathan, Mia.	3	1	0	0	1
Nicolas, Clev.	0	0	1	0	1
Norman, Den.	1	1	0	0	1
O'Brien, N.Y. Jets	4	2	0	0	2
Odom, Ind.	0	0	1	0	1
Owens, N.E.	0	0	1	0	1
Padjen, Ind.	1	0	0	0	0
Pagel, Ind.	4	1	0	0	1
Paige, N.Y. Jets	1	0	0	0	0
Petersen, Clev.-Ind.	0	1	0	0	1
Plunkett, L.A. Raiders	2	1	0	0	1
Pollard, Pitt.	9	2	0	0	2
T. Porter, Ind.	2	1	0	0	1
Pruitt, L.A. Raiders	9	2	0	0	2
Pruitt, Clev.	1	1	0	0	1
Puzzuoli, Clev.	0	0	1	0	1
Radachowsky, Ind.	1	0	0	0	0
Randle, Ind.	0	1	1	0	2
Ray, N.Y. Jets	0	0	0	52	0
Razzano, Cin.	0	0	1	0	1
Riddick, Buff.	1	0	0	0	0
Roaches, Hou.	1	1	0	0	1
Robbins, Den.	0	0	1	0	1
Robinson, N.E.	0	1	0	0	1
Robinson, Sea.	0	0	4	3	4
Romano, Raid-Hou.	1	0	0	-11	0
Romes, Buff.	0	0	1	0	1
Ross, K.C.	0	0	1	0	1
Rudolph, N.Y. Jets	0	0	1	0	1
Ryan, Den.	0	0	1	0	1
Ryan, N.Y. Jets	4	1	0	0	1
Sampson, Den.	1	0	0	0	0
Sanford, Buff.	0	0	2	46	2
Sawyer, Den.	0	2	0	0	2
Schlichter, Ind.	4	3	0	1	3
Scholtz, Sea.	0	0	1	0	1
Schonert, Cin.	2	0	0	0	0
Schroy, N.Y. Jets	0	0	2	0	2
Shuler, N.Y. Jets	1	0	0	0	0
Sievers, S.D.	1	0	1	0	1
Simpkins, Cin.	0	0	1	0	1
Simpson, Sea.	0	0	2	0	2
Smerlas, Buff.	0	0	2	0	2
A. Smith, Den.	1	0	0	0	0
B.R. Smith, S.D.	0	0	3	0	3
D. Smith, Den.	0	0	1	64	1
J.T. Smith, K.C.	1	0	0	0	0
L. Smith, Buff.-S.D.	1	0	0	0	0
P. Smith, Ind.	1	0	0	0	0
Smith, Hou.	0	1	0	0	1
Snell, Pitt.	0	1	0	0	1
Solt, Ind.	0	1	0	0	1
Sowell, Mia.	0	1	0	0	1
Spencer, Pitt.	5	2	0	0	2
Springs, N.Y. Jets	3	1	1	4	2
Squirek, L.A. Raiders	0	0	1	0	1
Stallworth, Pitt.	1	0	0	0	0
Stankavage, Den.	0	1	0	0	1
Stark, Ind.	0	1	0	0	1
Starring, N.E.	1	1	0	8	1
Stensrud, Hou.	0	0	1	0	1
Stephenson, Mia.	0	1	0	0	1
Still, K.C.	0	0	1	3	1
Strock, Mia.	1	0	0	-2	0
Summers, Den.	0	1	0	0	1
Talley, Buff.	0	0	1	0	1
Tatupu, N.E.	4	1	0	0	1
Thomas, S.D.	1	1	0	0	1
Thomas, Mia.	0	1	0	0	1
Thompson, Pitt.	1	0	0	0	0
Tongue, Buff.	0	0	1	0	1
Townsend, Den.	0	0	1	0	1
Tullis, Hou.	1	1	0	0	1
Turner, Cin.	0	0	1	0	1
Turner, S.D.	0	0	1	0	1
Utt, Ind.	0	1	0	0	1
Veals, Pitt.	0	1	0	0	1
Waldemore, N.Y. Jets	0	0	1	0	1
Walker, Clev.	1	0	0	0	0
Walker, Mia.	2	0	0	0	0
Wilkerson, S.D.	0	1	0	0	1
Willhite, Den.	3	1	1	0	2
E. Williams, N.E.	0	0	1	0	1
E. Williams, Pitt.	0	1	0	6	1
E. Williams, S.D.	0	0	1	0	1
J. Williams, Hou.	2	1	0	0	1
L. Williams, N.E.	0	0	1	0	1
T. Williams, N.E.	0	0	1	0	1
Va. Williams, Buff.	1	1	0	0	1
Willis, Pitt.	0	0	1	0	1
Wilson, Buff.	3	0	1	40	1
Wilson, L.A. Raiders	11	3	0	-11	3
Wilson, Den.	1	0	1	0	1
Winder, Den.	5	2	0	0	2
Winslow, S.D.	1	0	0	0	0
Winter, Ind.	0	0	1	0	1
Wisniewski, Ind.	0	0	1	0	1
Woodley, Pitt.	5	2	0	-4	2
Woodring, N.Y. Jets	0	0	1	0	1
Woodruff, Pitt.	0	0	1	65	1
L. Wright, Den.	0	0	2	27	2
Young, S.D.	1	0	1	0	1
C. Young, Sea.	1	0	0	0	0

Touchdowns: Baumhower, Mia.; Bostic, Hou.; Buttle, Jets; Byner, Cleve.; Foley, Den.; Gastineau, Jets; Hinkle, Pitt.; Jones, N.E.; R. Jones, Den.; Keating, Buff.; Martin, Raiders; Nash, Sea.; Sanford, Buff.; D. Smith, Den.; Woodruff, Pitt.; L. Wright, Den., 1 each.

NFC—INDIVIDUALS

Player—Team	Fum.	Own Rec.	Opp. Rec.	Yds.	Tot. Rec.
Albritton, Dall.	0	1	1	0	2
Allen, Dall.	2	1	0	0	1
Allerman, St.L.	0	0	1	2	1
Anderson, Minn.	8	2	0	0	2
Anderson, G.B.	0	0	1	0	1
Anderson, St.L.	8	1	0	0	1
Andrews, L.A. Rams	0	0	4	9	4
Anthony, N.O.	1	1	0	0	1
Archer, Atl.	1	0	0	0	0
Armstrong, T.B.	1	1	0	0	1
Ayers, S.F.	0	1	0	0	1
Bailey, Atl.	1	0	0	0	0
Baker, Phila.	0	1	0	0	1
Banks, N.Y. Giants	0	0	1	0	1
Barber, L.A. Rams	1	0	0	0	0
Bartkowski, Atl.	7	4	0	—11	4
Baschnagel, Chi.	1	2	0	0	2
Bates, Dall.	0	0	1	0	1
Beasley, Wash.	0	0	1	0	1
J. Bell, T.B.	0	1	0	0	1
T. Bell, T.B.	1	0	0	0	0
Bell, Chi.	0	0	2	4	2
Bess, Minn.	1	1	1	0	2
Black, Det.	0	1	0	0	1
Blair, Minn.	0	0	1	0	1
Board, S.F.	0	0	1	0	1
Bostic, Wash.	0	1	1	0	2
Brantley, T.B.	0	0	2	0	2
Bright, T.B.	2	1	0	0	1
Brown, Phila.	0	0	1	0	1
T. Brown, Minn.	2	0	0	0	0
Browner, Minn.	0	0	3	63	3
Browner, T.B.	0	0	1	0	1
Burt, N.Y. Giants	0	0	2	0	2
Butler, Atl.	0	0	1	10	1
Butz, Wash.	0	0	1	0	1
Cain, Atl.	2	0	0	0	0
Campbell, Hou.-N.O.	2	2	0	1	2
Campbell, G.B.	1	0	0	0	0
Cannon, T.B.	0	0	1	0	1
Carpenter, N.Y. Giants	2	1	0	0	1
Carroll, T.B.	0	0	1	0	1
Carson, N.Y. Giants	0	0	1	0	1
Carter, T.B.	1	0	1	0	1
Carver, T.B.	0	0	0	0	0
Castille, T.B.	0	0	2	16	2
B. Clark, N.O.	0	0	2	5	2
Clark, G.B.	2	0	0	0	0
M. Clark, S.F.	0	0	1	0	1
Clark, St.L.	0	1	1	0	2
Clinkscale, Dall.	0	0	2	0	2
Cofer, Det.	0	0	1	0	1
Coffey, Wash.	0	0	1	0	1
Coffman, G.B.	1	1	0	0	1
Coleman, Wash.	0	0	1	0	1
Collins, L.A. Rams	1	0	2	17	2
Cooper, S.F.	0	1	0	0	1
Cosbie, Dall.	1	0	0	0	0
Cotney, T.B.	0	0	2	3	2
Covert, Chi.	0	2	0	0	2
Cox, Atl.	1	0	0	0	0
Craig, S.F.	3	1	0	0	1
Cromwell, L.A. Rams	0	0	1	0	1
Croudip, L.A. Rams	0	0	2	0	2
Crutchfield, L.A. Rams	1	0	0	0	0
Cumby, G.B.	0	0	2	0	2
Curran, Atl.	2	1	0	0	1
Curry, Atl.	0	0	1	4	1
Danielson, Det.	7	2	0	—5	2
Davis, T.B.	0	0	1	0	1
DeBerg, T.B.	15	2	0	—8	2
Dean, Wash.	0	0	1	6	1
Dent, Chi.	0	0	1	0	1
Dickerson, Dall.	0	0	1	0	1
Dickerson, L.A. Rams	14	4	0	15	4
Dickey, G.B.	3	1	0	—11	1
Dodge, Det.	0	0	1	0	1
Dorsett, Dall.	12	1	0	—21	1
Doss, L.A.	0	0	1	0	1
Douglass, G.B.	0	1	1	0	2
Downs, Dall.	0	0	2	28	2
Duda, St.L.	0	0	1	0	1
Ekern, L.A. Rams	0	0	1	0	1
Ellard, L.A. Rams	4	2	0	0	2
Ellis, G.B.	2	0	0	0	0
Ellis, Phila.	1	0	1	0	1
Elshire, Minn.	0	0	1	0	1
English, Det.	0	0	1	0	1
Epps, G.B.	1	1	0	0	1
Farrell, T.B.	0	2	0	0	2
Fellows, Dall.	3	0	1	12	1
Fencik, Chi.	1	1	0	0	1
Ferrell, St.L.	3	0	0	0	0
Fields, N.O.	2	1	0	0	1
Fisher, Chi.	4	1	0	0	1
Flynn, G.B.	1	0	3	3	3
Francis, S.F.	1	2	0	0	2
Frye, Atl.	0	0	2	0	2
Gaison, Atl.	0	1	0	0	1
Gary, N.O.	0	0	1	5	1
Gault, Chi.	1	0	0	0	0
Gay, Det.	0	0	2	30	2
Giacomarro, Atl.	1	1	0	0	1
Graham, Det.	0	0	2	0	2
Granger, Dall.	0	0	1	0	1
Grant, Wash.	0	0	4	22	4
Greco, Det.	0	1	0	0	1
Green, L.A. Rams	0	0	1	0	1
Green, St.L.	1	0	0	0	0
Griffin, Wash.	7	0	0	0	0
Grimm, Wash.	0	2	0	0	2
Guman, L.A. Rams	0	1	0	0	1
Haddix, Phila.	2	0	0	0	0
Haines, Minn.	0	0	1	6	1
Hall, Det.	3	1	0	0	1
Hallstrom, G.B.	0	2	0	1	2
Hampton, Chi.	0	0	3	0	3
Harmon, S.F.	1	1	1	0	2
Harris, L.A. Rams	0	0	1	0	1
Harris, Atl.	0	0	1	0	1
Harrison, Phila.	0	0	1	0	1
Hartenstine, Chi.	0	0	2	0	2
Hasselbeck, Minn.	0	0	1	0	1
Hayes, Wash.	2	1	0	0	1
Hayes, Phila.	2	1	0	0	1
Haynes, N.Y. Giants	0	0	2	12	2
Headen, N.Y. Giants	0	0	1	81	1
Hegman, Dall.	0	0	1	0	1
Hicks, S.F.	1	1	2	6	3
Da. Hill, L.A. Rams	2	1	0	0	1
Hoage, N.O.	0	0	1	0	1
Hodge, Atl.	1	0	0	0	0
Hogeboom, Dall.	8	4	0	—3	4
Holloway, Minn.-St.L.	0	0	3	0	3
Holt, T.B.	0	0	1	0	1
Hopkins, Phila.	0	0	3	0	3
House, T.B.	0	1	0	0	1
Howard, St.L.	0	0	1	29	1
Huckleby, G.B.	1	1	0	0	1
Huff, Wash.	0	3	0	0	3
Hunt, N.Y. Giants	0	0	2	0	2
Irwin, Minn.	0	1	0	2	1
Ivery, G.B.	1	0	0	0	0
A. Jackson, Atl.	0	1	0	0	1
J. Jackson, Atl.	0	1	0	0	1
Jackson, N.O.	1	1	3	4	4
Jacoby, Wash.	0	1	0	0	1
Jaworski, Phila.	5	2	0	0	2
Jeffcoat, Dall.	0	0	1	0	1
Jenkins, Det.	1	1	0	0	1
B. Johnson, Atl.	1	0	0	0	0
Johnson, Det.	0	0	1	0	1
D. Johnson, Minn.	0	0	1	0	1
G. Johnson, S.D.-S.F.	0	0	3	36	3
K. Johnson, Atl.	2	0	0	0	0
A.J. Jones, L.A. Rams	0	0	1	0	1
D. Jones, G.B.	0	1	2	0	3
E. Jones, Dall.	0	0	2	0	2

Player—Team	Fum.	Own Rec.	Opp. Rec.	Yds.	Tot. Rec.
Jones, Det.	6	3	0	—21	3
Jones, Minn.	1	2	0	0	2
T. Jones, G.B.	0	0	1	0	1
Jordan, Wash.	0	0	1	29	1
Jordan, Chi.	1	1	2	0	3
Jordan, Minn.	0	0	1	0	1
Junkin, Buff.-Wash.	0	0	1	0	1
Kane, Wash.	3	0	0	0	0
Kaufman, Wash.	0	0	1	0	1
Kemp, L.A. Rams	8	3	0	—16	3
Kinard, N.Y. Giants	1	0	1	0	1
Korte, N.O.	0	1	0	0	1
Kramer, Minn.	10	3	0	—5	3
Kuykendall, Atl.	0	0	2	9	2
Landrum, Atl.	0	1	0	0	1
Latimer, Det.	0	0	1	0	1
Lee, Minn.	0	0	1	0	1
L. Lee, Det.	2	1	0	—24	1
Lee, G.B.	0	0	2	0	2
Lewis, Det.	2	2	0	0	2
Lewis, Minn.	1	3	0	0	3
Lisch, Chi.	5	1	0	—6	1
Lockhart, Dall.	0	0	1	0	1
Lofton, G.B.	1	0	0	0	0
Lomax, St.L.	11	2	0	—5	2
Love, St.L.	1	0	0	0	0
Mandley, Det.	2	2	0	0	2
Manley, Wash.	0	0	1	0	1
Mann, Wash.	0	0	1	0	1
Manning, Minn.	4	2	0	0	2
Manuel, N.Y. Giants	2	0	0	0	0
C. Martin, Minn.	0	0	1	8	1
Martin, N.Y. Giants	0	0	1	0	1
Martin, Det.	5	3	1	0	4
McConkey, N.Y. Giants	2	1	0	0	1
McKinnon, Chi.	1	0	0	0	0
McLaughlin, Giants	0	0	1	0	1
McLemore, S.F.	1	0	0	0	0
McLeod, G.B.	0	0	1	0	1
McMahon, Chi.	1	0	0	0	0
McNeill, Minn.	0	0	2	0	2
McSwain, Dall.	2	0	0	0	0
Meade, Det.	1	0	0	0	0
Meisner, L.A. Rams	0	0	1	0	1
Mitchell, St.L.	6	2	0	0	2
Monk, Wash.	1	0	0	0	0
Monroe, S.F.	2	0	0	0	0
Montana, S.F.	4	2	0	—3	2
Montgomery, S.F.	0	1	0	0	1
Montgomery, Phila.	5	1	0	0	1
Moore, Wash.	1	0	0	0	0
Moroski, Atl.	6	2	0	0	2
Morris, N.Y. Giants	1	0	0	0	0
Morton, T.B.	3	2	0	0	2
Muhammad, Wash.	1	1	1	0	2
Mularkey, Minn.	1	1	0	0	1
Murphy, G.B.	1	0	1	2	1
Nelms, Wash.	1	0	0	0	0
Dar. Nelson, Minn.	4	3	0	0	3
Newsome, Dall.	3	0	0	0	0
Nichols, Det.	0	1	0	0	1
Noga, St.L.	0	0	1	0	1
Oliver, Phila.	0	1	0	0	1
Olkewicz, Wash.	0	0	2	0	2
Owens, L.A. Rams	0	0	2	0	2
Paris, S.F.	0	1	0	0	1
Payton, Chi.	5	1	0	0	1
Perrin, St.L.	0	0	2	16	2
Peters, Wash.	0	0	1	0	1
Pillers, S.F.	0	0	1	0	1
Pisarcik, Phila.	4	0	0	0	0
Pittman, St.L.	1	1	0	0	1
Pitts, Atl.	0	0	2	0	2
Prather, G.B.	0	0	1	0	1
Pridemore, Atl.	0	0	2	0	2
Provence, Atl.	0	0	1	0	1
Rade, Atl.	0	0	1	0	1
Rafferty, Dall.	0	2	0	0	2
Reasons, N.Y. Giants	0	0	3	0	3
Reed, L.A. Rams	0	0	1	2	1
Reichenbach, Phila.	0	1	1	0	2
Rice, Minn.	1	2	0	0	2
Richards, Dall.	0	1	0	0	1
Richardson, Atl.	0	0	3	0	3
Richardson, Chi.	0	0	1	0	1
Riggins, Wash.	7	0	0	0	0
Riggs, Atl.	11	2	0	0	2
Roberts, N.Y. Giants	0	1	0	0	1
Robinson, Phila.	0	0	1	0	1
Rodgers, G.B.	1	0	0	0	0
G. Rogers, N.O.	2	1	0	0	1
Rohrer, Dall.	1	0	1	5	1
Rouse, Minn.	0	1	0	0	1
Saldi, Chi.	2	0	0	0	0
Salonen, Dall.	0	1	0	0	1
Sams, Minn.	1	0	0	—17	0
Scott, N.O.	1	0	0	0	0
V. Scott, Dall.	0	1	1	0	2
Scully, Atl.	0	1	0	0	1
Selmon, T.B.	0	0	2	0	2
Sharpe, St.L.	0	1	0	0	1
Shell, S.F.	0	0	1	0	1
Simms, N.Y. Giants	8	4	0	—5	4
Sims, Det.	6	2	0	0	2
Singletary, Chi.	0	0	1	0	1
Smith, Atl.	0	0	2	0	2
J. Smith, Wa-Rai-GB	0	0	1	0	1
L. Smith, St.L.	0	0	1	0	1
W. Smith, St.L.	0	1	2	12	3
Spagnola, Phila.	2	0	0	0	0
Springs, Dall.	1	0	0	0	0
Stabler, N.O.	1	0	0	0	0
Stamps, Atl.	2	0	0	0	0
Stieve, St.L.	0	1	0	2	1
Suhey, Chi.	6	2	0	0	2
Sully, L.A. Rams	0	0	1	0	1
Swain, Minn.	0	0	1	0	1
Tate, Atl.	1	1	0	0	1
Teal, Minn.	1	0	0	0	0
Theismann, Wash.	7	6	0	5	6
Thielemann, Atl.	0	1	0	0	1
C. Thomas, Chi.	1	0	1	0	1
Z. Thomas, Den.-T.B.	3	2	0	0	2
J. Thompson, T.B.	1	1	0	0	1
L. Thompson, Det.	1	1	0	0	1
Thurman, Dall.	0	1	0	0	1
Tilley, St.L.	1	0	0	0	0
Todd, N.O.	9	3	0	—16	3
Tuiasosopo, S.F.	0	0	2	6	2
Tyler, S.F.	13	2	0	0	2
Tyrrell, Atl.	0	1	2	0	3
Vann, L.A. Rams	0	0	2	0	2
Waddy, Minn.	1	1	0	0	1
Walker, Wash.	0	1	0	0	1
A. Washington, Wash.	0	0	1	0	1
J. Washington, Wash.	3	0	0	0	0
Washington, St.L.	0	0	1	0	1
Waters, Phila.	1	0	1	0	1
Wattelet, N.O.	0	1	1	22	2
West, G.B.	0	1	0	0	1
D. White, Dall.	2	1	0	—3	1
White, Minn.	1	0	0	0	0
Wilder, T.B.	10	4	0	0	4
Wilks, N.O.	0	0	1	0	1
G. Williams, Wash.	0	0	1	0	1
Williams, Det.	0	0	1	0	1
J. Williams, Phila.	0	0	2	0	2
M. Williams, Phila.	1	0	0	0	0
P. Williams, N.Y.	0	0	1	0	1
D. Wilson, N.O.	2	0	0	0	0
Wilson, T.B.	1	0	0	0	0
Wilson, Minn.	2	0	0	0	0
W. Wilson, N.O.	2	0	0	0	0
Winston, N.O.	0	0	1	0	1
Witkowski, Det.	1	0	0	0	0
Witte, T.B.	0	1	0	0	1
Woolfolk, N.Y. Giants	1	1	0	0	1
Wright, G.B.	1	1	0	0	1
Young, N.O.	1	0	0	0	0
Ja. Youngblood, L.A.	0	0	1	9	1

Touchdowns: Browner, Minn.; Grant, Wash.; Headen, Giants; Howard, St. L.; Jacoby, Wash.; Jeffcoat, Dall.; G. Johnson, S.D.-S.F.; Jordan, Wash.; C. Martin, Minn.; Wattelet, N.O., 1 each.

1984 SACKS

AFC—TEAM

	Sacks	Yds.
L.A. Raiders	64	516
Denver	57	430
New England	55	452
Seattle	55	398
Kansas City	50	364
Pittsburgh	47	390
N.Y. Jets	44	360
Cleveland	43	353
Indianapolis	42	320
Miami	42	339
Cincinnati	40	298
San Diego	33	218
Houston	32	267
Buffalo	26	191

NFC—TEAM

	Sacks	Yds.
Chicago	72	583
Washington	66	529
Philadelphia	60	456
Dallas	57	390
New Orleans	55	420
St. Louis	55	403
San Francisco	51	363
N.Y. Giants	48	361
Green Bay	44	324
L.A. Rams	43	298
Atlanta	38	287
Detroit	37	271
Tampa Bay	32	239
Minnesota	25	175

AFC—INDIVIDUALS

Player—Team	Sacks	Player—Team	Sacks
Gastineau, N.Y. Jets	22.0	Bowyer, Denver	3.0
Tippett, New England	18.5	Brudzinski, Miami	3.0
Merriweather, Pittsburgh	15.0	Carter, Denver	3.0
J. Bryant, Seattle	14.5	Carter, N.Y. Jets	3.0
Still, Kansas City	14.5	Charles, Miami	3.0
Betters, Miami	14.0	Collins, Cincinnati	3.0
Camp, Cleveland	14.0	Dennison, Denver	3.0
Bell, Kansas City	13.5	Klecko, N.Y. Jets	3.0
Green, Seattle	13.0	Lowe, San Diego	3.0
Pickel, L.A. Raiders	12.5	McNanie, Buffalo	3.0
Long, L.A. Raiders	12.0	Odom, Indianapolis	3.0
Matthews, Cleveland	12.0	Ryan, Denver	3.0
Cooks, Indianapolis	11.5	B.R. Smith, San Diego	3.0
Baker, Houston	11.0	Woodard, Denver	3.0
R. Jones, Denver	11.0	Banks, Cleveland	2.5
Martin, L.A. Raiders	11.0	Goodman, Pittsburgh	2.5
Bowser, Miami	9.0	Kremer, Kansas City	2.5
Edwards, Cincinnati	9.0	Millen, N.Y. Raiders	2.5
R. Williams, Cincinnati	9.0	Riley, Houston	2.5
Maxwell, Indianapolis	8.5	Ackerman, S.D.-L.A. Raiders	2.0
Browner, Cincinnati	8.0	Barnett, Miami	2.0
Ferguson, San Diego	8.0	Baumhower, Miami	2.0
Chavous, Denver	7.5	Bingham, Houston	2.0
Fanning, Seattle	7.0	Bostic, Houston	2.0
Mecklenburg, Denver	7.0	Bracelin, Indianapolis	2.0
Nash, Seattle	7.0	Brazile, Houston	2.0
Nelson, Pittsburgh	7.0	Cole, Pittsburgh	2.0
Townsend, L.A. Raiders	7.0	Ehin, San Diego	2.0
Wisniewski, Indianapolis	7.0	Faurot, N.Y. Jets	2.0
Owens, New England	6.5	Frazier, Cincinnati	2.0
Alzado, L.A. Raiders	6.0	Freeman, Buffalo	2.0
T. Jackson, Denver	6.0	Golic, Cleveland	2.0
T. Williams, New England	6.0	Hamm, Houston	2.0
M. Davis, L.A. Raiders	5.5	Henson, New England	2.0
Hinkle, Pittsburgh	5.5	Keating, Buffalo	2.0
Blackmon, New England	5.0	Kush, Buffalo	2.0
Krumrie, Cincinnati	5.0	Lindstrom, Kansas City	2.0
Maas, Kansas City	5.0	Lyons, N.Y. Jets	2.0
Mehl, N.Y. Jets	5.0	Puzzuoli, Cleveland	2.0
Talley, Buffalo	5.0	Rogers, New England	2.0
Townsend, Denver	5.0	Schuh, Cincinnati	2.0
Willis, Pittsburgh	5.0	Simpson, Seattle	2.0
Baldwin, Cleveland	4.5	Smerlas, Buffalo	2.0
Daniels, Kansas City	4.5	Squirek, L.A. Raiders	2.0
Robinson, San Diego	4.5	White, Indianapolis	2.0
Stensrud, Houston	4.5	B. Williams, Buffalo	2.0
Adams, New England	4.0	Williams, Pittsburgh	2.0
Bennett, N.Y. Jets	4.0	Winter, Indianapolis	2.0
Bokamper, Miami	4.0	Baldwin, N.Y. Jets	1.5
Gary, Pittsburgh	4.0	Edwards, Seattle	1.5
Hairston, Cleveland	4.0	Elko, San Diego	1.5
King, San Diego	4.0	Franks, Cleveland	1.5
McAlister, Kansas City	4.0	Nelson, L.A. Raiders	1.5
Nelson, New England	4.0	Rudolph, N.Y. Jets	1.5
Thompson, Indianapolis	4.0	L. Williams, New England	1.5
Gaines, Seattle	3.5	Barnes, L.A. Raiders	1.0
Haslett, Buffalo	3.5	Benson, Miami	1.0
K. Johnson, Buffalo	3.5	M. Brown, Miami	1.0
Sims, New England	3.5	Busick, Denver	1.0
Sochia, Houston	3.5	K. Butler, Seattle	1.0

Player—Team	Sacks	Player—Team	Sacks
Cameron, Cincinnati	1.0	Manor, T.B.-Den.	1.0
Clayton, Pittsburgh	1.0	Marion, New England	1.0
Comeaux, Denver	1.0	McKinney, L.A. Raiders	1.0
David, Buffalo	1.0	Moyer, Seattle	1.0
Dawson, Kansas City	1.0	Parker, Indianapolis	1.0
Duhe, Miami	1.0	Rhone, Miami	1.0
Dunn, Pittsburgh	1.0	Robbins, Denver	1.0
Eason, Houston	1.0	D. Smith, Denver	1.0
Foster, Houston	1.0	Spani, Kansas City	1.0
Fox, San Diego	1.0	Thomas, Miami	1.0
Garnett, Denver	1.0	L. Williams, San Diego	1.0
Green, San Diego	1.0	Young, San Diego	1.0
Greene, San Diego	1.0	F. Young, Seattle	1.0
J. Harris, Seattle	1.0	Blanton, Kansas City	0.5
Horton, Cincinnati	1.0	Holle, Kansas City	0.5
M. Jackson, Seattle	1.0	E. Johnson, Cleveland	0.5
Jones, L.A. Raiders	1.0	Johnson, Houston	0.5
Krauss, Indianapolis	1.0	McGrew, New England	0.5
Lewis, Kansas City	1.0	Rembert, New England	0.5
Little, Pittsburgh	1.0	Robinson, Seattle	0.5
Mangiero, Seattle	1.0	Wilson, Denver	0.5

NFC—INDIVIDUALS

Player—Team	Sacks	Player—Team	Sacks
Dent, Chicago	17.5	Green, Tampa Bay	4.0
Brown, Philadelphia	16.0	C. Johnson, Minnesota	4.0
Greer, St. Louis	14.0	T. Jones, Green Bay	4.0
Manley, Washington	13.5	McColl, San Francisco	4.0
R. White, Dallas	12.5	Milot, Washington	4.0
Harrison, Philadelphia	12.0	Tuiasosopo, San Francisco	4.0
Jackson, New Orleans	12.0	Warren, New Orleans	4.0
Hampton, Chicago	11.5	Anderson, Green Bay	3.5
Jeffcoat, Dallas	11.5	Cannon, Tampa Bay	3.5
Taylor, N.Y. Giants	11.5	Downs, Dallas	3.5
B. Clark, New Orleans	10.5	Elshire, Minnesota	3.5
Clarke, Philadelphia	10.5	Hegman, Dallas	3.5
Coleman, Washington	10.5	Mays, St. Louis	3.5
A. Baker, St. Louis	10.0	Meisner, L.A. Rams	3.5
Board, San Francisco	10.0	Owens, L.A. Rams	3.5
Gay, Detroit	10.0	Richardson, Atlanta	3.5
McMichael, Chicago	10.0	Singletary, Chicago	3.5
Junior, St. Louis	9.5	Armstrong, Philadelphia	3.0
Paul, New Orleans	9.5	Banks, N.Y. Giants	3.0
Ja. Youngblood, L.A. Rams	9.5	Carreker, Green Bay	3.0
Douglass, Green Bay	9.0	Cobb, Detroit	3.0
Doss, L.A. Rams	8.5	DeJurnett, L.A. Rams	3.0
Green, Detroit	8.5	Duda, St. Louis	3.0
Merrill, N.Y. Giants	8.5	Duerson, Chicago	3.0
Grant, Washington	8.0	Griggs, Philadelphia	3.0
E. Jones, Dallas	8.0	Martin, Green Bay	3.0
Selmon, Tampa Bay	8.0	Nelson, St. Louis	3.0
Wilks, New Orleans	7.5	Scott, Green Bay	3.0
Burt, N.Y. Giants	7.0	Stuckey, San Francisco	3.0
Cofer, Detroit	7.0	Cumby, Green Bay	2.5
Hartenstine, Chicago	7.0	Dutton, Dallas	2.5
E. Johnson, Green Bay	7.0	Keys, Chicago	2.5
Mann, Washington	7.0	Lockhart, Dallas	2.5
Holloway, Minn.-St. L.	6.5	Provence, Atlanta	2.5
Marshall, N.Y. Giants	6.5	Beasley, Washington	2.0
Wilson, Chicago	6.5	T. Benson, Atlanta	2.0
Andrews, L.A. Rams	6.0	Browner, Tampa Bay	2.0
Geathers, New Orleans	6.0	Bryan, Atlanta	2.0
Smith, Atlanta	6.0	Cotney, Tampa Bay	2.0
Brooks, Washington	5.5	Dickerson, Dallas	2.0
Galloway, St. Louis	5.5	Ellison, San Francisco	2.0
Kaufman, Washington	5.5	Frye, Atlanta	2.0
Logan, Tampa Bay	5.5	Green, L.A. Rams	2.0
Martin, N.Y. Giants	5.5	Grooms, St. Louis	2.0
Pitts, Atlanta	5.5	Haines, Minnesota	2.0
Bates, Dallas	5.0	Harris, Chicago	2.0
Brown, Green Bay	5.0	Harris, St. Louis	2.0
Burley, Atlanta	5.0	J. Jackson, Atlanta	2.0
Darby, Philadelphia	5.0	Re. Lewis, New Orleans	2.0
English, Detroit	5.0	Moore, New Orleans	2.0
G. Johnson, S.D.-S.F.	5.0	Murphy, Green Bay	2.0
Washington, Tampa Bay	5.0	Pillers, San Francisco	2.0
Bell, Chicago	4.5	Sally, N.Y. Giants	2.0
Butz, Washington	4.5	Shell, San Francisco	2.0
McGee, Washington	4.5	Strauthers, Philadelphia	2.0
Carter, San Francisco	4.0	Turner, San Francisco	2.0
Dean, San Francisco	4.0	Waechter, Ind.-Chi.	2.0

Player—Team	Sacks	Player—Team	Sacks
Wilcher, L.A. Rams	2.0	K. Johnson, Atlanta	1.0
Wilkes, Philadelphia	2.0	Kovach, New Orleans	1.0
Williams, Detroit	2.0	Kuykendall, Atlanta	1.0
Yeates, Atlanta	2.0	Lott, San Francisco	1.0
Fantetti, Detroit	1.5	C. Martin, Minnesota	1.0
Fuller, San Francisco	1.5	D. Martin, Minnesota	1.0
Hopkins, Philadelphia	1.5	McNeill, Minnesota	1.0
Schulz, Philadelphia	1.5	Mularkey, Minnesota	1.0
Stover, San Francisco	1.5	Mullaney, Minnesota	1.0
J. Williams, Philadelphia	1.5	Neill, Green Bay	1.0
Albritton, Dallas	1.0	Newsome, L.A. Rams	1.0
Benish, Atlanta	1.0	Olkewicz, Washington	1.0
Bess, Minnesota	1.0	Osborne, Chicago	1.0
Blair, Minnesota	1.0	Reasons, N.Y. Giants	1.0
Brantley, Tampa Bay	1.0	Reed, L.A. Rams	1.0
Browner, Minnesota	1.0	Robinson, Philadelphia	1.0
Bunz, San Francisco	1.0	Sendlein, Minnesota	1.0
M. Clark, San Francisco	1.0	Smerek, Dallas	1.0
Clinkscale, Dallas	1.0	L. Smith, St. Louis	1.0
Cobb, Minnesota	1.0	Thurman, Dallas	1.0
Ekern, L.A. Rams	1.0	Tuinei, Dallas	1.0
Fencik, Chicago	1.0	Walter, San Francisco	1.0
Ferrari, San Francisco	1.0	Williamson, San Francisco	1.0
Harris, Atlanta	1.0	Arbubakrr, Minnesota	0.5
Headen, N.Y. Giants	1.0	Collins, L.A. Rams	0.5
Hill, N.Y. Giants	1.0	Curry, Atlanta	0.5
Humphrey, Green Bay	1.0	Harris, L.A. Rams	0.5
Hunt, N.Y. Giants	1.0	Winston, New Orleans	0.5
Jeter, L.A. Rams	1.0		

CLUB RANKINGS BY YARDS

	OFFENSE			DEFENSE		
	Total	Rush	Pass	Total	Rush	Pass
Atlanta	19	15	20	15	21	7
Buffalo	27	26	25	23	19	19
Chicago	7	*1	26	*1	*1	2
Cincinnati	5	†6	†13	13	11	18
Cleveland	24	21	18	2	15	3
Dallas	11	20	6	7	24	5
Denver	22	10	23	25	5	27
Detroit	12	14	†13	17	8	21
Green Bay	6	13	9	16	20	8
Houston	23	23	17	27	28	11
Indianapolis	28	12	28	22	17	22
Kansas City	17	27	7	24	16	23
L.A. Raiders	15	17	12	3	13	4
L.A. Rams	21	2	27	14	3	24
Miami	*1	16	*1	19	22	14
Minnesota	25	18	22	28	27	26
New England	14	11	16	9	12	12
New Orleans	20	8	24	4	26	*1
N.Y. Giants	13	22	5	11	9	16
N.Y. Jets	16	5	21	21	18	20
Philadelphia	26	28	11	12	23	6
Pittsburgh	8	†6	15	5	4	15
St. Louis	3	9	3	8	14	9
San Diego	4	24	2	26	10	28
San Francisco	2	3	4	10	7	17
Seattle	18	25	10	6	6	10
Tampa Bay	10	19	8	20	25	13
Washington	9	4	19	18	2	25

*League leader
†Tie for position

CLUB LEADERS

	Offense	Defense
First Downs	Miami 387	Chicago 216
Rushing	Chicago 164	Chicago 72
Passing	Miami 243	Chicago 122
Penalty	New Orleans 30	Miami 12
Rushes	Chicago 674	Chicago 378
Net Yards Gained	Chicago 2974	Chicago 1377
Average Gain	L.A. Rams 5.3	Detroit 3.5
Passes Attempted	San Diego 662	New Orleans 422
Completed	San Diego 401	Chicago 198
Percent Completed	Miami 64.2	Chicago 45.5
Total Yards Gained	Miami 5146	New Orleans 2873
Times Sacked	Miami 14	Chicago 72
Yards Lost	Miami 128	Chicago 583
Net Yards Gained	Miami 5018	New Orleans 2453
Net Yards per Pass Play	Miami 8.56	L.A. Raid. & Dall. 4.81
Yards Gained per Completion	Pittsburgh 14.66	Green Bay 11.02
Combined Net Yards Gained	Miami 6936	Chicago 3863
Percent Total Yards Rushing	L.A. Rams 57.2	Denver 29.3
Percent Total Yards Passing	San Diego 73.7	New Orleans 49.9
Ball Control Plays	San Diego 1154	Chicago 885
Average Yards per Play	Miami 6.5	L.A. Raiders 4.3
Average Time of Possession	Chicago 35:08	
Third Down Efficiency	Miami 51.5	Chicago 26.4
Interceptions		Seattle 38
Yards Returned		Seattle 697
Returned for TD		Seattle 7
Punts	Dallas 108	
Yards Punted	Kansas City 4397	
Average Yards per Punt	Kansas City 44.9	
Punt Returns	L.A. Raiders 67	Miami 17
Yards Returned	Pittsburgh 696	Miami 138
Average Yards per Return	Cincinnati 12.4	Dallas 4.2
Returned for TD	L.A. Rams 2	
Kickoff Returns	Minnesota 86	Indianapolis 42
Yards Returned	Minnesota 1775	Indianapolis 849
Average Yards per Return	N.Y. Jets 23.0	Green Bay 16.0
Returned for TD	Five with 1	
Total Points Scored	Miami 513	San Francisco 227
Total TDs	Miami 70	San Francisco 24
TDs Rushing	Chicago 22	Dallas 8
TDs Passing	Miami 49	Chi. & S.F. 14
TDs on Returns and Recoveries	Seattle 9	Three with 0
Extra Points	Miami 66	San Francisco 24
Safeties	L.A. Rams 3	
Field Goals Made	Philadelphia 30	Miami 9
Field Goals Attempted	Philadelphia 37	Miami 17
Percent Successful	Minnesota 87.0	Miami 52.9

1984 NFL TEAM-BY-TEAM STATISTICS SUMMARY

AMERICAN FOOTBALL CONFERENCE

OFFENSE

	Buff.	Cin.	Clev.	Den.	Hou.	Ind.	K.C.	Raid.	Mia.	N.E.	N.Y.J.	Pitt.	S.D.	Sea.
First Downs	263	339	295	299	284	254	295	301	387	315	310	302	374	287
Rushing	98	135	89	121	95	117	88	114	115	104	118	117	106	94
Passing	149	179	180	152	164	117	178	162	243	186	176	167	240	171
Penalty	16	25	26	26	25	23	29	25	29	25	16	18	28	22
Rushes	398	540	489	508	433	510	408	516	484	482	504	574	456	495
Net Yards Gained	1643	2179	1696	2076	1656	2025	1527	1886	1918	2032	2189	2179	1654	1645
Average Gain	4.1	4.0	3.5	4.1	3.8	4.0	3.7	3.7	4.0	4.2	4.3	3.8	3.6	3.3
Average Yards per Game	102.7	136.2	106.0	129.8	103.5	126.6	95.4	117.9	119.9	127.0	136.8	136.2	103.4	102.8
Passes Attempted	588	496	495	475	487	411	593	491	572	500	488	443	662	497
Completed	298	306	273	263	282	206	305	266	367	292	272	240	401	283
Percent Completed	50.7	61.7	55.2	55.4	57.9	50.1	51.4	54.2	64.2	58.4	55.7	54.2	60.6	56.9
Total Yards Gained	3252	3659	3490	3116	3610	2543	3869	3718	5146	3685	3341	3519	4928	3751
Times Sacked	60	45	55	35	49	58	33	54	14	66	52	35	36	42
Yards Lost	554	358	358	257	382	436	301	360	128	454	382	278	285	328
Net Yards Gained	2698	3301	3132	2859	3228	2107	3568	3358	5018	3231	2959	3241	4643	3423
Average Yards per Game	168.6	206.3	195.8	178.7	201.8	131.7	223.0	209.9	313.9	201.9	184.9	202.6	290.2	213.9
Net Yards per Pass Play	4.16	6.10	5.69	5.61	6.02	4.49	5.70	6.16	8.56	5.71	5.48	6.78	6.65	6.35
Yards Gained per Completion	10.91	11.96	12.78	11.85	12.80	12.34	12.69	13.98	14.02	12.62	12.28	14.66	12.29	13.25
Combined Net Yards Gained	4341	5480	4828	4935	4884	4132	5095	5244	6936	5263	5148	5420	6297	5068
Percent Total Yards Rushing	37.8	39.8	35.1	42.1	33.9	49.0	30.0	36.0	27.7	38.6	42.5	40.2	26.3	32.5
Percent Total Yards Passing	62.2	60.2	64.9	57.9	66.1	51.0	70.0	64.0	72.3	61.4	57.5	59.8	73.7	67.5
Average Yards per Game	271.3	342.5	301.8	308.4	305.3	258.3	318.4	327.8	433.5	328.9	321.8	338.8	393.6	316.8
Ball Control Plays	1046	1081	1039	1018	969	979	1034	1061	1070	1048	1044	1052	1154	1034
Average Yards per Play	4.2	5.1	4.6	4.8	5.0	4.2	4.9	4.9	6.5	5.0	4.9	5.2	5.5	4.9
Average Time of Possession	28.43	30.50	30.53	28.56	28.02	27.24	27.25	29.26	30.18	29.51	30.02	30.33	31.43	30.46
Third Down Efficiency	35.4	44.1	39.0	32.5	33.2	29.9	32.7	35.9	51.5	39.6	41.5	40.3	47.1	37.8

AFC OFFENSE—Continued

	Buff.	Cin.	Clev.	Den.	Hou.	Ind.	K.C.	Raid.	Mia.	N.E.	N.Y.J.	Pitt.	S.D.	Sea.
Had Intercepted	30	22	23	17	15	22	22	28	18	14	21	25	21	26
Yards Opponent Returned	416	364	518	189	214	423	683	300	377	237	207	371	180	333
Returned by Opponent for TD	4	2	3	0	2	2	7	2	1	3	0	1	0	3
Punts	90	67	76	96	88	98	98	91	51	92	75	70	66	95
Yards Punted	3696	2832	3213	3850	3482	4383	4397	3809	2281	3904	2935	2883	2773	3567
Average Yards per Punt	41.1	42.3	42.3	40.1	39.6	44.7	44.9	41.9	44.7	42.4	39.1	41.2	42.0	37.5
Punt Returns	33	38	40	41	26	38	42	67	39	48	35	61	33	44
Yards Returned	297	473	322	318	152	278	346	667	365	430	324	696	212	484
Average Yards per Return	9.0	12.4	8.1	7.8	5.8	7.3	8.2	10.0	9.4	9.0	9.3	11.0	6.4	11.0
Returned for TD	1	0	0	0	0	0	0	1	0	0	0	1	1	1
Kickoff Returns	76	61	61	45	69	69	56	56	44	63	65	54	63	54
Yards Returned	1422	1155	1157	897	1352	1331	1061	1216	799	1246	1498	1026	1319	1007
Average Yards per Return	18.7	18.9	19.0	19.9	19.6	19.3	18.9	21.7	18.2	19.8	23.0	19.0	20.9	18.6
Returned for TD	0	0	0	0	0	1	0	0	0	0	1	0	0	0
Penalties	121	85	111	78	99	95	98	143	67	86	96	112	112	128
Yards Penalized	997	693	928	636	813	798	801	1209	527	674	779	948	1023	1179
Fumbles	31	32	31	36	36	35	34	42	26	29	26	40	35	24
Lost	14	17	16	17	16	17	15	20	10	15	13	15	17	13
Out of Bounds	6	2	1	1	1	4	3	2	0	2	1	2	4	3
Own Recovered for TD	0	0	1	0	0	0	0	0	0	1	0	0	0	0
Opponents Recovered by	21	15	15	24	11	13	11	14	12	8	18	10	17	25
Opponents Recovered for TD	2	0	0	4	1	0	0	1	1	0	2	2	0	1
Total Points Scored	250	339	250	353	240	239	314	368	513	362	332	387	394	418
Total TDs	31	39	25	42	28	28	35	44	70	42	40	45	48	51
TDs Rushing	9	18	10	12	13	13	12	19	18	15	17	13	18	10
TDs Passing	18	17	14	22	14	13	21	21	49	26	20	25	25	32
TDs on Return and Recovered	4	4	1	8	1	2	2	4	1	1	3	7	5	9
Extra Points	31	37	25	38	27	27	35	40	66	42	39	45	46	50
Safeties	0	1	0	0	0	0	0	2	1	1	1	0	0	1
Field Goals Made	11	22	25	21	15	14	23	20	9	22	17	24	20	20
Field Goals Attempted	21	31	35	28	19	23	33	27	19	28	24	32	29	24
Percent Successful	52.4	71.0	71.4	75.0	78.9	60.9	69.7	74.1	47.4	78.6	70.8	75.0	69.0	83.3

AMERICAN FOOTBALL CONFERENCE

DEFENSE

	Buff.	Cin.	Clev.	Den.	Hou.	Ind.	K.C.	Raid.	Mia.	N.E.	N.Y.J.	Pitt.	S.D.	Sea.
First Downs	345	322	270	311	345	343	335	297	314	311	341	282	322	288
Rushing	134	115	103	90	158	124	121	107	130	109	117	87	109	99
Passing	186	191	145	206	168	194	192	147	172	182	198	167	189	160
Penalty	25	16	22	15	19	25	22	43	12	20	26	28	24	29
Rushes	531	477	494	435	596	559	523	517	458	498	497	454	457	475
Net Yards Gained	2106	1868	1945	1664	2789	2007	1980	1892	2155	1886	2064	1617	1851	1789
Average Gain	4.0	3.9	3.9	3.8	4.7	3.6	3.8	3.7	4.7	3.8	4.2	3.6	4.1	3.8
Average Yards per Game	131.6	116.8	121.6	104.0	174.3	125.4	123.8	118.3	134.7	117.9	129.0	101.1	115.7	111.8
Passes Attempted	495	517	458	631	447	515	586	508	551	513	511	515	531	521
Completed	300	302	261	346	271	298	332	254	310	283	312	299	323	265
Percent Completed	60.6	58.4	57.0	54.8	60.6	57.9	56.7	50.0	56.3	55.2	61.1	58.1	60.8	50.9
Total Yards Gained	3667	3689	3049	4453	3446	3890	4009	3268	3604	3666	3862	3689	4303	3572
Times Sacked	26	40	43	57	32	42	50	64	42	55	44	47	33	55
Yards Lost	191	298	353	430	267	320	364	516	339	452	360	390	218	398
Net Yards Gained	3476	3391	2696	4023	3179	3570	3645	2752	3265	3214	3502	3299	4085	3174
Average Yards per Game	217.3	211.9	168.5	251.4	198.7	223.1	227.8	172.0	204.1	200.9	218.9	206.2	255.3	198.4
Net Yards per Pass Play	6.67	6.09	5.38	5.85	6.64	6.41	5.73	4.81	5.51	5.66	6.31	5.87	7.24	5.51
Yards Gained per Completion	12.22	12.22	11.68	12.87	12.72	13.05	12.08	12.87	11.63	12.95	12.38	12.34	13.32	13.48
Combined Net Yards Gained	5582	5259	4641	5687	5968	5577	5625	4644	5420	5100	5566	4916	5936	4963
Percent Total Yards Rushing	37.7	35.5	41.9	29.3	46.7	36.0	35.2	40.7	39.8	37.0	37.1	32.9	31.2	36.0
Percent Total Yards Passing	62.3	64.5	58.1	70.7	53.3	64.0	64.8	59.3	60.2	63.0	62.9	67.1	68.8	64.0
Average Yards per Game	348.9	328.7	290.1	355.4	373.0	348.6	351.6	290.3	338.8	318.8	347.9	307.3	371.0	310.2
Ball Control Plays	1052	1034	995	1123	1075	1116	1159	1089	1051	1066	1052	1016	1021	1051
Average Yards per Play	5.3	5.1	4.7	5.1	5.6	5.0	4.9	4.3	5.2	4.8	5.3	4.8	5.8	4.7
Third Down Efficiency	42.9	40.6	39.6	35.4	47.7	42.6	36.6	30.1	41.1	39.7	39.7	32.9	42.1	34.0
Intercepted by	16	25	20	31	13	18	30	20	24	17	15	31	19	38
Yards Returned by	233	368	236	510	139	190	465	339	478	210	152	433	499	697
Returned for TD	0	4	0	4	0	1	2	2	2	0	0	4	4	7

AFC DEFENSE—Continued

	Buff.	Cin.	Clev.	Den.	Hou.	Ind.	K.C.	Raid.	Mia.	N.E.	N.Y.J.	Pitt.	S.D.	Sea.
Punts	72	67	77	81	64	80	91	117	83	83	67	90	73	83
Yards Punted	2812	2771	3123	3361	2702	3363	3642	5071	3476	3347	2854	3818	2890	3345
Average Yards per Punt	39.1	41.4	40.6	41.5	42.2	42.0	40.0	43.3	41.9	40.3	42.6	42.4	39.6	40.3
Punt Returns	52	38	43	44	60	62	60	34	17	45	37	37	43	32
Yards Returned	597	310	489	335	618	600	461	345	138	442	242	351	399	205
Average Yards per Return	11.5	8.2	11.4	7.6	10.3	9.7	7.7	10.1	8.1	9.8	6.5	9.5	9.3	6.4
Returned for TD	0	0	0	0	0	0	0	0	0	1	0	1	0	1
Kickoff Returns	44	69	52	55	51	42	64	61	66	73	48	61	72	67
Yards Returned	958	1446	1159	1181	986	849	1354	1063	1368	1373	1030	1338	1437	1116
Average Yards per Return	21.8	21.0	22.3	21.5	19.3	20.2	21.2	17.4	20.7	18.8	21.5	21.9	20.0	16.7
Returned for TD	0	1	0	0	0	0	0	0	0	0	0	1	0	0
Penalties	87	90	108	104	105	98	108	121	93	87	87	107	108	114
Yards Penalized	734	743	765	891	876	813	951	1061	772	773	723	945	905	883
Fumbles	36	27	34	44	24	29	18	28	23	33	34	30	34	47
Lost	21	15	15	24	11	13	11	14	12	8	19	11	17	25
Out of Bounds	1	2	0	3	1	2	1	5	1	4	1	2	3	3
Own Recovered for TD	1	0	0	0	0	0	0	0	0	0	0	0	0	0
Opposition Recovered by	14	16	16	17	16	16	15	20	10	15	13	15	17	13
Opposition Recovered for TD	0	0	2	0	1	1	2	0	0	2	0	1	1	1
Total Points Scored	454	339	297	241	437	414	324	278	298	352	364	310	413	282
Total TDs	56	39	30	26	53	50	38	33	39	42	41	35	51	34
TDs Rushing	19	21	10	10	27	16	10	12	16	11	16	12	23	11
TDs Passing	32	15	15	16	23	31	19	19	22	25	24	19	27	18
TDs on Returns and Recoveries	5	3	5	3	3	3	9	2	1	6	1	4	1	5
Extra Points	56	37	30	26	51	47	37	29	37	37	40	34	50	34
Safeties	1	1	0	1	1	2	0	0	0	0	0	0	0	1
Field Goals Made	20	22	29	19	22	21	19	17	9	21	26	22	19	14
Field Goals Attempted	28	27	33	33	30	23	27	21	17	31	37	28	25	22
Percent Successful	71.4	81.5	87.9	57.6	73.3	91.3	70.4	81.0	52.9	67.7	70.3	78.6	76.0	63.6

NATIONAL FOOTBALL CONFERENCE

OFFENSE

	Atl.	Chi.	Dall.	Det.	G.B.	Rams	Minn.	N.O.	N.Y.G.	Phil.	St.L.	S.F.	T.B.	Wash.
First Downs	292	297	323	306	315	258	289	298	310	280	345	356	344	339
Rushing	123	164	93	118	120	140	111	131	97	83	129	138	114	154
Passing	151	115	202	170	168	100	150	137	198	176	200	204	209	164
Penalty	18	18	28	18	27	18	28	30	15	21	16	14	21	21
Rushes	489	674	469	446	461	541	444	523	493	381	488	534	483	588
Net Yards Gained	1994	2974	1714	2017	2019	2864	1844	2171	1660	1338	2088	2465	1776	2274
Average Gain	4.1	4.4	3.7	4.5	4.4	5.3	4.2	4.2	3.4	3.5	4.3	4.6	3.7	3.9
Average Yards per Game	124.6	185.9	107.1	126.1	126.2	179.0	115.3	135.7	103.8	83.6	130.5	154.1	111.0	142.1
Passes Attempted	478	390	604	531	506	358	533	476	535	606	566	496	563	485
Completed	294	226	322	298	281	176	281	246	288	331	347	312	334	286
Percent Completed	61.5	57.9	53.3	56.1	55.5	49.2	52.7	51.7	53.8	54.6	61.3	62.9	59.3	59.0
Total Yards Gained	3546	2695	3995	3787	3740	2382	3337	3198	4066	3823	4634	4079	3907	3417
Times Sacked	67	36	48	61	42	32	64	45	55	60	49	27	45	48
Yards Lost	496	232	389	486	310	240	465	361	434	463	377	178	362	341
Net Yards Gained	3050	2463	3606	3301	3430	2142	2872	2837	3632	3360	4257	3901	3545	3076
Average Yards per Game	190.6	153.9	225.4	206.3	214.4	133.9	179.5	177.3	227.0	210.0	266.1	243.8	221.6	192.3
Net Yards per Pass Play	5.60	5.78	5.53	5.58	6.26	5.49	4.81	5.45	6.16	5.05	6.92	7.46	5.83	5.77
Yards Gained per Completion	12.06	11.92	12.41	12.71	13.31	13.53	11.88	13.00	14.12	11.55	13.35	13.07	11.70	11.95
Combined Net Yards Gained	5044	5437	5320	5318	5449	5006	4716	5008	5292	4698	6345	6366	5321	5350
Percent Total Yards Rushing	39.5	54.7	32.2	37.9	37.1	57.2	39.1	43.4	31.4	28.5	32.9	38.7	33.4	42.5
Percent Total Yards Passing	60.5	45.3	67.8	62.1	62.9	42.8	60.9	56.6	68.6	71.5	67.1	61.3	66.6	57.5
Average Yards per Game	315.3	339.8	332.5	332.4	340.6	312.9	294.8	313.0	330.8	293.6	396.6	397.9	332.6	334.4
Ball Control Plays	1034	1100	1121	1038	1009	931	1041	1044	1083	1047	1103	1057	1091	1121
Average Yards per Play	4.9	4.9	4.7	5.1	5.4	5.4	4.5	4.8	4.9	4.5	5.8	6.0	4.9	4.8
Average Time of Possession	30:14	35:08	29:00	29:43	26:48	28:22	28:14	30:13	30:44	29:30	32:43	30:26	31:17	32:49
Third Down Efficiency	35.3	41.2	34.9	39.1	36.6	33.3	34.7	39.7	36.6	33.2	41.4	46.4	42.9	45.3
Had Intercepted	20	15	26	22	30	17	25	28	18	17	16	10	23	13
Yards Opponents Returned	304	241	372	251	317	240	344	420	222	211	219	155	249	159
Returned by Opponents for TD	2	3	4	1	2	2	2	3	1	1	0	0	0	0

NFC OFFENSE—Continued

	Atl.	Chi.	Dall.	Det.	G.B.	Rams	Minn.	N.O.	N.Y.G.	Phil.	St.L.	S.F.	T.B.	Wash.
Punts	70	85	108	76	85	74	82	70	94	92	68	62	68	73
Yards Punted	2855	3328	4123	3164	3596	2866	3473	3020	3598	3880	2594	2536	2849	2834
Average Yards per Punt	40.8	39.2	38.2	41.6	42.3	38.7	42.4	43.1	38.3	42.2	38.1	40.9	41.9	38.8
Punt Returns	41	63	54	36	48	40	31	33	55	40	47	45	34	55
Yards Returned	264	558	446	241	351	489	217	268	368	250	399	521	207	474
Average Yards per Return	6.4	8.9	8.3	6.7	7.3	12.2	7.0	8.1	6.7	6.3	8.5	11.6	6.1	8.6
Returned for TD	0	0	0	0	0	2	0	0	0	0	0	1	0	0
Kickoff Returns	70	49	63	74	67	58	86	72	61	59	74	47	68	60
Yards Returned	1367	896	1199	1347	1362	1244	1775	1465	1117	1156	1563	1039	1354	1174
Average Yards per Return	19.5	18.3	19.0	18.2	20.3	21.4	20.6	20.3	18.3	19.6	21.1	22.1	19.9	19.6
Returned for TD	0	0	0	1	1	1	0	0	0	1	0	0	0	0
Penalties	125	114	100	138	110	93	90	101	79	77	109	100	118	80
Yards Penalized	1011	851	947	1165	915	830	762	849	703	632	904	884	875	723
Fumbles	39	31	35	36	17	31	39	22	17	23	32	26	36	33
Lost	21	16	17	14	7	18	16	13	9	16	20	12	20	15
Out of Bounds	0	4	4	1	0	2	1	0	0	0	2	1	0	2
Own Recovered for TD	0	0	0	0	0	0	0	0	0	0	0	0	0	1
Opponents Recovered by	20	13	16	11	15	22	17	10	16	11	12	12	14	21
Opponents Recovered for TD	0	0	1	0	0	0	2	1	1	0	1	1	0	2
Total Points Scored	281	325	308	283	390	346	276	298	299	278	423	475	335	426
Total TDs	31	37	34	32	51	38	31	34	36	27	51	57	40	51
TDs Rushing	16	22	12	13	18	16	10	9	12	6	21	21	17	20
TDs Passing	14	14	19	19	30	16	18	21	22	19	28	32	22	24
TDs on Returned and Recovered	1	1	3	0	3	6	3	4	2	2	2	4	1	7
Extra Points	31	35	33	31	48	37	30	34	32	26	48	56	38	48
Safeties	2	1	1	0	0	3	0	0	0	0	0	1	0	0
Field Goals Made	20	22	23	20	12	25	20	20	17	30	23	25	19	24
Field Goals Attempted	27	28	29	27	21	33	23	27	33	37	35	35	26	31
Percent Successful	74.1	78.6	79.3	74.1	57.1	75.8	87.0	74.1	51.5	81.1	65.7	71.4	73.1	77.4

NATIONAL FOOTBALL CONFERENCE

DEFENSE

	Atl.	Chi.	Dall.	Det.	G.B.	Rams	Minn.	N.O.	N.Y.G.	Phil.	St.L.	S.F.	T.B.	Wash.
First Downs	317	216	283	328	323	309	342	298	296	307	292	302	311	307
Rushing	131	72	106	120	136	108	144	134	107	123	108	101	139	91
Passing	162	122	155	177	166	179	182	142	174	171	157	173	157	194
Penalty	24	22	22	31	21	22	16	22	15	13	27	28	15	22
Rushes	538	378	510	519	545	449	547	549	474	556	442	432	511	390
Net Yards Gained	2153	1377	2226	1808	2145	1600	2573	2461	1818	2189	1923	1795	2233	1589
Average Gain	4.0	3.6	4.4	3.5	3.9	3.6	4.7	4.5	3.8	3.9	4.4	4.2	4.4	4.1
Average Yards per Game	134.6	86.1	139.1	113.0	134.1	100.0	160.8	153.8	113.6	136.8	120.2	112.2	139.6	99.3
Passes Attempted	443	435	527	466	551	566	490	422	529	492	494	546	490	575
Completed	262	198	250	288	315	346	319	239	288	262	251	298	286	318
Percent Completed	59.1	45.5	47.4	61.8	57.2	61.1	65.1	56.6	54.4	53.3	50.8	54.6	58.4	55.3
Total Yards Gained	3413	3069	3200	3782	3470	3964	3954	2873	3736	3506	3574	3744	3480	4301
Times Sacked	38	72	57	37	44	43	25	55	48	60	55	51	32	66
Yards Lost	287	583	390	271	324	298	175	420	361	456	403	363	239	529
Net Yards Gained	3126	2486	2810	3511	3146	3666	3779	2453	3375	3050	3171	3381	3241	3772
Average Yards per Game	195.4	155.4	175.6	219.4	196.6	229.1	236.2	153.3	210.9	190.6	198.2	211.3	202.6	235.8
Net Yards per Pass Play	6.50	4.90	4.81	6.98	5.29	6.02	7.34	5.14	5.85	5.53	5.78	5.66	6.21	5.88
Yards Gained per Completion	13.03	15.50	12.80	13.13	11.02	11.46	12.39	12.02	12.97	13.38	14.24	12.56	12.17	13.53
Combined Net Yards Gained	5279	3863	5036	5319	5291	5266	6352	4914	5193	5239	5094	5176	5474	5361
Percent Total Yards Rushing	40.8	35.6	44.2	34.0	40.5	30.4	40.5	50.1	35.0	41.8	37.8	34.7	40.8	29.6
Percent Total Yards Passing	59.2	64.4	55.8	66.0	59.5	69.6	59.5	49.9	65.0	58.2	62.2	65.3	59.2	70.4
Average Yards per Game	329.9	241.4	314.8	332.4	330.7	329.1	397.0	307.1	324.6	327.4	318.4	323.5	342.1	335.1
Ball Control Plays	1019	885	1094	1022	1140	1058	1062	1026	1051	1108	991	1029	1033	1031
Average Yards per Play	5.2	4.4	4.6	5.2	4.6	5.0	6.0	4.8	4.9	4.7	5.1	5.0	5.3	5.2
Third Down Efficiency	44.3	26.4	33.6	45.4	36.6	39.1	45.5	37.7	37.5	41.7	34.8	35.2	43.9	37.4
Intercepted by	12	21	28	14	27	17	11	13	19	20	21	25	18	21
Yards Returned by	147	290	297	87	338	399	120	213	182	287	163	345	308	391
Returned for TD	1	1	2	0	2	3	1	3	0	0	1	2	1	4

	Atl.	Chi.	Dall.	Det.	G.B.	Rams	Minn.	N.O.	N.Y.G.	Phil.	St.L.	S.F.	T.B.	Wash.
Punts	60	100	99	73	89	71	68	84	92	89	81	80	68	78
Yards Punted	2497	4160	4236	2921	3643	2949	2777	3492	3677	3497	3157	3239	2787	3114
Average Yards per Punt	41.6	41.6	42.8	40.0	40.9	41.5	40.8	41.6	40.0	39.3	39.0	40.5	41.0	39.9
Punt Returns	42	41	55	49	46	35	49	47	50	58	27	30	36	38
Yards Returned	450	249	230	516	368	196	435	550	479	486	239	190	310	187
Average Yards per Return	10.7	6.1	4.2	10.5	8.0	5.6	8.9	11.7	9.6	8.4	8.9	6.3	8.6	4.9
Returned for TD	1	0	0	1	0	0	1	1	2	0	0	0	0	0
Kickoff Returns	48	68	65	60	73	74	59	45	55	69	85	78	67	73
Yards Returned	1053	1443	1310	1250	1171	1288	1281	916	1088	1298	1549	1499	1336	1404
Average Yards per Return	21.9	21.2	20.2	20.8	16.0	17.4	21.7	20.4	19.8	18.8	18.2	19.2	19.9	19.2
Returned for TD	0	1	0	0	0	0	0	0	0	0	1	0	0	1
Penalties	93	86	95	107	145	115	113	119	93	96	75	91	136	84
Yards Penalized	820	698	868	978	1129	871	1047	1025	699	904	578	723	1078	803
Fumbles	36	33	35	28	33	42	35	28	24	32	20	28	27	32
Lost	20	13	16	11	15	22	18	10	16	11	12	13	14	22
Out of Bounds	0	0	2	0	2	3	2	1	0	6	0	1	0	1
Own Recovered for TD	0	0	0	0	0	0	1	0	0	1	0	0	0	0
Opponents Recovered by	21	16	17	13	7	17	15	13	9	16	20	12	20	15
Opponents Recovered for TD	2	1	1	2	2	0	1	1	1	0	1	0	0	0
Total Points Scored	382	248	308	408	309	316	484	361	301	320	345	227	380	310
Total TDs	48	29	36	48	34	36	59	41	35	36	39	24	47	39
TDs Rushing	16	10	8	17	14	15	20	13	10	12	11	10	27	13
TDs Passing	27	14	23	27	16	18	35	23	20	22	26	14	20	25
TDs on Returns and Recoveries	5	5	5	4	4	3	4	5	5	2	2	0	0	1
Extra Points	46	26	35	48	33	32	58	41	34	36	36	24	44	37
Safeties	0	0	0	0	0	1	0	1	3	1	1	1	0	0
Field Goals Made	16	16	19	24	24	22	24	24	17	22	25	19	18	13
Field Goals Attempted	30	22	28	29	31	31	28	33	26	35	38	25	27	20
Percent Successful	53.3	72.7	67.9	82.8	77.4	71.0	85.7	72.7	65.4	62.9	65.8	76.0	66.7	65.0

1984 NFC, AFC, AND NFL SUMMARY

	NFC Offense Total	NFC Offense Average	NFC Defense Total	NFC Defense Average	AFC Offense Total	AFC Offense Average	AFC Defense Total	AFC Defense Average	NFL Total	NFL Average
First Downs	4352	310.9	4231	302.2	4305	307.5	4426	316.1	8657	309.2
Rushing	1715	122.5	1620	115.7	1508	107.7	1603	114.5	3223	115.1
Passing	2344	167.4	2311	165.1	2464	176.0	2497	178.4	4808	171.7
Penalty	293	20.9	300	21.4	333	23.8	326	23.3	626	22.4
Rushes	7014	501.0	6840	488.6	6797	485.5	6971	497.9	13,811	493.3
Net Yards Gained	29,198	2085.6	27,890	1992.1	26,305	1878.9	27,613	1972.4	55,503	1982.3
Average Gain		4.2		4.1		3.9		4.0		4.0
Average Yards per Game		130.3		124.5		117.4		123.3		123.9
Passes Attempted	7127	509.1	7026	501.9	7198	514.1	7299	521.4	14,325	511.6
Completed	4022	287.3	3920	280.0	4054	289.6	4156	296.9	8076	288.4
Percent Completed		56.4		55.8		56.3		56.9		56.4
Total Yards Gained	50,606	3614.7	50,066	3576.1	51,627	3687.6	52,167	3726.2	102,233	3651.2
Times Sacked	679	48.5	683	48.8	634	45.3	630	45.0	1313	46.9
Yards Lost	5134	366.7	5099	364.2	4861	347.2	4896	349.7	9995	357.0
Net Yards Gained	45,472	3248.0	44,967	3211.9	46,766	3340.4	47,271	3376.5	92,238	3294.2
Average Yards per Game		203.0		200.7		208.8		211.0		205.9
Net Yards per Pass Play		5.83		5.83		5.97		5.96		5.90
Yards Gained per Completion		12.58		12.77		12.73		12.55		12.66
Combined Net Yards Gained	74,670	5333.6	72,857	5204.1	73,071	5219.4	74,884	5348.9	147,741	5276.5
Percent Total Yards Rushing		39.10		38.28		36.00		36.87		37.57
Percent Total Yards Passing		60.90		61.72		64.00		63.13		62.43
Average Yards per Game		333.3		325.3		326.2		334.3		329.8
Ball Control Plays	14,820	1058.6	14,549	1039.2	14,629	1044.9	14,900	1064.3	29,449	1051.8
Average Yards per Play		5.0		5.0		5.0		5.0		5.0
Third Down Efficiency		38.7		38.5		38.6		38.8		38.7
Interceptions	280	20.0	267	19.1	304	21.7	317	22.6	584	20.9
Yards Returned	3704	264.6	3567	254.8	4812	343.7	4949	353.5	8516	304.1
Returned for TD	21	1.5	21	1.5	30	2.1	30	2.1	51	1.8

1984 NFC, AFC, AND NFL SUMMARY—Continued

	AFC Offense Total	AFC Offense Average	AFC Defense Total	AFC Defense Average	NFC Offense Total	NFC Offense Average	NFC Defense Total	NFC Defense Average	NFL Total	NFL Average
Punts	1107		1132		1153		1128		2260	80.7
Yards Punted	44,716	3194.0	46,146	3296.1	48,005	3428.9	46,575	3326.8	92,721	3311.5
Average Yards per Punt		40.4		40.8		41.6		41.3		41.0
Punt Returns	622		603		585		604		1207	43.1
Yards Returned	5053	360.9	4885	348.9	5364	383.1	5532	395.1	10,417	372.0
Average Yards per Return		8.1		8.1		9.2		9.2		8.6
Returned for TD	3	0.2	5	0.4	5	0.4	3	0.2	8	0.3
Kickoff Returns	908		919		836		825		1744	62.3
Yards Returned	18,058	1289.9	17,886	1277.6	16,486	1177.6	16,658	1189.9	34,544	1233.7
Average Yards per Return		19.9		19.5		19.7		20.2		19.8
Returned for TD	3	0.2	3	0.2	2	0.1	2	0.1	5	0.2
Penalties	1434	102.4	1448	103.4	1431	102.2	1417	101.2	2865	102.3
Yards Penalized	12,051	860.8	12,221	872.9	12,005	857.5	11,835	845.4	24,056	859.1
Fumbles	417	29.8	433	30.9	457	32.6	441	31.5	874	31.2
Lost	214	15.3	213	15.2	215	15.4	216	15.4	429	15.3
Out of Bounds	17	1.2	20	1.4	32	2.3	29	2.1	49	1.8
Own Recovered for TD	1	0.1	2	0.1	2	0.1	1	0.1	3	0.1
Opponents Recovered	210	15.0	211	15.1	214	15.3	213	15.2	424	15.1
Opponents Recovered for TD	9	0.6	12	0.9	14	1.0	11	0.8	23	0.8
Total Points Scored	4743	338.8	4699	335.6	4759	339.9	4803	343.1	9502	339.4
Total TDs	550	39.3	551	39.4	568	40.6	567	40.5	1118	39.9
TDs Rushing	213	15.2	196	14.0	197	14.1	214	15.3	410	14.6
TDs Passing	298	21.3	310	22.1	317	22.6	305	21.8	615	22.0
TDs on Returns and Recoveries	39	2.8	45	3.2	54	3.9	48	3.4	93	3.3
Extra Points	527	37.6	530	37.9	548	39.1	545	38.9	1075	38.4
Safeties	8	0.6	7	0.5	7	0.5	8	0.6	15	0.5
Field Goals Made	300	21.4	283	20.2	263	18.8	280	20.0	563	20.1
Field Goals Attempted	412	29.4	403	28.8	373	26.6	382	27.3	785	28.0
Percent Successful		72.8		70.2		70.5		73.3		71.7

COACHES WITH 100 CAREER VICTORIES

(Ranked according to career wins)

	Yrs.	REGULAR SEASON				POST-SEASON			CAREER			
		Won	Lost	Tied	Pct.	Won	Lost	Pct.	Won	Lost	Tied	Pct.
George Halas	40	320	148	30	.673	6	3	.667	326	151	30	.673
Curley Lambeau	33	231	133	23	.627	3	2	.600	234	135	43	.626
*Tom Landry	25	223	126	6	.637	21	17	.553	244	143	6	.628
*Don Shula	22	227	82	6	.730	17	12	.586	244	94	6	.718
Paul Brown	21	166	100	6	.621	4	9	.308	170	109	6	.607
*Bud Grant	17	151	87	5	.632	10	13	.435	161	100	5	.615
Steve Owen	23	151	100	17	.595	3	8	.273	154	108	17	.582
*Chuck Noll	16	142	88	1	.617	15	7	.682	157	95	1	.623
Hank Stram	17	131	97	10	.571	5	3	.625	136	100	10	.573
Weeb Ewbank	20	130	129	7	.502	4	1	.800	134	130	7	.507
Sid Gillman	18	122	99	7	.550	1	5	.167	123	104	7	.541
George Allen	12	116	47	5	.705	4	7	.364	120	54	5	.684
USFL Total	2	22	14	0	.611	2	2	.500	24	16	0	.600
John Madden	10	103	32	7	.750	9	7	.563	112	39	7	.731
Buddy Parker	15	104	75	9	.577	3	2	.600	107	77	9	.578
*Chuck Knox	12	112	62	1	.643	7	9	.438	119	71	1	.626
Vince Lombardi	10	96	34	6	.728	8	2	.800	104	36	6	.733
*Don Coryell	12	102	68	1	.599	3	6	.333	105	74	1	.586

*Active NFL coaches in 1985.

ACTIVE COACHES CAREER RECORDS

(Ranked according to career percentages)

	Yrs.	REGULAR SEASON				POST-SEASON			CAREER			
		Won	Lost	Tied	Pct.	Won	Lost	Pct.	Won	Lost	Tied	Pct.
Joe Gibbs	4	41	16	0	.719	6	2	.750	47	18	0	.723
Don Shula	22	227	82	6	.730	17	12	.586	244	94	6	.718
Tom Flores	6	58	31	0	.652	8	2	.800	66	33	0	.667
Tom Landry	25	223	126	6	.637	21	17	.553	244	143	6	.628
Chuck Knox	12	112	62	1	.643	7	9	.438	119	71	1	.626
Chuck Noll	16	142	88	1	.617	15	7	.682	157	95	1	.623
Bud Grant	17	151	87	5	.632	10	13	.435	161	100	5	.615
Don Coryell	12	102	68	1	.599	3	6	.333	105	74	1	.586
Bill Walsh	6	49	40	0	.551	7	1	.875	56	41	0	.577
Dan Reeves	4	34	23	0	.596	0	2	.000	34	25	0	.576
John Robinson	2	19	13	0	.594	1	2	.333	20	15	0	.571
Bum Phillips	10	78	69	0	.531	4	3	.571	82	72	0	.532
Leeman Bennett	6	46	41	0	.529	1	3	.250	47	44	0	.516
Mike Ditka	3	21	20	0	.512	1	1	.500	22	21	0	.512
Forrest Gregg	8	58	56	0	.509	2	2	.500	60	58	0	.508
CFL Total	1	5	11	0	.313	0	0	.000	5	11	0	.313
Raymond Berry	1	4	4	0	.500	0	0	.000	4	4	0	.500
Marty Schottenheimer	1	4	4	0	.500	0	0	.000	4	4	0	.500
Sam Wyche	1	8	8	0	.500	0	0	.000	8	8	0	.500
Jim Hanifan	5	34	38	1	.473	0	1	.000	34	39	1	.466
John Mackovic	2	14	18	0	.438	0	0	.000	14	18	0	.438
Joe Walton	2	14	18	0	.438	0	0	.000	14	18	0	.438
Bill Parcells	2	12	19	1	.391	1	1	.500	13	20	1	.397
Dan Henning	2	11	21	0	.344	0	0	.000	11	21	0	.344
Kay Stephenson	2	10	22	0	.313	0	0	.000	10	22	0	.313
Marion Campbell	5	17	39	1	.307	0	0	.000	17	39	1	.307
Hugh Campbell	1	3	13	0	.188	0	0	.000	3	13	0	.188
CFL	6	70	21	5	.755	11	1	.917	81	22	5	.773
USFL	1	8	10	0	.444	0	0	.000	8	10	0	.444
Rod Dowhower	0	0	0	0	.000	0	0	.000	0	0	0	.000
Darryl Rogers	0	0	0	0	.000	0	0	.000	0	0	0	.000

LEADING AFC ACTIVE PASSERS

(Based on 1,000 or more attempts)

	Yrs.	Att.	Comp.	Pct.	Yds.	Avg. Gain	TD	Pct. TD	Int.	Pct. Int.	Pts.
Ken Anderson, Cin.	14	4420	2627	59.4	32497	7.35	194	4.4	158	3.6	81.9
Dan Fouts, S.D.	12	4380	2585	59.0	33854	7.73	201	4.6	185	4.2	81.3
Bill Kenney, K.C.	6	1397	776	55.5	10163	7.27	60	4.3	52	3.7	77.6
Gary Danielson, Clev.	8	1684	952	56.5	11885	7.06	69	4.1	71	4.2	74.8
Steve Grogan, N.E.	10	2681	1389	51.8	20270	7.56	139	5.2	162	6.0	69.1
Jim Zorn, Sea.	9	2990	1593	53.3	20122	6.73	107	3.6	133	4.4	68.2
David Woodley, Pitt.	5	1117	593	53.1	7201	6.45	42	3.8	49	4.4	67.6
Jim Plunkett, L.A.	14	3346	1739	52.0	23093	6.90	147	4.4	186	5.6	65.5
Bob Avellini, N.Y.	10	1110	560	50.5	7111	6.41	33	3.0	69	6.2	55.1

LEADING NFC ACTIVE PASSERS

(Based on 1,000 or more attempts)

	Yrs.	Att.	Comp.	Pct.	Yds.	Avg. Gain	TD	Pct. TD	Int.	Pct. Int.	Pts.
Joe Montana, S.F.	6	2077	1324	63.7	15609	7.52	106	5.1	54	2.6	92.7
Neil Lomax, St.L.	4	1355	782	57.7	10192	7.52	61	4.5	43	3.2	83.2
Danny White, Dallas	9	1943	1155	59.4	14754	7.59	109	5.6	90	4.6	81.8
Joe Theismann, Wash.	11	3301	1877	56.9	23432	7.10	152	4.6	122	3.7	79.0
Steve Bartkowski, Atl.	10	3219	1802	56.0	22732	7.06	149	4.6	140	4.3	75.6
Vince Ferragamo, L.A.	7	1288	730	56.7	9376	7.28	70	5.4	71	5.5	74.8
Ron Jaworski, Phila.	11	3313	1759	53.1	22827	6.89	151	4.6	133	4.0	73.7
Tommy Kramer, Minn.	8	2380	1326	55.7	15631	6.57	100	4.2	102	4.3	72.0
Lynn Dickey, G.B.	12	2811	1575	56.0	21116	7.51	126	4.5	162	5.8	70.9
Phil Simms, N.Y.	5	1529	792	51.8	10269	6.72	61	4.0	61	4.0	69.9
Steve DeBerg, T.B.	8	2256	1292	57.3	14593	6.47	78	3.5	102	4.5	69.7
Joe Ferguson, Det.	12	4166	2188	52.5	27590	6.62	181	4.3	190	4.6	68.6
Richard Todd, N.O.	9	2935	1594	54.3	20419	6.96	121	4.1	157	5.3	67.9
Archie Manning, Minn.	14	3642	2011	55.2	23911	6.57	125	3.4	173	4.8	66.8

LEADING AFC ACTIVE SCORERS

	Yrs.	TDs.	FGs.	XPs.	Pts.
Pat Leahy, New York	11	0	158	306	780
Chris Bahr, Los Angeles	9	0	146	321	759
Rolf Benirschke, San Diego	8	0	130	287	677
Uwe von Schamann, Miami	6	0	101	237	540
Tony Franklin, New England	6	0	102	214	520
Matt Bahr, Cleveland	6	0	104	203	515
Nick Lowery, Kansas City	6	0	112	177	513
Pete Johnson, Miami	8	82	0	0	492
Jim Breech, Cincinnati	7	0	96	202	490
Benny Ricardo, San Diego	7	0	92	171	447
Chuck Muncie, San Diego	9	74	0	0	444
Steve Largent, Seattle	9	73	0	0	438
Cliff Branch, Los Angeles	13	67	0	0	402
Nat Moore, Miami	11	61	0	0	366
Charlie Joiner, San Diego	16	56	0	0	336
John Stallworth, Pittsburgh	11	56	0	0	336
Isaac Curtis, Cincinnati	12	53	0	0	318
Dave Casper, Los Angeles	11	52	0	0	312
Mike Pruitt, Cleveland	9	52	0	0	312

LEADING NFC ACTIVE SCORERS

	Yrs.	TDs.	FGs.	XPs.	Pts.
Jan Stenerud, Minnesota	18	0	358	539	1613
Mark Moseley, Washington	14	0	266	426	1224
Ray Wersching, San Francisco	12	0	171	319	832
Rafael Septien, Dallas	8	0	146	335	773
John Riggins, Washington	13	108	0	0	648
Bob Thomas, Chicago	10	0	133	248	647
Walter Payton, Chicago	10	98	0	0	588
Neil O'Donoghue, St. Louis	8	0	102	221	527
Ed Murray, Detroit	5	0	108	166	490
Earl Campbell, New Orleans	7	73	0	0	438
Tony Dorsett, Dallas	8	68	0	0	408
Mick Luckhurst, Atlanta	4	0	68	146	350
Wilbert Montgomery, Philadelphia	8	58	0	0	348
Wendell Tyler, San Francisco	8	58	0	0	348
Freddie Solomon, San Francisco	10	56	0	0	336
Sammy White, Minnesota	9	50	0	0	300

LEADING AFC ACTIVE RUSHERS

	Yrs.	Att.	Yds.	TDs.		Yrs.	Att.	Yds.	TDs.
Chuck Muncie, S.D.	9	1561	6702	71	Tony Nathan, Miami	6	558	2653	11
Mike Pruitt, Cleve.	9	1595	6540	47	Charles Alexander, Cin.	6	704	2489	11
Greg Pruitt, L.A.	12	1196	5672	27	Kenny King, L.A.	6	563	2410	7
Pete Johnson, Miami	8	1489	5626	76	Randy McMillan, Ind.	4	611	2409	14
Curtis Dickey, Ind.	5	791	3456	26	Frank Pollard, Pitt.	5	537	2283	14
Wayne Morris, S.D.	9	899	3387	38	Andra Franklin, Miami	4	622	2232	22
Cullen Bryant, Sea.	12	848	3262	20	Ken Anderson, Cin.	14	396	2220	20
Freeman McNeil, N.Y.	4	677	3133	14	Sammy Winder, Den.	3	559	2169	8
Tony Collins, N.E.	4	725	3104	23	Steve Grogan, N.E.	10	377	2061	29
Marcus Allen, L.A.	3	701	2879	33	Theotis Brown, K.C.	6	549	2046	30

LEADING NFC ACTIVE RUSHERS

	Yrs.	Att.	Yds.	TDs.		Yrs.	Att.	Yds.	TDs.
Walter Payton, Chi.	10	3047	13309	89	Ted Brown, Minn.	6	961	3959	29
John Riggins, Wash.	13	2740	10675	96	Eric Dickerson, L.A.	2	769	3913	32
Tony Dorsett, Dallas	8	2136	9525	59	Tony Galbreath, N.Y.	9	976	3750	34
Earl Campbell, N.O.	7	2029	8764	73	Rickey Young, Minn.	9	1011	3666	23
Ottis Anderson, St.L.	6	1690	7364	40	Scott Dierking, T.B.	8	734	2915	18
W. Montgomery, Phila.	8	1465	6538	45	Gerry Ellis, G.B.	5	648	2910	18
William Andrews, Atl.	5	1263	5772	29	James Wilder, T.B.	4	758	2878	24
Wendell Tyler, S.F.	8	1142	5384	44	Eddie Lee Ivery, G.B.	6	531	2272	21
Billy Sims, Det.	5	1131	5106	42	Lynn Cain, Atl.	5	604	2263	19
Joe Washington, Atl.	8	1143	4629	11	Gerald Riggs, Atl.	3	531	2222	26
George Rogers, Wash.	4	995	4267	23	Archie Manning, Minn.	14	384	2197	18
Rob Carpenter, N.Y.	8	1110	4159	29	Ron Springs, Dallas	6	604	2180	28

LEADING AFC ACTIVE RECEIVERS

	Yrs.	No.	Yds.	TDs.		Yrs.	No.	Yds.	TDs.
Charlie Joiner, S.D.	16	657	10774	56	Stanley Morgan, N.E.	8	312	6441	42
Steve Largent, Sea.	9	545	8772	72	Wesley Walker, N.Y.	8	312	5735	46
Cliff Branch, L.A.	13	501	8685	67	Chuck Muncie, S.D.	9	263	2323	3
Ozzie Newsome, Cleve.	7	440	5570	34	Mike Pruitt, Cleve.	9	255	1761	5
Nat Moore, Miami	11	421	6414	60	Tony Nathan, Miami	6	253	2407	13
Isaac Curtis, Cin.	12	417	7106	53	Cris Collinsworth, Cin.	4	246	3828	20
Kellen Winslow, S.D.	6	399	5176	37	Steve Watson, Den.	6	236	4331	27
Wes Chandler, S.D.	7	393	6243	40	Jerry Butler, Buff.	5	222	3229	25
Charle Young, Sea.	12	390	4755	25	Todd Christensen, L.A.	6	222	2879	25
John Stallworth, Pitt.	11	387	6799	55	Bruce Harper, N.Y.	8	220	2409	12
Dave Casper, L.A.	11	378	5216	52	Preston Dennard, Buff.	7	219	3483	28
Henry Marshall, K.C.	9	335	5321	32	Dan Doornink, Sea.	7	201	1954	11
Greg Pruitt, L.A.	12	328	3069	18					

LEADING NFC ACTIVE RECEIVERS

	Yrs.	No.	Yds.	TDs.		Yrs.	No.	Yds.	TDs.
Pat Tilley, St.L.	9	416	6228	31	Paul Coffman, G.B.	7	273	3557	33
Rickey Young, Minn.	9	408	3285	16	William Andrews, Atl.	5	272	2612	11
Tony Galbreath, N.Y.	9	401	3223	8	Ottis Anderson, St.L.	6	266	2179	5
James Lofton, G.B.	7	397	7663	41	W. Montgomery, Phila.	8	266	2447	12
Sammy White, Minn.	9	385	6324	50	Billy Johnson, Atl.	10	261	3240	20
Walter Payton, Chi.	10	373	3456	9	John Riggins, Wash.	13	244	2072	12
Dwight Clark, S.F.	6	367	4961	31	Earnest Gray, N.Y.	6	243	3768	27
Joe Washington, Atl.	8	358	3085	17	James Wilder, T.B.	4	243	2038	4
Tony Hill, Dallas	8	356	6105	41	Jimmie Giles, T.B.	8	235	3596	25
John Jefferson, G.B.	7	348	5684	47	Kevin House, T.B.	5	231	3919	26
Freddie Solomon, S.F.	10	346	5587	47	Roy Green, St.L.	6	222	3958	33
David Hill, L.A.	9	304	3634	26	Ron Springs, Dallas	6	222	2028	10
Art Monk, Wash.	5	302	4256	22	Mike Barber, L.A.	9	220	2751	17
Duriel Harris, Dallas	9	299	5031	20	Gerry Ellis, G.B.	5	219	2050	10
Ted Brown, Minn.	6	294	2427	10	Earl Cooper, S.F.	5	209	1863	12
Tony Dorsett, Dallas	8	292	2539	8	Leonard Thompson, Det.	10	201	3626	25
Russ Francis, S.F.	9	275	3857	36					

LEADING AFC ACTIVE INTERCEPTORS

	Yrs.	No.	Yds.	TDs.		Yrs.	No.	Yds.	TDs.
Donnie Shell, Pitt.	11	43	371	1	Kenny Easley, Sea.	4	24	435	3
Dave Brown, Sea.	10	39	527	3	Tim Fox, S.D.	9	24	368	0
Steve Foley, Den.	9	39	536	1	Louis Breeden, Cin.	7	22	413	1
Mike Haynes, L.A.	9	35	613	2	Steve Freeman, Buff.	10	22	329	3
John Harris, Sea.	7	34	405	2	Gregg Bingham, Hous.	12	21	279	0
Lyle Blackwood, Miami	12	33	575	2	Darrol Ray, N.Y.	5	21	581	3
Lester Hayes, L.A.	8	33	538	3	Ray Clayborn, N.E.	8	20	382	0
Terry Jackson, Sea.	7	28	360	3	Tom Jackson, Den.	12	20	340	3
Jack Lambert, Pitt.	11	28	243	0					

LEADING NFC ACTIVE INTERCEPTORS

	Yrs.	No.	Yds.	TDs.		Yrs.	No.	Yds.	TDs.
Dennis Thurman, Dallas	7	31	541	3	Mark Murphy, Wash.	8	27	282	0
Herman Edwards, Phila.	8	30	90	0	Mario Clark, S.F.	9	26	438	0
Gary Fencik, Chi.	9	30	408	1	Dwight Hicks, S.F.	6	26	518	3
Cedric Brown, T.B.	9	29	593	2	Everson Walls, Dallas	4	25	276	0
Nolan Cromwell, L.A.	8	28	537	3	Gerald Small, Atl.	7	24	380	1
Gary Green, L.A.	8	27	418	1	Eric Harris, L.A.	5	21	329	1

TOP 1984 REGULAR-SEASON PERFORMANCES

*Denotes overtime game.

TOP 40 RUSHING PERFORMANCES BY YARDS

Player-Team	Opp. Date	Att.	Yds.	TDs.
Eric Dickerson, Rams vs. Houston, December 9		27	215	2
Eric Dickerson, Rams at St. Louis, November 4		21	208	0
Greg Bell, Buffalo vs. Dallas, November 18		27	206	1
Gerald Riggs, Atlanta at New Orleans, September 2		35	202	2
Eric Dickerson, Rams at Tampa Bay, November 25		28	191	3
Ernest Byner, Cleveland at Houston, December 16		21	188	2
Walter Payton, Chicago vs. Denver, September 9		20	179	1
Walter Payton, Chicago vs. Green Bay, December 9		35	175	1
James Wilder, Tampa Bay vs. Green Bay, September 30		*43	172	1
John Riggins, Washington vs. Dallas, October 14		32	165	0
Eric Dickerson, Rams at New Orleans, October 14		21	164	1
Boyce Green, Cleveland at Buffalo, November 4		29	156	0
Ernest Jackson, San Diego at Raiders, September 24		29	155	1
Walter Payton, Chicago vs. Dallas, September 30		25	155	1
Marcus Allen, Raiders at Miami, December 2		20	155	3
Walter Payton, Chicago vs. New Orleans, October 7		32	154	1
Freeman McNeil, Jets vs. Cincinnati, September 16		26	150	2
Eric Dickerson, Rams vs. Chicago, November 11		28	149	2
Eric Dickerson, Rams vs. New Orleans, December 2		33	149	1
James Wilder, Tampa Bay at Minnesota, November 4		30	146	2
Lynn Cain, Atlanta at Rams, October 7		35	145	3
Greg Bell, Buffalo at Indianapolis, September 30		29	144	0
Eric Dickerson, Rams at Atlanta, October 22		25	142	1
Billy Sims, Detroit at Atlanta, September 9		*23	140	1
John Riggins, Washington at New England, September 23		33	140	1
Sammy Winder, Denver vs. Kansas City, September 23		31	139	1
Eric Dickerson, Rams vs. Dallas, September 3		21	138	1
Larry Moriarty, Houston vs. Jets, November 18		23	138	1
Craig James, New England vs. Indianapolis, December 16		30	138	0
Gerald Riggs, Atlanta at San Francisco, September 30		28	136	0
Ottis Anderson, St. Louis at New England, December 2		30	136	1
Gerald Riggs, Atlanta at Washington, November 5		27	134	2
Gerald Riggs, Atlanta vs. San Francisco, December 2		30	133	1
Freeman McNeil, Jets vs. Miami, November 4		20	132	1
Eric Dickerson, Rams at Green Bay, November 18		25	132	0
Sammy Winder, Denver at Raiders, October 28		*34	126	0
James Wilder, Tampa Bay vs. Atlanta, December 9		28	125	1
Ernest Jackson, San Diego vs. Miami, November 18		*28	124	0
Boyce Green, Cleveland at Atlanta, November 18		30	121	0
Gerald Riggs, Atlanta vs. Houston, September 23		25	120	2
Alfred Anderson, Minnesota at Detroit, September 23		19	120	0
Eric Dickerson, Rams vs. Giants, September 30		22	120	0
Craig James, New England at Denver, November 4		20	120	0

TOP 40 PASSING PERFORMANCES BY YARDS

Player—Team	Opp. Date	Att.	Cmp.	Yds.	TDs.	Int.
Dan Marino, Miami vs. Raiders, December 2		57	35	470	4	2
Neil Lomax, St. Louis at Washington, December 16		46	37	468	2	1
Dan Marino, Miami at St. Louis, September 30		36	24	429	3	0
Dan Marino, Miami at Jets, November 4		42	23	422	2	2
Dan Fouts, San Diego vs. Raiders, October 21		45	24	410	3	3
Phil Simms, Giants vs. Philadelphia, September 2		30	23	409	4	0
Dave Krieg, Seattle at Denver, November 25		44	30	406	3	0
Dan Marino, Miami at Indianapolis, December 9		41	29	404	4	1
Neil Lomax, St. Louis vs. Dallas, November 11		52	27	388	2	2
Tommy Kramer, Minnesota at Tampa Bay, October 7		47	27	386	2	2
Lynn Dickey, Green Bay vs. San Diego, October 7		39	25	384	3	2
Joe Montana, San Francisco vs. Washington, September 10		40	24	381	2	0
Dan Fouts, San Diego vs. Miami, November 18		*56	37	380	4	1
Dan Fouts, San Diego at Green Bay, October 7		50	31	376	3	0
Lynn Dickey, Green Bay at Denver, October 15		37	27	371	1	1
Warren Moon, Houston vs. Indianapolis, September 9		43	23	365	0	0
Joe Montana, San Francisco at Rams, October 28		31	21	365	3	0
Lynn Dickey, Green Bay vs. Seattle, October 21		38	24	364	3	3
Jim Plunkett, Raiders vs. San Diego, September 24		33	24	363	1	1
Neil Lomax, St. Louis vs. Washington, October 21		38	20	361	3	0
Warren Moon, Houston vs. San Francisco, October 21		33	25	356	2	2
Tony Eason, New England at Jets, September 30		42	28	354	3	0
Neil Lomax, St. Louis at Dallas, October 7		29	19	354	3	0
Joe Montana, San Francisco at Houston, October 21		35	25	353	3	1
Ken O'Brien, Jets vs. Giants, December 2		41	28	351	1	1
Phil Simms, Giants at Washington, September 16		45	22	347	1	3
Gary Hogeboom, Dallas at Rams, September 3		47	33	343	1	1
Phil Simms, Giants vs. Kansas City, November 25		41	24	343	2	3
Neil Lomax, St. Louis vs. Rams, November 4		52	34	341	1	2
Joe Ferguson, Buffalo vs. Jets, September 23		46	31	340	2	0

TOP 40 PASSING PERFORMANCES BY YARDS

Player—Team Opp. Date	Att.	Cmp.	Yds.	TDs.	Int.
Ron Jaworski, Philadelphia vs. St. Louis, October 28	38	22	340	2	3
Dan Marino, Miami vs. Dallas, December 17	40	23	340	4	2
Phil Simms, Giants vs. Washington, October 28	29	18	339	2	0
Dan Marino, Miami at San Diego, November 18	*41	28	338	2	1
Dan Fouts, San Diego vs. Houston, September 16	37	26	336	0	1
Dave Krieg, Seattle vs. Denver, December 15	50	30	334	2	2
Joe Pisarcik, Philadelphia at Atlanta, December 16	46	24	334	1	0
Ed Luther, San Diego vs. Kansas City, December 16	44	24	333	1	0
Dan Fouts, San Diego at Seattle, September 9	40	23	332	2	4
Marc Wilson, Raiders at San Diego, October 21	37	24	332	5	1
Bill Kenney, Kansas City vs. Tampa Bay, October 28	46	26	332	2	2

TOP 40 RECEIVING PERFORMANCES BY YARDS

Player-Team Opp. Date	Rec.	Yds.	TDs.
James Lofton, Green Bay at Denver, October 15	11	206	1
Art Monk, Washington at San Francisco, September 10	10	200	0
Roy Green, St. Louis at Washington, December 16	8	196	2
Alfred Jackson, Atlanta vs. San Francisco, December 2	11	193	1
Ozzie Newsome, Cleveland vs. Jets, October 14	14	191	0
Steve Largent, Seattle at Denver, November 25	12	191	1
Roy Green, St. Louis at Dallas, October 7	8	189	2
Bobby Duckworth, San Diego vs. Chicago, December 3	3	185	1
Louis Lipps, Pittsburgh vs. Kansas City, September 2	6	183	2
Roy Green, St. Louis at Indianapolis, September 16	8	183	2
Mark Duper, Miami at Washington, September 2	6	178	2
Mark Clayton, Miami vs. Raiders, December 2	9	177	2
Mark Duper, Miami vs. Indianapolis, September 23	7	173	2
Marcus Allen, Raiders vs. Seattle, October 7	4	173	1
Mike Quick, Philadelphia vs. St. Louis, October 28	6	170	1
Byron Williams, Giants vs. Philadelphia, September 2	5	167	1
John Stallworth, Pittsburgh vs. Kansas City, September 2	8	167	1
Tim Smith, Houston vs. Cleveland, December 16	7	167	0
Roy Green, St. Louis vs. Chicago, October 14	6	166	0
Gerald Carter, Tampa Bay at San Francisco, November 18	9	166	1
Henry Marshall, Kansas City vs. Seattle, December 9	8	166	1
Carlos Carson, Kansas City vs. San Diego, October 14	7	165	0
Mark Duper, Miami at St. Louis, September 30	8	164	0
Roy Green, St. Louis vs. Washington, October 21	6	163	2
James Lofton, Green Bay vs. Seattle, October 21	5	162	2
Tim Smith, Houston at San Diego, September 16	5	159	1
Stacey Bailey, Atlanta at Rams, October 7	7	158	0
James Lofton, Green Bay vs. San Diego, October 7	5	158	1
Kellen Winslow, San Diego at Green Bay, October 7	15	157	0
Butch Johnson, Denver vs. New England, November 4	9	156	2
Mark Duper, Miami at Jets, November 4	7	155	1
Carlos Carson, Kansas City at Giants, November 25	5	153	1
Drew Hill, Rams at Pittsburgh, September 16	4	152	1
Mark Clayton, Miami vs. Dallas, December 17	4	150	3
M.L. Harris, Cincinnati at Jets, September 16	4	148	1
Henry Marshall, Kansas City at Denver, September 23	8	148	0
Mike Quick, Philadelphia at Giants, September 2	8	147	1
Kellen Winslow, San Diego vs. Houston, September 16	10	146	0
Mark Clayton, Miami at St. Louis, September 30	5	143	1
Cris Collinsworth, Cincinnati at Denver, September 2	10	141	0
Art Monk, Washington at Indianapolis, October 7	8	141	3

NATIONAL FOOTBALL CONFERENCE
INDIVIDUAL LEADERS, 1960-84
(National Football League, 1960-69)

RUSHING

Year	Player	Net Yds.	Att.	TD
1984	Eric Dickerson, LA	2,105	379	14
1983	Eric Dickerson, LA	1,808	390	18
1982	Tony Dorsett, Dallas	745	177	5
1981	George Rogers, NO	1,674	378	13
1980	Walter Payton, Chicago	1,460	317	6
1979	Walter Payton, Chicago	1,610	369	14
1978	Walter Payton, Chicago	1,395	333	11
1977	Walter Payton, Chicago	1,852	339	14
1976	Walter Payton, Chicago	1,390	311	13
1975	Jim Otis, St. Louis	1,076	269	5
1974	Lawrence McCutcheon, LA	1,109	236	3
1973	John Brockington, GB	1,144	265	3
1972	Larry Brown, Washington	1,216	285	8
1971	John Brockington, GB	1,105	216	4
1970	Larry Brown, Washington	1,125	237	5
1969	Gale Sayers, Chicago	1,032	236	8
1968	Leroy Kelly, Cleveland	1,239	248	16
1967	Leroy Kelly, Cleveland	1,205	235	11
1966	Gale Sayers, Chicago	1,231	229	8
1965	Jim Brown, Cleveland	1,544	289	17
1964	Jim Brown, Cleveland	1,446	280	7
1963	Jim Brown, Cleveland	1,863	291	12
1962	Jim Taylor, Green Bay	1,474	272	19
1961	Jim Brown, Cleveland	1,408	305	8
1960	Jim Brown, Cleveland	1,257	215	9

PASSING

Year	Player	Passes	Com.	Yds.	TD	Int.
1984	Joe Montana, San Francisco	432	279	3,630	28	10
1983	Steve Bartkowski, Atlanta	432	274	3,167	22	5
1982	Joe Theismann, Washington	252	161	2,033	13	9
1981	Joe Montana, San Francisco	488	311	3,565	19	12
1980	Ron Jaworski, Philadelphia	451	257	3,529	27	12
1979	Roger Staubach, Dallas	461	267	3,586	27	11
1978	Roger Staubach, Dallas	413	231	3,190	25	16
1977	Roger Staubach, Dallas	361	210	2,620	18	9
1976	James Harris, Los Angeles	158	91	1,460	8	6
1975	Fran Tarkenton, Minnesota	425	273	2,994	25	13
1974	Sonny Jurgensen, Washington	167	107	1,185	11	5
1973	Roger Staubach, Dallas	286	179	2,428	23	15
1972	Norm Snead, New York Giants	325	196	2,307	17	12
1971	Roger Staubach, Dallas	211	126	1,882	15	4
1970	John Brodie, San Francisco	378	223	2,941	24	10
1969	Sonny Jurgensen, Washington	442	274	3,102	22	15
1968	Earl Morrall, Baltimore	317	182	2,909	26	17
1967	Sonny Jurgensen, Washington	508	288	3,747	31	16
1966	Bart Starr, Green Bay	251	156	2,257	14	3
1965	Rudy Bukich, Chicago Bears	312	176	2,641	20	9
1964	Bart Starr, Green Bay	272	163	2,144	15	4
1963	Y. A. Tittle, New York	367	221	3,145	36	14
1962	Bart Starr, Green Bay	285	178	2,438	12	9
1961	Milt Plum, Cleveland	302	177	2,416	18	10
1960	Milt Plum, Cleveland	250	151	2,297	21	5

PASS RECEIVING

Year	Player	No.	Yds.	TD
1984	Art Monk, Washington	106	1,372	7
1983	Roy Green, St. Louis	78	1,227	14
1982	Dwight Clark, SF	60	913	5
1981	Dwight Clark, SF	85	1,105	4
1980	Earl Cooper, San Francisco	83	567	4
1979	Ahmad Rashad, Minnesota	80	1,156	9
1978	Rickey Young, Minnesota	88	704	5
1977	Ahmad Rashad, Minnesota	51	681	2
1976	Drew Pearson, Dallas	58	806	6
1975	Chuck Foreman, Minnesota	73	691	9
1974	Charles Young, Phila.	63	696	3
1973	Harold Carmichael, Phila.	67	1,116	9
1972	Harold Jackson, Phila.	62	1,048	4
1971	Bob Tucker, NY Giants	59	791	4
1970	Dick Gordon, Chicago	71	1,026	13
1969	Dan Abramowicz, NO	73	1,015	7
1968	Clifton McNeil, San Fran.	71	994	7
1967	Charley Taylor, Wash.	70	990	9
1966	Charley Taylor, Wash.	72	1,119	12
1965	Dave Parks, San Francisco	80	1,344	12
1964	Johnny Morris, Chicago	93	1,200	10
1963	Bobby Joe Conrad, St. Louis	73	967	10
1962	Bobby Mitchell, Wash.	72	1,384	11
1961	Jim Phillips, Los Angeles	78	1,092	5
1960	Raymond Berry, Baltimore	74	1,298	10

SCORING

Year	Player	TD	PAT	FG	Tot.
1984	Ray Wersching, SF	0	56	25	131
1983	Mark Moseley, Wash.	0	62	33	161
1982	Wendell Tyler, LA	13	0	0	78
1981	Ed Murray, Detroit	0	46	25	121
	Rafael Septien, Dallas	0	40	27	121
1980	Ed Murray, Detroit	0	35	27	116
1979	Mark Moseley, Wash.	0	39	25	114
1978	Frank Corral, Los Angeles	0	31	29	118
1977	Walter Payton, Chicago	16	0	0	96
1976	Mark Moseley, Wash.	0	31	22	97
1975	Chuck Foreman, Minn.	22	0	0	132
1974	Chester Marcol, GB	0	19	25	94
1973	David Ray, Los Angeles	0	40	30	130
1972	Chester Marcol, GB	0	29	33	128
1971	Curt Knight, Washington	0	27	29	114
1970	Fred Cox, Minnesota	0	35	30	125
1969	Fred Cox, Minnesota	0	43	26	121
1968	Leroy Kelly, Cleveland	20	0	0	120
1967	Jim Bakken, St. Louis	0	36	27	117
1966	Bruce Gossett, LA	0	29	28	113
1965	Gale Sayers, Chicago	22	0	0	132
1964	Lenny Moore, Baltimore	20	0	0	120
1963	Don Chandler, New York	0	52	18	106
1962	Jim Taylor, Green Bay	19	0	0	114
1961	Paul Hornung, GB	10	41	15	146
1960	Paul Hornung, GB	15	41	15	176

FIELD GOALS

1984—Paul McFadden, Philadelphia ...30	1971—Curt Knight, Washington...29
1983—Ali Haji-Sheikh, New York...35	1970—Fred Cox, Minnesota...30
1982—Mark Moseley, Washington...20	1969—Fred Cox, Minnesota...26
1981—Rafael Septien, Dallas...27	1968—Mac Percival, Chicago...25
1980—Ed Murray, Detroit...27	1967—Jim Bakken, St. Louis...27
1979—Mark Moseley, Washington...25	1966—Bruce Gossett, Los Angeles...28
1978—Frank Corral, Los Angeles...29	1965—Fred Cox, Minnesota...23
1977—Mark Moseley, Washington...21	1964—Jim Bakken, St. Louis...25
1976—Mark Moseley, Washington...22	1963—Jim Martin, Baltimore...24
1975—Toni Fritsch, Dallas...22	1962—Lou Michaels, Pittsburgh...26
1974—Chester Marcol, Green Bay...25	1961—Steve Myhra, Baltimore...21
1973—David Ray, Los Angeles...30	1960—Tommy Davis, San Francisco...19
1972—Chester Marcol, Green Bay...33	

PASS INTERCEPTIONS

	No.	Yds.		No.	Yds.
1984—Tom Flynn, Green Bay	9	106	1970—Dick Le Beau, Detroit	9	96
1983—Mark Murphy, Washington	9	127	1969—Mel Renfro, Dallas	10	118
1982—Everson Walls, Dallas	7	61	1968—Willie Williams, New York	10	103
1981—Everson Walls, Dallas	11	133	1967—Lem Barney, Detroit	10	232
1980—Nolan Cromwell, Los Angeles	8	140	Dave Whitsell, New Orleans	10	178
1979—Lemar Parrish, Washington	9	65	1966—Larry Wilson, St. Louis	10	180
1978—Ken Stone, St. Louis	9	139	1965—Bobby Boyd, Baltimore	9	78
Willie Buchanon, Green Bay	9	93	1964—Paul Krause, Washington	12	140
1977—Rolland Lawrence, Atlanta	7	138	1963—Dick Lynch, New York Giants	9	251
1976—Monte Jackson, Los Angeles	10	173	Rosie Taylor, Chicago	9	172
1975—Paul Krause, Minnesota	10	201	1962—Willie Wood, Green Bay	9	132
1974—Ray Brown, Atlanta	8	164	1961—Dick Lynch, New York Giants	9	60
1973—Bob Bryant, Minnesota	7	105	1960—Dave Baker, San Francisco	10	96
1972—Bill Bradley, Philadelphia	9	73	Jerry Norton, St. Louis	10	96
1971—Bill Bradley, Philadelphia	11	248			

PUNTING

	No.	Avg.		No.	Avg.
1984—Brian Hansen, New Orleans	69	43.8	1971—Tom McNeill, Philadelphia	73	42.0
1983—Frank Garcia, Tampa Bay	95	42.2	1970—Julian Fagan, New Orleans	77	42.5
1982—Carl Birdsong, St. Louis	54	43.8	1969—David Lee, Baltimore	50	45.3
1981—Tom Skladany, Detroit	64	43.5	1968—Billy Lothridge, Atlanta	75	44.3
1980—Dave Jennings, NY Giants	94	44.8	1967—Billy Lothridge, Atlanta	87	43.7
1979—Dave Jennings, New York	104	42.7	1966—David Lee, Baltimore	49	45.6
1978—Tom Skladany, Detroit	86	42.5	1965—Gary Collins, Cleveland	65	46.7
1977—Tom Blanchard, New Orleans	82	42.4	1964—Bobby Walden, Minnesota	72	46.4
1976—John James, Atlanta	101	42.1	1963—Yale Lary, Detroit	35	48.9
1975—Herman Weaver, Detroit	80	42.0	1962—Tommy Davis, San Francisco	48	45.8
1974—Tom Blanchard, New Orleans	88	42.1	1961—Yale Lary, Detroit	52	48.4
1973—Tom Wittum, San Francisco	79	43.7	1960—Jerry Norton, St. Louis	39	45.6
1972—Dave Chapple, Los Angeles	53	44.2			

PUNT RETURNS

	No.	Yds.	Avg.		No.	Yds.	Avg.
1984—Henry Ellard, Los Angeles	30	403	13.4	1971—Les Duncan, Washington	22	233	10.6
1983—Henry Ellard, Los Angeles	16	217	13.6	1970—Bruce Taylor, San Francisco	43	516	12.0
1982—Billy Johnson, Atlanta	24	273	11.4	1969—Alvin Haymond, Los Angeles	33	435	13.2
1981—LeRoy Irvin, Los Angeles	46	615	13.4	1968—Bob Hayes, Dallas	15	312	20.8
1980—Kenny Johnson, Atlanta	23	281	12.2	1967—Ben Davis, Cleveland	18	229	12.7
1979—John Sciarra, Philadelphia	16	182	11.4	1966—Johnny Roland, St. Louis	20	221	11.1
1978—Jackie Wallace, Los Angeles	52	618	11.9	1965—Leroy Kelly, Cleveland	17	265	15.6
1977—Larry Marshall, Philadelphia	46	489	10.6	1964—Tommy Watkins, Detroit	16	238	14.9
1976—Eddie Brown, Washington	48	646	13.5	1963—Dick James, Washington	16	214	13.4
1975—Terry Metcalf, St. Louis	23	285	12.4	1962—Pat Studstill, Detroit	29	457	15.8
1974—Dick Jauron, Detroit	17	286	16.8	1961—Willie Wood, Green Bay	14	225	16.1
1973—Bruce Taylor, San Francisco	15	207	13.8	1960—Abe Woodson, San Francisco	13	174	13.4
1972—Ken Ellis, Green Bay	14	215	15.4				

KICKOFF RETURNS

	No.	Yds.	Avg.		No.	Yds.	Avg.
1984—Barry Redden, Los Angeles	23	530	23.0	1971—Travis Williams, Los Angeles	25	743	29.7
1983—Darrin Nelson, Minnesota	18	445	24.7	1970—Cecil Turner, Chicago	23	752	32.7
1982—Alvin Hall, Detroit	16	426	26.6	1969—Bobby Williams, Detroit	17	563	33.1
1981—Mike Nelms, Washington	37	1099	29.7	1968—Preston Pearson, Baltimore	15	527	35.1
1980—Rich Mauti, New Orleans	31	798	27.6	1967—Travis Williams, Green Bay	18	739	41.1
1979—Jimmy Edwards, Minnesota	44	1103	25.1	1966—Gale Sayers, Chicago	23	718	31.2
1978—Steve Odom, Green Bay	25	677	27.1	1965—Tommy Watkins, Detroit	17	584	34.4
1977—Wilbert Montgomery, Phila.	23	619	26.9	1964—Clarence Childs, NYG	34	987	29.0
1976—Cullen Bryant, Los Angeles	16	459	28.7	1963—Abe Woodson, San Francisco	29	935	32.3
1975—Walter Payton, Chicago	14	444	31.7	1962—Abe Woodson, San Francisco	37	1157	31.3
1974—Terry Metcalf, St. Louis	20	623	31.2	1961—Dick Bass, Los Angeles	23	698	30.3
1973—Carl Garrett, Chicago	16	486	30.4	1960—Tom Moore, Green Bay	12	397	33.1
1972—Ron Smith, Chicago	30	924	30.8				

AMERICAN FOOTBALL CONFERENCE
INDIVIDUAL LEADERS, 1960-84
(American Football League, 1960-69)

RUSHING

	Net Yds.	Att.	TD		Net Yds.	Att.	TD
1984—Earnest Jackson, S.D.	1,179	296	8	1971—Floyd Little, Denver	1,133	284	6
1983—Curt Warner, Seattle	1,449	335	13	1970—Floyd Little, Denver	901	209	3
1982—Freeman McNeil, N.Y.	786	151	6	1969—Dick Post, San Diego	873	182	6
1981—Earl Campbell, Houston	1,376	361	10	1968—Paul Robinson, Cincinnati	1,023	238	8
1980—Earl Campbell, Houston	1,934	373	13	1967—Jim Nance, Boston	1,216	269	7
1979—Earl Campbell, Houston	1,697	368	19	1966—Jim Nance, Boston	1,458	299	11
1978—Earl Campbell, Houston	1,450	302	13	1965—Paul Lowe, San Diego	1,121	222	7
1977—Mark van Eeghen, Oakland.	1,273	324	7	1964—Cookie Gilchrist, Buffalo	981	230	6
1976—O. J. Simpson, Buffalo	1,503	290	8	1963—Clem Daniels, Oakland	1,099	215	3
1975—O. J. Simpson, Buffalo	1,817	329	16	1962—Cookie Gilchrist, Buffalo	1,096	214	13
1974—Otis Armstrong, Denver	1,407	263	9	1961—Billy Cannon, Houston	948	200	6
1973—O. J. Simpson, Buffalo	2,003	332	12	1960—Abner Haynes, Dallas	875	156	9
1972—O. J. Simpson, Buffalo	1,251	292	6				

PASSING

	Passes	Com.	Yds.	TD	Int.
1984—Dan Marino, Miami	564	362	5,084	48	17
1983—Dan Marino, Miami	296	173	2,210	20	6
1982—Ken Anderson, Cincinnati	309	218	2,495	12	9
1981—Ken Anderson, Cincinnati	479	300	3,754	29	10
1980—Brian Sipe, Cleveland	554	337	4,132	30	14
1979—Dan Fouts, San Diego	530	332	4,082	24	24
1978—Terry Bradshaw, Pittsburgh	368	207	2,915	28	20
1977—Bob Griese, Miami	307	180	2,252	22	13
1976—Ken Stabler, Oakland	291	194	2,737	27	17
1975—Ken Anderson, Cincinnati	377	228	3,169	21	11
1974—Ken Anderson, Cincinnati	328	213	2,667	18	10
1973—Ken Stabler, Oakland	260	163	1,997	14	10
1972—Earl Morrall, Miami	150	83	1,360	11	7
1971—Bob Griese, Miami	263	145	2,089	19	9
1970—Daryle Lamonica, Oakland	356	179	2,516	22	15
1969—Greg Cook, Cincinnati	197	106	1,854	15	11
1968—Len Dawson, Kansas City	224	131	2,109	17	9
1967—Daryle Lamonica, Oakland	425	220	3,228	30	20
1966—Len Dawson, Kansas City	284	159	2,527	26	10
1965—John Hadl, San Diego	348	174	2,798	20	21
1964—Len Dawson, Kansas City	354	199	2,879	30	18
1963—Tobin Rote, San Diego	286	170	2,510	20	17
1962—Len Dawson, Dallas	310	189	2,759	29	17
1961—George Blanda, Houston	362	187	3,330	36	22
1960—Jack Kemp, Los Angeles	406	211	3,018	20	25

PASS RECEIVING

	No.	Yds.	TD		No.	Yds.	TD
1984—Ozzie Newsome, Cleveland	89	1,001	5	1971—Fred Biletnikoff, Oakland	61	929	9
1983—Todd Christensen, LA	92	1,247	12	1970—Marlin Briscoe, Buffalo	57	1,036	8
1982—Kellen Winslow, San Diego.	54	721	6	1969—Lance Alworth, San Diego	64	1,003	4
1981—Kellen Winslow, San Diego..	88	1,075	10	1968—Lance Alworth, San Diego	68	1,312	10
1980—Kellen Winslow, San Diego.	89	1,290	9	1967—George Sauer, New York	75	1,189	6
1979—Joe Washington, Baltimore	82	750	3	1966—Lance Alworth, San Diego.	73	1,383	13
1978—Steve Largent, Seattle	71	1,168	8	1965—Lionel Taylor, Denver	85	1,131	6
1977—Lydell Mitchell, Baltimore	71	620	4	1964—Charley Hennigan, Houston.	101	1,546	8
1976—MacArthur Lane, KC	66	686	1	1963—Lionel Taylor, Denver	78	1,101	10
1975—Reggie Jackson, Cleveland...	60	770	3	1962—Lionel Taylor, Denver	77	908	4
1974—Lydell Mitchell, Baltimore	72	544	2	1961—Lionel Taylor, Denver	100	1,176	4
1973—Fred Willis, Houston	57	371	1	1960—Lionel Taylor, Denver	92	1,235	12
1972—Fred Biletnikoff, Oakland	58	802	7				

SCORING

	TD	PAT	FG	Tot.		TD	PAT	FG	Tot.
1984—Gary Anderson, Pitts.	0	45	24	117	1971—Garo Yepremian, Miami	0	33	28	117
1983—Gary Anderson, Pitts.	0	38	27	119	1970—Jan Stenerud, Kansas City	0	26	30	116
1982—Marcus Allen, Los Angeles	14	0	0	84	1969—Jim Turner, New York	0	33	32	129
1981—Jim Breech, Cincinnati	0	49	22	115	1968—Jim Turner, New York	0	43	34	145
Nick Lowery, Kansas City	0	37	26	115	1967—George Blanda, Oakland	0	56	20	116
1980—John Smith, New England	0	51	26	129	1966—Gino Cappelletti, Boston	6	35	16	119
1979—John Smith, New England	0	46	23	115	1965—Gino Cappelletti, Boston	9	27	17	132
1978—Pat Leahy, New York	0	41	22	107	1964—Gino Cappelletti, Boston	7	36	25	155
1977—Errol Mann, Oakland	0	39	20	99	1963—Gino Cappelletti, Boston	2	35	22	113
1975—O. J. Simpson, Buffalo	23	0	0	138	1962—Gene Mingo, Denver	4	32	27	137
1974—Roy Gerela, Pittsburgh	0	33	20	93	1961—Gino Cappelletti, Boston	8	48	17	147
1973—Roy Gerela, Pittsburgh	0	36	29	123	1960—Gene Mingo, Denver	6	33	18	123
1972—Bobby Howfield, NY Jets	0	40	27	121					

FIELD GOALS

1984—Gary Anderson, Pittsburgh.........................24	1972—Roy Gerela, Pittsburgh............................28
Matt Bahr, Cleveland...............................24	1971—Garo Yepremian, Miami.........................28
1983—Raul Allegre, Baltimore 30	1970—Jan Stenerud, Kansas City......................30
1982—Nick Lowery, Kansas City.........................19	1969—Jim Turner, New York..............................32
1981—Nick Lowery, Kansas City.........................26	1968—Jim Turner, New York..............................34
1980—John Smith, New England........................26	1967—Jan Stenerud, Kansas City......................21
Fred Steinfort, Denver 26	1966—Mike Mercer, Oakland-Kansas City 21
1979—John Smith, New England........................23	1965—Pete Gogolak, Buffalo.............................28
1978—Pat Leahy, New York................................22	1964—Gino Cappelletti, Boston........................25
1977—Errol Mann, Oakland................................20	1963—Gino Cappelletti, Boston........................22
1975—Jan Stenerud, Kansas City......................22	1962—Gene Mingo, Denver................................27
1974—Roy Gerela, Pittsburgh............................20	1961—Gino Cappelletti, Boston........................17
1973—Roy Gerela, Pittsburgh............................29	1960—Gene Mingo, Denver................................18

PASS INTERCEPTIONS

	No.	Yds.		No.	Yds.
1984—Kenny Easley, Seattle	10	126	1972—Mike Sensibaugh, Kansas City	8	65
1983—Ken Riley, Cincinnati	8	89	1971—Ken Houston, Houston...................	9	220
Vann McElroy, Los Angeles	8	68	1970—Johnny Robinson, Kansas City......	10	155
1982—Ken Riley, Cincinnati	5	88	1969—Emmitt Thomas, Kansas City.....	9	146
Bobby Jackson, New York	5	84	1968—Dave Grayson, Oakland...............	10	195
Dwayne Woodruff, Pittsburgh....	5	53	1967—Miller Farr, Houston....................	10	264
Donnie Shell, Pittsburgh	5	27	Tom Janik, Buffalo........................	10	222
1981—John Harris, Seattle	10	155	Dick Westmoreland, Miami	10	127
1980—Lester Hayes, Oakland	13	273	1966—Johnny Robinson, Kansas City.....	10	136
1979—Mike Reinfeldt, Houston	12	205	Bobby Hunt, Kansas City	10	113
1978—Thom Darden, Cleveland	10	200	1965—W. K. Hicks, Houston...................	9	156
1977—Lyle Blackwood, Baltimore..........	10	163	1964—Dainard Paulson, New York.......	12	157
1976—Ken Riley, Cincinnati	9	141	1963—Fred Glick, Houston	12	180
1975—Mel Blount, Pittsburgh	11	121	1962—Lee Riley, New York	11	122
1974—Emmitt Thomas, Kansas City.....	12	214	1961—Bill Atkins, Buffalo.....................	10	158
1973—Dick Anderson, Miami	8	136	1960—Austin Gonsoulin, Denver............	11	98
Mike Wagner, Pittsburgh.............	8	134			

PUNTING

	No.	Avg.		No.	Avg.
1984—Jim Arnold, Kansas City.............	98	44.9	1971—Dave Lewis, Cincinnati.................	72	44.8
1983—Rohn Stark, Baltimore	91	45.3	1970—Dave Lewis, Cincinnati.................	79	46.2
1982—Luke Prestridge, Denver	45	45.0	1969—Dennis Partee, San Diego	71	44.6
1981—Pat McInally, Cincinnati	72	45.4	1968—Jerrel Wilson, Kansas City	63	45.1
1980—Luke Prestridge, Denver	70	43.9	1967—Bob Scarpitto, Denver	105	44.9
1979—Bob Grupp, Kansas City..............	89	43.6	1966—Bob Scarpitto, Denver	76	45.8
1978—Pat McInally, Cincinnati	91	43.1	1965—Jerrel Wilson, Kansas City	69	45.4
1977—Ray Guy, Oakland.......................	59	43.4	1964—Jim Fraser, Denver	73	44.2
1976—Marv Bateman, Buffalo................	86	42.8	1963—Jim Fraser, Denver	81	44.4
1975—Ray Guy, Oakland.......................	68	43.8	1962—Jim Fraser, Denver	55	43.6
1974—Ray Guy, Oakland.......................	74	42.2	1961—Bill Atkins, Buffalo	85	44.5
1973—Jerrel Wilson, Kansas City	80	45.5	1960—Paul Maguire, Los Angeles..........	43	40.5
1972—Jerrel Wilson, Kansas City	66	44.8			

PUNT RETURNS

	No.	Yds.	Avg.		No.	Yds.	Avg.
1984—Mike Martin, Cincinnati	24	376	15.7	1971—Leroy Kelly, Cleveland	30	292	9.7
1983—Kirk Springs, New York	23	287	12.5	1970—Ed Podolak, Kansas City	23	311	13.5
1982—Rick Upchurch, Denver	15	242	16.1	1969—Bill Thompson, Denver	25	288	11.5
1981—James Brooks, San Diego	22	290	13.2	1968—Noland Smith, Kansas City....	18	270	15.0
1980—J. T. Smith, Kansas City	40	581	14.5	1967—Floyd Little, Denver	16	270	16.9
1979—Tony Nathan, Miami	28	306	10.9	1966—Leslie Duncan, San Diego	18	238	13.2
1978—Rick Upchurch, Denver	36	493	13.7	1965—Leslie Duncan, San Diego	30	464	15.5
1977—Billy Johnson, Houston	30	539	15.4	1964—Bobby Jancik, Houston...........	12	220	18.3
1976—Rick Upchurch, Denver	39	536	13.7	1963—Claude Gibson, Oakland	26	307	11.8
1975—Billy Johnson, Houston	40	612	18.8	1962—Dick Christy, New York	15	250	16.7
1974—Lemar Parrish, Cincinnati	18	338	18.8	1961—Dick Christy, New York	18	383	21.3
1973—Ron Smith, San Diego	27	352	15.0	1960—Abner Haynes, Dallas.............	14	215	15.4
1972—Chris Farasopolous, NYJ	17	179	10.5				

KICKOFF RETURNS

	No.	Yds.	Avg.		No.	Yds.	Avg.
1984—Bobby Humphery, New York	22	675	30.7	1971—Mercury Morris, Miami	15	423	28.2
1983—Fulton Walker, Miami	36	962	26.7	1970—Jim Duncan, Baltimore	20	707	35.4
1982—Mike Mosley, Buffalo..............	18	487	27.1	1969—Bill Thompson, Denver	19	594	31.3
1981—Carl Roaches, Houston	28	769	27.5	1968—George Atkinson, Oakland	32	802	25.1
1980—Horace Ivory, New England .	36	992	27.6	1967—Zeke Moore, Houston..............	14	405	28.9
1979—Larry Brunson, Oakland........	17	441	25.9	1966—Goldie Sellers, Denver	19	541	28.5
1978—Keith Wright, Cleveland	30	789	26.3	1965—Abner Haynes, Denver	34	901	26.5
1977—Raymond Clayborn, NE	20	869	31.0	1964—Bo Roberson, Oakland............	36	975	27.1
1976—Duriel Harris, Miami	17	559	32.9	1963—Bobby Jancik, Houston	45	1,317	29.3
1975—Harold Hart, Oakland	17	518	30.5	1962—Bobby Jancik, Houston	24	726	30.3
1974—Greg Pruitt, Cleveland............	22	606	27.5	1961—Dave Grayson, Dallas	16	453	28.3
1973—Wallace Francis, Buffalo........	23	687	29.9	1960—Ken Hall, Houston...................	19	594	31.3
1972—Bruce Laird, Baltimore...........	29	843	29.1				

ALL-TIME PRO FOOTBALL RECORDS

(Through 1984 season)

RUSHING

LEADING LIFETIME RUSHERS

(Courtesy of Pro Football's Hall of Fame, Canton, Ohio)

Player	League	Yrs.	Att.	Yards	Avg.	TD
WALTER PAYTON	NFL	10	3047	13309	4.4	89
JIM BROWN	NFL	9	2359	12312	5.2	106
FRANCO HARRIS	NFL	13	2949	12120	4.1	91
O.J. SIMPSON	AFL-NFL	11	2404	11236	4.7	61
JOHN RIGGINS	NFL	13	2740	10675	3.9	96
JOE PERRY	AAFC-NFL	16	1929	9723	5.0	71
TONY DORSETT	NFL	8	2136	9525	4.5	59
EARL CAMPBELL	NFL	7	2029	8764	4.3	73
JIM TAYLOR	NFL	10	1941	8597	4.4	83
LARRY CSONKA	AFL-NFL	11	1891	8081	4.3	64
O.J. ANDERSON	NFL	6	1690	7364	4.4	40
LEROY KELLY	NFL	10	1727	7274	4.2	74
JOHN HENRY JOHNSON	NFL-AFL	13	1571	6803	4.3	48
CHUCK MUNCIE	NFL	9	1561	6702	4.3	71
MARK VAN EEGHEN	NFL	10	1652	6651	4.0	37
LAWRENCE McCUTCHEON	NFL	10	1521	6578	4.3	26
MIKE PRUITT	NFL	9	1593	6540	4.1	47
WILBERT MONTGOMERY	NFL	8	1465	6538	4.5	45
LYDELL MITCHELL	NFL	9	1675	6534	3.9	30
FLOYD LITTLE	AFL-NFL	9	1641	6323	3.8	43

NOTE—Mike Pruitt and Wilbert Montgomery attained Top Twenty ranking during the 1984 season. They displaced Don Perkins (6217 yards) and Ken Willard (6105 yards). William Andrews (5772 yards) did not play in 1984 because of injury but stands next in line to reach the Top Twenty if he returns to action in 1985. Of those players active in 1984, Greg Pruitt (5672 yards) and Pete Johnson (5626 yards) stand next in line behind Andrews to enter the Top Twenty.

AAFC—All-America Football Conference

AFL—American Football League

NFL—National Football League

Most Yards Gained, Season

2,105—Eric Dickerson, Los Angeles Rams, 1984

1,000-Yard Rushing Seasons by First-Year Players

Beattie Feathers, Chicago Bears, 1934, 1,004 yards
Cookie Gilchrist, Buffalo Bills, 1962, 1,096 yards
Paul Robinson, Cincinnati Bengals, 1968, 1,023 yards
John Brockington, Green Bay Packers, 1971, 1,105 yards
Franco Harris, Pittsburgh Steelers, 1972, 1,055 yards
Larry McCutcheon, Los Angeles Rams, 1973, 1,097 yards. (McCutcheon considered a 1973 rookie as he played only 3 games in 1972 and did not carry the ball, playing only on special teams.)
Don Woods, San Diego Chargers, 1974, 1,162 yards
Tony Dorsett, Dallas Cowboys, 1977, 1,007 yards
Earl Campbell, Houston Oilers, 1978, 1,450 yards
Terry Miller, Buffalo Bills, 1978, 1,060 yards
Ottis Anderson, St. Louis Cardinals, 1979, 1,605 yards
William Andrews, Atlanta Falcons, 1979, 1,023 yards
Billy Sims, Detroit Lions, 1980, 1,303 yards
Joe Cribbs, Buffalo Bills, 1980, 1,185 yards
George Rogers, New Orleans Saints, 1981, 1,674 yards
Joe Delaney, Kansas City Chiefs, 1981, 1,121 yards
Eric Dickerson, Los Angeles Rams, 1983, 1,808 yards
Curt Warner, Seattle Seahawks, 1983, 1,449 yards
Greg Bell, Buffalo Bills, 1984, 1,100 yards

Most Yards Gained, Game

275—Walter Payton, Chicago Bears vs. Minnesota Vikings, November 20, 1977.

Longest Run From Scrimmage

99—Tony Dorsett, Dallas Cowboys vs. Minnesota Vikings, January 3, 1983.

Most Games, 100 Yards or More, Season

12—Eric Dickerson, Los Angeles Rams, 1984

Most Games, 100 Yards or More, Career

63—Walter Payton, Chicago Bears, 1975-1984

Most Games, 200 Yards or More, Career

6—O. J. Simpson, Buffalo Bills, 1969-1976

Most Games, 200 Yards or More, Season

4—Earl Campbell, Houston Oilers, 1980

Most Touchdowns Rushing, Career

106—Jim Brown, Cleveland Browns, 1957-1965

Most Touchdowns Rushing, Season

24—John Riggins, Washington Redskins, 1983.

Most Touchdowns Rushing, Game

6—Ernie Nevers, Chicago Cardinals vs. Chicago Bears, November 8, 1929

Most Rushing Attempts, Season

407—James Wilder, Tampa Bay Buccaneers, 1984

Most Rushing Attempts, Game

43—Butch Woolfolk, New York Giants vs. Philadelphia Eagles, November 20, 1983
James Wilder, Tampa Bay Buccaneers vs. Green Bay Packers, September 30, 1984

PASSING
LEADING LIFETIME PASSERS
Minimum 1500 attempts
(Courtesy of Pro Football's Hall of Fame, Canton, Ohio)

Player	League	Yrs.	Att.	Comp.	Yds.	TD	Int.	Rating Pts.
JOE MONTANA	NFL	6	2077	1324	15,609	106	54	92.7
OTTO GRAHAM	AAFC-NFL	10	2626	1464	23,584	174	135	86.6
ROGER STAUBACH	NFL	11	2958	1685	22,700	153	109	83.4
DANNY WHITE	NFL	9	1943	1155	14,754	109	90	82.7
SONNY JURGENSEN	NFL	18	4262	2433	32,224	255	189	82.6
LEN DAWSON	NFL-AFL	19	3741	2136	28,711	239	183	82.6
KEN ANDERSON	NFL	14	4420	2627	32,497	194	158	82.0
DAN FOUTS	NFL	12	4380	2585	33,854	201	185	81.2
BART STARR	NFL	16	3149	1808	24,718	152	138	80.5
FRAN TARKENTON	NFL	18	6467	3686	47,003	342	266	80.4
JOE THEISMANN	NFL	11	3301	1877	23,432	152	122	79.0
BERT JONES	NFL	10	2551	1430	18,190	124	101	78.2
JOHNNY UNITAS	NFL	18	5186	2830	40,239	290	253	78.2
FRANK RYAN	NFL	13	2133	1090	16,042	149	111	77.6
BOB GRIESE	AFL-NFL	14	3429	1926	25,092	192	172	77.1
STEVE BARTKOWSKI	NFL	10	3219	1802	22,732	149	140	75.5
KEN STABLER	AFL-NFL	15	3793	2270	27,938	194	222	75.3
NORM VAN BROCKLIN	NFL	12	2895	1553	23,611	173	178	75.1
SID LUCKMAN	NFL	12	1744	904	14,686	137	132	75.0
BRIAN SIPE	NFL	10	3439	1944	23,713	154	149	74.8

NOTE—Steve Bartkowski attained Top Twenty ranking during the 1984 season. He displaced Don Meredith (74.7). Of those players who were active in 1984 who are not in the Top Twenty, Gary Danielson (74.7), Ron Jaworski (73.7) and Tommy Kramer (72.0) rank the highest.

Rating points based on a combination of performances in the following four categories: percentage of completions, percentage of touchdown passes, percentage of interceptions and average gain per pass attempt.

AAFC—All-America Football Conference
AFL—American Football League
NFL—National Football League

Most Yards Gained, Season

5,084—Dan Marino, Miami Dolphins, 1984

Most Yards Gained, Game

554—Norm Van Brocklin, Los Angeles Rams vs. New York Yankees, September 28, 1951 (27 completions in 41 attempts)

Most Games, 300 or More Yards Passing, Season

9—Dan Marino, Miami Dolphins, 1984

Longest Pass Completion (99 Yards; All Touchdowns)

Frank Filchock to Andy Farkas, Washington Redskins vs. Pittsburgh Steelers, October 15, 1939
Otto Graham to Mac Speedie, Cleveland Browns vs. Buffalo Bills, November 2, 1947
George Izo to Bobby Mitchell, Washington Redskins vs. Cleveland Browns, September 15, 1963
Karl Sweetan to Pat Studstill, Detroit Lions vs. Baltimore Colts, October 16, 1966
Sonny Jurgensen to Gerry Allen, Washington Redskins vs. Chicago Bears, September 15, 1968
Jim Plunkett to Cliff Branch, Los Angeles Raiders vs. Washington Redskins, October 2, 1983

Most Touchdowns Passing, Career

342—Fran Tarkenton, Minnesota Vikings, 1961-65; New York Giants 1967-71; Minnesota Vikings, 1972-78.

Most Touchdowns Passing, Season

48—Dan Marino, Miami Dolphins, 1984

Most Touchdowns Passing, Game

7—Sid Luckman, Chicago Bears vs. New York Giants, November 14, 1943
Adrian Burk, Philadelphia Eagles vs. Washington Redskins, October 17, 1954
George Blanda, Houston Oilers vs. New York Titans, November 19, 1961
Y. A. Tittle, New York Giants vs. Washington Redskins, October 28, 1962
Joe Kapp, Minnesota Vikings vs. Baltimore Colts, September 28, 1969

Most Consecutive Games, Touchdown Passes
47—Johnny Unitas, Baltimore, 1956-60

Most Passing Attempts, Season
609—Dan Fouts, San Diego Chargers, 1981

Most Passing Attempts, Game
68—George Blanda, Houston Oilers vs. Buffalo Bills, November 1, 1964 (37 completions)

Most Passes Completed, Season
362—Dan Marino, Miami Dolphins, 1984

Most Passes Completed, Game
42—Richard Todd, New York Jets vs. San Francisco 49ers, September 21, 1980

Most Consecutive Passes Completed
20—Ken Anderson, Cincinnati Bengals vs. Houston Oilers, January 2, 1983

Highest Completion Percentage, Season (Qualifiers)
70.55—Ken Anderson, Cincinnati Bengals, 1982 (309-218)

Highest Completion Percentage, Game (20 attempts)
90.91—Ken Anderson, Cincinnati Bengals vs. Pittsburgh Steelers, November 10, 1974 (22-20)

Most Passes Had Intercepted, Game
8—Jim Hardy, Chicago Cardinals vs. Philadelphia Eagles, September 24, 1950 (39 attempts)

Most Passes Had Intercepted, Season
42—George Blanda, Houston Oilers, 1962 (418 attempts)

Most Passes Had Intercepted, Career
277—George Blanda, Chicago Bears, 1949, 1950-1958; Baltimore Colts 1950; Houston Oilers, 1960-1966; Oakland Raiders, 1967-1975 (4,007 attempts)

Most Consecutive Passes Attempted Without Interception
294—Bart Starr, Green Bay Packers, 1964-1965

PASS RECEIVING
LEADING LIFETIME RECEIVERS
(Courtesy of Pro Football's Hall of Fame, Canton, Ohio)

Player	League	Yrs.	No.	Yards	Avg.	TD
CHARLIE JOINER	AFL-NFL	16	657	10774	16.4	56
CHARLEY TAYLOR	NFL	13	649	9110	14.0	79
DON MAYNARD	NFL-AFL	15	633	11834	18.7	88
RAYMOND BERRY	NFL	13	631	9275	14.7	68
HAROLD CARMICHAEL	NFL	14	590	8985	15.2	79
FRED BILETNIKOFF	AFL-NFL	14	589	8974	15.2	76
HAROLD JACKSON	NFL	16	579	10372	17.9	76
LIONEL TAYLOR	NFL-AFL	10	567	7195	12.7	45
STEVE LARGENT	NFL	9	545	8772	16.1	72
LANCE ALWORTH	AFL-NFL	11	542	10266	18.9	85
BOBBY MITCHELL	NFL	11	521	7954	15.3	65
BILLY HOWTON	NFL	12	503	8459	16.8	61
CLIFF BRANCH	NFL	12	501	8685	17.3	67
TOMMY McDONALD	NFL	12	495	8410	17.0	84
AHMAD RASHAD	NFL	10	495	6831	13.8	44
DREW PEARSON	NFL	11	489	7822	16.0	48
DON HUTSON	NFL	11	488	7991	16.4	99
JACKIE SMITH	NFL	16	480	7918	16.5	40
ART POWELL	AFL-NFL	10	479	8046	16.8	81
BOYD DOWLER	NFL	12	474	7270	15.4	40

NOTE—There were no new players added to the Top Twenty receiving list in 1984. Of those players active in 1984, Ozzie Newsome (440 receptions), Nat Moore (421 receptions) and Isaac Curtis (416 receptions) stand next in line for the Top Twenty.

AFL—American Football League
NFL—National Football League

Most Yards Gained, Season
1,746—Charley Hennigan, Houston Oilers, 1961

Most Yards Gained, Game
303—Jim Benton, Cleveland Rams vs. Detroit Lions, November 22, 1945 (10 receptions)

Longest Pass Reception
(See receivers mentioned under Longest Pass Completion)

Most Pass Receptions, Season
106—Art Monk, Washington Redskins, 1984

Most Pass Receptions, Game
18—Tom Fears, Los Angeles Rams vs. Green Bay Packers, December 3, 1950 (189 yards)

Most Consecutive Games, Pass Receptions
127—Harold Carmichael, Philadelphia Eagles, 1971-1980 (streak ended December 21, 1980)

Most Touchdown Passes, Career
99—Don Hutson, Green Bay Packers, 1935-1945

Most Touchdown Passes, Season
18—Mark Clayton, Miami Dolphins, 1984

Most Touchdowns Passes, Game
5—Bob Shaw, Chicago Cardinals vs. Baltimore Colts, October 2, 1950
Kellen Winslow, San Diego Chargers vs. Oakland Raiders, November 22, 1981

Most Consecutive Games, Touchdown Passes
11—Elroy Hirsch, Los Angeles Rams, 1950-1951
Buddy Dial, Pittsburgh Steelers, 1957-1960

PASS INTERCEPTIONS

Most Interceptions, Game
4—Sammy Baugh, Washington Redskins vs. Detroit Lions, November 14, 1943
Dan Sandifer, Washington Redskins vs. Boston Yanks, October 31, 1948
Don Doll, Detroit Lions vs. Chicago Cardinals, October 23, 1949
Bob Nussbaumer, Chicago Cardinals vs. New York Bulldogs, November 13, 1949
Russ Craft, Philadelphia Eagles vs. Chicago Cardinals, September 24, 1950
Bob Dillon, Green Bay Packers vs. Detroit Lions, November 26, 1953
Jack Butler, Pittsburgh Steelers vs. Washington Redskins, December 13, 1953
Jerry Norton, St. Louis Cardinals vs. Washington Redskins, November 20, 1960; vs. Pittsburgh Steelers, November 26, 1961
Goose Gonsoulin, Denver Broncos vs. Buffalo Bills, September 18, 1960
Dave Baker, San Francisco 49ers vs. Los Angeles Rams, December 4, 1960
Bobby Ply, Dallas Texans vs. San Diego Chargers, December 16, 1962
Bobby Hunt, Kansas City Chiefs vs. Houston Oilers, October 4, 1964
Willie Brown, Denver Broncos vs. New York Jets, November 15, 1964
Dick Anderson, Miami Dolphins vs. Pittsburgh Steelers, December 3, 1973
Willie Buchanon, Green Bay Packers vs. San Diego Chargers, September 24, 1978.

Most Interceptions, Season
14—Dick Lane, Los Angeles Rams, 1952

Most Interceptions, Career
81—Paul Krause, Washington Redskins, 1964-1967; Minnesota Vikings, 1968- 1979

Most Consecutive Games, Passes Intercepted By
8—Tom Morrow, Oakland Raiders, 1962 (4), 1963 (4)

Most Yardage Gained via Pass Interceptions, Career
1,282—Emlen Tunnell, New York Giants, 1948-1958; Green Bay Packers, 1959- 1961

Most Yardage Gained via Pass Interceptions, Season
349—Charley McNeil, San Diego Chargers, 1961

Most Yardage Gained via Pass Interceptions, Game
177—Charley McNeil, San Diego Chargers vs. Houston Oilers, September 24, 1961

Longest Run With Intercepted Pass (All Touchdowns)
102—Bob Smith, Detroit Lions vs. Chicago Bears, November 24, 1949
Erich Barnes, New York Giants vs. Dallas Cowboys, October 22, 1961
Gary Barbaro, Kansas City Chiefs vs. Seattle Seahawks, December 11, 1977
Louis Breeden, Cincinnati Bengals vs. San Diego Chargers, November 8, 1981

Most Touchdowns Scored via Pass Interceptions, Lifetime
9—Ken Houston, Houston Oilers, 1967 (2), 1968 (2), 1969, 1971 (4)

Most Touchdowns Scored via Pass Interceptions, Season
4—Ken Houston, Houston Oilers, 1971
Jim Kearney, Kansas City Chiefs, 1972

Most Touchdowns Scored via Pass Interceptions, Game
2—Bill Blackburn, Chicago Cardinals vs. Boston Yanks, October 24, 1948
Dan Sandifer, Washington Redskins vs. Boston Yanks, October 31, 1948
Bob Franklin, Cleveland Browns vs. Chicago Bears, December 11, 1960
Bill Stacy, St. Louis Cardinals vs. Dallas Cowboys, November 5, 1961
Jerry Norton, St. Louis Cardinals vs. Pittsburgh Steelers, November 26, 1961
Miller Farr, Houston Oilers vs. Buffalo Bills, December 7, 1968
Ken Houston, Houston Oilers vs. San Diego Chargers, December 19, 1971
Jim Kearney, Kansas City Chiefs vs. Denver Broncos, October 1, 1972
Lemar Parrish, Cincinnati Bengals vs. Houston Oilers, December 17, 1972
Dick Anderson, Miami Dolphins vs. Pittsburgh Steelers, December 3, 1973
Prentice McCray, New England Patriots vs. New York Jets, November 21, 1976
Kenny Johnson, Atlanta Falcons vs. Green Bay Packers, November 27, 1983
Mike Kozlowski, Miami Dolphins vs. New York Jets, December 16, 1983
Dave Brown, Seattle Seahawks vs. Kansas City Chiefs, November 4, 1984

SCORING

LEADING LIFETIME SCORERS

(Courtesy of Pro Football's Hall of Fame, Canton, Ohio)

Player	League	Yrs.	TD	PAT	FG	Tot.
GEORGE BLANDA	NFL-AFL	26	9	943	335	2002
JAN STENERUD	AFL-NFL	18	0	539	358	1613
LOU GROZA	AAFC-NFL	21	1	810	264	1608
JIM TURNER	AFL-NFL	16	1	521	304	1439
JIM BAKKEN	NFL	17	0	534	282	1380
FRED COX	NFL	15	0	519	282	1365
MARK MOSELEY	NFL	14	0	426	266	1224
GINO CAPPELLETTI	AFL	11	42	350	176	1130
DON COCKROFT	NFL	13	0	432	216	1080
GARO YEPREMIAN	NFL-AFL	14	0	444	210	1074
BRUCE GOSSETT	NFL	11	0	374	219	1031
SAM BAKER	NFL	15	2	428	179	977
LOU MICHAELS	NFL	13	1	386	187	*955
ROY GERELA	AFL-NFL	11	0	351	184	903
BOBBY WALSTON	NFL	12	46	365	80	881
PETE GOGOLAK	AFL-NFL	10	0	344	173	863
ERROL MANN	NFL	11	0	315	177	846
RAY WERSCHING	NFL	12	0	319	171	832
DON HUTSON	NFL	11	105	172	7	823
PAT LEAHY	NFL	11	0	306	158	780

NOTE—Ray Wersching and Pat Leahy attained Top Twenty ranking during the 1984 season. They displaced Paul Hornung (760 points) and Tony Fritsch (758 points). Of those players active in 1984, Rafael Septien (773 points) and Chris Bahr (759 points) stand next in line for the Top Twenty.

*Includes safety.

AAFC—All-America Football Conference
AFL—American Football League
NFL—National Football League

Most Points, Season

176—Paul Hornung, Green Bay Packers, 1960 (15 TDs, 41 PATs, 15 FGs)

Most Points, Game

40—Ernie Nevers, Chicago Cardinals vs. Chicago Bears, November 28, 1929 (6 TDs, 4 PATs)

Most Touchdowns, Season

24—John Riggins, Washington Redskins, 1983 (all rushing)

Most Touchdowns, Game

6—Ernie Nevers, Chicago Cardinals vs. Chicago Bears, November 28, 1929 (6 rushing)
Dub Jones, Cleveland Browns vs. Chicago Bears, November 25, 1951 (4 rushing, 2 pass receptions)
Gale Sayers, Chicago Bears vs. San Francisco 49ers, December 12, 1965 (4 rushing, 1 pass reception, 1 punt return)

Most Points After Touchdown, Game

9—Pat Harder, Chicago Cardinals vs. New York Giants, October 17, 1948
Joe Vetrano, San Francisco 49ers vs. Brooklyn Dodgers, November 21, 1948
Bob Waterfield, Los Angeles Rams vs. Baltimore Colts, October 22, 1950
Charlie Gogolak, Washington Redskins vs. New York Giants, November 27, 1966

Most Points After Touchdown, Season

66—Uwe von Schamann, Miami Dolphins, 1984 (70 attempts)

Most Consecutive Points After Touchdown

234—Tommy Davis, San Francisco 49ers, 1959-1965

Most Points After Touchdown (no misses), Season

56—Danny Villanueva, Dallas Cowboys, 1966
Ray Wersching, San Francisco 49ers, 1984

Most Points After Touchdown (no misses), Game

9—Pat Harder, Chicago Cardinals vs. New York Giants, October 17, 1948
Joe Vetrano, San Francisco 49ers vs. Brooklyn Dodgers, November 21, 1948
Bob Waterfield, Los Angeles Rams vs. Baltimore Colts, October 22, 1950

Most Points After Touchdown Attempted, Season

70—Uwe von Schamann, Miami Dolphins, 1984 (66 successful)

Most Points After Touchdown Attempted, Game

10—Charlie Gogolak, Washington Redskins vs. New York Giants, November 27, 1966 (9 successful)

Most Field Goals, Game

7—Jim Bakken, St. Louis Cardinals vs. Pittsburgh Steelers, September 24, 1967

Most Field Goals, Season

35—Ali Haji-Sheikh, New York Giants, 1983

Most Field Goals Attempted, Season

49—Bruce Gossett, Los Angeles Rams, 1966
Curt Knight, Washington Redskins, 1971

Most Field Goals Attempted, Game

9—Jim Bakken, St. Louis Cardinals vs. Pittsburgh Steelers, September 24, 1967 (7 successful)

Most Consecutive Field Goals

23—Mark Moseley, Washington Redskins, 1981-82

Most Consecutive Games, Field Goal

31—Fred Cox, Minnesota, 1968-1970

Longest Field Goal

63—Tom Dempsey, New Orleans Saints vs. Detroit Lions, November 8, 1970

Highest Field Goal Completion Percentage, Season (20 attempts)

95.2—Mark Moseley, Washington Redskins, 1982 (20 FGs in 21 attempts)

Highest Field Goal Percentage, Game (6 attempts)

100—Gino Cappelletti, Boston Patriots vs. Denver Broncos, October 4, 1964 (6 FGs in 6 attempts)
Joe Danelo, New York Giants vs. Seattle Seahawks, October 18, 1981 (6 FGs in 6 attempts)
Ray Wersching, San Francisco 49ers vs. New Orleans Saints, October 16, 1983 (6 FGs in 6 attempts)

Most Safeties, Career

4—Ted Hendricks, Baltimore Colts, 1969-73; Green Bay Packers, 1974; Oakland Raiders, 1975-81; Los Angeles Raiders, 1982-83

Most Safeties, Season

2—Tom Nash, Green Bay Packers, 1932
Roger Brown, Detroit Lions, 1962
Ron McDole, Buffalo Bills, 1964
Alan Page, Minnesota Vikings, 1971
Benny Barnes, Dallas Cowboys, 1973
Fred Dryer, Los Angeles Rams, 1973
James Young, Houston Oilers, 1977
Tom Hannon, Minnesota Vikings, 1981
Doug English, Detroit Lions, 1983

Most Safeties, Game

2—Fred Dryer, Los Angeles Rams vs. Green Bay Packers, October 21, 1973

PUNT RETURNS

Most Yardage Returning Punts, Career

3,008—Rick Upchurch, Denver Broncos, 1975-1983

Most Yardage Returning Punts, Season

666—Greg Pruitt, Los Angeles Raiders, 1983

Most Yardage Returning Punts, Game

207—LeRoy Irvin, Los Angeles Rams vs. Atlanta Falcons, October 11, 1981

Most Touchdowns Scored via Punt Returns, Career

8—Jack Christiansen, Detroit Lions, 1951 (4), 1952 (2), 1954, 1956
Rick Upchurch, Denver Broncos, 1976 (4), 1977 (1), 1978 (1), 1982 (2)

Most Touchdowns Scored via Punt Returns, Season

4—Jack Christiansen, Detroit Lions, 1951
Rick Upchurch, Denver Broncos, 1976

Most Touchdowns Scored via Punt Returns, Game

2—Jack Christiansen, Detroit Lions vs. Los Angeles Rams, October 14, 1951; vs. Green Bay Packers, November 22, 1951
Dick Christy, New York Titans vs. Denver Broncos, September 24, 1961
Rick Upchurch, Denver Broncos vs. Cleveland Browns, September 26, 1976
LeRoy Irvin, Los Angeles Rams vs. Atlanta Falcons, October 11, 1981.

Most Punt Returns, Career

258—Emlen Tunnell, New York Giants, 1948-1958; Green Bay Packers, 1959- 1961

Most Punt Returns, Season

70—Danny Reece, Tampa Bay Buccaneers, 1979

Most Punt Returns, Game

11—Eddie Brown, Washington Redskins vs. Tampa Bay Buccaneers, October 9, 1977

Longest Punt Return (All Touchdowns)

98—Gil LeFebvre, Cincinnati Reds vs. Brooklyn Dodgers, December 3, 1933
Charlie West, Minnesota Vikings vs. Washington Redskins, November 3, 1968
Dennis Morgan, Dallas Cowboys vs. St. Louis Cardinals, October 13, 1974

KICKOFF RETURNS

Most Yardage Returning Kickoffs, Career
6,922—Ron Smith, Chicago Bears, 1965; Atlanta Falcons, 1966-67; Los Angeles Rams, 1968-1969; Chicago Bears, 1970-1972; San Diego Chargers, 1973; Oakland Raiders, 1974

Most Yardage Returning Kickoffs, Season
1,317—Bobby Jancik, Houston Oilers, 1963

Most Yardage Returning Kickoffs, Game
294—Wally Triplett, Detroit Lions vs. Los Angeles Rams, October 29, 1950 (4 returns)

Most Touchdowns Scored via Kickoff Returns, Career
6—Ollie Matson, Chicago Cardinals, 1952 (2), 1954, 1956, 1958 (2)
Gale Sayers, Chicago Bears, 1965, 1966 (2), 1967 (3)
Travis Williams, Green Bay Packers, 1967 (4), 1969; Los Angeles Rams, 1971

Most Touchdowns Scored via Kickoff Returns, Season
4—Travis Williams, Green Bay Packers, 1967
Cecil Turner, Chicago Bears, 1970

Most Touchdowns Scored via Kickoff Returns, Game
2—Tim Brown, Philadelphia Eagles vs. Dallas Cowboys, November 6, 1966
Travis Williams, Green Bay Packers vs. Cleveland Browns, November 12, 1967

Most Kickoff Returns, Career
275—Ron Smith, Chicago Bears, 1965; Atlanta Falcons, 1966-67; Los Angeles Rams, 1968-1969; Chicago Bears, 1970-1972; San Diego Chargers, 1973; Oakland Raiders, 1974

Most Kickoff Returns, Season
60—Drew Hill, Los Angeles Rams, 1981

Most Kickoff Returns, Game
9—Noland Smith, Kansas City Chiefs vs. Oakland Raiders, November 23, 1967
Dino Hall, Cleveland Browns vs. Pittsburgh Steelers, October 7, 1979

Longest Kickoff Return
106—Al Carmichael, Green Bay Packers vs. Chicago Bears, October 7, 1956
Noland Smith, Kansas City Chiefs vs. Denver Broncos, December 17, 1967
Roy Green, St. Louis Cardinals vs. Dallas Cowboys, October 21, 1979

PUNTING

Highest Punting Average, Career (300 Punts)
45.10—Sammy Baugh, Washington Redskins, 1937-1952 (338 punts)

Highest Punting Average, Season (Qualifiers)
51.4—Sammy Baugh, Washington Redskins, 1940 (35 punts)

Highest Punting Average, Game (4 Punts)
61.8—Bob Cifers, Detroit Lions vs. Chicago Bears, November 24, 1946

Longest Punt
98—Steve O'Neal, New York Jets vs. Denver Broncos, September 21, 1969

Most Punts, Career
1,083—John James, Atlanta Falcons, 1972-1981; Detroit Lions, 1982; Houston Oilers, 1982-1984

Most Punts, Season
114—Bob Parsons, Chicago Bears, 1981

Most Punts, Game
14—Dick Nesbitt, Chicago Cardinals vs. Chicago Bears, November 30, 1933
Keith Molesworth, Chicago Bears vs. Green Bay Packers, December 10, 1933
Sammy Baugh, Washington Redskins vs. Philadelphia Eagles, November 5, 1939
Carl Kinscherf, New York Giants vs. Detroit Lions, November 7, 1943
George Taliaferro, New York Yankees vs. Los Angeles Rams, September 28, 1951

MISCELLANEOUS RECORDS

Most Fumbles, Career
105—Roman Gabriel, Los Angeles Rams, 1962-72; Philadelphia Eagles, 1973-77

Most Fumbles, Season
17—Dan Pastorini, Houston Oilers, 1973
Warren Moon, Houston Oilers, 1984

Most Fumbles, Game
7—Len Dawson, Kansas City Chiefs vs. San Diego Chargers, November 15, 1964

Longest Run With Recovered Fumble
104—Jack Tatum, Oakland Raiders vs. Green Bay Packers, September 24, 1972

George Halas (1950 photo) coached the Chicago Bears on four different occasions for a total of 40 seasons, winning more games (326) than any other coach in NFL history.

Longest Winning Streak (Includes Post-Season Play)
  18—games, Chicago Bears 1933-34 and 1941-42; Cleveland Browns, 1947-48; Miami Dolphins, 1972-73.

Longest Winning Streak (Regular Season)
  17—games, Chicago Bears, 1933-1934

Longest Undefeated Streak (Includes Tie Games)
  29—games, Cleveland Browns, 1947-1949 (Won 27, Tied 2)

Most Games Won in One Season (Regular Season)
  15—games, San Francisco 49ers, 1984

Most Games Won in One Season (Includes Post-Season Play)
  18—games, San Francisco 49ers, 1984

Most Seasons, Active Player
  26—George Blanda, Chicago Bears, 1949, 1950-1958; Baltimore Colts, 1950; Houston Oilers, 1960-1966; Oakland Raiders, 1967-1975 (340 games)

Most Seasons, Coach
  40—George Halas, Chicago Bears, 1920-1929; 1933-1942; 1946-1955; 1958-1967

TEAM YEAR-BY-YEAR STANDINGS

ATLANTA FALCONS (1966-84)

Year	W.	L.	T.	Pct.	Pts.	Opp.	Head Coach
1984	4	12	0	.250	281	382	Dan Henning
1983	7	9	0	.438	370	389	Dan Henning
1982‡	5	4	0	.556	183	199	Leeman Bennett
1981	7	9	0	.438	426	355	Leeman Bennett
1980†	12	4	0	.750	405	272	Leeman Bennett
1979	6	10	0	.375	300	388	Leeman Bennett
1978*	9	7	0	.563	240	290	Leeman Bennett
1977	7	7	0	.500	179	129	Leeman Bennett
1976	4	10	0	.286	172	312	Marion Campbell, Pat Peppler
1975	4	10	0	.286	240	289	Marion Campbell
1974	3	11	0	.214	111	271	Norm Van Brocklin, Marion Campbell
1973	9	5	0	.643	318	224	Norm Van Brocklin
1972	7	7	0	.500	269	274	Norm Van Brocklin
1971	7	6	1	.538	274	277	Norm Van Brocklin
1970	4	8	2	.333	206	261	Norm Van Brocklin
1969	6	8	0	.429	276	268	Norm Van Brocklin
1968	2	12	0	.143	170	389	Norb Hecker, Norm Van Brocklin
1967	1	12	1	.077	175	422	Norb Hecker
1966	3	11	0	.214	204	437	Norb Hecker

*NFC wild-card team.
†NFC Western Division champion.
‡NFC playoff qualifier.

BUFFALO BILLS (1960-84)

Year	W.	L.	T.	Pct.	Pts.	Opp.	Head Coach
1984	2	14	0	.125	250	454	Kay Stephenson
1983	8	8	0	.500	283	351	Kay Stephenson
1982	4	5	0	.444	150	154	Chuck Knox
1981‡	10	6	0	.625	311	276	Chuck Knox
1980§	11	5	0	.688	320	260	Chuck Knox
1979	7	9	0	.438	268	279	Chuck Knox
1978	5	11	0	.313	302	354	Chuck Knox
1977	3	11	0	.214	160	313	Jim Ringo
1976	2	12	0	.143	245	363	Lou Saban, Jim Ringo
1975	8	6	0	.571	420	355	Lou Saban
1974‡	9	5	0	.643	264	244	Lou Saban
1973	9	5	0	.643	259	230	Lou Saban
1972	4	9	1	.321	257	377	Lou Saban
1971	1	13	0	.071	184	394	Harvey Johnson
1970	3	10	1	.231	204	337	John Rauch
1969	4	10	0	.286	230	359	John Rauch
1968	1	12	1	.077	199	367	Joel Collier, Harvey Johnson
1967	4	10	0	.286	237	285	Joel Collier
1966†	9	4	1	.692	358	255	Joel Collier
1965*	10	3	1	.769	313	226	Lou Saban
1964*	12	2	0	.857	400	242	Lou Saban
1963	7	6	1	.538	304	291	Lou Saban
1962	7	6	1	.538	309	272	Lou Saban
1961	6	8	0	.429	294	342	Garrard Ramsey
1960	5	8	1	.385	296	303	Garrard Ramsey

*AFL champion.
†AFL Eastern Division champion.
‡AFC wild-card team.
§AFC Eastern Division champion.

CHICAGO BEARS (1920-84)

Year	W.	L.	T.	Pct.	Pts.	Opp.	Head Coach
1984x	10	6	0	.625	325	248	Mike Ditka
1983	8	8	0	.500	311	301	Mike Ditka
1982	3	6	0	.333	141	174	Mike Ditka
1981	6	10	0	.375	253	324	Neill Armstrong
1980	7	9	0	.438	304	264	Neill Armstrong
1979§	10	6	0	.625	306	249	Neill Armstrong
1978	7	9	0	.438	253	274	Neill Armstrong
1977§	9	5	0	.643	255	253	Jack Pardee
1976	7	7	0	.500	253	216	Jack Pardee
1975	4	10	0	.286	191	379	Jack Pardee
1974	4	10	0	.286	152	279	Abe Gibron

Year	W.	L.	T.	Pct.	Pts.	Opp.	Head Coach
1973	3	11	0	.214	195	334	Abe Gibron
1972	4	9	1	.321	225	275	Abe Gibron
1971	6	8	0	.429	185	276	Jim Dooley
1970	6	8	0	.429	256	261	Jim Dooley
1969	1	13	0	.071	210	339	Jim Dooley
1968	7	7	0	.500	250	333	Jim Dooley
1967	7	6	1	.538	239	218	George Halas
1966	5	7	2	.417	234	272	George Halas
1965	9	5	0	.643	409	275	George Halas
1964	5	9	0	.357	260	379	George Halas
1963*	11	1	2	.917	301	144	George Halas
1962	9	5	0	.643	321	287	George Halas
1961	8	6	0	.571	326	302	George Halas
1960	5	6	1	.455	194	299	George Halas
1959	8	4	0	.667	252	196	George Halas
1958	8	4	0	.667	298	230	George Halas
1957	5	7	0	.417	203	211	John (Paddy) Driscoll
1956‡	9	2	1	.818	363	246	John (Paddy) Driscoll
1955	8	4	0	.667	294	251	George Halas
1954	8	4	0	.667	301	279	George Halas
1953	3	8	1	.273	218	262	George Halas
1952	5	7	0	.417	245	326	George Halas
1951	7	5	0	.583	286	282	George Halas
1950	9	3	0	.750	279	207	George Halas
1949	9	3	0	.750	332	218	George Halas
1948	10	2	0	.833	375	151	George Halas
1947	8	4	0	.667	363	241	George Halas
1946*	8	2	1	.800	289	193	George Halas
1945	3	7	0	.300	192	235	Hunk Anderson, Luke Johnsos (co-coaches)
1944	6	3	1	.667	258	172	Hunk Anderson, Luke Johnsos (co-coaches)
1943*	8	1	1	.889	303	157	Hunk Anderson, Luke Johnsos (co-coaches)
1942†	11	0	0	1.000	376	84	George Halas, Hunk Anderson, Luke Johnsos
1941*	10	1	0	.909	396	147	George Halas
1940*	8	3	0	.727	238	152	George Halas
1939	8	3	0	.727	298	157	George Halas
1938	6	5	0	.545	194	148	George Halas
1937†	9	1	1	.900	201	100	George Halas
1936	9	3	0	.750	222	94	George Halas
1935	6	4	2	.600	192	106	George Halas
1934†	13	0	0	1.000	286	86	George Halas
1933*	10	2	1	.833	133	82	George Halas
1932*	7	1	6	.875			Ralph Jones
1931	8	4	0	.667			Ralph Jones
1930	9	4	1	.692			Ralph Jones
1929	4	8	2	.333			George Halas
1928	7	5	1	.583			George Halas
1927	9	3	2	.750			George Halas
1926	12	1	3	.923			George Halas
1925	9	5	3	.643			George Halas
1924	6	1	4	.857			George Halas
1923	9	2	1	.818			George Halas
1922	9	3	0	.750			George Halas

Chicago Staleys

Year	W.	L.	T.	Pct.	Pts.	Opp.	Head Coach
1921*	10	1	1	.909			George Halas

Decatur Staleys

Year	W.	L.	T.	Pct.	Pts.	Opp.	Head Coach
1920	10	1	1	.909			George Halas

*NFL champion.
†NFL Western Division champion.
‡NFL Western Conference champion.
§NFC wild-card team.
xNFC Central Division champion.

CINCINNATI BENGALS (1968-84)

Year	W.	L.	T.	Pct.	Pts.	Opp.	Head Coach
1984	8	8	0	.500	339	339	Sam Wyche
1983	7	9	0	.438	346	302	Forrest Gregg
1982§	7	2	0	.778	232	177	Forrest Gregg
1981‡	12	4	0	.750	421	304	Forrest Gregg

Year	W.	L.	T.	Pct.	Pts.	Opp.	Head Coach
1980	6	10	0	.375	244	312	Forrest Gregg
1979	4	12	0	.250	337	421	Homer Rice
1978	4	12	0	.250	252	284	Bill Johnson, Homer Rice
1977	8	6	0	.571	238	235	Bill Johnson
1976	10	4	0	.714	335	210	Bill Johnson
1975†	11	3	0	.786	340	246	Paul Brown
1974	7	7	0	.500	283	259	Paul Brown
1973*	10	4	0	.714	286	231	Paul Brown
1972	8	6	0	.571	299	229	Paul Brown
1971	4	10	0	.286	284	265	Paul Brown
1970*	8	6	0	.571	312	255	Paul Brown
1969	4	9	1	.308	280	367	Paul Brown
1968	3	11	0	.214	215	329	Paul Brown

*AFC Central Division champion.
†AFC wild-card team.
‡AFC champion.
§AFC playoff qualifier.

CLEVELAND BROWNS (1946-84)

Year	W.	L.	T.	Pct.	Pts.	Opp.	Head Coach
1984	5	11	0	.313	250	297	Sam Rutigliano, Marty Schottenheimer
1983	9	7	0	.562	356	342	Sam Rutigliano
1982a	4	5	0	.444	140	182	Sam Rutigliano
1981	5	11	0	.313	276	375	Sam Rutigliano
1980y	11	5	0	.688	357	310	Sam Rutigliano
1979	9	7	0	.563	359	352	Sam Rutigliano
1978	8	8	0	.500	334	356	Sam Rutigliano
1977	6	8	0	.429	269	267	Forrest Gregg, Dick Modzelewski
1976	9	5	0	.643	267	287	Forrest Gregg
1975	3	11	0	.214	218	372	Forrest Gregg
1974	4	10	0	.286	251	344	Nick Skorich
1973	7	5	2	.571	234	255	Nick Skorich
1972z	10	4	0	.714	268	249	Nick Skorich
1971y	9	5	0	.643	285	273	Nick Skorich
1970	7	7	0	.500	286	265	Blanton Collier
1969‡	10	3	1	.769	351	300	Blanton Collier
1968‡	10	4	0	.714	394	273	Blanton Collier
1967x	9	5	0	.643	334	297	Blanton Collier
1966	9	5	0	.643	403	259	Blanton Collier
1965‡	11	3	0	.786	363	325	Blanton Collier
1964†	10	3	1	.769	415	293	Blanton Collier
1963	10	4	0	.714	343	262	Blanton Collier
1962	7	6	1	.538	291	257	Paul Brown
1961	8	5	1	.615	319	270	Paul Brown
1960	8	3	1	.727	362	217	Paul Brown
1959	7	5	0	.583	270	214	Paul Brown
1958	9	3	0	.750	302	217	Paul Brown
1957‡	9	2	1	.818	269	172	Paul Brown
1956	5	7	0	.417	167	177	Paul Brown
1955†	9	2	1	.818	349	218	Paul Brown
1954†	9	3	0	.750	336	162	Paul Brown
1953‡	11	1	0	.917	348	162	Paul Brown
1952§	8	4	0	.667	310	213	Paul Brown
1951‡	11	1	0	.917	331	152	Paul Brown
1950†	10	2	0	.833	310	144	Paul Brown
1949*	9	1	2	.900	339	171	Paul Brown
1948*	14	0	0	1.000	389	190	Paul Brown
1947*	12	1	1	.923	410	185	Paul Brown
1946*	12	2	0	.857	423	137	Paul Brown

*AAFC champion.
†NFL champion.
‡NFL Eastern Conference champion.
§NFL American Conference champion.
xNFL Century Division champion.
yAFC Central Division champion.
zAFC wild-card team.
aAFC playoff qualifier.

DALLAS COWBOYS (1960-84)

Year	W.	L.	T.	Pct.	Pts.	Opp.	Head Coach
1984	9	7	0	.563	308	308	Tom Landry
1983x	12	4	0	.750	479	360	Tom Landry
1982z	6	3	0	.667	226	145	Tom Landry
1981y	12	4	0	.750	367	277	Tom Landry
1980x	12	4	0	.750	454	311	Tom Landry

Year	W.	L.	T.	Pct.	Pts.	Opp.	Head Coach
1979y	11	5	0	.688	371	313	Tom Landry
1978‡	12	4	0	.750	384	208	Tom Landry
1977§	12	2	0	.857	345	212	Tom Landry
1976y	11	3	0	.786	296	194	Tom Landry
1975‡	10	4	0	.714	350	266	Tom Landry
1974	8	6	0	.571	297	235	Tom Landry
1973*	10	4	0	.714	382	203	Tom Landry
1972x	10	4	0	.714	319	240	Tom Landry
1971§	11	3	0	.786	406	222	Tom Landry
1970‡	10	4	0	.714	299	221	Tom Landry
1969†	11	2	1	.846	369	223	Tom Landry
1968†	12	2	0	.857	431	186	Tom Landry
1967*	9	5	0	.643	342	268	Tom Landry
1966*	10	3	1	.769	445	239	Tom Landry
1965	7	7	0	.500	325	280	Tom Landry
1964	5	8	1	.385	250	289	Tom Landry
1963	4	10	0	.286	305	378	Tom Landry
1962	5	8	1	.385	398	402	Tom Landry
1961	4	9	1	.308	236	380	Tom Landry
1960	0	11	1	.000	177	369	Tom Landry

*NFL Eastern Conference champion.
†NFL Capitol Division champion.
‡NFC champion.
§Super Bowl champion.
xNFC wild-card team.
yNFC Eastern Division champion.
zNFC playoff qualifier.

DENVER BRONCOS (1960-84)

Year	W.	L.	T.	Pct.	Pts.	Opp.	Head Coach
1984†	13	3	0	.813	353	241	Dan Reeves
1983‡	9	7	0	.562	302	327	Dan Reeves
1982	2	7	0	.222	148	226	Dan Reeves
1981	10	6	0	.625	321	289	Dan Reeves
1980	8	8	0	.500	310	323	Red Miller
1979‡	10	6	0	.625	289	262	Red Miller
1978†	10	6	0	.625	282	198	Red Miller
1977*	12	2	0	.857	274	148	Red Miller
1976	9	5	0	.643	315	206	John Ralston
1975	6	8	0	.429	254	307	John Ralston
1974	7	6	1	.586	302	294	John Ralston
1973	7	5	2	.571	354	296	John Ralston
1972	5	9	0	.357	325	350	John Ralston
1971	4	9	1	.308	203	275	Lou Saban, Jerry Smith
1970	5	8	1	.385	253	264	Lou Saban
1969	5	8	1	.385	297	344	Lou Saban
1968	5	9	0	.357	255	404	Lou Saban
1967	3	11	0	.214	256	409	Lou Saban
1966	4	10	0	.286	196	381	Mac Speedie, Ray Malavasi
1965	4	10	0	.286	303	392	Mac Speedie
1964	2	11	1	.154	240	438	Jack Faulkner, Mac Speedie
1963	2	11	1	.154	301	473	Jack Faulkner
1962	7	7	0	.500	353	334	Jack Faulkner
1961	3	11	0	.214	251	432	Frank Filchock
1960	4	9	1	.308	309	393	Frank Filchock

*AFC champion.
†AFC Western Division champion.
‡AFC wild-card team.

DETROIT LIONS (1930-84)

Year	W.	L.	T.	Pct.	Pts.	Opp.	Head Coach
1984	4	11	1	.281	283	408	Monte Clark
1983x	9	7	0	.562	347	286	Monte Clark
1982§	4	5	0	.444	181	176	Monte Clark
1981	8	8	0	.500	397	322	Monte Clark
1980	9	7	0	.563	334	272	Monte Clark
1979	2	14	0	.125	219	365	Monte Clark
1978	7	9	0	.438	290	300	Monte Clark
1977	6	8	0	.429	183	252	Tommy Hudspeth
1976	6	8	0	.429	262	220	Rick Forzano, Tommy Hudspeth
1975	7	7	0	.500	245	262	Rick Forzano
1974	7	7	0	.500	256	270	Rick Forzano
1973	6	7	1	.464	271	247	Don McCafferty
1972	8	5	1	.607	339	290	Joe Schmidt
1971	7	6	1	.538	341	286	Joe Schmidt

Year	W.	L.	T.	Pct.	Pts.	Opp.	Head Coach
1970‡	10	4	0	.714	347	202	Joe Schmidt
1969	9	4	1	.692	259	188	Joe Schmidt
1968	4	8	2	.333	207	241	Joe Schmidt
1967	5	7	2	.417	260	259	Joe Schmidt
1966	4	9	1	.308	206	317	Harry Gilmer
1965	6	7	1	.462	257	295	Harry Gilmer
1964	7	5	2	.583	280	260	George Wilson
1963	5	8	1	.385	326	265	George Wilson
1962	11	3	0	.786	315	177	George Wilson
1961	8	5	1	.615	270	258	George Wilson
1960	7	5	0	.583	239	212	George Wilson
1959	3	8	1	.273	203	275	George Wilson
1958	4	7	1	.364	261	276	George Wilson
1957*	8	4	0	.667	251	231	George Wilson
1956	9	3	0	.750	300	188	Buddy Parker
1955	3	9	0	.250	230	275	Buddy Parker
1954†	9	2	1	.818	337	189	Buddy Parker
1953*	10	2	0	.833	271	205	Buddy Parker
1952*	9	3	0	.750	344	192	Buddy Parker
1951	7	4	1	.636	336	259	Buddy Parker
1950	6	6	0	.500	321	285	Alvin (Bo) McMillin
1949	4	8	0	.333	237	259	Alvin (Bo) McMillin
1948	2	10	0	.167	200	407	Alvin (Bo) McMillin
1947	3	9	0	.250	231	305	Gus Dorais
1946	1	10	0	.091	142	310	Gus Dorais
1945	7	3	0	.700	195	194	Gus Dorais
1944	6	3	1	.667	216	151	Gus Dorais
1943	3	6	1	.333	178	218	Gus Dorais
1942	0	11	0	.000	38	263	Bill Edwards, John Karcis
1941	4	6	1	.400	121	195	Bill Edwards
1940	5	5	1	.500	138	153	George (Potsy) Clark
1939	6	5	0	.545	145	150	Elmer (Gus) Henderson
1938	7	4	0	.636	119	108	Earl (Dutch) Clark
1937	7	4	0	.636	180	105	Earl (Dutch) Clark
1936	8	4	0	.667	235	102	George (Potsy) Clark
1935*	7	3	2	.700	191	111	George (Potsy) Clark
1934	10	3	0	.769	238	59	George (Potsy) Clark

Portsmouth Spartans

Year	W.	L.	T.	Pct.	Pts.	Opp.	Head Coach
1933	6	5	0	.545	128	87	George (Potsy) Clark
1932	6	2	4	.750			George (Potsy) Clark
1931	11	3	0	.786			George (Potsy) Clark
1930	5	6	3	.455			George (Potsy) Clark

*NFL champion.
†NFL Western Conference champion.
‡NFC wild-card team.
§NFC playoff qualifier.
xNFC Central Division champion.

GREEN BAY PACKERS (1921-84)

Year	W.	L.	T.	Pct.	Pts.	Opp.	Head Coach
1984	8	8	0	.500	390	309	Forrest Gregg
1983	8	8	0	.500	429	439	Bart Starr
1982x	5	3	1	.611	226	169	Bart Starr
1981	8	8	0	.500	324	361	Bart Starr
1980	5	10	1	.44	231	371	Bart Starr
1979	5	11	0	.313	246	316	Bart Starr
1978	8	7	1	.531	249	269	Bart Starr
1977	4	10	0	.286	134	219	Bart Starr
1976	5	9	0	.357	218	299	Bart Starr
1975	4	10	0	.286	226	285	Bart Starr
1974	6	8	0	.429	210	206	Dan Devine
1973	5	7	2	.429	202	259	Dan Devine
1972§	10	4	0	.714	304	226	Dan Devine
1971	4	8	2	.333	274	298	Dan Devine
1970	6	8	0	.429	196	293	Phil Bengtson
1969	8	6	0	.5710	269	221	Phil Bengtson
1968	6	7	1	.462	281	227	Phil Bengtson
1967‡	9	4	1	.692	332	209	Vince Lombardi
1966‡	12	2	0	.857	335	163	Vince Lombardi
1965*	10	3	1	.769	316	224	Vince Lombardi
1964	8	5	1	.615	342	245	Vince Lombardi
1963	11	2	1	.846	369	206	Vince Lombardi
1962*	13	1	0	.929	415	148	Vince Lombardi
1961*	11	3	0	.786	391	223	Vince Lombardi
1960†	8	4	0	.667	332	209	Vince Lombardi
1959	7	5	0	.583	248	246	Vince Lombardi
1958	1	10	1	.091	193	382	Ray (Scooter) McLean
1957	3	9	0	.250	218	311	Lisle Blackbourn
1956	4	8	0	.333	264	342	Lisle Blackbourn
1955	6	6	0	.500	258	276	Lisle Blackbourn
1954	4	8	0	.333	234	251	Lisle Blackbourn
1953	2	9	1	.182	200	338	Gene Ronzani
1952	6	6	0	.500	295	312	Gene Ronzani
1951	3	9	0	.250	254	375	Gene Ronzani
1950	3	9	0	.250	244	406	Gene Ronzani
1949	2	10	0	.167	114	329	Earl (Curly) Lambeau
1948	3	9	0	.250	154	290	Earl (Curly) Lambeau
1947	6	5	1	.545	274	210	Earl (Cruly) Lambeau
1946	6	5	0	.545	148	158	Earl (Curly) Lambeau
1945	6	4	0	.600	258	173	Earl (Curly) Lambeau
1944*	8	2	0	.800	238	141	Earl (Curly) Lambeau
1943	7	2	1	.778	264	172	Earl (Curly) Lambeau
1942	8	2	1	.800	300	215	Earl (Curly) Lambeau
1941	10	1	0	.909	258	120	Earl (Curly) Lambeau
1940	6	4	1	.600	238	155	Earl (Curly) Lambeau
1939*	9	2	0	.818	233	153	Earl (Curly) Lambeau
1938†	7	4	0	.636	220	122	Earl (Curly) Lambeau
1937	7	4	0	.636	220	122	Earl (Curly) Lambeau
1936*	10	1	1	.909	248	118	Earl (Curly) Lambeau
1935	8	4	0	.667	181	96	Earl (Curly) Lambeau
1934	7	6	0	.538	156	112	Earl (Curly) Lambeau
1933	5	7	1	.417	170	107	Earl (Curly) Lambeau
1932	10	3	1	.769			Earl (Curly) Lambeau
1931*	12	2	0	.857			Earl (Curly) Lambeau
1930*	10	3	1	.769			Earl (Curly) Lambeau
1929*	12	0	1	1.000			Earl (Curly) Lambeau
1928	6	4	3	.600			Earl (Curly) Lambeau
1927	7	2	1	.778			Earl (Curly) Lambeau
1926	7	3	3	.700			Earl (Curly) Lambeau
1925	8	5	0	.615			Earl (Curly) Lambeau
1924	8	4	0	.667			Earl (Curly) Lambeau
1923	7	2	1	.778			Earl (Curly) Lambeau
1922	4	3	3	.571			Earl (Curly) Lambeau
1921	6	2	2	.750			Earl (Curly) Lambeau

*NFL champion.
†NFL Western Conference champion.
‡Super Bowl champion.
§NFC Central Division champion.
xNFC playoff qualifier.

HOUSTON OILERS (1960-84)

Year	W.	L.	T.	Pct.	Pts.	Opp.	Head Coach
1984	3	13	0	.188	240	437	Hugh Campbell
1983	2	14	0	.125	288	460	Ed Biles, Chuck Studley
1982	1	8	0	.111	136	245	Ed Biles
1981	7	9	0	.438	281	355	Ed Biles
1980‡	11	5	0	.688	295	251	O.A. (Bum) Phillips
1979‡	11	5	0	.688	362	331	O.A. (Bum) Phillips
1978‡	10	6	0	.625	283	298	O.A. (Bum) Phillips
1977	8	6	0	.571	299	230	O.A. (Bum) Phillips
1976	5	9	0	.357	222	273	O.A. (Bum) Phillips
1975	10	4	0	.714	293	226	O.A. (Bum) Phillips
1974	7	7	0	.500	236	282	Sid Gillman
1973	1	13	0	.071	199	447	Bill Peterson, Sid Gillman
1972	1	13	0	.071	164	380	Bill Peterson
1971	4	9	1	.308	251	330	Ed Hughes
1970	3	10	1	.231	217	352	Wally Lemm
1969	6	6	2	.500	278	279	Wally Lemm
1968	7	7	0	.500	303	248	Wally Lemm
1967†	9	4	1	.692	258	199	Wally Lemm
1966	3	11	0	.214	335	396	Wally Lemm
1965	4	10	0	.286	298	429	Hugh (Bones) Taylor
1964	4	10	0	.286	310	355	Sammy Baugh
1963	6	8	0	.429	302	372	Frank (Pop) Ivy
1962†	11	3	0	.786	387	270	Frank (Pop) Ivy
1961*	10	3	1	.769	513	242	Lou Rymkus, Wally Lemm
1960*	10	4	0	.714	379	285	Lou Rymkus

*AFL champion.
†AFL Eastern Division champion.
‡AFC wild-card team.

INDIANAPOLIS COLTS (1953-84)

Year	W.	L.	T.	Pct.	Pts.	Opp.	Head Coach
1984	4	12	0	.250	239	414	Frank Kush
							Hal Hunter

Baltimore Colts

Year	W.	L.	T.	Pct.	Pts.	Opp.	Head Coach
1983	7	9	0	.438	264	354	Frank Kush
1982	0	8	1	.056	113	236	Frank Kush
1981	2	14	0	.125	259	533	Mike McCormack
1980	7	9	0	.438	355	387	Mike McCormack
1979	5	11	0	.313	271	351	Ted Marchibroda
1978	5	11	0	.313	239	421	Ted Marchibroda
1977x	10	4	0	.714	295	221	Ted Marchibroda
1976x	11	3	0	.786	417	246	Ted Marchibroda
1975x	10	4	0	.714	395	269	Ted Marchibroda
1974	2	12	0	.143	190	329	Howard Schn'lenberger, Joe Thomas
1973	4	10	0	.286	226	341	Howard Schnellenberger
1972	5	9	0	.357	235	252	Don McCafferty, John Sandusky
1971§	10	4	0	.714	313	140	Don McCafferty
1970‡	11	2	1	.846	321	234	Don McCafferty
1969	8	5	1	.615	279	268	Don Shula
1968*	13	1	0	.929	402	144	Don Shula
1967	11	1	2	.917	398	198	Don Shula
1966	9	5	0	.643	314	226	Don Shula
1965	10	3	1	.769	389	284	Don Shula
1964†	12	2	0	.857	428	225	Don Shula
1963	8	6	0	.571	316	285	Don Shula
1962	7	7	0	.500	293	288	Weeb Ewbank
1961	8	6	0	.571	302	307	Weeb Ewbank
1960	6	6	0	.500	288	234	Weeb Ewbank
1959*	9	3	0	.750	374	251	Weeb Ewbank
1958*	9	3	0	.750	381	203	Weeb Ewbank
1957	7	5	0	.583	303	235	Weeb Ewbank
1956	5	7	0	.417	270	322	Weeb Ewbank
1955	5	6	1	.455	214	239	Weeb Ewbank
1954	3	9	0	.250	131	279	Weeb Ewbank
1953	3	9	0	.250	182	350	Keith Molesworth

*NFL champion.
†Western Conference champion.
‡Super Bowl champion.
§AFC wild-card team.
xAFC Eastern Division champion.

KANSAS CITY CHIEFS (1960-84)

Year	W.	L.	T.	Pct.	Pts.	Opp.	Head Coach
1984	8	8	0	.500	314	324	John Mackovic
1983	6	10	0	.375	386	367	John Mackovic
1982	3	6	0	.333	176	184	Marv Levy
1981	9	7	0	563	343	290	Marv Levy
1980	8	8	0	.500	319	336	Marv Levy
1979	7	9	0	.438	238	262	Marv Levy
1978	4	12	0	.250	243	327	Marv Levy
1977	2	12	0	.143	225	349	Paul Wiggin, Tom Bettis
1976	5	9	0	.357	290	376	Paul Wiggin
1975	5	9	0	.357	282	341	Paul Wiggin
1974	5	9	0	.357	233	293	Hank Stram
1973	7	5	2	.583	231	192	Hank Stram
1972	8	6	0	.571	287	254	Hank Stram
1971§	10	3	1	.769	302	208	Hank Stram
1970	7	5	2	.583	272	244	Hank Stram
1969‡	11	3	0	.786	359	177	Hank Stram
1968†	12	2	0	.857	371	170	Hank Stram
1967	9	5	0	.643	408	254	Hank Stram
1966*	11	2	1	.846	448	276	Hank Stram
1965	7	5	2	.583	322	285	Hank Stram
1964	7	7	0	.500	366	306	Hank Stram
1963	5	7	2	.417	347	263	Hank Stram

Dallas Texans

Year	W.	L.	T.	Pct.	Pts.	Opp.	Head Coach
1962*	11	3	0	.786	389	233	Hank Stram
1961	6	8	0	.429	334	343	Hank Stram
1960	8	6	0	.571	362	253	Hank Stram

*AFL champion.
†AFL Western Division co-champion.
‡Super Bowl champion.
§AFC Western Division champion.

LOS ANGELES RAIDERS (1960-84)

Year	W.	L.	T.	Pct.	Pts.	Opp.	Head Coach
1984x	11	5	0	.688	368	278	Tom Flores
1983§	12	4	0	.750	442	338	Tom Flores
1982y	8	1	0	.889	260	200	Tom Flores

Oakland Raiders

Year	W.	L.	T.	Pct.	Pts.	Opp.	Head Coach
1981	7	9	0	.438	273	343	Tom Flores
1980§	11	5	0	.688	364	306	Tom Flores
1979	9	7	0	.563	365	337	Tom Flores
1978	9	7	0	.563	311	283	John Madden
1977x	11	3	0	.786	351	230	John Madden
1976§	13	1	0	.929	350	237	John Madden
1975‡	11	3	0	.786	375	255	John Madden
1974‡	12	2	0	.857	355	228	John Madden
1973‡	9	4	1	.679	292	175	John Madden
1972‡	10	3	1	.750	365	248	John Madden
1971	8	4	2	.667	344	278	John Madden
1970‡	8	4	2	.667	300	293	John Madden
1969†	12	1	1	.923	377	242	John Madden
1968†	12	2	0	.857	453	233	John Rauch
1967*	13	1	0	.929	468	233	John Rauch
1966	8	5	1	.615	315	288	John Rauch
1966	8	5	1	.615	315	288	John Rauch
1965	8	5	1	.615	298	239	Al Davis
1964	5	7	2	.417	303	350	Al Davis
1963	10	4	0	.714	363	288	Al Davis
1962	1	13	0	.071	213	370	Marty Feldman, William Conkright
1961	2	12	0	.143	237	458	Eddie Erdelatz, Marty Feldman
1960	6	8	0	.429	319	388	Eddie Erdelatz

*AFL champion.
†AFL Western Division champion.
‡AFC Western Division champion.
§Super Bowl champion.
xAFC wild-card team.
yAFC playoff qualifier.

LOS ANGELES RAMS (1937-84)

Year	W.	L.	T.	Pct.	Pts.	Opp.	Head Coach
1984y	10	6	0	.625	346	316	John Robinson
1983y	9	7	0	.562	361	344	John Robinson
1982	2	7	0	.222	200	250	Ray Malavasi
1981	6	10	0	.375	303	351	Ray Malavasi
1980y	11	5	0	.688	424	289	Ray Malavasi
1979x	9	7	0	.563	323	309	Ray Malavasi
1978§	12	4	0	.750	316	245	Ray Malavasi
1977§	10	4	0	.714	302	146	Chuck Knox
1976§	10	3	1	.750	351	190	Chuck Knox
1975§	12	2	0	.857	312	135	Chuck Knox
1974§	10	4	0	.714	263	181	Chuck Knox
1973§	12	2	0	.857	388	178	Chuck Knox
1972	6	7	1	.464	291	286	Tommy Prothro
1971	8	5	1	.615	313	260	Tommy Prothro
1970	9	4	1	.692	325	202	George Allen
1969‡	11	3	0	.786	320	243	George Allen
1968	10	3	1	.769	312	200	George Allen
1967‡	11	1	2	.917	398	196	George Allen
1966	8	6	0	.571	289	212	George Allen
1965	4	10	0	.286	269	328	Harland Svare
1964	5	7	2	.417	283	339	Harland Svare
1963	5	9	0	.357	210	350	Harland Svare
1962	1	12	1	.077	220	334	Bob Waterfield, Harland Svare
1961	4	10	0	.286	263	333	Bob Waterfield
1960	4	7	1	.364	265	297	Bob Waterfield
1959	2	10	0	.167	242	315	Sid Gillman
1958	8	4	0	.667	344	278	Sid Gillman
1957	6	6	0	.500	307	278	Sid Gillman
1956	4	8	0	.333	291	307	Sid Gillman
1955†	8	3	1	.727	260	231	Sid Gillman
1954	6	5	1	.545	314	285	Hampton Pool
1953	8	3	1	.727	366	236	Hampton Pool
1952	9	3	0	.750	349	234	Hampton Pool
1951*	8	4	0	.667	392	261	Joe Stydahar
1950†	9	3	0	.750	466	309	Joe Stydahar
1949†	8	2	2	.800	360	239	Clark Shaughnessy
1948	6	5	1	.545	327	269	Clark Shaughnessy
1947	6	6	0	.500	259	214	Bob Snyder
1946	6	4	1	.600	277	257	Adam Walsh

Cleveland Rams

Year	W.	L.	T.	Pct.	Pts.	Opp.	Head Coach
1945*	9	1	0	.900	244	136	Adam Walsh
1944	4	6	0	.400	188	224	Aldo (Buff)Donelli
1943				(Rams did not play in 1943)			

Year	W.	L.	T.	Pct.	Pts.	Opp.	Head Coach
1942	5	6	0	.455	150	207	Earl (Dutch) Clark
1941	2	9	0	.182	116	244	Earl (Dutch) Clark
1940	4	6	1	.400	171	191	Earl (Dutch) Clark
1939	5	5	1	.500	195	164	Earl (Dutch) Clark
1938	4	7	0	.363	131	215	Hugo Bezdek, Art Lewis
1937	1	10	0	.091	75	207	Hugo Bezdek

*NFL champion.
†NFL Western Conference champion.
‡NFL Coastal Division champion.
§NFC Western Division champion.
xNFC champion.
yNFC wild-card team.

MIAMI DOLPHINS (1966-84)

Year	W.	L.	T.	Pct.	Pts.	Opp.	Head Coach
1984†	14	2	0	.875	513	298	Don Shula
1983§	12	4	0	.750	389	250	Don Shula
1982†	7	2	0	.778	198	131	Don Shula
1981§	11	4	1	.719	345	275	Don Shula
1980	8	8	0	.500	266	305	Don Shula
1979§	10	6	0	.625	341	257	Don Shula
1978*	11	5	0	.688	372	254	Don Shula
1977	10	4	0	.714	313	197	Don Shula
1976	6	8	0	.429	263	264	Don Shula
1975	10	4	0	.714	357	222	Don Shula
1974§	11	3	0	.786	327	216	Don Shula
1973‡	12	2	0	.857	343	150	Don Shula
1972‡	14	0	0	1.000	385	171	Don Shula
1971†	10	3	1	.769	315	174	Don Shula
1970*	10	4	0	.714	297	228	Don Shula
1969	3	10	1	.231	233	332	George Wilson
1968	5	8	1	.385	276	355	George Wilson
1967	4	10	0	.286	219	407	George Wilson
1966	3	11	0	.214	213	362	George Wilson

*AFC wild-card team.
†AFC champion.
‡Super Bowl champion.
§AFC Eastern Division champion.

MINNESOTA VIKINGS (1961-84)

Year	W.	L.	T.	Pct.	Pts.	Opp.	Head Coach
1984	3	13	0	.188	276	484	Les Steckel
1983	8	8	0	.500	316	348	Harry (Bud) Grant
1982x	5	4	0	.556	187	198	Harry (Bud) Grant
1981	7	9	0	.438	325	369	Harry (Bud) Grant
1980‡	9	7	0	.563	317	308	Harry (Bud) Grant
1979	7	9	0	.438	259	337	Harry (Bud) Grant
1978‡	8	7	1	.531	294	306	Harry (Bud) Grant
1977‡	9	5	0	.643	231	227	Harry (Bud) Grant
1976§	11	2	1	.821	305	176	Harry (Bud) Grant
1975‡	12	2	0	.857	377	180	Harry (Bud) Grant
1974§	10	4	0	.714	310	195	Harry (Bud) Grant
1973§	12	2	0	.857	296	168	Harry (Bud) Grant
1972	7	7	0	.500	301	252	Harry (Bud) Grant
1971‡	11	3	0	.786	245	139	Harry (Bud) Grant
1970‡	12	2	0	.857	335	143	Harry (Bud) Grant
1969†	12	2	0	.857	379	133	Harry (Bud) Grant
1968*	8	6	0	.571	282	242	Harry (Bud) Grant
1967	3	8	3	.273	233	294	Harry (Bud) Grant
1966	4	9	1	.308	292	304	Norm Van Brocklin
1965	7	7	0	.500	383	403	Norm Van Brocklin
1964	8	5	1	.615	355	296	Norm Van Brocklin
1963	5	8	1	.385	309	390	Norm Van Brocklin
1962	2	11	1	.154	254	410	Norm Van Brocklin
1961	3	11	0	.214	285	407	Norm Van Brocklin

*NFL Central Division champion.
†NFL champion.
‡NFC Central Division champion.
§NFC champion.
xNFC playoff qualifier.

NEW ENGLAND PATRIOTS (1960-84)

Year	W.	L.	T.	Pct.	Pts.	Opp.	Head Coach
1984	9	7	0	.563	362	352	Ron Meyer, Raymond Berry
1983	8	8	0	.500	274	289	Ron Meyer
1982§	5	4	0	.556	143	157	Ron Meyer
1981	2	14	0	.125	322	370	Ron Erhardt
1980	10	6	0	.625	441	325	Ron Erhardt
1979	9	7	0	.563	411	326	Ron Erhardt
1978‡	11	5	0	.688	358	286	C. Fairbanks, R. Erhardt, Hank Bullough
1977	9	5	0	.643	278	217	Chuck Fairbanks
1976†	11	3	0	.786	376	236	Chuck Fairbanks
1975	3	11	0	.214	258	358	Chuck Fairbanks
1974	7	7	0	.500	348	289	Chuck Fairbanks
1973	5	9	0	.357	258	300	Chuck Fairbanks
1972	3	11	0	.214	192	446	John Mazur, Phil Bengtson
1971	6	8	0	.429	238	325	John Mazur

Boston Patriots

Year	W.	L.	T.	Pct.	Pts.	Opp.	Head Coach
1970	2	12	0	.143	149	361	Clive Rush, John Mazur
1969	4	10	0	.286	266	316	Clive Rush
1968	4	10	0	.286	229	406	Mike Holovak
1967	3	10	1	.231	280	389	Mike Holovak
1966	8	4	2	.667	315	283	Mike Holovak
1965	4	8	2	.333	244	302	Mike Holovak
1964	10	3	1	.769	365	297	Mike Holovak
1963*	8	7	1	.538	327	257	Mike Holovak
1962	9	4	1	.692	346	295	Mike Holovak
1961	9	4	1	.692	413	313	Lou Saban, Mike Holovak
1960	5	9	0	.357	286	349	Lou Saban

*AFL Eastern Division champion.
†AFC wild-card team.
‡AFC Eastern Division champion.
§AFC playoff qualifier.

NEW ORLEANS SAINTS (1967-84)

Year	W.	L.	T.	Pct.	Pts.	Opp.	Head Coach
1984	7	9	0	.438	298	361	O.A. (Bum) Phillips
1983	8	8	0	.500	319	337	O.A. (Bum) Phillips
1982	4	5	0	.444	129	160	O.A. (Bum) Phillips
1981	4	12	0	.250	207	378	O.A. (Bum) Phillips
1980	1	15	0	.063	291	487	Dick Nolan, Dick Stanfel
1979	8	8	0	.500	370	360	Dick Nolan
1978	7	9	0	.438	281	298	Dick Nolan
1977	3	11	0	.214	232	336	Hank Stram
1976	4	10	0	.286	253	346	Hank Stram
1975	2	12	0	.143	165	360	John North, Ernie Hefferle
1974	5	9	0	.357	166	263	John North
1973	5	9	0	.357	163	312	John North
1972	2	11	1	.154	215	361	J.D. Roberts
1971	4	8	2	.333	266	347	J.D. Roberts
1970	2	11	1	.154	172	347	Tom Fears, J.D. Roberts
1969	5	9	0	.357	311	393	Tom Fears
1968	4	9	1	.308	246	327	Tom Fears
1967	3	11	0	.214	233	379	Tom Fears

NEW YORK GIANTS (1925-84)

Year	W.	L.	T.	Pct.	Pts.	Opp.	Head Coach
1984§	9	7	0	.563	299	301	Bill Parcells
1983	3	12	1	.219	267	347	Bill Parcells
1982	4	5	0	.444	164	160	Ray Perkins
1981§	9	7	0	.563	295	257	Ray Perkins
1980	4	12	0	.250	249	425	Ray Perkins
1979	6	10	0	.375	237	323	Ray Perkins
1978	6	10	0	.375	264	298	John McVay
1977	5	9	0	.357	181	265	John McVay
1976	3	11	0	.214	170	250	Bill Arnsparger, John McVay
1975	5	9	0	.357	216	306	Bill Arnsparger
1974	2	12	0	.143	195	299	Bill Arnsparger
1973	2	11	1	.179	226	362	Alex Webster

Year	W.	L.	T.	Pct.	Pts.	Opp.	Head Coach
1972	8	6	0	.571	331	247	Alex Webster
1971	4	10	0	.286	228	362	Alex Webster
1970	9	5	0	.643	301	270	Alex Webster
1969	6	8	0	.429	264	298	Alex Webster
1968	7	7	0	.500	294	325	Allie Sherman
1967	7	7	0	.500	369	379	Allie Sherman
1966	1	12	1	.077	263	501	Allie Sherman
1965	7	7	0	.500	270	338	Allie Sherman
1964	2	10	2	.167	241	399	Allie Sherman
1963‡	11	3	0	.786	448	280	Allie Sherman
1962‡	12	2	0	.857	398	283	Allie Sherman
1961‡	10	3	1	.769	368	220	Allie Sherman
1960	6	4	2	.600	271	261	Jim Lee Howell
1959‡	10	2	0	.833	284	170	Jim Lee Howell
1958‡	9	3	0	.750	246	183	Jim Lee Howell
1957	7	5	0	.583	254	211	Jim Lee Howell
1956*	8	3	1	.727	264	197	Jim Lee Howell
1955	6	5	1	.545	267	223	Jim Lee Howell
1954	7	5	0	.583	293	184	Jim Lee Howell
1953	3	9	0	.250	179	277	Steve Owen
1952	7	5	0	.583	234	231	Steve Owen
1951	9	2	1	.818	254	161	Steve Owen
1950	10	2	0	.833	268	150	Steve Owen
1949	6	6	0	.500	287	298	Steve Owen
1948	4	8	0	.333	297	388	Steve Owen
1947	2	8	2	.200	190	309	Steve Owen
1946†	7	3	1	.700	236	162	Steve Owen
1945	3	6	1	.333	179	198	Steve Owen
1944†	8	1	1	.889	206	75	Steve Owen
1943	6	3	1	.667	197	170	Steve Owen
1942	5	5	1	.500	155	139	Steve Owen
1941†	8	3	0	.727	238	114	Steve Owen
1940	6	4	1	.600	131	133	Steve Owen
1939†	9	1	1	.900	168	85	Steve Owen
1938*	8	2	1	.800	194	79	Steve Owen
1937	6	3	2	.667	128	109	Steve Owen
1936	5	6	1	.455	115	163	Steve Owen
1935†	9	3	0	.750	180	96	Steve Owen
1934*	8	5	0	.615	147	107	Steve Owen
1933†	11	3	0	.786	244	101	Steve Owen
1932	4	6	2	.400	93	113	Steve Owen
1931	7	6	1	.538	154	100	Steve Owen
1930	13	4	0	.765	308	98	LeRoy Andrews
1929	13	1	1	.929	312	86	LeRoy Andrews
1928	4	7	2	.364	79	136	Earl Potteiger
1927*	11	1	1	.917	197	20	Earl Potteiger
1926	8	4	1	.667	147	51	Joe Alexander
1925	8	4	0	.667	122	67	Robert Folwell

*NFL champion.
†NFL Eastern Division champion.
‡NFL Eastern Conference champion.
§NFC wild-card team.

NEW YORK JETS (1960-84)

Year	W.	L.	T.	Pct.	Pts.	Opp.	Head Coach
1984	7	9	0	.438	332	364	Joe Walton
1983	7	9	0	.438	313	331	Joe Walton
1982§	6	3	0	.667	245	166	Walt Michaels
1981‡	10	5	1	.656	355	287	Walt Michaels
1980	4	12	0	.250	302	395	Walt Michaels
1979	8	8	0	.500	337	383	Walt Michaels
1978	8	8	0	.500	359	364	Walt Michaels
1977	3	11	0	.214	191	300	Walt Michaels
1976	3	11	0	.214	169	383	Lou Holtz, Mike Holovak
1975	3	11	0	.214	256	433	Charley Winner, Ken Shipp
1974	7	7	0	.500	279	300	Charley Winner
1973	4	10	0	.286	240	306	Weeb Ewbank
1972	7	7	0	.500	367	324	Weeb Ewbank
1971	6	8	0	.429	212	299	Weeb Ewbank
1970	4	10	0	.286	255	286	Weeb Ewbank
1969†	10	4	0	.714	353	269	Weeb Ewbank
1968*	11	3	0	.786	419	280	Weeb Ewbank
1967	8	5	1	.615	371	329	Weeb Ewbank
1966	6	6	2	.500	322	312	Weeb Ewbank
1965	5	8	1	.385	285	303	Weeb Ewbank
1964	5	8	1	.385	278	315	Weeb Ewbank
1963	5	8	1	.385	249	399	Weeb Ewbank

New York Titans

Year	W.	L.	T.	Pct.	Pts.	Opp.	Head Coach
1962	5	9	0	.357	278	423	Clyde (Bulldog) Turner
1961	7	7	0	.500	301	390	Sammy Baugh
1960	7	7	0	.500	382	399	Sammy Baugh

*Super Bowl champion.
†AFL Eastern Division champion.
‡AFC wild-card team.
§AFC playoff qualifier.

PHILADELPHIA EAGLES (1933-84)

Year	W.	L.	T.	Pct.	Pts.	Opp.	Head Coach
1984	6	9	1	.406	278	320	Marion Campbell
1983	5	11	0	.313	233	322	Marion Campbell
1982	3	6	0	.333	191	195	Dick Vermeil
1981‡	10	6	0	.625	368	221	Dick Vermeil
1980§	12	4	0	.750	384	222	Dick Vermeil
1979‡	11	5	0	.688	339	282	Dick Vermeil
1978‡	9	7	0	.563	270	250	Dick Vermeil
1977	5	9	0	.357	220	207	Dick Vermeil
1976	4	10	0	.286	165	286	Dick Vermeil
1975	4	10	0	.286	225	302	Mike McCormack
1974	7	7	0	.500	242	217	Mike McCormack
1973	5	8	1	.393	310	393	Mike McCormack
1972	2	11	1	.179	145	352	Ed Khayat
1971	6	7	1	.462	221	302	Jerry Williams, Ed Khayat
1970	3	10	1	.231	241	332	Jerry Williams
1969	4	9	1	.308	279	377	Jerry Williams
1968	2	12	0	.143	202	351	Joe Kuharich
1967	6	7	1	.462	351	409	Joe Kuharich
1966	9	5	0	.643	326	340	Joe Kuharich
1965	5	9	0	.357	363	359	Joe Kuharich
1964	6	8	0	.429	312	313	Joe Kuharich
1963	2	10	2	.167	242	381	Nick Skorich
1962	3	10	1	.231	282	356	Nick Skorich
1961	10	4	0	.714	361	297	Nick Skorich
1960†	10	2	0	.833	321	246	Lawrence (Buck) Shaw
1959	7	5	0	.583	268	278	Lawrence (Buck) Shaw
1958	2	9	1	.182	235	306	Lawrence (Buck) Shaw
1957	4	8	0	.333	173	230	Hugh Devore
1956	3	8	1	.273	143	215	Hugh Devore
1955	4	7	1	.364	248	231	Jim Trimble
1954	7	4	1	.636	284	230	Jim Trimble
1953	7	4	1	.636	352	215	Jim Trimble
1952	7	5	0	.583	252	271	Jim Trimble
1951	4	8	0	.333	234	264	Alvin (Bo) McMillin, Wayne Millner
1950	6	6	0	.500	254	141	Earle (Greasy) Neale
1949†	11	1	0	.917	364	134	Earle (Greasy) Neale
1948†	9	2	1	.818	376	156	Earle (Greasy) Neale
1947*	8	4	0	.667	308	242	Earle (Greasy) Neale
1946	6	5	0	.545	231	220	Earle (Greasy) Neale
1945	7	3	0	.700	272	133	Earle (Greasy) Neale
1944	7	1	2	.875	267	131	Earle (Greasy) Neale

Phil-Pitt Steagles
(Combined Philadelphia and Pittsburgh squads.)

Year	W.	L.	T.	Pct.	Pts.	Opp.	Head Coach
1943	5	4	1	.556	225	230	Greasy Neale, Walt Kiesling (co-coaches)

Philadelphia Eagles

Year	W.	L.	T.	Pct.	Pts.	Opp.	Head Coach
1942	2	9	0	.182	134	239	Earle (Greasy) Neale
1941	2	8	1	.200	119	218	Earle (Greasy) Neale
1940	1	10	0	.091	111	211	Bert Bell
1939	1	9	1	.100	105	200	Bert Bell
1938	5	6	0	.455	154	164	Bert Bell
1937	2	8	1	.200	86	177	Bert Bell
1936	1	11	0	.083	51	206	Bert Bell
1935	2	9	0	.182	60	179	Lud Wray
1934	4	7	0	.364	127	85	Lud Wray
1933	3	5	1	.375	77	158	Lud Wray

*NFL Eastern Division champion.
†NFL champion.
‡NFC wild-card team.
§NFC champion.

PITTSBURGH STEELERS (1933-84)

Year	W.	L.	T.	Pct.	Pts.	Opp.	Head Coach
1984*	9	7	0	.563	387	310	Chuck Noll
1983*	10	6	0	.625	355	303	Chuck Noll
1982§	6	3	0	.667	204	146	Chuck Noll
1981	8	8	0	.500	356	297	Chuck Noll
1980	9	7	0	.563	352	313	Chuck Noll
1979‡	12	4	0	.750	416	262	Chuck Noll
1978‡	14	2	0	.875	356	195	Chuck Noll
1977*	9	5	0	.643	283	243	Chuck Noll
1976*	10	4	0	.714	342	138	Chuck Noll
1975‡	12	2	0	.857	373	162	Chuck Noll
1974‡	10	3	1	.750	305	189	Chuck Noll
1973†	10	4	0	.714	347	210	Chuck Noll
1972*	11	3	0	.786	343	175	Chuck Noll
1971	6	8	0	.429	246	292	Chuck Noll
1970	5	9	0	.357	210	272	Chuck Noll
1969	1	13	0	.071	218	404	Chuck Noll
1968	2	11	1	.154	244	397	Bill Austin
1967	4	9	1	.308	281	320	Bill Austin
1966	5	8	1	.385	316	347	Bill Austin
1965	2	12	0	.143	202	397	Mike Nixon
1964	5	9	0	.357	253	315	Buddy Parker
1963	7	4	3	.636	321	295	Buddy Parker
1962	9	5	0	.643	312	363	Buddy Parker
1961	6	8	0	.429	295	287	Buddy Parker
1960	5	6	1	.455	240	275	Buddy Parker
1959	6	5	1	.545	257	216	Buddy Parker
1958	7	4	1	.636	261	230	Buddy Parker
1957	6	6	0	.500	161	178	Buddy Parker
1956	5	7	0	.417	217	250	Walt Kiesling
1955	4	8	0	.333	195	285	Walt Kiesling
1954	5	7	0	.417	219	263	Walt Kiesling
1953	6	6	0	.500	211	263	Joe Bach
1952	5	7	0	.417	300	273	Joe Bach
1951	4	7	1	.364	183	235	John Michelosen
1950	6	6	0	.500	180	195	John Michelosen
1949	6	5	1	.545	224	214	John Michelosen
1948	4	8	0	.333	200	243	John Michelosen
1947	8	4	0	.667	240	259	Jock Sutherland
1946	5	5	1	.500	136	117	Jock Sutherland
1945	2	8	0	.200	79	220	Jim Leonard

Card-Pitt
(Combined Pittsburgh and Chicago Cardinals squads.)

Year	W.	L.	T.	Pct.	Pts.	Opp.	Head Coach
1944	0	10	0	.000	108	328	Walt Kiesling, Phil Handler (co-coaches)

Phil-Pitt Steagles
(Combined Pittsburgh and Philadelphia squads.)

Year	W.	L.	T.	Pct.	Pts.	Opp.	Head Coach
1943	5	4	1	.556	225	230	Walt Kiesling, Greasy Neale (co-coaches)

Pittsburgh Steelers

Year	W.	L.	T.	Pct.	Pts.	Opp.	Head Coach
1942	7	4	0	.636	167	119	Walt Kiesling
1941	1	9	1	.100	103	276	Bert Bell, Aldo (Buff) Donelli, Walt Kiesling

Pittsburgh Pirates

Year	W.	L.	T.	Pct.	Pts.	Opp.	Head Coach
1940	2	7	2	.222	60	178	Walt Kiesling
1939	1	9	1	.100	114	216	Johnny Blood (McNally), Walt Kiesling
1938	2	9	0	.182	79	169	Johnny Blood (McNally)
1937	4	7	0	.364	122	145	Johnny Blood (McNally)
1936	6	6	0	.500	98	187	Joe Bach
1935	4	8	0	.333	100	209	Joe Bach
1934	2	10	0	.167	51	206	Luby DiMelio
1933	3	6	2	.333	67	208	Forrest Douds

*AFC Central Division champion.
†AFC wild-card team.
‡Super Bowl champion.
§AFC playoff qualifier.

ST. LOUIS CARDINALS (1920-84)

Year	W.	L.	T.	Pct.	Pts.	Opp.	Head Coach
1984	9	7	0	.563	423	345	Jim Hanifan
1983	8	7	1	.531	374	428	Jim Hanifan
1982§	5	4	0	.556	135	170	Jim Hanifan
1981	7	9	0	.438	315	408	Jim Hanifan
1980	5	11	0	.313	299	350	Jim Hanifan
1979	5	11	0	.313	307	358	Bud Wilkinson, Larry Wilson
1978	6	10	0	.375	248	296	Bud Wilkinson
1977	7	7	0	.500	272	287	Don Coryell
1976	10	4	0	.714	309	267	Don Coryell
1975‡	11	3	0	.786	356	276	Don Coryell
1974‡	10	4	0	.714	285	218	Don Coryell
1973	4	9	1	.308	286	365	Don Coryell
1972	4	9	1	.308	193	303	Bob Hollway
1971	4	9	1	.308	231	279	Bob Hollway
1970	8	5	1	.615	325	228	Charley Winner
1969	4	9	1	.308	389	394	Charley Winner
1968	9	4	1	.692	325	289	Charley Winner
1967	6	7	1	.462	333	356	Charley Winner
1966	8	5	1	.615	264	265	Charley Winner
1965	5	9	0	.357	296	309	Wally Lemm
1964	9	3	2	.750	357	331	Wally Lemm
1963	9	5	0	.643	341	283	Wally Lemm
1962	4	9	1	.308	287	361	Wally Lemm
1961	7	7	0	.500	279	267	Frank (Pop) Ivy
1960	6	5	1	.545	288	230	Frank (Pop) Ivy

Chicago Cardinals

Year	W.	L.	T.	Pct.	Pts.	Opp.	Head Coach
1959	2	10	0	.167	234	324	Frank (Pop) Ivy
1958	2	9	1	.182	261	356	Frank (Pop) Ivy
1957	3	9	0	.250	200	299	Ray Richards
1956	7	5	0	.583	240	182	Ray Richards
1955	4	7	1	.364	224	252	Ray Richards
1954	2	10	0	.167	183	347	Joe Stydahar
1953	1	10	1	.091	190	337	Joe Stydahar
1952	4	8	0	.333	172	221	Joe Kuharich
1951	3	9	0	.250	210	287	Earl (Curly) Lambeau
1950	5	7	0	.417	233	287	Earl (Curly) Lambeau
1949	6	5	1	.545	360	301	Phil Handler, Buddy Parker (co-coaches)
1948†	11	1	0	.917	395	226	Jimmy Conzelman
1947*	9	3	0	.750	306	231	Jimmy Conzelman
1946	6	5	0	.545	260	198	Jimmy Conzelman
1945	1	9	0	.100	98	228	Phil Handler

Card-Pitt
(Combined Chicago Cardinals and Pittsburgh squads.)

Year	W.	L.	T.	Pct.	Pts.	Opp.	Head Coach
1944	0	10	0	.000	108	328	Phil Handler, Walt Kiesling (co-coaches)

Chicago Cardinals

Year	W.	L.	T.	Pct.	Pts.	Opp.	Head Coach
1943	0	10	0	.000	95	238	Phil Handler
1942	3	8	0	.273	98	209	Jimmy Conzelman
1941	3	7	1	.300	127	197	Jimmy Conzelman
1940	2	7	2	.222	139	222	Jimmy Conzelman
1939	1	10	0	.091	84	254	Ernie Nevers
1938	2	9	0	.182	111	168	Milan Creighton
1937	5	5	1	.500	135	165	Milan Creighton
1936	3	8	1	.273	74	143	Milan Creighton
1935	6	4	2	.600	99	97	Milan Creighton
1934	5	6	0	.455	80	84	Paul Schissler
1933	1	9	1	.100	52	101	Paul Schissler
1932	2	6	2	.250			Jack Chevigny
1931	5	4	0	.556			LeRoy Andrews, Ernie Nevers
1930	5	6	2	.455			Ernie Nevers
1929	6	6	1	.500			Ernie Nevers
1928	1	5	0	.167			Guy Chamberlin
1927	3	7	1	.300			Fred Gillies
1926	5	6	1	.455			Norman Barry
1925*	11	2	1	.846			Norman Barry
1924	5	4	1	.556			Arnold Horween
1923	8	4	0	.667			Arnold Horween
1922	8	3	0	.727			John (Paddy) Driscoll
1921	2	3	2	.400			John (Paddy) Driscoll
1920	5	2	1	.714			Marshall Smith

*NFL champion.
†NFL Western Division champion.
‡NFC Eastern Division champion.
§NFC playoff qualifier.

SAN DIEGO CHARGERS (1960-84)

Year	W.	L.	T.	Pct.	Pts.	Opp.	Head Coach
1984	7	9	0	.438	394	413	Don Coryell
1983	6	10	0	.375	358	462	Don Coryell
1982§	6	3	0	.667	288	221	Don Coryell
1981‡	10	6	0	.625	478	390	Don Coryell
1980‡	11	5	0	.688	418	327	Don Coryell
1979‡	12	4	0	.750	411	246	Don Coryell
1978	9	7	0	.563	355	309	Tommy Prothro, Don Coryell
1977	7	7	0	.500	222	205	Tommy Prothro
1976	6	8	0	.429	248	285	Tommy Prothro
1975	2	12	0	.143	189	345	Tommy Prothro
1974	5	9	0	.357	212	285	Tommy Prothro
1973	2	11	1	.179	188	386	Harland Svare, Ron Waller
1972	4	9	1	.308	264	344	Harland Svare
1971	6	8	0	.429	311	341	Sid Gillman, Harland Svare
1970	5	6	3	.455	282	278	Charlie Waller
1969	8	6	0	.571	288	276	Sid Gillman, Charlie Waller
1968	9	5	0	.643	382	310	Sid Gillman
1967	8	5	1	.615	360	352	Sid Gillman
1966	7	6	1	.538	335	284	Sid Gillman
1965*	9	2	3	.818	340	227	Sid Gillman
1964*	8	5	1	.615	341	300	Sid Gillman
1963†	11	3	0	.786	399	256	Sid Gillman
1962	4	10	0	.286	314	392	Sid Gillman
1961*	12	2	0	.857	396	219	Sid Gillman

Los Angeles Chargers

Year	W.	L.	T.	Pct.	Pts.	Opp.	Head Coach
1960*	10	4	0	.714	373	336	Sid Gillman

*AFL Western Division champion.
†AFL champion.
‡AFC Western Division champion.
§AFC playoff qualifier.

SAN FRANCISCO 49ers (1946-84)

Year	W.	L.	T.	Pct.	Pts.	Opp.	Head Coach
1984†	15	1	0	.938	475	227	Bill Walsh
1983*	10	6	0	.625	432	293	Bill Walsh
1982	3	6	0	.333	209	206	Bill Walsh
1981†	13	3	0	.813	357	250	Bill Walsh
1980	6	10	0	.375	320	415	Bill Walsh
1979	2	14	0	.125	308	416	Bill Walsh
1978	2	14	0	.125	219	350	Pete McCulley, Fred O'Connor
1977	5	9	0	.357	220	260	Ken Meyer
1976	8	6	0	.571	270	190	Monte Clark
1975	5	9	0	.357	255	286	Dick Nolan
1974	6	8	0	.429	226	236	Dick Nolan
1973	5	9	0	.357	262	319	Dick Nolan
1972*	8	5	1	.607	353	249	Dick Nolan
1971*	9	5	0	.643	300	216	Dick Nolan
1970*	10	3	1	.769	352	267	Dick Nolan
1969	4	8	2	.333	277	319	Dick Nolan
1968	7	6	1	.538	303	310	Dick Nolan
1967	7	7	0	.500	273	337	Jack Christiansen
1966	6	6	2	.500	320	325	Jack Christiansen
1965	7	6	1	.538	421	402	Jack Christiansen
1964	4	10	0	.286	236	330	Jack Christiansen
1963	2	12	0	.143	198	391	Howard (Red) Hickey, Jack Christiansen
1962	6	8	0	.429	282	331	Howard (Red) Hickey
1961	7	6	1	.538	346	272	Howard (Red) Hickey
1960	7	5	0	.583	208	205	Howard (Red) Hickey
1959	7	5	0	.583	255	237	Howard (Red) Hickey
1958	6	6	0	.500	257	324	Frankie Albert
1957	8	4	0	.667	260	264	Frankie Albert
1956	5	6	1	.455	233	284	Frankie Albert
1955	4	8	0	.333	216	298	Norman (Red) Strader
1954	7	4	1	.636	313	251	Lawrence (Buck) Shaw
1953	9	3	0	.750	372	237	Lawrence (Buck) Shaw
1952	7	5	0	.583	285	221	Lawrence (Buck) Shaw
1951	7	4	1	.636	255	205	Lawrence (Buck) Shaw
1950	3	9	0	.250	213	300	Lawrence (Buck) Shaw
1949	9	3	0	.750	416	227	Lawrence (Buck) Shaw
1948	12	2	0	.857	495	248	Lawrence (Buck) Shaw
1947	8	4	2	.667	327	264	Lawrence (Buck) Shaw
1946	9	5	0	.643	307	189	Lawrence (Buck) Shaw

*NFC Western Division champion.
†Super Bowl champion.

SEATTLE SEAHAWKS (1976-84)

Year	W.	L.	T.	Pct.	Pts.	Opp.	Head Coach
1984*	12	4	0	.750	418	282	Chuck Knox
1983*	9	7	0	.562	403	397	Chuck Knox
1982	4	5	0	.444	127	147	Jack Patera, Mike McCormack
1981	6	10	0	.375	322	388	Jack Patera
1980	4	12	0	.250	291	408	Jack Patera
1979	9	7	0	.563	378	372	Jack Patera
1978	9	7	0	.563	345	358	Jack Patera
1977	5	9	0	.357	282	373	Jack Patera
1976	2	12	0	.143	229	429	Jack Patera

*AFC wild-card team.

TAMPA BAY BUCCANEERS (1976-84)

Year	W.	L.	T.	Pct.	Pts.	Opp.	Head Coach
1984	6	10	0	.375	335	380	John McKay
1983	2	14	0	.125	241	380	John McKay
1982†	5	4	0	.556	158	178	John McKay
1981*	9	7	0	.563	315	268	John McKay
1980	5	10	1	.344	271	341	John McKay
1979*	10	6	0	.625	273	237	John McKay
1978	5	11	0	.313	241	259	John McKay
1977	2	12	0	.143	103	223	John McKay
1976	0	14	0	.000	125	412	John McKay

*NFC Central Division champion.
†NFC playoff qualifier.

WASHINGTON REDSKINS (1932-84)

Year	W.	L.	T.	Pct.	Pts.	Opp.	Head Coach
1984y	11	5	0	.688	426	310	Joe Gibbs
1983§	14	2	0	.875	541	332	Joe Gibbs
1982x	8	1	0	.889	190	128	Joe Gibbs
1981	8	8	0	.500	347	349	Joe Gibbs
1980	6	10	0	.375	261	293	Jack Pardee
1979	10	6	0	.625	348	295	Jack Pardee
1978	8	8	0	.500	273	283	Jack Pardee
1977	9	5	0	.643	196	189	George Allen
1976‡	10	4	0	.714	291	217	George Allen
1975	8	6	0	.571	325	276	George Allen
1974‡	10	4	0	.714	320	196	George Allen
1973‡	10	4	0	.714	325	198	George Allen
1972§	11	3	0	.786	336	218	George Allen
1971‡	9	4	1	.692	276	190	George Allen
1970	6	8	0	.429	297	314	Bill Austin
1969	7	5	2	.583	307	319	Vince Lombardi
1968	5	9	0	.357	249	358	Otto Graham
1967	5	6	3	.455	347	353	Otto Graham
1966	7	7	0	.500	351	355	Otto Graham
1965	6	8	0	.429	257	301	Bill McPeak
1964	6	8	0	.429	307	305	Bill McPeak
1963	3	11	0	.214	279	398	Bill McPeak
1962	5	7	2	.417	305	376	Bill McPeak
1961	1	12	1	.077	174	392	Bill McPeak
1960	1	9	2	.100	178	309	Mike Nixon
1959	3	9	0	.250	185	350	Mike Nixon
1958	4	7	1	.364	214	268	Joe Kuharich
1957	5	6	1	.455	251	230	Joe Kuharich
1956	6	6	0	.500	183	225	Joe Kuharich
1955	8	4	0	.667	246	222	Joe Kuharich
1954	3	9	0	.250	207	432	Joe Kuharich
1953	6	5	1	.545	208	215	Earl (Curly) Lambeau
1952	4	8	0	.333	240	287	Earl (Curly) Lambeau
1951	5	7	0	.417	183	296	Herman Ball, Dick Todd
1950	3	9	0	.250	232	326	Herman Ball
1949	4	7	1	.364	268	339	John Whelchel, Herman Ball
1948	7	5	0	.583	291	287	Glen (Turk) Edwards
1947	4	8	0	.333	295	367	Glen (Turk) Edwards

Coach Tom Landry's Dallas Cowboys, who reached their peak with Super Bowl championships following the 1971 and 1977 seasons, finished 9-7 and out of the playoffs for the first time in 10 years in 1984.

Year	W.	L.	T.	Pct.	Pts.	Opp.	Head Coach
1946	5	5	1	.500	171	191	Glen (Turk) Edwards
1945*	8	2	0	.800	209	121	Dudley DeGroot
1944	6	3	1	.667	169	180	Dudley DeGroot
1943*	6	3	1	.667	229	137	Arthur Bergman
1942†	10	1	0	.909	227	102	Ray Flaherty
1941	6	5	0	.545	176	174	Ray Flaherty
1940*	9	2	0	.818	245	142	Ray Flaherty
1939	8	2	1	.800	242	94	Ray Flaherty
1938	6	3	2	.667	148	154	Ray Flaherty
1937†	8	3	0	.727	195	120	Ray Flaherty

*NFL Eastern Division champion.
†NFL champion.
‡NFC wild-card team.

Boston Redskins

Year	W.	L.	T.	Pct.	Pts.	Opp.	Head Coach
1936*	7	5	0	.583	149	110	Ray Flaherty
1935	2	8	1	.200	65	123	Eddie Casey
1934	6	6	0	.500	107	94	William Dietz
1933	5	5	2	.500	103	97	William Dietz

Boston Braves

Year	W.	L.	T.	Pct.	Pts.	Opp.	Head Coach
1932	4	4	2	.500	55	79	Lud Wray

§NFC champion.
xSuper Bowl champion.
yNFC Eastern Division champion.

ALL-TIME SERIES RECORDS

Listed below are the all-time regular-season series records for all 28 NFL teams. The date to the right indicates the last time the two teams met in regular-season play. Although many current teams have played in different cities (in parentheses) and with different nicknames, for the purpose of this section franchises are recognized to have started in the following years: Atlanta, 1966; Buffalo, 1960; Chicago, 1920 (Decatur); Cincinnati, 1968; Cleveland, 1950; Dallas, 1960; Denver, 1960; Detroit, 1934; Green Bay, 1921; Houston, 1960; Indianapolis, 1953 (Baltimore); Kansas City, 1960 (Dallas); Los Angeles Raiders, 1960 (Oakland); Los Angeles Rams, 1946; Miami, 1966; Minnesota, 1961; New England, 1960 (Boston); New Orleans, 1967; New York Giants, 1925; New York Jets, 1960; Philadelphia, 1933; Pittsburgh, 1933; St. Louis, 1920 (Chicago); San Diego, 1960 (Los Angeles); San Francisco, 1950; Seattle, 1976; Tampa Bay, 1976; Washington, 1937. American Football League results (1960-69) are recognized; All-America Football Conference results (1946-49) are not.

Atlanta vs. Buffalo (1983)
(Series tied, 2-2)

Atlanta vs. Chicago (1983)
(Atlanta leads series, 9-4)

Atlanta vs. Cincinnati (1984)
(Cincinnati leads series, 4-1)

Atlanta vs. Cleveland (1984)
(Cleveland leads series, 6-1)

Atlanta vs. Dallas (1976)
(Dallas leads series, 5-1)

Atlanta vs. Denver (1982)
(Atlanta leads series, 3-2)

Atlanta vs. Detroit (1984)
(Detroit leads series, 11-4)

Atlanta vs. Green Bay (1983)
(Green Bay leads series, 8-6)

Atlanta vs. Houston (1984)
(Atlanta leads series, 4-1)

Atlanta vs. Indianapolis (1974)
(Indianapolis leads series, 8-0)

Atlanta vs. Kansas City (1972)
(Kansas City leads series, 1-0)

Atlanta vs. Los Angeles Raiders (1982)
(Raiders leads series, 3-1)

Atlanta vs. Los Angeles Rams (1984)
(Rams lead series, 27-7-2)

Atlanta vs. Miami (1983)
(Miami leads series, 4-0)

Atlanta vs. Minnesota (1984)
(Minnesota leads series, 8-5)

Atlanta vs. New England (1983)
(Series tied, 2-2)

Atlanta vs. New Orleans (1984)
(Atlanta leads series, 21-11)

Atlanta vs. New York Giants (1984)
(Atlanta leads series, 6-5)

Atlanta vs. New York Jets (1983)
(Atlanta leads series, 2-1)

Atlanta vs. Philadelphia (1984)
(Series tied, 5-5-1)

Atlanta vs. Pittsburgh (1984)
(Pittsburgh leads series, 6-1)

Atlanta vs. St. Louis (1982)
(St. Louis leads series, 6-3)

Atlanta vs. San Diego (1979)
(Atlanta leads series, 2-0)

Atlanta vs. San Francisco (1984)
(San Francisco leads series, 19-17)

Atlanta vs. Seattle (1979)
(Seattle leads series, 2-0)

Atlanta vs. Tampa Bay (1984)
(Tampa Bay leads series, 3-2)

Atlanta vs. Washington (1984)
(Washington leads series, 8-2-1)

Buffalo vs. Chicago (1979)
(Chicago leads series, 2-1)

Buffalo vs. Cincinnati (1984)
(Cincinnati leads series, 7-5)

Buffalo vs. Cleveland (1984)
(Cleveland leads series, 4-2)

Buffalo vs. Dallas (1984)
(Dallas leads series, 3-1)

Buffalo vs. Denver (1984)
(Buffalo leads series, 13-9-1)

Buffalo vs. Detroit (1979)
(Series tied, 1-1-1)

Buffalo vs. Green Bay (1982)
(Buffalo leads series, 2-1)

Buffalo vs. Houston (1983)
(Houston leads series, 17-8)

Buffalo vs. Indianapolis (1984)
(Series tied, 14-14-1)

Buffalo vs. Kansas City (1983)
(Buffalo leads series, 14-10-1)

Buffalo vs. Los Angeles Raiders (1983)
(Raiders lead series, 12-11)

Buffalo vs. Los Angeles Rams (1983)
(Rams lead series, 3-1)

Buffalo vs. Miami (1984)
(Miami leads series, 30-7-1)

Buffalo vs. Minnesota (1982)
(Minnesota leads series, 3-1)

Buffalo vs. New England (1984)
(New England leads series, 25-23-1)

Buffalo vs. New Orleans (1983)
(Buffalo leads series, 2-1)

Buffalo vs. New York Giants (1978)
(Giants lead series, 2-1)

Buffalo vs. New York Jets (1984)
(Buffalo leads series, 25-23)

Buffalo vs. Philadelphia (1984)
(Philadelphia leads series, 2-1)

Buffalo vs. Pittsburgh (1982)
(Pittsburgh leads series, 4-3)

Buffalo vs. St. Louis (1984)
(St. Louis leads series, 3-1)

Buffalo vs. San Diego (1981)
(San Diego leads series, 14-7-2)

Buffalo vs. San Francisco (1983)
(Buffalo leads series, 2-1)

Buffalo vs. Seattle (1984)
(Seattle leads series, 2-0)

Buffalo vs. Tampa Bay (1982)
(Tampa Bay leads series, 2-1)

Buffalo vs. Washington (1984)
(Series tied, 2-2)

Chicago vs. Cincinnati (1980)
(Cincinnati leads series, 2-0)

Chicago vs. Cleveland (1980)
(Cleveland leads series, 6-2)

Chicago vs. Dallas (1984)
(Dallas leads series, 7-3)

Chicago vs. Denver (1984)
(Chicago leads series, 4-3)

Chicago vs. Detroit (1984)
(Chicago leads series, 57-42-3)

Chicago vs. Green Bay (1984)
(Chicago leads series, 68-55-6)

Chicago vs. Houston (1980)
(Houston leads series, 2-1)

Chicago vs. Indianapolis (1983)
(Indianapolis leads series, 21-13)

Chicago vs. Kansas City (1981)
(Chicago leads series, 2-1)

Chicago vs. Los Angeles Raiders (1984)
(Raiders lead series, 3-2)

Chicago vs. Los Angeles Rams (1984)
(Chicago leads series, 31-21-3)

Chicago vs. Miami (1979)
(Miami leads series, 3-0)

Chicago vs. Minnesota (1984)
(Minnesota leads series, 25-20-2)

Chicago vs. New England (1982)
(New England leads series, 2-1)

Chicago vs. New Orleans (1984)
(Chicago leads series, 7-4)

Chicago vs. New York Giants (1977)
(Chicago leads series, 22-14-2)

Chicago vs. New York Jets (1979)
(Series tied, 1-1)

Chicago vs. Philadelphia (1983)
(Chicago leads series, 20-3-1)

Chicago vs. Pittsburgh (1980)
(Chicago leads series, 16-4-1)

Chicago vs. St. Louis (1984)
(Chicago leads series, 52-25-6)

Chicago vs. San Diego (1984)
(San Diego leads series, 4-1)

Chicago vs. San Francisco (1983)
(Chicago leads series, 23-22-1)

Chicago vs. Seattle (1984)
(Seattle leads series, 3-1)

Chicago vs. Tampa Bay (1984)
(Chicago leads series, 10-4)

Chicago vs. Washington (1981)
(Chicago leads series, 12-8)

Cincinnati vs. Cleveland (1984)
(Cincinnati leads series, 15-14)

Cincinnati vs. Dallas (1979)
(Dallas leads series, 2-0)

Cincinnati vs. Denver (1984)
(Denver leads series, 8-6)

Cincinnati vs. Detroit (1983)
(Detroit leads series, 2-1)

Cincinnati vs. Green Bay (1983)
(Cincinnati leads series, 3-2)

Cincinnati vs. Houston (1984)
(Cincinnati leads series, 19-12-1)

Cincinnati vs. Indianapolis (1983)
(Indianapolis leads series, 5-4)

Cincinnati vs. Kansas City (1984)
(Kansas City leads series, 8-7)

Cincinnati vs. Los Angeles Raiders (1983)
(Raiders lead series, 10-4)

Cincinnati vs. Los Angeles Rams (1984)
(Cincinnati leads series, 3-2)

Cincinnati vs. Miami (1983)
(Miami leads series, 7-3)

Cincinnati vs. Minnesota (1983)
(Series tied, 2-2)

Cincinnati vs. New England (1984)
(New England leads series, 5-3)

Cincinnati vs. New Orleans (1984)
(Cincinnati leads series, 3-2)

Cincinnati vs. New York Giants (1977)
(Cincinnati leads series, 2-0)

Cincinnati vs. New York Jets (1984)
(Jets lead series, 5-3)

Cincinnati vs. Philadelphia (1982)
(Cincinnati leads series, 4-0)

Cincinnati vs. Pittsburgh (1984)
(Pittsburgh leads series, 17-12)

Cincinnati vs. St. Louis (1979)
(Cincinnati leads series, 2-0)

Cincinnati vs. San Diego (1982)
(San Diego leads series, 9-6)

Cincinnati vs. San Francisco (1984)
(San Francisco leads series, 3-1)

Cincinnati vs. Seattle (1984)
(Cincinnati leads series, 3-1)

Cincinnati vs. Tampa Bay (1983)
(Cincinnati leads series, 2-1)

Cincinnati vs. Washington (1979)
(Washington leads series, 2-1)

Cleveland vs. Dallas (1982)
(Cleveland leads series, 13-7)

Cleveland vs. Denver (1984)
(Denver leads series, 8-3)

Cleveland vs. Detroit (1983)
(Detroit leads series, 9-2)

Cleveland vs. Green Bay (1983)
(Green Bay leads series, 6-5)

Cleveland vs. Houston (1984)
(Cleveland leads series, 18-11)

Cleveland vs. Indianapolis (1983)
(Cleveland leads series, 9-3)

Cleveland vs. Kansas City (1984)
(Kansas City leads series, 5-4-1)

Cleveland vs. Los Angeles Raiders (1979)
(Raiders lead series, 6-1)

Cleveland vs. Los Angeles Rams (1984)
(Series tied, 6-6)

Cleveland vs. Miami (1979)
(Cleveland leads series, 3-1)

Cleveland vs. Minnesota (1983)
(Minnesota leads series, 6-1)

Cleveland vs. New England (1984)
(Cleveland leads series, 5-2)

Cleveland vs. New Orleans (1984)
(Cleveland leads series, 8-1)

Cleveland vs. New York Giants (1977)
(Cleveland leads series, 24-15-2)

Cleveland vs. New York Jets (1984)
(Cleveland leads series, 7-2)

Cleveland vs. Philadelphia (1982)
(Cleveland leads series, 29-11-1)

Cleveland vs. Pittsburgh (1984)
(Cleveland leads series, 40-30)

Cleveland vs. St. Louis (1979)
(Cleveland leads series, 30-9-3)

Cleveland vs. San Diego (1983)
(San Diego leads series, 5-3-1)

Cleveland vs. San Francisco (1984)
(Cleveland leads series, 8-4)

Cleveland vs. Seattle (1984)
(Seattle leads series, 6-2)

Cleveland vs. Tampa Bay (1983)
(Cleveland leads series, 3-0)

Cleveland vs. Washington (1979)
(Cleveland leads series, 31-7-1)

Dallas vs. Denver (1980)
(Dallas leads series, 2-1)

Dallas vs. Detroit (1981)
(Dallas leads series, 5-2)

Dallas vs. Green Bay (1984)
(Green Bay leads series, 7-3)

Dallas vs. Houston (1982)
(Dallas leads series, 3-1)

Dallas vs. Indianapolis (1984)
(Dallas leads series, 6-2)

Dallas vs. Kansas City (1983)
(Dallas leads series, 2-1)

Dallas vs. Los Angeles Raiders (1983)
(Raiders lead series, 2-1)

Dallas vs. Los Angeles Rams (1984)
(Series tied, 6-6)

Dallas vs. Miami (1984)
(Miami leads series, 3-1)

Dallas vs. Minnesota (1983)
(Dallas leads series, 7-4)

Dallas vs. New England (1984)
(Dallas leads series, 5-0)

Dallas vs. New Orleans (1984)
(Dallas leads series, 11-1)

Dallas vs. New York Giants (1984)
(Dallas leads series, 30-13-2)

Dallas vs. New York Jets (1978)
(Dallas leads series, 3-0)

Dallas vs. Philadelphia (1984)
(Dallas leads series, 33-15)

Dallas vs. Pittsburgh (1982)
(Series tied, 10-10)

Dallas vs. St. Louis (1984)
(Dallas leads series, 28-16-1)

Dallas vs. San Diego (1983)
(Dallas leads series, 2-1)

Dallas vs. San Francisco (1983)
(San Francisco leads series, 6-5-1)

Dallas vs. Seattle (1983)
(Dallas leads series, 3-0)

Dallas vs. Tampa Bay (1983)
(Dallas leads series, 4-0)

Dallas vs. Washington (1984)
(Dallas leads series, 28-18-2)

Denver vs. Detroit (1984)
(Denver leads series, 3-2)

Denver vs. Green Bay (1984)
(Denver leads series, 3-1)

Denver vs. Houston (1983)
(Houston leads series, 17-9-1)

Denver vs. Indianapolis (1983)
(Denver leads series, 5-1)

Denver vs. Kansas City (1984)
(Kansas City leads series, 33-16)

Denver vs. Los Angeles Raiders (1984)
(Raiders lead series, 34-13-2)

Denver vs. Los Angeles Rams (1982)
(Series tied, 2-2)

Denver vs. Miami (1975)
(Miami leads series, 4-2-1)

Denver vs. Minnesota (1984)
(Series tied, 2-2)

Denver vs. New England (1984)
(New England leads series, 12-11)

Denver vs. New Orleans (1979)
(Denver leads series, 3-0)

Denver vs. New York Giants (1980)
(Denver leads series, 2-1)

Denver vs. New York Jets (1980)
(Series tied, 10-10-1)

Denver vs. Philadelphia (1983)
(Philadelphia leads series, 3-1)

Denver vs. Pittsburgh (1983)
(Denver leads series, 5-3-1)

Denver vs. St. Louis (1977)
(Denver leads series, 1-0-1)

Denver vs. San Diego (1984)
(San Diego leads series, 26-23-1)

Denver vs. San Francisco (1982)
(Series tied, 2-2)

Denver vs. Seattle (1984)
(Denver leads series, 9-6)

Denver vs. Tampa Bay (1981)
(Denver leads series, 2-0)

Denver vs. Washington (1980)
(Washington leads series, 2-1)

Detroit vs. Green Bay (1984)
(Green Bay leads series, 52-45-6)

Detroit vs. Houston (1983)
(Houston leads series, 2-1)

Detroit vs. Indianapolis (1980)
(Detroit leads series, 17-16-2)

Detroit vs. Kansas City (1981)
(Series tied, 2-2)

Detroit vs. Los Angeles Raiders (1984)
(Raiders lead series, 3-2)

Detroit vs. Los Angeles Rams (1983)
(Rams lead series, 29-25-1)

Detroit vs. Miami (1979)
(Miami leads series, 2-0)

Detroit vs. Minnesota (1984)
(Minnesota leads series, 29-16-2)

Detroit vs. New England (1979)
(Detroit leads series, 2-1)

Detroit vs. New Orleans (1980)
(Series tied, 4-4-1)

Detroit vs. New York Giants (1983)
(Detroit leads series, 13-8-1)

Detroit vs. New York Jets (1982)
(Jets lead series, 2-1)

Detroit vs. Philadelphia (1984)
(Detroit leads series, 10-9-2)

Detroit vs. Pittsburgh (1983)
(Detroit leads series, 13-8-1)

Detroit vs. St. Louis (1980)
(Detroit leads series, 26-13-3)

Detroit vs. San Diego (1984)
(Detroit leads series, 3-2)

Detroit vs. San Francisco (1984)
(Detroit leads series, 24-22-1)

Detroit vs. Seattle (1984)
(Seattle leads series, 2-1)

Detroit vs. Tampa Bay (1984)
(Detroit leads series, 8-6)

Detroit vs. Washington (1984)
(Washington leads series, 17-3)

Green Bay vs. Houston (1983)
(Series tied, 2-2)

Green Bay vs. Indianapolis (1982)
(Green Bay leads series, 17-16-1)

Green Bay vs. Kansas City (1977)
(Kansas City leads series, 1-0-1)

Green Bay vs. Los Angeles Raiders (1984)
(Raiders lead series, 4-0)

Green Bay vs. Los Angeles Rams (1984)
(Rams lead series, 35-21-1)

Green Bay vs. Miami (1979)
(Miami leads series, 3-0)

Green Bay vs. Minnesota (1984)
(Minnesota leads series, 24-22-1)

Green Bay vs. New England (1979)
(Series tied, 1-1)

Green Bay vs. New Orleans (1984)
(Green Bay leads series, 9-2)

Green Bay vs. New York Giants (1983)
(Green Bay leads series, 20-17-2)

Green Bay vs. New York Jets (1982)
(Jets lead series, 3-1)

Green Bay vs. Philadelphia (1979)
(Green Bay leads series, 17-4)

Green Bay vs. Pittsburgh (1983)
(Green Bay leads series, 19-10)

Green Bay vs. St. Louis (1984)
(Green Bay leads series, 39-20-4)

Green Bay vs. San Diego (1984)
(Green Bay leads series, 3-1)

Green Bay vs. San Francisco (1981)
(San Francisco leads series, 22-20-1)

Green Bay vs. Seattle (1984)
(Green Bay leads series, 3-1)

Green Bay vs. Tampa Bay (1984)
(Series tied, 6-6-1)

Green Bay vs. Washington (1983)
(Series tied, 9-9)

Houston vs. Indianapolis (1984)
(Indianapolis leads series, 4-3)

Houston vs. Kansas City (1984)
(Kansas City leads series, 19-11)

Houston vs. Los Angeles Raiders (1984)
(Raiders lead series, 18-10)

Houston vs. Los Angeles Rams (1984)
(Rams lead series, 3-1)

Houston vs. Miami (1984)
(Miami leads series, 9-8)

Houston vs. Minnesota (1983)
(Minnesota leads series, 2-1)

Houston vs. New England (1982)
(New England leads series, 14-12-1)

Houston vs. New Orleans (1984)
(Series tied, 2-2-1)

Houston vs. New York Giants (1982)
(Giants lead series, 2-0)

Houston vs. New York Jets (1984)
(Houston leads series, 15-10-1)

Houston vs. Philadelphia (1982)
(Philadelphia leads series, 3-0)

Houston vs. Pittsburgh (1984)
(Pittsburgh leads series, 20-9)

Houston vs. St. Louis (1979)
(St. Louis leads series, 3-0)

Houston vs. San Diego (1984)
(San Diego leads series, 16-8-1)

Houston vs. San Francisco (1984)
(San Francisco leads series, 3-2)

Houston vs. Seattle (1982)
(Houston leads series, 3-2)

Houston vs. Tampa Bay (1983)
(Houston leads series, 2-1)

Houston vs. Washington (1979)
(Houston leads series, 2-1)

Indianapolis vs. Kansas City (1980)
(Kansas City leads series, 5-3)

Indianapolis vs. Los Angeles Raiders (1984)
(Raiders lead series, 3-1)

Indianapolis vs. Los Angeles Rams (1975)
(Indianapolis leads series, 20-15-2)

Indianapolis vs. Miami (1984)
(Miami leads series, 21-9)

Indianapolis vs. Minnesota (1982)
(Indianapolis leads series, 11-5-1)

Indianapolis vs. New England (1984)
(Indianapolis leads series, 15-14)

Indianapolis vs. New Orleans (1973)
(Indianapolis leads series, 3-0)

Indianapolis vs. New York Giants (1979)
(Indianapolis leads series, 5-3)

Indianapolis vs. New York Jets (1984)
(Indianapolis leads series, 16-13)

Indianapolis vs. Philadelphia (1984)
(Series tied, 5-5)

Indianapolis vs. Pittsburgh (1984)
(Pittsburgh leads series, 7-4)

Indianapolis vs. St. Louis (1984)
(St. Louis leads series, 5-4)

Indianapolis vs. San Diego (1984)
(San Diego leads series, 4-2)

Indianapolis vs. San Francisco (1972)
(Indianapolis leads series, 21-14)

Indianapolis vs. Seattle (1978)
(Indianapolis leads series, 2-0)

Indianapolis vs. Tampa Bay (1979)
(Series tied, 1-1)

Indianapolis vs. Washington (1984)
(Indianapolis leads series, 15-6)

Kansas City vs. Los Angeles Raiders (1984)
(Raiders lead series, 28-19-2)

Kansas City vs. Los Angeles Rams (1982)
(Rams lead series, 2-0)

Kansas City vs. Miami (1983)
(Kansas City leads series, 7-4)

Kansas City vs. Minnesota (1981)
(Minnesota leads series, 2-1)

Kansas City vs. New England (1981)
(Kansas City leads series, 11-7-3)

Kansas City vs. New Orleans (1982)
(New Orleans leads series, 2-1)

Kansas City vs. New York Giants (1984)
(Giants lead series, 4-1)

Kansas City vs. New York Jets (1984)
(Kansas City leads series, 12-11)

Kansas City vs. Philadelphia (1972)
(Philadelphia leads series, 1-0)

Kansas City vs. Pittsburgh (1984)
(Pittsburgh leads series, 8-4)

Kansas City vs. St. Louis (1983)
(Kansas City leads series, 3-0-1)

Kansas City vs. San Diego (1984)
(San Diego leads series, 25-23-1)

Kansas City vs. San Francisco (1982)
(San Francisco leads series, 2-1)

Kansas City vs. Seattle (1984)
(Kansas City leads series, 7-6)

Kansas City vs. Tampa Bay (1984)
(Kansas City leads series, 3-2)

Kansas City vs. Washington (1983)
(Kansas City leads series, 2-1)

L. A. Raiders vs. L. A. Rams (1982)
(Raiders lead series, 3-1)

Los Angeles Raiders vs. Miami (1984)
(Raiders lead series, 12-2-1)

Los Angeles Raiders vs. Minnesota (1984)
(Raiders lead series, 4-1)

Los Angeles Raiders vs. New England (1981)
(New England leads series, 11-10-1)

Los Angeles Raiders vs. New Orleans (1979)
(Raiders lead series, 2-0-1)

L. A. Raiders vs. N. Y. Giants (1983)
(Raiders lead series, 3-0)

Los Angeles Raiders vs. New York Jets (1979)
(Raiders lead series, 11-9-2)

Los Angeles Raiders vs. Philadelphia (1980)
(Raiders lead series, 2-1)

Los Angeles Raiders vs. Pittsburgh (1984)
(Raiders lead series, 6-3)

Los Angeles Raiders vs. St. Louis (1983)
(Series tied, 1-1)

Los Angeles Raiders vs. San Diego (1984)
(Raiders lead series, 31-17-2)

Los Angeles Raiders vs. San Francisco (1982)
(Raiders lead series, 3-1)

Los Angeles Raiders vs. Seattle (1984)
(Series tied, 7-7)

Los Angeles Raiders vs. Tampa Bay (1981)
(Raiders lead series, 2-0)

Los Angeles Raiders vs. Washington (1983)
(Raiders lead series, 3-1)

Los Angeles Rams vs. Miami (1983)
(Miami leads series, 3-1)

Los Angeles Rams vs. Minnesota (1979)
(Minnesota leads series, 11-10-2)

Los Angeles Rams vs. New England (1983)
(New England leads series, 2-1)

Los Angeles Rams vs. New Orleans (1984)
(Rams lead series, 22-8)

Los Angeles Rams vs. New York Giants (1984)
(Rams lead series, 14-4)

Los Angeles Rams vs. New York Jets (1983)
(Series tied, 2-2)

Los Angeles Rams vs. Philadelphia (1983)
(Rams lead series, 13-8-1)

Los Angeles Rams vs. Pittsburgh (1984)
(Rams lead series, 14-3-2)

Los Angeles Rams vs. St. Louis (1984)
(Rams lead series, 11-8-2)

Los Angeles Rams vs. San Diego (1979)
(Rams lead series, 2-1)

Los Angeles Rams vs. San Francisco (1984)
(Rams lead series, 43-25-2)

Los Angeles Rams vs. Seattle (1979)
(Rams lead series, 2-0)

Los Angeles Rams vs. Tampa Bay (1984)
(Rams lead series, 3-2)

Los Angeles Rams vs. Washington (1983)
(Washington leads series, 12-4-1)

Miami vs. Minnesota (1982)
(Miami leads series, 3-1)

Miami vs. New England (1984)
(Miami leads series, 23-13)

Miami vs. New Orleans (1983)
(Miami leads series, 3-1)

Miami vs. New York Giants (1972)
(Miami leads series, 1-0)

Miami vs. New York Jets (1984)
(Miami leads series, 20-17-1)

Miami vs. Philadelphia (1984)
(Miami leads series, 3-2)

Miami vs. Pittsburgh (1984)
(Miami leads series, 4-2)

Miami vs. St. Louis (1984)
(Miami leads series, 5-0)

Miami vs. San Diego (1984)
(San Diego leads series, 7-4)

Miami vs. San Francisco (1983)
(Miami leads series, 4-0)

Miami vs. Seattle (1979)
(Miami leads series, 2-0)

Miami vs. Tampa Bay (1982)
(Series tied, 1-1)

Miami vs. Washington (1984)
(Miami leads series, 3-1)

Minnesota vs. New England (1979)
(New England leads series, 2-1)

Minnesota vs. New Orleans (1983)
(Minnesota leads series, 8-3)

Minnesota vs. New York Giants (1976)
(Minnesota leads series, 6-1)

Minnesota vs. New York Jets (1982)
(Jets lead series, 3-1)

Minnesota vs. Philadelphia (1984)
(Minnesota leads series, 8-2)

Minnesota vs. Pittsburgh (1983)
(Minnesota leads series, 5-3)

Minnesota vs. St. Louis (1983)
(St. Louis leads series, 7-2)

Minnesota vs. San Diego (1984)
(San Diego leads series, 3-2)

Minnesota vs. San Francisco (1984)
(Minnesota leads series, 12-11-1)

Minnesota vs. Seattle (1984)
(Seattle leads series, 2-1)

Minnesota vs. Tampa Bay (1984)
(Minnesota leads series, 9-5)

Minnesota vs. Washington (1984)
(Series tied, 3-3)

New England vs. New Orleans (1983)
(New England leads series, 4-0)

New England vs. New York Giants (1974)
(Series tied, 1-1)

New England vs. New York Jets (1984)
(Jets lead series, 28-20-1)

New England vs. Philadelphia (1984)
(Philadelphia leads series, 3-2)

New England vs. Pittsburgh (1983)
(Pittsburgh leads series, 5-2)

New England vs. St. Louis (1984)
(St. Louis leads series, 4-1)

New England vs. San Diego (1983)
(New England leads series, 13-11-2)

New England vs. San Francisco (1983)
(San Francisco leads series, 3-1)

New England vs. Seattle (1984)
(New England leads series, 4-1)

New England vs. Tampa Bay (1976)
(New England leads series, 1-0)

New England vs. Washington (1984)
(Washington leads series, 3-1)

New Orleans vs. New York Giants (1984)
(Series tied, 5-5)

New Orleans vs. New York Jets (1983)
(Jets lead series, 3-1)

New Orleans vs. Philadelphia (1983)
(Philadelphia leads series, 8-5)

New Orleans vs. Pittsburgh (1984)
(Series tied, 4-4)

New Orleans vs. St. Louis (1984)
(St. Louis leads series, 8-4)

New Orleans vs. San Diego (1979)
(San Diego leads series, 3-0)

New Orleans vs. San Francisco (1984)
(San Francisco leads series, 21-8-2)

New Orleans vs. Seattle (1979)
(Series tied, 1-1)

New Orleans vs. Tampa Bay (1984)
(New Orleans leads series, 4-3)

New Orleans vs. Washington (1982)
(Washington leads series, 7-4)

New York Giants vs. New York Jets (1984)
(Series tied, 2-2)

New York Giants vs. Philadelphia (1984)
(Giants lead series, 53-45-2)

New York Giants vs. Pittsburgh (1976)
(Giants lead series, 42-27-3)

New York Giants vs. St. Louis (1984)
(Giants lead series, 52-31-2)

New York Giants vs. San Diego (1983)
(Series tied, 2-2)

New York Giants vs. San Francisco (1984)
(Giants lead series, 9-5)

New York Giants vs. Seattle (1983)
(Giants lead series, 3-1)

New York Giants vs. Tampa Bay (1984)
(Giants lead series, 5-3)

New York Giants vs. Washington (1984)
(Giants lead series, 50-42-2)

New York Jets vs. Philadelphia (1978)
(Philadelphia leads series, 3-0)

New York Jets vs. Pittsburgh (1984)
(Pittsburgh leads series, 8-0)

New York Jets vs. St. Louis (1978)
(St. Louis leads series, 2-1)

New York Jets vs. San Diego (1983)
(San Diego leads series, 14-7-1)

New York Jets vs. San Francisco (1983)
(San Francisco leads series, 3-1)

New York Jets vs. Seattle (1983)
(Seattle leads series, 7-0)

New York Jets vs. Tampa Bay (1984)
(Jets lead series, 2-1)

New York Jets vs. Washington (1978)
(Washington leads series, 3-0)

Philadelphia vs. Pittsburgh (1979)
(Philadelphia leads series, 41-25-3)

Philadelphia vs. St. Louis (1984)
(St. Louis leads series, 39-32-4)

Philadelphia vs. San Diego (1980)
(Series tied, 1-1)

Philadelphia vs. San Francisco (1984)
(San Francisco leads series, 9-4-1)

Philadelphia vs. Seattle (1980)
(Philadelphia leads series, 2-0)

Philadelphia vs. Tampa Bay (1981)
(Philadelphia leads series, 2-0)

Philadelphia vs. Washington (1984)
(Washington leads series, 52-40-6)

Pittsburgh vs. St. Louis (1979)
(Pittsburgh leads series, 28-20-3)

Pittsburgh vs. San Diego (1984)
(Pittsburgh leads series, 8-2)

Pittsburgh vs. San Francisco (1984)
(Series tied, 6-6)

Pittsburgh vs. Seattle (1983)
(Pittsburgh leads series, 3-2)

Pittsburgh vs. Tampa Bay (1983)
(Pittsburgh leads series, 3-0)

Pittsburgh vs. Washington (1979)
(Washington leads series, 36-24-4)

St. Louis vs. San Diego (1983)
(San Diego leads series, 2-1)

St. Louis vs. San Francisco (1983)
(St. Louis leads series, 7-6)

St. Louis vs. Seattle (1983)
(St. Louis leads series, 2-0)

St. Louis vs. Tampa Bay (1983)
(Tampa Bay leads series, 2-1)

St. Louis vs. Washington (1984)
(Washington leads series, 44-30-1)

San Diego vs. San Francisco (1982)
(San Diego leads series, 3-1)

San Diego vs. Seattle (1984)
(San Diego leads series, 9-4)

San Diego vs. Tampa Bay (1981)
(San Diego leads series, 2-0)

San Diego vs. Washington (1983)
(Washington leads series, 3-0)

San Francisco vs. Seattle (1979)
(Series tied, 1-1)

San Francisco vs. Tampa Bay (1984)
(San Francisco leads series, 5-1)

San Francisco vs. Washington (1984)
(San Francisco leads series, 6-5-1)

Seattle vs. Tampa Bay (1977)
(Seattle leads series, 2-0)

Seattle vs. Washington (1983)
(Washington leads series, 2-1)

Tampa Bay vs. Washington (1982)
(Washington leads series, 2-0)

NFL ANNUAL SELECTION MEETING

APRIL 30, 1985

FIRST ROUND

1. Buffalo	SMITH, Bruce (1)	DE	Virginia Tech
2. Atlanta	FRALIC, Bill (2)	T	Pittsburgh
from Houston through Minnesota			
3. Houston	CHILDRESS, Ray (3)	DE	Texas A&M
from Minnesota			
4. Minnesota	DOLEMAN, Chris (4)	LB	Pittsburgh
from Atlanta			
5. Indianapolis	BICKETT, Duane (5)	LB	Southern Cal
6. Detroit	BROWN, Lomas (6)	T	Florida
7. Green Bay	RUETTGERS, Ken (7)	T	Southern Cal
from Cleveland through Buffalo			
8. Tampa Bay	HOLMES, Ron (8)	DE	Washington
9. Philadelphia	ALLEN, Kevin (9)	T	Indiana
10. New York Jets	TOON, Al (10)	WR	Wisconsin
11. Houston	JOHNSON, Richard (11)	DB	Wisconsin
from New Orleans			
12. San Diego	LACHEY, Jim (12)	G	Ohio State
13. Cincinnati	BROWN, Eddie (13)	WR	Miami, Fla.
14. Buffalo	BURROUGHS, Derrick (14)	DB	Memphis State
from Green Bay			
15. Kansas City	HORTON, Ethan (15)	RB	North Carolina
16. San Francisco	RICE, Jerry (16)	WR	Mississippi Valley
from New England			
17. Dallas	BROOKS, Kevin (17)	DE	Michigan
18. St. Louis	NUNN, Freddie Joe (18)	LB	Mississippi
19. New York Giants	ADAMS, George (19)	RB	Kentucky
20. Pittsburgh	SIMS, Darryl (20)	DE	Wisconsin
21. Los Angeles Rams	GRAY, Jerry (21)	DB	Texas
22. Chicago	PERRY, William (22)	DT	Clemson
23. Los Angeles Raiders	HESTER, Jessie (23)	WR	Florida State
24. New Orleans	TOLES, Alvin (24)	LB	Tennessee
from Washington			
25. Cincinnati	KING, Emanuel (25)	LB	Alabama
from Seattle			
26. Denver	SEWELL, Steve (26)	RB	Oklahoma
27. Miami	HAMPTON, Lorenzo (27)	RB	Florida
28. New England	MATICH, Trevor (28)	C	Brigham Young
from San Francisco			

End of Round:	Time of Round:	Elapsed Time:
11:38 a.m.	3 hours, 36 minutes	3 hours, 36 minutes

NFL ANNUAL SELECTION MEETING

APRIL 30, 1985

SECOND ROUND

1. Buffalo   TRAYNOWICZ, Mark (29)   T   Nebraska
2. Minnesota   HOLT, Issiac (30)   DB   Alcorn State
3. Denver   JOHNSON, Vance (31)   WR   Arizona
   from Houston
4. Indianapolis   ANDERSON, Don (32)   DB   Purdue
5. Washington   NIXON, Tory (33)   DB   San Diego St.
   from Atlanta
6. Detroit   GLOVER, Kevin (34)   C   Maryland
7. Cleveland   ALLEN, Greg (35)   RB   Florida State
8. Houston   BYRD, Richard (36)   DE   So. Mississippi
   from Tampa Bay through Denver
9. Philadelphia   CUNNINGHAM, Randall (37)   QB   Nevada-Las Vegas
10. New Orleans   GILBERT, Daren (38)   T   Cal St.-Fullerton
11. San Diego   DAVIS, Wayne (39)   DB   Indiana State
12. New York Jets   LYLES, Lester (40)   DB   Virginia
13. Kansas City*   HAYES, Jonathan (41)   TE   Iowa
14. Buffalo   BURKETT, Chris (42)   WR   Jackson State
    from Green Bay
15. Cincinnati   ZANDER, Carl (43)   LB   Tennessee
16. Dallas   PENN, Jesse (44)   LB   Virginia Tech
17. Atlanta   GANN, Mike (45)   DE   Notre Dame
    from St. Louis
18. New York Giants   ROBINSON, Stacy (46)   WR   North Dakota St.
19. Pittsburgh   BEHNING, Mark (47)   T   Nebraska
20. New England   VERIS, Garin (48)   DE   Stanford
21. Chicago   PHILLIPS, Reggie (49)   DB   So. Methodist
22. Los Angeles Rams   SCOTT, Chuck (50)   WR   Vanderbilt
23. St. Louis   BERGOLD, Scott (51)   T   Wisconsin
    from Washington through Atlanta
24. New England   BOWMAN, Jim (52)   DB   Central Michigan
    from Los Angeles Raiders
25. Seattle   GILL, Owen (53)   RB   Iowa
26. Denver   FLETCHER, Simon (54)   DE   Houston
27. San Diego   DALE, Jeffery (55)   DB   Louisiana State
    from Miami
28. New England   THOMAS, Ben (56)   DE   Auburn
    from San Francisco

*Selected ahead of Buffalo, which passed.

End of Round: **Time of Round:**   **Elapsed Time:**
3:02 p.m.   3 hours, 24 minutes   7 hours, 0 minutes

NFL ANNUAL SELECTION MEETING

APRIL 30, 1985

THIRD ROUND

1. Buffalo	REICH, Frank (57)	QB	Maryland
2. New York Giants from Houston	DAVIS, Tyrone (58)	DB	Clemson
3. Minnesota	LOWDERMILK, Kirk (59)	C	Ohio State
4. Minnesota from Atlanta	MEAMBER, Tim (60)	LB	Washington
5. Indianapolis	YOUNG, Anthony (61)	DB	Temple
6. Detroit	JOHNSON, James (62)	LB	San Diego State
7. Buffalo from Cleveland	GARNER, Hal (63)	LB	Utah State
8. Tampa Bay	RANDLE, Ervin (64)	LB	Baylor
9. Miami from Philadelphia	LITTLE, George (65)	DT	Iowa
10. Minnesota from San Diego	LONG, Tim (66)	T	Memphis State
11. New York Jets	ELDER, Donnie (67)	DB	Memphis State
12. New Orleans	DEL RIO, Jack (68)	LB	Southern Cal.
13. San Diego from Kansas City	HENDY, John (69)	DB	Cal St.-Long Beach
14. Cincinnati	THOMAS, Sean (70)	DB	Texas Christian
15. Green Bay	MORAN, Rich (71)	G	San Diego State
16. St. Louis	SMITH, Lance (72)	T	Louisiana State
17. New York Giants	JOHNSTON, Brian (73)	C	North Carolina
18. Pittsburgh	HOBLEY, Liffort (74)	DB	Louisiana State
19. San Francisco from New England	MOORE, Ricky (75)	RB	Alabama
20. Dallas	KER, Crawford (76)	G	Florida
21. Los Angeles Rams	HATCHER, Dale (77)	P	Clemson
22. Chicago	MANESS, James (78)	WR	Texas Christian
23. Los Angeles Raiders	MOFFETT, Tim (79)	WR	Mississippi
24. Los Angeles Raiders from Washington through Houston	ADAMS, Stefon (80)	DB	East Carolina
25. Seattle	GREENE, Danny (81)	WR	Washington
26. Houston from Denver	KELLEY, Mike (82)	C	Notre Dame
27. Miami	MOYER, Alex (83)	LB	Northwestern
28. New England from San Francisco	McMILLIAN, Audrey (84)	DB	Houston

End of Round:
4:17 p.m.   **Time of Round:**   **Elapsed Time:**
                1 hour, 15 minutes   8 hours, 15 minutes

NFL ANNUAL SELECTION MEETING

APRIL 30, 1985

FOURTH ROUND

1. Minnesota*	RHYMES, Buster (85)	WR	Oklahoma
2. Buffalo	REED, Andre (86)	WR	Kutztown, Pa.
3. Houston	BRIEHL, Tom (87)	LB	Stanford
4. Indianapolis	BROUGHTON, Willie (88)	DE	Miami, Fla.
5. Atlanta	HARRY, Emile (89)	WR	Stanford
6. Detroit	HANCOCK, Kevin (90)	LB	Baylor
7. Miami from Cleveland	SMITH, Mike (91)	DB	Texas-El Paso
8. Tampa Bay	HEAVEN, Mike (92)	DB	Illinois
9. Philadelphia	NARON, Greg (93)	G	North Carolina
10. New York Jets	ALLEN, Doug (94)	WR	Arizona State
11. New Orleans	ALLEN, Billy (95)	DB	Florida State
12. San Diego	MOJSIEJENKO, Ralf (96)	K	Michigan State
13. Cincinnati	TUGGLE, Anthony (97)	DB	Nicholls State
14. Green Bay	STANLEY, Walter (98)	WR	Mesa, Colo.
15. Kansas City	OLDERMAN, Bob (99)	G	Virginia
16. New York Giants	BAVARO, Mark (100)	TE	Notre Dame
17. Pittsburgh	TURK, Dan (101)	C	Wisconsin
18. New England	TOTH, Tom (102)	T	Western Michigan
19. Dallas	LAVETTE, Robert (103)	RB	Georgia Tech
20. St. Louis	WOLFLEY, Ron (104)	RB	West Virginia
21. Chicago	BUTLER, Kevin (105)	K	Georgia
22. Minnesota from Los Angeles Rams	MORRELL, Kyle (106)	DB	Brigham Young
23. Los Angeles Raiders from Washington	KIMMEL, Jamie (107)	LB	Syracuse
24. New England from Los Angeles Raiders	PHELAN, Gerard (108)	WR	Boston College
25. Seattle	DAVIS, Tony (109)	TE	Missouri
26. Denver	McGREGOR, Keli (110)	TE	Colorado State
27. Miami	DELLENBACH, Jeff (111)	T	Wisconsin
28. Buffalo from San Francisco	HELLESTRAE, Dale (112)	T	So. Methodist

*Selected ahead of Buffalo, which passed.

End of Round:
5:32 p.m.

Time of Round:
1 hour, 15 minutes

Elapsed Time:
9 hours, 30 minutes

NFL ANNUAL SELECTION MEETING
APRIL 30, 1985

Start of Round:
5:32 p.m.

FIFTH ROUND

1. Los Angeles Rams from Buffalo	GREENE, Kevin (113)	LB	Auburn
2. Dallas from Houston	WALKER, Herschel (114)	RB	Georgia
3. Minnesota	MacDONALD, Mark (115)	G	Boston College
4. St. Louis from Atlanta	DUNN, K.D. (116)	TE	Clemson
5. Indianapolis	CARON, Roger (117)	T	Harvard
6. Detroit	McINTOSH, Joe (118)	RB	N. Carolina State
7. Dallas from Cleveland through Buffalo	DARWIN, Matt (119)	C	Texas A & M
8. New York Jets from Tampa Bay	BENSON, Troy (120)	LB	Pittsburgh
9. Philadelphia	JILES, Dwayne (121)	LB	Texas Tech
10. Washington from New Orleans	CHERRY, Raphel (122)	RB	Hawaii
11. Seattle from San Diego	NAPOLITAN, Mark (123)	C	Michigan State
12. New York Jets	LUFT, Brian (124)	DT	S'thern California
13. Green Bay	NOBLE, Brian (125)	LB	Arizona State
14. Kansas City	KING, Bruce (126)	RB	Purdue
15. Cincinnati	DEGRATE, Tony (127)	DT	Texas
16. Seattle from Pittsburgh	BROWN, Arnold (128)	DB	N. Car. Central
17. Cincinnati from New England	DAVIS, Lee (129)	DB	Mississippi
18. Buffalo from Dallas	TEAL, Jimmy (130)	WR	Texas A & M
19. St. Louis	WONG, Louis (131)	G	Brigham Young
20. New York Giants	HENDERSON, Tracy (132)	WR	Iowa State
21. Houston from Los Angeles Rams through Kansas City	BUSH, Frank (133)	LB	N. Carolina St.
22. New York Jets from Chicago	SMITH, Tony (134)	WR	San Jose State
23. Los Angeles Raiders	REEDER, Dan (135)	RB	Delaware
24. Pittsburgh from Washington	JACOBS, Cam (136)	LB	Kentucky
25. Seattle	JONES, Johnnie (137)	RB	Tennessee
26. Houston from Denver	JOHNSON, Lee (138)	K	Brigham Young
27. Denver from Miami	HINSON, Billy (139)	G	Florida
28. San Francisco	COLLIE, Bruce (140)	T	Texas-Arlington

End of Round:
6:40 p.m.

Time of Round:
1 hour, 8 minutes

Elapsed Time:
10 hours, 38 minutes

NFL ANNUAL SELECTION MEETING

APRIL 30, 1985

Start of Round:
6:40 p.m.

SIXTH ROUND

1. Buffalo	HAMBY, Mike (141)	DT	Utah State
2. Minnesota	BONO, Steve (142)	QB	UCLA
3. Los Angeles Raiders from Houston	HILGER, Rusty (143)	QB	Oklahoma State
4. Dallas from Indianapolis	PLOEGER, Kurt (144)	DE	G. Adolphus, Minn.
5. Miami from Atlanta	SHORTHOSE, George (145)	WR	Missouri
6. Detroit	SHORT, Stan (146)	G	Penn State
7. Cleveland	KREROWICZ, Mark (147)	G	Ohio State
8. Cincinnati from Tampa Bay	STOKES, Eric (148)	T	Northeastern
9. Kansas City from Philadelphia	BOSTIC, Jonathan (149)	DB	Bethune-Cookman
10. San Diego	LEWIS, Terry (150)	DB	Michigan State
11. New York Jets	DEATON, Jeff (151)	G	Stanford
12. Atlanta from New Orleans	PLEASANT, Reggie (152)	DB	Clemson
13. Houston from Kansas City	KRAKOSKI, Joe (153)	LB	Washington
14. Cincinnati	LESTER, Keith (154)	TE	Murray State
15. Green Bay	LEWIS, Mark (155)	TE	Texas A&M
16. Philadelphia from New England	REEVES, Ken (156)	T	Texas A&M
17. Dallas	MORAN, Matt (157)	G	Stanford
18. St. Louis	NOVACEK, Jay (158)	WR	Wyoming
19. New York Giants	OLIVER, Jack (159)	G	Memphis State
20. Pittsburgh	CARR, Gregg (160)	LB	Auburn
21. Los Angeles Rams from Chicago	YOUNG, Mike (161)	WR	UCLA
22. Los Angeles Rams	JOHNSON, Damone (162)	TE	Cal Poly-Obispo
23. Washington	LEE, Danzell (163)	TE	Lamar
24. Minnesota from Los Angeles Raiders	NEWTON, Tim (164)	NT	Florida
25. New York Giants from Seattle	PEMBROOK, Mark (165)	DB	Cal St.-Fullerton
26. New York Jets from Denver	MIANO, Rich (166)	DB	Hawaii
27. Miami	DAVENPORT, Ron (167)	RB	Louisville
28. San Francisco	BARRY, Scott (168)	QB	Cal-Davis

End of Round:
7:55 p.m.

Time of Round:
1 hour, 15 minutes

Elapsed Time:
11 hours, 53 minutes

NFL ANNUAL SELECTION MEETING

APRIL 30, 1985

SEVENTH ROUND

1. Buffalo	PITTS, Ron (169)	DB	UCLA
2. Houston	AKIU, Mike (170)	WR	Hawaii
3. Green Bay from Minnesota	WILSON, Eric (171)	LB	Maryland
4. Cincinnati from Atlanta	LOCKLIN, Kim (172)	RB	New Mexico State
5. Indianapolis	HARBOUR, James (173)	WR	Mississippi
6. Detroit	STATEN, Tony (174)	DB	Angelo State
7. Cleveland	LANGHORNE, Reginald (175)	WR	Elizabeth City St.
8. Tampa Bay	PRIOR, Mike (176)	DB	Illinois State
9. Washington from Philadelphia	HARRIS, Jamie (177)	KR	Oklahoma State
10. Dallas from New York Jets through Kansas City	POWE, Karl (178)	WR	Alabama State
11. New Orleans	MARTIN, Eric (179)	WR	Louisiana State
12. Kansas City from San Diego	THOMSON, Vince (180)	DE	Missouri Western
13. Cincinnati	WALTER, Joe (181)	T	Texas Tech
14. Green Bay	ELLERSON, Gary (182)	RB	Wisconsin
15. Kansas City	HEFFERNAN, Dave (183)	G	Miami, Fla.
16. Dallas	HERRMANN, Jim (184)	DE	Brigham Young
17. Washington from St. Louis through Kansas City	VITAL, Lionel (185)	RB	Nicholls State
18. Los Angeles Raiders from New York Giants	BELCHER, Kevin (186)	T	Wisconsin
19. Pittsburgh	ANDREWS, Alan (187)	TE	Rutgers
20. Los Angeles Raiders from New England	PATTISON, Mark (188)	WR	Washington
21. Los Angeles Rams	BRADLEY, Danny (189)	RB	Oklahoma
22. Chicago	BENNETT, Charles (190)	DE	S.W. Louisiana
23. Los Angeles Raiders	CLARK, Bret (191)	DB	Nebraska
24. Los Angeles Raiders from Washington through New England	HADEN, Nick (192)	C	Penn State
25. Seattle	MATTES, Ron (193)	T	Virginia
26. Denver	CAMERON, Dallas (194)	NT	Miami, Fla.
27. Miami	REVEIZ, Fuad (195)	K	Tennessee
28. San Diego from San Francisco	FELLOWS, Mark (196)	LB	Montana State

End of Round:
9:07 p.m.

Time of Round:
1 hour, 12 minutes

Elapsed Time:
13 hours, 5 minutes

— 367 —

NFL ANNUAL SELECTION MEETING
APRIL 30, 1985

EIGHTH ROUND

1. Buffalo	ROBINSON, Jacque (197)	RB	Washington
2. Minnesota	BLAIR, Nikita (198)	LB	Texas-El Paso
3. Houston	THOMAS, Chuck (199)	C	Oklahoma
4. Indianapolis	NICHOLS, Ricky (200)	WR	East Carolina
5. Atlanta	LEE, Ashley (201)	DB	Virginia Tech
6. Detroit	CALDWELL, Scotty (202)	RB	Texas-Arlington
7. Cleveland	BANKS, Fred (203)	WR	Liberty Baptist
8. Tampa Bay	FREEMAN, Phil (204)	WR	Arizona
9. Philadelphia	POLLEY, Tom (205)	LB	Nevada-Las Vegas
10. New Orleans	KOHLBRAND, Joe (206)	DE	Miami, Fla.
11. San Diego	ADAMS, Curtis (207)	RB	Central Michigan
12. New York Jets	MONGER, Matt (208)	LB	Oklahoma State
13. Green Bay	STILLS, Ken (209)	DB	Wisconsin
14. Kansas City	HILLARY, Ira (210)	WR	South Carolina
15. Cincinnati	STROBEL, Dave (211)	LB	Iowa
16. St. Louis	MONACO, Rob (212)	G	Vanderbilt
17. New York Giants	ROUSON, Lee (213)	RB	Colorado
18. Pittsburgh	NEWSOME, Harry (214)	P	Wake Forest
19. Atlanta from New England	WASHINGTON, Ronnie (215)	LB	N.E. Louisiana
20. Dallas	GONZALES, Leon (216)	WR	Bethune-Cookman
21. Chicago	BUXTON, Steve (217)	T	Indiana State
22. Los Angeles Rams	McINTYRE, Marlon (218)	RB	Pittsburgh
23. Washington	WILBURN, Barry (219)	DB	Mississippi
24. Los Angeles Raiders	WINGATE, Leonard (220)	DT	South Carolina St.
25. Seattle	LEWIS, Judious (221)	WR	Arkansas State
26. Denver	RILEY, Eric (222)	DB	Florida State
27. Miami	SHARP, Dan (223)	TE	Texas Christian
28. New England from San Francisco	HODGE, Milford (224)	DT	Washington State

End of Round:
10:23 p.m.

Time of Round:
1 hour, 16 minutes

Elapsed Time:
14 hours, 21 minutes

— 368 —

NFL ANNUAL SELECTION MEETING
APRIL 30, 1985

NINTH ROUND

1. Buffalo	JONES, Glenn (225)	DB	Norfolk State
2. Houston	TASKER, Steve (226)	KR	Northwestern
3. Minnesota	COVINGTON, Jaime (227)	RB	Syracuse
4. Atlanta	MOON, Micah (228)	LB	North Carolina
5. Indianapolis	BOYER, Mark (229)	TE	Southern Cal
6. Detroit	JAMES, June (230)	LB	Texas
7. Philadelphia from Cleveland	TOUB, Dave (231)	C	Texas-El Paso
8. Tampa Bay	CALABRIA, Steve (232)	QB	Colgate
9. Philadelphia	DRAKE, Joe (233)	DT	Arizona
10. San Diego	BERNER, Paul (234)	QB	Pacific
11. New York Jets	WATERS, Mike (235)	RB	San Diego State
12. New Orleans	JOHNSON, Earl (236)	DB	South Carolina
13. Kansas City	ARMENTROUT, Mike (237)	DB	S.W. Missouri
14. Cincinnati	CRUISE, Keith (238)	DE	Northwestern
15. Green Bay	JOHNSON, Morris (239)	G	Alabama A&M
16. New York Giants	WRIGHT, Frank (240)	NT	South Carolina
17. Pittsburgh	SMALL, Fred (241)	LB	Washington
18. Pittsburgh from New England	HARRIS, Andre (242)	DB	Minnesota
19. Dallas	STRASBURGER, Scott (243)	LB	Nebraska
20. St. Louis	WILLIAMS, Scott (244)	TE	Georgia
21. Los Angeles Rams	SWANSON, Gary (245)	LB	Cal Poly-Obispo
22. Los Angeles Raiders*	SYDNOR, Chris (246)	DB	Penn State
23. Washington*	GEIER, Mitch (247)	G	Troy State
24. Seattle*	OTTO, Bob (248)	DE	Idaho State
25. Denver*	SMITH, Daryl (249)	DB	North Alabama
26. Chicago	SANDERS, Thomas (250)	RB	Texas A&M
27. Miami	HINDS, Adam (251)	DB	Oklahoma State
28. San Diego from San Francisco	REMSBERG, Dan (252)	T	Abilene Christian

*Los Angeles Raiders, Washington, Seattle and Denver selected ahead of Chicago, which passed.

End of Round:	Time of Round:	Elapsed Time:
11:30 p.m.	1 hour, 7 minutes	15 hours, 28 minutes

NFL ANNUAL SELECTION MEETING
APRIL 30-MAY 1, 1985

Start of Round:
11:30 p.m.

TENTH ROUND

1. Buffalo	BABYAR, Chris (253)	G	Illinois
2. Minnesota	JOHNSON, Juan (254)	WR	Langston, Okla.
3. Houston	GOLIC, Mike (255)	DE	Notre Dame
4. Indianapolis	PINESETT, Andre (256)	DT	Cal St.-Fullerton
5. Atlanta	MARTIN, Brent (257)	C	Stanford
6. Detroit	BEAUFORD, Clayton (258)	WR	Auburn
7. Cleveland	WILLIAMS, Larry (259)	G	Notre Dame
8. Tampa Bay	IGWEBUIKE, Donald (260)	K	Clemson
9. Philadelphia	KELSO, Mark (261)	DB	William & Mary
10. New York Jets	GLENN, Kerry (262)	DB	Minnesota
11. Washington from New Orleans	ORR, Terry (263)	RB	Texas
12. San Diego	KING, David (264)	DB	Auburn
13. Cincinnati	KING, Bernard (265)	LB	Syracuse
14. Green Bay	BURGESS, Ronnie (266)	DB	Wake Forest
15. Kansas City	SMITH, Jeff (267)	RB	Nebraska
16. Pittsburgh	WHITE, Oliver (268)	TE	Kentucky
17. Denver from New England	FUNCK, Buddy (269)	QB	New Mexico
18. Dallas	JONES, Joe (270)	TE	Virginia Tech
19. St. Louis	WILLIAMS, Dennis (271)	RB	Furman
20. New York Giants	DUBROC, Gregg (272)	LB	Louisiana State
21. Chicago	CORYATT, Pat (273)	DT	Baylor
22. Los Angeles Rams	LOVE, Duval (274)	G	UCLA
23. Los Angeles Raiders from Washington	McKENZIE, Reggie (275)	LB	Tennessee
24. Los Angeles Raiders	MYRES, Albert (276)	DB	Tulsa
25. Seattle	CONNER, John (277)	QB	Arizona
26. Denver	ANDERSON, Ron (278)	LB	SMU
27. Miami	PENDLETON, Mike (279)	DB	Indiana
28. Seattle from San Francisco	BOWERS, James (280)	DB	Memphis State

End of Round:
12:37 a.m.

Time of Round:
1 hour, 7 minutes

Elapsed Time:
16 hours, 35 minutes

NFL ANNUAL SELECTION MEETING

MAY 1, 1985

Start of Round:
12:37 a.m.

ELEVENTH ROUND

1. Houston*	DREWREY, Willie (281)	KR	West Virginia
2. Buffalo	SEAWRIGHT, James (282)	LB	South Carolina
3. Minnesota	WILLIAMS, Tim (283)	DB	No. Carolina A & T
4. Atlanta	AYRES, John (284)	DB	Illinois
5. Los Angeles Rams from Indianapolis	FLUTIE, Doug (285)	QB	Boston College
6. Detroit	HARRIS, Kevin (286)	DB	Georgia
7. Cleveland	TUCKER, Travis (287)	TE	So. Connecticut
8. Tampa Bay	WILLIAMS, James (288)	RB	Memphis State
9. Philadelphia	HUNTER, Herman (289)	RB	Tennessee State
10. Washington from New Orleans	McKENZIE, Raleigh (290)	G	Tennessee
11. San Diego	SMITH, Jeff (291)	NT	Kentucky
12. New York Jets	WHITE, Brad (292)	DE	Texas Tech
13. Kansas City*	JACKSON, Chris (293)	C	SMU
14. Green Bay	SHIELD, Joe (294)	QB	Trinity, Conn.
15. New England*	LEWIS, Paul (295)	RB	Boston U.
16. Cincinnati	STANFIELD, Harold (296)	TE	Mississippi College
17. Dallas	DELLOCONO, Neal (297)	LB	UCLA
18. St. Louis	ANDERSON, Ricky (298)	K	Vanderbilt
19. New York Giants	YOUNG, Allen (299)	DB	Virginia Tech
20. Pittsburgh	MATICHAK, Terry (300)	DB	Missouri
21. Los Angeles Rams	BROWN, Kevin (301)	DB	Northwestern
22. Chicago	MORRISSEY, James (302)	LB	Michigan State
23. Los Angeles Raiders	STRACHAN, Steve (303)	RB	Boston College
24. Washington	KIMBLE, Garry (304)	DB	Sam Houston State
25. Seattle	COOPER, Louis (305)	LB	Western Carolina
26. Denver	ROLLE, Gary (306)	WR	Florida
27. Miami	JONES, Mike (307)	RB	Tulane
28. San Francisco	WOOD, David (308)	DE	Arizona

*Houston selected ahead of Buffalo, which passed. Kansas City selected ahead of Green Bay, which passed. New England selected ahead of Cincinnati, which passed.

End of Round:	**Time of Round:**	**Elapsed Time:**
1:38 a.m.	1 hour, 1 minute	17 hours, 36 minutes

NFL ANNUAL SELECTION MEETING

MAY 1, 1985

Start of Round:
1:38 a.m.

TWELFTH ROUND

1.	Washington from Buffalo	HAMEL, Dean (309)	DT	Tulsa
2.	Minnesota	JONES, Byron (310)	NT	Tulsa
3.	Houston	VONDER HAAR, Mark (311)	DT	Minnesota
4.	Indianapolis	BURNETTE, Dave (312)	T	Central Arkansas
5.	Atlanta	WHISENHUNT, Ken (313)	TE	Georgia Tech
6.	Detroit	WEAVER, Mike (314)	G	Georgia
7.	Cleveland	SWANSON, Shane (315)	WR	Nebraska
8.	Tampa Bay	ROCKFORD, Jim (316)	DB	Oklahoma
9.	Philadelphia	RUSSELL, Todd (317)	DB	Boston College
10.	San Diego	SIMMONS, Tony (318)	DE	Tennessee
11.	New York Jets	WALLACE, Bill (319)	WR	Pittsburgh
12.	New Orleans	SONGY, Treg (320)	DB	Tulane
13.	Kansas City	LeBEL, Harper (321)	C	Colorado State
14.	Cincinnati	GARZA, Louis (322)	T	New Mexico State
15.	Green Bay	MEYER, Jim (323)	P	Arizona State
16.	Dallas	JORDAN, Karl (324)	LB	Vanderbilt
17.	St. Louis	YOUNG, Lonnie (325)	DB	Michigan State
18.	New York Giants	WELCH, Herb (326)	DB	UCLA
19.	Pittsburgh	SANCHEZ, Jeff (327)	DB	Georgia
20.	New England	MUMFORD, Tony (328)	RB	Penn State
21.	San Diego from Chicago	PEARSON, Bret (329)	TE	Wisconsin
22.	Tampa Bay from Los Angeles Rams	MELKA, Jim (330)	LB	Wisconsin
23.	Washington	WINN, Bryant (331)	LB	Houston
24.	Los Angeles Raiders	POLK, Raymond (332)	DB	Oklahoma State
25.	Buffalo from Seattle	WOODSIDE, Paul (333)	K	West Virginia
26.	Denver	LYNCH, Dan (334)	G	Washington State
27.	Miami	NOBLE, Ray (335)	DB	California
28.	San Francisco	CHUMLEY, Donald (336)	DT	Georgia

End of Round:
2:29 a.m.

Time of Round:
0 hours, 51 minutes

Elapsed Time:
18 hours, 27 minutes

TEAM-BY-TEAM NO. 1 DRAFT CHOICES

*—Designates first player chosen in draft.

ATLANTA FALCONS

1985—Bill Fralic, T, Pittsburgh
1984—Rick Bryan, DT, Oklahoma
1983—Mike Pitts, DE, Alabama
1982—Gerald Riggs, RB, Arizona State
1981—Bobby Butler, DB, Florida State
1980—Junior Miller, TE, Nebraska
1979—Don Smith, DE, Miami (Fla.)
1978—Mike Kenn, T, Michigan
1977—Warren Bryant, T, Kentucky
    Wilson Faumuina, DT, San Jose State
1976—Bubba Bean, RB, Texas A&M
1975—Steve Bartkowski, QB, California*
1974—(No Number One Selection)
1973—(No Number One Selection)
1972—Clarence Ellis, DB, Notre Dame
1971—Joe Profit, RB, Northeast Louisiana
1970—John Small, LB, Citadel
1969—George Kunz, T, Notre Dame
1968—Claude Humphrey, DE, Tennessee State
1967—(No Number One Selection)
1966—Tommy Nobis, LB, Texas*
    Randy Johnson, QB, Texas A&I

BUFFALO BILLS

1985—Bruce Smith, DT, Virginia Tech*
    Derrick Burroughs, DB, Memphis State
1984—Greg Bell, RB, Notre Dame
1983—Tony Hunter, TE, Notre Dame
    Jim Kelly, QB, Miami (Fla.)
1982—Perry Tuttle, WR, Clemson
1981—Booker Moore, RB, Penn State
1980—Jim Ritcher, C, North Carolina State
1979—Tom Cousineau, LB, Ohio State*
    Jerry Butler, WR, Clemson
1978—Terry Miller, RB, Oklahoma State
1977—Phil Dokes, DT, Oklahoma State
1976—Mario Clark, DB, Oregon
1975—Tom Ruud, LB, Nebraska
1974—Reuben Gant, TE, Oklahoma State
1973—Paul Seymour, T, Michigan
    Joe DeLamielleure, G, Michigan State
1972—Walt Patulski, DE, Notre Dame*
1971—J.D. Hill, WR, Arizona State
1970—Al Cowlings, DE, Southern California
1969—O.J. Simpson, RB, Southern California*
1968—Haven Moses, WR, San Diego State
1967—John Pitts, DB, Arizona State
1966—Mike Dennis, RB, Mississippi
1965—Jim Davidson, T, Ohio State
1964—Carl Eller, DE, Minnesota
1963—Dave Behrman, C, Michigan State
1962—Ernie Davis, RB, Syracuse
1961—Ken Rice, T, Auburn* (AFL)
1960—Richie Lucas, QB, Penn State

CHICAGO BEARS

1985—William Perry, DT, Clemson
1984—Wilber Marshall, LB, Florida
1983—Jimbo Covert, T, Pittsburgh
    Willie Gault, WR, Tennessee
1982—Jim McMahon, QB, Brigham Young
1981—Keith Van Horne, T, Southern California
1980—Otis Wilson, LB, Louisville
1979—Dan Hampton, DT, Arkansas
    Al Harris, DE, Arizona State
1978—(No Number One Selection)
1977—Ted Albrecht, T, California
1976—Dennis Lick, T, Wisconsin
1975—Walter Payton, RB, Jackson State
1974—Waymond Bryant, LB, Tennessee State
    Dave Gallagher, DE, Michigan
1973—Wally Chambers, DE, Eastern Kentucky
1972—Lionel Antoine, T, Southern Illinois
    Craig Clemons, DB, Iowa
1971—Joe Moore, RB, Missouri
1970—(No Number One Selection)

1969—Rufus Mayes, T, Ohio State
1968—Mike Hull, RB, Southern California
1967—Loyd Phillips, DE, Arkansas
1966—George Rice, DT, Louisiana State
1965—Dick Butkus, LB, Illinois
    Gale Sayers, RB, Kansas
    Steve DeLong, DE, Tennessee
1964—Dick Evey, DT, Tennessee
1963—Dave Behrman, C, Michigan State
1962—Ron Bull, RB, Baylor
1961—Mike Ditka, E, Pittsburgh
1960—Roger Davis, G, Syracuse
1959—Don Clark, B, Ohio State
1958—Chuck Howley, LB, West Virginia
1957—Earl Leggett, DT, Louisiana State
1956—Menan (Tex) Schriewer, E, Texas
1955—Ron Drzewiecki, B, Marquette
1954—Stan Wallace, B, Illinois
1953—Billy Anderson, B, Compton (Calif.) JC
1952—Jim Dooley, B, Miami
1951—Bob Williams, B, Notre Dame
    Billy Stone, B, Bradley
1950—Chuck Hunsinger, B, Florida
1949—Dick Harris, C, Texas
1948—Bobby Layne, QB, Texas
    Max Baumgardner, E, Texas
1947—Bob Fenimore, B, Oklahoma A&M*
1946—Johnny Lujack, QB, Notre Dame
1945—Don Lund, B, Michigan
1944—Ray Evans, B, Kansas
1943—Bob Steuber, B, Missouri
1942—Frankie Albert, B, Stanford
1941—Tom Harmon, B, Michigan*
    Norm Standlee, B, Stanford
    Don Scott, B, Ohio State
1940—Clyde Turner, C, Hardin-Simmons
1939—Sid Luckman, B, Columbia
    Bill Osmanski, B, Holy Cross
1938—Joe Gray, B, Oregon State
1937—Les McDonald, E, Nebraska
1936—Joe Stydahar, T, West Virginia

CINCINNATI BENGALS

1985—Eddie Brown, WR, Miami (Fla.)
    Emanuel King, LB, Alabama
1984—Ricky Hunley, LB, Arizona
    Pete Koch, DE, Maryland
    Brian Blados, T, North Carolina
1983—Dave Rimington, C, Nebraska
1982—Glen Collins, DE, Mississippi State
1981—David Verser, WR, Kansas
1980—Anthony Munoz, T, Southern California
1979—Jack Thompson, QB, Washington State
    Charles Alexander, RB, Louisiana State
1978—Ross Browner, DE, Notre Dame
    Blair Bush, C, Washington
1977—Eddie Edwards, DT, Miami
    Wilson Whitley, DT, Houston
    Mike Cobb, TE, Michigan State
1976—Billy Brooks, WR, Oklahoma
    Archie Griffin, RB, Ohio State
1975—Glenn Cameron, LB, Florida
1974—Bill Kollar, DT, Montana State
1973—Issac Curtis, WR, San Diego State
1972—Sherman White, DE, California
1971—Vernon Holland, T, Tennessee State
1970—Mike Reid, DT, Penn State
1969—Greg Cook, QB, Cincinnati
1968—Bob Johnson, C, Tennessee

CLEVELAND BROWNS

1985—(No Number One Selection)
1984—Don Rogers, DB, UCLA
1983—(No Number One Selection)
1982—Chip Banks, LB, Southern California
1981—Hanford Dixon, CB, Southern Mississippi
1980—Charles White, RB, Southern California

1979—Willis Adams, WR, Houston
1978—Clay Matthews, LB, Southern California
      Ozzie Newsome, WR, Alabama
1977—Robert Jackson, LB, Texas A&M
1976—Mike Pruitt, RB, Purdue
1975—Mack Mitchell, DE, Houston
1974— (No Number One Selection)
1973—Steve Holden, WR, Arizona State
      Pete Adams, G, Southern California
1972—Thom Darden, DB, Michigan
1971—Clarence Scott, DB, Kansas State
1970—Mike Phipps, QB, Purdue
      Bob McKay, T, Texas
1969—Ron Johnson, RB, Michigan
1968—Marvin Upshaw, DE, Trinity (Tex.)
1967—Bob Matheson, LB, Duke
1966—Milt Morin, TE, Massachusetts
1965— (No Number One Selection)
1964—Paul Warfield, WR, Ohio State
1963—Tom Hutchinson, TE, Kentucky
1962—Gary Collins, WR, Maryland
      Leroy Jackson, B, Western Illinois
1961— (No Number One Selection)
1960—Jim Houston, DE, Ohio State
1959—Rich Kreitling, DE, Illinois
1958—Jim Shofner, DB, Texas Christian
1957—Jim Brown, B, Syracuse
1956—Preston Carpenter, B, Arkansas
1955—Kent Burris, C, Oklahoma
1954—Bobby Garrett, QB, Stanford*
      John Bauer, G, Illinois
1953—Doug Atkins, DT, Tennessee
1952—Bert Rechichar, DB, Tennessee
      Harry Agganis, QB, Boston U.
1951—Ken Konz, B, Louisiana State
1950—Ken Carpenter, B, Oregon State

DALLAS COWBOYS

1985—Kevin Brooks, DE, Michigan
1984—Billy Cannon, Jr., LB, Texas A&M
1983—Jim Jeffcoat, DE, Arizona State
1982—Rod Hill, DB, Kentucky State
1981—Howard Richards, T, Missouri
1980— (No Number One Selection)
1979—Robert Shaw, C, Tennessee
1978—Larry Bethea, DE, Michigan State
1977—Tony Dorsett, RB, Pittsburgh
1976—Aaron Kyle, DB, Wyoming
1975—Randy White, LB, Maryland
      Thomas Henderson, LB, Langston
1974—Ed Jones, DE, Tennessee State*
      Charles Young, RB, North Carolina State
1973—Billy Joe DuPree, TE, Michigan State
1972—Bill Thomas, RB, Boston College
1971—Tody Smith, DE, Southern California
1970—Duane Thomas, RB, West Texas State
1969—Calvin Hill, RB, Yale
1968—Dennis Homan, WR, Alabama
1967— (No Number One Selection)
1966—John Niland, G, Iowa
1965—Craig Morton, QB, California
1964—Scott Appleton, DT, Texas
1963—Lee Roy Jordan, LB, Alabama
1962— (No Number One Selection)
1961—Bob Lilly, DT, Texas Christian

DENVER BRONCOS

1985—Steve Sewell, RB, Oklahoma
1984— (No Number One Selection)
1983—Chris Hinton, G, Northwestern
1982—Gerald Willhite, RB, San Jose State
1981—Dennis Smith, DB, Southern California
1980— (No Number One Selection)
1979—Kelvin Clark, T, Nebraska
1978—Don Latimer, DT, Miami (Fla.)
1977—Steve Schindler, G, Boston College
1976—Tom Glassic, G, Virginia
1975—Louis Wright, DB, San Jose State
1974—Randy Gradishar, LB, Ohio State
1973—Otis Armstrong, RB, Purdue
1972—Riley Odoms, TE, Houston
1971—Marv Montgomery, T, Southern California

1970—Bob Anderson, RB, Colorado
1969— (No Number One Selection)
1968— (No Number One Selection)
1967—Floyd Little, RB, Syracuse
1966—Jerry Shay, DT, Purdue
1965— (No Number One Selection)
1964—Bob Brown, T, Nebraska
1963—Kermit Alexander, DB, UCLA
1962—Merlin Olsen, DT, Utah State
1961—Bob Gaiters, RB, New Mexico State
1960—Roger Leclerc, C, Trinity (Conn.)

DETROIT LIONS

1985—Lomas Brown, T, Florida
1984—David Lewis, TE, California
1983—James Jones, RB, Florida
1982—Jimmy Williams, LB, Nebraska
1981—Mark Nichols, WR, San Jose State
1980—Billy Sims, RB, Oklahoma*
1979—Keith Dorney, T, Penn State
1978—Luther Bradley, DB, Notre Dame
1977— (No Number One Selection)
1976—James Hunter, DB, Grambling
1975—Lynn Boden, G, South Dakota State
1974—Ed O'Neil, LB, Penn State
1973—Ernie Price, DE, Texas A&I
1972—Herb Orvis, DE, Colorado
1971—Bob Bell, DT, Cincinnati
1970—Steve Owens, RB, Oklahoma
1969— (No Number One Selection)
1968—Greg Landry, QB, Massachusetts
1967—Mel Farr, RB, UCLA
1966— (No Number One Selection)
1965—Tom Nowatzke, RB, Indiana
1964—Pete Beathard, QB, Southern California
1963—Daryl Sanders, T, Ohio State
1962—John Hadl, QB, Kansas
1961— (No Number One Selection)
1960—John Robinson, DB, Louisiana State
1959—Nick Pietrosante, B, Notre Dame
1958—Alex Karras, DT, Iowa
1957—Bill Glass, G, Baylor
1956—Howard Cassidy, B, Ohio State
1955—Dave Middleton, B, Auburn
1954—Dick Chapman, T, Rice
1953—Harley Sewell, G, Texas
1952— (No Number One Selection)
1951— (No Number One Selection)
1950—Leon Hart, E, Notre Dame*
1949—John Rauch, B, Georgia
1948—Y.A. Tittle, B, Louisiana State
1947—Glenn Davis, B, Army
1946—Bill Dellastatious, B, Missouri
1945—Frank Szymanski, B, Notre Dame
1944—Otto Graham, B, Northwestern
1943—Frank Sinkwich, B, Georgia*
1942—Bob Westfall, B, Michigan
1941—Jim Thomason, B, Texas A&M
1940—Doyle Nave, B, Southern California
1939—John Pingel, B, Michigan State
1938—Alex Wojciechowicz, C, Fordham
1937—Lloyd Cardwell, B, Nebraska
1936—Sid Wagner, G, Michigan State

GREEN BAY PACKERS

1985—Ken Ruettgers, T, Southern California
1984—Alphonso Carreker, DT, Florida State
1983—Tim Lewis, DB, Pittsburgh
1982—Ron Hallstrom, G, Iowa
1981—Rich Campbell, QB, California
1980—Bruce Clark, DT, Penn State
      George Cumby, LB, Oklahoma
1979—Eddie Lee Ivery, RB, Georgia Tech
1978—James Lofton, WR, Stanford
      John Anderson, LB, Michigan
1977—Mike Butler, DE, Kansas
      Ezra Johnson, DE, Morris Brown
1976—Mark Koncar, T, Colorado
1975— (No Number One Selection)
1974—Barty Smith, RB, Richmond
1973—Barry Smith, WR, Florida State

1972—Willie Buchanon, DB, San Diego State
    Jerry Tagge, QB, Nebraska
1971—John Brockington, RB, Ohio State
1970—Mike McCoy, DT, Notre Dame
    Rich McGeorge, TE, Elon
1969—Rich Moore, DT, Villanova
1968—Fred Carr, LB, Texas-El Paso
    Bill Lueck, G, Arizona
1967—Bob Hyland, C, Boston College
    Don Horn, QB, San Diego State
1966—Gale Gillingham, G, Minnesota
    Jim Grabowski, RB, Illinois
1965—Donny Anderson, RB, Texas Tech
    Larry Elkins, E, Baylor
1964—Lloyd Voss, DT, Nebraska
1963—Dave Robinson, LB, Penn State
1962—Earl Gros, RB, Louisiana State
1961—Herb Adderley, DB, Michigan State
1960—Tom Moore, RB, Vanderbilt
1959—Randy Duncan, B, Iowa*
1958—Dan Currie, C, Michigan State
1957—Paul Hornung, B, Notre Dame*
    Ron Kramer, E, Michigan
1956—Jack Losch, B, Miami
1955—Tom Bettis, G, Purdue
1954—Art Hunter, T, Notre Dame
1953—Al Carmichael, B, Southern California
1952—Babe Parilli, QB, Kentucky
1951—Bob Gain, T, Kentucky
1950—Clayton Tonnemaker, G, Minnesota
1949—Stan Heath, B, Nevada
1948—Earl Girard, B, Wisconsin
1947—Ernie Case, B, UCLA
1946—Johnny Strzykalski, B, Marquette
1945—Walt Schlinkman, G, Texas Tech
1944—Merv Pregulman, G, Michigan
1943—Dick Wildung, T, Minnesota
1942—Urban Odson, T, Minnesota
1941—George Paskvan, B, Wisconsin
1940—Hal Van Every, B, Marquette
1939—Larry Buhler, B, Minnesota
1938—Cecil Isbell, B, Purdue
1937—Ed Jankowski, B, Wisconsin
1936—Russ Letlow, G, San Francisco

HOUSTON OILERS

1985—Ray Childress, DE, Texas A & M
    Richard Johnson, DB, Wisconsin
1984—Dean Steinkuhler, G, Nebraska
1983—Bruce Matthews, G, Southern California
1982—Mike Munchak, G, Penn State
1981— (No Number One Selection)
1980— (No Number One Selection)
1979— (No Number One Selection)
1978—Earl Campbell, RB, Texas*
1977—Morris Towns, T, Missouri
1976— (No Number One Selection)
1975—Robert Brazile, LB, Jackson State
    Don Hardeman, RB, Texas A & I
1974— (No Number One Selection)
1973—John Matuszak, DE, Tampa*
    George Amundson, RB, Iowa State
1972—Greg Sampson, DE, Stanford
1971—Dan Pastorini, QB, Santa Clara
1970—Doug Wilkerson, G, North Carolina Central
1969—Ron Pritchard, LB, Arizona State
1968— (No Number One Selection)
1967—George Webster, LB, Michigan State
    Tom Regner, G, Notre Dame
1966—Tommy Nobis, LB, Texas
1965—Lawrence Elkins, WR, Baylor* (AFL)
1964—Scott Appleton, DT, Texas
1963—Danny Brabham, LB, Arkansas
1962—Ray Jacobs, DT, Howard Payne
1961—Mike Ditka, E, Pittsburgh
1960—Billy Cannon, RB, Louisiana State

INDIANAPOLIS COLTS

1985—Duane Bickett, LB, Southern California
1984—Leonard Coleman, DB, Vanderbilt
    Ron Solt, G, Maryland
1983—John Elway, QB, Stanford*

1982—Johnie Cooks, LB, Mississippi State
    Art Schlichter, QB, Ohio State
1981—Randy McMillan, RB, Pittsburgh
    Donnell Thompson, DT, North Carolina
1980—Curtis Dickey, RB, Texas A & M
    Derrick Hatchett, DB, Texas
1979—Barry Krauss, LB, Alabama
1978—Reese McCall, TE, Auburn
1977—Randy Burke, WR, Kentucky
1976—Ken Novak, DT, Purdue
1975—Ken Huff, G, North Carolina
1974—John Dutton, DE, Nebraska
    Roger Carr, WR, Louisiana Tech
1973—Bert Jones, QB, Louisiana State
    Joe Ehrmann, DT, Syracuse
1972—Tom Drougas, T, Oregon
1971—Don McCauley, RB, North Carolina
    Leonard Dunlap, DB, North Texas State
1970—Norm Bulaich, RB, Texas Christian
1969—Eddie Hinton, WR, Oklahoma
1968—John Williams, G, Minnesota
1967—Bubba Smith, DT, Michigan State*
    Jim Detwiler, RB, Michigan
1966—Sam Ball, T, Kentucky
1965—Mike Curtis, LB, Duke
1964—Marv Woodson, DB, Indiana
1963—Bob Vogel, T, Ohio State
1962—Wendell Harris, DB, Louisiana State
1961—Tom Matte, RB, Ohio State
1960—Ron Mix, T, Southern California
1959—Jackie Burkett, C, Auburn
1958—Lenny Lyles, B, Louisville
1957—Jim Parker, T, Ohio State
1956—Lenny Moore, B, Penn State
1955—George Shaw, B, Oregon*
    Alan Ameche, B, Wisconsin
1954—Cotton Davidson, B, Baylor
1953—Billy Vessels, B, Oklahoma

KANSAS CITY CHIEFS

1985—Ethan Horton, RB, North Carolina
1984—Bill Maas, DT, Pittsburgh
    John Alt, T, Iowa
1983—Todd Blackledge, QB, Penn State
1982—Anthony Hancock, WR, Tennessee
1981—Willie Scott, TE, South Carolina
1980—Brad Budde, G, Southern California
1979—Mike Bell, DE, Colorado State
    Steve Fuller, QB, Clemson
1978—Art Still, DE, Kentucky
1977—Gary Green, DB, Baylor
1976—Rod Walters, G, Iowa
1975— (No Number One Selection)
1974—Woody Green, RB, Arizona State
1973— (No Number One Selection)
1972—Jeff Kinney, RB, Nebraska
1971—Elmo Wright, WR, Houston
1970—Sid Smith, T, Southern California
1969—Jim Marsalis, DB, Tennessee State
1968—Mo Moorman, G, Texas A & M
    George Daney, G, Texas-El Paso
1967—Gene Trosch, DE, Miami
1966—Aaron Brown, DE, Minnesota
1965—Gale Sayers, RB, Kansas
1964—Pete Beathard, QB, Southern California
1963—Buck Buchanan, DT, Grambling* (AFL)
    Ed Budde, G, Michigan State
1962—Ronnie Bull, RB, Baylor
1961—E.J. Holub, C, Texas Tech
1960—Don Meredith, QB, Southern Methodist

LOS ANGELES RAIDERS

1985—Jessie Hester, WR, Florida State
1984— (No Number One Selection)
1983—Don Mosebar, T, Southern California
1982—Marcus Allen, RB, Southern California
1981—Ted Watts, DB, Texas Tech
    Curt Marsh, G, Washington
1980—Marc Wilson, QB, Brigham Young
1979— (No Number One Selection)
1978— (No Number One Selection)
1977— (No Number One Selection)

1976— (No Number One Selection)
1975—Neal Colzie, DB, Ohio State
1974—Henry Lawrence, T, Florida A & M
1973—Ray Guy, P, Southern Mississippi
1972—Mike Siani, WR, Villanova
1971—Jack Tatum, DB, Ohio State
1970—Raymond Chester, TE, Morgan State
1969—Art Thoms, DT, Syracuse
1968—Eldridge Dickey, QB, Tennessee State
1967—Gene Upshaw, G, Texas A & I
1966—Rodger Bird, DB, Kentucky
1965—Harry Schuh, T, Memphis State
1964—Tony Lorick, RB, Arizona State
1963— (No Number One Selection)
1962—Roman Gabriel, QB, N.C. State* (AFL)
1961—Joe Rutgens, DT, Illinois
1960—Dale Hackbart, DB, Wisconsin

LOS ANGELES RAMS

1985—Jerry Gray, DB, Texas
1984— (No Number One Selection)
1983—Eric Dickerson, RB, Southern Methodist
1982—Barry Redden, RB, Richmond
1981—Mel Owens, LB, Michigan
1980—Johnnie Johnson, DB, Texas
1979—George Andrews, LB, Nebraska
      Kent Hill, G, Georgia Tech
1978—Elvis Peacock, RB, Oklahoma
1977—Bob Brudzinski, LB, Ohio State
1976—Kevin McLain, LB, Colorado State
1975—Mike Fanning, DT, Notre Dame
      Dennis Harrah, G, Miami
      Doug France, T, Ohio State
1974—John Cappelletti, RB, Penn State
1973— (No Number One Selection)
1972— (No Number One Selection)
1971—Isiah Robertson, LB, Southern
      Jack Youngblood, DE, Florida
1970—Jack Reynolds, LB, Tennessee
1969—Larry Smith, RB, Florida
      Jim Seymour, E, Notre Dame
      Bob Klein, TE, Southern California
1968— (No Number One Selection)
1967— (No Number One Selection)
1966—Tom Mack, G, Michigan
1965—Clancy Williams, DB, Washington State
1964—Bill Munson, QB, Utah State
1963—Terry Baker, QB, Oregon State*
      Rufus Guthrie, G, Georgia Tech
1962—Roman Gabriel, QB, North Carolina State
      Merlin Olsen, DT, Utah State
1961—Marlin McKeever, LB, Southern California
1960—Billy Cannon, RB, Louisiana State*
1959—Paul Dickson, G, Baylor
      Dick Bass, B, Pacific
1958—Lou Michaels, T, Kentucky
      Jim Phillips, E, Auburn
1957—Jon Arnett, B, Southern California
      Del Shofner, B, Baylor
1956—Joe Marconi, B, West Virginia
      Charlie Horton, B, Vanderbilt
1955—Larry Morris, C, Georgia Tech
1954—Ed Beatty, C, Cincinnati
1953—Donn Moomaw, C, UCLA
      Ed Barker, E, Washington State
1952—Bill Wade, B, Vanderbilt*
      Bob Carey, E, Michigan State
1951—Bud McFadin, G, Texas
1950—Ralph Pasquariello, B, Villanova
      Stan West, G, Oklahoma
1949—Bobby Thomason, B, Virginia Military
1948— (No Number One Selection)
1947—Herman Wedemeyer, B, St. Mary's (Calif.)
1946—Emil Sitko, B, Notre Dame
1945—Elroy Hirsch, B, Wisconsin
1944—Tony Butkovich, B, Illinois
1943—Mike Holovak, B, Boston College
1942—Jack Wilson, B, Baylor
1941—Rudy Mucha, C, Washington
1940—Ollie Cordill, B, Rice
1939—Parker Hall, B, Mississippi
1938—Corbett Davis, B, Indiana*
1937—Johnny Drake, B, Purdue

MIAMI DOLPHINS

1985—Lorenzo Hampton, RB, Florida
1984—Jackie Shipp, LB, Oklahoma
1983—Dan Marino, QB, Pittsburgh
1982—Roy Foster, G, Southern California
1981—David Overstreet, RB, Oklahoma
1980—Don McNeal, DB, Alabama
1979—Jon Giesler, T, Michigan
1978— (No Number One Selection)
1977—A.J. Duhe, DE, Louisiana State
1976—Larry Gordon, LB, Arizona State
      Kim Bokamper, LB, San Jose State
1975—Darryl Carlton, T, Tampa
1974—Don Reese, DE, Jackson State
1973— (No Number One Selection)
1972—Mike Kadish, DT, Notre Dame
1971— (No Number One Selection)
1970— (No Number One Selection)
1969—Bill Stanfill, DE, Georgia
1968—Larry Csonka, RB, Syracuse
      Doug Crusan, T, Indiana
1967—Bob Griese, QB, Purdue
1966—Jim Grabowski, RB, Illinois*
      Rick Norton, QB, Kentucky

MINNESOTA VIKINGS

1985—Chris Doleman, LB, Pittsburgh
1984—Keith Millard, DE, Washington State
1983—Joey Browner, DB, Southern California
1982—Darrin Nelson, RB, Stanford
1981— (No Number One Selection)
1980—Doug Martin, DT, Washington
1979—Ted Brown, RB, North Carolina State
1978—Randy Holloway, DE, Pittsburgh
1977—Tommy Kramer, QB, Rice
1976—James White, RB, Oklahoma State
1975—Mark Mullaney, DE, Colorado State
1974—Fred McNeill, LB, UCLA
      Steve Riley, T, Southern California
1973—Chuck Foreman, RB, Miami (Fla.)
1972—Jeff Siemon, LB, Stanford
1971—Leo Hayden, RB, Ohio State
1970—John Ward, DT, Oklahoma State
1969— (No Number One Selection)
1968—Ron Yary, T, Southern California*
1967—Clint Jones, RB, Michigan State
      Gene Washington, WR, Michigan State
      Alan Page, DT, Notre Dame
1966—Jerry Shay, DT, Purdue
1965—Jack Snow, WR, Notre Dame
1964—Carl Eller, DE, Minnesota
1963—Jim Dunaway, T, Mississippi
1962— (No Number One Selection)
1961—Tommy Mason, RB, Tulane*

NEW ENGLAND PATRIOTS

1985—Trevor Matich, C, Brigham Young
1984—Irving Fryar, WR, Nebraska*
1983—Tony Eason, QB, Illinois
1982—Kenneth Sims, DT, Texas*
1981—Brian Holloway, T, Stanford
1980—Roland James, DB, Tennessee
      Vagas Ferguson, RB, Notre Dame
1979—Rick Sanford, DB, South Carolina
1978—Bob Cryder, G, Alabama
1977—Raymond Clayborn, DB, Texas
      Stanley Morgan, WR, Tennessee
1976—Mike Haynes, DB, Arizona State
      Pete Brock, C, Colorado
      Tim Fox, DB, Ohio State
1975—Russ Francis, TE, Oregon
1974— (No Number One Selection)
1973—John Hannah, G, Alabama
      Sam Cunningham, RB, Southern California
      Darryl Stingley, WR, Purdue
1972— (No Number One Selection)
1971—Jim Plunkett, QB, Stanford*
1970—Phil Olsen, DT, Utah State
1969—Ron Sellers, WR, Florida State
1968—Dennis Byrd, DE, North Carolina State
1967—John Charles, DB, Purdue

1966—Karl Singer, T, Purdue
     Willie Townes, T, Tulsa
1965—Jerry Rush, DE, Michigan State
     Dave McCormick, T, Louisiana State
1964—Jack Concannon, QB, Boston Col* (AFL)
1963—Art Graham, E, Boston College
1962—Gary Collins, WR, Maryland
1961—Tommy Mason, RB, Tulane
1960—Ron Burton, RB, Northwestern

NEW ORLEANS SAINTS

1985—Alvin Toles, LB, Tennessee
1984—(No Number One Selection)
1983—(No Number One Selection)
1982—Lindsay Scott, WR, Georgia
1981—George Rogers, RB, South Carolina*
1980—Stan Brock, T, Colorado
1979—Russell Erxleben, P, Texas
1978—Wes Chandler, WR, Florida
1977—Joe Campbell, DE, Maryland
1976—Chuck Muncie, RB, California
1975—Larry Burton, WR, Purdue
     Kurt Schumacher, G, Ohio State
1974—Rick Middleton, LB, Ohio State
1973—(No Number One Selection)
1972—Royce Smith, G, Georgia
1971—Archie Manning, QB, Mississippi
1970—Ken Burrough, WR, Texas Southern
1969—John Shinners, G, Xavier (Ohio)
1968—Kevin Hardy, DE, Notre Dame
1967—Les Kelley, RB, Alabama

NEW YORK GIANTS

1985—George Adams, RB, Kentucky
1984—Carl Banks, LB, Michigan State
     Bill Roberts, T, Ohio State
1983—Terry Kinard, DB, Clemson
1982—Butch Woolfolk, RB, Michigan
1981—Lawrence Taylor, LB, North Carolina
1980—Mark Haynes, DB, Colorado
1979—Phil Simms, QB, Morehead State
1978—Gordon King, T, Stanford
1977—Gary Jeter, DT, Southern California
1976—Troy Archer, DE, Colorado
1975—(No Number One Selection)
1974—John Hicks, G, Ohio State
1973—(No Number One Selection)
1972—Eldridge Small, DB, Texas A & I
1971—Rocky Thompson, RB, West Texas State
1970—Jim Files, LB, Oklahoma
1969—Fred Dryer, DE, San Diego State
1968—(No Number One Selection)
1967—(No Number One Selection)
1966—Francis Peay, T, Missouri
1965—Tucker Frederickson, RB, Auburn*
1964—Joe Don Looney, RB, Oklahoma
1963—(No Number One Selection)
1962—Jerry Hillebrand, LB, Colorado
1961—(No Number One Selection)
1960—Lou Cordileone, G, Clemson
1959—Lee Grosscup, B, Utah
1958—Phil King, B, Vanderbilt
1957—(No Number One Selection)
1956—Henry Moore, B, Arkansas
1955—Joe Heap, B, Notre Dame
1954—(No Number One Selection)
1953—Bobby Marlow, B, Alabama
1952—Frank Gifford, B, Southern California
1951—Kyle Rote, B, Southern Methodist*
1950—Travis Tidwell, B, Auburn
1949—Paul Page, B, Southern Methodist
1948—Tony Minisi, B, Pennsylvania
1947—Vic Schwall, B, Northwestern
1946—George Connor, T, Notre Dame
1945—Elmer Barbour, B, Wake Forest
1944—Billy Hillenbrand, B, Indiana
1943—Steve Filipowicz, B, Fordham
1942—Merle Hapes, B, Mississippi
1941—George Franck, B, Minnesota
1940—Grenville Lansdell, B, Southern California
1939—Walt Nielson, B, Arizona
1938—George Karamatic, B, Gonzaga

1937—Ed Widseth, T, Minnesota
1936—Art Lewis, T, Ohio

NEW YORK JETS

1985—Al Toon, WR, Wisconsin
1984—Russell Carter, DB, Southern Methodist
     Ron Faurot, DE, Arkansas
1983—Ken O'Brien, QB, California-Davis
1982—Bob Crable, LB, Notre Dame
1981—Freeman McNeil, RB, UCLA
1980—Lam Jones, WR, Texas
1979—Marty Lyons, DT, Alabama
1978—Chris Ward, T, Ohio State
1977—Marvin Powell, T, Southern California
1976—Richard Todd, QB, Alabama
1975—(No Number One Selection)
1974—Carl Barzilauskas, DT, Indiana
1973—Burgess Owens, DB, Miami
1972—Jerome Barkum, WR, Jackson State
     Mike Taylor, LB, Michigan
1971—John Riggins, RB, Kansas
1970—Steve Tannen, DB, Florida
1969—Dave Foley, T, Ohio State
1968—Lee White, RB, Weber State
1967—Paul Seiler, G, Notre Dame
1966—Bill Yearby, DT, Michigan
1965—Joe Namath, QB, Alabama
     Tom Nowatzke, RB, Indiana
1964—Matt Snell, RB, Ohio State
1963—Jerry Stovall, RB, Louisiana State
1962—Sandy Stephens, QB, Minnesota
1961—Tom Brown, G, Minnesota
1960—George Izo, QB, Notre Dame

PHILADELPHIA EAGLES

1985—Kevin Allen, T, Indiana
1984—Kenny Jackson, WR, Penn State
1983—Michael Haddix, RB, Mississippi State
1982—Mike Quick, WR, North Carolina State
1981—Leonard Mitchell, DE, Houston
1980—Roynell Young, DB, Alcorn State
1979—Jerry Robinson, LB, UCLA
1978—(No Number One Selection)
1977—(No Number One Selection)
1976—(No Number One Selection)
1975—(No Number One Selection)
1974—(No Number One Selection)
1973—Jerry Sisemore, T, Texas
     Charle Young, TE, Southern California
1972—John Reaves, QB, Florida
1971—Richard Harris, DE, Grambling
1970—Steve Zabel, E, Oklahoma
1969—Leroy Keyes, RB, Purdue
1968—Tim Rossovich, DE, Southern California
1967—Harry Jones, RB, Arkansas
1966—Randy Beisler, T, Indiana
1965—(No Number One Selection)
1964—Bob Brown, T, Nebraska
1963—Ed Budde, T, Michigan State
1962—(No Number One Selection)
1961—Art Baker, B, Syracuse
1960—Ron Burton, B, Northwestern
1959—(No Number One Selection)
1958—Walter Kowalczyk, B, Michigan State
1957—Clarence Peaks, B, Michigan State
1956—Bob Pellegrini, C, Maryland
1955—Dick Bielski, B, Maryland
1954—Neil Worden, B, Notre Dame
1953—(No Number One Selection)
1952—John Bright, B, Drake
1951—Ebert Van Buren, B, Louisiana State
1950—Harry Grant, E, Minnesota
1949—Chuck Bednarik, C, Pennsylvania*
     Frank Tripucka, QB, Notre Dame
1948—Clyde Scott, B, Arkansas
1947—Neil Armstrong, E, Oklahoma A & M
1946—Leo Riggs, B, Southern California
1945—John Yonaker, E, Notre Dame
1944—Steve Van Buren, B, Louisiana State
1943—Joe Muha, B, Virginia Military
1942—Pete Kmetovic, B, Stanford
1941—(No Number One Selection)

1940—Wes McAfee, B, Duke
1939—Davey O'Brien, QB, Texas Christian
1938—John McDonald, B, Nebraska
1937—Sam Francis, B, Nebraska*
1936—Jay Berwanger, B, Chicago*

PITTSBURGH STEELERS

1985—Darryl Sims, DT, Wisconsin
1984—Louis Lipps, WR, Southern Mississippi
1983—Gabriel Rivera, DT, Texas Tech
1982—Walter Abercrombie, RB, Baylor
1981—Keith Gary, DE, Oklahoma
1980—Mark Malone, QB, Arizona State
1979—Greg Hawthorne, RB, Baylor
1978—Ron Johnson, DB, Eastern Michigan
1977—Robin Cole, LB, New Mexico
1976—Bennie Cunningham, TE, Clemson
1975—Dave Brown, DB, Michigan
1974—Lynn Swann, WR, Southern California
1973—James Thomas, DB, Florida State
1972—Franco Harris, RB, Penn State
1971—Frank Lewis, WR, Grambling
1970—Terry Bradshaw, QB, Louisiana Tech*
1969—Joe Greene, DT, North Texas State
1968—Mike Taylor, T, Southern California
1967—(No Number One Selection)
1966—Dick Leftridge, RB, West Virginia
1965—(No Number One Selection)
1964—Paul Martha, RB, Pittsburgh
1963—(No Number One Selection)
1962—Bob Ferguson, RB, Ohio State
1961—(No Number One Selection)
1960—Jack Spikes, B, Texas Christian
1959—(No Number One Selection)
1958—(No Number One Selection)
1957—Len Dawson, QB, Purdue
1956—Gary Glick, B, Colorado State*
 Art Davis, B, Mississippi State
1955—Frank Varrichione, T, Notre Dame
1954—John Lattner, B, Notre Dame
1953—Ted Marchibroda, QB, St. Bonaventure
1952—Ed Modzelewski, B, Maryland
1951—Clarence Avinger, B, Alabama
1950—Lynn Chandnois, B, Michigan State
1949—Bobby Gage, B, Clemson
1948—Dan Edwards, E, Georgia
1947—Hub Bechtol, E, Texas
1946—Doc Blanchard, B, Army
1945—Paul Duhart, B, Florida
1944—Johnny Podesto, B, St. Mary's (Calif.)
1943—Bill Daley, B, Minnesota
1942—Bill Dudley, B, Virginia*
1941—Chet Gladchuk, C, Boston College
1940—Kay Eakin, B, Arkansas
1939—(No Number One Selection)
1938—Byron White, B, Colorado
 Frank Filchock, B, Indiana
1937—Mike Basrak, C, Duquesne
1936—Bill Shakespeare, B, Notre Dame

ST. LOUIS CARDINALS

1985—Freddie Joe Nunn, LB, Mississippi
1984—Clyde Duncan, WR, Tennessee
1983—Leonard Smith, DB, McNeese State
1982—Luis Sharpe, T, UCLA
1981—E.J. Junior, LB, Alabama
1980—Curtis Greer, DE, Michigan
1979—Ottis Anderson, RB, Miami (Fla.)
1978—Steve Little, K, Arkansas
 Ken Greene, DB, Washington State
1977—Steve Pisarkiewicz, QB, Missouri
1976—Mike Dawson, DT, Arizona
1975—Tim Gray, DB, Texas A&M
1974—J.V. Cain, TE, Colorado
1973—Dave Butz, DT, Purdue
1972—Bobby Moore, RB, Oregon
1971—Norm Thompson, DB, Utah
1970—Larry Stegent, RB, Texas A&M
1969—Roger Wehrli, DB, Missouri
1968—MacArthur Lane, RB, Utah State
1967—Dave Williams, WR, Washington
1966—Carl McAdams, LB, Oklahoma

1965—Joe Namath, QB, Alabama
1964—Ken Kortas, DT, Louisville
1963—Jerry Stovall, DB, Louisiana State
 Don Brumm, E, Purdue
1962—Fate Echols, DT, Northwestern
 Irv Goode, C, Kentucky
1961—Ken Rice, T, Auburn
1960—George Izo, QB, Notre Dame
1959—Billy Stacy, B, Mississippi State
1958—King Hill, B, Rice*
1957—Jerry Tubbs, C, Oklahoma
1956—Joe Childress, B, Auburn
1955—Max Boydston, E, Oklahoma
1954—Lamar McHan, B, Arkansas
1953—Johnny Olszewski, QB, California
1952—Ollie Matson, B, San Francisco
1951—Jerry Groom, C, Notre Dame
1950—(No Number One Selection)
1949—Bill Fischer, G, Notre Dame
1948—Jim Spavital, B, Oklahoma A&M
1947—DeWitt (Tex) Coulter, T, Army
1946—Dub Jones, B, Louisiana State
1945—Charley Trippi, B, Georgia*
1944—Pat Harder, B, Wisconsin
1943—Glenn Dobbs, B, Tulsa
1942—Steve Lach, B, Duke
1941—John Kimbrough, B, Texas A&M
1940—George Cafego, B, Tennessee*
1939—Charles Aldrich, C, Texas Christian*
1938—Jack Robbins, B, Arkansas
1937—Ray Buivid, B, Marquette
1936—Jim Lawrence, B, Texas Christian

SAN DIEGO CHARGERS

1985—Jim Lachey, G, Ohio State
1984—Mossy Cade, DB, Texas
1983—Billy Ray Smith, LB, Arkansas
 Gary Anderson, WR, Arkansas
 Gill Byrd, DB, San Jose State
1982—(No Number One Selection)
1981—James Brooks, RB, Auburn
1980—(No Number One Selection)
1979—Kellen Winslow, TE, Missouri
1978—John Jefferson, WR, Arizona State
1977—Bob Rush, C, Memphis State
1976—Joe Washington, RB, Oklahoma
1975—Gary Johnson, DT, Grambling
 Mike Williams, DB, Louisiana State
1974—Bo Matthews, RB, Colorado
 Don Goode, LB, Kansas
1973—Johnny Rodgers, WR, Nebraska
1972—(No Number One Selection)
1971—Leon Burns, RB, Long Beach State
1970—Walker Gillette, WR, Richmond
1969—Marty Domres, QB, Columbia
 Bob Babich, LB, Miami (Ohio)
1968—Russ Washington, T, Missouri
 Jim Hill, DB, Texas A&I
1967—Ron Billingsley, DT, Wyoming
1966—Don Davis, T, Los Angeles State
1965—Steve DeLong, DE, Tennessee
1964—Ted Davis, E, Georgia Tech
1963—Walt Sweeney, E, Syracuse
1962—Bob Ferguson, RB, Ohio State
1961—Earl Faison, E, Indiana
1960—Monty Stickles, E, Notre Dame

SAN FRANCISCO 49ers

1985—Jerry Rice, WR, Mississippi Valley
1984—Todd Shell, LB, Brigham Young
1983—(No Number One Selection)
1982—(No Number One Selection)
1981—Ronnie Lott, DB, Southern California
1980—Earl Cooper, RB, Rice
 Jim Stuckey, DE, Clemson
1979—(No Number One Selection)
1978—Ken McAfee, TE, Notre Dame
 Dan Bunz, LB, Long Beach State
1977—(No Number One Selection)
1976—(No Number One Selection)
1975—Jimmy Webb, DT, Mississippi State

1974—Wilbur Jackson, RB, Alabama
    Bill Sandifer, DT, UCLA
1973—Mike Holmes, DB, Texas Southern
1972—Terry Beasley, WR, Auburn
1971—Tim Anderson, DB, Ohio State
1970—Cedrick Hardman, DE, North Texas State
    Bruce Taylor, DB, Boston U.
1969—Ted Kwalick, TE, Penn State
    Gene Washington, WR, Stanford
1968—Forrest Blue, C, Auburn
1967—Steve Spurrier, QB, Florida
    Cas Banaszek, LB, Northwestern
1966—Stan Hindman, DE, Mississippi
1965—Ken Willard, RB, North Carolina
    George Donnelly, DB, Illinois
1964—Dave Parks, E, Texas Tech*
1963—Kermit Alexander, RB, UCLA
1962—Lance Alworth, RB, Arkansas
1961—Jim Johnson, RB, UCLA
    Bernie Casey, RB, Bowling Green
    Bill Kilmer, QB, UCLA
1960—Monty Stickles, E, Notre Dame
1959—Dave Baker, RB, Oklahoma
    Dan James, C, Ohio State
1958—Jim Pace, RB, Michigan
    Charles Krueger, T, Texas A&M
1957—John Brodie, QB, Stanford
1956—Earl Morrall, QB, Michigan State
1955—Dick Moegel, HB, Rice
1954—Bernie Faloney, QB, Maryland
1953—Harry Babcock, E, Georgia*
    Tom Stolhandske, E, Texas
1952—Hugh McElhenny, RB, Washington
1951—Y.A. Tittle, QB, Louisiana State
1950—Leo Nomellini, T, Minnesota

SEATTLE SEAHAWKS

1985— (No Number One Selection)
1984—Terry Taylor, DB, Southern Illinois
1983—Curt Warner, RB, Penn State
1982—Jeff Bryant, DE, Clemson
1981—Kenny Easley, DB, UCLA
1980—Jacob Green, DE, Texas A&M
1979—Manu Tuiasosopo, DT, UCLA
1978—Keith Simpson, DB, Memphis State
1977—Steve August, G, Tulsa
1976—Steve Niehaus, DT, Notre Dame

TAMPA BAY BUCCANEERS

1985—Ron Holmes, DE, Washington
1984— (No Number One Selection)
1983— (No Number One Selection)
1982—Sean Farrell, G, Penn State
1981—Hugh Green, LB, Pittsburgh
1980—Ray Snell, T, Wisconsin
1979— (No Number One Selection)
1978—Doug Williams, QB, Grambling
1977—Ricky Bell, RB, Southern California*
1976—Lee Roy Selmon, DE, Oklahoma*

WASHINGTON REDSKINS

1985— (No Number One Selection)
1984— (No Number One Selection)
1983—Darrell Green, DB, Texas A&I
1982— (No Number One Selection)
1981—Mark May, T, Pittsburgh
1980—Art Monk, WR, Syracuse
1979— (No Number One Selection)
1978— (No Number One Selection)
1977— (No Number One Selection)
1976— (No Number One Selection)
1975— (No Number One Selection)
1974— (No Number One Selection)
1973— (No Number One Selection)
1972— (No Number One Selection)
1971— (No Number One Selection)
1970— (No Number One Selection)
1969— (No Number One Selection)
1968—Jim Smith, DB, Oregon
1967—Ray McDonald, RB, Idaho
1966—Charlie Gogolak, K, Princeton
1965— (No Number One Selection)
1964—Charley Taylor, RB, Arizona State
1963—Pat Richter, TE, Wisconsin
1962—Ernie Davis, RB, Syracuse*
    Leroy Jackson, RB, Illinois Central
1961—Joe Rutgens, T, Illinois
    Norm Snead, QB, Wake Forest
1960—Richie Lucas, QB, Penn State
1959—Don Allard, QB, Boston College
1958— (No Number One Selection)
1957—Don Bosseler, RB, Miami (Fla.)
1956—Ed Vereb, RB, Maryland
1955—Ralph Guglielmi, QB, Notre Dame
1954—Steve Meilinger, TE, Kentucky
1953—Jack Scarbath, QB, Maryland
1952—Larry Isbell, QB, Baylor
1951—Leon Heath, RB, Oklahoma
1950—George Thomas, RB, Oklahoma
1949—Rob Goode, RB, Texas A&M
1948—Harry Gilmer, QB, Alabama*
1947—Cal Rossi, B, UCLA
1946—Cal Rossi, B, UCLA
1945—Jim Hardy, B, Southern California
1944—Mike Micka, B, Colgate
1943—Jack Jenkins, B, Missouri
1942—Orban Sanders, B, Texas
1941—Forrest Evashevski, B, Michigan
1940—Ed Boell, B, New York U.
1939—I.B. Hale, T, Texas Christian
1938—Andy Farkas, B, Detroit
1937—Sammy Baugh, QB, Texas Christian
1936—Riley Smith, QB, Alabama

1984-85 INTERCONFERENCE TRADES

(Covering July 1984 through June 1985)

Tackle JERRY BAKER from Denver to Minnesota for a draft choice (7/3).

Cornerback MARIO CLARK from Buffalo to San Francisco for 4th-round choice in 1985 draft (7/16). Buffalo subsequently selected tackle DALE HELLESTRAE (Southern Methodist).

Running back PERRY HARRINGTON from Philadelphia to Cleveland for a draft choice (7/23).

Running back ROBERT ALEXANDER from Los Angeles Rams to San Diego for a draft choice (7/24).

Tackle DON SWAFFORD from Cincinnati to Tampa Bay for 6th-round choice in 1985 draft (7/24). Cincinnati subsequently selected tackle ERIC STOKES (Northeastern).

Quarterback JEFF CHRISTENSEN from Cincinnati to Los Angeles Rams for a draft choice (7/25).

Guard STEVE COURSON from Pittsburgh to Tampa Bay for guard RAY SNELL (7/30).

Wide receiver PRESTON DENNARD from Los Angeles Rams to Buffalo for 5th-round choice in 1985 draft (8/1). Los Angeles Rams subsequently selected linebacker KEVIN GREENE (Auburn).

Cornerback CHRIS WILLIAMS from Buffalo to Los Angeles Rams for a draft choice (8/1).

Tackle BILLY SHIELDS from San Diego to Minnesota for safety JOHN TURNER (8/10). Minnesota received 3rd-round choice in 1985 draft when SHIELDS did not report. Minnesota subsequently selected tackle TIM LONG (Memphis State).

Defensive end BRISON MANOR from Denver to Tampa Bay for a 1986 draft choice (8/13).

Punter DAVID FINZER from San Diego to Chicago for 12th-round choice in 1985 draft (8/15). San Diego subsequently selected tight end BRET PEARSON (Wisconsin).

Offensive lineman RICK DONNALLEY from Pittsburgh to Washington for 5th-round choice in 1985 draft (8/20). Pittsburgh subsequently selected linebacker CAM JACOBS (Kentucky).

Wide receiver PERRY TUTTLE from Buffalo to Tampa Bay for a draft choice (8/21).

Cornerback ROD HILL and 5th-round choice in 1985 draft from Dallas to Buffalo for 5th-round choice in 1985 draft and 1986 draft choice (8/23). Buffalo subsequently

selected wide receiver JIMMY TEAL (Texas A&M). Dallas subsequently selected center MATT DARWIN (Texas A&M).

Defensive tackle GARY BURLEY from Cincinnati to Atlanta for 7th-round choice in 1985 draft (8/23). Cincinnati subsequently selected running back KIM LOCKLIN (New Mexico State).

Cornerback GERALD SMALL from Miami to Atlanta for offensive lineman RONNIE LEE and 6th-round choice in 1985 draft (8/26). Miami subsequently selected wide receiver GEORGE SHORTHOSE (Missouri).

Defensive back GEORGE RADACHOWSKY from Los Angeles Rams to Indianapolis for 11th-round choice in 1985 draft (8/27). Los Angeles Rams subsequently selected quarterback DOUG FLUTIE (Boston College).

Cornerback ROD McSWAIN from Atlanta to New England for 8th-round choice in 1985 draft (8/27). Atlanta subsequently selected linebacker RONNIE WASHINGTON (Northeast Louisiana).

Defensive back KENNY HILL from Los Angeles Raiders to New York Giants for 7th-round choice in 1985 draft (8/27). Los Angeles Raiders subsequently selected tackle KEVIN BELCHER (Wisconsin).

Tackle MORRIS TOWNS from Los Angeles Raiders to Washington for 10th-round choice in 1985 draft (8/30). Los Angeles Raiders subsequently selected linebacker REGGIE McKENZIE (Tennessee).

Linebacker THOMAS HOWARD from Kansas City to St. Louis for 7th-round choice in 1985 draft (9/1).

Defensive back RICKY SMITH from New England to Washington for 7th-round choice in 1985 draft (9/11).

Defensive back BRIAN CARPENTER from Washington to Buffalo for 12th-round choice in 1985 draft (9/19). Washington subsequently selected defensive tackle DEAN HAMEL (Tulsa).

Defensive tackle GARY JOHNSON from San Diego to San Francisco for 5th- and 11th-round choices in 1986 draft (9/28).

Wide receiver CALVIN MUHAMMAD from Los Angeles Raiders to Washington for 4th-round choice in 1985 draft (10/3). Los Angeles Raiders subsequently selected linebacker JAMIE KIMMEL (Syracuse).

Running back EARL CAMPBELL from Houston to New Orleans for 1st-round choice in 1985 draft (10/9). Houston subsequently selected defensive back RICHARD JOHNSON (Wisconsin).

Linebacker BRAD VAN PELT from Minnesota to Los Angeles Raiders for 6th-round choice in 1985 draft and 2nd-round choice in 1986 draft (10/9). Minnesota subsequently selected nose tackle TIM NEWTON (Florida).

Running back BUTCH WOOLFOLK from New York Giants to Houston for 3rd-round choice in 1985 draft (3/21). New York Giants subsequently selected defensive back TYRONE DAVIS (Clemson).

Quarterback SCOTT BRUNNER from Denver to Green Bay for 1986 draft choice (4/25).

Green Bay traded 1st- and 2nd-round choices in 1985 draft to Buffalo for 1st-round choice in 1985 draft and 4th-round choice in 1986 draft (4/30). Buffalo subsequently selected defensive back DERRICK BURROUGHS (Memphis State) and wide receiver CHRIS BURKETT (Jackson State). Green Bay subsequently selected tackle KEN RUETTGERS (Southern California).

San Francisco traded 1st-, 2nd- and 3rd-round choices in 1985 draft to New England for 1st- and 3rd-round choices in 1985 draft (4/30). New England subsequently selected center TREVOR MATICH (Brigham Young), defensive end BEN THOMAS (Auburn) and defensive back AUDREY McMILLIAN (Houston). San Francisco subsequently selected wide receiver JERRY RICE (Mississippi Valley State) and running back RICKY MOORE (Alabama).

Quarterback JOE FERGUSON from Buffalo to Detroit for 1986 draft choice (4/30).

Kansas City traded 7th-round choice in 1985 draft to Washington for 6th-round choice in 1986 draft (4/30). Washington subsequently selected running back LIONEL VITAL (Nicholls State).

Quarterback GARY DANIELSON from Detroit to Cleveland for 1986 draft choice (5/1).

Tackle SCOTT RARIDON from Philadelphia to Denver for 1986 draft choice (5/8).

Quarterback RICH CAMPBELL from Green Bay to Los Angeles Raiders for 1986 draft choice (6/10).

1984-85 NATIONAL CONFERENCE TRADES
(Covering July 1984 through June 1985)

Linebacker BRAD VAN PELT from New York Giants to Minnesota for running back TONY GALBREATH (7/12).

Kicker JAN STENERUD from Green Bay to Minnesota for 7th-round choice in 1985 draft (7/17). Green Bay subsequently selected linebacker ERIC WILSON (Maryland).

Linebacker JOHN HARPER from Atlanta to St. Louis for a draft choice (8/13).

Quarterback BOB HOLLY from Washington to Philadelphia for 7th-round choice in 1985 draft (8/14). Washington subsequently selected wide receiver JAMIE HARRIS (Oklahoma State).

Tight end JUNIOR MILLER from Atlanta to New Orleans for 6th-round choice in 1985 draft (8/26). Atlanta subsequently selected defensive back REGGIE PLEASANT (Clemson).

Linebacker ANGELO KING from Dallas to Detroit for 1986 draft choice (8/27).

Defensive end BOOKER REESE from Tampa Bay to Los Angeles Rams for 12th-round choice in 1985 draft (9/4). Tampa Bay subsequently selected linebacker JIM MELKA (Wisconsin).

Quarterback STEVE DILS from Minnesota to Los Angeles Rams for 4th-round choice in 1985 draft (9/18). Minnesota subsequently selected defensive back KYLE MORRELL (Brigham Young).

Running back GEORGE ROGERS and 5th-, 10th- and 11th-round choices in 1985 draft from New Orleans to Washington for 1st-round choice in 1985 draft (4/26). Washington subsequently selected running back RAPHEL CHERRY (Hawaii), running back TERRY ORR (Texas) and guard RALEIGH McKENZIE (Tennessee). New Orleans subsequently selected linebacker ALVIN TOLES (Tennessee).

Atlanta traded 1st- and 3rd-round choices in 1985 draft to Minnesota for 1st-round choice in 1985 draft (4/30). Minnesota subsequently selected linebacker CHRIS DOLEMAN (Pittsburgh) and linebacker TIM MEAMBER (Washington). Atlanta subsequently selected tackle BILL FRALIC (Pittsburgh).

Running back JOE WASHINGTON, 2nd-round choice in 1985 draft and 1st-round choice in 1986 draft from Washington to Atlanta for 2nd-round choice in 1985 draft and 2nd- and 6th-round choices in 1986 draft (4/30). Washington subsequently selected defensive back TORY NIXON (San Diego State).

Atlanta traded 2nd- and 5th-round

choices in 1985 draft to St. Louis for 2nd-round choice in 1985 draft (4/30). Atlanta subsequently selected defensive end MIKE GANN (Notre Dame). St. Louis subse- quently selected tackle SCOTT BERGOLD (Wisconsin) and tight end K.D. DUNN (Clemson).

1984-85 AMERICAN CONFERENCE TRADES
(Covering July 1984 through June 1985)

Rights to kicker STU CRUM from New York Jets to Kansas City for a draft choice (7/17).

Tackle BOB CRYDER from New England to Seattle for 2nd-round choice in 1986 draft (7/31).

Wide receiver BUTCH JOHNSON from Houston to Denver for 3rd-round choice in 1985 draft (8/20). Houston subsequently selected center MIKE KELLEY (Notre Dame).

Punter LUKE PRESTRIDGE from Denver to New England for 10th-round choice in 1985 draft (8/20). Denver subsequently selected quarterback BUDDY FUNCK (New Mexico).

Wide receiver GREG HAWTHORNE from Pittsburgh to New England for 9th-round choice in 1985 draft (8/21). Pittsburgh subsequently selected defensive back ANDRE HARRIS (Minnesota).

Running back PETE JOHNSON from San Diego to Miami for rights to defensive tackle DEWEY FORTE and 2nd-round choice in 1985 draft (9/22). San Diego subsequently selected defensive back JEFFERY DALE (Louisiana State).

Rights to linebacker RICKY HUNLEY from Cincinnati to Denver for 1st- and 3rd-round choices in 1986 draft and 5th-round choice in 1987 draft (10/9).

Cornerback LAWRENCE JOHNSON from Cleveland to Buffalo for a draft choice (10/9).

Center JIM ROMANO from Los Angeles Raiders to Houston for 3rd- and 6th-round choices in 1985 draft (10/9). Los Angeles Raiders subsequently selected defensive back STEFON ADAMS (East Carolina) and quarterback RUSTY HILGER (Oklahoma State).

Tackle STEVE AUGUST from Seattle to Pittsburgh for 5th-round choice in 1985 draft (10/9). Seattle subsequently selected defensive back ARNOLD BROWN (North Carolina Central).

Quarterback MARK HERRMANN from Indianapolis to San Diego for 1986 draft choice (3/27).

Buffalo traded 1st-round choice in 1985 supplemental draft to Cleveland for 1st- and 3rd-round choices in 1985 draft and 1st- and 6th-round choices in 1986 draft (4/9).

Linebacker CHARLES JACKSON from Kansas City to New York Jets for 7th-round choice in 1985 draft (4/25).

Offensive lineman JON BORCHARDT from Buffalo to Seattle for 1986 draft choice (4/26).

Denver traded 2nd- and 5th-round choices in 1985 draft to Houston for 2nd-round choice in 1985 draft (4/30). Houston subsequently selected defensive end RICHARD BYRD (Southern Mississippi) and kicker LEE JOHNSON (Brigham Young). Denver subsequently selected wide receiver VANCE JOHNSON (Arizona).

Defensive end BOB HAMM and 1986 draft choice from Houston to Kansas City for 5th- and 6th-round choices in 1985 draft (4/30). Houston subsequently selected linebacker FRANK BUSH (North Carolina State) and linebacker JOE KRAKOSKI (Washington).

Quarterback BRYAN CLARK from Cincinnati to Miami for 1986 draft choice (5/6).

Wide receiver VICTOR OATIS from Indianapolis to Cleveland for 1986 draft choice (5/16).

The New Orleans Saints dealt running back George Rogers and three draft picks to Washington just prior to the 1985 NFL draft.

1985 NATIONAL FOOTBALL LEAGUE SCHEDULE

(All times local)

FIRST WEEK

SUNDAY, SEPTEMBER 8

1. Denver at Los Angeles Rams 1:00
2. Detroit at Atlanta 1:00
3. Green Bay at New England 1:00
4. Indianapolis at Pittsburgh 1:00
5. Kansas City at New Orleans 12:00
6. Miami at Houston 12:00
7. New York Jets at Los Angeles Raiders 1:00
8. Philadelphia at New York Giants 1:00
9. St. Louis at Cleveland 1:00
10. San Diego at Buffalo 4:00
11. San Francisco at Minnesota 12:00
12. Seattle at Cincinnati 1:00
13. Tampa Bay at Chicago 12:00

MONDAY, SEPTEMBER 9

14. Washington at Dallas 8:00

SECOND WEEK

THURSDAY, SEPTEMBER 12

15. Los Angeles Raiders at Kansas City 7:00

SUNDAY, SEPTEMBER 15

16. Atlanta at San Francisco 1:00
17. Buffalo at New York Jets 1:00
18. Cincinnati at St. Louis 12:00
19. Dallas at Detroit 1:00
20. Houston at Washington 1:00
21. Indianapolis at Miami 4:00
22. Los Angeles Rams at Philadelphia 1:00
23. Minnesota at Tampa Bay 4:00
24. New England at Chicago 12:00
25. New Orleans at Denver 2:00
26. New York Giants at Green Bay 3:00
27. Seattle at San Diego 1:00

MONDAY, SEPTEMBER 16

28. Pittsburgh at Cleveland 9:00

THIRD WEEK

THURSDAY, SEPTEMBER 19

29. Chicago at Minnesota 7:00

SUNDAY, SEPTEMBER 22

30. Cleveland at Dallas 12:00
31. Denver at Atlanta 1:00
32. Detroit at Indianapolis 12:00
33. Houston at Pittsburgh 1:00
34. Kansas City at Miami 4:00
35. New England at Buffalo 1:00
36. New York Jets vs. Green Bay at Milw. 3:00
37. Philadelphia at Washington 1:00
38. St. Louis at New York Giants 1:00
39. San Diego at Cincinnati 1:00
40. San Francisco at Los Angeles Raiders 1:00
41. Tampa Bay at New Orleans 12:00

MONDAY, SEPTEMBER 23

42. Los Angeles Rams at Seattle 6:00

FOURTH WEEK

SUNDAY, SEPTEMBER 29

43. Atlanta at Los Angeles Rams 1:00
44. Cleveland at San Diego 1:00
45. Dallas at Houston 12:00
46. Green Bay at St. Louis 12:00
47. Indianapolis at New York Jets 4:00
48. Los Angeles Raiders at New England 1:00
49. Miami at Denver 2:00
50. Minnesota at Buffalo 1:00
51. New Orleans at San Francisco 1:00
52. New York Giants at Philadelphia 1:00
53. Seattle at Kansas City 12:00
54. Tampa Bay at Detroit 1:00
55. Washington at Chicago 12:00

MONDAY, SEPTEMBER 30

56. Cincinnati at Pittsburgh 9:00

FIFTH WEEK

SUNDAY, OCTOBER 6

57. Buffalo at Indianapolis 12:00
58. Chicago at Tampa Bay 1:00
59. Dallas at New York Giants (night) 8:00
60. Detroit at Green Bay 12:00
61. Houston at Denver 2:00
62. Kansas City at Los Angeles Raiders 1:00
63. Minnesota at Los Angeles Rams 1:00
64. New England at Cleveland 1:00
65. New York Jets at Cincinnati 4:00
66. Philadelphia at New Orleans 12:00
67. Pittsburgh at Miami 1:00
68. San Diego at Seattle 1:00
69. San Francisco at Atlanta 1:00

MONDAY, OCTOBER 7

70. St. Louis at Washington 9:00

SIXTH WEEK

SUNDAY, OCTOBER 13

71. Atlanta at Seattle 1:00
72. Buffalo at New England 1:00
73. Chicago at San Francisco 1:00
74. Cleveland at Houston 12:00
75. Denver at Indianapolis 12:00
76. Detroit at Washington 1:00
77. Kansas City at San Diego 1:00
78. Los Angeles Rams at Tampa Bay 1:00
79. Minnesota vs. Green Bay at Milwaukee 12:00
80. New Orleans at Los Angeles Raiders 1:00
81. New York Giants at Cincinnati 1:00
82. Philadelphia at St. Louis 12:00
83. Pittsburgh at Dallas 12:00

MONDAY, OCTOBER 14

84. Miami at New York Jets 9:00

SEVENTH WEEK

SUNDAY, OCTOBER 20

85. Cincinnati at Houston 12:00
86. Dallas at Philadelphia 1:00
87. Indianapolis at Buffalo 1:00
88. Los Angeles Raiders at Cleveland 1:00
89. Los Angeles Rams at Kansas City 12:00
90. New Orleans at Atlanta 1:00
91. New York Jets at New England 4:00
92. St. Louis at Pittsburgh 1:00
93. San Diego at Minnesota 12:00
94. San Francisco at Detroit 1:00
95. Seattle at Denver 2:00
96. Tampa Bay at Miami 4:00
97. Washington at New York Giants 1:00

MONDAY, OCTOBER 21

98. Green Bay at Chicago 8:00

EIGHTH WEEK

SUNDAY, OCTOBER 27

99. Atlanta at Dallas 12:00
100. Buffalo at Philadelphia 1:00
101. Denver at Kansas City 12:00
102. Green Bay at Indianapolis 1:00
103. Houston at St. Louis 12:00
104. Miami at Detroit 1:00
105. Minnesota at Chicago 12:00
106. New England at Tampa Bay 1:00
107. New York Giants at New Orleans 3:00
108. Pittsburgh at Cincinnati 4:00
109. San Francisco at Los Angeles Rams 1:00
110. Seattle at New York Jets 1:00
111. Washington at Cleveland 1:00

MONDAY, OCTOBER 28

112. San Diego at Los Angeles Raiders 6:00

NINTH WEEK

SUNDAY, NOVEMBER 3
113. Chicago at Green Bay 12:00
114. Cincinnati at Buffalo 1:00
115. Cleveland at Pittsburgh 1:00
116. Denver at San Diego 1:00
117. Detroit at Minnesota 12:00
118. Kansas City at Houston 12:00
119. Los Angeles Raiders at Seattle 1:00
120. Miami at New England 1:00
121. New Orleans at Los Angeles Rams 1:00
122. New York Jets at Indianapolis 4:00
123. Philadelphia at San Francisco 1:00
124. Tampa Bay at New York Giants 1:00
125. Washington at Atlanta 1:00

MONDAY, NOVEMBER 4
126. Dallas at St. Louis 8:00

TENTH WEEK

SUNDAY, NOVEMBER 10
127. Atlanta at Philadelphia 1:00
128. Cleveland at Cincinnati 1:00
129. Dallas at Washington 4:00
130. Detroit at Chicago 12:00
131. Green Bay at Minnesota 12:00
132. Houston at Buffalo 1:00
133. Indianapolis at New England 1:00
134. Los Angeles Raiders at San Diego 1:00
135. Los Angeles Rams at New York Giants 1:00
136. New York Jets at Miami 4:00
137. Pittsburgh at Kansas City 12:00
138. St. Louis at Tampa Bay 1:00
139. Seattle at New Orleans 12:00

MONDAY, NOVEMBER 11
140. San Francisco at Denver 7:00

ELEVENTH WEEK

SUNDAY, NOVEMBER 17
141. Buffalo at Cleveland 1:00
142. Chicago at Dallas 12:00
143. Cincinnati at Los Angeles Raiders 1:00
144. Kansas City at San Francisco 1:00
145. Los Angeles Rams at Atlanta 1:00
146. Miami at Indianapolis 1:00
147. Minnesota at Detroit 4:00
148. New England at Seattle 1:00
149. New Orleans vs. Green Bay at Milw. 12:00
150. Pittsburgh at Houston 12:00
151. St. Louis at Philadelphia 1:00
152. San Diego at Denver 2:00
153. Tampa Bay at New York Jets 1:00

MONDAY, NOVEMBER 18
154. New York Giants at Washington 9:00

TWELFTH WEEK

SUNDAY, NOVEMBER 24
155. Atlanta at Chicago 12:00
156. Cincinnati at Cleveland 1:00
157. Denver at Los Angeles Raiders 1:00
158. Detroit at Tampa Bay 1:00
159. Green Bay at Los Angeles Rams 1:00
160. Indianapolis at Kansas City 3:00
161. Miami at Buffalo 1:00
162. New England at New York Jets 1:00
163. New Orleans at Minnesota 12:00
164. New York Giants at St. Louis 3:00
165. Philadelphia at Dallas 3:00
166. San Diego at Houston 12:00
167. Washington at Pittsburgh 1:00

MONDAY, NOVEMBER 25
168. Seattle at San Francisco 6:00

THIRTEENTH WEEK

THURSDAY, NOVEMBER 28
169. New York Jets at Detroit 12:30
170. St. Louis at Dallas 3:00

SUNDAY, DECEMBER 1
171. Buffalo at San Diego 1:00
172. Cleveland at New York Giants 1:00
173. Denver at Pittsburgh 1:00
174. Houston at Cincinnati 1:00
175. Kansas City at Seattle 1:00
176. Los Angeles Raiders at Atlanta 4:00
177. Los Angeles Rams at New Orleans 12:00
178. Minnesota at Philadelphia 1:00
179. New England at Indianapolis 1:00
180. San Francisco at Washington 4:00
181. Tampa Bay at Green Bay 12:00

MONDAY, DECEMBER 2
182. Chicago at Miami 9:00

FOURTEENTH WEEK

THURSDAY, DECEMBER 5
183. Pittsburgh at San Diego 5:00

SUNDAY, DECEMBER 8
184. Atlanta at Kansas City 12:00
185. Cleveland at Seattle 1:00
186. Dallas at Cincinnati 1:00
187. Detroit at New England 1:00
188. Indianapolis at Chicago 12:00
189. Los Angeles Raiders at Denver 2:00
190. Miami at Green Bay 12:00
191. New Orleans at St. Louis 12:00
192. New York Giants at Houston 3:00
193. New York Jets at Buffalo 1:00
194. Tampa Bay at Minnesota 3:00
195. Washington at Philadelphia 1:00

MONDAY, DECEMBER 9
196. Los Angeles Rams at San Francisco 6:00

FIFTEENTH WEEK

SATURDAY, DECEMBER 14
197. Chicago at New York Jets 12:30
198. Kansas City at Denver 2:00

SUNDAY, DECEMBER 15
199. Buffalo at Pittsburgh 1:00
200. Cincinnati at Washington 1:00
201. Green Bay at Detroit 1:00
202. Houston at Cleveland 1:00
203. Indianapolis at Tampa Bay 1:00
204. Minnesota at Atlanta 1:00
205. New York Giants at Dallas 12:00
206. Philadelphia at San Diego 1:00
207. St. Louis at Los Angeles Rams 1:00
208. San Francisco at New Orleans 12:00
209. Seattle at Los Angeles Raiders 1:00

MONDAY, DECEMBER 16
210. New England at Miami 9:00

SIXTEENTH WEEK

FRIDAY, DECEMBER 20
211. Denver at Seattle 5:00

SATURDAY, DECEMBER 21
212. Pittsburgh at New York Giants 12:30
213. Washington at St. Louis 3:00

SUNDAY, DECEMBER 22
214. Atlanta at New Orleans 12:00
215. Buffalo at Miami 1:00
216. Chicago at Detroit 1:00
217. Cincinnati at New England 1:00
218. Cleveland at New York Jets 1:00
219. Dallas at San Francisco 1:00
220. Green Bay at Tampa Bay 1:00
221. Houston at Indianapolis 4:00
222. Philadelphia at Minnesota 12:00
223. San Diego at Kansas City 12:00

MONDAY, DECEMBER 23
224. Los Angeles Raiders at L.A. Rams 6:00

NFL PRESEASON GAMES

(All times local)

HALL OF FAME GAME

SATURDAY, AUGUST 3

Houston vs. New York Giants at Canton, O. 2:30

FIRST WEEK

FRIDAY, AUGUST 9

Buffalo at Detroit 7:00
Chicago at St. Louis 7:30

SATURDAY, AUGUST 10

Cleveland at San Diego 6:00
Green Bay at Dallas 8:00
Houston at Los Angeles Rams 7:00
Kansas City at Cincinnati 7:00
Minnesota at Miami 8:00
New Orleans at New England 4:00
New York Giants at Denver 7:00
Philadelphia at New York Jets 8:00
San Francisco at Los Angeles Raiders 6:00
Seattle at Indianapolis 7:30

SUNDAY, AUGUST 11

Pittsburgh at Tampa Bay 8:00
Washington at Atlanta 7:00

SECOND WEEK

THURSDAY, AUGUST 15

St. Louis at Los Angeles Rams 7:00

FRIDAY, AUGUST 16

Detroit at Seattle 7:30

SATURDAY, AUGUST 17

Atlanta at Tampa Bay 8:00
Buffalo at Miami 8:00
Dallas at San Diego 6:00
Green Bay at New York Giants 8:00
Houston at New Orleans 7:00
Indianapolis at Chicago 6:00
New England at Kansas City 7:00
New York Jets at Cincinnati 7:00
Philadelphia at Cleveland 7:30
Pittsburgh at Minnesota 7:00

SUNDAY, AUGUST 18

Washington at Los Angeles Raiders 1:00

MONDAY, AUGUST 19

Denver at San Francisco 7:00

THIRD WEEK

FRIDAY, AUGUST 23

Cincinnati at Detroit 8:00
New England at Washington 8:00
Pittsburgh at St. Louis 7:30

SATURDAY, AUGUST 24

Atlanta vs. Green Bay at Milwaukee 7:00
Cleveland at Buffalo 6:00
Indianapolis at Denver 7:00
Kansas City at Houston 8:00
Los Angeles Rams vs. Philadelphia .... NA
Miami at Los Angeles Raiders 6:00
New York Giants vs. New York Jets 8:00
San Diego at San Francisco 12:00
Seattle at Minnesota 7:00
Tampa Bay at New Orleans 7:00

MONDAY, AUGUST 26

Chicago at Dallas 7:00

FOURTH WEEK

THURSDAY, AUGUST 29

Detroit at Philadelphia 7:00

FRIDAY, AUGUST 30

Cincinnati at Indianapolis 7:30
Los Angeles Raiders at Cleveland 7:30
Miami at Atlanta 7:00
Minnesota at Denver 7:00
New Orleans at San Diego 7:00
New York Giants at Pittsburgh 7:30
San Francisco at Seattle 6:00
Washington at Tampa Bay 8:00

SATURDAY, AUGUST 31

Buffalo at Chicago 6:00
Houston at Dallas 8:00
New England at Los Angeles Rams 7:00
New York Jets at Green Bay 7:00
St. Louis at Kansas City 7:00

1985 NATIONALLY TELEVISED GAMES
(All games also carried on NBC Network Radio)

REGULAR SEASON

Monday,   Sept. 9—Washington at Dallas (night, ABC)
Thursday, Sept. 12—Los Angeles Raiders at Kansas City (night, ABC)
Monday,   Sept. 16—Pittsburgh at Cleveland (night, ABC)
Thursday, Sept. 19—Chicago at Minnesota (night, ABC)
Monday,   Sept. 23—Los Angeles Rams at Seattle (night, ABC)
Monday,   Sept. 30—Cincinnati at Pittsburgh (night, ABC)
Sunday,   Oct. 6—Dallas at New York Giants (night, ABC)
Monday,   Oct. 7—St. Louis at Washington (night, ABC)
Monday,   Oct. 14—Miami at New York Jets (night, ABC)
Monday,   Oct. 21—Green Bay at Chicago (night, ABC)
Monday,   Oct. 28—San Diego at Los Angeles Raiders (night, ABC)
Monday,   Nov. 4—Dallas at St. Louis (night, ABC)
Monday,   Nov. 11—San Francisco at Denver (night, ABC)
Monday,   Nov. 18—New York Giants at Washington (night, ABC)
Monday,   Nov. 25—Seattle at San Francisco (night, ABC)
Thursday, Nov. 28—(Thanksgiving) New York Jets at Detroit (day, NBC)
                             St. Louis at Dallas (day, CBS)
Monday,   Dec. 2—Chicago at Miami (night, ABC)
Thursday, Dec. 5—Pittsburgh at San Diego (night, ABC)
Monday,   Dec. 9—Los Angeles Rams at San Francisco (night, ABC)
Saturday, Dec. 14—Chicago at New York Jets (day, CBS)
                             Kansas City at Denver (day, NBC)
Monday,   Dec. 16—New England at Miami (night, ABC)
Friday,   Dec. 20—Denver at Seattle (night, ABC)
Saturday, Dec. 21—Pittsburgh at New York Giants (day, NBC)
                             Washington at St. Louis (day, CBS)
Monday,   Dec. 23—Los Angeles Raiders at Los Angeles Rams (night, ABC)

POSTSEASON

Sunday,   Dec. 29—AFC and NFC First Round Playoffs (NBC and CBS)
Saturday, Jan. 4—AFC and NFC Divisional Playoffs (NBC and CBS)
Sunday,   Jan. 5—AFC and NFC Divisional Playoffs (NBC and CBS)
Sunday,   Jan. 12—AFC and NFC Championship Games (NBC and CBS)
Sunday,   Jan. 26—Super Bowl XX at Louisiana Superdome, New Orleans (NBC)
Sunday,   Feb. 2—AFC-NFC Pro Bowl, Honolulu, Hawaii (ABC)

MONDAY NIGHT GAMES

(All times local; televised by ABC and broadcast by NBC Network Radio)

Sept. 9—Washington at Dallas	8:00
Sept. 16—Pittsburgh at Cleveland	9:00
Sept. 23—Los Angeles Rams at Seattle	6:00
Sept. 30—Cincinnati at Pittsburgh	9:00
Oct. 7—St. Louis at Washington	9:00
Oct. 14—Miami at New York Jets	9:00
Oct. 21—Green Bay at Chicago	8:00
Oct. 28—San Diego at Los Angeles Raiders	6:00
Nov. 4—Dallas at St. Louis	8:00
Nov. 11—San Francisco at Denver	7:00
Nov. 18—New York Giants at Washington	9:00
Nov. 25—Seattle at San Francisco	6:00
Dec. 2—Chicago at Miami	9:00
Dec. 9—Los Angeles Rams at San Francisco	6:00
Dec. 16—New England at Miami	9:00
Dec. 23—Los Angeles Raiders at Los Angeles Rams	6:00

SUNDAY, THURSDAY & FRIDAY NIGHT GAMES

(All times local; televised by ABC and broadcast by NBC Network Radio)

Thursday, Sept. 12—Los Angeles Raiders at Kansas City 7:00
Thursday, Sept. 19—Chicago at Minnesota 7:00
Sunday,　　Oct.　6—Dallas at New York Giants 8:00
Thursday, Dec.　5—Pittsburgh at San Diego... 5:00
Friday,　　 Dec. 20—Denver at Seattle.. 5:00

NFL POST-SEASON PLAN,
1985 TIE-BREAKING PROCEDURES

DIVISION TIES

Two Clubs

1. Head-to-head (best won-lost-tied percentage in games between the clubs).
2. Best won-lost-tied percentage in games played within the division.
3. Best won-lost-tied percentage in games played within the conference.
4. Best won-lost-tied percentage in common games, if applicable.
5. Best net points in division games.
6. Best net points in all games.
7. Strength of schedule.
8. Best net touchdowns in all games.
9. Coin toss.

Three or More Clubs

(Note: If two clubs remain tied after other clubs are eliminated during any step, tie-breaker reverts to step 1 of two-club format.)

1. Head-to-head (best won-lost-tied percentage in games among the clubs).
2. Best won-lost-tied percentage in games played within the division.
3. Best won-lost-tied percentage in games played within the conference.
4. Best won-lost-tied percentage in common games.
5. Best net points in division games.
6. Best net points in all games.
7. Strength of schedule.
8. Best net touchdowns in all games.
9. Coin toss.

WILD CARD TIES

If necessary to break ties to determine the two wild card clubs from each conference, the following steps will be taken:

1. If all the tied clubs are from the same division, apply division tie-breaker.
2. If the tied clubs are from different divisions, apply the following steps:

Two Clubs

1. Head-to-head, if applicable.
2. Best won-lost-tied percentage in games played within the conference.
3. Best won-lost-tied percentage in common games, minimum of four.
4. Best net points in conference games.
5. Best net points in all games.
6. Strength of schedule.
7. Best net touchdowns in all games.
8. Coin toss.

Three or More Clubs

(Note: If two clubs remain tied after other clubs are eliminated, tie-breaker reverts to step 1 of applicable two-club format.)

1. Head-to-head sweep (applicable only if one club has defeated each of the others or one club has lost to each of the others).
2. Best won-lost-tied percentage in games within the conference.
3. Best won-lost-tied percentage in common games, minimum of four.
4. Best net points in conference games.
5. Best net points in all games.
6. Strength of schedule.
7. Best net touchdowns in all games.
8. Coin toss.

1985 AFC-NFC INTERCONFERENCE GAMES

(All times local. All games Sunday unless noted otherwise.)

Sept.	8—Denver at Los Angeles Rams	1:00
	Green Bay at New England	1:00
	Kansas City at New Orleans	12:00
	St. Louis at Cleveland	1:00
Sept.	15—Cincinnati at St. Louis	12:00
	Houston at Washington	1:00
	New England at Chicago	12:00
	New Orleans at Denver	2:00
Sept.	22—Cleveland at Dallas	12:00
	Denver at Atlanta	1:00
	Detroit at Indianapolis	12:00
	New York Jets vs. Green Bay at Milwaukee	3:00
	San Francisco at Los Angeles Raiders	1:00
Sept.	23—Los Angeles Rams at Seattle (Monday night)	6:00
Sept.	29—Dallas at Houston	12:00
	Minnesota at Buffalo	1:00
Oct.	13—Atlanta at Seattle	1:00
	New Orleans at Los Angeles Raiders	1:00
	New York Giants at Cincinnati	1:00
	Pittsburgh at Dallas	12:00
Oct.	20—Los Angeles Rams at Kansas City	12:00
	St. Louis at Pittsburgh	1:00
	San Diego at Minnesota	12:00
	Tampa Bay at Miami	4:00
Oct.	27—Buffalo at Philadelphia	1:00
	Green Bay at Indianapolis	1:00
	Houston at St. Louis	12:00
	Miami at Detroit	1:00
	New England at Tampa Bay	1:00
	Washington at Cleveland	1:00
Nov.	10—Seattle at New Orleans	12:00
Nov.	11—San Francisco at Denver (Monday night)	7:00
Nov.	17—Kansas City at San Francisco	1:00
	Tampa Bay at New York Jets	1:00
Nov.	24—Washington at Pittsburgh	1:00
Nov.	25—Seattle at San Francisco (Monday night)	6:00
Nov.	28—New York Jets at Detroit (Thanksgiving)	12:30
Dec.	1—Cleveland at New York Giants	1:00
	Los Angeles Raiders at Atlanta	4:00
Dec.	2—Chicago at Miami (Monday night)	9:00
Dec.	8—Atlanta at Kansas City	12:00
	Detroit at New England	1:00
	Dallas at Cincinnati	1:00
	Indianapolis at Chicago	12:00
	Miami at Green Bay	12:00
	New York Giants at Houston	3:00
Dec.	14—Chicago at New York Jets (Saturday)	12:30
Dec.	15—Cincinnati at Washington	1:00
	Indianapolis at Tampa Bay	1:00
	Philadelphia at San Diego	1:00
Dec.	21—Pittsburgh at New York Giants (Saturday)	12:30
Dec.	23—Los Angeles Raiders at Los Angeles Rams (Monday night)	6:00

1984 NFL AVERAGE PAID ATTENDANCE OF 59,813 WAS 2ND HIGHEST EVER

National Football League attendance exceeded 13 million for the fifth consecutive complete season in 1984 when the per-game average was 59,813, the second highest in the 65-year history of the league.

Official NFL figures revealed total paid attendance for 224 regular season games to be 13,398,112. The 1984 total represents 88.43 percent of stadia capacity. The 1984 total marked an increase of 120,890 over the 1983 total of 13,277,222, which was the third highest ever for an average of 59,273.

The NFL paid attendance first exceeded 13 million in 1979. In 1981, the league set a regular season record of 13,606,990 for an average of 60,745. The 1982 regular season was reduced to 126 games by the eight-week players' strike that wiped out 98 games and total paid attendance was 7,367,438 for an average of 58,472.

Paid attendance for all 1984 games—including exhibition, regular season and post-season—was 16,824,691 for an average of 57,817 for 291 games.

Paid attendance for 10 postseason games was 665,194. Super Bowl XIX, in which NFC Champion San Francisco defeated AFC Champion Miami, 38-16, at Stanford (Calif.) Stadium, drew a sellout crowd of 84,059.

The New York Giants led the NFL in home paid attendance with a total of 605,296. The New York Jets were second with 602,588. Other teams which sold more than 500,000 tickets were: Denver, 595,016; Los Angeles Raiders, 542,357; Miami, 532,337; New Orleans, 519,610; Philadelphia, 512,520; Seattle, 511,599; Dallas, 508,918; Chicago, 504,395, and Detroit 503,495.

In the 12th season during which NFL games were made available to local television after selling out 72 hours in advance of kickoff, 118 of the 224 regular season games were televised in the home-team area. The total number of unused tickets was 1,227,922, or nine percent of the 13,649,084 tickets distributed.

1984 ATTENDANCE BREAKDOWN

	G.	Attendance	Avg.
AFC Exhibition Games	11	473,453	43,041
NFC Exhibition Games	11	562,381	51,126
Interconference Exhibition Games	35	1,725,551	49,301
NFL Exhibition Total	57	2,761,385	48,445
AFC Regular Season	86	5,124,275	59,585
NFC Regular Season	86	5,219,911	60,697
Interconference Games	52	3,053,926	58,729
NFL Regular Season Total	224	13,398,112	59,813
AFC First Round Playoff	1		
(Los Angeles Raiders-Seattle)		64,291	
AFC Divisional Playoffs	2		
(Seattle-Miami)		74,291	
(Pittsburgh-Denver)		74,502	
AFC Championship	1		
(Pittsburgh-Miami)		74,588	
NFC First Round Playoff	1		
(New York Giants-Los Angeles Rams)		66,919	
NFC Divisional Playoffs	2		
(New York Giants-San Francisco)		60,373	
(Chicago-Washington)		54,450	
NFC Championship	1		
(Chicago-San Francisco)		61,336	
Super Bowl XIX at Stanford, Calif.	1		
(Miami-San Francisco)		84,059	
AFC-NFC Pro Bowl at Honolulu, Haw.	1		
		50,385	
Postseason Total	10	655,194	66,519
NFL All Games Total	291	16,824,691	57,817

PAID ATTENDANCE
NATIONAL FOOTBALL LEAGUE

	Regular Season		Average	*Post-Season	
1984	13,398,112	(224 games)	59,813	614,809	(9)
1983	13,277,222	(224 games)	59,273	625,068	(9)
1982†	7,367,438	(126 games)	58,472	985,952	(15)
1981	13,606,990	(224 games)	60,745	587,361	(9)
1980	13,392,230	(224 games)	59,787	577,186	(9)
1979	13,182,039	(224 games)	58,848	582,266	(9)
1978	12,771,800	(224 games)	57,017	578,107	(9)
1977	11,018,632	(196 games)	56,218	483,588	(7)
1976	11,070,543	(196 games)	56,482	428,733	(7)
1975	10,213,193	(182 games)	56,116	443,811	(7)
1974	10,236,322	(182 games)	56,224	412,180	(7)
1973	10,730,933	(182 games)	58,961	458,515	(7)
1972	10,445,827	(182 games)	57,395	435,466	(7)
1971	10,076,035	(182 games)	55,363	430,244	(7)
1970	9,533,333	(182 games)	52,381	410,371	(7)
1969	6,096,127	(112 games)	54,430	242,841	(4)
1968	5,882,313	(112 games)	52,521	291,279	(4)
1967	5,938,924	(112 games)	53,026	241,754	(4)
1966	5,337,044	(105 games)	50,829	135,098	(2)
1965	4,634,021	(98 games)	47,296	100,304	(2)
1964	4,563,049	(98 games)	46,562	79,544	(1)
1963	4,163,643	(98 games)	42,486	45,801	(1)
1962	4,003,421	(98 games)	40,851	64,892	(1)
1961	3,986,159	(98 games)	40,675	39,029	(1)
1960	3,128,296	(78 games)	40,106	67,325	(1)
1959	3,140,000	(72 games)	43,617	57,545	(1)
1958	3,006,124	(72 games)	41,752	123,659	(2)
1957	2,836,318	(72 games)	39,393	119,579	(2)
1956	2,551,263	(72 games)	35,434	56,836	(1)
1955	2,521,836	(72 games)	35,026	85,693	(1)
1954	2,190,571	(72 games)	30,425	43,827	(1)
1953	2,164,585	(72 games)	30,064	54,577	(1)
1952	2,052,126	(72 games)	28,502	97,507	(2)
1951	1,913,019	(72 games)	26,570	57,522	(1)
1950	1,977,753	(78 games)	25,356	136,647	(3)
1949	1,391,735	(60 games)	23,196	27,980	(1)
1948	1,525,243	(60 games)	25,421	36,309	(1)
1947	1,837,437	(60 games)	30,624	66,268	(2)
1946	1,732,135	(55 games)	31,493	58,346	(1)
1945	1,270,401	(50 games)	25,408	32,178	(1)
1944	1,019,649	(50 games)	20,393	46,016	(1)
1943	969,128	(50 games)	19,383	71,315	(2)
1942	887,920	(55 games)	16,144	36,006	(1)
1941	1,108,615	(55 games)	20,157	55,870	(2)
1940	1,063,025	(55 games)	19,328	36,034	(1)
1939	1,071,200	(55 games)	19,476	32,279	(1)
1938	937,197	(55 games)	17,040	48,120	(1)
1937	963,039	(55 games)	17,510	15,878	(1)
1936	816,007	(54 games)	15,111	29,545	(1)
1935	638,178	(53 games)	12,041	15,000	(1)
1934	492,684	(60 games)	8,211	35,059	(1)

*Includes conference and league championship and AFL-NFL championship (Super Bowl) games; number of post-season games in parentheses. Pro Bowl not included.

†A 57-day players' strike reduced 224-game schedule to 126 games.

NATIONAL PROFESSIONAL FOOTBALL
HALL OF FAME

The Pro Football Hall of Fame in Canton, Ohio.

FIVE NEW INDUCTEES IN 1985
Frank Gatski, Joe Namath, Pete Rozelle, O.J. Simpson and Roger Staubach were inducted into Pro Football's Hall of Fame in 1985, expanding the list of former stars honored at Canton, Ohio, to 128.

Pro Football Hall of Fame

The National Professional Football Hall of Fame is located in Canton, Ohio, site of the organizational meeting in 1920 from which the National Football League grew.

The League recognized Canton as the Hall of Fame site on April 27, 1961, and ground was broken for the Hall on August 11, 1962. Dedication ceremonies were held September 7, 1963.

The National Board of Selectors, consisting of representatives from professional football cities, elected 17 charter members to the Hall. The selections were announced on January 29, 1963.

Subsequent selections were announced on February 28, 1964, January 19, 1965, March 23, 1966, February 8, 1967, February 19, 1968, February 6, 1969, February 2, 1970, February 4, 1971, February 8, 1972, February 6, 1973, February 5, 1974, January 20, 1975, January 26, 1976, January 17, 1977, January 23, 1978, January 30, 1979, January 26, 1980, January 31, 1981, January 28, 1982, February 5, 1983, January 28, 1984 and January 22, 1985.

ROSTER OF MEMBERS (128)

*Deceased member.

HERB ADDERLEY (Michigan State), 1980, cornerback, Green Bay Packers (1961-69), Dallas Cowboys (1970-72).

LANCE ALWORTH (Arkansas), 1978, wide receiver, San Diego Chargers (1962-70), Dallas Cowboys (1971-72).

DOUG ATKINS (Tennessee), 1982, defensive end, Cleveland Browns (1953-54), Chicago Bears (1955-66), New Orleans Saints (1967-69).

MORRIS (RED) BADGRO (Southern California), 1981, end, New York Yankees (1926), New York Giants (1930-35).

*CLIFF BATTLES (West Virginia Wesleyan), 1968, halfback-quarterback, Boston Braves, Boston Redskins, Washington Redskins (1932-37); coach, Brooklyn Dodgers (1946-47).

SAMMY BAUGH (Texas Christian), Charter 1963, quarterback, Washington Redskins (1937-52); coach, New York Titans (1960-61); Houston Oilers (1964).

CHUCK BEDNARIK (Pennsylvania), 1967, center and linebacker, Philadelphia Eagles (1949-62).

*BERT BELL (Pennsylvania), Charter 1963, NFL Commissioner (1946-59).

BOBBY BELL (Minnesota), 1983, linebacker, Kansas City Chiefs (1963-74).

RAYMOND BERRY (Southern Methodist), 1973, offensive end, Baltimore Colts (1955-67).

*CHARLES W. BIDWILL (Loyola), 1967, owner, Chicago Cardinals (1933-47).

GEORGE BLANDA (Kentucky), 1981, quarterback-placekicker, Chicago Bears (1949-58), Baltimore Colts (1950), Houston Oilers (1960-66), Oakland Raiders (1967-73).

JIM BROWN (Syracuse), 1971, fullback, Cleveland Browns (1957-65).

PAUL BROWN (Miami, Ohio), 1967, coach, Cleveland Browns (1946-62), Cincinnati Bengals (1968-75).

ROOSEVELT BROWN (Morgan State), 1975, tackle, New York Giants (1953-66).

WILLIE BROWN (Grambling), 1984, defensive back, Denver Broncos (1963-66), Oakland Raiders (1967-78).

DICK BUTKUS (Illinois), 1979, linebacker, Chicago Bears (1965-73).

TONY CANADEO (Gonzaga), 1974, halfback, Green Bay Packers (1941-44, 1946-52).

*JOE CARR, Charter 1963, NFL President (1921-39).

*GUY CHAMBERLIN (Nebraska), 1965, player-coach, Canton Bulldogs, Cleveland, Frankford Yellowjackets, Chicago Bears, and Chicago Cardinals (1919-28).

JACK CHRISTIANSEN (Colorado A&M), 1970, defensive back, Detroit Lions (1951-58); coach, San Francisco 49ers (1963-67).

*DUTCH CLARK (Colorado College), Charter 1963, quarterback, Portsmouth Spartans and Detroit Lions (1931-38).

GEORGE CONNOR (Notre Dame), 1975, tackle and linebacker, Chicago Bears (1948-55).

*JIMMY CONZELMAN (Washington, Mo.), 1964, halfback, coach, executive, Decatur, Rock Island, Milwaukee, Detroit, Providence, Chicago Cardinals (1920-48).

WILLIE DAVIS (Grambling), 1981, defensive end, Cleveland Browns (1958-59), Green Bay Packers (1960-69).

ART DONOVAN (Boston College), 1968, defensive tackle, Baltimore Colts, New York Yanks, Dallas Texans, Baltimore Colts (1950-61).

*PADDY DRISCOLL (Northwestern), 1965, player-coach, Chicago Cardinals and Chicago Bears (1919-31, 1941-68).

BILL DUDLEY (Virginia), 1966, halfback, Pittsburgh Steelers, Detroit Lions and Washington Redskins (1942-53).

*TURK EDWARDS (Washington State), 1969, tackle, Boston Braves, Boston Redskins, Washington Redskins (1932-40).

WEEB EWBANK (Miami, O.), 1978, coach, Baltimore Colts (1954-1962) and New York Jets (1963-1973).

TOM FEARS (Santa Clara, UCLA), 1970, end, Los Angeles Rams (1948-56), coach, New Orleans Saints (1967-70).

RAY FLAHERTY (Gonzaga), 1976, player-coach, Los Angeles Wildcats, New York Yankees (AFL), New York Giants, Boston Redskins, Washington Redskins, New York Yankees (AAFC), Chicago Hornets (1926-1949).

*LEN FORD (Michigan), 1976, end, Los Angeles Dons and Cleveland Browns (1948-1958).

DANNY FORTMANN (Colgate), 1965, guard, Chicago Bears (1936-43).

FRANK GATSKI (Marshall), 1985, center, Cleveland Browns (1946-56), Detroit Lions (1957).

*BILL GEORGE (Wake Forest), 1974, linebacker, Chicago Bears, and Los Angeles Rams (1952-66).

FRANK GIFFORD (Southern California), 1977, halfback and end, New York Giants (1952-60 and 1962-64).

SID GILLMAN (Ohio State), 1983, end, Cleveland Rams (1936); coach, Los Angeles Rams (1955-59), Los Angeles Chargers (1960), San Diego Chargers (1961-69, 71), Houston Oilers (1973-74).

OTTO GRAHAM (Northwestern), 1965, quarterback, Cleveland Browns (1946-55), coach, Washington Redskins (1966-68).

RED GRANGE (Illinois), Charter 1963, halfback, Chicago Bears (1925; 1929-34), New York Yankees (1926-27).

FORREST GREGG (Southern Methodist), 1977, tackle, Green Bay Packers and Dallas Cowboys (1956; 1958-71); coach, Cleveland Browns (1975-77), and Cincinnati Bengals (1980-82).

LOU GROZA (Ohio State), 1974, offensive tackle and placekicker, Cleveland Browns (1946-59, 1961-67).

*JOE GUYON (Carlisle, Georgia Tech), 1966, halfback, Canton Bulldogs, Cleveland Indians, Oorang Indians, Rock Island Independents, Kansas City Cowboys and New York Giants (1918-27).

*GEORGE HALAS (Illinois), Charter 1963, player, coach, founder, Chicago Bears (1920-82).

*ED HEALEY (Dartmouth), 1964, tackle, Rock Island and Chicago Bears (1920-27).

MEL HEIN (Washington State), Charter 1963, center, New York Giants (1931-45).

*WILBUR HENRY (Washington & Jefferson), Charter 1963, tackle, Canton Bulldogs, Akron Indians, New York Giants, Pottsville Maroons, Pittsburgh Steelers (1920-30).

*ARNIE HERBER (Regis), 1966, halfback, Green Bay Packers and New York Giants (1930-45).

*BILL HEWITT (Michigan), 1971, end, Chicago Bears (1932-36), Philadelphia Eagles (1937-39), Philadelphia-Pittsburgh (1943).

CLARKE HINKLE (Bucknell), 1964, fullback, Green Bay Packers (1932-41).

ELROY (CRAZYLEGS) HIRSCH (Wisconsin), 1968, end-halfback, Chicago Rockets, Los Angeles Rams (1946-57).

*CAL HUBBARD (Centenary, Geneva), Charter 1963, tackle and end, New York Giants, Green Bay Packers and Pittsburgh Steelers (1927-36).

SAM HUFF (West Virginia), 1982, linebacker, New York Giants (1956-63), Washington Redskins (1964-67, 69).

LAMAR HUNT (Southern Methodist), 1972, founder, American Football League, 1959; president, Dallas Texans (1960-62), Kansas City Chiefs (1963-82).

DON HUTSON (Alabama), Charter 1963, end, Green Bay Packers (1935-45).

DEACON JONES (South Carolina State), 1980, defensive end, Los Angeles Rams (1961-71), San Diego Chargers (1972-73), Washington Redskins (1974).

SONNY JURGENSEN (Duke), 1983, quarterback, Philadelphia Eagles (1957-63), Washington Redskins (1964-74).

*WALTER KIESLING (St. Thomas), 1966, player-coach, Duluth Eskimos, Pottsville Maroons, Boston Braves, Chicago Cardinals, Chicago Bears, Green Bay Packers and Pittsburgh Steelers (1926-56).

FRANK (BRUISER) KINARD (Mississippi), 1971, tackle, Brooklyn Dodgers (1938-45) New York Yankees (1946-47).

*CURLY LAMBEAU (Notre Dame), Charter 1963, founder, player, coach, Green Bay Packers (1919-49).

DICK (NIGHT TRAIN) LANE (Scottsbluff Jr. Coll.), 1974, defensive back, Los Angeles Rams, Chicago Cardinals, Detroit Lions (1952-65).

YALE LARY (Texas A & M), 1979, defensive back, Detroit Lions (1952-53, 1956-64).

DANTE LAVELLI (Ohio State), 1975, end, Cleveland Browns (1946-56).

BOBBY LAYNE (Texas), 1967, quarterback, Chicago Bears, New York Bulldogs, Detroit Lions, Pittsburgh Steelers (1948-62).

*TUFFY LEEMANS (George Washington), 1978, fullback, New York Giants (1936-1943).

BOB LILLY (Texas Christian), 1980, defensive tackle, Dallas Cowboys (1961-1974).

*VINCE LOMBARDI (Fordham), 1971, coach, Green Bay Packers (1959-67), Washington Redskins (1969).

SID LUCKMAN (Columbia), 1965, quarterback, Chicago Bears (1939-50).

*ROY (LINK) LYMAN, 1964, tackle, Canton Bulldogs, Cleveland, Chicago Bears (1922-34).

*TIM MARA, Charter 1963, founder, New York Giants (1925-65).

GINO MARCHETTI (San Francisco), 1972, defensive end, Dallas Cowboys (1952), Baltimore Colts (1953-66).

*GEORGE PRESTON MARSHALL, Charter 1963, founder, Washington Redskins (1932-1965).

OLLIE MATSON (San Francisco), 1972, halfback, Chicago Cardinals (1952, 1954-58), Los Angeles Rams (1959-62), Detroit Lions (1963), Philadelphia Eagles (1964-66).

GEORGE McAFEE (Duke), 1966, halfback, Chicago Bears (1940-41, 1945-50).

MIKE McCORMACK (Kansas), 1984, tackle, New York Yanks (1951), Cleveland Browns (1954-62).

HUGH McELHENNY (Washington), 1970, halfback, San Francisco 49ers, Minnesota Vikings, New York Giants and Detroit Lions (1952-64).

JOHNNY BLOOD (McNALLY) (St. John's, Minn.), Charter 1963, halfback, Milwaukee Badgers, Duluth Eskimos, Pottsville Maroons, Green Bay Packers, Pittsburgh Steelers (1925-39).

AUGUST (MIKE) MICHALSKE (Penn State), 1964, guard, New York Yankees and Green Bay Packers (1927-37).

*WAYNE MILLNER (Notre Dame), 1968, end, Boston Redskins, Washington Redskins (1936-41, 1945).

BOBBY MITCHELL (Illinois), 1983, running back and receiver, Cleveland Browns (1958-61), Washington Redskins (1962-68).

RON MIX (Southern California), 1979, offensive tackle, Los Angeles Chargers (1960), San Diego Chargers (1961-69), Oakland Raiders (1971).

LENNY MOORE (Penn State), 1975, halfback, Baltimore Colts (1956-67).

MARION MOTLEY (Nevada), 1968, fullback-linebacker, Cleveland Browns, Pittsburgh Steelers (1946-1955).

GEORGE MUSSO (Millikin), 1982, offensive guard and defensive tackle, Chicago Bears (1933-44).

BRONKO NAGURSKI (Minnesota), Charter 1963, fullback and tackle, Chicago Bears (1930-37, 1943).

JOE NAMATH (Alabama), 1985, quarterback, New York Jets (1965-76), Los Angeles Rams (1977).

*EARLE (GREASY) NEALE (West Virginia Wesleyan), 1969, coach, Philadelphia Eagles (1941-50).

*ERNIE NEVERS (Stanford), Charter 1963, fullback, Duluth Eskimos and Chicago Cardinals (1926-37).

RAY NITSCHKE (Illinois), 1978, linebacker, Green Bay Packers (1958-72).

LEO NOMELLINI (Minnesota), 1969, defensive tackle, San Francisco 49ers (1953-63).

MERLIN OLSEN (Utah State), 1982, defensive tackle, Los Angeles Rams (1962-76).

JIM OTTO (Miami, Fla.), 1980, center, Oakland Raiders (1960-1974).

*STEVE OWEN (Phillips), 1966, player-coach, Kansas City Cowboys and New York Giants (1924-53).

CLARENCE (ACE) PARKER (Duke), 1972, halfback, Brooklyn Dodgers (1937-41), Boston Yanks (1945), New York Yankees (1946).

JIM PARKER (Ohio State), 1973, guard, Baltimore Colts (1957-67).

JOE PERRY (Compton J. C.), 1969, fullback, San Francisco 49ers, Baltimore Colts (1948-63).

PETE PIHOS (Indiana), 1970, end, Philadelphia Eagles (1947-55).

*HUGH (SHORTY) RAY (Illinois), 1966, NFL technical adviser and supervisor of officials (1938-56).

*DANIEL F. REEVES (Georgetown), 1967, founder, Los Angeles Rams (1941-71).

JIM RINGO (Syracuse), 1981, center, Green Bay Packers (1953-63), Philadelphia Eagles (1964-67).

ANDY ROBUSTELLI (Arnold), 1971, defensive end, Los Angeles Rams (1951-55), New York Giants (1956-64).

ARTHUR J. ROONEY (Georgetown), 1964, founder, Pittsburgh Steelers (1933-82).

PETE ROZELLE (San Francisco), 1985, NFL Commissioner (1960-present).

GALE SAYERS (Kansas), 1977, running back, Chicago Bears (1965-71).

JOE SCHMIDT (Pittsburgh), 1973, linebacker, Detroit Lions (1953-65); coach, Detroit Lions (1967-72).

O.J. SIMPSON (Southern California), 1985, running back, Buffalo Bills (1969-77), San Francisco 49ers (1978).

BART STARR (Alabama), 1977, quarterback, Green Bay Packers (1956-71); coach, Green Bay Packers (1975-82).

ROGER STAUBACH (Navy), 1985, quarterback, Dallas Cowboys (1969-79).

ERNIE STAUTNER (West Virginia), 1969, defensive tackle, Pittsburgh Steelers (1950-63).

*KEN STRONG (New York U.), 1967, halfback-placekicker, Staten Island Stapletons, New York Yankees and New York Giants (1929-39, 1944-47).

*JOE STYDAHAR (West Virginia), 1967, tackle, Chicago Bears (1936-42, 1945-46).

CHARLEY TAYLOR (Arizona State), 1984, wide receiver, Washington Redskins (1964-75, 77).

JIM TAYLOR (Louisiana State), 1976, fullback, Green Bay Packers (1958-1966), New Orleans Saints (1967).

*JIM THORPE (Carlisle), Charter 1963, halfback, Canton Bulldogs, Oorang Indians, Cleveland Indians, Toledo Maroons, Rock Island Independents, New York Giants (1915-26, 1929).

Y.A. TITTLE (Louisiana State), 1971, quarterback, Baltimore Colts (1948-50), San Francisco 49ers (1951-60), New York Giants (1961-64).

*GEORGE TRAFTON (Notre Dame), 1964, center, Chicago Bears (1920-32).

CHARLIE TRIPPI (Georgia), 1968, halfback, Chicago Cardinals (1947-55).

*EMLEN TUNNELL (Iowa), 1967, defensive back, New York Giants and Green Bay Packers (1948-61).

CLYDE (BULLDOG) TURNER (Hardin-Simmons), 1966, center-linebacker, Chicago Bears (1940-52); coach, New York Titans (1962).

JOHN UNITAS (Louisville), 1979, quarterback, Baltimore Colts (1956-72), San Diego Chargers (1973).

*****NORM VAN BROCKLIN** (Oregon), 1971, quarterback, Los Angeles Rams (1949-57), Philadelphia Eagles (1958-60), coach, Minnesota Vikings (1961-66), Atlanta Falcons (1968-74).

STEVE VAN BUREN (Louisiana State), 1965, halfback, Philadelphia Eagles (1944-51).

PAUL WARFIELD (Ohio State), 1983, receiver, Cleveland Browns (1964-69, 76-77), Miami Dolphins (1970-74).

*****BOB WATERFIELD** (UCLA), 1965, quarterback, Cleveland Rams and Los Angeles Rams (1945-52); coach, Los Angeles Rams (1960-62).

ARNIE WEINMEISTER (Washington), 1984, tackle, New York Yankees (1948-49), New York Giants (1950-53).

BILL WILLIS (Ohio State), 1977, guard, Cleveland Browns (1946-53).

LARRY WILSON (Utah), 1978, defensive back, St. Louis Cardinals (1960-72).

ALEX WOJCIECHOWICZ (Fordham), 1968, center-linebacker Detroit Lions, Philadelphia Eagles (1938-50).

Former Buffalo star O.J. Simpson (left) joined fellow 1985 inductee Roger Staubach as the first Heisman Trophy winners ever elected to the Pro Football Hall of Fame. Simpson won the award in 1968 at Southern California; Staubach in 1963 at Navy.

Frank Gatski

Joe Namath

Pete Rozelle

Roger Staubach

1985 ROSTER OF OFFICIALS

Art McNally, Supervisor of Officials
Jack Reader, Assistant Supervisor of Officials
Nick Skorich, Assistant Supervisor of Officials

Mark Burns, Officiating Assistant
Joe Gardi, Officiating Assistant
Tony Veteri, Officiating Assistant

REFEREES

No.	Name	College	Yrs.
14	Gene Barth	St. Louis	15
43	Red Cashion	Texas A & M	14
6	Tom Dooley	VMI	8
12	Ben Dreith	Colorado State	26
71	Bob Frederic	Colorado	18
40	Pat Haggerty	Colorado State	21
46	Chuck Heberling	Wash. & Jefferson	21
60	Dick Jorgensen	Wisconsin	18
9	Jerry Markbreit	Illinois	10
48	Gordon McCarter	Western Reserve	19
95	Bob McElwee	Navy	10
70	Jerry Seeman	Winona State	11
7	Fred Silva	San Jose State	19
32	Jim Tunney	Occidental	26
11	Fred Wyant	West Virginia	20

LINE JUDGES

No.	Name	College	Yrs.
59	Bob Beeks	Lincoln	18
83	Ron Blum	Marin	1
45	Ron DeSouza	Morgan State	6
39	Jack Fette	No College	21
15	Bama Glass	Colorado	7
112	Joe Haynes	Alcorn State	2
54	Jack Johnson	Pacific Lutheran	10
94	Vern Marshall	Linfield College	10
41	Dick McKenzie	Ashland	8
51	Dale Orem	Louisville	6
44	Walt Peters	Indiana State, Pa.	18
53	Bill Reynolds	West Chester State	11
33	Howard Roe	Wichita State	2
56	Carver Shannon	Southern Illinois	3
3	Boyce Smith	Vanderbilt	5
30	Dan Wilford	Mississippi	3

UMPIRES

No.	Name	College	Yrs.
115	Hendi Ancich	Harbor College	4
110	Ron Botchan	Occidental	6
101	Bob Boylston	Alabama	8
27	Al Conway	Army	17
78	Art Demmas	Vanderbilt	18
57	Ed Fiffick	Marquette	7
50	Neil Gereb	California	5
42	Dave Hamilton	Utah	11
19	Tommy Hensley	Tennessee	19
67	John Keck	Cornell	14
117	Ben Montgomery	Morehouse	4
88	Dave Moss	Dartmouth	6
103	Rex Stuart	Appalachian St.	2
100	Bob Wagner	Penn State	1
89	Gordon Wells	Occidental	14

BACK JUDGES

No.	Name	College	Yrs.
22	Paul Baetz	Heidelberg	8
24	Roy Clymer	New Mexico State	6
105	Dick Hantak	Southeast Missouri	8
106	Al Jury	S. Bernardino Valley	8
107	Jim Kearney	Pennsylvania	8
25	Tom Kelleher	Holy Cross	26
21	Pete Liske	Penn State	3
36	Bob Moore	Dayton	2
92	Jim Poole	San Diego State	11
98	Jimmy Rosser	Auburn	9
29	J.W. Sanders	Southern Illinois	6
38	Bill Swanson	Lake Forest	22
52	Ben Tompkins	Texas	15
28	Don Wedge	Ohio Wesleyan	14
99	Banks Williams	Houston	8

HEAD LINESMEN

No.	Name	College	Yrs.
81	Dave Anderson	Salem College	2
17	Jerry Bergman	Duquesne	20
111	Earnie Frantz	No College	5
72	Terry Gierke	Portland State	5
85	Frank Glover	Morris Brown	14
63	Ligouri Hagerty	Syracuse	10
104	Dale Hamer	California St., Pa.	8
114	Tom Johnson	Miami-Ohio	4
65	Norm Kragseth	Northwestern	12
26	Ed Marion	Pennsylvania	26
35	Leo Miles	Virginia State	17
10	Ron Phares	Virginia Polytechnic	1
109	Sid Semon	Southern California	3
37	Burl Toler	San Francisco	21
8	Dale Williams	California State	6

SIDE JUDGES

No.	Name	College	Yrs.
34	Gerald Austin	Western Carolina	4
16	Royal Cathcart	Calif.-Santa Barb.	15
61	Dick Creed	Louisville	8
74	Ray Dodez	Wooster	18
102	Merrill Douglas	Utah	5
47	Tom Fincken	Kansas State	2
62	Duwayne Gandy	Tulsa	5
66	Dave Hawk	Southern Methodist	14
97	Nate Jones	Lewis and Clark	9
120	Gary Lane	Missouri	4
49	Dean Look	Michigan State	14
90	Gil Mace	Westminster	12
20	Larry Menners	Upper Iowa	1
64	Dave Parry	Wabash	11
58	William Quinby	Iowa State	8
80	Bob Rice	Denison	17

FIELD JUDGES

No.	Name	College	Yrs.
31	Dick Dolack	Ferris State	20
23	Johnny Grier	D.C. Teachers	5
75	Don Habel	Western Oregon	2
96	Don Hakes	Bradley	9
86	Barney Kukar	St. John's	2
18	Bob Lewis	No College	10
82	Pat Mallette	Nebraska	17
116	Chuck McCallum	Michigan State	4
76	Ed Merrifield	Missouri	11
77	Don Orr	Vanderbilt	15
73	Bob Skelton	Alabama	1
119	Ron Spitler	Panhandle State	4
91	Bill Stanley	Redlands	12
93	Jack Vaughn	Mississippi State	10
84	Bob Wortman	Findlay	20